CYBERSPACE LAW

ASPEN PUBLISHERS

CYBERSPACE LAW

CASES AND MATERIALS

THIRD EDITION

RAYMOND S. R. KU
Professor of Law
Co-Director, Center for Law, Technology and the Arts
Case Western Reserve University School of Law

JACQUELINE LIPTON
Professor of Law
Associate Dean for Faculty Development and Research
Co-Director, Center for Law, Technology and the Arts
Associate Director, Frederick K. Cox International Center
Case Western Reserve University School of Law

Wolters Kluwer
Law & Business

AUSTIN   BOSTON   CHICAGO   NEW YORK   THE NETHERLANDS

>
> Aspen Publishers
> Attn: Permissions Department
> 76 Ninth Avenue, 7th Floor
> New York, NY 10011-5201

To contact Customer Care, e-mail customer.care@aspenpublishers.com, call 1-800-234-1660, fax 1-800-901-9075, or mail correspondence to:

> Aspen Publishers
> Attn: Order Department
> PO Box 990
> Frederick, MD 21705

Printed in the United States of America.

1 2 3 4 5 6 7 8 9 0

ISBN 978-0-7355-8933-9

Library of Congress Cataloging-in-Publication Data

Ku, Raymond S. R., 1970-
    Cyberspace law : cases and materials / Raymond S.R. Ku, Jacqueline
Lipton. — 3rd ed.
        p. cm.
    Includes bibliographical references and index.
    ISBN 978-0-7355-8933-9 (alk. paper)
    1. Computer networks — Law and legislation — United States — Cases. 2.
Internet — Law and legislation — United States — Cases. I. Lipton,
Jacqueline D. II. Title.

KF390.5.C6K8 2010
343.7309'944 — dc22

                                                                    2010001866

About Wolters Kluwer Law & Business

Wolters Kluwer Law & Business is a leading provider of research information and workflow solutions in key specialty areas. The strengths of the individual brands of Aspen Publishers, CCH, Kluwer Law International and Loislaw are aligned within Wolters Kluwer Law & Business to provide comprehensive, in-depth solutions and expert-authored content for the legal, professional and education markets.

CCH was founded in 1913 and has served more than four generations of business professionals and their clients. The CCH products in the Wolters Kluwer Law & Business group are highly regarded electronic and print resources for legal, securities, antitrust and trade regulation, government contracting, banking, pension, payroll, employment and labor, and healthcare reimbursement and compliance professionals.

Aspen Publishers is a leading information provider for attorneys, business professionals and law students. Written by preeminent authorities, Aspen products offer analytical and practical information in a range of specialty practice areas from securities law and intellectual property to mergers and acquisitions and pension/benefits. Aspen's trusted legal education resources provide professors and students with high-quality, up-to-date and effective resources for successful instruction and study in all areas of the law.

Kluwer Law International supplies the global business community with comprehensive English-language international legal information. Legal practitioners, corporate counsel and business executives around the world rely on the Kluwer Law International journals, loose-leafs, books and electronic products for authoritative information in many areas of international legal practice.

Loislaw is a premier provider of digitized legal content to small law firm practitioners of various specializations. Loislaw provides attorneys with the ability to quickly and efficiently find the necessary legal information they need, when and where they need it, by facilitating access to primary law as well as state-specific law, records, forms and treatises.

Wolters Kluwer Law & Business, a unit of Wolters Kluwer, is headquartered in New York and Riverwoods, Illinois. Wolters Kluwer is a leading multinational publisher and information services company.

We wish to dedicate this book
to our respective families for their
love and support:

Melissa
Ronen
Nya

■

Patrick
Sean
Brianne

SUMMARY OF CONTENTS

Contents

4. CONTENT AS PROPERTY IN CYBERSPACE   271

PREFACE TO THE THIRD EDITION

Much has happened in the field of cyberlaw since the publication of the second edition. In particular, Web 2.0 technologies have emerged. This term is used to refer to the more participatory, user-generated nature of much that happens on the modern Internet. From social networking sites like Facebook, to blogs, wikis, and sophisticated multiplayer online games, more people are interacting with one another globally in forums very different from those that characterized the early Internet.

These technological developments raise significant new challenges for law and policy makers, both domestically and globally. Professor Lawrence Lessig's comments regarding the need to appreciate multimodal approaches to cyberspace regulation take on new significance in this context. Where legal regulation becomes more difficult in the context of virtual worlds and other online forums, more emphasis needs to be placed on other modes of regulation, including code, norms, and market forces. Importantly, however, lawyers need to understand how legal regulation interacts with these other modes of regulation in cyberspace, and how law can both shape and respond to online behavior.

While we have retained the basic framework of our previous editions, we have revised it in certain important respects with new technological developments in mind. We still maintain that the study of cyberspace law deals with the regulation of *information*, rather than of specific *technologies*. Thus, our approach to Web 2.0 technologies focuses on their impact on the regulation of information exchanged by online participants in new online forums. As in the previous editions, we also aim to assist students develop legal reasoning methodologies based on both doctrinal and non-doctrinal approaches to particular cyberspace problems. Thus, we have retained the structure of comparing "real world" cases to newer digital examples of legal regulation. However, in the context of the digital examples, we have supplemented early Internet cases with more recent problems involving newer technologies, such as sophisticated search engines, modern online payments systems, and online social networks. We have also updated the original problem sets and supplemented them with a new series of Web 2.0–focused problem sets. This enables students to compare issues arising in the early days of the Internet with more recent issues involving blogging and other more recent forms of online communication.

In terms of coverage, we have retained the structure of the previous editions in ranging through jurisdictional questions, free speech issues involving the Internet, property and intellectual property rights online, privacy issues online, and issues relating to the private ordering of cyberspace. We have broadened the scope of some of these issues by including new issues arising in recent cases both in the United States and in other jurisdictions. In particular, in Chapter 5 we have included some European and British cases dealing with online privacy rights. We have also extended the coverage of intellectual property issues by incorporating details of recent litigation relating to the use of trademarks and copyrights by search engines, by including in the patent coverage discussion of the recent *Bilski* litigation, and by adding updated material on *sui generis* online property rights. We have also revised the notes and comments sections throughout the text and provided new notes on trade secrets, net neutrality, and political cyberfraud.

The authors would like to thank Aspen's editorial staff for their hard work during the publication process on this edition. Barbara Roth and Troy Froebe deserve a special mention for all their efforts. We would also like to thank Case Western Reserve University School of Law and, in particular, the support and encouragement we received from Dean Gary Simson and, subsequently, from Interim Dean Robert Rawson.

Raymond S. R. Ku
Jacqueline D. Lipton

February 2010

PREFACE TO THE SECOND EDITION

"This instrument can teach, it can illuminate; yes, and it can even inspire, but it can do so only to the extent that humans are determined to use it to those ends. Otherwise it is merely wires and lights in a box."

Edwin R. Murrow

While Murrow was describing the emerging technology of his day — the television — his sentiments are equally applicable to the vast global network of the Internet, and our purpose is to introduce students to the ends that we may achieve and the means for achieving them. In approaching the second edition, we naturally had to ask ourselves what was new since the first edition. Did we agree that cyberspace law is still the study of the regulation of information in a world interlinked and moderated by computer networks as noted in the preface to the first edition? Moreover, are we today more or less convinced that cyberspace law is a distinct field of law, or is cyberlaw at least more of a law of the horse than it seemed in 2002?

Law of the horse or not, both of us remain convinced that there is a value to studying the regulation of information disseminated on an increasingly global scale over the Internet and other new global communications media. We still take the view that focusing on the regulation of *information* over these networks, rather than the regulation of specific *technologies*, is the appropriate way to approach this subject matter. As in the first edition, our focus here is to help students develop legal reasoning methodologies as well as doctrinal and nondoctrinal approaches to resolving specific kinds of problems in new contexts. We have retained the structure of comparing real world case examples to newer digital media examples to facilitate this process.

Again, we range through fields such as jurisdictional questions, issues relating to freedom of expression on the Internet, the development of property rights and specifically intellectual property rights within this medium, and varying attempts to privately order what might be defined as cyberspace. The second edition retains the basic structure of the first edition. However, we have included a number of new developments and perspectives.

The addition of Professor Lipton as a co-author brings a comparative and international flavor to the text, particularly in areas concerning the protection of digital data against unauthorized use both through intellectual property law and other legal means. Additionally, there have been a number of specific legislative and judicial developments since the first edition including a number of digital copyright cases such as MGM v. Grokster, Perfect 10 v. Google, Chamberlain v. Skylink, and Lexmark v. Static Control Components. The European Union Database Directive has undergone substantive critical review and Congress has introduced several new database protection bills, none of which have yet been enacted. The U.S. Supreme Court has ruled on several free speech issues, including the cases of Ashcroft v. ACLU and United States v. American Libraries Association.

We have retained and updated the narrative problem sets that were utilized in the first edition and updated the extensive Notes and Comments sections to facilitate class discussions. A number of professors have also used these problems and comments effectively to foster online discussions between classes.

The authors would like to thank Aspen's editorial staff for their hard work during the publication process as well as the anonymous reviewers who commented on the first edition. We would also like to thank our various research assistants for their contributions to the book and to Case School of Law and, in particular, the support and encouragement we received from Dean Gerald Korngold and subsequently from Dean Gary Simson.

Raymond S. R. Ku
Jacqueline D. Lipton

October 2006

PREFACE TO THE FIRST EDITION

This casebook is organized under the unifying principle that cyberspace law is the study of the regulation of information in a world interlinked and mediated by computer networks. Today, we live in a world in which information is increasingly distributed through computers rather than traditional mediums such as paper, broadcast, or film, and the interlinking of computers that make up the Internet has increased our ability to communicate and distribute information. Correspondingly, because information is distributed through computers capable of copying, filtering, or altering information, it is now possible to control and manipulate information at various levels throughout the network in ways and to an extent that were otherwise impossible or impractical.

While existing doctrines such as freedom of speech, intellectual property, and privacy are used as familiar doctrinal and theoretical starting points, cyberspace allows, and often requires, a re-examination of the values underlying those areas of law. This re-examination is necessary not only to translate those values into cyberspace applications, but to alter existing rules and legal institutions in real space as well. To give one example, the value of studying cyberspace law is not only about answering whether data stored in random access memory should be considered a copy under copyright law, but whether copyright protection or the control of information in any form is necessary in a world in which information can be perfectly reproduced and distributed globally at almost no expense.

Our approach to this subject matter differs significantly from the existing books on the market. We believe that the study of cyberspace law is fundamentally the study of the rules and norms governing the control and dissemination of information in a computer mediated world. While computers, routers, and fiber optics are all needed to make Internet communication possible, we have chosen not to rely upon technology or any particular substantive area of law to tie together what might otherwise appear to be unrelated cases. It is our belief that the characteristics of information transmission presented by computer mediated communications are what make Internet law unique and not the underlying technology, which is constantly changing. Moreover, this approach requires students not only to examine whether new technology requires the modification of existing contract or copyright law, it requires students to examine and question our existing conceptual and legal categorization of information problems into separate fields, such as freedom of speech, intellectual property, and privacy.

Given the pace at which Internet cases are decided and frequently overruled, one of the greatest challenges for a cyberspace law casebook is to keep the materials from becoming obsolete even before the book is published. Any approach that treats Internet-related cases under the traditional casebook formula (presenting the so-called majority position with some discussion of minority views) is especially susceptible to becoming rapidly outdated. How does one present the doctrine when the doctrine is still being developed? How does one hold a byte or an electron in one's hand? While some see this doctrinal indeterminacy as an obstacle or problem to be avoided by limiting the materials to include to those decisions that present black letter law, we embrace the indeterminacy.

Recognizing that the law is in a state of flux, we endeavored to organize our materials around the competing approaches and theories for any given issue rather than so-called current leading cases. This approach has several important pedagogical benefits. First, by emphasizing the competing theories offered by different courts, different jurisdictions, scholars, and policymakers, this approach provides students with the necessary foundation for handling the next generation of legal controversies in an area of law where the only guaranty is that the technology and case law will change. Second, this organization allows professors the flexibility to present the materials from the perspectives of legislative/policy making, private regulation and bargaining, judicial doctrine, or some combination. Lastly, this organization facilitates the development of advanced legal reasoning and argument by requiring students to confront and employ both doctrinal and nondoctrinal authorities in an effort to resolve legal problems.

In addition to principal materials and explanatory text throughout the casebook, materials are presented with narrative problems. We have found that many students find it beneficial to approach materials from the perspective of addressing a "real world" problem rather than reading materials in the abstract. The problems further reinforce the idea that these materials are tools and not answers.

The authors would like to thank Aspen's editorial staff for their assistance and patience in seeing this project through to completion, and the various outside reviewers whose comments and criticisms helped make this a better book. We would also like to thank our various research assistants for their contributions to the casebook. Professors Ku and Farber would like to say a special thank you to Seton Hall Law School and to Richard Mixter for his faith in this project.

Raymond S. R. Ku
Michele A. Farber
Arthur J. Cockfield

April 2002

ACKNOWLEDGMENTS

Barlow, John Perry, Cyberspace Declaration of Independence, 1996.

Barron, Jerome A., Access to the Press—A New First Amendment Right, 80 Harv. L. Rev. 1641 (1967). Copyright © 1967 by Harvard Law Review. Reprinted by permission.

Boyle, James, Focault in Cyberspace: Surveillance, Sovereignty, and Hardwired Censors, 66 U. Cin. L. Rev. 177 (1997). Copyright © 1997 by University of Cincinnati Law Review. Reprinted by permission.

Branscomb, Ann W., Anonymity, Autonomy and Accountability: Challenges to the First Amendment in Cyberspace, 104 Yale L.J. 1639 (1995). Copyright © 1995 by Yale Law Journal. Reprinted by permission.

Burk, Dan, The Trouble with Trespass, 4 J. Small & Emerging Bus. L. 27 (2000). Copyright © 2000 by the Journal of Small & Emerging Business Law. Reprinted by permission.

Cohen, Julie E., Examined Lives: Informational Privacy and the Subject as Object, 52 Stan. L. Rev. 1373, 1406-08 (2000). Copyright © 2000 by Stanford Law Review. Reprinted by permission.

Easterbrook, Frank H., Cyberspace and the Law of the Horse, 1996 U. Chi. Legal F. 20, 207 (1996). Copyright © 1996 by University of Chicago Law Review. Reprinted by permission.

Froomkin, Michael A., The Metaphor is the Key: Cryptography, the Clipper Ship and the Constitution, 143 U. Pa. L. Rev. 709, 7.81 (1995). Copyright © 1995 by University of Pennsylvania Law Review and Michael A. Froomkin. Reprinted by permission.

Froomkin, Michael A., Wrong Turn in Cyberspace: Using ICANN to Route Around the APA and the Constitution, 50 Duke L.J. 17 (2000). Copyright © 2000 by Duke Law Journal and Michael A. Froomkin. Reprinted by permission.

Goldsmith, Jack L., Against Cyberanarchy, 65 U. Chi. L. Rev. 1199 (1998). Copyright © 1998 by University of Chicago Law Review. Reprinted by permission.

Hunter, Dan, Cyberspace as Place and the Tragedy of the Digital Anticommons, 91 Cal. L. Rev. 17 (2003). Copyright © 2003 by the California Law Review, Inc. Reprinted from California Law Review Vol. 91, No. 2, by permission of the Regents of the University of California.

Johnson and Post, Law and Borders—The Rise of Law in Cyberspace, 48 Stan. L. Rev. 1367 (1996). Copyright © 1996 by Stanford Law Review. Reprinted by permission.

Kang, Jerry, Information Privacy in Cyberspace Transactions, 50 Stan. L. Rev. 1193 (1998). Copyright © 1998 by Stanford Law Review. Reprinted by permission.

Kerr, Orin S., The Fourth Amendment in Cyberspace, Can Encryption Create a Reasonable Expectation of Privacy?, 33 Conn. L. Rev. 503 (2001). Copyright © 2001 by Connecticut Law Review. Reprinted by permission.

Ku, Raymond S., Forward: A Brave New Cyberworld?, 22 T. Jefferson L. Rev. 125 (2000). Copyright © 2000 by Thomas Jefferson Law Review. Reprinted by Permission.

Ku, Raymond S., Irreconcilable Differences? Congressional Treatment of Internet Service Providers as Speakers, 3 Van. J. Ent. Law & Prac. 70 (2001). Copyright © 2001 by Raymond S. Ku and Vanderbilt Journal of Entertainment Law & Practice. Reprinted by permission.

Ku, Raymond S., Open Internet Access and Freedom of Speech: A First Amendment Catch-22, and originally published in 75 Tul. L. Rev. 87-135 (2000). Reprinted with the permission of the Tulane Law Review Association, which holds the copyright.

Ku, Raymond S., Think Twice Before You Type, 163 N.J. L.J. 23 (2001). Copyright © NL IP Company. Reprinted with permission. This article was first published in the February 19, 2001, issue of the New Jersey Law Journal. Further duplication without permission is prohibited. All rights reserved.

Lessig, Lawrence, The Law of the Horse: What Cyberlaw Might Teach, 113 Harv. L. Rev. 501 (1999). Copyright © 1999 by Harvard Law Review. Reprinted by permission.

Lessig, Lawrence, The Limits in Open Code: Regulatory Standards and the Future of the Net, 14 Berkeley Tech. L. J., 759, 764-766 (1999). Copyright © 1999 by Berkeley Technical Law Journal. Reprinted by permission.

Murphy, Richard S., Property Rights in Personal Information: An Economic Defense of Privacy, 84 Geo. L.J. 2381, 2382 (1996). Reprinted with permission of the publisher, Georgetown Law Journal © 1996.

Rotenberg, Marc, Fair Information Practices and the Architecture of Privacy (What Larry Doesn't Get), 2001 Stan. Tech. L. Rev. 1, 72-89 (2001). Copyright © 2001 by Stanford Law Review. Reprinted by permission.

Samuelson, Pamela, The Copyright Grab, Wired (Jan. 1996). Copyright © 1996 by Conde Nast and Pamela Samuelson. Reprinted by permission. Courtesy of The Conde-Nast Publications Inc.

Schwartz, Paul, Privacy and Democracy in Cyberspace, 52 Vand. L. Rev. 1609, 1620 (1999). Copyright © 1999 by Vanderbilt Law Review. Reprinted by permission.

Solove, Daniel J., Privacy and Power: Computer Databases and Metaphors for Informational Privacy, 53 Stan. L. Rev. 1393, 1397-98 (2001). Copyright © 2001 by Stanford Law Review. Reprinted by permission.

Tien, Lee, Publishing Software as a Speech Act, 15 Berkeley Tech L. J. 629, 665-686 (2000). Copyright © 2000 by Lee Tien. Reprinted by permission.

CYBERSPACE LAW

1

INTRODUCTION TO THE STUDY OF CYBERSPACE LAW

As with any course, we must begin with the question: Why study this subject matter? Is it worth studying? What do we hope to gain? This is especially true with respect to cyberspace law because not only is the area relatively new, but it is constantly changing and evolving. This section begins by providing an overview of how the Internet works. This overview is deliberately short and general. The study of cyberspace law does not require a detailed understanding of computer or telecommunications technology. Like the study of law in general, the focus is on how society is responding and should respond to certain activities and events. This section then introduces the reader to three of the principal approaches to the question of why study cyberspace law, and concludes by introducing the reader to the approach taken by this casebook.

A. INTERNET BASICS

RAYMOND SHIH RAY KU
OPEN INTERNET ACCESS AND FREEDOM OF SPEECH:
A FIRST AMENDMENT CATCH-22

75 Tul. L. Rev. 87 (2000)

In essence, the Internet is simply a collection of computers, a network, in which the computers are capable of communicating with each other. What makes the Internet special is its reach as the largest network in the world. . . . Through this network you can send e-mail to friends and colleagues, do research, play computer games with people from around the world, shop, read the *New York Times*, listen to radio stations, and watch video programming. All of this is made possible by shared communication protocols, such as the Transmission Control Protocol (TCP) and Internet Protocol (IP) or

1

TCP/IP, which allows information to be transmitted quickly from computer to computer and the hardware that links the computers together.

1. TCP/IP PROTOCOLS

The TCP/IP protocols break down information transmitted to the Internet into packets and reassemble it at its destination. This allows the Internet to operate as a packet-switched network where the various data packets may travel different routes to reach the same destination. This design allows information to be transmitted through the Internet at faster speeds than circuit-switched networks [like a traditional telephone line], where, once a connection is made, that part of the network is dedicated only to that connection. [Packet-switched networks monopolize available wire space only for the time it takes to transmit the individual packet of information. Originally designed by the United States military as a means of communicating in the event of war, transmitting information in packets is a more efficient method of using the telecommunications infrastructure and makes it possible for information to travel from sender to recipient even if portions of the network are blocked or even destroyed.]

2. THE HARDWARE LINKS

As the Internet exists today, one cannot simply plug a personal computer into the Internet through a telephone or cable line any more than one can obtain telephone or cable television service by plugging a telephone into an outlet or hooking your television up to coaxial cable. Just as you contract with the telephone or cable company for telephone and cable service, to connect to the Internet you must have an ISP. Currently, four different groups provide the vast majority of Americans with access to the Internet: federal, state, and local governments; schools; private employers; and private service providers. While government, businesses, and schools provide many individuals with access outside of the home, most do not provide service to the general public or to residential users, who must contract with a private provider. Understanding why an Internet service provider is necessary requires a brief explanation of the Internet's architecture and the method by which information is transmitted across this global network of networks.

Accessing the full resources of the Internet from a personal computer requires passing through multiple layers of hardware and telecommunications services. Imagine you are sending a friend an e-mail. First, you must prepare the e-mail on your personal computer or handheld device, and that device must typically be connected to a local area network (LAN). The connection can be established either through local wiring, as in an office, or through telephone, cable, or similar services to a local ISP. When connecting through an ISP, the ISP acts as your LAN. Once connected to the LAN, your computer interacts with the LAN's internal router/server, a more powerful computer and switching device capable of interacting with the multiple computers in a LAN simultaneously and translating different data formats. The server acts as a repository for various data and applications that allow the user to send and retrieve information on the Internet. In the case of e-mail, the server translates your e-mail through the TCP/IP protocol and sends it as various data packets. The LAN's server, in turn, must be connected to a router. Routers connect networks and direct the flow of data on the Internet. The router looks at the Internet addresses in the data packets and sends them on the best path to the recipient.

Through routers, LANs are connected into midlevel networks or regional networks. To communicate with other LANs, each LAN must be linked together through privately leased communication services such as telephone lines, T1 lines, Integrated Services Digital Network (ISDN) lines, Digital Subscriber Lines (DSL), coaxial cable, satellite, microwave, or fiber-optic cable. These types of connections are often leased from local exchange carriers such as Pacific Bell or MCI WorldCom. If the recipient of your e-mail is within the midlevel network, a router or series of routers delivers the e-mail message to the recipient's local network server where it is reassembled and eventually downloaded onto the recipient's personal computer. If the recipient is outside the midlevel network, the data packets are sent to a Network Access Point (NAP) where they are sent along high-speed backbones, capable of transmitting data at speeds of 155 Mbps (megabits per second) and higher, to another NAP and regional network, either across the country or around the world. Consequently, what people think of as the Internet is, in reality, computer equipment and telecommunications connections representing three different layers of networks.

Given the multiple layers of the Internet, it may already be apparent that in order to access what people commonly think of as the Internet one must have access to all three layers of networks: local, regional, and national/international. More importantly, given the current architecture, access fees are inescapable. Individual users must pay an ISP to be connected to a local network. Local ISPs must pay regional ISPs, such as MidWestnet or East-Coastnet, for connecting at the regional level, and regional ISPs must pay National Backbone Providers (NBPs) such as MCI WorldCom or PSINet for national and international access. While some users — for example, universities and large corporations — avoid local ISP fees by purchasing the necessary equipment, such as a router and a modem pool, thereby becoming their own ISPs, they must ultimately pay to tap into a regional ISP. Similarly, while regional ISPs may avoid paying fees to NBPs by tapping into NAPs directly, they must then pay the NAP, which is typically run by a Regional Bell Operating Company. Therefore, given the Internet's current topography, tolls on the information superhighway are unavoidable.

In addition to the limitations upon access imposed by the Internet's architecture, access to the Internet is limited by the technology used to transmit data and connect us to the Internet. Typically, the computers and computer networks of the Internet are physically connected together through copper wire, coaxial cable, or fiber optics. Computers can also be connected through a variety of technologies that do not require direct physical connections. The type of connection between computers and networks determines the maximum speed at which information may be transmitted. For example, regular telephone lines typically transmit data at a maximum of 56 Kbps (kilobits per second). Special leased telephone lines are capable of transmitting data at even higher speeds. For example, ISDN lines can carry data at 128 Kbps and DSL can carry data at 1.5 Mbps; T1 lines can carry data at 1.5 Mbps and T3 lines can carry data at 44 Mbps; and fiber-optic cable can carry data at 600 Mbps. Similarly, cable typically transmits data at 3 Mbps. In the near future, high-speed wireless systems promise data speeds up to 100 Mbps.

[W]hat do these differences in speed mean in practical terms? The bandwidth available to a residential user influences both Internet performance and function. In short, downloading the latest version of AOL with a traditional telephone line and 56 Kpbs modem takes approximately one hour. In contrast, with a high-speed T1 line or cable modem running at 1.5 Mbps, it would only take two minutes to download the same software. The speed of data transmission translates, therefore, into the amount of time someone must spend on-line to perform even the simplest of functions such as retrieving e-mail. Additionally, bandwidth translates into more types of informational services practically available to the residential user. At slower rates of transmission, while it is possible to change webpages, download video and music, or watch streaming programming, the process can be painfully slow, making it either unappealing or practically impossible. In contrast, the high-speed data transmission promised by cable and other services makes it possible for information providers to deliver true multimedia programming. With high-speed access, individuals can change webpages as easily as changing channels on a television. They can communicate with loved ones through telephony with audio and real-time video. Broadband Internet access would permit us to watch the latest CNN report without purchasing a special video card, listen to radio stations outside their areas of service, or download the latest hit movie for home viewing in a matter of minutes. In short, broadband technology has the potential to radically transform the ways in which we receive, send, and manipulate information.

In its current form, the Internet's infrastructure and packet-switched design carry information regardless of the computer operating system used or the applications involved. This means that computers operating under different operating systems from Palm OS to Microsoft Windows to Linux can all be linked together. Similarly, the Internet is not designed to run any particular application. Applications are the computer programs that we use to access the Internet for activities including World Wide Web surfing, e-mail,

Internet telephony, or interactive games. The Internet's open design means that anyone may write a program capable of using the Internet to share, transmit, or manipulate data. Finally, the Internet's current architecture also permits access across a wide array of platforms from supercomputers to personal computers and from electronic book readers to smartphones.

For detailed discussions of the origins of the Internet or for further explanations of how the Internet works see Preston Gralla, *How the Internet Works* (Millennium Edition, 2002); Barry M. Leiner et al., *A Brief History of the Internet*, at *http://www.isoc.org/internet/history/brief.shtml*; David Post, *In Search of Jefferson's Moose: Notes on the Study of Cyberspace*, at 24-30 (2009).

In recent years, while the basic operation of the Internet has remained unchanged, the technologies utilized for transmitting information at ever greater speeds have developed at a rapid pace, causing issues for regulators of telecommunications and related services, such as the Federal Communications Commission. For a recent discussion of these developments, both technological and regulatory, see Daniel Spulber & Christopher Yoo, *Rethinking Broadband Internet Access*, 22 Harv. J.L. & Tech. 1 (2008).

B. The Study of Cyberspace Law

Because the Internet is a medium for communication, should one study "Internet Law" or should one study courses like contracts, property, and torts and explore how the doctrines developed in those "substantive" fields apply to this new technology? Is there such a thing as Internet or cyberspace law? What does the study of cyberspace law have to offer?

FRANK H. EASTERBROOK
CYBERSPACE AND THE LAW OF THE HORSE

1996 U. Chi. Legal F. 207

When he was dean of this law school, Gerhard Casper was proud that the University of Chicago did not offer a course in "The Law of the Horse." He did not mean by this that Illinois specializes in grain rather than livestock. His point, rather, was that "Law and . . ." courses should be limited to subjects that could illuminate the entire law. . . .

. . . We are at risk of multidisciplinary dilettantism, or, as one of my mentors called it, the cross-sterilization of ideas. Put together two fields about which you know little and get the worst of both worlds. . . . Beliefs lawyers hold about computers, and predictions they make about new technology, are highly likely to be false. . . . The blind are not good trailblazers.

Dean Casper's remark had a second meaning—that the best way to learn the law applicable to specialized endeavors is to study general rules. Lots of cases deal with sales of horses; others deal with people kicked by horses; still more deal with the licensing and racing of horses, or with the care veterinarians give to horses, or with prizes at horse shows. Any effort to collect these strands into a course on "The Law of the Horse" is doomed to be shallow and to miss unifying principles. Teaching 100 percent of the cases on people kicked by horses will not convey the law of torts very well. Far better for most students—better, even, for those who plan to go into the horse trade—to take courses in property, torts, commercial transactions, and the like, adding to the diet of horse cases a smattering of transactions in cucumbers, cats, coal, and cribs. Only by putting the law of the horse in the context of broader rules about commercial endeavors could one really understand the law about horses.

Now you can see the meaning of my title. When asked to talk about "Property in Cyberspace," my immediate reaction was, "Isn't this just the law of the horse?" I don't know much about cyberspace; what I do know will be outdated in five years (if not five months!); and my predictions about the direction of change are worthless, making any effort to tailor the law to the subject futile. And if I did know something about computer networks, all I could do in discussing "Property in Cyberspace" would be to isolate the subject from the rest of the law of intellectual property, making the assessment weaker. . . .

Well, then, what can we do? By and large, nothing. If you don't know what is best, let people make their own arrangements.

Next after nothing is: keep doing what you have been doing. Most behavior in cyberspace is easy to classify under current property principles. . . . What else is there to do? I offer three themes.

1. Make rules clearer, to promote bargains. "We" don't know what is best, but in a Coasean world the affected parties will by their actions establish what is best.

The federal government's Working Group on Intellectual Property Rights recently issued a report called Intellectual Property and the National Information Infrastructure. In addition to the pompous title and the standard drumbeat of calls for more studies, this report contains a few concrete proposals. One, which I gather is controversial, is to amend the Copyright Act to beef up the distribution right. The Working Group recommends that the law recognize that dissemination of copyrighted works via electronic transmission is one of the rights the copyright proprietor possesses.

One may say in response that this change gives too much to the copyright proprietor or restricts unduly the ability to disseminate works. Some people believe that copyright proprietors should be delighted to have a throng willing to transmit their works to consumers who will pay royalties for them (as a recipient clearly must do—for they get a copy whether or not a transmission is a "distribution" of the work). Perhaps so; but if this is so, the author or owner will permit the transmission, just as song writers license the transmission of their works over the radio to people who may choose to turn on their tape recorders. An author could give this permission at large, while retaining the right to charge for the keeping of copies.

Simply put, it is awfully hard to know what the optimal compensation package for authors is, unless the property rights are clear. If something about the nature of cyberspace has made application of the distribution right cloudy, then by all means clear it up again, so that people may make their own arrangements. And on balance it is best to give these rights to authors. Why? Because if the best arrangement turns out to be free distribution, then private transactions may produce this result when the statute assigns the rights to authors; but if the best arrangement turns out to be some fee for distribution and a lower price for copying, it is extremely hard to reach this state of affairs if the statute cancels the distribution right. Private transactions could shift the right back to authors only if the parties have contractual relations (for example, patrons of the opera may agree not to tape the performances). We must bear in mind the high possibility of error in the original specification of entitlements — a risk especially high in a legislative world dominated by interest-group politics. (The copy law contains a special provision for agricultural fairs and exhibitions, still another allusion to the law of the horse!) The risk of error should lead to initial assignments that are easy to reverse, so that people may find their own way with the least interference.

2. Create property rights, where now there are none — again to make bargains possible.

Property rights in domain names is an example of what I have in mind. Until recently, domain names on the Internet were assigned by the government (rather, by a firm under contract to do the government's bidding). Allocation was first-come, first-served, with no effort to purge unused names. That led to people storing up domain names. Intellectual-property law rightly has been hostile to such maneuvers. Domain names have some of the attributes of trademarks; but one can't get a trademark by just filing. A firm must use a mark to obtain rights in it; must use the mark continuously; and once this occurs, latecomers stand behind it in line. Similarly, corporate names are registered with the states, and new arrivals cannot duplicate existing names.

The allocation of domain names is now in private hands, and the $50 annual fee will abate the snatch-and-grab incentive to a limited degree. But the allocation of names remains first-come, first-served, with the result that people lay claims to famous corporate and political names. Today you can point your browser to www.clinton96.org and find, not the home page for the Clinton reelection campaign, but a satire of that campaign, with a big picture of the President holding up one finger and a caption claiming that he has a single accomplishment — election. Dick Tuck has come to cyberspace. This is nonpartisan harassment: www.dole96.org also is a satire page.

Property rights need to be better specified than that. Appropriation of names and trademarks would not be tolerated in the rest of the commercial or political world; why so for Internet addresses? In other words, we need to bring the Internet into the world of property law. I grant that, with search facilities, you can find the American Broadcasting Corporation even if someone else has www.abc.com. Nodes are in the end numbers, and conversion to letters is arbitrary. But the search process is costly and can be avoided by correct allocation in the first place.

By "correct" allocation I certainly do not mean allocation according to some government formula. We have tried that approach with broadcast licenses, and it has failed. Indeed, even in the world of over-the-air communications, the Federal Communications Commission has moved in the direction Ronald Coase and Leo Herzel pointed in the 1950s: sell frequencies at auctions. So it can be with domain names. Let people bid for symbols, then sell them in a developed aftermarket. Perhaps initial allocations could be made by corporate names or product trademarks. Details are far less important than the principle that it is important to establish property rights, without which welfare-increasing bargains cannot occur. . . .

3. Create bargaining institutions.

Computers offer many opportunities to do, at next to no cost, the sort of thing the Copyright Clearance Center has tried and failed to do for photocopies. Consider, for example, the question whether a publisher of content on the Internet wants to authorize the making of copies and, if so, the making of copies that can be recopied, or a single copy for use on a local computer. Or does the publisher only want to authorize viewing on screen? All are logical possibilities, each rational for some authors, or for any given author at different times. How is it possible to specify which is which, and to collect payment? — especially in a world where Netscape Navigator is making cache copies behind everyone's back and turning all of you into persistent infringers!

The answer, it seems to me, is a convention—a protocol under which each file contains its own instructions on this question, and programs know how to interpret them. You are familiar with such conventions. When your modem calls a remote modem, the two devices engage in elaborate interrogation to discover what speed to use and what compression and error-correction algorithms are in place. An international standards-setting organization agreed on the language; private firms all over the world have decided whether, and to what extent, to use this agreed language for communications. Some firms have come up with their own extensions, outside the organization's framework. Encryption technology is similar. You may notice that when Netscape enters a particular corner of the web, a solid key appears in the lower left of the screen; this shows that the client and the server have agreed on an encryption protocol, securing the session.

There are several available protocols. So can it be with copying. A standards-setting organization could prescribe, say, twenty different copying rules—sets of permission and payment terms. There could be competing organizations, with their own standards. Each Internet server and client would understand these terms and carry out the negotiation automatically, remitting any payment to an agreed depository by secure methods. . . .

A quick summary: Error in legislation is common, and never more so than when the technology is galloping forward. Let us not struggle to match an imperfect legal system to an evolving world that we understand poorly. Let us instead do what is essential to permit the participants in this evolving world to make their own decisions. That means three things: make rules clear; create property rights where now there are none; and facilitate the formation of bargaining institutions. Then let the world of cyberspace evolve as it will, and enjoy the benefits.

LAWRENCE LESSIG
THE LAW OF THE HORSE:
WHAT CYBERLAW MIGHT TEACH

113 Harv. L. Rev. 501 (1999)

[Judge] Easterbrook's concern is a fair one. Courses in law school, Easterbrook argued, "should be limited to subjects that could illuminate the entire law." "[T]he best way to learn the law applicable to specialized endeavors," he argued, "is to study general rules." This "the law of cyberspace," conceived of as torts in cyberspace, contracts in cyberspace, property in cyberspace, etc., was not.

My claim is to the contrary. I agree that our aim should be courses that "illuminate the entire law," but unlike Easterbrook, I believe that there is an important general point that comes from thinking in particular about how law and cyberspace connect.

This general point is about the limits on law as a regulator and about the techniques for escaping those limits. This escape, both in real space and in cyberspace, comes from recognizing the collection of tools that a society has at hand for affecting constraints upon behavior. Law in its traditional sense — an order backed by a threat directed at primary behavior — is just one of these tools. The general point is that law can affect these other tools — that they constrain behavior themselves, and can function as tools of the law. The choice among tools obviously depends upon their efficacy. But importantly, the choice will also raise a question about values. By working through these examples of law interacting with cyberspace, we will throw into relief a set of general questions about law's regulation outside of cyberspace.

I do not argue that any specialized area of law would produce the same insight. I am not defending the law of the horse. My claim is specific to cyberspace. We see something when we think about the regulation of cyberspace that other areas would not show us. . . .

Many believe that cyberspace simply cannot be regulated. Behavior in cyberspace, this meme insists, is beyond government's reach. The anonymity and multi-jurisdictionality of cyberspace makes control by government in cyberspace impossible. The nature of the space makes behavior there unregulable.

This belief about cyberspace is wrong, but wrong in an interesting way. It assumes either that the nature of cyberspace is fixed — that its architecture, and the control it enables, cannot be changed — or that government cannot take steps to change this architecture.

Neither assumption is correct. Cyberspace has no nature; it has no particular architecture that cannot be changed. Its architecture is a function of its design — or, as I will describe it in the section that follows, its code. This code can change, either because it evolves in a different way, or because government or business pushes it to evolve in a particular way. And while particular versions of cyberspace do resist effective regulation, it does not follow that every version of cyberspace does so as well. Or alternatively, there are versions of cyberspace where behavior can be regulated, and the government can take steps to increase this regulability.

To see just how, we should think more broadly about the question of regulation. What does it mean to say that someone is "regulated"? How is that regulation achieved? What are its modalities? . . .

FOUR MODALITIES OF REGULATION IN REAL SPACE AND CYBERSPACE

Behavior, we might say, is regulated by four kinds of constraints. Law is just one of those constraints. Law (in at least one of its aspects) orders people to behave in certain ways; it threatens punishment if they do not obey. The law tells me not to buy certain drugs, not to sell cigarettes without a license, and not to trade across international borders without first filing a customs form. It promises strict punishments if these orders are not followed. In this way, we say that law regulates.

But not only law regulates in this sense. Social norms do as well. Norms control where I can smoke; they affect how I behave with members of the opposite sex; they limit what I may wear; they influence whether I will pay my taxes. Like law, norms regulate by threatening punishment ex post. But unlike law, the punishments of norms are not centralized. Norms are enforced (if at all) by a community, not by a government. In this way, norms constrain, and therefore regulate.

Markets, too, regulate. They regulate by price. The price of gasoline limits the amount one drives — more so in Europe than in the United States. The price of subway tickets affects the use of public transportation — more so in Europe than in the United States. Of course the market is able to constrain in this manner only because of other constraints of law and social norms: property and contract law govern markets; markets operate within the domain permitted by social norms. But given these norms, and given this law, the market presents another set of constraints on individual and collective behavior.

And finally, there is a fourth feature of real space that regulates behavior — "architecture." By "architecture" I mean the physical world as we find it, even if "as we find it" is simply how it has already been made. That a highway divides two neighborhoods limits the extent to which the neighborhoods integrate. That a town has a square, easily accessible with a diversity of shops, increases the integration of residents in that town. That Paris has large boulevards limits the ability of revolutionaries to protest. That the Constitutional Court in Germany is in Karlsruhe, while the capital is in Berlin, limits the influence of one branch of government over the other. These constraints function in a way that shapes behavior. In this way, they too regulate.

Norms regulate behavior in cyberspace as well: talk about democratic politics in the alt.knitting newsgroup, and you open yourself up to "flaming" (an angry, text-based response). "Spoof" another's identity in a "MUD" (a text-based virtual reality), and you may find yourself "toaded" (your character removed). Talk too much on a discussion list, and you are likely to wind up on a common "bozo" filter (blocking messages from you). In each case norms constrain behavior, and, as in real space, the threat of ex post (but decentralized) sanctions enforce these norms.

Markets regulate behavior in cyberspace too. Price structures often constrain access, and if they do not, then busy signals do. (America Online (AOL) learned this lesson when it shifted from an hourly to a flat-rate pricing plan.) Some sites on the web charge for access, as on-line services like AOL have for some time. Advertisers reward popular sites; on-line services drop unpopular forums. These behaviors are all a function of market constraints and market opportunity, and they all reflect the regulatory role of the market.

And finally the architecture of cyberspace, or its code, regulates behavior in cyberspace. The code, or the software and hardware that make cyberspace the way it is, constitutes a set of constraints on how one can behave. The substance of these constraints varies — cyberspace is not one place. But what distinguishes the architectural constraints from other constraints is how they are experienced. As with the constraints of architecture in real space — railroad tracks that divide neighborhoods, bridges that block the access of buses, constitutional courts located miles from the seat of the government — they are experienced as conditions on one's access to areas of cyberspace. The conditions, however, are different. In some places, one must enter a password before one gains access; in other places, one can enter whether identified or not. In some places, the transactions that one engages in produce traces, or "mouse droppings," that link the transactions back to the individual; in other places, this link is achieved only if the individual consents. In some places, one can elect to speak a language that only the recipient can understand (through encryption); in other places, encryption is not an option. Code sets these features; they are features selected by code writers; they constrain some behavior (for example, electronic eavesdropping) by making other behavior possible (encryption). They embed certain values, or they make the realization of certain values impossible. In this sense, these features of cyberspace also regulate, just as architecture in real space regulates.

These four constraints — both in real space and in cyberspace — operate together. For any given policy, their interaction may be cooperative, or competitive. Thus, to understand how a regulation might succeed, we must view these four modalities as acting on the same field, and understand how they interact.

RAYMOND KU
FOREWORD: A BRAVE NEW CYBERWORLD?

22 T. Jefferson L. Rev. 125 (2000)

[C]yberspace is here, and it falls upon this generation to explore and understand what has been called the electronic frontier.

Equating cyberspace with an electronic frontier invokes a mythology deeply ingrained in this Nation's collective imagination and character. As Frederick Jackson Turner recognized, the frontier, as a metaphor and reality, played an important role in this Nation's early history and development. The dictionary defines frontier as "[a] region just beyond or at the edge of a settled area," or "[a]n undeveloped area or field for discovery or research." The American West and outer space clearly fit the former definition while the human genome project clearly fits the latter. With respect to the Internet, many have argued that cyberspace is in fact a region just beyond real space. According to this school of thought, the Internet is not only a place, it is many different places. As a place, it has its own rules and some have suggested should have its own sovereignty.

We are asked to accept a description of cyberspace as a world much like the one depicted in the science fiction movie The Matrix, a computer generated world where human beings interact with one another just as they do in the real world, but through the filters of technology. In the Matrix, one experiences emotions such as pain, joy, and sadness, participates in activities such as work, study, and recreation, and lives life indistinguishable from life in the real world. If you die in the Matrix, you die in the real world. In fact, the movie's premise is that human beings are tricked into believing that the computer generated virtual world is the real world. While it may be that someday we will generate virtual realities that not only have a psychic but a physical effect upon us, that day is not yet upon us.

Moreover, cyberspace is more than email, the World Wide Web or the world between the wires; it encompasses the ever-present mingling of technology in our everyday lives as well, an ever growing real world mediated by microprocessors — a cyberworld. From smart credit cards which tell stores not only whether we can make the purchase but what we have purchased in the past, to cellular telephones that allow us to reach out to anyone around the world while making it possible for others to reach us, to on-board automobile navigation systems that help us to find a friend's home and which also allow others to track our movements, to home security systems that not only sound an alarm when someone tries to enter the home, but allow us to turn lights on and off from remote locations, we live in a world increasingly interconnected by technology. Accordingly even if cyberspace is its own place, it is also increasingly part of the cyberworld of real space. Fortunately, to appreciate its impact upon our society in general and our law in particular, it does not matter whether cyberspace should be treated as a place or not. It is not what cyberspace is (especially since cyberspace changes quicker than pundits can write), but what cyberspace and our cyberworld represent that matters.

What does the electronic frontier represent? In his seminal work, Frederick Jackson Turner described the value of the frontier in American life as much more than the addition of new territory or the exploration of a new body of knowledge. According to Turner, "[w]hat the Mediterranean Sea was to the Greeks, breaking the bond of custom, offering new experiences, calling out new institutions and activities, that and more, the ever retreating frontier has been to the United States." Like the American frontier of the 19th century, therefore, cyberspace is important because is represents an opportunity to examine and perhaps to reinvent ourselves and our society. Cyberspace presents us with an opportunity to break the bonds of existing law and customs, to create new institutions, and yes, to create new experiences.

As lawyers, judges, lawmakers, and scholars we have an obligation to examine the law and cyberspace and to take part in the discourse on how our cyberworld will be regulated. While Judge Easterbrook is clearly right that this effort requires a general understanding of the laws of intellectual property, antitrust, or the First Amendment, I disagree with his conclusion that the study of cyberspace does not "illuminate the entire law." With each inevitable controversy involving the Internet, the law is forced to confront cyberspace on two levels. On one level, we will be asked such questions as: what real space rules and legal regimes, if any, should be applied to cyberspace? Do the issues arising from cyber-conflicts fit into existing regimes or must new rules and perhaps new institutions be created to resolve these cyber-conflicts? At this level, we are asked to translate where possible our existing values and legal principles into values and principles applicable to cyberspace. While some like Judge Easterbrook may find these problems rather mundane or argue that this process of translation is not unique to cyberspace, few would consider them simple. For example, does the use of a meta-tag represent the use of a trademark? Is the process and code of one click shopping entitled to patent protection? Are Internet service providers public accommodations? Are the free speech rights of ISPs violated by regulations requiring open access? While the answer to these questions depends upon a thorough understanding of existing legal doctrine, that understanding must still be applied to a technology that many still do not comprehend and which may not fit into existing paradigms. As Judge Buckwalter recognized in American Civil Liberties Union v. Reno, in cyberspace "even commonly understood terms may have different connotations or parameters. . . ." Consequently, even skilled practitioners and legal experts may find themselves through the proverbial looking glass when it comes to applying existing law to the new and rapidly changing cyberworld.

More importantly, pioneering our cyberworld and determining the rules and laws that will govern, forces us to examine our pre-cyberworld rules as well as our commitment to the values that form the foundation for those laws. As a new frontier, cyberspace, like the Western frontier, reopens "the debate over values that always precede the formation of principles and always infuses the effort to implement and interpret" law and legal principles. In other words, before we can coherently apply existing law to the challenges posed by cyberspace, we must resolve conflicting values and clarify the latent ambiguities that justify existing legal rules. In so doing, we may ultimately be forced to alter the laws of real space in light of our new understanding. For example, in order to resolve whether data mining violates consumer privacy, we must understand the values protected by current real space privacy laws. By the time we reach consensus on the values these laws are meant to uphold, we may ultimately conclude that the existing rules must be discarded as inconsistent with those values. Our concerns today about invasion of privacy in cyberspace, therefore, may not represent anything unique to cyberspace, but instead reflect our discomfort and concern over the loss of privacy in real space. By creating new activities and experiences, cyberspace sheds new light on old conflicts demanding their resolution. Accordingly, the resolution of these value conflicts will have an impact that extends far beyond the borders of cyberspace. As we take part in the discourse over how cyberspace should be regulated, we will ultimately come to better understand how real space should be regulated as well.

COMMENTS AND QUESTIONS

1. Is Easterbrook's assumption that lawyers do not understand technology, and, therefore, that they are "blind" trailblazers accurate? To what extent does this represent a generational gap? If it is purely a generational gap, can we expect to see this changing over time?

2. Even if Easterbrook's assumption is correct with respect to some lawyers, does it matter? Is a Nobel Prize in computer science (or economics for that matter) necessary before one can study a body of law from a multi-disciplinary perspective?

3. Must every course illuminate the study of law in general? For example, to what degree does a course in property illuminate the entire law? Is property law merely a compilation of separate legal doctrines that all revolve around real property?

4. Easterbrook concludes his comments (extracted above) with the suggestion that we should not match an imperfect legal system to an evolving world that we understand poorly. The solution, in his words, is to: "make rules clear; create property rights where now there are none; and facilitate the formation of bargaining institutions." Could this approach itself be described as a

framework for a new field of law called cyberlaw or Internet law? Might a new field of law be characterized by these kinds of principles applied to cyberspace activities?

5. Do the responses provided by Lessig and Ku address Easterbrook's concerns? Do they necessarily reject Easterbrook's primary concern? Ku suggests, for example, that resolving some issues in cyberspace — such as personal privacy rights — might also illuminate related issues in the "real world." Does this suggestion confirm Easterbrook's concerns?

6. Recognizing that computer code regulates human behavior, how does that fact illuminate the entire law? For an extended discussion of Lessig's theory, see Lawrence Lessig, *Code Version 2.0* (Basic Books, 2006). See also Andrew L. Shapiro, *The Control Revolution* (Public Affairs Council for Education, 1999); Joel R. Reidenberg, *Lex Informatica: The Formulation of Information Policy Rules Through Technology*, 76 Tex. L. Rev. 553 (1998).

7. Since the above articles were written, a number of commentators have entered the debate about the nature of the Internet and cyberspace, and how/ whether digital information, or digital information systems, might be effectively regulated. Some of these issues are taken up in more detail in Chapter 2. Different perspectives on these questions arise in the following articles: Alfred Yen, *Western Frontier or Feudal Society? Metaphors and Perceptions of Cyberspace*, 17 Berkeley Tech. L.J. 1207 (2002); Orin Kerr, *The Problem of Perspective in Internet Law*, 91 Geo. L.J. 357 (2003); Dan Hunter, *Cyberspace as Place and the Tragedy of the Digital Anticommons*, 91 Cal. L. Rev. 439 (2003); Mark Lemley, *Place and Cyberspace*, 91 Cal. L. Rev. 521 (2003); Jacqueline Lipton, *Mixed Metaphors in Cyberspace: Property in Information and Information Systems*, 35 Loy. U. Chi. L.J. 235 (2003); Jacqueline Lipton, *A Framework for Information Law and Policy*, 82 Or. L. Rev. 695 (2003).

8. Another important development since the early days of the Internet has been the move from the early "passive" Internet to what has been described as Web 2.0. Web 2.0 is characterized by a high degree of interactivity between participants, as opposed to Web 1.0 — the early Internet — which tended to be characterized by Internet users passively receiving information posted by governments, educational institutions, businesses, and large media organizations. Examples of Web 2.0 technologies include virtual worlds like Second Life (www.secondlife.com), digital video sharing services such as YouTube (www.youtube.com), online social networking services, such as MySpace (www.myspace.com) and Facebook (www.facebook.com), and online wikis where groups of people collectively contribute information to a shared common enterprise, such as Wikipedia (www.wikipedia.org). As described by Tapscott and Williams: "The new Web is fundamentally different in both its architecture and applications. Instead of a digital newspaper, think of a shared canvas where every splash of paint contributed by one user provides a richer tapestry for the next user to modify or build on. Whether people are creating, sharing, or socializing, the new Web is principally about participating

rather than about passively receiving information." (Donald Tapscott & Anthony D. Williams, *Wikinomics: How Mass Collaboration Changes Everything*, 37 (Portfolio, 2006/2008). Does this evolution of the Internet change how we think about the early views by Easterbrook, Lessig, and Ku in relation to the nature of cyberlaw? Does Web 2.0 potentially make cyberlaw less a "law of the horse" than initially contemplated by Easterbrook? Does Web 2.0 raise the significance of the interaction between the four regulatory modalities identified by Lessig?

Note: Cyberspace and the Regulation of Information

Ever since Judge Easterbrook compared Internet law classes with teaching the Law of the Horse (in other words, Internet law has no truly distinct value aside from being one of many potential areas for applying every legal discipline from antitrust to zoning law), scholars who teach and work in this area of law have felt the need to respond to this charge. In fact, the criticism is accurate to a certain extent if the only unifying theme of a course on "Internet law" are the keywords: Internet or cyberspace.

We believe that it is a mistake to treat Internet law as a smorgasbord of controversial cases or a survey through all the areas of law that touch upon the Internet. Every area of law will eventually be forced to address Internet issues. (To provide a grand tour would entail condensing all of law into one course.) Titling this book *Cyberspace Law* is in part a linguistic attempt at separating this casebook from such an approach. More importantly, however, our use of cyberspace rather than Internet represents a shift in the substantive focus of the materials and why these courses should be taught.

Cyberspace law is inherently about the regulation, control, and dissemination of information in a world mediated by computers. The Internet is after all simply a global network of computers designed for the high-speed transmission of data within and among its constituent networks. What we generally refer to as the Internet (e-mail, the World Wide Web, newsgroups, etc.) represents only a portion of the communications enabled by this global network. The convergence of print, audio, and video programming into a single medium, the monitoring of consumer spending habits on both the Web and in real space, the ability to monitor and bill individuals for the number of times they listen to a song or operate a particular computer program, and even video surveillance linked to computers capable of face recognition to identify individuals from anywhere in the nation are other activities made possible by this global communications medium. All of these activities involve the dissemination and control of information in a networked world.

The study of cyberspace law is, therefore, the study of the regulation of information in a world interlinked and mediated by computer networks. While existing doctrines such as freedom of speech, intellectual property, and privacy are starting points, cyberspace allows and often requires a reexamination of the values underlying those areas of law not only to translate those values into cyberspace applications, but to alter existing rules and legal institutions in real space as well. While this book is organized according to preexisting categories of information law, students should question whether those categories can and should remain discrete. In other words, the study of cyberspace law is the study of whether traditionally separate substantive laws that dealt with information should give way to a new overarching category of information law.

The study of cyberspace law is also a vehicle for exposing students to other important lessons. These include the limits of judicial and legislative responses to new technology, the malleability of computer code, the public and private regulation of behavior in the information age, and the challenges of regulating information across borders. Our goal is to provide materials that will foster lively discussion on the significant Internet cases, help students to translate existing legal rules to cyberspace, and provide materials and an organization that facilitate discourse on the larger question of information regulation.

2

REGULATING CYBERSPACE

A. CYBERANARCHY VS. CYBERORDER

Unlike the other subjects that you have studied during law school where it was assumed that laws can and should be enacted and judge-made rules created to regulate the actions in question, the birth of the Internet was followed by a fundamental debate over whether the Internet can and should be regulated. To many, the early Internet represented a lawless frontier. Communications were unregulated. Free speech reigned supreme. Government regulation was shunned. Groups advocating freedom of expression in digital media were formed. One of these groups, The Electronic Frontier Foundation, was cofounded in 1990 by John Perry Barlow, a retired Wyoming cattle rancher and former lyricist for the Grateful Dead. He wrote exclusively on cyberspace issues, including freedom from government cyberspace regulation. But the rapid growth and commercialization of cyberspace raised many questions. Could or should cyberspace be regulated?

JOHN PERRY BARLOW
CYBERSPACE DECLARATION OF INDEPENDENCE

http://homes.eff.org/~barlow/Declaration-Final.html (1996)

Governments of the Industrial World, you weary giants of flesh and steel, I come from Cyberspace, the new home of Mind. On behalf of the future, I ask you of the past to leave us alone. You are not welcome among us. You have no sovereignty where we gather.

We have no elected government, nor are we likely to have one, so I address you with no greater authority than that with which liberty itself always speaks. I declare the global social space we are building to be naturally independent of the tyrannies you seek to impose on us. You have no moral right to rule us nor do you possess any methods of enforcement we have true reason to fear.

Governments derive their just powers from the consent of the governed. You have neither solicited nor received ours. We did not invite you. You do not know us, nor do you know our world. Cyberspace does not lie within your borders. Do not think that you can build it, as though it were a public construction project. You cannot. It is an act of nature and it grows itself through our collective actions.

You have not engaged in our great and gathering conversation, nor did you create the wealth of our marketplaces. You do not know our culture, our ethics, or the unwritten codes that already provide our society more order than could be obtained by any of your impositions.

You claim there are problems among us that you need to solve. You use this claim as an excuse to invade our precincts. Many of these problems don't exist. Where there are real conflicts, where there are wrongs, we will identify them and address them by our means. We are forming our own Social Contract. This governance will arise according to the conditions of our world, not yours. Our world is different.

Cyberspace consists of transactions, relationships, and thought itself, arrayed like a standing wave in the web of our communications. Ours is a world that is both everywhere and nowhere, but it is not where bodies live.

We are creating a world that all may enter without privilege or prejudice accorded by race, economic power, military force, or station of birth.

We are creating a world where anyone, anywhere may express his or her beliefs, no matter how singular, without fear of being coerced into silence or conformity.

Your legal concepts of property, expression, identity, movement, and context do not apply to us. They are based on matter. There is no matter here.

Our identities have no bodies, so, unlike you, we cannot obtain order by physical coercion. We believe that from ethics, enlightened self-interest, and the commonweal, our governance will emerge. Our identities may be distributed across many of your jurisdictions. The only law that all our constituent cultures would generally recognize is the Golden Rule. We hope we will be able to build our particular solutions on that basis. But we cannot accept the solutions you are attempting to impose.

In the United States, you have today created a law, the Telecommunications Reform Act, which repudiates your own Constitution and insults the dreams of Jefferson, Washington, Mill, Madison, de Tocqueville, and Brandeis. These dreams must now be born anew in us.

You are terrified of your own children, since they are natives in a world where you will always be immigrants. Because you fear them, you entrust your bureaucracies with the parental responsibilities you are too cowardly to confront yourselves. In our world, all the sentiments and expressions of humanity, from the debasing to the angelic, are parts of a seamless whole, the global conversation of bits. We cannot separate the air that chokes from the air upon which wings beat.

In China, Germany, France, Russia, Singapore, Italy and the United States, you are trying to ward off the virus of liberty by erecting guard posts at the frontiers of Cyberspace. These may keep out the contagion for a small time, but they will not work in a world that will soon be blanketed in bit-bearing media.

Your increasingly obsolete information industries would perpetuate themselves by proposing laws, in America and elsewhere, that claim to own speech itself throughout the world. These laws would declare ideas to be another industrial product, no more noble than pig iron. In our world, whatever the human mind may create can be reproduced and distributed infinitely at no cost. The global conveyance of thought no longer requires your factories to accomplish.

These increasingly hostile and colonial measures place us in the same position as those previous lovers of freedom and self-determination who had to reject the authorities of distant, uninformed powers. We must declare our virtual selves immune to your sovereignty, even as we continue to consent to your rule over our bodies. We will spread ourselves across the Planet so that no one can arrest our thoughts.

We will create a civilization of the Mind in Cyberspace. May it be more humane and fair than the world your governments have made before.

Unlike Barlow, many supported legislative reforms. Despite Barlow's eloquent attempts to declare cyberspace independent, today geographically based governments do regulate activities that occur through the Internet. The United States of America has made it illegal to transmit obscenity. The Republic of France has required Yahoo! to block the sale of Nazi memorabilia within its borders. The People's Republic of China has created the great firewall blocking content that the government deems inappropriate, and nations have cooperated in efforts to investigate and prosecute international hackers. While the debate over whether cyberspace *can* be effectively regulated is now largely an interesting milestone in the evolution of efforts to regulate the Internet, many of the concerns raised by early commentators in the area still linger. The history of this debate is summarized nicely in the following extract.

DAN HUNTER
CYBERSPACE AS PLACE AND THE TRAGEDY OF THE
DIGITAL ANTICOMMONS

91 Cal. L. Rev. 439 (2003)

Cyberspace was once thought to be the modern equivalent of the Western Frontier. It was a place, albeit an abstract place, where land was free for the taking, explorers could roam, and communities could form with their own rules. It was an endless expanse of space: open, free, replete with possibility. No longer. As with the Western Frontier, settlers have entered this new land, charted the territory, fenced off their own little claims, and erected "No Trespassing" signs. Cyberspace is being subdivided. Suburbs and SUVs cannot be far off.

Since cyberspace seems like a place, this trend seems preordained: the progression of property interests over the last five hundred years shows that places tend to be enclosed and privately exploited. However, it is a surprising trend because legal commentators have convinced us that cyberspace is not a place at all. Some early scholars argued that cyberspace was a separate space for the purposes of law and regulation, but they were quickly derided for their naïveté. By the end of the last century, the received wisdom ordained that no one could be foolish enough to argue that cyberspace was a place.

However, the received wisdom has confused the descriptive question of whether we think of cyberspace as a place with the normative question of whether we should regulate cyberspace as a regime independent of national laws. These are two conceptually distinct questions. Whatever the answer to the normative question, cognitive science investigations provide ample evidence that, purely as a descriptive observation, we do think of cyberspace as a place.

Thinking of cyberspace as a place has led judges, legislators, and legal scholars to apply physical assumptions about property in this new, abstract space. Owners of Internet resources think of their systems as their own little claims in cyberspace, which must be protected against the typical encroachments that we find in the physical property world. This has led to a series of cases and statutes that enshrine the idea of property interests in cyberspace.

The effect of this is to take the hitherto commons-like character of cyberspace and splinter it into millions of tiny landholdings. Privatization in this form is not, of itself, a problem: private interests are the dominant forms of resource allocation in our world. However, modern property theorists have demonstrated the dangers of splintering interests: the undesirable consequence is the creation of "anticommons property." Anticommons property emerges where multiple people hold rights of exclusion to a property such that no one has an effective right of use. As a result, a "tragedy of the anticommons" occurs, where property is locked into suboptimal and wasteful uses because the holders of the exclusion rights block the best use of the resource.

. . .

I. Cyberspace as Autonomous Legal Place

I think of cyberspace as a place. It may be virtual and abstract, but I conceive of it as a place nonetheless. Let me be bolder: though you may have never consciously thought about the proposition, you also conceive of cyberspace as a place. Let me go further and suggest that all legislators, judges, and lawyers unconsciously think that cyberspace is a place, even though at times they may argue vehemently that it is not.

These are dangerous claims. For those aware of the development of Internet and cyberspace law, arguing that cyberspace is a place will appear either ill-informed or quixotic. Even arguing that we think of cyberspace as a place goes against accepted views. For a brief moment, the legal conception of cyberspace as place flared, and then was gone. As a legal argument it peaked around 1996, was attacked soon thereafter, and, as one commentator has noted, by the year 2000 one was hard pressed to find anyone foolish enough to subscribe to this theory. The reason I am foolish enough to defend this theory—indeed to base this entire Article around it—requires an understanding of history.

A. The History of Cyberspace as a Legal Place

The idea that cyberspace might be regulated as a place stemmed from the early cyberlibertarian conception that cyberspace was different from "here" and so should be accorded some form of autonomy from physical world— or so-called "meatspace"—sovereigns. At its high point the rhetoric was amusing and intentionally overblown:

> Governments of the Industrial World, you weary giants of flesh and steel, I come from Cyberspace, the new home of Mind. On behalf of the future, I ask you of the past to leave us alone. You are not welcome among us. You have no sovereignty where we gather. [John Perry Barlow, A Declaration of the Independence of Cyberspace (Feb. 8, 1996), at *http://homes.eff.org/~barlow/Declaration-Final.html.*]

The legal reflection of this idea, shorn of its rhetorical excesses, asked: "What is the appropriate mechanism for cyberspace regulation?" The initial answer was that self-regulation was the only appropriate governance structure. Within scholarly discourse, this cyberspace self-governance movement was championed most notably by David Johnson and David Post in a seminal 1996 article. [David R Johnson & David Post, *Law and Borders: The Rise of Law in Cyberspace,* 48 Stan. L. Rev. 1367 (1996)] They argued that the Internet challenged the power of the nation-state to regulate online behavior, as well as its legitimacy to do so, because there was no longer an obvious method to connect an electronic transaction or communication to a particular nation-state jurisdiction. As a result, from both the descriptive and normative perspectives, it was no longer obvious that national laws should apply to cyberspace transactions. They concluded that cyberspace should be left to develop its own self-regulatory structures, and that national sovereigns should, under certain circumstances, defer to this new legal environment.

At around the same time, other theorists developed similar arguments in favor of internal self-regulatory structures. These arguments included suggestions that online transactions might be better regulated by a system of norms similar to the Lex Mercatoria, the set of norms that governed merchant transactions in medieval times, or that we might see the rise of the "United States District Court for the District of Cyberspace," among other surprising claims. . . . Another defining characteristic was that cyberspace should be regulated independently of physical, geographically-delimited sovereigns. As a result, there was a strong trend, circa 1996-97, suggesting that cyberspace was, or should have been, an autonomous place for the purposes of regulation.

By 1998 the tide had turned. Jack Goldsmith mounted an influential attack on those he labeled cyberspace "regulation skeptics." His argument was, essentially, that cyberspace created no problems that had not already been resolved by unexceptional jurisdictional rules and legal mechanisms derived from conflict of laws. Goldsmith challenged the descriptive argument underlying cyberspace self-regulatory theories: cyberspace was not, he argued, descriptively different from "real space." He concluded that transactions in cyberspace were no different from those occurring in the space of physical world transnational transactions. Goldsmith's challenge posed the question: Since we are able to regulate similar matters effectively and appropriately on a national basis, why should we treat cyberspace differently for the purposes of regulation and governance?

Following Goldsmith's descriptive challenge, Neil Weinstock Netanel attacked the normative basis for cyberspace self-regulation. The core of the normative argument in favor of self-regulation was that "governments derive their just powers from the consent of the governed." Netanel identified two specific normative claims that arose in the cyberspace environment based on this social-contractarian, bottom-up governance approach. First was the claim that cyberspace self-regulation is the perfection of liberal rule since it "embodies the liberal democratic goals of individual liberty, popular sovereignty, and consent of the governed." Second was the claim that a truly liberal state grants autonomy to groups that seek it: if cyberspace is a self-defining community, intrusion by a state amounts to a "colonial" usurpation of group norms and authority. Netanel demonstrated that both of these claims were unfounded. He argued that an "unregulated" cyberspace would prove inimical to liberal democratic ideals, in part due to the usual countermajoritarian and tyrannical government concerns, pragmatic concerns with popular referenda, and theoretical problems with direct democracy. As a result, state intervention would be warranted under democratic theory in order to protect the ideals of liberalism. Even if this did not occur, Netanel argued, cyberspace would develop its own quasi-state institutions in the absence of a state regulatory structure. These institutions would demonstrate the same democratic deficits that formed the basis of the cyberlibertarian challenge to the state's regulatory legitimacy. Far from being the perfection of liberal democratic ideals, he argued that cyberspace self-governance would lead to a breeding ground for illiberal activities such as status discrimination, narrowing of content access, systematic invasions of privacy, and gross inequality.

Though these two scholars remain the most influential critics of the idea that cyberspace is, or should be, an autonomous regulatory sphere, other commentators fleshed out additional reasons why the early self-regulation approach was problematic. Most of these theorists did not argue directly against the cyberspace as place metaphor, confining themselves to discussing problems with the idea of online self-regulation. However, most of the approaches assumed that cyberspace self-governance arose because the self-regulation advocates considered cyberspace to be a separate place. Furthermore, two theorists, Andrew Shapiro and Timothy Wu, directly attacked the conception of cyberspace as a place. Shapiro, author of the influential cyberspace policy work, *The Control Revolution*, argued against the metaphor of cyberspace as an autonomous place. His argument mirrors much of what was said elsewhere by cyberspace self-governance critics: what happens in cyberspace happens in the physical world also, and cyberspace is not a real place but just a medium that we may control. He suggested that we are not well served by the idea that cyberspace is an autonomous "place," and that "cyberspace is not elsewhere."

Timothy Wu argued much the same, suggesting that it is no longer possible to conceive of cyberspace as an autonomous place — "the general sense of Cyberspace as one place is missing" — and further that the metaphor of cyberspace as place was dead:

> The metaphor of place did not exactly stand the test of time. For the Internet, as a whole, did not develop into a kind of other-world kingdom inhabited by netizens; or even, more modestly, develop a real "commons." Yes, many years ago, the mainstay of Internet usage was community-based and somewhat place-like. Users were fewer, more similar in personality, and there was little reason to log on if it wasn't to interact (there was nothing else to do). But the early users of the Internet notwithstanding, the Internet was never designed to be "like" a place. It was designed to be a multiple-use network, capable of supporting any kind of application anyone wanted to run on it. . . . The metaphor and the technology never matched. [Timothy Wu, *When Law & The Internet First Met*, 3 Green Bag 2d 171, 172-173 (1999-2000)]

It now should be clear why defending the idea that "cyberspace is a place" appears quixotic. It goes against the recent argument that cyberspace is not a place, and should not be regulated separately from physical space. As Wu pointed out, the metaphor just did not seem to stand the test of time.

B. Reconsidering Autonomy and Place

The scholars who present the received wisdom are, I think, wrong. They conflate the idea that cyberspace has the characteristics of a place with the debate about cyberspace regulatory autonomy. I do not argue here that cyberspace should be self-regulated. I do argue, however, that judges, legislators, practitioners, and lay people treat cyberspace as if it were a physical place. Examining how people discuss their online interactions, we find a vast amount of evidence that people think about online communications and transactions as occurring in some place. This place may be inchoate and virtual, but no less real in our minds.

If we set aside the issue of how we regulate cyberspace, we still must ask what evidence there is for us thinking of cyberspace as though it were a place. . . .

First consider how everyone employs physical vocabulary to talk about events, transactions, and systems that exist or occur online. At its most fundamental, think of the term WEB, an allusion to the "web-like" connections between computers. Then there is the NET, referring to the network of connections as well as the net-like character of the material caught in the network. We SURF this WEB, MOVING from one SITE to the next, ENTERING or VISITING the site, or, in the slightly old-fashioned nomenclature, we access someone's HOMEPAGE. We HANG OUT IN CHATROOMS communicating with our ONLINE buddies. We ROAM AROUND Multiple User DUNGEONS and DOMAINS ("MUDs") and MUDs Object Oriented ("MOOs"). Software programs called ROBOTS, AGENTS, or SPIDERS are allowed to CRAWL over websites unless they are barred by terms and conditions of ENTRY or ACCESS, or by the robot EXCLUSION standard. We NAVIGATE the WEB using computer programs with names like NAVIGATOR and EXPLORER. We use Uniform Resource LOCATORS ("URLs") and DOMAIN names to find our way. Information is sent to us using hypertext TRANSPORT protocol ("http") or simple mail TRANSPORT protocol. We use email ADDRESSES to send messages to others, and the machines themselves use Internet Protocol ("IP") ADDRESSES to locate other computers. We log INTO or log ONTO our Internet Service Provider ("ISP"). Malignant wrongdoers ACCESS our accounts by hacking INTO the system using BACKDOORS, TRAPDOORS, or stolen KEYS, and engage in computer TRESPASSES.

C.   City of Bits, Sense of Place

Apart from linguistic usage, other evidence from "sense of place" geographers teach us to think that cyberspace is a place. In 1990 Mitch Kapor and John Perry Barlow penned a manifesto that led to the creation of the Electronic Frontier Foundation, an online civil liberties group. Entitled Across the Electronic Frontier, the manifesto adopted the term "cyberspace" as well as a series of spatial metaphors for aspects of the Internet. During this early phase of cyberspace evolution, the development of electronic communities was the subject of significant description and discussion. The "frontier" was pushed back by electronic homesteaders, and they were eager to provide their accounts of this new virtual place and the communities inhabiting it. Howard Rheingold's The Virtual Community (subtitled Homesteading on the Electronic Frontier) explained the construction of new kinds of virtual places, the emergence of community structures, and other early examples of how spatially based community expectations were moved into cyberspace.

Apart from first-person accounts of the lives lived in that abstract space, a number of theorists — usually geographers, architects, or urban planners — began examining the spatial characteristics of the online world. These scholars explained how we generate a sense of place in the physical world, and how this sense of place mapped to the virtual world. The most influential theorist was the dean of Massachusetts Institute of Technology's School of Architecture and Planning, William Mitchell, who provided the fundamental roadmap of the online world in his seminal book, *City of Bits.*

Mitchell's work demonstrated how we effortlessly transpose an enormous number of our physical understandings of our environment into our understanding of the online world. He showed, for example, the presence of public and private spaces online: the Web is public, as are many chatrooms, whereas email is private. He examined how our use of the space is similar to our uses of physical world space. We promenade along the public spaces. We explore frontier regions, urban neighborhoods, and imaginary worlds. We name the spaces we inhabit with titles that reflect our personality or the usage of the space: chatrooms are called "The Flirt's Nook" or "StarFleet Academy" and the like. He described the various physical spaces that were being directly "moved" into the online environment. These ranged from schools to stock exchanges to prisons.

Identifying spatial characteristics led quickly to the mapping of cyberspace. On one hand, designers of abstract spaces adopted a map-like metaphor as an interface to the various services they provided. Early examples included Apple Computer's eWorld and the city of Cleveland's FreeNet. In eWorld the various services available were displayed on the screen as a kind of small town. For example, email services were available from the building labeled "Post Office" and administrative functions were found at "City Hall." In FreeNet, the online services offered by Cleveland were found in different "buildings" available online. Many other examples are familiar from the earliest days of the network: virtual libraries were often visualized exactly like their physical counterparts (with stacks, reference sections, help desks, and so forth) in order to assist navigation, searching, and use. More recently we have begun seeing spatial visualizations of online resources that attempt to reflect features of the physical world to make human interaction more meaningful. . . .

The mapping of cyberspace is by no means confined to this appropriation of explicit physical references, nor is it confined to the Cartesian or Newtonian mapping of objects. Abstract spaces can now be readily mapped and visualized. Online objects, users, services, and relationships are now the subject of cartographic experiments. Examples of maps of cyberspace now include infrastructure and network maps, IP address space diagrams, maps of domain name concentrations, Usenet traffic flow visualizations, network congestion diagrams, "topological" maps of the concentrations of materials around particular news topics, and arc-relation diagrams of real-time messaging relationships. There are even "satellite" maps and "urban density" maps of online multiuser spaces.

The point here is not to document exhaustively all of the evidence that supports the notion that we conceive of cyberspace as a place. Rather, it is merely to demonstrate that the language that we use to discuss cyberspace is shot through with physical references and implications, and that geographers have mapped out these places. Even those who argue against the cyberspace as place metaphor find it impossible to talk about Internet regulation without invoking spatial references. For example, while arguing in favor of setting aside public forums on the Internet, Andrew Shapiro specifically applied the cyberspace as place metaphor—including references to online bookstores, online shopping malls, meandering down the cyberspace boulevards, and so on. The physical world of stores, places, and roads was translated online into an abstract space that shared all the spatial characteristics of the physical world.

. . .

[Hunter goes on to argue that the use of the property metaphor in cyberspace potentially leads to a situation where a digital "anticommons" ensues because of the enclosure of too many online resources as a result of over-propertization and fragmentation of property interests in information and information systems. To avoid this outcome he suggests either changing the metaphors we use to describe cyberspace or becoming more aware of the potential impact of property metaphors in cyberspace.]

COMMENTS AND QUESTIONS

1. Hunter suggests that previous commentators have confused the descriptive question of thinking about cyberspace as a "place" with the normative question of whether cyberspace can be regulated independent of national laws. Do you agree with his assessment? Is the separation of the normative and descriptive questions helpful in determining whether and how cyberspace might be regulated? If we don't use spatial terminology to describe cyberspace, what descriptive language should we use?

2. Hunter suggests that initially cyberspace had a "commons-like" character. What did he mean by this? What is the "tragedy of the anticommons"?

3. On what basis did commentators such as Barlow, Johnson, and Post suggest that cyberspace was beyond national legal regulation? How did Goldsmith counter these claims? Which view has been borne out in practice in subsequent years? For more recent views on the ability of cyberspace to be regulated, see Jack Goldsmith & Tim Wu, *Who Controls the Internet: Illusions of a Borderless World* (updated edition, OUP, 2006/2008); Lawrence Lessig, *Code Version 2.0* (Basic Books, 2006); David Post, *In Search of Jefferson's Moose: Notes on the Study of Cyberspace* (OUP, 2009).

4. What are some of the other arguments raised by past commentators both for and against describing cyberspace as a place? For a recent analysis of the "cyberspace as place" literature, see Julie Cohen, *Cyberspace As/And Space*, 107 Colum. L. Rev. 210 (2007).

5. Barlow's Declaration of Independence invoked the concept of popular sovereignty. In order to regulate the Internet or activities that occur through the Internet, do territorial sovereigns require the consent of those whom they seek to govern in cyberspace? How is that consent absent? With respect to cyberspace, how do we define or identify who "the people" are and whose consent must be obtained? As the Internet becomes more global in practice, and more and more people become connected, does this change the equation about the type of consent required by the governed? Recently, Professor David Post made the following comments about Internet governance: "We have created, all of a sudden, in the space of a couple of decades . . . a global place, where the people of the world have gotten all mixed up together, interacting with one another in ways unimaginable a mere two decades ago. We often disagree — quite fundamentally — about the kind of law we want to have, about what the Law is, and where it comes from. Nobody has the right answer, because these are not the sorts of questions that have right and wrong answers. And nobody has the right to impose his or her vision on others who do not share it, because all are created equal." (David Post, *In Search of Jefferson's Moose: Notes on the Study of Cyberspace*, 206 (OUP, 2009). Do Post's words illuminate issues about the need for consent of the governed and whose consent must be obtained to govern cyberspace? Do they suggest that central cyberspace governance is impossible because of the scope and scale of consent that would be required for any kind of sovereign government?

6. Assuming that Goldsmith is correct that many Internet transactions involve similar "spillover" effects as real space business transactions, does it matter who the parties to the transaction are? While it may be legitimate to require Yahoo to comply with the laws of France, what about Jane Doe? What about a small, one-man business enterprise? Does the rise of Web 2.0 online services (such as Second Life, YouTube, Wikipedia, Facebook, and Flickr) change anything in this respect? If more and more private individuals are interacting online for less "transactional" and more "social" and "community" purposes, does this change the way we think about spillover effects? Does the fact that many online environments, such as Second Life, resemble "places" where individuals interact on a social level suggest that there should be a law for a place called "cyberspace"? Or perhaps that there should be different laws for different kinds of virtual worlds? In other words, might it be possible to be a citizen of, say, Second Life or Facebook? If so, how would the citizens ascertain the law of the virtual world? Who has the right to impose law, and on what basis? In this context, would the sheer scale of the virtual world and the physically dispersed nature of its inhabitants in the real world create problems for regulation and enforcement of regulation? As Professor Sánchez Abril noted in 2007, "If MySpace alone were a country and each of its profiles a person, it would be the 12th most populous nation in the world." (Patricia Sánchez Abril, *A (My)Space of One's Own: On Privacy and Online Social Networks*, 6 Nw. J. Tech. & Intell. Prop. 73, 74 (2007)). Presumably, by now, MySpace

and Facebook are amongst the most populous "countries" in the world, due to the exponential growth of participation in online social networks.

7. Is the focus on public regulation of conduct appropriate? In his article, *Foucault in Cyberspace: Surveillance, Sovereignty, and Hardwired Censors,* 66 U. Cin. L. Rev. 177 (1997), James Boyle suggests that the debate over whether the Internet can and should be regulated assumes a positivist view of law as "commands backed by threats." According to Boyle:

> [O]ne of Foucault's most interesting contributions was to challenge a particular notion of power, power-as-sovereignty, and to juxtapose against it a vision of "surveillance" and "discipline." . . . Foucault argued that, rather than the public and formal triangle of sovereign, citizen, and right, we should focus on a series of subtler private, informal, and material forms of coercion organized around the concepts of surveillance and discipline. The paradigm for the idea of surveillance was the Panopticon, Bentham's plan for a prison constructed in the shape of a wheel around the hub of an observing warden. At any moment the warden might have the prisoner under observation through a nineteenth century version of the closed-circuit TV. Unsure when authority might in fact be watching, the prisoner would strive always to conform his behavior to its presumed desires. Bentham had hit upon a behavioralist equivalent of the superego, formed from uncertainty about when one was being observed by the powers that be. The echo of contemporary laments about the "privacy-free state" is striking. To this, Foucault added the notion of discipline — crudely put, the multitudinous private methods of regulation of individual behavior ranging from workplace time-and-motion efficiency directives to psychiatric evaluation.
>
> Foucault pointed out the apparent conflict between a formal language of politics organized around relations between sovereign and citizen, expressed through rules backed by sanctions, and an actual experience of power being exercised through multitudinous non-state sources, often dependent on material or technological means of enforcement.

What do the concepts of surveillance and private power add to the debate over whether the Internet can and should be regulated? Under this view, is Microsoft a regulator of the Internet? Is regulation by private parties any more legitimate than government regulation?

8. In his article, *Google's Law*, 73 Brook. L. Rev. 1327, 1328-29 (2008), Greg Lastowka talks about the regulatory role Google has acquired as a result of society's reliance on it as the predominant search engine: "Google has become, for the majority of Americans, the index of choice for online information. Through dynamically generated results keyed to a near-infinite variety of search terms, Google steers our thoughts and our learning online. It tells us what words mean, what things look like, where to buy things, and who and what is most important to us. Google's control over search results constitutes an awesome ability to set the course of human knowledge. It is not surprising that the commercial exploitation of results is also the primary source of Google's wealth. . . . [F]ortunes are won and lost based on Google's results pages, including the fortunes of Google itself. . . . If, as Lawrence Lessig has argued, computer code has a regulatory force tantamount to law, the absence of any state involvement in the shape of

Google's results will effectively cede the structure of our primary online index to 'Google's law.' Given Google's meteoric rise to prominence and its current role as our primary online index, the law should be vigilant. Google may enjoy substantial public goodwill, but what is best for Google will not always be what is best for society." Lastowka raises concerns about unfettered private regulation of online information by powerful online service providers. Do you agree with his concerns? Are they specific to Google, or might they apply more broadly to other popular online service providers, such as popular social networking sites (MySpace, Facebook, blogs), or community projects, such as Wikipedia?

Note: ICANN and Regulation

To what extent should private groups regulate the Internet? For example, the Internet Corporation for Assigned Names and Numbers (ICANN) promulgated the Uniform Domain Name Dispute Resolution Policy (UDRP) in response to the growing number of disputes involving domain names. Because ICANN controls the assignment of domain names, it has the power to control who can and cannot register. Under what circumstances should such a private entity exercise such power? While this form of private regulation may avoid some of the problems associated with governmental regulation, is it legitimate? Consider Lawrence R. Helfer & Graeme B. Dinwoodie, *Designing Non-national Systems: The Case of the Uniform Domain Name Dispute Resolution Policy*, 43 Wm. & Mary L. Rev. 141 (2001) (arguing that the UDRP is a significant step toward developing a nonnational regulatory mechanism, but suggesting the need to adopt safeguards); A. Michael Froomkin, *Wrong Turn in Cyberspace: Using ICANN to Route Around the APA and the Constitution*, 50 Duke L.J. 17 (2000) (arguing that the Department of Commerce's relationship with ICANN violates either the Administrative Procedures Act or the Constitution's Nondelegation Doctrine); Jonathan Weinberg, *ICANN and the Problem of Legitimacy*, 50 Duke L.J. 187 (2000) (questioning ICANN's legitimacy as a public policymaking body in the absence of meaningful judicial review or representation).

In 2000, ICANN experimented briefly with allowing direct public participation in the governance of the infrastructure of the Internet. At the time of the formation of the ICANN Board of Directors in 2000, five of the 19 seats were reserved for representatives of the noncommercial, Internet-using public. These board members were elected through global online elections. The remaining board members were appointed by ICANN's own Nomination Committee. The ICANN elections were originally set up to allow anybody over the age of 16 with a valid e-mail address to vote for board members, leading to charges that the system made it too easy for parties to set up multiple e-mail accounts in order to vote more than once.

This experiment was short-lived. In 2002, then-president of ICANN, Stuart Lynn, called for a dramatic reconfiguring of the organization's policy-making apparatus, including among other things the elimination of the public representative board seats. At a press conference accompanying the release of this report, Lynn stated that "The ICANN is not an exercise in Global Democracy" and argued that as representatives of their respective publics, board members from various government agencies would serve the public interest more effectively.

The ICANN board of directors voted the publicly elected positions out of existence at a meeting in Shanghai in October of 2002, eliminating future publicly elected board positions and allowing the terms of the existing publicly elected members to expire. In its place, ICANN has established an ombudsman position to represent the public and allows selected organizations to be considered "at-large" groups and provide their input to decisions facing the board of directors.

Critics contend that the elimination of the publicly elected board seats has helped lead to an ICANN that promotes the interests of business and government over that of the general Internet-surfing public. Critics point to the board's 2006 decision to refuse requests to create a ".xxx" top-level domain name for use by the adult entertainment industry as an example of the ICANN bowing to political pressure. ICANN's 2006 agreement with VeriSign, which will allow the company to retain control of the ".com" top-level domain name until 2012, has also come under fire as being anti-small business. For further reading, see Michael Froomkin, *Habermas@discourse.net: Toward a Critical Theory of Cyberspace*, 116 Harv. L. Rev. 751 (2003); Dr. Milton Mueller, *Dancing the Quango: ICANN and the Privatization of International Governance*, remarks to Conference on New Technologies and Internet Government, Paul H. Nitze School of Advanced International Relations, Johns Hopkins University, *http://istweb.syr.edu/~mueller/quango.pdf* (2002); ICANN Watch, *www.icannwatch.org* (last visited June 12, 2009); ICANN, *www.icann.org* (last visited June 12, 2009); Milton Mueller, *Ruling the Root: Internet Governance and the Taming of Cyberspace* (MIT Press, 2004); David Lindsay, *International Domain Name Law: ICANN and the UDRP*, Chapter 2 (Hart Publishing, 2007); David Post, *In Search of Jefferson's Moose: Notes on the State of Cyberspace*, 155-62 (OUP, 2009)

B. PERSONAL JURISDICTION

Historically, one of the most troubling aspects of regulating the Internet was personal jurisdiction. When is it legitimate for a jurisdiction to apply its rules to an individual when the individual's contacts are based upon transactions that occur over a global electronic network? As the following materials illustrate, the courts addressing this question have taken a variety of different positions.

Before examining the Internet cases, this chapter begins by introducing the principal U.S. Supreme Court decisions involving personal jurisdiction and the limits of personal jurisdiction under the U.S. Constitution.

Problem 1.0

In this casebook, we shall use the fictitious company name, The StarttUp Company, solely for the purpose of illustration. The StarttUp Company, hereinafter referred to as StarttUp, is an Internet start-up company based in New Jersey. StarttUp has hired you as General Counsel. You are the third employee joining the two founders, Alan and Barbara. While you have no Internet-related experience, Alan and Barbara and the venture capitalists funding the company have faith in your analytical skills and are comforted by the fact that you are a quick study. Moreover, outside counsel has put together a series of materials to introduce you to cyberspace law and will provide you with materials as necessary.

The business plan for StarttUp is to build an all-purpose global online community. While the company currently has a small network of subscribers in New Jersey acquired from an old local Internet Service provider, its plan is to become a national and ultimately a global online community in which users will not only be able to interact with one another through chat rooms, e-mail, and instant messaging, but also be able to shop, plan vacations, and download the latest news and entertainment. In short, StarttUp's goal is to provide its subscribers with every conceivable service and activity available on the Internet.

Until now, StarttUp has predominantly been doing business in New Jersey. Its subscriber base of 1,000 was created when StarttUp was originally a local Internet service provider. Back then, it did not have to worry about multijurisdictional issues because it only advertised in New Jersey and subscribers could only access its services through a local telephone number.

Because the current business plan calls for StarttUp's expansion to a global Internet community, Alan and Barbara are planning a Web site to introduce the company, provide information about the proposed community, and provide e-mail and other contact information for potential subscribers and investors. They have shown you the beta (test) version of the site, and it is highly interactive. It provides users with a simulated Web experience to give them an idea of what StarttUp's online community will look and feel like. Users are also given the option to receive e-mail updates about the new service. You are told that the initial e-mail will contain a detailed explanation of why the recipient should subscribe to StarttUp.

After the initial Web site goes online, StarttUp plans to offer subscription packages to the public. The current plan calls for several levels of access:

1) **Free Access.** Anyone visiting the Web site will have access to an extremely limited amount of content and no access to services. This level is primarily a means of exposing interested subscribers to the service.

2) **Registered Free Access.** By providing certain personal and demographic information, registered users will be able to access more of StarttUp's content, and will be able to view message boards and enter chat rooms.

3) **Regular Subscriber Access.** For a monthly fee and after agreeing to an online subscription agreement, subscribers are given access to all of StarttUp's content and services, including e-mail and instant messaging. Certain premium services, such as streaming music and video, are available on a pay-per-use basis.

4) **Premium Subscriber Access.** For a higher monthly fee and after agreeing to an online subscription agreement, premium subscribers are given access to all of the services as regular subscribers plus unlimited access to the premium services.

Given that StarttUp currently has only limited funds, Alan and Barbara want to know if they go forward with the current Web site, can the company be sued successfully in states other than New Jersey or in countries outside of the United States. If they have any problems with subscribers, can they sue the subscribers in New Jersey? They also want to know what they can do to minimize the risk of being sued elsewhere and maximize their chances of being able to sue in New Jersey.

Problem 1.1

While you are working for StarttUp, Barbara has asked if you would mind giving some legal advice to her daughter, Cora. Cora wants to create a group blog with some friends from college. The blog would be operated from servers located at Barbara and Cora's home in New Jersey. Most of the regular group bloggers reside in New Jersey and live in local college dorms, although some of them go home for the holidays to other states. One of the bloggers — Demi — lives in Canada. Cora and her friends plan to blog predominantly about pop culture issues with a feminist slant. They plan to enable comment feeds on their posts to encourage their readers to interact on the blog. They plan to name the blog Gals On-Line ("GOL" for short). Cora wants to know if she has any problems with people commenting on the blog, whether she would be able to sue them in New Jersey. She also wants to know what she and her fellow bloggers might do to minimize their risk of being sued elsewhere.

1. The Supreme Court and Due Process

You may recall from your Civil Procedure class that a court may only hear a lawsuit and render a judgment if the court has personal jurisdiction over the defendant. Such personal jurisdiction, over a nonresident defendant, may be either general or specific. General jurisdiction usually exists when the cause of action is unrelated to the defendant's activity and the defendant's activities in the forum state are either "substantial" or "continuous and systematic."[1] On the other hand, specific jurisdiction exists when the defendant's activities arise from or relate to the defendant's actions within the forum.[2]

No matter which form of jurisdiction is claimed, a defendant's connection with the forum must satisfy the Due Process Clause of the Fourteenth Amendment. According to the Supreme Court:

> Due process requires only that in order to subject defendant to a judgment in personam, if he be not present within the territory of the forum, he have certain minimum contacts with it such that the maintenance of the suit does not offend "traditional notions of fair play and substantial justice."[3]

In other words, due process requires that "individuals have 'fair warning that a particular activity may subject [them] to the jurisdiction of a foreign sovereign. . . .'"[4] With respect to the minimum contacts prong, the "'fair warning' requirement is satisfied if the defendant has 'purposefully directed' his activities at residents of the forum."[5]

As you may recall, there is still uncertainty with respect to what acts may represent sufficient minimum contacts. For example, the Supreme Court has stated that a contract with an out-of-state party alone cannot automatically establish sufficient minimum contacts.[6] Instead, a court must look to other facts, including "prior negotiations and contemplated future consequences, along with the terms of the contract and the parties' actual course of dealing. . . ."[7] In World-Wide Volkswagen Corp. v. Woodson, the Supreme Court rejected the argument that a state could assert jurisdiction over an out-of-state auto retailer merely because it was foreseeable that its vehicles might be driven in the forum as a result of the plaintiff's unilateral activity.[8] In contrast, the Supreme Court has held that the writer and editor of an allegedly defamatory publication were subject to jurisdiction in the plaintiff's state because they "knew that the brunt of that injury would be felt by respondent in the State in which she lives and works and in which the *National Enquirer* has its

1. Burger King Corp. v. Rudzewicz, 471 U.S. 462, 473 (1985).
2. *Id.*
3. International Shoe Co. v. Washington, 326 U.S. 310, 316 (1945).
4. *Burger King*, 471 U.S. at 472 (quoting Shaffer v. Heitner, 433 U.S. 186 (1977) (Stevens, J., concurring)).
5. *Id.*
6. *Id.* at 478.
7. *Id.* at 479.
8. 444 U.S. 286, 296-97 (1980).

largest circulation."[9] According to the Court, "An individual injured in California need not go to Florida to seek redress from persons who, though remaining in Florida, knowingly cause the injury in California."[10]

More recently, the justices split on whether a defendant's awareness that a product would reach the forum state through the stream of commerce constitutes sufficient minimum contacts with the forum. In Asahi Metal Industry Co. v. Superior Court of California, Justice O'Connor, writing for a plurality of four justices, concluded that "[t]he placement of a product into the stream of commerce, without more, is not an act of the defendant purposefully directed toward the forum state."[11]

> Additional conduct of the defendant may indicate an intent or purpose to serve the market in the forum State, for example, designing the product for the market in the forum State, advertising in the forum State, establishing channels for providing regular advice to customers in the forum State, or marketing the product through a distributor who has agreed to serve as the sales agent in the forum State. But a defendant's awareness that the stream of commerce may or may not sweep the product into the forum state does not convert the mere act of placing the product into the stream into an act purposefully directed toward the forum State.[12]

In contrast, Justice Brennan, in his concurrence, concluded that no other "additional conduct" was necessary.[13] According to Justice Brennan:

> The stream of commerce refers not to unpredictable currents or eddies, but to the regular and anticipated flow of products from manufacture to distribution in retail sale. As long as a participant in this process is aware that the final product is being marketed in the forum State, the possibility of a lawsuit there cannot come as a surprise.[14]

The Court was, however, unanimous in its conclusion that California's exercise of jurisdiction over a dispute between a Japanese and Taiwanese company did not comport with "fair play and substantial justice."

2. Purposeful Availment and the Internet

In light of the Supreme Court's minimum contacts analysis, when does the display of a Web page or participation in online activities subject a person to personal jurisdiction? While a great deal has been written on the subject by lawyers, scholars, and students, the courts have still not reached a consensus on these questions. In part, this is due to the sensitive nature of jurisdiction analysis as well as the variety of different activities one may engage in over the

---

9. Calder v. Jones, 465 U.S. 783, 789-90 (1984).
10. *Id.* at 790.
11. 480 U.S. 102, 112 (1987).
12. *Id.*
13. *Id.* at 117 (Brennan, J., concurring).
14. *Id.*

Internet. The following materials provide the reader with the various approaches to this question. Are they consistent with the Supreme Court's decisions discussed above? Are the technical differences highlighted by the decisions relevant?

a) In General

INSET SYSTEMS, INC. v. INSTRUCTION SET, INC.

937 F. Supp. 161 (D. Conn. 1996)

COVELLO, District Judge. . . .

The plaintiff, Inset Systems, Inc. ("Inset"), is a corporation organized under the laws of the state of Connecticut, with its office and principal place of business in Brookfield, Connecticut. Inset develops and markets computer software and other related services throughout the world. The defendant, Instruction Set, Inc. ("ISI"), is a corporation organized under the laws of the state of Massachusetts, with its office and principal place of business in Natick, Massachusetts. ISI provides computer technology and support to thousands of organizations throughout the world. ISI does not have any employees, nor offices within Connecticut, and it does not conduct business in Connecticut on a regular basis.

On August 23, 1985, Inset filed for registration as the owner of the federal trademark INSET. . . .

Thereafter, ISI obtained "INSET.COM" as its Internet domain address. ISI uses this domain address to advertise its goods and services. . . .

Domain addresses are similar to street addresses, in that it is through this domain address that Internet users find one another. A domain address consists of three parts: the first part identifies the part of the Internet desired, such as world wide web (www), the second part is usually the name of the company or other identifying words, and the third part identifies the type of institution, such as government (.gov) or commercial (.com), etc. If a company uses a domain which is identical to the name or trademark of a company, an Internet user may inadvertently access an unintended company. Thereafter, the Internet user may not realize that the advertisement is actually from an unintended company, or the Internet user may erroneously assume that the source of information is the intended company. As a result, confusion in the marketplace could develop.

Unlike television and radio, in which advertisements are broadcast at certain times only, or newspapers in which advertisements are often disposed of quickly, advertisements over the Internet are available to Internet users continually, at the stroke of a few keys of a computer. At this time there are at least 10,000 Internet connected computer users in the state of Connecticut. . . .

Inset . . . argues that the requirement of the Connecticut long-arm statute has been satisfied because ISI has repeatedly solicited business within Connecticut via its Internet advertisement and the availability of its toll-free number. The Connecticut long-arm statute, C.G.S. §33-411(c)(2) states that "Every foreign corporation shall be subject to suit in this state, by a resident of this state . . . on any cause of action arising . . . out of any business solicited in this state . . . if the corporation has repeatedly so solicited business, whether the orders or offers relating thereto were accepted within or without the state. . . ."

In McFaddin v. National Executive Search, Inc., 354 F. Supp. 1166, 1169 (D. Conn. 1973), the court held that "the placing of at least six franchise ads over a six-month period in a newspaper whose circulation clearly includes Connecticut (citation omitted) demonstrates a sufficiently repetitious pattern to satisfy subsection (c)(2)" of the Connecticut long-arm statute, C.G.S. §33-411. . . .

Similarly, since March 1995, ISI has been continuously advertising over the Internet, which includes at least 10,000 access sites in Connecticut. Further, unlike hard-copy advertisements noted in the above two cases, which are often quickly disposed of and reach a limited number of potential consumers, Internet advertisements are in electronic printed form so that they can be accessed again and again by many more potential consumers.

The court concludes that advertising via the Internet is solicitation of a sufficient repetitive nature to satisfy subsection (c)(2) of the Connecticut long-arm statute, C.G.S. §33-411, thereby conferring Connecticut's long-arm jurisdiction upon ISI. . . .

The defendant claims that personal jurisdiction is lacking here because it does not have sufficient minimum contacts within Connecticut to satisfy constitutional precepts concerning due process. Minimum contacts are lacking, according to the defendant, because it is a Massachusetts corporation with its office and principal place of business in Natick, Massachusetts, "it does not conduct business in Connecticut on a regular basis," and it "does not maintain an office in Connecticut, nor does it have a sales force or employees in the State."

The plaintiff responds that minimum contacts comporting with due process have been satisfied because the defendant has used the Internet, as well as its toll-free number to try to conduct business within the state of Connecticut. . . .

The essence of the minimum contacts test is "that there be some act by which the defendant purposefully avails itself of the privilege of conducting activities within the forum State, thus invoking the benefits and protections of its laws." This "due process inquiry rests upon the totality of the circumstances rather than any mechanical criteria. . . ."

In *Whelen Eng'g Co.*, the court concluded that because "[the defendant] readily supplied interested potential customers with catalogs advertised in periodicals having Connecticut circulation, provided products on order . . . , and demonstrated its readiness to initiate telephone solicitation of Connecticut customers," it purposefully availed itself of the privilege of doing business within the state and therefore, could reasonably be expected to be hailed into court.

In the present case, Instruction has directed its advertising activities via the Internet and its toll-free number toward not only the state of Connecticut, but to all states. The Internet as well as toll-free numbers are designed to communicate with people and their businesses in every state. Advertisement on the Internet can reach as many as 10,000 Internet users within Connecticut alone. Further, once posted on the Internet, unlike television and radio advertising, the advertisement is available continuously to any Internet user. ISI has therefore, purposefully availed itself of the privilege of doing business within Connecticut.

The court concludes that since ISI purposefully directed its advertising activities toward this state on a continuing basis since March, 1995, it could reasonably anticipate the possibility of being hailed into court here. . . .

ZIPPO MANUFACTURING CO. V. ZIPPO DOT COM, INC.

952 F. Supp. 1119 (W.D. Pa. 1997)

McLAUGHLIN, District Judge.

This is an Internet domain name dispute. At this stage of the controversy, we must decide the Constitutionally permissible reach of Pennsylvania's Long Arm Statute, 42 Pa. C.S.A. 5322, through cyberspace. Plaintiff Zippo Manufacturing Corporation ("Manufacturing") has filed a five count complaint against Zippo Dot Com, Inc. ("Dot Com") alleging trademark dilution, infringement, and false designation. . . . Dot Com has moved to dismiss for lack of personal jurisdiction and improper venue. . . .

The facts relevant to this motion are as follows. Manufacturing is a Pennsylvania corporation with its principal place of business in Bradford, Pennsylvania. Manufacturing makes, among other things, well known "Zippo" tobacco lighters. Dot Com is a California corporation with its principal place of business in Sunnyvale, California. Dot Com operates an Internet Web site and an Internet news service and has obtained the exclusive right to use the domain names "zippo.com", "zippo.net" and "zipponews.com" on the Internet.

Dot Com's Web site contains information about the company, advertisements and an application for its Internet news service. The news service itself consists of three levels of membership—public/free, "Original" and "Super." Each successive level offers access to a greater number of Internet newsgroups. A customer who wants to subscribe to either the "Original" or "Super" level of service, fills out an on-line application that asks for a variety of information, including the person's name and address. Payment is made by credit card over

the Internet or the telephone. The application is then processed and the subscriber is assigned a password which permits the subscriber to view and/or
download Internet newsgroup messages that are stored on the Defendant's
server in California.

Dot Com's contacts with Pennsylvania have occurred almost exclusively
over the Internet. Dot Com's offices, employees and Internet servers are
located in California. Dot Com maintains no offices, employees or agents in
Pennsylvania. Dot Com's advertising for its service to Pennsylvania residents
involves posting information about its service on its Web page, which is accessible to Pennsylvania residents via the Internet. Defendant has approximately
140,000 paying subscribers worldwide. Approximately two percent (3,000) of
those subscribers are Pennsylvania residents. These subscribers have contracted
to receive Dot Com's service by visiting its Web site and filling out the application. Additionally, Dot Com has entered into agreements with seven Internet access providers in Pennsylvania to permit their subscribers to access Dot
Com's news service. Two of these providers are located in the Western District
of Pennsylvania.

The basis of the trademark claims is Dot Com's use of the word "Zippo"
in the domain names it holds, in numerous locations in its Web site and in the
heading of Internet newsgroup messages that have been posted by Dot Com
subscribers. When an Internet user views or downloads a newsgroup message
posted by a Dot Com subscriber, the word "Zippo" appears in the "Message-
ID" and "Organization" sections of the heading. The news message itself,
containing text and/or pictures, follows. Manufacturing points out that some
of the messages contain adult oriented, sexually explicit subject matter.

1.   THE TRADITIONAL FRAMEWORK

... Pennsylvania's long arm jurisdiction statute is codified at 42 Pa.
C.S.A. 5322(a). The portion of the statute authorizing us to exercise jurisdiction here permits the exercise of jurisdiction over non-resident defendants
upon: Contracting to supply services or things in this Commonwealth.

It is undisputed that Dot Com contracted to supply Internet news services
to approximately 3,000 Pennsylvania residents and also entered into agreements with seven Internet access providers in Pennsylvania. Moreover, even
if Dot Com's conduct did not satisfy a specific provision of the statute, we
would nevertheless be authorized to exercise jurisdiction to the "fullest extent
allowed under the Constitution of the United States." ...

A three-pronged test has emerged for determining whether the exercise of
specific personal jurisdiction over a non-resident defendant is appropriate:
(1) the defendant must have sufficient "minimum contacts" with the forum
state, (2) the claim asserted against the defendant must arise out of those
contacts, and (3) the exercise of jurisdiction must be reasonable.
The "Constitutional touchstone" of the minimum contacts analysis is

embodied in the first prong, "whether the defendant purposefully established" contacts with the forum state. *Burger King Corp*. Defendants who " 'reach out beyond one state' and create continuing relationships and obligations with the citizens of another state are subject to regulation and sanctions in the other State for consequences of their actions." Id. "[T]he foreseeability that is critical to the due process analysis is . . . that the defendant's conduct and connection with the forum State are such that he should reasonably expect to be haled into court there." World-Wide Volkswagen Corp. v. Woodson, 444 U.S. 286, 297 (1980). This protects defendants from being forced to answer for their actions in a foreign jurisdiction based on "random, fortuitous or attenuated" contacts. "Jurisdiction is proper, however, where contacts proximately result from actions by the defendant himself that create a 'substantial connection' with the forum State." *Burger King*.

The "reasonableness" prong exists to protect defendants against unfairly inconvenient litigation. Under this prong, the exercise of jurisdiction will be reasonable if it does not offend "traditional notions of fair play and substantial justice." *International Shoe*. When determining the reasonableness of a particular forum, the court must consider the burden on the defendant in light of other factors including: "the forum state's interest in adjudicating the dispute; the plaintiff's interest in obtaining convenient and effective relief, at least when that interest is not adequately protected by the plaintiff's right to choose the forum; the interstate judicial system's interest in obtaining the most efficient resolution of controversies; and the shared interest of the several states in furthering fundamental substantive social policies."

2. THE INTERNET AND JURISDICTION

In Hanson v. Denckla, the Supreme Court noted that "[a]s technological progress has increased the flow of commerce between States, the need for jurisdiction has undergone a similar increase." Twenty-seven years later, the Court observed that jurisdiction could not be avoided "merely because the defendant did not physically enter the forum state." *Burger King*. The Court observed that:

> [I]t is an inescapable fact of modern commercial life that a substantial amount of commercial business is transacted solely by mail and wire communications across state lines, thus obviating the need for physical presence within a State in which business is conducted.

Enter the Internet, a global "'super-network' of over 15,000 computer networks used by over 30 million individuals, corporations, organizations, and educational institutions worldwide." . . . "In recent years, businesses have begun to use the Internet to provide information and products to consumers and other businesses." The Internet makes it possible to conduct business throughout the world entirely from a desktop. With this global revolution looming on the horizon, the development of the law concerning the permissible scope of personal jurisdiction based on Internet use is in its infant stages. The cases are scant. Nevertheless, our review of the available cases and materials reveals that the likelihood that personal jurisdiction can be constitutionally exercised is directly proportionate to the nature and quality of commercial activity that an entity conducts over the Internet. This sliding scale is consistent with well-developed personal jurisdiction principles. At one end of the spectrum are situations where a defendant clearly does business over the Internet. If the defendant enters into contracts with residents of a foreign jurisdiction that involve the knowing and repeated transmission of computer files over the Internet, personal jurisdiction is proper. E.g. CompuServe, Inc. v. Patterson, [*infra*]. At the opposite end are situations where a defendant has simply posted information on an Internet Web site which is accessible to users in foreign jurisdictions. A passive Web site that does little more than make information available to those who are interested in it is not grounds for the exercise of personal jurisdiction. E.g. Bensusan Restaurant Corp. v. King, 937 F. Supp. 295 (S.D.N.Y. 1996). The middle ground is occupied by interactive Web sites where a user can exchange information with the host computer. In these cases, the exercise of jurisdiction is determined by examining the level of interactivity and commercial nature of the exchange of information that occurs on the Web site.

Traditionally, when an entity intentionally reaches beyond its boundaries to conduct business with foreign residents, the exercise of specific jurisdiction is proper. Different results should not be reached simply because business is conducted over the Internet. [The court's discussion of *CompuServe* is omitted.]

In Maritz, Inc. v. Cybergold, Inc., 947 F. Supp. 1328 (E.D. Mo. 1996), the defendant had put up a Web site as a promotion for its upcoming Internet service. The service consisted of assigning users an electronic mailbox and then forwarding advertisements for products and services that matched the users' interests to those electronic mailboxes. The defendant planned to charge advertisers and provide users with incentives to view the advertisements. Although the service was not yet operational, users were encouraged to add their address to a mailing list to receive updates about the service. The court rejected the defendant's contention that it operated a "passive Web site." The court reasoned that the defendant's conduct amounted to "active solicitations" and "promotional activities" designed to "develop a mailing list of Internet users" and that the defendant "indiscriminately responded to every user" who accessed the site.

[The court's discussion of *Inset* and *Bensusan* are omitted].

3.   APPLICATION TO THIS CASE

First, we note that this is not an Internet advertising case in the line of *Inset Systems* and *Bensusan*, Dot Com has not just posted information on a Web site that is accessible to Pennsylvania residents who are connected to the Internet. This is not even an interactivity case in the line of *Maritz*, supra. Dot Com has done more than create an interactive Web site through which it exchanges information with Pennsylvania residents in hopes of using that information for commercial gain later. We are not being asked to determine whether Dot Com's Web site alone constitutes the purposeful availment of doing business in Pennsylvania. This is a "doing business over the Internet" case in the line of *CompuServe*, supra. We are being asked to determine whether Dot Com's conducting of electronic commerce with Pennsylvania residents constitutes the purposeful availment of doing business in Pennsylvania. We conclude that it does. Dot Com has contracted with approximately 3,000 individuals and seven Internet access providers in Pennsylvania. The intended object of these transactions has been the downloading of the electronic messages that form the basis of this suit in Pennsylvania.

We find Dot Com's efforts to characterize its conduct as falling short of purposeful availment of doing business in Pennsylvania wholly unpersuasive. At oral argument, Defendant repeatedly characterized its actions as merely "operating a Web site" or "advertising." Dot Com also cites to a number of cases from this Circuit which, it claims, stand for the proposition that merely advertising in a forum, without more, is not a sufficient minimal contact. This argument is misplaced. Dot Com has done more than advertise on the Internet in Pennsylvania. Defendant has sold passwords to approximately 3,000 subscribers in Pennsylvania and entered into seven contracts with Internet access providers to furnish its services to their customers in Pennsylvania.

Dot Com also contends that its contacts with Pennsylvania residents are "fortuitous" within the meaning of *World-Wide Volkswagen*. Defendant argues that it has not "actively" solicited business in Pennsylvania and that any business it conducts with Pennsylvania residents has resulted from contacts that were initiated by Pennsylvanians who visited the Defendant's Web site. The fact that Dot Com's services have been consumed in Pennsylvania is not "fortuitous" within the meaning of *World-Wide Volkswagen*. In *World-Wide Volkswagen*, a couple that had purchased a vehicle in New York, while they were New York residents, were injured while driving that vehicle through Oklahoma and brought suit in an Oklahoma state court. The manufacturer did not sell its vehicles in Oklahoma and had not made an effort to establish business relationships in Oklahoma. The Supreme Court characterized the manufacturer's ties with Oklahoma as fortuitous because they resulted entirely out of the fact that the plaintiffs had driven their car into that state.

Here, Dot Com argues that its contacts with Pennsylvania residents are fortuitous because Pennsylvanians happened to find its Web site or heard about its news service elsewhere and decided to subscribe. This argument misconstrues the concept of fortuitous contacts embodied in *World-Wide Volkswagen*. Dot Com's contacts with Pennsylvania would be fortuitous within the meaning of *World-Wide Volkswagen* if it had no Pennsylvania subscribers and an Ohio subscriber forwarded a copy of a file he obtained from Dot Com to a friend in Pennsylvania or an Ohio subscriber brought his computer along on a trip to Pennsylvania and used it to access Dot Com's service. That is not the situation here. Dot Com repeatedly and consciously chose to process Pennsylvania residents' applications and to assign them passwords. Dot Com knew that the result of these contracts would be the transmission of electronic messages into Pennsylvania. The transmission of these files was entirely within its control. Dot Com cannot maintain that these contracts are "fortuitous" or "coincidental" within the meaning of *World-Wide Volkswagen*. When a defendant makes a conscious choice to conduct business with the residents of a forum state, "it has clear notice that it is subject to suit there." Dot Com was under no obligation to sell its services to Pennsylvania residents. It freely chose to do so, presumably in order to profit from those transactions. If a corporation determines that the risk of being subject to personal jurisdiction in a particular forum is too great, it can choose to sever its connection to the state. If Dot Com had not wanted to be amenable to jurisdiction in Pennsylvania, the solution would have been simple — it could have chosen not to sell its services to Pennsylvania residents.

Next, Dot Com argues that its forum-related activities are not numerous or significant enough to create a "substantial connection" with Pennsylvania. Defendant points to the fact that only two percent of its subscribers are Pennsylvania residents. However, the Supreme Court has made clear that even a single contact can be sufficient. The test has always focused on the "nature and quality" of the contacts with the forum and not the quantity of those contacts. . . .

We also conclude that the cause of action arises out of Dot Com's forum-related conduct in this case. . . .

In the instant case, both a significant amount of the alleged infringement and dilution, and resulting injury have occurred in Pennsylvania. The object of Dot Com's contracts with Pennsylvania residents is the transmission of the messages that Plaintiff claims dilute and infringe upon its trademark. When these messages are transmitted into Pennsylvania and viewed by Pennsylvania residents on their computers, there can be no question that the alleged infringement and dilution occur in Pennsylvania. Moreover, since Manufacturing is a Pennsylvania corporation, a substantial amount of the injury from the alleged wrongdoing is likely to occur in Pennsylvania. Thus, we conclude that the cause of action arises out of Dot Com's forum-related activities under the authority of both *Tefal* and *Indianapolis Colts*, supra.

Finally, Dot Com argues that the exercise of jurisdiction would be unreasonable in this case. We disagree. There can be no question that Pennsylvania has a strong interest in adjudicating disputes involving the alleged infringement of trademarks owned by resident corporations. We must also give due regard to the Plaintiff's choice to seek relief in Pennsylvania. These concerns outweigh the burden created by forcing the Defendant to defend the suit in Pennsylvania, especially when Dot Com consciously chose to conduct business in Pennsylvania, pursuing profits from the actions that are now in question.

The Due Process Clause is not a "territorial shield to interstate obligations that have been voluntarily assumed." *Burger King.*

We conclude that this Court may appropriately exercise personal jurisdiction over the Defendant. . . .

ALS Scan, Inc. v. Digital Service Consultants, Inc.

293 F.3d 707 (4th Cir. 2002)

Niemeyer, Circuit Judge. . . .

I

ALS Scan, Inc., a Maryland corporation with its place of business in Columbia, Maryland, commenced this action for copyright infringement against Digital Service Consultants, Inc. ("Digital"), and Digital's customers, Robert Wilkins and Alternative Products, Inc. (collectively, "Alternative Products"). ALS Scan, which creates and markets adult photographs of female models for distribution over the Internet, claims that Alternative Products appropriated copies of hundreds of ALS Scan's copyrighted photographs and placed them on its websites, *www.abpefarc.net* and *www.abpeuarc.com,* thereby gaining revenue from them through membership fees and advertising. ALS Scan further alleges that Digital, as the Internet Service Provider ("ISP") for Alternative Products, "enabled" Alternative Products to publish ALS Scan's copyrighted photographs on the Internet by providing Alternative Products with the bandwidth service needed to maintain its websites. ALS Scan thus alleges that all of the defendants have infringed and are infringing its copyrights within Maryland and elsewhere by selling, publishing, and displaying its copyrighted photographs.

Digital filed a motion to dismiss the complaint against it under Federal Rule of Civil Procedure 12(b)(2), asserting that the district court lacked personal jurisdiction over it. In support of its motion, Digital provided affidavits demonstrating that Digital is a Georgia corporation with its only place of business in Atlanta. Digital asserts that it is an ISP which provided bandwidth service to Alternative Products as a customer but that it is not affiliated in any way with Alternative Products except through an arms-length customer relationship. In addition, Digital states that it did not select the infringing photographs for publication; it did not have knowledge that they were posted on Alternative Products' website; and it received no income from Alternative Products' subscribers. Digital acknowledges that it does maintain its own website, *www.dscga.com,* but asserts that its website "contains no means for any person to enter into a contract with, transfer funds to, or otherwise transact business with, Digital."

Digital also states that, other than through the Internet, it has no contacts with the State of Maryland. It avers that it conducts no business and has no offices in Maryland; that it has no contracts with any persons or entities in Maryland; that it derives no income from any clients or business in Maryland; that it does not advertise in Maryland (other than through its website); and that it owns no property in Maryland.

In a responding affidavit, ALS Scan asserts that copies of its copyrighted photographs have appeared on Alternative Products' two websites, *www. abpefarc.net* and *www.abpeuarc.com*. It also alleges that one of its employees in Maryland purchased an "on-line" membership to *www.abpefarc.net,* using a credit card, and, by obtaining that membership, the employee received a "user name" and a "password" to access the website. That website, it asserts, displayed ALS Scan's copyrighted photographs, allegedly in violation of the Copyright Act.

The district court granted Digital's motion to dismiss for lack of personal jurisdiction. The court found that it had neither specific nor general jurisdiction over Digital because "Digital does not engage in any continuous and systematic activities within Maryland, and there is no evidence that [ALS Scan's] claim arises out of any contacts which Digital may have with Maryland." . . .

III

In this case, ALS Scan argues that Digital's activity in enabling Alternative Products' publication of the infringing photographs on the Internet, thereby causing ALS Scan injury in Maryland, forms a proper basis for the district court's specific jurisdiction over Digital. The question thus becomes whether a person electronically transmitting or enabling the transmission of information via the Internet to Maryland, causing injury there, subjects the person to the jurisdiction of a court in Maryland, a question of first impression in the Fourth Circuit.

Applying the traditional due process principles governing a State's jurisdiction over persons outside of the State based on Internet activity requires some adaptation of those principles because the Internet is omnipresent — when a person places information on the Internet, he can communicate with persons in virtually every jurisdiction. If we were to conclude as a general principle that a person's act of placing information on the Internet subjects that person to personal jurisdiction in each State in which the information is accessed, then the defense of personal jurisdiction, in the sense that a State has geographically limited judicial power, would no longer exist. The person placing information on the Internet would be subject to personal jurisdiction in every State.

But under current Supreme Court jurisprudence, despite advances in technology, State judicial power over persons appears to remain limited to persons within the State's boundaries and to those persons outside of the State who have minimum contacts with the State such that the State's exercise of judicial power over the person would not offend traditional notions of fair play and substantial justice. . . . But even under the limitations articulated in *International Shoe* and retained by *Hanson,* the argument could still be made that the Internet's electronic signals are surrogates for the person and that Internet users conceptually enter a State to the extent that they send their electronic signals into the State, establishing those minimum contacts sufficient to subject the sending person to personal jurisdiction in the State where the signals are received. Under this argument, the electronic transmissions "symbolize those activities . . . within the state which courts will deem to be sufficient to satisfy the demands of due process." *Int'l Shoe,* 326 U.S. at 316-17. But if that broad interpretation of minimum contacts were adopted, State jurisdiction over persons would be universal, and notions of limited State sovereignty and personal jurisdiction would be eviscerated. . . .

Until the due process concepts of personal jurisdiction are reconceived and rearticulated by the Supreme Court in light of advances in technology, we must develop, under existing principles, the more limited circumstances when it can be deemed that an out-of-state citizen, through electronic contacts, has conceptually "entered" the State via the Internet for jurisdictional purposes. Such principles are necessary to recognize that a State does have limited judicial authority over out-of-state persons who use the Internet to contact persons within the State. . . .

. . . [W]e conclude that a State may, consistent with due process, exercise judicial power over a person outside of the State when that person (1) directs electronic activity into the State, (2) with the manifested intent of engaging in business or other interactions within the State, and (3) that activity creates, in a person within the State, a potential cause of action cognizable in the State's courts. Under this standard, a person who simply places information on the Internet does not subject himself to jurisdiction in each State into which the electronic signal is transmitted and received. Such passive Internet activity does not generally include directing electronic activity into the State with the manifested intent of engaging business or other interactions in the State thus creating in a person within the State a potential cause of action cognizable in courts located in the State.

This standard for reconciling contacts through electronic media with standard due process principles is not dissimilar to that applied by the Supreme Court in *Calder v. Jones,* 465 U.S. 783 (1984). In *Calder,* the Court held that a California court could constitutionally exercise personal jurisdiction over a Florida citizen whose only material contact with California was to write a libelous story in Florida, directed at a California citizen, for a publication circulated in California, knowing that the "injury would be felt by [the Californian] in the State in which she lives and works." *Id.* at 789-90. Analogously, under the standard we adopt and apply today, specific jurisdiction in the Internet context may be based only on an out-of-state person's Internet activity directed at Maryland and causing injury that gives rise to a potential claim cognizable in Maryland.

Applying this standard to the present case, we conclude that Digital's activity was, at most, passive and therefore does not subject it to the judicial power of a Maryland court even though electronic signals from Digital's facility were concededly received in Maryland. Digital functioned from Georgia as an ISP, and in that role provided bandwidth to Alternative Products, also located in Georgia, to enable Alternative Products to create a website and send information over the Internet. It did not select or knowingly transmit infringing photographs specifically to Maryland with the intent of engaging in business or any other transaction in Maryland. Rather, its role as an ISP was at most passive. Surely, it cannot be said that Digital "purposefully availed" itself of the privilege of conducting business or other transactions in Maryland.

Indeed, the only *direct* contact that Digital had with Maryland was through the general publication of its website on the Internet. But that website is unrelated to ALS Scan's claim in this case because Digital's website was not involved in the publication of any infringing photographs.

Thus, under the standard articulated in this case, Digital did not direct its electronic activity specifically at any target in Maryland; it did not manifest an intent to engage in a business or some other interaction in Maryland; and none of its conduct in enabling a website created a cause of action in Maryland, although on this last point, facts would have to be developed about whether Digital continued to enable the website after receiving notice. This factual issue, however, need not be resolved because Digital's conduct does not satisfy the first two prongs of the test.

Accordingly, we agree with the district court that Digital's contacts in Maryland do not justify a Maryland court's exercise of specific jurisdiction over Digital.

IV

It is not clear whether ALS Scan contends that, even if it is unable to establish specific jurisdiction over Digital, a Maryland court should nevertheless assert *general* jurisdiction over Digital. At one point in its brief, ALS Scan acknowledged that Digital's contacts with Maryland are "perhaps not extensive enough" to justify a finding of general jurisdiction. But, somewhat in tension with this acknowledgment, ALS Scan continues to argue that Digital's general contacts with Maryland through the maintenance of its own website are sufficient to justify the district court's exercise of general jurisdiction over Digital. . . .

We are not prepared at this time to recognize that a State may obtain general jurisdiction over out-of-state persons who regularly and systematically transmit electronic signals into the State via the Internet based solely on those transmissions. Something more would have to be demonstrated. And we need not decide today what that "something more" is because ALS Scan has shown no more.

Other than maintain its website on the Internet, Digital has engaged in no activity in Maryland, and its only contacts with the State occur when persons in Maryland access Digital's website. Even though electronic transmissions from maintenance of a website on the Internet may have resulted in numerous and repeated electronic connections with persons in Maryland, such transmissions do not add up to the quality of contacts necessary for a State to have jurisdiction over the person for all purposes. . . .

COMMENTS AND QUESTIONS

1. Following the *Zippo* court's sliding scale analysis and distinguishing Calder v. Jones, the Ninth Circuit held that an "ostensibly passive homepage" was insufficient to establish purposeful availment. *See* Cybersell, Inc. v. Cybersell, Inc., 130 F.3d 414 (9th Cir. 1997). According to the court, the defendant "did nothing to encourage people in Arizona to access its site, and there is no evidence that any part of its business (let alone a continuous part of its business) was sought or achieved in Arizona." *Id.* at 419. *See also* Toys R Us v. Step Two S.A., 318 F.3d 446 (3d Cir. 2003) (holding that the existence of a commercial and interactive site alone is insufficient to establish that the defendant purposefully availed itself in the forum state).

2. Considering the *Zippo* three-part test, what would you advise a client in setting up her Web site? Would a disclaimer on the Web site be prudent? If so, what should it state? Should it state that the site is only intended for users of X state? Should you counsel the client to use a toll-free number on the site? Should the number of hits a Web site receives from a jurisdiction matter?

3. Why should the level of interactivity of a Web site influence the due process analysis? Is there a relationship between the interactivity of a Web site and the "foreseeability" that the site is reaching individuals from that jurisdiction? Is interactivity evidence that the defendant intentionally directed activities to a particular forum? *See* Hsin Ten Enterprise USA, Inc. v. Clark Enterprises, 138 F. Supp. 2d 449 (S.D.N.Y. 2000) (stating that courts associate interactive Web sites with advertising purposefully directed toward the forum state). *Consider* Millennium Enterprises, Inc. v. Millennium Music, LP, 33 F. Supp. 2d 907, 913 (D. Or. 1999) in which the court decided whether a Web site in which customers could purchase compact discs, request franchising information, and join a discount club was sufficiently interactive to justify jurisdiction. According to the court:

> On its face, the site would appear to suffice for personal jurisdiction under the middle category in *Zippo*; the level of potential interactivity, while not necessarily high, is not insubstantial. Further, the potential exchange of information can be commercial in nature. However, the court finds that the middle interactive category of Internet contacts as described in *Zippo* needs further refinement to include the fundamental requirement of personal jurisdiction: "deliberate action" within the forum state in the form of

> transactions between the defendant and residents of the forum or conduct of the defendant purposefully directed at residents of the forum state. . . .
>
> Defendants' Internet Web site, interactive though it may be, is not "conduct and connection" with Oregon giving defendants "fair warning" so that they would reasonably anticipate being "haled" into court here. Defendants have not taken action creating "a substantial connection" with Oregon, or deliberately engaged in "significant activities" within Oregon, or created "ongoing obligations" with residents of Oregon in a manner related to plaintiff's claims. See *Burger King*, 471 U.S. at 473, 475-76. Rather, defendants have published information on an Internet Web site that is accessible to whomever may find it. See *Bensusan*, 937 F. Supp. at 301. The fact that someone who accesses defendants' Web site can purchase a compact disc does not render defendants' actions "purposefully directed" at this forum. Id. . . . It is the conduct of the defendants, rather than the medium utilized by them, to which the parameters of specific jurisdiction apply. *World-Wide Volkswagen*, 444 U.S. at 297.

33 F. Supp. 2d at 921.

As in *ALS Scan*, under this approach, a plaintiff must show that the Web site was "intentionally or purposefully" targeted at the forum state. 33 F. Supp. 2d at 922.

4. Is *Inset* consistent with the Supreme Court's interpretation of purposeful availment? If so, then why the need for any other test?

5. How does the owner of a Web page know where potential viewers are located? Is it more accurate to describe the contact as fortuitous based upon users "pulling" the data that comprise a Web page to their jurisdiction instead of a defendant "sending" the data to the user? *Cf.* World-Wide Volkswagen Corp. v. Woodson, 444 U.S. 286 (1980) (holding that unilateral actions of the plaintiff are insufficient to establish jurisdiction over a defendant if they were reasonably foreseeable).

6. A different question is raised when Web sites or individuals using Web sites enter into contractual agreements. Under those circumstances, the agreement itself represents evidence that the party purposefully availed itself of the benefits of the forum. The classic Internet case on this is CompuServe, Inc. v. Patterson, 89 F.3d 1257 (1996), in which jurisdiction in Ohio was upheld based upon the defendant transmitting software to and entering into an ongoing contractual relationship with CompuServe which was headquartered in Ohio. In *CompuServe*, the court also concluded that the defendant's letters and telephone calls to CompuServe threatening litigation were evidence that he purposefully availed himself of the Ohio forum. Should the same conclusion be reached for e-mail complaints?

7. Should the sale of a single product or service from a Web site justify specific jurisdiction? *See* Mattel, Inc. v. Adventure Apparel, No. 00 CIV. 4085 (RWS) (Mar. 22, 2001) (holding that single sale to plaintiff's investigator was sufficient to support jurisdiction); Ty Inc. v. Baby Me Inc., No. 00 C 6016 (N.D. Ill. Apr. 20, 2001) (same). *But see* Millennium Enterprises, Inc. v. Millennium Music, LP, 33 F. Supp. 2d 907, 911 (D. Or. 1999) (concluding that the sale of a single CD into the jurisdiction was insufficient).

8. Should it matter whether the transaction involved "snail" mail requiring a delivery address, or if it was merely electronic? Should a single e-mail represent sufficient minimum contacts for the exercise of specific jurisdiction? *See* Internet Doorway Inc. v. Parks, 138 F. Supp. 2d 773 (S.D. Miss. 2001) (holding that a single e-mail is sufficient to create specific jurisdiction and that the "sliding scale" applies only to Web sites).

9. To what extent do analogies to advertising in different media help to inform the jurisdictional inquiry? Is the Internet more like a telephone or print advertising? In what respects?

10. The Hague Conference on Private International Law is attempting to resolve some of these jurisdictional issues at the international level. For example, the draft Convention on Jurisdiction and Foreign Judgments in Civil and Commercial Matters provides that contracting states would recognize a consumer's right to "bring a claim in the courts of the State in which it is habitually resident," and that claims against consumers may only be brought in the State of habitual residence of the consumer. *See id.* Article 7. Similarly, with respect to contracts, the draft provides that a plaintiff may bring an action in the courts of a State: (1) in matters relating to the supply of goods, in the State in which the goods were supplied; (2) contracts for services, where the services were provided; or (3) when both goods and services are provided, in the State in which performance of the principal obligation took place. *See id.* Article 6. To what extent do these approaches differ from the case law in the United States? What are the advantages and disadvantages of following the approach adopted by the Hague Conference versus the minimum contact approach?

b) Tortious Conduct

BOCHAN v. LA FONTAINE

68 F. Supp. 2d 692 (E.D. Va. 1999)

ELLIS, District Judge. . . .

Plaintiff, a devoté of John F. Kennedy (JFK) conspiracy theories, is the district manager of a group of theaters in Northern Virginia. Journalists Ray and Mary La Fontaine are Texas residents who wrote a book on the JFK assassination entitled Oswald Talked: The New Evidence in the JFK Assassination. Defendant Robert Harris, who is yet another JFK conspiracy devoté, is a resident of Albuquerque, New Mexico, where he owns Computer Works, a New Mexico-based computer systems business. Plaintiff purchased the La Fontaines' book at Borders Bookstore in Fairfax, Va., sometime after it was published in 1996. He became a vocal critic of the book, often expressing his criticisms via the Internet, specifically by posting his critiques to the interactive newsgroup alt.conspiracy.jfk. These postings provoked defendants to post responses to the newsgroup, which responsive postings are the alleged defamations in this action.

The principal precipitating event occurred on October 12, 1998, when plaintiff posted a message to the La Fontaines that contained the following quote from the acknowledgments of the La Fontaine's book: "'We thank Charlotte and Eugenia for putting up with weird parents.'" The next day, Ray La Fontaine responded from Dallas, Texas, by posting a message to alt. conspiracy.jfk. This October 13, 1998, posting was labeled "The scum posts of Bochan," and stated, "I know you like kids, Bochan, but I suggest you limit your interest to trolling in alt.sex.festish.tinygirls and leave our children out of it." La Fontaine then went on in this posting to provide "for anyone interested" what La Fontaine claimed was Bochan's October 1997 author profile with Deja News, an Internet discussion network. This author profile, as provided by Bochan, listed 238 articles, allegedly posted by Bochan, identifying the individual newsgroups to which each article was posted. The majority of the articles were listed as posted to various conspiracy theory sites, but according to La Fontaine's version of the author profile, Bochan also posted articles to three apparently pornographic sites: alt.sex.fetish.tinygirls, alt.sex.pictures. male, and alt.sex.snuff.cannibalism. La Fontaine followed the alleged profile with the following additional editorial comment directed to Bochan: "How come you only posted once to alt.sex.fetish.tinygirls and alt.sex.pictures.male, Bochan? Did you get lucky the first time around?" . . .

Harris also entered the fray on October 14, 1998, stating, in a posting to alt.conspiracy.jfk, that although Harris's children were grown, he could imagine how the La Fontaines must feel to have a "sicko" like plaintiff making "not very subtle references" to their children, and further, expressing the hope that Bochan's "tastes run more to sex.pictures.male than to tinygirls." On October 17, 1998, Harris posted another message to alt.conspiracy.jfk which called alt.sex.fetish.tinygirls "Bochan's newsgroup."

On the basis of these postings, Bochan sues both the La Fontaines and Harris in the Eastern District of Virginia for defamation and for intentional infliction of emotional distress, alleging that all defendants have publicly accused him of being a pedophile.

At the threshold, defendants assert a lack of personal jurisdiction. In support of this contention, the La Fontaines state that they i) have not been in Virginia since 1993, when they drove from National Airport to the District of Columbia, ii) have not participated in any book promotions in Virginia, iii) receive no royalties from Virginia sales as they do not directly sell their book in Virginia, nor do they directly receive royalties on books sold by others in Virginia, but rather receive royalties on the total books sold by their publisher to national chains, and iv) have never derived any revenue that they are aware of from Virginia. Moreover, they note as significant that they i) do not have their own Web site, ii) do not conduct commercial activity over the Internet, and iii) made the allegedly defamatory postings by accessing the Internet through a California-based Internet service provider.

Harris, in support of his personal jurisdiction defense, states that he i) has never conducted any business in Virginia, ii) has only visited Virginia once, in 1994, to attend a Washington, D.C. conference and visit some historic sites in Virginia, iii) did not use any Virginia-based company in posting the allegedly defamatory comments, but instead used either California or New Mexico-based Internet service providers, and iv) did not direct his Internet postings to any Virginia resident. He further notes as significant that i) his Web site specifically states that Computer Works sells computers only in New Mexico, and ii) Computer Works has never sold any computers or computer products to anyone in Virginia. Bochan responds that the La Fontaines posted the allegedly defamatory messages using an account with AOL, a Virginia-based company, and moreover, that the La Fontaines have advertised, promoted and sold their book in Virginia. As to Harris, Bochan notes i) that the Web site for his business, Computer Works, is interactive, contains contact information and advertisements, and is accessible to Virginia residents 24 hours a day, and ii) that Harris has advertised specific computers in a variety of newsgroups, suggesting that he would take credit cards over the Internet, and that there were no geographical limitations on buyers. Bochan moreover states that all defendants knew that he resides and works in Virginia, and that the reputational harm, as well as the emotional distress, would be suffered in Virginia.

A. THE LA FONTAINE DEFENDANTS

Analysis properly begins with the question whether the La Fontaines' conduct fits within the reach of §8.01-328.1(A)(3). Put more concretely, the question is whether the La Fontaines committed a tort (i.e. libel) in Virginia by posting certain messages to an Internet newsgroup via AOL and Earthlink.net. This, as it happens, is a novel question in Virginia and there do not appear to be any decisions from other jurisdictions that are factually identical. There are, however, factually analogous cases that shed some light on how the Supreme Court of Virginia would analyze this issue. In Krantz v. Air Line Pilots Association, Int'l, 427 S.E.2d 326, 245 Va. 202 (1993), the defendant airline pilot posted a message from New York to ACCESS, a computer bulletin board physically located in Virginia. This message called for other pilots to pass the word that plaintiff was a "scab," apparently in an attempt to sabotage plaintiff's prospective employment at another airline. The Supreme Court of Virginia concluded that defendant's use of a bulletin board based in a Virginia facility satisfied §8.01-328.1(A)(3). In reaching this conclusion, the court stated that "[w]ithout the use of ACCESS, a Virginia facility, [defendant] could not have obtained those recruits, and there would have been no interference with [plaintiff's] prospective contract, the third required element for a prima facie showing of this sort." See Krantz, 427 S.E.2d at 328.

Several federal district courts have applied the principles enunciated in Krantz to cases alleging Internet torts. In Telco Communications v. An Apple a Day, 977 F. Supp. 404 (E.D. Va. 1997), the court, in dicta, concluded that jurisdiction existed under §8.01-328.1(A)(3) on the ground that "[b]ut for the Internet service providers [AOL] and users present in Virginia, the alleged tort of defamation would not have occurred in Virginia." Thus, the court concluded that those defendants fell "under the jurisdictional net cast by *Krantz.*" In contrast, the court in Mitchell v. McGowan, Civ. No. 98-1026-A, 1998 U.S. Dist. LEXIS 18587 (E.D. Va. September 18, 1998) (unpublished disposition), concluded that the defendant "appears to escape [the 'net' cast by *Krantz*] because the computer bulletin board he accessed is based in Texas," noting that this distinction, though rather "fine," was dispositive. Thus, since *Krantz* courts have focused in large measure on the location of the Internet service provider or the server on which the bulletin board is stored and the role played by this service or hardware in facilitating the alleged tort.

Under this analysis, a prima facie showing of a sufficient act by the La Fontaines in Virginia follows from their use of the AOL account, a Virginia-based service, to publish the allegedly defamatory statements. According to Bochan's expert, because the postings were accomplished through defendant's AOL account, they were transmitted first to AOL's USENET server hardware, located in Loudon County, Virginia.[23] There, the message was apparently both stored temporarily and transmitted to other USENET servers around the world. Thus, as to the La Fontaines, because publication is a required element of defamation, and a prima facie showing has been made that the use of USENET server in Virginia was integral to that publication, there is a sufficient act in Virginia to satisfy §8.01-328.1(A)(3).

B.   DEFENDANT HARRIS

Because Harris did not use an AOL account after accessing the Internet, or use any Virginia-based service, but instead used only the Internet service providers Earthlink, located in California, or High Fiber, located in New Mexico, there is nothing in the record to suggest that Harris committed any tortious act in Virginia within the meaning of §8.01-328.1(A)(3). Therefore, personal jurisdiction over Harris, if it exists at all, must be based on §8.01-328.1(A)(4). In this regard, because there is no dispute that the alleged injury occurred in Virginia, the question is whether Harris regularly does or solicits business in Virginia or engages in any persistent course of conduct in Virginia.

Courts determining personal jurisdiction primarily on the basis of Internet activity generally focus on "the nature and quality of activity that a defendant conducts over the Internet." A judicial consensus has generally emerged that

23. Defendants' expert notes that the newsgroup alt.conspiracy.jfk was created in Clearwater, Florida, that many newsgroups are unrelated to any specific physical or geographical area, and that the vast majority of messages posted to newgroups via AOL are not specifically targeted at any particular geographical area. These statements do not, however, clarify where and how storage and transmission of the postings on the newsgroup actually occur.

personal jurisdiction exists when Internet activities involve the conduct of business over the Internet, including on-line contracting with residents of the jurisdiction or other kinds of substantial commercial interactivity. Federal courts in Virginia in particular have generally found that Internet advertising accessible to Virginia residents 24 hours a day constitutes solicitation of business in Virginia sufficient to satisfy the requirements of §8.01-328.1(A)(4). Thus, in *Telco*, the district court, addressing §8.01-328.1(A)(4), found that jurisdiction existed over defendants who had issued press releases on the Internet that allegedly caused the plaintiffs' stock prices to fall. In that case, the district court concluded that defendants were conducting business over the Internet because they were advertising their firm and soliciting investment banking assistance when they posted the press releases. See *Telco*, 977 F. Supp. at 406. The court's reasoning was that "[b]ecause [defendants] conducted their advertising and soliciting over the Internet, which could be accessed by a Virginia resident 24 hours a day" the defendants conducted their business "regularly" under the terms of the long-arm statute sufficient to satisfy 8.01-328.1(A)(4). Id. at 407.

Here, Harris, as the owner of Computer Works, has solicited business in Virginia by promoting and advertising his computer hardware company on the Internet through its Web site, accessible to Virginia Internet users 24 hours a day. This Web site is interactive in several ways, although no sales are concluded through it. Moreover, even if the Web site contains sufficient geographic limitations to diminish its jurisdictional significance outside those geographic areas, Harris's own advertisements of specific computers on Internet newsgroups include his name, company and telephone numbers so that he can be contacted, and state that there are no surcharges for Visa or Mastercard, occasionally specifically request reply by e-mail, and in no way appear to place geographical limits on buyers. Under these circumstances, Harris sufficiently advertises and solicits business within Virginia to find personal jurisdiction within the meaning of §8.01-328.1(A)(4) of the Virginia long-arm. . . .

Given that §8.01-328.1(A)(3) reaches the La Fontaines and that §8.01-328.1(A)(4) reaches Harris, the next question is whether these reaches exceed the constitutional grasp of the provisions. In this regard, the Due Process Clause requires that no defendant shall be haled into court unless defendant has "certain minimum contacts [with the state] . . . such that the maintenance of the suit does not offend traditional notions of fair play and substantial justice." *International Shoe Co.* And the constitutional analysis, unlike the statutory analysis, is virtually identical with respect to both the La Fontaines and Harris. The statements made by all defendants posted on the Internet concerned the presumably local activities of an individual each knew was a Virginia citizen. Bochan, and several of his Virginia friends, accessed the postings in Virginia, and the reputational harm resulting from defendants' actions and allegations of pedophilia and sexual deviancy, if any, has been primarily suffered in Virginia, where Bochan lives and works. Under these circumstances, because the predominant "effects" of the La Fontaines' and Harris's conduct are in Virginia, these defendants could reasonably foresee being haled into court in this jurisdiction. See Calder v. Jones. Thus, the constitutional prong of the inquiry is satisfied as to all defendants.

COMMENTS AND QUESTIONS

1. To what extent is the jurisdictional analysis for torts consistent with the analysis for business-related activities? Is the knowledge and foreseeability necessary to establish personal jurisdiction with respect to business-related activities the same as the knowledge and foreseeability required in tort cases?

2. Should the noncommercial nature of the activity change the purposeful availment inquiry? Should it matter that businesses and individuals engaged in commercial activities may have greater financial resources to limit the reach of their Internet activities? Are the harms created by torts sufficiently different from those caused by other transactions to justify a separate rule?

3. While a forum may decide that reputational injuries are entitled to greater protection than contract damages, is there a constitutional basis for distinguishing between such injuries for jurisdictional purposes? Should jurisdiction turn on the type of injury involved or the severity of the injuries suffered?

4. To what extent does *Bochan* relax, if not eliminate, the requirement of purposeful availment? Why is the forum's interest in providing a remedy for an injury that "occurred" within its borders sufficient to satisfy minimum contacts? *Consider* Gutnick v. Dow Jones & Co. Inc., VSC 305 (28 Aug. 2001), at *http://www.austlii.edu.au/cgi-bin/disp.pl/au/cases/vic/VSC/2001/305.html?query=%7e/plgutnick*, aff'd Dow Jones & Co, Inc. v. Gutnick [2002] HCA 56 (10 Dec. 2002), at *http://www.austlii.edu.au/au/cases/cth/HCA/2002/56.html* in which the High Court of Australia affirmed the holding of the Supreme Court of Victoria, that it had jurisdiction over the defendant Dow Jones for an allegedly defamatory publication available through its *Barrons* Internet subscription service. In rejecting the defendant's argument that Australia lacked jurisdiction over the publication because it was prepared and uploaded in the United States, the Supreme Court of Victoria stated:

> To say that the country where the article is written, edited and uploaded and where the publisher does its business, must be the forum is an invitation to entrench the United States, the primary home of much Internet publishing, as the forum. The applicant's argument that it would be unfair for publishers to have to litigate in the multitude of jurisdictions in which its statements are downloaded and read, must be balanced against the world-wide inconvenience caused to litigants, from Outer Mongolia to the Outer Barcoo, frequently not of notable means, who would at enormous expense and inconvenience have to embark upon the formidable task of suing in the USA. . . . Dow Jones controls access to its materials by reason of the imposition of charges, passwords and the like, and the conditions of supply of material on the Internet. It can, if it chooses to do

so, restrict the dissemination of its publication of Barrons on the Internet in a number of respects. . . .

Gutnick v. Dow Jones & Co. Inc., VSC 305 (28 Aug. 2001), at ¶73.

Judge Callinan in his concurring opinion in the High Court decision reflected these sentiments:

> I agree with the respondent's submission that what the appellant seeks to do, is to impose upon Australian residents for the purposes of this and many other cases, an American legal hegemony in relation to Internet publications. The consequence, if the appellant's submission were to be accepted would be to confer upon one country, and one notably more benevolent to the commercial and other media than this one, an effective domain over the law of defamation, to the financial advantage of publishers in the United States, and the serious disadvantage of those unfortunate enough to be reputationally damaged outside the United States. A further consequence might be to place commercial publishers in this country at a disadvantage to commercial publishers in the United States.

Dow Jones & Co., Inc. v. Gutnick, [2002] HCA 56 (10 Dec. 2002), at ¶200.

As noted by the court in *Gutnick*, the jurisdictional analysis often determines who bears the expense of litigating in a distant forum.

5. As the preceding materials demonstrate, the most troubling question with respect to personal jurisdiction is whether the defendant has purposefully availed herself of the forum. Concerned that the Internet allows out-of-state individuals or entities to cause serious harm with little effort or expense, Martin Redish argues for the elimination of purposeful availment. *See Of New Wine and Old Bottles: Personal Jurisdiction, the Internet, and the Nature of Constitutional Evolution*, 38 Jurimetrics J. 575 (1998). Instead, Redish suggests that courts should focus on the interests of the state and procedural fairness. If the state interest in asserting jurisdiction is strong, courts should be willing to tolerate greater procedural burdens on out-of-state defendants. In light of the preceding materials, is this proposal a departure from the existing case law or does it simply make what has been occurring implicitly explicit?

6. Would the creation and acceptance of avenues for online dispute resolution resolve the problems raised by these cases? Would it avoid the need to revise jurisdictional doctrine as suggested by Redish? One example of a successful online dispute resolution procedure that we will examine in more detail in Chapter 4 is the UDRP promulgated by ICANN with respect to Internet domain name disputes. Online dispute resolution procedures have also been suggested in other areas: for example, in *Health Privacy in a Techno-Social World: A Cyber-Patient's Bill of Rights*, 6 Nw. J. Tech. & Intell. Prop. 244, 274 (2008), Patricia Sánchez Abril and Anita Cava argue in favor of the development of online dispute resolution procedures with respect to disputes involving unauthorized uses of sensitive personal health information online.

7. In response to the large number of disputes over domain names in the 1990s, Congress passed the Anti-Cybersquatting Consumer Protection Act (ACPA). Consider how the Act deals with the question of situs as you read an excerpt of the statute and the case interpreting it.

ANTI-CYBERSQUATTING CONSUMER PROTECTION ACT

15 U.S.C. §1125(d)(2)(A)

The owner of a mark may file an in rem civil action against a domain name in the judicial district in which the domain name registrar, domain name registry, or other domain name authority that registered or assigned the domain name is located if:

(i) the domain name violates any right of the owner of a mark registered in the Patent and Trademark Office, or protected under subsection (a) and (c); and

(ii) the court finds that the owner:

(I) is not able to obtain in personam jurisdiction over a person who would have been a defendant and in a civil action under paragraph (i); or

(II) through due diligence was not able to find a person who would have been a defendant in a civil action under paragraph (i) by:

(aa) sending a notice of the alleged violation and intent to proceed under this paragraph to the registrant of the domain name at the postal and e-mail address provided by the registrant to the registrar; and

(bb) publishing notice of the action as the court may direct promptly after filing the action.

CABLE NEWS NETWORK L.P. v. CNNEWS.COM

162 F. Supp. 2d 484 (E.D. Va. 2001)

ELLIS, District Judge.

I.

Plaintiff, Cable News Network L.P., L.L.L.P., is a Delaware limited liability limited partnership with its principal place of business in Atlanta, Georgia. It is engaged in the business of providing news and information services throughout the world via a variety of electronic media. It is also the owner of the trademark "CNN," which plaintiff has registered in this country and dozens of others, including China. Since at least 1980, plaintiff has used its registered CNN trademark in connection with providing news and information services to people worldwide through a variety of cable and satellite television networks, private networks, radio networks, Web sites, and syndicated news services. Some of these services are accessible in China and provided in the Chinese language. Since adopting the CNN mark, plaintiff has used the mark "CNN" in the names of all of its broadcast networks, the best known of which include CNN Headline News, CNN En Espanol, CNNSI, CNNFN, and CNN International. Plaintiff's services are also accessible worldwide via the Internet at the domain name "cnn.com." There can be no doubt that plaintiff's CNN mark is famous.

Maya Online Broadband Network (HK) Co. Ltd. ("Maya") is a Chinese company that is a subsidiary of a second Chinese company, Shanghai On-line Broadband Network Co. Ltd. On November 12, 1999, Maya's general manager, Heyu Wang, registered the domain name "cnnews.com" with Network Solutions, Inc. ("NSI"), a domain name registrar and registry, located in Herndon, Virginia.

Maya operates the cnnews.com Web site, which is designed to provide news and information to Chinese-speaking individuals worldwide. This Web site is part of Maya's comprehensive on-line services system that includes video on demand, broadband services, and a variety of e-business services. The cnnews.com Web site is one of many sites linked to Maya's main Web site, cnmaya.com. The "cn" prefix apparently refers to "China," where the characters "cn" are widely used and understood as an abbreviation for the country name "China." The top level Internet domain for China is "cn." Given this, Maya, the respondent in this action, asserts that its choice of the domain name cnnews.com was entirely reasonable and that it did not select or use this domain name in bad faith. And Maya further points out that most people who access the cnnews.com Web site in China likely have never heard of CNN, as most Chinese citizens lack access to plaintiff's television stations and Web sites.

Maya asserts that the target audience of its on-line services, including cnnews.com, is located entirely within China. Maya also asserts that it does not advertise any of its services outside of China, sells no products or services to persons outside of China, does not ship goods outside of China, or accept payments from any source outside of China. In confirmation of these assertions, Maya proffers statistics reflecting that 99.5% of the registered users of Maya's Web sites are located within Chinese cities. It appears, moreover, that all of Maya's business is conducted in the Chinese language and that it transacts no business in the United States.

Plaintiff acted promptly on discovering that Wang had registered the cnnews.com domain name with NSI and that Maya had posted news information on that site. First, plaintiff notified Wang of its service mark rights and demanded that he transfer the domain name cnnews.com to plaintiff. Plaintiff also warned that it would pursue an ACPA *in rem* action in the Eastern District of Virginia to acquire control over the cnnews.com domain name if he failed to comply. Maya responded to plaintiff's communications with Wang, indicating that it did not intend to comply with plaintiff's demands. Next, plaintiff suggested that Maya change the domain name of its news Web site to "cn-news.-com" and use the new domain name only in Chinese characters. Maya rejected this proposal and plaintiff subsequently filed this complaint. . . .

II.

At the outset, it is necessary to confirm that this action meets the ACPA criteria for an *in rem* action. These criteria, found in 15 U.S.C. §1125(d)(2)(A), make clear that the owner of a mark, like plaintiff, may maintain an *in rem* action against an infringing domain name (i) if the action is brought in the jurisdiction where the registrar or registry of the infringing domain name is located, and (ii) if *in personam* jurisdiction over the registrant does not exist. This action fits squarely within these criteria. The registry for the allegedly infringing domain name is located in this jurisdiction and it is clear on this record that there is no *in personam* jurisdiction over Wang or Maya, the former and current registrants of cnnews.com. Thus, *in rem* jurisdiction is proper.

But the analysis cannot end here, for if it is clear that this action meets the ACPA criteria for an *in rem* action against a domain name, it is less clear that such an action comports with due process in light of *Shaffer v. Heitner*, 433 U.S. 186 (1977). Put another way, the question is whether judicial disposition of an absent registrant's substantive rights to an infringing domain name in an ACPA *in rem* action is consistent with due process.

III.

More than twenty years ago, the Supreme Court, in a close and controversial decision, cast doubt on the constitutionality of certain *in rem* proceedings. *See Shaffer v. Heitner*, 433 U.S. 186 (1977). Properly understood, *Shaffer* is no bar to an ACPA *in rem* action.

In *Shaffer*, the Supreme Court held unconstitutional a Delaware statute that provided *in rem* jurisdiction by allowing the sequestration of stock of a Delaware corporation so as to compel the personal appearance of nonresident corporate managers who owned shares of the stock and were facing a shareholders' derivative lawsuit in Delaware state court. *See Shaffer*, 433 U.S. at 193. In *Shaffer*, *in rem* jurisdiction was invoked solely to compel the appearance of the defendants in a matter unrelated to the property upon which *in rem* jurisdiction was based. *See id.*

To understand *Shaffer*, it is necessary to distinguish three types of *in rem* actions, as does *Hanson v. Denckla*, 357 U.S. 235, 246 n. 12 (1958), and then to understand *Shaffer*'s effect on each type. The first of the three, usually called simply "*in rem*" or "true *in rem*," arises when a court adjudicates the property rights corresponding to a particular *res* for every potential rights holder, whether each rights holder is named in the proceeding or not. *See Hanson*, 357 U.S. at 246 n. 12. ACPA *in rem* actions, including the case at bar, are of the "true *in rem*" genre because they involve the rights of a disputed mark for every potential rights holder. The second type of *in rem* action is the "quasi *in rem*" or "quasi *in rem* I" action, which allocates property rights as against particular named persons. *See id*. Examples of this type of litigation include actions to remove a cloud on a land title or actions seeking quiet title against another individual's claim. The third type of *in rem* proceeding, "quasi *in rem* II," concerns the rights of a particular person or persons in a thing, but is distinguished from quasi *in rem* I claims because the underlying claim in a quasi *in rem* II matter is unrelated to the *res* that provides jurisdiction. *Shaffer* was a quasi *in rem* II matter because the suit itself (a shareholders' derivative action alleging misconduct against a corporation's directors and officers) was unrelated to the *res* that established jurisdiction (the stock certificates owned by the managers of the corporation). *See Shaffer*, 433 U.S. at 193.

   Shaffer clearly holds that quasi *in rem* II and *in personam* proceedings require the same minimum contacts so as to satisfy due process, as discussed in *International Shoe Co. v. Washington*, 326 U.S. 310, 316 (1945). *See Shaffer*, 433 U.S. at 209. It is less clear, however, how, if at all, *Shaffer* affects true *in rem* and quasi *in rem* I cases. To be sure, there is language in *Shaffer* that could be read to require that *all in rem* cases conform to the same due process constraints as *in personam* cases. For instance, the *Shaffer* opinion states that "[t]he standard for determining whether an exercise of jurisdiction over the interest of persons is consistent with the Due Process Clause is the minimum-contacts standard elucidated in *International Shoe*." *Shaffer*, 433 U.S. at 207. Some courts, therefore, have held that *Shaffer* commands that all types of *in rem* actions must have the same minimum contacts as required for *in personam* actions. *See, e.g., Fleetboston*, 138 F. Supp. 2d at 133-34. Yet, the greater weight of (and more persuasive) authority holds that the language of *Shaffer* requires minimum contacts only for quasi *in rem* II — type cases. . . . Thus, where, as here, the action is properly categorized as "true *in rem*," there is no requirement that the owner or claimant of the *res* have minimum contacts with the forum. More particularly, in an ACPA *in rem* action, it is not necessary that the allegedly infringing registrant have minimum contacts with the forum; it is enough, as here, that the registry is located in the forum.

IV.

   Maya argues that plaintiff in this ACPA *in rem* action must plead and prove a registrant's bad faith to withstand a threshold jurisdictional challenge. This argument fails, for it confuses a jurisdictional requirement with a substantive element of a cause of action. The bad faith requirement in Section 1125(d)(1)(A)(i) is, at most, the latter, but in no event, the former.

While courts have debated whether the ACPA's bad faith requirement applies at all to the statute's *in rem* actions, no court has held that a showing of bad faith is or could be a jurisdictional requirement. This is so as a matter of definition and settled legal doctrine. . . .

Further, because bad faith is not a jurisdictional requirement, plaintiff's claim may be dismissed for lack of subject matter jurisdiction only if the claim "is so insubstantial, implausible, foreclosed by prior decisions of this Court, or otherwise completely devoid of merit as not to involve a federal controversy." [Steel Co. v. Citizens for a Better Env't, 523 U.S. 83, 89 (1998)] (citations omitted). This stringent standard is not met here; plaintiff's amended complaint presents a plausible trademark infringement claim under the ACPA. . . .

COMMENTS AND QUESTIONS

1. Why is it consistent with Due Process to allow *in rem* proceedings against domain names? *See* Porsche Cars North America, Inc. v. Porsche.net, 302 F.3d 248, 260 (4th Cir. 2002) (rejecting a constitutional challenge to the ACPA on the basis that a domain name is merely an address, instead "Congress may treat a domain name registration as property subject to in rem jurisdiction if it chooses, without violating the Constitution."). For additional judicial interpretation of the *in rem* proceedings of the ACPA, see Fleetboston Financial Corp v. Fleetbostonfinancial.com, 138 F. Supp. 2d 121 (D. Mass. 2001).

2. According to the court in Lucent Technologies v. Lucentsucks. com, 95 F. Supp. 2d 528 (E.D. Va. 2000), Congress enacted the *in rem* provision of the ACPA to provide trademark owners with a remedy against anonymous cybersquatters. Is the use of *in rem* jurisdiction in *CNNews.com* consistent with Congress's intent?

In *Lucent Technologies*, the court interpreted the ACPA as denying *in rem* jurisdiction when the plaintiff knows the identity of the defendant and can obtain jurisdiction over the defendant. Does this suggest that defendants can always defeat *in rem* jurisdiction by appearing after an action has already commenced? Would there be any reason for a defendant to delay such an appearance?

3. Can an argument be made that CNNews.com purposefully directed its activities to Virginia with respect to the domain name? What policies, if any, justify such a result?

4. The *in rem* provisions of the ACPA are perhaps not as useful today, at least to American trademark holders, as they were in 1999 when the legislation was first enacted. Since the enactment of the ACPA, ICANN has entered into arrangements to open up competition in the popular ".com", ".net", and ".org" domains so that they are now not always registered by Network

Solutions in Reston, Virginia. A list of ICANN-accredited domain name registrars is available at *http://www.icann.org/en/registrars/accredited-list.html*. At
the time the *CNNews.com* case was decided, all ".com" names were registered
by Network Solutions in Reston, Virginia. If a case like *CNNews.com*
was decided today, and the domain name was registered with a Chinese
".com" registry, would the result on jurisdiction be different?

5. Another reason why the ACPA is less important in practice today than
when it was first enacted has been the proven success and increasing popularity
of the Uniform Domain Name Dispute Resolution Policy (UDRP) as an avenue for domain name dispute resolution. The operation of the UDRP is discussed in Chapter 4. The UDRP avoids jurisdictional problems because it is a
form of private arbitration contractually mandated by domain name registration agreements. Arbitrations under the UDRP are conducted remotely with
most proceedings taking place online. Thus, there is no need for either party to
be concerned about having to litigate in the other party's chosen forum. While
the UDRP does not oust the jurisdiction of domestic courts, most parties in
practice are satisfied with UDRP outcomes and do not take their domain name
complaints before domestic courts.

3. Contractual Forum Selection and Choice of Law

One potential way to avoid the conceptual and doctrinal difficulties of
personal jurisdiction is for the defendant to consent to jurisdiction. Contractual forum selection and choice of law provisions would appear to be the
favored means for obtaining this consent. Practically every Web site's subscription agreement or terms and conditions of use contain forum selection
and choice of law provisions. The following materials explore whether these
clauses are valid. Questions of the validity and enforceability of these terms
of use take on particular significance in the Web 2.0 environment characterized by extremely large, global, online communities, most of whom have
apparently agreed to a service provider's online terms of use. Interested
readers should consider the terms of use of Web 2.0 service providers
such as Facebook, MySpace, YouTube, Second Life, Flickr, Wikipedia,
and see how easy it is to find forum selection and choice of law provisions
in these terms.

CARNIVAL CRUISE LINES, INC. v. SHUTE

499 U.S. 585 (1991)

Justice BLACKMUN delivered the opinion of the Court.

In this admiralty case we primarily consider whether the United States Court
of Appeals for the Ninth Circuit correctly refused to enforce a forum-selection

clause contained in tickets issued by petitioner Carnival Cruise Lines, Inc., to respondents Eulala and Russel Shute.

I

The Shutes, through an Arlington, Wash., travel agent, purchased passage for a 7-day cruise on petitioner's ship, the *Tropicale*. Respondents paid the fare to the agent who forwarded the payment to petitioner's headquarters in Miami, Fla. Petitioner then prepared the tickets and sent them to respondents in the State of Washington. The face of each ticket, at its left-hand lower corner, [directed the ticket holder to read the conditions on the last page, including that all disputes shall be litigated in the state of Florida].

II

Respondents boarded the *Tropicale* in Los Angeles, Cal. The ship sailed to Puerto Vallarta, Mexico, and then returned to Los Angeles. While the ship was in international waters off the Mexican coast, respondent Eulala Shute was injured when she slipped on a deck mat during a guided tour of the ship's galley. Respondents filed suit against petitioner in the United States District Court for the Western District of Washington, claiming that Mrs. Shute's injuries had been caused by the negligence of Carnival Cruise Lines and its employees.

Petitioner moved for summary judgment, contending that the forum clause in respondents' tickets required the Shutes to bring their suit against petitioner in a court in the State of Florida. . . .

III

We begin by noting the boundaries of our inquiry. First, this is a case in admiralty, and federal law governs the enforceability of the forum-selection clause we scrutinize. Second, we do not address the question whether respondents had sufficient notice of the forum clause before entering the contract for passage. Respondents essentially have conceded that they had notice of the forum-selection provision. Additionally, the Court of Appeals evaluated the enforceability of the forum clause under the assumption, although "doubtful," that respondents could be deemed to have had knowledge of the clause.

Within this context, respondents urge that the forum clause should not be enforced because, contrary to this Court's teachings in [The Bremen v. Zapata Off-Shore Co., 407 U.S. 1 (1972)], the clause was not the product of negotiation, and enforcement effectively would deprive respondents of their day in court. . . .

IV

A

In *The Bremen*, this Court addressed the enforceability of a forum-selection clause in a contract between two business corporations. An American corporation, Zapata, made a contract with Unterweser, a German corporation, for the towage of Zapata's oceangoing drilling rig from Louisiana to a point in the Adriatic Sea off the coast of Italy. The agreement provided that any dispute arising under the contract was to be resolved in the London Court of Justice. After a storm in the Gulf of Mexico seriously damaged the rig, Zapata ordered Unterweser's ship to tow the rig to Tampa, Fla., the nearest point of refuge. Thereafter, Zapata sued Unterweser in admiralty in federal court at Tampa. Citing the forum clause, Unterweser moved to dismiss. . . .

This Court vacated and remanded, stating that, in general, "a freely negotiated private international agreement, unaffected by fraud, undue influence, or overweening bargaining power, such as that involved here, should be given full effect." The Court further generalized that "in the light of present-day commercial realities and expanding international trade we conclude that the forum clause should control absent a strong showing that it should be set aside." The Court did not define precisely the circumstances that would make it unreasonable for a court to enforce a forum clause. Instead, the Court discussed a number of factors that made it reasonable to enforce the clause at issue in *The Bremen* and that, presumably, would be pertinent in any determination whether to enforce a similar clause.

In this respect, the Court noted that there was "strong evidence that the forum clause was a vital part of the agreement, and [that] it would be unrealistic to think that the parties did not conduct their negotiations, including fixing the monetary terms, with the consequences of the forum clause figuring prominently in their calculations." Further, the Court observed that it was not "dealing with an agreement between two Americans to resolve their essentially local disputes in a remote alien forum," and that in such a case, "the serious inconvenience of the contractual forum to one or both of the parties might carry greater weight in determining the reasonableness of the forum clause." The Court stated that even where the forum clause establishes a remote forum for resolution of conflicts, "the party claiming [unfairness] should bear a heavy burden of proof."

In applying *The Bremen*, the Court of Appeals in the present litigation took note of the foregoing "reasonableness" factors and rather automatically decided that the forum-selection clause was unenforceable because, unlike the parties in *The Bremen*, respondents are not business persons and did not negotiate the terms of the clause with petitioner. Alternatively, the Court of Appeals ruled that the clause should not be enforced because enforcement effectively would deprive respondents of an opportunity to litigate their claim against petitioner. . . .

In evaluating the reasonableness of the forum clause at issue in this case, we must refine the analysis of *The Bremen* to account for the realities of form passage contracts. As an initial matter, we do not adopt the Court of Appeals' determination that a nonnegotiated forum-selection clause in a form ticket contract is never enforceable simply because it is not the subject of bargaining. Including a reasonable forum clause in a form contract of this kind well may be permissible for several reasons: First, a cruise line has a special interest in limiting the fora in which it potentially could be subject to suit. Because a cruise ship typically carries passengers from many locales, it is not unlikely that a mishap on a cruise could subject the cruise line to litigation in several different fora. Additionally, a clause establishing *ex ante* the forum for dispute resolution has the salutary effect of dispelling any confusion about where suits arising from the contract must be brought and defended, sparing litigants the time and expense of pretrial motions to determine the correct forum and conserving judicial resources that otherwise would be devoted to deciding those motions. Finally, it stands to reason that passengers who purchase tickets containing a forum clause like that at issue in this case benefit in the form of reduced fares reflecting the savings that the cruise line enjoys by limiting the fora in which it may be sued.

We also do not accept the Court of Appeals' "independent justification" for its conclusion that *The Bremen* dictates that the clause should not be enforced because "[t]here is evidence in the record to indicate that the Shutes are physically and financially incapable of pursuing this litigation in Florida." We do not defer to the Court of Appeals' findings of fact. In dismissing the case for lack of personal jurisdiction over petitioner, the District Court made no finding regarding the physical and financial impediments to the Shutes' pursuing their case in Florida. The Court of Appeals' conclusory reference to the record provides no basis for this Court to validate the finding of inconvenience. Furthermore, the Court of Appeals did not place in proper context this Court's statement in *The Bremen* that "the serious inconvenience of the contractual forum to one or both of the parties might carry greater weight in determining the reasonableness of the forum clause." The Court made this statement in evaluating a hypothetical "agreement between two Americans to resolve their essentially local disputes in a remote alien forum." In the present case, Florida is not a "remote alien forum," nor — given the fact that Mrs. Shute's accident occurred off the coast of Mexico — is this dispute an essentially local one inherently more suited to resolution in the State of Washington than in Florida. In light of these distinctions, and because respondents do not claim lack of notice of the forum clause, we conclude that they have not satisfied the "heavy burden of proof," required to set aside the clause on grounds of inconvenience.

It bears emphasis that forum-selection clauses contained in form passage contracts are subject to judicial scrutiny for fundamental fairness. In this case, there is no indication that petitioner set Florida as the forum in which disputes were to be resolved as a means of discouraging cruise passengers from pursuing legitimate claims. Any suggestion of such a bad-faith motive is belied by two facts: Petitioner has its principal place of business in Florida, and many of its cruises depart from and return to Florida ports. Similarly, there is no evidence that petitioner obtained respondents' accession to the forum clause by fraud or overreaching. Finally, respondents have conceded that they were given notice of the forum provision and, therefore, presumably retained the option of rejecting the contract with impunity. In the case before us, therefore, we conclude that the Court of Appeals erred in refusing to enforce the forum-selection clause. . . .

Justice STEVENS, with whom Justice MARSHALL joins, dissenting.

The Court prefaces its legal analysis with a factual statement that implies that a purchaser of a Carnival Cruise Lines passenger ticket is fully and fairly notified about the existence of the choice of forum clause in the fine print on the back of the ticket. Even if this implication were accurate, I would disagree with the Court's analysis. But, given the Court's preface, I begin my dissent by noting that only the most meticulous passenger is likely to become aware of the forum-selection provision. . . .

Of course, many passengers, like the respondents in this case, will not have an opportunity to read [the forum-selection provision] until they have actually purchased their tickets. By this point, the passengers will already have accepted the condition set forth in paragraph 16(a), which provides that "[t]he Carrier shall not be liable to make any refund to passengers in respect of . . . tickets wholly or partly not used by a passenger." Not knowing whether or not that provision is legally enforceable, I assume that the average passenger would accept the risk of having to file suit in Florida in the event of an injury, rather than canceling—without a refund—a planned vacation at the last minute. The fact that the cruise line can reduce its litigation costs, and therefore its liability insurance premiums, by forcing this choice on its passengers does not, in my opinion, suffice to render the provision reasonable. . . .

Forum-selection clauses in passenger tickets involve the intersection of two strands of traditional contract law that qualify the general rule that courts will enforce the terms of a contract as written. Pursuant to the first strand, courts traditionally have reviewed with heightened scrutiny the terms of contracts of adhesion, form contracts offered on a take-or-leave basis by a party with stronger bargaining power to a party with weaker power. Some commentators have questioned whether contracts of adhesion can justifiably be enforced at all under traditional contract theory because the adhering party generally enters into them without manifesting knowing and voluntary consent to all their terms.

The common law, recognizing that standardized form contracts account for a significant portion of all commercial agreements, has taken a less extreme position and instead subjects terms in contracts of adhesion to scrutiny for reasonableness. Judge J. Skelly Wright set out the state of the law succinctly in *Williams v. Walker-Thomas Furniture*, 350 F.2d 445, 449-450 (1965) (footnotes omitted):

> Ordinarily, one who signs an agreement without full knowledge of its terms might be held to assume the risk that he has entered a one-sided bargain. But when a party of little bargaining power, and hence little real choice, signs a commercially unreasonable contract with little or no knowledge of its terms, it is hardly likely that his consent, or even an objective manifestation of his consent, was ever given to all of the terms. In such a case the usual rule that the terms of the agreement are not to be questioned should be abandoned and the court should consider whether the terms of the contract are so unfair that enforcement should be withheld.

The second doctrinal principle implicated by forum-selection clauses is the traditional rule that "contractual provisions, which seek to limit the place or court in which an action may . . . be brought, are invalid as contrary to public policy." Although adherence to this general rule has declined in recent years, particularly following our decision in *The Bremen*, the prevailing rule is still that forum-selection clauses are not enforceable if they were not freely bargained for, create additional expense for one party, or deny one party a remedy. A forum-selection clause in a standardized passenger ticket would clearly have been unenforceable under the common law before our decision in *The Bremen*, and, in my opinion, remains unenforceable under the prevailing rule today.

The Bremen, which the Court effectively treats as controlling this case, had nothing to say about stipulations printed on the back of passenger tickets. That case involved the enforceability of a forum-selection clause in a freely negotiated international agreement between two large corporations providing for the towage of a vessel from the Gulf of Mexico to the Adriatic Sea. The Court recognized that such towage agreements had generally been held unenforceable in American courts, but held that the doctrine of those cases did not extend to commercial arrangements between parties with equal bargaining power. . . .

CASPI V. THE MICROSOFT NETWORK, L.L.C.

323 N.J. Super. 118 (App. Div. 1999)

KESTIN, J.A.D.

We are here called upon to determine the validity and enforceability of a forum selection clause contained in an on-line subscriber agreement of the Microsoft Network (MSN), an on-line computer service.

The amended class action complaint in eighteen counts sought diverse relief against two related corporate entities, The Microsoft Network, L.L.C. and Microsoft Corporation (collectively, Microsoft). . . . Among the claims was an accusation that Microsoft had engaged in "unilateral negative option billing," a practice condemned by the attorneys general of twenty-one states, including New Jersey's, with regard to a Microsoft competitor, America Online, Inc. Under the practice as alleged, Microsoft, without notice to or permission from MSN members, unilaterally charged them increased membership fees attributable to a change in service plans.

The four named plaintiffs are members of MSN. Two reside in New Jersey; the others in Ohio and New York. Purporting to represent a nationwide class of 1.5 million similarly aggrieved MSN members, plaintiffs, in May 1997, moved for multi-state class action certification.

Shortly thereafter, defendants moved to dismiss the amended complaint for lack of jurisdiction and improper venue by reason of the forum selection clause which, defendants contended, was in every MSN membership agreement and bound all the named plaintiffs and all members of the class they purported to represent. That clause, paragraph 15.1 of the MSN membership agreement, provided:

> This agreement is governed by the laws of the State of Washington, USA, and you consent to the exclusive jurisdiction and venue of courts in King County, Washington, in all disputes arising out of or relating to your use of MSN or your MSN membership. . . .

Before becoming an MSN member, a prospective subscriber is prompted by MSN software to view multiple computer screens of information, including a membership agreement which contains the above clause. MSN's membership agreement appears on the computer screen in a scrollable window next to blocks providing the choices "I Agree" and "I Don't Agree." Prospective members assent to the terms of the agreement by clicking on "I Agree" using a computer mouse. Prospective members have the option to click "I Agree" or "I Don't Agree" at any point while scrolling through the agreement. Registration may proceed only after the potential subscriber has had the opportunity to view and has assented to the membership agreement, including MSN's forum selection clause. No charges are incurred until after the membership agreement review is completed and a subscriber has clicked on "I Agree."

The trial court observed:

> Generally, forum selection clauses are prima facie valid and enforceable in New Jersey. New Jersey courts will decline to enforce a clause only if it fits into one of three exceptions to the general rule: (1) the clause is a result of fraud or "overweening" bargaining power; (2) enforcement would violate the strong public policy of New Jersey; or (3) enforcement would seriously inconvenience trial. The burden falls on the party objecting to enforcement to show that the clause in question fits within one of these exceptions. Plaintiffs have failed to meet that burden here.

Judge Fitzpatrick correctly discerned that:

> New Jersey follows the logic of the United States Supreme Court decision in *Carnival Cruise Lines v. Shute*. In *Carnival*, cruise ship passengers were held to a forum selection clause which appeared in their travel contract. The clause enforced in *Carnival* was very similar in nature to the clause in question here, the primary difference being that the

Carnival clause was placed in small print in a travel contract while the clause in the case *sub judice* was placed on-line on scrolled computer screens.

The trial court opinion went on to analyze plaintiffs' contentions:

Plaintiffs' consent to MSN's clause does not appear to be the result of fraud or over-weening bargaining power. In New Jersey, fraud consists of (1) material misrepresentation of a past or present fact; (2) knowledge or belief by the declarant of its falsity; (3) an intention that the recipient rely on it; (4) reasonable reliance by the recipient; and (5) result-ing damages. Plaintiffs have not shown that MSN's forum selection clause constitutes fraud. The clause is reasonable, clear and contains no material misrepresentation.

Further, plaintiffs were not subjected to overweening bargaining power in dealing with Microsoft and MSN. The Supreme Court has held that a corporate vendor's inclu-sion of a forum selection clause in a consumer contract does not in itself constitute overweening bargaining power. *Carnival.* In order to invalidate a forum selection clause, something more than merely size difference must be shown. A court's focus must be whether such an imbalance in size resulted in an inequality of bargaining power that was unfairly exploited by the more powerful party.

Plaintiffs have shown little more than a size difference here. The on-line computer service industry is not one without competition, and therefore consumers are left with choices as to which service they select for Internet access, e-mail and other information services. Plaintiffs were not forced into a situation where MSN was the only available server. Additionally, plaintiffs and the class which they purport to represent were given ample opportunity to affirmatively assent to the forum selection clause. Like *Carnival*, plaintiffs here "retained the option of rejecting the contract with impunity." In such a case, this court finds it impossible to perceive an overwhelming bargaining situation.

. . . The only viable issues that remain bear upon the argument that plain-tiffs did not receive adequate notice of the forum selection clause, and therefore that the clause never became part of the membership contract which bound them. A related, alternative argument is that the question of notice is a factual matter that should be submitted to a jury. Defendants respond by arguing that 1) in the absence of fraud, a contracting party is bound by the provisions of a form contract even if he or she never reads them; 2) this clause met all reason-able standards of conspicuousness; and 3) the sign-up process gave plaintiffs ample opportunity to review and reject the agreement. Defendants also con-tend that notice is a question of law, decidable by a court, not a jury.

The holding in *Carnival Cruise Lines v. Shute* does not dispose of the notice question because the plaintiffs there had "essentially . . . conceded that they had notice of the forum-selection provision[,]" by stating that they "'[did] not contest . . . that the forum selection clause was reasonably communicated to [them], as much a three pages of fine print can be communicated.'" The dissenting justices described the format in which the forum selection clause had been presented as "in the fine print on the back of the [cruise] ticket."

The scenario presented here is different because of the medium used, electronic versus printed; but, in any sense that matters, there is no significant distinction. The plaintiffs in *Carnival* could have perused all the fine-print provisions of their travel contract if they wished before accepting the terms by purchasing their cruise ticket. The plaintiffs in this case were free to scroll through the various computer screens that presented the terms of their contracts before clicking their agreement.

Also, it seems clear that there was nothing extraordinary about the size or placement of the forum selection clause text. By every indication we have, the clause was presented in exactly the same format as most other provisions of the contract. It was the first item in the last paragraph of the electronic document. We note that a few paragraphs in the contract were presented in uppercase typeface, presumably for emphasis, but most provisions, including the forum selection clause, were presented in lowercase typeface. We discern nothing about the style or mode of presentation, or the placement of the provision, that can be taken as a basis for concluding that the forum selection clause was proffered unfairly, or with a design to conceal or de-emphasize its provisions. To conclude that plaintiffs are not bound by that clause would be equivalent to holding that they were bound by no other clause either, since all provisions were identically presented. Plaintiffs must be taken to have known that they were entering into a contract; and no good purpose, consonant with the dictates of reasonable reliability in commerce, would be served by permitting them to disavow particular provisions or the contracts as a whole. . . .

Affirmed.

COMMENTS AND QUESTIONS

1.   In light of these decisions, what should an online service provider do to minimize the risk of being sued in other jurisdictions? How should the provisions be presented to the consumer? Should the kind of online service provided have any bearing on this question? For example, should a popular social networking service be treated any differently to, say, an electronic commerce Web site in this respect?

2.   Under *Carnival Cruise Lines* and *Caspi*, when would it be unfair to enforce a forum selection clause against a consumer?

3.   The Uniform Computer Information Transactions Act (UCITA) has been adopted in Maryland and Virginia. It contains rules for governing computer transactions proposed by the National Conference of Commissioners on Uniform State Laws. UCITA has been controversial and has not been widely adopted throughout the United States partly because UCITA recognizes the validity of so-called "click wrap" agreements in which consumers agree to the contractual terms of a Web site or for software by using the service or product or by clicking on "I Agree." The validity of these types of agreements is covered in detail in Chapter 7. With respect to choice of forum, §110 of UCITA provides:

(a) The parties in their agreement may choose an exclusive judicial forum unless the choice is unreasonable and unjust.

(b) A judicial forum specified in an agreement is not exclusive unless the agreement expressly so provides.

Similarly, §109 provides with respect to choice of law:

(a) The parties in their agreement may choose the applicable law. However, the choice is not enforceable in a consumer contract to the extent it would vary a rule that may not be varied by agreement under the law of the jurisdiction whose law would apply under subsections (b) and (c) in the absence of the agreement.

(b) In the absence of an enforceable agreement on choice of law, the following rules determine which jurisdiction's law governs in all respects for purposes of contract law:

1. An access contract or contract providing for electronic delivery of a copy is governed by the law of the jurisdiction in which the licensor was located when the agreement was entered into.

2. A consumer contract that requires delivery of a copy on a tangible medium is governed by the law of the jurisdiction in which the copy is or should have been delivered to the consumer.

3. In all other cases, the contract is governed by the law of the jurisdiction having the most significant relationship to the transaction.

(c) In cases governed by subsection (b), if the jurisdiction whose law governs is outside the United States, the laws of that jurisdiction governs only if it provides substantially similar protections and rights to a party not located in the jurisdiction as are provided under this [Act]. Otherwise, the law of the State that has the most significant relationship to the transaction governs. . . .

How does UCITA deal with choice of forum and choice of law? What limitations, if any, does UCITA recognize for contractual choice of forum and law?

C. REGULATORY AUTHORITY

In addition to the problem of whose courts may exercise personal jurisdiction over a defendant, the Internet raises the larger question of whose laws, if any, should apply to activities that occur in cyberspace. When can a particular government regulate activities that occur in cyberspace, especially when the person engaged in the activity is located in another nation? It is in this context that Johnson's and Post's concerns over "spillover" are most apparent. The following materials are divided into three separate sections. The first examines the limits of state regulatory power because cyberspace may be considered a separate place, or more accurately, because cyber-activities may not have any local effects that justify governmental regulation. The second set of materials examines the extent to which the U.S. Constitution requires a basic level of uniformity in local and state efforts to regulate the Internet. Lastly, we will examine local efforts to regulate international conduct.

1. State Regulation of Cyberspace in the United States

a) Cyberspace as a Separate Place?

VOYEUR DORM, L.C. v. CITY OF TAMPA, FLA.

265 F.3d 1232 (11th Cir. 2001)

DUBINA, Circuit Judge: . . .

As alleged in its complaint, Voyeur Dorm is a Florida limited liability company that maintains offices and conducts its business in Hillsborough County, Florida. Voyeur Dorm operates an internet based web site that provides a 24 hour a day internet transmission portraying the lives of the residents of 2312 West Farwell Drive, Tampa, Florida. Throughout its existence, Voyeur Dorm has employed 25 to 30 different women, most of whom entered into a contract that specifies, among other things, that they are "employees," on a "stage and filming location," with "no reasonable expectation of privacy," for "entertainment purposes." Subscribers to "voyeurdorm.com" pay a subscription fee of $34.95 a month to watch the women employed at the premises and pay an added fee of $16.00 per month to "chat" with the women. From August 1998 to June 2000, Voyeur Dorm generated subscriptions and sales totaling $3,166,551.35. . . .

[The City of Tampa concluded that Voyeur Dorm's activities violated the City Code. Section 27-523 defines adult entertainment as:

> Any premises, except those businesses otherwise defined in this chapter, on which is offered to members of the public or any person, for a consideration, entertainment featuring or in any way including specified sexual activities, as defined in this section, or entertainment featuring the displaying or depicting of specified anatomical areas, as defined in this section; "entertainment" as used in this definition shall include, but not be limited to, books, magazines, films, newspapers, photographs, paintings, drawings, sketches or other publications or graphic media, filmed or live plays, dances or other performances distinguished by their display or depiction of specified anatomical areas or specified anatomical activities, as defined in this section.

This conclusion was upheld by the district court.]

The threshold inquiry is whether section 27-523 of Tampa's City Code applies to the alleged activities occurring at 2312 West Farwell Drive. . . .

Tampa argues that Voyeur Dorm is an adult use business pursuant to the express and unambiguous language of Section 27-523 and, as such, cannot operate in a residential neighborhood. In that regard, Tampa points out: that members of the public pay to watch women employed on the premises; that the

Employment Agreement refers to the premises as "a stage and filming location"; that certain anatomical areas and sexual activities are displayed for entertainment; and that the entertainers are paid accordingly. Most importantly, Tampa asserts that nothing in the City Code limits its applicability to premises where the adult entertainment is actually consumed.

In accord with Tampa's arguments, the district court specifically determined that the "plain and unambiguous language of the City Code . . . does not expressly state a requirement that the members of the public paying consideration be *on* the premises viewing the adult entertainment." *Voyeur Dorm, L.C., et al., v. City of Tampa, Fla.*, 121 F. Supp. 2d 1373 (M.D. Fla. 2000) (order granting summary judgment to Tampa). While the public does not congregate to a specific edifice or location in order to enjoy the entertainment provided by Voyeur Dorm, the district court found 2312 West Farwell Drive to be "a premises on which is offered to members of the public for consideration entertainment featuring specified sexual activities within the plain meaning of the City Code." *Id.*

Moreover, the district court relied on Supreme Court and Eleventh Circuit precedent that trumpets a city's entitlement to protect and improve the quality of residential neighborhoods. *See City of Renton v. Playtime Theatres, Inc.*, 475 U.S. 41, 50 (1986) ("[A] city's 'interest in attempting to preserve the quality of urban life is one that must be accorded high respect.'") (quoting *Young v. American Mini Theatres, Inc.*, 427 U.S. 50, 71 (1976)); *Sammy's of Mobile, Ltd. v. City of Mobile*, 140 F.3d 993, 996-97 (11th Cir. 1998) (noting that it is well established that the regulation of public health, safety and morals is a valid and substantial state interest); *Corn v. City of Lauderdale Lakes*, 997 F.2d 1369, 1375 (11th Cir. 1993) (noting that the "Supreme Court has held [that] restrictions may be imposed to protect 'family values, youth values and the blessings of quiet seclusion'") (internal citations omitted).

In opposition, Voyeur Dorm argues that it is not an adult use business. Specifically, Voyeur Dorm contends that section 27-523 applies to locations or premises wherein adult entertainment is actually offered to the public. Because the public does not, indeed cannot, physically attend 2312 West Farwell Drive to enjoy the adult entertainment, 2312 West Farwell Drive does not fall within the purview of Tampa's zoning ordinance. We agree with this argument.

The residence of 2312 West Farwell Drive provides no "offer[ing] [of adult entertainment] to members of the public." The offering occurs when the videotaped images are dispersed over the internet and into the public eye for consumption. The City Code cannot be applied to a location that does not, itself, offer adult entertainment to the public. As a practical matter, zoning restrictions are indelibly anchored in particular geographic locations. Residential areas are often cordoned off from business districts in order to promote a State's interest. *See e.g., City of Renton*, 475 U.S. at 50 ("A city's interest in attempting to preserve the quality of urban life is one that must be accorded high respect."). It does not follow, then, that a zoning ordinance designed to restrict facilities that offer adult entertainment can be applied to a particular location that does not, at that location, offer adult entertainment. Moreover, the case law relied upon by Tampa and the district court concern adult entertainment in which customers *physically attend* the premises wherein the entertainment is performed.[2] Here, the audience or consumers of the adult entertainment do not go to 2312 West Farwell Drive or congregate anywhere else in Tampa to enjoy the entertainment. Indeed, the public offering occurs over the internet in "virtual space." While the district court read Section 27-523 in a literal sense, finding no requirement that the paying public be *on the premises*, we hold that section 27-523 does not apply to a residence at which there is no public offering of adult entertainment. . . .

COMMENTS AND QUESTIONS

1. What is the argument that Voyeur Dorm offered adult entertainment at 2312 West Farwell Drive? In rejecting that argument, does the court in *Voyeur Dorm* treat cyberspace as a separate place? If not, how does the court explain its conclusion that Tampa cannot regulate the activities of Voyeur Dorm?

2. Does the decision stand for the proposition that Tampa could never regulate the activities at 2312 West Farwell? What if the city amended the City Code to specifically include businesses that offer entertainment exclusively over the Internet?

3. Why does the court refer to the U.S. Supreme Court's decisions involving the "secondary effects doctrine"? It is possible to interpret the decision in *Voyeur Dorm* as consistent with recent decisions recognizing limits to a state's police power (i.e., the power to regulate public health, safety, and morals). *See generally* Raymond Ku, *Swingers: Morality Legislation and the Limits of State Police Power,* 12 St. Thomas L. Rev. 1, 31 (1999) (discussing the limits of state police powers to regulate conduct "when that conduct does not invade the rights of others" and state court decisions raising the issue). Can an argument be made that the conduct of Voyeur Dorm invades the rights of citizens in the city of Tampa?

---

2. The body of case law applying legislative restrictions to adult entertainment establishments relies on adverse effects that debase adjacent properties. *See, e.g., City of Erie v. Pap's A.M.*, 529 U.S. 277 (2000) (relying on the negative secondary effects doctrine to uphold a city's ordinance as applied to an erotic dancing establishment); *City of Renton v. Playtime Theatres, Inc.*, 475 U.S. 41 (1986) (upholding a zoning ordinance that prohibited adult motion picture theaters from operating in certain locations based upon the negative secondary effects created by such theaters); *Young v. American Mini Theatres, Inc.*, 427 U.S. 50 (1976); *Flanigan's Enterprises, Inc. v. Fulton County*, 242 F.3d 976 (11th Cir. 2001) (holding that a local ordinance failed to further the county's purported concern with negative secondary effects and was thus unconstitutionally applied). . . .

b) Due Process and the Dormant Commerce Clause

AMERICAN LIBRARY ASSOCIATION V. PATAKI

969 F. Supp. 160 (S.D.N.Y. 1997)

[The State of New York made it illegal to distribute material harmful to minors over the Internet. The plaintiffs, including the American Library Association representing a broad group of individuals and entities that send information over the Internet challenged the law under the First Amendment and the Commerce Clause of the U.S. Constitution.]

PRESKA, District Judge:

. . . The borderless world of the Internet raises profound questions concerning the relationship among the several states and the relationship of the federal government to each state, questions that go to the heart of "our federalism." The Act at issue in the present case is only one of many efforts by state legislators to control the chaotic environment of the Internet. For example, the Georgia legislature has enacted a recent law prohibiting Internet users from "falsely identifying" themselves on-line. Similar legislation is pending in California. Texas and Florida have concluded that law firm web pages (apparently including those of out of state firms) are subject to the rules of professional conduct applicable to attorney advertising. Further, states have adopted widely varying approaches in the application of general laws to communications taking place over the Internet. Minnesota has aggressively pursued out-of-state advertisers and service providers who reach Minnesotans via the Internet; Illinois has also been assertive in using existing laws to reach out-of-state actors whose connection to Illinois occurs only by virtue of an Internet communication. Florida has taken the opposite route, declining to venture into on-line law enforcement until various legal issues (including, perhaps, the one discussed in the present opinion) have been determined. . . .

The unique nature of the Internet highlights the likelihood that a single actor might be subject to haphazard, uncoordinated, and even outright inconsistent regulation by states that the actor never intended to reach and possibly was unaware were being accessed. Typically, states' jurisdictional limits are related to geography; geography, however, is a virtually meaningless construct on the Internet. The menace of inconsistent state regulation invites analysis under the Commerce Clause of the Constitution, because that clause represented the framers' reaction to overreaching by the individual states that might jeopardize the growth of the nation — and in particular, the national infrastructure of communications and trade — as a whole. *See Quill Corp.* ("Under the Articles of Confederation, state taxes and duties hindered and suppressed interstate commerce; the Framers intended the Commerce Clause as a cure for these structural ills."); *see also* The Federalist Nos. 7, 11 (A. Hamilton).

The Commerce Clause is more than an affirmative grant of power to Congress. As long ago as 1824, Justice Johnson in his concurring opinion in *Gibbons v. Ogden*, recognized that the Commerce Clause has a negative sweep as well. In what commentators have come to term its negative or "dormant" aspect, the Commerce Clause restricts the individual states' interference with the flow of interstate commerce in two ways. The Clause prohibits discrimination aimed directly at interstate commerce, and bars state regulations that, although facially nondiscriminatory, unduly burden interstate commerce. Moreover, courts have long held that state regulation of those aspects of commerce that by their unique nature demand cohesive national treatment is offensive to the Commerce Clause. . . .

A.   THE ACT CONCERNS INTERSTATE COMMERCE

[According to the court, the Act clearly applies to interstate communications.]

The conclusion that the Act must apply to interstate as well as intrastate communications receives perhaps its strongest support from the nature of the Internet itself. The Internet is wholly insensitive to geographic distinctions. In almost every case, users of the Internet neither know nor care about the physical location of the Internet resources they access. Internet protocols were designed to ignore rather than document geographic location; while computers on the network do have "addresses," they are logical addresses on the network rather than geographic addresses in real space. The majority of Internet addresses contain no geographic clues and, even where an Internet address provides such a clue, it may be misleading. . . .

Moreover, no aspect of the Internet can feasibly be closed off to users from another state. An internet user who posts a Web page cannot prevent New Yorkers or Oklahomans or Iowans from accessing that page and will not even know from what state visitors to that site hail. Nor can a participant in a chat room prevent other participants from a particular state from joining the conversation. Someone who uses a mail exploder is similarly unaware of the precise contours of the mailing list that will ultimately determine the recipients of his or her message, because users can add or remove their names from a mailing list automatically. Thus, a person could choose a list believed not to include any New Yorkers, but an after-added New Yorker would still receive the message. . . .

E-mail, because it is a one-to-one messaging system, stands on a slightly different footing than the other aspects of the Internet. Even in the context of e-mail, however, a message from one New Yorker to another New Yorker may well pass through a number of states en route. The Internet is, as described above, a redundant series of linked computers. Thus, a message from an Internet user sitting at a computer in New York may travel via one or more other states before reaching a recipient who is also sitting at a terminal in New York.

The system is further complicated by two Internet practices: packet switching and caching. "Packet switching" protocols subdivide individual messages into smaller packets that are then sent independently to the destination, where they are automatically reassembled by the receiving computer. If computers along the route become overloaded, packets may be rerouted to computers with greater capacity. A single message may—but does not always—travel several different pathways before reaching the receiving computer. "Caching" is the Internet practice of storing partial or complete duplicates of materials from frequently accessed sites to avoid repeatedly requesting copies from the original server. The recipient has no means of distinguishing between the cached materials and the original. Thus, the user may be accessing materials at the original site, or he may be accessing copies of those materials cached on a different machine located anywhere in the world.

The New York Act, therefore, cannot effectively be limited to purely intrastate communications over the Internet because no such communications exist. No user could reliably restrict her communications only to New York recipients. Moreover, no user could avoid liability under the New York Act simply by directing his or her communications elsewhere, given that there is no feasible way to preclude New Yorkers from accessing a Web site, receiving a mail exploder message or a newsgroup posting, or participating in a chat room. Similarly, a user has no way to ensure that an e-mail does not pass through New York even if the ultimate recipient is not located there, or that a message never leaves New York even if both sender and recipient are located there. . . .

The Act is therefore necessarily concerned with interstate communications. The next question that requires an answer as a threshold matter is whether the types of communication involved constitute "commerce" within the meaning of the Clause. . . .

[According to the court, the] non-profit nature of certain entities that use the Internet or of certain transactions that take place over the Internet does not take the Internet outside the Commerce Clause.

The Supreme Court has expressly held that the dormant commerce clause is applicable to activities undertaken without a profit motive. . . .

Commercial use of the Internet, moreover, is a growing phenomenon. In addition, many of those users who are communicating for private, noncommercial purposes are nonetheless participants in interstate commerce by virtue of their Internet consumption. Many users obtain access to the Internet by means of an on-line service provider, such as America Online, which charges a fee for its services. "Internet service providers," including plaintiffs Panix, Echo, and NYC NET, also offer Internet access for a monthly or hourly fee. Patrons of storefront "computer coffee shops," such as New York's own CyberCafe, similarly pay for their access to the Internet, in addition to partaking of food and beverages sold by the cafe. Dial-in bulletin board systems often charge a fee for access. *See Katzenbach v. McClung,* 379 U.S. 294, 300-01 (1964) (holding that an entity that purchases goods used in the provision of its services from interstate sources is an actor in interstate commerce even in connection with the provision of services within a single state).

The courts have long recognized that railroads, trucks, and highways are themselves "instruments of commerce," because they serve as conduits for the transport of products and services. The Internet is more than a means of communication; it also serves as a conduit for transporting digitized goods, including software, data, music, graphics, and videos which can be downloaded from the provider's site to the Internet user's computer. For example, plaintiff BiblioBytes and members of plaintiff IDSA both sell and deliver their products over the Internet.

The inescapable conclusion is that the Internet represents an instrument of interstate commerce, albeit an innovative one; the novelty of the technology should not obscure the fact that regulation of the Internet impels traditional Commerce Clause considerations. The New York Act is therefore closely concerned with interstate commerce, and scrutiny of the Act under the Commerce Clause is entirely appropriate. As discussed in the following sections, the Act cannot survive such scrutiny, because it places an undue burden on interstate traffic, whether that traffic be in goods, services, or ideas.

B. NEW YORK HAS OVERREACHED BY ENACTING LAW THAT SEEKS TO REGULATE CONDUCT OCCURRING OUTSIDE ITS BORDERS

The interdiction against direct interference with interstate commerce by state legislative overreaching is apparent in a number of the Supreme Court's decisions. In *Baldwin v. G.A.F. Seelig, Inc.*, 294 U.S. 511, 521 (1935), for example, Justice Cardozo authored an opinion enjoining enforcement of a law that prohibited a dealer from selling within New York milk purchased from the producer in Vermont at less than the minimum price fixed for milk produced in New York. Justice Cardozo sternly admonished, "New York has no power to project its legislation into Vermont by regulating the price to be paid in that state for milk," finding that "[s]uch a power, if exerted, [would] set a barrier to traffic between one state and another as effective as if customs duties, equal to the price differential, had been laid upon the thing transported."

The Court has more recently confirmed that the Commerce Clause precludes a state from enacting legislation that has the practical effect of exporting that state's domestic policies. In *Edgar v. MITE*, 457 U.S. 624 (1982), the Court examined the constitutionality of an Illinois anti-takeover statute that required a tender offeror to notify the Secretary of State and the target company of its intent to make a tender offer and the terms of the offer 20 days before the offer became effective. . . . In striking the law as violative of the Commerce Clause, the Court found particularly egregious the fact that the Illinois law on its face would apply to a transaction that would not affect a single Illinois shareholder if a corporation fit within the definition of a "target company." The Court concluded "the Illinois statute is a direct restraint on interstate commerce and has a sweeping extraterritorial effect," because the statute would prevent a tender offeror from communicating its offer to shareholders both within and outside Illinois. Acceptance of the offer by any of the shareholders would result in interstate transactions; the Illinois statute effectively stifled such transactions during the waiting period and thereby disrupted prospective interstate commerce. Under the Commerce Clause, the projection of these extraterritorial "practical effect[s]," regardless of the legislators' intentions, "'exceeded the inherent limits of the State's power.'"

In the present case, a number of witnesses testified to the chill that they felt as a result of the enactment of the New York statute; these witnesses refrained from engaging in particular types of interstate commerce. . . .

[The] extraterritoriality analysis rests on the premise that the Commerce Clause has two aspects: it subordinates each state's authority over interstate commerce to the federal power of regulation (a vertical limitation), and it embodies a principle of comity that mandates that one state not expand its regulatory powers in a manner that encroaches upon the sovereignty of its fellow states (a horizontal limitation). . . .

The need to contain individual state overreaching thus arises not from any disrespect for the plenary authority of each state over its own internal affairs but out of a recognition that true protection of each state's respective authority is only possible when such limits are observed by all states.

The nature of the Internet makes it impossible to restrict the effects of the New York Act to conduct occurring within New York. An Internet user may not intend that a message be accessible to New Yorkers, but lacks the ability to prevent New Yorkers from visiting a particular Web site or viewing a particular newsgroup posting or receiving a particular mail exploder. Thus, conduct that may be legal in the state in which the user acts can subject the user to prosecution in New York and thus subordinate the user's home state's policy — perhaps favoring freedom of expression over a more protective stance — to New York's local concerns. New York has deliberately imposed its legislation on the Internet and, by doing so, projected its law into other states whose citizens use the Net. This encroachment upon the authority which the Constitution specifically confers upon the federal government and upon the sovereignty of New York's sister states is per se violative of the Commerce Clause.

C. The Burdens the Act Imposes on Interstate Commerce Exceed Any Local Benefit

Even if the Act were not a per se violation of the Commerce Clause by virtue of its extraterritorial effects, the Act would nonetheless be an invalid indirect regulation of interstate commerce, because the burdens it imposes on interstate commerce are excessive in relation to the local benefits it confers. The Supreme Court set forth the balancing test applicable to indirect regulations of interstate commerce in *Pike v. Bruce Church*, 397 U.S. 137,

142 (1970). *Pike* requires a two-fold inquiry. The first level of examination is directed at the legitimacy of the state's interest. The next, and more difficult, determination weighs the burden on interstate commerce in light of the local benefit derived from the statute.

In the present case, I accept that the protection of children against pedophilia is a quintessentially legitimate state objective — a proposition with which I believe even the plaintiffs have expressed no quarrel. . . .

[According to the court, "The local benefits likely to result from the New York Act are not overwhelming." In the court's view the law could not reach communications that occurred outside of the state and would do little to achieve the state's objective.]

Balanced against the limited local benefits resulting from the Act is an extreme burden on interstate commerce. The New York Act casts its net worldwide; moreover, the chilling effect that it produces is bound to exceed the actual cases that are likely to be prosecuted, as Internet users will steer clear of the Act by significant margin. . . .

Moreover, as both three-judge panels that struck the federal statute have found, the costs associated with Internet users' attempts to comply with the terms of the defenses that the Act provides are excessive. . . .

The severe burden on interstate commerce resulting from the New York statute is not justifiable in light of the attenuated local benefits arising from it. The alternative analysis of the Act as an indirect regulation on interstate commerce therefore also mandates the issuance of the preliminary injunction sought by plaintiffs.

D.   THE ACT UNCONSTITUTIONALLY SUBJECTS INTERSTATE USE OF
     THE INTERNET TO INCONSISTENT REGULATIONS

Finally, a third mode of Commerce Clause analysis further confirms that the plaintiffs are likely to succeed on the merits of their claim that the New York Act is unconstitutional. The courts have long recognized that certain types of commerce demand consistent treatment and are therefore susceptible to regulation only on a national level. The Internet represents one of those areas; effective regulation will require national, and more likely global, cooperation. Regulation by any single state can only result in chaos, because at least some states will likely enact laws subjecting Internet users to conflicting obligations. Without the limitation's imposed by the Commerce Clause, these inconsistent regulatory schemes could paralyze the development of the Internet altogether. . . .

The Internet, like the rail and highway traffic . . . requires a cohesive national scheme of regulation so that users are reasonably able to determine their obligations. Regulation on a local level, by contrast, will leave users lost in a welter of inconsistent laws, imposed by different states with different priorities. . . .

As discussed at length above, an Internet user cannot foreclose access to her work from certain states or send differing versions of her communication to different jurisdictions. In this sense, the Internet user is in a worse position than the truck driver or train engineer who can steer around Illinois or Arizona, or change the mudguard or train configuration at the state line; the Internet user has no ability to bypass any particular state. The user must thus comply with the regulation imposed by the state with the most stringent standard or forego Internet communication of the message that might or might not subject her to prosecution. . . .

Further development of the Internet requires that users be able to predict the results of their Internet use with some degree of assurance. Haphazard and uncoordinated state regulation can only frustrate the growth of cyberspace. The need for uniformity in this unique sphere of commerce requires that New York's law be stricken as a violation of the Commerce Clause.

STATE OF WASHINGTON V. HECKEL

122 Wash. App. 60; 93 P.3d 189 (2004)

KENNEDY J.: [GROSSE J. and COX C.J. concurring]

In 1998, the Washington State Attorney General's office filed suit against Oregon resident Jason Heckel, alleging violations of Washington's Commercial Electronic Mail Act (the Act). . . . The ACT does not prohibit spam as such; rather, it prohibits misrepresentation in the subject line or transmission path of any unsolicited commercial e-mail message sent from a computer located in Washington, or sent to an e-mail address that the sender knows or has reason to know is held by a Washington resident. It also prohibits use of a third party's Internet domain name without permission of that party. In 2000, on cross-motions for summary judgment, the trial court dismissed the State's claims, concluding that the Act violated the Commerce Clause of the United States Constitution. In State v. Heckel, 143 Wn. 2d 824, 24 P.3d 404, cert. denied, 534 U.S. 997, 122 S. Ct. 467, 151 L. Ed. 2d 383 (2001) (*Heckel I*) our Supreme Court held that the Act does not unduly burden interstate commerce, reversed the dismissal, and remanded the case to the trial court.

In August 2002, the State moved for partial summary judgment. On September 13, 2002, the trial court granted summary judgment to the State, and on October 18, 2002, entered a judgment and decree imposing permanent injunctions and a civil penalty on Heckel, and awarding attorney fees and costs to the State.

Heckel appeals, contending (1) that the State failed to show that he knew or had reason to know that his spam — which contained misrepresentations in the subject lines and used a third party's domain name without permission — had been sent to a particular e-mail address held by a Washington resident, (2) that the Act as applied to him in this case violates the Commerce Clause, and (3) that there is a factual issue for trial regarding whether his subject lines were "misleading" under First Amendment analysis of commercial speech. We reject these contentions and affirm the trial court's judgment and decree.

FACTS

In 1997, Jason Heckel developed a 46-page on-line booklet entitled "How to Profit from the Internet," which included information on setting up an on-line promotional business, acquiring free e-mail accounts, and obtaining software to build basic websites and send bulk e-mail. From June to October 1998, Heckel sent between 100,000 and 1,000,000 unsolicited commercial e-mail, or "spam," messages over the Internet each week. Each message used one of two subject lines: "Did I get the right e-mail address?" and "For your review—HANDS OFF!" . . . The text of each message was a sales pitch for his booklet, priced at $39.95, and included an order form listing the mailing address for Heckel's Salem, Oregon business, Natural Instincts.

In June 1998, after receiving complaints from Washington recipients of Heckel's messages, David Hill of the Attorney General's Office sent Heckel a letter advising him of Washington's new law regarding commercial e-mail. On or around June 25, 1998, Heckel telephoned Hill for more information. During their conversation, Hill explained the provisions of the Act and procedures that bulk e-mailers can use to identify Washington e-mail address holders. Hill specifically referred Heckel to the Washington Association of Internet Providers on-line registry, where Washington residents who do not wish to receive spam can register their e-mail addresses, and thus where responsible e-commerce businesses can find lists of Washington e-mail addresses. After this conversation, Heckel did nothing to change his spamming procedure, and consumers continued to file complaints with the Attorney General's Office regarding Heckel's spam. Hill created a complaint matrix detailing 20 such complaints, and indicating that at least 16 involved messages received from Heckel after June 26. At least one of these complainants had previously registered her e-mail address at the on-line registry above mentioned, before she received Heckel's spam.

To send his spam, Heckel used at least 12 different Internet addresses with the domain name "juno.com," which accounts were generally cancelled by Juno within two days of his bulk e-mail transmissions. When Juno would shut down one of Heckel's accounts, Heckel would simply open a new one, and send out more batches of spam. Some recipients attempted to reply to Heckel's spam and failed—in some cases because Juno had already terminated the account or accounts from which the spam had been sent.

Some recipients stated that the domain name Heckel used to send the spam was different from the domain identified in the message. In particular, 9 messages indicated that they originated from "13.com" but the "message-ID" display demonstrated that they had actually been transmitted from a different domain. The owner of the inactive domain name of "13.com" since 1995 submitted an unrebutted declaration stating that he had never authorized Heckel to use the domain name.

Heckel sold 17 copies of his booklet to Washington residents before the State filed its suit. In September 1998, Heckel cashed a check sent by a Washington resident in response to one of his spam messages.

In response to the State's motion for summary judgment, Heckel did not contest any of the facts above described. . . .

ANALYSIS

. . .

The Commercial Electronic Mail Act provides in pertinent part:

(1) No person may initiate the transmission, conspire with another to initiate the transmission, or assist the transmission, of a commercial electronic mail message from a computer located in Washington or to an electronic mail address that the sender knows, or has reason to know, is held by a Washington resident that:

(a) Uses a third party's internet domain name without permission of the third party, or otherwise misrepresents or obscures any information in identifying the point of origin or the transmission path of a commercial electronic mail message; or

(b) Contains false or misleading information in the subject line.

(2) For purposes of this section, a person knows that the intended recipient of a commercial electronic mail message is a Washington resident if that information is available, upon request, from the registrant of the internet domain name contained in the recipient's electronic mail address.

. . .

Heckel does not deny that he violated [the Act] by using the domain name "13.com" without the permission of the name's owner, thereby misrepresenting or obscuring the point of origin or the transmission path of at least 9 of his spam messages sent to Washington residents. Instead, Heckel contends that the State failed to present evidence that he sent any e-mail "to an electronic mail address that [he knew], or [had] reason to know, [was] held by a Washington resident."

In support of this assertion, Heckel first argues that the *only* way the State could prove that he had a "reason to know" is by proving facts to satisfy [the Act's requirements], that is, by presenting evidence to demonstrate that the information regarding Washington residency was available from the registrant of the Internet domain name of each particular e-mail address at issue.

Not only does Heckel fail to cite any authority for this position, but also we find his proposed reading of the statute absurd. [Subsection (2) of the Act] states that a person knows — in other words, actual knowledge is imputed — if residency information is available from the domain name registrant. The statute does not state that proof that the residency information is available from the Internet domain name registrant is the exclusive means of proving knowledge under the statute. Moreover, this section says nothing about what evidence is sufficient to demonstrate that a sender had a "reason to know" that an e-mail address was held by a Washington resident. Finally, there is nothing in the record to indicate that the State intended to rely on [subsection (2)] to show Heckel's knowledge here.

Relying on our Supreme Court's analysis in *Heckel I* of American Libraries Ass'n v. Pataki, 969 F. Supp. 160 (1997), Heckel next contends that the Act and the Commerce Clause required the State to prove he had knowledge as to *specific e-mail addresses*. In *American Libraries*, the court held that a New York statute that made it a felony to use a computer communication system to display or distribute sexually explicit content to minors violated the Commerce Clause. 969 F. Supp. at 169. The statute was overreaching in that it applied to any type of Internet activity — even websites or chat rooms where individuals posting content that would be legitimate for adults have no control over future access by minors, in New York or anywhere else. As our Supreme Court observed in *Heckel I*, that case is distinguishable because here, the Act is limited to deceptive unsolicited commercial e-mail messages sent to a Washington resident — in other words, the sender actually intends the recipient to access the content. *Heckel I*, 143 Wn. 2d at 840.

Heckel argues that the Court's statement, "the Act reaches only those deceptive UCE messages directed to a Washington resident," *Heckel I*, 143 Wn. 2d at 840, indicates that to satisfy the Act and the Commerce Clause the State must prove that he knew that *specific e-mail addresses* were registered to Washington residents and that here, although he knew based on his conversation with Hill on June 25 that some of his e-mails had been received by unidentified Washington residents, the State failed to prove that he had specific knowledge that any particular addresses belonged to Washington residents as required by the statute.

Again, if we were to interpret the Act the way Heckel suggests, no spammer sending deceptive e-mail could ever violate the Act as long as he were to use a bulk e-mail program to harvest large numbers of addresses without regard to residence of the owners, because he could always claim that he had no specific knowledge about particular recipients. But Heckel does not dispute that he actually intended to send his message to each person who received it. He also does not dispute that Hill advised him about the Act and that the Attorney General's Office had received complaints from Washington residents who had received his e-mail. He also does not dispute the State's evidence that more Washington residents actually received his e-mails *after* his conversation with Hill. Despite his knowledge that the bulk e-mail software he was using to send out his spam had gathered addresses and sent e-mail to Washington residents, Heckel failed to take any action whatsoever to determine whether any of his intended bulk e-mail recipients were Washington residents or to change his practices to comply with the Act, and in fact he continued to send the same e-mail messages to more Washington residents. The trial court properly found that these facts were sufficient to demonstrate Heckel's knowledge that he was in fact directing deceptive spam to Washington residents.

The State urges this court to adopt the reasoning of the trial court and at least two federal district courts and hold that a spammer sending millions of e-mails over the Internet has reason to know that he could be "ha[u]led into court in a distant jurisdiction to answer for the ramifications of that solicitation." Internet Doorway, Inc. v. Parks, 138 F. Supp. 2d 773, 779-80 (S.D. Miss. 2001); Verizon Online Servs., Inc. v. Ralsky, 203 F. Supp. 2d 601, 618 (E.D. Va. 2002). Heckel urges a rejection of this "statistical argument," arguing that the Act requires a "particular" or "specific" e-mail address of a Washington resident and that reasonable minds could differ on whether sending any particular number of e-mail messages must statistically impose a conclusive presumption that some of those would be directed to the addresses of Washington residents. But Heckel does not dispute that he sent between 100,000 and 1,000,000 messages *per week* over a period of at least four months. Based on these numbers, we agree with the State and conclude that Heckel had reason to know that his spam would be directed to Washington residents.

The State also contends that Heckel had reason to know that his spam was reaching Washington residents because some of them were listed at the website of the Washington Association of Internet Service Providers (WAISP), where Washington residents who do not want to receive spam can register. See, *Heckel I*, 143 Wn. 2d at 837 n.13. Heckel responds that evidence that recipients of his spam were registered with WAISP is insufficient to prove that he had reason to know they were Washington residents because there was no evidence in the record on how the registry works and reasonable minds could differ on whether accessing the registry is unduly burdensome or whether an advertiser ought to be required to check one or more registries before sending out e-mail.

Again, we agree with the State. As of June 25, Heckel knew that his spam was reaching Washington residents and that they were complaining to the Attorney General. He knew that the Act prohibited the kinds of e-mail he was sending. He also knew, based on his conversation with Hill, that the WAISP registry listed Washington residents that did not want unsolicited commercial e-mail. Because Heckel fails to identify any material fact for trial regarding his knowledge as above described, and because reasonable minds could not find that he did not have reason to know that he was sending e-mail to Washington residents, summary judgment was proper.

Heckel acknowledges in his reply brief that our Supreme Court has held that the Act does not facially violate the Commerce Clause but argues that it failed to consider whether it violates the clause as applied in this case. Relying on Quill Corp. v. North Dakota, 504 U.S. 298, 112 S. Ct. 1904, 119 L. Ed. 2d 91 (1992), Heckel contends that his lack of ties with the State of

Washington—no employees, representatives, or physical facilities—indicates a lack of a sufficient nexus with the State, such that he cannot be subject to the Act. But as the State points out, in *Quill*, the question was whether North Dakota violated the Commerce Clause by imposing an excise tax on an out-of-state company operating a mail order business. Because the Act does not involve taxation and the burden it imposes is slight in comparison, *Quill* is inapposite.

Moreover, Heckel reads *Heckel I* too narrowly. In *Heckel I*, 143 Wn. 2d at 833, the court explained not only that the Act is not facially discriminatory but also that it applies evenhandedly to both instate and out-of-state spammers.

Finally, Heckel makes no reasoned argument showing how an act that prohibits only deceptive spam and that does not thereby violate the Commerce Clause on its face could possibly violate the Commerce Clause as applied to Heckel's deceptive spam. We conclude that the Act, as applied to Heckel in this case, does not violate the Commerce Clause.

Heckel also contends that the Act violates the First Amendment because it is vague and overbroad. Heckel also attempts to create an issue of material fact for trial by asserting that the subject lines on his e-mails were not misleading, particularly when viewed with the body of the e-mail.

Commercial speech is entitled to First Amendment protection if it is not misleading. Central Hudson Gas & Elec. Corp. v. Public Serv. Comm'n of New York, 447 U.S. 557, 566, 100 S. Ct. 2343, 65 L. Ed. 2d 341 (1980). The Act prohibits unsolicited commercial e-mail with false or misleading information in the subject line. RCW 19.190.020(1)(b). The trial court concluded that reasonable minds could not differ with the conclusion that Heckel's two subject lines, "Did I get the right e-mail address?" and "For your review— HANDS OFF!", were deceptive and misleading when the body of the e-mail consisted of an unsolicited advertisement. We agree with the trial court.

Heckel does not claim that his spam was anything other than commercial speech. To demonstrate that the subject line is not misleading, Heckel urges this court to consider the first line of the body of the e-mail or the whole message of the e-mail rather than viewing the subject line alone, "artificially segregating the subject line from the rest of the communication and banning creative advertising to entice potential customers to read the rest of the commercial speech.". . . . But the Act does not regulate the body of the e-mail, only the subject line. Here, the subject line was clearly designed to entice the recipient to open the message, not with creative advertising as Heckel contends, but by enticing the recipient to believe that the message might be from a friend or acquaintance or business contact who is trying to "get the right e-mail address" or who is sending something confidential, rather than a commercial advertisement. The trial court did not err.

. . .

Because the Act is narrowly tailored to regulate only deceptive commercial speech, which is not protected by the First Amendment, the Act is not overly broad. Neither is the Act unconstitutionally vague. Contrary to Heckel's

argument, the Act's prohibition against "misleading" subject lines or transmission paths is not vague. Indeed, the United States Supreme Court used the
word "misleading" in *Central Hudson*, 447 U.S. at 566, as part of the appropriate standard in determining when commercial speech is constitutionally
protected: "For commercial speech to come within [the protection of the First
Amendment] it at least must concern lawful activity and not be misleading."
Id. See also City of Yakima v. Irving, 70 Wn. App. 1, 851 P.2d 724 (1993),
(holding that an ordinance that prohibited making "misleading" police reports
not unconstitutionally vague).

Conclusion

The trial court did not err in granting summary judgment to the State.
Heckel's spam clearly fell within the hard core of the prohibitions contained in
the Act: The spam was accompanied by misleading subject lines; was transmitted along misleading paths, and 9 of the spam messages used the domain name
of a third party who had not given permission to Heckel to use that inactive
domain name. Heckel received actual notice from the Attorney General that his
spam violated Washington's Act and that it was in fact being received by
Washington residents. Mr. Hill explained to Heckel how he could go about
learning the e-mail addresses of Washington residents who do not wish to
receive spam at all — let alone deceptive spam. Not only did Heckel fail to
change his procedures for disseminated spam, but he also failed to change
his misleading subject lines, a means by which he could have brought his
advertisements within the parameters of the Act — insofar as misleading
subject lines are concerned, anyhow. The Act does not violate the Commerce
Clause, either facially or as applied to Heckel. The Act does not violate the First
Amendment, either facially or as applied. The Act is not unconstitutionally
vague. We affirm the trial court's summary judgment ruling and the decree
that was subsequently entered.

COMMENTS AND QUESTIONS

1. To what extent does the court's decision in *Pataki* depend upon its
conclusion that "no aspect of the Internet can feasibly be closed off to users
from another state"? Why is that conclusion relevant to whether New York
could regulate speech on the Internet consistently with the Dormant Commerce Clause? What if the New York statute only applied when the sender of a
message and the recipient are both located in New York?
2. Why does it matter whether the speech in question can be considered
commercial? How is an e-mail exchange between parent and child commercial?
Are the *Pataki* court's examples of nonprofit activities or its treatment of the
Internet as an instrumentality of interstate commerce persuasive?

3. To the extent that speech reaches New York through the Internet, how is the state regulating conduct that occurs exclusively outside of its borders?

4. According to the court in *Pataki*, why should courts be concerned about the extraterritorial effects of state regulation? Does this decision create a virtually *per se* rule that state regulation of the Internet unduly burdens interstate commerce?

5. How are the benefits of regulating speech on the Internet attenuated? What are the burdens upon interstate commerce? How do the requirements of the New York law subject Internet speakers to inconsistent obligations?

6. A conclusion similar to the one in *Pataki* was reached with respect to state regulation of privacy in Quintiles v. WebMD, No. 5:01-CV-180-Bo(3) (E.D.N.C. Mar. 21, 2001), which involved a dispute over the transmission of patient medical data between Quintiles and WebMD. WebMD claimed to have suspended the transmission of certain data to Quintiles because the data could be used to identify individual patients in violation of state privacy laws. Quintiles argued that WebMD was contractually obligated to continue the data transmissions. According to the court, even if the data transmissions violated state privacy law, the commerce clause would prevent the states from regulating the interstate transmission of data. Data transmittal is "an article of commerce" and "[a] long line of Supreme Court cases has firmly entrenched the principle that a State statute that regulates commerce wholly outside of the boundaries of the State is in violation of the Commerce Clause." The court went on: "Furthermore, a State has no interest in this data once outside of its borders, and the State's laws do not attach themselves to that data even if said data originated in the State." Therefore, the court concluded that WebMD was not relieved of its obligations based upon state privacy laws.

7. According to the court in *Heckel*, why is the Washington statute consistent with the Dormant Commerce Clause? Why is the statute consistent with the First Amendment?

8. Is it possible to reconcile *Heckel* and *Pataki*? How does the court in *Heckel* distinguish *Pataki*?

9. Congress has now enacted legislation in an attempt to regulate unsolicited commercial e-mail more uniformly across the States. The Controlling the Assault of Non-Solicited Pornography and Marketing Act of 2003 (also referred to as the CAN-SPAM Act) takes a similar approach to the Washington legislation discussed in *Heckel*, although the Federal Trade Commission has decided not to implement a centralized "do-not-email" list because of concerns that it would not be feasible to administer such a list and it may raise security concerns. To what extent does a federal law such as CAN-SPAM potentially resolve the problems associated with regulating unsolicited commercial e-mail?

10. Taxation of online transactions raises some of the same Commerce Clause issues as the laws under consideration in *Pataki* and *Heckel*. In the early days of electronic commerce, there were concerns that the potential application

of multiple state tax laws to Internet transactions would chill the development of electronic commerce. With over 7,500 taxing jurisdictions at the state and local level, federal legislators initially feared that state and local taxing authorities would force many Internet companies out of business due to the high costs of complying with the tax laws of potentially hundreds of taxing jurisdictions. Thus, in 1998 Congress enacted the Internet Tax Freedom Act that prevented any state or local government from enacting a discriminatory tax on e-commerce until October 21, 2001. This period was subsequently amended until November 1, 2007, under the Internet Tax Nondiscrimination Act of 2004, and then again extended until November 1, 2014, under the Internet Tax Freedom Act Amendment Acts of 2007. For a review of tax issues and the Internet, see Charles E. McLure, Jr., *Taxation of Electronic Commerce: Economic Objectives, Technological Constraints, and Tax Law*, 52 Tax L. Rev. 269 (1997); Walter Hellerstein, *U.S. State Taxation of Electronic Commerce: Preliminary Thoughts on Model Uniform Legislation*, 75 Tax Notes 819 (1997); Arthur J. Cockfield, *Transforming the Internet into a Taxable Forum: A Case Study in E-Commerce Taxation*, 85 Minn. L. Rev. 1171 (2001); Arthur J. Cockfield, *Balancing National Interests in the Taxation of Electronic Commerce Business Profits*, 74 Tul. L. Rev. 133-217 (1999); Streamlined Sales Tax Project (information available at *http://www.streamlinedsalestax.org/*).

2. International Regulation of Cyberspace

Dow Jones & Co. v. Gutnick

[2002] HCA 56 (10 Dec. 2002)

Gleeson C.J., McHugh, Gummow and Hayne JJ: [Gaudron, Kirby, and Callinan J.J. concurring]

1. . . . The appellant, Dow Jones & Company Inc ("Dow Jones"), prints and publishes the *Wall Street Journal* newspaper and *Barron's* magazine. Since 1996, Dow Jones has operated WSJ.com, a subscription news site on the World Wide Web. Those who pay an annual fee (set, at the times relevant to these proceedings, at $US59, or $US29 if they are subscribers to the printed editions of either the *Wall Street Journal* or *Barron's*) may have access to the information to be found at WSJ.com. Those who have not paid a subscription may also have access if they register, giving a user name and a password. The information at WSJ.com includes *Barron's Online* in which the text and pictures published in the current printed edition of *Barron's* magazine are reproduced.

2. The edition of *Barron's Online* for 28 October 2000 (and the equivalent edition of the magazine which bore the date 30 October 2000) contained an article entitled "Unholy Gains" in which several references were

made to the respondent, Mr. Joseph Gutnick, Mr. Gutnick contends that part of the article defamed him. He has brought an action in the Supreme Court of Victoria against Dow Jones claiming damages for defamation. Mr. Gutnick lives in Victoria. He has his business headquarters there. Although he conducts business outside Australia, including in the United States of America, and has made significant contributions to charities in the United States and Israel, much of his social and business life could be said to be focused in Victoria.

. . .

4. The principal issue debated in the appeal to this Court was where was the material of which Mr. Gutnick complained published? Was it published in Victoria? The answer to these questions was said to affect, even determine, whether proceedings in the Supreme Court of Victoria should, as Dow Jones contended, be stayed on the ground that that Court was a clearly inappropriate forum for determination of the action.

. . .

WIDELY DISSEMINATED PUBLICATIONS

38. In the course of argument much emphasis was given to the fact that the advent of the World Wide Web is a considerable technological advance. So it is. But the problem of widely disseminated communications is much older than the Internet and the World Wide Web. The law has had to grapple with such cases ever since newspapers and magazines came to be distributed to large numbers of people over wide geographic areas. Radio and television presented the same kind of problem as was presented by widespread dissemination of printed material, although international transmission of material was made easier by the advent of electronic means of communication.

39. It was suggested that the World Wide Web was different from radio and television because the radio or television broadcaster could decide how far the signal was to be broadcast. It must be recognised, however, that satellite broadcasting now permits very wide dissemination of radio and television and it may, therefore, be doubted that it is right to say that the World Wide Web has a uniquely broad reach. It is no more or less ubiquitous than some television services. In the end, pointing to the breadth or depth of reach of particular forms of communication may tend to obscure one basic fact. However broad may be the reach of any particular means of communication, those who make information accessible by a particular method do so knowing of the reach that their information may have. In particular, those who post information on the World Wide Web do so knowing that the information they make available is available to all and sundry without any geographic restriction.

40. Because publication is an act or event to which there are at least two parties, the publisher and a person to whom material is published, publication

to numerous persons may have as many territorial connections as there are those to whom particular words are published. It is only if one starts from a premise that the publication of particular words is necessarily a *singular* event which is to be located by reference *only* to the conduct of the publisher that it would be right to attach no significance to the territorial connections provided by the several places in which the publication is available for comprehension.

41. Other territorial connections may also be identified. In the present case, Dow Jones began the process of making material available at WSJ.com by transmitting it from a computer located in New York city. For all that is known, the author of the article may have composed it in another State. Dow Jones is a Delaware corporation. Consideration has been given to these and indeed other bases of territorial connection in identifying the law that might properly be held to govern an action for defamation where the applicable choice of law rule was what came to be known as the proper law of the tort.

42. Many of these territorial connections are irrelevant to the inquiry which the Australian common law choice of law rule requires by its reference to the law of the place of the tort. In that context, it is defamation's concern with reputation, and the significance to be given to damage (as being of the gist of the action) that require rejection of Dow Jones's contention that publication is necessarily a singular event located by reference only to the publisher's conduct. Australian common law choice of law rules do not require locating the place of publication of defamatory material as being necessarily, and only, the place of the publisher's conduct (in this case, being Dow Jones uploading the allegedly defamatory material onto its servers in New Jersey).

43. Reference to decisions such as *Jackson v. Spittall, Distillers Co (Bio-chemicals) Ltd v. Thompson* and *Voth v. Manildra Flour Mills Pty Ltd* show that locating the place of commission of a tort is not always easy. Attempts to apply a single rule of location (such as a rule that intentional torts are committed where the tortfeasor acts, or that torts are committed in the place where the last event necessary to make the actor liable has taken place) have proved unsatisfactory if only because the rules pay insufficient regard to the different kinds of tortious claims that may be made. Especially is that so in cases of omission. In the end the question is "where in substance did this cause of action arise"? In cases, like trespass or negligence, where some quality of the defendant's conduct is critical, it will usually be very important to look to where the defendant acted, not to where the consequences of the conduct were felt.

44. In defamation, the same considerations that require rejection of locating the tort by reference only to the publisher's conduct, lead to the conclusion that, ordinarily, defamation is to be located at the place where the damage to reputation occurs. Ordinarily that will be where the material which is alleged to be defamatory is available in comprehensible form assuming, of course, that the person defamed has in that place a reputation which is thereby damaged. It is only when the material is in comprehensible form that the damage to reputation is done and it is damage to reputation which is the principal focus of defamation, not any quality of the defendant's conduct. In the case of material

on the World Wide Web, it is not available in comprehensible form until down-loaded on to the computer of a person who has used a web browser to pull the material from the web server. It is where that person downloads the material that the damage to reputation may be done. Ordinarily then, that will be the place where the tort of defamation is committed. . . .

53. Three other matters should be mentioned. In considering what further development of the common law defences to defamation may be thought desirable, due weight must be given to the fact that a claim for damage to reputation will warrant an award of substantial damages only if the plaintiff has a reputation in the place where the publication is made. Further, plaintiffs are unlikely to sue for defamation published outside the forum unless a judgment obtained in the action would be of real value to the plaintiff. The value that a judgment would have may be much affected by whether it can be enforced in a place where the defendant has assets.

54. Finally, if the two considerations just mentioned are not thought to limit the scale of the problem confronting those who would make information available on the World Wide Web, the spectre which Dow Jones sought to conjure up in the present appeal, of a publisher forced to consider every article it publishes on the World Wide Web against the defamation laws of every country from Afghanistan to Zimbabwe is seen to be unreal when it is recalled that in all except the most unusual of cases, identifying the person about whom material is to be published will readily identify the defamation law to which that person may resort.

COMMENTS AND QUESTIONS

1. What policy reasons are given in *Gutnick* for locating the action for defamation at the place where reputational injury occurs? Why does the majority take the view that this is unlikely to subject the defendant to actions in multiple jurisdictions, except in unusual cases?

2. On what basis does the court distinguish the jurisdictional result in a defamation case from the rule usually applying in tort cases involving trespass or negligence? Why is the place of the defendant's conduct regarded as being more relevant to jurisdiction in trespass or negligence than in defamation? Do you agree with the court's analysis on this point?

3. To what extent should differences between "push" versus "pull" technology lead to different jurisdictional results? In *Gutnick*, Dow Jones argued that the readers who download content from a Web site control where that content will go and not the Web site operators. Under those circumstances, readers of Dow Jones's publications are arguably pulling that content to their nation. Is this the type of unilateral activity that the Supreme Court of the United States found insufficient to support jurisdiction in *World Wide Volkswagen*? Does *Dow Jones* differ from the United States cases dealing with tortious conduct?

4. Does Internet publication create new issues for the legal system, particularly in terms of tortious conduct like defamation or invasion of privacy (see Chapter 5)? Was Easterbrook incorrect in suggesting that "cyberlaw" is like the "law of the horse" with respect to online torts related to liability for online speech?

PLAYBOY ENTERPRISES, INC. v. CHUCKLEBERRY PUBLISHING, INC.

939 F. Supp. 1032 (S.D.N.Y. 1996)

SCHEINDLIN, District Judge:

Plaintiff, Playboy Enterprises, Inc. ("PEI"), has moved for a finding of contempt against Defendant, Tattilo Editrice, S.p.A. ("Tattilo"). PEI alleges that by operating an Internet site from Italy under the PLAYMEN label, Tattilo has violated a judgment dated June 26, 1981, enjoining it from publishing, printing, distributing or selling in the United States an English language male sophisticate magazine under the name "PLAYMEN" ("Injunction"). . . .

In 1967, Tattilo began publishing a male sophisticate magazine in Italy under the name PLAYMEN. Although the magazine carried an English title, it was written entirely in Italian. In July 1979, Tattilo announced plans to publish an English language version of PLAYMEN in the United States. Shortly thereafter, PEI brought suit against Tattilo to enjoin Tattilo's use of the name PLAYMEN in connection with a male sophisticate magazine and related products. PEI has published the well-known male entertainment magazine "PLAYBOY" since 1953, which is sold throughout the world in a multitude of foreign languages. Plaintiff's suit for injunctive relief alleged trademark infringement, false designation of origin, unfair competition based on infringement of Plaintiff's common law trademark rights, and violations of the New York Anti-Dilution Statute. . . .

A permanent injunction was awarded on April 1, 1981, and a judgment subsequently entered on June 26, 1981, permanently enjoining Tattilo from [using the word "Playmen" as a mark in the United States.] . . . PEI was similarly successful in enjoining the use of the PLAYMEN name in the courts of England, France and West Germany. However, the Italian courts ruled that "lexically" PLAYBOY was a weak mark and not entitled to protection in that country. The publication of PLAYMEN in Italy continues to the present day.

On approximately January 22, 1996, PEI discovered that Tattilo had created an Internet site featuring the PLAYMEN name. This Internet site makes available images of the cover of the Italian magazine, as well as its "Women of the Month" feature and several other sexually explicit photographic images. Users of the Internet site also receive "special discounts" on other Tattilo products, such as CD ROMs and Photo CDs. Tattilo created this site by uploading these images onto a World Wide Web server located in Italy.

These images can be accessed at the Internet address "http://www. playmen.it."[3] . . .

In order to access the Lite version of the PLAYMEN Internet service, the prospective user must first contact Tattilo. The user will then receive a temporary user name and password via e-mail. To subscribe to PLAYMEN Pro, the prospective user must fill out a form and send it via fax to Tattilo. Within 24 hours, the user receives by e-mail a unique password and login name that enable the user to browse the PLAYMEN Pro service.

The PLAYMEN Internet site is widely available to patrons living in the United States. More to the point, *anyone* in the United States with access to the Internet has the capacity to browse the PLAYMEN Internet site, review, and obtain print and electronic copies of sexually explicit pages of PLAYMEN magazine. All that is required to establish the account is the brief contact with Tattilo outlined above. . . .

In order to violate the Injunction, however, Defendant must distribute the pictorial images within the United States. Defendant argues that it is merely posting pictorial images on a computer server in Italy, rather than distributing those images to anyone within the United States. A computer operator wishing to view these images must, in effect, transport himself to Italy to view Tattilo's pictorial displays. The use of the Internet is akin to boarding a plane, landing in Italy, and purchasing a copy of PLAYMEN magazine, an activity permitted under Italian law. Thus Defendant argues that its publication of pictorial images over the Internet cannot be barred by the Injunction despite the fact that computer operators can view these pictorial images in the United States.

Once more, I disagree. Defendant has actively solicited United States customers to its Internet site, and in doing so has distributed its product within the United States. When a potential subscriber faxes the required form to Tattilo, he receives back via e-mail a password and user name. By this process, Tattilo distributes its product within the United States.

Defendant's analogy of "flying to Italy" to purchase a copy of the PLAY-MEN magazine is inapposite. Tattilo may of course maintain its Italian Internet site. The Internet is a world-wide phenomenon, accessible from every corner of the globe. Tattilo cannot be prohibited from operating its Internet site merely because the site is accessible from within one country in which its product is banned. To hold otherwise "would be tantamount to a declaration that this Court, and every other court throughout the world, may assert jurisdiction over all information providers on the global World Wide Web." Such a holding would have a devastating impact on those who use this global service. The Internet deserves special protection as a place where public discourse may

---

3. Internet addresses, such as the one at issue here, typically include a final extension to their "uniform resource locator" ("URL"). To United States users of the Internet, the most familiar URL extensions are ".com" (indicating that the accessed computer is commercial); ".edu" (educational); ".org" (non-profit organization); ".gov" (government agency); and ".net" (networking organization). In comparison, ".it" — such as appears in the PLAYMEN Internet site address "http://www.playmen.it" — indicates that the accessed computer is located in Italy.

be conducted without regard to nationality, religion, sex, age, or to monitors of community standards of decency.

However, this special protection does not extend to ignoring court orders and injunctions. If it did, injunctions would cease to have meaning and intellectual property would no longer be adequately protected. In the absence of enforcement, intellectual property laws could be easily circumvented through the creation of Internet sites that permit the very distribution that has been enjoined. Our long-standing system of intellectual property protections has encouraged creative minds to be productive. Diluting those protections may discourage that creativity.

While this Court has neither the jurisdiction nor the desire to prohibit the creation of Internet sites around the globe, it may prohibit access to those sites in *this* country. Therefore, while Tattilo may continue to operate its Internet site, it must refrain from accepting subscriptions from customers living in the United States. In accord with this holding, an Italian customer who subsequently moves to the United States may maintain his or her subscription to the Internet site. . . .

COMMENTS AND QUESTIONS

1.   If Chuckleberry Publishing has a right to use the term "Playmen" in Italy, why should U.S. law limit its use on the Internet? Is this an example of extraterritorial legislation? Does the court's limited remedy alleviate any extraterritorial concerns?

2.   Should it matter that some U.S. citizens may misrepresent their country of origin?

3.   If the court rejects Chuckleberry's analogy of Internet access as a user flying to Italy, why does it allow Italian subscribers to maintain their subscription when they move to the United States?

4.   Both *Dow Jones* and *Chuckleberry Publishing* involved Web sites that only provided access to subscribers. As such, the Web site operators had already undertaken some affirmative steps to screen users. What if a Web site has not taken steps to screen users? Consider the following:

LIGUE CONTRE LE RACISME ET L'ANTISEMITISME V. YAHOO!, INC.

Superior Ct. of Paris (Nov. 20, 2000) (Translation available at
http://www.lapres.net/yahen.html)

In *Yahoo!*, a French court ordered Yahoo! to implement screening technology to block individuals located within French territory from accessing auctions involving Nazi memorabilia. According to Yahoo!, its French subsidiary sites do not permit such postings, but its U.S. based site allows the postings because any restrictions might infringe upon the First Amendment to the U.S. Constitution.

Yahoo! challenged the jurisdiction of the French court on the grounds that:

1. its services are destined essentially to Internet users located within the United States of America;
2. its servers are located on the same territory;
3. a coercive measure against the company could not be applied in the United States because such a measure would contravene the first amendment of the Constitution of the United States which guarantees to all citizens freedom of speech and expression.

In rejecting Yahoo!'s argument the court concluded that French jurisdiction over Yahoo! for activities occurring on its general auction site was appropriate because "the company directs its services to a French audience because the company responds to visitors to its auction site from a computer located in France by posting advertising banners in French. . . ."

Yahoo! also argued that it was technologically impossible to block access to its Web site based upon geography. Yahoo!'s expert, Vinton Cerf, co-founder of the TCP/IP protocal, testified:

"It has been proposed that users identify where they are at the request of the web server, such as the one(s) serving yahoo.fr—or yahoo.com. There are several potential problems with this approach. For one thing, users can choose to lie about their locations. For another, every user of the web site would have to be asked to identify his or her location since the web server would have no way to determine a priori whether the user is French or is using the Internet from a French location. Some users consider such questions to be an invasion of privacy. While I am not completely acquainted with privacy provisions in the Europe Union, it might be considered a violation of the rights of privacy of European users, including French users to request this information. Of course if this information is required solely because of the French Court Order, one might wonder on what grounds all other users all over the world are required to comply.

Another complaint about the idea of asking user for their location in that this might have to be done repeatedly by each web site that the user accesses—yahoo cannot force every web site to make this request. When a user first contacts the server(s) at yahoo.fr— or yahoo.com, one might imagine that the question of geographic location might be asked and then a piece of data called a cookie might be stored on the user's computer disk. Repeated visits to Yahoo sites might then refer to this cookie for user location information. The problem with this idea is that cookies are considered by many to be an invasion of privacy also, as a result many users either configure browsers to reject storage of cookies on their disk drives or they clear them away after each session on the Internet—thus forcing the query about geographical location each time the user encounters a Yahoo-controlled web site. Again, Yahoo would have no way to force a web site net under its control to either ask the location question or to request a copy of the cookie containing the location. Indeed, it would open up a vulnerability for each user if arbitrary web sites were told how to retrieve the cookie placed there by the Yahoo sites.

It has been suggested that the filtering need only apply to users accessing the Internet from French Territories or by users who are French citizens. It is not clear whether the jurisdiction of the French Court extends to actions taken by French citizens who are not in

French territory at the time of their access to Internet. For these and many other reasons, it does not appear to be very feasible to rely on discovering the geographic location of users for purposes of imposing filtering of the kind described in the Court Order."

In rejecting these arguments, the court concluded that according to the court expert testimony from both parties demonstrated, it was possible to determine the geographic location of an IP address with approximately 70% reliability. Likewise:

"it is appropriate to recall that Yahoo! Inc. has already identifies the geographic location of French Internet users and those Internet users connecting from French territory because Yahoo! Inc. systematically posts advertising banners in the French language directed at such Internet users, which Yahoo! Inc. apparently hast has the means to locate; that Yahoo! Inc. cannot validly argue that the technology to be implemented in this case would be 'crude' without any reliability, unless it was assumed that Yahoo! Inc. had decided to waste its own money or cheat its advertisers on the quality of the services to which it has committed itself, which does not appear to be the case here. . . ."

"Whereas, in addition to the geographical identification which is already being used by Yahoo! Inc., the report of the experts suggests that for cases where the geographic location of the IP address is ambiguous, Internet visitors users can declare their nationality, which is actually a declaration of the geographic origin of the Internet user, which could be required either at the time when the web page is opened or, in the case of a search for nazi objects, if the word "nazi" appears in search term from the user, right before the search is processed by the search engine; . . .

Whereas the experts, who contest the allegations of Yahoo Inc. with respect to the adverse effects of such control on the performance levels and the response time of the server hosting the auction sale site, estimate that the combination of the two procedures, geographical identification and declaration of nationality make it possible to achieve a filtering rate close to 90%. . . ."

In addition, the court noted that Yahoo! also has the ability to control where objects purchased in its auctions were delivered, and does have a policy of refusing to auction "human organs, drugs, works or objects related to pedophilia, cigarettes or live animals" the court concluded that "the combination of technical and of the initiatives which it can implement if only for the sake of social morality therefore make it possible to comply with the injunctions contained in the order of May 22, 2000, concerning filtering access to the auction sites of Nazi objects. . . ."

COMMENTS AND QUESTIONS

1. According to Joel Reidenberg, the *Yahoo!* decision represents the maturing of efforts to regulate the Internet; see Joel Reidenberg, *The Yahoo! Case and the International Democratization of the Internet*, available at the Social Science Research Network, at *<http://papers.ssrn.com/sol3/papers. cfm?abstract_id=267148>*. How might the case represent an evolution in the ways in which courts and society think about the Internet?

2.   Is Yahoo!'s argument that it is impossible or impracticable to comply with the French order convincing? What is wrong with asking users to identify their country of origin?

3.   Following the French decision against them, Yahoo! filed suit against La Ligue Contre Le Racisme Et, L'Antisemitisme in the United States seeking a declaratory judgment that the order was unenforceable. *See* Yahoo! Inc. v. La Ligue Contre le Racisme et L'Antisemitisme, 145 F. Supp. 2d 1168 (N.D. Cal. 2001). In that action, the French defendants argued that the California court lacked personal jurisdiction over them. Relying upon the Supreme Court's decision in *Calder*, the district court concluded that the French defendants purposefully availed themselves to California by attempting to have Yahoo! comply with the French decision. As such, they "engaged in actions intentionally targeted at its Santa Clara headquarters for the express purpose of causing the consequences of such actions to be felt in California." 145 F. Supp. 2d at 1174. The court treated the French lawsuit as the potential equivalent of a tort stating that:

> While filing a lawsuit in a foreign jurisdiction may be entirely proper under the laws of that jurisdiction, such an act nonetheless may be "wrongful" from the standpoint of a court in the United States if its primary purpose or intended effect is to deprive a United States resident of its constitutional rights.

145 F. Supp. 2d at 1175. On appeal, the United States Court of Appeals for the Ninth Circuit split both on the question of purposeful availment and on the question as to whether the case should be dismissed for lack of ripeness: Yahoo! Inc. v. La Ligue Contre Le Racisme Et L'Antisemitisme, 2006 U.S. App. LEXIS 668 (2006). The result was that the decision of the lower court was reversed and the matter was remanded with directions to dismiss the action without prejudice. For a detailed discussion of the Yahoo! litigation in France and the aftermath of that litigation with respect to Yahoo's business practices, see Jack Goldsmith & Tim Wu, *Who Controls the Internet? Illusions of a Borderless World*, Chapter 1 (OUP, 2006/2008); David Post, *In Search of Jefferson's Moose: Notes on the State of Cyberspace*, 164-71 (OUP, 2009).

4.   The reasoning in *Yahoo!* is similar to the famous German decision against CompuServe. In *People v. Somm*, a German court found the Managing Director of CompuServe guilty of disseminating materials to minors because the company failed to block access to those materials in Germany. While CompuServe USA could block offending newsgroups in their entirety, it argued that it could not limit its blocking to Germany. Instead, it provided German users with software that would allow parents to block access to the newsgroups in question. The judgment against Felix Somm was overturned on appeal partly because it was not technologically possible for CompuServe USA to block the publication of the pornographic materials in Germany alone.

5.   As preceding cases and materials illustrate, efforts to regulate the Internet at the international level have primarily focused upon imposing

liability upon the publishers of information to the extent that they fail to prevent their communications from reaching the residents of a particular nation. As illustrated by the *Yahoo!* controversy, whether these efforts will be successful depends both upon the technological capabilities of a particular Internet entity initiating Internet communications (the topic debated in *Gutnick*) and the nation's ability to enforce its judgment against that entity when it is outside its geographical borders. China's effort to regulate Internet communications represents an alternative approach. Instead of relying upon legal rules backed by threats alone, China seeks to control the Internet through its architecture creating the digital equivalent of the Great Wall. By limiting the country's telecommunications connections with the outside world to a handful of official gateways, China is able to implement the Great Firewall that filters Internet traffic the government deems inappropriate from entering its borders. Similarly, the Chinese government requires all Internet users to register with the government before they may obtain access to the Internet, and users must agree not to use the Internet to threaten state security or to access obscene or pornographic material. Additionally, ISPs are required to implement their own filters and to monitor user activity. *See generally* Geremie R. Barme & Sang Ye, *The Great Firewall of China*, WIRED (June 1997). How have the Chinese chosen to address the "spillover" effects of the Internet? Why might Internet content providers prefer the Chinese approach to the approaches developing in Australia, Europe, and the United States? For a more detailed discussion of the Chinese attempts to regulate the Internet, see Jack Goldsmith & Tim Wu, *Who Controls the Internet? Illusions of a Borderless World*, Chapter 6 (OUP, 2006/2008).

6. In light of the preceding materials, how do the international efforts to regulate cyberspace differ from the jurisdictional and regulatory concerns within the United States? Can you identify any themes or trends in these decisions?

7. How have the preceding materials responded to the challenge that it is both technologically impossible and unjust for territorial governments to regulate cyberspace? Have these responses adequately addressed the "regulation skeptics'" concerns?

8. In discussing scholarly responses to the *Yahoo!* litigation, David Post has identified two distinct perspectives on the outcome—the "cyberspace unexceptionalists" and the "exceptionalists." According to Post, the unexceptionalists "see nothing illegitimate in France's exercise of legal authority over Yahoo!'s website." Unexceptionalists take the view that "the Yahoo! problem is just like the many old-fashioned border-crossing problems that have been around for centuries. Yahoo! might just as well have been conducting its auctions, and displaying the prohibited items, by sending catalogs or magazines or newspapers or television signals into France." On this view, "there are well-settled principles of international law to deal with these problems . . . and it is perfectly reasonable to apply those principles here." Post, *supra* note 3, at 166. On the other hand, exceptionalists, according to Post, will argue that the

Internet is not functionally equivalent to mail, telephone, television, or other preceding real space analogs. Exceptionalists take the view that it is not appropriate to apply those real space jurisdictional rules to the Internet. In fact, the application of these principles would lead to troubling and absurd results. Post, *supra* note 3, at 167 (OUP, 2009). Consider the following extract from a recent article by Post based on this work.

DAVID POST
GOVERNING CYBERSPACE LAW

24 Santa Clara Computer & High Tech. L.J. 883 (2008)

Code may be law in cyberspace, but law — ordinary law, the rules contained in the statutes and ordinances and municipal regulations and constitutions and court decisions and all the rest — is also law in cyberspace. It, too, constrains — at the very top of the protocol stack, as it were — what you may or may not do on the inter-network.

The tricky part, though, is: Which law? Whose law? The international legal system is premised, at bottom, on the existence and mutual recognition of the physical boundaries that separate sovereign and independent law-making communities — nation-states — from one another. These boundaries matter, in that system, and they matter a great deal. But on the inter-network, information moves in ways that seem to pay scant regard to those boundaries, and mapping them onto network activity is a profoundly difficult challenge.

. . .

A. The Unexceptionalists

Cyberspace Unexceptionalists . . . see nothing illegitimate in France's exercise of legal authority over Yahoo!'s website. To Unexceptionalists, as their name suggests, there is nothing exceptional — nothing warranting an exception — in the fact that this interaction is taking place on the Internet. Here's how a leading Unexceptionalist, Prof. Jack Goldsmith, put it:

> Transactions in cyberspace involve real people in one territorial jurisdiction either (i) transacting with real people in other territorial jurisdictions or (ii) engaging in activity in one jurisdiction that causes real-world effects in another territorial jurisdiction. To this extent, activity in cyberspace is functionally identical to transnational activity mediated by other means, such as mail or telephone or smoke signal.
>
> A government's responsibility for redressing local harms caused by a foreign source does not change because the harms are caused by an Internet communication. Cross-border harms that occur via the Internet are not any different than those outside the Net. . . . Nations have a right and a duty to protect their citizens from harm, whatever the source and whatever the medium.

For all intents and purposes, say the Unexceptionalists, the Yahoo! Problem is just like the many old-fashioned border-crossing problems that have been around for centuries. Yahoo! might just as well have been conducting its auctions, and displaying the prohibited items, by means of catalogs, or magazines, or newspapers, or television signals, sent into France. There are well-settled principles of international law to deal with these problems, the Unexceptionalists point out, and it is perfectly reasonable to apply those principles here.

One of those well-settled principles permits nations to regulate conduct occurring outside their borders — "extraterritorial conduct" — if that conduct has "significant effects" within those borders. . . .

In the Unexceptionalist view . . . the Yahoo! Problem isn't really all that difficult. Yahoo!'s conduct, though taking place outside of French borders, caused harm, as defined by French law, in France; French law provides a remedy for that harm; French citizens have a right, recognized under international law, to protect themselves against those who have caused them harm, even if they are standing outside of French territory when they did so. It is therefore reasonable and just to demand that Yahoo! take steps to comply with French law, and to punish it if it fails to do so.

B. THE EXCEPTIONALISTS

On the other hand . . . [t]o Exceptionalists, it does matter that Yahoo!'s actions took place on the Internet. Yahoo!'s website is not the "functional equivalent of mail, or telephone, or smoke signals," (or television broadcasts, catalogs, magazines, newspapers, or other realspace analogues), and applying jurisdictional principles that were developed to deal with realspace border-crossing transactions to network transactions leads to troubling, and perhaps even absurd, results.

The problem is that everything on the Web can affect everyone else simultaneously; website content appearing anywhere on the inter-network can have "significant effects" anywhere else on the inter-network, i.e., pretty much anywhere else on the planet.

It's not really a "problem," of course — not a bug but a feature, one of the things that makes the Web so extraordinary a medium for human communication. But it is a problem for the Unexceptionalist view of things. A place where just about everybody can have significant effects on just about everyone else, everywhere, simultaneously, is a place where the "significant effects principle" can't sensibly resolve jurisdictional questions. Unexceptionalist logic leads inexorably to the conclusion that (just about) everything you do on the Web may be subject to (just about) everybody's law. . . .

Unexceptionalists are well aware of this problem of multiple overlapping simultaneous jurisdictional claims, of course — they just don't think that it matters very much, as a practical matter. They acknowledge that courts in

Malaysia, and Mexico, and Latvia, might each (simultaneously) do what the French court did in the Yahoo! case: assert that its law applies to the auction website (or your daughter's newsletter), enter a judgment that the "wrong-doers" are violating that law, and order (on pain of some punishment) the offending conduct to cease immediately. But, Unexceptionalists contend, that's not really a problem, because Malaysia, and Mexico, and Latvia have no way to enforce those judgments and orders (unless the wrongdoer is located in, or has assets (property, or a bank account, or the like) located in, Malaysia, Mexico, or Latvia). For those of us who aren't located in, and don't have assets located in, Malaysia, Mexico, or Latvia, the mere "theoretical possibility" that Malaysia or Mexico or Latvia can take action against us can, for all intents and purposes, be ignored. . . .

It's not, to my eyes, a terribly satisfying resolution of the problem. It turns law, and the question of legal obligation, into something that looks more like a game — 3-Card Monte, or Jurisdictional Whack-a-Mole: If you (or your assets) pop up in Singapore, . . . Wham!! Singaporean law can be — can legitimately be — applied to you. Once posted to the Web, your daughter's junior high school newsletter is subject to Malaysian and Mexican and Latvian law simultaneously, because it may indeed be having "significant effects" in each country, and each of them can legitimately apply its coercive powers against the school or its officers or the newsletter editors (if it turns out to be in a position to do so); the school's obligation to comply with those laws is defined by the likelihood that it has assets in any one of them, or that any of its officers might travel to any of them.

It's a strange kind of law being served up by the Unexceptionalists — law that only gets revealed to the interacting parties ex post, and which can therefore no longer guide the behavior of those subject to it in any meaningful way.

. . .

What, though, is the alternative? What other answers might there be? There is one obvious and straightforward "solution" to the Yahoo! Problem, but it is one that few people on either side of this debate think much of: international harmonization, a single global law for copyright, or "hate speech," or fraud, or libel, or pornography, or consumer protection, or data privacy, or . . . [i]f the nations of the world were to agree, by treaty or some other multi-lateral act, to such law, the entire Yahoo! Problem disappears; no more conflicts between the laws of different jurisdictions, no more concerns about the difficulties of complying with 175 different legal regimes. Global law for a global Internet.

There has been a good deal of movement in the international legal system in recent years in the direction of increasing global harmonization, and it is almost certain to pick up speed in the future. But, most Unexceptionalists and Exceptionalists agree, this cure is worse than the disease. Countries have different laws because people have different histories, different cultures, different customs, and different views on important matters. . . .

. . .

I'm reasonably certain that millions of people, perhaps hundreds of millions of people . . . are going to be entering virtual places of one kind or another, most for the first time, over the next few years. And some of them, at least, are going to be looking for — demanding, even — something that looks more like "law," something that more effectively helps them do the things they'd like to do there, than anything the Unexceptionalists, clinging to their "bordered Internet" and the law of geographically-based sovereigns like a drowning man to a life raft, can provide.

It would be a shame, the waste of a global resource of potentially enormous value, if Jurisdictional Whack-a-Mole is the best we can come up with, and I don't think it is. There is an alternative, staring us right in the face; as complicated as the jurisdictional problem is on the Web, it is so much more complicated in virtual world space that, paradoxically, it is easier to solve. The Unexceptionalists are right about one thing: it's all just people in one place interacting and communicating with other people in other places. So why not begin by recognizing their right — perhaps even their inalienable right? — to govern themselves as they see fit? Why not let those who choose to enter, and to interact within, these online communities make their own law, deciding for themselves how they'd like to order their affairs?

What a crazy idea — self-governing communities!

Perhaps it is crazy . . . [b]ut it doesn't seem so crazy to me. Indeed, asking those who spend their time in Second Life for the answer to those questions ("Are Ponzi schemes 'frauds' in Second Life?" "Is a seller obligated to reveal defects when selling something in Second Life?" etc.) seems a lot more reasonable to me than asking the people of Malaysia how Malaysian law answers those same questions.

It doesn't seem so crazy to me because there's a "place-ness" to these virtual places — not just in the way they look but in the way they persist through time, and in the way they present opportunities for an infinite variety of repeated interactions between individuals, for collective decision-making, and for common enterprise — that enables us to think about them and talk about them the way that the people who spend lots of time there often do: as true communities, with shared norms and customs and expectations characteristic of each and continually being created and re-created by the members within each. I don't see why they are somehow inherently less deserving of less respect than the other communities — Topeka, Kansas, say, or Leicester, U.K., or Sri Lanka — within the international legal order.

. . .

That is, to be sure, just the beginning of the conversation. At the moment, there is no law of the place — nothing that can fairly be called "Second Life law" or "There.com law" or "Lineage II law" — because no institutions or processes for making "law" have been developed in any of these virtual worlds. They are, at the moment, truly law-less places — or, more precisely, places where code, and only code, is law.

But I'd be very surprised if that were a permanent condition. Like I said, there's real gold in those hills, and much of it can be unlocked only with a functioning legal system in place. I'm hardly the only one who realizes this; so there will be plenty of "law entrepreneurs" who will seize on this problem and get to work; some have already begun.

I don't know, to be honest, what they'll come up with, what those law-making institutions and processes will look like, or should look like, in a virtual world — whether they'll have representative assemblies or not, whether they'll use juries or not, whether they'll separate executive and legislative powers or not, whether they'll have paid judges or not, whether they'll have different tribunals for different kinds of actions or not. . . .

What I do know is that people have the right to make those decisions and answer those questions for themselves.

And I just wish the Unexceptionalists would stop telling us that we don't, that we've somehow given up our right to create new communities and to live under law of our own devising, or that we've somehow finished designing legal institutions, and are stuck, forevermore, with the ones we happen to have come up with by 1995.

COMMENTS AND QUESTIONS

1. In this passage, Post identifies three distinct approaches to cyberspace regulation: (a) unexceptionalism; (b) exceptionalism; (c) global harmonization of law. What are Post's major criticisms of the unexceptionalist approach to cyberspace regulation? Do you find these criticisms convincing?

2. As an exceptionalist, Post suggests the development of self-governing cyberspace communities. Do you find this proposal realistic?

3. Is the idea of self-governing cyberspace communities advocated by Post the same as the idea of cyberspace governance set forth in John Perry Barlow's *Cyberspace Declaration of Independence* (see above)? In what respects might it differ?

4. Is Post's notion of a self-governing cyberspace community simply a re-emphasizing of Lessig's earlier identification of social norms as an important aspect of cyberspace regulation? *See* Lessig, *The Law of the Horse: What Cyberlaw Might Teach* (excerpted in Chapter 1).

5. Post quickly dismisses the possibility of international harmonization of laws as a solution to problems of cyberspace regulation. On what grounds? Do you find his arguments convincing on this point?

6. Consider Professor Post's arguments as you read the following case involving a plaintiff in Texas attempting to establish personal jurisdiction over an Australian defendant. The case particularly raises aspects of Web 2.0 technology — in this case user-generated contact on the popular Flickr photograph sharing website. As the Internet becomes more of a collaborative forum with personal and commercial interests overlapping and increasing numbers of

people generating content, how should we resolve the jurisdictional questions that arise in greater numbers, and that involve the interests of often multiple parties in different jurisdictions?

CHANG v. VIRGIN MOBILE USA, L.L.C.

2009 U.S. Dist. LEXIS 3051 (2009)

SIDNEY A. FITZWATER, Chief Judge, United States District Court for the Northern District of Texas (Dallas Division).

. . . Plaintiffs Susan Chang ("Chang"), as next friend of Alison Chang ("Alison"), a minor, and Justin Ho-Wee Wong ("Wong") sued defendant Virgin Mobile Pty Ltd. ("Virgin Australia"), an Australian-based company, in Texas state court on claims for invasion of privacy, libel, breach of contract, and copyright infringement based on Virgin Australia's use of an image of Alison ("the photograph") in its "Are You With Us or What" advertising campaign (the "Campaign"). The case was removed to this court based on diversity jurisdiction, and Virgin Australia now moves to dismiss for lack of personal jurisdiction and insufficient service of process.

Virgin Australia is an Australian company with its principal place of business in Sydney, New South Wales, Australia. Virgin Australia provides a range of mobile phone products and services, including prepaid and postpaid mobile phones. Its geographical area of operation is limited to the area of domestic Australia covered by the Optus telecommunications network. [In a footnote, the court notes that Virgin USA and Virgin Australia are completely separate legal entities with no business connections and no common parent company ownership.]

In 2007 Virgin Australia launched the Campaign in select Australian cities, such as Sydney and Adelaide. The Campaign featured a collection of over 100 photographs downloaded at no cost to Virgin Australia from Yahoo!'s ("Yahoo's") public photo-sharing website, Flickr. Alison's photograph was taken by her church counselor, Wong, a resident of Fort Worth, Texas, who then published the photograph on Flickr under a Creative Commons Attribution 2.0 license agreement that provides for the most unrestricted use available to any worldwide user (including commercial use and no monetary payment). Virgin Australia used the photograph in an advertisement encouraging viewers to "DUMP YOUR PEN FRIEND" and advertising "FREE VIRGIN TO VIRGIN TEXTING." The advertisement was placed on bus shelter ad shells in major metropolitan areas in Australia. Virgin Australia never distributed the advertisement incorporating Alison's image in the United States, including Texas, and it never posted the photograph on its website or on any other website.

Several weeks after Wong uploaded the photograph onto Flickr, Alison received an email from one of her friends with a picture of her on a billboard affixed to a bus shelter in Adelaide, Australia. A member of the Flickr online blogger community then posted the picture of the billboard to the World Wide Web. The advertisement eventually garnered the interest of news stations, legal commentators, and website bloggers.

Virgin Australia moves to dismiss, contending that it lacks minimum contacts with the state of Texas and that it was not properly served. Plaintiffs respond that they have re-served Virgin Australia and that the court has personal jurisdiction because of Virgin Australia's purposeful contacts with Flickr's Texas servers, its contract with Wong, and the intrastate effect of its conduct.

II

A

The determination whether a federal district court has personal jurisdiction over a nonresident defendant is bipartite. The court first decides whether the long-arm statute of the state in which it sits confers personal jurisdiction over the defendant. If it does, the court then resolves whether the exercise of jurisdiction is consistent with the Due Process Clause of the Fourteenth Amendment. *See Mink v. AAAA Dev. LLC*, 190 F.3d 333, 335 (5th Cir. 1999). Because the Texas long-arm statute extends to the limits of due process, the court's statutory and constitutional inquiries are identical. *See, e.g., Kelly v. Syria Shell Petroleum Dev. B.V.*, 213 F.3d 841, 854 (5th Cir. 2000).

The Due Process Clause permits a court to exercise personal jurisdiction over a nonresident defendant if

> (1) that defendant has purposefully availed himself of the benefits and protections of the forum state by establishing "minimum contacts" with the forum state; and (2) the exercise of jurisdiction over that defendant does not offend "traditional notions of fair play and substantial justice." To comport with due process, the defendant's conduct in connection with the forum state must be such that he "should reasonably anticipate being haled into court" in the forum state.

Latshaw v. Johnston, 167 F.3d 208, 211 (5th Cir. 1999) (footnotes omitted). Minimum contacts include either "contacts sufficient to assert specific jurisdiction, or contacts sufficient to assert general jurisdiction." *Alpine View Co. v. Atlas Copco AB*, 205 F.3d 208, 215 (5th Cir. 2000). Specific jurisdiction is appropriate when a nonresident corporation "has purposefully directed its activities at the forum state and the 'litigation results from alleged injuries that "arise out of or relate to" those activities.'" *Id.* (quoting *Burger King Corp. v. Rudzewicz*, 471 U.S. 462, 472 (1985); *Helicopteros Nacionales de Colombia, S.A. v. Hall*, 466 U.S. 408, 414 (1984)). "General jurisdiction, on the other hand, will attach where the nonresident defendant's contacts with the forum state, although not related to the plaintiff's cause of action, are 'continuous and systematic.'" *Id.* (quoting *Helicopteros*, 466 U.S. at 415-16).

To determine whether exercising jurisdiction would satisfy traditional notions of fair play and substantial justice, the court examines "(1) the defendant's burden; (2) the forum state's interests; (3) the plaintiffs' interest in convenient and effective relief; (4) the judicial system's interest in efficient resolution of controversies; and (5) the state's shared interest in furthering fundamental social policies." *Ruston Gas Turbines, Inc. v. Donaldson Co.*, 9 F.3d 415, 421 (5th Cir. 1993).

. . .

III

Plaintiffs do not contend that the court has general jurisdiction over Virgin Australia. They maintain instead that the sole determinative issue is whether specific jurisdiction extends to a nonresident defendant who uses a website owned by a United States company to contract with a Texas resident and obtain from a Texas server a picture of a Texas resident via a computer located in Australia. Plaintiffs essentially argue that Virgin Australia is amenable to personal jurisdiction in Texas based on three contacts with the state: (1) Virgin Australia's accessing a Flickr server located in Texas; (2) Virgin Australia's contract with a Texas resident; and (3) the intrastate effects of Virgin Australia's use of Alison's photograph in the Campaign.

A

Plaintiffs maintain that Virgin Australia had contact with a Flickr server located in Texas, and they argue that this constitutes sufficient minimum contact to satisfy due process. Assuming *arguendo* that contact with a computer server fortuitously located in the state of Texas can establish personal jurisdiction here, plaintiffs have failed to make a prima facie showing that the server in this case was in fact located in Texas. Plaintiffs have only shown (through an affidavit from Yahoo's Compliance Paralegal) that Flickr's parent company, Yahoo, maintains servers in Texas that are used to process, transmit, or store images for Flickr users. Plaintiffs have not made a prima facie showing that the Texas servers were actually or necessarily used to process, transmit, or store images for Flickr users at the time Virgin Australia acquired the photograph. Plaintiffs recognize that Yahoo maintains servers in California and Virginia, yet they have failed to show that these were not the servers used to process, transmit, or store images for Flickr at the time Virgin Australia acquired the photograph. Especially after having granted plaintiffs *three* extensions to conduct jurisdictional discovery, the court is not required to credit plaintiffs' conclusory assertion that the photograph was stored on a server located in Texas. *See Panda Brandywine Corp.*, 2000 U.S. Dist. LEXIS 22714, 2000 WL 35615925, at *2. Consequently, because plaintiffs have not made a prima facie showing that Virgin Australia's alleged contact with the server storing Alison's photograph actually represents a contact with the state of Texas, this contact is insufficient to establish personal jurisdiction. *Cf. TravelJungle v. Am. Airlines, Inc.,* 212 S.W.3d 841, 848 (Tex. App. 2006, no pet.) (holding that plaintiff showed that accessed website servers were located in forum state); *Internet Doorway, Inc. v. Parks,* 138 F. Supp. 2d 773, 777 (S.D. Miss. 2001) (concluding there was no question that spam email allegedly sent by defendant was received, opened, and read by residents in forum state).

B

Alternatively, even if the court assumes that plaintiffs made the prima facie showing of contact with a Texas server, they cannot rely on the fortuitous location of Flickr's servers to establish personal jurisdiction over Virgin Australia. . . .

Citing *TravelJungle* and spam-email cases, plaintiffs contend that, by virtue of the fact that Virgin Australia (through its vendors) deliberately directed its activity toward Flickr.com (i.e., by visiting the website and downloading the photograph from Flickr.com), Virgin Australia can be haled into any forum where Flickr.com's servers are located. The cases plaintiffs cite, however, are readily distinguishable, either because they arise in the context of spam-email or because the harm alleged in the complaint was directed toward the plaintiff's server. *See TravelJungle,* 212 S.W.3d at 850 (defendant allegedly sent electronic spiders to plaintiff's website, accessing the site 2,972 times in one day and using valuable computer capacity); *Verizon Online Servs., Inc. v. Ralsky,* 203 F. Supp. 2d 601, 604 (E.D. Va. 2002) (defendant allegedly bombarded plaintiff's servers with spam, overwhelming the servers and causing delays in processing legitimate emails); *D.C. Micro Dev., Inc. v. Lange,* 246 F. Supp. 2d 705, 710 (W.D. Ky. 2003) (defendant allegedly hacked into a database of a Kentucky server, stole client information, and used the information to send spam-emails). Therefore, even if plaintiffs had made a prima facie showing that Virgin Australia made contact with a Flickr server located in Texas, such contact would be insufficient to establish minimum contacts.

C

Assuming *arguendo* that Virgin Australia contracted with Wong (a Texas resident) to use Alison's photograph under the terms of the license agreement and then breached the contract, this conduct does not establish specific personal jurisdiction over Virgin Australia. "[M]erely contracting with a resident of the forum state does not establish minimum contacts." *Moncrief Oil Int'l Inc. v. Oao Gazprom,* 481 F.3d 309, 311 (5th Cir. 2007) (citing cases). Furthermore, "a plaintiff's unilateral activities in Texas do not constitute minimum contacts [in a breach of contract case] where the defendant did not perform any of its obligations in Texas, the contract did not require performance in Texas, and the contract is centered outside of Texas." *Id. at 312* (citing *Hydrokinetics, Inc. v. Alaska Mech., Inc.,* 700 F.2d 1026 (5th Cir. 1983)).

Here, the license agreement did not require Virgin Australia to perform any of its obligations in Texas; on the contrary, the license permitted Alison's photograph to be used anywhere in the world. . . . Furthermore, plaintiffs have failed to show that Virgin Australia performed any of its obligations in Texas. It used the photograph solely in Australia, the one place that, according to Virgin Australia's evidence, it is authorized to sell its products and services. Finally, because Virgin Australia only used the photograph in Australia, the contract that permits the use of the photograph is centered in Australia, not Texas. *See Holt Oil & Gas Corp. v. Harvey,* 801 F.2d 773, 778 (5th Cir. 1986) (holding that performance of contract regarding oil and gas drilling venture in Oklahoma was centered in Oklahoma); *Moncrief,* 481 F.3d at 312-13 (concluding that contract to develop Russian gas field was centered in Russia). Consequently, the unilateral activity of Wong—i.e., taking the photograph and publishing it in Texas on Flickr under the Creative Commons Attribution 2.0 license agreement—does not satisfy the requirement of contact between Virgin Australia and the state of Texas. *See Hydrokinetics,* 700 F.2d at 1029. Because the only contact with Texas that remains is the mere act of contracting with Wong, this is insufficient to establish minimum contacts. *See Moncrief,* 481 F.3d at 312 ("[M]erely contracting with a resident of Texas is not enough to establish minimum contacts.").

Virgin Australia's vendor searched through hundreds of millions of Flickr photographs publicly available on the Internet and fortuitously selected Alison's photograph. Neither the nationality or residence of the photographed individual nor the location where the photograph was taken are clear from the image itself, and even if Virgin Australia should have known, based on Wong's Flickr profile, that Wong was a Texas resident, Wong's Texas location was irrelevant to the contract. . . . The mere fortuity that a party to a contract happens to be a Texas resident, coupled with that party's unilateral performance in the forum state, is not enough to confer jurisdiction. *See Holt Oil,* 801 F.2d at 778 (holding that in a contract to drill for oil and gas in Oklahoma, it was a "mere fortuity" that defendant happened to be a resident of Texas); *Renoir,* 230 Fed. Appx. at 360 ("[Defendant's] only contact with Texas came about by the fortuity that [the] collection [it contracted to auction in Maryland] happened to be owned by the [plaintiffs] in Texas."). Thus the facts of plaintiffs' breach of contract claim will not support a finding of specific personal jurisdiction over Virgin Australia.

D

Plaintiffs invoke the effects test articulated by the Supreme Court in *Calder v. Jones,* 465 U.S. 783, 104 S. Ct. 1482, 79 L. Ed. 2d 804 (1984), contending that, with respect to plaintiffs' intentional tort claims, personal jurisdiction is established by the intrastate effects of Virgin Australia's conduct. "In *Calder*, the Supreme Court held that when an alleged tort-feasor's intentional actions are expressly aimed at the forum state, and the tort-feasor knows that the brunt of the injury will be felt by a particular resident in the forum, the tort-feasor must reasonably anticipate being haled into court there to answer for its tortious actions." *Southmark Corp. v. Life Investors, Inc.*, 851 F.2d 763, 772 (5th Cir. 1988) (citing *Calder*, 465 U.S. at 789-790). This holds true even if the tortfeasor's conduct occurred in a state other than the forum state. *See id.*

In *Noonan v. Winston Co.*, 135 F.3d 85 (1st Cir. 1998), the *Calder* effects test was applied to a substantially analogous case. Noonan, a Massachusetts resident, brought an action alleging misappropriation, defamation, invasion of privacy, and related claims against French advertising agency Lintas:Paris, French cigarette manufacturer RJR France, and others based on the unauthorized use of his photograph in a cigarette advertising campaign in France. The advertisement pictured Noonan in his Boston Police uniform on horseback at Faneuil Hall in Boston. Without the knowledge of Lintas:Paris, several hundred copies of various French magazines containing the advertisement were distributed to, and sold from, retail magazine outlets in the Boston area. Noonan became aware of the advertisement when several of his acquaintances, some of whom had seen the advertisment in France and some of whom had seen it in Boston, told Noonan about it. After some people denounced him for supporting the cigarette industry, Noonan filed suit.

Holding that the exercise of personal jurisdiction over Lintas:Paris and RJR France would offend due process, the First Circuit reasoned that while Noonan had satisfied the injurious-effects part of the *Calder* test, Lintas:Paris and RJR France had not acted with "sufficient intent to make them reasonably anticipate being haled into court [in Massachusetts]." *Id.* at 90 (internal quotation marks omitted).

> Like [the plaintiff in *Calder*], [Noonan] felt a tortious effect in the forum state where [he] lived and worked. Moreover, the content of the picture — a Boston Police Officer in uniform, sitting on a saddle blanket decorated with the Boston Police insignia, in front of a distinctive Boston landmark — indicated where any injury would be felt.
>
> For the first part of *Calder*'s framework to be satisfied, however, the defendants must have acted toward the forum state with sufficient intent to make them "reasonably anticipate being haled into court there." In *Calder*, the court found that the defendants' intentional conduct was "*calculated* to cause injury to respondent in California." There is no analogous intentional behavior here. . . .
>
> The defendants did not direct their actions toward Massachusetts. That the advertisement contains French text and a French phone number suggests Lintas:Paris created it for a French audience. This interpretation is corroborated, without contradiction, by a Lintas:Paris representative who stated that "[t]he advertisement was aimed solely at the French consumer market." Furthermore, Lintas:Paris "was not aware that some copies of the magazines bearing the advertisement" would reach Massachusetts.

Id. at 90-91 (citations omitted; emphasis and brackets in original).

Here, as in *Noonan*, plaintiffs have satisfied the injurious-effects part of the *Calder* test but have failed to make a prima facie showing of intent. Although Alison felt a tortious effect in Texas after the advertisement incorporating her picture garnered the interest of news stations, legal commentators, and website bloggers, Virgin Australia did not direct its actions toward Texas. Like the defendants in *Noonan*, who aimed their advertisement solely at the French consumer market and did not intentionally target Massachusetts, Virgin Australia aimed the Campaign solely at Australia and did not intentionally target Texas.

If anything, the lack of intentional behavior aimed at the forum state is even more pronounced here than in *Noonan*. The advertisement in *Noonan* was placed in publications with international circulations, and although the defendants in *Noonan* claimed ignorance of the distribution, 305 copies of various French magazines containing the advertisement were distributed to retailers in the Boston area. Here, by contrast, Alison's photograph was only used on billboards at bus stations in Australian cities, and Alison only learned about the use of her image in Virgin Australia's Campaign after a third party saw the billboard at a bus station in Adelaide, Australia, took a picture of it, and then posted it on the Internet. The nondescript content of Alison's photograph, moreover, unlike the picture in *Noonan*, did not clearly indicate where any injury would be felt.

Alison's Texas injury — i.e., her distress at seeing her image used in an allegedly disparaging way — is insufficient to support personal jurisdiction in the state of Texas over Virgin Australia. *See id.* at 92; *Revell v. Lidov*, 317 F.3d 467, 473 (5th Cir. 2002) ("[P]laintiff's residence in the forum, and suffering of harm there, will not alone support jurisdiction under *Calder*."); *Archer & White, Inc. v. Tishler*, 2003 U.S. Dist. LEXIS 19010, 2003 WL 22456806, at *3 (N.D. Tex. Oct. 23, 2003) (Fitzwater, J.) (holding that tortious effects felt in forum state were insufficient to establish personal jurisdiction where there is no evidence that defendant intended to target forum state). "To find otherwise would inappropriately credit random, isolated, or fortuitous contacts and negate the reason for the purposeful availment requirement." *Noonan*, 135 F.3d at 92.

E

Because none of the three contacts on which plaintiffs rely establishes sufficient minimum contacts between Virgin Australia and the state of Texas, the court cannot constitutionally exercise personal jurisdiction over Virgin Australia. "Because [the court] find[s] that the first due process condition of minimum contacts was not satisfied, [the court] need not address whether the exercise of personal jurisdiction in this case would offend traditional notions of fair play and substantial justice." . . .

COMMENTS AND QUESTIONS

1. What are the plaintiff's arguments in favor of the defendant's purposeful availment of the state of Texas? Does the court find these arguments convincing? Do you agree with the court's reasoning?

2. In the court's view, when would the fortuitous use by a defendant of a server located in the forum state be sufficient as a basis for finding personal jurisdiction? Are you convinced by the court's reasoning on this point?

3. On the court's reasoning, when would a contract with a resident of Texas be a sufficient basis for the court to exercise jurisdiction over a defendant residing outside the state of Texas?

4. Do you find the court's analogy with the *Noonan* case useful here? Does *Noonan* clearly support the finding in *Chang*? The court suggests that in *Chang* the lack of intentional behavior aimed at the forum state is even more pronounced than in *Noonan* because, unlike the magazines in *Noonan*, Virgin Australia's publications were only available on public transport venues physically situated within Australia. The court notes that it was fortuitous that Australian friends notified Chang of the advertisement, and that photographs of the Australian advertisements were posted online. Was it unforeseeable that this would occur and that Chang would as a result suffer injury in Texas? In the Web 2.0 world, can a defendant ever really say that it had no knowledge or intent that a particular image will be photographed and posted online, and thereby made accessible to the whole world? Does the potential for this to occur require a new approach to personal jurisdiction?

5. Does the finding on jurisdiction effectively settle the case? In other words, does the plaintiff have any other recourse against the defendant? Wong (the photographer) was the copyright holder in this case and was a plaintiff along with Chang. While copyright infringement claims may be substantially the same if brought in an Australian court, torts relating to invasions of privacy are much less globally harmonized. Thus, it is possible that if Chang attempted to bring an action against the Australian defendants in Australia, she would have no substantive grounds to do so. Does this suggest that Professor Post is correct in his assessment that we need a new approach to jurisdiction in cyberspace?

3

SPEECH IN CYBERSPACE

While the Internet may be many things, it is principally a medium for communication. Admittedly, the Internet's global reach and the ability to gather and filter information are unique characteristics, giving rise to many of the problems discussed in Chapter 2. The network of networks has also introduced new forms of speech and new speakers. Electronic mailing lists, e-mail, Web pages, social networking services such as Facebook and MySpace, wikis, blogs, and many other forms of e-communication are changing the way we communicate with one another and require us to examine what it means to speak in a world interconnected by computers. Similarly, in this new medium, Web site operators, bulletin board moderators, and Internet service providers could influence how we experience cyberspace: determining in some measure what we can see and hear and establishing the parameters of what we may do. How this new technology and these new forms of speech fit within our existing First Amendment values and the appropriateness of those values will be the focus of this chapter. We begin by exploring whether the Internet and its various communicative tools change the nature of speech. This chapter then examines efforts to regulate the content of speech on the Internet, ensure access to this new medium, and determine who can be held responsible for the harmful effects of speech on the Internet.

A. A NEW FORM OF SPEECH?

ANNE WELLS BRANSCOMB
ANONYMITY, AUTONOMY, AND ACCOUNTABILITY:
CHALLENGES TO THE FIRST AMENDMENT IN CYBERSPACE

104 Yale L.J. 1639 (1995)

. . . In this Essay, I examine some of the ways in which cultural behavior developing in cyberspaces is challenging the First Amendment. In addition,

I explore the manner in which intrusion by real-world communities may inhibit the free flow of information in cybercommunities and threaten not only the independence of such communities but also the value of electronic communication as a vehicle for democratic discourse. Given the development of new cybercommunities seeking to engage in self-governance, there is a very real possibility that the nation-state as a mediator or determinant of socially and legally acceptable behavior may be displaced by smaller "virtual communities" on-line that create their own behavioral norms. If so, then the First Amendment may have little effect on the practices and procedures employed within the Networld. . . .

In order to examine the conflicts and questions that the First Amendment will provoke in cyberspaces, I focus upon three areas of controversy: anonymity, autonomy, and accountability. These three subjects represent interlocking and competing forces. The elevation of one of these forces has important implications for the other two. For example, a right of absolute anonymity may foreclose accountability, whereas full accountability of users may mean the prohibition of anonymity. Similarly, full autonomy and control over the flow of information may isolate one from access to information upon which democratic discourse and a healthy exercise of the functions of self-governance in a democratic society depend. Therefore, it is necessary to explore how these forces interact in the context of actual cyberconflicts. In order to ensure that we are exploring these forces with a common understanding, I briefly define the forces of anonymity, autonomy, and accountability in the following Sections.

A. ANONYMITY

True anonymity in the Networld would mean that no one could trace the source of an electronic message. The First Amendment prevents the outlawing of true anonymity, although it only prevents governmental interference with anonymous messages. For this reason, the new cybercommunities as well as commercial providers of electronic environments must grapple with the propriety of anonymity. The possibility of genuine anonymity implicates both the positive value in protecting the sources of certain information as well as the danger inherent in allowing individuals to speak and write without detection. For some computer users, anonymity is merely fun and games. For other anonymous posters, however, the ability to remain unknown removes many of the layers of civilized behavior as they realize that they can escape responsibility for negligent or abusive postings.

There are numerous situations in which anonymity seems entirely appropriate and even desirable. Psychologists and sociologists point out that people benefit from being able to assume different personae. It is therefore natural that individuals use electronic communication to disguise themselves, as in costume balls in the multiuser dungeons (MUDs) that Howard

Rheingold describes. As one student admitted, "It's my hallucinogen of choice. . . . I love being able to slip into another body, another persona, another world."

There are many other valid justifications for preserving a limited right to anonymity. The media often cite "a prominent source" who does not wish to be identified, and pseudonymous authors have long been with us, sometimes in the past to prevent disclosure that the writer was female for fear her work would not be published were her gender known. Usually, in these cases, the publisher or journalist knows the source and vouches for its integrity. Anonymity has also been protected in cases in which actual retaliation or harm may ensue if the source of the writing is known, as in the case of whistle-blowers or political dissidents under authoritarian regimes.

Yet, there are also many valid reasons supporting prohibition of anonymity. Disguising the sources of messages or postings relieves their authors from responsibility for any harm that may ensue. This often encourages outrageous behavior without any opportunity for recourse to the law for redress of grievances. Law enforcement officials or lawyers seeking to file a civil suit might not be able to identify an individual to hold responsible.

Many providers of computer-mediated facilities do not permit genuine anonymity. They keep records of the real identity of pseudonymous traffic so that abusers can be identified and reprimanded. Recent years, however, have witnessed the development of a trend towards the establishment of "anonymous re-mailers" who provide a guarantee that messages cannot be traced back to their sources; diverting traffic through several of these re-mailers can effectively render an audit trail impossible, once again raising the specter of true anonymity.

B. Autonomy

Autonomy means the right to exert some modicum of control over one's electronic environment. Efforts to devise some rules to preserve autonomy must include consideration of several challenging questions. First, is there a right to prevent access to, or control the timing and terms of disclosure of, information about oneself, one's corporation, or one's institutional entity? Second, may certain cyberspaces be maintained as private spaces in which the users themselves determine the governing rules? Third, how can one ensure the confidentiality of messages posted to trusted colleagues? Such issues of autonomy over communications present difficult challenges in the cyberspaces. . . .

Control over personal information may appear to be the flip side of freedom of speech, that is, the freedom not to speak. This freedom not to speak simply protects the right not to have information disclosed without consent or in a manner that may be contrary to one's interests. This has become a matter of considerable concern; the opportunities for unwitting disclosure in cyberspaces range from uses of electronic identification for access to the system, to uses of credit cards for purchases, identification of viewer preferences, communication of medical records, and countless ways in which computerized identification is coupled with personal preferences and behavior. . . .

C. ACCOUNTABILITY

Accountability refers to the acceptance of responsibility for one's actions. Without accountability, there is no basis upon which an injured party can initiate a tort action to redress grievances. Technically, the law would hold the initiator of a defamatory message accountable for any deleterious consequences associated with it. If one cannot hold the poster of an abusive message responsible, because it is anonymous or the poster is judgment-proof, the defendant must be the provider of the electronic space containing the message. Potential litigants and their legal counsel have not hesitated to seek the source of the deepest pockets.

The complexity of the relationships between anonymity, autonomy, and accountability is most apparent when attention is focused upon accountability. For example, anonymity or pseudonymity on the electronic highways is rampant and seems to strip users of the civility that the face-to-face encounter has engendered in most modern societies. It also facilitates the distribution of false information that may have detrimental consequences. Although the users of anonymous messages seem adamant in claiming an absolute right to their anonymity, this anonymity prevents the legal system from holding them accountable for abuses of the privilege.

This lack of accountability throws the legal responsibility back upon the providers of the cyberspaces and transforms them into censors, a role none of them wishes to play. Being required to monitor all digital traffic would place an undue burden upon these information providers, all of which are still in their infancy. This would be especially true for the smaller bulletin board operators (sysops), who are, for the most part, judgment-proof. There is as yet no consensus regarding where to place the burden for behavior that contravenes well-established legal restrictions. . . .

COMMENTS AND QUESTIONS

1.   While we now know that we are not as anonymous in cyberspace as we once thought, because it is possible for Internet service providers, Web site operators, and others to identify and monitor user behavior, see *infra* Chapter 5, Branscomb's description of anonymity as it relates to Internet behavior is still useful in general. The ability to use aliases and pseudonyms online still provides users with some means to define or hide their identities. According to the Branscomb essay, why is the anonymity she describes valuable? Aside from obvious examples in which anonymity is used to facilitate criminal behavior,

why is anonymity troublesome? Consider the following example from Branscomb's essay:

> The "Strange Case of the Electronic Lover" involved an alleged female who suggested the establishment of an all-female bulletin board on CompuServe in which women could talk frankly with one another. The female who suggested the special interest group was allegedly confined to a wheelchair. She identified herself as Joan Sue Green and claimed she was a New York neuropsychologist who had been injured in an automobile accident caused by a drunk driver. The women on the electronic discussion confided their innermost sentiments to her. Indeed, Joan discussed her sexual inclinations quite openly and encouraged others to do the same. "Joan" also quite openly suggested that they meet a "friend" of hers, a psychiatrist named Alex. As it turned out, Alex, a prominent New York psychiatrist, was in reality the "Joan" of the discussion group. When the other participants realized how they had been fooled by the psychiatrist, they felt violated and betrayed. Nonetheless, they had to admit that "Joan" had been able to help many of them sort out their problems.

104 Yale L.J. at 1664. Is "Joan's" use of anonymity under these circumstances deceptive? Does it matter that "Joan" was able to help people on the bulletin board because they did not know "her" true identity? Some have suggested that this form of anonymity may allow individuals to transcend gender and racial discrimination by allowing people to interact in an environment in which those traits cannot be readily determined. *See* Jerry Kang, *Cyber-Race*, 113 Harv. L. Rev. 1130 (2000). According to Kang, "Perhaps cyber-passing could teach us that the bodies we have been given need not dictate the identities we embrace." *Id*. at 1136-37.

How might an interest in accountability undermine the positive benefits of cyber-passing? If we desire to create online forums in which women, men, or children feel comfortable that they are interacting with people that they have chosen to interact with, can cyber-passing be permitted? Are the interests in anonymity and accountability under these circumstances irreconcilable?

2. Many online social networking services, such as Facebook, incorporate terms of service that attempt to negate anonymity by requiring participants not to use false identities. Facebook's terms of service, for example, provide that users of the service agree not to use it to: "create a false identity on the Service or the Site" (see Facebook, Terms of Use, available at *http://www.facebook.com/terms.php*). How effective are these terms in practice? Should services like Facebook affirmatively attempt to encourage online norms that negate anonymity? Is there a difference between social networking services like Facebook and other Internet services, such as blogs and chat groups, with respect to anonymity? In other words, would it make sense to discourage anonymity on Facebook, while encouraging—or at least tolerating—it in the blogosphere? What about in the context of an online group project such as Wikipedia? Should wikis allow those who edit wiki pages to be anonymous or should they require individual page editors to identify themselves?

3. When should brick and mortar community norms and rules govern speech in cyberspace? In her essay, Branscomb describes a controversy that arose at Santa Rosa Junior College in California in which a faculty advisor had established a male-only bulletin board in response to student requests:

> The bulletin board, which was available to only ten males, was intended to be operated under a pledge of confidentiality. One of the male participants broke the pledge and informed two women of derogatory remarks made about them on the board. Because no women were involved in bulletin board conversation, however, the women who were allegedly harassed were not participants on the board. . . .

104 Yale. L.J. at 1654. Subsequently, two male high school students were arrested in Westchester, New York, after school officials discovered that they had posted their sexual exploits with various female classmates on a Web site that was accessible only by the boys and those to whom they had given a password. Once again, the complaint was one of sexual harassment. Since the women who were the subjects of these postings, or any women for that matter, could not read the postings or participate in the online discussions, how were they harmed? Does the fact that these statements were made in cyberspace make them more harmful than communications that take place through telephones, notes, or face to face?

Is there a claim that the speakers' interests in autonomy were implicated by these cases? How important is the fact that the participants had taken steps to keep their speech confidential?

In the Westchester case, the charges were ultimately dropped against the boys, and in the Santa Rosa example, the faculty advisor was forced to take administrative leave.

4. To what extent should computer network providers be responsible for policing what occurs on their networks? For example, why should Santa Rosa be able to punish individuals for statements made on an all-male or all-female bulletin board? Because the school owns the computer network? Because it had an obligation under state and federal law to prevent its computer facilities from being used in a discriminatory manner? Should private Internet service providers have the same duty to investigate and eliminate harassing speech on their networks? What about concerns about censorship? If we impose such obligations on private ISPs who are not generally subject to First Amendment scrutiny, do we risk creating undesirable censorship online? In other words, might risk-averse ISPs choose to filter content too rigorously if they are worried about legal liability for content shared over their networks? We will come back to these issues later in this chapter when we consider §230 of the Communications Decency Act of 1996 which limits the liability of ISPs for information shared over their services.

5. Assuming that some degree of self-regulation and autonomy is desirable, what are the problems of self-regulation? Consider the following example from Branscomb's essay:

A case in point is the virtual rape on the LambdaMOO (MOO). Mr. Bungle (a pseudonym) committed sexually explicit verbal rape on a female in a public space and was appropriately chastised for his behavior. In actuality, the Mr. Bungle persona took over the characters created by other participants in the MOO and attributed to them sadistic fantasies that highly offended them and others. After much discussion and consternation, especially with respect to what constituted a proper trial and due process, the Wizards (the skilled computer literati) in the MOO decided that there was a consensus that Mr. Bungle should be "toaded" (in fairy-tale terms, turned into a frog). As many as fifty or so of the MOOers verbally seconded the motion to "toad" Mr. Bungle, with only a dozen or so hard-liners objecting. As a result of his punishment, Mr. Bungle was banished from the MOO into oblivion.

What concerned the members of the LambdaMOO after the incident was resolved was how to handle such aberrant behavior in the future. The first question they faced was what constituted a community of citizens in the cyberspaces. Moreover, they needed to determine how to empower themselves to set standards of behavior within the community they defined. The experience of witnessing and rejecting the behavior of Mr. Bungle precipitated a crisis in governance that prompted the group to consider what kind of social organization they wished to live under in the future. Some users, "parliamentarian legalist types," argued that Mr. Bungle should not have been "toaded" because he had not broken any preexisting rules but also urged that a regimented system be inaugurated. Others argued that behavioral standards were a matter of individual choice, and that those who objected to Mr. Bungle's behavior should merely close their eyes or "hit the @gag command," blocking all of the messages from Mr. Bungle from their screens. The latter alternative, however, merely eliminates the message from the view of the offended but leaves the real individuals using the "Starsinger" and "legba" identities unprotected from the misrepresentation that they were the sources of the reprehensible language.

104 Yale L.J. at 1662-63. Even in a self-defined virtual community like LambdaMOO, how does one define the relevant community for purposes of self-regulation? Does it matter whether the self-regulator is a small online community or a commercial Internet service provider? Should we be concerned that speech in cyberspace may be limited by private censors, or does government intervention violate a countervailing principle of autonomy?

6. Beyond anonymity, cyberspace also dramatically changes the costs associated with speech. Prior to the Internet, reaching large audiences, especially national and global audiences, was an expensive proposition. Either one had to own print, broadcast, or similar facilities capable of reaching those numbers, or afford to pay those who did. Today, anyone with a computer and Internet connection can become a global speaker or publisher of information.

This change in the economics of speech has important social consequences. For example, early in the Internet's development, Eugene Volokh suggested that "cheap speech" will lead to a greater democratization and diversification of speech. *See* Eugene Volokh, *Cheap Speech and What It Will Do*, 104 Yale L.J. 1805, 1833-43 (1995). In other words, because it is easier and less expensive to speak either through voice, print, music, or video, we will be exposed to a greater diversity of speech than we have experienced before. This will be especially beneficial for those whose tastes do not fall within the mainstream. The proliferation of Web sites, newsgroups, and chatrooms on just about every topic imaginable is certainly evidence of this trend. Moreover, Volokh predicted that because anyone can speak and publish, control over what the pubic listens to, reads, and watches would shift from the large companies that dominate the current media in all its forms to the public. *Id.* at 1834-38.

7. Not everyone believes that the greater democratization and diversification of speech is a positive development. For one thing, as anyone who uses the Internet can tell you, one of the side effects of cheaper speech is information overload. There are simply too many files, Web pages, newsgroups, chatrooms, etc., available through the Internet for an individual to visit, let alone evaluate. With all of this information out there, how does one determine what to experience through the Web? The easiest solution is simply to experience what we find the most agreeable, and filter out the rest. Cass Sunstein argues that the fragmentation of the speech market in a world in which individuals are only exposed to what they want to hear is a threat to democracy. *See* Cass R. Sunstein, *Republic.com* (Princeton University Press, 2001). Because the Internet makes it possible for people to restrict their online experiences and the information they receive to only those groups and sites with whom they agree, Sunstein suggests that society will become increasingly polarized and fragmented. To overcome this problem, Sunstein proposes that government regulate the Internet by requiring, among other things, that Web sites carry links exposing visitors to important information and different views.

Is the proliferation of hate groups on the Internet and the use of the Internet by these groups to recruit new followers evidence that Sunstein's concerns are well-founded? Is the power of the Internet user to filter the information she receives any different from more traditional media? If so, how is the Internet different?

8. As Branscomb notes in her essay, "there is a very real possibility that the nation-state as a mediator or determinant of socially and legally acceptable behavior may be displaced by smaller "virtual communities" online that create their own behavioral norms. If so, then the First Amendment may have little effect on the practices and procedures employed within the Networld." Some would argue that this possibility has actually come to fruition under the current state of First Amendment law online.

9. To what extent does it make sense to draw the public/private distinction for speech regulation on the Internet when most online experiences occur over privately owned computer networks? Consider this question in light of the "access to cyberspace" cases in Part 3.D, *infra*.

10. Can the First Amendment be meaningfully applied in cyberspace? Would it be fair to apply American free speech principles to an effectively global medium? Consider some of the comments on the problems of imposing one

society's standards on Internet communications more generally raised in Reno v. ACLU and Ashcroft v. ACLU, below.

B. CONTENT REGULATION

Assuming that American courts will apply American law to conduct in cyberspace, at least where they are able to exercise jurisdiction over the parties, we must consider the extent to which American constitutional principles will impact the development of American law in this area. In the United States, efforts to regulate the potential problems posed by Internet speech will inevitably be analyzed under the First Amendment to the U.S. Constitution. Before we examine how the principles of freedom of speech embodied in the First Amendment apply to specific efforts to address the problems of anonymity, autonomy, and accountability in cyberspace, we must first determine how the First Amendment will apply to this new medium. This inquiry is required because the Supreme Court has adopted a media-specific interpretation of the First Amendment. According to the Court, the media-specific inquiry is required because each medium, namely print, broadcast, cable, and the Internet, may have unique characteristics and problems that require it to be treated differently from the print medium that receives full First Amendment protection.

For example, in Red Lion Broadcasting Co. v. FCC, 395 U.S. 367 (1969), the Supreme Court upheld the Federal Communication Commission's decision to require broadcasters to discuss public issues giving both sides fair coverage and requiring individuals attacked or opposed by a broadcaster to be given a reasonable opportunity to reply. The Court distinguished its decision in Miami Herald Publishing Co. v. Tornillo, *infra*, in which it struck down a similar requirement for newspaper publishers based upon the unique physical characteristics of the broadcast medium (i.e., the scarcity of radio frequencies). According to Justice White, public use of the electromagnetic spectrum for broadcasting had to be regulated to prevent "the chaos" and interference that would ensue if anyone was permitted "to use any frequency at whatever power level he wished. . . ." Because "[t]here are substantially more individuals who want to broadcast than there are frequencies to be allocated, it is idle to posit an unabridgeable First Amendment right to broadcast comparable to the right of every individual to speak, write, or publish." According to Justice White, those who are licensed stand in no better position than those denied licenses. While a license permits the licensee to broadcast, "the licensee has no constitutional right to be the one who holds the license or to monopolize a radio frequency to the exclusion of his fellow citizens."

Similarly, in FCC v. Pacifica Foundation, 438 U.S. 726 (1978), the Supreme Court allowed the FCC to regulate indecent radio broadcasts because of the pervasiveness of the medium. In *Pacifica*, a radio listener complained about the broadcasting of George Carlin's "Filthy Words" monologue on a weekday afternoon, and the FCC concluded that the station "could have been subject to administrative sanctions" for broadcasting the monologue when it did. In upholding the FCC's decision, the Court once again concluded that broadcast presented unique problems that justified treating it differently from face-to-face communications or print under the First Amendment. According to Justice Stevens, broadcast is particularly intrusive with programming "confront[ing] the citizen, not only in public, but also in the privacy of the home, where the individual's right to be left alone plainly outweighs the First Amendment rights of an intruder." Likewise, it is "uniquely accessible to children, even those too young to read." In dissent, Justice Brennan criticized the intrusiveness justification because radio listeners not only voluntarily open their homes to radio broadcasts, they may avoid programming that they find offensive simply be changing the station or turning off the receiver.

As you study efforts to regulate content or ensure access, consider whether this media-specific inquiry is justified. What differences justify less rigorous First Amendment scrutiny? Can the Internet be distinguished from print, broadcast, or cable? Are there problems unique to the Internet that may warrant special treatment from the general rule against content-based restrictions of speech?

Problem 2.0

As part of the Internet community created by StarttUp, your Web site offers users the opportunity to post messages and files on community bulletin boards. These boards are organized by countless topics. Alan and Barbara have come to you because they are concerned that some of the most popular bulletin boards address sexual topics. The content available on these bulletin boards includes text, pictures, and video about sexuality that ranges from frank, but academic, discussions about sexuality, to all kinds of the most explicit forms of pornography. Many of these groups require users to take some affirmative step either in subscribing or joining the group before they have access to the content. Alan and Barbara have recently seen a news report that Congress is intending to draft new legislation to restrict the availability of indecent and obscene content to minors on the Internet. No details of the new legislation have yet been released. Assuming that StarttUp can be held responsible for distributing the materials on their bulletin boards (a topic which we will address later in this chapter), they want to know if StarttUp should take steps to prohibit, block, and/or remove the content of some of their more popular bulletin boards. Because these groups are the most popular among StarttUp's users, they will deny users' access to these materials only if they can be banned by law.

Problem 2.1

Cora and Demi are also concerned about the proposed new legislation as some of the content that appears on their blog does address sexual and sexually explicit topics. Some of this content is posted by the bloggers themselves and some appears in the comment sections. Cora and Demi want to know if they should alter their practices about what they blog for fear of contravening this new legislation. They also want to know if they should develop some kind of use policy for commenters to ensure that comments do not infringe the legislation, assuming, of course, that Cora and Demi could be held liable for comments posted on the blog. Naturally, Cora and Demi would prefer not to impose any kind of censorship on themselves or their commenters, so they only want to alter their current practices if some of those practices are in danger of being banned by the new law.

---

1. Indecency

RENO v. ACLU

521 U.S. 844 (1997)

Justice STEVENS delivered the opinion of the Court. . . .

At issue is the constitutionality of two statutory provisions enacted to protect minors from "indecent" and "patently offensive" communications on the Internet. . . .

. . . [In this decision, the Supreme Court examined whether two provisions of the Communications Decency Act of 1996 were consistent with the First Amendment guarantee of freedom of speech. The first, 47 U.S.C. §223(a) (1994 ed., Supp. II), provides in pertinent part:

> "(a) Whoever—
> "(1) in interstate or foreign communications— . . .
> "(B) by means of a telecommunications device knowingly—
> "(i) makes, creates, or solicits, and
> "(ii) initiates the transmission of,
> "any comment, request, suggestion, proposal, image, or other communication which is obscene or indecent, knowing that the recipient of the communication is under 18 years of age, regardless of whether the maker of such communication placed the call or initiated the communication; . . .
> "(2) knowingly permits any telecommunications facility under his control to be used for any activity prohibited by paragraph (1) with the intent that it be used for such activity,

"shall be fined under Title 18, or imprisoned not more than two years, or both."

The second provision, §223(d), provides:

"(d) Whoever—
    "(1) in interstate or foreign communications knowingly—
        "(A) uses an interactive computer service to send to a specific person or persons under 18 years of age, or
        "(B) uses any interactive computer service to display in a manner available to a person under 18 years of age,
    "any comment, request, suggestion, proposal, image, or other communication that, in context, depicts or describes, in terms patently offensive as measured by contemporary community standards, sexual or excretory activities or organs, regardless of whether the user of such service placed the call or initiated the communication; or
        "(2) knowingly permits any telecommunications facility under such person's control to be used for an activity prohibited by paragraph (1) with the intent that it be used for such activity,
    "shall be fined under Title 18, or imprisoned not more than two years, or both."

The breadth of these prohibitions is qualified by two affirmative defenses. See §223(e)(5). One covers those who take "good faith, reasonable, effective, and appropriate actions" to restrict access by minors to the prohibited communications. §223(e)(5)(A). The other covers those who restrict access to covered material by requiring certain designated forms of age proof, such as a verified credit card or an adult identification number or code. §223(e)(5)(B). . . ."

The district court enjoined, "the Government from enforcing the prohibitions in §223(a)(1)(B) insofar as they relate to 'indecent' communications, but expressly preserves the Government's right to investigate and prosecute the obscenity or child pornography activities prohibited therein. The injunction against enforcement of §§223(d)(1) and (2) is unqualified because those provisions contain no separate reference to obscenity or child pornography."]

I

. . . Sexually explicit material on the Internet includes text, pictures, and chat and "extends from the modestly titillating to the hardest-core." These files are created, named, and posted in the same manner as material that is not sexually explicit, and may be accessed either deliberately or unintentionally during the course of an imprecise search. "Once a provider posts its content on the Internet, it cannot prevent that content from entering any community." . . .

Though such material is widely available, users seldom encounter such content accidentally. "A document's title or a description of the document will usually appear before the document itself . . . and in many cases the user will receive detailed information about a site's content before he or she need take the step to access the document. Almost all sexually explicit images are preceded by warnings as to the content." For that reason, the "odds are slim" that a user would enter a sexually explicit site by accident. Unlike communications received by radio or television, "the receipt of information on the Internet requires a series of affirmative steps more deliberate and directed than merely turning a dial. A child requires some sophistication and some ability to read to retrieve material and thereby to use the Internet unattended." . . .

Systems have been developed to help parents control the material that may be available on a home computer with Internet access. A system may either limit a computer's access to an approved list of sources that have been identified as containing no adult material, it may block designated inappropriate sites, or it may attempt to block messages containing identifiable objectionable features. "Although parental control software currently can screen for certain suggestive words or for known sexually explicit sites, it cannot now screen for sexually explicit images." Nevertheless, the evidence indicates that "a reasonably effective method by which parents can prevent their children from accessing sexually explicit and other material which parents may believe is inappropriate for their children will soon be widely available."

Age Verification

The problem of age verification differs for different uses of the Internet. The District Court categorically determined that there "is no effective way to determine the identity or the age of a user who is accessing material through e-mail, mail exploders, newsgroups or chat rooms." The Government offered no evidence that there was a reliable way to screen recipients and participants in such forums for age. Moreover, even if it were technologically feasible to block minors' access to newsgroups and chat rooms containing discussions of art, politics, or other subjects that potentially elicit "indecent" or "patently offensive" contributions, it would not be possible to block their access to that material and "still allow them access to the remaining content, even if the overwhelming majority of that content was not indecent."

Technology exists by which an operator of a Web site may condition access on the verification of requested information such as a credit card number or an adult password. Credit card verification is only feasible, however, either in connection with a commercial transaction in which the card is used, or by payment to a verification agency. Using credit card possession as a surrogate for proof of age would impose costs on noncommercial Web sites that would require many of them to shut down. For that reason, at the time of the trial, credit card verification was "effectively unavailable to a substantial number of Internet content providers." Moreover, the imposition of such a requirement "would completely bar adults who do not have a credit card and lack the resources to obtain one from accessing any blocked material."

Commercial pornographic sites that charge their users for access have assigned them passwords as a method of age verification. The record does not contain any evidence concerning the reliability of these technologies. Even if passwords are effective for commercial purveyors of indecent material, the District Court found that an adult password requirement would impose significant burdens on noncommercial sites, both because they would discourage users from accessing their sites and because the cost of creating and maintaining such screening systems would be "beyond their reach." . . .

V.

In Southeastern Promotions, Ltd. v. Conrad, 420 U.S. 546, 557 (1975), we observed that "[e]ach medium of expression . . . may present its own problems." Thus, some of our cases have recognized special justifications for regulation of the broadcast media that are not applicable to other speakers, see Red Lion Broadcasting Co. v. FCC, 395 U.S. 367 (1969); FCC v. Pacifica Foundation, 438 U.S. 726 (1978). In these cases, the Court relied on the history of extensive Government regulation of the broadcast medium, see, e.g., *Red Lion*, 395 U.S., at 399-400; the scarcity of available frequencies at its inception, see, e.g., Turner Broadcasting System, Inc. v. FCC, 512 U.S. 622, 637-638 (1994); and its "invasive" nature, see Sable Communications of Cal., Inc. v. FCC, 492 U.S. 115, 128 (1989).

Those factors are not present in cyberspace. Neither before nor after the enactment of the CDA have the vast democratic forums of the Internet been subject to the type of government supervision and regulation that has attended the broadcast industry. Moreover, the Internet is not as "invasive" as radio or television. The District Court specifically found that "[c]ommunications over the Internet do not 'invade' an individual's home or appear on one's computer screen unbidden. Users seldom encounter content 'by accident.'" . . . It also found that "[a]lmost all sexually explicit images are preceded by warnings as to the content," and cited testimony that " 'odds are slim' that a user would come across a sexually explicit sight by accident."

We distinguished *Pacifica* in *Sable*, 492 U.S., at 128, on just this basis. In *Sable*, a company engaged in the business of offering sexually oriented prerecorded telephone messages (popularly known as "dial-a-porn") challenged the constitutionality of an amendment to the Communications Act of 1934 that imposed a blanket prohibition on indecent as well as obscene interstate commercial telephone messages. We held that the statute was constitutional insofar as it applied to obscene messages but invalid as applied to indecent messages. In attempting to justify the complete ban and criminalization of indecent commercial telephone messages, the Government relied on *Pacifica*, arguing that the ban was necessary to prevent children from gaining access to such messages. We agreed that "there is a compelling interest in protecting the physical and psychological well-being of minors" which extended to shielding them from indecent messages that are not obscene by adult standards, 492 U.S., at 126, but distinguished our "emphatically narrow holding" in *Pacifica* because it did not involve a complete ban and because it involved a different medium of communication, id., at 127. We explained that "the dial-it medium requires the listener to take affirmative steps to receive the communication." Id., at 127-128. "Placing a telephone call," we continued, "is not the same as turning on a radio and being taken by surprise by an indecent message." Id., at 128.

Finally, unlike the conditions that prevailed when Congress first authorized regulation of the broadcast spectrum, the Internet can hardly be considered a "scarce" expressive commodity. It provides relatively unlimited, low-cost capacity for communication of all kinds. The Government estimates that "[a]s many as 40 million people use the Internet today, and that figure is expected to grow to 200 million by 1999." This dynamic, multifaceted category of communication includes not only traditional print and news services, but also audio, video, and still images, as well as interactive, real-time dialogue. Through the use of chat rooms, any person with a phone line can become a town crier with a voice that resonates farther than it could from any soapbox. Through the use of Web pages, mail exploders, and newsgroups, the same individual can become a pamphleteer. As the District Court found, "the content on the Internet is as diverse as human thought." We agree with its conclusion that our cases provide no basis for qualifying the level of First Amendment scrutiny that should be applied to this medium. . . .

[After concluding that the characteristics of the Internet did not justify reduced First Amendment scrutiny, the court then distinguished its prior decisions in Ginsberg v. New York, 390 U.S. 629 (1968); FCC v. Pacifica Foundation, 438 U.S. 726 (1978); and Renton v. Playtime Theatres, Inc., 475 U.S. 41 (1986), and concluded that the indecency provision is unconstitutionally vague.]

VII

We are persuaded that the CDA lacks the precision that the First Amendment requires when a statute regulates the content of speech. In order to deny minors access to potentially harmful speech, the CDA effectively suppresses a large amount of speech that adults have a constitutional right to receive and to address to one another. That burden on adult speech is unacceptable if less restrictive alternatives would be at least as effective in achieving the legitimate purpose that the statute was enacted to serve.

In evaluating the free speech rights of adults, we have made it perfectly clear that "[s]exual expression which is indecent but not obscene is protected by the First Amendment." *Sable*, 492 U.S., at 126. . . . Indeed, *Pacifica* itself admonished that "the fact that society may find speech offensive is not a sufficient reason for suppressing it." 438 U.S., at 745. . . .

In arguing that the CDA does not so diminish adult communication, the Government relies on the incorrect factual premise that prohibiting a transmission whenever it is known that one of its recipients is a minor would not interfere with adult-to-adult communication. The findings of the District Court make clear that this premise is untenable. Given the size of the potential audience for most messages, in the absence of a viable age verification process, the sender must be charged with knowing that one or more minors will likely view it. Knowledge that, for instance, one or more members of a 100-person chat group will be a minor — and therefore that it would be a crime to send the group an indecent message — would surely burden communication among adults.

The District Court found that at the time of trial existing technology did not include any effective method for a sender to prevent minors from obtaining access to its communications on the Internet without also denying access to adults. The Court found no effective way to determine the age of a user who is accessing material through e-mail, mail exploders, newsgroups, or chat rooms. As a practical matter, the Court also found that it would be prohibitively expensive for noncommercial — as well as some commercial — speakers who have Web sites to verify that their users are adults. These limitations must inevitably curtail a significant amount of adult communication on the Internet. By contrast, the District Court found that "[d]espite its limitations, currently available user-based software suggests that a reasonably effective method by which parents can prevent their children from accessing sexually explicit and other material which parents may believe is inappropriate for their children will soon be widely available."

The breadth of the CDA's coverage is wholly unprecedented. Unlike the regulations upheld in *Ginsberg* and *Pacifica*, the scope of the CDA is not limited to commercial speech or commercial entities. Its open-ended prohibitions embrace all nonprofit entities and individuals posting indecent messages or displaying them on their own computers in the presence of minors. The general, undefined terms "indecent" and "patently offensive" cover large amounts of nonpornographic material with serious educational or other value. Moreover, the "community standards" criterion as applied to the Internet means that any communication available to a nation wide audience will be judged by the standards of the community most likely to be offended by the message. The regulated subject matter includes any of the seven "dirty words" used in the *Pacifica* monologue, the use of which the Government's expert acknowledged could constitute a felony. It may also extend to discussions about prison rape or safe sexual practices, artistic images that include nude subjects, and arguably the card catalog of the Carnegie Library.

For the purposes of our decision, we need neither accept nor reject the Government's submission that the First Amendment does not forbid a blanket prohibition on all "indecent" and "patently offensive" messages communicated to a 17-year-old — no matter how much value the message may contain and regardless of parental approval. It is at least clear that the strength of the Government's interest in protecting minors is not equally strong throughout the coverage of this broad statute. Under the CDA, a parent allowing her

17-year-old to use the family computer to obtain information on the Internet that she, in her parental judgment, deems appropriate could face a lengthy prison term. See 47 U.S.C. §223(a)(2) (1994 ed., Supp. II). Similarly, a parent who sent his 17-year-old college freshman information on birth control via e-mail could be incarcerated even though neither he, his child, nor anyone in their home community found the material "indecent" or "patently offensive," if the college town's community thought otherwise.

The breadth of this content-based restriction of speech imposes an especially heavy burden on the Government to explain why a less restrictive provision would not be as effective as the CDA. It has not done so. The arguments in this Court have referred to possible alternatives such as requiring that indecent material be "tagged" in a way that facilitates parental control of material coming into their homes, making exceptions for messages with artistic or educational value, providing some tolerance for parental choice, and regulating some portions of the Internet — such as commercial Web sites — differently from others, such as chat rooms. Particularly in the light of the absence of any detailed findings by the Congress, or even hearings addressing the special problems of the CDA, we are persuaded that the CDA is not narrowly tailored if that requirement has any meaning at all. . . .

VIII

. . . The Government also asserts that the "knowledge" requirement of both §§223(a) and (d), especially when coupled with the "specific child" element found in §223(d), saves the CDA from overbreadth. Because both sections prohibit the dissemination of indecent messages only to persons known to be under 18, the Government argues, it does not require transmitters to "refrain from communicating indecent material to adults; they need only refrain from disseminating such materials to persons they know to be under 18." This argument ignores the fact that most Internet forums — including chat rooms, newsgroups, mail exploders, and the Web — are open to all comers. The Government's assertion that the knowledge requirement somehow protects the communications of adults is therefore untenable. Even the strongest reading of the "specific person" requirement of §223(d) cannot save the statute. It would confer broad powers of censorship, in the form of a "heckler's veto," upon any opponent of indecent speech who might simply log on and inform the would-be discoursers that his 17-year-old child — a "specific person . . . under 18 years of age," 47 U.S.C.A. §223(d)(1)(A) (Supp. 1997) — would be present. . . .

IX

The Government's three remaining arguments focus on the defenses provided in §223(e)(5). First, relying on the "good faith, reasonable, effective, and appropriate actions" provision, the Government suggests that "tagging" provides a defense that saves the constitutionality of the CDA. The suggestion assumes that transmitters may encode their indecent communications in a way that would indicate their contents, thus permitting recipients to block their reception with appropriate software. It is the requirement that the good-faith action must be "effective" that makes this defense illusory. The Government recognizes that its proposed screening software does not currently exist. Even if it did, there is no way to know whether a potential recipient will actually block the encoded material. Without the impossible knowledge that every guardian in America is screening for the "tag," the transmitter could not reasonably rely on its action to be "effective."

For its second and third arguments concerning defenses — which we can consider together — the Government relies on the latter half of §223(e)(5), which applies when the transmitter has restricted access by requiring use of a verified credit card or adult identification. Such verification is not only technologically available but actually is used by commercial providers of sexually explicit material. These providers, therefore, would be protected by the defense. Under the findings of the District Court, however, it is not economically feasible for most noncommercial speakers to employ such verification. Accordingly, this defense would not significantly narrow the statute's burden on noncommercial speech. Even with respect to the commercial pornographers that would be protected by the defense, the Government failed to adduce any evidence that these verification techniques actually preclude minors from posing as adults. Given that the risk of criminal sanctions "hovers over each content provider, like the proverbial sword of Damocles," the District Court correctly refused to rely on unproven future technology to save the statute. The Government thus failed to prove that the proffered defense would significantly reduce the heavy burden on adult speech produced by the prohibition on offensive displays.

We agree with the District Court's conclusion that the CDA places an unacceptably heavy burden on protected speech, and that the defenses do not constitute the sort of "narrow tailoring" that will save an otherwise patently invalid unconstitutional provision. In *Sable*, 492 U.S., at 127, we remarked that the speech restriction at issue there amounted to " 'burn[ing] the house to roast the pig.' " The CDA, casting a far darker shadow over free speech, threatens to torch a large segment of the Internet community. . . .

XI

In this Court, though not in the District Court, the Government asserts that — in addition to its interest in protecting children — its "[e]qually significant" interest in fostering the growth of the Internet provides an independent basis for upholding the constitutionality of the CDA. The Government apparently assumes that the unregulated availability of "indecent" and "patently offensive" material on the Internet is driving countless citizens away from the medium because of the risk of exposing themselves or their children to harmful material.

We find this argument singularly unpersuasive. The dramatic expansion of this new marketplace of ideas contradicts the factual basis of this contention. The record demonstrates that the growth of the Internet has been and continues to be phenomenal. As a matter of constitutional tradition, in the absence of evidence to the contrary, we presume that governmental regulation of the content of speech is more likely to interfere with the free exchange of ideas than to encourage it. The interest in encouraging freedom of expression in a democratic society outweighs any theoretical but unproven benefit of censorship. . . .

Justice O'CONNOR, with whom THE CHIEF JUSTICE joins, concurring in the judgment in part and dissenting in part.

I write separately to explain why I view the Communications Decency Act of 1996 (CDA) as little more than an attempt by Congress to create "adult zones" on the Internet. Our precedent indicates that the creation of such zones can be constitutionally sound. Despite the soundness of its purpose, however, portions of the CDA are unconstitutional because they stray from the blueprint our prior cases have developed for constructing a "zoning law" that passes constitutional muster. . . .

The creation of "adult zones" is by no means a novel concept. States have long denied minors access to certain establishments frequented by adults. States have also denied minors access to speech deemed to be "harmful to minors." The Court has previously sustained such zoning laws, but only if they respect the First Amendment rights of adults and minors. That is to say, a zoning law is valid if (i) it does not unduly restrict adult access to the material; and (ii) minors have no First Amendment right to read or view the banned material. As applied to the Internet as it exists in 1997, the "display" provision and some applications of the "indecency transmission" and "specific person" provisions fail to adhere to the first of these limiting principles by restricting adults' access to protected materials in certain circumstances. Unlike the Court, however, I would invalidate the provisions only in those circumstances.

I

Our cases make clear that a "zoning" law is valid only if adults are still able to obtain the regulated speech. If they cannot, the law does more than simply keep children away from speech they have no right to obtain — it interferes with the rights of adults to obtain constitutionally protected speech and effectively "reduce[s] the adult population . . . to reading only what is fit for children." Butler v. Michigan, 352 U.S. 380, 383 (1957). The First Amendment does not tolerate such interference. . . . If the law does not unduly restrict adults' access to constitutionally protected speech, however, it may be valid. In Ginsberg v. New York, 390 U.S. 629, 634 (1968), for example, the Court sustained a New York law that barred store owners from selling pornographic magazines to minors in part because adults could still buy those magazines.

The Court in *Ginsberg* concluded that the New York law created a constitutionally adequate adult zone simply because, on its face, it denied access only to minors. The Court did not question—and therefore necessarily assumed—that an adult zone, once created, would succeed in preserving adults' access while denying minors' access to the regulated speech. Before today, there was no reason to question this assumption, for the Court has previously only considered laws that operated in the physical world, a world that with two characteristics that make it possible to create "adult zones": geography and identity. . . . A minor can see an adult dance show only if he enters an establishment that provides such entertainment. And should he attempt to do so, the minor will not be able to conceal completely his identity (or, consequently, his age). Thus, the twin characteristics of geography and identity enable the establishment's proprietor to prevent children from entering the establishment, but to let adults inside.

The electronic world is fundamentally different. Because it is no more than the interconnection of electronic pathways, cyberspace allows speakers and listeners to mask their identities. Cyberspace undeniably reflects some form of geography; chat rooms and Web sites, for example, exist at fixed "locations" on the Internet. Since users can transmit and receive messages on the Internet without revealing anything about their identities or ages, however, it is not currently possible to exclude persons from accessing certain messages on the basis of their identity.

Cyberspace differs from the physical world in another basic way: Cyberspace is malleable. Thus, it is possible to construct barriers in cyberspace and use them to screen for identity, making cyberspace more like the physical world and, consequently, more amenable to zoning laws. This transformation of cyberspace is already underway. Internet speakers (users who post material on the Internet) have begun to zone cyberspace itself through the use of "gateway" technology. Such technology requires Internet users to enter information about themselves—perhaps an adult identification number or a credit card number—before they can access certain areas of cyberspace much like a bouncer checks a person's driver's license before admitting him to a nightclub. Internet users who access information have not attempted to zone cyberspace itself, but have tried to limit their own power to access information in cyberspace, much as a parent controls what her children watch on television by installing a lock box. This user-based zoning is accomplished through the use of screening software (such as Cyber Patrol or SurfWatch) or browsers with screening capabilities, both of which search addresses and text for keywords that are associated with "adult" sites and, if the user wishes, blocks access to such sites. The Platform for Internet Content Selection project is designed to facilitate user-based zoning by encouraging Internet speakers to rate the content of their speech using codes recognized by all screening programs.

Despite this progress, the transformation of cyberspace is not complete. Although gateway technology has been available on the World Wide Web for some time now, it is not available to all Web speakers, and is just now becoming technologically feasible for chat rooms and USENET newsgroups. Gateway technology is not ubiquitous in cyberspace, and because without it "there is no means of age verification," cyberspace still remains largely unzoned — and unzoneable. User-based zoning is also in its infancy. For it to be effective, (i) an agreed-upon code (or "tag") would have to exist; (ii) screening software or browsers with screening capabilities would have to be able to recognize the "tag"; and (iii) those programs would have to be widely available — and widely used — by Internet users. At present, none of these conditions is true. Screening software "is not in wide use today" and "only a handful of browsers have screening capabilities." There is, moreover, no agreed-upon "tag" for those programs to recognize.

Although the prospects for the eventual zoning of the Internet appear promising, I agree with the Court that we must evaluate the constitutionality of the CDA as it applies to the Internet as it exists today. Given the present state of cyberspace, I agree with the Court that the "display" provision cannot pass muster. Until gateway technology is available throughout cyberspace, and it is not in 1997, a speaker cannot be reasonably assured that the speech he displays will reach only adults because it is impossible to confine speech to an "adult zone." Thus, the only way for a speaker to avoid liability under the CDA is to refrain completely from using indecent speech. But this forced silence impinges on the First Amendment right of adults to make and obtain this speech and, for all intents and purposes, "reduce[s] the adult population [on the Internet] to reading only what is fit for children." *Butler*, 352 U.S., at 383. As a result, the "display" provision cannot withstand scrutiny. Accord, *Sable Communications*, 492 U.S., at 126-131.

The "indecency transmission" and "specific person" provisions present a closer issue, for they are not unconstitutional in all of their applications. As discussed above, the "indecency transmission" provision makes it a crime to transmit knowingly an indecent message to a person the sender knows is under 18 years of age. 47 U.S.C.A. §223(a)(1)(B) (May 1996 Supp.). The "specific person" provision proscribes the same conduct, although it does not as explicitly require the sender to know that the intended recipient of his indecent message is a minor. §223(d)(1)(A). The Government urges the Court to construe the provision to impose such a knowledge requirement, and I would do so. . . .

So construed, both provisions are constitutional as applied to a conversation involving only an adult and one or more minors — e.g., when an adult speaker sends an e-mail knowing the addressee is a minor, or when an adult and minor converse by themselves or with other minors in a chat room. In this context, these provisions are no different from the law we sustained in *Ginsberg*. Restricting what the adult may say to the minors in no way restricts the adult's ability to communicate with other adults. He is not prevented from speaking indecently to other adults in a chat room (because there are no other adults participating in the conversation) and he remains free to send indecent e-mails to other adults. The relevant universe contains only one adult, and the adult in that universe has the power to refrain from using indecent speech and consequently to keep all such speech within the room in an "adult" zone.

The analogy to *Ginsberg* breaks down, however, when more than one adult is a party to the conversation. If a minor enters a chat room otherwise occupied by adults, the CDA effectively requires the adults in the room to stop using indecent speech. If they did not, they could be prosecuted under the "indecency transmission" and "specific person" provisions for any indecent statements they make to the group, since they would be transmitting an indecent message to specific persons, one of whom is a minor. The CDA is therefore akin to a law that makes it a crime for a bookstore owner to sell pornographic magazines to anyone once a minor enters his store. Even assuming such a law might be constitutional in the physical world as a reasonable alternative to excluding minors completely from the store, the absence of any means of excluding minors from chat rooms in cyberspace restricts the rights of adults to engage in indecent speech in those rooms. The "indecency transmission" and "specific person" provisions share this defect. . . .

I would therefore sustain the "indecency transmission" and "specific person" provisions to the extent they apply to the transmission of Internet communications where the party initiating the communication knows that all of the recipients are minors. . . .

COMMENTS AND QUESTIONS

1.   As the preceding materials demonstrate, the Supreme Court's First Amendment jurisprudence treats each medium for communication differently depending upon the medium's characteristics. Why should the varying characteristics matter? Are the characteristics used simply to mask an underlying conclusion that government regulation is more or less justified? What characteristics are important? When the Supreme Court determines whether to qualify the level of First Amendment scrutiny, what specifically does it consider with respect to the medium?

2.   In *Reno*, the Supreme Court relied heavily upon an understanding that the Internet is not invasive and individuals must take affirmative steps to receive information. Is this accurate in light of unsolicited e-mail, pop-up windows, and Internet broadcasting? If not, does it change the Court's conclusion?

3. To what extent should First Amendment scrutiny depend upon the service being offered rather than the medium in which it is carried? Should we evaluate Web pages under the same standards as e-mail or as radio broadcasts retransmitted though the Internet? *See* Timothy Wu, *Application-Centered Internet Analysis*, 85 Va. L. Rev. 1163 (1999) (arguing that First Amendment analysis should vary depending upon the application involved).

4. Another problem created by the Supreme Court's media-specific First Amendment analysis is the fact that information transmitted through the Internet is in fact carried by many different media including broadcast, copper telephone wire, fiber optics, and cable. Which medium's characteristics should we consider? Should it depend upon whether you connect to the Internet through cable, telephone, or satellite?

5. Why is the unprecedented scope of the CDA troubling? Is it because the CDA violates the First Amendment or because regulating noncommercial speech may be beyond Congress's enumerated powers? *See* United States v. Lopez, 514 U.S. 549 (1995); Ashcroft v. ACLU, 542 U.S. 656 (2004), *infra*.

6. In the Supreme Court's opinion, if the CDA were limited only to commercial content providers, could Congress require them to employ some form of gateway technology? *See* Ashcroft v. ACLU, 542 U.S. 656 (2004), *infra*.

7. Both the majority and Justice O'Connor found it important that existing age verification technologies were either inadequate or too costly making cyberspace "unzoned and unzoneable." In light of the debates over regulation of the Internet in general, why must age verification be perfect before Congress can regulate indecent speech? Could Congress prohibit the display of a defined category of indecent speech unless the content provider used some form of technology to restrict access including a simple warning page?

8. If a "perfect" form of gateway technology becomes available that requires a Internet user to pay a fee, could Congress require content providers to adopt that technology?

9. Justice O'Connor contemplates that some parts of the CDA could pass constitutional muster in circumstances where, say, an adult speaker is aware that she is only communicating with children online either by e-mail or in a chat room. How likely is this situation to arise in practice? This is an issue with online anonymity. How do we ever know precisely who we are talking to online?

10. Has the state of gateway technology changed significantly enough since this decision for Congress to effectively draft a law that protects minors from inappropriate speech? To what extent is the state of such technology relevant to Congress' ability to regulate in this way? After *Reno*, Congress enacted the Child Online Protection Act (COPA) to regulate Internet posting of material that might be harmful to minors. This legislation was also challenged on constitutional grounds. Consider the following extract.

ASHCROFT v. ACLU

542 U.S. 656 (2004)

Justice KENNEDY delivered the opinion of the Court.

This case presents a challenge to a statute enacted by Congress to protect minors from exposure to sexually explicit materials on the Internet, the Child Online Protection Act (COPA). 112 Stat. 2681-736, codified at 47 U.S.C. §231. We must decide whether the Court of Appeals was correct to affirm a ruling by the District Court that enforcement of COPA should be enjoined because the statute likely violates the First Amendment.

In enacting COPA, Congress gave consideration to our earlier decisions on this subject, in particular the decision in *Reno v. American Civil Liberties Union,* 521 U.S. 844 (1997). . . .

Content-based prohibitions, enforced by severe criminal penalties, have the constant potential to be a repressive force in the lives and thoughts of a free people. To guard against that threat the Constitution demands that content-based restrictions on speech be presumed invalid, *R.A.V. v. St. Paul,* 505 U.S. 377, 382 (1992), and that the Government bear the burden of showing their constitutionality. *United States v. Playboy Entertainment Group, Inc.,* 529 U.S. 803, 817 (2000). This is true even when Congress twice has attempted to find a constitutional means to restrict, and punish, the speech in question. . . .

I

A

. . . In response to the Court's decision in *Reno,* Congress passed COPA. COPA imposes criminal penalties of a $50,000 fine and six months in prison for the knowing posting, for "commercial purposes," of World Wide Web content that is "harmful to minors." §231(a)(1). Material that is "harmful to minors" is defined as:

any communication, picture, image, graphic image file, article, recording, writing, or other matter of any kind that is obscene or that—

"(A) the average person, applying contemporary community standards, would find, taking the material as a whole and with respect to minors, is designed to appeal to, or is designed to pander to, the prurient interest;

"(B) depicts, describes, or represents, in a manner patently offensive with respect to minors, an actual or simulated sexual act or sexual contact, an actual or simulated normal or perverted sexual act, or a lewd exhibition of the genitals or post-pubescent female breast; and

"(C) taken as a whole, lacks serious literary, artistic, political, or scientific value for minors." §231(e)(6).

"Minors" are defined as "any person under 17 years of age." §231(e)(7). A person acts for "commercial purposes only if such person is engaged in the business of making such communications." "Engaged in the business," in turn,

> means that the person who makes a communication, or offers to make a communication, by means of the World Wide Web, that includes any material that is harmful to minors, devotes time, attention, or labor to such activities, as a regular course of such person's trade or business, with the objective of earning a profit as a result of such activities (although it is not necessary that the person make a profit or that the making or offering to make such communications be the person's sole or principal business or source of income). §231(e)(2).

While the statute labels all speech that falls within these definitions as criminal speech, it also provides an affirmative defense to those who employ specified means to prevent minors from gaining access to the prohibited materials on their Web site. A person may escape conviction under the statute by demonstrating that he

> has restricted access by minors to material that is harmful to minors —
>
> "(A) by requiring use of a credit card, debit account, adult access code, or adult personal identification number;
> "(B) by accepting a digital certificate that verifies age, or
> "(C) by any other reasonable measures that are feasible under available technology."
> §231(c)(1). . . .

B

Respondents, Internet content providers and others concerned with protecting the freedom of speech, filed suit in the United States District Court for the Eastern District of Pennsylvania. They sought a preliminary injunction against enforcement of the statute. After considering testimony from witnesses presented by both respondents and the Government, the District Court issued an order granting the preliminary injunction. The court first noted that the statute would place a burden on some protected speech. *American Civil Liberties Union v. Reno,* 31 F. Supp. 2d 473, 495 (E.D. Pa. 1999). The court then concluded that respondents were likely to prevail on their argument that there were less restrictive alternatives to the statute: "On the record to date, it is not apparent . . . that [petitioner] can meet its burden to prove that COPA is the least restrictive means available to achieve the goal of restricting the access of minors" to harmful material. *Id.,* at 497. In particular, it noted that "[t]he record before the Court reveals that blocking or filtering technology may be at least as successful as COPA would be in restricting minors' access to harmful material online without imposing the burden on constitutionally protected speech that COPA imposes on adult users or Web site operators." *Ibid.*

. . .

II

A

. . .

The District Court, in deciding to grant the preliminary injunction, concentrated primarily on the argument that there are plausible, less restrictive alternatives to COPA. A statute that "effectively suppresses a large amount of speech that adults have a constitutional right to receive and to address to one another . . . is unacceptable if less restrictive alternatives would be at least as effective in achieving the legitimate purpose that the statute was enacted to serve." *Reno,* 521 U.S., at 874. When plaintiffs challenge a content-based speech restriction, the burden is on the Government to prove that the proposed alternatives will not be as effective as the challenged statute. *Id.,* at 874.

In considering this question, a court assumes that certain protected speech may be regulated, and then asks what is the least restrictive alternative that can be used to achieve that goal. The purpose of the test is not to consider whether the challenged restriction has some effect in achieving Congress' goal, regardless of the restriction it imposes. The purpose of the test is to ensure that speech is restricted no further than necessary to achieve the goal, for it is important to assure that legitimate speech is not chilled or punished. For that reason, the test does not begin with the status quo of existing regulations, then ask whether the challenged restriction has some additional ability to achieve Congress' legitimate interest. Any restriction on speech could be justified under that analysis. Instead, the court should ask whether the challenged regulation is the least restrictive means among available, effective alternatives. . . .

The primary alternative considered by the District Court was blocking and filtering software. Blocking and filtering software is an alternative that is less restrictive than COPA, and, in addition, likely more effective as a means of restricting children's access to materials harmful to them. The District Court, in granting the preliminary injunction, did so primarily because the plaintiffs had proposed that filters are a less restrictive alternative to COPA and the Government had not shown it would be likely to disprove the plaintiffs' contention at trial. *Ibid.*

Filters are less restrictive than COPA. They impose selective restrictions on speech at the receiving end, not universal restrictions at the source. Under a filtering regime, adults without children may gain access to speech they have a right to see without having to identify themselves or provide their credit card information. Even adults with children may obtain access to the same speech on the same terms simply by turning off the filter on their home computers. Above all, promoting the use of filters does not condemn as criminal any category of speech, and so the potential chilling effect is eliminated, or at least much diminished. All of these things are true, moreover, regardless of how broadly or narrowly the definitions in COPA are construed.

Filters also may well be more effective than COPA. First, a filter can prevent minors from seeing all pornography, not just pornography posted to the Web from America. The District Court noted in its factfindings that one witness estimated that 40% of harmful-to-minors content comes from overseas. *Id.*, at 484.

COPA does not prevent minors from having access to those foreign harmful materials. That alone makes it possible that filtering software might be more effective in serving Congress' goals. Effectiveness is likely to diminish even further if COPA is upheld, because the providers of the materials that would be covered by the statute simply can move their operations overseas. It is not an answer to say that COPA reaches some amount of materials that are harmful to minors; the question is whether it would reach more of them than less restrictive alternatives. In addition, the District Court found that verification systems may be subject to evasion and circumvention, for example by minors who have their own credit cards. See *id.*, at 484, 496-497. Finally, filters also may be more effective because they can be applied to all forms of Internet communication, including e-mail, not just communications available via the World Wide Web.

That filtering software may well be more effective than COPA is confirmed by the findings of the Commission on Child Online Protection, a blue-ribbon commission created by Congress in COPA itself. Congress directed the Commission to evaluate the relative merits of different means of restricting minors' ability to gain access to harmful materials on the Internet. Note following 47 U.S.C. §231. It unambiguously found that filters are more effective than age-verification requirements. See Commission on Child Online Protection (COPA), Report to Congress, at 19-21, 23-25, 27 (Oct. 20, 2000) (assigning a score for "Effectiveness" of 7.4 for server-based filters and 6.5 for client-based filters, as compared to 5.9 for independent adult-ID verification, and 5.5 for credit card verification). Thus, not only has the Government failed to carry its burden of showing the District Court that the proposed alternative is less effective, but also a Government Commission appointed to consider the question has concluded just the opposite. That finding supports our conclusion that the District Court did not abuse its discretion in enjoining the statute.

Filtering software, of course, is not a perfect solution to the problem of children gaining access to harmful-to-minors materials. It may block some materials that are not harmful to minors and fail to catch some that are. See 31 F. Supp. 2d, at 492. Whatever the deficiencies of filters, however, the Government failed to introduce specific evidence proving that existing technologies are less effective than the restrictions in COPA. The District Court made a specific factfinding that "[n]o evidence was presented to the Court as to the percentage of time that blocking and filtering technology is over- or underinclusive." *Ibid.* In the absence of a showing as to the relative effectiveness of COPA and the alternatives proposed by respondents, it was not an abuse of discretion for the District Court to grant the preliminary injunction. The Government's burden is not merely to show that a proposed less restrictive alternative has some flaws; its burden is to show that it is less effective. *Reno*, 521 U.S., at 874. It is not enough for the Government to show that COPA has some effect. Nor do respondents bear a burden to introduce, or offer to introduce, evidence that their proposed alternatives are more effective. The Government has the burden to show they are less so. The Government having failed to carry its burden, it was not an abuse of discretion for the District Court to grant the preliminary injunction.

One argument to the contrary is worth mentioning — the argument that filtering software is not an available alternative because Congress may not require it to be used. That argument carries little weight, because Congress undoubtedly may act to encourage the use of filters. We have held that Congress can give strong incentives to schools and libraries to use them. *United States v. American Library Assn., Inc.*, 539 U.S. 194 (2003). It could also take steps to promote their development by industry, and their use by parents. It is incorrect, for that reason, to say that filters are part of the current regulatory status quo. The need for parental cooperation does not automatically disqualify a proposed less restrictive alternative. *Playboy Entertainment Group*, 529 U.S., at 824. ("A court should not assume a plausible, less restrictive alternative would be ineffective; and a court should not presume parents, given full information, will fail to act.") In enacting COPA, Congress said its goal was to prevent the "widespread availability of the Internet" from providing "opportunities for minors to access materials through the World Wide Web in a manner that can frustrate parental supervision or control." Congressional Findings, note following 47 U.S.C. §231 (quoting Pub. L. 105-277, Tit. XIV, §1402(1), 112 Stat. 2681-736). COPA presumes that parents lack the ability, not the will, to monitor what their children see. By enacting programs to promote use of filtering software, Congress could give parents that ability without subjecting protected speech to severe penalties.

B

... The Government has not shown that the less restrictive alternatives proposed by respondents should be disregarded. Those alternatives, indeed, may be more effective than the provisions of COPA. The District Court did not abuse its discretion when it entered the preliminary injunction. The judgment of the Court of Appeals is affirmed, and the case is remanded for proceedings consistent with this opinion.

It is so ordered.

Justice STEVENS, with whom Justice GINSBURG joins, concurring.

When it first reviewed the constitutionality of the Child Online Protection Act (COPA), the Court of Appeals held that the statute's use of "contemporary community standards" to identify materials that are "harmful to minors" was a

serious, and likely fatal, defect. *American Civil Liberties Union v. Reno,*
217 F.3d 162 (C.A.3 2000). I have already explained at some length why
I agree with that holding. See *Ashcroft v. American Civil Liberties Union,*
535 U.S. 564, 603 (2002) (dissenting opinion) ("In the context of the
Internet, ... community standards become a sword, rather than a shield. If
a prurient appeal is offensive in a puritan village, it may be a crime to post it on
the World Wide Web"). I continue to believe that the Government may not
penalize speakers for making available to the general World Wide Web audience that which the least tolerant communities in America deem unfit for their
children's consumption, cf. *Reno v. American Civil Liberties Union,* 521 U.S.
844, 878 (1997), and consider that principle a sufficient basis for deciding this
case.

But COPA's use of community standards is not the statute's only
constitutional defect. Today's decision points to another: that, as far as the
record reveals, encouraging deployment of user-based controls, such as filtering software, would serve Congress' interest in protecting minors from sexually
explicit Internet materials as well or better than attempting to regulate the vast
content of the World Wide Web at its source, and at a far less significant cost to
First Amendment values.

In registering my agreement with the Court's less-restrictive-means analysis, I wish to underscore just how restrictive COPA is. COPA is a content-
based restraint on the dissemination of constitutionally protected speech. It
enforces its prohibitions by way of the criminal law, threatening noncompliant
Web speakers with a fine of as much as $50,000, and a term of imprisonment as
long as six months, for each offense. 47 U.S.C. §231(a). Speakers who "intentionally" violate COPA are punishable by a fine of up to $50,000 for each day
of the violation. *Ibid.* And because implementation of the various adult-
verification mechanisms described in the statute provides only an affirmative
defense, §231(c)(1), even full compliance with COPA cannot guarantee freedom from prosecution. Speakers who dutifully place their content behind age
screens may nevertheless find themselves in court, forced to prove the lawful-
ness of their speech on pain of criminal conviction. Cf. *Ashcroft v. Free Speech
Coalition,* 535 U.S. 234, 255 (2002).

Criminal prosecutions are, in my view, an inappropriate means to regulate the universe of materials classified as "obscene," since "the line between
communications which 'offend' and those which do not is too blurred to
identify criminal conduct." *Smith v. United States,* 431 U.S. 291, 316 (1977)
(Stevens, J., dissenting). See also *Marks v. United States,* 430 U.S. 188,
198 (1977) (Stevens, J., concurring in part and dissenting in part). COPA's
creation of a new category of criminally punishable speech that is "harmful to
minors" only compounds the problem. It may be, as Justice Breyer contends,
that the statute's coverage extends "only slightly" beyond the legally
obscene, and therefore intrudes little into the realm of protected expression.
But even with Justice Breyer's guidance, I find it impossible to identify just
how far past the already ill-defined territory of "obscenity" he thinks the

statute extends. Attaching criminal sanctions to a mistaken judgment about the contours of the novel and nebulous category of "harmful to minors" speech clearly imposes a heavy burden on the exercise of First Amendment freedoms.

COPA's criminal penalties are, moreover, strong medicine for the ill that the statute seeks to remedy. To be sure, our cases have recognized a compelling interest in protecting minors from exposure to sexually explicit materials. See, e.g., Ginsberg v. New York, 390 U.S. 629, 640 (1968). As a parent, grandparent, and great-grandparent, I endorse that goal without reservation. As a judge, however, I must confess to a growing sense of unease when the interest in protecting children from prurient materials is invoked as a justification for using criminal regulation of speech as a substitute for, or a simple backup to, adult oversight of children's viewing habits.

In view of the gravity of the burdens COPA imposes on Web speech, the possibility that Congress might have accomplished the goal of protecting children from harmful materials by other, less drastic means is a matter to be considered with special care. With that observation, I join the opinion of the Court.

Justice BREYER, with whom THE CHIEF JUSTICE and Justice O'CONNOR join, dissenting. [Justice SCALIA delivered a separate dissenting judgment largely agreeing with Justice BREYER on the constitutionality of COPA.]

The Child Online Protection Act (Act), 47 U.S.C. §231, seeks to protect children from exposure to commercial pornography placed on the Internet. It does so by requiring commercial providers to place pornographic material behind Internet "screens" readily accessible to adults who produce age verification. The Court recognizes that we should " 'proceed . . . with care before invalidating the Act,' " while pointing out that the "imperative of according respect to the Congress . . . does not permit us to depart from well-established First Amendment principles." I agree with these generalities. Like the Court, I would subject the Act to "the most exacting scrutiny," *Turner Broadcasting System, Inc. v. FCC,* 512 U.S. 622, 642 (1994), requiring the Government to show that any restriction of nonobscene expression is "narrowly drawn" to further a "compelling interest" and that the restriction amounts to the "least restrictive means" available to further that interest, *Sable Communications of Cal., Inc. v. FCC,* 492 U.S. 115, 126 (1989). See also *Denver Area Ed. Telecommunications Consortium, Inc. v. FCC,* 518 U.S. 727, 755-756 (1996).

Nonetheless, my examination of (1) the burdens the Act imposes on protected expression, (2) the Act's ability to further a compelling interest, and (3) the proposed "less restrictive alternatives" convinces me that the Court is wrong. I cannot accept its conclusion that Congress could have accomplished its statutory objective — protecting children from commercial pornography on the Internet — in other, less restrictive ways. . . .

II

I turn next to the question of "compelling interest," that of protecting minors from exposure to commercial pornography. No one denies that such an interest is "compelling." . . . Rather, the question here is whether the Act, given its restrictions on adult access, significantly advances that interest. In other words, is the game worth the candle?

The majority argues that it is not, because of the existence of "blocking and filtering software." The majority refers to the presence of that software as a "less restrictive alternative." But that is a misnomer — a misnomer that may lead the reader to believe that all we need do is look to see if the blocking and filtering software is less restrictive; and to believe that, because in one sense it is (one can turn off the software), that is the end of the constitutional matter.

But such reasoning has no place here. Conceptually speaking, the presence of filtering software is not an *alternative* legislative approach to the problem of protecting children from exposure to commercial pornography. Rather, it is part of the status quo, *i.e.,* the backdrop against which Congress enacted the present statute. It is always true, by definition, that the status quo is less restrictive than a new regulatory law. It is always less restrictive to do *nothing* than to do *something.* But "doing nothing" does not address the problem Congress sought to address — namely that, despite the availability of filtering software, children were still being exposed to harmful material on the Internet.

Thus, the relevant constitutional question is not the question the Court asks: Would it be less restrictive to do nothing? Of course it would be. Rather, the relevant question posits a comparison of (a) a status quo that includes filtering software with (b) a change in that status quo that adds to it an age-verification screen requirement. Given the existence of filtering software, does the problem Congress identified remain significant? Does the Act help to address it? These are questions about the relation of the Act to the compelling interest. Does the Act, compared to the status quo, significantly advance the ball? (An affirmative answer to these questions will not justify "[a]ny restriction on speech," as the Court claims, for a final answer in respect to constitutionality must take account of burdens and alternatives as well.)

The answers to these intermediate questions are clear: Filtering software, as presently available, does not solve the "child protection" problem. It suffers from four serious inadequacies that prompted Congress to pass legislation instead of relying on its voluntary use. First, its filtering is faulty, allowing some pornographic material to pass through without hindrance. Just last year, in American Library Assn., Justice Stevens described "fundamental defects in the filtering software that is now available or that will be available in the foreseeable future." 539 U.S., at 221 (dissenting opinion). He pointed to the problem of underblocking: "Because the software relies on key words or phrases to block undesirable sites, it does not have the capacity to exclude a precisely defined category of images." *Ibid.* That is to say, in the absence of words, the software alone cannot distinguish between the most obscene pictorial image and the Venus de Milo. No Member of this Court disagreed.

Second, filtering software costs money. Not every family has the $40 or so necessary to install it. . . . By way of contrast, age screening costs less. See *supra*, at 7 (citing costs of up to 20 cents per password or $20 per user for an identification number).

Third, filtering software depends upon parents willing to decide where their children will surf the Web and able to enforce that decision. As to millions of American families, that is not a reasonable possibility. More than 28 million school age children have both parents or their sole parent in the work force, at least 5 million children are left alone at home without supervision each week, and many of those children will spend afternoons and evenings with friends who may well have access to computers and more lenient parents. . . .

Fourth, software blocking lacks precision, with the result that those who wish to use it to screen out pornography find that it blocks a great deal of material that is valuable. As Justice Stevens pointed out, "the software's reliance on words to identify undesirable sites necessarily results in the blocking of thousands of pages that contain content that is completely innocuous for both adults and minors, and that no rational person could conclude matches the filtering companies' category definitions, such as pornography or sex." *American Library Assn., supra*, at 222 (internal quotation marks and citations omitted). . . .

In sum, a "filtering software status quo" means filtering that underblocks, imposes a cost upon each family that uses it, fails to screen outside the home, and lacks precision. Thus, Congress could reasonably conclude that a system that relies entirely upon the use of such software is not an effective system. And a law that adds to that system an age-verification screen requirement significantly increases the system's efficacy. That is to say, at a modest additional cost to those adults who wish to obtain access to a screened program, that law will bring about better, more precise blocking, both inside and outside the home. . . .

III

I turn, then, to the actual "less restrictive alternatives" that the Court proposes. The Court proposes two real alternatives, *i.e.*, two potentially less restrictive ways in which Congress might alter the status quo in order to achieve its "compelling" objective.

First, the Government might "act to encourage" the use of blocking and filtering software. The problem is that any argument that rests upon this alternative proves too much. If one imagines enough government resources devoted to the problem and perhaps additional scientific advances, then, of course, the use of software might become as effective and less restrictive. Obviously, the Government could give all parents, schools, and Internet cafes free computers with filtering programs already installed, hire federal employees to train parents and teachers on their use, and devote millions of dollars to the development of better software. The result might be an alternative that is extremely effective.

But the Constitution does not, because it cannot, require the Government to disprove the existence of magic solutions, *i.e.,* solutions that, put in general terms, will solve any problem less restrictively but with equal effectiveness. Otherwise, "the undoubted ability of lawyers and judges," who are not constrained by the budgetary worries and other practical parameters within which Congress must operate, "to imagine *some* kind of slightly less drastic or restrictive an approach would make it impossible to write laws that deal with the harm that called the statute into being." . . . Perhaps that is why no party has argued seriously that additional expenditure of government funds to encourage the use of screening is a "less restrictive alternative."

Second, the majority suggests decriminalizing the statute, noting the "chilling effect" of criminalizing a category of speech. . . . To remove a major sanction, however, would make the statute less effective, virtually by definition. . . .

COMMENTS AND QUESTIONS

1. What are the main reasons behind the differences of opinion between the majority and dissenting judges in Ashcroft v. ACLU? Do you think these divergences have more to do with how the judges see the current state of filtering technology than with their interpretation of the constitutional questions at issue in the case? Is filtering part of the "status quo" as the dissenting judges suggest, or a viable less restrictive alternative to the legislation? In this context, Justice Breyer stated that: "Conceptually speaking, the presence of filtering software is not an *alternative* legislative approach to the problem of protecting children from exposure to commercial pornography. Rather, it is part of the status quo, *i.e.,* the backdrop against which Congress enacted the present statute. It is always true, by definition, that the status quo is less restrictive than a new regulatory law. It is always less restrictive to do *nothing* than to do *something*. But 'doing nothing' does not address the problem Congress sought to address — namely that, despite the availability of filtering software, children were still being exposed to harmful material on the Internet." Do you agree with his view?

2. Given that neither legislation nor technology is currently able to completely protect minors from harmful speech, how should this problem be addressed? Should Congress encourage the use of filtering technologies, or place sanctions on the dissemination of harmful material, or both? Is it possible to develop an effective approach to the problem that combines both legal and technological solutions?

3. In regulating harmful speech, should the government focus on regulating the receipt of information or the dissemination of information online? Is either approach more effective? Why/why not?

4.   Justice Breyer seems to be suggesting that the case is really a matter of statutory interpretation and that, properly interpreted, COPA does not go much beyond sanctioning speech that is nonprotected in any event. What are the key differences between the CDA and COPA in this respect? Would there have been any more effective way for Congress to have drafted the relevant provisions in COPA to avoid the constitutional concerns that arose in Reno v. ACLU?

5.   Do *Reno* and *Ashcroft*, taken together, stand for the proposition that government may never prohibit indecent content on the Internet? If not, under what circumstances can the government regulate indecent speech?

6.   What about obscene speech that is not protected by the First Amendment? Can Congress ever prohibit obscene conduct on the Internet in light of *Reno* and *Ashcroft*? What about other kinds of undesirable speech, such as hate speech?

2. Filtering

While the First Amendment restrains government actions to punish Internet speakers based upon the content of the speech, does it prohibit governments from restricting access to speech when it provides access to the Internet? In other words, can local, state, and federal governments use filtering technology to restrict access to content available on public computers?

UNITED STATES v. AMERICAN LIBRARY ASSOCIATION, INC.

539 U.S. 194 (2003)

Chief Justice REHNQUIST announced the judgment of the Court and delivered an opinion, in which Justice O'CONNOR, Justice SCALIA, and Justice THOMAS joined. [Justice KENNEDY concurred in a separate judgment.]

To address the problems associated with the availability of Internet pornography in public libraries, Congress enacted the Children's Internet Protection Act (CIPA), 114 Stat. 2763A-335. Under CIPA, a public library may not receive federal assistance to provide Internet access unless it installs software to block images that constitute obscenity or child pornography, and to prevent minors from obtaining access to material that is harmful to them. . . .

. . . [CIPA] provides that a library may not receive E-rate or LSTA assistance unless it has "a policy of Internet safety for minors that includes the operation of a technology protection measure . . . that protects against access" by all persons to "visual depictions" that constitute "obscen[ity]" or "child pornography," and that protects against access by minors to "visual depictions" that are "harmful to minors." The statute defines a "[t]echnology protection measure" as "a specific technology that blocks or filters Internet access to material covered by" CIPA. CIPA also permits the library to "disable" the filter "to enable access for bona fide research or other lawful purposes." Under the E-rate program, disabling is permitted "during use by an adult." Under the LSTA program, disabling is permitted during use by any person.

. . .

Congress has wide latitude to attach conditions to the receipt of federal assistance in order to further its policy objectives. *South Dakota v. Dole*, 483 U.S. 203, 206 (1987). But Congress may not "induce" the recipient "to engage in activities that would themselves be unconstitutional." *Id.*, at 210. . . .

. . . A public library does not acquire Internet terminals in order to create a public forum for Web publishers to express themselves, any more than it collects books in order to provide a public forum for the authors of books to speak. It provides Internet access, not to "encourage a diversity of views from private speakers," *Rosenberger, supra,* at 834, but for the same reasons it offers other library resources: to facilitate research, learning, and recreational pursuits by furnishing materials of requisite and appropriate quality. . . . As Congress recognized, "[t]he Internet is simply another method for making information available in a school or library." It is "no more than a technological extension of the book stack." *Ibid.*

The District Court disagreed because, whereas a library reviews and affirmatively chooses to acquire every book in its collection, it does not review every Web site that it makes available. Based on this distinction, the court reasoned that a public library enjoys less discretion in deciding which Internet materials to make available than in making book selections. We do not find this distinction constitutionally relevant. A library's failure to make quality-based judgments about all the material it furnishes from the Web does not somehow taint the judgments it does make. A library's need to exercise judgment in making collection decisions depends on its traditional role in identifying suitable and worthwhile material; it is no less entitled to play that role when it collects material from the Internet than when it collects material from any other source. Most libraries already exclude pornography from their print collections because they deem it inappropriate for inclusion. We do not subject these decisions to heightened scrutiny; it would make little sense to treat libraries' judgments to block online pornography any differently, when these judgments are made for just the same reason.

Moreover, because of the vast quantity of material on the Internet and the rapid pace at which it changes, libraries cannot possibly segregate, item by item, all the Internet material that is appropriate for inclusion from all that is not. . . .

Like the District Court, the dissents fault the tendency of filtering software to "overblock" — that is, to erroneously block access to constitutionally protected speech that falls outside the categories that software users intend to block. . . . Assuming that such erroneous blocking presents constitutional difficulties, any such concerns are dispelled by the ease with which patrons may have the filtering software disabled. When a patron encounters a blocked site, he need only ask a librarian to unblock it or (at least in the case of adults) disable the filter. As the District Court found, libraries have the capacity to permanently unblock any erroneously blocked site, and the Solicitor General stated at oral argument that a "library may . . . eliminate the filtering with respect to specific sites . . . at the request of a patron." With respect to adults, CIPA also expressly authorizes library officials to "disable" a filter altogether "to enable access for bona fide research or other lawful purposes." The Solicitor General confirmed that a "librarian can, in response to a request from a patron, unblock the filtering mechanism altogether," and further explained that a patron would not "have to explain . . . why he was asking a site to be unblocked or the filtering to be disabled." The District Court viewed unblocking and disabling as inadequate because some patrons may be too embarrassed to request them. But the Constitution does not guarantee the right to acquire information at a public library without any risk of embarrassment. . . .

Because public libraries' use of Internet filtering software does not violate their patrons' First Amendment rights, CIPA does not induce libraries to violate the Constitution, and is a valid exercise of Congress' spending power. Nor does CIPA impose an unconstitutional condition on public libraries. Therefore, the judgment of the District Court for the Eastern District of Pennsylvania is reversed.

Justice BREYER, concurring in the judgment.

In ascertaining whether the statutory provisions are constitutional, I would apply a form of heightened scrutiny, examining the statutory requirements in question with special care. The Act directly restricts the public's receipt of information. . . . And it does so through limitations imposed by outside bodies (here Congress) upon two critically important sources of information — the Internet as accessed via public libraries. . . . For that reason, we should not examine the statute's constitutionality as if it raised no special First Amendment concern — as if, like tax or economic regulation, the First Amendment demanded only a "rational basis" for imposing a restriction. Nor should we accept the Government's suggestion that a presumption in favor of the statute's constitutionality applies.

At the same time, in my view, the First Amendment does not here demand application of the most limiting constitutional approach — that of "strict scrutiny." The statutory restriction in question is, in essence, a kind of "selection" restriction (a kind of editing). It affects the kinds and amount of materials that the library can present to its patrons. And libraries often properly engage in the selection of materials, either as a matter of necessity (*i.e.,* due to the scarcity of resources) or by design (*i.e.,* in accordance with collection development policies). To apply "strict scrutiny" to the "selection" of a library's collection (whether carried out by public libraries themselves or by other community bodies with a traditional legal right to engage in that function) would unreasonably interfere with the discretion necessary to create, maintain, or select a library's "collection" (broadly defined to include all the information the library makes available). Cf. *Miami Herald Publishing Co. v. Tornillo,* 418 U.S. 241, 256-258 (1974) (protecting newspaper's exercise of editorial control and judgment). That is to say, "strict scrutiny" implies too limiting and rigid a test for me to believe that the First Amendment requires it in this context.

Instead, I would examine the constitutionality of the Act's restrictions here as the Court has examined speech-related restrictions in other contexts where circumstances call for heightened, but not "strict," scrutiny — where, for example, complex, competing constitutional interests are potentially at issue or speech-related harm is potentially justified by unusually strong governmental interests. Typically the key question in such instances is one of proper fit. . . .

In such cases the Court has asked whether the harm to speech-related interests is disproportionate in light of both the justifications and the potential alternatives. It has considered the legitimacy of the statute's objective, the extent to which the statute will tend to achieve that objective, whether there are other, less restrictive ways of achieving that objective, and ultimately whether the statute works speech-related harm that, in relation to that objective, is out of proportion. . . .

The Act's restrictions satisfy these constitutional demands. The Act seeks to restrict access to obscenity, child pornography, and, in respect to access by minors, material that is comparably harmful. These objectives are "legitimate," and indeed often "compelling." . . . As the District Court found, software filters "provide a relatively cheap and effective" means of furthering these goals. Due to present technological limitations, however, the software filters both "overblock," screening out some perfectly legitimate material, and "under-block," allowing some obscene material to escape detection by the filter. But no one has presented any clearly superior or better fitting alternatives.

At the same time, the Act contains an important exception that limits the speech-related harm that "overblocking" might cause. As the plurality points out, the Act allows libraries to permit any adult patron access to an "over-blocked" Web site; the adult patron need only ask a librarian to unblock the specific Web site or, alternatively, ask the librarian, "Please disable the entire filter."

The Act does impose upon the patron the burden of making this request. But it is difficult to see how that burden (or any delay associated with compliance) could prove more onerous than traditional library practices associated with segregating library materials in, say, closed stacks, or with interlibrary lending practices that require patrons to make requests that are not anonymous and to wait while the librarian obtains the desired materials from elsewhere. Perhaps local library rules or practices could further restrict the ability of patrons to obtain "overblocked" Internet material. . . . But we are not now considering any such local practices. We here consider only a facial challenge to the Act itself.

Given the comparatively small burden that the Act imposes upon the library patron seeking legitimate Internet materials, I cannot say that any speech-related harm that the Act may cause is disproportionate when considered in relation to the Act's legitimate objectives. I therefore agree with the plurality that the statute does not violate the First Amendment, and I concur in the judgment.

Justice STEVENS, dissenting.

. . . Rather than allowing local decisionmakers to tailor their responses to local problems, the Children's Internet Protection Act (CIPA) operates as a blunt nationwide restraint on adult access to "an enormous amount of valuable information" that individual librarians cannot possibly review. Most of that information is constitutionally protected speech. In my view, this restraint is unconstitutional. . . .

I

The unchallenged findings of fact made by the District Court reveal fundamental defects in the filtering software that is now available or that will be available in the foreseeable future. Because the software relies on key words or phrases to block undesirable sites, it does not have the capacity to exclude a precisely defined category of images. As the District Court explained:

> [T]he search engines that software companies use for harvesting are able to search text only, not images. This is of critical importance, because CIPA, by its own terms, covers only "visual depictions." Image recognition technology is immature, ineffective, and unlikely to improve substantially in the near future. None of the filtering software companies deposed in this case employs image recognition technology when harvesting or categorizing URLs. Due to the reliance on automated text analysis and the absence of image recognition technology, a Web page with sexually explicit images and no text cannot be harvested using a search engine. This problem is complicated by the fact that Web site publishers may use image files rather than text to represent words, i.e., they may use a file that computers understand to be a picture, like a photograph of a printed word, rather than regular text, making automated review of their textual content impossible. For example, if the Playboy Web site displays its name using a logo rather than regular text, a search engine would not see or recognize the Playboy name in that logo.

Given the quantity and ever-changing character of Web sites offering free sexually explicit material, it is inevitable that a substantial amount of such material will never be blocked. Because of this "underblocking," the statute will provide parents with a false sense of security without really solving the problem that motivated its enactment. Conversely, the software's reliance on words to identify undesirable sites necessarily results in the blocking of thousands of pages that "contain content that is completely innocuous for both adults and minors, and that no rational person could conclude matches the filtering companies' category definitions, such as 'pornography' or 'sex.'" In my judgment, a statutory blunderbuss that mandates this vast amount of "overblocking" abridges the freedom of speech protected by the First Amendment.

The effect of the overblocking is the functional equivalent of a host of individual decisions excluding hundreds of thousands of individual constitutionally protected messages from Internet terminals located in public libraries throughout the Nation. Neither the interest in suppressing unlawful speech nor the interest in protecting children from access to harmful materials justifies this overly broad restriction on adult access to protected speech. "The Government may not suppress lawful speech as the means to suppress unlawful speech." . . .

Although CIPA does not permit any experimentation, the District Court expressly found that a variety of alternatives less restrictive are available at the local level:

> [L]ess restrictive alternatives exist that further the government's legitimate interest in preventing the dissemination of obscenity, child pornography, and material harmful to minors, and in preventing patrons from being unwillingly exposed to patently offensive, sexually explicit content. To prevent patrons from accessing visual depictions that are obscene and child pornography, public libraries may enforce Internet use policies that make clear to patrons that the library's Internet terminals may not be used to access illegal speech. Libraries may then impose penalties on patrons who violate these policies, ranging from a warning to notification of law enforcement, in the appropriate case. Less restrictive alternatives to filtering that further libraries' interest in preventing minors from exposure to visual depictions that are harmful to minors include requiring parental consent to or presence during unfiltered access, or restricting minors' unfiltered access to terminals within view of library staff. Finally, optional filtering, privacy screens, recessed monitors, and placement of unfiltered Internet terminals outside of sight-lines provide less restrictive alternatives for libraries to prevent patrons from being unwillingly exposed to sexually explicit content on the Internet. 201 F. Supp. 2d, at 410.

Those findings are consistent with scholarly comment on the issue arguing that local decisions tailored to local circumstances are more appropriate than a mandate from Congress. The plurality does not reject any of those findings. Instead, "[a]ssuming that such erroneous blocking presents constitutional difficulties," it relies on the Solicitor General's assurance that the statute permits individual librarians to disable filtering mechanisms whenever a patron so requests. In my judgment, that assurance does not cure the constitutional infirmity in the statute. . . .

Until a blocked site or group of sites is unblocked, a patron is unlikely to know what is being hidden and therefore whether there is any point in asking for the filter to be removed. It is as though the statute required a significant part of every library's reading materials to be kept in unmarked, locked rooms or cabinets, which could be opened only in response to specific requests. Some curious readers would in time obtain access to the hidden materials, but many would not. Inevitably, the interest of the authors of those works in reaching the widest possible audience would be abridged. Moreover, because the procedures that different libraries are likely to adopt to respond to unblocking requests will no doubt vary, it is impossible to measure the aggregate effect of the statute on patrons' access to blocked sites. Unless we assume that the statute is a mere symbolic gesture, we must conclude that it will create a significant prior restraint on adult access to protected speech. A law that prohibits reading without official consent, like a law that prohibits speaking without consent, "constitutes a dramatic departure from our national heritage and constitutional tradition." *Watchtower Bible & Tract Soc. of N.Y., Inc. v. Village of Stratton*, 536 U.S. 150, 166 (2002). . . .

Justice SOUTER, with whom Justice GINSBURG joins, dissenting.

. . .

[W]e are here to review a statute, and the unblocking provisions simply cannot be construed, even for constitutional avoidance purposes, to say that a library must unblock upon adult request, no conditions imposed and no questions asked. First, the statute says only that a library "may" unblock, not that it must. In addition, it allows unblocking only for a "bona fide research or other lawful purposes," and if the "lawful purposes" criterion means anything that would not subsume and render the "bona fide research" criterion superfluous, it must impose some limit on eligibility for unblocking. There is therefore necessarily some restriction, which is surely made more onerous by the uncertainty of its terms and the generosity of its discretion to library staffs in deciding who gets complete Internet access and who does not. . . .

We therefore have to take the statute on the understanding that adults will be denied access to a substantial amount of nonobscene material harmful to children but lawful for adult examination, and a substantial quantity of text and pictures harmful to no one. As the plurality concedes, this is the inevitable consequence of the indiscriminate behavior of current filtering mechanisms, which screen out material to an extent known only by the manufacturers of the blocking software.

We likewise have to examine the statute on the understanding that the restrictions on adult Internet access have no justification in the object of protecting children. Children could be restricted to blocked terminals, leaving other unblocked terminals in areas restricted to adults and screened from casual glances. And of course the statute could simply have provided for unblocking at adult request, with no questions asked. The statute could, in other words, have protected children without blocking access for adults or subjecting adults to anything more than minimal inconvenience, just the way (the record shows) many librarians had been dealing with obscenity and indecency before imposition of the federal conditions. Instead, the Government's funding conditions engage in overkill to a degree illustrated by their refusal to trust even a library's staff with an unblocked terminal, one to which the adult public itself has no access.

The question for me, then, is whether a local library could itself constitutionally impose these restrictions on the content otherwise available to an adult patron through an Internet connection, at a library terminal provided for public use. The answer is no. A library that chose to block an adult's Internet access to material harmful to children (and whatever else the undiscriminating filter might interrupt) would be imposing a content-based restriction on communication of material in the library's control that an adult could otherwise lawfully see. This would simply be censorship. . . .

II

. . .

A

Public libraries are indeed selective in what they acquire to place in their stacks, as they must be. There is only so much money and so much shelf space, and the necessity to choose some material and reject the rest justifies the effort to be selective with an eye to demand, quality, and the object of maintaining the library as a place of civilized enquiry by widely different sorts of people. Selectivity is thus necessary and complex, and these two characteristics explain why review of a library's selection decisions must be limited: the decisions are made all the time, and only in extreme cases could one expect particular choices to reveal impermissible reasons (reasons even the plurality would consider to be illegitimate), like excluding books because their authors are Democrats or their critiques of organized Christianity are unsympathetic. See *Board of Ed., Island Trees Union Free School Dist. No. 26 v. Pico*, 457 U.S. 853, 870-871 (1982) (plurality opinion). Review for rational basis is probably the most that any court could conduct, owing to the myriad particular selections that might be attacked by someone, and the difficulty of untangling the play of factors behind a particular decision.

At every significant point, however, the Internet blocking here defies comparison to the process of acquisition. Whereas traditional scarcity of money and space require a library to make choices about what to acquire, and the choice to be made is whether or not to spend the money to acquire something, blocking is the subject of a choice made after the money for Internet access has been spent or committed. Since it makes no difference to the cost of Internet access whether an adult calls up material harmful for children or the Articles of Confederation, blocking (on facts like these) is not necessitated by scarcity of either money or space. In the instance of the Internet, what the library acquires is electronic access, and the choice to block is a choice to limit access that has already been acquired. Thus, deciding against buying a book means there is no book (unless a loan can be obtained), but blocking the Internet is merely blocking access purchased in its entirety and subject to unblocking if the librarian agrees. The proper analogy therefore is not to passing up a book that might have been bought; it is either to buying a book and then keeping it from adults lacking an acceptable "purpose," or to buying an encyclopedia and then cutting out pages with anything thought to be unsuitable for all adults. . . .

MAINSTREAM LOUDOUN V. BD. OF TRUSTEES
OF THE LOUDOUN CO. LIBRARY (*LOUDOUN I*)

2 F. Supp. 2d 783 (E.D. Va. 1998)

BRINKEMA, District Judge.

[P]laintiffs in this case are an association, Mainstream Loudoun, and ten individual plaintiffs, all of whom are both members of Mainstream Loudoun and adult patrons of Loudoun County public libraries. Defendants are the Board of Trustees of the Loudoun County Public Library, five individual Board members, and Douglas Henderson, Loudoun County's Director of Library Services. The Loudoun County public library system . . . provides patrons with access to the Internet and the World Wide Web. . . .

On October 20, 1997, the Library Board voted to adopt a "Policy on Internet Sexual Harassment" (the "Policy"), which requires that "[s]ite-blocking software . . . be installed on all [library] computers" so as to: "a. block child pornography and obscene material (hard core pornography)"; and "b. block material deemed Harmful to Juveniles under applicable Virginia statutes and legal precedents (soft core pornography)." To implement the Policy, the Library Board chose "X-Stop," a commercial software product intended to limit access to sites deemed to violate the Policy.

Plaintiffs allege that the Policy impermissibly blocks their access to protected speech such as the Quaker Home Page, the Zero Population Growth Web site, and the site for the American Association of University Women — Maryland. They also claim that there are no clear criteria for blocking decisions and that defendants maintain an unblocking policy that unconstitutionally chills plaintiffs' receipt of constitutionally protected materials. . . .

In their Motion to Dismiss for Failure to State a Claim, or, in the Alternative, for Summary Judgment, defendants concede that the Policy prohibits access to speech on the basis of its content. However, defendants argue that the "First Amendment does not in any way limit the decisions of a public library on whether to provide access to information on the Internet." Indeed, at oral argument, defendants went so far as to claim that a public library could constitutionally prohibit access to speech simply because it was authored by African-Americans, or because it espoused a particular political viewpoint, for example pro-Republican. Thus, the central question before this Court is whether a public library may, without violating the First Amendment, enforce content-based restrictions on access to Internet speech.

No cases directly address this issue. However, the parties agree that the most analogous authority on this issue is Board of Education v. Pico, 457 U.S. 853 (1982), in which the Supreme Court reviewed the decision of a local board of education to remove certain books from a high school library based on the board's belief that the books were "anti-American, anti-Christian, anti-Sem[i]tic, and just plain filthy." Id. 457 U.S. at 856. The Second Circuit had reversed the district court's grant of summary judgment to the school board on plaintiff's First Amendment claim. A sharply-divided Court voted to affirm the Court of Appeal's decision to remand the case for a determination of the school board's motives. However, the Court did not render a majority opinion . . . Justice Brennan[, joined by three Justices,] held that the First Amendment necessarily limits the government's right to remove materials on the basis of their content from a high school library. See id. at 864-69 (plurality op.). Justice Brennan reasoned that the right to receive information is inherent in the right to speak and that "the State may not, consistently with the spirit of the First Amendment, contract the spectrum of available knowledge." Id. at 866 (quoting Griswold v. Connecticut, 381 U.S. 479, 482 (1965)); see also Stanley v. Georgia, 394 U.S. 557, 564 (1969) ("the Constitution protects the right to receive information and ideas"). . . . At the same time, Justice Brennan recognized that public high schools play a crucial inculcative role in "the prep-aration of individuals for participation as citizens" and are therefore entitled to great discretion "to establish and apply their curriculum in such a way as to transmit community values." Id. at 863-64 (quoting Ambach v. Norwick, 441 U.S. 68, 76-77 (1979) (internal quotation marks omitted)). Accordingly, Justice Brennan held that the school board members could not remove books "simply because they dislike the ideas contained [in them]," thereby "prescrib[ing] what shall be orthodox in politics, nationalism, religion, or other matters of opinion," but that the board might remove books for reasons of educational suitability, for example pervasive vulgarity. Id. 457 U.S. at 872 (quoting West Va. Bd. of Educ. v. Barnette, 319 U.S. 624, 642 (1943)) (internal quotation marks omitted).

In a concurring opinion, Justice Blackmun focused not on the right to receive information recognized by the plurality, but on the school board's dis-crimination against disfavored ideas. Justice Blackmun explicitly recognized that *Pico*'s facts invoked two significant, competing interests: the inculcative mission of public high schools and the First Amendment's core proscription against content-based regulation of speech. See id. 457 U.S. at 876-79 (Blackmun, J., concurring). . . . Balancing the two principles above, Justice Blackmun agreed with the plurality that the school board could not remove books based on mere disapproval of their content but could limit its collection for reasons of educa-tional suitability or budgetary constraint. See id. at 879.

Dissenting, Chief Justice Burger, joined by three Justices, concluded that any First Amendment right to receive speech did not affirmatively obligate the government to provide such speech in high school libraries. See id. at 888 (Burger, C.J., dissenting). Chief Justice Burger reasoned that although the State could not constitutionally prohibit a speaker from reaching an intended audience, nothing in the First Amendment requires public high schools to act as a conduit for particular speech. See id. at 885-89. . . .

Defendants contend that the *Pico* plurality opinion has no application to this case because it addressed only decisions to remove materials from libraries and specifically declined to address library decisions to acquire materials. See id.

at 861-63, 871-72 (plurality op.). Defendants liken the Internet to a vast Interlibrary Loan system, and contend that restricting Internet access to selected materials is merely a decision not to acquire such materials rather than a decision to remove them from a library's collection. . . .

In response, plaintiffs argue that, unlike a library's collection of individual books, the Internet is a "single, integrated system." As plaintiffs explain, "[t]hough information on the Web is contained in individual computers, the fact that each of these computers is connected to the Internet through [World Wide Web] protocols allows all of the information to become part of a single body of knowledge." Accordingly, plaintiffs analogize the Internet to a set of encyclopedias, and the Library Board's enactment of the Policy to a decision to "black out" selected articles considered inappropriate for adult and juvenile patrons.

After considering both arguments, we conclude that defendants have misconstrued the nature of the Internet. By purchasing Internet access, each Loudoun library has made all Internet publications instantly accessible to its patrons. Unlike an Interlibrary loan or outright book purchase, no appreciable expenditure of library time or resources is required to make a particular Internet publication available to a library patron. In contrast, a library must actually expend resources to restrict Internet access to a publication that is otherwise immediately available. In effect, by purchasing one such publication, the library has purchased them all. The Internet therefore more closely resembles plaintiffs' analogy of a collection of encyclopedias from which defendants have laboriously redacted portions deemed unfit for library patrons. As such, the Library Board's action is more appropriately characterized as a removal decision. We therefore conclude that the principles discussed in the *Pico* plurality are relevant and apply to the Library Board's decision to promulgate and enforce the Policy. . . .

Defendants argue that any limitation on their discretion to remove materials would force them to act as an unwilling conduit of information, and urge this Court to adopt the position of the *Pico* dissent. Defendants interpret the dissent to mean that they are entitled to unfettered discretion in deciding what materials to make available to library patrons.

Adopting defendants' position, however, would require this Court to ignore the *Pico* plurality's decision to remand the case. . . . Moreover, all of the *Pico* Justices, including the dissenters, recognized that any discretion accorded to school libraries was uniquely tied to the public school's role as educator. . . . Of even more significance to our case is Justice Rehnquist's observation that high school libraries must be treated differently from public libraries. See id. at 915 (Rehnquist, J., dissenting) ("Unlike university or public libraries, elementary and secondary school libraries are not designed for free-wheeling inquiry."). Indeed, Chief Justice Burger and Justice Rehnquist justified giving public schools broad discretion to remove books in part by noting that such materials remained available in public libraries. See id. at 892 (Burger, C.J., dissenting) ("Books may be acquired from . . . public libraries, or other alternative sources unconnected with the unique environment of the local public schools."); 915 (Rehnquist, J., dissenting) ("[T]he most obvious reason that petitioners' removal of the books did not violate respondents' right to receive information is the ready availability of the books elsewhere. . . . The books may be borrowed from a public library."). Accordingly, neither the dissent nor the plurality of *Pico* can be said to support defendants' argument that public libraries enjoy unfettered discretion to remove materials from their collections.

To the extent that *Pico* applies to this case, we conclude that it stands for the proposition that the First Amendment applies to, and limits, the discretion of a public library to place content-based restrictions on access to constitutionally protected materials within its collection. Consistent with the mandate of the First Amendment, a public library, "like other enterprises operated by the State, may not be run in such a manner as to 'prescribe what shall be orthodox in politics, nationalism, religion, or other matters of opinion.'" Id. at 876 (Blackmun, J., concurring) (quoting *Barnette*, 319 U.S. at 642).

Furthermore, the factors which justified giving high school libraries broad discretion to remove materials in *Pico* are not present in this case. The plaintiffs in this case are adults rather than children. Children, whose minds and values are still developing, have traditionally been afforded less First Amendment protection, particularly within the context of public high schools. See Tinker v. Des Moines Sch. Dist., 393 U.S. 503, 506 (1969). In contrast, adults are deemed to have acquired the maturity needed to participate fully in a democratic society, and their right to speak and receive speech is entitled to full First Amendment protection. Accordingly, adults are entitled to receive categories of speech, for example "pervasively vulgar" speech, which may be inappropriate for children. See Reno v. ACLU, 521 U.S. 844 (1997); Sable Communications v. FCC, 492 U.S. 115, 126 (1989).

More importantly, the tension Justice Blackmun recognized between the inculcative role of high schools and the First Amendment's prohibition on content-based regulation of speech does not exist here. See *Pico*, 457 U.S. at 876-80 (Blackmun, J., concurring). Public libraries lack the inculcative mission that is the guiding purpose of public high schools. Instead, public libraries are places of freewheeling and independent inquiry. See id. at 914 (Rehnquist, J., dissenting). Adult library patrons are presumed to have acquired already the "fundamental values" needed to act as citizens, and have come to the library to pursue their personal intellectual interests rather than the curriculum of a high school classroom. As such, no curricular motive justifies a public library's decision to restrict access to Internet materials on the basis of their content.

Finally, the unique advantages of Internet speech eliminate any resource-related rationale libraries might otherwise have for engaging in content-based discrimination. The Supreme Court has analogized the Internet to a "vast library including millions of readily available and indexed publications," the content of which "is as diverse as human thought." *Reno*, 117 S. Ct. at 2335. Unlike more traditional libraries, however, there is no marginal cost associated with acquiring Internet publications. Instead, all, or nearly all, Internet publications are jointly available for a single price. Indeed, it costs a library more to restrict the content of its collection by means of blocking software than it does for the library to offer unrestricted access to all Internet publications. Nor do Internet publications, which exist only in "cyberspace," take up shelf space or require physical maintenance of any kind. Accordingly, considerations of cost or physical resources cannot justify a public library's decision to restrict access to Internet materials. Cf. *Pico*, 457 U.S. at 909 (Rehnquist, J., dissenting) (budgetary considerations force schools to choose some books over others); 879 n.1 (Blackmun, J., concurring) (same).

In sum, there is "no basis for qualifying the level of First Amendment scrutiny" that must be applied to a public library's decision to restrict access to Internet publications. *Reno*, 117 S. Ct. at 2344. We are therefore left with the First Amendment's central tenet that content-based restrictions on speech must be justified by a compelling governmental interest and must be narrowly tailored to achieve that end. See Simon & Schuster, Inc. v. Members of the N.Y. State Crime Victims Bd., 502 U.S. 105, 118 (1991). This principle was recently affirmed within the context of Internet speech. See *Reno*, 117 S. Ct. at 2343-48. Accordingly, we hold that the Library Board may not adopt and enforce content-based restrictions on access to protected Internet speech absent a compelling state interest and means narrowly drawn to achieve that end.

This holding does not obligate defendants to act as unwilling conduits of information, because the Library Board need not provide access to the Internet at all. Having chosen to provide access, however, the Library Board may not thereafter selectively restrict certain categories of Internet speech because it disfavors their content. . . .

Mainstream Loudoun v. Bd. of Trustees of the Loudoun Co. Library (*Loudoun II*)

24 F. Supp. 2d 552 (E.D. Va. 1998)

[Having concluded that the Library's decision to provide Internet access was subject to the limits of the First Amendment, the court then examined whether the filtering of Web sites violated the First Amendment.]

Brinkema, District Judge.

Background

At issue in this civil action is whether a public library may enact a policy prohibiting the access of library patrons to certain content-based categories of Internet publications. . . .

To [implement its policy], the library has purchased X-Stop, commercial site-blocking software manufactured by Log-On Data Corporation. While the method by which X-Stop chooses sites to block has been kept secret by its developers, it is undisputed that it has blocked at least some sites that do not contain any material that is prohibited by the Policy.[2]

If a patron is blocked from accessing a site that she feels should not be blocked under the Policy, she may request that defendant unblock the site by filing an official, written request with the librarian stating her name, the site she wants unblocked, and the reason why she wants to access the site. The librarian will then review the site and manually unblock it if he determines that the site should not be blocked under the Policy. There is no time limit in which a request must be handled and no procedure for notifying the patron of the outcome of a request.

Plaintiffs and intervenors both allege that the Policy, as written and as implemented, violates their First Amendment rights because it impermissibly discriminates against protected speech on the basis of content and constitutes an unconstitutional prior restraint. . . .

Defendant contends that even if we conclude that strict scrutiny is the appropriate standard of review, the Policy is constitutional because it is the least restrictive means to achieve two compelling government interests: "1) minimizing access to illegal pornography; and 2) avoidance of creation of a sexually hostile environment. . . ."

A content-based limitation on speech will be upheld only where the state demonstrates that the limitation "is necessary to serve a compelling state interest and that it is narrowly drawn to achieve that end." Perry Educ. Ass'n v. Perry Local Educators' Ass'n, 460 U.S. 37, 45 (1983) (citing Carey v. Brown, 447 U.S. 455, 461 (1980)). This test involves three distinct inquiries: (1) whether the interests asserted by the state are compelling; (2) whether the limitation is necessary to further those interests; and (3) whether the limitation is narrowly drawn to achieve those interests.

A. Whether the Defendant's Interests Are Compelling . . .

For the purposes of this analysis, therefore, we assume that minimizing access to illegal pornography and avoidance of creation of a sexually hostile environment are compelling government interests.

B. Whether the Policy Is Necessary to Further Those Interests

To satisfy strict scrutiny, defendant must do more than demonstrate that it has a compelling interest; it must also demonstrate that the Policy is necessary to further that interest. In other words, defendant must demonstrate that in the absence of the Policy, a sexually hostile environment might

---

2. Defendant admits to having blocked the Safer Sex Page, the Books for Gay and Lesbian Teens/Youth page, and the Renaissance Transgender Association page, even though it recognizes that none of them contain prohibited material.

exist and/or there would be a problem with individuals accessing child pornography or obscenity or minors accessing materials that are illegal as to them. . . . The defendant bears this burden because "[t]he interest in encouraging freedom of expression in a democratic society outweighs any theoretical but unproven benefit of censorship." Reno v. ACLU, 521 U.S. 844 (1997).

The only evidence to which defendant can point in support of its argument that the Policy is necessary consists of a record of a single complaint arising from Internet use in another Virginia library and reports of isolated incidents in three other libraries across the country. In the Bedford County Central Public Library in Bedford County, Virginia, a patron complained that she had observed a boy viewing what she believed were pornographic pictures on the Internet. This incident was the only one defendant discovered within Virginia and the only one in the 16 months in which the Bedford County public library system had offered unfiltered public access to the Internet. After the incident, the library merely installed privacy screens on its Internet terminals which, according to the librarian, "work great."

The only other evidence of problems arising from unfiltered Internet access is described by David Burt, defendant's expert, who was only able to find three libraries that allegedly had experienced such problems, one in Los Angeles County,[17] another in Orange County, Florida,[18] and one in Austin, Texas.[19] There is no evidence in the record establishing that any other libraries have encountered problems; rather, Burt's own statements indicate that such problems are practically nonexistent. . . . As a matter of law, we find this evidence insufficient to sustain defendant's burden of showing that the Policy is reasonably necessary. . . .

C.   Whether the Policy Is Narrowly Tailored to Achieve the Compelling Government Interests

Even if defendant could demonstrate that the Policy was reasonably necessary to further compelling state interests, it would still have to show that the Policy is narrowly tailored to achieve those interests. The parties disagree about several issues relating to whether the Policy is narrowly tailored: (1) whether less restrictive means are available; (2) whether the Policy is over-inclusive; and (3) whether X-Stop, the filtering software used by defendant, is the least restrictive filtering software available.

17. Quoting a newspaper article, Burt reported that library computers "are regularly steered to on-line photos of naked women, digitized videos of sex acts and ribald chat-room discussions," causing legitimate researchers to have to wait in line while others read "personal ads or X-rated chat rooms." Burt Rep. at 14 (quoting Public Libraries Debating How to Handle Net Porn, August Chron., July 3, 1997).

18. Burt alleges that filters had to be installed in Orange County libraries after patrons were accessing hard-core porn sites "for hours on end." Id. (quoting Pamela Mendels, A Library That Would Rather Block Than Offend, N.Y. Times, Jan.18, 1997).

19. The Austin library installed filters after two incidents. In the first, a librarian caught a patron printing child pornography on the library printer. In the second incident, at a different branch, an adult patron was caught teaching children how to access pornography on the Internet.

1. Whether Less Restrictive Means are Available

Defendant alleges that the Policy is constitutional because it is the least restrictive means available to achieve its interests. The only alternative to filtering, defendant contends, is to have librarians directly monitor what patrons view. Defendant asserts this system would be far more intrusive than using filtering software. Plaintiffs and intervenors respond that there are many less restrictive means available, including designing an acceptable use policy, using privacy screens, using filters that can be turned off for adult use, changing the location of Internet terminals, educating patrons on Internet use, placing time limits on use, and enforcing criminal laws when violations occur.

We find that the Policy is not narrowly tailored because less restrictive means are available to further defendant's interests and, as in Sable, there is no evidence that defendant has tested any of these means over time. First, the installation of privacy screens is a much less restrictive alternative that would further defendant's interest in preventing the development of a sexually hostile environment. . . . Second, there is undisputed evidence in the record that charging library staff with casual monitoring of Internet use is neither extremely intrusive nor a change from other library policies. . . . Third, filtering software could be installed on only some Internet terminals and minors could be limited to using those terminals. Alternately, the library could install filtering software that could be turned off when an adult is using the terminal. While we find that all of these alternatives are less restrictive than the Policy, we do not find that any of them would necessarily be constitutional if implemented. That question is not before us.

2. Whether the Policy Is Overinclusive . . .

In examining the specific Policy before us, we find it overinclusive because, on its face, it limits the access of all patrons, adult and juvenile, to material deemed fit for juveniles. It is undisputed that the Policy requires that "[i]f the Library Director considers a particular Web site to violate . . . [the Virginia Harmful to Juveniles Statute], the Web site should be blocked under the policy for adult as well as juvenile patrons." . . . It has long been a matter of settled law that restricting what adults may read to a level appropriate for minors is a violation of the free speech guaranteed by the First Amendment and the Due Process Clause of the Fourteenth Amendment. See Reno v. ACLU, 521 U.S. 844 (1997) ("It is true that we have repeatedly recognized the governmental interest in protecting children from harmful materials but that interest does not justify an unnecessarily broad suppression of speech addressed to adults.") (citations omitted); Butler v. Michigan, 352 U.S. 380, 383 (1957) (restricting adults to what is appropriate for juveniles is "not reasonably restricted to the evil with which it is said to deal"). . . .

3. Whether X-Stop Is the Least Restrictive Filtering Software

Defendant claims that X-Stop is the least restrictive filtering software currently available and, therefore, the Policy is narrowly tailored as applied. Our finding that the Policy is unconstitutional on its face makes this argument moot. . . .

Plaintiffs and intervenors allege that even if the Policy were to survive strict scrutiny analysis, the Court would have to find it unconstitutional under the doctrine of prior restraint because it provides neither sufficient standards to limit the discretion of the decisionmaker nor adequate procedural safeguards. Defendant responds that the Policy is not a prior restraint because it only prohibits viewing certain sites in Loudoun County public libraries, and not in the whole of Loudoun County.

Preventing prior restraints of speech is an essential component of the First Amendment's free speech guarantee. See Freedman v. Maryland, 380 U.S. 51, 58 (1965). . . .

It is undisputed that the Policy lacks any provision for prior judicial determinations before material is censored. . . . We find that the Policy includes neither sufficient standards nor adequate procedural safeguards. As to the first issue, the defendant's discretion to censor is essentially unbounded. The Policy itself speaks only in the broadest terms about child pornography, obscenity, and material deemed harmful to juveniles and fails to include any guidelines whatsoever to help librarians determine what falls within these broad categories. . . . There are no standards by which a reviewing authority can determine if the decisions made were appropriate.

The degree to which the Policy is completely lacking in standards is demonstrated by the defendant's willingness to entrust all preliminary blocking decisions — and, by default, the overwhelming majority of final decision — to a private vendor, Log-On Data Corp. Although the defendant argues that X-Stop is the best available filter, a defendant cannot avoid its constitutional obligation by contracting out its decision[-]making to a private entity. Such abdication of its obligation is made even worse by the undisputed facts here. Specifically, defendant concedes that it does not know the criteria by which Log-On Data makes its blocking decisions. . . . It is also undisputed that Log-On Data does not base its blocking decisions on any legal definition of obscenity or even on the parameters of defendant's Policy. . . . Thus, on this record, we find that the defendant has not satisfied the first prong of prior restraint analysis, establishing adequate standards.

In addition, the Policy also fails to include adequate procedural safeguards. The three minimum procedural safeguards required are (1) a specific brief time period of imposition before judicial review; (2) expeditious judicial review; and (3) the censor bearing the burden of proof. The Policy, even including the alleged protections of the unofficial "unblocking policy," is inadequate in each of these respects. . . .

COMMENTS AND QUESTIONS

1. Is a library's decision to filter Internet content more like a limited acquisition decision or a decision to censor content? Is it the same as purchasing

a set of Encyclopedia and then removing certain volumes, or rather a decision only to purchase certain volumes in the first place? Does it matter? If filtering is the same as censorship, is it a problem that private entities can make these decisions without worrying about the First Amendment?

2. Is it possible to reconcile the *American Library Association* case with the *Reno* and *Ashcroft* cases?

3. Is the problem raised by the *Loudoun* decisions "filtering" or the purported government interest in protecting its employees from a hostile work environment?

4. Under these decisions, can *Loudoun* take steps to implement a filtering policy consistent with the First Amendment? What steps could a public library take?

5. Would the result be different if instead of purchasing "unlimited" Internet access and then employing a filter, Loudoun County subscribed to an Internet service provider that specialized in "family friendly" Internet access?

6. Could a state adopt a policy of filtering for computers used by state employees in government offices? *See* Urofsky v. Gilmore, 216 F.3d 401 (4th Cir. 2000) (upholding a Virginia statute restricting state employees from accessing sexually explicit materials on government computers).

7. What if the state itself is the Internet service provider? Could it filter objectionable content? Would it depend upon whether private Internet service providers had the same power? *Consider* Lehman v. Shaker Heights, 418 U.S. 298, 304 (1974) (upholding a city ordinance prohibiting city public transportation from selling political advertising because the government was involved in a "commercial venture" and advertising spaces on buses are not a public forum).

8. What if a library refuses to block access to Internet content? Could it be subject to damages if minors view material that is considered harmful? *Consider* Kathleen R. v. City of Livermore, 87 Cal. App. 4th 684, 104 Cal. Rptr. 2d 772 (Cal. Ct. App. 2001) (concluding that 47 U.S.C. §230(c)(1) immunized a library as an information service provider). Section 230 immunity is examined in greater detail in Section E of this chapter.

9. The majority of the court in United States v. American Library Association held CIPA to be constitutionally valid. Is this reconcilable with the *Loudon* decisions?

10. What are the problems with the legislation in the *American Library Association* case identified by the dissenting judges?

11. In his dissent in United States v. American Library Association, Justice Stevens suggested that there were a number of less restrictive alternatives to achieve Congress's aims in enacting CIPA. What were the alternatives, and were his arguments convincing on this point?

3. Violence

VIDEO SOFTWARE DEALERS v. SCHWARZENEGGER

No. 07-16620 (9th Cir., Feb. 20, 2009)

Judge CALLAHAN, Circuit Judge:

[This appeal concerned the constitutionality of a Californian state law that imposed labeling requirements on violent video games, as well as restrictions on sales and licensing of those games to minors. In affirming the district court's grant of summary judgment, the court held that the statute was a presumptively invalid content-based restriction on speech, subject to strict scrutiny. It further held that the state had failed to establish a compelling state interest or that the law was sufficiently narrowly tailored to pass strict scrutiny.]

IV.

[The court rejected a claim by the state that it should change the standard of review for the violent video games in line with a series of cases that lowered the standard of review for certain kinds of obscene speech addressed to minors. The court held that the violent speech contained in the video games did not amount to the kind of speech that would justify a lower standard of scrutiny.]

V.

Accordingly, we review the Act's content-based prohibitions under strict scrutiny. As noted above, "[c]ontent-based regulations are presumptively invalid," *R.A.V.*, 505 U.S. at 382, and to survive the Act "must be narrowly tailored to promote a compelling Government interest." *Playboy Entm't Group, Inc.*, 529 U.S. at 813. Further, "[i]f a less restrictive alternative would serve the Government's purpose, the legislature must use that alternative." *Id.*

A.

The Legislature stated that it had two compelling interests in passing the Act: (1) "preventing violent, aggressive, and antisocial behavior"; and (2) "preventing psychological or neurological harm to minors who play violent video games." Although there was some early confusion over whether the State was relying on both of these interests, the State subsequently clarified that "[t]he physical and psychological wellbeing of children is the concern of the Act," as distinguished from the interest of protecting third parties from violent behavior. The State's focus is on the actual harm to the brain of the child playing the video game. Therefore, we will not assess the Legislature's purported interest in the prevention of "violent, aggressive, and antisocial behavior."

The Supreme Court has recognized that "there is a compelling interest in protecting the physical and psychological well-being of minors." *Sable Commc'ns of Cal., Inc.*, 492 U.S. at 126; *see also Entm't Software Ass'n v. Swanson*, 519 F.3d 768, 771 (8th Cir. 2008); *Interactive Digital Software Ass'n*, 329 F.3d at 958; *Nunez by Nunez v. City of San Diego*, 114 F.3d 935, 944 (9th Cir. 1997); *Maleng*, 325 F. Supp. 2d at 1186-87. Notwithstanding this abstract compelling interest, when the government seeks to restrict speech "[i]t must demonstrate that the recited harms are real, not merely conjectural, and that the regulation will in fact alleviate these harms in a direct and material way." *Turner Broad. Sys., Inc. v. FCC*, 512 U.S. 622, 664 (1994) (plurality op.); *Swanson*, 519 F.3d at 771; *Interactive Digital Software Ass'n*, 329 F.3d at 958-59. Although we must accord deference to the predictive judgments of the legislature, our "obligation is to assure that, in formulating its judgments, [the legislature] has drawn reasonable inferences based on substantial evidence." *Turner Broad. Sys., Inc. v. FCC*, 520 U.S. 180, 195 (1997) (citations and quotation marks omitted); *see also Playboy Entm't Group, Inc.*, 529 U.S. at 822 ("This is not to suggest that a 10,000-page record must be compiled in every case or that the Government must delay in acting to address a real problem; but the Government must present more than anecdote and supposition. The question is whether an actual problem has been proved. . . .").

In evaluating the State's asserted interests, we must distinguish the State's interest in protecting minors from actual psychological or neurological harm from the State's interest in controlling minors' thoughts. The latter is not legitimate. The Supreme Court has warned that the

> government cannot constitutionally premise legislation on the desirability of controlling a person's private thoughts. First Amendment freedoms are most in danger when the government seeks to control thought or to justify its laws for that impermissible end. The right to think is the beginning of freedom, and speech must be protected from the government because speech is the beginning of thought.

Ashcroft, 535 U.S. at 253 (citation and internal quotation marks omitted.) In *Kendrick*, the Seventh Circuit commented on a psychological harm rationale in the violent video game context:

> Violence has always been and remains a central interest of humankind and a recurrent, even obsessive theme of culture both high and low. It engages the interest of children from an early age, as anyone familiar with the classic fairy tales collected by Grimm, Andersen, and Perrault is aware. To shield children right up to the age of 18 from exposure to violent descriptions and images would not only be quixotic, but deforming; it would leave them unequipped to cope with the world as we know it.

244 F.3d at 579; *see also Interactive Digital Software Ass'n*, 329 F.3d at 960 ("Speech that is neither obscene as to youths nor subject to some other legitimate proscription cannot be suppressed solely to protect the young from

ideas or images that a legislative body thinks unsuitable for them.") (citation and quotation marks omitted). Because the government may not restrict speech in order to control a minor's thoughts, we focus on the State's psychological harm rationale in terms of some actual effect on minors' psychological health.

Whether the State's interest in preventing psychological or neurological harm to minors is legally compelling depends on the evidence the State proffers of the effect of video games on minors. Although the Legislature is entitled to some deference, the courts are required to review whether the Legislature has drawn reasonable inferences from the evidence presented. *See Turner Broad. Sys., Inc.*, 520 U.S. at 195. Here, the State relies on a number of studies in support of its argument that there is substantial evidence of a causal effect between minors playing violent video games and actual psychological harm.

The State relies heavily on the work of Dr. Craig Anderson, pointing to Dr. Anderson's 2004 updated meta-analysis called *An update on the effects of playing violent video games.* Craig A. Anderson, *An update on the effects of playing violent video games*, 27 J. Adolescence 113 (2004). This article states that it "reveals that exposure to violent video games is significantly linked to increases in aggressive behaviour, aggressive cognition, aggressive affect, and cardiovascular arousal, and to decreases in helping behaviour." Even upon lay review, however, the disclaimers in this article, alone, significantly undermine the inferences drawn by the State in support of its psychological harm rationale. First, Dr. Anderson remarks on the relative paucity of the video game literature and concedes that the violent video game literature is not sufficiently large to conduct a detailed meta-analysis of the specific methodological features of other studies, many of which were themselves flawed. Second, he further states that "[t]here is not a large enough body of samples . . . for truly sensitive tests of potential age difference in susceptibility to violent video game effects," and jettisons mid-article his exploration of the effect of age differences (i.e., over-eighteen versus under-eighteen). It appears that he abandoned the age aspect of the study, in part, because "there was a hint that the aggressive behaviour [sic] results might be slightly larger for the 18 and over group." He concludes the meta-analysis with the admission that there is a "glaring empirical gap" in video game violence research due to "the lack of longitudinal studies."

Thus, Dr. Anderson's research has readily admitted flaws that undermine its support of the State's interest in regulating video games sales and rentals to minors, perhaps most importantly its retreat from the study of the psychological effects of video games as related to the age of the person studied. Although not dispositive of this case, we note that other courts have either rejected Dr. Anderson's research or found it insufficient to establish a causal link between violence in video games and psychological harm. *See Kendrick*, 244 F.3d at 578; *Granholm*, 426 F. Supp. 2d at 653; *Entm't Software Ass'n v. Hatch*, 443 F. Supp. 2d 1065, 1069 & n.1 (D. Minn. 2006); *Blagojevich*, 404 F. Supp. 2d at 1063.

The State also relies on a study of the effects of video game violence on adolescents, conducted by Dr. Douglas Gentile, which studied eighth and ninth graders and concluded that "[a]dolescents who expose themselves to greater amounts of video game violence were more hostile" and reported getting into more arguments and fights and performing poorly in school. Douglas A. Gentile et al., *The effects of violent video game habits on adolescent hostility, aggressive behaviors, and school performance*, 27 J. Adolescence 5 (2004). The extent to which this study supports the State's position is suspect for similar reasons as Dr. Anderson's work. First, this study states that due to its "correlational nature" it could not directly answer the following question: "Are young adolescents more hostile and aggressive because they expose themselves to media violence, or do previously hostile adolescents prefer violent media?" Second, this study largely relates to the player's violent or aggressive behavior toward others — which, as noted above, is not the interest relied on by the State here — rather than the psychological or neurological harm to the player. Moreover, the study glaringly states that "[i]t is important to note . . . that this study is limited by its correlational nature. *Inferences about causal direction should be viewed with caution*" (emphasis added). Finally, Dr. Gentile's study suggests that "[a]dditional experimental and longitudinal research is needed."

Additionally, the State relies on a study by Dr. Jeanne Funk for the proposition that video games can lead to desensitization to violence in minors. Jeanne B. Funk et al., *Violence exposure in real-life, video games, television, movies, and the internet: is there desensitization?*, 27 J. Adolescence 23 (2004). Like the others, this study presents only an attenuated path between video game violence and desensitization. It specifically disclaims that it is based on correlation principles and that "causality was not studied."

Finally, the State relies on a two-page press release from Indiana University regarding the purported connection between violent video games and altered brain activity in the frontal lobe. Press Release, Indiana University School of Medicine, Aggressive Youths, Violent Video Games Trigger Unusual Brain Activity (Dec. 2, 2002). The research described, conducted in part by Dr. Kronenberger, has been criticized by courts that have reviewed it in depth. *See Blagojevich*, 404 F. Supp. 2d at 1063-65 ("Dr. Kronenberger conceded that his studies only demonstrate a correlative, not a causal, relationship between high media violence exposure and children who experience behavioral disorders [or] decreased brain activity. . . ."); *Granholm*, 426 F. Supp. 2d at 653 ("Dr. Kronenberger's research not only fails to provide concrete evidence that there is a connection between violent media and aggressive behavior, it also fails to distinguish between video games and other forms of media.").

In sum, the evidence presented by the State does not support the Legislature's purported interest in preventing psychological or neurological harm. Nearly all of the research is based on correlation, not evidence of causation, and most of the studies suffer from significant, admitted flaws in methodology as they relate to the State's claimed interest. None of the research establishes or suggests a causal link between minors playing violent video games and actual psychological or neurological harm, and inferences to that effect would not be reasonable. In fact, some of the studies caution against inferring causation. Although we do not require the State to demonstrate a "scientific certainty," the State must come forward with more than it has. As a result, the State has not met its burden to demonstrate a compelling interest.

B.

Even if we assume that the State demonstrated a compelling interest in preventing psychological or neurological harm, the State still has the burden of demonstrating that the Act is narrowly tailored to further that interest, and that there are no less restrictive alternatives that would further the Act. *Playboy Entm't Group, Inc.*, 529 U.S. at 813. We hold that the State has not demonstrated that less restrictive alternative means are not available.

Instead of focusing its argument on the possibility of less restrictive means, the State obscures the analysis by focusing on the "most effective" means, which it asserts is the one thousand dollar penalty imposed for each violation. Specifically, the State argues that the ESRB rating system, a voluntary system without the force of law or civil penalty, is not a less-restrictive alternative means of furthering the Legislature's purported compelling interest. Acknowledging that the industry has implemented new enforcement mechanisms, the State nevertheless argues that the ESRB does not adequately prevent minors from purchasing M-rated games. The State also dismisses the notion that parental controls on modern gaming systems could serve the government's purposes, arguing that there is no evidence that this technology existed at the time the Act was passed. *But see Foti*, 451 F. Supp. 2d at 833 (suggesting that such controls could be a less-restrictive measure); *cf. Reno*, 521 U.S. at 876-77 (finding relevant the fact that a reasonably effective method by which parents could prevent children from accessing internet material which parents believed to be inappropriate "will soon be widely available").

Further, the State does not acknowledge the possibility that an enhanced education campaign about the ESRB rating system directed at retailers and parents would help achieve government interests. *See also Playboy*, 529 U.S. at 816 ("When a plausible, less restrictive alternative is offered to a content based speech restriction, it is the Government's obligation to prove that the alternative will be ineffective to achieve its goals."); *44 Liquormart, Inc. v. Rhode Island*, 517 U.S. 484, 507-08 (1996) (plurality op.) (striking down ban on advertising alcohol prices because of less restrictive alternatives, such as an educational campaign or counter-speech). The State appears to be singularly focused on the "most effective" way to further its goal, instead of the "least restrictive means," and has not shown why the less-restrictive means would be ineffective.

Even assuming that the State's interests in enacting the Act are sufficient, the State has not demonstrated why less restrictive means would not forward its interests. The Act, therefore, is not narrowly tailored. Based on the foregoing, and in light of the presumptive invalidity of content-based restrictions, we conclude that the Act fails under strict scrutiny review.

VI.

Finally, we evaluate the constitutionality of the Act's labeling provision, which requires that the front side of the package of a "violent video game" be labeled with a four squareinch [sic] label that reads "18." Cal. Civ. Code §1746.2. Plaintiffs argue that section 1746.2 unconstitutionally forces video game retailers to carry the State of California's subjective opinion, a message with which it disagrees. The State counters that the "labeling provision impacts the purely commercial aspect regarding retail sales of the covered video games" and, under the resulting rational basis analysis, the labeling requirement is rationally related to the State's "self-evident purpose of communicating to consumers and store clerks that the video game cannot be legally purchased by anyone under 18 years of age."

Generally, "freedom of speech prohibits the government from telling people what they must say." *Rumsfeld v. Forum for Academic & Institutional Rights, Inc.*, 547 U.S. 47, 61 (2006); *see also United States v. United Foods, Inc.*, 533 U.S. 405, 410 (2001); *Riley v. Nat'l Fed'n of the Blind*, 487 U.S. 781, 795 (1988). Commercial speech, however, is generally accorded less protection than other expression. *See United Foods, Inc.*, 533 U.S. at 409. The Court has upheld compelled commercial speech where the state required inclusion of "purely factual and uncontroversial information" in advertising. *See Zauderer v. Office of Disciplinary Counsel*, 471 U.S. 626, 651 (1985) (upholding state's requirement that attorney include in his advertisements a disclosure that clients may be responsible for litigation costs); *see also United States v. Schiff*, 379 F.3d 621, 630-31 (9th Cir. 2004) (holding that the government could compel website operator to post factual information about potential criminal liability if patrons used website to evade taxes); *Nat'l Elec. Mfrs. Ass'n v. Sorrell*, 272 F.3d 104, 113-15 (2d Cir. 2001) (upholding state labeling law that required manufacturers of mercury-containing products to disclose on packaging factual and uncontroversial information about the disposal of mercury-containing products). Compelled disclosures, justified by the need to "dissipate the possibility of consumer confusion or deception," are permissible if the "disclosure requirements are reasonably related to the State's interest in preventing deception of customers." *Zauderer*, 471 U.S. at 651.

Ordinarily, we would initially decide whether video game packaging constitutes separable commercial speech or commercial speech that is "inextricably intertwined" with otherwise fully-protected speech. *See Riley*, 487 U.S. at 795-96 (stating that "[i]t is not clear that . . . speech is necessarily commercial whenever it relates to [a] person's financial motivation for speaking"). That analysis would direct what level of scrutiny to apply to the labeling requirement. However, we need not decide that question because the labeling requirement fails even under the factual information and deception prevention standards set forth in *Zauderer*. Our holding above, that the Act's sale and rental prohibition is unconstitutional, negates the State's argument that the labeling provision only requires that video game retailers carry "purely factual and uncontroversial information" in advertising. *Zauderer*, 471 U.S. at 651. Unless the Act can clearly and legally characterize a video game as "violent" and not subject to First Amendment protections, the "18" sticker does not convey factual information.

Moreover, the labeling requirement fails *Zauderer*'s rational relationship test, which asks if the "disclosure requirements are reasonably related to the State's interest in preventing deception of customers." *Id.* at 651. Our determination that the Act is unconstitutional eliminates the alleged deception that the State's labeling requirement would purportedly prevent: the misleading of consumers and retailers by the ESRB age ratings that already appear on the video games' packaging. Since the Act is invalid and, as a result, there is no state-mandated age threshold for the purchase or rental of video games, there is no chance for deception based on the possibly conflicting ESRB rating labels. In fact, the State's mandated label would arguably now convey a false statement that certain conduct is illegal when it is not, and the State has no legitimate reason to force retailers to affix false information on their products. *See Hatch*, 443 F. Supp. 2d at 1072, *aff'd on other grounds*, *Swanson*, 519 F.3d 768.

VII.

... [T]he district court's grant of summary judgment to Plaintiffs and denial of the State's cross-motion for summary judgment is AFFIRMED.

COMMENTS AND QUESTIONS

1. What was the compelling state interest claimed by the state in the *Video Software Dealers* case? Was the court convinced of the state's argument? Do you find the court's analysis compelling?

2. How does the court describe the relationship between freedom of speech and freedom of private thought? Is freedom of private thought an aspect of First Amendment protection? On the importance of freedom of thought as an aspect of First Amendment Protection, see also Neil Richards, *Intellectual Privacy*, 87 Tex. L. Rev. 387 (2008).

3. What evidence does the state put forward to support its argument that the legislation is supported by a compelling state interest? How does the court view this evidence? Do you agree with the court's reasoning on this point? What other evidence might the state have brought to support its claim of a compelling state interest?

4. On what basis does the court hold that the statute is not sufficiently narrowly tailored to pass the strict scrutiny test? Do you agree? How does this analysis compare with the analyses in *Reno* and *Ashcroft, supra*? Should it be permissible for courts to compare a legislative alternative with other kinds of alternatives, such as technology and public education, when considering whether legislation is the least restrictive alternative available to the state? Why/why not?

5. How does the court deal with the labeling provisions of the statute? What is the constitutional concern about "compelled speech"? We will come back to this issue in *Pruneyard v. Robins, infra*.

C. Anonymous Communications

As discussed in the Branscomb essay at the beginning of this chapter, anonymity is an important feature of Internet communications. Through the use of aliases and pseudonyms, individuals may mask their true identities in cyberspace. In addition to allowing individuals to experiment, some studies have revealed that the anonymity provided by Internet transactions has helped to eliminate discrimination against women and minorities when purchasing automobiles. Of course, anonymity also raises the potential for abuse, permitting individuals to defame, defraud, and harass individuals in cyberspace. The following materials examine anonymity and its role under the First Amendment and the legal limits to maintaining anonymity in cyberspace. Once again, we will begin by examining pre-Internet cases before examining whether the Internet changes such inquiry.

Problem 3.0

As General Counsel to StarttUp, you receive a subpoena demanding the production of documents identifying a StarttUp subscriber who uses the alias — Citizen X. After calling the attorney issuing the subpoena, you discover that Citizen X apparently posted a very critical message about the plaintiff, a large computer software manufacturer, on one of StarttUp's message boards. The plaintiff, who desires to remain anonymous, is now suing Citizen X for, among other things, defamation.

Alan and Barbara both believe that you should take steps to challenge the subpoena because subscriber privacy is extremely important to the long-term success of your business. StarttUp's privacy policy, however, clearly states that you will turn over subscriber information if required to do so by law. What should you do? What steps should you take? Does the law require you to notify Citizen X? Should the law require that such notification be given? Does your position change if the party seeking the identity of the subscriber is the government and not a private litigant?

> **Problem 3.1**
>
> After you deal with the subpoena issue for Alan and Barbara, Cora comes to see you and mentions that she has been speaking to Barbara about the subpoena issued to StarttUp. Cora is now concerned that she may receive a subpoena with respect to her GOL blog. She is concerned that some of the anonymous commenters on the blog might post material that could lead to legal action either because it criticizes public or private organizations, or because it is potentially defamatory of individuals discussed on the blog. Cora currently has no policy about protecting the anonymity of commenters on the blog. She seeks your advice as to whether she should develop such a policy and, if so, what it should say. She also wants to know what she should do if she does receive a subpoena seeking identifying information about any of her commenters? Should she notify the commenter whose identity has been sought?

1. The Right to Speak Anonymously

TALLEY v. CALIFORNIA

362 U.S. 60 (1960)

Mr. Justice BLACK delivered the opinion of the Court.

The question presented here is whether the provisions of a Los Angeles City ordinance restricting the distribution of handbills "abridge the freedom of speech and of the press secured against state invasion by the Fourteenth Amendment of the Constitution." The ordinance, [prohibited the distribution of any handbill that did not disclose the identity of the drafter and distributor].

The petitioner was arrested and tried in a Los Angeles Municipal Court for violating this ordinance [by distributing handbills]. . . .

The handbills urged readers to help the organization carry on a boycott against certain merchants and businessmen, whose names were given, on the ground that, as one set of handbills said, they carried products of "manufacturers who will not offer equal employment opportunities to Negroes, Mexicans, and Orientals." There also appeared a blank, which, if signed, would request enrollment of the signer as a "member of National Consumers Mobilization," and which was preceded by a statement that: "I believe that every man should have an equal opportunity for employment no matter what his race, religion, or place of birth." . . .

The broad ordinance now before us, barring distribution of "any hand-bill in any place under any circumstances," falls precisely under the ban of our prior cases unless this ordinance is saved by the qualification that handbills can be distributed if they have printed on them the names and addresses of the persons who prepared, distributed or sponsored them. . . . Counsel has urged that this ordinance is aimed at providing a way to identify those responsible for fraud, false advertising and libel. Yet the ordinance is in no manner so limited, nor have we been referred to any legislative history indicating such a purpose. Therefore we do not pass on the validity of an ordinance limited to prevent these or any other supposed evils. This ordinance simply bars all handbills under all circumstances anywhere that do not have the names and addresses printed on them in the place the ordinance requires. . . .

Anonymous pamphlets, leaflets, brochures and even books have played an important role in the progress of mankind. Persecuted groups and sects from time to time throughout history have been able to criticize oppressive practices and laws either anonymously or not at all. The obnoxious press licensing law of England, which was also enforced on the Colonies was due in part to the knowledge that exposure of the names of printers, writers and distributors would lessen the circulation of literature critical of the government. The old seditious libel cases in England show the lengths to which government had to go to find out who was responsible for books that were obnoxious to the rulers. John Lilburne was whipped, pilloried and fined for refusing to answer questions designed to get evidence to convict him or someone else for the secret distribution of books in England. Two Puritan Ministers, John Penry and John Udal, were sentenced to death on charges that they were responsible for writing, printing or publishing books. Before the Revolutionary War colonial patriots frequently had to conceal their authorship or distribution of literature that easily could have brought down on them prosecutions by English-controlled courts. Along about that time the Letters of Junius were written and the identity of their author is unknown to this day. Even the Federalist Papers, written in favor of the adoption of our Constitution, were published under fictitious names. It is plain that anonymity has sometimes been assumed for the most constructive purposes.

We have recently had occasion to hold in two cases that there are times and circumstances when States may not compel members of groups engaged in the dissemination of ideas to be publicly identified. Bates v. City of Little Rock, 361 U.S. 51 (1960); N.A.A.C.P. v. State of Alabama, 357 U.S. 449, 462 (1958). The reason for those holdings was that identification and fear of reprisal might deter perfectly peaceful discussions of public matters of importance. This broad Los Angeles ordinance is subject to the same infirmity. We hold that it . . . is void on its face. . . .

[Concurring opinion of HARLAN, J., omitted.]

Mr. Justice CLARK, whom Mr. Justice FRANKFURTER and Mr. Justice WHITTAKER join, dissenting.

To me, Los Angeles' ordinance cannot be read as being void on its face. . . . As I read it, the ordinance here merely prohibits the distribution of a handbill which does not carry the identification of the name of the person who "printed, wrote, compiled . . . manufactured (or) . . . caused" the distribution of it. There could well be a compelling reason for such a requirement. . . .

Therefore, before passing upon the validity of the ordinance, I would weigh the interests of the public in its enforcement against the claimed right of Talley. The record is barren of any claim, much less proof, that he will suffer any injury whatever by identifying the handbill with his name. Unlike N.A.A.C.P. v. State of Alabama, 357 U.S. 449 (1958) which is relied upon, there is neither allegation nor proof that Talley or any group sponsoring him would suffer "economic reprisal, loss of employment, threat of physical coercion (or) other manifestations of public hostility." 357 U.S. at 462. Talley makes no showing whatever to support his contention that a restraint upon his freedom of speech will result from the enforcement of the ordinance. The existence of such a restraint is necessary before we can strike the ordinance down.

But even if the State had this burden, which it does not, the substantiality of Los Angeles' interest in the enforcement of the ordinance sustains its validity. Its chief law enforcement officer says that the enforcement of the ordinance prevents "fraud, deceit, false advertising, negligent use of words, obscenity, and libel," and, as we have said, that such was its purpose. In the absence of any showing to the contrary by Talley, this appears to me entirely sufficient.

I stand second to none in supporting Talley's right of free speech — but not his freedom of anonymity. The Constitution says nothing about freedom of anonymous speech. In fact, this Court has approved laws requiring no less than Los Angeles' ordinance. . . . First, Lewis Publishing Co. v. Morgan, 229 U.S. 288 (1913), upheld an Act of Congress requiring any newspaper using the second-class mails to publish the names of its editor, publisher, owner, and stockholders. 39 U.S.C. §233, 39 U.S.C.A. §233. Second, in the Federal Regulation of Lobbying Act, 2 U.S.C. §267, 2 U.S.C.A. §267, Congress requires those engaged in lobbying to divulge their identities and give "a modicum of information" to Congress. United States v. Harriss, 347 U.S. 612, 625 (1954). Third, the several States have corrupt practices acts outlawing, inter alia, the distribution of anonymous publications with reference to political candidates. While these statutes are leveled at political campaign and election practices, the underlying ground sustaining their validity applies with equal force here. . . .

All that Los Angeles requires is that one who exercises his right of free speech through writing or distributing handbills identify himself just as does one who speaks from the platform. The ordinance makes for the responsibility in writing that is present in public utterance. When and if the application of such an ordinance in a given case encroaches on First Amendment freedoms, then will be soon enough to strike that application down. But no such restraint has been shown here. . . .

McIntyre v. Ohio Elections Commission

514 U.S. 334 (1995)

Justice STEVENS delivered the opinion of the Court.

The question presented is whether an Ohio statute that prohibits the distribution of anonymous campaign literature is a "law . . . abridging the freedom of speech" within the meaning of the First Amendment. . . .

Ohio maintains that the statute under review is a reasonable regulation of the electoral process. The State does not suggest that all anonymous publications are pernicious or that a statute totally excluding them from the marketplace of ideas would be valid. This is a wise (albeit implicit) concession, for the anonymity of an author is not ordinarily a sufficient reason to exclude her work product from the protections of the First Amendment.

"Anonymous pamphlets, leaflets, brochures and even books have played an important role in the progress of mankind." Talley v. California, 362 U.S. [60, 64 (1960)]. Great works of literature have frequently been produced by authors writing under assumed names. Despite readers' curiosity and the public's interest in identifying the creator of a work of art, an author generally is free to decide whether or not to disclose his or her true identity. The decision in favor of anonymity may be motivated by fear of economic or official retaliation, by concern about social ostracism, or merely by a desire to preserve as much of one's privacy as possible. Whatever the motivation may be, at least in the field of literary endeavor, the interest in having anonymous works enter the marketplace of ideas unquestionably outweighs any public interest in requiring disclosure as a condition of entry. Accordingly, an author's decision to remain anonymous, like other decisions concerning omissions or additions to the content of a publication, is an aspect of the freedom of speech protected by the First Amendment.

The freedom to publish anonymously extends beyond the literary realm. In *Talley*, the Court held that the First Amendment protects the distribution of unsigned handbills urging readers to boycott certain Los Angeles merchants who were allegedly engaging in discriminatory employment practices. Writing for the Court, Justice Black noted that "[p]ersecuted groups and sects from time to time throughout history have been able to criticize oppressive practices and laws either anonymously or not at all." . . . Justice Black recalled England's abusive press licensing laws and seditious libel prosecutions, and he reminded us that even the arguments favoring the ratification of the Constitution advanced in the Federalist Papers were published under fictitious names. . . . On occasion, quite apart from any threat of persecution, an advocate may believe her ideas will be more persuasive if her readers are unaware of her identity. Anonymity thereby provides a way for a writer who may be personally unpopular to ensure that readers will not prejudge her message simply because they do not like its proponent. Thus, even in the field of political rhetoric, where "the identity of the speaker is an important component of many attempts to persuade," City of Ladue v. Gilleo, 512 U.S. 43, 56 (1994) (footnote omitted), the most effective advocates have sometimes opted for anonymity. The specific holding in *Talley* related to advocacy of an economic boycott, but the Court's reasoning embraced a respected tradition of anonymity in the advocacy of political causes. This tradition is perhaps best exemplified by the secret ballot, the hard-won right to vote one's conscience without fear of retaliation. . . .

Nevertheless, the State argues that, even under the strictest standard of review, the disclosure requirement . . . is justified by two important and legitimate state interests. Ohio judges its interest in preventing fraudulent and libelous statements and its interest in providing the electorate with relevant information to be sufficiently compelling to justify the anonymous speech ban. These two interests necessarily overlap to some extent, but it is useful to discuss them separately.

Insofar as the interest in informing the electorate means nothing more than the provision of additional information that may either buttress or undermine the argument in a document, we think the identity of the speaker is no different from other components of the document's content that the author is free to include or exclude.[11] We have already held that the State may not compel a newspaper that prints editorials critical of a particular candidate to provide space for a reply by the candidate. Miami Herald Publishing Co. v. Tornillo, 418 U.S. 241 (1974). The simple interest in providing voters with additional relevant information does not justify a state requirement that a writer make statements or disclosures she would otherwise omit. Moreover, in the case of a handbill written by a private citizen who is not known to the recipient, the name and address of the author add little, if anything, to the reader's ability to evaluate the document's message. Thus, Ohio's informational interest is plainly insufficient to support the constitutionality of its disclosure requirement.

The state interest in preventing fraud and libel stands on a different footing. We agree with Ohio's submission that this interest carries special weight during election campaigns when false statements, if credited, may have serious adverse consequences for the public at large. Ohio does not, however, rely solely on [the disclosure requirements] to protect that interest. Its Election Code includes detailed and specific prohibitions against making or disseminating false statements during political campaigns. Ohio Rev. Code Ann. §§3599.09.1(B), 3599.09.2(B) (1988). These regulations apply both

---

11. "Of course, the identity of the source is helpful in evaluating ideas. But 'the best test of truth is the power of the thought to get itself accepted in the competition of the market' (Abrams v. United States, [250 U.S. 616, 630 (1919) (Holmes, J., dissenting)])." Don't underestimate the common man. People are intelligent enough to evaluate the source of an anonymous writing. They can see it is anonymous. They know it is anonymous. They can evaluate its anonymity along with its message, as long as they are permitted, as they must be, to read that message.

to candidate elections and to issue-driven ballot measures. Thus, Ohio's prohibition of anonymous leaflets plainly is not its principal weapon against fraud. Rather, it serves as an aid to enforcement of the specific prohibitions and as a deterrent to the making of false statements by unscrupulous prevaricators. Although these ancillary benefits are assuredly legitimate, we are not persuaded that they justify [the statute's] extremely broad prohibition. . . .

Under our Constitution, anonymous pamphleteering is not a pernicious, fraudulent practice, but an honorable tradition of advocacy and of dissent. Anonymity is a shield from the tyranny of the majority. See generally J. Mill, On Liberty and Considerations on Representative Government 1, 3-4 (R. McCallum ed. 1947). It thus exemplifies the purpose behind the Bill of Rights, and of the First Amendment in particular: to protect unpopular individuals from retaliation — and their ideas from suppression — at the hand of an intolerant society. The right to remain anonymous may be abused when it shields fraudulent conduct. But political speech by its nature will sometimes have unpalatable consequences, and, in general, our society accords greater weight to the value of free speech than to the dangers of its misuse. . . . Ohio has not shown that its interest in preventing the misuse of anonymous election-related speech justifies a prohibition of all uses of that speech. The State may, and does, punish fraud directly. But it cannot seek to punish fraud indirectly by indiscriminately outlawing a category of speech, based on its content, with no necessary relationship to the danger sought to be prevented. One would be hard pressed to think of a better example of the pitfalls of Ohio's blunderbuss approach than the facts of the case before us.

[Concurring opinions of Ginsburg, J., and Thomas, J., omitted.]

[Justice Scalia, joined by Chief Justice Rehnquist, dissented, arguing that the traditions and long established practices of the United States did not support a constitutional right to anonymous electioneering.]

American Civil Liberties Union v. Miller

977 F. Supp. 1228 (N.D. Ga. 1997)

Shoob, Senior District Judge.

. . . Plaintiffs bring this action for declaratory and injunctive relief challenging the constitutionality of Act No. 1029, Ga. Laws 1996, p. 1505, codified at O.C.G.A. §16-9-93.1 ("act" or "statute"). The act makes it a crime for

> any person . . . knowingly to transmit any data through a computer network . . . for the purpose of setting up, maintaining, operating, or exchanging data with an electronic mailbox, home page, or any other electronic information storage bank or point of access to electronic information if such data uses any individual name . . . to falsely identify the person . . .

and for

> any person . . . knowingly to transmit any data through a computer network . . . if such
> data uses any . . . trade name, registered trademark, logo, legal or official seal, or copy-
> righted symbol . . . which would falsely state or imply that such person . . . has permission
> or is legally authorized to use [it] for such purpose when such permission or authorization
> has not been obtained. . . .

Plaintiffs argue that the act has tremendous implications for internet users, many of whom "falsely identify" themselves on a regular basis for the purpose of communicating about sensitive topics without subjecting themselves to ostracism or embarrassment. . . .

Defendants contend that the act prohibits a much narrower class of communications. They interpret it as forbidding only fraudulent transmissions or the appropriation of the identity of another person or entity for some improper purpose. . . .

[T]he Court concludes that plaintiffs are likely to prevail on the merits of their claim. It appears from the record that plaintiffs are likely to prove that the statute imposes content-based restrictions which are not narrowly tailored to achieve the state's purported compelling interest. Furthermore, plaintiffs are likely to show that the statute is overbroad and void for vagueness.

First, because "the identity of the speaker is no different from other components of [a] document's contents that the author is free to include or exclude," McIntyre v. Ohio Elections Comm'n, 514 U.S. 334, 340-42 (1995), the statute's prohibition of internet transmissions which "falsely identify" the sender constitutes a presumptively invalid content-based restriction. See R.A.V. v. St. Paul, 505 U.S. 377, 382 (1992). The state may impose content-based restrictions only to promote a "compelling state interest" and only through use of "the least restrictive means to further the articulated interest." Sable Communications of California, Inc. v. FCC, 492 U.S. 115, 126 (1989). Thus, in order to overcome the presumption of invalidity, defendants must demonstrate that the statute furthers a compelling state interest and is narrowly tailored to achieve it.

Defendants allege that the statute's purpose is fraud prevention, which the Court agrees is a compelling state interest. However, the statute is not narrowly tailored to achieve that end and instead sweeps innocent, protected speech within its scope. Specifically, by its plain language the criminal prohibition applies regardless of whether a speaker has any intent to deceive or whether deception actually occurs. Therefore, it could apply to a wide range of transmissions which "falsely identify" the sender, but are not "fraudulent" within the specific meaning of the criminal code.

Defendants respond that the act does not mean what it says and that, instead, a variety of limiting concepts should be engrafted onto it. First, defendants propose to add an element of fraud, or a specific intent requirement of "intent to defraud" or "intent to deceive" to the act. None of these terms or phrases appears in the statute, however, although they are expressly included in other Georgia criminal statutes which require proof of specific intent. See, e.g., O.C.G.A. §§10-1-453, 16-9-1(a), 16-9-2, and 16-8-3.

Second, defendants contend that the act applies only to persons who misappropriate the identity of another specific entity or person. Again, there is nothing in the language of the act from which a reasonable person would infer such a requirement, and the General Assembly has specifically included analogous elements when it meant to do so. See O.C.G.A. §10-1-453.

Third, defendants seek to limit the restriction on use of trade names, marks, and seals by collapsing the act's two clauses — suggesting that "use" of a mark is prohibited only when it would "falsely identify" the user. Without explanation, this construction borrows the "false identification" portion of the first clause and applies it to the second. In addition to not making sense grammatically, the interpretation also imports into the second clause all of the previously discussed interpretive problems with the phrase "falsely identify."

In construing a statute, the Court must "follow the literal language of the statute 'unless it produces contradiction, absurdity or such an inconvenience as to insure that the legislature meant something else.'" Telecom*USA, Inc. v. Collins, 260 Ga. 362, 363 (1990) (citing Department of Transp. v. City of Atlanta, 255 Ga. 124, 137 (1985)). Only if a statute is "readily susceptible to a narrowing construction" may such an interpretation be applied to save a questionable law. . . . The words and phrases defendants seek to add to the act appear nowhere in it. Moreover, defendants' attempt to interpret the act is so confusing and contradictory that it could not possibly constitute grounds for rejecting the act's plain language. Even if the Court could impose a limiting construction on the act, defendants' brief provides no real guidance on what that construction should be, but instead offers a variety of very different possible interpretations in hopes that the Court will select one. The Court concludes, therefore, that the act is not readily susceptible to a limiting construction and that its plain language is not narrowly tailored to promote a compelling state interest. . . .

The Court concludes that the statute was not drafted with the precision necessary for laws regulating speech. On its face, the act prohibits such protected speech as the use of false identification to avoid social ostracism, to prevent discrimination and harassment, and to protect privacy, as well as the use of trade names or logos in non-commercial educational speech, news, and commentary — a prohibition with well-recognized first amendment problems. Therefore, even if the statute could constitutionally be used to prosecute persons who intentionally "falsely identify" themselves in order to deceive or defraud the public, or to persons whose commercial use of trade names and logos creates a substantial likelihood of confusion or the dilution of a famous mark, the statute is nevertheless overbroad because it operates unconstitutionally for a substantial category of the speakers it covers. Village of Schaumburg v. Citizens for a Better Environment, 444 U.S. 620, 634 (1980).

[The Court also finds the Georgia statute void-for-vagueness, among other reasons, because of its failure to adequately define "falsely identify."]

COMMENTS AND QUESTIONS

1. Why is anonymity considered a right protected by the First Amendment? How is anonymity related to speech?

2. Should anonymity be protected regardless of the type of speech involved? For example, should the First Amendment treat anonymity differently when used as part of a plea for social or political change as opposed to an anonymous e-mail? What constitutional interests are implicated by individual correspondences?

3. Even if the state has a compelling state interest in the identity of an anonymous Internet user, could prohibiting anonymity ever be considered the least restrictive alternative?

4. Do the decisions in *Talley, McIntrye*, and *Miller* guarantee a right to remain anonymous? In other words, does the right to anonymity apply only to the initial publication of the message? To the extent that anonymity is based upon the right to speak, how is that right implicated by postpublication disclosures of identity?

2. The Right to Remain Anonymous

While the preceding materials recognize a general constitutional right to speak anonymously, under what circumstances can the government and other citizens discover the identity of anonymous speakers? In Columbia Ins. Co. v. SeesCandy.Com, 185 F.R.D. 573 (N.D. Cal. 1999), a domain name cybersquatting dispute, the district court noted that on the Internet a "tortfeasor can act pseudonymously or anonymously and may give fictitious or incomplete identifying information. Parties who have been injured by these acts are likely to find themselves chasing the tortfeasor from Internet Service Provider (ISP) to ISP, with little or no hope of actually discovering the identity of the tortfeasor. . . ." In an effort to balance the interests of allowing injured parties to seek redress and the right to speak anonymously, the court suggested the following safeguards:

> First, the plaintiff should identify the missing party with sufficient specificity such that the Court can determine that defendant is a real person or entity who could be sued in federal court. . . .
> Second, the party should identify all previous steps taken to locate the elusive defendant. This element is aimed at ensuring that plaintiffs make a good faith effort to comply with the requirements of service of process and specifically identifying defendants. . . .
> Third, plaintiff should establish to the Court's satisfaction that plaintiff's suit against defendant could withstand a motion to dismiss. . . . A conclusory pleading will never be sufficient to satisfy this element. Pre-service discovery is akin to the process used during criminal investigations to obtain warrants. The requirement that the government show probable cause is, in part, a protection against the misuse of *ex parte* procedures to invade the privacy of one who has done no wrong. A similar requirement is necessary here to

prevent abuse of this extraordinary application of the discovery process and to ensure that plaintiff has standing to pursue an action against defendant. . . .

   Lastly, the plaintiff should file a request for discovery with the Court, along with a statement of reasons justifying the specific discovery requested as well as identification of a limited number of persons or entities on whom discovery process might be served and for which there is a reasonable likelihood that the discovery process will lead to identifying information about defendant that would make service of process possible. . . .

Since *SeesCandy, id.* at 578-580, other courts have confronted this issue each providing its own interpretation. Are the differences between these rules significant? Do they adequately address the concerns raised by efforts to identify anonymous online speakers?

IN RE SUBPOENA DUCES TECUM TO AMERICA ONLINE, INC.

52 Va. Cir. 26 (2000)

KLEIN, J.

   This matter is before the Court on America Online, Inc.'s ("AOL") Motion to Quash Subpoena seeking disclosure of identifying information for four AOL Internet service subscribers.

   Plaintiff Anonymous Publicly Traded Company ("APTC") seeks to learn the identities of the subscribers so that it can properly name them as defendants in an action it has instituted in the state of Indiana. AOL asserts that the First Amendment rights of its subscribers preclude APTC from obtaining the relief it seeks in this Court. For the reasons set forth in this opinion, the Motion To Quash is denied. . . .

   APTC argues that if the subpoena unreasonably burdens the First Amendment rights of the John Does, then the John Does are the proper parties to seek relief from the subpoena, not AOL. APTC's argument ignores longstanding precedent upholding the standing of third parties to seek vindication of First Amendment rights of others in situations analogous to the circumstances presented herein. . . .

   It can not be seriously questioned that those who utilize the "chat rooms" and "message boards" of AOL do so with an expectation that the anonymity of their postings and communications generally will be protected. If AOL did not uphold the confidentiality of its subscribers, as it has contracted to do, absent extraordinary circumstances, one could reasonably predict that AOL subscribers would look to AOL's competitors for anonymity. As such, the *subpoena duces tecum* at issue potentially could have an oppressive effect on AOL. . . .

   This Court must now decide whether the First Amendment right to anonymity should be extended to communications by persons utilizing chat rooms and message boards on the information superhighway. It is beyond question that thousands, perhaps millions, of people communicating by way of the Internet do so with a "desire to preserve as much of [their] privacy as possible."

McIntyre v. Ohio Elections Comm'n, 514 U.S. 334, 342 (1995). "Through the use of chat rooms, any person with a phone line can become a town crier with a voice that resonates farther than it could from any soapbox. Through the use of Web pages, mail exploders and newsgroups, the same individual can become a pamphleteer." Reno v. ACLU, 521 U.S. 844 (1997). To fail to recognize that the First Amendment right to speak anonymously should be extended to communications on the Internet would require this Court to ignore either United States Supreme Court precedent or the realities of speech in the twenty-first century. This Court declines to do either and holds that the right to communicate anonymously on the Internet falls within the scope of the First Amendment's protections.

As AOL conceded at oral argument, however, the right to speak anonymously is not absolute. In that the Internet provides a virtually unlimited, inexpensive, and almost immediate means of communication with tens, if not hundreds, of millions of people, the dangers of its misuse cannot be ignored. The protection of the right to communicate anonymously must be balanced against the need to assure that those persons who choose to abuse the opportunities presented by this medium can be made to answer for such transgressions. Those who suffer damages as a result of tortious or other actionable communications on the Internet should be able to seek appropriate redress by preventing the wrongdoers from hiding behind an illusory shield of purported First Amendment rights. . . .

Nonetheless, before a court abridges the First Amendment right of a person to communicate anonymously on the Internet, a showing, sufficient to enable that court to determine that a true, rather than perceived, cause of action may exist, must be made. AOL proposes that this Court adopt the following two prong test to determine when a subpoena request is reasonable and accordingly would require AOL to identify its subscribers: (1) the party seeking the information must have pled with specificity a prima facie claim that it is the victim of particular tortious conduct and (2) the subpoenaed identity information must be centrally needed to advance that claim. APTC responds that this Court should not, in any way, address the merits of its claim and should merely follow the procedures that APTC asserts are compelled by Va. Code §8.01-411. Although this Court agrees with AOL that APTC must establish that there is a legitimate basis to believe that it may have *bona fide* claims against the John Does before compliance with the *subpoena duces tecum* is ordered, it agrees with APTC that AOL's proposed test is unduly cumbersome. What is sufficient to plead a prima facie case varies from state to state and, sometimes, from court to court. This Court is unwilling to establish any precedent that would support an argument that judges of one state could be required to determine the sufficiency of pleadings from another state when ruling on matters such as the instant motion. . . .

[T]his Court holds that, when a subpoena is challenged under a rule akin to Virginia Supreme Court Rule 4:9(c), a court should only order a non-party, Internet service provider to provide information concerning the identity of a subscriber (1) when the court is satisfied by the pleadings or evidence supplied to that court (2) that the party requesting the subpoena has a legitimate, good faith basis to contend that it may be the victim of conduct actionable in the jurisdiction where suit was filed and (3) the subpoenaed identity information is centrally needed to advance that claim. A review of the Indiana pleadings and the subject Internet postings satisfies this Court that all three prongs of the above-stated test have been satisfied as to the identities of the subscribers utilizing the four e-mail addresses in question.

DOE I AND DOE II v. INDIVIDUALS, WHOSE TRUE NAMES ARE UNKNOWN

Civil Action No. 3:07 CV 909 (CFD), 2008 WL 2428206 (D. Conn. June 13, 2008)

DRONEY, District Judge.

[This case concerned an action brought by two female Yale students who had been targeted on a publicly accessible law school admissions website with derogatory, defamatory, and threatening statements posted by anonymous users of the service. The substantive complaint alleged libel, invasion of privacy, negligent and intentional infliction of emotional distress, and copyright violations in relation to unauthorized use of photographs of the plaintiffs. The plaintiffs issued a subpoena to AT&T for information relating to the identity of a person posting some of the comments in question. The potential defendant used the pseudonym "AK47" on AutoAdmit.com, the online service. Having determined that the potential defendant has a First Amendment right of anonymity, the court turned to the issue of the subpoena.]

The forgoing principles and decisions make clear that Doe 21 has a First Amendment right to anonymous Internet speech, but that the right is not absolute and must be weighed against Doe II's need for discovery to redress alleged wrongs. Courts have considered a number of factors in balancing these two competing interests. This balancing analysis ensures that the First Amendment rights of anonymous Internet speakers are not lost unnecessarily, and that plaintiffs do not use discovery to "harass, intimidate or silence critics in the public forum opportunities presented by the Internet." Dendrite Intern. Inc. v. Doe No. 3, 775 A.2d 756, 771 (N.J. Super. 2001). The Court will address each factor in turn.

First, the Court should consider whether the plaintiff has undertaken efforts to notify the anonymous posters that they are the subject of a subpoena and withheld action to afford the fictitiously named defendants a reasonable opportunity to file and serve opposition to the application. See Krinsky v. Doe 6, 159 Cal. Rptr. 3d 231 (Cal. App. 2008); Dendrite Intern. Inc. v. Doe No. 3, 775 A.2d 756, 760 (N.J. Super. 2001). In this case, the plaintiffs have satisfied this factor by posting notice regarding the subpoenas on AutoAdmit in January of 2008, which allowed the posters ample time to respond, as evidenced by Doe 21's activity in this action.

Second, the Court should consider whether the plaintiff has identified and set forth the exact statements purportedly made by each anonymous poster that the plaintiff alleges constitutes actionable speech. *Dendrite*, 775 A.2d at 760. Doe II has identified the allegedly actionable statements by AK47/Doe 21: the first such statement is "Alex Atkind, Stephen Reynolds, [Doe II], and me: GAY LOVERS;" and the second such statement is "Women named Jill and Doe II should be raped." . . .

The Court should also consider the specificity of the discovery request and whether there is an alternative means of obtaining the information called for in the subpoena. *Sony Music*, 326 F. Supp at 565; Columbia Inc. v. SeesCandy. com, 185 F.R.D. 573, 578, 580 (N.D. Cal. 1999). Here, the subpoena sought, and AT&T provided, only the name, address, telephone number, and email address of the person believed to have posted defamatory or otherwise tortious content about Doe II on AutoAdmit, and is thus sufficiently specific. Furthermore, there are no other adequate means of obtaining the information because AT&T's subscriber data is the plaintiffs' only source regarding the identity of AK47.

Similarly, the Court should consider whether there is a central need for the subpoenaed information to advance the plaintiffs' claims. *America Online, Inc.*, 2000 WL 1210372 at *7; *Dendrite*, 775 A.2d at 760-61. Here, clearly the defendant's identity is central to Doe II's pursuit of her claims against him.

Next, the Court should consider the subpoenaed party's expectation of privacy at the time the online material was posted. *Sony Music*, 326 F. Supp. 2d at 566-67; *Verizon Internet Services*, 257 F. Supp. 2d 244, 267-68 (D.D.C. 2003), rev'd on other grounds, 351 F.3d 1229 (D.C. Cir. 2003). Doe 21's expectation of privacy here was minimal because AT&T's Internet Services Privacy Policy states, in pertinent part: "We may, where permitted or required by law, provide personal identifying information to third parties . . . without your consent . . . To comply with court orders, subpoenas, or other legal or regulatory requirements." Thus, Doe 21 has little expectation of privacy in using AT&T's service to engage in tortious conduct that would subject him to discovery under the federal rules.

Finally, and most importantly, the Court must consider whether the plaintiffs have made an adequate showing as to their claims against the anonymous defendant. Courts have differed on what constitutes such an adequate showing. Several courts have employed standards fairly deferential to the plaintiff, requiring that the plaintiff show a "good faith basis" to contend it may be the victim of conduct actionable in the jurisdiction where the suit was filed; *America Online*, 2000 WL 1213072, at *8; or to show that there is probable cause for a claim against the anonymous defendant; La Societe Metro Cash & Carry France v. Time Warner Cable, No.030197400, 2003 WL 22962857, *7 (Conn. Super. 2003). The Court finds these standards set the threshold for disclosure too low to adequately protect the First Amendment rights of anonymous defendants, and thus declines to follow these approaches. Other courts have required that a plaintiff show its claims can withstand a motion to dismiss. *SeesCandy.com*, 185 F.R.D. at 579; Lassa v. Rongstad, 718 N.W. 2d 673, 687 (Wis. 2006). However, other courts have rejected this procedural label as potentially confusing because of the variations in the motion to dismiss standard in different jurisdictions. See *Krinsky*, 72 Cal Rptr. at 244. Similarly, but more burdensome, some courts have used a standard which required plaintiffs to show their claims could withstand a motion for summary judgment. Best Western Intern., Inc. v. Doe, No. CV-06-1537, 2006 WL 2091695, *4 (D. Ariz. 2006); Doe v. Cahill, 884 A.2d 451, 461 (Del. Supr. 2005). The Court finds this standard to be both potentially confusing and also difficult for a plaintiff to satisfy when she has been unable to conduct any discovery at this juncture. Indeed, it would be impossible to meet this standard for any cause of action which required evidence within the control of the defendant.

Several courts have required that a plaintiff make a concrete showing as to each element of a prima facie case against the defendant. Highfields Capital Management L.P. v. Doe, 385 F. Supp. 2d 969, 976 (N.D. Cal. 2005); *Sony Music*, 326 F. Supp. 2d at 565; *Krinksy* v. Doe 6, 72 Cal. Rptr. 3d at 245; *Dendrite*, 775 A.2d at 760-61. Under such a standard, "[w]hen there is a factual and legal basis for believing [actionable speech] has occurred, the writer's message will not be protected by the First Amendment." *Krinsky*, 72 Cal. Rptr. at 245. The Court finds such a standard strikes the most appropriate balance between the First Amendment rights of the defendant and the interest in the plaintiffs of pursuing their claims, ensuring that the plaintiff "is not merely seeking to harass or embarrass the speaker or stifle legitimate criticism." Id. at 244. Doe II has presented evidence constituting a concrete showing as to each element of a prima facie case of libel against Doe 21. Libel is written defamation. To establish a prima facie case of defamation under Connecticut law, the Doe II must demonstrate that: (1) Doe 21 published a defamatory statement; (2) the defamatory statement identified the plaintiff to a third person; (3) the defamatory statement was published to a third person; and (4) the plaintiff's reputation suffered injury as a result of the statement. Cweklinsky v. Mobil Chem. Co., 837 A.2d 759, 763-64 (Conn. 2004), citing QSP, Inc. v. Aetna Casualty & Surety Co., 773 A.2d 906, 916 (Conn. 2001); 3 Restatement (Second), Torts §558, 580B, at 155, 221-22 (1977); W. Prosser & W. Keeton, Torts (5th Ed. 1984) §113, at 802.

A defamatory statement is defined as a communication that tends to "harm the reputation of another as to lower him in the reputation of the community or to deter third persons from associating or dealing with him. . . ." *QSP, Inc*, 773 A.2d at 916 (internal quotation marks omitted). Doe II alleges, and has presented evidence tending to show that, AK47's statement, "Alex Atkind, Stephen Reynolds, [Doe II], and me: GAY LOVERS," is defamatory, because any discussion of Doe II's sexual behavior on the internet tends to lower her reputation in the community, particular in the case of any potential employers who might search for her name online. . . .

Doe II has also alleged and presented evidence that Doe 21's statement clearly identified Doe II by name and was available to a large number of third persons (peers, colleagues, potential employers), whether they were on Auto-admit for their own purposes, or searched for Doe II via a search engine. Finally, Doe II has alleged and provided evidence that her reputation did suffer injury because of this comment. In her interviews with potential employers in the Fall of 2007, Doe II felt she needed to disclose that existence of this and other such comments on AutoAdmit and explain that she had been targeted by pseudonymous online posters. In addition, this statement has contributed to difficulties in Doe II's relationships with her family, friends, and classmates at Yale Law School.

Thus, the plaintiff has shown sufficient evidence supporting a prima facie case for libel, and thus the balancing test of the plaintiff's interest in pursuing discovery in this case outweighs the defendant's First Amendment right to speak anonymously. The defendant's motion to quash is denied.

III. Defendant's Motion to Proceed Anonymously

Parties to a lawsuit must generally identify themselves. Fed. R. Civ. P. 10(a) (complaint must "include the names of all the parties"). This rule protects the public's legitimate interest in knowing all of the facts involved, including the identities of the parties. K.D. v. City of Norwalk, No. 3:06cv406, 2006 WL 1662905, at *1 (D. Conn. 2006). Thus, "[c]ourts should not permit parties to proceed pseudonymously just to protect the parties' professional or economic life." Doe v. United Services Life Ins. Co., 123 F.R.D. 437, 439 n.1 (S.D.N.Y. 1988). A party may proceed anonymously only after demonstrating "a substantial privacy right which outweighs the customary and constitutionally embedded presumption of openness in judicial proceedings." K.D. v. City of Norwalk, 2006 WL 1662905, at *1 (citing Fed. R. Civ. P. 10(a); Doe v. Stegall, 653 F.2d 180 (5th Cir. 1981)).

Doe 21 has not made a showing of any substantial privacy right or of any potential physical or mental harm as a result of being a named party to this litigation. He argues that other named defendants have been subjected to ridicule on AutoAdmit or lost employment. However, even if Doe 21 could show he was likely to receive the same alleged treatment, which he has not, these harms are not the special harms required in order to proceed anonymously, but rather social stigma, embarrassment, and economic harm, none of which are grounds for proceeding anonymously. See James v. Jacobson, 6. F.3d 233, 238-39 (4th Cir. 1993) (citing cases); *Frank*, 251 F.2d at 324; Guerrilla Girls Inc. v. Kaz, 224 F.R.D. 571, 573 (S.D.N.Y. 2004). In addition, Doe 21's argument that he should be allowed to proceed anonymously because the plaintiffs have been allowed to do so is also without merit and irrelevant to the defendant's status.

Thus, the defendant's motion to proceed anonymously is denied.

DOE v. 2THEMART.COM, INC.

140 F. Supp. 2d 1088 (W.D. Wa. 2001)

ZILLY, District Judge.

This matter comes before the Court on the motion of J. Doe (Doe) to proceed under a pseudonym and to quash a subpoena issued by 2TheMart.com (TMRT) to a local internet service provider, Silicon Investor/InfoSpace, Inc. (InfoSpace). The motion raises important First Amendment issues regarding Doe's right to speak anonymously on the Internet and to proceed in this Court using a pseudonym in order to protect that right. . . .

There is a federal court lawsuit pending in the Central District of California in which the shareholders of TMRT have brought a shareholder derivative class action against the company and its officers and directors alleging fraud on the market. In that litigation, the defendants have asserted as an affirmative defense that no act or omission by the defendants caused the plaintiffs' injury. By subpoena, TMRT seeks to obtain the identity of twenty-three speakers who have participated anonymously on Internet message boards operated by Info-Space. That subpoena is the subject of the present motion to quash.

InfoSpace is a Seattle based Internet company that operates a Web site called "Silicon Investor." The Silicon Investor site contains a series of electronic bulletin boards, and some of these bulletin boards are devoted to specific publically traded companies. InfoSpace users can freely post and exchange messages on these boards. Many do so using Internet pseudonyms, the often fanciful names that people choose for themselves when interacting on the Internet. By using a pseudonym, a person who posts or responds to a message on an Internet bulletin board maintains anonymity.

One of the Internet bulletin boards on the Silicon Investor Web site is specifically devoted to TMRT. According to the brief filed on behalf of J. Doe, "[t]o date, almost 1500 messages have been posted on the TMRT board, covering an enormous variety of topics and posters. Investors and members of the public discuss the latest news about the company, what new businesses it may develop, the strengths and weaknesses of the company's operations, and what its managers and its employees might do better." . . . Past messages posted on the site are archived, so any new user can read and print copies of prior postings.

Some of the messages posted on the TMRT site have been less than flattering to the company. In fact, some have been downright nasty. . . .

TMRT, the defendant in the California lawsuit, issued the present subpoena to InfoSpace pursuant to Fed. R. Civ. P. 45(a)(2). The subpoena seeks, among other things, "[a]ll identifying information and documents, including, but not limited to, computerized or computer stored records and logs, electronic mail (E-mail), and postings on your on-line message boards," concerning a list of twenty-three InfoSpace users, including Truthseeker, Cuemaster, and the current J. Doe, who used the pseudonym NoGuano. These users have posted messages on the TMRT bulletin board or have communicated via the Internet with users who have posted such messages. The subpoena would require InfoSpace to disclose the subscriber information for these twenty-three users, thereby stripping them of their Internet anonymity.

InfoSpace notified these users by e-mail that it had received the subpoena, and gave them time to file a motion to quash. One such user who used the Internet pseudonym NoGuano now seeks to quash the subpoena.[2] . . .

The Internet represents a revolutionary advance in communication technology. It has been suggested that the Internet may be the "greatest innovation in speech since the invention of the printing press[.]" See Raymond Shih Ray Ku, Open Internet Access and Freedom of Speech: A First Amendment Catch-22, 75 Tul. L. Rev. 87, 88 (2000). It allows people from all over the world to exchange ideas and information freely and in "real-time." Through the use of the Internet, "any person with a phone line can become a town crier with a voice that resonates farther than it could from any soapbox." Reno v. ACLU, 521 U.S. 844, 870 (1997). . . .

The free exchange of ideas on the Internet is driven in large part by the ability of Internet users to communicate anonymously. If Internet users could be stripped of that anonymity by a civil subpoena enforced under the liberal rules of civil discovery, this would have a significant chilling effect on Internet communications and thus on basic First Amendment rights. Therefore, discovery requests seeking to identify anonymous Internet users must be subjected to careful scrutiny by the courts.

As InfoSpace has urged, "[u]nmeritorious attempts to unmask the identities of on-line speakers . . . have a chilling effect on" Internet speech. The "potential chilling effect imposed by the unmasking of anonymous speakers would diminish if litigants first were required to make a showing in court of their need for the identifying information." . . .

In the context of a civil subpoena issued pursuant to Fed. R. Civ. P. 45, this Court must determine when and under what circumstances a civil litigant will be permitted to obtain the identity of persons who have exercised their First Amendment right to speak anonymously. There is little in the way of persuasive authority to assist this Court. However, courts that have addressed

---

2. NoGuano has moved anonymously to quash the subpoena. At oral argument, counsel for all parties agreed that NoGuano was entitled to appear before this Court anonymously on the motion to quash. When an individual wishes to protect their First Amendment right to speak anonymously, he or she must be entitled to vindicate that right without disclosing their identity. Accordingly, this Court grants NoGuano's request to proceed under a pseudonym for the purposes of this motion. However, this Court does not hold that a person would be allowed to proceed anonymously in all cases or under any circumstances. The Court need not reach this issue in light of the parties' agreement to allow Doe to proceed anonymously before this Court.

related issues have used balancing tests to decide when to protect an individual's First Amendment rights. . . .

The courts in *SeesCandy.Com* and *America Online, Inc.* . . . required a showing of, at least, a good faith basis for bringing the lawsuit, and both required some showing of the compelling need for the discovery sought. In both cases, the need for the information was especially great because the information sought concerned J. Doe *defendants.* Without the identifying information, the litigation against those defendants could not have continued.

The standard for disclosing the identity of a non-party *witness* must be higher than that articulated in *SeesCandy.Com* and *America Online, Inc.* When the anonymous Internet user is not a party to the case, the litigation can go forward without the disclosure of their identity. Therefore, non-party disclosure is only appropriate in the exceptional case where the compelling need for the discovery sought outweighs the First Amendment rights of the anonymous speaker. Accordingly, this Court adopts the following standard for evaluating a civil subpoena that seeks the identity of an anonymous Internet user who is not a party to the underlying litigation. The Court will consider four factors in determining whether the subpoena should issue. These are whether: (1) the subpoena seeking the information was issued in good faith and not for any improper purpose, (2) the information sought relates to a core claim or defense, (3) the identifying information is directly and materially relevant to that claim or defense, and (4) information sufficient to establish or to disprove that claim or defense is unavailable from any other source.[5]

This test provides a flexible framework for balancing the First Amendment rights of anonymous speakers with the right of civil litigants to protect their interests through the litigation discovery process. The Court shall give weight to each of these factors as the court determines is appropriate under the circumstances of each case. . . .

In the present case, TMRT seeks information it says will validate its defense that "changes in [TMRT] stock prices were *not* caused by the Defendants but by the illegal actions of individuals who manipulated the [TMRT] stock price using the Silicon Investor message boards." This Court must evaluate TMRT's stated need for the information in light of the four factors outlined above. . . .

[After concluding that the subpoenas were sought in good faith, the court examined whether the information sought related to a core claim or defense.] Only when the identifying information is needed to advance core claims or defenses can it be sufficiently material to compromise First Amendment rights. See Silkwood v. Kerr-McGee Corp., 563 F.2d 433, 438 (10th Cir. 1977) (in

5. This Court is aware that many civil subpoenas seeking the identifying information of Internet users may be complied with, and the identifying information disclosed, without notice to the Internet users themselves. This is because some Internet service providers do not notify their users when such a civil subpoena is received. The standard set forth in this Order may guide Internet service providers in determining whether to challenge a specific subpoena on behalf of their users. However, this will provide little solace to Internet users whose Internet service company does not provide them notice when a subpoena is received.

order to overcome the journalistic privilege of maintaining confidential sources, a party seeking to identify those sources must demonstrate, *inter alia,* that the "information goes to the heart of the matter"). If the information relates only to a secondary claim or to one of numerous affirmative defenses, then the primary substance of the case can go forward without disturbing the First Amendment rights of the anonymous Internet users.

The information sought by TMRT does not relate to a core defense. Here, the information relates to only one of twenty-seven affirmative defenses raised by the defendant, the defense that "no act or omission of any of the Defendants was the cause in fact or the proximate cause of any injury or damage to the plaintiffs." This is a generalized assertion of the lack of causation. Defendants have asserted numerous other affirmative defenses that go more "to the heart of the matter," such as the lack of material misstatements by the defendants, actual disclosure of material facts by the defendants, and the business judgment defense. Therefore, this factor also weighs in favor of quashing the subpoena.

Even when the claim or defense for which the information is sought is deemed core to the case, the identity of the Internet users must also be materially relevant to that claim or defense. Under the Federal Rules of Civil Procedure discovery is normally very broad, requiring disclosure of any relevant information that "appears reasonably calculated to lead to the discovery of admissible evidence." . . . But when First Amendment rights are at stake, a higher threshold of relevancy must be imposed. Only when the information sought is directly and materially relevant to a core claim or defense can the need for the information outweigh the First Amendment right to speak anonymously. . . .

TMRT has failed to demonstrate that the identity of the Internet users is directly and materially relevant to a core defense. These Internet users are not parties to the case and have not been named as defendants as to any claim, cross-claim or third-party claim. Therefore, unlike in *SeesCandy.Com* and *America Online, Inc.*, their identity is not needed to allow the litigation to proceed. . . .

[Lastly,] TMRT has failed to demonstrate that the information it needs to establish its defense is unavailable from any other source. The chat room messages are archived and are available to anyone to read and print. TMRT obtained copies of some of these messages and submitted them to this Court. TMRT can therefore demonstrate what was said, when it was said, and can compare the timing of those statements with information on fluctuations in the TMRT stock price. The messages are available for use at trial, and TMRT can factually support its defense without encroaching on the First Amendment rights of the Internet users.

COMMENTS AND QUESTIONS

1. Are the tests articulated in *SeesCandy* and *America Online* the same as suggested by the court in *Doe I and Doe II*? Do these tests differ from the test in *2TheMart*?

2. How does the test articulated in *2TheMart* differ from the earlier decisions? Should the test used to reveal the identity of the speaker vary depending upon whether the speaker is a defendant or third party?

3. What is the relevance of AT&T's privacy policy in *Doe I and Doe II*?

4. How does the court in *Doe I and Doe II* deal with the potential defendant's arguments that he should be allowed to proceed anonymously? What policy issues does the defendant raise in support of his arguments? Were you persuaded by his point of view?

5. The courts addressing this issue all agree that the party seeking the identity of a speaker must satisfy the court that the plaintiff presents a *prima facia* cause of action. How rigorous is this requirement? *Consider* Dendrite Int'l, Inc. v. Doe No. 3, 342 N.J. Super. 134, 775 A.2d 756 (N.J. Super. A.D. 2001), in which plaintiffs sought the identity of several anonymous defendants for statements made on various bulletin and message boards. According to the New Jersey Appellate Division:

> [T]he trial court should first require the plaintiff to undertake efforts to notify the anonymous posters that they are the subject of a subpoena or application for an order of disclosure, and withhold action to afford the fictitiously-named defendants a reasonable opportunity to file and serve opposition to the application. These notification efforts should include posting a message of notification of the identity discovery request to the anonymous user on the ISP's pertinent message board.
>
> The court shall also require the plaintiff to identify and set forth the exact statements purportedly made by each anonymous poster that plaintiff alleges constitutes actionable speech.
>
> The complaint and all information provided to the court should be carefully reviewed to determine whether plaintiff has set forth a prima facie cause of action against the fictitiously-named anonymous defendants. In addition to establishing that its action can withstand a motion to dismiss for failure to state a claim upon which relief can be granted . . . , the plaintiff must produce sufficient evidence supporting each element of its cause of action, on a prima facie basis, prior to a court ordering the disclosure of the identity of the unnamed defendant.
>
> Finally, assuming the court concludes that the plaintiff has presented a prima facie cause of action, the court must balance the defendant's First Amendment right of anonymous free speech against the strength of the prima facie case presented and the necessity for the disclosure of the anonymous defendant's identity to allow the plaintiff to properly proceed.
>
> The application of these procedures and standards must be undertaken and analyzed on a case-by-case basis. The guiding principle is a result based on a meaningful analysis and a proper balancing of the equities and rights at issue.

Id. at 141-142. With respect to the sufficiency of the pleadings, the court emphasized that, "a strict application of our rules surrounding motions to dismiss is not the appropriate litmus test to apply in evaluating the disclosure issue." *Id.* at 156. Instead, "a more probing evaluation into the 'bona fides of [plaintiff's] claim was necessary,' " to ensure "that plaintiffs do not use discovery procedures to ascertain the identities of unknown defendants in order to harass, intimidate or silence critics." *Id.* at 156-157. The Virginia Supreme Court upheld a lower court decision ordering AOL to reveal information on an anonymous subscriber in a case involving libel and unfair business practice claims resulting from a posting on a Yahoo! chat board. *See* America Online v. Nam Tai Electronics, Inc. (Va. Sup. Ct. Nov. 1, 2002), *http://www.courts.state.va.us/txtops/1012761.txt.*

6. In *Doe I and Doe II*, Judge Droney notes that: "Courts . . . recognize that anonymity is a particularly important component of Internet speech. . . . However, the right to speak anonymously, on the internet [sic] or otherwise, is not absolute and does not protect speech that otherwise would be unprotected." (p. 7 of the judgment). How have courts attempted to strike this balance in the cases you have considered? Do you think courts are striking the right balance? Does the Internet raise new concerns about this balancing exercise?

7. So far the cases we have been studying have examined when an Internet service provider can be required to disclose the identity of an Internet user. What happens if the ISP voluntarily discloses the identity of the user? As the court in *2TheMart* recognized, ISPs are not necessarily under any obligation to notify the subscribers that their identities are being requested let alone disclosed.

8. The Digital Millennium Copyright Act of 1998 included a provision for plaintiff copyright owners to seek identifying information about potential copyright infringers from ISPs. Consider the following.

IN RE VERIZON INTERNET SERVICES, INC.

257 F. Supp. 2d 244 (D.D.C. 2003)

BATES, District Judge.

Before the Court is the motion of Verizon Internet Services ("Verizon") to quash the February 4, 2003 subpoena served on it by the Recording Industry Association of America ("RIAA") pursuant to the Digital Millennium Copyright Act of 1998 ("DMCA"), 17 U.S.C. §512. On behalf of copyright owners, RIAA seeks the identity of an anonymous user of the conduit functions of Verizon's Internet service who is alleged to have infringed copyrights by offering hundreds of songs for downloading over the Internet. In an earlier action, this Court rejected Verizon's statutory challenges to a similar subpoena, holding that Verizon's conduit functions were within the scope of the subpoena authority of §512(h) of the DMCA. *See In re: Verizon Internet Services, Inc., Subpoena Enforcement Matter*, 240 F. Supp. 2d 24 (D.D.C.2003). Verizon now claims that [among other things] §512(h) violates the First Amendment rights of Internet users. . . .

[After rejecting Verizon's argument that §512(h) violated Article III of the U.S. Constitution as an impermissible delegation of judicial power, the court went on to consider Verizon's First Amendment argument.] Verizon also contends that the subpoena authority in 512(h) violates the First Amendment rights of Internet users — by piercing their anonymity — both because it does not provide sufficient procedural protection for expressive and associational rights and because it is overbroad and sweeps in protected expression. Although these are certainly important considerations, the Court concludes that §512(h) does not offend the First Amendment. . . .

The Supreme Court has recognized a right of anonymity within the First Amendment. *Buckley v. American Constitutional Law Found.*, 525 U.S. 182, 200 (1999) (invalidating, on First Amendment grounds, a Colorado statute that required initiative petitioners to wear identification badges); *McIntyre v. Ohio Elections Comm'n*, 514 U.S. 334, 357 (1995) (overturning Ohio law that prohibited distribution of campaign literature without name and address of the person issuing the literature; "anonymous pamphleteering is not a pernicious, fraudulent practice, but an honorable tradition of advocacy and of dissent"); *Talley v. California*, 362 U.S. 60, 65 (1960) (invalidating California statute prohibiting distribution of handbills without name and address of preparer). Courts have also recognized that the protections of the First Amendment reach expression on the Internet. *See, e.g., Reno v. ACLU*, 521 U.S. 844, 870 (1997) ("Through the use of chat rooms, any person with a phone line can become a town crier with a voice that resonates further than it could from any soapbox."); *2TheMart.Com*, 140 F. Supp. 2d at 1092 ("First Amendment protections extend to speech via the Internet.").

An individual's anonymity may be important for encouraging the type of expression protected by the First Amendment. "The decision in favor of anonymity may be motivated by fear of economic or official retaliation, by concern about social ostracism, or merely by a desire to preserve as much of one's privacy as possible." *McIntyre*, 514 U.S. at 341-42. Indeed, "quite apart from any threat of persecution, an advocate may believe her ideas will be more persuasive if her readers are unaware of her identity." *Id.* at 342. As stated in *Talley*, "[a]nonymous pamphlets, leaflets, brochures and even books have played an important role in the progress of mankind." 362 U.S. at 64. Hence, several lower court cases have found that First Amendments rights, particularly the right to anonymity, extend to expression on the Internet. *See, e.g., 2TheMart.Com*, 140 F. Supp. 2d at 1097 ("the constitutional rights of Internet users, including the right to speak anonymously, must be carefully safeguarded"); *ACLU v. Johnson*, 4 F. Supp. 2d 1029, 1033 (D.N.M.1998) (striking law "that prevents people from communicating and accessing information anonymously"); *Columbia Ins. Co. v. SeesCandy.Com*, 185 F.R.D. 573, 578 (N.D. Cal. 1999) (recognizing "legitimate and valuable right to participate in online forums anonymously or pseudonymously").

But when the Supreme Court has held that the First Amendment protects anonymity, it has typically done so in cases involving core First Amendment expression. . . .

The DMCA, however, does not directly impact core political speech, and thus may not warrant the type of "exacting scrutiny" reserved for that context.

Section 512(h) deals strictly with copyright infringement. Verizon concedes, as it must, that there is no First Amendment defense to copyright violations. The "Supreme Court . . . has made it unmistakably clear that the First Amendment does not shield copyright infringement." *Universal City Studios, Inc. v. Reimerdes,* 82 F. Supp. 2d 211, 220 (S.D.N.Y. 2000); *see Harper & Row Publishers, Inc. v. Nation Enterprises,* 471 U.S. 539, 568, (1985) (rejecting First Amendment challenge to copyright infringement action); *Zacchini v. Scripps-Howard,* 433 U.S. 562, 574-78 (1977). In other words, "the First Amendment is not a license to trammel on legally recognized rights in intellectual property." *In re Capital Cities/ABC, Inc.,* 918 F.2d 140, 143 (11th Cir. 1990) (quotations omitted). Indeed, copyrights serve as important incentives to encourage and protect expression: "the Framers intended copyright itself to be the engine of free expression." *Eldred,* 123 S. Ct. at 788 (quoting *Harper & Row,* 471 U.S. at 558). "By establishing a marketable right to the use of one's expression, copyright supplies the economic incentive to create and disseminate ideas." *Id.* Nonetheless, the Court concludes for present purposes that there is some level of First Amendment protection that should be afforded to anonymous expression on the Internet, even though the degree of protection is minimal where alleged copyright infringement is the expression at issue. . . .

Verizon maintains that the DMCA does not provide adequate safeguards to protect Internet users' rights of expression and association. In this regard, Verizon relies heavily on the Supreme Court's decision in *Blount v. Rizzi,* 400 U.S. 410 (1971), which overturned a federal statute authorizing prior restraint and censorship of obscene materials sent through the mail. The Court in *Blount* held that "the line between speech unconditionally guaranteed and speech which may legitimately be regulated . . . is finely drawn," and thus "[t]he separation of legitimate from illegitimate speech calls for sensitive tools." *Id.* at 417 (quoting *Speiser v. Randall,* 357 U.S. 513, 525 (1958)). The strictures in *Blount* and its progeny, however, do not apply outside the obscenity realm; moreover, even if they did, the DMCA contains adequate safeguards to ensure that the First Amendment rights of Internet users will not be curtailed.

Blount struck down a statute that authorized the Postmaster General to halt the use of the mails for commerce in allegedly obscene materials and permitted detention of mail pending resolution of an obscenity determination.

> Since §4006 on its face, and §4007 as applied, are procedures designed to deny use of the mails to commercial distributors of obscene literature, those procedures violate the First Amendment unless they include built-in safeguards against curtailment of constitutionally protected expression, for Government is not free to adopt whatever procedures it pleases for dealing with obscenity . . . without regard to the possible consequences for constitutionally protected speech. Rather, the First Amendment requires that procedures be incorporated that ensure against the curtailment of constitutionally protected expression, which is often separate from obscenity only by a dim and uncertain line.

400 U.S. at 416 (citations omitted). Because the government was censoring speech and regulating obscenity, the Court "insist[ed] that regulations of obscenity scrupulously embody the most rigorous procedural safeguards." *Id.* "[T]he fatal flaw of the [statute's] procedure," the Court explained, was that it "fail[ed] to require that the Postmaster General seek to obtain a prompt judicial determination of the obscenity of the material." *Id.* at 418.

The Supreme Court's decision in *Blount* cannot be read as broadly as Verizon would like. The statute challenged in *Blount* authorized government censorship and prior restraint of allegedly obscene material sent through the mail, without any judicial determination of obscenity. In such circumstances, the Court emphasized, "the censor's business is to censor." *Id.* at 419. "The teaching of our cases is that, because only a judicial determination in an adversary proceeding ensures the necessary sensitivity to freedom of expression, only a procedure requiring a judicial determination suffices to impose a valid final restraint." *Id.* (quoting *Freedman v. Maryland,* 380 U.S. 51, 58 (1965)). The Court emphasized that "it is vital that prompt judicial review on the issue of obscenity — rather than merely probable cause — be assured on the Government's initiative before the severe restrictions in [the statute] are invoked." *Id.* at 420.

Unlike the statute in *Blount,* however, the DMCA neither authorizes governmental censorship nor involves prior restraint of potentially protected expression. Section 512(h) merely allows a private copyright owner to obtain the identity of an alleged copyright infringer in order to protect constitutionally-recognized rights in creative works; it does not even directly seek or restrain the underlying expression (the sharing of copyrighted material). Thus, the DMCA does not regulate protected expression or otherwise permit prior restraint of protected speech. It only requires production of the identity of one who has engaged in unprotected conduct sharing copyrighted material on the Internet. . . . The DMCA places no limits on protected activity; it governs unprotected copyright piracy, and §512(h) reaches only the identity of the subscriber (already known to the service provider), not any underlying expression. Moreover, the content of §512(h) is not obscenity but copyright legislation, where "[t]he wisdom of Congress' action . . . is not within [the Court's] province to second guess." *Eldred,* 123 S. Ct. at 790. . . .

Even if such safeguards were required, however, the DMCA includes sufficient procedures to prevent any substantial encroachment on the First Amendment rights of Internet users. Before a copyright owner (or its agent) can obtain a §512(h) subpoena, for example, one must have a "good faith belief" that the use of copyrighted material is not authorized by the owner. 17 U.S.C. §512(c)(3)(A)(v). Moreover, the DMCA requires a copyright owner to submit

> a sworn declaration to the effect that the purpose for which the subpoena is sought is to obtain the identity of an alleged infringer and that such information will only be used for the purpose of protecting rights under this title.

Id. §512(h)(2)(c). The DMCA also requires a person seeking a subpoena to state, under penalty of perjury, that he is authorized to act on behalf of the copyright owner. *Id.* §512(c)(3)(A)(vi). These provisions provide substantial protection for Internet users against baseless or abusive subpoenas. In fact, the statute contains an important disincentive for false representations, thereby further protecting against abusive or harassing subpoenas. *See id.* §512(f) (any person who "knowingly materially misrepresents" that activity is infringing "shall be liable for damages, including costs and attorneys' fees, incurred by the alleged infringer" as a result of the misrepresentation). With all these protections, it is unlikely that §512(h) will require disclosure, to any significant degree, of the identity of individuals engaged in protected anonymous speech, as opposed to those engaged in unprotected copyright infringement.

Verizon asserts that, under the DMCA, a copyright owner does not have to demonstrate that the allegation of copyright infringement could withstand a motion to dismiss. However, in order to obtain a subpoena, the copyright owner must, in effect, plead a prima facie case of copyright infringement. *See Feist Publ'ns, Inc. v. Rural Tel. Svc. Co.,* 499 U.S. 340, 361, 111 S. Ct. 1282, 113 L. Ed. 2d 358 (1991) (the elements of a prima facie case of copyright infringement are "(1) ownership of a valid copyright, and (2) copying of constituent elements of the work that are original"); *accord, Lulirama, Ltd. v. Axcess Broadcast Svcs.,* 128 F.3d 872, 884 (5th Cir. 1997). Under §512, one must assert ownership of an exclusive copyright, §512(c)(3)(A)(i), and a good faith belief that the use of copyrighted material is not authorized, §512(c)(3)(A)(v). In other words, the subpoena notification must establish ownership and unauthorized use — a prima facie case of copyright infringement.

Lastly, the DMCA provides that the Federal Rules of Civil Procedure govern the issuance, service, enforcement, and compliance of subpoenas. 17 U.S.C. §512(h)(6). Hence, access to the courts and the judicial supervision Verizon urges to protect Internet users is available. Service providers or their subscribers, for example, can employ Fed. R. Civ. P. 45 to object to, modify or move to quash a subpoena, or even to seek sanctions. *See, e.g.,* Fed. R. Civ. P. 45(c)(1) (authorizing sanctions for overbroad, burdensome, or vexatious subpoenas). This adds yet another layer of protection for Internet users. Thus, in sum, the Court rejects Verizon's contention that §512 does not provide sufficient safeguards or judicial supervision to protect Internet users' First Amendment rights, including anonymity. . . .

COMMENTS AND QUESTIONS

1. Why does the court in *Verizon* take the view that §512 does not run afoul of the First Amendment?

2. Can you foresee a situation in which the disclosure of the identity of an alleged copyright infringer might implicate First Amendment rights?

3. Should ISPs include specific provisions in their privacy policies to cover situations where they may be compelled to disclose the identities of subscribers under §512? If so, what should such provisions say?

4. Does §512 allow copyright holders to go on "fishing expeditions" in an attempt to identify potential avenues for litigation? In other words, does it give them too much leeway to seek identities of Internet subscribers from ISPs?

5. The *Verizon* decision was reconsidered in Recording Industry Association of America, Inc. v. Verizon Internet Services, Inc., 351 F.3d 1229 (D.C. Cir. 2003). The court there held that the text and overall structure of §512 does not authorize the issuance of a subpoena to an ISP acting as a mere conduit for the transmission of information sent by others, as in a peer-to-peer file-sharing situation. Thus, §512 is still regarded as constitutionally valid, but it was found not to apply to the facts of this case, so the result was that the subpoena against Verizon was ultimately quashed.

D. ACCESS TO CYBERSPACE

The question of whether there should be a First Amendment right of access to cyberspace becomes increasingly more important every day. Access to the Internet is increasingly provided by private entities. They include cable providers and telephone companies, as well as traditional ISPs. As we attempt to bridge the digital divide, to what degree can we require these private entities to provide access?

Similarly, to what extent should government be able to dictate what information and services may be available online? As discussed earlier, some argue that certain Internet sites should be required to provide links to issues of public concern and to opposing viewpoints to prevent group polarization. Additionally, as private Internet service providers such as AOL and Microsoft become increasingly larger and more powerful, to what extent can government prohibit them from blocking competing services, critical comment, or speech that they find offensive?

Access to media has been a topic of much debate for more than 30 years. This section begins by examining the argument for the right of access and the Supreme Court's treatment of access rights to other media before examining the question of Internet access. The preceding materials addressed areas that were generally understood to implicate the freedom of speech protected under the First Amendment. Beginning with the question of access to cyberspace, we will now examine several areas in which one of the central problems is determining whether the First Amendment is implicated at all. As you study the materials, ask yourself to what extent does this question involve access, content discrimination, property rights, or perhaps a combination of competing interests.

Problem 4.0

As General Counsel for StarttUp, you receive a letter from a Web site operator. The letter claims that StarttUp uses technology to prevent its users from accessing his Web site. According to the Web site's publisher, StarttUp's action is preventing its message from reaching an important segment of the Internet community, and demands that StarttUp stop blocking access to the Web site.

Unaware that your company has been blocking any sites, you approach Alan and Barbara. They explain that StarttUp has an unofficial policy of blocking sites it considers to be offensive. Barbara explains that she and Alan have ordered several sites to be blocked, including the one in question, usually because a user complained about the site. Some complaints arose because the site distributed pornographic files; others arose because the site allegedly misused credit card information. Alan admits, however, that in one case, he asked the tech staff to block a site because he disagreed with its political message.

Your tech staff explains that when StarttUp blocks access to a site, its users are unaware that any blocking is occurring. This means that unless the user knows that the site exists from some other source, StarttUp users will not only be unable to access the site, they will not know that the blocked site exists.

As you study the following material, consider how you should respond to the complaining Web site operator. Does it matter why the Web site is being blocked? Is there a technological compromise? Would your conclusion be different if AOL and other Internet service providers like yourself all blocked access to the site?

Problem 4.1

Cora has similar concerns about access. She recently discovered that Demi routinely deleted comments from the GOL blog made by a person identifying herself as "Flower Child." According to Demi, Flower Child's comments tended to be derogatory and bullying of women. However, some of her comments appeared to be politically biased or motivated and Demi objected to the political bias of the comments, and removed them on that basis. Demi generally removes the comments so quickly that no one notices they were posted. Cora only realized that Demi was deleting the comments when Flower Child emailed Cora to complain about her lack of ability to comment on Demi's posts. Moreover, after a particularly offensive comment, Demi suggested permanently blocking "Flower Child" from posting to the blog. What action, if any, should Cora take?

1. The Precedent

In his landmark article, *Access to the Press: A New First Amendment Right*, Jerome Barron argued:

> There is an anomaly in our constitutional law. While we protect expression once it has come to the fore, our law is indifferent to creating opportunities for expression. Our constitutional theory is in the grip of a romantic conception of free expression, a belief that the "marketplace of ideas" is freely accessible. But if ever there were a self-operating marketplace of ideas, it has long ceased to exist. The mass media's development of an antipathy to ideas requires legal intervention if novel and unpopular ideas are to be assured a forum — unorthodox points of view which have no claim on broadcast time and newspaper space as a matter of right are in poor position to compete with those aired as a matter of grace.

80 Harv. L. Rev. 1641 (1967). According to Barron, the solution to this problem was to create a right of access to the various media. *Id.* at 1667-78. Barron and others were concerned that in the modern marketplace of ideas, the mass media had become an obstacle to free expression. Corporate control over the marketplace resulted in part from the significant costs of running newspapers and broadcast stations. Unless the owners of these media agreed to convey a particular message, it would be unlikely for that message to reach a broad or nationwide audience. After the publication of Barron's article, Barron and other lawyers began lobbying for legislation to implement access and litigating these issues in the courts. Before we examine how the issue of access applies in cyberspace, we will examine the Supreme Court's decisions with regard to other media. In those cases, has the access movement succeeded?

MIAMI HERALD PUBLISHING COMPANY v. TORNILLO

418 U.S. 241 (1974)

Mr. Chief Justice BURGER delivered the opinion of the Court.

The issue in this case is whether a state statute granting a political candidate a right to equal space to reply to criticism and attacks on his record by a newspaper violates the guarantees of a free press. . . .

The appellee and supporting advocates of an enforceable right of access to the press vigorously argue that government has an obligation to ensure that a wide variety of views reach the public.[8] The contentions of access proponents will be set out in some detail. It is urged that at the time the First Amendment to the Constitution was ratified in 1791 as part of our Bill of Rights the press was broadly representative of the people it was serving. While many of the

---

8. See generally Barron, Access to the Press — A New First Amendment Right, 80 Harv. L. Rev. 1641 (1967).

newspapers were intensely partisan and narrow in their views, the press collectively presented a broad range of opinions to readers. Entry into publishing was inexpensive; pamphlets and books provided meaningful alternatives to the organized press for the expression of unpopular ideas and often treated events and expressed views not covered by conventional newspapers. A true marketplace of ideas existed in which there was relatively easy access to the channels of communication.

Access advocates submit that although newspapers of the present are superficially similar to those of 1791 the press of today is in reality very different from that known in the early years of our national existence. In the past half century a communications revolution has seen the introduction of radio and television into our lives, the promise of a global community through the use of communications satellites, and the spectre of a "wired" nation by means of an expanding cable television network with two-way capabilities. The printed press, it is said, has not escaped the effects of this revolution. Newspapers have become big business and there are far fewer of them to serve a larger literate population. Chains of newspapers, national newspapers, national wire and news services, and one-newspaper towns, are the dominant features of a press that has become noncompetitive and enormously powerful and influential in its capacity to manipulate popular opinion and change the course of events. Major metropolitan newspapers have collaborated to establish news services national in scope. Such national news organizations provide syndicated "interpretive reporting" as well as syndicated features and commentary, all of which can serve as part of the new school of "advocacy journalism."

The elimination of competing newspapers in most of our large cities, and the concentration of control of media that results from the only newspaper's being owned by the same interests which own a television station and a radio station, are important components of this trend toward concentration of control of outlets to inform the public.

The result of these vast changes has been to place in a few hands the power to inform the American people and shape public opinion. Much of the editorial opinion and commentary that is printed is that of syndicated columnists distributed nationwide and, as a result, we are told, on national and world issues there tends to be a homogeneity of editorial opinion, commentary, and interpretive analysis. The abuses of bias and manipulative reportage are, likewise, said to be the result of the vast accumulations of unreviewable power in the modern media empires. In effect, it is claimed, the public has lost any ability to respond or to contribute in a meaningful way to the debate on issues. The monopoly of the means of communication allows for little or no critical analysis of the media except in professional journals of very limited readership. . . .

The obvious solution, which was available to dissidents at an earlier time when entry into publishing was relatively inexpensive, today would be to have additional newspapers. But the same economic factors which have caused the disappearance of vast numbers of metropolitan newspapers, have made entry into the marketplace of ideas served by the print media almost impossible. It is urged that the claim of newspapers to be "surrogates for the public" carries with it a concomitant fiduciary obligation to account for that stewardship. From this premise it is reasoned that the only effective way to insure fairness and accuracy and to provide for some accountability is for government to take affirmative action. The First Amendment interest of the public in being informed is said to be in peril because the "marketplace of ideas" is today a monopoly controlled by the owners of the market.

Proponents of enforced access to the press take comfort from language in several of this Court's decisions which suggests that the First Amendment acts as a sword as well as a shield, that it imposes obligations on the owners of the press in addition to protecting the press from government regulation. In Associated Press v. United States, 326 U.S. 1, 20 (1945), the Court, in ejecting the argument that the press is immune from the antitrust laws by virtue of the First Amendment, stated:

> "The First Amendment, far from providing an argument against application of the Sherman Act, here provides powerful reasons to the contrary. That Amendment rests on the assumption that the widest possible dissemination of information from diverse and antagonistic sources is essential to the welfare of the public, that a free press is a condition of a free society. Surely a command that the government itself shall not impede the free flow of ideas does not afford non-governmental combinations a refuge if they impose restraints upon that constitutionally guaranteed freedom. Freedom to publish means freedom for all and not for some. Freedom to publish is guaranteed by the Constitution, but freedom to combine to keep others from publishing is not. Freedom of the press from governmental interference under the First Amendment does not sanction repression of that freedom by private interests." (Footnote omitted.)

In New York Times Co. v. Sullivan, 376 U.S. 254, 270 (1964), the Court spoke of "a profound national commitment to the principle that debate on public issues should be uninhibited, robust, and wide-open." It is argued that the "uninhibited, robust" debate is not "wide-open" but open only to a monopoly in control of the press. Appellee cites the plurality opinion in Rosenbloom v. Metromedia, Inc., 403 U.S. 29, 47, and n.15 (1971), which he suggests seemed to invite experimentation by the State in right-to-access regulation of the press. . . .

However much validity may be found in these arguments, at each point the implementation of a remedy such as an enforceable right of access necessarily calls for some mechanism, either governmental or consensual. If it is governmental coercion, this at once brings about a confrontation with the express provisions of the First Amendment and the judicial gloss on that Amendment developed over the years.

The Court foresaw the problems relating to government-enforced access as early as its decision in Associated Press v. United States, supra. There it carefully contrasted the private "compulsion to print" called for by the Association's bylaws with the provisions of the District Court decree against appellants which "does not compel AP or its members to permit publication of anything which their 'reason' tells them should not be published." 326 U.S., at 20 n.18. In Branzburg v. Hayes, 408 U.S. 665, 681, we emphasized that the cases then before us "involve no intrusions upon speech or assembly, no prior restraint or restriction on what the press may publish, and no express or implied command that the press publish what it prefers to withhold." In Columbia Broadcasting System, Inc. v. Democratic National Committee, 412 U.S. 94, 117, the plurality opinion as to Part III noted:

> "The power of a privately owned newspaper to advance its own political, social, and economic views is bounded by only two factors: first, the acceptance of a sufficient number of readers — and hence advertisers — to assure financial success; and, second, the journalistic integrity of its editors and publishers."

An attitude strongly adverse to any attempt to extend a right of access to newspapers was echoed by other Members of this Court in their separate opinions in that case. Recently, while approving a bar against employment advertising specifying "male" or "female" preference, the Court's opinion in Pittsburgh Press Co. v. Human Relations Comm'n, 413 U.S. 376, 391 (1973), took pains to limit its holding within narrow bounds:

> "Nor, a fortiori, does our decision authorize any restriction whatever, whether of content or layout, on stories or commentary originated by Pittsburgh Press, its columnists, or its contributors. On the contrary, we reaffirm unequivocally the protection afforded to editorial judgment and to the free expression of views on these and other issues, however controversial."

Dissenting in Pittsburgh Press, Mr. Justice Stewart, joined by Mr. Justice Douglas, expressed the view that no "government agency — local, state, or federal — can tell a newspaper in advance what it can print and what it cannot." Id., at 400.

We see the beginning with Associated Press, supra, the Court has expressed sensitivity as to whether a restriction or requirement constituted the compulsion exerted by government on a newspaper to print that which it would not otherwise print. The clear implication has been that any such compulsion to publish that which " 'reason' tells them should not be published" is unconstitutional. A responsible press is an undoubtedly desirable goal, but press responsibility is not mandated by the Constitution and like many other virtues it cannot be legislated.

Appellee's argument that the Florida statute does not amount to a restriction of appellant's right to speak because "the statute in question here has not prevented the Miami Herald from saying anything it wished" begs the core question. Compelling editors or publishers to publish that which " 'reason' tells them should not be published" is what is at issue in this case. The Florida statute operates as a command in the same sense as a statue or regulation forbidding appellant to publish specified matter. Governmental restraint on publishing need not fall into familiar or traditional patterns to be subject to constitutional limitations on governmental powers. Grosjean v. American Press Co., 297 U.S. 233, 244-245 (1936). The Florida statute exacts a penalty on the basis of the content of a newspaper. The first phase of the penalty resulting from the compelled printing of a reply is exacted in terms of the cost in printing and composing time and materials and in taking up space that could be devoted to other material the newspaper may have preferred to print. It is correct, as appellee contends, that a newspaper is not subject to the finite technological limitations of time that confront a broadcaster but it is not correct to say that, as an economic reality, a newspaper can proceed to infinite expansion of its column space to accommodate the replies that a government agency determines or a statute commands the readers should have available.

Faced with the penalties that would accrue to any newspaper that published news or commentary arguably within the reach of the right-of-access statute, editors might well conclude that the safe course is to avoid controversy. . . .

Even if a newspaper would face no additional costs to comply with a compulsory access law and would not be forced to forgo publication of news or opinion by the inclusion of a reply, the Florida statute fails to clear the barriers of the First Amendment because of its intrusion into the function of editors. A newspaper is more than a passive receptacle or conduit for news, comment, and advertising. The choice of material to go into a newspaper, and the decisions made as to limitations on the size and content of the paper, and treatment of public issues and public officials — whether fair or unfair — constitute the exercise of editorial control and judgment. It has yet to be demonstrated how governmental regulation of this crucial process can be exercised consistent with First Amendment guarantees of a free press as they have evolved to this time. Accordingly, the judgment of the Supreme Court of Florida is reversed. . . .

[Concurring opinions by BRENNAN, J., and WHITE, J., omitted.]

TURNER BROADCASTING SYSTEM, INC. v. FCC

512 U.S. 622 (1994)

Justice KENNEDY announced the judgment of the Court and delivered the opinion of the Court, except as to Part III-B. . . .

At issue in this case is the constitutionality of the so-called must-carry provisions, contained in §§4 and 5 of the [Cable Television Consumer Protection and Competition Act of 1992], which require cable operators to carry the signals of a specified number of local broadcast television stations.

Section 4 requires carriage of "local commercial television stations," defined to include all full power television broadcasters, other than those qualifying as "noncommercial educational" stations under §5, that operate within the same television market as the cable system. §4, 47 U.S.C. §534(b)(1)(B), (h)(1)(A) (1988 ed., Supp. IV). Cable systems with more than 12 active channels, and more than 300 subscribers, are required to set aside up to one-third of their channels for commercial broadcast stations that request carriage. §534(b)(1)(B). Cable systems with more than 300 subscribers, but only 12 or fewer active channels, must carry the signals of three commercial broadcast stations. §534(b)(1)(A). . . .

Section 5 of the Act imposes similar requirements regarding the carriage of local public broadcast television stations, referred to in the Act as local "noncommercial educational television stations." 47 U.S.C. §535(a) (1988 ed., Supp. IV). . . .

Taken together, therefore, §§4 and 5 subject all but the smallest cable systems nationwide to must-carry obligations, and confer must-carry privileges on all full power broadcasters operating within the same television market as a qualified cable system. . . .

Congress enacted the 1992 Cable Act after conducting three years of hearings on the structure and operation of the cable television industry. . . . The conclusions Congress drew from its factfinding process are recited in the text of the Act itself. In brief, Congress found that the physical characteristics of cable transmission, compounded by the increasing concentration of economic power in the cable industry, are endangering the ability of over-the-air broadcast television stations to compete for a viewing audience and thus for necessary operating revenues. Congress determined that regulation of the market for video programming was necessary to correct this competitive imbalance.

In particular, Congress found that over 60 percent of the households with television sets subscribe to cable, §2(a)(3), and for these households cable has replaced over-the-air broadcast television as the primary provider of video programming, §2(a)(17). This is so, Congress found, because "[m]ost subscribers to cable television systems do not or cannot maintain antennas to receive broadcast television services, do not have input selector switches to convert from a cable to antenna reception system, or cannot otherwise receive broadcast television services." Ibid. In addition, Congress concluded that due to "local franchising requirements and the extraordinary expense of constructing more than one cable television system to serve a particular geographic area," the overwhelming majority of cable operators exercise a monopoly over cable service. §2(a)(2). "The result," Congress determined, "is undue market power for the cable operator as compared to that of consumers and video programmers." Ibid.

According to Congress, this market position gives cable operators the power and the incentive to harm broadcast competitors. The power derives from the cable operator's ability, as owner of the transmission facility, to "terminate the retransmission of the broadcast signal, refuse to carry new signals, or reposition a broadcast signal to a disadvantageous channel position." §2(a)(15). The incentive derives from the economic reality that "[c]able television systems and broadcast television stations increasingly compete for television advertising revenues." §2(a)(14). By refusing carriage of broadcasters' signals, cable operators, as a practical matter, can reduce the number of households that have access to the broadcasters' programming, and thereby capture advertising dollars that would otherwise go to broadcast stations. §2(a)(15). . . .

In light of these technological and economic conditions, Congress concluded that unless cable operators are required to carry local broadcast stations, "[t]here is a substantial likelihood that . . . additional local broadcast signals will be deleted, repositioned, or not carried," §2(a)(15); the "marked shift in market share" from broadcast to cable will continue to erode the advertising revenue base which sustains free local broadcast television, §§2(a)(13)-(14); and that, as a consequence, "the economic viability of free local broadcast television and its ability to originate quality local programming will be seriously jeopardized," §2(a)(16). . . .

II

There can be no disagreement on an initial premise: Cable programmers and cable operators engage in and transmit speech, and they are entitled to the protection of the speech and press provisions of the First Amendment. Leathers v. Medlock, 499 U.S. 439, 444 (1991). Through "original programming or by exercising editorial discretion over which stations or programs to include in its repertoire," cable programmers and operators "see[k] to communicate messages on a wide variety of topics and in a wide variety of formats." Los Angeles v. Preferred Communications, Inc., 476 U.S. 488, 494 (1986). By requiring cable systems to set aside a portion of their channels for local broadcasters, the must-carry rules regulate cable speech in two respects: The rules reduce the number of channels over which cable operators exercise unfettered control, and they render it more difficult for cable programmers to compete for carriage on the limited channels remaining. Nevertheless, because not every interference with speech triggers the same degree of scrutiny under the First Amendment, we must decide at the outset the level of scrutiny applicable to the must-carry provisions. . . .

B

At the heart of the First Amendment lies the principle that each person should decide for himself or herself the ideas and beliefs deserving of expression, consideration, and adherence. Our political system and cultural life rest upon this ideal. See Leathers v. Medlock, 499 U.S., at 449 (citing Cohen v. California, 403 U.S. 15, 24 (1971)); West Virginia Bd. of Ed. v. Barnette, 319 U.S. 624, 638, 640-642 (1943). Government action that stifles speech on account of its message, or that requires the utterance of a particular message favored by the Government, contravenes this essential right. Laws of this sort pose the inherent risk that the Government seeks not to advance a legitimate regulatory goal, but to suppress unpopular ideas or information or manipulate the public debate through coercion rather than persuasion. These restrictions "rais[e] the specter that the Government may effectively drive certain ideas or viewpoints from the marketplace." Simon & Schuster, Inc. v. Members of State Crime Victims Bd., 502 U.S. 105, 116 (1991).

For these reasons, the First Amendment, subject only to narrow and well-understood exceptions, does not countenance governmental control over the content of messages expressed by private individuals. R.A.V. v. St. Paul, 505 U.S. 377, 382-383 (1992); Texas v. Johnson, 491 U.S. 397, 414 (1989). Our precedents thus apply the most exacting scrutiny to regulations that suppress, disadvantage, or impose differential burdens upon speech because of its content. See *Simon & Schuster*, 502 U.S., at 115; id., at 125-126 (Kennedy, J., concurring in judgment); Perry Ed. Assn. v. Perry Local Educators' Assn., 460 U.S. 37, 45 (1983). Laws that compel speakers to utter or distribute speech bearing a particular message are subject to the same rigorous scrutiny. See Riley v. National Federation for Blind of N.C., Inc., 487 U.S., at 798; West Virginia Bd. of Ed. v. Barnette, supra. In contrast, regulations that are unrelated to the content of speech are subject to an intermediate level of scrutiny, see Clark v. Community for Creative Non-Violence, 468 U.S. 288, 293 (1984), because in most cases they pose a less substantial risk of excising certain ideas or viewpoints from the public dialogue.

Deciding whether a particular regulation is content based or content neutral is not always a simple task. We have said that the "principal inquiry in determining content neutrality . . . is whether the government has adopted a regulation of speech because of [agreement or] disagreement with the message it conveys." Ward v. Rock Against Racism, 491 U.S. 781, 791 (1989). See *R.A.V.*, supra, 505 U.S., at 386 ("The government may not regulate [speech] based on hostility — or favoritism — towards the underlying message expressed"). The purpose, or justification, of a regulation will often be evident on its face. See Frisby v. Schultz, 487 U.S. 474, 481(1988). But while a content-based purpose may be sufficient in certain circumstances to show that a regulation is content based, it is not necessary to such a showing in all cases. Cf. *Simon & Schuster*, supra, 502 U.S., at 117 ("'[I]llicit legislative intent is not the sine qua non of a violation of the First Amendment'") (quoting *Minneapolis Star & Tribune*, supra, 460 U.S., at 592). Nor will the mere assertion of a content-neutral purpose be enough to save a law which, on its face, discriminates based on content. *Arkansas Writers' Project*, 481 U.S., at 231-232; Carey v. Brown, 447 U.S. 455, 464-469 (1980).

As a general rule, laws that by their terms distinguish favored speech from disfavored speech on the basis of the ideas or views expressed are content based. . . . By contrast, laws that confer benefits or impose burdens on speech without reference to the ideas or views expressed are in most instances content neutral. . . .

C

Insofar as they pertain to the carriage of full-power broadcasters, the must-carry rules, on their face, impose burdens and confer benefits without reference to the content of speech. Although the provisions interfere with cable operators' editorial discretion by compelling them to offer carriage to a certain minimum number of broadcast stations, the extent of the interference does not depend upon the content of the cable operators' programming. The rules impose obligations upon all operators, save those with fewer than 300 subscribers, regardless of the programs or stations they now offer or have offered in the past. Nothing in the Act imposes a restriction, penalty, or burden by reason of the views, programs, or stations the cable operator has selected or will select. The number of channels a cable operator must set aside depends only on the operator's channel capacity, hence, an operator cannot avoid or mitigate its obligations under the Act by altering the programming it offers to subscribers.

The must-carry provisions also burden cable programmers by reducing the number of channels for which they can compete. But, again, this burden is unrelated to content, for it extends to all cable programmers irrespective of the programming they choose to offer viewers. . . . And finally, the privileges conferred by the must-carry provisions are also unrelated to content. The rules benefit all full power broadcasters who request carriage — be they commercial or noncommercial, independent or network affiliated, English or Spanish language, religious or secular. The aggregate effect of the rules is thus to make every full power commercial and noncommercial broadcaster eligible for must-carry, provided only that the broadcaster operates within the same television market as a cable system.

It is true that the must-carry provisions distinguish between speakers in the television programming market. But they do so based only upon the manner in which speakers transmit their messages to viewers, and not upon the messages they carry: Broadcasters, which transmit over the airwaves, are favored, while cable programmers, which do not, are disfavored. Cable operators, too, are burdened by the carriage obligations, but only because they control access to the cable conduit. So long as they are not a subtle means of exercising a content preference, speaker distinctions of this nature are not presumed invalid under the First Amendment.

That the must-carry provisions, on their face, do not burden or benefit speech of a particular content does not end the inquiry. Our cases have recognized that even a regulation neutral on its face may be content based if its manifest purpose is to regulate speech because of the message it conveys. . . .

Appellants contend, in this regard, that the must-carry regulations are content based because Congress' purpose in enacting them was to promote speech of a favored content. We do not agree. Our review of the Act and its various findings persuades us that Congress' overriding objective in enacting must-carry was not to favor programming of a particular subject matter, viewpoint, or format, but rather to preserve access to free television programming for the 40 percent of Americans without cable. . . .

By preventing cable operators from refusing carriage to broadcast television stations, the must-carry rules ensure that broadcast television stations will retain a large enough potential audience to earn necessary advertising revenue — or, in the case of noncommercial broadcasters, sufficient viewer contributions, see §2(a)(8)(B) — to maintain their continued operation. In so doing, the provisions are designed to guarantee the survival of a medium that has become a vital part of the Nation's communication system, and to ensure that every individual with a television set can obtain access to free television programming.

This overriding congressional purpose is unrelated to the content of expression disseminated by cable and broadcast speakers. Indeed, our precedents have held that "protecting noncable households from loss of regular television broadcasting service due to competition from cable systems," is not only a permissible governmental justification, but an "important and substantial federal interest." Capital Cities Cable, Inc. v. Crisp, 467 U.S. 691, 714 (1984); see also United States v. Midwest Video Corp., 406 U.S. 649, 661-662, 664 (1972) (plurality opinion).

The design and operation of the challenged provisions confirm that the purposes underlying the enactment of the must-carry scheme are unrelated to the content of speech. The rules, as mentioned, confer must-carry rights on all full power broadcasters, irrespective of the content of their programming. They do not require or prohibit the carriage of particular ideas or points of view. They do not penalize cable operators or programmers because of the content of their programming. They do not compel cable operators to affirm points of view with which they disagree. They do not produce any net decrease in the amount of available speech. And they leave cable operators free to carry whatever programming they wish on all channels not subject to must-carry requirements.

Appellants and Justice O'Connor make much of the fact that, in the course of describing the purposes behind the Act, Congress referred to the value of broadcast programming. In particular, Congress noted that broadcast television is "an important source of local news[,] public affairs programming and other local broadcast services critical to an informed electorate," §2(a)(11); see also §2(a)(10), and that noncommercial television "provides educational and informational programming to the Nation's citizens," §2(a)(8). We do not think, however, that such references cast any material doubt on the content-neutral character of must-carry. That Congress acknowledged the local orientation of broadcast programming and the role that noncommercial stations have played in educating the public does not indicate that Congress regarded broadcast programming as more valuable than cable programming. Rather, it reflects nothing more than the recognition that the services provided by broadcast television have some intrinsic value and, thus, are worth preserving against the threats posed by cable. . . .

In short, Congress' acknowledgment that broadcast television stations make a valuable contribution to the Nation's communications system does not render the must-carry scheme content based. The scope and operation of the challenged provisions make clear, in our view, that Congress designed the must-carry provisions not to promote speech of a particular content, but to prevent cable operators from exploiting their economic power to the detriment of broadcasters, and thereby to ensure that all Americans, especially those unable to subscribe to cable, have access to free television programming—whatever its content. . . .

[D.1]

Appellants maintain that the must-carry provisions trigger strict scrutiny because they compel cable operators to transmit speech not of their choosing. Relying principally on Miami Herald Publishing Co. v. Tornillo, 418 U.S. 241, appellants say this intrusion on the editorial control of cable operators amounts to forced speech which, if not per se invalid, can be justified only if narrowly tailored to a compelling government interest.

Tornillo affirmed an essential proposition: The First Amendment protects the editorial independence of the press. The right-of-reply statute at issue in *Tornillo* required any newspaper that assailed a political candidate's character to print, upon request by the candidate and without cost, the candidate's reply in equal space and prominence. Although the statute did not censor speech in the traditional sense—it only required newspapers to grant access to the messages of others—we found that it imposed an impermissible content-based burden on newspaper speech. Because the right of access at issue in *Tornillo* was triggered only when a newspaper elected to print matter critical of political candidates, it "exact[ed] a penalty on the basis of . . . content." Id., at 256. We found, and continue to recognize, that right-of-reply statutes of this sort are an impermissible intrusion on newspapers' "editorial control and judgment." Id., at 258.

We explained that, in practical effect, Florida's right-of-reply statute would deter newspapers froms peaking in unfavorable terms about political candidates:

> "Faced with the penalties that would accrue to any newspaper that published news or commentary arguably within the reach of the right-of-access statute, editors might well conclude that the safe course is to avoid controversy. Therefore, under the operation of the Florida statute, political and electoral coverage would be blunted or reduced." Id., at 257.

Moreover, by affording mandatory access to speakers with which the newspaper disagreed, the law induced the newspaper to respond to the candidates' replies when it might have preferred to remain silent. See Pacific Gas & Elec. Co. v. Public Util. Comm'n of Cal., 475 U.S. 1, 11 (1986) (plurality opinion).

Tornillo [does] not control this case for the following reasons. First, unlike the access rules struck down in those cases, the must-carry rules are content neutral in application. They are not activated by any particular message spoken by cable operators and thus exact no content-based penalty. . . .

Second, appellants do not suggest, nor do we think it the case, that must-carry will force cable operators to alter their own messages to respond to the broadcast programming they are required to carry. . . . Given cable's long history of serving as a conduit for broadcast signals, there appears little risk that cable viewers would assume that the broadcast stations carried on a cable system convey ideas or messages endorsed by the cable operator. Indeed, broadcasters are required by federal regulation to identify themselves at least once every hour, and it is a common practice for broadcasters to disclaim any identity of viewpoint between the management and the speakers who use the broadcast facility. Cf. PruneYard Shopping Center v. Robins, 447 U.S. 74, 87, (1980) (noting that the views expressed by speakers who are granted a right of access to a shopping center would "not likely be identified with those of the owner"). Moreover, in contrast to the statute at issue in *Tornillo*, no aspect of the must-carry provisions would cause a cable operator or cable programmer to conclude that "the safe course is to avoid controversy," *Tornillo*, 418 U.S., at 257, and by so doing diminish the free flow of information and ideas.

Finally, the asserted analogy to *Tornillo* ignores an important technological difference between newspapers and cable television. Although a daily newspaper and a cable operator both may enjoy monopoly status in a given locale, the cable operator exercises far greater control over access to the relevant medium. A daily newspaper, no matter how secure its local monopoly, does not possess the power to obstruct readers' access to other competing publications — whether they be weekly local newspapers, or daily newspapers published in other cities. Thus, when a newspaper asserts exclusive control over its own news copy, it does not thereby prevent other newspapers from being distributed to willing recipients in the same locale.

The same is not true of cable. When an individual subscribes to cable, the physical connection between the television set and the cable network gives the cable operator bottleneck, or gatekeeper, control over most (if not all) of the television programming that is channeled into the subscriber's home. Hence, simply by virtue of its ownership of the essential pathway for cable speech, a cable operator can prevent its subscribers from obtaining access to programming it chooses to exclude. A cable operator, unlike speakers in other media, can thus silence the voice of competing speakers with a mere flick of the switch.[8]

The potential for abuse of this private power over a central avenue of communication cannot be overlooked. . . . The First Amendment's command

---

8. As one commentator has observed: "The central dilemma of cable is that it has unlimited capacity to accommodate as much diversity and as many publishers as print, yet all of the producers and publishers use the same physical plant. . . . If the cable system is itself a publisher, it may restrict the circumstances under which it allows others also to use its system." I. de Sola Pool, Technologies of Freedom 168 (1983).

that government not impede the freedom of speech does not disable the government from taking steps to ensure that private interests not restrict, through physical control of a critical pathway of communication, the free flow of information and ideas. See Associated Press v. United States, 326 U.S., at 20. We thus reject appellants' contention that *Tornillo* and *Pacific Gas & Electric* require strict scrutiny of the access rules in question here. . . .

III

A

In sum, the must-carry provisions do not pose such inherent dangers to free expression, or present such potential for censorship or manipulation, as to justify application of the most exacting level of First Amendment scrutiny. We agree with the District Court that the appropriate standard by which to evaluate the constitutionality of must-carry is the intermediate level of scrutiny applicable to content-neutral restrictions that impose an incidental burden on speech. See Ward v. Rock Against Racism, 491 U.S. 781 (1989); United States v. O'Brien, 391 U.S. 367 (1968).

Under *O'Brien*, a content-neutral regulation will be sustained if:

"it furthers an important or substantial governmental interest; if the governmental interest is unrelated to the suppression of free expression; and if the incidental restriction on alleged First Amendment freedoms is no greater than is essential to the furtherance of that interest." Id., at 377.

To satisfy this standard, a regulation need not be the least speech-restrictive means of advancing the Government's interests. "Rather, the requirement of narrow tailoring is satisfied 'so long as the . . . regulation promotes a substantial government interest that would be achieved less effectively absent the regulation.'" *Ward*, supra, 491 U.S., at 799. Narrow tailoring in this context requires, in other words, that the means chosen do not "burden substantially more speech than is necessary to further the government's legitimate interests." *Ward*, supra, 491 U.S., at 799.

Congress declared that the must-carry provisions serve three interrelated interests: (1) preserving the benefits of free, over-the-air local broadcast television, (2) promoting the widespread dissemination of information from a multiplicity of sources, and (3) promoting fair competition in the market for television programming. None of these interests is related to the "suppression of free expression," or to the content of any speakers' messages. And viewed in the abstract, we have no difficulty concluding that each of them is an important governmental interest. . . .

As we recognized in *Southwestern Cable*, the importance of local broadcasting outlets "can scarcely be exaggerated, for broadcasting is demonstrably a principal source of information and entertainment for a great part of the

Nation's population." The interest in maintaining the local broadcasting structure does not evaporate simply because cable has come upon the scene. Although cable and other technologies have ushered in alternatives to broadcast television, nearly 40 percent of American households still rely on broadcast stations as their exclusive source of television programming. And as we said in Capital Cities Cable, Inc. v. Crisp, "protecting noncable households from loss of regular television broadcasting service due to competition from cable systems" is an important federal interest. 467 U.S., at 714.

Likewise, assuring that the public has access to a multiplicity of information sources is a governmental purpose of the highest order, for it promotes values central to the First Amendment. Indeed, " 'it has long been a basic tenet of national communications policy that "the widest possible dissemination of information from diverse and antagonistic sources is essential to the welfare of the public." ' " United States v. Midwest Video Corp., 406 U.S., at 668, n.27 (plurality opinion) (quoting Associated Press v. United States, 326 U.S., at 20, 65 S. Ct., at 1424-1425). Finally, the Government's interest in eliminating restraints on fair competition is always substantial, even when the individuals or entities subject to particular regulations are engaged in expressive activity protected by the First Amendment. See Lorain Journal Co. v. United States, 342 U.S. 143 (1951); Associated Press v. United States, supra; cf. FTC v. Superior Court Trial Lawyers Assn., 493 U.S. 411, 431-432 (1990).

B

That the Government's asserted interests are important in the abstract does not mean, however, that the must-carry rules will in fact advance those interests. When the Government defends a regulation on speech as a means to redress past harms or prevent anticipated harms, it must do more than simply "posit the existence of the disease sought to be cured." Quincy Cable TV, Inc. v. FCC, 768 F.2d 1434, 1455 (CADC 1985). It must demonstrate that the recited harms are real, not merely conjectural, and that the regulation will in fact alleviate these harms in a direct and material way. . . .

Thus, in applying O'Brien scrutiny we must ask first whether the Government has adequately shown that the economic health of local broadcasting is in genuine jeopardy and in need of the protections afforded by must-carry. Assuming an affirmative answer to the foregoing question, the Government still bears the burden of showing that the remedy it has adopted does not "burden substantially more speech than is necessary to further the government's legitimate interests." Ward, 491 U.S., at 799. On the state of the record developed thus far, and in the absence of findings of fact from the District Court, we are unable to conclude that the Government has satisfied either inquiry. . . .

We agree that courts must accord substantial deference to the predictive judgments of Congress. See, e.g., Columbia Broadcasting System, Inc. v.

Democratic National Committee, 412 U.S., at 103 (The "judgment of the Legislative Branch" should not be ignored "simply because [appellants] cas[t] [their] claims under the umbrella of the First Amendment"). Sound policy-making often requires legislators to forecast future events and to anticipate the likely impact of these events based on deductions and inferences for which complete empirical support may be unavailable. See FCC v. National Citizens Comm. for Broadcasting, supra, 436 U.S., at 814; FPC v. Transcontinental Gas Pipe Line Corp., 365 U.S. 1, 29 (1961). As an institution, moreover, Congress is far better equipped than the judiciary to "amass and evaluate the vast amounts of data" bearing upon an issue as complex and dynamic as that presented here. And Congress is not obligated, when enacting its statutes, to make a record of the type that an administrative agency or court does to accommodate judicial review.

That Congress' predictive judgments are entitled to substantial deference does not mean, however, that they are insulated from meaningful judicial review altogether. On the contrary, we have stressed in First Amendment cases that the deference afforded to legislative findings does "not foreclose our independent judgment of the facts bearing on an issue of constitutional law." Sable Communications of Cal., Inc. v. FCC, 492 U.S. 115, 129 (1989); see also Landmark Communications, Inc. v. Virginia, 435 U.S. 829, 843 (1978). This obligation to exercise independent judgment when First Amendment rights are implicated is not a license to reweigh the evidence de novo, or to replace Congress' factual predictions with our own. Rather, it is to assure that, in formulating its judgments, Congress has drawn reasonable inferences based on substantial evidence. . . .

The judgment below is vacated, and the case is remanded for further proceedings consistent with this opinion.

It is so ordered.

[Concurring opinions of BLACKMUN, J., and STEVENS, J., omitted.]

Justice O'CONNOR, with whom Justice SCALIA and Justice GINSBURG join, and with whom Justice THOMAS joins as to Parts I and III, concurring in part and dissenting in part.

. . . The 1992 Cable Act implicates the First Amendment rights of two classes of speakers. First, it tells cable operators which programmers they must carry, and keeps cable operators from carrying others that they might prefer. Though cable operators do not actually originate most of the programming they show, the Court correctly holds that they are, for First Amendment purposes, speakers. Selecting which speech to retransmit is, as we know from the example of publishing houses, movie theaters, bookstores, and Reader's Digest, no less communication than is creating the speech in the first place.

Second, the Act deprives a certain class of video programmers — those who operate cable channels rather than broadcast stations — of access to over one-third of an entire medium. Cable programmers may compete only for those channels that are not set aside by the must-carry provisions. A cable programmer that might otherwise have been carried may well be denied access in favor of a broadcaster that is less appealing to the viewers but is favored by the must-carry rules. It is as if the Government ordered all movie theaters to reserve at least one-third of their screening for films made by American production companies, or required all bookstores to devote one-third of their shelf space to nonprofit publishers. As the Court explains in Parts I, II-A, and II-B of its opinion, which I join, cable programmers and operators stand in the same position under the First Amendment as do the more traditional media.

Under the First Amendment, it is normally not within the government's power to decide who may speak and who may not, at least on private property or in traditional public fora. The government does have the power to impose content-neutral time, place, and manner restrictions, but this is in large part precisely because such restrictions apply to all speakers. Laws that treat all speakers equally are relatively poor tools for controlling public debate, and their very generality creates a substantial political check that prevents them from being unduly burdensome. Laws that single out particular speakers are substantially more dangerous, even when they do not draw explicit content distinctions.

I agree with the Court that some speaker-based restrictions — those genuinely justified without reference to content — need not be subject to strict scrutiny. But looking at the statute at issue, I cannot avoid the conclusion that its preference for broadcasters over cable programmers is justified with reference to content.. . .

Preferences for diversity of viewpoints, for localism, for educational programming, and for news and public affairs all make reference to content. They may not reflect hostility to particular points of view, or a desire to suppress certain subjects because they are controversial or offensive. They may be quite benignly motivated. But benign motivation, we have consistently held, is not enough to avoid the need for strict scrutiny of content-based justifications. Simon & Schuster, Inc. v. Members of N.Y. State Crime Victims Bd., 502 U.S. 105, 117 (1991); Arkansas Writers' Project, Inc. v. Ragland, 481 U.S. 221, 228 (1987). The First Amendment does more than just bar government from intentionally suppressing speech of which it disapproves. It also generally prohibits the government from excepting certain kinds of speech from regulation because it thinks the speech is especially valuable. . . .

C

Content-based speech restrictions are generally unconstitutional unless they are narrowly tailored to a compelling state interest. Boos v. Barry, 485 U.S. 312, 321 (1988). This is an exacting test. It is not enough that the goals of the law be legitimate, or reasonable, or even praiseworthy. There must be some pressing public necessity, some essential value that has to be preserved; and even then the law must restrict as little speech as possible to serve the goal.

The interest in localism, either in the dissemination of opinions held by the listeners' neighbors or in the reporting of events that have to do with the local community, cannot be described as "compelling" for the purposes of the compelling state interest test. It is a legitimate interest, perhaps even an important one — certainly the government can foster it by, for instance, providing subsidies . . . — but it does not rise to the level necessary to justify content-based speech restrictions. It is for private speakers and listeners, not for the government, to decide what fraction of their news and entertainment ought to be of a local character and what fraction ought to be of a national (or international) one. And the same is true of the interest in diversity of viewpoints: While the government may subsidize speakers that it thinks provide novel points of view, it may not restrict other speakers on the theory that what they say is more conventional. . . .

II

Even if I am mistaken about the must-carry provisions being content based, however, in my view they fail content-neutral scrutiny as well. Assuming, arguendo, that the provisions are justified with reference to the content-neutral interests in fair competition and preservation of free television, they nonetheless restrict too much speech that does not implicate these interests.

Sometimes, a cable system's choice to carry a cable programmer rather than a broadcaster may be motivated by anticompetitive impulses, or might lead to the broadcaster going out of business. That some speech within a broad category causes harm, however, does not justify restricting the whole category. If Congress wants to protect those stations that are in danger of going out of business, or bar cable operators from preferring programmers in which the operators have an ownership stake, it may do that. But it may not, in the course of advancing these interests, restrict cable operators and programmers in circumstances where neither of these interests is threatened. . . .

III

Having said all this, it is important to acknowledge one basic fact: The question is not whether there will be control over who gets to speak over cable — the question is who will have this control. Under the FCC's view, the answer is Congress, acting within relatively broad limits. Under my view, the answer is the cable operator. Most of the time, the cable operator's decision will be largely dictated by the preferences of the viewers; but because many cable operators are indeed monopolists, the viewers' preferences will not always prevail. Our recognition that cable operators are speakers is bottomed in large part on the very fact that the cable operator has editorial discretion.

I have no doubt that there is danger in having a single cable operator decide what millions of subscribers can or cannot watch. And I have no doubt that Congress can act to relieve this danger. In other provisions of the Act, Congress has already taken steps to foster competition among cable systems. Congress can encourage the creation of new media, such as inexpensive satellite broadcasting, or fiber-optic networks with virtually unlimited channels, or even simple devices that would let people easily switch from cable to over-the-air broadcasting. And of course Congress can subsidize broadcasters that it thinks provide especially valuable programming.

Congress may also be able to act in more mandatory ways. If Congress finds that cable operators are leaving some channels empty—perhaps for ease of future expansion—it can compel the operators to make the free channels available to programmers who otherwise would not get carriage. Congress might also conceivably obligate cable operators to act as common carriers for some of their channels, with those channels being open to all through some sort of lottery system or time-sharing arrangement. Setting aside any possible Takings Clause issues, it stands to reason that if Congress may demand that telephone companies operate as common carriers, it can ask the same of cable companies; such an approach would not suffer from the defect of preferring one speaker to another.

But the First Amendment as we understand it today rests on the premise that it is government power, rather than private power, that is the main threat to free expression; and as a consequence, the Amendment imposes substantial limitations on the Government even when it is trying to serve concededly praiseworthy goals. Perhaps Congress can to some extent restrict, even in a content-based manner, the speech of cable operators and cable programmers. But it must do so in compliance with the constitutional requirements, requirements that were not complied with here. Accordingly, I would reverse the judgment below.

[Opinion of GINSBURG, J., concurring in part and dissenting in part omitted.]

PRUNEYARD SHOPPING CENTERS V. ROBINS

447 U.S. 74 (1980)

Mr. Justice REHNQUIST delivered the opinion of the Court.

We postponed jurisdiction of this appeal from the Supreme Court of California to decide the important federal constitutional questions it presented. Those are whether state constitutional provisions, which permit individuals to exercise free speech and petition rights on the property of a privately owned shopping center to which the public is invited, violate the shopping center owner's property rights under the Fifth and Fourteenth Amendments or his free speech rights under the First and Fourteenth Amendments.

I

Appellant PruneYard is a privately owned shopping center in the city of Campbell, Cal. It covers approximately 21 acres — 5 devoted to parking and 16 occupied by walkways, plazas, sidewalks, and buildings that contain more than 65 specialty shops, 10 restaurants, and a movie theater. The PruneYard is open to the public for the purpose of encouraging the patronizing of its commercial establishments. It has a policy not to permit any visitor or tenant to engage in any publicly expressive activity, including the circulation of petitions, that is not directly related to its commercial purposes. This policy has been strictly enforced in a nondiscriminatory fashion. The PruneYard is owned by appellant Fred Sahadi.

Appellees are high school students who sought to solicit support for their opposition to a United Nations resolution against "Zionism." On a Saturday afternoon they set up a card table in a corner of PruneYard's central courtyard. They distributed pamphlets and asked passersby to sign petitions, which were to be sent to the President and Members of Congress. Their activity was peaceful and orderly and so far as the record indicates was not objected to by PruneYard's patrons.

Soon after appellees had begun soliciting signatures, a security guard informed them that they would have to leave because their activity violated PruneYard regulations. The guard suggested that they move to the public sidewalk at the PruneYard's perimeter. Appellees immediately left the premises and later filed this lawsuit in the California Superior Court of Santa Clara County. They sought to enjoin appellants from denying them access to the PruneYard for the purpose of circulating their petitions.

[The California Supreme Court held that appellees' activities were protected expression under the California Constitution. On appeal, the shopping center argued that requiring them to permit appellees' activities violated its speech rights.]

V

Appellants . . . contend that a private property owner has a First Amendment right not to be forced by the State to use his property as a forum for the speech of others. They state that in Wooley v. Maynard, 430 U.S. 705 (1977), this Court concluded that a State may not constitutionally require an individual to participate in the dissemination of an ideological message by displaying it on his private property in a manner and for the express purpose that it be observed and read by the public. This rationale applies here, they argue, because the message of Wooley is that the State may not force an individual to display any message at all.

Wooley, however, was a case in which the government itself prescribed the message, required it to be displayed openly on appellee's personal property that was used "as part of his daily life," and refused to permit him to take any measures to cover up the motto even though the Court found that the display of the motto served no important state interest. Here, by contrast, there are a number of distinguishing factors. Most important, the shopping center by choice of its owner is not limited to the personal use of appellants. It is instead a business establishment that is open to the public to come and go as they please. The views expressed by members of the public in passing out pamphlets or seeking signatures for a petition thus will not likely be identified with those of the owner. Second, no specific message is dictated by the State to be displayed on appellants' property. There consequently is no danger of governmental discrimination for or against a particular message. Finally, as far as appears here appellants can expressly disavow any connection with the message by simply posting signs in the area where the speakers or handbillers stand. Such signs, for example, could disclaim any sponsorship of the message and could explain that the persons are communicating their own messages by virtue of state law.

Appellants also argue that their First Amendment rights have been infringed in light of West Virginia State Board of Education v. Barnette, 319 U.S. 624 (1943) and Miami Herald Publishing v. Tornillo, 418 U.S. 241 (1974). *Barnette* is inapposite because it involved the compelled recitation of a message containing an affirmation of belief. This Court held such compulsion unconstitutional because it "require[d] the individual to communicate by word and sign his acceptance" of government-dictated political ideas, whether or not he subscribed to them. Appellants are not similarly being compelled to affirm their belief in any governmentally prescribed position or view, and they are free to publicly dissociate themselves from the views of the speakers or handbillers.

Tornillo struck down a Florida statute requiring a newspaper to publish a political candidate's reply to criticism previously published in that newspaper. It rests on the principle that the State cannot tell a newspaper what it must print. The Florida statute contravened this principle in that it "exact[ed] a penalty on the basis of the content of a newspaper." There also was a danger in *Tornillo* that the statute would "dampe[n] the vigor and limi[t] the variety of public debate" by deterring editors from publishing controversial political statements that might trigger the application of the statute. Thus, the statute was found to be an "intrusion into the function of editors." These concerns obviously are not present here.

We conclude that neither appellants' federally recognized property rights nor their First Amendment rights have been infringed by the California Supreme Court's decision recognizing a right of appellees to exercise state-protected rights of expression and petition on appellants' property. The judgment of the Supreme Court of California is therefore

Affirmed.

[Concurring opinions of MARSHALL, J., and WHITE, J., omitted.]

Mr. Justice POWELL, with whom Mr. Justice WHITE joins, concurring in part and in the judgment. . . .

Restrictions on property use, like other state laws, are invalid if they infringe the freedom of expression and belief protected by the First and Fourteenth Amendments. In . . . today's opinion, the Court rejects appellants' contention that "a private property owner has a First Amendment right not to be forced by the State to use his property as a forum for the speech of others." I agree that the owner of this shopping center has failed to establish a cognizable First Amendment claim in this case. But some of the language in the Court's opinion is unnecessarily and perhaps confusingly broad. In my view, state action that transforms privately owned property into a forum for the expression of the public's views could raise serious First Amendment questions.

The State may not compel a person to affirm a belief he does not hold. See [Wooley v. Maynard and West Vigrinia State Board of Edcuation v. Barnett]. Whatever the full sweep of this principle, I do not believe that the result in Wooley v. Maynard, would have changed had the State of New Hampshire directed its citizens to place the slogan "Live Free or Die" in their shop windows rather than on their automobiles. In that case, we said that "[a] system which secures the right to proselytize religious, political, and ideological causes must also guarantee the concomitant right to decline to foster such concepts." 430 U.S., at 714. This principle on its face protects a person who refuses to allow use of his property as a marketplace for the ideas of others. And I can find no reason to exclude the owner whose property is "not limited to [his] personal use. . . ." A person who has merely invited the public onto his property for commercial purposes cannot fairly be said to have relinquished his right to decline "to be an instrument for fostering public adherence to an ideological point of view he finds unacceptable." Wooley v. Maynard, *supra*, 430 U.S., at 715.

As the Court observes, this case involves only a state-created right of limited access to a specialized type of property. But even when no particular message is mandated by the State, First Amendment interests are affected by state action that forces a property owner to admit third-party speakers. In many situations, a right of access is no less intrusive than speech compelled by the State itself. For example, a law requiring that a newspaper permit others to use its columns imposes an unacceptable burden upon the newspaper's First Amendment right to select material for publication. [Miami Herald Publishing Co. v. Tornillo]. See also Columbia Broadcasting System, Inc. v. Democratic National Committee, 412 U.S. 94, 117 (1973) (plurality opinion). Such a right of access burdens the newspaper's "fundamental right to decide what to print or omit." Wooley v. Maynard, 430 U.S., at 714; see Miami Herald

Publishing v. Tornillo. As such, it is tantamount to compelled affirmation and, thus, presumptively unconstitutional.[2]

The selection of material for publication is not generally a concern of shopping centers. But similar speech interests are affected when listeners are likely to identify opinions expressed by members of the public on commercial property as the views of the owner. If a state law mandated public access to the bulletin board of a freestanding store, hotel, office, or small shopping center, customers might well conclude that the messages reflect the view of the proprietor. The same would be true if the public were allowed to solicit or distribute pamphlets in the entrance area of a store or in the lobby of a private building. The property owner or proprietor would be faced with a choice: he either could permit his customers to receive a mistaken impression or he could disavow the messages. Should he take the first course, he effectively has been compelled to affirm someone else's belief. Should he choose the second, he had been forced to speak when he would prefer to remain silent. In short, he has lost control over his freedom to speak or not to speak on certain issues. The mere fact that he is free to dissociate himself from the views expressed on his property, cannot restore his "right to refrain from speaking at all." Wooley v. Maynard, 430 U.S., at 714.

A property owner also may be faced with speakers who wish to use his premises as a platform for views that he finds morally repugnant. Numerous examples come to mind. A minority-owned business confronted with leaflet distributers from the American Nazi Party or the Ku Klux Klan, a church-operated enterprise asked to host demonstrations in favor of abortion, or a union compelled to supply a forum to right-to-work advocates could be placed in an intolerable position if state law requires it to make its private property available to anyone who wishes to speak. The strong emotions evoked by speech in such situations may virtually compel the proprietor to respond.

The pressure to respond is particularly apparent when the owner has taken a position opposed to the view being expressed on his property. But an owner who strongly objects to some of the causes to which the state-imposed right of access would extend may oppose ideological activities "of *any* sort" that are not related to the purposes for which he has invited the public onto his property. See Abood v. Detroit Board of Education, 431 U.S. 209, 231, 241 (1977). To require the owner to specify the particular ideas he finds objectionable enough to compel a response would force him to relinquish his "freedom to maintain his own beliefs without public disclosure." *Ibid*. Thus, the right to control one's own speech may be burdened impermissibly even when listeners will not assume that the messages expressed on private property are those of the owner. . . .

---

2. Even if a person's own speech is not affected by a right of access to his property, a requirement that he lend support to the expression of a third party's views may burden impermissibly the freedoms of association and belief protected by the First and Fourteenth Amendments. . . . To require a landowner to supply a forum for causes he finds objectionable also might be an unacceptable "compelled subsidization" in some circumstances.

COMMENTS AND QUESTIONS

1.   Scarcity is clearly an important factor in determining whether government can impose access requirements upon the owner of a medium. In light of the preceding cases, does the Supreme Court distinguish economic scarcity from technological scarcity? In other words, how does the Court distinguish between newspaper publishing in which there may only be a single newspaper serving a city versus broadcast and cable?

2.   By lowering the costs of publishing and distributing content globally, does the growth of the Internet undermine the argument for access to other media? If a speaker can always send their message out across the Internet, does she need a right of access to newspapers or televisions?

3.   How does the monopoly like status of most cable operators enter into the access equation? Does it matter that until 1992 local municipalities were allowed to award cable systems exclusive franchises? *See* 47 U.S.C. §541(a)(1) (prohibiting a franchising authority from granting exclusive franchises and from unreasonably refusing to award an additional competitive franchise). *Consider* the Supreme Court's decision in Red Lion Broadcasting Co. v. FCC, 315. U.S. 367 (1969) (upholding a right of access to broadcasting stations, despite the fact the spectrum scarcity was, in part, created by law).

4.   In *Tornillo*, would the Supreme Court reach a different result if the statute required the publisher to accept the response as an advertisement with the government paying the full advertising fee? Would it matter if the newspaper had a policy of accepting all advertisements?

5.   What factors made the newspaper editor, broadcaster, and cable operator speakers under the First Amendment? Is the mall owner considered a speaker in *PruneYard*? Why is it acceptable to limit the free speech rights of certain speakers in order to provide access, but not others?

6.   What is the relationship between speech and property ownership? While this issue will be explored in greater detail in Chapter 6, is the newspaper editor's right based upon her ownership of the paper and ink that make up a newspaper? If so, then why is the mall owner not entitled to exclude leafleters?

7.   What is the relationship between access and content regulation? If access is justified because it promotes diversity of viewpoints, is it a content-based regulation of speech deserving strict scrutiny? In *Turner*, what is the majority's reasoning for concluding that Congress's interest in local programming was not based upon the content? How do the must-carry provisions differ from the right of reply statute at issue in *Tornillo*?

8.   Considering Problem 4.0, would StarttUp have a First Amendment defense if Congress or a local government passed legislation prohibiting ISPs from blocking access to Web sites or e-mail?

9.   What if StarttUp is ultimately successful in its efforts to become the world's largest Internet community? Could Congress or a state government require StarttUp to provide access to low-income families at reduced

rates? Could Congress require StarttUp to provide Web-hosting services to nonprofit organizations?

2. Open Access

In the early days of Internet regulation, a significant controversy over Internet access arose between Internet service providers and cable operators providing Internet access. Spurred, in part, by mergers in the cable industry and cable operators' plans to offer competing Internet services, Internet service providers argued that they should be entitled to provide consumers with access to the Internet through cable operators' high-speed cable networks. Known as "Open Access," to what extent did this claim raise the same First Amendment concerns as traditional media access cases?

The two cases extracted here provide early examples of this debate. They involve situations where local regulations required cable operators to allow competitors equal access to their systems. The debate about access to cyberspace has grown more complex in recent years as cable services and DSL services have become more powerful and more consolidated. Additionally, the advent of new fiber optic networks will raise new challenges for regulating access to online content. For a detailed examination of the development of these different kinds of networks, see Daniel Spulber & Christopher Yoo, *Rethinking Broadband Internet Access*, 22 Harv. J.L. & Tech. 1, 6-10 (2008). Spulber and Yoo note that in recent years, with the development and deployment of these new technologies, the regulatory questions about access have become much more complex than in the early days of the Internet. In particular, questions arise about whether local regulations, such as those discussed in the *Broward* and *Portland* cases excerpted below, are effectively preempted by federal laws governing common carriage and nondiscriminatory access requirements. Spulber & Yoo, *supra*, at 10-11.

Ultimately, a series of judicial decisions held that local authorities lacked the jurisdiction to compel access by ISPs to cable service. Spulber & Yoo, *supra*, at 15. Thus, while the cases extracted below provide some history about ways in which local courts dealt with open access issues in the early days of the Internet, the regulations examined in the cases have little relevance to future regulation of these questions. While many of the intricacies of federal regulation of cable modem, DSL, and fiber optic networks are too complex for consideration in this casebook, Spulber and Yoo provide a useful summary of the current state of regulation and suggested future directions for access regulation. They argue against heavy-handed regulation that might impact negatively on economic incentives for companies to provide these services.

COMCAST CABLEVISION OF BROWARD CO., INC. v. BROWARD COUNTY

124 F. Supp. 2d 685 (S.D. Fla. 2000)

MIDDLEBROOKS, District Judge. . . .

I. INTRODUCTION

The issue presented in this case is whether the First Amendment to the United States Constitution restricts the authority of local government to require a cable television system which offers its subscribers high-speed Internet service to allow competitors equal access to its system. Broward County, a political subdivision of the State of Florida, has adopted an ordinance that requires any cable system franchisee to provide any requesting Internet service provider access to its broadband Internet transport services on rates, terms, and conditions at least as favorable as those on which it provides such access to itself. . . .

C.

The Broward County ordinance operates to impose a significant constraint and economic burden directly on a cable operator's means and methodology of expression. The ordinance singles out cable operators from all other speakers and discriminates further against those cable operators who choose to provide Internet content. The ordinance has no application to wireless, satellite, or telephone transmission or other providers of Internet service. In these respects, the ordinance operates in much the same manner as the use tax held to violate the First Amendment in Minneapolis Star and Tribune Co. v. Minnesota Com'r of Revenue, 460 U.S. 573 (1983); *see also* Arkansas Writers' Project, Inc. v. Ragland, 481 U.S. 221 (1987); Grosjean v. American Press Co., 297 U.S. 233 (1936). But see Leathers v. Medlock, 499 U.S. 439 (1991). . . .

Under the First Amendment, government should not interfere with the process by which preferences for information evolve. Not only the message, but also the messenger receives constitutional protection.

The Broward County ordinance invidiously impacts a cable operator's ability to participate in the information market. The cable operator, unlike a telephone service, does not sell transmission but instead offers a collection of content. Like a newspaper, a cable operator sells advertising to defray the costs of its service. Advertising allows an operator to keep subscriber rates lower than would otherwise be the case, an attraction in obtaining the critical mass of subscribers necessary to pay for the sizable investment in physical plant.

The business plan adopted by the cable operators is not the only one possible and may not succeed. Some Internet service providers, for example,

Altavista, offer free access to the Internet relying only on advertising for revenues. This model is more similar to that used by broadcast television or radio. . . . Others may rely solely on subscriber fees. The imposition of an equal access provision by operation of the Broward County ordinance both deprives the cable operator of editorial discretion over its programming and harms its ability to market and finance its service, thereby curtailing the flow of information to the public. It distorts and disrupts the integrity of the information market by interfering with the ability of market participants to use different cost structures and economic approaches based upon the inherent advantages and disadvantages of their respective technology.

D.

The impact of the access requirement on a cable operator and the application of First Amendment analysis to the ordinance can be demonstrated by slightly changing the hypothetical posed by the County in its memorandum supporting summary judgment. Suppose the Broward County Commission, concerned about the ability of consumers to gain access to classified advertising and other sources of information, adopted an ordinance requiring *The Ft. Lauderdale News and Sun Sentinel* to deliver *The Miami Herald, The New York Times,* and the printed material of anyone who made a request on the same terms as it delivered its own newspaper. Could such an ordinance withstand scrutiny under the First Amendment?

Since Broward County's access regulation is only triggered by a cable operator's decision to offer an Internet information channel, it is very similar to the Florida law which led to the Supreme Court's decision in Miami Herald Pub. Co. v. Tornillo. . . . The argument of the proponents of that measure are echoed by the County's arguments here — that government has an obligation to ensure that a wide variety of views reach the public. It was argued that concentration of ownership and the expense of entry into publishing had resulted in a loss of any ability by the public to respond or contribute in any meaningful way to debate on issues. One newspaper towns had become the rule, said access proponents, with effective competition operating in only four percent of large cities.

The Supreme Court unanimously rejected these arguments finding that an enforceable right of access brings about a direct confrontation with the express provisions of the First Amendment. . . . It is ironic that a technology, which is permitting citizens greater ease of access to channels of communication than has existed at any time throughout history, is being subjected to the same arguments rejected by the Supreme Court in *Tornillo.* Broward County's ordinance intrudes upon the ability of the cable operator to choose the content of the cable system and imposes a cost in time and materials in order to make available the space that may be demanded. The result has been that cable operators have not provided Internet service in unincorporated Broward County. Compelled access like that ordered by the Broward County ordinance both penalizes expression and forces the cable operators to alter their content to conform to an agenda they do not set. See generally Pacific Gas and Elec. Co. v. Public Utilities Com'n of California, 475 U.S. 1 (1986). . . .

F.

In *Turner I*, the Supreme Court held that cable operators are generally entitled to the same First Amendment protection as the print media. The standard adopted by the Court in *Red Lion Broadcasting*, which was grounded on the scarcity of broadcasting frequencies, was held inapplicable to cable. "[T]he rationale for applying a less rigorous standard of First Amendment scrutiny to broadcast regulation . . . does not apply in the context of cable regulation." "[A]pplication of the more relaxed standard of scrutiny adopted in *Red Lion* and the other broadcast cases is inapt when determining the First Amendment validity of cable regulation."

Nevertheless, in *Turner I*, the Court upheld the must-carry provisions adopted by the FCC which require carriage of local broadcast stations on cable systems. The Court determined that the applicable standard to evaluate the must-carry provisions was the intermediate level of scrutiny applicable to content-neutral restrictions that impose an incidental burden on speech. However, the reasons given by the Court for applying intermediate rather than strict scrutiny do not apply in this case.

First, unlike the must-carry rules which applied to virtually all cable operators in the country, the Broward County ordinance applies only to the select few that seek to operate broadband Internet service. This ordinance is targeted only at the Plaintiffs, and it is likely to result in the elimination of broadband cable Internet service in unincorporated Broward County. The ordinance was adopted at the behest of a telephone company seeking to eliminate or hamper a competitor.

Moreover, differential treatment is not justified by some special characteristic of the medium being regulated. . . .

Cable operators control no bottleneck monopoly over access to the Internet. Today, most customers reach the Internet by telephone. Those who obtain access through cable can use the Internet to reach any Internet information provider. After inquiry, the FCC has concluded that it does not foresee monopoly, or even duopoly in broadband Internet services. The "bottleneck" theory offers no justification for less than heightened scrutiny of the Broward County ordinance.

Finally, the Court found that the must-carry regulations did not force the cable operators to alter their own message or create a risk that a cable viewer might assume that ideas or messages of the broadcaster were endorsed by the cable operator. The Court pointed out that cable had a long history of serving as a conduit for broadcast signals and that broadcasters were required by FCC regulation to identify themselves at least once every hour. The Court stated that no aspect of must-carry would cause a cable operator to avoid controversy and by so doing diminish the free flow of information and ideas. *See Turner I*, 512 U.S. at 655-56.

In contrast, there is no history of cable operators serving as a conduit for Internet service providers. During oral argument, counsel for Broward County estimated that there may be around 5,000 Internet service providers at present, and unlike broadcasters, there is no limit on the number that might demand access. Nor is there any reason to expect that Internet information services granted access to the cable system would not be offensive to the operator and its subscribers. The cable operator under the ordinance would be required to adopt technology which would allow its system to identify each subscriber's choice of Internet service provider so that equal access could be provided and accommodate the demands of the service providers, all in contravention of existing contracts. The Broward County ordinance, unlike the must-carry regulations of the FCC, threaten to diminish the free flow of information and ideas.

For these reasons, I believe this case falls within the rule of [*Tornillo*] and therefore strict scrutiny is required. However, if I am mistaken, the ordinance fails content-neutral scrutiny as well.

G.

. . . When the government defends a regulation on speech it must demonstrate that the harm it seeks to prevent is real, not merely conjectural, and that the regulation will alleviate the harm in a direct and material way. See Edenfield v. Fane, 507 U.S. 761, 770-71 (1993). A court may not simply assume that an ordinance will advance the asserted state interests sufficiently to justify its abridgment of expressive activity. See *Preferred Communications*, 476 U.S. at 496. While a legislative body is entitled to substantial deference, in First Amendment cases the deference afforded to legislative findings does not foreclose independent judgment of the facts bearing on an issue of constitutional law. See Landmark Communications, Inc. v. Virginia, 435 U.S. 829, 843 (1978).

Broward County argues that its ordinance is necessary to ensure competition by providing ISP's access to the "essential facility" operated by the cable operations. *See, e.g.,* Defendant Broward County's Memorandum of Law in Support of the County's Motion for Summary Judgment at 4, 6. According to the County, its ordinance was designed to ensure "competition" and "diversity" in cable broadband Internet services, and the cable operators "are thwarting such competition and diversity by using their exclusive control over the cable 'pipeline'. . . ."

However, the harm the ordinance is purported to address appears to be non-existent. Cable possesses no monopoly power with respect to Internet access. Most Americans now obtain Internet access through use of the telephone. Local telephone companies provide dial up Internet access to over 46.5 million customers, whereas all cable companies combined currently provide Internet services to only about two million customers. . . . The FCC has predicted that traditional telephone lines "will remain the principal means of accessing the Internet" in the near term. AOL, the most dominant ISP with over 24 million subscribers, and other predominantly dial-up ISPs have more than 90% of residential Internet users as customers.

With respect to advanced telecommunications capability or broadband, the FCC estimated that there were approximately one million subscribers as of December 31, 1999. Of these, approximately 875,000 subscribed to cable based services, 115,000 subscribed to asymmetric DSL, with the remaining attributed to other media. Since late 1998, cable increased subscribers approximately three-fold and local telephone companies increased their DSL subscribership approximately four-fold.

The FCC, the agency charged by Congress with the responsibility of monitoring the deployment of broadband technology, has concluded that the preconditions for monopoly in the consumer market for broadband appear absent. According to the FCC, there are, or likely will soon be, a large number of potential entrants into the residential market using different technologies such as DSL, cable modems, and utility fiber to the home, satellite, and radio. The FCC does not foresee the consumer market for broadband becoming a sustained monopoly or duopoly.

In contrast to the FCC, Broward County has conducted no inquiry. The County has proffered no substantial evidence demonstrating that actual harm exists that could justify infringement of First Amendment interests. "[T]he mere assertion of a dysfunction or failure in a speech market, without more is not sufficient to shield a speech regulation from the First Amendment. . . ." *Turner* I, 512 U.S. at 640. It has not been demonstrated that the Broward County ordinance furthers a substantial governmental interest. Therefore, even applying content-neutral intermediate scrutiny, the ordinance violates the First Amendment.

AT&T CORP. v. CITY OF PORTLAND

43 F. Supp. 2d 1146 (D. Or. 1999), *rev'd on other grounds,*
216 F.3d 871 (9th Cir. 2000)

[In *City of Portland*, the court examined an open access mandate imposed by the local municipality and county similar to the one struck down in *Broward County*. In the Portland case, the local Cable Regulatory Commission concluded that the exclusive contract between AT&T and @Home would drive many local Internet service providers out of the market because they would not be able to compete with the high-speed service. "The Commission intended that the open access requirement allow customers of unaffiliated ISPs to 'obtain direct access to their [ISP] of choice without having to pay the full

@Home retail rate.' Unaffiliated ISPs would not get a free ride on the cable modem platform. They would pay AT&T for access."]

PANNER, District Judge. . . .

Plaintiffs contend that the mandatory access provision violates their First Amendment rights. There is no free speech violation, however, because AT&T volunteered to give cable subscribers access to competing ISPs. See PruneYard Shopping Center v. Robins, 447 U.S. 74, 87 (1980) (requirement that shopping center owner allow protesters access did not violate owner's First Amendment rights because shopping center was "open to the public to come and go as they please. The views expressed by members of the public in passing out pamphlets or seeking signatures for a petition thus will not likely be identified with those of the owner.").

The open access requirement is an economic regulation. It does not force plaintiffs to carry any particular speech. See id. ("[N]o specific message is dictated by the State to be displayed on appellants' property. There consequently is no danger of governmental discrimination for or against a particular message."). Plaintiffs have not presented evidence that cable subscribers accessing the Internet through AT&T's cable modem platform would associate AT&T with the speech of unaffiliated ISPs. See AMSAT Cable, Ltd. v. Cablevision of Connecticut, 6 F.3d 867, 874 (2d Cir. 1993) (no evidence that transmission of cable system's programming into apartments would cause tenants to associate apartment owner with cable system).

Even if the open access requirement could be said to affect plaintiffs' free speech rights, the requirement passes the Supreme Court test for reasonableness. See United States v. O'Brien, 391 U.S. 367, 377 (1968); Chicago Cable Communications v. Chicago Cable Com'n, 879 F.2d 1540, 1548 (7th Cir. 1989) ("O'Brien is an appropriate standard-bearer for dealing with questions of local regulation of cable television."). The open access provision is within constitutional power of the City and County, it furthers the substantial governmental interest in preserving competition, the governmental interest is unrelated to the suppression of free speech, and the incidental restriction on free speech is no greater than necessary.

Note: Network Neutrality

Concerns about the ability of network providers to control content have been raised since the early days of the Internet. *See* Mark A. Lemley & Lawrence Lessig, *The End of End-to-End: Preserving the Architecture of the Internet in the Broadband Era*, 48 UCLA L. Rev. 925 (2001); Raymond Shih Ray Ku, *Open Internet Access and Freedom of Speech: A First Amendment Catch-22*, 75 Tul. L. Rev. 87 (2000). Many of these concerns have now been rolled into a debate known as "net neutrality," which is short for network neutrality. This has become a major issue in telecommunications law and policy in the United States. In fact, the popular search engine provider, Google, devotes a section of its Web site to a discussion of net neutrality issues, available at *http://www.google.com/help/netneutrality.html.* Google explains the concept of net neutrality in the following way:

> "Network neutrality is the principle that Internet users should be in control of what content they view and what applications they use on the Internet. The Internet has operated according to this neutrality principle since its earliest days. Indeed, it is this neutrality that has allowed many companies, including Google, to launch, grow, and innovate. Fundamentally, net neutrality is about equal access to the Internet. In our view, the broadband carriers should not be permitted to use their market power to discriminate against competing applications or content. Just as telephone companies are not permitted to tell consumers who they can call or what they can say, broadband carriers should not be allowed to use their market power to control activity online. Today, the neutrality of the Internet is at stake as the broadband carriers want Congress's permission to determine what content gets to you first and fastest. Put simply, this would fundamentally alter the openness of the Internet." *http://www.google.com/help/netneutrality.html*

Concerns about network neutrality arise in a variety of contexts, including that noted by Google — that is, the idea that customers could be enticed to pay more to have their packets of information prioritized along the cables that provide Internet access. Additionally, there is a possibility that cable and DSL providers could monitor content and report to government agencies in the context of, say, criminal investigations. A number of scholars have recently written about the benefits and disadvantages of the idea of promoting net neutrality: Tim Wu & Christopher Yoo, *Keeping the Internet Neutral,* 59 Fed. Comm. L.J. 575 (2007); Douglas Hass, *The Never-Was-Neutral Net and Why Informed End Users Can End the Net Neutrality Debates,* 22 Berkeley Tech. L.J. 1565 (2007); Kai Zhu, *Bringing Neutrality to Network Neutrality,* 22 Berkeley Tech. L.J. 615 (2007); Sascha Meinrath & Victor W Pickard, *The New Network Neutrality: Criteria for Internet Freedom,* 12 Int'l J. Comm. L. & Pol'y 225 (2008); Christopher Yoo, *Network Neutrality and the Economics of Congestion,* 94 Geo. L.J. 1847 (2006).

COMMENTS AND QUESTIONS

1. Is it possible to separate the medium from the message? According to the court in *Comcast,* is the transmission of data through cable speech? What is the connection?

2. How does the district court in *AT&T* approach the question of whether the medium can be separated from the message?

3. Should Internet service providers be considered speakers? Does the First Amendment permit treating the various services provided by ISPs as separate and distinct services? If so, under what circumstances? For an excellent discussion of how the First Amendment has evolved with respect to electronic

communications from the telegraph to computer networks, see Ithiel de Sola Pool, *Technologies of Freedom* (Belknap Press, 1983).

4.   Does the issue of Open Access differ from the question of an ISP blocking access to a Web site presented by Problem 4.0? Can an argument be made that even ISPs like AOL or MSN or AT&T should be treated as carriers of data similar to a telephone company instead of speakers?

5.   Consider the issues of preserving the open nature of the Internet and a First Amendment right of access in the context of instant messaging. Popular messaging services such as MSN Instant Messenger and AOL's Instant Messenger are designed to be incompatible with competing services. As such, they encourage users to become part of those communities as opposed to competing online communities. Is this a First Amendment access issue? This also occurred in the early days of text messaging—many cellphone companies did not provide access to text messages sent from other mobile phone networks.

E. INTERNET SERVICE PROVIDER LIABILITY FOR SPEECH

Problem 4.2

After completing your research on access and discussing StarttUp's blocking policy with Alan and Barbara in greater detail, you decide to maintain your policy. As General Counsel, you have taken the position that StarttUp is protected under the First Amendment because you exercise editorial control over your computer network. In other words, like a newspaper publisher, cable operator, or station manager, you decide what your users can and cannot read, watch, or listen to through your service. Having made this decision, StarttUp now examines complaints made by its users and determines whether in its judgment the offending posting, site, or e-mailer should be blocked from the network.

(a) After you implement this policy, you receive a particularly troubling letter from an attorney who claims that you have defamed her client. According to the letter, an allegedly defamatory statement about her client was posted on one of StarttUp's bulletin boards. The posting claimed that this individual defrauded various members of the StarttUp community by offering products for sale, accepting payment, and then not delivering the product. The letter claims that the client complained in writing to StarttUp demanding that the posting be removed, and StarttUp failed to remove it. You do, in fact, remember this complaint, because you looked into the matter personally, and decided to leave the

---

posting in place because you thought it might have some merit and because you thought the way the post was written was quite humorous.

(b) Alan and Barbara have also asked you to consider a proposal they have to set up a "classified ads" service through StarttUp, that would compete with businesses like Craigslist and Angie's List. They want to start out with a prototype of the service that would be limited to attempting to match local service providers with clients, with a focus on handyman services and home help. They intend to allow people with small home service businesses (handyman services, childcare, home tutors, mothers' helpers, etc.) to establish online profiles that potential customers can search to find the kind of help they are looking for. Alan and Barbara are also considering including as a feature of this service a place where customers can leave feedback about the home service businesses. They want to know if they might face any potential liability for defamatory or other objectionable content if they proceed with the prototype of this service. Additionally, might they face any liability if they eventually extend the service to cover other kinds of classified advertisements — such as a dating service, a housemate matching service, or an online auction service along the lines of eBay.

Problem 4.3

On the GOL blog, Demi has decided to write a post explaining why she deleted the comments by Flower Child (see Problem 4.1). In the post, she makes some rather uncomplimentary comments about Flower Child suggesting that Flower Child is sexist and racist. In the post, Demi also accuses Flower Child of purposely hiding her true identity for fear that readers of the blog might identify her as being involved in some recently well publicized hate crimes. In the comment section following the post, a new commenter, identifying herself only as "GG" has applauded Demi's actions and has added that she is fairly sure that Flower Child is indeed a person recently named in the news as being involved in hate crimes. GG adds in the comment that even if Flower Child is not the person named in the news reports, she is clearly "just as bad" as that person and "should be ashamed of herself."

A week or so later, Cora receives a letter from an attorney claiming to represent Flower Child, but declining to divulge Flower Child's true identity. The attorney has threatened Cora with a defamation action, as the organizer of the GOL blog. Cora has asked your advice as to how to respond to the attorney's letter.

Consider the following materials as you determine how to respond to these concerns.

1. Common Law Liability: Distributor or Publisher

CUBBY, INC. v. COMPUSERVE, INC.

776 F. Supp. 135 (S.D.N.Y. 1991)

LEISURE, District Judge:

. . . CompuServe develops and provides computer-related products and services, including CompuServe Information Service ("CIS"), an on-line general information service or "electronic library" that subscribers may access from a personal computer or terminal. Subscribers to CIS pay a membership fee and on-line time usage fees, in return for which they have access to the thousands of information sources available on CIS. Subscribers may also obtain access to over 150 special interest "forums," which are comprised of electronic bulletin boards, interactive on-line conferences, and topical databases.

One forum available is the Journalism Forum, which focuses on the journalism industry. Cameron Communications, Inc. ("CCI"), which is independent of CompuServe, has contracted to "manage, review, create, delete, edit and otherwise control the contents" of the Journalism Forum "in accordance with editorial and technical standards and conventions of style as established by CompuServe."

One publication available as part of the Journalism Forum is Rumorville USA ("Rumorville"), a daily newsletter that provides reports about broadcast journalism and journalists. Rumorville is published by Don Fitzpatrick Associates of San Francisco ("DFA"), which is headed by defendant Don Fitzpatrick. CompuServe has no employment, contractual, or other direct relationship with either DFA or Fitzpatrick; DFA provides Rumorville to the Journalism Forum under a contract with CCI. The contract between CCI and DFA provides that DFA "accepts total responsibility for the contents" of Rumorville. The contract also requires CCI to limit access to Rumorville to those CIS subscribers who have previously made membership arrangements directly with DFA.

CompuServe has no opportunity to review Rumorville's contents before DFA uploads it into CompuServe's computer banks, from which it is immediately available to approved CIS subscribers. CompuServe receives no part of any fees that DFA charges for access to Rumorville, nor does CompuServe compensate DFA for providing Rumorville to the Journalism Forum; the compensation CompuServe receives for making Rumorville available to its subscribers is the standard on-line time usage and membership fees charged to all CIS subscribers, regardless of the information services they use. CompuServe maintains that, before this action was filed, it had no notice of any complaints about the contents of the Rumorville publication or about DFA.

In 1990, plaintiffs Cubby, Inc. ("Cubby") and Robert Blanchard ("Blanchard") (collectively, "plaintiffs") developed Skuttlebut, a computer database designed to publish and distribute electronically news and gossip in the television news and radio industries. Plaintiffs intended to compete with Rumorville; subscribers gained access to Skuttlebut through their personal computers after completing subscription agreements with plaintiffs.

Plaintiffs claim that, on separate occasions in April 1990, Rumorville published false and defamatory statements relating to Skuttlebut and Blanchard, and that CompuServe carried these statements as part of the Journalism Forum. The allegedly defamatory remarks included a suggestion that individuals at Skuttlebut gained access to information first published by Rumorville "through some back door"; a statement that Blanchard was "bounced" from his previous employer, WABC; and a description of Skuttlebut as a "new start-up scam." . . .

Plaintiffs base their libel claim on the allegedly defamatory statements contained in the Rumorville publication that CompuServe carried as part of the Journalism Forum. CompuServe argues that, based on the undisputed facts, it was a distributor of Rumorville, as opposed to a publisher of the Rumorville statements. CompuServe further contends that, as a distributor of Rumorville, it cannot be held liable on the libel claim because it neither knew nor had reason to know of the allegedly defamatory statements. Plaintiffs, on the other hand, argue that the Court should conclude that CompuServe is a publisher of the statements and hold it to a higher standard of liability.

Ordinarily, " 'one who repeats or otherwise republishes defamatory matter is subject to liability as if he had originally published it.' " Cianci v. New Times Publishing Co., 639 F.2d 54, 61 (2d Cir. 1980) (Friendly, J.) (quoting Restatement (Second) of Torts §578 (1977)). With respect to entities such as news vendors, book stores, and libraries, however, "New York courts have long held that vendors and distributors of defamatory publications are not liable if they neither know nor have reason to know of the defamation."

The requirement that a distributor must have knowledge of the contents of a publication before liability can be imposed for distributing that publication is deeply rooted in the First Amendment, made applicable to the states through the Fourteenth Amendment. "[T]he constitutional guarantees of the freedom of speech and of the press stand in the way of imposing" strict liability on distributors for the contents of the reading materials they carry. Smith v. California, 361 U.S. 147, 152-53 (1959). In *Smith*, the Court struck down an ordinance that imposed liability on a bookseller for possession of an obscene book, regardless of whether the bookseller had knowledge of the book's contents. The Court reasoned that:

> "Every bookseller would be placed under an obligation to make himself aware of the contents of every book in his shop. It would be altogether unreasonable to demand so near an approach to omniscience." And the bookseller's burden would become the public's burden, for by restricting him the public's access to reading matter would be restricted. If the contents of bookshops and periodical stands were restricted to material of which their proprietors had made an inspection, they might be depleted indeed.

Id. at 153. Although *Smith* involved criminal liability, the First Amendment's guarantees are no less relevant to the instant action: "What a State may not constitutionally bring about by means of a criminal statute is likewise beyond the reach of its civil law of libel. The fear of damage awards . . . may be markedly more inhibiting than the fear of prosecution under a criminal statute." *New York Times Co. v. Sullivan,* 376 U.S. 254, 277 (1964).

CompuServe's CIS product is in essence an electronic, for-profit library that carries a vast number of publications and collects usage and membership fees from its subscribers in return for access to the publications. CompuServe and companies like it are at the forefront of the information industry revolution. High technology has markedly increased the speed with which information is gathered and processed; it is now possible for an individual with a personal computer, modem, and telephone line to have instantaneous access to thousands of news publications from across the United States and around the world. While CompuServe may decline to carry a given publication altogether, in reality, once it does decide to carry a publication, it will have little or no editorial control over that publication's contents. This is especially so when CompuServe carries the publication as part of a forum that is managed by a company unrelated to CompuServe.

With respect to the Rumorville publication, the undisputed facts are that DFA uploads the text of Rumorville into CompuServe's data banks and makes it available to approved CIS subscribers instantaneously. CompuServe has no more editorial control over such a publication than does a public library, book store, or newsstand, and it would be no more feasible for CompuServe to examine every publication it carries for potentially defamatory statements than it would be for any other distributor to do so. "First Amendment guarantees have long been recognized as protecting distributors of publications. . . . Obviously, the national distributor of hundreds of periodicals has no duty to monitor each issue of every periodical it distributes. Such a rule would be an impermissible burden on the First Amendment." . . .

Technology is rapidly transforming the information industry. A computerized database is the functional equivalent of a more traditional news vendor, and the inconsistent application of a lower standard of liability to an electronic news distributor such as CompuServe than that which is applied to a public library, book store, or newsstand would impose an undue burden on the free flow of information. Given the relevant First Amendment considerations, the appropriate standard of liability to be applied to CompuServe is whether it knew or had reason to know of the allegedly defamatory Rumorville statements.

B. CompuServe's Liability as a Distributor

CompuServe contends that it is undisputed that it had neither knowledge nor reason to know of the allegedly defamatory Rumorville statements, especially given the large number of publications it carries and the speed with which DFA uploads Rumorville into its computer banks and makes the publication available to CIS subscribers. Plaintiffs have not set forth anything other than conclusory allegations as to whether CompuServe knew or had reason to know of the Rumorville statements, and have failed to meet their burden on this issue. Plaintiffs do contend that CompuServe was informed that persons affiliated with Skuttlebut might be "hacking" in order to obtain unauthorized access to Rumorville, but that claim is wholly irrelevant to the issue of whether CompuServe was put on notice that the Rumorville publication contained statements accusing the Skuttlebut principals of engaging in "hacking."

Plaintiffs have not set forth any specific facts showing that there is a genuine issue as to whether CompuServe knew or had reason to know of Rumorville's contents. Because CompuServe, as a news distributor, may not be held liable if it neither knew nor had reason to know of the allegedly defamatory Rumorville statements, summary judgment in favor of CompuServe on the libel claim is granted.

Stratton Oakmont, Inc. v. Prodigy Services Company

1995 WL 323710 (N.Y. Sup. May 24, 1995)

[In an action for defamation, plaintiffs argued that Prodigy was the publisher of various statements appearing on Prodigy computer bulletin boards. The statements giving rise to the controversy were posted by an unidentified user, and accused the securities investment banking firm and its president of engaging in criminal and fraudulent behavior.]

Stuart L. Ain, Justice.

. . . Plaintiffs commenced this action against [Prodigy Services Co.] PRODIGY, the owner and operator of the computer network on which the statements appeared, and the unidentified party who posted the aforementioned statements. The second amended complaint alleges ten (10) causes of action, including claims for per se libel. On this motion, . . . Plaintiffs seek partial summary judgment on two issues, namely:

1. whether PRODIGY may be considered a "publisher" of the aforementioned statements; and,
2. whether Epstein, the Board Leader for the computer bulletin board on which the statements were posted, acted with actual and apparent authority as PRODIGY's "agent" for the purposes of the claims in this action. By way of background, it is undisputed that PRODIGY's computer network has at least two million subscribers who communicate with each other and with the general subscriber population on

PRODIGY's bulletin boards. "Money Talk" the board on which the aforementioned statements appeared, is allegedly the leading and most widely read financial computer bulletin board in the United States, where members can post statements regarding stocks, investments and other financial matters. PRODIGY contracts with bulletin Board Leaders, who, among other things, participate in board discussions and undertake promotional efforts to encourage usage and increase users. The Board Leader for "Money Talk" at the time the alleged libelous statements were posted was Charles Epstein. . . .

PRODIGY commenced operations in 1990. Plaintiffs base their claim that PRODIGY is a publisher in large measure on PRODIGY's stated policy, starting in 1990, that it was a family oriented computer network. In various national newspaper articles written by Geoffrey Moore, PRODIGY's Director of Market Programs and Communications, PRODIGY held itself out as an on-line service that exercised editorial control over the content of messages posted on its computer bulletin boards, thereby expressly differentiating itself from its competition and expressly likening itself to a newspaper. In one article PRODIGY stated:

"We make no apology for pursuing a value system that reflects the culture of the millions of American families we aspire to serve. Certainly no responsible newspaper does less when it chooses the type of advertising it publishes, the letters it prints, the degree of nudity and unsupported gossip its editors tolerate."

Plaintiffs characterize the aforementioned articles by PRODIGY as admissions and argue that, together with certain documentation and deposition testimony, these articles establish Plaintiffs' prima facie case. In opposition, PRODIGY insists that its policies have changed and evolved since 1990 and that the latest article on the subject, dated February, 1993, did not reflect PRODIGY's policies in October, 1994, when the allegedly libelous statements were posted. Although the eighteen month lapse of time between the last article and the aforementioned statements is not insignificant, and the Court is wary of interpreting statements and admissions out of context, these considerations go solely to the weight of this evidence.

Plaintiffs further rely upon the following additional evidence in support of their claim that PRODIGY is a publisher:

A. promulgation of "content guidelines" (the "Guidelines" found at Plaintiffs' Exhibit F) in which, inter alia, users are requested to refrain from posting notes that are "insulting" and are advised that "notes that harass other members or are deemed to be in bad taste or grossly repugnant to community standards, or are deemed harmful to maintaining a harmonious on-line community, will be removed when brought to PRODIGY's attention"; the Guidelines all expressly state that although

"Prodigy is committed to open debate and discussion on the bulletin boards, . . . this doesn't mean that 'anything goes' ";

B. use of a software screening program which automatically prescreens all bulletin board postings for offensive language;

C. the use of Board Leaders such as Epstein whose duties include enforcement of the Guidelines, according to Jennifer Ambrozek, the Manager of Prodigy's bulletin boards and the person at PRODIGY responsible for supervising the Board Leaders; and

D. testimony by Epstein as to a tool for Board Leaders known as an "emergency delete function" pursuant to which a Board Leader could remove a note and send a previously prepared message of explanation "ranging from solicitation, bad advice, insulting, wrong topic, off topic, bad taste, etcetera." . . .

A finding that PRODIGY is a publisher is the first hurdle for Plaintiffs to overcome in pursuit of their defamation claims, because one who repeats or otherwise republishes a libel is subject to liability as if he had originally published it. In contrast, distributors such as book stores and libraries may be liable for defamatory statements of others only if they knew or had reason to know of the defamatory statement at issue. [Cubby Inc. v. CompuServe Inc., 776 F. Supp. 135, 139.] A distributor, or deliverer of defamatory material is considered a passive conduit and will not be found liable in the absence of fault. . . . However, a newspaper, for example, is more than a passive receptacle or conduit for news, comment and advertising. [Miami Herald Publishing Co. v. Tornillo, 418 U.S. 241, 258.] The choice of material to go into a newspaper and the decisions made as to the content of the paper constitute the exercise of editorial control and judgment (Id.), and with this editorial control comes increased liability. (See *Cubby*, supra.) In short, the critical issue to be determined by this Court is whether the foregoing evidence establishes a prima facie case that PRODIGY exercised sufficient editorial control over its computer bulletin boards to render it a publisher with the same responsibilities as a newspaper.

Again, PRODIGY insists that its former policy of manually reviewing all messages prior to posting was changed "long before the messages complained of by Plaintiffs were posted." However, no documentation or detailed explanation of such a change, and the dissemination of news of such a change, has been submitted. In addition, PRODIGY argues that in terms of sheer volume—currently 60,000 messages a day are posted on PRODIGY bulletin boards—manual review of messages is not feasible. While PRODIGY admits that Board Leaders may remove messages that violate its Guidelines, it claims in conclusory manner that Board Leaders do not function as "editors." Furthermore, PRODIGY argues generally that this Court should not decide issues that can directly impact this developing communications medium without the benefit of a full record, although it fails to describe what further facts remain to be developed on this issue of whether it is a publisher.

As for legal authority, PRODIGY relies on the *Cubby* case, supra. . . .

The key distinction between CompuServe and PRODIGY is twofold. First, PRODIGY held itself out to the public and its members as controlling the content of its computer bulletin boards. Second, PRODIGY implemented this control through its automatic software screening program, and the Guidelines which Board Leaders are required to enforce. By actively utilizing technology and manpower to delete notes from its computer bulletin boards on the basis of offensiveness and "bad taste", for example, PRODIGY is clearly making decisions as to content (see, Miami Herald Publishing Co. v. Tornillo, supra), and such decisions constitute editorial control. (Id.) That such control is not complete and is enforced both as early as the notes arrive and as late as a complaint is made, does not minimize or eviscerate the simple fact that PRODIGY has uniquely arrogated to itself the role of determining what is proper for its members to post and read on its bulletin boards. Based on the foregoing, this Court is compelled to conclude that for the purposes of Plaintiffs' claims in this action, PRODIGY is a publisher rather than a distributor.

An interesting comparison may be found in Auvil v. CBS 60 Minutes [800 F. Supp. 928 (E.D. Wash. 1992)], where apple growers sued a television network and local affiliates because of an allegedly defamatory investigative report generated by the network and broadcast by the affiliates. The record established that the affiliates exercised no editorial control over the broadcast although they had the power to do so by virtue of their contract with CBS, they had the opportunity to do so by virtue of a three hour hiatus for the west coast time differential, they had the technical capability to do so, and they in fact had occasionally censored network programming in the past, albeit never in connection with "60 Minutes." The *Auvil* court found:

> It is argued that these features, coupled with the power to censor, triggered the duty to censor. That is a leap which the Court is not prepared to join in. . . .
> . . . [P]laintiffs' construction would force the creation of full time editorial boards at local stations throughout the country which possess sufficient knowledge, legal acumen and access to experts to continually monitor incoming transmissions and exercise on-the-spot discretionary calls or face $75 million dollar lawsuits at every turn. That is not realistic. . . .
> More than merely unrealistic in economic terms, it is difficult to imagine a scenario more chilling on the media's right of expression and the public's right to know.

Consequently, the court dismissed all claims against the affiliates on the basis of "conduit liability," which could not be established therein absent fault, which was not shown.

In contrast, here PRODIGY has virtually created an editorial staff of Board Leaders who have the ability to continually monitor incoming transmissions and in fact do spend time censoring notes. Indeed, it could be said that PRODIGY's current system of automatic scanning, Guidelines and Board Leaders may have a chilling effect on freedom of communication in Cyberspace, and it appears that this chilling effect is exactly what PRODIGY wants, but for the legal liability that attaches to such censorship.

Let it be clear that this Court is in full agreement with *Cubby* and *Auvil*. Computer bulletin boards should generally be regarded in the same context as bookstores, libraries and network affiliates. It is PRODIGY's own policies, technology and staffing decisions which have altered the scenario and mandated the finding that it is a publisher.

PRODIGY's conscious choice, to gain the benefits of editorial control, has opened it up to a greater liability than CompuServe and other computer networks that make no such choice. For the record, the fear that this Court's finding of publisher status for PRODIGY will compel all computer networks to abdicate control of their bulletin boards, incorrectly presumes that the market will refuse to compensate a network for its increased control and the resulting increased exposure. Presumably PRODIGY's decision to regulate the content of its bulletin boards was in part influenced by its desire to attract a market it perceived to exist consisting of users seeking a "family-oriented" computer service. This decision simply required that to the extent computer networks provide such services, they must also accept the concomitant legal consequences. In addition, the Court also notes that the issues addressed herein may ultimately be preempted by federal law if the Communications Decency Act of 1995, several versions of which are pending in Congress, is enacted. . . .

COMMENTS AND QUESTIONS

1. What factors distinguish the results in *Cubby* and *Stratton Oakmont*? Under the common law, should ISPs be accountable for the speech of others? If so, why?

2. If both CompuServe and Prodigy have the right to control the content available over their computer networks, should they both be held responsible at least under a theory of distributor liability?

3. Following the decision in *Cubby* and *Stratton Oakmont*, Congress passed the Communications Decency Act. Section 230 of the Act addressed ISP liability. As you study the following materials, to what extent does the CDA change ISP liability? What policy concerns justify these changes, if any?

4. The CDA, 47 U.S.C.A. §230, provides in pertinent part:

(a) Findings
   The Congress finds the following:
      (1) The rapidly developing array of Internet and other interactive computer services available to individual Americans represent an extraordinary advance in the availability of educational and informational resources to our citizens.
      (2) These services offer users a great degree of control over the information that they receive, as well as the potential for even greater control in the future as technology develops.
      (3) The Internet and other interactive computer services offer a forum for a true diversity of political discourse, unique

opportunities for cultural development, and myriad avenues for intellectual activity.

(4) The Internet and other interactive computer services have flourished, to the benefit of all Americans, with a minimum of government regulation.

(5) Increasingly Americans are relying on interactive media for a variety of political, educational, cultural, and entertainment services.

(b) Policy

It is the policy of the United States —

(1) to promote the continued development of the Internet and other interactive computer services and other interactive media;

(2) to preserve the vibrant and competitive free market that presently exists for the Internet and other interactive computer services, unfettered by Federal or State regulation;

(3) to encourage the development of technologies which maximize user control over what information is received by individuals, families, and schools who use the Internet and other interactive computer services;

(4) to remove disincentives for the development and utilization of blocking and filtering technologies that empower parents to restrict their children's access to objectionable or inappropriate on-line material; and

(5) to ensure vigorous enforcement of Federal criminal laws to deter and punish trafficking in obscenity, stalking, and harassment by means of computer.

(c) Protection for "good samaritan" blocking and screening of offensive material

(1) Treatment of publisher or speaker

No provider or user of an interactive computer service shall be treated as the publisher or speaker of any information provided by another information content provider.

(2) Civil liability

No provider or user of an interactive computer service shall be held liable on account of —

(A) any action voluntarily taken in good faith to restrict access to or availability of material that the provider or user considers to be obscene, lewd, lascivious, filthy, excessively violent, harassing, or otherwise objectionable, whether or not such material is constitutionally protected; or

(B) any action taken to enable or make available to information content providers or others the technical means to restrict access to material described in paragraph (1).

(d) Obligations of interactive computer service

A provider of interactive computer service shall, at the time of entering an agreement with a customer for the provision of interactive computer service and in a manner deemed appropriate by the provider, notify such customer that parental control protections (such as computer hardware, software, or filtering services) are commercially available that may assist the customer in limiting access to material that is harmful to minors. Such notice shall identify, or provide the customer with access to information identifying, current providers of such protections. . . .

(f) Definitions

As used in this section:

(1) Internet: The term "Internet" means the international computer network of both Federal and non-Federal interoperable packet switched data networks.

(2) Interactive computer service: The term "interactive computer service" means any information service, system, or access software provider that provides or enables computer access by multiple users to a computer server, including specifically a service or system that provides access to the Internet and such systems operated or services offered by libraries or educational institutions.

(3) Information content provider: The term "information content provider" means any person or entity that is responsible, in whole or in part, for the creation or development of information provided through the Internet or any other interactive computer service.

(4) Access software provider: The term "access software provider" means a provider of software (including client or server software), or enabling tools that do any one or more of the following:

(A) filter, screen, allow, or disallow content;

(B) pick, choose, analyze, or digest content; or

(C) transmit, receive, display, forward, cache, search, subset, organize, reorganize, or translate content.

2. Liability after the Communications Decency Act

ZERAN v. AMERICA ONLINE, INC.

129 F.3d 327 (4th Cir. 1997)

WILKINSON, Chief Judge:

. . . On April 25, 1995, an unidentified person posted a message on an [American On-line] AOL bulletin board advertising "Naughty Oklahoma T-Shirts." The posting described the sale of shirts featuring offensive and tasteless slogans related to the April 19, 1995, bombing of the Alfred P. Murrah Federal Building in Oklahoma City. Those interested in purchasing the shirts were instructed to call "Ken" at Zeran's home phone number in Seattle, Washington. As a result of this anonymously perpetrated prank, Zeran received a high volume of calls, comprised primarily of angry and derogatory messages, but also including death threats. Zeran could not change his phone number because he relied on its availability to the public in running his business out of his home. Later that day, Zeran called AOL and informed a company representative of his predicament. The employee assured Zeran that the posting would be removed from AOL's bulletin board but explained that as a matter of policy AOL would not post a retraction. The parties dispute the date that AOL removed this original posting from its bulletin board.

On April 26, the next day, an unknown person posted another message advertising additional shirts with new tasteless slogans related to the Oklahoma City bombing. Again, interested buyers were told to call Zeran's phone number, to ask for "Ken," and to "please call back if busy" due to high demand. The angry, threatening phone calls intensified. Over the next four days, an unidentified party continued to post messages on AOL's bulletin board, advertising additional items including bumper stickers and key chains with still more offensive slogans. During this time period, Zeran called AOL repeatedly and was told by company representatives that the individual account from which the messages were posted would soon be closed. Zeran also reported his case to Seattle FBI agents. By April 30, Zeran was receiving an abusive phone call approximately every two minutes.

Meanwhile, an announcer for Oklahoma City radio station KRXO received a copy of the first AOL posting. On May 1, the announcer related the message's contents on the air, attributed them to "Ken" at Zeran's phone number, and urged the listening audience to call the number. After this radio broadcast, Zeran was inundated with death threats and other violent calls from Oklahoma City residents. Over the next few days, Zeran talked to both KRXO and AOL representatives. He also spoke to his local police, who subsequently surveilled his home to protect his safety. By May 14, after an Oklahoma City newspaper published a story exposing the shirt advertisements as a hoax and after KRXO made an on-air apology, the number of calls to Zeran's residence finally subsided to fifteen per day.

Zeran first filed suit on January 4, 1996, against radio station KRXO in the United States District Court for the Western District of Oklahoma. On April 23, 1996, he filed this separate suit against AOL in the same court. Zeran did not bring any action against the party who posted the offensive messages. After Zeran's suit against AOL was transferred to the Eastern District of Virginia pursuant to 28 U.S.C. §1404(a), AOL answered Zeran's complaint and interposed 47 U.S.C. §230 as an affirmative defense. AOL then moved for judgment on the pleadings pursuant to Fed. R. Civ. P. 12(c). The district court granted AOL's motion, and Zeran filed this appeal.

II.

A.

Because §230 was successfully advanced by AOL in the district court as a defense to Zeran's claims, we shall briefly examine its operation here. Zeran seeks to hold AOL liable for defamatory speech initiated by a third party. He argued to the district court that once he notified AOL of the unidentified third party's hoax, AOL had a duty to remove the defamatory posting promptly, to notify its subscribers of the message's false nature, and to effectively screen future defamatory material. Section 230 entered this litigation as an affirmative defense pled by AOL. The company claimed that Congress immunized interactive computer service providers from claims based on information posted by a third party.

The relevant portion of §230 states: "No provider or user of an interactive computer service shall be treated as the publisher or speaker of any information provided by another information content provider." 47 U.S.C. §230(c)(1). By its plain language, §230 creates a federal immunity to any cause of action that would make service providers liable for information originating with a third-party user of the service. Specifically, §230 precludes courts from entertaining claims that would place a computer service provider in a publisher's role. Thus, lawsuits seeking to hold a service provider liable for its exercise of a publisher's traditional editorial functions — such as deciding whether to publish, withdraw, postpone or alter content — are barred.

The purpose of this statutory immunity is not difficult to discern. Congress recognized the threat that tort-based lawsuits pose to freedom of speech in the new and burgeoning Internet medium. The imposition of tort liability on service providers for the communications of others represented, for Congress, simply another form of intrusive government regulation of speech. Section 230 was enacted, in part, to maintain the robust nature of Internet communication and, accordingly, to keep government interference in the medium to a minimum. In specific statutory findings, Congress recognized the Internet and interactive computer services as offering "a forum for a true diversity of political discourse, unique opportunities for cultural development, and myriad avenues for intellectual activity." Id. §230(a)(3). It also found that the Internet and interactive computer services "have flourished, to the benefit of all Americans, with a minimum of government regulation." Id. §230(a)(4). Congress further stated that it is "the policy of the United States . . . to preserve the vibrant and competitive free market that presently exists for the Internet and other interactive computer services, unfettered by Federal or State regulation." Id. §230(b)(2).

None of this means, of course, that the original culpable party who posts defamatory messages would escape accountability. While Congress acted to keep government regulation of the Internet to a minimum, it also found it to be the policy of the United States "to ensure vigorous enforcement of Federal criminal laws to deter and punish trafficking in obscenity, stalking, and harassment by means of computer." Id. §230(b)(5). Congress made a policy choice, however, not to deter harmful on-line speech through the separate route of imposing tort liability on companies that serve as intermediaries for other parties' potentially injurious messages.

Congress' purpose in providing the §230 immunity was thus evident. Interactive computer services have millions of users. See Reno v. ACLU, 521 U.S. at, 117 S. Ct. at 2334 (noting that at time of district court trial, "commercial on-line services had almost 12 million individual subscribers"). The amount of information communicated via interactive computer services is therefore staggering. The specter of tort liability in an area of such prolific speech would have an obvious chilling effect. It would be impossible for service providers to screen each of their millions of postings for possible problems. Faced with potential liability for each message republished by their services, interactive computer service providers might choose to severely restrict the number and type of messages posted. Congress considered the weight of the speech interests implicated and chose to immunize service providers to avoid any such restrictive effect.

Another important purpose of §230 was to encourage service providers to self-regulate the dissemination of offensive material over their services. In this respect, §230 responded to a New York state court decision, Stratton Oakmont, Inc. v. Prodigy Servs. Co., 1995 WL 323710 (N.Y. Sup. Ct. May 24, 1995). . . .

Congress enacted §230 to remove the disincentives to self regulation created by the *Stratton Oakmont* decision. Under that court's holding, computer service providers who regulated the dissemination of offensive material on their services risked subjecting themselves to liability, because such regulation cast the service provider in the role of a publisher. Fearing that the specter of liability would therefore deter service providers from blocking and screening offensive material, Congress enacted §230's broad immunity "to remove disincentives for the development and utilization of blocking and filtering technologies that empower parents to restrict their children's access to objectionable or inappropriate on-line material." 47 U.S.C. §230(b)(4). In line with this purpose, §230 forbids the imposition of publisher liability on a service provider for the exercise of its editorial and self-regulatory functions.

B.

Zeran argues, however, that the §230 immunity eliminates only publisher liability, leaving distributor liability intact. Publishers can be held liable for defamatory statements contained in their works even absent proof that they had specific knowledge of the statement's inclusion. W. Page Keeton et al., Prosser and Keeton on the Law of Torts §113, at 810 (5th ed. 1984). According to Zeran, interactive computer service providers like AOL are normally considered instead to be distributors, like traditional news vendors or book sellers. Distributors cannot be held liable for defamatory statements contained in the materials they distribute unless it is proven at a minimum that they have actual knowledge of the defamatory statements upon which liability is predicated. Id. at 811 (explaining that distributors are not liable "in the absence of proof that they knew or had reason to know of the existence of defamatory matter contained in matter published"). Zeran contends that he provided AOL with sufficient notice of the defamatory statements appearing on the company's bulletin board. This notice is significant, says Zeran, because AOL could be held liable as a distributor only if it acquired knowledge of the defamatory statements' existence.

Because of the difference between these two forms of liability, Zeran contends that the term "distributor" carries a legally distinct meaning from the term "publisher." Accordingly, he asserts that Congress' use of only the term "publisher" in §230 indicates a purpose to immunize service providers only from publisher liability. He argues that distributors are left unprotected by §230 and, therefore, his suit should be permitted to proceed against AOL. We disagree. Assuming arguendo that Zeran has satisfied the requirements for imposition of distributor liability, this theory of liability is merely a subset, or a species, of publisher liability, and is therefore also foreclosed by §230.

The terms "publisher" and "distributor" derive their legal significance from the context of defamation law. Although Zeran attempts to artfully plead his claims as ones of negligence, they are indistinguishable from a garden variety defamation action. Because the publication of a statement is a necessary element in a defamation action, only one who publishes can be subject to this form of tort liability. Restatement (Second) of Torts §558(b) (1977); Keeton et al., supra, §113, at 802. Publication does not only describe the choice by an author to include certain information. In addition, both the negligent communication of a defamatory statement and the failure to remove such a statement when first communicated by another party — each alleged by Zeran here under a negligence label — constitute publication. Restatement (Second) of Torts §577. In fact, every repetition of a defamatory statement is considered a publication. Keeton et al., supra, §113, at 799.

In this case, AOL is legally considered to be a publisher. "[E]very one who takes part in the publication . . . is charged with publication." Id. Even distributors are considered to be publishers for purposes of defamation law:

> Those who are in the business of making their facilities available to disseminate the writings composed, the speeches made, and the information gathered by others may also be regarded as participating to such an extent in making the books, newspapers, magazines, and information available to others as to be regarded as publishers. They are intentionally making the contents available to others, sometimes without knowing all of the contents — including the defamatory content — and sometimes without any opportunity to ascertain, in advance, that any defamatory matter was to be included in the matter published. . . .

Id. at 803. AOL falls squarely within this traditional definition of a publisher and, therefore, is clearly protected by §230's immunity.

Zeran contends that decisions like *Stratton Oakmont* and Cubby, Inc. v. CompuServe Inc., 776 F. Supp. 135 (S.D.N.Y. 1991), recognize a legal distinction between publishers and distributors. He misapprehends, however, the significance of that distinction for the legal issue we consider here. It is undoubtedly true that mere conduits, or distributors, are subject to a different standard of liability. As explained above, distributors must at a minimum have knowledge of the existence of a defamatory statement as a prerequisite to liability. But this distinction signifies only that different standards of liability may be applied within the larger publisher category, depending on the specific type of publisher concerned. See Keeton et al., supra, §113, at 799-800 (explaining that every party involved is charged with publication, although degrees of legal responsibility differ). To the extent that decisions like *Stratton* and *Cubby* utilize the terms "publisher" and "distributor" separately, the decisions correctly describe two different standards of liability. *Stratton* and *Cubby* do not, however, suggest that distributors are not also a type of publisher for purposes of defamation law.

Zeran simply attaches too much importance to the presence of the distinct notice element in distributor liability. The simple fact of notice surely cannot transform one from an original publisher to a distributor in the eyes of the law. To the contrary, once a computer service provider receives notice of a potentially defamatory posting, it is thrust into the role of a traditional publisher. The computer service provider must decide whether to publish, edit, or withdraw the posting. In this respect, Zeran seeks to impose liability on AOL for assuming the role for which §230 specifically proscribes liability — the publisher role.

Our view that Zeran's complaint treats AOL as a publisher is reinforced because AOL is cast in the same position as the party who originally posted the offensive messages. According to Zeran's logic, AOL is legally at fault because it communicated to third parties an allegedly defamatory statement. This is precisely the theory under which the original poster of the offensive messages would be found liable. If the original party is considered a publisher of the offensive messages, Zeran certainly cannot attach liability to AOL under the same theory without conceding that AOL too must be treated as a publisher of the statements.

Zeran next contends that interpreting §230 to impose liability on service providers with knowledge of defamatory content on their services is consistent with the statutory purposes outlined in Part IIA. Zeran fails, however, to understand the practical implications of notice liability in the interactive computer service context. Liability upon notice would defeat the dual purposes advanced by §230 of the CDA. Like the strict liability imposed by the *Stratton Oakmont* court, liability upon notice reinforces service providers' incentives to restrict speech and abstain from self-regulation.

If computer service providers were subject to distributor liability, they would face potential liability each time they receive notice of a potentially defamatory statement — from any party, concerning any message. Each notification would require a careful yet rapid investigation of the circumstances surrounding the posted information, a legal judgment concerning the information's defamatory character, and an on-the-spot editorial decision whether to risk liability by allowing the continued publication of that information. Although this might be feasible for the traditional print publisher, the sheer number of postings on interactive computer services would create an impossible burden in the Internet context. Cf. Auvil v. CBS 60 Minutes, 800 F. Supp. 928, 931 (E.D. Wash. 1992) (recognizing that it is unrealistic for network affiliates to "monitor incoming transmissions and exercise on-the-spot discretionary calls"). Because service providers would be subject to liability only for the publication of information, and not for its removal, they would have a natural incentive simply to remove messages upon notification, whether the contents were defamatory or not. Thus, like strict liability, liability upon notice has a chilling effect on the freedom of Internet speech.

Similarly, notice-based liability would deter service providers from regulating the dissemination of offensive material over their own services. Any efforts by a service provider to investigate and screen material posted on its service would only lead to notice of potentially defamatory material more frequently and thereby create a stronger basis for liability. Instead of subjecting themselves to further possible lawsuits, service providers would likely eschew any attempts at self-regulation.

More generally, notice-based liability for interactive computer service providers would provide third parties with a no-cost means to create the basis for future lawsuits. Whenever one was displeased with the speech of another party conducted over an interactive computer service, the offended party could simply "notify" the relevant service provider, claiming the information to be legally defamatory. In light of the vast amount of speech communicated through interactive computer services, these notices could produce an impossible burden for service providers, who would be faced with ceaseless choices of suppressing controversial speech or sustaining prohibitive liability. Because the probable effects of distributor liability on the vigor of Internet speech and on service provider self-regulation are directly contrary to §230's statutory purposes, we will not assume that Congress intended to leave liability upon notice intact. . . .

BLUMENTHAL v. DRUDGE

992 F. Supp. 44 (D.D.C. 1998)

[Plaintiffs, Plaintiffs Sidney Blumenthal and Jacqueline Jordan Blumenthal sued Matt Drudge and America Online for statements made in the Drudge Report in which Drudge accused Sidney Blumenthal, a Clinton White House appointee, of abusing his wife in the past.]

PAUL L. FRIEDMAN, District Judge.

This is a defamation case revolving around a statement published on the Internet by defendant Matt Drudge. . . .

Access to defendant Drudge's world wide web site is available at no cost to anyone who has access to the Internet at the Internet address of "www. drudgereport.com." . . . In addition, during the time period relevant to this case, Drudge had developed a list of regular readers or subscribers to whom he e-mailed each new edition of the Drudge Report. By March 1995, the Drudge Report had 1,000 e-mail subscribers, and plaintiffs allege that by 1997 Drudge had 85,000 subscribers to his e-mail service. . . .

In late May or early June of 1997 . . . defendant Drudge entered into a written license agreement with AOL.[3] The agreement made the Drudge Report available to all members of AOL's service for a period of one year. In exchange, defendant Drudge received a flat monthly "royalty payment" of $3,000 from AOL. During the time relevant to this case, defendant Drudge has had no other source of income. Under the licensing agreement, Drudge is to create, edit, update and "otherwise manage" the content of the Drudge Report, and AOL may "remove content that AOL reasonably determine[s] to violate AOL's then standard terms of service." Drudge transmits new editions of the Drudge Report by e-mailing them to AOL. AOL then posts the new editions on the AOL service. Drudge also has continued to distribute each new edition of the Drudge Report via e-mail and his own web site.

Late at night on the evening of Sunday, August 10, 1997 (Pacific Daylight Time), defendant Drudge wrote and transmitted the edition of the Drudge Report that contained the alleged defamatory statement about the Blumenthals. Drudge transmitted the report from Los Angeles, California by e-mail to his direct subscribers and by posting both a headline and the full text of the Blumenthal story on his world wide web site. He then transmitted the text but not the headline to AOL, which in turn made it available to AOL subscribers. . . .

The near instantaneous possibilities for the dissemination of information by millions of different information providers around the world to those with access to computers and thus to the Internet have created ever-increasing opportunities for the exchange of information and ideas in "cyberspace." This information revolution has also presented unprecedented challenges relating to rights of privacy and reputational rights of individuals, to the control of obscene and pornographic materials, and to competition among journalists and news organizations for instant news, rumors and other information that is communicated so quickly that it is too often unchecked and unverified.

---

3. According to AOL, it operates "the world's largest interactive computer service. AOL's more than nine million subscribers use the AOL service as a conduit to receive and disseminate vast quantities of information by means of modern connections to AOL's computer network."

Needless to say, the legal rules that will govern this new medium are just beginning to take shape. . . .

In February of 1996, Congress made an effort to deal with some of these challenges in enacting the Communications Decency Act of 1996. While various policy options were open to the Congress, it chose to "promote the continued development of the Internet and other interactive computer services and other interactive media" and "to preserve the vibrant and competitive free market" for such services, largely "unfettered by Federal or State regulation. . . ." 47 U.S.C. §230(b)(1) and (2). Whether wisely or not, it made the legislative judgment to effectively immunize providers of interactive computer services from civil liability in tort with respect to material disseminated by them but created by others. In recognition of the speed with which information may be disseminated and the near impossibility of regulating information content, Congress decided not to treat providers of interactive computer services like other information providers such as newspapers, magazines or television and radio stations, all of which may be held liable for publishing or distributing obscene or defamatory material written or prepared by others. While Congress could have made a different policy choice, it opted not to hold interactive computer services liable for their failure to edit, withhold or restrict access to offensive material disseminated through their medium. . . .

Plaintiffs concede that AOL is a "provider . . . of an interactive computer service" for purposes of Section 230, and that if AOL acted exclusively as a provider of an interactive computer service it may not be held liable for making the Drudge Report available to AOL subscribers. They also concede that Drudge is an "information content provider" because he wrote the alleged defamatory material about the Blumenthals contained in the Drudge Report. While plaintiffs suggest that AOL is responsible along with Drudge because it had some role in writing or editing the material in the Drudge Report, they have provided no factual support for that assertion. Indeed, plaintiffs affirmatively state that "no person, other than Drudge himself, edited, checked, verified, or supervised the information that Drudge published in the Drudge Report." It also is apparent to the Court that there is no evidence to support the view originally taken by plaintiffs that Drudge is or was an employee or agent of AOL, and plaintiffs seem to have all but abandoned that argument.

AOL acknowledges both that Section 230(c)(1) would not immunize AOL with respect to any information AOL developed or created entirely by itself and that there are situations in which there may be two or more information content providers responsible for material disseminated on the Internet — joint authors, a lyricist and a composer, for example. While Section 230 does not preclude joint liability for the joint development of content, AOL maintains that there simply is no evidence here that AOL had any role in creating or developing any of the information in the Drudge Report. The Court agrees. It is undisputed that the Blumenthal story was written by Drudge without any substantive or editorial involvement by AOL. Drudge

Decl. II §§46-47. AOL was nothing more than a provider of an interactive computer service on which the Drudge Report was carried, and Congress has said quite clearly that such a provider shall not be treated as a "publisher or speaker" and therefore may not be held liable in tort. 47 U.S.C. §230(c)(1). . . .

Plaintiffs make the additional argument, however, that Section 230 of the Communications Decency Act does not provide immunity to AOL in this case because Drudge was not just an anonymous person who sent a message over the Internet through AOL. He is a person with whom AOL contracted, whom AOL paid $3,000 a month — $36,000 a year, Drudge's sole, consistent source of income — and whom AOL promoted to its subscribers and potential subscribers as a reason to subscribe to AOL. Furthermore, the license agreement between AOL and Drudge by its terms contemplates more than a passive role for AOL; in it, AOL reserves the "right to remove, or direct [Drudge] to remove, any content which, as reasonably determined by AOL . . . violates AOL's then-standard Terms of Service. . . ." By the terms of the agreement, AOL also is "entitled to require reasonable changes to . . . content, to the extent such content will, in AOL's good faith judgment, adversely affect operations of the AOL network."

In addition, shortly after it entered into the licensing agreement with Drudge, AOL issued a press release making clear the kind of material Drudge would provide to AOL subscribers — gossip and rumor — and urged potential subscribers to sign onto AOL in order to get the benefit of the Drudge Report. The press release was captioned: "AOL Hires Runaway Gossip Success Matt Drudge." It noted that "[m]averick gossip columnist Matt Drudge has teamed up with America On-line," and stated: "Giving the Drudge Report a home on America On-line (keyword: Drudge) opens up the floodgates to an audience ripe for Drudge's brand of reporting. . . . AOL has made Matt Drudge instantly accessible to members who crave instant gossip and news breaks." Why is this different, the Blumenthals suggest, from AOL advertising and promoting a new purveyor of child pornography or other offensive material? Why should AOL be permitted to tout someone as a gossip columnist or rumor monger who will make such rumors and gossip "instantly accessible" to AOL subscribers, and then claim immunity when that person, as might be anticipated, defames another?

If it were writing on a clean slate, this Court would agree with plaintiffs. AOL has certain editorial rights with respect to the content provided by Drudge and disseminated by AOL, including the right to require changes in content and to remove it; and it has affirmatively promoted Drudge as a new source of unverified instant gossip on AOL. Yet it takes no responsibility for any damage he may cause. AOL is not a passive conduit like the telephone company, a common carrier with no control and therefore no responsibility for what is said over the telephone wires. Because it has the right to exercise editorial control over those with whom it contracts and whose words it disseminates, it would seem only fair to hold AOL to the liability standards applied to a publisher or, at least, like a book store owner or library, to the liability standards applied to a distributor. But Congress has made a different policy choice by providing immunity even where the interactive service provider has an active, even aggressive role in making available content prepared by others. In some sort of tacit quid pro quo arrangement with the service provider community, Congress has conferred immunity from tort liability as an incentive to Internet service providers to self-police the Internet for obscenity and other offensive material, even where the self-policing is unsuccessful or not even attempted.

. . . While it appears to this Court that AOL in this case has taken advantage of all the benefits conferred by Congress in the Communications Decency Act, and then some, without accepting any of the burdens that Congress intended, the statutory language is clear: AOL is immune from suit, and the Court therefore must grant its motion for summary judgment.

COMMENTS AND QUESTIONS

1. Under what circumstances does §230 of the CDA provide ISPs with a safe harbor from liability?

2. Is the *Zeran* court's rejection of distributor liability compelled by §230? Is this conclusion undermined by the fact that Congress was willing to impose a distributor liability in the context of copyright infringement under 17 U.S.C. §512, which will be studied in Chapter 4?

3. Why does §230 immunize ISPs from liability for defamation? According to the Supreme Court in *Reno*, the CDA was enacted to restrict access to sexual material on the Internet. While Congress may have wanted ISPs to voluntarily block these materials and not be held responsible, is it clear that defamation claims fall within the scope of the statute? The decisions in both *Zeran* and *Drudge* rely upon the House Conference report for the conclusion that §230 was intended to preclude suits for defamation. The Conference Report states:

> One of the specific purposes of this section is to overrule Stratton Oakmont v. Prodigy and any other similar decisions which have treated such providers and users as publishers or speakers of content that is not their own because they have restricted access to objectionable material. The conferees believe that such decisions create serious obstacles to the important federal policy of empowering parents to determine the content of communications their children receive through interactive computer services.

H.R. Conf. Rep. No. 104-458, at 194 (1996). How does a policy of enabling parents to filter content support defamation immunity for ISPs?

4. *Drudge* also raised the question of when is speech the ISP's speech. As someone who received royalty payments from AOL, why is Drudge not an employee of, or contractor for, AOL? According to *Zeran* and *Drudge*, when can an ISP be sued for defamation?

5. As a result of §230, is there anything to prevent an ISP from blocking any content it desires? Is that result consistent with the statute's stated goal of preserving the Internet as a "vibrant forum for a true diversity of political discourse, unique opportunities for cultural development, and myriad avenues for intellectual activity"?

6. Other courts have also interpreted §230 as immunizing interactive computer service providers from liability even when they take no steps to block offensive content. *See* Kathleen R. v. City of Livermore, 87 Cal. App. 4th 684, 104 Cal. Rptr. 2d 772 (Cal. Ct. App. 2001) (holding that §230 immunized a library from liability for failing to block material harmful to minors); Doe v. America Online, Inc., 783 So. 2d 1010 (Fla. 2001) (holding that §230 immunized an Internet service provider who had allegedly received notice of objectionable material and failed to block); Stoner v. eBay, Inc., 56 U.S.P.Q.2d 1852 (Cal. Super. Ct. Nov. 1, 2000) (holding that §230 immunized eBay from liability for allegedly reaping profits from the sale of unauthorized sound recordings).

7. The preceding cases dealt with situations involving one-way communications between an internet service provider and an Internet user. In other words, they dealt with material transmitted from a website to a user, where the website was, for the most part, a passive conduit of that information. As the Internet has evolved in recent years, we have moved into an age of what has been described as Web 2.0 technologies. These web services are more interactive than previous Web 1.0 services in that content now tends to be collaboratively created rather than created by one person and transmitted to users. In other words, users play a much more interactive and collaborative role in creating online content. They collaborate both with each other and with online services such as Wikipedia, Facebook, MySpace, YouTube, Flickr, Craigslist, Angie's List, eBay, and the like. Courts have recently started to confront questions of Internet service provider immunity under section 230 of the Communications Decency Act in the context of more interactive online services where content is created collaboratively by service providers and their users. Consider the following case.

FAIR HOUSING COUNCIL OF SAN FERNANDO VALLEY; THE FAIR HOUSING COUNCIL OF SAN DIEGO v. ROOMMATE.COM, LLC

521 F.3d 1157 (9th Cir. 2008)

KOZINSKI, Circuit Judge.

... Defendant Roommate.com, LLC ("Roommate") operates a website designed to match people renting out spare rooms with people looking for a place to live. ... Roommate seeks to profit by collecting revenue from advertisers and subscribers.

Before subscribers can search listings or post housing opportunities on Roommate's website, they must create profiles, a process that requires them to answer a series of questions. In addition to requesting basic information — such as name, location and email address — Roommate requires each subscriber to disclose his sex, sexual orientation and whether he would bring children to a household. Each subscriber must also describe his preferences in roommates with respect to the same three criteria: sex, sexual orientation and whether they will bring children to the household. The site also encourages subscribers to provide "Additional Comments" describing themselves and their desired roommate in an open-ended essay. After a new subscriber completes the application, Roommate assembles his answers into a "profile page." The profile page displays the subscriber's pseudonym, his description and his preferences, as divulged through answers to Roommate's questions.

Subscribers can choose between two levels of service: Those using the site's free service level can create their own personal profile page, search the profiles of others and send personal email messages. They can also receive periodic emails from Roommate, informing them of available housing opportunities matching their preferences. Subscribers who pay a monthly fee also gain the ability to read emails from other users, and to view other subscribers' "Additional Comments."

The Fair Housing Councils of the San Fernando Valley and San Diego ("Councils") sued Roommate in federal court, alleging that Roommate's business violates the federal Fair Housing Act ("FHA"), 42 U.S.C. §3601 et seq., and California housing discrimination laws [prohibiting certain forms of discrimination on the basis of race, color, religion, sex, familial status, or national origin]. Councils claim that Roommate is effectively a housing broker doing online what it may not lawfully do off-line. The district court held that Roommate is immune under section 230 of the CDA, 47 U.S.C. §230(c), and dismissed the federal claims without considering whether Roommate's actions violated the FHA. . . .

ANALYSIS

. . .

A website operator can be both a service provider and a content provider [for the purposes of §230, CDA]: If it passively displays content that is created entirely by third parties, then it is only a service provider with respect to that content. But as to content that it creates itself, or is "responsible, in whole or in part" for creating or developing, the website is also a content provider. Thus, a website may be immune from liability for some of the content it displays to the public but be subject to liability for other content.

[The majority then summarized the details of the *Stratton Oakmont* case, excerpted above.]

In passing section 230, Congress sought to [allow Internet service providers] to perform some editing on user-generated content without thereby becoming liable for all defamatory or otherwise unlawful messages that they didn't edit or delete. In other words, Congress sought to immunize the *removal* of user-generated content, not the *creation* of content: "[S]ection [230] provides 'Good Samaritan' protections from civil liability for providers . . . of an interactive computer service for actions to *restrict* . . . access to objectionable online material. One of the specific purposes of this section is to overrule *Stratton-Oakmont* [sic] *v. Prodigy* and any other similar decisions which have treated such providers . . . as publishers or speakers of content that is not their own *because they have restricted access* to objectionable material." H.R. Rep. No. 104-458 (1996) (Conf. Rep.), *as reprinted in* 1996 U.S.C.C.A.N. 10 (emphasis added). Indeed, the section is titled "Protection for 'good samaritan' blocking and screening of offensive material" and, as the Seventh Circuit recently held, the substance of section 230(c) can and should be interpreted consistent with its caption. *Chi. Lawyers' Comm. for Civ. Rights Under Law, Inc. v. Craigslist, Inc.*, 519 F.3d 666, (7th Cir. Mar. 14, 2008) (quoting *Doe v. GTE Corp.*, 347 F.3d 655, 659-60 (7th Cir. 2003)).

With this backdrop in mind, we examine three specific functions performed by Roommate that are alleged to violate the Fair Housing Act and California law.

1. Councils first argue that the questions Roommate poses to prospective subscribers during the registration process violate the Fair Housing Act and the analogous California law. Councils allege that requiring subscribers to disclose their sex, family status and sexual orientation "indicates" an intent to discriminate against them, and thus runs afoul of both the FHA and state law.

Roommate created the questions and choice of answers, and designed its website registration process around them. Therefore, Roommate is undoubtedly the "information content provider" as to the questions and can claim no immunity for posting them on its website, or for forcing subscribers to answer them as a condition of using its services.

Here, we must determine whether Roommate has immunity under the CDA because Councils have at least a plausible claim that Roommate violated state and federal law by merely posing the questions. . . . We note that asking questions certainly *can* violate the Fair Housing Act and analogous laws in the physical world. For example, a real estate broker may not inquire as to the race of a prospective buyer, and an employer may not inquire as to the religion of a prospective employee. If such questions are unlawful when posed face-to-face or by telephone, they don't magically become lawful when asked electronically online. The Communications Decency Act was not meant to create a lawless no-man's-land on the Internet.

Councils also claim that requiring subscribers to answer the questions as a condition of using Roommate's services unlawfully "cause[s]" subscribers to make a "statement . . . with respect to the sale or rental of a dwelling that indicates [a] preference, limitation, or discrimination," in violation of

42 U.S.C. §3604(c). The CDA does not grant immunity for inducing third parties to express illegal preferences. Roommate's own acts—posting the questionnaire and requiring answers to it—are entirely its doing and thus section 230 of the CDA does not apply to them. Roommate is entitled to no immunity.

2. . . . The dissent tilts at windmills when it shows, quite convincingly, that Roommate's *subscribers* are information content providers who create the profiles by picking among options and providing their own answers. . . . There is no disagreement on this point. But, the fact that users are information content providers does not preclude Roommate from *also* being an information content provider by helping "develop" at least "in part" the information in the profiles. As we explained in *Batzel*, the party responsible for putting information online may be subject to liability, even if the information originated with a user. *See Batzel v. Smith*, 333 F.3d 1018, 1033 (9th Cir. 2003).

Here, the part of the profile that is alleged to offend the Fair Housing Act and state housing discrimination laws—the information about sex, family status and sexual orientation—is provided by subscribers in response to Roommate's questions, which they cannot refuse to answer if they want to use defendant's services. By requiring subscribers to provide the information as a condition of accessing its service, and by providing a limited set of pre-populated answers, Roommate becomes much more than a passive transmitter of information provided by others; it becomes the developer, at least in part, of that information. And section 230 provides immunity only if the interactive computer service does not "creat[e] or develop" the information "in whole or in part." *See* 47 U.S.C. §230(f)(3).

Our dissenting colleague takes a much narrower view of what it means to "develop" information online, and concludes that Roommate does not develop the information because "[a]ll Roommate does is to provide a form with options for standardized answers." . . . But Roommate does much more than provide options. To begin with, it asks discriminatory questions that even the dissent grudgingly admits are not entitled to CDA immunity. . . . The FHA makes it unlawful to ask certain discriminatory questions for a very good reason: Unlawful questions solicit (a.k.a. "develop") unlawful answers. Not only does Roommate ask these questions, Roommate makes answering the discriminatory questions a condition of doing business. This is no different from a real estate broker in real life saying, "Tell me whether you're Jewish or you can find yourself another broker." When a business enterprise extracts such information from potential customers as a condition of accepting them as clients, it is no stretch to say that the enterprise is responsible, at least in part, for developing that information. For the dissent to claim that the information in such circumstances is "created solely by" the customer, and that the business has not helped in the least to develop it . . . strains both credulity and English.

. . .

Roommate's search function is similarly designed to steer users based on discriminatory criteria. Roommate's search engine thus differs materially from generic search engines such as Google, Yahoo! and MSN Live Search, in that Roommate designed its system to use allegedly unlawful criteria so as to limit the results of each search, and to force users to participate in its discriminatory process. In other words, Councils allege that Roommate's search is designed to make it more difficult or impossible for individuals with certain protected characteristics to find housing—something the law prohibits. By contrast, ordinary search engines do not use unlawful criteria to limit the scope of searches conducted on them, nor are they designed to achieve illegal ends—as Roommate's search function is alleged to do here. Therefore, such search engines play no part in the "development" of any unlawful searches. See 47 U.S.C. §230(f)(3).

. . .

In an abundance of caution, and to avoid the kind of misunderstanding the dissent seems to encourage, we offer a few examples to elucidate what does and does not amount to "development" under section 230 of the Communications Decency Act: If an individual uses an ordinary search engine to query for a "white roommate," the search engine has not contributed to any alleged unlawfulness in the individual's conduct; providing *neutral* tools to carry out what may be unlawful or illicit searches does not amount to "development" for purposes of the immunity exception. A dating website that requires users to enter their sex, race, religion and marital status through drop-down menus, and that provides means for users to search along the same lines, retains its CDA immunity insofar as it does not contribute to any alleged illegality; this immunity is retained even if the website is sued for libel based on these characteristics because the website would not have contributed materially to any alleged defamation. Similarly, a housing website that allows users to specify whether they will or will not receive emails by means of *user-defined* criteria might help some users exclude email from other users of a particular race or sex. However, that website would be immune, so long as it does not require the use of discriminatory criteria. A website operator who edits user-created content—such as by correcting spelling, removing obscenity or trimming for length—retains his immunity for any illegality in the user-created content, provided that the edits are unrelated to the illegality. However, a website operator who edits in a manner that contributes to the alleged illegality—such as by removing the word "not" from a user's message reading "[Name] did *not* steal the artwork" in order to transform an innocent message into a libelous one—is directly involved in the alleged illegality and thus not immune. . . .

3. Councils finally argue that Roommate should be held liable for the discriminatory statements displayed in the "Additional Comments" section of profile pages. At the end of the registration process, on a separate page from the other registration steps, Roommate prompts subscribers to "tak[e] a moment to personalize your profile by writing a paragraph or two describing yourself and what you are looking for in a roommate." The subscriber is presented with a blank text box, in which he can type as

much or as little about himself as he wishes. Such essays are visible only to paying subscribers.

. . .

Roommate publishes these comments as written. It does not provide any specific guidance as to what the essay should contain, nor does it urge subscribers to input discriminatory preferences. Roommate is not responsible, in whole or in part, for the development of this content, which comes entirely from subscribers and is passively displayed by Roommate. Without reviewing every essay, Roommate would have no way to distinguish unlawful discriminatory preferences from perfectly legitimate statements. Nor can there be any doubt that this information was tendered to Roommate for publication online. . . . This is precisely the kind of situation for which section 230 was designed to provide immunity. . . .

The message to website operators is clear: If you don't encourage illegal content, or design your website to require users to input illegal content, you will be immune.

We believe that this distinction is consistent with the intent of Congress to preserve the free-flowing nature of Internet speech and commerce without unduly prejudicing the enforcement of other important state and federal laws. When Congress passed section 230 it didn't intend to prevent the enforcement of all laws online; rather, it sought to encourage interactive computer services that provide users *neutral* tools to post content online to police that content without fear that through their "good samaritan . . . screening of offensive material," 47 U.S.C. §230(c), they would become liable for every single message posted by third parties on their website.

* * *

In light of our determination that the CDA does not provide immunity to Roommate for all of the content of its website and email newsletters, we remand for the district court to determine in the first instance whether the alleged actions for which Roommate is not immune violate the Fair Housing Act, 42 U.S.C. §3604(c). . . .

McKEOWN, Circuit Judge, with whom RYMER and BEA, Circuit Judges, join, concurring in part and dissenting in part:

. . .

The majority's unprecedented expansion of liability for Internet service providers threatens to chill the robust development of the Internet that Congress envisioned. The majority condemns Roommate's "search system," a function that is the heart of interactive service providers. My concern is not an empty Chicken Little "sky is falling" alert. By exposing every interactive service provider to liability for sorting, searching, and utilizing the all too familiar drop-down menus, the majority has dramatically altered the landscape of Internet liability. Instead of the "robust" immunity envisioned by Congress, interactive service providers are left scratching their heads and wondering where immunity ends and liability begins.

To promote the unfettered development of the Internet, Congress adopted the Communications Decency Act of 1996 ("CDA"), which provides that interactive computer service providers will not be held legally responsible for publishing information provided by third parties. 47 U.S.C. §230(c)(1). Even though traditional publishers retain liability for performing essentially equivalent acts in the "non-virtual world," Congress chose to treat interactive service providers differently by immunizing them from liability stemming from sorting, searching, and publishing third-party information. . . .

To be sure, the statute, which was adopted just as the Internet was beginning a surge of popular currency, is not a perfect match against today's technology. The Web 2.0 version is a far cry from web technology in the mid-1990s. Nonetheless, the basic message from Congress has retained its traction, and there should be a high bar to liability for organizing and searching third-party information. The bipartisan view in Congress was that the Internet, as a new form of communication, should not be impeded by the transference of regulations and principles developed from traditional modes of communication. The majority repeatedly harps that if something is prohibited in the physical world, Congress could not have intended it to be legal in cyberspace. Yet that is precisely the path Congress took with the CDA: the anomaly that a webhost may be immunized for conducting activities in cyberspace that would traditionally be cause for liability is exactly what Congress intended by enacting the CDA.

In the end, the majority offers interactive computer service providers no bright lines and little comfort in finding a home within §230(c)(1). . . .

. . .

Roommate's users are "information content providers" because they are responsible for creating the information in their user profiles and, at their option — not the website's choice — in expressing preferences as to roommate characteristics. §230(f)(3). The critical question is whether Roommate is itself an "information content provider," such that it cannot claim that the information at issue was "provided by another information content provider." A close reading of the statute leads to the conclusion that Roommate is not an information content provider for two reasons: (1) providing a drop-down menu does not constitute "creating" or "developing" information; and (2) the structure and text of the statute make plain that Congress intended to immunize Roommate's sorting, displaying, and transmitting of third-party information.

Roommate neither "creates" nor "develops" the information that is challenged by the Councils, i.e., the information provided by the users as to their protected characteristics and the preferences expressed as to roommate characteristics. All Roommate does is to provide a form with options for standardized answers. Listing categories such as geographic location, cleanliness, gender and number of occupants, and transmitting to users profiles of other users whose expressed information matches their expressed preferences, can hardly be said to be creating or developing information. Even adding standardized options does not "develop" information. Roommate, with its prompts, is merely "selecting material for publication," which we have stated does not constitute the "development" of information. *Batzel*, 333 F.3d at 1031. The profile is created solely by the user, not the provider of the interactive website. Indeed, without user participation, there is no information at all. The drop-down menu is simply a precategorization of user information before the electronic sorting and displaying that takes place via an algorithm. If a user has identified herself as a non-smoker and another has expressed a preference for a non-smoking roommate, Roommate's sorting and matching of user information are no different than that performed by a generic search engine.

. . .

Millions of websites use prompts and drop-down menus. . . . The majority's definition of "development" would transform every interactive site into an information content provider and the result would render illusory any immunity under §230(c). Virtually every site could be responsible in part for developing content.

. . .

Anticipating the morphing of the Internet and the limits of creative genius and entrepreneurship that fuel its development is virtually impossible. However, Congress explicitly drafted the law to permit this unfettered development of the Internet. Had Congress discovered that, over time, courts across the country have created more expansive immunity than it originally envisioned under the CDA, Congress could have amended the law. But it has not. In fact, just six years ago, Congress approved of the broad immunity that courts have uniformly accorded interactive webhosts under §230(c).

[Dissent describes H.R. Rep No. 107-449 of 2002 in which Congress expressly approved past judicial interpretations of §230 of the Communications Decency Act that granted a broad immunity to online service providers.]

This express Congressional approval of the courts' interpretation of §230(c)(1), six years after its enactment, advises us to stay the course of "robust" webhost immunity.

The consequences of the majority's interpretation are far-reaching. Its position will chill speech on the Internet and impede "the continued development of the Internet and other interactive computer services and other interactive media." §230(b)(1). . . .

COMMENTS AND QUESTIONS

1. Do Web 2.0 technologies change the way we think about the immunities granted under section 230 of the Communications Decency Act for Internet service providers? Should they?

2. The majority in *Roommate.com* says that section 230 "was not meant to create a lawless no-mans-land on the Internet." Do you think the majority

was concerned about previous judicial interpretations of the statute, like those in the *Zeran* and *Drudge* cases? Are those concerns well-founded?

3. How does the majority distinguish Roommate's search function from more generic search engines like Yahoo! and Google? Are you convinced by this distinction?

4. The majority holds that Roommate should not be liable for "additional comments" posted by users, as opposed to the profile questions for which they are liable. Do you agree with their reasoning?

5. On what basis does the dissent in *Roommate.com* differ from the majority? What policy arguments do the dissenting judges raise in favor of greater immunity for online service providers?

6. Would the majority have held differently if Roommate used blank text boxes for user profiles instead of drop-down menus? In other words, is it the provision of the potentially discriminatory terms in the drop-down menus that makes Roommate a content provider in the eyes of the majority?

7. What are the dissenting judges' main concerns about the majority's decision with respect to the future of Internet regulation more generally? Are their concerns realistic?

F. CODE AS SPEECH

While the preceding materials on Open Access and the liability of Internet service providers examine the novel question of who can be considered a speaker in a world connected by computers, this section asks the related question of: What can be considered speech? In particular, can computer code be considered speech? The answer to this question has significant consequences for cyberspace because code makes the Internet and all its applications possible. If government's ability to regulate code is limited because code is considered protected expression, its ability to regulate cyberspace will also be limited. As you study the following materials, keep in mind that code can encompass many different forms of computer programming, functions, and commands from the commands that allow a computer to perform word processing to the links that allow us to download files or jump to another Web page. For the purposes of the First Amendment, should the kind of code matter?

BERNSTEIN V. UNITED STATES DEPARTMENT OF JUSTICE

176 F.3d 1132 (9th Cir. 1999)

FLETCHER, Circuit Judge.

... Bernstein is currently a professor in the Department of Mathematics, Statistics, and Computer Science at the University of Illinois at Chicago. As a doctoral candidate at the University of California, Berkeley, he developed an encryption method ... that he dubbed "Snuffle." Bernstein described his method in two ways: in a paper containing analysis and mathematical equations (the "Paper") and in two computer programs written in "C," a high-level computer programming language ("Source Code"). Bernstein later wrote a set of instructions in English (the "Instructions") explaining how to program a computer to encrypt and decrypt data utilizing a one-way hash function, essentially translating verbatim his Source Code into prose form.

Seeking to present his work on Snuffle within the academic and scientific communities, Bernstein asked the State Department whether he needed a license to publish Snuffle in any of its various forms. The State Department responded that Snuffle was a munition under the International Traffic in Arms Regulations ("ITAR"), and that Bernstein would need a license to "export" the Paper, the Source Code, or the Instructions. . . .

Bernstein ultimately filed this action, challenging the constitutionality of the ITAR regulations. . . .

Cryptography is the science of secret writing, a science that has roots stretching back hundreds, and perhaps thousands, of years. See generally David Kahn, The Codebreakers (2d ed. 1996). For much of its history, cryptography has been the jealously guarded province of governments and militaries. In the past twenty years, however, the science has blossomed in the civilian sphere, driven on the one hand by dramatic theoretical innovations within the field, and on the other by the needs of modern communication and information technologies. As a result, cryptography has become a dynamic academic discipline within applied mathematics. It is the cryptographer's primary task to find secure methods to encrypt messages, making them unintelligible to all except the intended recipients:

[The court then described how technological encryption works, and noted that it has a variety of applications, including secrecy applications that may be of interest to the military, as well as more domestic applications such as ensuring data integrity and authenticating user identities online.]

It is, of course, encryption's secrecy applications that concern the government. The interception and deciphering of foreign communications has long played an important part in our nation's national security efforts. . . . As increasingly sophisticated and secure encryption methods are developed, the government's interest in halting or slowing the proliferation of such methods has grown keen. . . .

The EAR contain specific regulations to control the export of encryption software, expressly including computer source code. . . .

If encryption software falls within the ambit of the relevant EAR provisions, the "export" of such software requires a prepublication license. When a prepublication license is requested, the relevant agencies undertake a "case-by-case" analysis to determine if the export is "consistent with U.S. national security and foreign policy interests." 15 C.F.R. §742.15(b). All applications must be "resolved or referred to the President no later than 90 days" from the date an application is entered into the BXA's electronic license processing system. 15 C.F.R. §750.4(a). There is no time limit, however, that applies once an application is referred to the President. Although the regulations do provide for an internal administrative appeal procedure, such appeals are governed only by the exhortation that they be completed "within a reasonable time." 15 C.F.R. §756.2(c)(1). Final administrative decisions are not subject to judicial review. 15 C.F.R. §756.2(c)(2).

. . . We are called on to determine whether encryption source code is expression for First Amendment purposes.

We begin by explaining what source code is. "Source code," at least as currently understood by computer programmers, refers to the text of a program written in a "high-level" programming language, such as "PASCAL" or "C." The distinguishing feature of source code is that it is meant to be read and understood by humans and that it can be used to express an idea or a method. A computer, in fact, can make no direct use of source code until it has been translated ("compiled") into a "low-level" or "machine" language, resulting in computer-executable "object code." That source code is meant for human eyes and understanding, however, does not mean that an untutored layperson can understand it. Because source code is destined for the maw of an automated, ruthlessly literal translator — the compiler — a programmer must follow stringent grammatical, syntactical, formatting, and punctuation conventions. As a result, only those trained in programming can easily understand source code.

. . .

[C]ryptographers use source code to express their scientific ideas in much the same way that mathematicians use equations or economists use graphs. Of course, both mathematical equations and graphs are used in other fields for many purposes, not all of which are expressive. But mathematicians and economists have adopted these modes of expression in order to facilitate the precise and rigorous expression of complex scientific ideas. Similarly, the undisputed record here makes it clear that cryptographers utilize source code in the same fashion.

In light of these considerations, we conclude that encryption software, in its source code form and as employed by those in the field of cryptography, must be viewed as expressive for First Amendment purposes, and thus is entitled to the protections of the prior restraint doctrine. If the government required that mathematicians obtain a prepublication license prior to publishing material that included mathematical equations, we have no doubt that such a regime would be subject to scrutiny as a prior restraint. . . .

The government, in fact, does not seriously dispute that source code is used by cryptographers for expressive purposes. Rather, the government maintains that source code is different from other forms of expression (such as blueprints, recipes, and "how-to" manuals) because it can be used to control directly the operation of a computer without conveying information to the user. In the government's view, by targeting this unique functional aspect of source code, rather than the content of the ideas that may be expressed therein, the export regulations manage to skirt entirely the concerns of the First Amendment. This argument is flawed for at least two reasons.

First, it is not at all obvious that the government's view reflects a proper understanding of source code. As noted earlier, the distinguishing feature of source code is that it is meant to be read and understood by humans, and that it cannot be used to control directly the functioning of a computer. While source code, when properly prepared, can be easily compiled into object code by a user, ignoring the distinction between source and object code obscures the important fact that source code is not meant solely for the computer, but is rather written in a language intended also for human analysis and understanding.

Second, and more importantly, the government's argument, distilled to its essence, suggests that even one drop of "direct functionality" overwhelms any constitutional protections that expression might otherwise enjoy. This cannot be so. The distinction urged on us by the government would prove too much in this era of rapidly evolving computer capabilities. The fact that computers will soon be able to respond directly to spoken commands, for example, should not confer on the government the unfettered power to impose prior restraints on speech in an effort to control its "functional" aspects. The First Amendment is concerned with expression, and we reject the notion that the admixture of functionality necessarily puts expression beyond the protections of the Constitution.

[Having concluded that the source code at issue is speech, the court then concludes that the challenged regulations represent an unconstitutional prior restraint upon speech.]

We emphasize the narrowness of our First Amendment holding. We do not hold that all software is expressive. Much of it surely is not. Nor need we resolve whether the challenged regulations constitute content-based restrictions, subject to the strictest constitutional scrutiny, or whether they are, instead, content-neutral restrictions meriting less exacting scrutiny. We hold merely that because the prepublication licensing regime challenged here applies directly to scientific expression, vests boundless discretion in government officials, and lacks adequate procedural safeguards, it constitutes an impermissible prior restraint on speech. . . .

[Concurring judgment of BRIGHT, Circuit Judge, omitted.]

T.G. NELSON, Circuit Judge, Dissenting:

Bernstein was not entitled to bring a facial First Amendment challenge to the EAR, and the district court improperly granted an injunction on the basis of a facial challenge. I therefore respectfully dissent.

The basic error which sets the majority and the district court adrift is the failure to fully recognize that the basic function of encryption source code is to act as a method of controlling computers. As defined in the EAR regulations, encryption source code is "[a] precise set of operating instructions to a computer, that when compiled, allows for the execution of an encryption function on a computer." 15 C.F.R. pt. 722. Software engineers generally do not create software in object code — the series of binary digits (1's and 0's) — which tells a computer what to do because it would be enormously difficult, cumbersome and time-consuming. Instead, software engineers use high-level computer programming languages such as "C" or "Basic" to create source code as a shorthand method for telling the computer to perform a desired function. In this respect, lines of source code are the building blocks or the tools used to create an encryption machine. See, e.g., Patrick Ian Ross, Bernstein v. United States Department of State, 13 Berkeley Tech. L.J. 405, 410-11 (1998) ("[E]lectronic source code that is ready to compile merely needs a few keystrokes to generate object code — the equivalent of flipping an 'on' switch. Code used for this purpose can fairly easily be characterized as 'essentially functional.'"); Pamela Samuelson et al., A Manifesto Concerning Legal Protection of Computer Programs, 94 Colum. L. Rev. 2308, 2315-30 (1994) ("[P]rograms are, in fact, machines (entities that bring about useful results, i.e., behavior) that have been constructed in the medium of text (source code and object code)."). Encryption source code, once compiled, works to make computer communication and transactions secret; it creates a lockbox of sorts around a message that can only be unlocked by someone with a key. It is the function or task that encryption source code performs which creates its value in most cases. This functional aspect of encryption source code contains no expression; it is merely the tool used to build the encryption machine.

This is not to say that this very same source code is not used expressively in some cases. Academics, such as Bernstein, seek to convey and discuss their ideas concerning computer encryption. As noted by the majority, Bernstein must actually use his source code textually in order to discuss or teach cryptology. In such circumstances, source code serves to express Bernstein's scientific methods and ideas.

While it is conceptually difficult to categorize encryption source code under our First Amendment framework, I am still inevitably led to conclude that encryption source code is more like conduct than speech. Encryption source code is a building tool. Academics and computer programmers can convey this source code to each other in order to reveal the encryption machine they have built. But, the ultimate purpose of encryption code is, as its name suggests, to perform the function of encrypting messages. Thus, while encryption source code may occasionally be used in an expressive manner, it is inherently a functional device. . . .

It cannot seriously be argued that any form of computer code may be regulated without reference to First Amendment doctrine. The path from idea to human language to source code to object code is a continuum. As one moves from one to the other, the levels of precision and, arguably, abstraction increase, as does the level of training necessary to discern the idea from the expression. Not everyone can understand each of these forms. Only English speakers will understand English formulations. Principally those familiar with the particular programming language will understand the source code expression. And only a relatively small number of skilled programmers and computer scientists will understand the machine readable object code. But each form expresses the same idea, albeit in different ways.

COMMENTS AND QUESTIONS

1. How do you understand the difference between source code and object code for First Amendment purposes? Is the majority right in considering at least source code to have some expressive elements?

2. Can object code ever be considered expressive for First Amendment purposes? In other words, can the resulting computer program be considered expressive?

3. According to Judge Nelson's dissent in *Bernstein*, why does "functionality" of code reduce its First Amendment value? Isn't all speech inherently functional (i.e., intended to accomplish a given task)? Consider *Universal City Studios, Inc. v. Reimerdes* in Chapter 4, upholding provisions of the Digital Millennium Copyright Act that prohibited the trafficking in software that allowed users to defeat copyright protection technology).

4. Is there a difference between describing code as "functional" and describing it as "conduct"? Judge Nelson describes code in both ways interchangeably. Can you see any logical difficulties with this approach?

5. The *Bernstein* case was dismissed after the Bush administration said it would no longer enforce relevant parts of the regulations. *See* Declan McCullagh, *Cold War Encryption Laws Stand, but Not as Firmly*, CNET, news.com, Oct. 15, 2003 (available at *http://news.com.com/2100-1028_3-5092154.html*).

6. Should the expressiveness of software depend upon the intent of the programmer? *See* Lee Tien, *Publishing Software as a Speech Act*, 15 Berkeley Tech. L.J. 629 (2000) (arguing that First Amendment analysis should focus on whether publishing software is intended as a speech act rather than focusing on what is used to convey the message). Tien notes that "functionality" has never been part of First Amendment doctrine. *Id.* at 684-85. According to Tien:

> If the case law recognized a functionality doctrine, what would it look like? Functionality cannot merely mean that the work of speech is useful, since instructions, recipes and manuals are both useful and covered by the First Amendment. Indeed, the First Amendment partly covers commercial speech because consumers can benefit from widespread information. Similarly, functionality cannot simply mean that a form of speech could cause harm since much speech — chemistry books teaching bomb-making or calls to revolution — could cause harm.
>
> To state that software "functions" only means that one can use software to do something. Yet, many forms of "speech" can be used to do things. For instance, although charitable solicitations "function" to raise money, the First Amendment covers charitable appeals because they involve important interests like the communication of information, the dissemination and propagation of ideas, and the advocacy of causes. To push the

analogy further, erotic works "function" to sexually arouse people, seditious libel "functions" to subvert government, defamation "functions" to damage reputation, and textbooks "function" to confer knowledge and abilities. In short, there is no doctrinal foundation for not treating software as speech simply because it "functions." This idea encompasses so much speech that it is useless as an analytical tool.

Id. at 685-86.

7. Can laws that target the end results of computer code be considered content neutral? What is the governmental objective behind laws prohibiting encryption or decryption? Is it to prevent the act itself or to keep people from learning how to commit the act? *Consider* Rice v. Paladin Enterprises, Inc., 128 F.3d 233 (4th Cir. 1997) (concluding that publisher could be held responsible under the First Amendment for publishing a book that purported to be a guide to becoming a killer for hire). Could Congress prohibit popular video games like "Doom" or "Mortal Kombat" or hold the publishers of those games responsible for the acts of game players under the theory that the games train people to kill other people? What if the distributor of a computer program knows that it may be used for an illegal act?

8. Around the same time that the Ninth Circuit Court was deciding *Bernstein*, the Sixth Circuit was asked to consider similar issues arising under the Export Administration Regulations. On the question of First Amendment protection for encryption code, the court in Junger v. Daley, 209 F.3d 481 (2000) noted:

The issue of whether or not the First Amendment protects encryption source code is a difficult one because source code has both an expressive feature and a functional feature. The United States does not dispute that it is possible to use encryption source code to represent and convey information and ideas about cryptography and that encryption source code can be used by programmers and scholars for such informational purposes. Much like a mathematical or scientific formula, one can describe the function and design of encryption software by a prose explanation; however, for individuals fluent in a computer programming language, source code is the most efficient and precise means by which to communicate ideas about cryptography.

The district court concluded that the functional characteristics of source code overshadow its simultaneously expressive nature. The fact that a medium of expression has a functional capacity should not preclude constitutional protection. Rather, the appropriate consideration of the medium's functional capacity is in the analysis of permitted government regulation.

The Supreme Court has explained that "all ideas having even the slightest redeeming social importance," including those concerning "the advancement of truth, science, morality, and arts" have the full protection of the First Amendment. Roth v. United States, 354 U.S. 476, 484 (1957). This protection is not reserved for purely expressive communication. The Supreme Court has recognized First Amendment protection for symbolic conduct, such as draft-card burning, that has both functional and expressive features. . . .

The Supreme Court has expressed the versatile scope of the First Amendment by labeling as "unquestionably shielded" the artwork of Jackson Pollack, the music of Arnold Schoenberg, or the Jabberwocky verse of Lewis Carroll. . . . Though unquestionably expressive, these things identified by the Court are not traditional speech. Particularly, a musical score cannot be read by the majority of the public but can be used as a means of communication among musicians. Likewise, computer source code, though unintelligible to many, is the preferred method of communication among computer programmers.

Because computer source code is an expressive means for the exchange of information and ideas about computer programming, we hold that it is protected by the First Amendment.

The functional capabilities of source code, and particularly those of encryption source code, should be considered when analyzing the governmental interest in regulating the exchange of this form of speech. Under intermediate scrutiny, the regulation of speech is valid, in part, if "it furthers an important or substantial governmental interest." *O'Brien*, 391 U.S. at 377. In Turner Broadcasting System v. FCC, 512 U.S. 622, 664 (1994), the Supreme Court noted that although an asserted governmental interest may be important, when the government defends restrictions on speech "it must do more than simply 'posit the existence of the disease sought to be cured.'" Id. (quoting Quincy Cable TV, Inc. v. FCC, 248 U.S. App. D.C. 1, 768 F.2d 1434, 1455 (D.C. Cir. 1985)). The government "must demonstrate that the recited harms are real, not merely conjectural, and that the regulation will in fact alleviate these harms in a direct and material way." Id. We recognize that national security interests can outweigh the interests of protected speech and require the regulation of speech. In the present case, the record does not resolve whether the exercise of presidential power in furtherance of national security interests should overrule the interests in allowing the free exchange of encryption source code. [The matter was then remanded to the District Court for further consideration.]

The court here compares software code with other forms of expression that are more abstract than literal speech — such as the artwork of Jackson Pollock or a musical score. Do these comparisons usefully illuminate the question whether computer code should be protected by the First Amendment?

9. If code can be considered speech, what else may it represent? As you study the following chapters on intellectual property, privacy, etc., consider to what extent we may be over- or underprotecting expression in cyberspace. Under what circumstances should the value of communication outweigh other values, such as privacy, or vice versa?

4

Content as Property in Cyberspace

Chapter 3 explored the principles and values of free speech in cyberspace. The remaining materials explore the extent to which communications through the Internet may be limited by other principles and values. This chapter explores the role that property rights in content play in regulating information in cyberspace. In particular, we will focus on efforts to translate and import traditional intellectual property principles from trademark, copyright, and patent law to electronic communications. As you study these materials, consider the following questions: To what degree should existing property regimes be translated for use in cyberspace? What are the benefits of applying trademark, copyright, and patent principles to the online world? What are the costs? Would the recognition of intellectual property rights in cyberspace respond to the policy considerations that justify such rights in general, or are there problems and opportunities unique to cyberspace? Is it necessary to develop new *sui generis* forms of intellectual property in cyberspace? If so, what are the policy justifications for such developments?

A. Trademarks, Domain Names, and Internet Search Engines

One of the most frequently debated issues since the advent of the Internet is to what degree does trademark law apply to the different features of the Internet. In general, trademarks are a means for identifying the source of a good or service. Under the common law, trademark law arose as a means of preventing trademark infringement, the most common example of which is "palming off" where a competitor uses the competition's mark on its goods in order to mislead consumers. For example, palming off occurs when a manufacturer of athletic shoes other than Nike affixes the Nike swoosh to its shoes in the hopes that consumers interested in purchasing Nike shoes will purchase its shoes instead. Another aspect of trademark law is trademark dilution, in which the law protects some aspects of the goodwill or value of the trademark. Today, trademarks are protected by a combination of common law and statutes. For example, at the federal level, trademark infringement is governed by sections 32 and 43 of the Lanham Act. Section 32 provides in pertinent part:

(1) Any person who shall, without the consent of the registrant —
(a) use in commerce any reproduction, counterfeit, copy, or color-able imitation of a registered mark in connection with the sale . . . or advertising of any goods or services on or in connection with which such use is likely to cause confusion, or to cause mistake, or to deceive . . . shall be liable in a civil action by the registrant. . . .[1]

Similarly, section 43(a) of the Act provides:

Any person who, on or in connection with any goods or services, or any container for goods, uses in commerce any word, term, name, symbol, or device, or any combination thereof, or any false designation of origin, false or misleading description of fact, or false or misleading representation of fact, which —
(A) is likely to cause confusion, or to cause mistake, or to deceive as to the affiliation, connection, or association of such person with another person, or as to the origin, sponsorship, or approval of his or her goods, services, or commercial activities by another person, or
(B) in commercial advertising or promotion, misrepresents the nature, characteristics, qualities, or geographic origin of his or her or another person's goods, services, or commercial activities, shall be liable in a civil action by any person who believes that he or she is or is likely to be damaged by such act.[2]

Additionally, under Federal law, dilution of famous marks is governed by 15 U.S.C. §1125(c), which prohibits dilution by blurring and dilution by tarnishment of a famous mark. 15 U.S.C. §1125(c)(1). Dilution by blurring is defined as: "association arising from the similarity between a mark or trade name and a famous mark that impairs the distinctiveness of the famous mark". 15 U.S.C. §1125(c)(2)(B). Dilution by tarnishment was included in the federal legislation in 2006 under the Trademark Dilution Revision Act (TDRA). "Tarnishment" is now defined in this context as: "association arising from the similarity between a mark or trade name and a famous mark that

1. 15 U.S.C. §1114(1)(a).
2. 15 U.S.C. §1125(a)(1).

harms the reputation of the famous mark." 15 U.S.C. §1125(c)(2)(C). Statutory defenses to a dilution action were also revised in 2006 under the TDRA. 15 U.S.C. §1125(c)(3) now provides that:

> The following shall not be actionable as dilution by blurring or dilution by tarnishment under this subsection:
>
> (A) Any fair use, including a nominative or descriptive fair use, or facilitation of such fair use, of a famous mark by another person other than as a designation of source for the person's own goods or services, including use in connection with —
>
> (i) advertising or promotion that permits consumers to compare goods or services; or
>
> (ii) identifying and parodying, criticizing, or commenting upon the famous mark owner or the goods or services of the famous mark owner.
>
> (B) All forms of news reporting and news commentary.
>
> (C) Any noncommercial use of a mark.

Under trademark infringement, a person or business generally obtains the right to prevent others from using the same or similar marks by being the first to use a distinctive mark, which is capable of distinguishing the user's goods from the goods of others in a geographic market. Under the common law, a second user may adopt the same or similar mark if there was no evidence of confusion and the mark was adopted in good faith. Today, under federal law, the senior user of a mark may generally prevent subsequent adoptions if the user registers the mark on the Principal Register, which, in addition to providing additional statutory rights and remedies against infringement, provides constructive notice to those considering adopting the same or similar mark.

Whether trademark law should apply online is especially daunting because one of the dominant features of trademark law is the limited territorial protection afforded marks. In the brick and mortar world, users of the same or similar marks may use their mark in their respective locations so long as there is no consumer confusion. However, the Internet knows no geographic boundaries once someone is online. Further, the application of trademark law to cyberspace communications challenges other basic trademark principles including what constitutes trademark use and consumer confusion.

The following materials explore efforts to apply trademark law to search engines, domain names, and metatags. Unlike the use of distinctive words, sounds, and symbols on Web pages or in e-mails, which fall readily under traditional trademark principles, search engines, domain names, and metatags are important parts of the Internet's architecture and have few brick and mortar analogs.

Although the importance of domain names and metatags as Internet search tools has decreased since the advent of sophisticated search engines like Google, domain name trading continues to be big business, and disputes involving trademark holders complaining about domain name registration and use continue to arise in increasing numbers every year: *see Domain Name Disputes Doubled Since 2003, Origin of Most Cases in US* (Dec. 31, 2008), CircleID, available at *http://www.circleid.com/posts/domain_disputes_doubled_ since_2003/*.

1. Domain Names and Trademark Infringement

As suggested by the materials in the preceding chapters, the Internet is a revolutionary medium for communication, but if you want to send an e-mail to a friend or visit a Web page, how does your computer send or receive the information it needs from the proper computer in networks made up of millions of computers? The answer is the Domain Name System (DNS). Every computer connected to the Internet is assigned an Internet Protocol (IP) address, which is a series of numbers separated by periods such as 123.45.678.90. Because these numeric addresses are difficult for people to remember and may change, the DNS was developed.

The DNS allows users to select a combination of letters, numbers, and characters and translates that combination to a purely numerical IP address and then connects the users to the numerical address. An Internet address is divided into several parts. The username, the host name (or second-level domain), and the top-level domain (TLD) such as .com, .edu, .gov, or country code top-level domains, such as .uk (for United Kingdom), or .fr (for France), or .us (for the United States). In 2000, ICANN approved the addition of seven new TLDs, namely .biz, .info, .name, .pro, .museum, .aero, and .coop. In 2008, ICANN started work on a new system that would open up the generic TLD (gTLD) space by providing for registration of any new string of characters as a gTLD on application of a proposed registrar for the string(s). *See http://www.icann. org/en/topics/new-gtld-program.htm.*

Domain names are obtained on a first-come, first-served basis by paying a nominal fee and registering with one of several domain name registrars such as Verisign, Inc., formerly known as Network Solutions, Inc. In the Internet's initial development, Network Solutions was the exclusive domain name registry for top-level domain names, but now there are many others. Further information concerning the history of the DNS and the Internet can be found at www.WIPO.org and www.ICANN.org. Interested readers might also consult Milton Mueller, *Ruling the Root: Internet Governance and the Taming of Cyberspace (2004); David Lindsay, International Domain Name Law: ICANN and the UDRP* (2007).

Problem 5.0

Customer service has brought to your attention approximately 20 e-mails raising troubling complaints. A sample of one reads as follows:

Dear StarttUp Customer Service:

I have been in search of a new Internet service provider after my local provider closed. Several friends of mine recommended your service so I decided to check it out through work. When I attempted to go to your site, I was directed to a pornographic site featuring highly offensive material. Upon viewing this material, I was immediately turned off by your service, and signed up with America Online. After the initial shock, I tried several possible variations of Start_Up including .net, .com, and .org, but kept ending up at the same pornographic site. It was only after I searched for "StarttUp.com" that I realized that there was more than one Web site, and that your correct address was specifically StarttUp.com.

Is there a relationship between these sites? If not, I would suggest you do something about it because many people do not appreciate that kind of smut!

Lost Customer

The other e-mails were similar, each describing the difficulty potential customers had in reaching your Web page. According to Alan and Barbara, when the company started, they only registered "StarttUp.com." They did not think to register "Startt-Up.com," "Start_Up.com," "StartUp.net," or any other variants. All of these domain names were subsequently registered to a pornographic company. Because they registered the service mark StarttUp.com, Alan called the domain name registrant of the other sites. She claims that she registered those domain names and used StarttUp as a metatag because people often get confused about the exact name of her Web site, StarttUsUp, and will not give up those domain names.

To make matters worse, the head of StarttUp's technology department informs you that entering the term StarttUp in a search engine results in several hundred hits. The vast majority of these hits are not links to your Web site. Most lead to StarttUsUp, but others lead to Web sites critical of your service, including BoycottStarttUp.org and StarttUpSucks.com.

Concerned that they are losing customers as a result of these other domain names, Alan and Barbara want to know what you can do. Given the imminence of a new product launch, they are particularly concerned that the accompanying ad campaign will fail if potential customers cannot find your site.

Problem 5.1

While you are working on your advice to StarttUp, Cora contacts you with some domain name issues of her own. She has received a letter from America Online, complaining about her recent registration of the domain name "GOL.com" for the Gals On-Line blog. Originally, Cora operated the blog under the domain name "galsonline.com", but she additionally registered "gol.com" at the suggestion of some of her co-bloggers who were concerned that "galsonline.com" was too wordy and difficult to find. America Online is concerned that the gol.com domain name might confuse its customers who are looking for its official website at aol.com. In particular, America Online has noted in its letter that when some of its legal officers did a Google search for "AOL," the search results often placed a reference to the GOL blog somewhere in the top 50 results listings. America Online has requested that Cora transfer the domain name and, if she fails to do so, they will take formal action against the blog.

Cora is also concerned about a complaint letter she has received from Dell Computers in relation to a series of blog posts in which bloggers and commenters — mostly college students — wrote about their experiences with different brands of computers. Many of the comments about Dell were less than complimentary. Dell has threatened action in trademark infringement and dilution unless Cora agrees to remove the posts, or at least the references to Dell that appear in the posts. Cora wants to know how she should respond to Dell.

---

a) Traditional Trademark Law

In the brick and mortar world, identifying when someone is using a trademark is generally an easy task. We see them affixed to advertisements and products. However, even before the growth of the Internet, advances in technology required courts to ask whether a certain combination of letters, numbers, sounds, etc. can be considered use of a trademark. That is, are these distinctive combinations being used to identify the source of goods and services? For example, courts have concluded that telephone numbers may be considered trademarks. *See* Dial-A-Mattress Franchise Corp. v. Page, 880 F.2d 675, 678 (2d Cir. 1989). Should the use of a combination of letters and numbers as a domain name be considered the use of a trademark?

i) Trademark Prerequisites

To obtain relief, a trademark owner must establish that the defendant has used the owner's trademark as a trademark and that such use was either in commerce or commercial. Under what circumstances should the use of a similar combination of letters and characters be considered trademark use or "in commerce"? What values, if any, would be served by concluding that domain names should not be treated as trademarks? Consider a decision involving the use of vanity telephone numbers. In Holiday Inns, Inc. v. 800 Reservation, Inc., the Sixth Circuit concluded that Holiday Inns's trademark rights in its vanity telephone number 1-800-HOLIDAY were not infringed by the use and registration of 1-800-405-4329, which corresponds with Holiday Inns's telephone number in all respects except the letter "o" was replaced by a zero. 86 F.3d 619 (6th Cir. 1996). The defendant admitted that "his 'sole purpose' in choosing the 405 number was to intercept calls from misdialed customers who were attempting to reach Holiday Inns, and he acknowledged that his company reaped benefits in direct proportion to Holiday Inns's efforts at marketing 1-800-HOLIDAY for securing reservations." Nonetheless, the court concluded that Holiday Inns failed to establish a claim for infringement because even though the defendant used the 405 telephone number, they never used or advertised the vanity telephone number or any of Holiday Inns's marks. According to the court, "the defendant's use of a protected mark or their use of a misleading representation is a prerequisite to the finding of a Lanham Act violation. Absent such a finding, the eight-factor test [for trademark infringement] is irrelevant." Furthermore, to the extent that any consumers were actually confused by the defendant's use of the telephone number, the court concluded that the confusion was not created by the defendants who merely took advantage of the existing consumer confusion caused by misdialed telephone numbers. Can similar arguments be made with respect to domain names?

PANAVISION INT'L, L.P. V. TOEPPEN

141 F.3d 1316 (9th Cir. 1998)

DAVID R. THOMPSON, Circuit Judge:

I.

... Panavision attempted to register a web site on the Internet with the domain name Panavision.com. It could not do that, however, because Toeppen had already established a web site using Panavision's trademark as his domain name. Toeppen's web page for this site displayed photographs of the City of Pana, Illinois.

On December 20, 1995, Panavision's counsel sent a letter from California to Toeppen in Illinois informing him that Panavision held a trademark in the name Panavision and telling him to stop using that trademark and the domain name Panavision.com. Toeppen responded by mail to Panavision in California, stating he had the right to use the name Panavision.com on the Internet as his domain name. Toeppen stated:

> If your attorney has advised you otherwise, he is trying to screw you. He wants to blaze new trails in the legal frontier at your expense. Why do you want to fund your attorney's purchase of a new boat (or whatever) when you can facilitate the acquisition of "Pana-Vision.com" cheaply and simply instead?

Toeppen then offered to "settle the matter" if Panavision would pay him $13,000 in exchange for the domain name. Additionally, Toeppen stated that if Panavision agreed to his offer, he would not "acquire any other Internet addresses which are alleged by Panavision Corporation to be its property."

After Panavision refused Toeppen's demand, he registered Panavision's other trademark with NSI as the domain name Panaflex.com. Toeppen's web page for Panaflex.com simply displays the word "Hello."

Toeppen has registered domain names for various other companies including Delta Airlines, Neiman Marcus, Eddie Bauer, Lufthansa, and over 100 other marks. Toeppen has attempted to "sell" domain names for other trademarks such as intermatic.com to Intermatic, Inc. for $10,000 and americanstandard.com to American Standard, Inc. for $15,000....

II.

... Toeppen argues that his use of Panavision's trademarks simply as his domain names cannot constitute a commercial use under the [Federal Trademark Dilution] Act.... Developing this argument, Toeppen contends that a domain name is simply an address used to locate a web page. He asserts that entering a domain name on a computer allows a user to access a web page, but a domain name is not associated with information on a web page. If a user were to type Panavision.com as a domain name, the computer screen would display Toeppen's web page with aerial views of Pana, Illinois. The screen would not provide any information about "Panavision," other than a "location window" which displays the domain name. Toeppen argues that a user who types in Panavision.com, but who sees no reference to the plaintiff Panavision on Toeppen's web page, is not likely to conclude the web page is related in any way to the plaintiff, Panavision.

Toeppen's argument misstates his use of the Panavision mark. His use is not as benign as he suggests. Toeppen's "business" is to register trademarks as domain names and then sell them to the rightful trademark owners. He "act[s] as a 'spoiler,' preventing Panavision and others from doing business on the Internet under their trademarked names unless they pay his fee." Panavision, 938 F. Supp. at 621. This is a commercial use. See Intermatic Inc. v. Toeppen, 947 F. Supp. 1227, 1230 (N.D. Ill. 1996) (stating that "[o]ne of Toeppen's business objectives is to profit by the resale or licensing of these domain names, presumably to the entities who conduct business under these names").

As the district court found, Toeppen traded on the value of Panavision's marks. So long as he held the Internet registrations, he curtailed Panavision's exploitation of the value of its trademarks on the Internet, a value which Toeppen then used when he attempted to sell the Panavision.com domain name to Panavision. . . .

Toeppen argues he is not diluting the capacity of the Panavision marks to identify goods or services. He contends that even though Panavision cannot use Panavision.com and Panaflex.com as its domain name addresses, it can still promote its goods and services on the Internet simply by using some other "address" and then creating its own web page using its trademarks.

We reject Toeppen's premise that a domain name is nothing more than an address. A significant purpose of a domain name is to identify the entity that owns the web site.[8] "A customer who is unsure about a company's domain name will often guess that the domain name is also the company's name." Cardservice Int'l v. McGee, 950 F. Supp. 737, 741 (E.D. Va. 1997). "[A] domain name mirroring a corporate name may be a valuable corporate asset, as it facilitates communication with a customer base." MTV Networks, Inc. v. Curry, 867 F. Supp. 202, 203-204 n.2 (S.D.N.Y. 1994).

Using a company's name or trademark as a domain name is also the easiest way to locate that company's web site. Use of a "search engine" can turn up hundreds of web sites, and there is nothing equivalent to a phone book or directory assistance for the Internet. See *Cardservice*, 950 F. Supp. at 741.

Moreover, potential customers of Panavision will be discouraged if they cannot find its web page by typing in "Panavision.com," but instead are forced to wade through hundreds of web sites. This dilutes the value of Panavision's trademark. We echo the words of Judge Lechner, quoting Judge Wood: "Prospective users of plaintiff's services who mistakenly access defendant's Web site may fail to continue to search for plaintiff's own home page, due to anger, frustration or the belief that plaintiff's home page does not exist." Jews for Jesus v. Brodsky, 993 F. Supp. 282, 306-07 (D.N.J. 1998) (Lechner, J., quoting Wood, J. in Planned Parenthood v. Bucci, 1997 WL 133313 at *4); see also *Teletech*, 977 F. Supp. at 1410 (finding that use of a search engine can generate as many as 800 to 1000 matches and it is "likely to deter web browsers from searching for Plaintiff's particular Web site").

Toeppen's use of Panavision.com also puts Panavision's name and reputation at his mercy. See *Intermatic*, 947 F. Supp. at 1240 ("If Toeppen were allowed to use 'intermatic.com,' Intermatic's name and reputation would be at

---

8. This point was made in a recent legal periodical:

> The domain name serves a dual purpose. It marks the location of the site within cyberspace, much like a postal address in the real world, but it may also indicate to users some information as to the content of the site, and, in instances of well-known trade names or trademarks, may provide information as to the origin of the contents of the site.

Peter Brown, *New Issues in Internet Litigation*, 17th Annual Institute on Computer Law: The Evolving Law of the Internet-Commerce, Free Speech, Security, Obscenity and Entertainment, 471 Prac. L. Inst. 151 (1997).

Toeppen's mercy and could be associated with an unimaginable amount of messages on Toeppen's web page.").

We conclude that Toeppen's registration of Panavision's trademarks as his domain names on the Internet diluted those marks within the meaning of the Federal Trademark Dilution Act, 15 U.S.C. §1125(c), and the California Anti-dilution statute, Cal. Bus. & Prof. Code §14330. . . .

COMMENTS AND QUESTIONS

1. What does Toeppen argue to support his position that Panavision.com is not a trademark use of Panavision's mark? Is the court's response persuasive? Would the result be different if Toeppen had not been attempting to sell the various domain names he registered? What if a citizen of Pana had registered the name for purposes of displaying a picture of their town?

2. Does *Panavision* establish a per se rule that use of someone else's trademark in a domain name is trademark use?

3. Should the availability of a virtually unlimited number of alternative domain names such as "PanavisionInternational.com" influence whether a domain name should be considered use of a trademark?

4. Should the defendant's registration of a number of alternative domain names corresponding to the plaintiff's trademarks be evidence of the defendant's intention to commit trademark infringement? Toeppen had, in fact, registered various domain names corresponding to Panavision's registered trademark, including "panaflex.com."

5. Toeppen had also registered many domain names corresponding with other companies' well-known trademarks. Should this pattern of behavior be relevant to a finding of trademark infringement in an action against Toeppen by any of the registered trademark holders?

6. Is *Panavision* consistent with *Holiday Inns*? If you were Toeppen's attorney, how would you argue that *Holiday Inns* supports your client?

7. *Panavision* is an example of cybersquatting in which an individual registers a domain name for the purpose of selling the name to another, usually the trademark owner. Domain name disputes also arise in circumstances in which the registrant also has rights to the mark, is unaware that someone else has rights to the mark, or desires to make some statement about the owner of the trademark. How should courts evaluate trademark claims under each of those circumstances?

PLANNED PARENTHOOD FEDERATION OF AMERICA, INC. v. BUCCI

42 U.S.P.Q.2d 1430 (S.D.N.Y. 1997)

WOOD, J.

Plaintiff Planned Parenthood Federation of America, Inc. ("Planned Parenthood") has moved to preliminarily enjoin defendant Richard Bucci

("Bucci"), doing business as Catholic Radio, from using the domain name "plannedparenthood.com," and from identifying his Web site on the Internet under the name "www.plannedparenthood.com."

I.   Undisputed Facts

The parties do not dispute the following facts. Plaintiff Planned Parenthood, founded in 1922, is a non-profit, reproductive health care organization that has used its present name since 1942.

Defendant Bucci is the host of "Catholic Radio," a daily radio program broadcast on the WVOA radio station in Syracuse, New York. Bucci is an active participant in the anti-abortion movement. Bucci operates web sites at "www.catholicradio.com" and at "lambsofchrist.com." On August 28, 1996, Bucci registered the domain name "plannedparenthood.com" with Network Solutions, Inc. ("NSI"), a corporation that administers the assignment of domain names on the Internet. After registering the domain name, Bucci set up a web site and home page on the Internet at the address "www.plannedparenthood.com."

Internet users who type in the address "www.plannedparenthood.com," or who use a search engine such as Yahoo or Lycos to find web sites containing the term "planned parenthood," can reach Bucci's web site and home page. Once a user accesses Bucci's home page, she sees on the computer screen the words "Welcome to the PLANNED PARENTHOOD HOME PAGE!" These words appear on the screen first, because the text of a home page downloads from top to bottom. Once the whole home page has loaded, the user sees a scanned image of the cover of a book entitled The Cost of Abortion, by Lawrence Roberge ("Roberge"), under which appear several links: "Foreword," "Afterword," "About the Author," "Book Review," and "Biography."

After clicking on a link, the user accesses text related to that link. By clicking on "Foreword" or "Afterword," the Internet user simply accesses the foreword or afterword of the book The Cost of Abortion. That text eventually reveals that The Cost of Abortion is an anti-abortion book. The text entitled "About the Author" contains the curriculum vitae of author Roberge. It also notes that "Mr. Roberge is available for interview and speaking engagements," and provides his telephone number. The "Book Review" link brings the Internet user to a selection of quotations by various people endorsing The Cost of Abortion. Those quotations include exhortations to read the book and obtain the book. "Biography" offers more information about Roberge's background.

II.   Disputed Facts

The parties dispute defendant's motive in choosing plaintiff's mark as his domain name. Plaintiff alleges that defendant used plaintiff's mark with the "specific intent to damage Planned Parenthood's reputation and to confuse unwitting users of the Internet." Discussing the difference between the domain name at issue here and defendant's other Web sites, defendant's counsel states that "[t]he WWW.PLANNEDPARENTHOOD.COM [sic] website . . . enables Defendant's message to reach a broader audience." Defendant's counsel made the following statement to the Court regarding defendant's use of plaintiff's mark to designate his web site:

> My belief is that it was intended to reach people who would be sympathetic to the proabortion position . . . [I]t is an effort to get the . . . political and social message to people we might not have been otherwise able to reach. I think it's analogous to putting an advertisement in the New York Times rather than The National Review. You are more likely to get people who are sympathetic to the proabortion position, and that's who you want to reach. I believe that is exactly what Mr. Bucci did when he selected Planned Parenthood.

Defendant did not dispute that his counsel was correct in that statement. Defendant's counsel also admitted that Bucci was trying to reach Internet users who thought, in accessing his web site, that they would be getting information from plaintiff.

Defendant stated that his motive in using plaintiff's mark as his domain name was "to reach, primarily, Catholics that are disobedient to the natural law." In an affidavit submitted to the Court, defendant stated that he wanted his "anti-abortion message to reach as many people as possible, and particularly the people who do not think that abortion has an inimical effect on society." . . . Defendant demonstrated full knowledge of plaintiff's name and activities, and admitted to an understanding that using plaintiff's mark as his domain name would attract "pro-abortion" Internet users to his web site because of their misapprehension as to the site's origin. . . . [D]efendant's motive in choosing plaintiff's mark as his domain name was, at least in part, to attract to his home page Internet users who sought plaintiff's home page.

III.   ANALYSIS

B.   Whether the Lanham Act Is Applicable

Defendant argues that his use of plaintiff's mark cannot be reached under the Lanham Act because it is non-commercial speech. Planned Parenthood has brought suit under Sections 1114, 1125(a), and 1125(c) of the Lanham Act, Title 15, United States Code. Section 1114 of the Lanham Act forbids a party to "use in commerce any reproduction, counterfeit, copy, or colorable imitation of a registered mark in connection with the sale, offering for sale, distribution, or advertising of any goods or services on or in connection with which such use is likely to cause confusion, or to cause mistake, or to deceive." An injunction under Section 1125(c) is proper to stop "commercial use in commerce of a mark or trade name" if that use causes dilution of a famous mark. Finally, with respect to Section 1125(a), defendant may be liable if he has used the plaintiff's mark "in commerce" in a way that either "is likely to cause confusion, or to cause mistake, or to deceive as to the affiliation, connection, or association of such person with another person, or as to the origin, sponsorship, or approval of his or her goods, services, or commercial activities by another person," Section 1125(a)(1)(A), or "in commercial advertising or promotion, misrepresents the nature, characteristics, qualities, or geographic origin of his or her or another person's goods, services, or commercial activities," Section 1125(a)(1)(B). Section 1125(c)(4)(B) specifically exempts from the scope of all provisions of Section 1125 the "noncommercial use of a mark."

[D]efendant now argues that his activities are not subject to the Lanham Act because they are not "in commerce." I find this argument meritless. The "use in commerce" requirement of the Lanham Act is a jurisdictional predicate to any law passed by Congress. It is well settled that the scope of "in commerce" as a jurisdictional predicate of the Lanham Act is broad and has a sweeping reach. . . . The activity involved in this action meets the "in commerce" standard for two reasons. First, defendant's actions affect plaintiff's ability to offer plaintiff's services, which, as health and information services offered in forty-eight states and over the Internet, are surely "in commerce." Thus, even assuming, arguendo, that defendant's activities are not in interstate commerce for Lanham Act purposes, the effect of those activities on plaintiff's interstate commerce activities would place defendant within the reach of the Lanham Act. . . . Second, Internet users constitute a national, even international, audience, who must use interstate telephone lines to access defendant's web site on the Internet. The nature of the Internet indicates that establishing a typical home page on the Internet, for access to all users, would satisfy the Lanham Act's "in commerce" requirement. . . . Therefore, I conclude that defendant's actions are "in commerce" within the meaning of that term for jurisdictional purposes. I now turn to the specific language of each provision of the Lanham Act under which plaintiff has brought suit.

1. Section 1114

Notwithstanding its jurisdictional "in commerce" requirement, Section 1114 contains no commercial activity requirement; rather, it prohibits any person from, without consent of the registrant of a mark, using the mark "in connection with the sale, offering for sale, distribution, or advertising of any good or services on or in connection with which such use is likely to cause confusion, or to cause mistake, or to deceive." The question the Court must decide, then, is whether defendant's use of plaintiff's mark is properly viewed as in connection with the distribution or advertising of goods or services.

Defendant's use of plaintiff's mark satisfies the requirement of Section 1114 in a variety of ways. First, defendant has stated that he chose to place materials about The Cost of Abortion on the "www.plannedparenthood. com" web site because he wanted to help Roberge "plug" his book. . . . Although defendant receives no money from any sales of the book that result from its exposure on his home page, there is no personal profit requirement in Section 1114. The materials on the home page, which are similar to a publisher's publicity kit, certainly relate to the advertisement and distribution of The Cost of Abortion.

Second, defendant's home page is merely one portion of his, and Catholic Radio's, broader effort to educate Catholics about the anti-abortion movement. With respect to that effort, defendant solicits funds and encourages supporters to join him in his protest activities. Much like plaintiff, defendant has a practical as well as a political motive. While plaintiff seeks to make available what it terms "reproductive services," including, inter alia, birth control and abortion services, defendant offers informational services for use in convincing people that certain activities, including the use of plaintiff's services, are morally wrong. In this way, defendant offers his own set of services, and his use of plaintiff's mark is in connection with the distribution of those services over the Internet. . . .

In addition, defendant's use of plaintiff's mark is "in connection with the distribution of services" because it is likely to prevent some Internet users from reaching plaintiff's own Internet web site. Prospective users of plaintiff's services who mistakenly access defendant's web site may fail to continue to search for plaintiff's own home page, due to anger, frustration, or the belief that plaintiff's home page does not exist. One witness explained, "We didn't resume the search [for plaintiff's web site] after [finding defendant's web site] because . . . we were pretty much thrown off track." Therefore, defendant's action in appropriating plaintiff's mark has a connection to plaintiff's distribution of its services. For these reasons, Section 1114 is applicable to defendant's use of plaintiff's mark.

2. Section 1125(c)

[The Court concludes that the defendant's conduct satisfies the "commercial use" requirement of Section 1125(c) for the same reasons it satisfies the "in commerce" requirement under Section 1114. According to the court, "defendant's use is commercial because of its effect on plaintiff's activities. First, defendant has appropriated plaintiff's mark in order to reach an audience of Internet users who want to reach plaintiff's services and viewpoint, intercepting them and misleading them in an attempt to offer his own political message. Second, defendant's appropriation not only provides Internet users with competing and directly opposing information, but also prevents those users from reaching plaintiff and its services and message. In that way, defendant's use is classically competitive: he has taken plaintiff's mark as his own in order to purvey his Internet services — his Web site — to an audience intending to access plaintiff's services."]

3. Section 1125(a)(1)(A)

In relevant part, Section 1125(a)(1)(A) prohibits a person from using in commerce any term or false designation of origin which "is likely to cause confusion . . . as to the affiliation, connection, or association of such person with another person, or as to the origin, sponsorship, or approval of his or her goods, services, or commercial activities by another person." Section 1125(a)(1) is also limited by Section 1125(c)(4)(B), which states that "noncommercial use of a mark" is not actionable under the Lanham Act.

Here, as discussed above, defendant offers informational services relating to the anti-abortion and anti-birth control movement, specifically providing his audience with relevant literature and the means to contact Roberge. In addition, defendant's solicitation of funds in relation to his anti-abortion efforts are commercial in nature. Therefore, because defendant's labeling of his web site with plaintiff's mark relates to the "origin, sponsorship, or approval" by plaintiff of defendant's web site, I find that Section 1125(a)(1)(A) may govern defendant's actions in this case.

I therefore determine that Section 1114, Section 1125(c), and 1125(a)(1)(a) of the Lanham Act are applicable here. . . .

[The court subsequently finds that Bucci's use of the domain name is likely to cause confusion.]

COMMENTS AND QUESTIONS

1. As discussed in *Planned Parenthood*, to successfully raise either a trademark infringement or dilution claim, the plaintiff must establish that the mark was used "in commerce." Does *Planned Parenthood* establish a per se rule that use of a mark on the Internet is "in commerce"? Does it establish a per se rule with respect to "commercial use"?

2. Is there a difference between commercial use of a domain name and commercial use of a trademark? Consider Avery Dennison Corp. v. Sumpton, 51 U.S.P.Q.2d 1801 (9th Cir. 1999), in which the defendants registered the domain names "Avery.net" and "Dennison.net" in order to offer vanity e-mail addresses to individuals for a fee. In rejecting the company's argument that this use diluted its trademark "Avery Dennison," the court reasoned:

Commercial Use under the Federal Trademark Dilution Act requires the defendant to be using the trademark as a trademark, capitalizing on its trademark status. See *Panavision*, 141 F.3d at 1325. Courts have phrased this requirement in various ways. In a classic "cybersquatter" case, one court referenced the defendant's "intention to arbitrage" the registration which included the plaintiff's trademark. *Intermatic*, 947 F. Supp. at 1239. Another court, whose decision we affirmed, noted that the defendant "traded on the value of marks as marks." Panavision Int'l, L.P. v. Toeppen, 945 F. Supp. 1296, 1303 (C.D. Cal. 1996), aff'd, 141 F.3d 1316 (9th Cir. 1998). In our *Panavision* decision, we considered the defendant's "attempt to sell the trademarks themselves." 141 F.3d at 1325.

All evidence in the record indicates that Appellants register common surnames in domain-name combinations and license e-mail addresses using those surnames, with the consequent intent to capitalize on the surname status of "Avery" and "Dennison." Appellants do not use trademarks qua trademarks as required by the case to establish commercial use. Rather, Appellants use words that happen to be trademarks for their non-trademark value.

Can *Avery Dennison* and *Planned Parenthood* be reconciled? Was Bucci using Planned Parenthood as a trademark?

3. Should Bucci's promotion of *The Cost of Abortion* and his overall fund-raising efforts be relevant to the commercial use analysis? Is posting a resume on a Web site in the hopes that potential employers may hire you commercial?

4. To what extent should the "in commerce" and "commercial use" requirements be influenced by First Amendment considerations? In *Planned Parenthood*, Bucci used the domain name as a means of reaching his intended audience, individuals seeking information about abortion who might not otherwise receive his message. Assuming that the Web page itself clearly identified that it was not affiliated with Planned Parenthood, is there an argument that this should be an acceptable method of communication? Consider further the case of Bosley Medical Institute, Inc. v. Kremer, 403 F.3d 672 (2005), in which the defendant, a dissatisfied customer of the plaintiff, registered a domain name corresponding to the plaintiff's registered trademark for the purposes of criticizing the plaintiff. The Ninth Circuit Court of Appeals held that the defendant's activities did not constitute a commercial use for the purposes of a trademark infringement action. The court noted that:

> Kremer is not Bosley's competitor; he is their critic. His use of the Bosley mark is not in connection with a sale of goods or services — it is in connection with the expression of his opinion *about* Bosley's goods and services.
>
> The dangers that the Lanham Act was designed to address are simply not at issue in this case. The Lanham Act, expressly enacted to be applied in commercial contexts, does not prohibit all unauthorized uses of a trademark. Kremer's use of the Bosley Medical mark simply cannot mislead consumers into buying a competing product — no customer will mistakenly purchase a hair replacement service from Kremer under the belief that the service is being offered by Bosley. Neither is Kremer capitalizing on the good will Bosley has created in its mark. Any harm to Bosley arises not from a competitor's sale of a similar product under Bosley's mark, but from Kremer's criticism of their services. Bosley cannot use the Lanham Act either as a shield from Kremer's criticism, or as a sword to shut Kremer up.

Compare this decision with the Fourth Circuit Court of Appeals decision in People for the Ethical Treatment of Animals v. Doughney, 263 F.3d 359 (2001). In that case, the Fourth Circuit did not support the defendant's alleged First Amendment right to utilize a domain name corresponding with the plaintiff's registered "PETA" trademark to host a parody of the plaintiff's activities. The Fourth Circuit affirmed the District Court's order for summary judgment for trademark infringement. For a further discussion of potential First Amendment concerns arising in relation to Internet domain name disputes, see Jacqueline Lipton, *Beyond Cybersquatting: Taking Domain Name Disputes Past Trademark Policy*, 40 Wake Forest L. Rev. 1361, 1392-1404 (2005); Jacqueline Lipton, *Commerce versus Commentary: Gripe Sites,*

Parody, and the First Amendment in Cyberspace, 84 Wash. U. L. Rev. 1327 (2006).

Interestingly, when the issue of free speech has arisen in UDRP determinations, UDRP arbitrators have often attempted to protect free speech under the "legitimate interest" defense in the UDRP — see below for discussion of the operation of the UDRP and the legitimate interest defense. In the case of *Bridgestone Firestone v. Myers,* for example, a UDRP arbitrator noted that: "Although free speech is not listed as one of the [UDRP's] examples of a right or legitimate interest in a domain name, the list is not exclusive, and the Panel concludes that the exercise of free speech for criticism and commentary . . . demonstrates a right or legitimate interest in the domain name under Paragraph 4(c)(iii). The Internet is above all a framework for global communication, and the right to free speech should be one of the foundations of Internet law." WIPO Case No. D2000-0190, WIPO Arbitration and Mediation Center, July 6, 2000, at ¶6, see *http://www.wipo.int/amc/en/domains/decisions/html/2000/d2000-0190.html.*

ii) Likelihood of Confusion and Dilution

Assuming that a defendant's use of a trademark satisfies the statutory prerequisites, is that use likely to cause confusion or does it dilute the trademark? As the following materials illustrate, a principal debate with respect to confusion turns upon whether trademark law should prevent "initial interest confusion" where a user is drawn to a site not owned or affiliated with a trademark owner because the user assumed that some form of the trademark would be used as the owner's domain name.

BROOKFIELD COMMUNICATIONS, INC. v. WEST COAST ENTM'T CORP.

174 F.3d 1036 (9th Cir. 1999)

O'SCANNLAIN, Circuit Judge:

We must venture into cyberspace to determine whether federal trademark and unfair competition laws prohibit a video rental store chain from using an entertainment-industry information provider's trademark in the domain name of its web site and in its web site's metatags.

Brookfield Communications, Inc. ("Brookfield") appeals the district court's denial of its motion for a preliminary injunction prohibiting West Coast Entertainment Corporation ("West Coast") from using in commerce terms confusingly similar to Brookfield's trademark, "MovieBuff." Brookfield gathers and sells information about the entertainment industry. . . .

Brookfield expanded into the broader consumer market with computer software featuring a searchable database containing entertainment-industry related information marketed under the "MovieBuff" mark around December 1993. Brookfield's "MovieBuff" software now targets smaller companies and individual consumers who are not interested in purchasing Brookfield's professional level alternative. . . .

Sometime in 1996, Brookfield attempted to register the World Wide Web ("the Web") domain name "moviebuff.com" with Network Solutions, Inc. ("Network Solutions"), but was informed that the requested domain name had already been registered by West Coast. . . .

In October 1998, Brookfield learned that West Coast—one of the nation's largest video rental store chains with over 500 stores—intended to launch a web site at "moviebuff.com" containing, inter alia, a searchable entertainment database similar to "MovieBuff." West Coast had registered "moviebuff.com" with Network Solutions on February 6, 1996, and claims that it chose the domain name because the term "Movie Buff" is part of its service mark, "The Movie Buff's Movie Store," on which a federal registration issued in 1991 covering "retail store services featuring video cassettes and video game cartridges" and "rental of video cassettes and video game cartridges." West Coast notes further that, since at least 1988, it has also used various phrases including the term "Movie Buff" to promote goods and services available at its video stores in Massachusetts. . . .

To resolve whether West Coast's use of "moviebuff.com" constitutes trademark infringement or unfair competition, we must first determine whether Brookfield has a valid, protectable trademark interest in the "Movie-Buff" mark. Brookfield's registration of the mark on the Principal Register in the Patent and Trademark Office constitutes prima facie evidence of the validity of the registered mark and of Brookfield's exclusive right to use the mark on the goods and services specified in the registration. See 15 U.S.C. §§1057(b); 1115(a). Nevertheless, West Coast can rebut this presumption by showing that it used the mark in commerce first, since a fundamental tenet of trademark law is that ownership of an inherently distinctive mark such as "MovieBuff" is governed by priority of use. . . . The first to use a mark is deemed the "senior" user and has the right to enjoin "junior" users from using confusingly similar marks in the same industry and market or within the senior user's natural zone of expansion. . . .

[Assuming that the relevant inquiry is who used the term MovieBuff with respect to Internet related databases, the court concludes that Brookfield was the senior user of the mark. In so doing, the court rejected West Coast's argument that registration of a domain name was sufficient use. According to the court

> The purpose of a trademark is to help consumers identify the source, but a mark cannot serve a source-identifying function if the public has never seen the mark and thus is not meritorious of trademark protection until it is used in public in a manner that creates an association among consumers between the mark and the mark's owner.

Similarly, the court concluded that West Coast's use of moviebuff.com in limited e-mail between lawyers and some customers was insufficient use because the "purported 'use' is akin to putting one's mark 'on a business office door sign, letterheads, architectural drawings, etc.' or on a prototype displayed to a potential buyer, both of which have been held to be insufficient to establish trademark rights."]

Establishing seniority, however, is only half the battle. Brookfield must also show that the public is likely to be somehow confused about the source or sponsorship of West Coast's "moviebuff.com" web site — and somehow to associate that site with Brookfield. See 15 U.S.C. §§1114(1); 1125(a). The Supreme Court has described "the basic objectives of trademark law" as follows: "trademark law, by preventing others from copying a source-identifying mark, 'reduce[s] the customer's costs of shopping and making purchasing decisions,' for it quickly and easily assures a potential customer that this item — the item with this mark — is made by the same producer as other similarly marked items that he or she liked (or disliked) in the past. At the same time, the law helps assure a producer that it (and not an imitating competitor) will reap the financial, reputation-related rewards associated with a desirable product." Where two companies each use a different mark and the simultaneous use of those marks does not cause the consuming public to be confused as to who makes what, granting one company exclusive rights over both marks does nothing to further the objectives of the trademark laws; in fact, prohibiting the use of a mark that the public has come to associate with a company would actually contravene the intended purposes of the trademark law by making it more difficult to identify and to distinguish between different brands of goods.

"The core element of trademark infringement is the likelihood of confusion, i.e., whether the similarity of the marks is likely to confuse customers about the source of the products." We look to the following factors for guidance in determining the likelihood of confusion: similarity of the conflicting designations; relatedness or proximity of the two companies' products or services; strength of Brookfield's mark; marketing channels used; degree of care likely to be exercised by purchasers in selecting goods; West Coast's intent in selecting its mark; evidence of actual confusion; and likelihood of expansion in product lines. See Dr. Seuss Enters. v. Penguin Books USA, Inc., 109 F.3d 1394, 1404 (9th Cir. 1997), petition for cert. dismissed by, 521 U.S. 1146, 118 S. Ct. 27, 138 L. Ed. 2d 1057 (1997); *Sleekcraft*, 599 F.2d at 348-49; see also Restatement (Third) of Unfair Competition §§20-23 (1995). These eight factors are often referred to as the *Sleekcraft* factors.

A word of caution: this eight-factor test for likelihood of confusion is pliant. Some factors are much more important than others, and the relative importance of each individual factor will be case-specific. Although some factors — such as the similarity of the marks and whether the two companies are direct competitors — will always be important, it is often possible to reach a conclusion with respect to likelihood of confusion after considering only a subset of the factors. Moreover, the foregoing list does not purport to be exhaustive, and non-listed variables may often be quite important. We must be acutely aware of excessive rigidity when applying the law in the Internet context; emerging technologies require a flexible approach. . . .

We begin by comparing the allegedly infringing mark to the federally registered mark. The similarity of the marks will always be an important factor. Where the two marks are entirely dissimilar, there is no likelihood of confusion. "Pepsi" does not infringe Coca-Cola's "Coke." Nothing further need be said. Even where there is precise identity of a complainant's and an alleged infringer's mark, there may be no consumer confusion — and thus no trademark infringement — if the alleged infringer is in a different geographic area or in a wholly different industry. . . . Nevertheless, the more similar the marks in terms of appearance, sound, and meaning, the greater the likelihood of confusion. In analyzing this factor, "[t]he marks must be considered in their entirety and as they appear in the marketplace," with similarities weighed more heavily than differences.

In the present case, the district court found West Coast's domain name "moviebuff.com" to be quite different than Brookfield's domain name "moviebuffonline.com." Comparison of domain names, however, is irrelevant as a matter of law, since the Lanham Act requires that the allegedly infringing mark be compared with the claimant's trademark, see 15 U.S.C. §§1114(1), 1125(a), which here is "MovieBuff," not "moviebuffonline.com." Properly framed, it is readily apparent that West Coast's allegedly infringing mark is essentially identical to Brookfield's mark "MovieBuff." In terms of appearance, there are differences in capitalization and the addition of ".com" in West Coast's complete domain name, but these differences are inconsequential in light of the fact that Web addresses are not caps-sensitive and that the ".com" top-level domain signifies the site's commercial nature.

Looks aren't everything, so we consider the similarity of sound and meaning. The two marks are pronounced the same way, except that one would say "dot com" at the end of West Coast's mark. Because many companies use domain names comprised of ".com" as the top-level domain with their corporate name or trademark as the second-level domain, the addition of ".com" is of diminished importance in distinguishing the mark. The irrelevance of the ".com" becomes further apparent once we consider similarity in meaning. The domain name is more than a mere address: like trademarks, second-level domain names communicate information as to source. [M]any Web users are likely to associate "moviebuff.com" with the trademark "MovieBuff," thinking that it is operated by the company that makes "MovieBuff" products and services.[17] Courts, in fact, have routinely concluded that marks were essentially identical in similar contexts. . . . As "MovieBuff" and "moviebuff.com" are,

17. In an analogous context, courts have granted trademark protection to phone numbers that spell out a corporation's name, trademark, or slogan. See Dial-A-Mattress Franchise Corp. v. Page, 880 F.2d 675, 677-78 (2d Cir. 1989) (granting trademark protection to "(area code)-MATTRES"); American Airlines,

for all intents and purposes, identical in terms of sight, sound, and meaning, we conclude that the similarity factor weighs heavily in favor of Brookfield.

The similarity of marks alone, as we have explained, does not necessarily lead to consumer confusion. Accordingly, we must proceed to consider the relatedness of the products and services offered. Related goods are generally more likely than unrelated goods to confuse the public as to the producers of the goods. In light of the virtual identity of marks, if they were used with identical products or services likelihood of confusion would follow as a matter of course. If, on the other hand, Brookfield and West Coast did not compete to any extent whatsoever, the likelihood of confusion would probably be remote. A Web surfer who accessed "moviebuff.com" and reached a Web site advertising the services of Schlumberger Ltd. (a large oil drilling company) would be unlikely to think that Brookfield had entered the oil drilling business or was sponsoring the oil driller. At the least, Brookfield would bear the heavy burden of demonstrating (through other relevant factors) that consumers were likely to be confused as to source or affiliation in such a circumstance.

[The court concludes that the products are related because "[j]ust as Brookfield's 'MovieBuff' is a searchable database with detailed information on films, West Coast's Web site features a similar searchable database, which Brookfield points out is licensed from a direct competitor of Brookfield. Undeniably then, the products are used for similar purposes. . . . The use of similar marks to offer similar products accordingly weighs heavily in favor of likelihood of confusion."]

In addition to the relatedness of products, West Coast and Brookfield both utilize the Web as a marketing and advertising facility, a factor that courts have consistently recognized as exacerbating the likelihood of confusion. Both companies, apparently recognizing the rapidly growing importance of Web commerce, are maneuvering to attract customers via the Web. Not only do they compete for the patronage of an overlapping audience on the Web, both "MovieBuff" and "moviebuff.com" are utilized in conjunction with Web-based products.

Given the virtual identity of "moviebuff.com" and "MovieBuff," the relatedness of the products and services accompanied by those marks, and the companies' simultaneous use of the Web as a marketing and advertising tool, many forms of consumer confusion are likely to result. People surfing the Web for information on "MovieBuff" may confuse "MovieBuff" with the searchable entertainment database at "moviebuff.com" and simply assume that they have reached Brookfield's Web site. In the Internet context, in particular, entering a Web site takes little effort—usually one click from a linked site or a search engine's list; thus, Web surfers are more likely to be confused as to the ownership of a Web site than traditional patrons of a brick-and-mortar store would

---

Inc. v. A 1-800-A-M-E-R-I-C-A-N Corp., 622 F. Supp. 673, 683-84 (N.D. Ill. 1985); see also Dranoff-Perlstein Assocs. v. Sklar, 967 F.2d 852, 856-58 (3d Cir. 1992). But see Holiday Inns, Inc. v. 800 Reservation, Inc., 86 F.3d 619, 622 (6th Cir. 1996).

be of a store's ownership. Alternatively, they may incorrectly believe that West Coast licensed "MovieBuff" from Brookfield, or that Brookfield otherwise sponsored West Coast's database. Other consumers may simply believe that West Coast bought out Brookfield or that they are related companies.

Yet other forms of confusion are likely to ensue. Consumers may wrongly assume that the "MovieBuff" database they were searching for is no longer offered, having been replaced by West Coast's entertainment database, and thus simply use the services at West Coast's Web site. And even where people realize, immediately upon accessing "moviebuff.com," that they have reached a site operated by West Coast and wholly unrelated to Brookfield, West Coast will still have gained a customer by appropriating the goodwill that Brookfield has developed in its "MovieBuff" mark. A consumer who was originally looking for Brookfield's products or services may be perfectly content with West Coast's database (especially as it is offered free of charge); but he reached West Coast's site because of its use of Brookfield's mark as its second-level domain name, which is a misappropriation of Brookfield's goodwill by West Coast. . . .

[The court finds the likelihood-of-confusion conclusion to be consistent with the remaining factors as well. The court's discussion of metatags and initial interest confusion are discussed *infra*.]

HASBRO, INC. v. CLUE COMPUTING, INC.

66 F. Supp. 2d 117 (D. Mass. 1999)

WOODLOCK, District Judge.

Plaintiff Hasbro, Inc. brings this suit against Clue Computing, Inc., a Colorado company, for trademark infringement upon and dilution of the CLUE® trademark. Hasbro, which owns the CLUE® mark corresponding to the game CLUE, alleges that Clue Computing has infringed upon its trademark rights and diluted its famous mark through the use of a World Wide Web site at the address of "clue.com."

Clue Computing, Inc. is a Colorado corporation located in Longmont, Colorado. It is in the business of computer consulting. Created in 1994 as a partnership, Clue Computing is now owned by Eric Robison. Clue Computing was incorporated in Colorado as Clue Computing, Inc. on May 22, 1996. Robison is the sole full-time employee of Clue Computing. According to the defendant, Robison and Dieter Muller, Robison's friend and co-founder of Clue Computing, chose the name Clue Computing for reasons unrelated to the game of CLUE®. Defendant asserts that the name came about as a joke when Robison and Muller were both employed at another company. When individuals would call themselves "clueless" in conversation, Muller and Robison would hand them a card with the word "clue" on it.

The partnership Clue Computing, predecessor to Clue Computing, Inc., registered the Web domain "clue.com" with Network Solutions, Inc. ("NSI") on June 13, 1994, and the company has used the Web site at that address ever since. The company uses the Web site to advertise its business, including Internet consulting, training, system administration, and network design and implementation. The Web site offers the address, phone number, and e-mail address for the company. In addition, those Internet users who view the site can instantly e-mail the company by clicking on the page. . . .

Hasbro claims that Clue Computing infringed its CLUE® trademark under 15 U.S.C. §1125(a). . . .

Trademark law seeks to prevent one seller from using a "mark" identical or similar to that used by another seller in a way that confuses the public about the actual source of the goods or services in question. Such confusion may prevent the buyer from obtaining the goods he seeks or may endanger the reputation of the first user of the mark by association with the subsequent user. To prevail on a trademark infringement claim, a plaintiff must show 1) use and therefore ownership of the mark 2) use by the defendant of the same mark or a similar one, and 3) likelihood that the defendant's use will confuse the public, thereby harming the plaintiff. The first two components of this test are not in contention in this case; thus the key to Hasbro's infringement claim is the element of confusion.[4]

With respect to the element of confusion, the First Circuit has held:

> We require evidence of a "substantial" likelihood of confusion — not a mere possibility — and typically refer to eight factors in making the assessment: (1) the similarity of the marks; (2) the similarity of the goods [or services]; (3) the relationship between the parties' channels of trade; (4) the relationship between the parties' advertising; (5) the classes of prospective purchasers; (6) evidence of actual confusion; (7) the defendant's intent in adopting the mark; (8) the strength of the plaintiff's mark.

I will analyze these factors in turn to determine whether there are sufficient facts to create a dispute as to the likelihood of confusion.

[While the court finds that the marks are "essentially identical" and that Clue is a sufficiently strong mark, it concludes that the remaining factors weigh against finding a substantial likelihood of confusion. With respect to actual confusion, the court concluded:] . . . From the more than four years since Clue Computing began using the "clue.com" domain name, Hasbro has produced only a few scraps of evidence of actual confusion between Clue Computing's Web site and Hasbro's trademark. Plaintiff has produced three e-mails, including two sent three minutes apart by the same person, directed to the e-mail address link on Clue Computing's Web site asking about the game CLUE.

---

4. The First Circuit has also set out three prerequisite elements which the plaintiff must satisfy to be entitled to any form of trademark protection, whether on infringement or dilution grounds. These elements are that the "marks (a) must be used in commerce, (b) must be non-functional, and (c) must be distinctive." I.P. Lund Trading v. Kohler Co., 163 F.3d 27, 36 (1st Cir. 1998). Neither party has disputed these prerequisites, but I note that both the plaintiff's trademark and the defendant's domain name are clearly used in commerce and both are in themselves non-functional. Further, as explained in my discussion of strength of the mark, Hasbro's CLUE® trademark is either suggestive or descriptive and in any case has secondary meaning. As such, it meets the level of distinctiveness required for trademark protection.

There is no way to verify the source or authenticity of two of the e-mails, so they are of limited value as evidence. Hasbro has produced an affidavit from the author of the third e-mail saying that she was confused by the defendant's Web site and thought that it was connected to technical support for Plaintiff's CLUE CD-ROM. Hasbro also submitted an *affidavit* from one other customer who contacted the company after apparently searching for Hasbro's Web site without success and briefly becoming confused by Clue Computing's "clue.com" site.

The fact that one, two or three people over four years may have expressed confusion between Clue Computing's Web site and Hasbro's game does not constitute the level of actual confusion necessary to support a general finding of likelihood of confusion. "[A] single misdirected communication is very weak evidence of consumer confusion."

Furthermore, to the extent that Ms. Magestro's and Mr. Britt's affidavits show actual confusion, they do not show reasonable confusion, which is required to find infringement. "[T]he law has long demanded a showing that the allegedly infringing conduct carries with it a likelihood of confounding an appreciable number of reasonably prudent purchasers exercising ordinary care. This means, of course, that confusion resulting from the consuming public's carelessness, indifference, or ennui will not suffice." Considering the vast difference between Clue Computing's services and Hasbro's game and the explicitness of Clue Computing's Web site as to the nature of its business, any confusion shown by Hasbro seems to fit into the latter category of "carelessness, indifference, or ennui."

Finally, the kind of confusion that is more likely to result from Clue Computing's use of the "clue.com" domain name — namely, that consumers will realize they are at the wrong site and go to an Internet search engine to find the right one — is not substantial enough to be legally significant. "[A]n initial confusion on the part of Web browsers . . . is not cognizable under trademark law." But see Interstellar Starship Services, Ltd. v. Epix Inc., 184 F.3d 1107 (9th Cir. 1999) (recognizing "a brand of confusion called 'initial interest' confusion which permits a finding of a likelihood of confusion although the consumer quickly becomes aware of the source's actual identity."); Panavision Int'l, L.P. v. Toeppen, 141 F.3d 1316, 1327 (9th Cir. 1998) (finding that, when trademark is used as another entity's domain name, use of search engine to find the Web site sought may be time-consuming and frustrating and may deter customers). Indeed, the parties dispute the ease of finding Hasbro's site for CLUE. I conclude that, although the need to search for Hasbro's site may rise to the level of inconvenience, it is not sufficient to raise a dispute as to actual confusion. The paucity of evidence of reasonable and actual confusion weighs heavily against Hasbro's ability to show a likelihood of confusion. . . .

The FTDA defines dilution as "the lessening of the capacity of a famous mark to identify and distinguish goods or services, regardless of the presence or absence of (1) competition between the owner of the famous mark and other parties, or (2) the likelihood of confusion, mistake or deception." 15 U.S.C. §1127. The two kinds of dilution traditionally recognized are blurring and tarnishment. Hasbro, however, urges me to join several other courts in recognizing what would be essentially a third, "per se," category of dilution — use of another's trademark as a domain name. One such court, whose decision was recently reversed, asserted, "Courts presented with the question have held unanimously that it does 'lessen the capacity of a famous mark to identify and distinguish goods or services,' when someone other than the trademark holder registers the trademark name as an Internet domain name." Avery Dennison Corp. v. Sumpton, 999 F. Supp. 1337, 1340 (C.D. Cal. 1998), rev'd, 189 F.3d 868 (9th Cir. 1999); see also Panavision Int'l, L.P. v. Toeppen, 141 F.3d 1316, 1326-27 (9th Cir. 1998); *Lozano*, 44 U.S.P.Q.2d at 1769. These courts seem to suggest that simply preventing a plaintiff from using his own famous trademark as a domain name dilutes the plaintiff's ability to identify his goods and services and may frustrate or deter potential consumers. *Avery*, 999 F. Supp. at 1340-41; *Panavision*, 141 F.3d at 1326-27. Indeed, Senator Patrick Leahy said in reference to the FTDA, "[I]t is my hope that this antidilution statute can help stem the use of deceptive Internet addresses taken by those who are choosing marks that are associated with the products and reputations of others." 141 Cong. Rec. ¶19312091 (daily ed. Dec. 29, 1995). Although cited in Panavision, 141 F.3d at 1326, in support of something akin to a per se rule, the Leahy quotation suggests a more limited proposition, namely finding dilution only where the use of another's trademark as a domain name is deceptive or intentional. [The references in this judgment to the federal trademark legislation are to the version of the legislation that predated the Trademark Dilution Revision Act of 2006, see above.]

The statement of the District Court in Avery to the contrary notwithstanding, several courts have rejected such a per se rule. In Lockheed Martin Corp. v. Network Solutions Inc., 43 U.S.P.Q.2d 1056, 1058 (C.D. Cal. 1997), Judge Pregerson of the Central District of California wrote:

> [T]he law does not per se prohibit the use of trademarks or service marks as domain names. Rather, the law prohibits only uses that infringe or dilute a trademark or service mark owner's mark. Moreover, innocent third party users of a trademark or service mark have no duty to police the mark for the benefit of the mark's owner.

Another court differentiated a cybersquatter who took another's mark as a domain name in order to sell it back to the owner for profit — which the court found to be dilution — from "a situation where there were competing uses of the same name by competing parties and a race to the Internet between them," which would not necessarily be dilution. Intermatic Inc. v. Toeppen, 947 F. Supp. 1227, 1240 (N.D. Ill. 1996).

I join those courts finding that, while use of a trademark as a domain name to extort money from the markholder or to prevent that markholder from using the domain name may be per se dilution, a legitimate competing use of the domain name is not. Holders of a famous mark are not automatically entitled to use that mark as their domain name; trademark law does not support such a monopoly. If another Internet user has an innocent and legitimate reason for using the famous mark as a domain name and is the first to register it, that user should be able to use the domain name, provided that it has not otherwise infringed upon or diluted the trademark. I reject Hasbro's request for a per se dilution rule and instead turn to whether Clue Computing has diluted Hasbro's CLUE® mark under existing dilution standards. . . .

COMMENTS AND QUESTIONS

1.   With respect to domain names, one could argue that the adoption of a similar or identical domain name is likely to cause confusion. Under *Holiday Inns*, however, would the plaintiff be required to show that the defendant advertised or otherwise used the domain name as a trademark? Does *Brookfield* address this question? How does that decision treat domain names?

2.   Does the "use in commerce" requirement for purposes of establishing a trademark differ from the use in commerce requirement for determining whether a mark has been infringed? If so, is the difference justified?

3.   Is use of the traditional trademark likelihood of confusion analysis for domain name disputes appropriate? Are the problems created by the use of confusingly similar domain names increased because, as the court recognized in *Brookfield*, the parties will both be using the Internet as a means of marketing?

4.   When determining whether the use of a domain name infringes another's trademark, should the domain name be viewed in isolation or together with the Web page? What do *Brookfield* and *Hasbro* suggest?

5.   *Hasbro* rejects what has been described as "initial interest confusion," in which trademark infringement is based upon the consumer's initial confusion upon ending up at a Web site other than the one for which they were looking. For a more detailed discussion of "initial interest confusion," see *Brookfield, supra*. Are the court's reasons for rejecting "initial interest confusion" persuasive? For a recent critique of the initial interest confusion doctrine as applied online, see Greg Lastowka, *Google's Law*, 73 Brook. L. Rev. 1327, 1369-71 (2008).

Note: Liability of Domain Name Registrars for Assigning Infringing Domain Names

Paragraph 2 of the Uniform Domain Name Dispute Resolution Policy now requires registrants to make representations to domain name registrars that the registration will not infringe on others' rights or be otherwise unlawful. Paragraph 6 further prohibits a registrant from naming a registrar as a party in a domain name dispute. However, issues have arisen in the past about the extent to which domain name registrars should be liable for assigning domain names that infringe another's trademark rights, or any other legal rights. In Lockheed Martin Corp. v. Network Solutions, Inc., 194 F.3d 980 (9th Cir. 1999), for example, Network Solutions was sued for contributory service mark infringement and dilution on the basis that it allowed registration to an applicant of domain names corresponding with service marks owned by the plaintiff. In this case, the court held that Network Solutions was not liable for contributory service mark infringement because it did not exercise sufficient control and monitoring of the registrant's activities to support such a claim. This may be contrasted with the case of Kremen v. Cohen, 337 F.3d 1024 (2003), in which the Ninth Circuit Court of Appeals, in overturning a decision of the District Court for the Northern District of California, held that imposing liability on Network Solutions under Californian conversion law for wrongful transfer of a domain name from a rightful registrant to a con man would be appropriate. The case was then remanded for further proceedings. This case did not involve a trademark dispute as the domain name in question was "sex.com." However, it is interesting for its approach to registrar liability. The court noted:

> Network Solutions made no effort to contact Kremen before giving away his domain name, despite receiving a facially suspect letter from a third party [Cohen]. A jury would be justified in finding it was unreasonably careless.
>
> [T]here is nothing unfair about holding a company responsible for giving away someone else's property even if it was not at fault. Cohen is obviously the guilty party here, and the one who should in all fairness pay for his theft. But he's skipped the country, and his money is stashed in some offshore bank account. Unless Kremen's luck with his bounty hunters improves, Cohen is out of the picture. The question becomes whether Network Solutions should be open to liability for its decision to hand over Kremen's domain name. Negligent or not, it was Network Solutions that gave away Kremen's property. Kremen never did anything. It would not be unfair to hold Network Solutions responsible and force it to try to recoup its losses by chasing down Cohen. This, at any rate, is the logic of the common law, and we do not lightly discard it.
>
> The district court was worried that "the threat of litigation threatens to stifle the registration system by requiring further regulations by [Network Solutions] and potential increases in fees." Kremen, 99 F. Supp. 2d at 1174. Given that Network Solutions's "regulations" evidently allowed it to hand over a registrant's domain name on the basis of a facially suspect letter without even contacting him, "further regulations" don't seem like such a bad idea. And the prospect of higher fees presents no issue here that it doesn't in any other context. A bank could lower its ATM fees if it didn't have to pay security guards, but we doubt most depositors would think that was a good idea.

Should Internet domain name registrars be exempted from liability for all wrongful registrations and transfers of domain names? What are the policy arguments for and against such liability?

b) Anti-Cybersquatting Laws

Beginning in 1992, the growing popularity of the Internet spurred a tremendous proliferation of domain name registrations. Around 1995, the "commercial Internet" emerged. Individuals rushed to register company names and company trademarks as domain names and to sell the domain names back to the respective name and trademark owners. Commonly known as cybersquatters, these individuals registered the domain names using the trademarks of large companies, generic words, and even famous individuals and presidential candidates.

The problem faced by the commercial entities or individuals who then sought to launch their own Web pages was that users would use "guessability" to locate Web sites on the Internet. They would type in the company name or its brand name in an attempt to locate the company. And, instead of reaching the intended company, they would reach an unintended third party or a blank page. As time went on, the cybersquatters became more daring, stating "Domain Name for Sale!" on the Web sites corresponding to these domain names. Moreover, many cybersquatters were so bold as to record fictitious names as the registrant owner, such as "Domain for Sale"!

It was a true gold rush. Articles appeared in the media announcing that cybersquatters were requesting (and obtaining) millions of dollars for domain names. Commercial entities believed cybersquatting was nothing more than a shakedown to purchase their own intellectual property. Moreover, it was time-consuming to locate the cybersquatters who often used false identifying information in registering the domain. Further, it was expensive to investigate the registration and registrant and buy or have the domain name transferred back to the trademark owner. Many commercial entities were outraged.

Private working groups and associations were formed to lobby the U.S. Congress to legislate change. The result was the Anticybersquatting Consumer Protection Act of 1999 (ACPA).[3] The ACPA established a civil action for a person with a bad faith intent to profit from a mark who "registers, traffics in, or uses a domain name" that: (1) "in the case of a mark that is distinctive at the time of registration of the domain name, is identical or confusingly similar to that mark"; (2) "in the case of a famous mark that is famous at the time of registration of the domain name, is identical or confusingly similar to or dilutive of that mark."

To determine whether the registrant acted in bad faith, the ACPA lists the following nonexclusive factors:

(I)   the trademark or other intellectual property rights of the person, if any, in the domain name;

(II) the extent to which the domain name consists of the legal name of the person or a name that is otherwise commonly used to identify that person;

(III) the person's prior use, if any, of the domain name in connection with the bona fide offering of any goods or services;

(IV) the person's bona fide noncommercial or fair use of the mark in a site accessible under the domain name;

3. 15 U.S.C. §1125(d).

(V) the person's intent to divert customers from the mark owner's online location to a site accessible under the domain name that could harm the goodwill represented by the mark, either for commercial gain or with the intent to tarnish or disparage the mark, by creating a likelihood of confusion as to the source, sponsorship, affiliation, or endorsement of the site;

(VI) the person's offer to transfer, sell, or otherwise assign the domain name to the mark owner or any third party for financial gain without having used, or having an intent to use, the domain name in the bona fide offering of any goods or services, or the person's prior conduct indicating a pattern of such conduct;

(VII) the person's provision of material and misleading false contact information when applying for the registration of the domain name, the person's intentional failure to maintain accurate contact information, or the person's prior conduct indicating a pattern or such conduct;

(VIII) the person's registration or acquisition of multiple domain names which the person knows are identical or confusingly similar to marks of others that are distinctive at the time of registration of such domain names, or dilutive of famous marks of others that are famous at the time of registration of such domain names, without regard to the goods or services of the parties; and

(IX) the extent to which the mark incorporated in the person's domain name registration is or is not distinctive and famous . . .

A bad faith intent may not be found if the registrant "believed and had reasonable grounds to believe that the use of the domain name was a fair use or otherwise lawful."

With respect to the registering of the name of a person, Congress provided for injunctive relief as follows:

> Any person who registers a domain name that consists of the name of another living person, or a name substantially and confusingly similar thereto, without that person's consent, with the specific intent to profit from such name by selling the domain name for financial gain to that person or any third party, shall be liable in a civil action by such person.

15 U.S.C.A. §1129(1)(A).

Does the ACPA address the issues raised by the cases brought under traditional trademark law? What is the relationship between the ACPA and traditional trademark law? Does the ACPA differ from traditional trademark infringement or dilution law? Does a plaintiff have to prove a likelihood of consumer confusion or dilution? The advantage of the ACPA would be if it resolved or at least clarified what constitutes trademark use. Does it? Consider the following case.

ELECTRONICS BOUTIQUE HOLDINGS CORP. V. ZUCCARINI

56 U.S.P.Q.2d 1705 (E.D. Pa. 2000)

SCHILLER.

Presently before the court is plaintiff Electronics Boutique Holding Corporation's action for Internet cybersquatting against defendant John Zuccarini. . . . ["Mr. Zuccarini failed to obtain counsel and refused to appear himself for the October 10, 2000, hearing."]

. . . EB, a specialty retailer in video games and personal computer software, operates more than 600 retail stores, primarily in shopping malls, and also sells its products via the Internet. EB has registered several service marks on the principal register of the United States Patent and Trademark Office for goods and services of electric and computer products, including "EB" and "Electronics Boutique." . . .

EB's online store can be accessed via the Internet at "www.ebworld.com" and "www.electronicsboutique.com." EB registered its "EBWorld" domain name on December 19, 1996, and its "Electronics Boutique" domain name on December 30, 1997. EB has invested heavily in promoting its web site to online customers. EB has expended a considerable amount of resources towards making its web site consumer friendly. An easy-to-use web site is critical to EB's ability to generate revenue directly through Internet customers and indirectly as support for EB's "brick and mortar" stores. Over the last eight months, online purchases have yielded an average of more than 1.1 million in sales per month and EB has logged more than 2.6 million online visitors.

On May 23, 2000, Mr. Zuccarini registered the domain names "www.electronicboutique.com," and "www.electronicbotique.com." One week later, Mr. Zuccarini registered the domain names "www.ebwold.com" and "www.ebworl.com." When a potential or existing online customer, attempting to access EB's web site, mistakenly types one of Mr. Zuccarini's domain misspellings, he is "mousetrapped" in a barrage of advertising windows, featuring a variety of products, including credit cards, internet answering machines, games, and music. The Internet user cannot exit the Internet without clicking on the succession of advertisements that appears. Simply clicking on the "X" in the top right-hand corner of the screen, a common way to close a web browser window, will not allow a user to exit. Mr. Zuccarini is paid between 10 and 25 cents by the advertisers for every click. Sometimes, after wading through as many as 15 windows, the Internet user could gain access to EB's web site.

. . . Under the ACPA, a person who registers, traffics in, or uses a domain name that is identical or confusingly similar to a distinctive or famous mark registered to someone else with a bad-faith intent to profit from that mark is subject to suit. *See* 15 U.S.C. §1125(d)(1)(A). In order to determine whether EB is entitled to relief under the ACPA, this Court must evaluate the following: (1) whether EB's service marks are distinctive or famous; (2) whether

Mr. Zuccarini's domain misspellings are identical or confusingly similar to EB's marks; and (3) whether Mr. Zuccarini registered the domain misspellings with a bad-faith intent to profit from them. . . . In addition, I must determine whether Mr. Zuccarini is entitled to protection under the safe harbor provided by 15 U.S.C. §1125(d)(1)(B)(ii). See id. . . .

B. "IDENTICAL OR CONFUSINGLY SIMILAR"

[After concluding that EB's marks were sufficiently famous] I must consider whether the domain misspellings are identical or confusingly similar to EB's marks. I note at the outset that the profitability of Mr. Zuccarini's enterprise is completely dependent on his ability to create and register domain names that are confusingly similar to famous names. As the similarity in the spellings of Mr. Zuccarini's domain names to popular or famous names increases, the likelihood that an Internet user will inadvertently type one of Mr. Zuccarini's misspellings (and Mr. Zuccarini will be compensated) increases. Through an e-mail message it received, EB is aware of at least one customer who was in fact confused by the domain misspellings and who believes that EB is associated with the domain misspelling "www.electronic-botique.com." Thus, it is without hesitation that I find that the domain misspellings are confusingly similar to EB's marks.

C. BAD-FAITH INTENT TO PROFIT

Finally, I must consider whether Mr. Zuccarini acted with a bad-faith intent to profit from EB's marks, and if so, whether he is entitled to the protection of the safe harbor of §1125(d)(1)(B)(2). . . .

Mr. Zuccarini's bad-faith intent to profit from the domain misspellings is abundantly clear. Mr. Zuccarini registered the domain misspellings in order to generate advertising revenue for himself, despite being aware of the Electronics Boutique stores and Web site. Mr. Zuccarini believes that Internet users will misspell the domain names of the web sites they intend to access and instead access one of Mr. Zuccarini's web sites. Mr. Zuccarini then profits each time an Internet user makes a typing or spelling mistake which Mr. Zuccarini correctly forecasts.

In addition, the domain misspellings quite obviously do not consist of names used to identify Mr. Zuccarini, legally or otherwise. Also, Mr. Zuccarini has no bona fide business purpose for registering the domain misspellings, as he does not and has not offered any goods or services that relate to EB or electronic products. Lastly, Mr. Zuccarini has no intellectual property rights at issue in this matter. I find that Mr. Zuccarini specifically intended to prey on the confusion and typographical and/or spelling errors of Internet users to divert Internet users from EB's web site for his own commercial gain.

Section 1125(d)(1)(B)(ii) provides a safe harbor available to Mr. Zuccarini if he establishes that he reasonably believed that his use of the domain misspellings was fair and lawful. Mr. Zuccarini declined to claim the protections of the safe harbor by refusing to participate in this matter.[14] . . .

COMMENTS AND QUESTIONS

1. How would Electronics Boutique have fared without the ACPA? Would it have been able to establish trademark use or that Zuccarini caused the consumer confusion? Would a trademark dilution action have been available? Why/why not?

2. Aside from the different mediums involved, is *Zuccarini* distinguishable from *Holiday Inns, supra*? Could reliance upon *Holiday Inns* be considered a good faith defense?

3. One highly publicized domain name dispute involved a boy, nicknamed "Pokey," who registered "pokey.org" for his personal Web site, and the company that owned the trademarks "Gumby" and "Pokey." While the company eventually dropped its complaint, would it have prevailed under trademark infringement or dilution prior to the ACPA? Who would prevail under the ACPA?

4. Was cybersquatting being addressed by traditional trademark law? Why was the ACPA necessary? What else does it add? Is it an effort to establish clear property rights in order to facilitate bargaining? If so, why was the first-come, first-serve registration rule not a sufficiently clear rule?

5. The *Electronics Boutique* case involved what has come to be known as "typosquatting": that is, registering a common misspelling of someone else's mark as a domain name in the hopes of diverting customers who accidentally mistype the trademark holder's mark into the URL bar. Is typosquatting less of a problem now that search engines are much more sophisticated than they were in 1999? Is any legal rule necessary to deal with typosquatting, or does the technology now solve the problem in practice?

6. Does the ACPA deal effectively with situations that involve personal names registered in the domain space? Consider both 15 U.S.C. §1125(d) and §1129. Are there any situations involving personal names in the domain space that are not covered by one or both of these provisions? For a further discussion of this issue, see Jacqueline Lipton, *Celebrity in Cyberspace: A Personality Rights Paradigm for Personal Domain Name Disputes*, 65 Wash. & Lee L. Rev. 1445 (2008).

---

14. I note that even if Mr. Zuccarini had been present or had retained counsel to act on his behalf, the facts suggest that he would have been unable to demonstrate that he reasonably believed his use of the domain misspellings was lawful. Mr. Zuccarini registered the domain misspellings at issue in the instant matter after being preliminarily enjoined from using similar misspellings in another action. *See* Shields v. Zuccarini, 89 F. Supp. 2d 634, 642-43 (E.D. Pa. 2000). In addition, at the time that Mr. Zuccarini registered the domain misspellings, suit for similar conduct had been commenced against him in the Southern District of New York.

c) *Private Dispute Resolution*

At the same time that Congress enacted the ACPA, there was also pressure at the international level to address domain name dispute resolution, particularly with respect to concerns about bad faith cybersquatting. While the ACPA included some *in rem* jurisdictional provisions (discussed in Chapter 2) to assist plaintiffs in asserting jurisdiction against foreign defendants in a domain name dispute, there was a perceived need to create a more international and accessible online forum for domain name dispute resolution. In response to these concerns, the Internet Corporation for Assigned Names and Numbers (ICANN) adopted an alternative Uniform Dispute Resolution Policy (UDRP) to handle these disputes. ICANN is a private, nonprofit corporation assigned the responsibility for developing policies for managing the Internet's domain name system and the allocation of IP addresses. The UDRP has been extremely successful in practice and has become a popular method for resolving Internet domain name disputes, even some that do not apparently involve obvious trademark interests. Many more disputes are heard by private arbitrators under the UDRP than in American courts under the ACPA. This is probably because of the distinct time, cost, and jurisdictional advantages of the UDRP as compared with the ACPA. The UDRP is a fast, efficient, predominantly online procedure that does not require the retention of legal counsel by the parties. Matters are decided quickly by domain name experts, rather than judges who may or may not be well versed in trademark law and/or the domain name system.

As you study the UDRP, what factors are the arbitrators to consider in domain name disputes? Do these factors differ from traditional trademark law or the ACPA? We will make a more detailed comparison of the ACPA with the UDRP at the end of the material on UDRP disputes.

UNIFORM DOMAIN NAME DISPUTE RESOLUTION POLICY

(as approved by ICANN on October 24, 1999)

. . .

2. Your Representations. By applying to register a domain name, or by asking us to maintain or renew a domain name registration, you hereby represent and warrant to us that (a) the statements that you made in your Registration Agreement are complete and accurate; (b) to your knowledge, the registration of the domain name will not infringe upon or otherwise violate the rights of any third party; (c) you are not registering the domain name for an unlawful purpose; and (d) you will not knowingly use the domain name in violation of any applicable laws or regulations. It is your responsibility to determine whether your domain name registration infringes or violates someone else's rights.

3. Cancellations, Transfers, and Changes. We will cancel, transfer or otherwise make changes to domain name registrations under the following circumstances:

a. subject to the provisions of Paragraph 8, our receipt of written or appropriate electronic instructions from you or your authorized agent to take such action;

b. our receipt of an order from a court or arbitral tribunal, in each case of competent jurisdiction, requiring such action; and/or

c. our receipt of a decision of an Administrative Panel requiring such action in any administrative proceeding to which you were a party and which was conducted under this Policy or a later version of this Policy adopted by ICANN. (See Paragraph 4(i) and (k) below.)

We may also cancel, transfer or otherwise make changes to a domain name registration in accordance with the terms of your Registration Agreement or other legal requirements.

4. Mandatory Administrative Proceeding. This Paragraph sets forth the type of disputes for which you are required to submit to a mandatory administrative proceeding. . . .

a. Applicable Disputes. You are required to submit to a mandatory administrative proceeding in the event that a third party (a "complainant") asserts to the applicable Provider, in compliance with the Rules of Procedure, that

(i) your domain name is identical or confusingly similar to a trademark or service mark in which the complainant has rights; and

(ii) you have no rights or legitimate interests in respect of the domain name; and

(iii) your domain name has been registered and is being used in bad faith.

In the administrative proceeding, the complainant must prove that each of these three elements are present.

b. Evidence of Registration and Use in Bad Faith. For the purposes of Paragraph 4(a)(iii), the following circumstances, in particular but without limitation, if found by the Panel to be present, shall be evidence of the registration and use of a domain name in bad faith:

(i) circumstances indicating that you have registered or you have acquired the domain name primarily for the purpose of selling, renting, or otherwise transferring the domain name registration to the complainant who is the owner of the trademark or service mark or to a competitor of that complainant, for valuable consideration in excess of your documented out-of-pocket costs directly related to the domain name; or

(ii) you have registered the domain name in order to prevent the owner of the trademark or service mark from reflecting the mark in a corresponding domain name, provided that you have engaged in a pattern of such conduct; or

(iii) you have registered the domain name primarily for the purpose of disrupting the business of a competitor; or

(iv) by using the domain name, you have intentionally attempted to attract, for commercial gain, Internet users to your Web site or other on-line location, by creating a likelihood of confusion with the complainant's mark as to the source, sponsorship, affiliation, or endorsement of your Web site or location or of a product or service on your Web site or location.

c. How to Demonstrate Your Rights to and Legitimate Interests in the Domain Name in Responding to a Complaint. When you receive a complaint, you should refer to Paragraph 5 of the Rules of Procedure in determining how your response should be prepared. Any of the following circumstances, in particular but without limitation, if found by the Panel to be proved based on its evaluation of all evidence presented, shall demonstrate your rights or legitimate interests to the domain name for purposes of Paragraph 4(a)(ii):

(i) before any notice to you of the dispute, your use of, or demonstrable preparations to use, the domain name or a name corresponding to the domain name in connection with a bona fide offering of goods or services; or

(ii) you (as an individual, business, or other organization) have been commonly known by the domain name, even if you have acquired no trademark or service mark rights; or

(iii) you are making a legitimate noncommercial or fair use of the domain name, without intent for commercial gain to misleadingly divert consumers or to tarnish the trademark or service mark at issue. . . .

i. Remedies. The remedies available to a complainant pursuant to any proceeding before an Administrative Panel shall be limited to requiring the cancellation of your domain name or the transfer of your domain name registration to the complainant. . . .

k. Availability of Court Proceedings. The mandatory administrative proceeding requirements set forth in Paragraph 4 shall not prevent either you or the complainant from submitting the dispute to a court of competent jurisdiction for independent resolution before such mandatory administrative proceeding is commenced or after such proceeding is concluded. If an Administrative Panel decides that your domain name registration should be canceled or transferred, we will wait ten (10) business days (as observed in the location of our principal office) after we are informed by the applicable Provider of the Administrative Panel's decision before implementing that decision. We will then implement the decision unless we have received from you during that ten (10) business day period official documentation (such as a copy of a complaint, file-stamped by the clerk of the court) that you have commenced a lawsuit against the complainant in a jurisdiction to which the complainant has submitted. . . .

COMMENTS AND QUESTIONS

1. The UDRP and associated rules can be found at *www.icann.org/udrp/udrp.htm*.

2. Under what circumstances does the UDRP require the transfer of a domain name to a complaining trademark holder? What defenses does a domain name registrant have under the UDRP? Does the UDRP differ from the ACPA? Traditional trademark law?

3. Who has the burden of proving that the registrant has "no rights or legitimate interests" in the domain name?

4. What principles or precedents may the administrative panel rely upon in resolving disputes under the UDRP? Is judicial review of an administrative panel's decision available? *See* Parisi v. Netlearning, Inc., 139 F. Supp. 2d 745 (E.D. Va. 2001) (holding that the Federal Arbitration Act's restrictions upon judicial review of arbitration decisions do not apply to decisions under the UDRP).

5. While the UDRP has been heralded by some as an effective mechanism for resolving domain name disputes, others have questioned the ICANN's legitimacy in establishing these policies. *See* A. Michael Froomkin, *Wrong Turn in Cyberspace: Using ICANN to Route Around the APA and the Constitution*, 50 Duke L.J. 17 (2000) (arguing that the Department of Commerce's relationship with ICANN violates either the Administrative Procedures Act or the Constitution's Nondelegation doctrine); Jonathan Weinberg, *ICANN and the Problem of Legitimacy*, 50 Duke L.J. 187 (2000) (questioning ICANN's legitimacy as a public policymaking body in the absence of meaningful judicial review or representation). According to Michael Froomkin, by delegating important policy decisions to ICANN, a private entity, the Department of Commerce "(1) reduced public participation in decisionmaking over public issues, (2) vested key decisionmaking power in an essentially unaccountable private body that many feel has already abused its authority in at least small ways and is indisputably capable of abusing it in big ways, and (3) nearly (but . . . not quite) eliminated the possibilities for judicial review of critical decisions regarding the DNS." 50 Duke L.J. at 29. As you study the following materials, to what extent should a private entity be allowed to establish rules that govern the entire Internet community? Does it matter that ICANN's authority is established by contract during the domain name registration process? ICANN's significant role over domain name governance again came into prominence at the end of 2008 as it proposed the introduction of a system whereby registrars could petition for the addition of new gTLDs that would be approved by ICANN, after which the petitioning registrar would implement the relevant gTLD. This has raised a number of concerns about the appropriateness of a private body having such significant power over the use of words and phrases in the domain space. *See* ICANN, New gTLD Program Web page, *http://www.icann.org/en/topics/new-gtld-program.htm*.

6.   Concerns have also been raised that both ACPA and the UDRP overly focus the attention of the Internet community on protecting commercial trademark interests in cyberspace. It has been suggested that more work needs to be done to create an Internet domain name system that can cater to other important interests outside the trademark system. What other kinds of interests in Internet domain names might be protected by the global legal and regulatory system? *See* Jacqueline Lipton, *Beyond Cybersquatting: Taking Domain Name Disputes Past Trademark Policy*, 40 Wake Forest L. Rev. 1361 (2005); Margreth Barrett, *Domain Names, Trademarks, and the First Amendment: Searching for Meaningful Boundaries*, 39 Conn. L. Rev. 973 (2007); Jacqueline Lipton, *Commerce versus Commentary: Gripe Sites, Parody, and the First Amendment in Cyberspace*, 34 Wash. U. L. Rev. 1327 (2006).

7.   The arbitration involving the domain name brucespringsteen.com is a good example of the way in which a UDRP arbitration panel interprets the various elements of a UDRP complaint. It is particularly interesting in that it raises the contentious issue of the trademarkability of personal names for UDRP purposes. It also exemplifies a panel decision in which the arbitrators were not unanimous in the way they applied the elements of the UDRP to the complaint. As you read through the panel's determination, consider whether you think it evidences problematic gaps in the reach of the UDRP. If you do see such gaps, how do you think they should be addressed in the future? With respect to the protection of personal names in the domain space generally, see Jacqueline Lipton, *Celebrity in Cyberspace: A Personality Rights Paradigm for Personal Domain Name Disputes*, 65 Wash. & Lee L. Rev. 1445 (2008) (dealing with the protection of celebrities' names, politicians' names, and private individuals' names in the domain space); Jacqueline Lipton, *Who Owns "Hillary.com"? Political Speech and the First Amendment in Cyberspace*, 49 B.C. L. Rev. 55 (2008) (dealing with politicians' names in the domain space).

BRUCE SPRINGSTEEN v. JEFF BURGAR AND BRUCE SPRINGSTEEN CLUB

WIPO Arbitration and Mediation Center Case No. D2000-1532 (Jan. 2001)

The Complainant is the famous, almost legendary, recording artist and composer, Bruce Springsteen. Since the release of his first album in 1972 he has been at the top of his profession, selling millions of recordings throughout the world. As a result, his name is instantly recognisable in almost every part of the globe. There is no assertion made on behalf of Bruce Springsteen that his name has been registered as a trade mark but he rather relies upon common law rights acquired as a result of his fame and success.

The domain name at issue [BruceSpringsteen.com] was registered by Mr. Burgar apparently on 26 November 1996 . . .

Representatives of Bruce Springsteen have succinctly addressed the requirements under the UDRP and commented as follows.

In relation to the issue of "identical or substantially similar" marks, they have asserted the common law rights of Bruce Springsteen in his name and drawn analogy with previous cases, for example, the "Julia Roberts" case to support their contention.

In relation to the question of whether Mr. Burgar has any right or legitimate interest in the name, they indicate that no permission was given by Bruce Springsteen for the name to allow the domain name at issue to be used. They point out that Mr. Burgar has never been known as "Bruce Springsteen," and assert that the use of the name creates a misleading impression of association which is not based in fact.

In relation to the issue of bad faith, Mr. Springsteen's representatives point to the fact that Mr. Burgar is the owner of around 1,500 names, and that many of those names, including the domain name at issue, take the internet user to his own site, "celebrity1000.com." They therefore point to the fact that this constitutes bad faith under paragraphs 4(b)(ii) and (iv) of the UDRP.

They further assert that he has registered this domain name, and others, using a fictitious name. In this case the fictitious name is "Bruce Springsteen Club."

Bruce Springsteen's representatives rely heavily on authorities, and produce copies of a number of previous decisions and court cases which they believe to be relevant.

Mr. Burgar, on his own behalf, has produced a substantial response . . .

In relation to the question of identicality of name, Mr. Burgar says that Bruce Springsteen's representatives have given no evidence of any common law rights. He points to the fact that the name has already been registered in a domain name, namely "brucespringsteen.net" and, that his use does not besmirch or denigrate the name of Bruce Springsteen to any extent.

He refers to other Web sites which feature the name in question, including, for example, "artistplace.com/brucespringsteen."

He also claims in relation to this heading that there has been and can be no confusion.

In relation to the question of rights or legitimate interests, he counters the statement of Mr. Springsteen's representatives by saying that there was no suggestion that permission is needed from Bruce Springsteen or anyone in relation to the registration of a domain name. He uses, for the first time, an analogy with magazines, indicating that the mere use of the name of a celebrity on the front page of a magazine does not mean that the magazine is claiming any kind of specific rights in relation to the name, but merely that it features an article about the individual in question. He asserts that the internet is of a similar nature.

He refers to the habits of internet users, and the relative unlikelihood that they would be typing in the full domain name, namely "brucespringsteen.com," and that if they did so they would be sufficiently sophisticated users to understand that the disclaimer contained on his site indicates that it is not an "official" Bruce Springsteen site.

He avers that he does not operate this domain name for profit or gain, and indeed has made none, and that he is not misleadingly directing people to his site.

In relation to the question of bad faith, he says that there has been no evidence submitted that he intended to stop Bruce Springsteen from registering the domain name "brucespringsteen.com" himself. He points to the fact that the domain name "brucespringsteen.net" has been registered by Mr. Springsteen's record company for some years and that, presumably, that should have sufficed.

In relation to the question of fictitious names, he denies that he owns 1,500 celebrity names, and that any of them have been registered in a fictitious name pointing out that he personally is identified as the administrative contact in relation to all the domain names which he has registered.

In relation to paragraph 4(b)(iv) of the UDRP, he denies that he has "intentionally attempted to attract, for commercial gain, internet users to his web site or other on-line location, by creating a likelihood of confusion with the Complainant's mark as to the source, sponsorship, affiliation or endorsement of his web site." He points to the nature of the internet and the volume of sites available, to indicate that it is most unlikely that confusion could have occurred in the minds of an internet user. He asserts that confusion is a necessary factor in paragraph 4(b)(iv).

He repeats his analogy regarding magazines, and refers to the fact that he has over 200 "mini sites" accessible from his principal site, "www. celebrity1000.com."

He points out that he now has a working, functioning web site at the domain name in issue in these proceedings.

Under paragraph 4 of the UDRP, the Complainant's burden is to prove in relation to the complaint, that:

    i. The domain name at issue is identical or confusingly similar to a trade mark or service mark in which the Complainant has rights;

    ii. The Respondent has no rights or legitimate interests in respect of the domain name; and

    iii. The domain name has been registered as being used in bad faith.

The Complainant must prove that each of these three elements are present in order to make out a successful case.

The first question to be considered is whether the domain name at issue is identical or confusingly similar to trade marks or service marks in which the Complainant has rights.

It is common ground that there is no registered trade mark in the name "Bruce Springsteen." In most jurisdictions where trade marks are filed it would be impossible to obtain a registration of a name of that nature. Accordingly, Mr. Springsteen must rely on common law rights to satisfy this element of the three part test.

It appears to be an established principle from cases such as Jeanette Winterson, Julia Roberts, and Sade that in the case of very well known celebrities, their names can acquire a distinctive secondary meaning giving rise to rights equating to unregistered trade marks, notwithstanding the non-registerability of the name itself. It should be noted that no evidence has been given of the name "Bruce Springsteen" having acquired a secondary meaning; in other words a recognition that the name should be associated with activities beyond the primary activities of Mr. Springsteen as a composer, performer and recorder of popular music.

In the view of this Panel, it is by no means clear from the UDRP that it was intended to protect proper names of this nature. As it is possible to decide the case on other grounds, however, the Panel will proceed on the assumption that the name Bruce Springsteen is protected under the policy; it then follows that the domain name at issue is identical to that name. . . .

The second limb of the test requires the Complainant to show that the domain name owner has no rights or legitimate interests in respect of the domain name. The way in which the UDRP is written clearly requires the Complainant to demonstrate this, and the mere assertion that the Respondent has no such rights does not constitute proof, although the panel is free to make reasonable inferences. That said, a Respondent would be well advised to proffer some evidence to the contrary in the face of such an allegation. Paragraph 4(c) of the UDRP sets out specific circumstances to assist the Respondent in demonstrating that he or she has legitimate rights or legitimate interests in the domain name. The circumstances are stated to be nonexclusive, but are helpful in considering this issue.

Dealing with each in turn as follows:

(i) The first circumstance is that, before any notice of the dispute to the Respondent, the Respondent had shown demonstrable preparations to use the domain name in connection with a bona fide offering of goods or services. In this case, there is no suggestion that the domain name <brucespringsteen.com> had in fact been used in this way prior to notification of the complaint. Instead, the domain name resolved to another web site belonging to Mr. Burgar, namely "celebrity1000.com."

(ii) The second circumstance is that the Respondent has "been commonly known by the domain name, even if he has acquired no trade mark or service mark rights". This is much more problematic. Mr. Burgar would say that the domain name at issue was registered in the name of "Bruce Springsteen Club" and consequently that the proprietor of the domain name has "been commonly known by the domain name" as required in the UDRP. The question in this case involves the meaning of the words "commonly" and "known by."

(iii) It is hard to say that the mere use of the name "Bruce Springsteen Club" can give rise to an impression in the minds of internet users that the proprietor was effectively "known as" Bruce Springsteen. It is even more remote that it could be said that the proprietor was "commonly" recognised in that fashion. Accordingly the Panel finds that this circumstance in paragraph 4(c) is not met.

The third circumstance is that the Respondent is "making a legitimate non-commercial or fair use of the domain name, without intent for commercial gain to misleadingly divert customers or to tarnish the trade mark or service mark at issue."

There are a number of concepts contained within this "circumstance" which make it a complex issue to resolve. For example, at what point does use of a domain name become "commercial" or alternatively what amounts to "fair use" since those concepts appear to be in the alternative.

An internet search using the words "Bruce Springsteen" gives rise to literally thousands of hits. It is perfectly apparent to any internet user that not all of those hits are "official" or "authorised" sites. The user will browse from one search result to another to find the information and material which he or she is looking for in relation to a search item, in this case the celebrity singer Bruce Springsteen. It is therefore hard to see how it can be said that the registration of the domain name at issue can be "misleading" in its diversion of consumers to the "celebrity1000.com" web site.

There have been examples in other cases of blatant attempts, for example, by the use of minor spelling discrepancies to entrap internet users onto sites which have absolutely no connection whatsoever with the name which is being used in its original or slightly altered form. In this case, the internet user, coming upon the "celebrity1000.com" web site would perhaps be unsurprised to have arrived there via a search under the name "Bruce Springsteen." If the internet user wished to stay longer at the site he or she could do so, or otherwise they could clearly return to their search results to find more instructed material concerning Bruce Springsteen himself.

Accordingly, it is hard to infer from the conduct of the Respondent in this case an intent, for commercial gain, to misleadingly divert consumers. There is certainly no question of the common law rights of Mr. Springsteen being "tarnished" by association with the "celebrity1000.com" web site. The Panelists' own search of that site indicates no links which would have that effect, for example connections to sites containing pornographic or other regrettable material.

Accordingly the Panel finds that Bruce Springsteen has not satisfied the second limb of the three part test in the UDRP.

Moving on to the question of bad faith, once again the UDRP contains helpful guidance as to how the Complainant may seek to demonstrate bad faith on the part of the Registrant. The four, non-exclusive, circumstances are set out in paragraph 4(b) of the UDRP, and can be dealt with as follows:

(i) The first circumstance is that there is evidence that the Registrant obtained the domain name primarily for the purpose of selling, renting or otherwise transferring it to the Complainant or to a competitor. This can be dealt with swiftly. There is simply no evidence put forward by the Complainant that there has been any attempt by Mr. Burgar to sell the domain name, either directly or indirectly.

(ii) The second circumstance is that the Registrant obtained the domain name in order to prevent the owner of the trade mark or service mark from reflecting that mark in a corresponding domain name, provided that there has been a pattern of such conduct. In this case, Bruce Springsteen's representatives point to the many other celebrity domain names registered by Mr. Burgar as evidence that he has indulged in a pattern of this conduct.

However, Mr. Burgar is clearly experienced in the ways of the internet. When he registered the domain name at issue in 1996, he would have been well aware that if he had wanted to block the activities of Bruce Springsteen or his record company in order to extract a large payment, or for whatever other reason there may be in creating such a blockage, he could, at nominal cost, have also registered the domain names <brucespringsteen.net> and <brucespringsteen.org>. He did not do so, and indeed subsequently in 1998 Mr. Springsteen's record company registered the name <brucespringsteen.net> which has been used as the host site for the official Bruce Springsteen web site since that time. It appears in the top five items in a search on the internet under the name "Bruce Springsteen."

It is trite to say that, by registering the domain name at issue, the Registrant has clearly prevented Bruce Springsteen from owning that name himself. However, that does not have the effect required in paragraph 4(b)(ii) of the UDRP. That paragraph indicates that the registration should have the effect of preventing the owner of a trade mark or service mark from reflecting the mark "in a corresponding domain name." In these circumstances what is meant by the word "corresponding"? Nothing that has been done by Mr. Burgar has prevented Bruce Springsteen's official web site at <brucespringsteen.net> being registered and used in his direct interests. That is surely a "corresponding domain name" for these purposes, as the expression "corresponding domain name" clearly refers back to the words "trade mark or service mark" rather than the domain name at issue referred to in the first line of paragraph 4(b)(ii).

It is perhaps pertinent to observe that the so-called "official" site at <brucespringsteen.net> was registered in 1998. It seems unlikely that, at that time, the existence of the domain name at issue did not become apparent. Whilst this is pure surmise, and consequently in no way relevant to the findings of the Panel, it might be thought that the alleged "blocking" effect of the domain name at issue might have given rise to a complaint at that time, if only in correspondence.

This Panel believes that previous Panels have all too readily concluded that the mere registration of the mark, and indeed other marks of a similar nature, is evidence of an attempt to prevent the legitimate owner of registered or common law trade mark rights from obtaining a "corresponding domain name." This is an issue which should be looked at more closely, and for the purposes of this complaint, the Panel finds that the "circumstance" in paragraph 4(b)(ii) does not arise for the purpose of demonstrating bad faith on the part of the Registrant.

(i) The third circumstance is that the Registrant has obtained the domain name "primarily for the purpose of disrupting the business of a competitor." This can be dealt with very swiftly as there is no suggestion that that is the case in the present complaint.

(ii) The fourth circumstance is that, by using the domain name, the Registrant has "intentionally attempted to attract, for commercial gain, internet users to his web site or other on-line location, by creating a likelihood of confusion with the Complainant's mark as to the source, sponsorship, affiliation or endorsement of the web site or location or of a product or a service on the Web site or location."

Once again, this sub-paragraph contains a number of concepts which render it complex to analyse and apply. However, the key issue appears to be the requirement that the use of the domain name must "create a likelihood of confusion with the Complainant's mark." As indicated above, a simple search under the name "Bruce Springsteen" on the internet gives rise to many thousands of hits. As also indicated above, even a relatively unsophisticated user would be clearly aware that not all of those hits would be directly associated in an official and authorized capacity with Bruce Springsteen himself, or his agents or record company. The nature of an internet search does not reveal the exact notation of the domain name. Accordingly, the search result may read "Bruce Springsteen — discography," but will not give the user the exact address. That only arises on a screen once the user has gone to that address. The relevance of this is that it is relatively unlikely that any user would seek to go straight to the internet and open the site <brucespringsteen.com> in the optimistic hope of reaching the official Bruce Springsteen web site. If anyone sufficiently sophisticated in the use of the internet were to do that, they would very soon realise that the site they reached was not the official site, and consequently would move on, probably to conduct a fuller search.

Accordingly, it is hard to see that there is any likelihood of confusion can arise in these circumstances. . . .

Before moving on to the final decision, it is perhaps appropriate in a case of this complexity and profile that the Panel should briefly consider the authorities which have been referred to, in particular by the Complainant. . . .

The case of Daniel C. Marino Jnr. -v- Video Images Productions (WIPO case number D2000-0598) contains a passage highlighted when annexed to the complaint in this case in the following terms:

> "in fact, in light of the uniqueness of the name <danmarino.com>, which is virtually identical to the Complainant's personal name and common law trade mark, it would

be extremely difficult to foresee any justifiable use that the Respondent could claim. On the contrary, selecting this name gives rise to the impression of an association with the Complainant which is not based in fact."

This Panel contends that that assertion is erroneous. For all the reasons set out above, the users of the internet do not expect all sites bearing the name of celebrities or famous historical figures or politicians to be authorised or in some way connected with the figure themselves. The internet is an instrument for purveying information, comment, and opinion on a wide range of issues and topics. It is a valuable source of information in many fields, and any attempt to curtail its use should be strongly discouraged. Users fully expect domain names incorporating the names of well known figures in any walk of life to exist independently of any connection with the figure themselves, but having been placed there by admirers or critics as the case may be.

Accordingly, in all the circumstances the Panel does not believe that Bruce Springsteen has met the necessary criteria to sustain a complaint under the UDRP. . . .

DISSENT

Paragraph 4(a)(i) of the UDRP requires a Complainant to show the existence of "a trade mark or service mark in which Complainant has rights." The majority has presumed (and should have concluded) that the personal name "Bruce Springsteen" has acquired distinctive secondary meaning giving rise to common law trademark rights in the "famous, almost legendary, recording artist and composer, Bruce Springsteen." . . .

Regardless of commentary that personal names (presumably without secondary meaning) are not protected, the language of paragraph 4(a)(i) does not exclude any specific type of common law trademarks from protection. The majority further concludes that the disputed domain name is identical with the common law mark. Therefore, Complainant has met the requirements of paragraph 4(a)(i).

Paragraph 4(a)(ii) requires a Complainant to show Respondent has no rights or legitimate interest in the disputed domain name. Although the way in which the UDRP is written requires the Complainant to demonstrate this, the logic of this burden of proof is questionable in that it requires the Complainant to prove the nonexistence of certain facts. In effect the assertion by Complainant that Respondent has no rights in the mark, through permission or consent of the Complainant or otherwise is sufficient to shift the burden to Respondent.

Paragraphs 4(c)(i)-(iii) describe the nonexclusive circumstances which may be used to prove that Respondent has rights or legitimate interest in the disputed domain name. The majority bases its decision on a finding that Complainant has failed to disprove 4(c)(iii). This circumstance allows Respondent rights or legitimate interest upon a showing of noncommercial or fair use without misleading diversion of customers. Specifically, the majority finds that Respondent has not misleadingly diverted customers to Respondent's Web site www.celebrity1000.com. The majority assumes that the internet user will search literally thousands of hits on "Bruce Springsteen" without going directly to <brucespringsteen.com> and without concluding that "brucespringsteen.com" resolves to a web site sanctioned by Complainant. Apparently the Presiding Panelist conducted his independent search in this manner and concludes that a hypothetical internet user would search in the same manner. This is an insufficient basis to conclude that resolution of the domain name <brucespringsteen.com> into Respondent's web site www.celebrity1000.com is not misleading.

The Dissenting Panelist concludes that the average internet user would not sift through thousands of hits searching for information on Bruce Springsteen. Instead, the internet user would devise shortcuts. One obvious shortcut is to go directly to <brucespringsteen.com> with the expectation that it would lead to the official web site. Respondent alludes to the phenomenon that "postponing the creation of other Tld's until the '.com' name space dominated the world just sort of happened." The dominance of the ".com" name space is reflected in the common usage of the phrase ".com" as being synonymous with commercial activity on the Internet. Given a vast array of information on the performer Bruce Springsteen, the internet user is more likely than not to associate <brucespringsteen.com> with commercial activity and with an official domain name, resolving to an official web site. Therefore, the Dissenting Panelist concludes that resolution of the domain name <brucespringsteen.com> into Respondent's web site www.celebrity1000. com is misleading. . . .

The Dissenting Panelist would rule that Complainant has met his burden and that the disputed domain name should be transferred.

COMMENTS AND QUESTIONS

1. Under what circumstances must a registrant submit to an administrative proceeding under the UDRP? Do UDRP proceedings differ from either traditional trademark cases or ACPA proceedings? What defenses may a registrant raise?

2. Why do the panelists consider the question whether the name "Bruce Springsteen" has acquired a secondary meaning? What does this mean in the context of trademark law? Why is it important in a UDRP dispute involving a personal name?

3. The dissenting panelist places some weight on the significance of the ".com" gTLD as supporting an inference that ".com" names should be reserved to "rightful" domain name holders. This issue has been raised in other domain name arbitrations. *See, e.g.,* Bridgestone Firestone v. Myers (UDRP decision, available at *http://www.wipo.int/amc/en/domains/decisions/html/2000/d2000-0190.html*). In this decision, the arbitrator excused as a legitimate

use the registration of a ".net" version of a company name for the purposes of a gripesite about the company. The arbitrator noted several times the significance of the fact that the registrant had not utilized a ".com" version of the company name for the gripesite, suggesting that the ".com" version of a domain name incorporating a trademark has a specific significance in the minds of Internet users and should perhaps be reserved to a rightful trademark owner, while at the same time, other gTLDs should not necessarily be able to be monopolized by a trademark holder. This issue is discussed further in Jacqueline Lipton, *Commerce vs Commentary: Gripe Sites, Parody and the First Amendment in Cyberspace*, 84 Wash. U. L. Rev. 1327, 1359-64 (2006). Do you think there is an argument for protecting ".com" domains in the hands of trademark holders as a special case? Why/why not? If so, should this be reflected in the ACPA and/or the UDRP?

4. What evidence should be considered in determining whether a registrant has "intentionally attempted to attract, for commercial gain, Internet users to your Web site or other on-line location, by creating a likelihood of confusion with the complainant's mark as to the source, sponsorship, affiliation, or endorsement of your Web site or location or of a product or service on your Web site or location"? *See* UDRP ¶4(b)(iv). Would setting up a "clickfarm" using someone else's trademark in the domain name be an example of such conduct? *See, e.g.*, discussion in Jacqueline Lipton, *Clickfarming: The New Cybersquatting?*, J. Internet L. (2008).

5. Who has the burden of proof that the registration was made in bad faith? According to the dissent in *Springsteen*, what was the majority's error with respect to the burden of proof?

6. Compare *Springsteen* with Madonna v. Dan Parisi and Madonna. com, WIPO Arbitration and Mediation Center Case No. D2000-0847 (Oct. 2000), in which a panel concluded that the registrant of Madonna.com registered a mark identical to the registered trademark of the famous performer and that the registrant did not have any legitimate interest in the domain name despite the fact that it refers to the Virgin Mary and is a personal name. In particular, the court rejected the registrant's argument that his use of the domain name was in good faith because of the existence of a disclaimer denying any affiliation or authorization from the performer. According to the panel:

> Respondent's use of a disclaimer on its Web site is insufficient to avoid a finding of bad faith. First, the disclaimer may be ignored or misunderstood by Internet users. Second, a disclaimer does nothing to dispel initial interest confusion that is inevitable from Respondent's actions. Such confusion is a basis for finding a violation of Complainant's rights.

Is it possible to reconcile *Madonna* and *Springsteen*? Why does the panel conclude that there is no likelihood of confusion in *Springsteen*? Does the majority of the panel accept the concept of initial interest confusion?

7. Consider also the case of Julia Fiona Roberts v. Russell Boyd, WIPO Arbitration and Mediation Center Case No. D2000-0210 (May 2000).

The respondent had registered the domain name "juliaroberts.com" and was attempting to sell it for a profit on the eBay online auction Web site. The movie actress, Julia Roberts, successfully arbitrated for a transfer of the name, although she herself did not intend to use it. She apparently wanted to avoid unauthorized use of the name. The panel found that the domain name in question was identical to the complainant's common law trademark rights in her name, and that the respondent had registered the name in bad faith. In particular, the panel noted that the UDRP does not require a complainant to establish registered trademark rights corresponding to a domain name. Common law rights supporting a passing off action will suffice. This is particularly important with respect to personal names which cannot be registered as trademarks under national trademark laws in a number of jurisdictions. Note that the majority panelists in the *Springsteen* arbitration were not convinced that Bruce Springsteen could establish even common law trademark rights in his personal name, but were prepared to proceed as if he could establish such rights. Part of the problem here is that, unlike the ACPA, the UDRP is not geared to protect personal names, even famous personal names. It focuses largely on commercial trademark rights. Given the popularity of the ".com" gTLD, as opposed to the newer ".name" gTLD, is it necessary for a new approach to disputes involving personal names to be developed? If so, what should such an approach look like? Should there be revisions to the UDRP to incorporate protections for personal names, or something else? *See, e.g.,* Jacqueline Lipton, *Celebrity in Cyberspace: A Personality Rights Paradigm for Personal Domain Name Disputes,* 65 Wash. & Lee L. Rev. 1445 (2008) (dealing with the protection of celebrities' names, politician's names, and private individuals names in the domain space).

8. As discussed earlier, in dealing with domain name cases under traditional trademark law analysis, courts differ over initial interest confusion. Does the UDRP suggest whether initial interest confusion violates registration policies?

9. To what extent can the threat of actions brought under the ACPA and the UDRP be used as a means of pressuring legitimate domain name holders into giving up those domain names otherwise known as "reverse hijacking"? According to the Rules for Uniform Domain Name Dispute Resolution Policy, reverse hijacking "means using the Policy in bad faith to attempt to deprive a registered domain-name holder of a domain name." UDRP Rule 1. However, aside from authorizing the panel to declare that an action was brought in bad faith, the UDRP does not provide for any other remedies. *See* UDRP Rule 15(e).

Consider Goldline Int'l Inc. v. Goldline, WIPO Case No. D2000-1151 (Jan. 2001):

Respondent has asked the Panel to make a finding of attempted reverse domain name hijacking. Rule 1 defines reverse domain name hijacking as "using the Policy in bad faith to attempt to deprive a registered domain-name holder of a domain name." See also Rule

15(e). To prevail on such a claim, Respondent must show that Complainant knew of Respondent's unassailable right or legitimate interest in the disputed domain name or the clear lack of bad faith registration and use, and nevertheless brought the Complaint in bad faith. See, e.g., Sydney Opera House Trust v. Trilynx Pty. Ltd., Case No. D2000-1224 (WIPO, Oct. 31, 2000).

Instructive is the Panel's decision in *Smart Design LLC v. Hughes*, Case No. D2000-0993 (WIPO October 18, 2000), in which the Panel found attempted reverse domain name hijacking in a similar, though not identical, situation, in which the domain name reflected a mark that was likely to have multiple legitimate uses. Taking account of the complainant's delay in bringing its claim and apparent initial acknowledgement that the respondent was the bona fide owner of the domain name, the Panel ruled that it was unreasonable for the complainant to have brought the complaint given the objective unlikelihood of success. In other words, bad faith was found to encompass both malicious intent and recklessness or knowing disregard of the likelihood that the respondent possessed legitimate interests. *Cf. Loblaws, Inc. v. Presidentchoice.inc/Presidentchoice.com*, Case Nos. AF-0170a to -0170c (eResolution, June 7, 2000) (suggesting that, "in a case where the trademark, although a well-known supermarket brand, is a common English phrase used as a mark by other businesses, the failure to conduct a cursory investigation seems especially unreasonable," though declining to find bad faith because the Policy was so new).

Under these standards, Complainant's actions in this case constitute bad faith. Prior to filing its Complaint, Complainant had to know that Complainant's mark was limited to a narrow field, and that Respondent's registration and use of the domain name could not, under any fair interpretation of the facts, constitute bad faith. Not only would a reasonable investigation have revealed these weaknesses in any potential ICANN complaint, but also, Respondent put Complainant on express notice of these facts and that any further attempt to prosecute this matter would be abusive and would constitute reverse domain name "hijack[ing]." . . . Complainant's decision to file its Complaint in the face of those facts was in bad faith. Accordingly, the Panel finds that Complainant has engaged in Reverse Domain Name Hijacking.

What constitutes a "bad faith attempt" to take a domain name or an "unassailable" right to the domain name? What can be done to deter reverse domain name hijacking? Can the threat of actions brought under the ACPA and the UDRP be used to halt cybersquatting, trademark infringement, and dilution? What are the respective benefits of the ACPA and UDRP?

Note: Which to Use: The ACPA or the UDRP?

In deciding whether to proceed under the ACPA or the UDRP, a trademark owner has to carefully weigh a number of important considerations. One of the most daunting problems facing trademark owners is obtaining personal jurisdiction over foreign residents or over cybersquatters who provide false registration contact information (including name and address). In rem provisions in the ACPA were added to address this issue. Section 43(d) of the ACPA allows limited in rem proceedings where personal jurisdiction would otherwise not be found. See discussion in Chapter 2.

Another benefit of the ACPA is the statutory damages provision, Section 43(d)(1), which permits the trademark owner to collect statutory damages in lieu of actual damages. Any statutory damages incurred must be in an amount of not less than $1,000 and not more than $100,000 per domain name, as the court considers just.

On the other hand, many believe the UDRP is advantageous when the domain name is not in use and a trademark owner desires a quick, cost effective means to have the domain name transferred back to the trademark owner. Further, in a majority of proceedings to date, Administrative Panels have found in favor of the trademark owners in proceedings commenced under the UDRP.

The ACPA is also much more helpful than the UDRP with respect to the protection of personal names, particularly in situations where such names do not necessarily correspond with a registered or common law trademark, despite being well known names. The ACPA contains specific protections for personal names — 15 U.S.C. §1129(1)(A) — while the UDRP only protects names that correspond to trademarks as noted in the *Bruce Springsteen* and *Julia Roberts* arbitrations.

This can be particularly problematic in arbitrations relating to lesser known celebrities whose personal names have not achieved common law trademark status. It can also be problematic with respect to other well known names that do not function as trademarks. An obvious example here is politicians' names. In a WIPO Arbitration concerning the politician, Kathleen Kennedy Townsend, who was running in an election for Governor for the State of Maryland in 2002, a WIPO panel found that Townsend had no rights under the UDRP to have a domain name transferred to her that corresponded to her personal name: Kathleen Kennedy Townsend v. Birt, Administrative Panel Decision No. D2002-0030, WIPO Arbitration and Mediation Center (2002). The panel noted that it was possible that a political organization, as distinct from a politician herself, might have sufficient trademark rights in some politicians' names or political slogans to support a successful action against the registrant of a domain name corresponding to that name or person. It was also suggested that the politician herself might proceed under §1129(1)(A) of the Lanham Act. In these kinds of situations, the ACPA may therefore hold some advantages over the UDRP.

Political Cyberfraud

With respect to political names and slogans in particular, some states have enacted specific "political cyberfraud" legislation to prevent wrongful registrations of domain names corresponding to political names and slogans, as well as other wrongful activities relating to political Web sites. California's Political Cyberfraud Abatement Act, for example, creates civil liability for engaging in an act of "political cyberfraud": see California Elections Code, §§18320-18323. "Political cyberfraud" is defined in the legislation to mean:

> "[A] knowing or willful [sic] act concerning a political Web site that is committed with the intent to deny a person access to a political Web site, deny a person the opportunity to

> register a domain name for a political Web site, or cause a person reasonably to believe that a political Web site has been posted by a person other than the person who posted the Web site, and would cause a reasonable person, after reading the Web site, to believe the site actually represents the views of the proponent or opponent of a ballot measure."

The definition provides some examples of political cyberfraud including: (a) intentionally diverting or redirecting access to a political Web site by using, *inter alia*, a similar domain name — §18320(a)(1)(A); (b) registering a domain name that is similar to another domain name for a political website — §18320(a)(1)(B); and (c) intentionally preventing the use of a domain name for a political Web site by registering and holding the domain name or by reselling it to another with the intent of preventing its use — §18320(a)(1)(D). "Political Web site" is defined for the purposes of this legislation as: "a Web site that urges or appears to urge the support or opposition of a ballot measure" — §18320(a)(3).

Cases of political cyberfraud will tend to fall through the gaps of both the ACPA and the UDRP because they often do not involve registered or common law trademark rights. This suggests that, even though the protection of trademark interests is extremely important as a matter of policy in the domain name context, there are also other important interests that need to be protected with respect to the domain name system.

COMMENTS AND QUESTIONS

1. What are the policy justifications underlying the enactment of legislation such as California's Political Cyberfraud Abatement Act? Do you think the legislation as currently drafted is likely to achieve its policy aims in practice? Should such legislation be more widely adopted on the federal and, ultimately, the international level? For a more detailed discussion of the problems inherent in the current system with respect to politicians' names in particular, see Jacqueline Lipton, *Who Owns "Hillary.com"? Political Speech and the First Amendment in Cyberspace*, 49 B.C. L. Rev. 55 (2008).

2. Has the focus on protecting commercial trademark interests in cyberspace distracted attention from other equally serious problems relating to domain name registrations and transfers? What are some of these problems? Does the domain name system require some modification to take some of these other interests into account? If so, should any changes to the domain name system be achieved through international governmental cooperation? Federal and/or state legislation? Private arrangements through bodies such as ICANN?

3. How effective are the ACPA and the UDRP in resolving situations where two or more parties have legitimate competing trademark interests in the same domain name? For example, could the ACPA or the UDRP have been

useful in resolving conflicts between Delta Airlines, Delta Financial, and Delta-Comm Internet Services, each of which had a legitimate trademark interest in aspects of the word "Delta" and, therefore, arguably in the "delta.com" domain name? This domain name was originally registered to DeltaComm, who then sold it to Delta Financial when it could not reach a satisfactory transfer agreement with Delta Airlines. Ultimately, Delta Airlines obtained the name from Delta Financial. For a more detailed discussion of problems involving competitions between multiple legitimate trademark holders for the same or a similar domain name, see Jacqueline Lipton, *A Winning Solution for YouTube and Utube? Corresponding Trademarks and Domain Name Sharing*, 21 Harv. J.L. & Tech. 509 (2008).

4. In 2009, former President Bill Clinton brought UDRP proceedings against a company called Web of Deception (represented by Mr. Joseph Culligan) with respect to the registration of the following domain names: *williamclinton.com*, *williamjclinton.com*, and *presidentbillclinton.com*. Mr. Culligan had directed the domain names to the GOP's official Web site. He had not sought to sell the domain names to President Clinton or to anyone else, and he had not made any money from his registration or use of the names. A UDRP panel denied relief to President Clinton on the basis that, although Clinton had established common law trademark rights in his name, he was unable to establish that Mr Culligan had used the domain names in bad faith as contemplated in the UDRP. Do you agree with this decision? (*See http://domains.adrforum.com/domains/decisions/1256123.htm.*) Would President Clinton have fared any better under any of the other laws discussed above, including the California Elections Code, §§18320-18323. Why/why not?

5. Professor Jacqueline Lipton has suggested a new way of categorizing domain name disputes in order to identify gaps in the existing regulatory structure, as well as to make suggestions for how these gaps should be addressed.

> Domain name disputes that have arisen in recent years might be classified as follows.
>
> (1) "Classic" Cybersquatting: This category of disputes covers situations in which a person has registered one or more domain names that correspond to well-known trademarks with a view to commercial profit by offering to transfer the domain name(s) to a party interested in the trademark for valuable consideration. This has been considered a bad-faith practice and has been relatively successfully regulated by the ACPA and the UDRP since 1999. . . .
>
> (2) "Noncommercial" Cybersquatting: This category refers to situations in which a person has registered usually only one domain name, but possibly more, for a predominantly noncommercial purpose. An obvious example might be where a person has registered a domain name corresponding to another person's trademark in order to use the domain name in a Web site that comments on the activities of the trademark holder. Recent examples in the United States have involved registrations of a domain name corresponding to the Planned Parenthood trademark, the People for the Ethical Treatment of Animals ("PETA") trademark, and the Bosley Medical Institute trademark. Such conduct is perhaps not truly cybersquatting in the "classic" sense of the term, because the

registrant is actually using the name herself for a particular purpose — commentary, parody, etc. — rather than for purposes of extorting money from a person with an interest in a corresponding trademark. This may, or may not, justify separate treatment in the dispute resolution arena than "classic" cybersquatting cases, depending on the circumstances.

"Noncommercial" in this context is not a term of art. A person who registers a domain name with a purpose of making commentary on a particular issue may have a secondary purpose of commercial profit. . . . This category of disputes might more appropriately be referred to as "First Amendment Cybersquatting." . . .

(3) Contest between Multiple Legitimate Interests: This category covers situations in which two or more people have what might be called a "legitimate" interest in the same domain name, which would occur, for example, when two or more companies have a similar trademark that corresponds with a particular domain name. Thus, it encompasses those situations where multiple legitimate interest holders are competing for the same domain name.

(4) Disputes Involving Personal Names: This category of disputes may be further subcategorized into: (i) disputes involving celebrity names (for example, actors, musicians, sports stars, etc.); (ii) disputes involving politician names; and (iii) disputes involving names of private individuals.

(5) Culturally Significant Names, Geographical Locators, etc.: This is a somewhat miscellaneous category of disputes for which there may be little data in records of existing arbitrations and litigation, at least in comparison to the other classes of disputes identified above. This category of disputes contemplates some of the issues recently addressed by Professor Chander in terms of the failure of the current system to take into account cultural and often noncommercial interests in domain names such as geographical place names or culturally significant words and phrases. . . . Jacqueline Lipton, *Beyond Cybersquatting: Taking Domain Name Disputes Past Trademark Practice*, 40 Wake Forest L. Rev. 1361 (2005).

Do you agree with this categorization of domain name disputes? Are there other categories you would add? Which categories of dispute will be covered by the existing regulatory structures? Should more regulatory action be taken to deal with any of these categories?

2. Domain Names as Speech

Closely related to the question of whether a domain name is being used as a trademark is the relationship between trademark law and freedom of speech. As one court has noted, it is not a violation of trademark law to use a trademark in a descriptive sense even for commercial purposes because, "sometimes there is no descriptive substitute. . . . For example, one might refer to 'the two-time world champions' or 'the professional basketball team from Chicago,' but it's far simpler (and more likely to be understood) to refer to the Chicago Bulls." New Kids on the Block v. News America Publishing, Inc., 971 F.2d 302, 306 (9th Cir. 1992). Before examining domain names, this issue is explored with respect to the visible text of a Web page. In both contexts, when can trademark owners prohibit others from using their marks to communicate a message?

PLAYBOY ENTERPRISES, INC. v. TERRI WELLES, INC.

279 F.3d 796 (9th Cir. 2002)

T.G. NELSON, Circuit Judge.

Playboy Enterprises, Inc. (PEI), appeals the district court's grant of summary judgment as to its claims of trademark infringement, unfair competition, and breach of contract against Terri Welles; Terri Welles, Inc.; Pippi, Inc.; and Welles' current and former "webmasters," Steven Huntington and Michael Mihalko. . . .

BACKGROUND

Terri Welles was on the cover of Playboy in 1981 and was chosen to be the Playboy Playmate of the Year for 1981. Her use of the title "Playboy Playmate of the Year 1981," and her use of other trademarked terms on her web site are at issue in this suit. During the relevant time period, Welles' web site offered information about and free photos of Welles, advertised photos for sale, advertised memberships in her photo club, and promoted her services as a spokesperson. A biographical section described Welles' selection as Playmate of the Year in 1981 and her years modeling for PEI. After the lawsuit began, Welles included discussions of the suit and criticism of PEI on her web site and included a note disclaiming any association with PEI.

PEI complains of four different uses of its trademarked terms on Welles' web site: (1) the terms "Playboy" and "Playmate" in the metatags of the web site; (2) the phrase "Playmate of the Year 1981" on the masthead of the web site; (3) the phrases "Playboy Playmate of the Year 1981" and "Playmate of the Year 1981" on various banner ads, which may be transferred to other web sites; and (4) the repeated use of the abbreviation "PMOY '81" as the watermark on the pages of the web site. PEI claimed that these uses of its marks constituted trademark infringement, dilution, false designation of origin, and unfair competition. . . .

DISCUSSION

A. Trademark Infringement

Except for the use of PEI's protected terms in the wallpaper of Welles' web site, we conclude that Welles' uses of PEI's trademarks are permissible, nominative uses. They imply no current sponsorship or endorsement by PEI. Instead, they serve to identify Welles as a past PEI "Playmate of the Year."

We articulated the test for a permissible, nominative use in *New Kids On The Block v. New America Publishing, Inc.*[, 971 F.2d 302 (9th Cir. 1992)]. The band, New Kids On The Block, claimed trademark infringement arising from the use of their trademarked name by several newspapers. The newspapers had conducted polls asking which member of the band New Kids On The Block was the best and most popular. The papers' use of the trademarked term did not fall within the traditional fair use doctrine. Unlike a traditional fair use scenario, the defendant newspaper was using the trademarked term to describe not its own product, but the plaintiff's. Thus, the factors used to evaluate fair use were inapplicable. The use was nonetheless permissible, we concluded, based on its nominative nature.

We adopted the following test for nominative use:

> First, the product or service in question must be one not readily identifiable without use of the trademark; second, only so much of the mark or marks may be used as is reasonably necessary to identify the product or service; and third, the user must do nothing that would, in conjunction with the mark, suggest sponsorship or endorsement by the trademark holder.

We noted in *New Kids* that a nominative use may also be a commercial one.

In cases in which the defendant raises a nominative use defense, the above three-factor test should be applied instead of the test for likelihood of confusion set forth in *Sleekcraft*. The three-factor test better evaluates the likelihood of confusion in nominative use cases. When a defendant uses a trademark nominally, the trademark will be identical to the plaintiff's mark, at least in terms of the words in question. Thus, application of the *Sleekcraft* test, which focuses on the similarity of the mark used by the plaintiff and the defendant, would lead to the incorrect conclusion that virtually all nominative uses are confusing. The three-factor test — with its requirements that the defendant use marks only when no descriptive substitute exists, use no more of the mark than necessary, and do nothing to suggest sponsorship or endorsement by the mark holder — better addresses concerns regarding the likelihood of confusion in nominative use cases.

1. Headlines and Banner Advertisements.

To satisfy the first part of the test for nominative use, "the product or service in question must be one not readily identifiable without use of the trademark[.]" This situation arises "when a trademark also describes a person, a place or an attribute of a product" and there is no descriptive substitute for the trademark. In such a circumstance, allowing the trademark holder exclusive rights would allow the language to "be depleted in much the same way as if generic words were protectable." In *New Kids*, we gave the example of the trademarked term, "Chicago Bulls." We explained that "one might refer to the 'two-time world champions' or 'the professional basketball team from Chicago,' but it's far simpler (and more likely to be understood) to refer to the Chicago Bulls." Moreover, such a use of the trademark would "not imply sponsorship or endorsement of the product because the mark is used only to describe the thing, rather than to identify its source." Thus, we concluded, such uses must be excepted from trademark infringement law.

The district court properly identified Welles' situation as one which must also be excepted. No descriptive substitute exists for PEI's trademarks in this context. The court explained:

> [T]here is no other way that Ms. Welles can identify or describe herself and her services without venturing into absurd descriptive phrases. To describe herself as the "nude model selected by Mr. Hefner's magazine as its number-one prototypical woman for the year 1981" would be impractical as well as ineffectual in identifying Terri Welles to the public.

We agree. Just as the newspapers in *New Kids* could only identify the band clearly by using its trademarked name, so can Welles only identify herself clearly by using PEI's trademarked title.

The second part of the nominative use test requires that "only so much of the mark or marks may be used as is reasonably necessary to identify the product or service[.]" *New Kids* provided the following examples to explain this element: "[A] soft drink competitor would be entitled to compare its product to Coca-Cola or Coke, but would not be entitled to use Coca-Cola's distinctive lettering." Similarly, in a past case, an auto shop was allowed to use the trademarked term "Volkswagen" on a sign describing the cars it repaired, in part because the shop "did not use Volkswagen's distinctive lettering style or color scheme, nor did he display the encircled 'VW' emblem." Welles' banner advertisements and headlines satisfy this element because they use only the trademarked words, not the font or symbols associated with the trademarks.

The third element requires that the user do "nothing that would, in conjunction with the mark, suggest sponsorship or endorsement by the trademark holder." As to this element, we conclude that aside from the wallpaper, which we address separately, Welles does nothing in conjunction with her use of the marks to suggest sponsorship or endorsement by PEI. The marks are clearly used to describe the title she received from PEI in 1981, a title that helps describe who she is. It would be unreasonable to assume that the Chicago Bulls sponsored a Web site of Michael Jordan's simply because his name appeared with the appellation "former Chicago Bull." Similarly, in this case, it would be unreasonable to assume that PEI currently sponsors or endorses someone who describes herself as a "Playboy Playmate of the Year in 1981." The designation of the year, in our case, serves the same function as the "former" in our example. It shows that any sponsorship or endorsement occurred in the past.

In addition to doing nothing in conjunction with her use of the marks to suggest sponsorship or endorsement by PEI, Welles affirmatively disavows any sponsorship or endorsement. Her site contains a clear statement disclaiming any connection to PEI. Moreover, the text of the site describes her ongoing legal battles with the company.

For the foregoing reasons, we conclude that Welles' use of PEI's marks in her headlines and banner advertisements is a nominative use excepted from the law of trademark infringement. . . .

[The court's discussion with respect to metatags is excerpted, *infra*, and the court concludes that Welles's use of PMOY '81 in the Web page's background wallpaper was not nominative use because it was not necessary to describe Welles.]

COMMENTS AND QUESTIONS

1. Under what circumstances is the use of another's trademark nominative? Should nominative use be considered as an alternative to the likelihood of confusion factors usually applied in a trademark infringement case, as the court did in *Welles*, or is it better conceived as a defense to a trademark infringement action?

2. In *Welles*, the district court noted that even if a particular trademark use could satisfy the requirements for fair use, that is the trademark was not being used as a trademark, it may nonetheless violate trademark law if there is a likelihood of confusion. In contrast, the Ninth Circuit's decision in *New Kids* recognizes that some uses of trademarks must be considered fair regardless of likelihood of confusion. If there is evidence of likelihood of confusion, why should the nominative use of the mark exempt the user from trademark liability? Is the Ninth Circuit's conclusion that there can never be a likelihood of confusion as to the source, origin, or affiliation of a product or service if the trademark is not being used to signify source, origin, or affiliation? Consider the case of Century 21 Real Estate v. Lendingtree, 425 F.3d 211 (2005), in which the Third Circuit Court of Appeals favored a test in nominative use cases that combines a streamlined likelihood of confusion test with a more specific version of the nominative use test applied in *Welles* and *New Kids on the Block*. In *Century 21*, the majority held that:

> the test for likelihood of confusion still has an important place in a trademark infringement case in which the defendant asserts the nominative fair use defense. In this case, the test should focus on the four relevant [likelihood of confusion] factors: (1) the price of the goods and other factors indicative of the care and attention expected of consumers when making a purchase; (2) the length of time the defendant has used the mark without evidence of actual confusion; (3) the intent of the defendant in adopting the mark; and (4) the evidence of actual confusion.
>
> Once plaintiff has met its burden of proving that confusion is likely, the burden then shifts to defendant to show that its nominative use of plaintiff's marks is nonetheless fair. In this Circuit, we have today adopted a test for nominative fair use in which a court will pose three questions: (1) Is the use of the plaintiff's mark necessary to describe both plaintiff's product or service and defendant's product or service? (2) Is only so much of the plaintiff's mark used as is necessary to describe plaintiff's products or services? (3) Does the defendant's conduct or language reflect the true and accurate relationship between plaintiff and defendant's products or services? If each of these questions can be answered

in the affirmative, the use will be considered a fair one, regardless of whether likelihood of confusion exists.

We adopt a bifurcated approach that tests for confusion and fairness in separate inquiries in order to distribute the burden of proof appropriately between the parties at each stage of the analysis. The defendant has no burden to show fairness until the plaintiff first shows confusion. Furthermore, by properly treating nominative fair use as an affirmative defense, our approach allows for the possibility that a district court could find a certain level of confusion, but still ultimately determine the use to be fair.

Century 21 Real Estate Corp. v. Lendingtree, Inc., 425 F.3d 211, 231 (2005). Do you agree with this analysis? Would the application of this bifurcated test have made any difference if applied to the facts of the *Welles* case?

3. While *Welles* did not use "Playboy" or "Playmate" in her domain name, under the court's reasoning, could she? If so, how could it be used?

4. Can an unauthorized use of another's mark in a domain name be justified under the First Amendment? Consider the following extract.

PLANNED PARENTHOOD FEDERATION OF AMERICA, INC. v. BUCCI

42 U.S.P.Q.2d 1430 (S.D.N.Y. 1997)

[The facts of the opinion are excerpted, *supra*.]

WOOD, J.

[After concluding that Planned Parenthood had demonstrated a likelihood of confusion, the court turned to the defendant's argument that his actions were nonetheless protected under the First Amendment.] Defendant . . . argues that his use of plaintiff's mark is protected from injunction because . . . it is protected speech under the First Amendment. I consider these arguments in turn. . . .

Defendant also argues that his use of the "planned parenthood" mark is protected by the First Amendment. As defendant argues, trademark infringement law does not curtail or prohibit the exercise of the First Amendment right to free speech. I note that plaintiff has not sought, in any way, to restrain defendant from speech that criticizes Planned Parenthood or its mission, or that discusses defendant's beliefs regarding reproduction, family, and religion. The sole purpose of the Court's inquiry has been to determine whether the use of the "planned parenthood" mark as defendant's domain name and home page address constitutes an infringement of plaintiff's trademark. Defendant's use of another entity's mark is entitled to First Amendment protection when his use of that mark is part of a communicative message, not when it is used to identify the source of a product. Yankee Publishing, Inc. v. News America Publishing, Inc., 809 F. Supp. 267, 275 (S.D.N.Y. 1992). By using the mark as a domain name and home page address and by welcoming Internet users to the home page with the message "Welcome to the Planned Parenthood Home

Page!" defendant identifies the web site and home page as being the product, or forum, of plaintiff. I therefore determine that, because defendant's use of the term "planned parenthood" is not part of a communicative message, his infringement on plaintiff's mark is not protected by the First Amendment.

Defendant argues that his use of the "Planned Parenthood" name for his web site is entitled to First Amendment protection, relying primarily on the holding of Yankee Publishing, 809 F. Supp. at 275. In that case, Judge Leval noted that the First Amendment can protect unauthorized use of a trademark when such use is part of an expression of a communicative message: "the Second Circuit has construed the Lanham Act narrowly when the unauthorized use of the trademark is for the purpose of a communicative message, rather than identification of product origin." Id. Defendant argues that his use of the "Planned Parenthood" name for his web site is a communicative message.

However, Yankee Publishing carefully draws a distinction between communicative messages and product labels or identifications:

> When another's trademark . . . is used without permission for the purpose of source identification, the trademark law generally prevails over the First Amendment. Free speech rights do not extend to labeling or advertising products in a manner that conflicts with the trademark rights of others.

Defendant offers no argument in his papers as to why the Court should determine that defendant's use of "plannedparenthood.com" is a communicative message rather than a source identifier. His use of "plannedparenthood.com" as a domain name to identify his web site is on its face more analogous to source identification than to a communicative message; in essence, the name identifies the web site, which contains defendant's home page. The statement that greets Internet users who access defendant's web site, "Welcome to the Planned Parenthood Home Page," is also more analogous to an identifier than to a communication. For those reasons, defendant's use of the trademarked term "planned parenthood" is not part of a communicative message, but rather, serves to identify a product or item, defendant's web site and home page, as originating from Planned Parenthood.

Defendant's use of plaintiff's mark is not protected as a title under Rogers v. Grimaldi, 875 F.2d 994, 998 (2d Cir. 1989). There, the Court of Appeals determined that the title of the film "Ginger and Fred" was not a misleading infringement, despite the fact that the film was not about Ginger Rogers and Fred Astaire, because of the artistic implications of a title. The Court of Appeals noted that "[f]ilmmakers and authors frequently rely on word-play, ambiguity, irony, and allusion in titling their works." Id. The Court of Appeals found that the use of a title such as the one at issue in Rogers was acceptable "unless the title has no artistic relevance to the underlying work"; even when the title has artistic relevance, it may not be used to "explicitly mislead[ ] [the consumer] as to the source or content of the work." Id. Here, even treating defendant's domain name and home page address as titles, rather than as source identifiers, I find that the title "plannedparenthood.com" has no artistic implications, and that the title is being used to attract some consumers by misleading them as to the web site's source or content. Given defendant's testimony indicating that he knew, and intended, that his use of the domain name "plannedparenthood.com" would cause some "pro-abortion" Internet users to access his Web site, he cannot demonstrate that his use of "planned parenthood" is entitled to First Amendment protection.

E.   Whether a Disclaimer Will Cure the Confusion

Defendant argues that a disclaimer, rather than an injunction, is the appropriate remedy here. I disagree. Due to the nature of Internet use, defendant's appropriation of plaintiff's mark as a domain name and home page address cannot adequately be remedied by a disclaimer. Defendant's domain name and home page address are external labels that, on their face, cause confusion among Internet users and may cause Internet users who seek plaintiff's web site to expend time and energy accessing defendant's web site. Therefore, I determine that a disclaimer on defendant's home page would not be sufficient to dispel the confusion induced by his home page address and domain name. . . .

Bally Total Fitness Holding Corp. v. Faber

29 F. Supp. 2d 1161 (C.D. Cal. 1998)

Pregerson, District Judge. . . .

Background

Bally Total Fitness Holding Corp. ("Bally") brings this action for trademark infringement, unfair competition, and dilution against Andrew S. Faber ("Faber") in connection with Bally's federally registered trademarks and service marks in the terms "Bally," "Bally's Total Fitness," and "Bally Total Fitness," including the name and distinctive styles of these marks. Bally is suing Faber based on his use of Bally's marks in a web site he designed.

Faber calls his site "Bally sucks." The web site is dedicated to complaints about Bally's health club business. When the web site is accessed, the viewer is presented with Bally's mark with the word "sucks" printed across it. Immediately under this, the web site states "Bally Total Fitness Complaints! Un-Authorized."

Faber has several web sites in addition to the "Bally sucks" site. The domain in which Faber has placed his web sites is "www.compupix.com." Faber's other web sites within "www.compupix.com" include the "Bally sucks" site (URL address "www.compupix.com/ballysucks"); "Images of Men," a web site displaying and selling photographs of nude males (URL address "www.compupix.com/index.html"); a web site containing information regarding the gay community

(URL address "www.compupix.com/gay"); a web site containing photographs of flowers and landscapes (URL address "www.compupix.com/fl/index.html"); and a web site advertising "Drew Faber Web Site Services" (URL address "www.compupix.com/biz.htm"). . . .

DISCUSSION

. . . Trademark Infringement

The Lanham Act provides the basic protections that a trademark owner receives. To find that Faber has infringed Bally's marks the Court would have to find that Bally has valid protectable trademarks and that Faber's use creates a likelihood of confusion. 15 U.S.C. §1114(1)(a). Faber asserts that Bally cannot meet this standard as a matter of law. . . .

In determining whether a defendant's use of a plaintiff's trademarks creates a likelihood of confusion, the courts apply an eight-factor test, including: (1) strength of the mark; (2) proximity of the goods; (3) similarity of the marks; (4) evidence of actual confusion; (5) marketing channels used; (6) type of goods and the degree of care likely to be exercised by the purchaser; (7) defendant's intent in selecting the mark; and (8) likelihood of expansion of the product lines.

See AMF Inc. v. Sleekcraft Boats, 599 F.2d 341, 348-49 (9th Cir. 1979). The Sleekcraft factors apply to related goods. Id. at 348. Bally is involved in the health club industry. Faber is an Internet web page designer who believes that Bally engages in unsatisfactory business practices. Faber operates a web site which is critical of Bally's operations. Bally, however, states that it uses the Internet to communicate with its members and to advertise its services. Consequently, Bally asserts that the parties have related goods because both parties use the Internet to communicate with current and potential Bally members.

"Related goods are those goods which, though not identical, are related in the minds of consumers." Levi Strauss & Co. v. Blue Bell, Inc., 778 F.2d 1352, 1363 (9th Cir. 1985). . . . The modern rule protects marks against "any product or service which would reasonably be thought by the buying public to come from the same source, or thought to be affiliated with, connected with, or sponsored by, the trademark owner." 3 J. Thomas McCarthy, McCarthy on Trademarks and Unfair Competition §24:6 at 24-13 (1997).

The Court finds that the goods here are not related. Web page design is a service based on computer literacy and design skills. This service is far removed from the business of managing health clubs. The fact that the parties both advertise their respective services on the Internet may be a factor tending to show confusion, but it does not make the goods related. The Internet is a communications medium. It is not itself a product or a service. Further, Faber's site states that it is "unauthorized" and contains the words "Bally sucks." No reasonable consumer comparing Bally's official web site with Faber's site would assume Faber's site "to come from the same source, or thought to be affiliated with, connected with, or sponsored by, the trademark owner." Therefore, Bally's claim for trademark infringement fails as a matter of law.

However, even assuming that these goods are related, Bally's claims also fail to satisfy the *Sleekcraft* factors.

a. Strength of Mark

This factor tips greatly toward Bally. Bally owns registered marks. Bally uses these marks extensively throughout the United States and Canada. Bally spends a significant amount of money each year to promote its marks. Finally, Bally asserts that no other company uses these marks in connection with health clubs, and that these marks are arbitrary. These facts demonstrate that Bally has strong marks.

b. Similarity of the Marks

Bally argues that the marks are identical. Bally argues that the only difference between the marks is that Faber attached the word "sucks" to Bally's marks. Bally argues that this is a minor difference.

"Sucks" has entered the vernacular as a word loaded with criticism. Faber has superimposed this word over Bally's mark. It is impossible to see Bally's mark without seeing the word "sucks." Therefore, the attachment cannot be considered a minor change. . . .

This factor cuts against Bally.

c. Competitive Proximity of the Goods

Bally argues that the goods are in close proximity because both parties use the Internet. Bally uses the Internet to generate revenue and disseminate information to its customers in support of its health clubs. Faber uses his web site to criticize Bally and to provide others with a forum for expressing their opinions of Bally. Faber does not attempt to pass-off his site as Bally's site. Faber states that his site is "unauthorized." Bally asserts that its site offers similar services because it has a complaints section and it provides information about Bally's services and products.

The Court finds that Faber's site does not compete with Bally's site. It is true that both sites provide Internet users with the same service — information about Bally. These sites, however, have fundamentally different purposes. Bally's site is a commercial advertisement. Faber's site is a consumer commentary. Having such different purposes demonstrates that these sites are not proximately competitive.

Therefore, this factor cuts against Bally.

d. Evidence of Actual Confusion

Bally does not offer evidence of actual confusion. Instead, Bally states, "consumer confusion is patently obvious in this case because of the strength of the Bally marks, combined with the obvious similarities in appearance and proximity of the marks, although there is no evidence of actual confusion."

Faber's states that his site is "unauthorized" and he has superimposed the word "sucks" over Bally's mark. The Court finds that the reasonably prudent user would not mistake Faber's site for Bally's official site.

Therefore, this factor cuts against Bally.

e. Marketing Channels Used

Bally argues that both parties use the Internet to reach current and potential Bally members. Bally states that it uses the Internet to disseminate information and generate revenue. Bally contends that it has spent over $500,000,000 in advertisements including the Internet, television, radio, billboards and signage since 1990. Therefore, Bally has a broad marketing strategy which includes the Internet.

Bally has not shown that Faber uses all of these channels for marketing. Instead, Bally has shown that Faber has one site which offers his services for web design, and this site included a reference to his "Bally sucks" site for some time. However, this site no longer includes this link.

Arguably, listing the "Bally sucks" site as one of many sites Faber has created in order to advertise his web design services is a form of marketing. This fact, however, does not change the primary purpose of the "Bally sucks" site which is consumer commentary. Bally's goods and Faber's goods are not related. Therefore, the fact that marketing channels overlap is irrelevant.

This factor is, at best, neutral, and likely cuts against Bally.

f. Degree of Care Likely to be Exercised

Bally argues that individual users may mistakenly access Faber's site rather than the official Bally site. Bally argues that this may happen when users employ an Internet search engine to locate Bally's site. Bally argues that the search result may list Faber's site and Bally's site. The result, it argues, will be that "[p]rospective users of plaintiff's services who mistakenly access defendant's Web site may fail to continue to search for plaintiff's own home page, due to anger, frustration or the belief that plaintiff's home page does not exist." (Bally's Mot. for Sum. Judg. 19:1-3, quoting Panavision Int'l, L.P. v. Toeppen, 141 F.3d 1316, 1327 (9th Cir. 1998).) The *Panavision* case, however, concerned an individual who engaged in commercial use of plaintiff's registered mark in his Internet domain name, "Panavision.com." See *Panavision*, 141 F.3d at 1324.

Here, Faber uses the Bally mark in the context of consumer criticism. He does not use Bally in his domain name. He communicates that the site is unauthorized and that it is not Bally's official site. Moreover, Faber's use of the Bally mark does not significantly add to the large volume of information that the average user will have to sift through in performing an average Internet search. See Teletech Customer Care Management (California), Inc. v. Tele-Tech Co., Inc., 977 F. Supp. 1407, 1410 (C.D. Cal. 1997) (noting that average search can result in 800 to 1000 "hits"). Whether the average user has to sift through 799 or 800 "hits" to find the official Bally site will not cause the frustration indicated in *Teletech* and *Panavision* because Faber is not using Bally's marks in the domain name. Moreover, even if Faber did use the mark as part of a larger domain name, such as "ballysucks.com", this would not necessarily be a violation as a matter of law.[2]

Further, the average Internet user may want to receive all the information available on Bally. The user may want to access the official Internet site to see how Bally sells itself. Likewise, the user may also want to be apprised of the opinions of others about Bally. This individual will be unable to locate sites containing outside commentary unless those sites include Bally's marks in the machine readable code upon which search engines rely. Prohibiting Faber from using Bally's name in the machine readable code would effectively isolate him from all but the most savvy of Internet users.

Therefore, this factor cuts against Bally.

g. Defendant's Intent in Selecting the Mark

Here, Faber purposely chose to use Bally's mark to build a "web site that is 'dedicated to complaint, issues, problems, beefs, grievances, grumblings, accusations, and gripes with Bally Total Fitness health clubs.'" Faber, however, is exercising his right to publish critical commentary about Bally. He cannot do this without making reference to Bally. . . .

Applying Bally's argument would extend trademark protection to eclipse First Amendment rights. The courts, however, have rejected this approach by holding that trademark rights may be limited by First Amendment concerns. . . .

Therefore, this factor is neutral.

h. Likelihood of Expansion of the Product Line

Bally essentially concedes that there is no likelihood that Bally will expand its product lines into the same areas in which Faber operates. However, Bally claims that Faber's intentional acts reduce the significance of this factor. Bally, though, relies on conclusions rejected by the Court.

---

2. The Court notes that there is a distinction between this example and cases like *Panavision* where an individual appropriates another's registered trademark as its domain name. In the "cybersquatter" cases like *Panavision*, there is a high likelihood of consumer confusion — reasonably prudent consumers would believe that the site using the appropriated name is the trademark owner's official site. Here, however, no reasonably prudent Internet user would believe that "Ballysucks.com" is the official Bally site or is sponsored by Bally.

It is apparent that the parties will not expand into the other's line of business. Bally intends to use the Internet as a means of increased communication. However, Bally has not represented that it intends to enter the web design business or that it intends to operate an official anti-Bally site. Further, Faber has not indicated that he intends to operate a health club.

Therefore, this factor also cuts against Bally.

3. Conclusion

Bally owns valuable marks. However, Faber has established that there is no likelihood of confusion as a matter of law. Therefore, the Court grants Faber's motion for summary judgment on trademark infringement.

C. Trademark Dilution . . .

Commercial use is an essential element of any dilution claim. Here, Bally argues that Faber has used Bally's mark to demonstrate his skills as a web site designer and to show current members how to effectively cancel their memberships with Bally. Bally asserts that Faber listed the "Bally sucks" web site on the "Drew Faber Web Site Services" site in an effort to advertise Faber's services.

Bally cites several "cybersquatting" cases in which individuals registered the trademarks of others as domain names for the purpose of selling or ransoming the domain name to the trademark owner. Bally asserts that these cases hold that using another's mark on the Internet is per se commercial use. The mere use of another's name on the Internet, however, is not per se commercial use. See 3 McCarthy, §24:97.2 at 24-172.

Here, Faber used Bally's marks in connection with a site devoted to consumer product review of Bally's services. In congressional hearings, Senator Orrin Hatch stated that the dilution statute "will not prohibit or threaten noncommercial expression, such as parody, satire, editorial and other forms of expression that are not a part of a commercial transaction." 141 Cong. Rec. S19306-10 (Daily ed. Dec. 29, 1995). Therefore, this exception encompasses both parodies and consumer product reviews. See Panavision Int'l, L.P. v. Toeppen, 945 F. Supp. 1296, 1303 (C.D. Cal. 1996).

Faber has shown that Bally cannot demonstrate that he is using Bally's mark in commerce. Bally argues that Faber's listing of the "Bally sucks" site, among others, in a site listing his available services and qualifications uses the Bally mark to promote a service. This argument is unpersuasive. Faber is not using the Bally mark to sell his services. Faber is not using Bally's mark to identify his goods in commerce. Faber merely listed the "Bally sucks" site as one of several web sites that he has designed so that those who are interested in his services may view his work. This is akin to an on-line resume.

Further, the courts have held that trademark owners may not quash unauthorized use of the mark by a person expressing a point of view. See *L.L. Bean*, 811 F.2d at 29, citing Lucasfilm Ltd. v. High Frontier, 622 F. Supp. 931,

933-35 (D.D.C. 1985). This is so even if the opinion may come in the form of a commercial setting. See Id. at 33 (discussing Maine's anti-dilution statute). In *L.L. Bean*, the First Circuit held that a sexually-oriented parody of L.L. Bean's catalog in a commercial adult-oriented magazine was non-commercial use of the trademark. See Id. The court stated:

> If the anti-dilution statute were construed as permitting a trademark owner to enjoin the use of his mark in a noncommercial context found to be negative or offensive, then a corporation could shield itself from criticism by forbidding the use of its name in commentaries critical of its conduct. The legitimate aim of the anti-dilution statute is to prohibit the unauthorized use of another's trademark in order to market incompatible products or services. The Constitution does not, however, permit the range of the anti-dilution statute to encompass the unauthorized use of a trademark in a noncommercial setting such as an editorial or artistic context.

Id.

Here, Bally wants to protect its valuable marks and ensure that they are not tarnished or otherwise diluted. This is an understandable goal. However, for the reasons set forth above, Faber's "Bally sucks" site is not a commercial use.

Even if Faber's use of Bally's mark is a commercial use, Bally also cannot show tarnishment. . . .

There are, however, two flaws with Bally's argument. First, none of the cases that Bally cites involve consumer commentary. In *Coca-Cola*, the court enjoined the defendant's publication of a poster stating "Enjoy Cocaine" in the same script as *Coca-Cola*'s trademark. See *Coca-Cola*, 346 F. Supp. at 1192. Likewise, in *Mutual of Omaha*, the court prohibited the use of the words "Mutual of Omaha," with a picture of an emaciated human head resembling the Mutual of Omaha's logo on a variety of products as a means of protesting the arms race. See *Mutual of Omaha*, 836 F.2d at 398. Here, however, Faber is using Bally's mark in the context of a consumer commentary to say that Bally engages in business practices which Faber finds distasteful or unsatisfactory. This is speech protected by the First Amendment. See *L.L. Bean*, 811 F.2d at 29; McCarthy, §24:105 at 24-191. As such, Faber can use Bally's mark to identify the source of the goods or services of which he is complaining. This use is necessary to maintain broad opportunities for expression. See Restatement (Third) of Unfair Competition §25(2), cmt. i (1995) (stating "extension of the antidilution statutes to protect against damaging nontrademark uses raises substantial free speech issues and duplicates other potential remedies better suited to balance the relevant interests").

The second problem with Bally's argument is that it is too broad in scope. Bally argues that the proximity of Faber's "Images of Men" site tarnishes the good will that Bally's mark enjoys because it improperly creates an association between Bally's mark and pornography. If the Court accepted this argument it would be an impossible task to determine dilution on the Internet. It is true that both sites are under the same domain name, "Compupix.com." Furthermore, it is also true that at a variety of times there were links between Faber's various sites. However, at no time was any pornographic material contained on Faber's "Bally sucks" site. From its inception, this site was devoted to consumer commentary. Looking beyond the "Bally sucks" site to other sites within the domain or to other linked sites would, to an extent, include the Internet in its entirety. The essence of the Internet is that sites are connected to facilitate access to information. Including linked sites as grounds for finding commercial use or dilution would extend the statute far beyond its intended purpose of protecting trademark owners from uses that have the effect of "lessening . . . the capacity of a famous mark to identify and distinguish goods or services." 15 U.S.C. §1127. Further, it is not logical that a reasonably prudent Internet user would believe that sites which contain no reference to a trademark and which are linked to, or within the same domain as, a site that is clearly not sponsored by the trademark owner are in some way sponsored by the trademark owner.

Therefore, the Court grants Faber's motion for summary judgment on the claim of trademark dilution. . . .

COMMENTS AND QUESTIONS

1. Given that Bucci's Web site welcomed users to the "Planned Parenthood Webpage," at the very least, he was using the Planned Parenthood trademark as a source identifier in the text of the Web site. If the text were removed and Bucci included a disclaimer, would the use of the domain name still be prohibited? Under what theory of likelihood of confusion?

2. Why does Judge Wood in *Planned Parenthood* reject the argument that a domain name is like a movie title in terms of First Amendment protections? Can you think of any circumstances in which the analogy might work as a defense to a trademark infringement or dilution action?

3. How easy is it to reconcile *Planned Parenthood* with *Faber*? Is the key distinction the fact that Bucci used Planned Parenthood's trademark within its domain name, while Faber only utilized Bally's mark in a sub-page identifier accessible via an unrelated domain name?

4. Compare these cases with Bosley Medical Institute v. Kremer (see discussion, *supra*). In that case, the Ninth Circuit Court of Appeals held that the defendant's registration of a domain name corresponding to the plaintiff's trademark for the purposes of establishing a "gripe site" about the plaintiff was not an infringement of general trademark law, as opposed to the ACPA. The court noted that this use of the trademark was not a commercial use and could not mislead consumers about the source of the plaintiff's services. Additionally, the court raised concerns that trademark law should not be used to prevent criticism and comment.

5. Would the results in any of these cases be different if they were brought under the ACPA or UDRP? (The ACPA issues in Bosley v. Kremer were remitted to the lower court for further consideration as the Ninth Circuit Court held that the lower court had erred in assuming a commercial use requirement under the ACPA that mirrored the commercial use

requirement in trademark infringement and dilution law. The question as to whether Kremer had infringed the ACPA has not been judicially resolved.)

6.   Consider the WIPO arbitration in Societé Air France v. Virtual Dates Inc., WIPO Arbitration and Mediation Center, Administrative Panel Decision Case No. D2005-0168 (May 24, 2005). This was a case involving a "gripe site" about Air France that was established under the domain name: "airfrancesucks. com." The majority panelists ordered transfer of the name to Air France on the basis the domain name was confusingly similar to the Air France trademark, the registrant had no legitimate rights in the name, and that the registrant had registered the domain name in bad faith. However, a dissenting panelist felt that domain names utilizing a trademark plus a pejorative word like "sucks" would not confuse consumers about the source of information on the Web site. Which view is correct?

Note: Are Domain Names Property?

As the preceding materials demonstrate, under some circumstances, domain names and other elements of Internet communication may be governed by intellectual property law. To what extent do other rules governing property apply? What purpose would they serve? If domain names are not property rights, how should they be characterized by the legal system?

While domain names often correspond with trademarks and thus bring trademark law into play in resolving disputes about trademark registration and use, not all domain names correspond with trademarks or function as trademarks. The question as to whether domain names are some other form of intangible property has never been resolved, although it has arisen in a variety of situations. In Network Solutions Inc. v. Umbro International Inc, 529 S.E. 2d 80 (Va. 2000), for example, the court held that domain names are not to be regarded as property in the context of garnishment proceedings. The majority held that domain names should be legally characterized as a mere contractual license between the registering authority and the registrant, and not as a property interest. This may be contrasted with the case of Kremen v. Cohen, 337 F.3d 1024 (9th Cir. 2003), in which the Ninth Circuit Court of Appeals held that domain names are appropriately regarded as a species of intangible property for the purposes of California's conversion statute.

The legal status of domain names remains uncertain, particularly the question as to whether or not they are appropriately regarded as property. Nevertheless, the global market in transactions involving domain names continues to thrive, and domain names are routinely regarded as property or a quasi-proprietary commercial asset in the domain name market. For details on the operation of this market, see David Kesmodel, *The Domain Game* (2008).

3. Search Engines and Metatags

The Internet contains so much information it would be virtually impossible to find all the information one might want by relying upon domain names alone. In addition to entering domain names, users can use Internet search engines to find the information they desire. In fact, in recent years, commentators have suggested that domain names are unimportant as a search tool in the wake of the development of sophisticated search engine technology. Eric Goldman, *Deregulating Relevancy in Internet Trademark Law*, 54 Emory L.J. 507, 548 (2005). Search engines are massive databases of information gathered from the Internet by computer programs called crawlers or spiders that search the Web gathering information from Web pages. These search engines index the information making it possible for a user to search through the index. Search engines both extract and index information differently. Search algorithms employed in sophisticated search engines like Google tend to generate search results based on combinations of metatags, domain names, full text searches, and popularity rankings of web pages. Greg Lastowka: *Google's Law*, 73 Brook. L. Rev. 1327, 1336-37 (2008). Metatags are self-selected key words embedded in the Hypertext Markup Language (HTML) used to format Web documents that are invisible to the user. Consequently, when someone searches for the White House, they may find not only the White House's official Web site, but every Web site that contains the words White and House in its text, metatags, or domain name. In the early days of Internet search engines, some courts held that metatags cause "initial interest confusion," in which a user is diverted to a third-party site and may purchase the third party's alternative products over the trademark owner's products. Some courts concluded this constitutes misappropriation of goodwill. To what extent can trademark law be used to change these results? Is the presence of another's trademark on a Web page or in a metatag necessarily trademark use? Should metatags be treated differently from domain names? How should trademark law deal with searching algorithms used by search engines? Is use of a trademarked term in a keyword advertising program a "trademark use"?

BROOKFIELD COMMUNICATIONS, INC. v. WEST COAST ENTM'T CORP.

174 F.3d 1036 (9th Cir. 1999)

[The facts of the case and the court's discussion with respect to the use of domain names is excerpted, *supra*.]

O'SCANNLAIN, Circuit Judge:

[In addition to typing in a domain name directly, a] Web surfer's second option when he does not know the domain name is to utilize an Internet search engine, such as Yahoo, Altavista, or Lycos. When a keyword is entered, the search engine processes it through a self-created index of Web sites to generate a (sometimes long) list relating to the entered keyword. Each search engine uses its own algorithm to arrange indexed materials in sequence, so the list of Web sites that any particular set of keywords will bring up may differ depending on the search engine used. Search engines look for keywords in places such as domain names, actual text on the Web page, and metatags. Metatags are HTML code intended to describe the contents of the Web site. There are different types of metatags, but those of principal concern to us are the "description" and "keyword" metatags. The description metatags are intended to describe the Web site; the keyword metatags, at least in theory, contain keywords relating to the contents of the Web site. The more often a term appears in the metatags and in the text of the Web page, the more likely it is that the Web page will be "hit" in a search for that keyword and the higher on the list of "hits" the Web page will appear. . . .

B . . .

At first glance, our resolution of the infringement issues in the domain name context would appear to dictate a similar conclusion of likelihood of confusion with respect to West Coast's use of "moviebuff.com" in its metatags. Indeed, all eight likelihood of confusion factors outlined [above] — with the possible exception of purchaser care, which we discuss below — apply here as they did in our analysis of domain names; we are, after all, dealing with the same marks, the same products and services, the same consumers, etc. Disposing of the issue so readily, however, would ignore the fact that the likelihood of confusion in the domain name context resulted largely from the associational confusion between West Coast's domain name "moviebuff.com" and Brookfield's trademark "MovieBuff." The question in the metatags context is quite different. . . .

Although entering "MovieBuff" into a search engine is likely to bring up a list including "westcoastvideo.com" if West Coast has included that term in its metatags, the resulting confusion is not as great as where West Coast uses the "moviebuff.com" domain name. First, when the user inputs "MovieBuff" into an Internet search engine, the list produced by the search engine is likely to include both West Coast's and Brookfield's Web sites. Thus, in scanning such list, the Web user will often be able to find the particular Web site he is seeking. Moreover, even if the Web user chooses the Web site belonging to West Coast, he will see that the domain name of the web site he selected is "westcoastvideo. com." Since there is no confusion resulting from the domain address, and since West Coast's initial Web page prominently displays its own name, it is difficult to say that a consumer is likely to be confused about whose site he has reached or to think that Brookfield somehow sponsors West Coast's web site.

Nevertheless, West Coast's use of "moviebuff.com" in metatags will still result in what is known as initial interest confusion. Web surfers looking for Brookfield's "MovieBuff" products who are taken by a search engine to "westcoastvideo.com" will find a database similar enough to "MovieBuff" such that a sizeable number of consumers who were originally looking for Brookfield's product will simply decide to utilize West Coast's offerings instead. Although there is no source confusion in the sense that consumers know they are patronizing West Coast rather than Brookfield, there is nevertheless initial interest confusion in the sense that, by using "moviebuff.com" or "Movie-Buff" to divert people looking for "MovieBuff" to its Web site, West Coast improperly benefits from the goodwill that Brookfield developed in its mark. . . .

Using another's trademark in one's metatags is much like posting a sign with another's trademark in front of one's store. Suppose West Coast's competitor (let's call it "Blockbuster") puts up a billboard on a highway reading — "West Coast Video: 2 miles ahead at Exit 7" — where West Coast is really located at Exit 8 but Blockbuster is located at Exit 7. Customers looking for West Coast's store will pull off at Exit 7 and drive around looking for it. Unable to locate West Coast, but seeing the Blockbuster store right by the highway entrance, they may simply rent there. Even consumers who prefer West Coast may find it not worth the trouble to continue searching for West Coast since there is a Blockbuster right there. Customers are not confused in the narrow sense: they are fully aware that they are purchasing from Blockbuster and they have no reason to believe that Blockbuster is related to, or in any way sponsored by, West Coast. Nevertheless, the fact that there is only initial consumer confusion does not alter the fact that Blockbuster would be misappropriating West Coast's acquired goodwill. . . .

. . . West Coast argues that our holding conflicts with Holiday Inns, in which the Sixth Circuit held that there was no trademark infringement where an alleged infringer merely took advantage of a situation in which confusion was likely to exist and did not affirmatively act to create consumer confusion. See Holiday Inns, 86 F.3d at 622 (holding that the use of "1-800-405-4329" — which is equivalent to "1-800-H[zero]LIDAY" — did not infringe Holiday Inns's trademark, "1-800-HOLIDAY"). Unlike the defendant in Holiday Inns, however, West Coast was not a passive figure; instead, it acted affirmatively in placing Brookfield's trademark in the metatags of its Web site, thereby creating the initial interest confusion. Accordingly, our conclusion comports with Holiday Inns.

[The court goes on to explain that this holding does not infringe West Coast's First Amendment rights to use terms in metatags in a manner that would constitute fair use, but that "MovieBuff" is not a descriptive term protected in this manner. The court notes that the proper descriptive term for a "motion picture enthusiast" is a "Movie Buff" and not "MovieBuff." West Coast would be free to use "Movie Buff" in its metatags. The court further notes that West Coast could use the mark "MovieBuff" in comparative advertising: for example, "Why pay for MovieBuff when you can get the same thing here for FREE?" However, it cannot use the term to misdirect customers seeking Brookfield's Web site.]

PLAYBOY ENTERPRISES, INC. V. TERRI WELLES, INC.

78 F. Supp. 2d 1066 (S.D. Cal. 1999), *aff'd in part and rev'd in part*, 279 F.3d 796
(9th Cir. 2002)

[Playboy Enterprises, Inc. (PEI) sued Terri Welles, a former playmate, for trademark infringement, dilution, and unfair competition. The facts and the Court of Appeals' discussion of defendant's visible use of plaintiff's marks are excepted *supra*.]

KEEP, District Judge.

The description of Ms. Welles' site as it appears in the meta code is "Playboy Playmate of the Year 1981 Terri Welles web site featuring erotic nude photos, semi-nude photos, softcore and exclusive Members Club." The metatag keywords on Ms. Welles' web site reads, "terri, welles, playmate, playboy, model, models, semi-nudity, naked, breast, breasts, tit, tits, nipple, nipples, ass, butt." . . .

Plaintiff relies on *Brookfield Communications, Inc. v. West Coast Entertainment Corp.*, 174 F.3d 1036 (9th Cir. 1999), to support its contention in this case that Defendant's use of PEI's trademarks in the metatags in her Web site infringes on its trademark by causing "likelihood of confusion . . . shown on the basis of initial interest confusion." The metatag use at issue is the use of the terms "Playboy Playmate of the Year 1981" in the meta code descriptor and the terms "playboy" and "playmate" in the metatag keywords. The court will simultaneously refer to the use of these terms in the metatags as "the use of PEI terms." Although Plaintiff is correct in citing *Brookfield* for the proposition that "likelihood of confusion can be shown on the basis of initial interest confusion," Plaintiff's reliance on *Brookfield* is misplaced as applied to Ms. Welles' case.

In *Brookfield*, the Ninth Circuit has noted that "the few courts to consider whether the use of another's trademark in one's metatags constitutes trademark infringement have ruled in the affirmative." *Brookfield Communications, Inc.*, 174 F.3d at 1064. . . . None of the cases which *Brookfield* discusses, however, involved the fair use defense or a use of trademarks in the metatags which accurately and fairly describe the contents of the web page or web site. And although *Brookfield* concerned the use of the plaintiff's trademarked terms in the metatags of the defendant's web site, it did *not* involve the use of the fair use defense within the metatags context. . . . .

[Court explains that it must nevertheless conduct a likelihood of confusion analysis, and notes that the *Sleekcraft* factors do not work in this context for the reasons addressed in the earlier extract from this case, *supra*.] Here, Defendant has used the terms "playboy," and "playmate" in the meta tag keywords and the term "Playboy Playmate of the Year 1981," in the meta code descriptor for her site so that those using search engines on the Web can find her web site if they are looking for a Playboy Playmate. Plaintiff's only evidence regarding likelihood of confusion with respect to Defendant's use of PEI terms in her metatags . . . concerns the theory of initial interest confusion: a confusion of "consumer attention, even though no actual sale is finally completed as a result of the confusion" and even though, once reaching the site, the consumer is not actually confused or is not likely to be confused as to the correct sponsor of the site to which he or she was led initially. *See Dr. Seuss Enters. v. Penguin Books USA, Inc.*, 109 F.3d 1394, 1405 (9th Cir. 1997), *cert. denied*, 521 U.S. 1146 (1997). . . .

Other courts cited by the *Brookfield* court which acknowledged initial interest confusion as being actionable under the Lanham Act have indicated that other factors are relevant in a finding of a confusing trademark use, or infringement. Among these are: (1) evidence of the initial interest confusion as being "damaging and wrongful," . . . (2) evidence that confusion between two products "will mistakenly lead the consumer to believe there is some connection between the two and therefore develop an interest in the [defendant's] line that it would otherwise not have," . . . ; or (3) evidence that the "situation offers an opportunity for sale not otherwise available by enabling defendant to interest prospective customers by confusion with the plaintiff's product." . . . In the present case, Plaintiff has failed to present any facts indicating 1) any initial interest confusion was "damaging and wrongful"; 2) anyone believes or is likely to believe there is a connection between PEI's and Ms. Welles' site; 3) Ms. Welles received "opportunit[ies] for sale not otherwise available" by confusing web users; or 4) any of Ms. Welles' actual customers were in the "appreciable number," or majority of people who when plugging in one of Plaintiff's trademark terms into a web browser search engine, was "looking for Playboy's official site." . . . Furthermore, there is no evidence in this case that Ms. Welles has intended to divert Plaintiff's customers to her web site by trading on PEI's goodwill. . . . This intent is relevant since the court in *Brookfield* stated that "in *Dr. Seuss*, the Ninth Circuit explicitly recognized that the use of another's trademark in a manner *calculated* 'to capture initial consumer attention, even though no actual sale is finally completed as a result of the confusion, *may* be still an infringement.'" *Brookfield Communications, Inc.*, 174 F.3d at 1062 (citing *Dr. Seuss*, 109 F.3d at 1405) (emphasis added). . . .

In rendering an analysis which is flexible and reflective of "emerging technologies," this court is also mindful that it must not lose sight of either common sense or the important, foundational and underlying principles of trademark law. Finding that Ms. Welles' use of PEI's trademarked terms in the metatags of her web site is a fair use comports with the fact web users must utilize identifying words to find their intended site. Not all web searches utilizing the words "Playboy," "Playmate," and "Playboy Playmate of the Year 1981" are intended to find "Playboy" goods or the official "Playboy" site. Plaintiff has not addressed the fact that Ms. Welles' fame and recognition derive from her popularity as a Playboy model and Playmate of the Year. If a consumer cannot remember her name, the logical way to find her site on the Web is by using key words that identify her source of recognition to the public: "Playboy Playmate of the Year 1981," "Playboy," and "Playmate." . . . The World Wide Web is a commercial marketplace and a free speech marketplace. To give consumers access to it, the court must also be careful to give consumers the freedom to locate desired sites while protecting the integrity of trademarks and trade names. The court stresses that the underlying or foundational purpose of trademark protection is *not* to create a property interest in *all* words used in a commercial context, but rather "[t]he policies of free competition and free use of language dictate that trademark law cannot forbid the commercial use of terms in their descriptive sense." 1 J. McCarthy, Trademarks and Unfair Competition, §11.45, at 82 (1999). As Justice Holmes in *Prestonettes v. Coty*, 264 U.S. 359, 368 (1924), put more eloquently, "[w]hen the mark is used in a way that does not deceive the public we see no such sanctity in the word as to prevent its being used to tell the truth." . . .

[On appeal, the Ninth Circuit affirmed the district court's conclusion with respect to Welles's use of metatags because the court considered the use nominative.]

COMMENTS AND QUESTIONS

1. If metatags are not visible to the Internet user, how can their use be considered the use of a trademark? Who do they confuse? *Consider* Maureen A. O'Rourke, *Defining the Limits of Free-Riding in Cyberspace: Trademark Liability for Metatagging*, 33 Gonz. L. Rev. 277 (1997/1998) (suggesting that the use of metatags does not confuse consumers, but instead confuses search engines).

2. Is the *Brookfield* court's analogy to a misleading road sign accurate? If not, why? Even assuming that metatags are used to some extent to capitalize on the good will of a competitor, could their use still be permissible in the absence of genuine consumer confusion? Instead of a misleading road sign, is a closer analogy a business physically locating next to a competitor hoping that the competitor's customers will now frequent the new establishment instead?

3. What about users searching generically for movie buff but accidentally omitting the space? Does *Holiday Inns* provide support for the argument that West Coast should be allowed to include moviebuff in its metatags in order to reach those consumers? Is the *Brookfield* court's effort to distinguish *Holiday Inns* persuasive? In what way is the selection of a domain name more affirmative than the selection of a telephone number?

4. O'Rourke argues that while use of metatags should not be considered trademark infringement and unfair competition, it may represent trademark dilution by "creating enough noise around the mark to make it very difficult for a user to enter the trademark into a search engine and find the mark owner's site." Maureen A. O'Rourke, *Defining the Limits of Free-Riding*

in Cyberspace: Trademark Liability for Metatagging, 33 Gonz. L. Rev. 277, 301 (1997/1998). Is this what is happening in *Welles*? If a user searches for Playboy and hundreds of other sites are included in the search results, will it be harder to identify the official site? To what extent can this problem be avoided through strict rules with respect to domain names? To what extent can this be fixed by changing the way search engines return results? For example, should search engines be required to list "official" Web sites first? If so, how would you go about defining an "official" website? Is it the *trademark.com* version, as opposed to, say, the ".org", ".net", or *trademarksucks.com* versions? Or would some form of registry of "official" online presences for businesses be required?

5. Lastowka has recently noted that most modern search engines now ignore meta-tags to avoid concerns about secondary liability for trademark infringements in situations such as those described in *Brookfield* and *Welles*. Greg Lastowka, *Google's Law*, 73 Brook. L. Rev. 1327, 1372 (2008).

6. Consider the position of search engines who may utilize other people's trademarks in keyword-advertising schemes. See the following extracts.

PLAYBOY ENTERPRISES, INC. v. NETSCAPE COMMUNICATIONS CORP.

354 F.3d 1020 (9th Cir. 2004)

T.G. NELSON, Circuit Judge:

. . . This case involves a practice called "keying" that defendants use on their Internet search engines. Keying allows advertisers to target individuals with certain interests by linking advertisements to pre-identified terms. To take an innocuous example, a person who searches for a term related to gardening may be a likely customer for a company selling seeds. Thus, a seed company might pay to have its advertisement displayed when searchers enter terms related to gardening. After paying a fee to defendants, that company could have its advertisements appear on the page listing the search results for gardening-related terms: the ad would be "keyed" to gardening-related terms. Advertisements appearing on search result pages are called "banner ads" because they run along the top or side of a page much like a banner.

Defendants have various lists of terms to which they key advertisers' banner ads. Those lists include the one at issue in this case, a list containing terms related to sex and adult-oriented entertainment. Among the over-400 terms in this list are two for which PEI holds trademarks: "playboy" and "playmate." Defendants *require* adult-oriented companies to link their ads to this set of words. Thus, when a user types in "playboy," "playmate," or one of the other listed terms, those companies' banner ads appear on the search results page.

PEI introduced evidence that the adult-oriented banner ads displayed on defendants' search results pages are often graphic in nature and are confusingly labeled or not labeled at all. In addition, the parties do not dispute that buttons on the banner ads say "click here." When a searcher complies, the search results page disappears, and the searcher finds him or herself at the advertiser's website. PEI presented uncontroverted evidence that defendants monitor "click rates," the ratio between the number of times searchers click on banner ads and the number of times the ads are shown. Defendants use click rate statistics to convince advertisers to renew their keyword contracts. The higher the click rate, the more successful they deem a banner ad.

PEI sued defendants, asserting that they were using PEI's marks in a manner that infringed upon and diluted them. . . .

A. Trademark Infringement

With regard to PEI's trademark infringement claim, the parties disagree on three points. First, the parties dispute whether a direct or a contributory theory of liability applies to defendants' actions. We conclude that defendants are potentially liable under one theory and that we need not decide which one. Second, the parties disagree regarding whether PEI has successfully shown that a genuine issue of material fact exists regarding the likelihood of consumer confusion resulting from defendants' use of PEI's marks. We conclude that a genuine issue of material fact does exist. Finally, the parties dispute whether any affirmative defenses apply. We conclude that no defenses apply. We will address each dispute in turn . . . .

2. PEI's Case for Trademark Infringement.

The "core element of trademark infringement," the likelihood of confusion, lies at the center of this case. . . .

PEI's strongest argument for a likelihood of confusion is for a certain kind of confusion: initial interest confusion. Initial interest confusion is customer confusion that creates initial interest in a competitor's product. Although dispelled before an actual sale occurs, initial interest confusion impermissibly capitalizes on the goodwill associated with a mark and is therefore actionable trademark infringement.

PEI asserts that, by keying adult-oriented advertisements to PEI's trademarks, defendants actively create initial interest confusion in the following manner. Because banner advertisements appear immediately after users type in PEI's marks, PEI asserts that users are likely to be confused regarding the sponsorship of unlabeled banner advertisements. In addition, many of the advertisements instruct users to "click here." Because of their confusion, users may follow the instruction, believing they will be connected to a PEI cite. Even if they realize "immediately upon accessing" the competitor's site that they have reached a site "wholly unrelated to" PEI's, the damage has been done: Through initial consumer confusion, the competitor "will still have gained a customer by appropriating the goodwill that [PEI] has developed in its [ ] mark."

[The court then discusses the *Brookfield* case.]

Although analogies to *Brookfield* suggest that PEI will be able to show a likelihood of confusion sufficient to defeat summary judgment, we must test PEI's theory using this circuit's well-established eight-factor test for the likelihood of confusion to be certain. Accordingly, we turn to that test now.

The Ninth Circuit employs an eight-factor test, originally set forth in *AMF Inc. v. Sleekcraft Boats*, to determine the likelihood of confusion. The eight factors are:

1. strength of the mark;
2. proximity of the goods;
3. similarity of the marks;
4. evidence of actual confusion;
5. marketing channels used;
6. type of goods and the degree of care likely to be exercised by the purchaser;
7. defendant's intent in selecting the mark; and
8. likelihood of expansion of the product lines.

In the Internet context, courts must be flexible in applying the factors, as some may not apply. Moreover, some factors are more important than others. For example, a showing of actual confusion among significant numbers of consumers provides strong support for the likelihood of confusion. For that reason, we turn first to an examination of factor four: evidence of actual confusion.

a. Factor 4: Evidence of Actual Confusion

The expert study PEI introduced establishes a strong likelihood of initial interest confusion among consumers. Thus, factor four alone probably suffices to reverse the grant of summary judgment.

[The court discusses the reliability of the survey evidence presented by PEI's expert, Dr. Ford, on actual consumer confusion.]

. . . The presence of Dr. Ford's criticized (but uncontradicted) report, with its strong conclusions that a high likelihood of initial interest confusion exists among consumers, thus generates a genuine issue of material fact on the actual confusion issue.

Because actual confusion is at the heart of the likelihood of confusion analysis, Dr. Ford's report alone probably precludes summary judgment. In the interest of being thorough, however, we will examine the other seven *Sleekcraft* factors. On balance, they also support PEI.

b. Factor One: Strength of the Mark

PEI has established that strong secondary meanings for its descriptive marks exist, and that a genuine issue of material fact exists as to whether it created the secondary meanings. Thus, the first *Sleekcraft* factor favors PEI.

At this point, defendants concede that they use the marks for their secondary meanings. Thus, they concede that the marks have secondary meanings. They offer only a weak argument regarding the strength of the meanings. Given that defendants themselves use the terms precisely because they believe that Internet searchers associate the terms with their secondary meanings, disputing the strength of the secondary meanings is somewhat farfetched. . . .

c. Factor Two: Proximity of the Goods

From an Internet searcher's perspective, the relevant "goods" are the links to the websites being sought and the goods or services available at those sites. The proximity between PEI's and its competitor's goods provides the reason Netscape keys PEI's marks to competitor's banner advertisements in the first place. Accordingly, this factor favors PEI as well.

d. Factor Three: Similarity of the Marks

No doubt exists regarding this factor. Aside from their lack of capitalization, their font, and the fact that defendants use the plural form of "playmate," the terms defendants use are identical to PEI's marks. Thus, they are certainly similar.

e. Factor Five: Marketing Channels Used

This factor is equivocal. PEI and the advertisers use identical marketing channels: the Internet. More specifically, each of their sites appears on defendants' search results pages. Given the broad use of the Internet today, the same could be said for countless companies. Thus, this factor merits little weight.

f. Factor Six: Type of Goods and Degree of Consumer Care Expected

This factor favors PEI. Consumer care for inexpensive products is expected to be quite low. Low consumer care, in turn, increases the likelihood of confusion.

In addition to price, the content in question may affect consumer care as well. We presume that the average searcher seeking adult-oriented materials on the Internet is easily diverted from a specific product he or she is seeking if other options, particularly graphic ones, appear more quickly. Thus, the adult-oriented and graphic nature of the materials weighs in PEI's favor as well.

g. Factor Seven: Defendants' Intent in Selecting the Mark

This factor favors PEI somewhat. A defendant's intent to confuse constitutes probative evidence of likely confusion: Courts assume that the defendant's intentions were carried out successfully. In this case, the evidence does not definitively establish defendants' intent. At a minimum, however, it does suggest that defendants do nothing to prevent click-throughs that result from confusion. Moreover, they profit from such click-throughs . . . .

PEI introduced evidence suggesting that labeling the advertisements would reduce click-through rates. It would also reduce confusion. However, although defendants control the content of advertisements in other contexts, defendants do not require that advertisers identify themselves on their banner ads. Moreover, they do not label the advertisements themselves. Perhaps even more telling, defendants refuse to remove the highly-rated terms "playboy" and "playmate" from their lists of keywords, even when advertisers request that they do so. . . .

h.   Factor Eight: Likelihood of Expansion of Product Lines

Because the advertisers' goods and PEI's are already related, as discussed within factor two, this factor is irrelevant.

Having examined all of the *Sleekcraft* factors, we conclude that the majority favor PEI. Accordingly, we conclude that a genuine issue of material fact exists as to the substantial likelihood of confusion. We now proceed to the defenses advanced by defendants.

3.   Defenses

Defendants assert three defenses: fair use, nominative use, and functional use. Because we have found that a genuine issue of fact exists as to likelihood of confusion under *Sleekcraft*, we must deny summary judgment as to the fair use defense. A fair use may not be a confusing use. Accordingly, we turn to defendants' other asserted defenses.

Defendants assert that they make a nominative use of PEI's marks. We apply a slightly different test for confusion in the nominative use, as opposed to the fair use, context. To be considered a nominative use, the use of a mark must meet the following three-factor test:

> First, the product or service in question must be one not readily identifiable without use of the trademark; second, only so much of the mark or marks may be used as is reasonably necessary to identify the product or service; and third, the user must do nothing that would, in conjunction with the mark, suggest sponsorship or endorsement by the trademark holder.

Before we apply this test to the facts at hand, we would like to emphasize what facts are *not* at hand. We note that defendants' use of PEI's marks to trigger the listing of PEI sites, and other sites that legitimately use PEI's marks, is not at issue here. In addition, we note that we are not addressing a situation in which a banner advertisement clearly identifies its source with its sponsor's name, or in which a search engine clearly identifies a banner advertisement's source. We are also not addressing a situation in which advertisers or defendants overtly compare PEI's products to a competitor's—saying, for example "if you are interested in Playboy, you may also be interested in the following message from [a different, named company]." Rather, we are evaluating a situation in which defendants display competitors' unlabeled banner advertisements, with no label or overt comparison to PEI, after Internet users type in PEI's trademarks.

The situation with which we are dealing runs afoul of the first requirement for nominative use. Accordingly, we do not consider the other prongs.

Defendants could use other words, besides PEI's marks, to trigger adult-oriented banner advertisements. Indeed, they already do so. The list they sell to advertisers includes over 400 terms besides PEI's marks. There is nothing indispensable, in this context, about PEI's marks. Defendants do not wish to identify PEI or its products when they key banner advertisements to PEI's marks. Rather, they wish to identify consumers who are interested in adult-oriented entertainment so they can draw them to competitors' websites. Accordingly, their use is not nominative. . . .

[Court then holds that genuine issues of material fact exist regarding PEI's dilution claim, so defendants are not entitled to summary judgment on that issue.]

IV. CONCLUSION

Genuine issues of material fact exist as to PEI's trademark infringement and dilution claims. Accordingly, we reverse the district court's grant of summary judgment in favor of defendants and remand for further proceedings.

BERZON, Circuit Judge, concurring:

I concur in Judge Nelson's careful opinion in this case, as it is fully consistent with the applicable precedents. I write separately, however, to express concern that one of those precedents was wrongly decided and may one day, if not now, need to be reconsidered *en banc*.

I am struck by how analytically similar keyed advertisements are to the metatags found infringing in *Brookfield Communications v. West Coast Entertainment Corp.*, 174 F.3d 1036 (9th Cir. 1999). In *Brookfield*, the court held that the defendant could not use the trademarked term "moviebuff" as one of its metatags. Metatags are part of the HTML code of a web page, and therefore are invisible to internet users. Search engines use these metatags to pull out websites applicable to search terms. *See also Promatek Indus., Ltd. v. Equitrac Corp.*, 300 F.3d 808, 812-13 (7th Cir. 2002) (adopting the *Brookfield* holding).

Specifically, *Brookfield* held that the use of the trademarked terms in metatags violated the *Lanham Act* because it caused "initial interest confusion." *Brookfield*, 174 F.3d at 1062-66. . . .

As applied to this case, *Brookfield* might suggest that there could be a *Lanham Act* violation *even if* the banner advertisements were clearly labeled, either by the advertiser or by the search engine. I do not believe that to be so. So read, the metatag holding in *Brookfield* would expand the reach of initial interest confusion from situations in which a party is initially confused to situations in which a party is never confused. I do not think it is reasonable to find initial interest confusion when a consumer is never confused as to source or affiliation, but instead knows, or should know, from the outset that a product or web link is not related to that of the trademark holder because the list produced by the search engine so informs him.

There is a big difference between hijacking a customer to another website by making the customer think he or she is visiting the trademark holder's website (even if only briefly), which is what may be happening in this case when the banner advertisements are not labeled, and just distracting a potential customer with another *choice*, when it is clear that it is a choice. . . .

[S]uppose a customer walks into a bookstore and asks for Playboy magazine and is then directed to the adult magazine section, where he or she sees Penthouse or Hustler up front on the rack while Playboy is buried in back. One would not say that Penthouse or Hustler had violated Playboy's trademark. This conclusion holds true even if Hustler paid the store owner to put its magazines in front of Playboy's.

. . . If I went to Macy's website and did a search for a Calvin Klein shirt, would Macy's violate Calvin Klein's trademark if it responded (as does Amazon.com, for example) with the requested shirt and pictures of other shirts I might like to consider as well? I very much doubt it.

Accordingly, I simply cannot understand the broad principle set forth in *Brookfield*. Even the main analogy given in *Brookfield* belies its conclusion. The Court gives an example of Blockbuster misdirecting customers from a competing video store, West Coast Video, by putting up a highway billboard sign giving directions to Blockbuster but telling customers that a West Coast Video store is located there. *Brookfield*, 174 F.3d at 1064. Even though customers who arrive at the Blockbuster realize that it is not West Coast Video, they were initially misled and confused. *Id.*

But there was no similar misdirection in *Brookfield*, nor would there be similar misdirection in this case were the banner ads labeled or otherwise identified. The *Brookfield* defendant's website was described by the court as being accurately listed as westcoastvideo.com in the applicable search results. Consumers were free to choose the official moviebuff.com website and were not hijacked or misdirected elsewhere. I note that the billboard analogy has been widely criticized as inapplicable to the internet situation, given both the fact that customers were not misdirected and the minimal inconvenience in directing one's web browser back to the original list of search results. *See* J. Thomas McCarthy, McCarthy on Trademarks & Unfair Competition §25:69 (4th ed. 2003); *Shea, supra* at 552 . . . .

COMMENTS AND QUESTIONS

1. The court in *Netscape* finds it unnecessary to decide if it should consider Netscape's activities on the basis of direct or secondary liability. Do you agree with the court's assessment?

2. Does the use of keyword advertising amount to initial interest confusion? Can you distinguish the keyword advertising scenario from the metatag cases, notably *Brookfield*? The court in *Netscape* relies on the *Brookfield* court's finding of initial interest confusion. Is the court's analogy with *Brookfield* convincing?

3. Do you find the *Netscape* court's rejection of the nominative use test convincing?

4. Judge Berzon in her concurrence questions the roadside billboard analogy made in the *Brookfield* case, *supra*. Do you agree with her reasoning?

RESCUECOM CORP. v. GOOGLE INC.

2009 U.S. App LEXIS 7160 (2d Cir. 2009)

LEVAL, Circuit Judge (CALABRESI and WESLEY, Circuit Judges, concurring).

. . . Rescuecom's Complaint alleges that Google is liable under §§32 and 43 of the Lanham Act, 15 U.S.C. §§1114 & 1125, for infringement, false designation of origin, and dilution of Rescuecom's eponymous trademark. . . .

. . . Rescuecom is a national computer service franchising company that offers on-site computer services and sales. Rescuecom conducts a substantial amount of business over the Internet and receives between 17,000 to 30,000 visitors to its website each month. It also advertises over the Internet, using many web-based services, including those offered by Google. Since 1998, "Rescuecom" has been a registered federal trademark, and there is no dispute as to its validity.

Google operates a popular Internet search engine, which users access by visiting www.google.com. Using Google's website, a person searching for the website of a particular entity in trade (or simply for information about it) can enter that entity's name or trademark into Google's search engine and launch a search. Google's proprietary system responds to such a search request in two ways. First, Google provides a list of links to websites, ordered in what Google deems to be of descending relevance to the user's search terms based on its proprietary algorithms. . . .

The second way Google responds to a search request is by showing context-based advertising. When a searcher uses Google's search engine by submitting a search term, Google may place advertisements on the user's screen. Google will do so if an advertiser, having determined that its ad is likely to be of interest to a searcher who enters the particular term, has purchased from Google the placement of its ad on the screen of the searcher who entered that search term. What Google places on the searcher's screen is more than simply an advertisement. It is also a link to the advertiser's website, so that in response to such an ad, if the searcher clicks on the link, he will open the advertiser's website, which offers not only additional information about the advertiser, but also perhaps the option to purchase the goods and services of the advertiser over the Internet. Google uses at least two programs to offer such context-based links: AdWords and Keyword Suggestion Tool.

AdWords is Google's program through which advertisers purchase terms (or keywords). When entered as a search term, the keyword triggers the appearance of the advertiser's ad and link. An advertiser's purchase of a particular term causes the advertiser's ad and link to be displayed on the user's screen whenever a searcher launches a Google search based on the purchased search term. Advertisers pay Google based on the number of times Internet users "click" on the advertisement, so as to link to the advertiser's website. . . .

In addition to Adwords, Google also employs Keyword Suggestion Tool, a program that recommends keywords to advertisers to be purchased. The program is designed to improve the effectiveness of advertising by helping advertisers identify keywords related to their area of commerce, resulting in the placement of their ads before users who are likely to be responsive to it. . . .

Once an advertiser buys a particular keyword, Google links the keyword to that advertiser's advertisement. The advertisements consist of a combination of content and a link to the advertiser's webpage. Google displays these advertisements on the search result page either in the right margin or in a horizontal band immediately above the column of relevance-based search results. These advertisements are generally associated with a label, which says "sponsored link." Rescuecom alleges, however, that a user might easily be misled to believe that the advertisements which appear on the screen are in fact part of the relevance-based search result and that the appearance of a competitor's ad and link in response to a searcher's search for Rescuecom is likely to cause trademark confusion as to affiliation, origin, sponsorship, or approval of service. This can occur, according to the Complaint, because Google fails to label the ads in a manner which would clearly identify them as purchased ads rather than search results. The Complaint alleges that when the sponsored links appear in a horizontal bar at the top of the search results, they may appear to the searcher to be the first, and therefore the most relevant, entries responding to the search, as opposed to paid advertisements. . . .

Many of Rescuecom's competitors advertise on the Internet. Through its Keyword Suggestion Tool, Google has recommended the Rescuecom trademark to Rescuecom's competitors as a search term to be purchased. Rescuecom's competitors, some responding to Google's recommendation, have purchased Rescuecom's trademark as a keyword in Google's AdWords program, so that whenever a user launches a search for the term "Rescuecom," seeking to be connected to Rescuecom's website, the competitors' advertisement and link will appear on the searcher's screen. This practice allegedly allows Rescuecom's competitors to deceive and divert users searching for Rescuecom's website. According to Rescuecom's allegations, when a Google user launches a search for the term "Rescuecom" because the searcher wishes to purchase Rescuecom's services, links to websites of its competitors will appear on the searcher's screen in a manner likely to cause the searcher to believe mistakenly that a competitor's advertisement (and website link) is sponsored by, endorsed by, approved by, or affiliated with Rescuecom. . . .

I.   GOOGLE'S USE OF RESCUECOM'S MARK WAS A "USE IN COMMERCE"

Our court ruled in *1-800* that a complaint fails to state a claim under the Lanham Act unless it alleges that the defendant has made "use in commerce" of the plaintiff's trademark as the term "use in commerce" is defined in 15 U.S.C. §1127. The district court believed that this case was on all fours with *1-800*, and that its dismissal was required for the same reasons as given in *1-800*. We believe the cases are materially different. . . .

In *1-800*, the plaintiff alleged that the defendant infringed the plaintiff's trademark through its proprietary software, which the defendant freely distributed to computer users who would download and install the program on their computer. The program provided contextually relevant advertising to the user by generating pop-up advertisements to the user depending on the website or search term the user entered in his browser. *Id.* at 404-05. For example, if a user typed "eye care" into his browser, the defendant's program would randomly display a pop-up advertisement of a company engaged in the field of eye care. Similarly, if the searcher launched a search for a particular company engaged in eye care, the defendant's program would display the pop-up ad of a company associated with eye care. *See id.* at 412. The pop-up ad appeared in a separate browser window from the website the user accessed, and the defendant's brand was displayed in the window frame surrounding the ad, so that there was no confusion as to the nature of the pop-up as an advertisement, nor as to the fact that the defendant, not the trademark owner, was responsible for displaying the ad, in response to the particular term searched. *Id.* at 405. . . .

1-800 explained why the defendant's program, which might randomly trigger pop-up advertisements upon a searcher's input of the plaintiff's website address, did not constitute a "use in commerce," as defined in §1127. *Id.* at 408-09. In explaining why the plaintiff's mark was not "used or displayed in the sale or advertising of services," *1-800* pointed out that, under the defendant's program, advertisers could not request or purchase keywords to trigger their ads. *Id.* at 409, 412. Even if an advertiser wanted to display its advertisement to a searcher using the plaintiff's trademark as a search term, the defendant's program did not offer this possibility. In fact, the defendant "did not disclose the proprietary contents of [its] directory to its advertising clients. . . . " *Id.* at 409. In addition to not selling trademarks of others to its customers to trigger these ads, the defendant did not "otherwise manipulate which category-related advertisement will pop up in response to any particular terms on the internal directory." *Id.* at 411. The display of a particular advertisement was controlled by the category associated with the website or keyword, rather than the website or keyword itself. The defendant's program relied upon categorical associations such as "eye care" to select a pop-up ad randomly from a predefined list of ads appropriate to that category. To the extent that an advertisement for a competitor of the plaintiff was displayed when a user opened the plaintiff's website, the trigger to display the ad was not based on the defendant's sale or recommendation of a particular trademark.

The present case contrasts starkly with those important aspects of the *1-800* decision. First, in contrast to *1-800*, where we emphasized that the defendant made no use whatsoever of the plaintiff's trademark, here what Google is recommending and selling to its advertisers is Rescuecom's trademark. Second, in contrast with the facts of *1-800* where the defendant did not "use or display," much less sell, trademarks as search terms to its advertisers, here Google displays, offers, and sells Rescuecom's mark to Google's advertising customers when selling its advertising services. In addition, Google encourages the purchase of Rescuecom's mark through its Keyword Suggestion Tool. . . .

Google, supported by amici, argues that *1-800* suggests that the inclusion of a trademark in an internal computer directory cannot constitute trademark use. . . . This over-reads the *1-800* decision. First, regardless of whether Google's use of Rescuecom's mark in its internal search algorithm could constitute an actionable trademark use, Google's recommendation and sale of Rescuecom's mark to its advertising customers are not internal uses. Furthermore, *1-800* did not imply that use of a trademark in a software program's internal directory precludes a finding of trademark use. . . . We did not imply in *1-800* that an alleged infringer's use of a trademark in an internal software program insulates the alleged infringer from a charge of infringement, no matter how likely the use is to cause confusion in the marketplace. If we were to adopt Google and its amici's argument, the operators of search engines would be free to use trademarks in ways designed to deceive and cause consumer confusion. This is surely neither within the intention nor the letter of the Lanham Act.

[The court remands the case for discussion of the consumer confusion issues.]

COMMENTS AND QUESTIONS

1. The District Court in *Rescuecom* had held that the *1-800* precedent compelled a finding that Google did not infringe Rescuecom's trademarks. In particular, the District Court noted that the use of the marks by Google, even in recommending terms to advertisers, was an "internal use" and therefore not a "use in commerce" as contemplated by the Lanham Act. How does the Second Circuit Court of Appeals distinguish the *1-800* case in *Rescuecom*? Do you agree with the Second Circuit Court's approach, or the District Court's approach?

2. The Second Circuit court in *Rescuecom* does not decide whether Google's practices cause consumer confusion. Do you think there is a good argument in favor of a court finding consumer confusion for trademark infringement purposes on the facts of this case?

3. Does the Second Circuit in *Rescuecom* characterize Google's use of Rescuecom's trademark as an *internal* or an *external* use? What is the significance of the distinction?

4. In Tiffany (NJ) Inc. v. eBay, 576 F. Supp. 2d 463 (2008), the court held that it was possible that eBay could be prima facie liable for trademark infringement for purchasing sponsored advertising links using the "Tiffany" trademark, and by advertising Tiffany's products for sale on its auction site. However, the court held that eBay had a valid nominative use defense because there was no other way it could effectively refer to the availability of Tiffany's products on eBay.

5. Could you draft legislation to set out clear rules as to when keyword advertising schemes involving trademarked terms might constitute trademark infringements?

B. COPYRIGHT IN CYBERSPACE

1. Copyright Basics

In the preceding section, we explored the extent to which property rights could be created in the means for identifying people, businesses, and places in cyberspace. This section will explore the extent to which copyright law creates property rights in the content of cyberspace: text, graphics, sounds, and video. In the United States, Congress's authority to enact copyright and patent laws is derived from Article I, section 8, clause 8 of the U.S. Constitution, which grants Congress the power "to promote the progress of science and useful arts, by securing for limited times to authors and inventors the exclusive right to their respective writings and discoveries." Since 1790, Congress has chosen to exercise this constitutional power by recognizing limited monopolies for creators of copyrighted works.

The justification for these limited monopolies is based upon the "public good" characteristics of original works of authorship. A public good is generally defined by two traits. First, once produced, it is virtually inexhaustible. This means that additional people may enjoy a public good at no added cost. Second, it is difficult to exclude people from enjoying the good. Because of these characteristics, a public good is vulnerable to the problems of "free riding"; some might enjoy the benefits without internalizing the costs of producing the good. As a result, if the funding of the good is left to the private market, free riding may lead to the underproduction of the good.

As required by the Constitution, the copyright monopoly has always been restricted. Congress has only granted copyright owners specific exclusive rights; namely, the right to: (1) reproduce the copyrighted work; (2) prepare derivative works based upon the copyrighted work; (3) distribute copies of the copyrighted work to the public; (4) perform the copyrighted work publicly; (5) display the copyrighted work publicly; and (6) to digitally transmit performances.[4] These rights are limited in time. Further, these rights are balanced by other statutory and doctrinal limitations including the first sale and fair use doctrines. The first sale doctrine limits a copyright owner's ability to control a copyrighted work to the first sale of that work. Similarly, the doctrine of fair use permits certain uses of copyrighted works that would otherwise violate the copyright owner's exclusive rights. Fair use includes use of copyrighted works for the purposes of criticism, comment, news reporting, teaching, scholarship, research, and parody.

2. The Digital Dilemma

Digital technology and the exponential growth of the Internet threaten to upset copyright law's delicate balance. Once converted to digital files, many works of authorship including text, music, graphics, and video can be flawlessly copied at almost no cost. Subsequent copies can be made with no degradation in the quality of these copies as happens in the analog world. Once in digital form, these same files can then be distributed globally using the Internet at virtually no cost. Technology, therefore, makes it possible for anyone with a computer to become a global distributor of copyrighted works. The threat posed by digital technology was the focus of a report from the Clinton White House, Intellectual Property and the National Information Infrastructure (1995), also known as the "White Paper."

Digital technology, however, can also be used to protect copyrighted works to a degree never before imaginable. With the aid of encryption, digital files can be programmed to: (1) prevent copying; (2) play only a specified number of times; (3) erase after a certain date; or (4) automatically bill users' credit cards every time a file is accessed. Some, including the Clinton Administration in the White Paper, viewed the control that this technology offers as the logical next step in copyright's evolution by allowing copyright owners to control all uses of copyrighted works.[5] Others argue that in light of this control, the protection afforded by copyright is no longer necessary.[6] Technology rather than copyright will protect expression. Critics of this technology fear that it has the potential to give copyright owners too much control, upsetting the delicate balance between the copyright owners' incentives and the public right to access and use those works.[7]

---

4. 17 U.S.C. §106.

5. *See* Paul Goldstein, *Copyright's Highway: The Law and Lore of Copyright from Gutenberg to the Celestial Jukebox* (1994).

6. *See* Eric Schlachter, *The Intellectual Property Renaissance in Cyberspace: Why Copyright Law Could Be Unimportant on the Internet,* 12 Berkeley Tech. L.J. 15 (1997).

7. *See* Jessica Litman, *Digital Copyright* (2001); Jacqueline Lipton, *Solving the Digital Piracy Puzzle: Disaggregating Fair Use from the DMCA's Anti-Device Provisions,* 19 Harv. J.L. & Tech. 111 (2005);

The following materials explore the digital dilemma and how copyright law is currently being used to control content in cyberspace. As you study the materials, continue to ask yourself, to what extent can preexisting rules be applied to the Internet? Are new rules necessary? What are the underlying values and principles we are seeking to protect? Are those values and principles better served by other legal regimes? Technology? Emerging social norms? Market forces?

The debate over copyright's role in cyberspace is not an academic one. Since the advent of the Internet, Congress has taken steps to protect copyright in a digital world including passage of the Digital Millennium Copyright Act (DMCA).[8] This section begins with an article from Pamela Samuelson summarizing the so-called copyright maximalists' legislative agenda. As you study the materials in this section, consider whether Congress and the courts have adopted the agenda described by Samuelson.

PAMELA SAMUELSON
THE COPYRIGHT GRAB

Wired (Jan. 1996)

Browsing through a borrowed book, lending a magazine to a friend, copying a news article for your files — all seem innocuous enough. But the Clinton administration plans to make such activities illegal for works distributed via digital networks. If legislation recommended in its white paper "Intellectual Property and the National Information Infrastructure" is enacted, your traditional user rights to browse, share, or make private non-commercial copies of copyrighted works will be rescinded. Not only that, your online service provider will be forced to snoop through your files, ready to cut you off and turn you in if it finds any unlicensed material there. The white paper regards digital technology as so threatening to the future of the publishing industry that the public must be stripped of all the rights copyright law has long recognized — including the rights of privacy. Vice President Al Gore has promised that the National Information Infrastructure (NII) will dramatically enhance public access to information; now we find out that it will be available only on a pay-per-use basis. . . .

. . . In the three centuries of its existence, copyright law has focused on regulating public and commercial activities, such as the commercial reproduction of physical objects embodying the copyrighted work (books, for example) for intended dissemination to the public, the commercial distribution of physical copies to the public, and public performances of dramas, music, and the like. (Singing a copyrighted tune in the shower is not an infringement because it is a private performance of the music.)

Jerome Reichman, Graeme Dinwoodie, & Pamela Samuelson, *A Reverse Notice and Takedown Regime to Enable Public Interest Uses of Technically Protected Copyright Works*, 22 Berkeley Tech. L.J. 981 (2007), Jessica Litman, *Lawful Personal Use*, 85 Tex. L. Rev. 1871 (2007).
 8. Pub. L. No. 105-304, 112 Stat. 2860 (codified as amended in scattered sections of 17 U.S.C.).

Some publishers, however, want to control not only all public and commercial uses of their works, but all private uses as well. They assert that this would better fulfill the constitutional purpose of copyright, because the greater the financial return to them, the greater will be their incentive to make works available to the public. . . . Now a group of major motion picture producers, sound recording companies, and print publishers have figured out a way to turn the threat of digital technology into an opportunity. Under this plan, they would retain all of their rights under existing law and quietly attain a host of new ones. . . .

The white paper seeks to implement the maximalist agenda partly by rewriting the copyright statute and partly by aggressively interpreting existing law. . . .

1. The exclusive right to read: The white paper seeks to extend publisher rights to control browsing and other uses of copyrighted works in digital form by an expansive interpretation of existing law. It observes that in order to browse a digital work, the user's computer must make a temporary copy of that work in its random access memory; that temporary copy, it claims, is an infringing reproduction of the work unless it has been licensed or is otherwise privileged. The white paper relies on an appellate court decision that treated the unlicensed loading of a computer program in RAM as an infringing reproduction. But it knowingly omits reference to the legislative history of the current copyright statute, in which Congress specifically stated that the temporary storage of a copyrighted work in a computer's memory should not be regarded as an infringing reproduction. . . .

2. The exclusive right to transmit: Lehman has been leading the drive for adoption of the white paper's proposed NII Copyright Protection Act on the theory that it is unclear under existing law whether a digital transmission is a distribution of a copy to the public. . . . But the white paper admits that the courts have already regarded digital transmissions of copyrighted works as infringing distributions in some cases, so either there is an unstated purpose behind this proposal, or else it is just a smoke screen to deflect attention from the real kickers in the package. Lehman is probably seeking the digital transmission amendments because his pals among the maximalists want to be able to control all performances and displays of copyrighted works, not just the public performances and public displays that the existing law grants to copyright owners.

3. The end of fair-use rights: The white paper attempts to eliminate fair-use rights by interpreting existing law as though fair use has no application when a use can be licensed (. . . maximalists believe all uses can be licensed). Copyright maximalists, in fact, regard all unauthorized copying of copyrighted work as theft. This theory has, however, been rejected by the U.S. Supreme Court. Universal and Disney once sued Sony to stop distribution of its

videotape machines, arguing that private noncommercial copying of their motion pictures by purchasers of Betamax machines was no more excusable than the theft of a necklace because the thief intended to wear it only at home for noncommercial purposes. The Supreme Court pointed out that the person who steals a necklace deprives its owner of possession and use of the item, whereas the copying of programs off the air "does not even remotely entail comparable consequences for the copyright owner." The Court held that it was fair use for consumers to copy programs off the air for time-shifting purposes. Indeed, the Court said that private, noncommercial copying should be presumed fair use. . . .

The notion that fair-use rights apply only when no licensing market exists is neither historically accurate nor good public policy. It ignores some important free speech and related public interest functions of fair use that were recognized in [other] cases. . . .

4. Eliminating first-sale rights for digitally transmitted documents: Copyright owners have historically been entitled to control only the first sale of copies of a work to the public. After that, the consumer who has bought the copy can share it with a friend, give it away, or resell it. (Libraries rely on first-sale rights to lend copies of books to the public.) Consumers would expect the same rule to apply if the copy was electronic. But the white paper says that sharing your copy of an electronic work with a friend is illegal because, in order to send that copy to your friend, your computer will have to make a copy of the document; and since that copy hasn't been authorized by the copyright owner, an infringing reproduction of the work has taken place. . . .

5. Helping documents spy on you: The white paper anticipates that publishers will want to attach copyright management information to digital forms of their works. It defines copyright management information as "the name and other identifying information of the author of a work, the name and other identifying information of the copyright owner, terms and conditions for uses of the work, and such other information as the Register of Copyrights may prescribe by regulation." It proposes to protect this information against tampering by making it illegal to knowingly remove or alter copyright management information or to distribute copies of works whose information has been tampered with. Money damages and criminal penalties would await violators.

While one can question whether it's necessary to make tampering with copyright management information a crime (much less a felony), this provision seems relatively innocuous at first blush. I didn't start worrying about it until I heard proponents talking about how copyright management information systems might be implemented. Some favor making these systems "dumb," while others favor making them "smart." Dumb systems would simply identify the work with a digital equivalent of the ISBN numbers used in the book world today. Smart ones would, among other things, have the ability to secretly report back to the copyright owner via the network on what the user was doing with the work, and the ability to search the consumer's hard disk and report back on what else was there. The Microsoft registration wizard may be just the beginning of the intrusive snooping to which copyright owners will be prone—only, in the future, it won't be possible to say no, and any effort you make to block these intrusions may make you a felon.

Plans are also underway to develop secure processors that won't permit copying of digital works unless their copyright management information authorizes it. Some publishers are already talking about getting governments to mandate inclusion of these secure processors in all reprography technologies (including photocopy machines). The precedent they offer for this mandate is the serial copy management system requirement imposed on manufacturers of digital audio-tape machines. They conveniently forget that the law regulating these machines does not ban all unauthorized copying; it permits consumers to make first-generation copies but not multiple secondary reproductions identical in quality to the digital material from which they are derived. . . .

6. Outlawing decryption: Many copyright owners are planning to protect digital forms of their products by technological means such as encryption. To ensure the security of this technological protection, the white paper recommends the following legislation: "No person shall import, manufacture, or distribute any device, product or component incorporated into a device or product, or offer or perform any service, the primary purpose or effect of which is to avoid, bypass, remove, deactivate, or otherwise circumvent, without the authority of the copyright owner or the law, any process, treatment, mechanism, or system which prevents or inhibits the violation of any of the exclusive rights of the copyright owner under section 106."

Civil penalties for violation of this law will include having to pay statutorily established damages and having any equipment used in the process (your computer, for example) impounded. While one can understand the desire to prevent decryption for the purposes of redistribution and profit, the provision doesn't require either of these as a precondition for liability. Merely manufacturing or distributing a technology that can be used to undo a system that a copyright owner has adopted to protect its work seems sufficient to incur liability.

Although the white paper doesn't say so, this legislation would overturn a second ruling in the Supreme Court's Sony Betamax decision, which held that copyright owners cannot stop distribution of a technology as long as it has a substantial noninfringing use.

In addition, the language of this proposed law is so broad and so vague that it can be construed as outlawing many activities widely believed to be lawful. For example, some software publishers will argue that the decompilation of mass-marketed software in order to get access to interface information violates this provision, because the decompiler would be performing a service whose primary purpose and effect was to bypass the technological system the program's developer had adopted to protect its program (distribution of the program in object code form in order to maintain the contents of the program as a trade secret). Although Sega v. Accolade and another federal appellate court decision have affirmed the right of software developers to decompile software for compatibility purposes, the white paper doesn't mention the decompilation and interoperability case law. Lehman and the maximalist software publishers who used to be his clients insist that decompilation is and should be illegal. They are hoping to overturn the decompilation case law indirectly by the white paper's endorsement of some changes to commercial law that would validate common terms in shrink-wrap licenses, such as prohibitions on decompilation. . . .

What the white paper doesn't mention is that previous industry attempts to protect copyrighted works in digital form by technological means failed in the marketplace as well as the courts. Users, who often felt there were legitimate reasons for them to have access to an unrestricted version of a program, created a demand for programs that could defeat software copy-protection systems. Litigation soon ensued. Vault, whose copy-protection software could be defeated through use of Quaid's unlocking program, sued Quaid to try to stop distribution of the latter's software. Vault relied in part on a Louisiana law intended to validate common terms of software shrink-wrap licenses. But because Quaid's software allowed purchasers of application programs to exercise rights conferred on them by copyright law to make backup copies and modifications to the software, the court decided that what Quaid had done was lawful. To the extent that the Louisiana law might stop users from exercising their rights under copyright law, the court decided the state law conflicted with the purposes of federal law and was unenforceable. The message of the marketplace was equally clear: Software developers eventually abandoned the distribution of copy-protected software because it was unpopular with consumers. Even though the market for locking and unlocking software died out — making it easy to copy software in digital form — the software industry as a whole has thrived.

7. Turning online service providers into cops: The white paper asserts that every online service provider is already liable for all copyright infringement committed by its users, regardless of whether the service has reason to know about the infringement or takes reasonable steps to ensure that it won't occur. . . .

Some commentators have argued that imposing a strict liability rule on online service providers is inconsistent with the public policy purposes underlying copyright law because it will chill so many noninfringing online exchanges of information. If online service providers have to monitor everything users do, they will artificially impose centralized structures of control over user communications. The danger that overzealous copyright owners will sue online service providers in order to censor online communications has already evidenced itself in the ongoing Religious Technology Center and Bridge Publications Inc. v. Netcom case. (The copyright holder and publisher, respectively, of Church of Scientology materials have sued Netcom and a church dissident for copyright and trade secret violations because the dissident used his Netcom account to post church teachings. See *Wired* 3.12, at 172.)

The white paper is quite frank in its determination that online service providers should become centralized control centers to enforce copyright law. "They—and perhaps only they—are in a position to know the identity and activities of their subscribers and to stop unlawful activities. And, although indemnification from their subscribers may not reimburse them to the full extent of their liability and other measures may add to their costs of doing business, they are still in a better position to prevent or stop infringement than the copyright owner. Between these two relatively innocent parties, the best policy is to hold the service provider liable." This statement, however, ignores the privacy interests of users, as well as serious questions about whether it is technically feasible for online services with millions of subscribers to do the continuous monitoring of user accounts that copyright owners might like. The white paper acts as though the interests of copyright owners so override other, competing interests that it isn't even worth mentioning what the other interests are, let alone trying to balance them against the copyright owner interests.

8. Teaching children not to share: To ensure that future generations are broken of the habit of thinking that it's OK to share copies of copyrighted works with a friend, the white paper offers examples of lessons about copyright that could be taught as early as kindergarten and as late as college. The general theme of these lessons, in order not to be too negative, would be, "Just say yes" to licensing. (It actually says this.)

Problem 6.0

While you are still strategizing how to handle the various trademark issues, StarttUp's technology staff informs you of two new concerns. First, in light of the online music cases, your investors have expressed concern about the potential liability for users trading music and movies through StarttUp's services. While no one has complained to you about this, you are aware that file sharing occurs through the StarttUp network. In fact, many members of your staff play MP3 files at work that they received through your bulletin boards. As an Internet service provider, what is your responsibility?

Second, Alan and Barbara are considering whether they should implement sophisticated search engine technology into their online service packages. In particular, they want to emulate Google's search engine functionality to enable customers to conduct text-based searches as well as searches for online images, and eventually even video files. What legal issues would they have to consider in terms of potential copyright liability if they implemented such a service?

Problem 6.1

Cora has also sought your advice on some copyright issues relating to the Gals On-Line blog. First, she has been encouraging her co-bloggers to insert graphics and video files into their blog postings to make the blog more visually interesting. However, Barbara has suggested to her that she might want to think carefully about this policy in terms of concerns about potential copyright infringement.

Second, she has become aware that some other blogs are reproducing blog entries from Gals On-Line without attributing them to the original authors or to the Gals On-Line blog. This usually happens when the authors of another blog find a post on Cora's blog particularly interesting and decide to cut and paste it to their blog rather than hyperlinking to it. While Cora and her co-bloggers are flattered by the interest that the copied blog posts are generating, they would like to take advantage of this interest in terms of increased readership to their own blog, rather than to the copyists' blogs. Advise Cora on these issues.

3. Copyright Infringement

As discussed earlier, copyright law grants the owner of copyright six exclusive rights including the rights to reproduce and distribute copies of the copyrighted work.[9] When another person exercises any of these rights without the copyright owner's authorization, that person is considered to have infringed the owner's copyright unless the use is considered fair use or subject to another exception under copyright law. With respect to copyright infringement, Internet distribution of copyrighted works raises two principal questions for copyright law: 1) when is a work reproduced in cyberspace? and 2) who is responsible for the reproduction, distribution, and display of works that occur on the various computer networks that make up the Internet? The following materials explore these two questions.

a) Reproducing and Modifying Digital Works

For several decades, it has been accepted that computer software is copyrightable.[10] However, in the early days of the personal computer revolution, it was not inevitable that this would be the case. Many commentators critiqued the use of copyright as a legal protection for software code in the latter part of the twentieth century. In particular, there were concerns about what aspects of

---

9. 17 U.S.C. §106(1) & (3).
10. *See* discussion in Marshall Leaffer, *Understanding Copyright Law* 104-05 (2005).

software would be protected by copyright: source code, object code,[11] and/or graphical user interfaces generated by running software programs.[12] It is now apparent that all of these aspects of software are protected, at least to some degree, by copyright law.[13]

In the seminal case of MAI Systems Corp v. Peak Computer, Inc, 991 F.2d 511 (9th Cir. 1993), the court held that copies of software are made for the purposes of copyright law even when a computer runs the software in its internal memory. This is because, in order to run the software, a copy of the software must be generated in the computer's memory. In *MAI Systems*, the relevant copies were made in the course of a workshop running computer software to diagnose problems with computers and repair them. In coming to this determination, the court considered the definitions of "copies" in 17 U.S.C. §101 where copies are defined as: "material objects, other than phonorecords, in which a work is fixed by any method now known or later developed, and from which the work can be perceived, reproduced, or otherwise communicated, either directly or with the aid of a machine or device." For the purposes of this definition, the statute defines "fixed" as follows: "A work is "fixed" in a tangible medium of expression when its embodiment in a copy or phonorecord, by or under the authority of the author, is sufficiently permanent or stable to permit it to be perceived, reproduced, or otherwise communicated for a period of more than transitory duration." (17 U.S.C. §101). The court in *MAI* held that temporary copies of software run in a computer's Random Access Memory (or RAM) are sufficiently permanent and stable to meet the copyright act's concept of a "copy" for copyright infringement purposes. Thus, the upshot of the court's decision is that any copy of a program even temporarily loaded into a computer's memory is a copy for the purposes of the copyright act. This potentially gives copyright law a very broad reach online.

To alleviate concerns about copyright law potentially over-reaching into the area of computer technology as a result of decisions like *MAI*, Congress inserted new provisions into the copyright act to create exceptions from copyright liability for certain operations routinely performed on computers that involved incidental creation of copies of software. These provisions state that it is not an infringement of a copyright holder's exclusive rights in a

---

11. For a basic discussion of the difference between source code and object code, see *id.*, 106 (most computer software is written in source code which is intelligible to humans; this is then translated or compiled by the computer into object code which consists of digital zeroes and ones which is generally not intelligible to humans, but is the only way a computer can read relevant instructions).

12. *See*, for example, Pamela Samuelson, Randall Davis, Mitchell Kapor & Jerome Reichman, *A Manifesto Concerning the Legal Protection of Computer Programs*, 94 Colum. L. Rev. 2308 (1994); Jane Ginsburg, *Four Reasons and a Paradox: The Manifest Superiority of Copyright Over Sui Generis Protection of Computer Software*, 94 Colum. L. Rev. 2559 (1994); Peter Menell, *An Analysis of the Scope of Copyright Protection for Application Programs*, 41 Stan. L. Rev. 1045 (1989); John Swinson, *Copyright or Patent or Both: An Algorithmic Approach to Computer Software Protection*, 5 Harv. J.L. & Tech. 145 (1991); Arthur R. Miller, *Copyright Protection for Computer Programs, Databases and Computer-Generated Works: Is There Anything New Since CONTU?*, 106 Harv. L. Rev. 977 (1993); Jacqueline Lipton, *IP's Problem Child: Shifting the Paradigms for Software Protection*, 58 Hastings L.J. 205 (2006).

13. *See* discussion in Leaffer, *supra* note 10, at 105-11.

computer program to: (a) make a copy or adaptation of a computer program as an essential step in the utilization of the computer program in conjunction with a machine provided that the copy is used in no other manner;[14] (b) make a copy or adaptation of a computer program for archival purposes only provided that all archival copies are destroyed in the event that continued possession of the computer program should cease to be rightful;[15] or (c) make or authorize the making of a copy of a computer program if such copy is made solely by virtue of the activation of a machine that lawfully contains an authorized copy of the computer program, for purposes only of maintenance or repair of that machine, provided that the new copy is used in no other manner and is destroyed immediately after the maintenance or repair is completed.[16]

Although the Congressional intent in adopting these provisions appears straightforward, problems of statutory interpretation have arisen in applying them in practice. In Krause v. Titleserv, 402 F.3d 119 (2d Cir. 2005), for example, the court struggled to apply the provisions of §117(a)(1) dealing with a defendant company making updates to a program the plaintiff had written for them in order to effectively utilize the program after their relations with the contract programmer had ended. The court ultimately held that the defendant was authorized to make the updates and had not infringed the plaintiff's copyright, even where the defendants used the programs in servers that they shared with some third party clients. The third party clients were not making any independent new use of the programs but were merely using them for the purposes for which they had originally been designed by the plaintiff. The use of the programs in this way was the kind of use contemplated when the programs were first written for the defendants. Similarly, in Storage Technology Corp. v. Custom Hardware Engineering & Consulting, 421 F.3d 1307 (Fed. Cir. 2005), the copyright owner of software designed to run digital storage libraries attempted to distinguish between "functional code" and "maintenance code" arguing that only the former fell within the statutory exceptions created by §§117(a) & (c). In rejecting this argument, the court noted:

> In enacting *section 117(c)*, Congress gave some indication of what it considered to be "necessary for the machine to be activated." Specifically, the House Report on *section 117(c)* noted that software is necessary for the machine to be activated if it "need[s] to be so loaded in order for the machine to be turned on." H.R. Rep. No. 105-551, pt. 1, at 28. As examples of software that need not be loaded in order for the machine to function, the Report listed programs marketed as separate products that load into RAM along with the operating system or software that the owner of the machine has independently configured the computer to load during initialization. *Id*. Therefore, separate "freestanding programs" that load into RAM upon startup clearly may not be accessed under *section 117(c)(2)*.

---

14. 17 U.S.C. §117(a)(1).
15. 17 U.S.C. §117(a)(2).
16. 17 U.S.C. §117(c)(1).

Congress's clearest indication of what it considered to be "necessary for the machine to be activated," however, is found not in *section 117(c)*, but in *section 117(d)*. As we have noted, *section 117(d)* defines repair and maintenance in terms of allowing the system to work "in accordance with its original specifications and any changes to those specifications authorized for that machine." Thus, the service provider must be able to cause the machine to boot up in order to determine if it "works in accordance with its original specifications." Accessing software programs, such as freestanding diagnosis and utility programs, that are not needed to boot up the computer and make that determination, goes too far because access to those programs is not strictly necessary to verify that the computer is "working in accordance with its original specifications."

In some instances, it may be difficult to determine whether particular software is necessary to make the computer function and to ascertain whether the computer is working properly. In this case, however, both parties agree that the maintenance code is so entangled with the functional code that the entire code must be loaded into RAM for the machine to function at all. That is, loading the maintenance code into RAM is necessary for the Management or Control Unit "to be turned on." Contrary to the dissent's position, the fact that the maintenance code has other functions, such as diagnosing malfunctions in the equipment, is irrelevant. Moreover, the possibility that StorageTek could have written the maintenance code as a separate, "freestanding" program that would not have been needed to start the machine does not affect the statutory analysis of the system that StorageTek in fact created. Finally, although the maintenance code can be reconfigured to perform fewer functions, as the dissent points out, what StorageTek can do with the maintenance code after the system boots up is irrelevant. As the statutory text and legislative history make clear, the phrase "necessary for the machine to be activated" refers to the portion of code that must be copied in order for the machine "to be turned on." In this case, copying the maintenance code into RAM is indispensable for the machine to be turned on or activated; its functionality (or lack thereof) after bootup is moot.

421 F.3d at 1314.

THE CARTOON NETWORK AND CABLE NEWS NETWORK v. CSC HOLDINGS AND CABLEVISION SYSTEMS CORPORATION

536 F.3d 121 (2008)

JOHN M. WALKER, JR., Circuit Judge:

Defendant-Appellant Cablevision Systems Corporation ("Cablevision") wants to market a new "Remote Storage" Digital Video Recorder system ("RS-DVR"), using a technology akin to both traditional, set-top digital video recorders, like TiVo ("DVRs"), and the video-on-demand ("VOD") services provided by many cable companies. Plaintiffs-Appellees produce copyrighted movies and television programs that they provide to Cablevision pursuant to numerous licensing agreements. They contend that Cablevision, through the operation of its RS-DVR system as proposed, would directly infringe their copyrights both by making unauthorized reproductions, and by engaging in public performances, of their copyrighted works. . . .

Today's television viewers increasingly use digital video recorders ("DVRs") instead of video cassette recorders ("VCRs") to record television programs and play them back later at their convenience. DVRs generally store recorded programming on an internal hard drive rather than a cassette. But, as this case demonstrates, the generic term "DVR" actually refers to a growing number of different devices and systems. Companies like TiVo sell a stand-alone DVR device that is typically connected to a user's cable box and television much like a VCR. Many cable companies also lease to their subscribers "set-top storage DVRs," which combine many of the functions of a standard cable box and a stand-alone DVR in a single device.

In March 2006, Cablevision, an operator of cable television systems, announced the advent of its new "Remote Storage DVR System." As designed, the RS-DVR allows Cablevision customers who do not have a stand-alone DVR to record cable programming on central hard drives housed and maintained by Cablevision at a "remote" location. RS-DVR customers may then receive playback of those programs through their home television sets, using only a remote control and a standard cable box equipped with the RS-DVR software. Cablevision notified its content providers, including plaintiffs, of its plans to offer RS-DVR, but it did not seek any license from them to operate or sell the RS-DVR.

Plaintiffs, which hold the copyrights to numerous movies and television programs, sued Cablevision for declaratory and injunctive relief. They alleged that Cablevision's proposed operation of the RS-DVR would directly infringe their exclusive rights to both reproduce and publicly perform their copyrighted works. Critically for our analysis here, plaintiffs alleged theories only of direct infringement, not contributory infringement, and defendants waived any defense based on fair use. . . .

I. Operation of the RS-DVR System

Cable companies like Cablevision aggregate television programming from a wide variety of "content providers" — the various broadcast and cable channels that produce or provide individual programs — and transmit those programs into the homes of their subscribers via coaxial cable. At the outset of the transmission process, Cablevision gathers the content of the various television channels into a single stream of data. Generally, this stream is processed and transmitted to Cablevision's customers in real time. Thus, if a Cartoon Network program is scheduled to air Monday night at 8 p.m., Cartoon Network transmits that program's data to Cablevision and other cable companies nationwide at that time, and the cable companies immediately re-transmit the data to customers who subscribe to that channel.

Under the new RS-DVR, this single stream of data is split into two streams. The first is routed immediately to customers as before. The second stream flows into a device called the Broadband Media Router ("BMR"), which buffers the data stream, reformats it, and sends it to the "Arroyo Server," which consists, in relevant part, of two data buffers and a number of high-capacity hard disks.

The entire stream of data moves to the first buffer (the "primary ingest buffer"), at which point the server automatically inquires as to whether any customers want to record any of that programming. If a customer has requested a particular program, the data for that program move from the primary buffer into a secondary buffer, and then onto a portion of one of the hard disks allocated to that customer. As new data flow into the primary buffer, they overwrite a corresponding quantity of data already on the buffer. The primary ingest buffer holds no more than 0.1 seconds of each channel's programming at any moment. Thus, every tenth of a second, the data residing on this buffer are automatically erased and replaced. The data buffer in the BMR holds no more than 1.2 seconds of programming at any time. While buffering occurs at other points in the operation of the RS-DVR, only the BMR buffer and the primary ingest buffer are utilized absent any request from an individual subscriber.

As the district court observed, "the RS-DVR is not a single piece of equipment," but rather "a complex system requiring numerous computers, processes, networks of cables, and facilities staffed by personnel twenty-four hours a day and seven days a week." To the customer, however, the processes of recording and playback on the RS-DVR are similar to that of a standard set-top DVR. Using a remote control, the customer can record programming by selecting a program in advance from an on-screen guide, or by pressing the record button while viewing a given program. A customer cannot, however, record the earlier portion of a program once it has begun. To begin playback, the customer selects the show from an on-screen list of previously recorded programs. The principal difference in operation is that, instead of sending signals from the remote to an on-set box, the viewer sends signals from the remote, through the cable, to the Arroyo Server at Cablevision's central facility. In this respect, RS-DVR more closely resembles a VOD service, whereby a cable subscriber uses his remote and cable box to request transmission of content, such as a movie, stored on computers at the cable company's facility. But unlike a VOD service, RS-DVR users can only play content that they previously requested to be recorded.

Cablevision has some control over the content available for recording: a customer can only record programs on the channels offered by Cablevision (assuming he subscribes to them). Cablevision can also modify the system to limit the number of channels available and considered doing so during development of the RS-DVR.

II. The District Court's Decision

In the district court, plaintiffs successfully argued that Cablevision's proposed system would directly infringe their copyrights in three ways. First, by briefly storing data in the primary ingest buffer and other data buffers integral to the function of the RS-DVR, Cablevision would make copies of protected works and thereby directly infringe plaintiffs' exclusive right of reproduction under the Copyright Act. Second, by copying programs onto the Arroyo Server hard disks (the "playback copies"), Cablevision would again directly infringe the reproduction right. And third, by transmitting the data from the Arroyo Server hard disks to its RS-DVR customers in response to a "playback" request, Cablevision would directly infringe plaintiffs' exclusive right of public performance. *See id.* at 617. Agreeing with all three arguments, the district court awarded summary declaratory judgment to plaintiffs and enjoined Cablevision from operating the RS-DVR system without obtaining licenses from the plaintiff copyright holders.

As to the buffer data, the district court rejected defendants' arguments 1) that the data were not "fixed" and therefore were not "copies" as defined in the Copyright Act, and 2) that any buffer copying was de minimis because the buffers stored only small amounts of data for very short periods of time. In rejecting the latter argument, the district court noted that the "aggregate effect of the buffering" was to reproduce the entirety of Cablevision's programming, and such copying "can hardly be called de minimis."

On the issue of whether creation of the playback copies made Cablevision liable for direct infringement, the parties and the district court agreed that the dispositive question was "*who* makes the copies"? Emphasizing Cablevision's "unfettered discretion" over the content available for recording, its ownership and maintenance of the RS-DVR components, and its "continuing relationship" with its RS-DVR customers, the district court concluded that "the copying of programming to the RS-DVR's Arroyo servers . . . would be done not by the customer but by Cablevision, albeit at the customer's request."

Finally, as to the public performance right, Cablevision conceded that, during the playback, "the streaming of recorded programming in response to a customer's request is a performance." Cablevision contended, however, that the work was performed not by Cablevision, but by the customer, an argument the district court rejected "for the same reasons that [it] reject[ed] the argument that the customer is 'doing' the copying involved in the RS-DVR." Cablevision also argued that such a playback transmission was not "to the public," and therefore not a public performance as defined in the Copyright Act, because it "emanates from a distinct copy of a program uniquely associated with one customer's set-top box and intended for that customer's exclusive viewing in his or her home." The district court disagreed, noting that "Cablevision would transmit *the same program* to members of the public, who may receive the performance at different times, depending on whether they view the program in real time or at a later time as an RS-DVR playback."

DISCUSSION

I. The Buffer Data

. . . The question is whether, by buffering the data that make up a given work, Cablevision "reproduce[s]" that work "in copies," 17 U.S.C. §106(1), and thereby infringes the copyright holder's reproduction right.

"Copies," as defined in the Copyright Act, "are material objects . . . in which a work is fixed by any method . . . and from which the work can be . . . reproduced." *Id.* §101. The Act also provides that a work is " 'fixed' in a tangible medium of expression when its embodiment . . . is sufficiently permanent or stable to permit it to be . . . reproduced . . . *for a period of more than transitory duration." Id.* (emphasis added). We believe that this language plainly imposes two distinct but related requirements: the work must be embodied in a medium, i.e., placed in a medium such that it can be perceived, reproduced, etc., from that medium (the "embodiment requirement"), and it must remain thus embodied "for a period of more than transitory duration" (the "duration requirement"). *See* 2 Melville B. Nimmer & David Nimmer, *Nimmer on Copyright* §8.02[B][3], at 8-32 (2007). Unless both requirements are met, the work is not "fixed" in the buffer, and, as a result, the buffer data is not a "copy" of the original work whose data is buffered.

The district court mistakenly limited its analysis primarily to the embodiment requirement. As a result of this error, once it determined that the buffer data was "[c]learly . . . capable of being reproduced," i.e., that the work was embodied in the buffer, the district court concluded that the work was therefore "fixed" in the buffer, and that a copy had thus been made. *Cablevision I*, 478 F. Supp. 2d at 621-22. In doing so, it relied on a line of cases beginning with *MAI Systems Corp. v. Peak Computer Inc.*, 991 F.2d 511 (9th Cir. 1993). It also relied on the United States Copyright Office's 2001 report on the Digital Millennium Copyright Act, which states, in essence, that an embodiment is fixed "[u]nless a reproduction manifests itself so fleetingly that *it cannot be copied*." U.S. Copyright Office, *DMCA Section 104 Report* 111 (Aug. 2001) ("*DMCA Report*") (emphasis added), *available at* http://www.copyright.gov/reports/studies/dmca/sec-104-report-vol-1.pdf.

The district court's reliance on cases like *MAI Systems* is misplaced. In general, those cases conclude that an alleged copy is fixed without addressing the duration requirement; it does not follow, however, that those cases assume, much less establish, that such a requirement does not exist. Indeed, the duration requirement, by itself, was not at issue in *MAI Systems* and its progeny. As a result, they do not speak to the issues squarely before us here: If a work is only "embodied" in a medium for a period of transitory duration, can it be "fixed" in that medium, and thus a copy? And what constitutes a period "of more than transitory duration"?

In *MAI Systems*, defendant Peak Computer, Inc., performed maintenance and repairs on computers made and sold by MAI Systems. In order to service a customer's computer, a Peak employee had to operate the computer and run the computer's copyrighted operating system software. *See MAI Sys.*, 991 F.2d at 513. The issue in *MAI Systems* was whether, by loading the software into the computer's RAM, the repairman created a "copy" as defined in §101. *See id.* at 517. The resolution of this issue turned on whether the software's embodiment in the computer's RAM was "fixed," within the meaning of the same section. The Ninth Circuit concluded that by showing that Peak loads the software into the RAM and is then able to view the system error log and diagnose the problem with the computer, MAI has adequately shown that the representation created in the RAM is "sufficiently permanent or stable to permit it to be perceived, reproduced, or otherwise communicated for a period of more than transitory duration."

Id. at 518 (quoting 17 U.S.C. §101).

The *MAI Systems* court referenced the "transitory duration" language but did not discuss or analyze it. The opinion notes that the defendants "vigorously" argued that the program's embodiment in the RAM was not a copy, but it does not specify the arguments defendants made. *Id.* at 517. This omission suggests that the parties did not litigate the significance of the "transitory duration" language, and the court therefore had no occasion to address it. This is unsurprising, because it seems fair to assume that in these cases the program was embodied in the RAM for at least several minutes.

Accordingly, we construe *MAI Systems* and its progeny as holding that loading a program into a computer's RAM *can* result in copying that program. We do not read *MAI Systems* as holding that, as a matter of law, loading a program into a form of RAM *always* results in copying. Such a holding would read the "transitory duration" language out of the definition, and we do not believe our sister circuit would dismiss this statutory language without even discussing it. . . .

Cablevision does not seriously dispute that copyrighted works are "embodied" in the buffer. Data in the BMR buffer can be reformatted and transmitted to the other components of the RS-DVR system. Data in the primary ingest buffer can be copied onto the Arroyo hard disks if a user has requested a recording of that data. Thus, a work's "embodiment" in either buffer "is sufficiently permanent or stable to permit it to be perceived, reproduced," (as in the case of the ingest buffer) "or otherwise communicated" (as in the BMR buffer). 17 U.S.C. §101. The result might be different if only a single second of a much longer work was placed in the buffer in isolation. In such a situation, it might be reasonable to conclude that only a minuscule portion of a work, rather than "a work" was embodied in the buffer. Here, however, where every second of an entire work is placed, one second at a time, in the buffer, we conclude that the work is embodied in the buffer.

Does any such embodiment last "for a period of more than transitory duration"? No bit of data remains in any buffer for more than a fleeting 1.2 seconds. And unlike the data in cases like *MAI Systems*, which remained embodied in the computer's RAM memory until the user turned the computer off, each bit of data here is rapidly and automatically overwritten as soon as it is processed. . . . [T]hese facts strongly suggest that the works in this case are embodied in the buffer for only a "transitory" period, thus failing the duration requirement.

. . . Given that the data reside in no buffer for more than 1.2 seconds before being automatically overwritten, and in the absence of compelling arguments to the contrary, we believe that the copyrighted works here are not "embodied" in the buffers for a period of more than transitory duration, and are therefore not "fixed" in the buffers. Accordingly, the acts of buffering in the operation of the RS-DVR do not create copies, as the Copyright Act defines that term. Our resolution of this issue renders it unnecessary for us to determine whether any copies produced by buffering data would be de minimis, and we express no opinion on that question.

COMMENTS AND QUESTIONS

1.   What are the legal and policy implications of *MAI*'s definition of a copy in the networked environment of the Internet? When one considers the number of "copies" created when data is transmitted across the Internet, who may be subject to copyright liability? Why would Congress amend the Copyright Act to permit certain uses after *MAI*, but keep *MAI* in place?

2.   Both *MAI* and *Cablevision* addressed the concept of when a work is sufficiently fixed to constitute a copy under copyright law. *MAI* concludes a work can be sufficiently fixed in a computer's temporary memory, while *Cablevision* concludes that a work is not sufficiently fixed when it is "buffered" that is only a small portion of the work is present for fleeting periods of time.

3.   How does the *Cablevision* court distinguish *MAI* on the definition of the term "fixed" in the context of copyright works? Should the functional differences between Random Access Memory and data buffering lead to different legal implications?

4.   Keeping in mind how the TCP/IP protocol functions, does *Cablevision* change the potential liability of Internet intermediaries?

b) Direct and Indirect Copyright Infringement

Because courts and Congress have adopted a relatively expansive definition of copying in cyberspace, the question of who should be responsible for such copying is of particular importance. As earlier materials discussed, information is distributed throughout the Internet by copying and sending that information through multiple computer networks. While the person at the beginning of this distribution chain is clearly subject to copyright liability,[17] under what circumstances, should other parties to Internet communications be responsible for copyright infringement if at all? These questions become more complex as more and more different types of online intermediaries emerge. Recent cases have considered the extent to which parties such as Internet search

---

17. *See* Playboy Enterprises, Inc. v. Webbworld, Inc., 991 F. Supp. 543 (N.D. Tex. 1997) (holding that a business that gathered digital images from newsgroups and then sold access to those copyrighted images on its own Web site without the authorization of the copyright owner was directly liable for infringement).

engines and online payments systems can be liable indirectly for the primary infringements of those who benefit from their services. Consider the following case law.

PLAYBOY ENTERPRISES, INC. V. FRENA

839 F. Supp. 1552 (M.D. Fla. 1993)

SHLESINGER, District Judge.

Defendant George Frena operates a subscription computer bulletin board service, Techs Warehouse BBS ("BBS"), that distributed unauthorized copies of Plaintiff Playboy Enterprises, Inc.'s ("PEI") copyrighted photographs. BBS is accessible via telephone modem to customers. For a fee, or to those who purchase certain products from Defendant Frena, anyone with an appropriately equipped computer can log onto BBS. Once logged on subscribers may browse through different BBS directories to look at the pictures and customers may also download the high quality computerized copies of the photographs and then store the copied image from Frena's computer onto their home computer. Many of the images found on BBS include adult subject matter. One hundred and seventy of the images that were available on BBS were copies of photographs taken from PEI's copyrighted materials. . . .

Subscribers can upload material onto the bulletin board so that any other subscriber, by accessing their computer, can see that material. Defendant Frena states in his Affidavit filed August 4, 1993, that he never uploaded any of PEI's photographs onto BBS and that subscribers to BBS uploaded the photographs. . . . Defendant Frena states that as soon as he was served with a summons and made aware of this matter, he removed the photographs from BBS and has since that time monitored BBS to prevent additional photographs of PEI from being uploaded. . . .

I. COPYRIGHT INFRINGEMENT

The Copyright Act of 1976 gives copyright owners control over most, if not all, activities of conceivable commercial value. The statute provides that

> the owner of a copyright . . . has the exclusive rights to do and to authorize any of the following: (1) to reproduce the copyrighted work in copies . . . ; (2) to prepare derivative works based upon the copyrighted work; (3) to distribute copies . . . of the copyrighted work to the public . . . and (5) in the case of . . . pictorial . . . works . . . to display the copyrighted work publicly.

17 U.S.C. §106. Engaging in or authorizing any of these categories without the copyright owner's permission violates the exclusive rights of the copyright owner and constitutes infringement of the copyright. *See* 17 U.S.C. §501(a).

To establish copyright infringement, PEI must show ownership of the copyright and "copying" by Defendant Frena, *see Feist Publications, Inc. v. Rural Tel. Serv. Co.*, 499 U.S. 340 (1991); *Southern Bell Tel. & Tel. v. Assoc. Telephone Directory Publishers*, 756 F.2d 801, 810 (11th Cir. 1985).

There is no dispute that PEI owns the copyrights on the photographs in question. PEI owns copyright registrations for each of the 50 issues of Playboy publications that contain the photographs on BBS. . . .

Public distribution of a copyrighted work is a right reserved to the copyright owner, and usurpation of that right constitutes infringement. *See Cable/Home Communication Corp. v. Network Productions, Inc.*, 902 F.2d 829, 843 (11th Cir. 1990). PEI's right under 17 U.S.C. §106(3) to distribute copies to the public has been implicated by Defendant Frena. Section 106(3) grants the copyright owner "the exclusive right to sell, give away, rent or lend any material embodiment of his work." 2 Melville B. Nimmer, Nimmer on Copyright §8.11[A], at 8-124.1 (1993). There is no dispute that Defendant Frena supplied a product containing unauthorized copies of a copyrighted work. It does not matter that Defendant Frena claims he did not make the copies itself. *See* Jay Dratler, Jr., Intellectual Property Law: Commercial, Creative and Industrial Property §6.01[3], at 6-15 (1991).

Furthermore, the "display" rights of PEI have been infringed upon by Defendant Frena. *See* 17 U.S.C. §106(5). The concept of display is broad. *See* 17 U.S.C. §101. It covers "the projection of an image on a screen or other surface by any method, the transmission of an image by electronic or other means, and the showing of an image on a cathode ray tube, or similar viewing apparatus connected with any sort of information storage and retrieval system." H.R. Rep. No. 1476, 94th Cong., 2d Sess. 64 (Sept. 3, 1976), reprinted in 1976 U.S. Code Cong. & Admin. News 5659, 5677. The display right precludes unauthorized transmission of the display from one place to another, for example, by a computer system. . . .

"Display" covers any showing of a "copy" of the work, "either directly or by means of a film, slide, television image or any other device or process." 17 U.S.C. §101. However, in order for there to be copyright infringement, the display must be public. A "public display" is a display "at a place open to the public or . . . where a substantial number of persons outside of a normal circle of family and its social acquaintenances is gathered." 2 Melville B. Nimmer, Nimmer on Copyright §8.14[C], at 8-169 (1993). A place is "open to the public" in this sense even if access is limited to paying customers. 2 Melville B. Nimmer, Nimmer on Copyright §8.14[C], at 8-169 n. 36 (1993); *see Columbia Pictures Indus., Inc. v. Redd Horne Inc.*, 749 F.2d 154 (3d Cir. 1984).

Defendant's display of PEI's copyrighted photographs to subscribers was a public display. Though limited to subscribers, the audience consisted of "a substantial number of persons outside of a normal circle of family and its social acquaintances." 2 Melville B. Nimmer, Nimmer on Copyright §8.14[C], at 8-169 (1993). . . .

There is irrefutable evidence of direct copyright infringement in this case. It does not matter that Defendant Frena may have been unaware of the copyright infringement. Intent to infringe is not needed to find copyright infringement. Intent or knowledge is not an element of infringement, and thus even an innocent infringer is liable for infringement; rather, innocence is significant to a trial court when it fixes statutory damages, which is a remedy equitable in nature. *See D.C. Comics Inc. v. Mini Gift Shop*, 912 F.2d 29 (2d Cir. 1990).

RELIGIOUS TECHNOLOGY CENTER V. NETCOM ONLINE COMMUNICATION SERV., INC.

907 F. Supp. 1361 (N.D. Cal. 1995)

WHYTE, District Judge.

This case concerns an issue of first impression regarding intellectual property rights in cyberspace. Specifically, this order addresses whether the operator of a computer bulletin board service ("BBS"), and the large Internet access provider that allows that BBS to reach the Internet, should be liable for copyright infringement committed by a subscriber of the BBS.

Plaintiffs Religious Technology Center ("RTC") and Bridge Publications, Inc. ("BPI") hold copyrights in the unpublished and published works of L. Ron Hubbard, the late founder of the Church of Scientology ("the Church"). Defendant Dennis Erlich ("Erlich") is a former minister of Scientology turned vocal critic of the Church, whose pulpit is now the Usenet newsgroup alt.religion.scientology ("a.r.s."), an on-line forum for discussion and criticism of Scientology. Plaintiffs maintain that Erlich infringed their copyrights when he posted portions of their works on a.r.s. Erlich gained his access to the Internet through defendant Thomas Klemesrud's ("Klemesrud's") BBS "support.com." Klemesrud is the operator of the BBS, which is run out of his home and has approximately 500 paying users. Klemesrud's BBS is not directly linked to the Internet, but gains its connection through the facilities of defendant Netcom On-Line Communications, Inc. ("Netcom"), one of the largest providers of Internet access in the United States.

After failing to convince Erlich to stop his postings, plaintiffs contacted defendants Klemesrud and Netcom. Klemesrud responded to plaintiffs' demands that Erlich be kept off his system by asking plaintiffs to prove that they owned the copyrights to the works posted by Erlich. However, plaintiffs refused Klemesrud's request as unreasonable. Netcom similarly refused plaintiffs' request that Erlich not be allowed to gain access to the Internet through its system. Netcom contended that it would be impossible to prescreen Erlich's postings and that to kick Erlich off the Internet meant kicking off the hundreds of users of Klemesrud's BBS. Consequently, plaintiffs named Klemesrud and Netcom in their suit against Erlich, although only on the copyright infringement claims. . . .

I.   NETCOM'S MOTION FOR SUMMARY JUDGMENT
OF NONINFRINGEMENT . . .

B.   Copyright Infringement

To establish a claim of copyright infringement, a plaintiff must demonstrate (1) ownership of a valid copyright and (2) "copying" of protectable expression by the defendant. . . . Infringement occurs when a defendant violates one of the exclusive rights of the copyright holder. 17 U.S.C. §501(a). These rights include the right to reproduce the copyrighted work, the right to prepare derivative works, the right to distribute copies to the public, and the right to publicly display the work. 17 U.S.C. §§106(1)-(3) & (5). The court has already determined that plaintiffs have established that they own the copyrights to all of the Exhibit A and B works, except item 4 of Exhibit A. The court also found plaintiffs likely to succeed on their claim that defendant Erlich copied the Exhibit A and B works and was not entitled to a fair use defense. Plaintiffs argue that, although Netcom was not itself the source of any of the infringing materials on its system, it nonetheless should be liable for infringement, either directly, contributorily, or vicariously. Netcom disputes these theories of infringement and further argues that it is entitled to its own fair use defense.

1.   Direct Infringement

Infringement consists of the unauthorized exercise of one of the exclusive rights of the copyright holder delineated in section 106. 17 U.S.C. §501. Direct infringement does not require intent or any particular state of mind,[10] although willfulness is relevant to the award of statutory damages. 17 U.S.C. §504(c). . . .

a.   Undisputed Facts

The parties do not dispute the basic processes that occur when Erlich posts his allegedly infringing messages to a.r.s. Erlich connects to Klemesrud's BBS using a telephone and a modem. Erlich then transmits his messages to Klemesrud's computer, where they are automatically briefly stored. According to a prearranged pattern established by Netcom's software, Erlich's initial act of posting a message to the Usenet results in the automatic copying of Erlich's message from Klemesrud's computer onto Netcom's computer and onto other

---

10. The strict liability for copyright infringement is in contrast to another area of liability affecting online service providers: defamation. Recent decisions have held that where a BBS exercised little control over the content of the material on its service, it was more like a "distributor" than a "republisher" and was thus only liable for defamation on its system where it knew or should have known of the defamatory statements. *Cubby, Inc. v. CompuServe, Inc.*, 776 F. Supp. 135 (S.D.N.Y. 1991). By contrast, a New York state court judge found that Prodigy was a publisher because it held itself out to be controlling the content of its services and because it used software to automatically prescreen messages that were offensive or in bad taste. *Stratton Oakmont, Inc. v. Prodigy Services Co.*, 1995 WL 323710, THE RECORDER, June 1, 1995, at 7 (excerpting May 24, 1995 Order Granting Partial Summary Judgment to Plaintiffs).

computers on the Usenet. In order to ease transmission and for the convenience of Usenet users, Usenet servers maintain postings from newsgroups for a short period of time — eleven days for Netcom's system and three days for Klemesrud's system. Once on Netcom's computers, messages are available to Netcom's customers and Usenet neighbors, who may then download the messages to their own computers. Netcom's local server makes available its postings to a group of Usenet servers, which do the same for other servers until all Usenet sites worldwide have obtained access to the postings, which takes a matter of hours. Francis Decl. §5.

Unlike some other large on-line service providers, such as CompuServe, America Online, and Prodigy, Netcom does not create or control the content of the information available to its subscribers. It also does not monitor messages as they are posted. It has, however, suspended the accounts of subscribers who violated its terms and conditions, such as where they had commercial software in their posted files. Netcom admits that, although not currently configured to do this, it may be possible to reprogram its system to screen postings containing particular words or coming from particular individuals. Netcom, however, took no action after it was told by plaintiffs that Erlich had posted messages through Netcom's system that violated plaintiffs' copyrights, instead claiming that it could not shut out Erlich without shutting out all of the users of Klemesrud's BBS.

b. Creation of Fixed Copies

. . . In the present case, there is no question after *MAI* that "copies" were created, as Erlich's act of sending a message to a.r.s. caused reproductions of portions of plaintiffs' works on both Klemesrud's and Netcom's storage devices. Even though the messages remained on their systems for at most eleven days, they were sufficiently "fixed" to constitute recognizable copies under the Copyright Act. *See* Information Infrastructure Task Force, *Intellectual Property and the National Information Infrastructure: The Report of the Working Group on Intellectual Property Rights* 66 (1995) ("IITF Report").

c. Is Netcom Directly Liable for Making the Copies?

Accepting that copies were made, Netcom argues that Erlich, and not Netcom, is directly liable for the copying. *MAI* did not address the question raised in this case: whether possessors of computers are liable for incidental copies automatically made on their computers using their software as part of a process initiated by a third party. Netcom correctly distinguishes *MAI* on the ground that Netcom did not take any affirmative action that directly resulted in copying plaintiffs' works other than by installing and maintaining a system whereby software automatically forwards messages received from subscribers onto the Usenet, and temporarily stores copies on its system. Netcom's actions, to the extent that they created a copy of plaintiffs' works, were necessary to having a working system for transmitting Usenet postings to and from the Internet. Unlike the defendants in *MAI*, neither Netcom nor Klemesrud initiated the copying. The defendants in *MAI* turned on their customers' computers thereby creating temporary copies of the operating system, whereas Netcom's and Klemesrud's systems can operate without any human intervention. Thus, unlike *MAI*, the mere fact that Netcom's system incidentally makes temporary copies of plaintiffs' works does not mean Netcom has caused the copying. The court believes that Netcom's act of designing or implementing a system that automatically and uniformly creates temporary copies of all data sent through it is not unlike that of the owner of a copying machine who lets the public make copies with it.[12] Although some of the people using the machine may directly infringe copyrights, courts analyze the machine owner's liability under the rubric of contributory infringement, not direct infringement. . . . Plaintiffs' theory would create many separate acts of infringement and, carried to its natural extreme, would lead to unreasonable liability. It is not difficult to conclude that Erlich infringes by copying a protected work onto his computer and by posting a message to a newsgroup. However, plaintiffs' theory further implicates a Usenet server that carries Erlich's message to other servers regardless of whether that server acts without any human intervention beyond the initial setting up of the system. It would also result in liability for every single Usenet server in the worldwide link of computers transmitting Erlich's message to every other computer. These parties, who are liable under plaintiffs' theory, do no more than operate or implement a system that is essential if Usenet messages are to be widely distributed. There is no need to construe the Act to make all of these parties infringers. Although copyright is a strict liability statute, there should still be some element of volition or causation which is lacking where a defendant's system is merely used to create a copy by a third party.

Plaintiffs point out that the infringing copies resided for eleven days on Netcom's computer and were sent out from it onto the "Information Superhighway." However, under plaintiffs' theory, any storage of a copy that occurs in the process of sending a message to the Usenet is an infringement. While it is possible that less "damage" would have been done if Netcom had heeded plaintiffs' warnings and acted to prevent Erlich's message from being forwarded, this is not relevant to its *direct* liability for copying. The same argument is true of Klemesrud and any Usenet server. Whether a defendant makes a direct copy that constitutes infringement cannot depend on whether it received a warning to delete the message. *See D.C. Comics, Inc. v. Mini Gift*, 912 F.2d 29, 35 (2d Cir.

---

12. Netcom compares itself to a common carrier that merely acts as a passive conduit for information. In a sense, a Usenet server that forwards all messages acts like a common carrier, passively retransmitting every message that gets sent through it. Netcom would seem no more liable than the phone company for carrying an infringing facsimile transmission or storing an infringing audio recording on its voice mail. As Netcom's counsel argued, holding such a server liable would be like holding the owner of the highway, or at least the operator of a toll booth, liable for the criminal activities that occur on its roads. Since other similar carriers of information are not liable for infringement, there is some basis for exempting Internet access providers from liability for infringement by their users. . . . In any event, common carriers are granted statutory exemptions for liability that might otherwise exist. Here, Netcom does not fall under this statutory exemption, and thus faces the usual strict liability scheme that exists for copyright. Whether a new exemption should be carved out for online service providers is to be resolved by Congress, not the courts.

1990). This distinction may be relevant to contributory infringement, however, where knowledge is an element. . . .

2. Contributory Infringement

Netcom is not free from liability just because it did not directly infringe plaintiffs' works; it may still be liable as a contributory infringer. Although there is no statutory rule of liability for infringement committed by others,

> [t]he absence of such express language in the copyright statute does not preclude the imposition of liability for copyright infringement on certain parties who have not them-selves engaged in the infringing activity. For vicarious liability is imposed in virtually all areas of the law, and the concept of contributory infringement is merely a species of the broader problem of identifying the circumstances in which it is just to hold one individual accountable for the actions of another.

Sony Corp. v. Universal City Studios, Inc., 464 U.S. 417, 435 (1984) (footnote omitted). Liability for participation in the infringement will be established where the defendant, "with knowledge of the infringing activity, induces, causes or materially contributes to the infringing conduct of another." *Gershwin Publishing Corp. v. Columbia Artists Management, Inc.*, 443 F.2d 1159, 1162 (2d Cir. 1971).

a. Knowledge of Infringing Activity

Plaintiffs insist that Netcom knew that Erlich was infringing their copy-rights at least after receiving notice from plaintiffs' counsel indicating that Erlich had posted copies of their works onto a.r.s. through Netcom's system. Despite this knowledge, Netcom continued to allow Erlich to post messages to a.r.s. and left the allegedly infringing messages on its system so that Netcom's subscribers and other Usenet servers could access them. Netcom argues that it did not possess the necessary type of knowledge because (1) it did not know of Erlich's planned infringing activities when it agreed to lease its facilities to Klemesrud, (2) it did not know that Erlich would infringe prior to any of his postings, (3) it is unable to screen out infringing postings before they are made, and (4) its knowl-edge of the infringing nature of Erlich's postings was too equivocal given the difficulty in assessing whether the registrations were valid and whether Erlich's use was fair. The court will address these arguments in turn.

Netcom cites cases holding that there is no contributory infringement by the lessors of premises that are later used for infringement unless the lessor had knowledge of the intended use at the time of the signing of the lease. *See, e.g., Deutsch v. Arnold*, 98 F.2d 686, 688 (2d Cir. 1938). The contribution to the infringement by the defendant in *Deutsch* was merely to lease use of the prem-ises to the infringer. Here, Netcom not only leases space but also serves as an access provider, which includes the storage and transmission of information necessary to facilitate Erlich's postings to a.r.s. Unlike a landlord, Netcom retains some control over the use of its system. *See infra* part I.B.3.a. Thus, the relevant time frame for knowledge is not when Netcom entered into an agreement with Klemesrud. It should be when Netcom provided its services to allow Erlich to infringe plaintiffs' copyrights. . . . It is undisputed that Netcom did not know that Erlich was infringing before it received notice from plaintiffs. Netcom points out that the alleged instances of infringement occurring on Netcom's system all happened prior to December 29, 1994, the date on which Netcom first received notice of plaintiffs' infringement claim against Erlich. . . . Thus, there is no question of fact as to whether Netcom knew or should have known of Erlich's infringing activities that occurred more than 11 days before receipt of the December 28, 1994, letter.

However, the evidence reveals a question of fact as to whether Netcom knew or should have known that Erlich had infringed plaintiffs' copyrights following receipt of plaintiffs' letter. Because Netcom was arguably participating in Erlich's public distribution of plaintiffs' works, there is a genuine issue as to whether Netcom knew of any infringement by Erlich before it was too late to do anything about it. If plaintiffs can prove the knowledge element, Netcom will be liable for contributory infringement since its failure to simply cancel Erlich's infringing message and thereby stop an infringing copy from being distributed worldwide constitutes substantial participation in Erlich's public distribution of the message. *Cf.* R. T. Nimmer, THE LAW OF COMPUTER TECHNOLOGY §15.11B, at S15-42 (2d ed. 1994) (opining that "where information service is less directly involved in the enterprise of creating unauthorized copies, a finding of contributory infringement is not likely").

Netcom argues that its knowledge after receiving notice of Erlich's alleged infringing activities was too equivocal given the difficulty in assessing whether registrations are valid and whether use is fair. Although a mere unsupported allegation of infringement by a copyright owner may not automatically put a defendant on notice of infringing activity, Netcom's position that liability must be unequivocal is unsupportable. . . . Where works contain copyright notices within them, as here, it is difficult to argue that a defendant did not know that the works were copyrighted. To require proof of valid registrations would be impractical and would perhaps take too long to verify, making it impossible for a copyright holder to protect his or her works in some cases, as works are automatically deleted less than two weeks after they are posted. The court is more persuaded by the argument that it is beyond the ability of a BBS operator to quickly and fairly determine when a use is not infringement where there is at least a colorable claim of fair use. Where a BBS operator cannot reasonably verify a claim of infringement, either because of a possible fair use defense, the lack of copyright notices on the copies, or the copyright holder's failure to provide the necessary documentation to show that there is a likely infringement, the operator's lack of knowledge will be found reasonable and there will be no liability for contributory infringement for allowing the continued distribution of the works on its system. . . .

b. Substantial Participation

Where a defendant has knowledge of the primary infringer's infringing activities, it will be liable if it "induces, causes or materially contributes to the infringing conduct of" the primary infringer. *Gershwin Publishing*, 443 F.2d at 1162. Such participation must be substantial. . . .

Providing a service that allows for the automatic distribution of all Usenet postings, infringing and noninfringing, goes well beyond renting a premises to an infringer. *See Fonovisa, Inc. v. Cherry Auction, Inc.*, 847 F. Supp. 1492, 1496 (E.D. Cal. 1994) (finding that renting space at swap meet to known bootleggers not "substantial participation" in the infringers' activities). It is more akin to the radio stations that were found liable for rebroadcasting an infringing broadcast. *See, e.g., Select Theatres Corp. v. Ronzoni Macaroni Corp.*, 59 U.S.P.Q. 288, 291 (S.D.N.Y. 1943). Netcom allows Erlich's infringing messages to remain on its system and be further distributed to other Usenet servers worldwide. It does not completely relinquish control over how its system is used, unlike a landlord. Thus, it is fair, assuming Netcom is able to take simple measures to prevent further damage to plaintiffs' copyrighted works, to hold Netcom liable for contributory infringement where Netcom has knowledge of Erlich's infringing postings yet continues to aid in the accomplishment of Erlich's purpose of publicly distributing the postings. Accordingly, plaintiffs do raise a genuine issue of material fact as to their theory of contributory infringement as to the postings made after Netcom was on notice of plaintiffs' infringement claim.

3. Vicarious Liability

Even if plaintiffs cannot prove that Netcom is contributorily liable for its participation in the infringing activity, it may still seek to prove vicarious infringement based on Netcom's relationship to Erlich. A defendant is liable for vicarious liability for the actions of a primary infringer where the defendant (1) has the right and ability to control the infringer's acts and (2) receives a direct financial benefit from the infringement. *See Shapiro, Bernstein & Co. v. H.L. Green Co.*, 316 F.2d 304, 306 (2d Cir. 1963). Unlike contributory infringement, knowledge is not an element of vicarious liability. 3 NIMMER ON COPYRIGHT §12.04[A][1], at 12-70.

a. Right and Ability to Control

The first element of vicarious liability will be met if plaintiffs can show that Netcom has the right and ability to supervise the conduct of its subscribers. Netcom argues that it does not have the right to control its users' postings before they occur. Plaintiffs dispute this and argue that Netcom's terms and conditions, to which its subscribers must agree, specify that Netcom reserves the right to take remedial action against subscribers. . . . Plaintiffs argue that under "netiquette," the informal rules and customs that have developed on the

Internet, violation of copyrights by a user is unacceptable and the access provider has a duty take measures to prevent this; where the immediate service provider fails, the next service provider up the transmission stream must act. . . . Further evidence of Netcom's right to restrict infringing activity is its prohibition of copyright infringement and its requirement that its subscribers indemnify it for any damage to third parties. . . . Plaintiffs have thus raised a question of fact as to Netcom's right to control Erlich's use of its services.

Netcom argues that it could not possibly screen messages before they are posted given the speed and volume of the data that goes through its system. Netcom further argues that it has never exercised control over the content of its users' postings. Plaintiffs' expert opines otherwise, stating that with an easy software modification Netcom could identify postings that contain particular words or come from particular individuals. . . . Plaintiffs further dispute Netcom's claim that it could not limit Erlich's access to Usenet without kicking off all 500 subscribers of Klemesrud's BBS. As evidence that Netcom has in fact exercised its ability to police its users' conduct, plaintiffs cite evidence that Netcom has acted to suspend subscribers' accounts on over one thousand occasions. . . . Further evidence shows that Netcom can delete specific postings. . . . Whether such sanctions occurred before or after the abusive conduct is not material to whether Netcom can exercise control. The court thus finds that plaintiffs have raised a genuine issue of fact as to whether Netcom has the right and ability to exercise control over the activities of its subscribers, and of Erlich in particular.

b. Direct Financial Benefit

Plaintiffs must further prove that Netcom receives a direct financial benefit from the infringing activities of its users. For example, a landlord who has the right and ability to supervise the tenant's activities is vicariously liable for the infringements of the tenant where the rental amount is proportional to the proceeds of the tenant's sales. *Shapiro, Bernstein*, 316 F.2d at 306. However, where a defendant rents space or services on a fixed rental fee that does not depend on the nature of the activity of the lessee, courts usually find no vicarious liability because there is no direct financial benefit from the infringement. *See, e.g., Roy Export Co. v. Trustees of Columbia University*, 344 F. Supp. 1350, 1353 (S.D.N.Y. 1972) (finding no vicarious liability of university because no financial benefit from allowing screening of bootlegged films); *Fonovisa*, 847 F. Supp. at 1496 (finding swap meet operators did not financially benefit from fixed fee). . . .

COMMENTS AND QUESTIONS

1. Both *Frena* and *Netcom* involved the question of when Internet service providers (ISPs) can be held responsible for copyright infringement of material posted by their subscribers. Under *Frena*, is an ISP treated any

differently than someone who posts copyrighted pictures on a Web page? Why does the court in *Netcom* reject the logic of *Frena*? According to the court in *Netcom*, *Frena* is distinguishable because

> the *Playboy* court was looking only at the exclusive right to distribute copies to the public, where liability exists regardless of whether the defendant makes copies. Here, however, plaintiffs do not argue that Netcom is liable for its public distribution of copies. Instead, they claim that Netcom is liable because its computers in fact made copies. Therefore, the above-quoted language has no bearing on the issue of direct liability for unauthorized reproductions. Notwithstanding *Playboy*'s holding that a BBS operator may be directly liable for *distributing or displaying* to the public copies of protected works, this court holds that the storage on a defendant's system of infringing copies and retransmission to other servers is not a direct infringement by the BBS operator of the exclusive right to *reproduce* the work where such copies are uploaded by an infringing user. *Playboy* does not hold otherwise.

Is the court's effort to distinguish *Frena* persuasive? Why is the provider of a newsgroup like Netcom's not copying and distributing copies to the public?

2. According to the court in *Netcom*, if an ISP may not be held responsible as a direct infringer, what other theories might be used to determine an ISP's liability? How do these theories differ? For a discussion of ISP liability, see Alfred C. Yen, *Internet Service Provider Liability for Subscriber Copyright Infringement, Enterprise Liability, and the First Amendment*, 88 Geo. L.J. 1833 (2000).

3. Why should ISPs be held responsible for the infringing acts of others? Should liability be imposed because ISPs are in a better position to police the copying of digital works? Are there any costs associated with imposing contributory and vicarious liability upon ISPs?

4. Following these decisions, Congress enacted the Digital Millennium Copyright Act (DMCA). Title II of the DMCA, the Online Copyright Infringement Liability Limitations Act (OCILLA), creates new rules of liability for Internet service providers for the copyright infringements of others. These provisions create a "safe harbor" for Internet service providers, shielding them from liability for third-party copyright infringements if they comply with the provisions of the Act. The term "service provider" means "an entity offering the transmission, routing, or providing of connections for digital online communications, between or among points specified by a user, of material of the user's choosing, without modification to the content of the material as sent or received," and includes a "provider of online services or network access, or the operator of facilities therefore. . . ." A service provider falls within OCILLA's safe harbor for transitory data communications under section 512(a) if:

> (1) the transmission of the material was initiated by or at the direction of a person other than the service provider; (2) the transmission, routing, provision of connections, or storage is carried out through an automatic technical process without selection of the material by the service provider; (3) the service provider does not select the recipients of the material except as an automatic response to the request of another person; (4) no copy of the material made by the service provider in the course of such intermediate or transient

storage is maintained on the system or network in a manner ordinarily accessible to anyone other than anticipated recipients, and no such copy is maintained on the system or network in a manner ordinarily accessible to such anticipated recipients for a longer period than is reasonably necessary for the transmission, routing, or provision of connections; and (5) the material is transmitted through the system or network without modification of its content.

With respect to information residing on a system or network, section 512(c) immunizes a service provider if the provider:

(A)(i) does not have actual knowledge that the material or an activity using the material on the system or network is infringing;

(ii) in the absence of such actual knowledge, is not aware of facts or circumstances from which infringing activity is apparent; or

(iii) upon obtaining such knowledge or awareness, acts expeditiously to remove, or disable access to, the material;

(B) does not receive a financial benefit directly attributable to the infringing activity, in a case in which the service provider has the right and ability to control such activity; and

(C) upon notification of claimed infringement as described in paragraph (3), responds expeditiously to remove, or disable access to, the material that is claimed to be infringing or to be the subject of infringing activity. . . .

Anyone who knowingly misrepresents that material or activity is infringing or that materials were removed or disabled by mistake is liable for damages, including costs and attorneys' fees, incurred by the copyright owner or licensee or by the service provider in responding to the notice.

Section 512(g) also immunizes service providers from any liability for any claims arising from "good faith disabling of access to, or removal of, material or activity claimed to be infringing or based on facts or circumstances from which infringing activity is apparent, regardless of whether the material or activity is ultimately determined to be infringing."

Does Section 512 of the DMCA codify the liability regime adopted in *Netcom*? Under what circumstances does Section 512 of the DMCA hold Internet service providers responsible for the copyright infringement of others? Earlier we studied Congress's treatment of Internet service providers under the Communications Decency Act. Is this treatment consistent with the CDA? If copyright owners can always go sue the "direct" infringer, why should they be treated differently from victims of defamation? Will the imposition of contributory or vicarious liability under these circumstances chill speech in cyberspace?

5. How specific must notice be to trigger an ISP's duty to investigate and remove the allegedly infringing material? Must the copyright owner provide a detailed list of infringing works? *Consider* ALS Scan, Inc. v. Remarq Communities, Inc., 239 F.3d 619, 624 (4th Cir. 2001), in which the district court concluded that ALS Scan's notice was insufficient to trigger liability under Section 512 because its notice failed to comply strictly with listing the

infringing works and identifying those works with sufficient detail to allow the ISP to locate and disable them. ALS Scan notified Remarq that two news groups containing ALS as part of their names were created for the sole purpose of violating its copyrights. *Id.* at 620. In reversing the district court, the Court of Appeals concluded, "when a letter provides notice equivalent to a list of representative works that can be easily identified by the service providers, the notice substantially complies with the notification requirements." *Id.* at 625. Should substantial compliance be sufficient to trigger an ISP's duty to remove and disable material? Is *ALS Scan* a unique case because the newsgroups themselves were named after the plaintiff?

6. Under Section 512 of the DMCA, is an ISP responsible for evaluating whether the complainant's copyrights are valid or whether the allegedly infringing use is fair use? According to the court in *Netcom*:

> Where a BBS operator cannot reasonably verify a claim of infringement, either because of a possible fair use defense, the lack of copyright notices on the copies, or the copyright holder's failure to provide the necessary documentation to show that there is a likely infringement, the operator's lack of knowledge will be found reasonable and there will be no liability for contributory infringement for allowing the continued distribution of the works on its system.

907 F. Supp. at 1374. Does this portion of the *Netcom* decision survive under Section 512?

A&M RECORDING, INC. v. NAPSTER, INC.

239 F.3d 1004 (9th Cir. 2001)

BEEZER, Circuit Judge:

Plaintiffs are engaged in the commercial recording, distribution and sale of copyrighted musical compositions and sound recordings. The complaint alleges that Napster, Inc. ("Napster") is a contributory and vicarious copyright infringer. On July 26, 2000, the district court granted plaintiffs' motion for a preliminary injunction. The injunction was slightly modified by written opinion on August 10, 2000. *A & M Records, Inc. v. Napster, Inc.*, 114 F. Supp. 2d 896 (N.D. Cal. 2000). The district court preliminarily enjoined Napster "from engaging in, or facilitating others in copying, downloading, uploading, transmitting, or distributing plaintiffs' copyrighted musical compositions and sound recordings, protected by either federal or state law, without express permission of the rights owner." *Id.* at 927. . . .

I.

We have examined the papers submitted in support of and in response to the injunction application and it appears that Napster has designed and operates a system which permits the transmission and retention of sound recordings employing digital technology.

In 1987, the Moving Picture Experts Group set a standard file format for the storage of audio recordings in a digital format called MPEG-3, abbreviated as "MP3." Digital MP3 files are created through a process colloquially called "ripping." Ripping software allows a computer owner to copy an audio compact disk ("audio CD") directly onto a computer's hard drive by compressing the audio information on the CD into the MP3 format. The MP3's compressed format allows for rapid transmission of digital audio files from one computer to another by electronic mail or any other file transfer protocol.

Napster facilitates the transmission of MP3 files between and among its users. Through a process commonly called "peer-to-peer" file sharing, Napster allows its users to: (1) make MP3 music files stored on individual computer hard drives available for copying by other Napster users; (2) search for MP3 music files stored on other users' computers; and (3) transfer exact copies of the contents of other users' MP3 files from one computer to another via the Internet. These functions are made possible by Napster's MusicShare software, available free of charge from Napster's Internet site, and Napster's network servers and server-side software. Napster provides technical support for the indexing and searching of MP3 files, as well as for its other functions, including a "chat room," where users can meet to discuss music, and a directory where participating artists can provide information about their music. . . .

B. Listing Available Files

If a registered user wants to list available files stored in his computer's hard drive on Napster for others to access, he must first create a "user library" directory on his computer's hard drive. The user then saves his MP3 files in the library directory, using self-designated file names. He next must log into the Napster system using his user name and password. His MusicShare software then searches his user library and verifies that the available files are properly formatted. If in the correct MP3 format, the names of the MP3 files will be uploaded from the user's computer to the Napster servers. The content of the MP3 files remains stored in the user's computer.

Once uploaded to the Napster servers, the user's MP3 file names are stored in a server-side "library" under the user's name and become part of a "collective directory" of files available for transfer during the time the user is logged onto the Napster system. The collective directory is fluid; it tracks users who are connected in real time, displaying only file names that are immediately accessible.

C. Searching for Available Files

Napster allows a user to locate other users' MP3 files in two ways: through Napster's search function and through its "hotlist" function.

Software located on the Napster servers maintains a "search index" of Napster's collective directory. To search the files available from Napster users currently connected to the network servers, the individual user accesses a form in the MusicShare software stored in his computer and enters either the name of a song or an artist as the object of the search. The form is then transmitted to a Napster server and automatically compared to the MP3 file names listed in the server's search index. Napster's server compiles a list of all MP3 file names pulled from the search index which include the same search terms entered on the search form and transmits the list to the searching user. The Napster server does not search the contents of any MP3 file; rather, the search is limited to "a text search of the file names indexed in a particular cluster. Those file names may contain typographical errors or otherwise inaccurate descriptions of the content of the files since they are designated by other users." *Napster*, 114 F. Supp. 2d at 906.

To use the "hotlist" function, the Napster user creates a list of other users' names from whom he has obtained MP3 files in the past. When logged onto Napster's servers, the system alerts the user if any user on his list (a "hotlisted user") is also logged onto the system. If so, the user can access an index of all MP3 file names in a particular hotlisted user's library and request a file in the library by selecting the file name. The contents of the hotlisted user's MP3 file are not stored on the Napster system.

D. Transferring Copies of an MP3 File

To transfer a copy of the contents of a requested MP3 file, the Napster server software obtains the Internet address of the requesting user and the Internet address of the "host user" (the user with the available files). . . . The Napster servers then communicate the host user's Internet address to the requesting user. The requesting user's computer uses this information to establish a connection with the host user and downloads a copy of the contents of the MP3 file from one computer to the other over the Internet, "peer-to-peer." A downloaded MP3 file can be played directly from the user's hard drive using Napster's MusicShare program or other software. The file may also be transferred back onto an audio CD if the user has access to equipment designed for that purpose. In both cases, the quality of the original sound recording is slightly diminished by transfer to the MP3 format.

This architecture is described in some detail to promote an understanding of transmission mechanics as opposed to the content of the transmissions. The content is the subject of our copyright infringement analysis. . . .

[After affirming the district court's holding that the sharing of music by Napster's users represents direct copyright infringement, the court turns to contributory and vicarious liability. The fair use discussion is excerpted, *infra*.]

IV.

We first address plaintiffs' claim that Napster is liable for contributory copyright infringement. Traditionally, "one who, with knowledge of the infringing activity, induces, causes or materially contributes to the infringing conduct of another, may be held liable as a 'contributory' infringer." *Gershwin Publ'g Corp. v. Columbia Artists Mgmt., Inc.*, 443 F.2d 1159, 1162 (2d Cir. 1971); *see also Fonovisa, Inc. v. Cherry Auction, Inc.*, 76 F.3d 259, 264 (9th Cir. 1996). Put differently, liability exists if the defendant engages in "personal conduct that encourages or assists the infringement." *Matthew Bender & Co. v. West Publ'g Co.*, 158 F.3d 693, 706 (2d Cir. 1998).

The district court determined that plaintiffs in all likelihood would establish Napster's liability as a contributory infringer. The district court did not err; Napster, by its conduct, knowingly encourages and assists the infringement of plaintiffs' copyrights.

A. Knowledge

Contributory liability requires that the secondary infringer "know or have reason to know" of direct infringement. . . . *Religious Tech. Ctr. v. Netcom On-Line Communication Servs., Inc.*, 907 F. Supp. 1361, 1373-74 (N.D. Cal. 1995) (framing issue as "whether Netcom knew or should have known of" the infringing activities). The district court found that Napster had both actual and constructive knowledge that its users exchanged copyrighted music. The district court also concluded that the law does not require knowledge of "specific acts of infringement" and rejected Napster's contention that because the company cannot distinguish infringing from noninfringing files, it does not "know" of the direct infringement. 114 F. Supp. 2d at 917.

It is apparent from the record that Napster has knowledge, both actual and constructive,[5] of direct infringement. Napster claims that it is nevertheless protected from contributory liability by the teaching of *Sony Corp. v. Universal City Studios, Inc.*, 464 U.S. 417 (1984). We disagree. We observe that Napster's actual, specific knowledge of direct infringement renders *Sony*'s holding of limited assistance to Napster. We are compelled to make a clear distinction between the architecture of the Napster system and Napster's conduct in relation to the operational capacity of the system.

The *Sony* Court refused to hold the manufacturer and retailers of video tape recorders liable for contributory infringement despite evidence that such

5. The district court found actual knowledge because: (1) a document authored by Napster co-founder Sean Parker mentioned "the need to remain ignorant of users' real names and IP addresses 'since they are exchanging pirated music'"; and (2) the Recording Industry Association of America ("RIAA") informed Napster of more than 12,000 infringing files, some of which are still available. 114 F. Supp. 2d at 918. The district court found constructive knowledge because: (a) Napster executives have recording industry experience; (b) they have enforced intellectual property rights in other instances; (c) Napster executives have downloaded copyrighted songs from the system; and (d) they have promoted the site with "screen shots listing infringing files." *Id.* at 919.

machines could be and were used to infringe plaintiffs' copyrighted television shows. *Sony* stated that if liability "is to be imposed on petitioners in this case, it must rest on the fact that *they have sold equipment with constructive knowledge of the fact that their customers may use that equipment to make unauthorized copies* of copyrighted material." *Id.* at 439 (emphasis added). The *Sony* Court declined to impute the requisite level of knowledge where the defendants made and sold equipment capable of both infringing and "substantial noninfringing uses." *Id.* at 442 (adopting a modified "staple article of commerce" doctrine from patent law). *See also Universal City Studios, Inc. v. Sony Corp.*, 480 F. Supp. 429, 459 (C.D. Cal. 1979) ("This court agrees with defendants that their knowledge was insufficient to make them contributory infringers."), *rev'd*, 659 F.2d 963 (9th Cir. 1981), *rev'd*, 464 U.S. 417 (1984); Alfred C. Yen, *Internet Service Provider Liability for Subscriber Copyright Infringement, Enterprise Liability, and the First Amendment*, 88 Geo. L.J. 1833, 1874 & 1893 n.210 (2000) (suggesting that, after *Sony*, most Internet service providers lack "the requisite level of knowledge" for the imposition of contributory liability).

We are bound to follow *Sony*, and will not impute the requisite level of knowledge to Napster merely because peer-to-peer file sharing technology may be used to infringe plaintiffs' copyrights. *See* 464 U.S. at 436 (rejecting argument that merely supplying the " 'means' to accomplish an infringing activity" leads to imposition of liability). We depart from the reasoning of the district court that Napster failed to demonstrate that its system is capable of commercially significant noninfringing uses. *See Napster*, 114 F. Supp. 2d at 916, 917-18. The district court improperly confined the use analysis to current uses, ignoring the system's capabilities. *See generally Sony*, 464 U.S. at 442-43 (framing inquiry as whether the video tape recorder is "*capable* of commercially significant noninfringing uses") (emphasis added). Consequently, the district court placed undue weight on the proportion of current infringing use as compared to current and future noninfringing use. *See generally Vault Corp. v. Quaid Software Ltd.*, 847 F.2d 255, 264-67 (5th Cir. 1988) (single noninfringing use implicated *Sony*). . . . Regardless of the number of Napster's infringing versus noninfringing uses, the evidentiary record here supported the district court's finding that plaintiffs would likely prevail in establishing that Napster knew or had reason to know of its users' infringement of plaintiffs' copyrights.

This analysis is similar to that of *Religious Technology Center v. Netcom On-Line Communication Services, Inc.*, which suggests that in an online context, evidence of actual knowledge of specific acts of infringement is required to hold a computer system operator liable for contributory copyright infringement. . . .

We agree that if a computer system operator learns of specific infringing material available on his system and fails to purge such material from the system, the operator knows of and contributes to direct infringement. *See Netcom*, 907 F. Supp. at 1374. Conversely, absent any specific information which identifies infringing activity, a computer system operator cannot be liable for contributory infringement merely because the structure of the system allows for the exchange of copyrighted material. *See Sony*, 464 U.S. at 436, 442-43. To enjoin simply because a computer network allows for infringing use would, in our opinion, violate *Sony* and potentially restrict activity unrelated to infringing use.

We nevertheless conclude that sufficient knowledge exists to impose contributory liability when linked to demonstrated infringing use of the Napster system. . . . The record supports the district court's finding that Napster has *actual* knowledge that *specific* infringing material is available using its system, that it could block access to the system by suppliers of the infringing material, and that it failed to remove the material. *See Napster*, 114 F. Supp. 2d at 918, 920-21.

B.   Material Contribution

Under the facts as found by the district court, Napster materially contributes to the infringing activity. . . . We agree that Napster provides "the site and facilities" for direct infringement. *See Fonovisa*, 76 F.3d at 264. . . . We affirm the district court's conclusion that plaintiffs have demonstrated a likelihood of success on the merits of the contributory copyright infringement claim. We will address the scope of the injunction in part VIII of this opinion.

V.

We turn to the question whether Napster engages in vicarious copyright infringement. Vicarious copyright liability is an "outgrowth" of respondeat superior. *Fonovisa*, 76 F.3d at 262. In the context of copyright law, vicarious liability extends beyond an employer/employee relationship to cases in which a defendant "has the right and ability to supervise the infringing activity and also has a direct financial interest in such activities." *Id.* . . .

A.   Financial Benefit

The district court determined that plaintiffs had demonstrated they would likely succeed in establishing that Napster has a direct financial interest in the infringing activity. *Napster*, 114 F. Supp. 2d at 921-22. We agree. Financial benefit exists where the availability of infringing material "acts as a 'draw' for customers." *Fonovisa*, 76 F.3d at 263-64 (stating that financial benefit may be shown "where infringing performances enhance the attractiveness of a venue"). Ample evidence supports the district court's finding that Napster's future revenue is directly dependent upon "increases in userbase." More users register with the Napster system as the "quality and quantity of available music increases." 114 F. Supp. 2d at 902. We conclude that the district court did not err in determining that Napster financially benefits from the availability of protected works on its system.

B. Supervision

The district court determined that Napster has the right and ability to supervise its users' conduct. *Napster*, 114 F. Supp. 2d at 920-21 (finding that Napster's representations to the court regarding "its improved methods of blocking users about whom rights holders complain . . . is tantamount to an admission that defendant can, and sometimes does, police its service"). We agree in part.

The ability to block infringers' access to a particular environment for any reason whatsoever is evidence of the right and ability to supervise. *See Fonovisa*, 76 F.3d at 262 ("Cherry Auction had the right to terminate vendors for any reason whatsoever and through that right had the ability to control the activities of vendors on the premises."); *cf. Netcom*, 907 F. Supp. at 1375-76 (indicating that plaintiff raised a genuine issue of fact regarding ability to supervise by presenting evidence that an electronic bulletin board service can suspend subscriber's accounts). Here, plaintiffs have demonstrated that Napster retains the right to control access to its system. Napster has an express reservation of rights policy, stating on its Web site that it expressly reserves the "right to refuse service and terminate accounts in [its] discretion, including, but not limited to, if Napster believes that user conduct violates applicable law . . . or for any reason in Napster's sole discretion, with or without cause."

To escape imposition of vicarious liability, the reserved right to police must be exercised to its fullest extent. Turning a blind eye to detectable acts of infringement for the sake of profit gives rise to liability. *See, e.g., Fonovisa*, 76 F.3d at 261 ("There is no dispute for the purposes of this appeal that Cherry Auction and its operators were aware that vendors in their swap meets were selling counterfeit recordings."); *see also Gershwin*, 443 F.2d at 1161-62 (citing *Shapiro, Bernstein & Co. v. H.L. Green Co.*, 316 F.2d 304 (2d Cir. 1963), for the proposition that "failure to police the conduct of the primary infringer" leads to imposition of vicarious liability for copyright infringement).

The district court correctly determined that Napster had the right and ability to police its system and failed to exercise that right to prevent the exchange of copyrighted material. The district court, however, failed to recognize that the boundaries of the premises that Napster "controls and patrols" are limited. *See, e.g., Fonovisa*, 76 F.3d at 262-63 (in addition to having the right to exclude vendors, defendant "controlled and patrolled" the premises); *see also Polygram*, 855 F. Supp. at 1328-29 (in addition to having the contractual right to remove exhibitors, trade show operator reserved the right to police during the show and had its "employees walk the aisles to ensure 'rules compliance'"). Put differently, Napster's reserved "right and ability" to police is cabined by the system's current architecture. As shown by the record, the Napster system does not "read" the content of indexed files, other than to check that they are in the proper MP3 format.

Napster, however, has the ability to locate infringing material listed on its search indices, and the right to terminate users' access to the system. The file name indices, therefore, are within the "premises" that Napster has the ability to police. We recognize that the files are user-named and may not match copyrighted material exactly (for example, the artist or song could be spelled wrong). For Napster to function effectively, however, file names must reasonably or roughly correspond to the material contained in the files, otherwise no user could ever locate any desired music. As a practical matter, Napster, its users and the record company plaintiffs have equal access to infringing material by employing Napster's "search function."

Our review of the record requires us to accept the district court's conclusion that plaintiffs have demonstrated a likelihood of success on the merits of the vicarious copyright infringement claim. Napster's failure to police the system's "premises," combined with a showing that Napster financially benefits from the continuing availability of infringing files on its system, leads to the imposition of vicarious liability. . . .

VI.

B. Digital Millennium Copyright Act

Napster also interposes a statutory limitation on liability by asserting the protections of the "safe harbor" from copyright infringement suits for "Internet service providers" contained in the Digital Millennium Copyright Act, 17 U.S.C. §512. *See Napster*, 114 F. Supp. 2d at 919 n.24. The district court did not give this statutory limitation any weight favoring a denial of temporary injunctive relief. The court concluded that Napster "has failed to persuade this court that subsection 512(d) shelters contributory infringers." *Id.*

We need not accept a blanket conclusion that §512 of the Digital Millennium Copyright Act will never protect secondary infringers. *See* S. Rep. 105-190, at 40 (1998) ("The limitations in subsections (a) through (d) protect qualifying service providers from liability for all monetary relief for direct, vicarious, and contributory infringement."). . . .

We do not agree that Napster's potential liability for contributory and vicarious infringement renders the Digital Millennium Copyright Act inapplicable per se. We instead recognize that this issue will be more fully developed at trial. At this stage of the litigation, plaintiffs raise serious questions regarding Napster's ability to obtain shelter under §512, and plaintiffs also demonstrate that the balance of hardships tips in their favor. *See Prudential Real Estate*, 204 F.3d at 874; *see also Micro Star v. Formgen, Inc.*, 154 F.3d 1107, 1109 (9th Cir. 1998) ("A party seeking a preliminary injunction must show . . . 'that serious questions going to the merits were raised and the balance of hardships tips sharply in its favor.' ").

Plaintiffs have raised and continue to raise significant questions under this statute, including: (1) whether Napster is an Internet service provider as defined by 17 U.S.C. §512(d); (2) whether copyright owners must give a service provider "official" notice of infringing activity in order for it to have knowledge or awareness of infringing activity on its system; and (3) whether Napster complies with §512(i), which requires a service provider to timely establish a detailed copyright compliance policy. *See A & M Records, Inc. v. Napster, Inc.*, No. 99-05183, 2000 WL 573136 (N.D. Cal. May 12, 2000) (denying summary judgment to Napster under a different subsection of the Digital Millennium Copyright Act, §512(a)). . . .

VIII.

The district court correctly recognized that a preliminary injunction against Napster's participation in copyright infringement is not only warranted but required. We believe, however, that the scope of the injunction needs modification in light of our opinion. Specifically, we reiterate that contributory liability may potentially be imposed only to the extent that Napster: (1) receives reasonable knowledge of specific infringing files with copyrighted musical compositions and sound recordings; (2) knows or should know that such files are available on the Napster system; and (3) fails to act to prevent viral distribution of the works. *See Netcom*, 907 F. Supp. at 1374-75. The mere existence of the Napster system, absent actual notice and Napster's demonstrated failure to remove the offending material, is insufficient to impose contributory liability. *See Sony*, 464 U.S. at 442-43.

Conversely, Napster may be vicariously liable when it fails to affirmatively use its ability to patrol its system and preclude access to potentially infringing files listed in its search index. Napster has both the ability to use its search function to identify infringing musical recordings and the right to bar participation of users who engage in the transmission of infringing files.

The preliminary injunction which we stayed is overbroad because it places on Napster the entire burden of ensuring that no "copying, downloading, uploading, transmitting, or distributing" of plaintiffs' works occur on the system. As stated, we place the burden on plaintiffs to provide notice to Napster of copyrighted works and files containing such works available on the Napster system before Napster has the duty to disable access to the offending content. Napster, however, also bears the burden of policing the system within the limits of the system. Here, we recognize that this is not an exact science in that the files are user named. In crafting the injunction on remand, the district court should recognize that Napster's system does not currently appear to allow Napster access to users' MP3 files. . . .

COMMENTS AND QUESTIONS

1. What factors did the Ninth Circuit consider in determining that Napster was liable for contributory and vicarious infringement? Is the Ninth

Circuit's decision consistent with *Netcom*? Is the decision consistent with Section 512 of the DMCA?

2. Prior to receiving notification from the plaintiffs, did Napster know or have reason to know that its network was being used to infringe copyrighted materials? What was actually "copied" and distributed on Napster's computers? To the extent that Napster receives notice of infringement, how can it purge that infringement from its system?

3. While we will examine the individual users' fair use arguments in the following section, to what extent does a potential claim of fair use make Napster's decision not to block access to the allegedly infringing works reasonable under *Netcom*? If it is not reasonable, are there any limits on a copyright owner's ability to block access to material in cyberspace by threatening ISPs? In other words, who should determine whether a particular use of copyrighted material represents fair use?

4. Both *Napster* and *Netcom* recognize that ISPs may be subject to vicarious liability because of their ability to control what occurs over their computer networks. What kind of control justifies imposing vicarious liability upon ISPs? Why did the court of appeals in *Napster* conclude that Napster's control was limited? Could an ISP escape liability by disclaiming any authority to control the content that travels through its network even though it may be technically able to exercise such control? This issue arose in the United States Supreme Court case of Metro-Goldwyn-Mayer Studios v. Grokster, 125 S. Ct. 2764 (2005) (*see infra*).

5. The court of appeals in *Napster* agreed with the district court that there were questions of fact with respect to whether the DMCA safe harbor provisions would apply to Napster. Which provision of Section 512 might apply to Napster?

6. The liability concerning use of sound recordings in cyberspace is particularly relevant to Web-casting and making these recordings available at the Web sites. An owner of a sound recording has the exclusive right to publicly perform the sound recording via a digital audio transmission, 17 U.S.C. Section 106(6). The DMCA defines an exception to the copyright owner's Section 106(6) exclusive right for nonexempt, noninteractive, digital subscription transmissions. Accordingly, to determine whether a Web-caster is liable for copyright infringement, the question of whether the Web-casting is noninteractive must first be answered. The DMCA provides:

> An "eligible nonsubscription transmission" is a noninteractive nonsubscription digital audio transmission not exempt under subsection (d)(1) that is made as part of a service that provides audio programming consisting, in whole or in part, of performances of sound recordings, including retransmissions of broadcast transmissions, if the primary purpose of the service is to provide to the public such audio or other entertainment programming, and the primary purpose of the service is not to sell, advertise, or promote particular products or services other than sound recordings, live concerts, or other music related events.

17 U.S.C. §114(j)(6). Currently, the determination as to whether a Web-casting is noninteractive versus interactive is made on a case-by-case basis.

7. In light of the preceding materials, despite the combined threat of the Internet and digital technology, are traditional copyright principles capable of dealing with infringement in cyberspace? If not, why not?

METRO-GOLDWYN-MAYER STUDIOS, INC. V. GROKSTER, LTD.

125 S. Ct. 2764 (2005)

[SOUTER, J., delivered the opinion for a unanimous Court. GINSBURG, J., filed a concurring opinion, in which REHNQUIST, C.J., and KENNEDY, J., joined. BREYER, J., filed a concurring opinion, in which STEVENS and O'CONNOR, JJ., joined.]

SOUTER:

The question is under what circumstances the distributor of a product capable of both lawful and unlawful use is liable for acts of copyright infringement by third parties using the product. We hold that one who distributes a device with the object of promoting its use to infringe copyright, as shown by clear expression or other affirmative steps taken to foster infringement, is liable for the resulting acts of infringement by third parties.

I

A

Respondents, Grokster, Ltd., and StreamCast Networks, Inc., . . . distribute free software products that allow computer users to share electronic files through peer-to-peer networks, so called because users' computers communicate directly with each other, not through central servers. . . . Given [their] benefits in security, cost, and efficiency, peer-to-peer networks are employed to store and distribute electronic files by universities, government agencies, corporations, and libraries, among others.

Other users of peer-to-peer networks include individual recipients of Grokster's and StreamCast's software, and although the networks that they enjoy through using the software can be used to share any type of digital file, they have prominently employed those networks in sharing copyrighted music and video files without authorization. A group of copyright holders (MGM for short, but including motion picture studios, recording companies, songwriters, and music publishers) sued Grokster and StreamCast for their users' copyright infringements, alleging that they knowingly and intentionally distributed their software to enable users to reproduce and distribute the copyrighted works in violation of the Copyright Act, . . .

Although Grokster and StreamCast do not . . . know when particular files are copied, a few searches using their software would show what is available on the networks the software reaches. MGM commissioned a statistician to conduct a systematic search, and his study showed that nearly 90% of the files available for download ... were copyrighted works. Grokster and StreamCast dispute this figure, raising methodological problems and arguing that free copying even of copyrighted works may be authorized by the rightholders. They also argue that potential noninfringing uses of their software are significant in kind, even if infrequent in practice. Some musical performers, for example, have gained new audiences by distributing their copyrighted works for free across peer-to-peer networks, and some distributors of unprotected content have used peer-to-peer networks to disseminate files, Shakespeare being an example. . . .

Grokster and StreamCast concede the infringement in most downloads ... and it is uncontested that they are aware that users employ their software primarily to download copyrighted files, even if the decentralized FastTrack and Gnutella networks fail to reveal which files are being copied, and when. From time to time, moreover, the companies have learned about their users' infringement directly, as from users who have sent e-mail to each company with questions about playing copyrighted movies they had downloaded, to whom the companies have responded with guidance. And MGM notified the companies of 8 million copyrighted files that could be obtained using their software.

Grokster and StreamCast are not, however, merely passive recipients of information about infringing use. The record is replete with evidence that from the moment Grokster and StreamCast began to distribute their free software, each one clearly voiced the objective that recipients use it to download copyrighted works, and each took active steps to encourage infringement.

After the notorious file-sharing service, Napster, was sued by copyright holders for facilitation of copyright infringement ... StreamCast gave away a software program of a kind known as OpenNap, designed as compatible with the Napster program and open to Napster users for downloading files from other Napster and OpenNap users' computers. Evidence indicates that ... the OpenNap program was engineered " 'to leverage Napster's 50 million user base.' " . . .

StreamCast monitored both the number of users downloading its Open-Nap program and the number of music files they downloaded. . . . It also used the resulting OpenNap network to distribute copies of the Morpheus software and to encourage users to adopt it. . . . Internal company documents indicate that StreamCast hoped to attract large numbers of former Napster users if that company was shut down by court order or otherwise, and that StreamCast planned to be the next Napster. . . . A kit developed by StreamCast to be delivered to advertisers, for example, contained press articles about Stream-Cast's potential to capture former Napster users . . . and it introduced itself to some potential advertisers as a company "which is similar to what Napster was." . . . It broadcast banner advertisements to users of other Napster-compatible software, urging them to adopt its OpenNap. . . . An internal e-mail from a company executive stated: " 'We have put this network in place so that when Napster pulls the plug on their free service . . . or if the Court orders them to shut down prior to that . . . we will be positioned to capture the flood of their 32 million users that will be actively looking for an alternative.' " . . . StreamCast even planned to flaunt the illegal uses of its software; when it launched the OpenNap network, the chief technology officer of the company averred that "the goal is to get in trouble with the law and get sued. It's the best way to get in the news." . . .

The evidence that Grokster sought to capture the market of former Napster users is sparser but revealing, for Grokster launched its own OpenNap system called Swaptor and inserted digital codes into its Web site so that computer users using Web search engines to look for "Napster" or "free filesharing" would be directed to the Grokster Web site, where they could download the Grokster software. . . . And Grokster's name is an apparent derivative of Napster.

In addition to this evidence of express promotion, marketing, and intent to promote further, the business models employed by Grokster and Stream-Cast confirm that their principal object was use of their software to download copyrighted works. Grokster and StreamCast receive no revenue from users, who obtain the software itself for nothing. Instead, both companies generate income by selling advertising space, and they stream the advertising to Grokster and Morpheus users while they are employing the programs. As the number of users of each program increases, advertising opportunities become worth more. . . . While there is doubtless some demand for free Shakespeare, the evidence shows that substantive volume is a function of free access to copyrighted work. . . .

Finally, there is no evidence that either company made an effort to filter copyrighted material from users' downloads or otherwise impede the sharing of copyrighted files. Although Grokster appears to have sent e-mails warning users about infringing content when it received threatening notice from the copyright holders, it never blocked anyone from continuing to use its software to share copyrighted files. . . . StreamCast not only rejected another company's offer of help to monitor infringement. . . . but blocked the Internet Protocol addresses of entities it believed were trying to engage in such monitoring on its networks. . . .

B

. . . The District Court held that those who used the Grokster and Morpheus software to download copyrighted media files directly infringed MGM's copyrights, a conclusion not contested on appeal, but the court nonetheless granted summary judgment in favor of Grokster and StreamCast as to any liability arising from distribution of the then current versions of their software. Distributing that software gave rise to no liability in the court's view, because its use did not provide the distributors with actual knowledge of specific acts of infringement. . . .

The Court of Appeals affirmed. . . . In the court's analysis, a defendant was liable as a contributory infringer when it had knowledge of direct infringement and materially contributed to the infringement. But the court read *Sony Corp. of America* v. *Universal City Studios, Inc.*, 464 U.S. 417, 78 L. Ed. 2d 574, 104 S. Ct. 774 (1984), as holding that distribution of a commercial product capable of substantial noninfringing uses could not give rise to contributory liability for infringement unless the distributor had actual knowledge of specific instances of infringement and failed to act on that knowledge. The fact that the software was capable of substantial noninfringing uses in the Ninth Circuit's view meant that Grokster and StreamCast were not liable, because they had no such actual knowledge, owing to the decentralized architecture of their software. The court also held that Grokster and StreamCast did not materially contribute to their users' infringement because it was the users themselves who searched for, retrieved, and stored the infringing files, with no involvement by the defendants beyond providing the software in the first place.

The Ninth Circuit also considered whether Grokster and StreamCast could be liable under a theory of vicarious infringement. The court held against liability because the defendants did not monitor or control the use of the software, had no agreed-upon right or current ability to supervise its use, and had no independent duty to police infringement. We granted certiorari. . . .

II

A

MGM and many of the *amici* fault the Court of Appeals's holding for upsetting a sound balance between the respective values of supporting creative pursuits through copyright protection and promoting innovation in new communication technologies by limiting the incidence of liability for copyright infringement. The more artistic protection is favored, the more technological innovation may be discouraged; the administration of copyright law is an exercise in managing the trade-off. . . .

The tension between the two values is the subject of this case, with its claim that digital distribution of copyrighted material threatens copyright holders as never before, because every copy is identical to the original, copying is easy, and many people (especially the young) use file-sharing software to download copyrighted works. . . . As the case has been presented to us, these fears are said to be offset by the different concern that imposing liability, not only on infringers but on distributors of software based on its potential for unlawful use, could limit further development of beneficial technologies. . . .

The argument for imposing indirect liability in this case is, however, a powerful one, given the number of infringing downloads that occur every day using StreamCast's and Grokster's software. When a widely shared service or product is used to commit infringement, it may be impossible to enforce rights in the protected work effectively against all direct infringers, the only practical alternative being to go against the distributor of the copying device for secondary liability on a theory of contributory or vicarious infringement. . . .

B

[In Sony v. Universal City Studios, see *infra*, there] was no evidence that Sony had expressed an object of bringing about taping in violation of copyright or had taken active steps to increase its profits from unlawful taping. . . . Although Sony's advertisements urged consumers to buy the VCR to " 'record favorite shows' " or " 'build a library' " of recorded programs, . . . neither of these uses was necessarily infringing, . . .

On those facts, with no evidence of stated or indicated intent to promote infringing uses, the only conceivable basis for imposing liability was on a theory of contributory infringement arising from its sale of VCRs to consumers with knowledge that some would use them to infringe. . . . But because the VCR was "capable of commercially significant noninfringing uses," we held the manufacturer could not be faulted solely on the basis of its distribution. . . .

[The *Sony*] doctrine absolves the equivocal conduct of selling an item with substantial lawful as well as unlawful uses, and limits liability to instances of more acute fault than the mere understanding that some of one's products will be misused. It leaves breathing room for innovation and a vigorous commerce. . . .

The parties and many of the *amici* in this case think the key to resolving it is the *Sony* rule and, in particular, what it means for a product to be "capable of commercially significant noninfringing uses.". . . . Because the Circuit found the StreamCast and Grokster software capable of substantial lawful use, it concluded on the basis of its reading of *Sony* that neither company could be held liable, since there was no showing that their software, being without any central server, afforded them knowledge of specific unlawful uses.

This view of *Sony*, however, was error, converting the case from one about liability resting on imputed intent to one about liability on any theory. Because *Sony* did not displace other theories of secondary liability, and because we find below that it was error to grant summary judgment to the companies on MGM's inducement claim, we do not revisit *Sony* further . . . to add a more quantified description of the point of balance between protection and commerce when liability rests solely on distribution with knowledge that unlawful use will occur. It is enough to note that the Ninth Circuit's judgment rested on an erroneous understanding of *Sony* and to leave further consideration of the *Sony* rule for a day when that may be required.

C

Sony's rule limits imputing culpable intent as a matter of law from the characteristics or uses of a distributed product. But nothing in *Sony* requires courts to ignore evidence of intent if there is such evidence, and the case was never meant to foreclose rules of fault-based liability derived from the common law. . . . Thus, where evidence goes beyond a product's characteristics or the knowledge that it may be put to infringing uses, and shows statements or actions directed to promoting infringement, *Sony*'s staple-article rule will not preclude liability.

The classic case of direct evidence of unlawful purpose occurs when one induces commission of infringement by another, or "entices or persuades another" to infringe, Black's Law Dictionary 790 (8th ed. 2004), as by advertising. Thus at common law a copyright or patent defendant who "not only expected but invoked [infringing use] by advertisement" was liable for infringement "on principles recognized in every part of the law." *Kalem Co v. Harper Brothers*, 222 U.S., at 62-63, 56 L. Ed. 2d 92, 32 S. Ct. 20 (copyright infringement).

The rule on inducement of infringement as developed in the early cases is no different today. Evidence of "active steps . . . taken to encourage direct infringement," *Oak Industries Inc v. Zenith Electronics Corp.*, 697 F. Supp. 988, 992 (ND Ill. 1988), such as advertising an infringing use or instructing how to engage in an infringing use, show an affirmative intent that the product be used to infringe, and a showing that infringement was encouraged overcomes the law's reluctance to find liability when a defendant merely sells a commercial product suitable for some lawful use. . . .

For the same reasons that *Sony* took the staple-article doctrine of patent law as a model for its copyright safe-harbor rule, the inducement rule, too, is a sensible one for copyright. We adopt it here, holding that one who distributes a device with the object of promoting its use to infringe copyright, as shown by clear expression or other affirmative steps taken to foster infringement, is liable for the resulting acts of infringement by third parties. We are, of course, mindful of the need to keep from trenching on regular commerce or discouraging the development of technologies with lawful and unlawful potential. Accordingly, just as *Sony* did not find intentional inducement despite the knowledge of the VCR manufacturer that its device could be used to infringe. . . . mere knowledge of infringing potential or of actual infringing uses would not be enough here to subject a distributor to liability. Nor would ordinary acts incident to product distribution, such as offering customers technical support or product updates, support liability in themselves. The inducement rule, instead, premises liability on purposeful, culpable expression and conduct, and thus does nothing to compromise legitimate commerce or discourage innovation having a lawful promise.

III

A

The only apparent question about treating MGM's evidence as sufficient to withstand summary judgment under the theory of inducement goes to the need on MGM's part to adduce evidence that StreamCast and Grokster communicated an inducing message to their software users. The classic instance of inducement is by advertisement or solicitation that broadcasts a message designed to stimulate others to commit violations. MGM claims that such a message is shown here. It is undisputed that StreamCast beamed onto the computer screens of users of Napster-compatible programs ads urging the adoption of its OpenNap program, which was designed, as its name implied, to invite the custom of patrons of Napster, then under attack in the courts for facilitating massive infringement. Those who accepted StreamCast's OpenNap program were offered software to perform the same services, which a factfinder could conclude would readily have been understood in the Napster market as the ability to download copyrighted music files. Grokster distributed an electronic newsletter containing links to articles promoting its software's ability to access popular copyrighted music. And anyone whose Napster or free file-sharing searches turned up a link to Grokster would have understood Grokster to be offering the same file-sharing ability as Napster, and to the same people who probably used Napster for infringing downloads; that would also have been the understanding of anyone offered Grokster's suggestively named Swaptor software, its version of OpenNap. And both companies communicated a clear message by responding affirmatively to requests for help in locating and playing copyrighted materials.

In StreamCast's case, of course, the evidence just described was supplemented by other unequivocal indications of unlawful purpose in the internal communications and advertising designs aimed at Napster users. . . . Whether the messages were communicated is not to the point on this record. The function of the message in the theory of inducement is to prove by a defendant's own statements that his unlawful purpose disqualifies him from claiming protection. . . . Here, the summary judgment record is replete with other evidence that Grokster and StreamCast, unlike the manufacturer and distributor in *Sony*, acted with a purpose to cause copyright violations by use of software suitable for illegal use. . . .

Three features of this evidence of intent are particularly notable. First, each company showed itself to be aiming to satisfy a known source of demand for copyright infringement, the market comprising former Napster users. StreamCast's internal documents made constant reference to Napster, it initially distributed its Morpheus software through an OpenNap program compatible with Napster, it advertised its OpenNap program to Napster users, and its Morpheus software functions as Napster did except that it could be used to distribute more kinds of files, including copyrighted movies and software programs. Grokster's name is apparently derived from Napster, it too initially offered an OpenNap program, its software's function is likewise comparable to Napster's, and it attempted to divert queries for Napster onto its own Web site. Grokster and StreamCast's efforts to supply services to former Napster users, deprived of a mechanism to copy and distribute what were overwhelmingly infringing files, indicate a principal, if not exclusive, intent on the part of each to bring about infringement.

Second, this evidence of unlawful objective is given added significance by MGM's showing that neither company attempted to develop filtering tools or other mechanisms to diminish the infringing activity using their software. While the Ninth Circuit treated the defendants' failure to develop such tools as irrelevant because they lacked an independent duty to monitor their users' activity, we think this evidence underscores Grokster's and StreamCast's intentional facilitation of their users' infringement.

Third, there is a further complement to the direct evidence of unlawful objective. It is useful to recall that StreamCast and Grokster make money by selling advertising space, by directing ads to the screens of computers employing their software. As the record shows, the more the software is used, the more ads are sent out and the greater the advertising revenue becomes. Since the extent of the software's use determines the gain to the distributors, the commercial sense of their enterprise turns on high-volume use, which the record shows is infringing. This evidence alone would not justify an inference of unlawful intent, but viewed in the context of the entire record its import is clear.

The unlawful objective is unmistakable.

B

In addition to intent to bring about infringement and distribution of a device suitable for infringing use, the inducement theory of course requires evidence of actual infringement by recipients of the device, the software in this case. As the account of the facts indicates, there is evidence of infringement on a gigantic scale, and there is no serious issue of the adequacy of MGM's showing on this point in order to survive the companies' summary judgment requests. Although an exact calculation of infringing use, as a basis for a claim of damages, is subject to dispute, there is no question that the summary judgment evidence is at least adequate to entitle MGM to go forward with claims for damages and equitable relief.

COMMENTS AND QUESTIONS

1. The *Grokster* case was ultimately settled between the parties with no further proceedings. A visit to the Grokster Web site (*grokster.com*) shortly after the settlement showed the following message: "The United States Supreme Court unanimously confirmed that using this service to trade copyrighted material is illegal. Copying copyrighted motion picture and music files using unauthorized peer-to-peer services is illegal and is prosecuted by copyright owners. There are legal services for downloading music and movies. This service is not one of them. Grokster hopes to have a safe and legal service

available soon." Is this statement an accurate reflection of what was decided by the Supreme Court in *Grokster*?

2.   What factors does the Supreme Court rely on to suggest that there is strong evidence of inducement to infringe copyright in *Grokster*? Do you find this analysis convincing?

3.   Is the inducement test for secondary liability in *Grokster* consistent with the *Sony* test for secondary liability? Are you convinced by Judge Souter's explanation of the relationship between the two tests?

4.   Is it possible to reconcile the approaches taken to secondary liability in *Napster* and *Grokster*? The *Napster* court applied the *Sony* test and found that the defendant did have sufficient knowledge of infringing activities to support a contributory infringement claim. The *Grokster* court avoided direct application of the *Sony* test but came to a similar conclusion based on a more general "inducement" test of secondary liability. Why couldn't the Supreme Court apply the *Sony* test to find in favor of the plaintiffs? Does the *Grokster* decision increase uncertainty in the law of secondary liability for copyright infringement? *See* Advisory Committee to the Congressional Internet Caucus, *Interpreting Grokster: Protecting Copyright in the Age of Peer-to-Peer*, July 19, 2005 (available at *http://www.netcaucus.org/events/2005/grokster/*); Electronic Frontier Foundation, *What Grokster Means on the Ground*, July 13, 2005 (available at *http://www.eff.org/deeplinks/archives/003808.php*); Electronic Frontier Foundation, *Interpreting MGM v. Grokster: What Is the Practical Impact and What Is Left for Congress to Do?* (available at *http://www.eff.org/IP/P2P/MGM_v_Grokster/grokster_one_pager.pdf*).

5.   Various commentators have suggested alternate approaches to copyright liability involving peer-to-peer file sharing services. *See* Alfred Yen, *Sony, Tort Doctrines and the Puzzle of Peer-to-Peer*, 55 Case W. Res. L. Rev. 815 (2005) (detailed discussion of applying common law tort principles to digital file sharing scenarios); Mark Lemley & R. Anthony Reese, *Reducing Digital Copyright Infringement Without Restricting Innovation*, 56 Stan. L. Rev. 1345 (2004) (suggesting a simple and inexpensive dispute resolution procedure for copyright holders to bring actions against direct infringers — file sharers — and thus to avoid suits against third-party service providers, the idea being to reduce the impact of copyright enforcement on innovation in file sharing technologies); Jane Ginsburg, *Separating the* Sony *Sheep from the* Grokster *Goats: Reckoning the Future Business Plans of Copyright-Dependent Technology Entrepreneurs*, 50 Ariz. L. Rev. 577 (2008).

6.   Professor Raymond Shih Ray Ku has also considered the Grokster problem from a broader perspective, suggesting that the battle in *Grokster* between copyright holders and developers of file sharing technologies reflects a larger and more fundamental issue of differing approaches to the judicial creation and protection of property rights. Raymond Shih Ray Ku, *Grokking Grokster*, 2005 Wis. L. Rev. 1217 (2005).

7.   In 2007, the Ninth Circuit Court of Appeals considered some of the direct and indirect copyright liability questions in the context of a search

engine's potential liability for copyright infringement. The same court also considered the possibility of an electronic payment system provider being held liable for secondary infringement. Consider the following extracts.

PERFECT 10, INC., v. GOOGLE INC.

508 F.3d 1146 (9th Cir. 2007)

IKUTA, Circuit Judge:

In this appeal, we consider a copyright owner's efforts to stop an Internet search engine from facilitating access to infringing images. Perfect 10, Inc. sued Google Inc., for infringing Perfect 10's copyrighted photographs of nude models, among other claims. Perfect 10 brought a similar action against Amazon.com and its subsidiary A9.com (collectively, "Amazon.com"). The district court preliminarily enjoined Google from creating and publicly displaying thumbnail versions of Perfect 10's images, *Perfect 10 v. Google, Inc.*, 416 F. Supp. 2d 828 (C.D. Cal. 2006), but did not enjoin Google from linking to third-party websites that display infringing full-size versions of Perfect 10's images. Nor did the district court preliminarily enjoin Amazon.com from giving users access to information provided by Google. Perfect 10 and Google both appeal the district court's order . . .

I

Background

Google's computers, along with millions of others, are connected to networks known collectively as the "Internet." "The Internet is a world-wide network of networks . . . all sharing a common communications technology." *Religious Tech. Ctr. v. Netcom On-Line Commc'n Servs., Inc.*, 923 F. Supp. 1231, 1238 n.1 (N.D. Cal. 1995). Computer owners can provide information stored on their computers to other users connected to the Internet through a medium called a webpage. A webpage consists of text interspersed with instructions written in Hypertext Markup Language ("HTML") that is stored in a computer. No images are stored on a webpage; rather, the HTML instructions on the webpage provide an address for where the images are stored, whether in the webpage publisher's computer or some other computer. In general, webpages are publicly available and can be accessed by computers connected to the Internet through the use of a web browser.

Google operates a search engine, a software program that automatically accesses thousands of websites (collections of webpages) and indexes them within a database stored on Google's computers. When a Google user accesses the Google website and types in a search query, Google's software searches its database for websites responsive to that search query. Google then sends relevant information from its index of websites to the user's computer. Google's search engines can provide results in the form of text, images, or videos.

The Google search engine that provides responses in the form of images is called "Google Image Search." In response to a search query, Google Image Search identifies text in its database responsive to the query and then communicates to users the images associated with the relevant text. Google's software cannot recognize and index the images themselves. Google Image Search provides search results as a webpage of small images called "thumbnails," which are stored in Google's servers. The thumbnail images are reduced, lower-resolution versions of full-sized images stored on third-party computers.

When a user clicks on a thumbnail image, the user's browser program interprets HTML instructions on Google's webpage. These HTML instructions direct the user's browser to cause a rectangular area (a "window") to appear on the user's computer screen. The window has two separate areas of information. The browser fills the top section of the screen with information from the Google webpage, including the thumbnail image and text. The HTML instructions also give the user's browser the address of the website publisher's computer that stores the full-size version of the thumbnail. By following the HTML instructions to access the third-party webpage, the user's browser connects to the website publisher's computer, downloads the full-size image, and makes the image appear at the bottom of the window on the user's screen. Google does not store the images that fill this lower part of the window and does not communicate the images to the user; Google simply provides HTML instructions directing a user's browser to access a third-party website. However, the top part of the window (containing the information from the Google webpage) appears to frame and comment on the bottom part of the window. Thus, the user's window appears to be filled with a single integrated presentation of the full-size image, but it is actually an image from a third-party website framed by information from Google's website. The process by which the webpage directs a user's browser to incorporate content from different computers into a single window is referred to as "in-line linking." *Kelly v. Arriba Soft Corp.*, 336 F.3d 811, 816 (9th Cir. 2003). The term "framing" refers to the process by which information from one computer appears to frame and annotate the in-line linked content from another computer. *Perfect 10*, 416 F. Supp. 2d at 833-34.

Google also stores webpage content in its cache. For each cached webpage, Google's cache contains the text of the webpage as it appeared at the time Google indexed the page, but does not store images from the webpage. *Id.* at 833. Google may provide a link to a cached webpage in response to a user's search query. However, Google's cache version of the webpage is not automatically updated when the webpage is revised by its owner. So if the webpage owner updates its webpage to remove the HTML instructions for finding an infringing image, a browser communicating directly with the webpage would not be able to access that image. However, Google's cache copy of the webpage would still have the old HTML instructions for the infringing image. Unless the owner of the computer changed the HTML address of the infringing image, or otherwise rendered the image unavailable, a browser accessing Google's cache copy of the website could still access the image where it is stored on the website publisher's computer. In other words, Google's cache copy could provide a user's browser with valid directions to an infringing image even though the updated webpage no longer includes that infringing image.

In addition to its search engine operations, Google generates revenue through a business program called "AdSense." Under this program, the owner of a website can register with Google to become an AdSense "partner." The website owner then places HTML instructions on its webpages that signal Google's server to place advertising on the webpages that is relevant to the webpages' content. Google's computer program selects the advertising automatically by means of an algorithm. AdSense participants agree to share the revenues that flow from such advertising with Google.

Google also generated revenues through an agreement with Amazon.com that allowed Amazon.com to in-line link to Google's search results. Amazon.com gave its users the impression that Amazon.com was providing search results, but Google communicated the search results directly to Amazon.com's users. Amazon.com routed users' search queries to Google and automatically transmitted Google's responses (i.e., HTML instructions for linking to Google's search results) back to its users.

Perfect 10 markets and sells copyrighted images of nude models. Among other enterprises, it operates a subscription website on the Internet. Subscribers pay a monthly fee to view Perfect 10 images in a "members' area" of the site. Subscribers must use a password to log into the members' area. Google does not include these password-protected images from the members' area in Google's index or database. Perfect 10 has also licensed Fonestarz Media Limited to sell and distribute Perfect 10's reduced-size copyrighted images for download and use on cell phones.

Some website publishers republish Perfect 10's images on the Internet without authorization. Once this occurs, Google's search engine may automatically index the webpages containing these images and provide thumbnail versions of images in response to user inquiries. When a user clicks on the thumbnail image returned by Google's search engine, the user's browser accesses the third-party webpage and in-line links to the full-sized infringing image stored on the website publisher's computer. This image appears, in its original context, on the lower portion of the window on the user's computer screen framed by information from Google's webpage. . . .

III

Direct Infringement

Perfect 10 claims that Google's search engine program directly infringes two exclusive rights granted to copyright holders: its display rights and its distribution rights. "Plaintiffs must satisfy two requirements to present a prima facie case of direct infringement: (1) they must show ownership of the allegedly infringed material and (2) they must demonstrate that the alleged infringers violate at least one exclusive right granted to copyright holders under 17 U.S.C. §106." *Napster*, 239 F.3d at 1013; *see* 17 U.S.C. §501(a). Even if a plaintiff satisfies these two requirements and makes a prima facie case of direct infringement, the defendant may avoid liability if it can establish that its use of the images is a "fair use" as set forth in 17 U.S.C. §107. *See Kelly*, 336 F.3d at 817.

Perfect 10's ownership of at least some of the images at issue is not disputed. . . .

A. Display Right

In considering whether Perfect 10 made a prima facie case of violation of its display right, the district court reasoned that a computer owner that stores an image as electronic information and serves that electronic information directly to the user ("i.e., physically sending ones and zeroes over the [I]nternet to the user's browser," *Perfect 10*, 416 F. Supp. 2d at 839) is displaying the electronic information in violation of a copyright holder's exclusive display right. *Id.* at 843-45; *see* 17 U.S.C. §106(5). Conversely, the owner of a computer that does not store and serve the electronic information to a user is not displaying that information, even if such owner in-line links to or frames the electronic information. *Perfect 10*, 416 F. Supp. 2d at 843-45. The district court referred to this test as the "server test." *Id.* at 838-39.

Applying the server test, the district court concluded that Perfect 10 was likely to succeed in its claim that Google's thumbnails constituted direct infringement but was unlikely to succeed in its claim that Google's in-line linking to full-size infringing images constituted a direct infringement. *Id.* at 843-45. As explained below, because this analysis comports with the language of the Copyright Act, we agree with the district court's resolution of both these issues.

We have not previously addressed the question when a computer displays a copyrighted work for purposes of section 106(5). Section 106(5) states that a copyright owner has the exclusive right "to display the copyrighted work publicly." The Copyright Act explains that "display" means "to show a copy of it, either directly or by means of a film, slide, television image, or any other device or process. . . . " 17 U.S.C. §101. Section 101 defines "copies" as "material objects, other than phonorecords, in which a work is fixed by any method now known or later developed, and from which the work can be perceived, reproduced, or otherwise communicated, either directly or with the aid of a machine or device." *Id.* Finally, the Copyright Act provides that "[a] work is 'fixed' in a tangible medium of expression when its embodiment in a copy or phonorecord, by or under the authority of the author, is sufficiently permanent or stable to permit it to be perceived, reproduced, or otherwise communicated for a period of more than transitory duration." *Id.*

We must now apply these definitions to the facts of this case. A photographic image is a work that is " 'fixed' in a tangible medium of expression," for purposes of the Copyright Act, when embodied (i.e., stored) in a computer's server (or hard disk, or other storage device). The image stored in the computer is the "copy" of the work for purposes of copyright law. *See MAI Sys. Corp. v. Peak Computer, Inc.*, 991 F.2d 511, 517-18 (9th Cir. 1993) (a computer makes a "copy" of a software program when it transfers the program from a third party's computer (or other storage device) into its own memory, because the copy of the program recorded in the computer is "fixed" in a manner that is "sufficiently permanent or stable to permit it to be perceived, reproduced, or otherwise communicated for a period of more than transitory duration" (quoting 17 U.S.C. §101)). The computer owner shows a copy "by means of a . . . device or process" when the owner uses the computer to fill the computer screen with the photographic image stored on that computer, or by communicating the stored image electronically to another person's computer. 17 U.S.C. §101. In sum, based on the plain language of the statute, a person displays a photographic image by using a computer to fill a computer screen with a copy of the photographic image fixed in the computer's memory. There is no dispute that Google's computers store thumbnail versions of Perfect 10's copyrighted images and communicate copies of those thumbnails to Google's users. Therefore, Perfect 10 has made a prima facie case that Google's communication of its stored thumbnail images directly infringes Perfect 10's display right.

Google does not, however, display a copy of full-size infringing photographic images for purposes of the Copyright Act when Google frames in-line linked images that appear on a user's computer screen. Because Google's computers do not store the photographic images, Google does not have a copy of the images for purposes of the Copyright Act. In other words, Google does not have any "material objects . . . in which a work is fixed . . . and from which the work can be perceived, reproduced, or otherwise communicated" and thus cannot communicate a copy. 17 U.S.C. §101.

Instead of communicating a copy of the image, Google provides HTML instructions that direct a user's browser to a website publisher's computer that stores the full-size photographic image. Providing these HTML instructions is not equivalent to showing a copy. First, the HTML instructions are lines of text, not a photographic image. Second, HTML instructions do not themselves cause infringing images to appear on the user's computer screen. The HTML merely gives the address of the image to the user's browser. The browser then interacts with the computer that stores the infringing image. It is this interaction that causes an infringing image to appear on the user's computer screen. Google may facilitate the user's access to infringing images. However, such assistance raises only contributory liability issues, *see Metro-Goldwyn-Mayer Studios, Inc. v. Grokster, Ltd.*, 545 U.S. 913, 929-30, 125 S. Ct. 2764, 162 L. Ed. 2d 781 (2005), *Napster*, 239 F.3d at 1019, and does not constitute direct infringement of the copyright owner's display rights.

Perfect 10 argues that Google displays a copy of the full-size images by framing the full-size images, which gives the impression that Google is showing the image within a single Google webpage. While in-line linking and framing may cause some computer users to believe they are viewing a single Google webpage, the Copyright Act, unlike the Trademark Act, does not protect a copyright holder against acts that cause consumer confusion. . . .

Nor does our ruling that a computer owner does not display a copy of an image when it communicates only the HTML address of the copy erroneously collapse the display right in section 106(5) into the reproduction right set forth in section 106(1). Nothing in the Copyright Act prevents the various rights protected in *section 106* from overlapping. Indeed, under some circumstances, more than one right must be infringed in order for an infringement claim to arise. For example, a "Game Genie" device that allowed a player to alter features of a Nintendo computer game did not infringe Nintendo's right to prepare derivative works because the Game Genie did not incorporate any portion of the game itself. *See Lewis Galoob Toys, Inc. v. Nintendo of Am., Inc.*, 964 F.2d 965, 967 (9th Cir. 1992). We held that a copyright holder's right to create derivative works is not infringed unless the alleged derivative work "incorporate[s] a protected work in some concrete or permanent 'form.' " *Id.* In other words, in some contexts, the claimant must be able to claim infringement of its reproduction right in order to claim infringement of its right to prepare derivative works.

Because Google's cache merely stores the text of webpages, our analysis of whether Google's search engine program potentially infringes Perfect 10's display and distribution rights is equally applicable to Google's cache. Perfect 10 is not likely to succeed in showing that a cached webpage that in-line links to full-size infringing images violates such rights. For purposes of this analysis, it is irrelevant whether cache copies direct a user's browser to third-party images that are no longer available on the third party's website, because it is the website publisher's computer, rather than Google's computer, that stores and displays the infringing image.

B. Distribution Right

The district court also concluded that Perfect 10 would not likely prevail on its claim that Google directly infringed Perfect 10's right to distribute its full-size images. *Perfect 10*, 416 F. Supp. 2d at 844-45. The district court reasoned that distribution requires an "actual dissemination" of a copy. *Id.* at 844. Because Google did not communicate the full-size images to the user's computer, Google did not distribute these images. *Id.*

Again, the district court's conclusion on this point is consistent with the language of the Copyright Act. Section 106(3) provides that the copyright owner has the exclusive right "to distribute copies or phonorecords of the copyrighted work to the public by sale or other transfer of ownership, or by rental, lease, or lending." 17 U.S.C. §106(3). As noted, "copies" means "material objects . . . in which a work is fixed." 17 U.S.C. §101. The Supreme Court has indicated that in the electronic context, copies may be distributed electronically. *See N.Y. Times Co. v. Tasini*, 533 U.S. 483, 498, 121 S. Ct. 2381, 150 L. Ed. 2d 500 (2001) (a computer database program distributed copies of newspaper articles stored in its computerized database by selling copies of those articles through its database service). Google's search engine communicates HTML instructions that tell a user's browser where to find full-size images on a website publisher's computer, but Google does not itself distribute copies of the infringing photographs. It is the website publisher's computer that distributes copies of the images by transmitting the photographic image electronically to the user's computer. As in *Tasini*, the user can then obtain copies by downloading the photo or printing it.

Perfect 10 incorrectly relies on *Hotaling v. Church of Jesus Christ of Latter-Day Saints* and *Napster* for the proposition that merely making images "available" violates the copyright owner's distribution right. *Hotaling v. Church of Jesus Christ of Latter-Day Saints*, 118 F.3d 199 (4th Cir. 1997); *Napster*, 239 F.3d 1004. *Hotaling* held that the owner of a collection of works who makes them available to the public may be deemed to have distributed copies of the works. *Hotaling*, 118 F.3d at 203. Similarly, the distribution rights of the plaintiff copyright owners were infringed by Napster *users* (private individuals with collections of music files stored on their home computers) when they used the Napster software to make their collections available to all other Napster users. *Napster*, 239 F.3d at 1011-14.

This "deemed distribution" rule does not apply to Google. Unlike the participants in the *Napster* system or the library in *Hotaling*, Google does not own a collection of Perfect 10's full-size images and does not communicate these images to the computers of people using Google's search engine. Though Google indexes these images, it does not have a collection of stored full-size images it makes available to the public. Google therefore cannot be deemed to distribute copies of these images under the reasoning of *Napster* or *Hotaling*. Accordingly, the district court correctly concluded that Perfect 10 does not have a likelihood of success in proving that Google violates Perfect 10's distribution rights with respect to full-size images. . . .

IV

Secondary Liability for Copyright Infringement

We now turn to the district court's ruling that Google is unlikely to be secondarily liable for its in-line linking to infringing full-size images under the doctrines of contributory and vicarious infringement. The district court ruled that Perfect 10 did not have a likelihood of proving success on the merits of either its contributory infringement or vicarious infringement claims with respect to the full-size images. *See Perfect 10*, 416 F. Supp. 2d at 856, 858.

In reviewing the district court's conclusions, we are guided by the Supreme Court's recent interpretation of secondary liability, namely: "[o]ne infringes contributorily by intentionally inducing or encouraging direct infringement, and infringes vicariously by profiting from direct infringement while declining to exercise a right to stop or limit it." *Grokster*, 545 U.S. at 930 (internal citations omitted).

Direct Infringement by Third Parties. As a threshold matter, before we examine Perfect 10's claims that Google is secondarily liable, Perfect 10 must establish that there has been direct infringement by third parties. *See Napster*, 239 F.3d at 1013 n.2 ("Secondary liability for copyright infringement does not exist in the absence of direct infringement by a third party.").

Perfect 10 alleges that third parties directly infringed its images in three ways. First, Perfect 10 claims that third-party websites directly infringed its copyright by reproducing, displaying, and distributing unauthorized copies of Perfect 10's images. Google does not dispute this claim on appeal.

Second, Perfect 10 claims that individual users of Google's search engine directly infringed Perfect 10's copyrights by storing full-size infringing images on their computers. We agree with the district court's conclusion that Perfect 10 failed to provide sufficient evidence to support this claim. *See Perfect 10*, 416 F. Supp. 2d at 852. There is no evidence in the record directly establishing that users of Google's search engine have stored infringing images on their computers, and the district court did not err in declining to infer the existence of such evidence.

Finally, Perfect 10 contends that users who link to infringing websites automatically make "cache" copies of full-size images and thereby directly infringe Perfect 10's reproduction right. The district court rejected this argument, holding that any such reproduction was likely a "fair use." *Id.* at 852 n.17. The district court reasoned that "[l]ocal caching by the browsers of individual users is noncommercial, transformative, and no more than necessary to achieve the objectives of decreasing network latency and minimizing unnecessary bandwidth usage (essential to the [I]nternet). It has a minimal impact on the potential market for the original work. . . . " *Id.* We agree; even assuming such automatic copying could constitute direct infringement, it is a fair use in this context. The copying function performed automatically by a user's computer to assist in accessing the Internet is a transformative use. Moreover, as noted by the district court, a cache copies no more than is necessary to assist the user in Internet use. It is designed to enhance an individual's computer use, not to supersede the copyright holders' exploitation of their works. Such automatic background copying has no more than a minimal effect on Perfect 10's rights, but a considerable public benefit. Because the four fair use factors weigh in favor of concluding that cache copying constitutes a fair use, Google has established a likelihood of success on this issue. Accordingly, Perfect 10 has not carried its burden of showing that users' cache copies of Perfect 10's full-size images constitute direct infringement.

Therefore, we must assess Perfect 10's arguments that Google is second-arily liable in light of the direct infringement that is undisputed by the parties: third-party websites' reproducing, displaying, and distributing unauthorized copies of Perfect 10's images on the Internet. *Id.* at 852.

A. Contributory Infringement

In order for Perfect 10 to show it will likely succeed in its contributory liability claim against Google, it must establish that Google's activities meet the definition of contributory liability recently enunciated in *Grokster*. Within the general rule that "[o]ne infringes contributorily by intentionally inducing or encouraging direct infringement," *Grokster*, 545 U.S. at 930, the Court has defined two categories of contributory liability: "Liability under our jurisprudence may be predicated on actively encouraging (or inducing) infringement through specific acts (as the Court's opinion develops) or on distributing a product distributees use to infringe copyrights, if the product is not capable of 'substantial' or 'commercially significant' noninfringing uses." *Id.* at 942 (Ginsburg, J., concurring) (quoting *Sony*, 464 U.S. at 442); *see also id.* at 936-37.

Looking at the second category of liability identified by the Supreme Court (distributing products), Google relies on *Sony*, 464 U.S. at 442, to argue that it cannot be held liable for contributory infringement because liability does not arise from the mere sale of a product (even with knowledge that consumers would use the product to infringe) if the product is capable of substantial non-infringing use. Google argues that its search engine service is such a product. Assuming the principle enunciated in *Sony* is applicable to the operation of Google's search engine, then Google cannot be held liable for contributory infringement *solely* because the design of its search engine facilitates such infringement. *Grokster*, 545 U.S. at 931-32 (discussing *Sony*, 464 U.S. 417, 104 S. Ct. 774, 78 L. Ed. 2d 574). Nor can Google be held liable solely because it did not develop technology that would enable its search engine to automatically avoid infringing images. *See id.* at 939 n.12. However, Perfect 10 has not based its claim of infringement on the design of Google's search engine and the *Sony* rule does not immunize Google from other sources of contributory liability. *See id.* at 933-34.

We must next consider whether Google could be held liable under the first category of contributory liability identified by the Supreme Court, that is, the liability that may be imposed for intentionally encouraging infringement through specific acts. *Grokster* tells us that contribution to infringement must be intentional for liability to arise. *Grokster*, 545 U.S. at 930. However, *Grokster* also directs us to analyze contributory liability in light of "rules of fault-based liability derived from the common law," *id.* at 934-35, and common law principles establish that intent may be imputed. "Tort law ordinarily imputes to an actor the intention to cause the natural and probable consequences of his conduct." *DeVoto v. Pac. Fid. Life Ins. Co.*, 618 F.2d 1340, 1347 (9th Cir.

1980); RESTATEMENT (SECOND) OF TORTS §8A cmt. b (1965) ("If the actor knows that the consequences are certain, or substantially certain, to result from his act, and still goes ahead, he is treated by the law as if he had in fact desired to produce the result."). When the Supreme Court imported patent law's "staple article of commerce doctrine" into the copyright context, it also adopted these principles of imputed intent. *Grokster*, 545 U.S. at 932 ("The [staple article of commerce] doctrine was devised to identify instances in which it may be presumed from distribution of an article in commerce that the distributor intended the article to be used to infringe another's patent, and so may justly be held liable for that infringement."). Therefore, under *Grokster*, an actor may be contributorily liable for intentionally encouraging direct infringement if the actor knowingly takes steps that are substantially certain to result in such direct infringement.

Our tests for contributory liability are consistent with the rule set forth in *Grokster*. We have adopted the general rule set forth in *Gershwin Publishing Corp. v. Columbia Artists Management, Inc.*, namely: "one who, with knowledge of the infringing activity, induces, causes or materially contributes to the infringing conduct of another, may be held liable as a 'contributory' infringer," 443 F.2d 1159, 1162 (2d Cir. 1971). *See Ellison*, 357 F.3d at 1076; *Napster*, 239 F.3d at 1019; *Fonovisa, Inc. v. Cherry Auction, Inc.*, 76 F.3d 259, 264 (9th Cir. 1996).

[The court then sets out details of the *Napster* and *Netcom* cases — each extracted previously in this chapter.]

Although neither *Napster* nor *Netcom* expressly required a finding of intent, those cases are consistent with *Grokster* because both decisions ruled that a service provider's knowing failure to prevent infringing actions could be the basis for imposing contributory liability. Under such circumstances, intent may be imputed. In addition, *Napster* and *Netcom* are consistent with the longstanding requirement that an actor's contribution to infringement must be material to warrant the imposition of contributory liability. *Gershwin*, 443 F.2d at 1162. Both *Napster* and *Netcom* acknowledge that services or products that facilitate access to websites throughout the world can significantly magnify the effects of otherwise immaterial infringing activities. *See Napster*, 239 F.3d at 1022; *Netcom*, 907 F. Supp. at 1375. The Supreme Court has acknowledged that "[t]he argument for imposing indirect liability" is particularly "powerful" when individuals using the defendant's software could make a huge number of infringing downloads every day. *Grokster*, 545 U.S. at 929. Moreover, copyright holders cannot protect their rights in a meaningful way unless they can hold providers of such services or products accountable for their actions pursuant to a test such as that enunciated in *Napster*. *See id.* at 929-30 ("When a widely shared service or product is used to commit infringement, it may be impossible to enforce rights in the protected work effectively against all direct infringers, the only practical alternative being to go against the distributor of the copying device for secondary liability on a theory of contributory or vicarious infringement.").

Accordingly, we hold that a computer system operator can be held contributorily liable if it "has *actual* knowledge that *specific* infringing material is available using its system," *Napster*, 239 F.3d at 1022, and can "take simple
measures to prevent further damage" to copyrighted works, *Netcom*,
907 F. Supp. at 1375, yet continues to provide access to infringing works.

Here, the district court held that even assuming Google had actual knowledge of infringing material available on its system, Google did not materially
contribute to infringing conduct because it did not undertake any substantial
promotional or advertising efforts to encourage visits to infringing websites,
nor provide a significant revenue stream to the infringing websites. *Perfect 10*,
416 F. Supp. 2d at 854-56. This analysis is erroneous. There is no dispute that
Google substantially assists websites to distribute their infringing copies to a
worldwide market and assists a worldwide audience of users to access infringing
materials. We cannot discount the effect of such a service on copyright owners,
even though Google's assistance is available to all websites, not just infringing
ones. Applying our test, Google could be held contributorily liable if it had
knowledge that infringing Perfect 10 images were available using its search
engine, could take simple measures to prevent further damage to Perfect 10's
copyrighted works, and failed to take such steps.

The district court did not resolve the factual disputes over the adequacy of
Perfect 10's notices to Google and Google's responses to these notices. Moreover, there are factual disputes over whether there are reasonable and feasible
means for Google to refrain from providing access to infringing images. Therefore, we must remand this claim to the district court for further consideration
whether Perfect 10 would likely succeed in establishing that Google was contributorily liable for in-line linking to full-size infringing images under the test
enunciated today.

B. Vicarious Infringement

Perfect 10 also challenges the district court's conclusion that it is not likely
to prevail on a theory of vicarious liability against Google. *Perfect 10*, 416 F.
Supp. 2d at 856-58. *Grokster* states that one "infringes vicariously by profiting
from direct infringement while declining to exercise a right to stop or limit it."
Grokster, 545 U.S. at 930. As this formulation indicates, to succeed in imposing vicarious liability, a plaintiff must establish that the defendant exercises the
requisite control over the direct infringer and that the defendant derives a
direct financial benefit from the direct infringement. *See id*. *Grokster* further
explains the "control" element of the vicarious liability test as the defendant's
"right and ability to supervise the direct infringer." *Id*. at 930 n.9. Thus, under
Grokster, a defendant exercises control over a direct infringer when he has both
a legal right to stop or limit the directly infringing conduct, as well as the
practical ability to do so.

We evaluate Perfect 10's arguments that Google is vicariously liable in
light of the direct infringement that is undisputed by the parties, namely, the

third-party websites' reproduction, display, and distribution of unauthorized copies of Perfect 10's images on the Internet. *Perfect 10*, 416 F. Supp. 2d at 852. . . . In order to prevail at this preliminary injunction stage, Perfect 10 must demonstrate a likelihood of success in establishing that Google has the right and ability to stop or limit the infringing activities of third party websites. In addition, Perfect 10 must establish a likelihood of proving that Google derives a direct financial benefit from such activities. Perfect 10 has not met this burden.

With respect to the "control" element set forth in *Grokster*, Perfect 10 has not demonstrated a likelihood of showing that Google has the legal right to stop or limit the direct infringement of third-party websites. *See Grokster*, 545 U.S. at 930. Unlike *Fonovisa*, where by virtue of a "broad contract" with its vendors the defendant swap meet operators had the right to stop the vendors from selling counterfeit recordings on its premises, *Fonovisa*, 76 F.3d at 263, Perfect 10 has not shown that Google has contracts with third-party websites that empower Google to stop or limit them from reproducing, displaying, and distributing infringing copies of Perfect 10's images on the Internet. Perfect 10 does point to Google's AdSense agreement, which states that Google reserves "the right to monitor and terminate partnerships with entities that violate others' copyright[s]." *Perfect 10*, 416 F. Supp. 2d at 858. However, Google's right to terminate an AdSense partnership does not give Google the right to stop direct infringement by third-party websites. An infringing third-party website can continue to reproduce, display, and distribute its infringing copies of Perfect 10 images after its participation in the AdSense program has ended.

Nor is Google similarly situated to Napster. Napster users infringed the plaintiffs' reproduction and distribution rights through their use of Napster's proprietary music-file sharing system. *Napster*, 239 F.3d at 1011-14. There, the infringing conduct was the use of Napster's "service to download and upload copyrighted music." *Id.* at 1014 (internal quotation omitted). Because Napster had a closed system requiring user registration, and could terminate its users' accounts and block their access to the Napster system, Napster had the right and ability to prevent its users from engaging in the infringing activity of uploading file names and downloading Napster users' music files through the Napster system. *Id.* at 1023-24. By contrast, Google cannot stop any of the third-party websites from reproducing, displaying, and distributing unauthorized copies of Perfect 10's images because that infringing conduct takes place on the third-party websites. Google cannot terminate those third-party websites or block their ability to "host and serve infringing full-size images" on the Internet. *Perfect 10*, 416 F. Supp. 2d at 831.

Moreover, the district court found that Google lacks the practical ability to police the third-party websites' infringing conduct. *Id.* at 857-58. Specifically, the court found that Google's supervisory power is limited because "Google's software lacks the ability to analyze every image on the [I]nternet, compare each image to all the other copyrighted images that exist in the world . . . and determine whether a certain image on the web infringes some-one's copyright." *Id.* at 858. The district court also concluded that Perfect 10's suggestions regarding measures Google could implement to prevent its web crawler from indexing infringing websites and to block access to infringing images were not workable. *Id.* at 858 n.25. Rather, the suggestions suffered from both "imprecision and overbreadth." *Id.* We hold that these findings are not clearly erroneous. Without image-recognition technology, Google lacks the practical ability to police the infringing activities of third-party websites. This distinguishes Google from the defendants held liable in *Napster* and *Fonovisa. See Napster*, 239 F.3d at 1023-24 (Napster had the ability to identify and police infringing conduct by searching its index for song titles); *Fonovisa*, 76 F.3d at 262 (swap meet operator had the ability to identify and police infringing activity by patrolling its premises).

Perfect 10 argues that Google could manage its own operations to avoid indexing websites with infringing content and linking to third-party infringing sites. This is a claim of contributory liability, not vicarious liability. Although "the lines between direct infringement, contributory infringement, and vicarious liability are not clearly drawn," *Sony*, 464 U.S. at 435 n.17 (internal quotation omitted), in general, contributory liability is based on the defendant's failure to stop its own actions which facilitate third-party infringement, while vicarious liability is based on the defendant's failure to cause a third party to stop its directly infringing activities. *See, e.g., Ellison*, 357 F.3d at 1077-78; *Fonovisa*, 76 F.3d at 261-64. Google's failure to change its operations to avoid assisting websites to distribute their infringing content may constitute contributory liability. . . . However, this failure is not the same as declining to exercise a right and ability to make third-party websites stop their direct infringement. We reject Perfect 10's efforts to blur this distinction. . . .

V

Amazon.com

Perfect 10 claims that Amazon.com displays and distributes Perfect 10's copyrighted images and is also secondarily liable for the infringements of third-party websites and Amazon.com users. The district court concluded that Perfect 10 was unlikely to succeed in proving that Amazon.com was a direct infringer, because it merely in-line linked to the thumbnails on Google's servers and to the full-size images on third-party websites. *Perfect 10 v. Amazon*, No. 05-4753, consolidated with 04-9484 (C.D. Cal. Feb. 21, 2006) (order denying preliminary injunction). In addition, the district court concluded that Perfect 10's secondary infringement claims against Amazon.com were likely to fail because Amazon.com had no program analogous to AdSense, and thus did not provide any revenues to infringing sites. *Id.* Finally, the district court determined that Amazon.com's right and ability to control the infringing conduct of third-party websites was substantially less than Google's. *Id*. Therefore, the district court denied Perfect 10's motion for a preliminary injunction against Amazon.com. *Id*.

[The court holds that Perfect 10 has not shown any likelihood that it could prevail on a direct infringement claim against Amazon.com because Amazon.com does not display or distribute copies of any of Perfect 10's images to its users. The court further holds that the claim against Amazon.com in vicarious liability is unlikely to succeed because Amazon.com did not have the right and ability to supervise any infringing activities and did not clearly have any direct financial interest in infringing activities.]

However, the district court did not consider whether Amazon.com had "*actual* knowledge that *specific* infringing material is available using its system," *Napster*, 239 F.3d at 1022 (emphasis in original), and could have "take[n] simple measures to prevent further damage" to copyrighted works, *Netcom*, 907 F. Supp. at 1375, yet continued to provide access to infringing works. Perfect 10 has presented evidence that it notified Amazon.com that it was facilitating its users' access to infringing material. It is disputed whether the notices gave Amazon.com actual knowledge of specific infringing activities available using its system, and whether Amazon.com could have taken reasonable and feasible steps to refrain from providing access to such images, but failed to do so. Nor did the district court consider whether Amazon.com is entitled to limit its liability under title II of the DMCA. On remand, the district court should consider Amazon.com's potential contributory liability, as well as possible limitations on the scope of injunctive relief, in light of our rulings today. . . .

[Affirmed in part; reversed in part; remanded.]

COMMENTS AND QUESTIONS

1. What is the "server test" for infringement of a copyright holder's display right? Do you agree with the results obtained from applying this test in *Perfect 10*?

2. Could Perfect 10 claim trademark infringement for Google's framing and inline linking of its photographs?

3. How does the *Perfect 10* court distinguish *Napster* and *Hotaling* on the issue of direct infringement of Perfect 10's distribution right?

4. In *Perfect 10*, why is Google potentially liable as a direct copyright infringer with respect to the thumbnail images, but not with respect to the full sized images? Does the court's distinction here make sense? Is this an area where the activities of search engines do not fit neatly within existing copyright law paradigms? Does it suggest that we need new copyright principles to deal with new challenges posed by the Internet?

5. What does Perfect 10 argue are the direct infringements for which it wishes to hold Google indirectly liable? Does the court accept Perfect 10's arguments on this issue?

6.   How does the court in *Perfect 10* apply the *Grokster* test for contributory liability? Is this approach consistent with the Supreme Court's ruling in *Grokster*? In what ways does it differ?

7.   How does the *Perfect 10* court distinguish *Napster* on the question of vicarious liability? Do you agree with the distinction?

8.   How does the court in *Perfect 10* explain the difference between contributory and vicarious liability? Is this explanation consistent with your understanding of the two doctrines from the previous cases you have considered?

9.   How did Perfect 10's claims against Amazon.com differ from its claims against Google? Why does the court hold that Amazon.com is unlikely to be liable for direct infringement or for vicarious infringement? On what basis might Amazon.com nevertheless be liable for contributory infringement? Is the court's analysis of Amazon.com's potential liability consistent with previous case law on direct and indirect copyright infringement?

PERFECT 10, INC. v. VISA INTERNATIONAL SERVICE ASSOCIATION

494 F.3d 788 (9th Cir. 2007)

MILAN D. SMITH, Circuit Judge Jr. (STEPHEN REINHARDT, concurring).

. . .

FACTS AND PRIOR PROCEEDINGS

Perfect 10 publishes the magazine "PERFECT10" and operates the subscription website www.perfect10.com., both of which "feature tasteful copyrighted images of the world's most beautiful natural models." Perfect 10 claims copyrights in the photographs published in its magazine and on its website, federal registration of the "PERFECT 10" trademark and blanket publicity rights for many of the models appearing in the photographs. Perfect 10 alleges that numerous websites based in several countries have stolen its proprietary images, altered them, and illegally offered them for sale online.

Instead of suing the direct infringers in this case, Perfect 10 sued Defendants, financial institutions that process certain credit card payments to the allegedly infringing websites. The Visa and MasterCard entities are associations of member banks that issue credit cards to consumers, automatically process payments to merchants authorized to accept their cards, and provide information to the interested parties necessary to settle the resulting debits and credits. Defendants collect fees for their services in these transactions. Perfect 10 alleges that it sent Defendants repeated notices specifically identifying infringing websites and informing Defendants that some of their consumers use their payment cards to purchase infringing images. Defendants admit receiving some of these notices, but they took no action in response to the notices after receiving them. . . .

A. Secondary Liability for Copyright Infringement

Perfect 10 alleges that numerous websites based in several countries — and their paying customers — have directly infringed its rights under the Copyright Act, 17 U.S.C. §101, et seq. In the present suit, however, Perfect 10 has sued Defendants, not the direct infringers, claiming contributory and vicarious copyright infringement because Defendants process credit card charges incurred by customers to acquire the infringing images.

We evaluate Perfect 10's claims with an awareness that credit cards serve as the primary engine of electronic commerce and that Congress has determined it to be the "policy of the United States — (1) to promote the continued development of the Internet and other interactive computer services and other interactive media [and] (2) to preserve the vibrant and competitive free market that presently exists for the Internet and other interactive computer services, unfettered by Federal or State regulation." 47 U.S.C. §§230(b)(1), (2).

1. Contributory Copyright Infringement

. . . We understand [the] several [enunciated] criteria to be noncontradictory variations on the same basic test, i.e., that one contributorily infringes when he (1) has knowledge of another's infringement and (2) either (a) materially contributes to or (b) induces that infringement. Viewed in isolation, the language of the tests described is quite broad, but when one reviews the details of the actual "cases and controversies" before the relevant court in each of the test-defining cases and the actual holdings in those cases, it is clear that the factual circumstances in this case are not analogous. To find that Defendants' activities fall within the scope of such tests would require a radical and inappropriate expansion of existing principles of secondary liability and would violate the public policy of the United States.

a. Knowledge of the Infringing Activity

Because we find that Perfect 10 has not pled facts sufficient to establish that Defendants induce or materially contribute to the infringing activity, Perfect 10's contributory copyright infringement claim fails and we need not address the Defendants' knowledge of the infringing activity.

b. Material Contribution, Inducement, or Causation

To state a claim of contributory infringement, Perfect 10 must allege facts showing that Defendants induce, cause, or materially contribute to the infringing conduct. . . . Perfect 10 argues that by continuing to process credit card payments to the infringing websites despite having knowledge of ongoing infringement, Defendants induce, enable and contribute to the infringing activity in the same way the defendants did in *Fonovisa*, *Napster* and *Grokster*. We disagree.

1. *Material Contribution*

The credit card companies cannot be said to materially contribute to the infringement in this case because they have no direct connection to that infringement. Here, the infringement rests on the reproduction, alteration, display and distribution of Perfect 10's images over the Internet. Perfect 10 has not alleged that any infringing material passes over Defendants' payment networks or through their payment processing systems, or that Defendants' systems are used to alter or display the infringing images. In *Fonovisa*, the infringing material was physically located in and traded at the defendant's market. Here, it is not. Nor are Defendants' systems used to locate the infringing images. The search engines in *Amazon.com* provided links to specific infringing images, and the services in *Napster* and *Grokster* allowed users to locate and obtain infringing material. Here, in contrast, the services provided by the credit card companies do not help locate and are not used to distribute the infringing images. While Perfect 10 has alleged that Defendants make it easier for websites to profit from this infringing activity, the issue here is reproduction, alteration, display and distribution, which can occur without payment. Even if infringing images were not paid for, there would still be infringement. *See Napster*, 239 F.3d at 1014 (Napster users infringed the distribution right by uploading file names to the search index for others to copy, despite the fact that no money changed hands in the transaction).

Our analysis is fully consistent with this court's recent decision in *Perfect 10 v. Amazon.com*, where we found that "Google could be held contributorily liable if it had knowledge that infringing Perfect 10 images were available using its search engine, could take simple measures to prevent further damage to Perfect 10's copyrighted works, and failed to take such steps." 2007 U.S. App. LEXIS 11420, [WL] at *19. The dissent claims this statement applies squarely to Defendants if we just substitute "payment systems" for "search engine." Dissent at 7866. But this is only true if search engines and payment systems are equivalents for these purposes, and they are not. The salient distinction is that Google's search engine itself assists in the distribution of infringing content to Internet users, while Defendants' payment systems do not. The *Amazon.com* court noted that "Google substantially assists websites to distribute their infringing copies to a worldwide market and assists a worldwide audience of users to access infringing materials." *Id.* Defendants do not provide such a service. They in no way assist or enable Internet users to locate infringing material, and they do not distribute it. They do, as alleged, make infringement more profitable, and people are generally more inclined to engage in an activity when it is financially profitable. However, there is an additional step in the causal chain: Google may materially contribute to infringement by making it fast and easy for third parties to locate and distribute infringing material, whereas Defendants make it easier for infringement to be *profitable*, which tends to increase financial incentives to infringe, which in turn tends to increase infringement.

... Helping users to locate an image might substantially assist users to download infringing images, but processing payments does not. If users couldn't pay for images with credit cards, infringement could continue on a large scale because other viable funding mechanisms are available. For example, a website might decide to allow users to download some images for free and to make its profits from advertising, or it might develop other payment mechanisms that do not depend on the credit card companies. In either case, the unlicensed use of Perfect 10's copyrighted images would still be infringement. We acknowledge that Defendants' payment systems make it easier for such an infringement to be profitable, and that they therefore have the effect of increasing such infringement, but because infringement of Perfect 10's copyrights can occur without using Defendants' payment system, we hold that payment processing by the Defendants as alleged in Perfect 10's First Amended Complaint does not constitute a "material contribution" under the test for contributory infringement of copyrights.

Our holding is also fully consistent with and supported by this court's previous holdings in *Fonovisa* and *Napster*. . . . In *Fonovisa*, we held a flea market proprietor liable as a contributory infringer when it provided the facilities for and benefitted from the sale of pirated works. 76 F.3d 259. The court found that the primary infringers and the swap meet were engaged in a mutual enterprise of infringement and observed that "it would be difficult for the infringing activity to take place in the massive quantities alleged without the support services provided by the swap meet. These services include, among other things, the provision of space, utilities, parking, advertising, plumbing, and customers." 76 F.3d at 264. But the swap meet owner did more to encourage the enterprise. In 1991, the Fresno County Sheriff raided the swap meet and seized 38,000 counterfeit recordings. *Id.* at 261. The Sheriff sent a letter to the swap meet operator the following year notifying it that counterfeit sales continued and reminding it that it had agreed to provide the Sheriff with identifying information from each vendor, but had failed to do so. *Id.* The *Fonovisa* court found liability because the swap meet operator knowingly provided the "site and facilities" for the infringing activity. *Id.* at 264.

In *Napster*, this court found the designer and distributor of a software program liable for contributory infringement. 239 F.3d 1004. Napster was a file-sharing program which, while capable of non-infringing use, was expressly engineered to enable the easy exchange of pirated music and was widely so used. *See Napster*, 239 F.3d at 1020 n.5 (quoting document authored by Napster co-founder which mentioned "the need to remain ignorant of users' real names and IP addresses 'since they are exchanging pirated music' "). Citing the *Fonovisa* standard, the *Napster* court found that Napster materially contributes to the users' direct infringement by knowingly providing the "site and facilities" for that infringement. 239 F.3d at 1022. . . .

The swap meet operator in *Fonovisa* and the administrators of the Napster and Grokster programs increased the level of infringement by providing a centralized place, whether physical or virtual, where infringing works could be collected, sorted, found, and bought, sold, or exchanged. The provision of parking lots, plumbing and other accoutrements in *Fonovisa* was significant only because this was part of providing the environment and market for counterfeit recording sales to thrive.

Defendants, in contrast, do no such thing. While Perfect 10 has alleged that it is easy to locate images that infringe its copyrights, the Defendants' payment systems do not cause this. Perfect 10's images are easy to locate because of the very nature of the Internet — the website format, software allowing for the easy alteration of images, high-speed connections allowing for the rapid transfer of high-resolution image files, and perhaps most importantly, powerful search engines that can aggregate and display those images in a useful and efficient manner, without charge, and with astounding speed. Defendants play no role in any of these functions.

Perfect 10 asserts otherwise by arguing for an extremely broad conception of the term "site and facilities" that bears no relationship to the holdings in the actual "cases and controversies" decided in *Fonovisa* and *Napster*. Taken literally, Perfect 10's theory appears to include any tangible or intangible component related to any transaction in which infringing material is bought and sold. But *Fonovisa* and *Napster* do not require or lend themselves to such a construction. The actual display, location, and distribution of infringing images in this case occurs on websites that organize, display, and transmit information over the wires and wireless instruments that make up the Internet. The *websites* are the "site" of the infringement, not Defendants' payment networks. . . .

Perfect 10 seeks to side-step this reality by alleging that Defendants are still contributory infringers because they could refuse to process payments to the infringing websites and thereby undermine their commercial viability. Even though we must take this factual allegation as true, that Defendants have the power to undermine the commercial viability of infringement does not demonstrate that the Defendants materially contribute to that infringement. As previously noted, the direct infringement here is the reproduction, alteration, display and distribution of Perfect 10's images over the Internet. Perfect 10 has not alleged that any infringing material passes over Defendants' payment networks or through their payment processing systems, or that Defendants designed or promoted their payment systems as a means to infringe. While Perfect 10 has alleged that Defendants make it easier for websites to profit from this infringing activity, the infringement stems from the failure to obtain a license to distribute, not the processing of payments.

2. Vicarious Copyright Infringement

Vicarious infringement is a concept related to, but distinct from, contributory infringement. Whereas contributory infringement is based on tort-law principles of enterprise liability and imputed intent, vicarious infringement's roots lie in the agency principles of *respondeat superior*. *See Fonovisa*, 76 F.3d at 261-62. To state a claim for vicarious copyright infringement, a plaintiff must allege that the defendant has (1) the right and ability to supervise the infringing conduct and (2) a direct financial interest in the infringing activity. *Ellison*, 357 F.3d at 1078; *Napster*, 239 F.3d at 1022 (citations omitted). The Supreme Court has recently offered (in dictum) an alternate formulation of the test: "One . . . infringes vicariously by profiting from direct infringement while declining to exercise a right to stop or limit it." *Grokster*, 545 U.S. at 930 (internal citations omitted). Perfect 10 alleges that Defendants have the right and ability to control the content of the infringing websites by refusing to process credit card payments to the websites, enforcing their own rules and regulations, or both. We hold that Defendants' conduct alleged in Perfect 10's first amended complaint fails to state a claim for vicarious copyright infringement.

a. Right and Ability to Supervise the Infringing Activity

In order to join a Defendant's payment network, merchants and member banks must agree to follow that Defendant's rules and regulations. These rules, among other things, prohibit member banks from providing services to merchants engaging in certain illegal activities and require the members and member banks to investigate merchants suspected of engaging in such illegal activity and to terminate their participation in the payment network if certain illegal activity is found. Perfect 10 has alleged that certain websites are infringing Perfect 10's copyrights and that Perfect 10 sent notices of this alleged infringement to Defendants. Accordingly, Perfect 10 has adequately pled that (1) infringement of Perfect 10's copyrights was occurring, (2) Defendants were aware of the infringement, and (3) on this basis, Defendants could have stopped processing credit card payments to the infringing websites. These allegations are not, however, sufficient to establish vicarious liability because even with all reasonable inferences drawn in Perfect 10's favor, Perfect 10's allegations of fact cannot support a finding that Defendants have the right and ability to control the infringing activity.

In reasoning closely analogous to the present case, the *Amazon.com* court held that Google was not vicariously liable for third-party infringement that its search engine facilitates. In so holding, the court found that Google's ability to control its own index, search results, and webpages does not give Google the right to control the infringing acts of third parties even though that ability would allow Google to affect those infringing acts to some degree. *Amazon.com*, 2007 U.S. App. LEXIS 11420, 2007 WL 1428632, at *20-21. Moreover, and even more importantly, the *Amazon.com* court rejected a vicarious liability claim based on Google's policies with sponsored advertisers, which state that it reserves "the right to monitor and terminate partnerships with entities that violate others' copyright[s]." 2007 U.S. App. LEXIS 11420, [WL] at *20 (alteration in original). The court found that

> Google's right to terminate an AdSense partnership does not give Google the right to stop direct infringement by third-party websites. An infringing third-party website can

> continue to reproduce, display, and distribute its infringing copies of Perfect 10 images after its participation in the AdSense program has ended.

Id. This reasoning is equally applicable to the Defendants in this case. Just like Google, Defendants could likely take certain steps that may have the indirect effect of reducing infringing activity on the Internet at large. However, neither Google nor Defendants has any ability to directly control that activity, and the mere ability to withdraw a financial "carrot" does not create the "stick" of "right and ability to control" that vicarious infringement requires. A finding of vicarious liability here, under the theories advocated by the dissent, would also require a finding that Google is vicariously liable for infringement—a conflict we need not create, and radical step we do not take.

Perfect 10 argues that this court's decision in *Napster* compels a contrary result. . . . As pled by Perfect 10, Defendants also provide a system that allows the business of infringement for profit to operate on a larger scale than it otherwise might, and Defendants have the ability to deny users access to that payment system.

This argument fails. The Napster program's involvement with—and hence its "policing" power over—the infringement was much more intimate and directly intertwined with it than Defendants' payment systems are. . . . Defendants can block access to their payment system, but they cannot themselves block access to the Internet, to any particular websites, or to search engines enabling the location of such websites. Defendants are involved with the payment resulting from violations of the distribution right, but have no direct role in the actual reproduction, alteration, or distribution of the infringing images. They cannot take away the tools the offending websites use to reproduce, alter, and distribute the infringing images over the Internet. They can only take away the means the websites currently use to sell them.

Perfect 10 offers two counter-arguments. Perfect 10 first claims that Defendants' rules and regulations permit them to require member merchants to cease illegal activity—presumably including copyright infringement—as a condition to their continuing right to receive credit card payments from the relevant Defendant entities. Perfect 10 argues that these contractual terms effectively give Defendants contractual control over the *content* of their merchants' websites, and that contractual control over content is sufficient to establish the "right and ability" to control that content for purposes of vicarious liability. In the sense that economic considerations can influence behavior, these contractual rules and regulations do give Defendants some measure of control over the offending websites since it is reasonable to believe that fear of losing access to credit card payment processing services would be a sufficient incentive for at least some website operators to comply with a content-based suggestion from Defendants. But the ability to exert financial pressure does not give Defendants the right or ability to control the actual infringing activity at issue in this case. Defendants have no absolute right to stop that activity—they cannot stop websites from reproducing, altering, or distributing infringing images.

Rather, the credit card companies are analogous to Google, which we held was not liable for vicarious copyright infringement even though search engines could effectively cause a website to disappear by removing it from their search results, and reserve the right to do so. Like Google, the credit card companies "cannot stop any of the third-party websites from reproducing, displaying, and distributing unauthorized copies of Perfect 10's images because that infringing conduct takes place on the third-party websites." *Amazon.com*, 2007 U.S. App. LEXIS 11420, 2007 WL 1428632, at *20. Defendants can only refuse to process credit card payments to the offending merchant within their payment network, or they can threaten to do so if the merchant does not comply with a request to alter content. While either option would likely have some indirect effect on the infringing activity, as we discuss at greater length in our analysis of the *Grokster* "stop or limit" standard below, so might any number of actions by any number of actors. For vicarious liability to attach, however, the defendant must have the right and ability to *supervise* and *control* the infringement, not just affect it, and Defendants do not have this right or ability. . . .

Perfect 10 also argues that were infringing websites barred from accepting the Defendants' credit cards, it would be impossible for an online website selling adult images to compete and operate at a profit. While we must take this allegation as true, it still fails to state a claim because it conflates the power to stop profiteering with the right and ability to control infringement. Perfect 10's allegations do not establish that Defendants have the authority to prevent theft or alteration of the copyrighted images, remove infringing material from these websites or prevent its distribution over the Internet. Rather, they merely state that this infringing activity could not be *profitable* without access to Defendants' credit card payment systems. The alleged infringement does not turn on the payment; it turns on the reproduction, alteration and distribution of the images, which Defendants do not do, and which occurs over networks Defendants do not control. . . .

b. Obvious and Direct Financial Interest in the Infringing Activity

Because Perfect 10 has failed to show that Defendants have the right and ability to control the alleged infringing conduct, it has not pled a viable claim of vicarious liability. Accordingly, we need not reach the issue of direct financial interest.

[Majority then dismisses the claims for trademark infringement and Californian statutory and common law claims on unfair competition and false advertising, as well as the other tort law claims.]

CONCLUSION

We decline to create any of the radical new theories of liability advocated by Perfect 10 and the dissent and we affirm the district court's dismissal with prejudice of all causes of action in Perfect 10's complaint for failure to state a claim upon which relief can be granted.

ALEX KOZINSKI, Circuit Judge (dissenting):

. . .

Federal law gives copyright owners the exclusive right to "distribute copies [of their works] . . . to the public by sale." 17 U.S.C. §106(3). Plaintiff alleges that certain third parties it refers to as the "Stolen Content Websites" unlawfully copy its protected images and sell them to the public, using defendants' payment systems as financial intermediaries. According to plaintiff, the Stolen Content Websites "maintain no physical presence in the United States in order to evade criminal and civil liability for their illegal conduct." Plaintiff also claims that "Defendants do not enforce their own rules against [the] Stolen Content Websites because Defendants do not want to lose the substantial revenues and profits they receive from the websites." Plaintiff has repeatedly notified defendants that they are abetting the sale of stolen merchandise by "knowingly providing crucial transactional support services for the sale of millions of stolen photos and film clips worth billions of dollars," but to no avail. Frustrated in its effort to protect the rights Congress has given it, plaintiff turns to the federal courts for redress. We should not slam the courthouse door in its face.

Accepting the truth of plaintiff's allegations, as we must on a motion to dismiss, the credit cards are easily liable for indirect copyright infringement: They knowingly provide a financial bridge between buyers and sellers of pirated works, enabling them to consummate infringing transactions, while making a profit on every sale. If such active participation in infringing conduct does not amount to indirect infringement, it's hard to imagine what would. By straining to absolve defendants of liability, the majority leaves our law in disarray.

CONTRIBUTORY INFRINGEMENT

We have long held that a defendant is liable for contributory infringement if it "materially contributes to the infringing conduct." Our recent opinion in *Perfect 10, Inc. v. Amazon.com, Inc.*, 2007 U.S. App. LEXIS 11420, slip op. at 5751 (9th Cir. 2007), canvasses the caselaw in this area and concludes that Google "could be held contributorily liable if it had knowledge that infringing Perfect 10 images were available using its search engine, could take simple measures to prevent further damage to Perfect 10's copyrighted works, and failed to take such steps." *Amazon*, 2007 U.S. App. LEXIS 11420, slip op. at 5793. Substitute "payment systems" for "search engine" in this sentence, and it describes defendants here: If a consumer wishes to buy an infringing image from one of the Stolen Content Websites, he can do so by using Visa or MasterCard, just as he can use Google to find the infringing images in the first place.

My colleagues engage in wishful thinking when they claim that "Google's search engine itself assists in the distribution of infringing content to Internet users, while Defendants' payment systems do not" and that "[h]elping users to locate an image might substantially assist users to download infringing images, but processing payments does not." . . .

The majority struggles to distinguish *Amazon* by positing an "additional step in the causal chain" between defendants' activities and the infringing conduct. According to the majority, "Google may materially contribute to infringement by making it fast and easy for third parties to locate and distribute infringing material, whereas Defendants make it easier for infringement to be *profitable*, which tends to increase financial incentives to infringe, which in turn tends to increase infringement." The majority is mistaken; there is no "additional step." Defendants participate in every credit card sale of pirated images; the images are delivered to the buyer only after defendants approve the transaction and process the payment. This is not just an economic incentive for infringement; it's an essential step in the infringement process. . . .

My colleagues recognize, as they must, that helping consumers locate infringing content can constitute contributory infringement, but they consign the means of payment to secondary status. . . . But why is *locating* infringing images more central to infringement than *paying* for them? If infringing images can't be found, there can be no infringement; but if infringing images can't be paid for, there can be no infringement either. . . .

The majority dismisses the significance of credit cards by arguing that "infringement could continue on a large scale [without them] because other viable funding mechanisms are available." . . . Of course, the same could be said about Google. As the majority admits, if Google were unwilling or unable to serve up infringing images, consumers could use Yahoo!, Ask.com, Microsoft Live Search, A9.com or AltaVista instead. . . . Even if none of these were available, consumers could still locate websites with infringing images through e-mails from friends, messages on discussion forums, tips via online chat, "typo-squatting," peer-to-peer networking using BitTorrent or eDonkey, offline and online advertisements . . . disreputable search engines hosted on servers in far-off jurisdictions or even old-fashioned word of mouth. The majority's claim that search engines "could effectively cause a website to disappear by removing it from their search results," . . . is quite a stretch. . . .

. . . Material assistance turns on whether the activity in question "substantially assists" infringement. *Amazon*, 2007 U.S. App. LEXIS 11420, slip op. at 5793. It makes no difference whether the primary infringers might do without it by finding a workaround, which is why the majority can cite no case supporting its analysis. We presume that primary infringers have good reasons for selecting a particular means to infringe, and that other ways to do so will be more costly, more cumbersome and less efficient. Moreover, infringement can always be carried out by other means; if the existence of alternatives were a defense to contributory infringement then there could never be a case of contributory infringement based on material assistance. The majority makes some very new — and very bad — law here.

The majority also makes a slightly different argument: "While Perfect 10 has alleged that Defendants make it easier for websites to profit from this infringing activity, the issue here is reproduction, alteration, display and distribution, which can occur without payment. Even if infringing images were not paid for, there would still be infringement." . . . What the majority seems to be arguing here is that helping an infringer get paid cannot materially assist infringement because the actual process of infringement — "reproduction, alteration, display and distribution" — does not include payment. There are two problems with this argument. The first is that the Stolen Content Websites are alleged to infringe plaintiff's right of distribution "by sale." 17 U.S.C. §106(3). It's not possible to distribute by sale without receiving compensation, so payment is in fact part of the infringement process. Second, this argument runs head-on into *Amazon*, where we held that helping to find infringing images materially assists infringement, even though locating infringing images also isn't "reproduction, alteration, display [or] distribution." To be sure, locating images, like paying for them, makes it a lot easier to infringe, but neither is intrinsic to the infringement process, as the majority conceives it.

Nor can today's opinion be squared with *Fonovisa, Inc. v. Cherry Auction, Inc.*, 76 F.3d 259 (9th Cir. 1996). In *Fonovisa*, defendant allowed known infringers to sell pirated works from stalls at its swap meet. We found material assistance based on the fact that "it would [have been] difficult for the infringing activity to take place in the massive quantities alleged without the support services provided by the swap meet." 76 F.3d at 264. The pivotal role played by the swap meet in *Fonovisa* is played by the credit cards in cyberspace, in that they make "massive quantities" of infringement possible that would otherwise be impossible. Indeed, the assistance provided here is far more material than in *Fonovisa*. A pirate kicked out of a swap meet could still peddle his illicit wares through newspaper ads or by word of mouth, but you can't do business at all on the Internet without credit cards. Plaintiff thus plausibly alleges that the "Stolen Content Websites would be eradicated" if defendants withdrew their support. . . .

The majority rejects *Fonovisa* by pointing out that the swap meet there provided a "centralized place" for the infringement to take place . . . whereas defendants here "have no direct connection to [the] infringement." . . . But material assistance does not depend on physical contact with the infringing activity. If you lend money to a drug dealer knowing he will use it to finance a drug deal, you materially assist the transaction, even if you never see the drugs. Or, if you knowingly drive a principal to the scene of the crime, you provide material assistance, even if nothing happens during the ride. Material assistance turns on whether the conduct assists infringement in a significant way, not on pedantic factual distinctions unrelated to how much the activity facilitates infringement. . . .

The majority's concern that imposing liability on defendants here would implicate vast numbers of other actors who provide incidental services to infringers . . . is unfounded. Line-drawing is always a bit tricky, but courts have shown themselves adept at dealing with it from time out of mind, in resolving such issues as proximate causation and reasonable suspicion. Contributory infringement requires *material* assistance to the infringing activity, and those the majority worries about would doubtless be absolved of liability because their contribution to the infringing activity is insufficiently material.

VICARIOUS INFRINGEMENT

A party "infringes vicariously by profiting from direct infringement while declining to exercise a right to stop or limit it." *Amazon*, 2007 U.S. App. LEXIS 11420, slip op. at 5794 (quoting *Grokster*, 545 U.S. at 930) (internal quotation marks omitted). There is no doubt that defendants profit from the infringing activity of the Stolen Content Websites; after all, they take a cut of virtually every sale of pirated material. The majority does not dispute this point so I need not belabor it. . . .

Defendants here also have a right to stop or limit the infringing activity, a right they have refused to exercise. As the majority recognizes, "Perfect 10 . . . claims that Defendants' rules and regulations permit them to require member merchants to cease illegal activity — presumably including copyright infringement — as a condition to their continuing right to receive credit card payments from the relevant Defendant entities." . . . Assuming the truth of this allegation, the cards have the authority, given to them by contract, to force the Stolen Content Websites to remove infringing images from their inventory as a condition for using defendants' payment systems. If the merchants comply, their websites stop peddling stolen content and so infringement is stopped or limited. If they don't comply, defendants have the right — and under copyright law the duty — to kick the pirates off their payment networks, forcing them to find other means of getting paid or go out of business. In that case, too, infringement is stopped or limited. The swap meet in *Fonovisa* was held vicariously liable precisely because it did not force the pirates to stop infringing or leave; there is no reason to treat defendants here differently. . . .

Here, the Stolen Content Websites have chosen credit cards as a form of payment, and for good reason. Credit cards are ubiquitous and permit the transfer of funds electronically in a matter of seconds. Consumers need not wait days or weeks for a check to reach its destination and clear before gaining access to the salacious pictures they crave. Consumers also know that, if goods bought by credit card are not delivered, the cards will likely reverse the transaction. Credit cards thus act as informal escrow agents, effectively guaranteeing that their merchants will deliver the goods. Blocking the ability to accept credit cards would be a heavy blow to the Stolen Content Websites because cards are "overwhelmingly the primary way by which customers pay to view Stolen

Content Websites." Even if the pirates could find an alternative way of plying their illegal trade, being denied their preferred means of doing business would sharply curtail their unlawful activities.

The majority toils to resist this obvious conclusion but its arguments are not persuasive. For example, it makes no difference that defendants control only the means of payment, not the mechanics of transferring the material. . . . In a commercial environment, distribution and payment are (to use a quaint anachronism) like love and marriage — you can't have one without the other. If cards don't process payment, pirates don't deliver booty. The credit cards, in fact, control distribution of the infringing material.

The majority also disparages defendants' ability to control the Stolen Content Websites as just "financial pressure" which doesn't give them an "absolute right to stop [the infringing] activity — they cannot stop websites from reproducing, altering, or distributing infringing images." . . . But we have never required an "absolute right to stop [the infringing] activity" as a predicate for vicarious liability; it's enough if defendants have the "practical ability" to do so. . . .

To resolve this case . . . we need not adopt a rule holding all credit cards responsible for all infringing Internet sales because plaintiff has alleged far more than the ordinary credit card/merchant relationship. According to plaintiff, defendants have adopted special rules and practices that apply only to the Stolen Content Websites, and that are designed to make it easier for these websites to ply their illegal trade. Plaintiff claims that the credit cards have singled out the Stolen Content Websites for preferential treatment because of the unusual and substantial profits they make on such transactions. Read fully and fairly, the complaint alleges that defendants are not merely passive providers of services available on equal terms to legal and illegal businesses alike; they are actually in cahoots with the pirates to prop up their illegal businesses and share their ill-gotten gains. If this is not vicarious infringement, nothing is.

QUESTIONS AND COMMENTS

1. Who were the direct infringers of Perfect 10's copyrighted images in *Visa*? Why didn't Perfect 10 sue the direct infringers?

2. How does the *Visa* court formulate the test for contributory liability? Is this formulation consistent with other case law you have studied?

3. How does the majority in the *Visa* court distinguish the court's holding on contributory liability in *Perfect 10 v. Google*? Do you find the distinction convincing? Is there an underlying suggestion that it is more important to shield engines of commerce, such as e-payments systems, from secondary copyright liability than Internet search tools, such as Google?

4. How does the majority in *Visa* distinguish *Fonovisa* and *Napster* on the issue of contributory liability? Are these arguments convincing?

5. On what basis does the majority hold that the payments systems do not induce infringement for the purposes of the *Grokster* test on contributory liability?

6. How does the majority in *Visa* distinguish *Napster* on the question of vicarious liability?

7. Does the majority in *Visa* appear to be concerned about a possible "slippery slope" to the effect that if payments systems and search engines are indirectly held liable for their users' copyright infringements, the Internet would grind to a standstill? Who else does the majority identify as potential targets of secondary liability for copyright infringement if the view is taken that the *Grokster* and *Napster* tests for liability should be applied broadly? Are these concerns realistic? How does Judge Kozinski in his dissent in *Visa* respond to these concerns?

8. How does Judge Kozinski distinguish *Google v. Perfect 10* from the facts in the *Visa* case with respect to vicarious liability? Do you find this distinction convincing?

9. Is the real distinction between the majority and dissenting views in *Visa* explained on the basis of differing conceptions of what secondary liability doctrines in copyright law are supposed to achieve? Does the majority assume that it is necessary to show that the imposition of secondary liability would prevent direct copyright infringements altogether, while Judge Kozinski would justify the imposition of secondary liability on the basis that it would make direct infringements significantly more difficult?

10. In concluding his dissenting judgment in *Visa*, Judge Kozinski states that: "This is an easy case, squarely controlled by our precedent in all material respects. Fairly applying our cases to the facts alleged by Perfect 10, we should reverse the district court and give plaintiff an opportunity to prove its case through discovery and trial. In straining to escape the strictures of our case law, the majority draws a series of ephemeral distinctions that are neither required nor permitted; the opinion will prove to be no end of trouble." Are you convinced by his analysis? In what sense might the majority opinion be "no end of trouble" in future cases?

11. Why didn't the court in *Visa* consider whether the defendant payments systems might have a viable defense under section 512 of the Copyright Act (the ISP safe harbor provision)? Is the definition of information service provider insufficiently broad to cover such services? For a detailed discussion of the interplay between section 512 and the common law of secondary liability online, see Jane Ginsburg, *Separating the* Sony *Sheep from the* Grokster *Goats: Reckoning the Future Business Plans of Copyright-Dependent Technology Entrepreneurs*, 50 Ariz. L. Rev. 577 (2008).

12. The judges in *Visa* came to the same conclusions on secondary liability for trademark infringement as they did on secondary liability for copyright infringement. The majority held that the electronic payments system operators were not liable for secondary trademark infringement, while Judge Kozinski in his dissent held that they should be liable. These views may be

compared with the holding of the District Court for the Southern District of New York in Tiffany v. eBay, 576 F. Supp. 2d 463 (2008), where the court considered the potential liability for direct and secondary trademark infringement of the popular online auction site eBay for unauthorized uses of trademarks belonging to the famous Tiffany jewelers. Tiffany's main concern in the case was that counterfeit products were being sold on eBay and the use of its marks on eBay suggested that it endorsed these counterfeit goods. It also sought to impose a burden on eBay to monitor allegations of counterfeiting, as opposed to taking action after Tiffany notified it of instances of actual counterfeiting. Tiffany failed to established trademark infringement or secondary trademark infringement on the part of eBay. The trademark infringement claims failed largely on the basis of the nominative use defense raised by eBay. The contributory liability claims largely failed because the court held that eBay acted expeditiously and proactively when it became aware of sales of counterfeit goods online, but that eBay had no broader duty to monitor its website for potential infringements in a general way. At the conclusion of its judgment, the court stated: "The rapid development of the Internet and websites like eBay have created new ways for sellers and buyers to connect to each other and to expand their businesses beyond geographical limits. These new markets have also, however, given counterfeiters new opportunities to expand their reach. The Court is not unsympathetic to Tiffany and other rights owners who have invested enormous resources in developing their brands, only to see them illicitly and efficiently exploited by others on the Internet. Nevertheless, the law is clear: it is the trademark owner's burden to police its mark, and companies like eBay cannot be held liable for trademark infringement based solely on their generalized knowledge that trademark infringement might be occurring on their websites." Does this statement reflect the balancing act that the 9th Circuit court of appeals was attempting to undertake in *Perfect 10 v. Google* and *Perfect 10 v. Visa*? Could the *eBay* court's comments be equally applied to businesses like Perfect 10 seeking to protect their valuable copyrights and trademarks online? Why/why not?

13. Some courts have had difficulty identifying whether a given defendant should be potentially regarded as a direct or an indirect infringer. Consider the following extract.

THE CARTOON NETWORK AND CABLE NEWS NETWORK V. CSC HOLDINGS AND CABLEVISION SYSTEMS CORPORATION

536 F.3d 121 (2008)

JOHN M. WALKER, JR., Circuit Judge:

[The facts and court's discussion of the functioning of the RS-DVR and how that relates the to question of copying is excerpted earlier in this chapter.]

II. Direct Liability for Creating the Playback Copies

In most copyright disputes, the allegedly infringing act and the identity of the infringer are never in doubt. These cases turn on whether the conduct in question does, in fact, infringe the plaintiff's copyright. In this case, however, the core of the dispute is over the authorship of the infringing conduct. After an RS-DVR subscriber selects a program to record, and that program airs, a copy of the program-a copyrighted work-resides on the hard disks of Cablevision's Arroyo Server, its creation unauthorized by the copyright holder. The question is *who* made this copy. If it is Cablevision, plaintiffs' theory of direct infringement succeeds; if it is the customer, plaintiffs' theory fails because Cablevision would then face, at most, secondary liability, a theory of liability expressly disavowed by plaintiffs.

Few cases examine the line between direct and contributory liability. Both parties cite a line of cases beginning with *Religious Technology Center v. Netcom On-Line Communications Services*, 907 F. Supp. 1361 (N.D. Cal. 1995). In *Netcom*, a third-party customer of the defendant Internet service provider ("ISP") posted a copyrighted work that was automatically reproduced by the defendant's computer. The district court refused to impose direct liability on the ISP, reasoning that "[a]lthough copyright is a strict liability statute, there should still be some element of volition or causation which is lacking where a defendant's system is merely used to create a copy by a third party." *Id.* at 1370. . . .

When there is a dispute as to the author of an allegedly infringing instance of reproduction, *Netcom* and its progeny direct our attention to the volitional conduct that causes the copy to be made. There are only two instances of volitional conduct in this case: Cablevision's conduct in designing, housing, and maintaining a system that exists only to produce a copy, and a customer's conduct in ordering that system to produce a copy of a specific program. In the case of a VCR, it seems clear — and we know of no case holding otherwise — that the operator of the VCR, the person who actually presses the button to make the recording, supplies the necessary element of volition, not the person who manufactures, maintains, or, if distinct from the operator, owns the machine. We do not believe that an RS-DVR customer is sufficiently distinguishable from a VCR user to impose liability as a direct infringer on a different party for copies that are made automatically upon that customer's command.

The district court emphasized the fact that copying is "instrumental" rather than "incidental" to the function of the RS-DVR system. *Cablevision I*, 478 F. Supp. 2d at 620. While that may distinguish the RS-DVR from the ISPs in *Netcom* and *CoStar*, it does not distinguish the RS-DVR from a VCR, a photocopier, or even a typical copy shop. And the parties do not seem to contest that a company that merely makes photocopiers available to the public on its premises, without more, is not subject to liability for direct infringement for reproductions made by customers using those copiers. They only dispute whether Cablevision is similarly situated to such a proprietor.

The district court found Cablevision analogous to a copy shop that makes course packs for college professors. In the leading case involving such a shop, for example, "[t]he professor [gave] the copyshop the materials of which the coursepack [was] to be made up, and the copyshop [did] the rest." *Princeton Univ. Press v. Mich. Document Servs.*, 99 F.3d 1381, 1384 (6th Cir. 1996) (en banc). There did not appear to be any serious dispute in that case that the shop itself was directly liable for reproducing copyrighted works. The district court here found that Cablevision, like this copy shop, would be "doing" the copying, albeit "at the customer's behest." *Cablevision I*, 478 F. Supp. 2d at 620.

But because volitional conduct is an important element of direct liability, the district court's analogy is flawed. In determining who actually "makes" a copy, a significant difference exists between making a request to a human employee, who then volitionally operates the copying system to make the copy, and issuing a command directly to a system, which automatically obeys commands and engages in no volitional conduct. In cases like *Princeton University Press*, the defendants operated a copying device and sold the product they made using that device. *See* 99 F.3d at 1383 ("The corporate defendant . . . is a commercial copyshop that reproduced substantial segments of copyrighted works of scholarship, bound the copies into 'coursepacks,' and sold the coursepacks to students. . . . "). Here, by selling access to a system that automatically produces copies on command, Cablevision more closely resembles a store proprietor who charges customers to use a photocopier on his premises, and it seems incorrect to say, without more, that such a proprietor "makes" any copies when his machines are actually operated by his customers. *See Netcom*, 907 F. Supp. at 1369. . . .

The district court also emphasized Cablevision's "unfettered discretion in selecting the programming that it would make available for recording." *Cablevision I*, 478 F. Supp. 2d at 620. This conduct is indeed more proximate to the creation of illegal copying than, say, operating an ISP or opening a copy shop, where all copied content was supplied by the customers themselves or other third parties. Nonetheless, we do not think it sufficiently proximate to the copying to displace the customer as the person who "makes" the copies when determining liability under the Copyright Act. . . .

Most of the facts found dispositive by the district court — e.g., Cablevision's "continuing relationship" with its RS-DVR customers, its control over recordable content, and the "instrumental[ity]" of copying to the RS-DVR system, *Cablevision I*, 478 F. Supp. 2d at 618-20 — seem to us more relevant to the question of contributory liability. . . .

. . . We need not decide today whether one's contribution to the creation of an infringing copy may be so great that it warrants holding that party directly liable for the infringement, even though another party has actually made the copy. We conclude only that on the facts of this case, copies produced by the RS-DVR system are "made" by the RS-DVR customer, and Cablevision's contribution to this reproduction by providing the system does not warrant the imposition of direct liability. Therefore, Cablevision is entitled to summary judgment on this point, and the district court erred in awarding summary judgment to plaintiffs.

III. Transmission of RS-DVR Playback

Plaintiffs' final theory is that Cablevision will violate the Copyright Act by engaging in unauthorized public performances of their works through the playback of the RS-DVR copies. The Act grants a copyright owner the exclusive right, "in the case of . . . motion pictures and other audiovisual works, to perform the copyrighted work publicly." 17 U.S.C. §106(4). Section 101, the definitional section of the Act, explains that

> [t]o perform or display a work "publicly" means (1) to perform or display it at a place open to the public or at any place where a substantial number of persons outside of a normal circle of a family and its social acquaintances is gathered; or (2) to transmit or otherwise communicate a performance or display of the work to a place specified by clause (1) or to the public, by means of any device or process, whether the members of the public capable of receiving the performance or display receive it in the same place or in separate places and at the same time or at different times.

Id. §101.

The parties agree that this case does not implicate clause (1). Accordingly, we ask whether these facts satisfy the second, "transmit clause" of the public performance definition: Does Cablevision "transmit . . . a performance . . . of the work . . . to the public"? *Id.* No one disputes that the RS-DVR playback results in the transmission of a performance of a work — the transmission from the Arroyo Server to the customer's television set. Cablevision contends that (1) the RS-DVR customer, rather than Cablevision, does the transmitting and thus the performing and (2) the transmission is not "to the public" under the transmit clause.

As to Cablevision's first argument, we note that our conclusion in Part II that the customer, not Cablevision, "does" the copying does not dictate a parallel conclusion that the customer, and not Cablevision, "performs" the copyrighted work. The definitions that delineate the contours of the reproduction and public performance rights vary in significant ways. For example, the statute defines the verb "perform" and the noun "copies," but not the verbs "reproduce" or "copy." *Id.* We need not address Cablevision's first argument further because, even if we assume that Cablevision makes the transmission when an RS-DVR playback occurs, we find that the RS-DVR playback, as described here, does not involve the transmission of a performance "to the public."

The statute itself does not expressly define the term "performance" or the phrase "to the public." It does explain that a transmission may be "to the public . . . whether the members of the public capable of receiving the performance . . . receive it in the same place or in separate places and at the same time or at different times." *Id.* This plain language instructs us that, in determining whether a transmission is "to the public," it is of no moment that the potential recipients of the transmission are in different places, or that they may receive the transmission at different times. The implication from this same language, however, is that it *is* relevant, in determining whether a transmission is made to the public, to discern who is "capable of receiving" the performance being transmitted. The fact that the statute says "capable of receiving the performance," instead of "capable of receiving the transmission," underscores the fact that a transmission of a performance is itself a performance. *Cf. Buck v. Jewell-La Salle Realty Co.*, 283 U.S. 191, 197-98 (1931).

The legislative history of the transmit clause supports this interpretation. The House Report on the 1976 Copyright Act states that

> [u]nder the bill, as under the present law, a performance made available *by transmission to the public at large* is "public" even though the recipients are not gathered in a single place, and even if there is no proof that any of the *potential recipients* was operating his receiving apparatus at the time of the transmission. The same principles apply whenever the *potential recipients of the transmission* represent a limited segment of the public, such as the occupants of hotel rooms or the subscribers of a cable television service.

H.R. Rep. No. 94-1476, at 64-65 (1976), *reprinted in* 1976 U.S.C.C.A.N. 5659, 5678 (emphases added). . . .

[T]he transmit clause directs us to examine who precisely is "capable of receiving" a particular transmission of a performance. Cablevision argues that, because each RS-DVR transmission is made using a single unique copy of a work, made by an individual subscriber, one that can be decoded exclusively by that subscriber's cable box, only one subscriber is capable of receiving any given RS-DVR transmission. This argument accords with the language of the transmit clause, which, as described above, directs us to consider the potential audience of a given transmission. . . .

The district court, in deciding whether the RS-DVR playback of a program to a particular customer is "to the public," apparently considered all of Cablevision's customers who subscribe to the channel airing that program and all of Cablevision's RS-DVR subscribers who request a copy of that program. Thus, it concluded that the RS-DVR playbacks constituted public performances because "Cablevision would transmit the *same program* to members of the public, who may receive the performance at different times, depending on whether they view the program in real time or at a later time as an RS-DVR playback." *Cablevision I*, 478 F. Supp. 2d at 623 (emphasis added). In essence, the district court suggested that, in considering whether a transmission is "to the public," we consider not the potential audience of a particular transmission, but the potential audience of the underlying work (i.e., "the program") whose content is being transmitted.

We cannot reconcile the district court's approach with the language of the transmit clause. That clause speaks of people capable of receiving a particular "transmission" or "performance," and not of the potential audience of a particular "work." Indeed, such an approach would render the "to the public" language surplusage. Doubtless the *potential* audience for every copyrighted audiovisual work is the general public. As a result, any transmission of the content of a copyrighted work would constitute a public performance under the district court's interpretation. But the transmit clause obviously contemplates the existence of non-public transmissions; if it did not, Congress would have stopped drafting that clause after "performance." . . .

Although the transmit clause is not a model of clarity, we believe that when Congress speaks of transmitting a performance to the public, it refers to the performance created by the act of transmission. Thus, HBO transmits its own performance of a work when it transmits to Cablevision, and Cablevision transmits its own performance of the same work when it retransmits the feed from HBO. . . .

[W]e reject plaintiffs' contention that we examine the potential recipients of the content provider's initial transmission to determine who is capable of receiving the RS-DVR playback transmission. . . .

In sum, none of the arguments advanced by plaintiffs or the district court alters our conclusion that, under the transmit clause, we must examine the potential audience of a given transmission by an alleged infringer to determine whether that transmission is "to the public." And because the RS-DVR system, as designed, only makes transmissions to one subscriber using a copy made by that subscriber, we believe that the universe of people capable of receiving an RS-DVR transmission is the single subscriber whose self-made copy is used to create that transmission.

Plaintiffs contend that it is "wholly irrelevant, in determining the existence of a public performance, whether 'unique' *copies* of the same work are used to make the transmissions." Fox Br. at 27. But plaintiffs cite no authority for this contention. . . .

. . . [I]t seems quite consistent with the [Copyright] Act to treat a transmission made using Copy A as distinct from one made using Copy B, just as we would treat a transmission made by Cablevision as distinct from an otherwise identical transmission made by Comcast. Both factors — the identity of the transmitter and the source material of the transmission — limit the potential audience of a transmission in this case and are therefore germane in determining whether that transmission is made "to the public."

Indeed, we believe that *Columbia Pictures Industries, Inc. v. Redd Horne, Inc.*, 749 F.2d 154 (3d Cir. 1984), relied on by both plaintiffs and the district court, supports our decision to accord significance to the existence and use of distinct copies in our transmit clause analysis. In that case, defendant operated a video rental store, Maxwell's, which also housed a number of small private booths containing seats and a television. Patrons would select a film, enter the booth, and close the door. An employee would then load a copy of the requested movie into a bank of VCRs at the front of the store and push play, thereby transmitting the content of the tape to the television in the viewing booth. *See id.* at 156-57.

The Third Circuit found that defendants' conduct constituted a public performance under both clauses of the statutory definition. In concluding that Maxwell's violated the transmit clause, that court explicitly relied on the fact that defendants showed the same copy of a work seriatim to its clientele, and it quoted a treatise emphasizing the same fact:

> Professor Nimmer's examination of this definition is particularly pertinent: "*if the same copy* . . . of a given work is repeatedly played (*i.e.*, 'performed') by different members of the public, albeit at different times, this constitutes a 'public' performance." 2 M. Nimmer, §8.14 [C][3], at 8-142 (emphasis in original). . . . Although Maxwell's has only one copy of each film, it shows each copy repeatedly to different members of the public. This constitutes a public performance.

Id. at 159 (first omission in original).

Unfortunately, neither the *Redd Horne* court nor Prof. Nimmer explicitly explains *why* the use of a distinct copy affects the transmit clause inquiry. But our independent analysis confirms the soundness of their intuition: the use of a unique copy may limit the potential audience of a transmission and is therefore relevant to whether that transmission is made "to the public." Plaintiffs' unsupported arguments to the contrary are unavailing.

Given that each RS-DVR transmission is made to a given subscriber using a copy made by that subscriber, we conclude that such a transmission is not "to the public," without analyzing the contours of that phrase in great detail. No authority cited by the parties or the district court persuades us to the contrary.

In addition to *Redd Horne*, the district court also cited and analyzed *On Command Video Corp. v. Columbia Pictures Industries*, 777 F. Supp. 787 (N.D. Cal. 1991), in its transmit clause analysis. In that case, defendant On Command developed and sold "a system for the electronic delivery of movie video tapes," which it sold to hotels. *Id.* at 788. The hub of the system was a bank of video cassette players, each containing a copy of a particular movie. From his room, a hotel guest could select a movie via remote control from a list on his television. The corresponding cassette player would start, and its output would be transmitted to that guest's room. During this playback, the movie selected was unavailable to other guests. *See id.* The court concluded that the transmissions made by this system were made to the public "because the relationship between the transmitter of the performance, On Command, and the audience, hotel guests, is a commercial, 'public' one regardless of where the viewing takes place." *Id.* at 790.

Thus, according to the *On Command* court, any commercial transmission is a transmission "to the public." We find this interpretation untenable, as it completely rewrites the language of the statutory definition. If Congress had wished to make all commercial transmissions public performances, the transmit clause would read: "to perform a work publicly means . . . to transmit a performance for commercial purposes." In addition, this interpretation overlooks, as Congress did not, the possibility that even non-commercial transmissions to the public may diminish the value of a copyright. Finally, like *Redd Horne*,

On Command is factually distinguishable, as successive transmissions to different viewers in that case could be made using a single copy of a given work. Thus, at the moment of transmission, any of the hotel's guests was capable of receiving a transmission made using a single copy of a given movie. As a result, the district court in this case erred in relying on *On Command*. . . .

In sum, we find that the transmit clause directs us to identify the potential audience of a given transmission, i.e., the persons "capable of receiving" it, to determine whether that transmission is made "to the public." Because each RS-DVR playback transmission is made to a single subscriber using a single unique copy produced by that subscriber, we conclude that such transmissions are not performances "to the public," and therefore do not infringe any exclusive right of public performance. We base this decision on the application of undisputed facts; thus, Cablevision is entitled to summary judgment on this point.

This holding, we must emphasize, does not generally permit content delivery networks to avoid all copyright liability by making copies of each item of content and associating one unique copy with each subscriber to the network, or by giving their subscribers the capacity to make their own individual copies. We do not address whether such a network operator would be able to escape any other form of copyright liability, such as liability for unauthorized reproductions or liability for contributory infringement.

In sum, because we find, on undisputed facts, that Cablevision's proposed RS-DVR system would not directly infringe plaintiffs' exclusive rights to reproduce and publicly perform their copyrighted works, we grant summary judgment in favor of Cablevision with respect to both rights. . . .

COMMENTS AND QUESTIONS

1. Is the RS-DVR more like a set-top video recorder or a video-on-demand service? Why is the distinction significant for copyright infringement purposes?

2. On what basis does the plaintiff argue that the defendant has directly infringed its copyrights? Should there have been a claim for indirect infringement?

3. How does the Second Circuit court's analysis of the direct infringement claim differ from that of the District Court in *Cablevision*? Which court's reasoning do you find the most persuasive, and why?

4. Who does the Second Circuit court identify as the potential direct infringer(s) of the playback copies of the plaintiffs' copyrighted programs? Why is this such a difficult question to resolve on these facts?

5. Can you think of other contexts in which it might be difficult to draw the line between direct and indirect infringers? What other examples does the court consider in *Cablevision*?

6. Is the Second Circuit court correct in accepting that "volitional conduct is an important element of direct liability"? Why/why not? How is this different from the court reading a *mens rea* requirement into a strict liability statute?

7. On what basis does the Second Circuit court hold that the transmission of programs to the defendant's customers is not a public performance for the purposes of the Copyright Act? How does the court distinguish the *Redd Horne* and *On Command Video* cases on this point? Are the distinctions convincing?

8. Could the plaintiffs in *Cablevision* succeed on a secondary liability action against Cablevision? On what basis? Who would be the primary infringer(s) in such an action?

4. Fair Use

One of the principal limitations upon copyright liability is the fair use doctrine. Fair use has been considered by some to be "the most troublesome" in all of copyright law.[18] Traditionally, the doctrine of fair use permitted individuals to record television programming onto videotape, share a newspaper article with colleagues, or copy a scholarly article for research. While all of these uses technically infringe at least one of a copyright owner's exclusive rights, they were treated as noninfringing uses. In essence, the fair use doctrine attempts to balance the public's interest in access and use of copyrighted works with the copyright owner's exclusive rights. Why the doctrine exists will be explored in the following materials.

Originally a judicially recognized defense to copyright infringement, the doctrine is now codified in Section 107 of the 1976 Copyright Act. Section 107 provides:

> Notwithstanding the [exclusive rights protected under copyright law], the fair use of a copyrighted work . . . for purposes such as criticism, comment, news reporting, teaching (including multiple copies for classroom use), scholarship, or research, is not an infringement of copyright. In determining whether the use made of a work in any particular case is a fair use the factors to be considered shall include —
>
> (1) the purpose and character of the use, including whether such use is of a commercial nature or is for nonprofit educational purposes;
>
> (2) the nature of the copyrighted work;
>
> (3) the amount and substantiality of the portion used in relation to the copyright work as a whole; and
>
> (4) the effect of the use upon the potential market for or value of the copyright work. . . .

17 U.S.C. §107. These factors, however, are neither equal nor exhaustive. In light of Section 107, you may already realize that fair use is determined on a case-by-case basis.

As Professor Samuelson discussed at the beginning of this chapter, some believe that fair use has outlived its usefulness. These "copyright maximalists" argue that copyright owners should be permitted to use new technologies to

---

18. Dellar v. Samuel Goldwyn, Inc., 104 F.2d 661, 662 (2d Cir. 1939).

control all uses of copyrighted works.[19] As you study the following materials, consider why fair use was recognized before the Internet, and how fair use should apply in cyberspace, if at all. Moreover, as fair use is considered a limitation upon copyright law, consider the efficacy of using traditional and novel copyright principles to regulate information online. In particular, it has never been clear whether fair use is a guaranteed right of users of copyrighted works, or rather is a tolerated inconvenience to copyright holders. This question becomes important given that digital technology allows copyright holders to exert so much more actual control over their works than in previous generations. If fair use is a guaranteed right, then users should be in a stronger position to assert it against copyright holders employing powerful technological encryption measures to protect their works. Of course, this issue now becomes more complex because of the implementation of the anticircumvention provisions in the Digital Millennium Copyright Act — see *infra*. Some commentators have argued that some unauthorized uses of copyright works that do not technically fall within the idea of fair use should nevertheless not be regarded as copyright infringements because they should not even be regarded as being within the ambit of copyright law's protection in the first place. Jessica Litman, *Lawful Personal Use*, 85 Tex. L. Rev. 1871 (2007).

Problem 7.0

   While you are researching the copyright issues presented in Problem 6.0, you receive letters from the Recording Industry Association of America (RIAA) and the Motion Picture Association of America (MPAA). Both the RIAA and MPAA claim that copyrighted works of their members are being shared on one of your bulletin boards and in your chatrooms. They specifically identify alt.movielovers.mpeg and alt.musiclovers.mp3, as well as the "Latest movies" and "Cool new songs" chatrooms. They demand that you stop this activity immediately.

   In addition to these acts of file swapping, your research of copyright-related activity on StarttUp revealed that many people have music and movies available on their personal Web pages hosted by StarttUp. One of these individuals is your head of technology who explains that many people, including herself, use such Web pages to watch movies or listen to music that they own at home at the office. In her case, she has a password to protect the files.

   Alan and Barbara believe that music and movies should be free and want to know if StarttUp and its subscribers have a defense to the RIAA's and MPAA's demands.

---

19. *See, e.g.*, Paul Goldstein, *Copyright's Highway: The Law and Lore of Copyright from Gutenberg to the Celestial Jukebox* 236 (Hill & Wang, 1994) (arguing that copyright should be extended "into every corner where consumers derive value from literary and artistic works").

Problem 7.1

As noted in Problem 6.1, Cora has encouraged her co-bloggers to insert graphics and video files into the Gals On-Line blog. Recently, a number of the bloggers have been posting music video clips of a forthcoming recording by a popular new music group, Mad Cows. The group's manager has sent a cease-and-desist letter and has threatened to sue Cora and her co-bloggers for copyright infringement with respect to the clips. None of the clips posted on Cora's blog are more than 30 seconds in duration and the picture quality is not particularly good in most of the clips. It looks like a number of them were recorded with a cellphone or video camera in front of a television screen. Most of the clips are accompanied by commentary about the group and critiques by the bloggers of the new songs and how they compare to the band's last album. Cora wants to know whether a fair use defense might be available to the bloggers with respect to the threatened copyright infringement action.

a) Doctrine

The Internet is by no means the first invention to facilitate commercial and noncommercial copying of expression. History is replete with examples of devices that made it possible for humanity to record and duplicate various forms of expression. With each technological advance — from pens to printing presses to photocopying machine — came an increased ability to copy. More importantly, these technological advances facilitated private, noncommercial copying. With copying no longer limited to commercial entities competing with the copyright owner, copyright law was challenged with how to respond.

The first case to present the question of whether private copying could be considered fair use involved the photocopying of academic articles for research purposes.[20] In that case, the Court of Appeals concluded that this form of copying was considered fair use, and the judgment was affirmed without an opinion by an equally divided Supreme Court in which Justice Blackmun did not participate.[21] It was almost a decade before the Supreme Court would have another opportunity to address this question. This time, instead of the photocopying machine, the technology at issue was the videotape recorder.

---

20. *See* Williams & Wilkins v. The United States, 487 F.2d 1345 (Ct. Cl. 1973), *aff'd*, 420 U.S. 376 (1975).
21. *Id.*

SONY CORP. OF AMERICA V. UNIVERSAL CITY STUDIOS, INC.

464 U.S. 417 (1984)

Justice STEVENS delivered the opinion of the Court.

Petitioners manufacture and sell home video tape recorders. Respondents own the copyrights on some of the television programs that are broadcast on the public airwaves. Some members of the general public use video tape recorders sold by petitioners to record some of these broadcasts, as well as a large number of other broadcasts. The question presented is whether the sale of petitioners' copying equipment to the general public violates any of the rights conferred upon respondents by the Copyright Act. . . .

I

The two respondents in this action, Universal Studios, Inc. and Walt Disney Productions, produce and hold the copyrights on a substantial number of motion pictures and other audiovisual works. In the current marketplace, they can exploit their rights in these works in a number of ways: by authorizing theatrical exhibitions, by licensing limited showings on cable and network television, by selling syndication rights for repeated airings on local television stations, and by marketing programs on prerecorded videotapes or videodiscs. Some works are suitable for exploitation through all of these avenues, while the market for other works is more limited.

Petitioner Sony manufactures millions of Betamax video tape recorders and markets these devices through numerous retail establishments. . . .

The respondents and Sony both conducted surveys of the way the Betamax machine was used by several hundred owners during a sample period in 1978. Although there were some differences in the surveys, they both showed that the primary use of the machine for most owners was "time-shifting" — the practice of recording a program to view it once at a later time, and thereafter erasing it. . . . Both surveys also showed, however, that a substantial number of interviewees had accumulated libraries of tapes. Sony's survey indicated that over 80% of the interviewees watched at least as much regular television as they had before owning a Betamax. Respondents offered no evidence of decreased television viewing by Betamax owners.

Sony introduced considerable evidence describing television programs that could be copied without objection from any copyright holder, with special emphasis on sports, religious, and educational programming. For example, their survey indicated that 7.3% of all Betamax use is to record sports events, and representatives of professional baseball, football, basketball, and hockey testified that they had no objection to the recording of their televised events for home use.

Respondents offered opinion evidence concerning the future impact of the unrestricted sale of VTR's on the commercial value of their copyrights.

The District Court found, however, that they had failed to prove any likelihood of future harm from the use of VTR's for time-shifting. . . .

II

The monopoly privileges that Congress may authorize are neither unlimited nor primarily designed to provide a special private benefit. Rather, the limited grant is a means by which an important public purpose may be achieved. It is intended to motivate the creative activity of authors and inventors by the provision of a special reward, and to allow the public access to the products of their genius after the limited period of exclusive control has expired.

"The copyright law, like the patent statute, makes reward to the owner a secondary consideration. In Fox Film Corp. v. Doyal, 286 U.S. 123, 127, Chief Justice Hughes spoke as follows respecting the copyright monopoly granted by Congress, 'The sole interest of the United States and the primary object in conferring the monopoly lie in the general benefits derived by the public from the labors of authors.' It is said that reward to the author or artist serves to induce release to the public of the products of his creative genius." United States v. Paramount Pictures, 334 U.S. 131, 158.

As the text of the Constitution makes plain, it is Congress that has been assigned the task of defining the scope of the limited monopoly that should be granted to authors or to inventors in order to give the public appropriate access to their work product. Because this task involves a difficult balance between the interests of authors and inventors in the control and exploitation of their writings and discoveries on the one hand, and society's competing interest in the free flow of ideas, information, and commerce on the other hand, our patent and copyright statutes have been amended repeatedly.[10]

From its beginning, the law of copyright has developed in response to significant changes in technology.[11] Indeed, it was the invention of a new form

---

10. In its report accompanying the comprehensive revision of the Copyright Act in 1909, the Judiciary Committee of the House of Representatives explained this balance:

> "The enactment of copyright legislation by Congress under the terms of the Constitution is not based upon any natural right that the author has in his writings, . . . but upon the ground that the welfare of the public will be served and progress of science and useful arts will be promoted by securing to authors for limited periods the exclusive rights to their writings. . . .
>
> "In enacting a copyright law Congress must consider . . . two questions: First, how much will the legislation stimulate the producer and so benefit the public, and, second, how much will the monopoly granted be detrimental to the public? The granting of such exclusive rights, under the proper terms and conditions, confers a benefit upon the public that outweighs the evils of the temporary monopoly."

H.R. Rep. No. 2222, 60th Cong., 2d Sess. 7 (1909).

11. Thus, for example, the development and marketing of player pianos and perforated roles of music, see White-Smith Music Publishing Co. v. Apollo Co., 209 U.S. 1 (1908), preceded the enactment of the Copyright Act of 1909; innovations in copying techniques gave rise to the statutory exemption for library copying embodied in §108 of the 1976 revision of the Copyright law; the development of the technology that made it possible to retransmit television programs by cable or by microwave systems, see Fortnightly

of copying equipment—the printing press—that gave rise to the original need for copyright protection.[12] Repeatedly, as new developments have occurred in this country, it has been the Congress that has fashioned the new rules that new technology made necessary. Thus, long before the enactment of the Copyright Act of 1909, it was settled that the protection given to copyrights is wholly statutory. Wheaton v. Peters, 33 U.S. (8 Peters) 591, 661-662 (1834). The remedies for infringement "are only those prescribed by Congress." Thompson v. Hubbard, 131 U.S. 123, 151 (1889).

The judiciary's reluctance to expand the protections afforded by the copyright without explicit legislative guidance is a recurring theme. . . . Sound policy, as well as history, supports our consistent deference to Congress when major technological innovations alter the market for copyrighted materials. Congress has the constitutional authority and the institutional ability to accommodate fully the varied permutations of competing interests that are inevitably implicated by such new technology.

In a case like this, in which Congress has not plainly marked our course, we must be circumspect in construing the scope of rights created by a legislative enactment which never contemplated such a calculus of interests. In doing so, we are guided by Justice Stewart's exposition of the correct approach to ambiguities in the law of copyright:

> "The limited scope of the copyright holder's statutory monopoly, like the limited copyright duration required by the Constitution, reflects a balance of competing claims upon the public interest: Creative work is to be encouraged and rewarded, but private motivation must ultimately serve the cause of promoting broad public availability of literature, music, and the other arts. The immediate effect of our copyright law is to secure a fair return for an 'author's' creative labor. But the ultimate aim is, by this incentive, to stimulate artistic creativity for the general public good. 'The sole interest of the United States and the primary object in conferring the monopoly,' this Court has said, 'lie in the general benefits derived by the public from the labors of authors.'" Fox Film Corp. v. Doyal, 286 U.S. 123, 127. See Kendall v. Winsor, 21 How. 322, 327-328; Grant v. Raymond, 6 Pet. 218, 241-242. When technological change has rendered its literal terms ambiguous, the Copyright Act must be construed in light of this basic purpose.

Corp. v. United Artists, 392 U.S. 390 (1968), and Teleprompter Corp. v. CBS, 415 U.S. 394 (1974), prompted the enactment of the complex provisions set forth in 17 U.S.C. §111(d)(2)(B) and §111(d)(5) after years of detailed congressional study, see Eastern Microwave, Inc. v. Doubleday Sports, Inc., 691 F.2d 125, 129 (CA2 1982). By enacting the Sound Recording Amendment of 1971, 85 Stat. 391, Congress also provided the solution to the "record piracy" problems that had been created by the development of the audio tape recorder. Sony argues that the legislative history of that Act, see especially H. Rep. No. 487, 92nd Cong., 1st Sess., p. 7, indicates that Congress did not intend to prohibit the private home use of either audio or video tape recording equipment. In view of our disposition of the contributory infringement issue, we express no opinion on that question.

12. "Copyright protection became necessary with the invention of the printing press and had its early beginnings in the British censorship laws. The fortunes of the law of copyright have always been closely connected with freedom of expression, on the one hand, and with technological improvements in means of dissemination, on the other. Successive ages have drawn different balances among the interest of the writer in the control and exploitation of his intellectual property, the related interest of the publisher, and the competing interest of society in the untrammeled dissemination of ideas." Foreword to B. Kaplan, An Unhurried View of Copyright vii-viii (1967).

Twentieth Century Music Corp. v. Aiken, 422 U.S. 151, 156.

Copyright protection "subsists . . . in original works of authorship fixed in any tangible medium of expression." 17 U.S.C. §102(a). This protection has never accorded the copyright owner complete control over all possible uses of his work. Rather, the Copyright Act grants the copyright holder "exclusive" rights to use and to authorize the use of his work in five qualified ways, including reproduction of the copyrighted work in copies. Id., §106. All reproductions of the work, however, are not within the exclusive domain of the copyright owner; some are in the public domain. Any individual may reproduce a copyrighted work for a "fair use"; the copyright owner does not possess the exclusive right to such a use. Compare id., §106 with id., §107. . . .

The two respondents in this case do not seek relief against the Betamax users who have allegedly infringed their copyrights. Moreover, this is not a class action on behalf of all copyright owners who license their works for television broadcast, and respondents have no right to invoke whatever rights other copyright holders may have to bring infringement actions based on Betamax copying of their works. As was made clear by their own evidence, the copying of the respondents' programs represents a small portion of the total use of VTR's. It is, however, the taping of respondents own copyrighted programs that provides them with standing to charge Sony with contributory infringement. To prevail, they have the burden of proving that users of the Betamax have infringed their copyrights and that Sony should be held responsible for that infringement.

III

The Copyright Act does not expressly render anyone liable for infringement committed by another. . . .

The closest analogy is provided by the patent law cases to which it is appropriate to refer because of the historic kinship between patent law and copyright law. [Patent law "expressly provides that the sale of a 'staple article or commodity of commerce suitable for substantial noninfringing use' is not contributory infringement."]

When a charge of contributory infringement is predicated entirely on the sale of an article of commerce that is used by the purchaser to infringe a patent, the public interest in access to that article of commerce is necessarily implicated. A finding of contributory infringement does not, of course, remove the article from the market altogether; it does, however, give the patentee effective control over the sale of that item. Indeed, a finding of contributory infringement is normally the functional equivalent of holding that the disputed article is within the monopoly granted to the patentee.[21]

---

21. It seems extraordinary to suggest that the Copyright Act confers upon all copyright owners collectively, much less the two respondents in this case, the exclusive right to distribute VTR's simply because they may be used to infringe copyrights. That, however, is the logical implication of their claim. The request for an injunction below indicates that respondents seek, in effect, to declare VTR's contraband. Their

For that reason, in contributory infringement cases arising under the patent laws the Court has always recognized the critical importance of not allowing the patentee to extend his monopoly beyond the limits of his specific grant. These cases deny the patentee any right to control the distribution of unpatented articles unless they are "unsuited for any commercial noninfringing use." Dawson Chemical Co. v. Rohm & Hass Co., 448 U.S. 176, 198 (1980). . . .

We recognize there are substantial differences between the patent and copyright laws. But in both areas the contributory infringement doctrine is grounded on the recognition that adequate protection of a monopoly may require the courts to look beyond actual duplication of a device or publication to the products or activities that make such duplication possible. The staple article of commerce doctrine must strike a balance between a copyright holder's legitimate demand for effective — not merely symbolic — protection of the statutory monopoly, and the rights of others freely to engage in substantially unrelated areas of commerce. Accordingly, the sale of copying equipment, like the sale of other articles of commerce, does not constitute contributory infringement if the product is widely used for legitimate, unobjectionable purposes. Indeed, it need merely be capable of substantial noninfringing uses.

IV

The question is thus whether the Betamax is capable of commercially significant noninfringing uses. In order to resolve that question, we need not explore all the different potential uses of the machine and determine whether or not they would constitute infringement. Rather, we need only consider whether on the basis of the facts as found by the district court a significant number of them would be noninfringing. Moreover, in order to resolve this case we need not give precise content to the question of how much use is commercially significant. For one potential use of the Betamax plainly satisfies this standard, however it is understood: private, noncommercial time-shifting in the home. It does so both (A) because respondents have no right to prevent other copyright holders from authorizing it for their programs, and (B) because the District Court's factual findings reveal that even the unauthorized home time-shifting of respondents' programs is legitimate fair use.

A. Authorized Time Shifting

Each of the respondents owns a large inventory of valuable copyrights, but in the total spectrum of television programming their combined market share is small. The exact percentage is not specified, but it is well below 10%. If they

---

suggestion in this Court that a continuing royalty pursuant to a judicially created compulsory license would be an acceptable remedy merely indicates that respondents, for their part, would be willing to license their claimed monopoly interest in VTR's to petitioners in return for a royalty.

were to prevail, the outcome of this litigation would have a significant impact on both the producers and the viewers of the remaining 90% of the programming in the Nation. No doubt, many other producers share respondents' concern about the possible consequences of unrestricted copying. Nevertheless the findings of the District Court make it clear that time-shifting may enlarge the total viewing audience and that many producers are willing to allow private time-shifting to continue, at least for an experimental time period.

The District Court found:

> "Even if it were deemed that home-use recording of copyrighted material constituted infringement, the Betamax could still legally be used to record noncopyrighted material or material whose owners consented to the copying. An injunction would deprive the public of the ability to use the Betamax for this noninfringing off-the-air recording."
>
> "Defendants introduced considerable testimony at trial about the potential for such copying of sports, religious, educational and other programming. This included testimony from representatives of the Offices of the Commissioners of the National Football, Basketball, Baseball and Hockey Leagues and Associations, the Executive Director of National Religious Broadcasters and various educational communications agencies. Plaintiffs attack the weight of the testimony offered and also contend that an injunction is warranted because infringing uses outweigh noninfringing uses."
>
> "Whatever the future percentage of legal versus illegal home-use recording might be, an injunction which seeks to deprive the public of the very tool or article of commerce capable of some noninfringing use would be an extremely harsh remedy, as well as one unprecedented in copyright law." 480 F. Supp., at 468.

Although the District Court made these statements in the context of considering the propriety of injunctive relief, the statements constitute a finding that the evidence concerning "sports, religious, educational, and other programming" was sufficient to establish a significant quantity of broadcasting whose copying is now authorized, and a significant potential for future authorized copying. That finding is amply supported by the record. . . .

If there are millions of owners of VTR's who make copies of televised sports events, religious broadcasts, and educational programs such as Mister Rogers' Neighborhood, and if the proprietors of those programs welcome the practice, the business of supplying the equipment that makes such copying feasible should not be stifled simply because the equipment is used by some individuals to make unauthorized reproductions of respondents' works. The respondents do not represent a class composed of all copyright holders. Yet a finding of contributory infringement would inevitably frustrate the interests of broadcasters in reaching the portion of their audience that is available only through time-shifting.

Of course, the fact that other copyright holders may welcome the practice of time-shifting does not mean that respondents should be deemed to have granted a license to copy their programs. Third party conduct would be wholly irrelevant in an action for direct infringement of respondents' copyrights. But in an action for contributory infringement against the seller of copying equipment, the copyright holder may not prevail unless the relief that he seeks affects only his programs, or unless he speaks for virtually all copyright holders with an interest in the outcome. In this case, the record makes it perfectly clear that there are many important producers of national and local television programs who find nothing objectionable about the enlargement in the size of the television audience that results from the practice of time-shifting for private home use. The seller of the equipment that expands those producers' audiences cannot be a contributory infringer if, as is true in this case, it has had no direct involvement with any infringing activity.

B. Unauthorized Time-Shifting

Even unauthorized uses of a copyrighted work are not necessarily infringing. An unlicensed use of the copyright is not an infringement unless it conflicts with one of the specific exclusive rights conferred by the copyright statute. Twentieth Century Music Corp. v. Aiken, 422 U.S. 151, 154-155. Moreover, the definition of exclusive rights in §106 of the present Act is prefaced by the words "subject to sections 107 through 118." Those sections describe a variety of uses of copyrighted material that "are not infringements of copyright notwithstanding the provisions of §106." The most pertinent in this case is §107, the legislative endorsement of the doctrine of "fair use."[29]

That section identifies various factors that enable a Court to apply an "equitable rule of reason" analysis to particular claims of infringement. Although not conclusive, the first factor requires that "the commercial or nonprofit character of an activity" be weighed in any fair use decision. If the Betamax were used to make copies for a commercial or profit-making purpose, such use would presumptively be unfair. The contrary presumption is appropriate here, however, because the District Court's findings plainly establish that time-shifting for private home use must be characterized as a noncommercial, nonprofit activity. Moreover, when one considers the nature of a televised copyrighted audiovisual work, see 17 U.S.C. §107(2), and that time-shifting merely enables a viewer to see such a work which he had been invited to witness in its entirety free of charge, the fact that the entire work is reproduced, see id., at §107(3), does not have its ordinary effect of militating against a finding of fair use.[33]

---

29. The Copyright Act of 1909, 35 Stat. 1075, did not have a "fair use" provision. Although that Act's compendium of exclusive rights "to print, reprint, publish, copy, and vend the copyrighted work" was broad enough to encompass virtually all potential interactions with a copyrighted work, the statute was never so construed. The courts simply refused to read the statute literally in every situation. When Congress amended the statute in 1976, it indicated that it "intended to restate the present judicial doctrine of fair use, not to change, narrow, or enlarge it in any way." House Report No. 94-1476, 94th Cong., 2d Sess., p. 66, U.S. Code Code & Admin. News 1976, pp. 5659, 5679.

33. It has been suggested that "consumptive uses of copyrights by home VTR users are commercial even if the consumer does not sell the homemade tape because the consumer will not buy tapes separately sold by the copyrightholder." Home Recording of Copyrighted Works: Hearing before Subcommittee on Courts, Civil Liberties and the Administration of Justice of the House Committee on the Judiciary, 97th Congress, 2d Session, pt. 2, p. 1250 (1982) (memorandum of Prof. Laurence H. Tribe). Furthermore, "[t]he error in

This is not, however, the end of the inquiry because Congress has also directed us to consider "the effect of the use upon the potential market for or value of the copyrighted work." Id., at §107(4). The purpose of copyright is to create incentives for creative effort. Even copying for noncommercial purposes may impair the copyright holder's ability to obtain the rewards that Congress intended him to have. But a use that has no demonstrable effect upon the potential market for, or the value of, the copyrighted work need not be prohibited in order to protect the author's incentive to create. The prohibition of such noncommercial uses would merely inhibit access to ideas without any countervailing benefit.

Thus, although every commercial use of copyrighted material is presumptively an unfair exploitation of the monopoly privilege that belongs to the owner of the copyright, noncommercial uses are a different matter. A challenge to a noncommercial use of a copyrighted work requires proof either that the particular use is harmful, or that if it should become widespread, it would adversely affect the potential market for the copyrighted work. Actual present harm need not be shown; such a requirement would leave the copyright holder with no defense against predictable damage. Nor is it necessary to show with certainty that future harm will result. What is necessary is a showing by a preponderance of the evidence that some meaningful likelihood of future harm exists. If the intended use is for commercial gain, that likelihood may be presumed. But if it is for a noncommercial purpose, the likelihood must be demonstrated.

In this case, respondents failed to carry their burden with regard to home time-shifting. The District Court described respondents' evidence as follows:

> "Plaintiffs' experts admitted at several points in the trial that the time-shifting without librarying would result in 'not a great deal of harm.' Plaintiffs' greatest concern about time-shifting is with 'a point of important philosophy that transcends even commercial judgment.' They fear that with any Betamax usage, 'invisible boundaries' are passed: 'the copyright owner has lost control over his program.'" 480 F. Supp., at 467.

Later in its opinion, the District Court observed:

> "Most of plaintiffs' predictions of harm hinge on speculation about audience viewing patterns and ratings, a measurement system which Sidney Sheinberg, MCA's president,

---

excusing such theft as noncommercial," we are told, "can be seen by simple analogy: jewel theft is not converted into a noncommercial veniality if stolen jewels are simply worn rather than sold." Ibid. The premise and the analogy are indeed simple, but they add nothing to the argument. The use to which stolen jewelery is put is quite irrelevant in determining whether depriving its true owner of his present possessory interest in it is venial; because of the nature of the item and the true owner's interests in physical possession of it, the law finds the taking objectionable even if the thief does not use the item at all. Theft of a particular item of personal property of course may have commercial significance, for the thief deprives the owner of his right to sell that particular item to any individual. Time-shifting does not even remotely entail comparable consequences to the copyright owner. Moreover, the time-shifter no more steals the program by watching it once than does the live viewer, and the live viewer is no more likely to buy pre-recorded videotapes than is the time-shifter. Indeed, no live viewer would buy a pre-recorded videotape if he did not have access to a VTR.

calls a 'black art' because of the significant level of imprecision involved in the calculations." Id., at 469.

There was no need for the District Court to say much about past harm. "Plaintiffs have admitted that no actual harm to their copyrights has occurred to date." Id., at 451.

On the question of potential future harm from time-shifting, the District Court offered a more detailed analysis of the evidence. It rejected respondents' "fear that persons 'watching' the original telecast of a program will not be measured in the live audience and the ratings and revenues will decrease," by observing that current measurement technology allows the Betamax audience to be reflected. Id., at 466. It rejected respondents' prediction "that live television or movie audiences will decrease as more people watch Betamax tapes as an alternative," with the observation that "[t]here is no factual basis for [the underlying] assumption." Ibid. It rejected respondents' "fear that time-shifting will reduce audiences for telecast reruns," and concluded instead that "given current market practices, this should aid plaintiffs rather than harm them." Ibid. And it declared that respondents' suggestion "that theater or film rental exhibition of a program will suffer because of time-shift recording of that program" "lacks merit." 480 F. Supp., at 467.[39] . . .

The District Court's conclusions are buttressed by the fact that to the extent time-shifting expands public access to freely broadcast television programs, it yields societal benefits. Earlier this year . . . we acknowledged the public interest in making television broadcasting more available. Concededly, that interest is not unlimited. But it supports an interpretation of the concept of "fair use" that requires the copyright holder to demonstrate some likelihood of harm before he may condemn a private act of time-shifting as a violation of federal law.

When these factors are all weighed in the "equitable rule of reason" balance, we must conclude that this record amply supports the District Court's conclusion that home time-shifting is fair use.[40] . . .

---

39. "This suggestion lacks merit. By definition, time-shift recording entails viewing and erasing, so the program will no longer be on tape when the later theater run begins. Of course, plaintiffs may fear that the Betamax will keep the tapes long enough to satisfy all their interest in the program and will, therefore, not patronize later theater exhibitions. To the extent this practice involves librarying, it is addressed in section V.C., infra. It should also be noted that there is no evidence to suggest that the public interest in later theatrical exhibitions of motion pictures will be reduced any more by Betamax recording than it already is by the television broadcast of the film." 480 F. Supp., at 467.

40. The Court of Appeals chose not to engage in any "equitable rule of reason" analysis in this case. Instead, it assumed that the category of "fair use" is rigidly circumscribed by a requirement that every such use must be "productive." It therefore concluded that copying a television program merely to enable the viewer to receive information or entertainment that he would otherwise miss because of a personal scheduling conflict could never be fair use. That understanding of "fair use" was erroneous. Congress has plainly instructed us that fair use analysis calls for a sensitive balancing of interests. The distinction between "productive" and "unproductive" uses may be helpful in calibrating the balance, but it cannot be wholly determinative. Although copying to promote a scholarly endeavor certainly has a stronger claim to fair use than copying to avoid interrupting a poker game, the question is not simply two-dimensional. For one thing, it is not true that all copyrights are fungible. Some copyrights govern material with broad potential secondary markets. Such material may well have a broader claim to protection because of the greater potential for

V

One may search the Copyright Act in vain for any sign that the elected representatives of the millions of people who watch television every day have made it unlawful to copy a program for later viewing at home, or have enacted a flat prohibition against the sale of machines that make such copying possible.

It may well be that Congress will take a fresh look at this new technology, just as it so often has examined other innovations in the past. But it is not our job to apply laws that have not yet been written. Applying the copyright statute, as it now reads, to the facts as they have been developed in this case, the judgment of the Court of Appeals must be reversed.

It is so ordered.

Justice BLACKMUN, with whom Justice MARSHALL, Justice POWELL, and Justice REHNQUIST join, dissenting. . . .

[After rejecting the argument that personal or private uses of copyright works is exempted under copyright law, Blackmun turned to fair use.]

The doctrine of fair use has been called, with some justification, "the most troublesome in the whole law of copyright." Dellar v. Samuel Goldwyn, Inc., 104 F.2d 661, 662 (CA2 1939); see Triangle Publications, Inc. v. Knight-Ridder Newspapers, Inc., 626 F.2d 1171, 1174 (CA5 1980); Meeropol v. Nizer, 560 F.2d 1061, 1068 (CA2 1977), cert. denied, 434 U.S. 1013 (1978). Although courts have constructed lists of factors to be considered in determining whether a particular use is fair, no fixed criteria have emerged by which that determination can be made. This Court thus far has provided no guidance; although fair use issues have come here twice, on each occasion the Court was equally divided and no opinion was forthcoming. Williams & Wilkins Co. v. United States, 487 F.2d 1345 (1973), aff'd, 420 U.S. 376 (1975); Benny v. Loew's, Inc., 239 F.2d 532 (CA9 1956), aff'd sub nom. CBS, Inc. v. Loew's Inc., 356 U.S. 43 (1958).

---

commercial harm. Copying a news broadcast may have a stronger claim to fair use than copying a motion picture. And, of course, not all uses are fungible. Copying for commercial gain has a much weaker claim to fair use than copying for personal enrichment. But the notion of social "productivity" cannot be a complete answer to this analysis. A teacher who copies to prepare lecture notes is clearly productive. But so is a teacher who copies for the sake of broadening his personal understanding of his specialty. Or a legislator who copies for the sake of broadening her understanding of what her constituents are watching; or a constituent who copies a news program to help make a decision on how to vote. Making a copy of a copyrighted work for the convenience of a blind person is expressly identified by the House Committee Report as an example of fair use, with no suggestion that anything more than a purpose to entertain or to inform need motivate the copying. In a hospital setting, using a VTR to enable a patient to see programs he would otherwise miss has no productive purpose other than contributing to the psychological well-being of the patient. Virtually any time-shifting that increases viewer access to television programming may result in a comparable benefit. The statutory language does not identify any dichotomy between productive and nonproductive time-shifting, but does require consideration of the economic consequences of copying.

Nor did Congress provide definitive rules when it codified the fair use doctrine in the 1976 Act; it simply incorporated a list of factors "to be considered": the "purpose and character of the use," the "nature of the copyrighted work," the "amount and substantiality of the portion used," and, perhaps the most important, the "effect of the use upon the potential market for or value of the copyrighted work". . . . §107. No particular weight, however, was assigned to any of these, and the list was not intended to be exclusive. The House and Senate Reports explain that §107 does no more than give "statutory recognition" to the fair use doctrine; it was intended "to restate the present judicial doctrine of fair use, not to change, narrow, or enlarge it in any way." 1976 House Report 66, U.S. Code Cong. & Admin. News 1976, p. 5680. See 1975 Senate Report 62; S. Rep. No. 93-983, p. 116 (1974); H.R. Rep. No. 83, 90th Cong., 1st Sess., 32 (1967); H.R. Rep. No. 2237, 89th Cong., 2d Sess., 61 (1966).

A

Despite this absence of clear standards, the fair use doctrine plays a crucial role in the law of copyright. The purpose of copyright protection, in the words of the Constitution, is to "promote the Progress of Science and useful Arts." Copyright is based on the belief that by granting authors the exclusive rights to reproduce their works, they are given an incentive to create, and that "encouragement of individual effort by personal gain is the best way to advance public welfare through the talents of authors and inventors in 'Science and the useful Arts.'" Mazer v. Stein, 347 U.S. 201, 219 (1954). The monopoly created by copyright thus rewards the individual author in order to benefit the public. Twentieth Century Music Corp. v. Aiken, 422 U.S. 151, 156 (1975); Fox Film Corp. v. Doyal, 286 U.S. 123, 127-128 (1932); see H.R. Rep. No. 2222, 60th Cong., 2d Sess., 7 (1909).

There are situations, nevertheless, in which strict enforcement of this monopoly would inhibit the very "Progress of Science and useful Arts" that copyright is intended to promote. An obvious example is the researcher or scholar whose own work depends on the ability to refer to and to quote the work of prior scholars. Obviously, no author could create a new work if he were first required to repeat the research of every author who had gone before him. The scholar, like the ordinary user, of course could be left to bargain with each copyright owner for permission to quote from or refer to prior works. But there is a crucial difference between the scholar and the ordinary user. When the ordinary user decides that the owner's price is too high, and forgoes use of the work, only the individual is the loser. When the scholar forgoes the use of a prior work, not only does his own work suffer, but the public is deprived of his contribution to knowledge. The scholar's work, in other words, produces external benefits from which everyone profits. In such a case, the fair use doctrine acts as a form of subsidy — albeit at the first author's expense — to permit the second author to make limited use of the first author's work for the public good. See Latman, Fair Use Study 31; Gordon, Fair Use as Market Failure: A Structural Analysis of the Betamax Case and Its Predecessors, 82 Colum. L. Rev. 1600, 1630 (1982).

A similar subsidy may be appropriate in a range of areas other than pure scholarship. The situations in which fair use is most commonly recognized are listed in §107 itself; fair use may be found when a work is used "for purposes such as criticism, comment, news reporting, teaching . . . scholarship, or research." . . . Each of these uses, however, reflects a common theme: each is a productive use, resulting in some added benefit to the public beyond that produced by the first author's work. The fair use doctrine, in other words, permits works to be used for "socially laudable purposes." See Copyright Office, Briefing Papers on Current Issues, reprinted in 1975 House Hearings 2051, 2055. I am aware of no case in which the reproduction of a copyrighted work for the sole benefit of the user has been held to be fair use. . . .

The making of a videotape recording for home viewing is an ordinary rather than a productive use of the Studios' copyrighted works. The District Court found that "Betamax owners use the copy for the same purpose as the original. They add nothing of their own." 480 F. Supp., at 453. Although applying the fair use doctrine to home VTR recording, as Sony argues, may increase public access to material broadcast free over the public airwaves, I think Sony's argument misconceives the nature of copyright. Copyright gives the author a right to limit or even to cut off access to his work. Fox Film Corp. v. Doyal, 286 U.S. 123, 127 (1932). A VTR recording creates no public benefit sufficient to justify limiting this right. Nor is this right extinguished by the copyright owner's choice to make the work available over the airwaves. Section 106 of the 1976 Act grants the copyright owner the exclusive right to control the performance and the reproduction of his work, and the fact that he has licensed a single television performance is really irrelevant to the existence of his right to control its reproduction. Although a television broadcast may be free to the viewer, this fact is equally irrelevant; a book borrowed from the public library may not be copied any more freely than a book that is purchased.

It may be tempting, as, in my view, the Court today is tempted, to stretch the doctrine of fair use so as to permit unfettered use of this new technology in order to increase access to television programming. But such an extension risks eroding the very basis of copyright law, by depriving authors of control over their works and consequently of their incentive to create. . . .

B

I recognize, nevertheless, that there are situations where permitting even an unproductive use would have no effect on the author's incentive to create, that is, where the use would not affect the value of, or the market for, the author's work. Photocopying an old newspaper clipping to send to a friend may be an example; pinning a quotation on one's bulletin board may be another. In each of these cases, the effect on the author is truly de minimis.

Thus, even though these uses provide no benefit to the public at large, no purpose is served by preserving the author's monopoly, and the use may be regarded as fair.

Courts should move with caution, however, in depriving authors of protection from unproductive "ordinary" uses. As has been noted above, even in the case of a productive use, §107(4) requires consideration of "the effect of the use upon the potential market for or value of the copyrighted work." "[A] particular use which may seem to have little or no economic impact on the author's rights today can assume tremendous importance in times to come." Register's Supplementary Report 14. Although such a use may seem harmless when viewed in isolation, "[i]solated instances of minor infringements, when multiplied many times, become in the aggregate a major inroad on copyright that must be prevented." 1975 Senate Report 65.

I therefore conclude that, at least when the proposed use is an unproductive one, a copyright owner need prove only a potential for harm to the market for or the value of the copyrighted work. See 3 M. Nimmer, Copyright §13.05[E][4][c], p. 13-84 (1982). Proof of actual harm, or even probable harm, may be impossible in an area where the effect of a new technology is speculative, and requiring such proof would present the "real danger . . . of confining the scope of an author's rights on the basis of the present technology so that, as the years go by, his copyright loses much of its value because of unforeseen technical advances." Register's Supplementary Report 14. Infringement thus would be found if the copyright owner demonstrates a reasonable possibility that harm will result from the proposed use. When the use is one that creates no benefit to the public at large, copyright protection should not be denied on the basis that a new technology that may result in harm has not yet done so.

The Studios have identified a number of ways in which VTR recording could damage their copyrights. VTR recording could reduce their ability to market their works in movie theaters and through the rental or sale of pre-recorded videotapes or videodiscs; it also could reduce their rerun audience, and consequently the license fees available to them for repeated showings. Moreover, advertisers may be willing to pay for only "live" viewing audiences, if they believe VTR viewers will delete commercials or if rating services are unable to measure VTR use; if this is the case, VTR recording could reduce the license fees the Studios are able to charge even for first-run showings. Library-building may raise the potential for each of the types of harm identified by the Studios, and time-shifting may raise the potential for substantial harm as well.[35]

35. A VTR owner who has taped a favorite movie for repeated viewing will be less likely to rent or buy a tape containing the same movie, watch a televised rerun, or pay to see the movie at a theater. Although time-shifting may not replace theater or rerun viewing or the purchase of pre-recorded tapes or discs, it may well replace rental usage; a VTR user who has recorded a first-run movie for later viewing will have no need to rent a copy when he wants to see it. Both library-builders and time-shifters may avoid commercials; the library-builder may use the pause control to record without them, and all users may fast-forward through commercials on playback. The Studios introduced expert testimony that both time-shifting and librarying would tend to decrease their revenue from copyrighted works. See 480 F. Supp., at 440. The District Court's findings also show substantial library-building and avoidance of commercials. Both sides submitted surveys showing that the average Betamax user owns between 25 and 32 tapes. The Studios' survey showed that at

Although the District Court found no likelihood of harm from VTR use, 480 F. Supp., at 468, I conclude that it applied an incorrect substantive standard and misallocated the burden of proof. . . .

The District Court's reluctance to engage in prediction in this area is understandable, but, in my view, the court was mistaken in concluding that the Studios should bear the risk created by this uncertainty. The Studios have demonstrated a potential for harm, which has not been, and could not be, refuted at this early stage of technological development.

The District Court's analysis of harm, moreover, failed to consider the effect of VTR recording on "the potential market for or the value of the copyrighted work," as required by §107(4). The requirement that a putatively infringing use of a copyrighted work, to be "fair," must not impair a "potential" market for the work has two implications. First, an infringer cannot prevail merely by demonstrating that the copyright holder suffered no net harm from the infringer's action. Indeed, even a showing that the infringement has resulted in a net benefit to the copyright holder will not suffice. Rather, the infringer must demonstrate that he had not impaired the copyright holder's ability to demand compensation from (or to deny access to) any group who would otherwise be willing to pay to see or hear the copyrighted work. Second, the fact that a given market for a copyrighted work would not be available to the copyright holder were it not for the infringer's activities does not permit the infringer to exploit that market without compensating the copyright holder. See Iowa State University Research Foundation, Inc. v. American Broadcasting Cos., 621 F.2d 57 (CA2 1980).

In this case, the Studios and their amici demonstrate that the advent of the VTR technology created a potential market for their copyrighted programs. That market consists of those persons who find it impossible or inconvenient to watch the programs at the time they are broadcast, and who wish to watch them at other times. These persons are willing to pay for the privilege of watching copyrighted work at their convenience, as is evidenced by the fact that they are willing to pay for VTRs and tapes; undoubtedly, most also would be willing to pay some kind of royalty to copyright holders. The Studios correctly argue that they have been deprived of the ability to exploit this sizable market. . . .

V

Contributory Infringement

. . . I therefore conclude that if a significant portion of the product's use is noninfringing, the manufacturers and sellers cannot be held contributorily liable for the product's infringing uses. . . . If virtually all of the

least 40% of users had more than 10 tapes in a "library"; Sony's survey showed that more than 40% of users planned to view their tapes more than once; and both sides' surveys showed that commercials were avoided at least 25% of the time. Id., at 438-439.

product's use, however, is to infringe, contributory liability may be imposed; if no one would buy the product for noninfringing purposes alone, it is clear that the manufacturer is purposely profiting from the infringement, and that liability is appropriately imposed. In such a case, the copyright owner's monopoly would not be extended beyond its proper bounds; the manufacturer of such a product contributes to the infringing activities of others and profits directly thereby, while providing no benefit to the public sufficient to justify the infringement.

. . . The key question is not the amount of television programming that is copyrighted, but rather the amount of VTR usage that is infringing. Moreover, the parties and their amici have argued vigorously about both the amount of television programming that is covered by copyright and the amount for which permission to copy has been given. The proportion of VTR recording that is infringing is ultimately a question of fact, and the District Court specifically declined to make findings on the "percentage of legal versus illegal home-use recording." 480 F. Supp., at 468. In light of my view of the law, resolution of this factual question is essential. I therefore would remand the case for further consideration of this by the District Court. . . .

COMMENTS AND QUESTIONS

1. For an excellent history of both the *William & Wilkins* and *Sony* decisions, see Paul Goldstein, *Copyright's Highway: The Law and Lore of Copyright from Gutenberg to the Celestial Jukebox* (Hill & Wang, 1994).

2. In addressing the legality of the videotape recorder, the Supreme Court relies upon the staple article of commerce doctrine from patent law. What is that test?

3. What does substantial mean in the context of the staple article of commerce test? Is substantiality relative to the infringing uses, a large number of noninfringing uses, or can it represent a single but valuable noninfringing use? What were the substantial noninfringing uses identified by the majority?

4. According to the plaintiffs, how is private copying commercial use of a copyrighted work? What analogy do they rely upon? How does Justice Stevens respond to this argument? How is the nonrivalrous nature of copyrighted works relevant?

5. Under *Sony*, does the use of a copyrighted work have to be considered productive or transformative before it may be considered fair? How do the majority and dissent respond to this question? Which position is more persuasive?

6. Under the fair use doctrine, courts must consider the "effect of the use upon the potential market for or value of the copyrighted work." In conducting this inquiry, how does the Court in *Sony* define the potential markets? Is there any evidence that home videotape harmed the plaintiffs?

7. The majority and the dissent in *Sony* fundamentally differ over not only the elements for fair use, but the justifications for the doctrine. What are their competing justifications for fair use? Which is more persuasive as a matter of doctrine, history or policy?

8. Is fair use a guaranteed legal right? Does it matter?[22]

9. After *Sony*, can Congress prohibit home taping? What about recordings of large digital libraries of musical works downloaded from the Internet for personal use?

UMG RECORDINGS, INC. V. MP3.COM, INC.

92 F. Supp. 2d 349 (S.D.N.Y. 2000)

RAKOFF, District Judge.

The complex marvels of cyberspatial communication may create difficult legal issues; but not in this case. . . .

The technology known as "MP3" permits rapid and efficient conversion of compact disc recordings ("CDs") to computer files easily accessed over the Internet. See generally Recording Industry Ass'n of America v. Diamond Multimedia Systems Inc., 180 F.3d 1072, 1073-74 (9th Cir. 1999). Utilizing this technology, defendant MP3.com, on or around January 12, 2000, launched its "My.MP3.com" service, which is advertised as permitting subscribers to store, customize and listen to the recordings contained on their CDs from any place where they have an Internet connection. To make good on this offer, defendant purchased tens of thousands of popular CDs in which plaintiffs held the copyrights, and, without authorization, copied their recordings onto its computer servers so as to be able to replay the recordings for its subscribers.

Specifically, in order to first access such a recording, a subscriber to MP3.com must either "prove" that he already owns the CD version of the recording by inserting his copy of the commercial CD into his computer CD-ROM drive for a few seconds (the "Beam-it Service") or must purchase the CD from one of defendant's cooperating on-line retailers (the "instant Listening Service"). Thereafter, however, the subscriber can access via the Internet from a computer anywhere in the world the copy of plaintiffs' recording made by defendant. Thus, although defendant seeks to portray its service as the

---

22. One of the leading English copyright law texts suggests that it has always been assumed under English law that fair dealing (the English equivalent to fair use) is a constitutionally guaranteed legal right, although there has historically been little debate about it: William Cornish & David Llewelyn, *Intellectual Property: Patents, Copyrights, Trade Marks and Allied Rights* 808 (2003). *See also* 321 Studios v. MGM Studios, 307 F. Supp. 2d 1085, 1011 (2004) (despite obiter comments in Supreme Court cases, it is not clear that fair use is a constitutionally guaranteed right); Jacqueline Lipton, *Solving the Digital Piracy Puzzle: Disaggregating Fair Use from the DMCA's Anti-Device Provisions*, 19 Harv. J.L. & Tech. 111 (2005) (suggesting that even if fair use has not previously been accepted as a legal right in the United States, the advent of digital encryption technology requires its elevation to that status or the balance of rights and interests in digital copyright works will be tipped too far in favor of copyright holders). Digital encryption technology and its impact on copyright law is considered in more detail, *infra*.

"functional equivalent" of storing its subscribers' CDs, in actuality defendant is re-playing for the subscribers converted versions of the recordings it copied, without authorization, from plaintiffs' copyrighted CDs. On its face, this makes out a presumptive case of infringement under the Copyright Act of 1976 ("Copyright Act"), 17 U.S.C. §101 et seq.

Defendant argues, however, that such copying is protected by the affirmative defense of "fair use." See 17 U.S.C. §107. . . .

Regarding the first factor — "the purpose and character of the use" — defendant does not dispute that its purpose is commercial, for while subscribers to My.MP3.com are not currently charged a fee, defendant seeks to attract a sufficiently large subscription base to draw advertising and otherwise make a profit. Consideration of the first factor, however, also involves inquiring into whether the new use essentially repeats the old or whether, instead, it "transforms" it by infusing it with new meaning, new understandings, or the like. See, e.g., Campbell v. Acuff-Rose Music, Inc., 510 U.S. 569, 579 (1994); *Castle Rock*, 150 F.3d at 142; see also Pierre N. Leval, "Toward a Fair Use Standard," 103 Harv. L. Rev. 1105, 111 (1990). Here, although defendant recites that My.MP3.com provides a transformative "space shift" by which subscribers can enjoy the sound recordings contained on their CDs without lugging around the physical discs themselves, this is simply another way of saying that the unauthorized copies are being retransmitted in another medium — an insufficient basis for any legitimate claim of transformation. . . .

Here, defendant adds no new "new aesthetics, new insights and understandings" to the original music recordings it copies, see *Castle Rock*, 150 F.3d at 142 (internal quotation marks omitted), but simply repackages those recordings to facilitate their transmission through another medium. While such services may be innovative, they are not transformative.

Regarding the second factor — "the nature of the copyrighted work" — the creative recordings here being copied are "close[] to the core of intended copyright protection," *Campbell*, 510 U.S. at 586, and, conversely, far removed from the more factual or descriptive work more amenable to "fair use," see Nihon Keizai Shimbun, Inc. v. Comline Business Data, Inc., 166 F.3d 65, 72-73 (2d Cir. 1999); see also *Castle Rock*, 150 F.3d at 143-44.

Regarding the third factor — "the amount and substantiality of the portion [of the copyrighted work] used [by the copier] in relation to the copyrighted work as a whole" — it is undisputed that defendant copies, and replays, the entirety of the copyrighted works here in issue, thus again negating any claim of fair use. . . .

Regarding the fourth factor — "the effect of the use upon the potential market for or value of the copyrighted work" — defendant's activities on their face invade plaintiffs' statutory right to license their copyrighted sound recordings to others for reproduction. See 17 U.S.C. §106. Defendant, however, argues that, so far as the derivative market here involves is concerned, plaintiffs have not shown that such licensing is "traditional, reasonable, or likely to be developed." *American Geophysical*, 60 F.3d at 930 & n.17. Moreover, defendant argues, its activities can only enhance plaintiffs' sales, since subscribers cannot gain access to particular recordings made available by MP3.com unless they have already "purchased" (actually or purportedly), or agreed to purchase, their own CD copies of those recordings.

Such arguments — though dressed in the garb of an expert's "opinion" (that, on inspection, consists almost entirely of speculative and conclusory statements) — are unpersuasive. Any allegedly positive impact of defendant's activities on plaintiffs' prior market in no way frees defendant to usurp a further market that directly derives from reproduction of the plaintiffs' copyrighted works. This would be so even if the copyright holder had not yet entered the new market in issue, for a copyright holder's "exclusive" rights, derived from the Constitution and the Copyright Act, include the right, within broad limits, to curb the development of such a derivative market by refusing to license a copyrighted work or by doing so only on terms the copyright owner finds acceptable. Here, moreover, plaintiffs have adduced substantial evidence that they have in fact taken steps to enter that market by entering into various licensing agreements.

Finally, regarding defendant's purported reliance on other factors, this essentially reduces to the claim that My.MP3.com provides a useful service to consumers that, in its absence, will be served by "pirates." Copyright, however, is not designed to afford consumer protection or convenience but, rather, to protect the copyright holders' property interests. Moreover, as a practical matter, plaintiffs have indicated no objection in principle to licensing their recordings to companies like MP3.com; they simply want to make sure they get the remuneration the law reserves for them as holders of copyrights on creative works. Stripped to its essence, defendant's "consumer protection" argument amounts to nothing more than a bald claim that defendant should be able to misappropriate plaintiffs' property simply because there is a consumer demand for it. This hardly appeals to the conscience of equity.

In sum, on any view, defendant's "fair use" defense is indefensible and must be denied as a matter of law. . . .

A&M RECORDS, INC. v. NAPSTER, INC.

114 F. Supp. 2d 896 (N.D. Cal. 2000), *aff'd and rev'd in part,*
239 F.3d 1004 (9th Cir. 2001)

[The facts of *Napster* and the court of appeals discussion of contributory and vicarious liability are excerpted, *supra.*]

PATEL, Chief J.

[After concluding that plaintiffs had established a *prima facie* case of direct infringement on the part of Napster's users, the court considered whether the sharing of MP3 files could be considered fair use.]

Defendant asserts the affirmative defenses of fair use and substantial non-infringing use. The latter defense is also known as the staple article of commerce doctrine. See *Sony*, 464 U.S. at 442. *Sony* stands for the rule that a manufacturer is not liable for selling a "staple article of commerce" that is "capable of commercially significant noninfringing uses." *Id*. The Supreme Court also declared in *Sony*, "Any individual may reproduce a copyrighted work for a 'fair use'; the copyright holder does not possess the exclusive right to such a use." *Id*. at 433. Defendant bears the burden of proving these affirmative defenses.

For the reasons set forth below, the court finds that any potential non-infringing use of the Napster service is minimal or connected to the infringing activity, or both. The substantial or commercially significant use of the service was, and continues to be, the unauthorized downloading and uploading of popular music, most of which is copyrighted. . . .

In the instant action, the purpose and character of the use militates against a finding of fair use. Ascertaining whether the new work transforms the copyrighted material satisfies the main goal of the first factor. See Campbell v. Acuff-Rose Music, Inc., 510 U.S. 569, 579 (1994). Plaintiff persuasively argues that downloading MP3 files does not transform the copyrighted music. See UMG Recordings, Inc. v. MP3.com, Inc., 92 F. Supp. 2d 349, 351 (S.D.N.Y. 2000) (concluding that repackaging copyrighted recordings in MP3 format suitable for downloading "adds no 'new aesthetics, new insights and understandings' to the original").

Under the first factor, the court must also determine whether the use is commercial. In *Acuff-Rose*, the Supreme Court clarified that a finding of commercial use weighs against, but does not preclude, a determination of fairness. See *Acuff-Rose*, 510 U.S. at 584.

If a use is non-commercial, the plaintiff bears the burden of showing a meaningful likelihood that it would adversely affect the potential market for the copyrighted work if it became widespread. See *Sony*, 464 U.S. at 451.

Although downloading and uploading MP3 music files is not paradigmatic commercial activity, it is also not personal use in the traditional sense. Plaintiffs have not shown that the majority of Napster users download music to sell — that is, for profit. However, given the vast scale of Napster use among anonymous individuals, the court finds that downloading and uploading MP3 music files with the assistance of Napster are not private uses. At the very least, a host user sending a file cannot be said to engage in a personal use when distributing that file to an anonymous requester. Moreover, the fact that Napster users get for free something they would ordinarily have to buy suggests that they reap economic advantages from Napster use. . . .

The court finds that the copyrighted musical compositions and sound recordings are creative in nature; they constitute entertainment, which cuts against a finding of fair use under the second factor.

With regard to the third factor, it is undisputed that downloading or uploading MP3 music files involves copying the entirety of the copyrighted work . . . even after *Sony*, wholesale copying for private home use tips the fair use analysis in plaintiffs' favor if such copying is likely to adversely affect the market for the copyrighted material. See *Sony*, 464 U.S. at 449-50, 456.

The fourth factor, the effect on the potential market for the copyrighted work, also weighs against a finding of fair use. Plaintiffs have produced evidence that Napster use harms the market for their copyrighted musical compositions and sound recordings in at least two ways. First, it reduces CD sales among college students. Second, it raises barriers to plaintiffs' entry into the market for the digital downloading of music.

Defendant asserts several potential fair uses of the Napster service — including sampling, space-shifting, and the authorized distribution of new artists' work. Sampling on Napster is not a personal use in the traditional sense that courts have recognized — copying which occurs within the household and does not confer any financial benefit on the user. See, e.g., *Sony*, 464 U.S. at 423, 449-50. Instead, sampling on Napster amounts to obtaining permanent copies of songs that users would otherwise have to purchase; it also carries the potential for viral distribution to millions of people. Defendant ignores critical differences between sampling songs on Napster and VCR usage in Sony. First, while "time-shifting [TV broadcasts] merely enables a viewer to see . . . a work which he ha[s] been invited to witness in its entirety free of charge," plaintiffs in this action almost always charge for their music — even if it is downloaded song-by-song. *Sony*, 464 U.S. at 449-50. They only make promotional downloads available on a highly restricted basis. Copyright owners also earn royalties from streamed song samples on retail web sites like Amazon.com. Second, the majority of VCR purchasers in *Sony* did not distribute taped television broad-casts, but merely enjoyed them at home. In contrast, a Napster user who down-loads a copy of a song to her hard drive may make that song available to millions of other individuals, even if she eventually chooses to purchase the CD. So-called sampling on Napster may quickly facilitate unauthorized distribution at an expo-nential rate.

Defendant's argument that using Napster to sample music is akin to visit-ing a free listening station in a record store, or listening to song samples on a retail web site, fails to convince the court because Napster users can keep the music they download. Whether or not they decide to buy the CD, they still obtain a permanent copy of the song. In contrast, many retail sites only offer thirty-to-sixty-second samples in streaming audio format, and promotional downloads from the record company plaintiffs are often "timed-out."

The global scale of Napster usage and the fact that users avoid paying for songs that otherwise would not be free militates against a determination that sampling by Napster users constitutes personal or home use in the traditional sense.

Even if the type of sampling supposedly done on Napster were a non-commercial use, plaintiffs have demonstrated a substantial likelihood that it would adversely affect the potential market for their copyrighted works if it became widespread. See *Sony*, 464 U.S. at 451. Plaintiffs claim three general types of harm: a decrease in retail sales, especially among college students; an obstacle to the record company plaintiffs' future entry into the digital downloading market; and a social devaluing of music stemming from its free distribution. With regard to sampling, twenty-one percent of the Jay survey respondents indicated that Napster helps them decide what music to purchase. Nevertheless, Jay reached the overarching conclusion that the more songs Napster users download, the more likely they are to reveal that such use reduces their music buying. Jay's evidence suggests that sampling and building a free music library through unauthorized downloading are not mutually exclusive: it is likely that survey respondents who sample are primarily direct infringers. Napster users — not the record companies — control the music selection, the amount and the timing of the sampling activity, and they may keep many songs after deciding not to purchase the entire CD.

Defendant maintains that sampling does not decrease retail music sales and may even stimulate them. To support this assertion, it relies heavily on the Fader Report, which concludes that consumers do not view MP3 files as perfect substitutes for CDs. . . .

Any potential enhancement of plaintiffs' sales due to sampling would not tip the fair use analysis conclusively in favor of defendant. Indeed, courts have rejected the suggestion that a positive impact on sales negates the copyright holder's entitlement to licensing fees or access to derivative markets. . . .

The MP3.com opinion is especially instructive. Although MP3.com's activities arguably stimulated CD sales, the plaintiffs "adduced substantial evidence that they . . . [had] taken steps to enter [the digital downloading market]." *MP3.com*, 92 F. Supp. 2d at 352. The fourth factor thus weighed against a finding of fair use. Plaintiffs in the instant action similarly allege that Napster use impedes their entry into the on-line market. The record company plaintiffs have already expended considerable funds and effort to commence Internet sales and licensing for digital downloads. Plaintiffs' economic expert opined that the availability of free MP3 files will reduce the market for authorized, commercial downloading. This point is corroborated by the fact that all forty-nine songs available for purchase on Sony's web site can be obtained for free using Napster. If consumers choose to buy, rather than burn, entire CDs they are still more likely to obtain permanent copies of songs on Napster than buy them from Sony's site or listen to streamed samples at other on-line locations.

The court concludes that, even assuming the sampling alleged in this case is a non-commercial use, the record company plaintiffs have demonstrated a meaningful likelihood that it would adversely affect their entry into the on-line market if it became widespread. See *Sony*, 464 U.S. at 451. Moreover, it deprives the music publisher plaintiffs of royalties for individual songs. The unauthorized downloading of plaintiffs' music to sample songs would not constitute a fair use, even if it enhanced CD sales.

The court is also unconvinced that Sony applies to space-shifting. Defendant erroneously relies on the Ninth Circuit's assertion, in a case involving an inapplicable statute, that space-shifting constitutes non-commercial personal use. See Recording Indus. Ass'n of Am. v. Diamond Multimedia Sys., Inc., 180 F.3d 1072, 1079 (9th Cir. 1999) (discussing the applicability of the Audio Home Recording Act of 1992 to the Rio MP3 player). Defendant also implies that space-shifting music is sufficiently analogous to time-shifting television broadcasts to merit the protection of Sony. According to the gravely flawed Fader Report, space-shifting — like time-shifting — leaves the value of the copyrights unscathed because it does not displace sales. Defendant again cites Fader for the statistic that seventy percent of Napster users at least sometimes engage in space-shifting. In contrast, Jay opined that approximately forty-nine percent of her college-student survey respondents previously owned less than ten percent of the songs they downloaded, and about sixty-nine percent owned less than a quarter. The court has already held that the Jay Report bears greater indicia of reliability than the Fader Report. Moreover, under either analysis, the instant matter is distinguishable from *Sony* because the Supreme Court determined in *Sony* that time-shifting represented the principal, rather than an occasional use of VCRs. See *Sony*, 464 U.S. at 421.

Defendant argues that, if space-shifting is deemed a fair use, the staple article of commerce doctrine precludes liability for contributory or vicarious infringement. Under *Sony*, the copyright holder cannot extend his monopoly to products "capable of substantial noninfringing uses." *Sony*, 464 U.S. at 442. Defendant fails to show that space-shifting constitutes a commercially significant use of Napster. Indeed, the most credible explanation for the exponential growth of traffic to the web site is the vast array of free MP3 files offered by other users — not the ability of each individual to space-shift music she already owns. Thus, even if space-shifting is a fair use, it is not substantial enough to preclude liability under the staple article of commerce doctrine. . . .

This court also declines to apply the staple article of commerce doctrine because, as paragraphs (D)(6) and (E)(2) of the legal conclusions explain, Napster exercises ongoing control over its service. In *Sony*, the defendant's participation did not extend past manufacturing and selling the VCRs: "[t]he only contact between Sony and the users of the Betamax . . . occurred at the moment of sale." *Sony*, 464 U.S. at 438. Here, in contrast, Napster, Inc. maintains and supervises an integrated system that users must access to upload or download files. Courts have distinguished the protection Sony offers to the manufacture and sale of a device from scenarios in which the defendant continues to exercise control over the device's use. See *General Audio Video*, 948 F. Supp. at 1456-57 (finding *Sony* doctrine inapplicable to seller of blank tapes who "acted as a contact between his customers and suppliers of other material necessary for counterfeiting"); RCA Records v. All-Fast Sys., Inc., 594 F. Supp. 335, 339 (S.D.N.Y. 1984) (holding that defendant in position to control cassette-copying machine could not invoke *Sony*); see also Columbia Pictures Indus., Inc. v. Aveco, Inc., 800 F.2d 59, 62 & n.3 (3d Cir. 1986) (holding that business which rented rooms where public viewed copyrighted video cassettes engaged in contributory infringement, even when it was not source of cassettes). Napster, Inc.'s facilitation of unauthorized file-sharing smacks of the contributory infringement in these cases, rather than the legitimate conduct of the VCR manufacturers. Given defendant's control over the service, as opposed to mere manufacturing or selling, the existence of a potentially unobjectionable use like space-shifting does not defeat plaintiffs' claims.

Nor do other potential non-infringing uses of Napster preclude contributory or vicarious liability. Defendant claims that it engages in the authorized promotion of independent artists, ninety-eight percent of whom are not represented by the record company plaintiffs. However, the New Artist Program may not represent a substantial or commercially significant aspect of Napster. The evidence suggests that defendant initially promoted the availability of songs by major stars, as opposed to "page after page of unknown artists." Its purported mission of distributing music by artists unable to obtain record-label representation appears to have been developed later. . . .

In any event, Napster's primary role of facilitating the unauthorized copying and distribution established artists' songs renders *Sony* inapplicable.

Plaintiffs do not object to all of the supposedly non-infringing uses of Napster. They do not seek an injunction covering chat rooms or message boards, the New Artist Program or any distribution authorized by rights holders. Nor do they seek to enjoin applications unrelated to the music recording industry. Because plaintiffs do not ask the court to shut down such satellite activities, the fact that these activities may be non-infringing does not lessen plaintiffs' likelihood of success. The court therefore finds that plaintiffs have established a reasonable probability of proving third-party infringement. . . .

KELLY v. ARRIBA SOFT CORP.

366 F.3d 811 (9th Cir. 2003)

T.G. NELSON, Circuit Judge:

This case involves the application of copyright law to the vast world of the internet and internet search engines. The plaintiff, Leslie Kelly, is a professional photographer who has copyrighted many of his images of the American West. Some of these images are located on Kelly's web site or other web sites with which Kelly has a license agreement. The defendant, Arriba Soft Corp., operates an internet search engine that displays its results in the form of small pictures rather than the more usual form of text. Arriba obtained its database of pictures by copying images from other web sites. By clicking on one of these small pictures, called "thumbnails," the user can then view a large version of that same picture within the context of the Arriba web page.

When Kelly discovered that his photographs were part of Arriba's search engine database, he brought a claim against Arriba for copyright infringement. The district court found that Kelly had established a prima facie case of copyright infringement based on Arriba's unauthorized reproduction and display of Kelly's works, but that this reproduction and display constituted a non-infringing "fair use" under *Section 107 of the Copyright Act*. Kelly appeals that decision, and we affirm in part and reverse in part. The creation and use of the thumbnails in the search engine is a fair use. However, the district court should not have decided whether the display of the larger image is a violation of Kelly's exclusive right to publicly display his works. Thus, we remand for further proceedings consistent with this opinion.

I.

The search engine at issue in this case is unconventional in that it displays the results of a user's query as "thumbnail" images. When a user wants to search the internet for information on a certain topic, he or she types a search term into a search engine, which then produces a list of web sites that contain information relating to the search term. Normally, the list of results is in text format. The Arriba search engine, however, produces its list of results as small pictures.

To provide this service, Arriba developed a computer program that "crawls" the web looking for images to index. This crawler downloads full-sized copies of the images onto Arriba's server. The program then uses these copies to generate smaller, lower-resolution thumbnails of the images. Once the thumbnails are created, the program deletes the full-sized originals from the server. Although a user could copy these thumbnails to his computer or disk, he cannot increase the resolution of the thumbnail; any enlargement would result in a loss of clarity of the image.

The second component of the Arriba program occurs when the user double-clicks on the thumbnail. From January 1999 to June 1999, clicking on the thumbnail produced the "Images Attributes" page. This page used in-line linking to display the original full-sized image, surrounded by text describing the size of the image, a link to the original web site, the Arriba banner, and Arriba advertising.

In-line linking allows one to import a graphic from a source web site and incorporate it in one's own web site, creating the appearance that the in-lined graphic is a seamless part of the second web page. The in-line link instructs the user's browser to retrieve the linked-to image from the source web site and display it on the user's screen, but does so without leaving the linking document. Thus, the linking party can incorporate the linked image into its own content. As a result, although the image in Arriba's Images Attributes page came directly from the originating web site and was not copied onto Arriba's server, the user would not realize that the image actually resided on another web site.

From July 1999 until sometime after August 2000, the results page contained thumbnails accompanied by two links: "Source" and "Details."

The "Details" link produced a screen similar to the Images Attributes page but with a thumbnail rather than the full-sized image. Alternatively, by clicking on the "Source" link or the thumbnail from the results page, the site produced two new windows on top of the Arriba page. The window in the forefront contained solely the full-sized image. This window partially obscured another window, which displayed a reduced-size version of the image's originating web page. Part of the Arriba web page was visible underneath both of these new windows.

In January 1999, Arriba's crawler visited web sites that contained Kelly's photographs. The crawler copied thirty-five of Kelly's images to the Arriba database. Kelly had never given permission to Arriba to copy his images and objected when he found out that Arriba was using them. Arriba deleted the thumbnails of images that came from Kelly's own web sites and placed those sites on a list of sites that it would not crawl in the future. Several months later, Arriba received Kelly's complaint of copyright infringement, which identified other images of his that came from third-party web sites. Arriba subsequently deleted those thumbnails and placed those third-party sites on a list of sites that it would not crawl in the future.

The district court granted summary judgment in favor of Arriba. Kelly's motion for partial summary judgment asserted that Arriba's use of the thumbnail images violated his display, reproduction, and distribution rights. Arriba cross-moved for summary judgment. For the purposes of the motion, Arriba conceded that Kelly established a prima facie case of infringement. However, it limited its concession to the violation of the display and reproduction rights *as to the thumbnail images*. Arriba then argued that its use of the thumbnail images was a fair use.

The district court did not limit its decision to the thumbnail images alone. The court granted summary judgment to Arriba, finding that its use of both the thumbnail images and the full-size images was fair. In doing so, the court broadened the scope of Kelly's original motion to include a claim for infringement of the full-size images. The court also broadened the scope of Arriba's concession to cover the prima facie case for both the thumbnail images and the full-size images. The court determined that two of the fair use factors weighed heavily in Arriba's favor. Specifically, the court found that the character and purpose of Arriba's use was significantly transformative and the use did not harm the market for or value of Kelly's works. Kelly now appeals this decision.

II.

. . . The district court's decision in this case involves two distinct actions by Arriba that warrant analysis. The first action consists of the reproduction of Kelly's images to create the thumbnails and the use of those thumbnails in Arriba's search engine. The second action involves the display of Kelly's larger images when the user clicks on the thumbnails. We conclude that, as to the first action, the district court correctly found that Arriba's use was fair. However, as to the second action, we conclude that the district court should not have reached the issue because neither party moved for summary judgment as to the full-size images and Arriba's response to Kelly's summary judgment motion did not concede the prima facie case for infringement as to those images.

A.

An owner of a copyright has the exclusive right to reproduce, distribute, and publicly display copies of the work. To establish a claim of copyright infringement by reproduction, the plaintiff must show ownership of the copyright and copying by the defendant. As to the thumbnails, Arriba conceded that Kelly established a prima facie case of infringement of Kelly's reproduction rights.

A claim of copyright infringement is subject to certain statutory exceptions, including the fair use exception. This exception "permits courts to avoid rigid application of the copyright statute when, on occasion, it would stifle the very creativity which that law is designed to foster." The statute sets out four factors to consider in determining whether the use in a particular case is a fair use. We must balance these factors in light of the objectives of copyright law, rather than view them as definitive or determinative tests. We now turn to the four fair use factors.

1. Purpose and Character of the Use.

The Supreme Court has rejected the proposition that a commercial use of the copyrighted material ends the inquiry under this factor. Instead,

> [t]he central purpose of this investigation is to see . . . whether the new work merely supersede[s] the objects of the original creation, or instead adds something new, with a further purpose or different character, altering the first with new expression, meaning, or message; it asks, in other words, whether and to what extent the new work is transformative.

The more transformative the new work, the less important the other factors, including commercialism, become.

There is no dispute that Arriba operates its web site for commercial purposes and that Kelly's images were part of Arriba's search engine database. As the district court found, while such use of Kelly's images was commercial, it was more incidental and less exploitative in nature than more traditional types of commercial use. Arriba was neither using Kelly's images to directly promote its web site nor trying to profit by selling Kelly's images. Instead, Kelly's images were among thousands of images in Arriba's search engine data-base. Because the use of Kelly's images was not highly exploitative, the commercial nature of the use weighs only slightly against a finding of fair use.

The second part of the inquiry as to this factor involves the transformative nature of the use. We must determine if Arriba's use of the images merely superseded the object of the originals or instead added a further purpose or different character. We find that Arriba's use of Kelly's images for its thumbnails was transformative.

Although Arriba made exact replications of Kelly's images, the thumbnails were much smaller, lower-resolution images that served an entirely different function than Kelly's original images. Kelly's images are artistic works intended to inform and to engage the viewer in an aesthetic experience. His images are used to portray scenes from the American West in an aesthetic manner. Arriba's use of Kelly's images in the thumbnails is unrelated to any aesthetic purpose. Arriba's search engine functions as a tool to help index and improve access to images on the internet and their related web sites. In fact, users are unlikely to enlarge the thumbnails and use them for artistic purposes because the thumbnails are of much lower-resolution than the originals; any enlargement results in a significant loss of clarity of the image, making them inappropriate as display material.

Kelly asserts that because Arriba reproduced his exact images and added nothing to them, Arriba's use cannot be transformative. Courts have been reluctant to find fair use when an original work is merely retransmitted in a different medium. Those cases are inapposite, however, because the resulting use of the copyrighted work in those cases was the same as the original use. For instance, reproducing music CDs in computer MP3 format does not change the fact that both formats are used for entertainment purposes. Likewise, reproducing news footage into a different format does not change the ultimate purpose of informing the public about current affairs.

Even in *Infinity Broadcast Corp. v. Kirkwood*, where the retransmission of radio broadcasts over telephone lines was for the purpose of allowing advertisers and radio stations to check on the broadcast of commercials or on-air talent, there was nothing preventing listeners from subscribing to the service for entertainment purposes. Even though the intended purpose of the retransmission may have been different from the purpose of the original transmission, the result was that people could use both types of transmissions for the same purpose.

This case involves more than merely a retransmission of Kelly's images in a different medium. Arriba's use of the images serves a different function than Kelly's use — improving access to information on the internet versus artistic expression. Furthermore, it would be unlikely that anyone would use Arriba's thumbnails for illustrative or aesthetic purposes because enlarging them sacrifices their clarity. Because Arriba's use is not superseding Kelly's use but, rather, has created a different purpose for the images, Arriba's use is transformative.

Comparing this case to two recent cases in the Ninth and First Circuits reemphasizes the functionality distinction. In *Worldwide Church of God v. Philadelphia Church of God, Inc.*, we held that copying a religious book to create a new book for use by a different church was not transformative. The second church's use of the book was merely to make use of the same book for another church audience. The court noted that "where the use is for the same intrinsic purpose as [the copyright holder's] . . . such use seriously weakens a claimed fair use."

On the other hand, in *Nunez v. Caribbean International News Corp.*, the First Circuit found that copying a photograph that was intended to be used in a modeling portfolio and using it instead in a news article was a transformative use. By putting a copy of the photograph in the newspaper, the work was transformed into news, creating a new meaning or purpose for the work. The use of Kelly's images in Arriba's search engine is more analogous to the situation in *Nunez* because Arriba has created a new purpose for the images and is not simply superseding Kelly's purpose.

The Copyright Act was intended to promote creativity, thereby benefitting the artist and the public alike. To preserve the potential future use of artistic works for purposes of teaching, research, criticism, and news reporting, Congress created the fair use exception. Arriba's use of Kelly's images promotes the goals of the Copyright Act and the fair use exception. The thumbnails do not stifle artistic creativity because they are not used for illustrative or artistic purposes and therefore do not supplant the need for the originals. In addition, they benefit the public by enhancing information-gathering techniques on the internet.

In *Sony Computer Entertainment America, Inc. v. Bleem*, we held that when Bleem copied "screen shots" from Sony computer games and used them in its own advertising, it was a fair use. In finding that the first factor weighed in favor of Bleem, we noted that "comparative advertising redounds greatly to the purchasing public's benefit with very little corresponding loss to the integrity of Sony's copyrighted material." Similarly, this first factor weighs in favor of Arriba due to the public benefit of the search engine and the minimal loss of integrity to Kelly's images.

2. Nature of the Copyrighted Work.

"Works that are creative in nature are closer to the core of intended copyright protection than are more fact-based works." Photographs that are meant to be viewed by the public for informative and aesthetic purposes, such as Kelly's, are generally creative in nature. The fact that a work is published or unpublished also is a critical element of its nature. Published works are more likely to qualify as fair use because the first appearance of the artist's expression has already occurred. Kelly's images appeared on the internet before Arriba used them in its search image. When considering both of these elements, we find that this factor weighs only slightly in favor of Kelly.

3. Amount and Substantiality of Portion Used.

"While wholesale copying does not preclude fair use per se, copying an entire work militates against a finding of fair use." However, the extent of permissible copying varies with the purpose and character of the use. If the secondary user only copies as much as is necessary for his or her intended use, then this factor will not weigh against him or her.

This factor neither weighs for nor against either party because, although Arriba did copy each of Kelly's images as a whole, it was reasonable to do so in light of Arriba's use of the images. It was necessary for Arriba to copy the entire image to allow users to recognize the image and decide whether to pursue more information about the image or the originating web site. If Arriba only copied part of the image, it would be more difficult to identify it, thereby reducing the usefulness of the visual search engine.

4. Effect of the Use upon the Potential Market for or Value
   of the Copyrighted Work.

This last factor requires courts to consider "not only the extent of market harm caused by the particular actions of the alleged infringer, but also 'whether unrestricted and wide-spread conduct of the sort engaged in by the defendant . . . would result in a substantially adverse impact on the potential market for the original.'" A transformative work is less likely to have an adverse impact on the market of the original than a work that merely supersedes the copyrighted work.

Kelly's images are related to several potential markets. One purpose of the photographs is to attract internet users to his web site, where he sells advertising space as well as books and travel packages. In addition, Kelly could sell or license his photographs to other web sites or to a stock photo data-base, which then could offer the images to its customers.

Arriba's use of Kelly's images in its thumbnails does not harm the market for Kelly's images or the value of his images. By showing the thumbnails on its results page when users entered terms related to Kelly's images, the search engine would guide users to Kelly's web site rather than away from it. Even if users were more interested in the image itself rather than the information on the web page, they would still have to go to Kelly's site to see the full-sized image. The thumbnails would not be a substitute for the full-sized images because the thumbnails lose their clarity when enlarged. If a user wanted to view or download a quality image, he or she would have to visit Kelly's web site. This would hold true whether the thumbnails are solely in Arriba's database or are more widespread and found in other search engine databases.

Arriba's use of Kelly's images also would not harm Kelly's ability to sell or license his full-sized images. Arriba does not sell or license its thumbnails to other parties. Anyone who downloaded the thumbnails would not be successful selling full-sized images enlarged from the thumbnails because of the low resolution of the thumbnails. There would be no way to view, create, or sell a clear, full-sized image without going to Kelly's web sites. Therefore, Arriba's creation and use of the thumbnails does not harm the market for or value of Kelly's images. This factor weighs in favor of Arriba.

Having considered the four fair use factors and found that two weigh in favor of Arriba, one is neutral, and one weighs slightly in favor of Kelly, we conclude that Arriba's use of Kelly's images as thumbnails in its search engine is a fair use.

B.

As mentioned above, the district court granted summary judgment to Arriba as to the full-size images as well. However, because the court broadened the scope of both the parties' motions for partial summary judgment and Arriba's concession on the prima facie case, we must reverse this portion of the court's opinion.

With limited exceptions that do not apply here, a district court may not grant summary judgment on a claim when the party has not requested it. The parties did not move for summary judgment as to copyright infringement of the full-size images. Further, Arriba had no opportunity to contest the prima facie case for infringement as to the full-size images. Accordingly, we reverse this portion of the district court's opinion and remand for further proceedings.

CONCLUSION

We hold that Arriba's reproduction of Kelly's images for use as thumbnails in Arriba's search engine is a fair use under the Copyright Act. However, we hold that the district court should not have reached whether Arriba's display of Kelly's full-sized images is a fair use because the parties never moved for summary judgment on this claim and Arriba never conceded the prima facie case as to the full-size images. The district court's opinion is affirmed as to the thumbnails and reversed as to the display of the full-sized images. We remand for further proceedings consistent with this opinion. Each party shall bear its own costs and fees on appeal.

AFFIRMED in part, REVERSED in part, and REMANDED.

COMMENTS AND QUESTIONS

1. How did the courts in *MP3.com* and *Napster* interpret "the purpose and character of the use" prong of fair use in determining whether "space shifting" and "file-sharing" could be considered fair uses? Is their reasoning consistent with the Supreme Court's decision in *Sony*? If not, why not? Is *Arriba Soft* consistent with these decisions?

2. Following *Arriba Soft*, the Ninth Circuit concluded in Perfect 10 v. Google, 508 F.3d 1146 (9th Cir. 2007), that Google's use of thumbnail

images in search engines was fair. In so doing, the court rejected the district court's efforts to distinguish *Arriba Soft*.

> [T]he district court determined that the commercial nature of Google's use weighed against its transformative nature. Although *Kelly* held that the commercial use of the photographer's images by Arriba's search engine was less exploitative than typical commercial use, and thus weighed only slightly against a finding of fair use, *Kelly*, 336 F.3d at 818-20, the district court here distinguished *Kelly* on the ground that some website owners in the AdSense program had infringing Perfect 10 images on their websites, *Perfect 10*, 416 F. Supp. 2d at 846-47. The district court held that because Google's thumbnails "lead users to sites that directly benefit Google's bottom line," the AdSense program increased the commercial nature of Google's use of Perfect 10's images.
>
> In conducting our case-specific analysis of fair use in light of the purposes of copyright, *Campbell*, 510 U.S. at 581, we must weigh Google's superseding and commercial uses of thumbnail images against Google's significant transformative use, as well as the extent to which Google's search engine promotes the purposes of copyright and serves the interests of the public. Although the district court acknowledged the "truism that search engines such as Google Image Search provide great value to the public," the district court did not expressly consider whether this value outweighed the significance of Google's superseding use or the commercial nature of Google's use. The Supreme Court, however, has directed us to be mindful of the extent to which a use promotes the purposes of copyright and serves the interests of the public. *See Campbell*, 510 U.S. at 579; *Harper & Row*, 471 U.S. at 556-57; *Sony*, 464 U.S. at 431-32.
>
> We note that the superseding use in this case is not significant at present: the district court did not find that any downloads for mobile phone use had taken place. Moreover, while Google's use of thumbnails to direct users to AdSense partners containing infringing content adds a commercial dimension that did not exist in *Kelly*, the district court did not determine that this commercial element was significant. The district court stated that Google's AdSense programs as a whole contributed "$630 million, or 46% of total revenues" to Google's bottom line, but noted that this figure did not "break down the much smaller amount attributable to websites that contain infringing content."
>
> We conclude that the significantly transformative nature of Google's search engine, particularly in light of its public benefit, outweighs Google's superseding and commercial uses of the thumbnails in this case.

3.   According to the plaintiffs, how did the uses at issue in *MP3.com* and *Napster* affect "the potential market for or value of the copyrighted work"? In *MP3.com* and *Napster*, why do the courts consider irrelevent the fact that the services provided by the defendants might actually increase sales of compact discs?

4.   In *Napster*, the court concluded that there was a likelihood that Napster's use would threaten CD sales. In reaching this conclusion, the court relied upon a report that CD sales had declined around certain college campuses despite the fact that CD sales had risen in the same time period. Assuming that college students are more likely to use Napster as a replacement for purchasing CDs, why should their behavior be held against all other users who may not behave in the same manner? Is the court assuming that only college students are more likely to use Napster because they are more "Internet savvy"? Is this a permissible assumption? If so, is it also likely that college students would be more likely to purchase music online rather than going to a local store?

5. If the consumer and the service in *MP3.com* legally purchased CDs, why should the copyright holder be permitted to prohibit them from "space shifting"? Does it matter whether MP3.com may in fact be better than the recording industry when it comes to providing such a service? Should it matter whether the copyright owners are actually offering such a service, or whether they are even willing to offer it? Could it be argued that the copyright holders are using decisions like *MP3.com* to reserve a market that they have not yet decided to exploit? Would such a practice potentially impede technological innovation and run counter to the utilitarian aims of copyright law?

6. In *Napster*, why does the court reject the staple article of commerce defense from *Sony* when some artists agreed to have their music distributed through Napster? How does the court distinguish *Sony* with respect to whether Napster was capable of substantial noninfringing uses? Are you convinced by the court's basis for distinguishing *Sony*? It is clear that Napster could be used for noninfringing uses, potentially even substantial ones. The same is the case with the betamax video recorders. However, in *Sony*, the actual uses for the technology were not yet known at the time of the decision, whereas in *Napster* it was clear that most of the uses were copyright infringing. Should the court in *Napster* have given more weight to the possibility that the file sharing technology at issue could have been used for substantial noninfringing uses in the future?

7. In the preceding materials, you studied how Napster's ability to control how its subscribers used its services could potentially subject Napster to contributory and vicarious liability. Is that control relevant in the context of fair use? How did the Supreme Court in *Grokster, supra*, deal with the fact that Grokster and StreamCast alleged that they were unable to control how those who downloaded their software ultimately made use of it? Was fair use relevant to their decision?

8. Copyright holders have been criticized for focusing on indirect infringers of copyrights online and not putting the effort into acting against the direct infringers. Of course, copyright holders have brought actions against direct infringers where they have been able to locate them. Consider the following case.

BMG MUSIC v. GONZALEZ

2005 U.S. App. LEXIS 26903 (7th Cir. 2005)

EASTERBROOK, Circuit Judge.

Last June the Supreme Court held in *MGM Studios, Inc. v. Grokster, Ltd.*, 125 S. Ct. 2764 (2005), that a distributed file-sharing system is engaged in contributory copyright infringement when its principal object is the dissemination of copyrighted material. The foundation of this holding is a belief that people who post or download music files are primary infringers. *In re Aimster Copyright Litigation*, 334 F.3d 643, 645 (7th Cir. 2003), which anticipated *Grokster*, made the same assumption. In this appeal Cecilia Gonzalez, who downloaded copyrighted music through the KaZaA file-sharing network, denies the premise of *Grokster* and *Aimster*. She contends that her activities were fair use rather than infringement. The district court disagreed and granted summary judgment for the copyright proprietors (to which we refer collectively as BMG Music). 2005 U.S. Dist. LEXIS 910 (N.D. Ill. Jan. 7, 2005). The court enjoined Gonzalez from further infringement and awarded $22,500 in damages under 17 U.S.C. §504(c).

A "fair use" of copyrighted material is not infringement. Gonzalez insists that she was engaged in fair use under the terms of 17 U.S.C. §107 — or at least that a material dispute entitles her to a trial. It is undisputed, however, that she downloaded more than 1,370 copyrighted songs during a few weeks and kept them on her computer until she was caught. Her position is that she was just sampling music to determine what she liked enough to buy at retail. Because this suit was resolved on summary judgment, we must assume that Gonzalez is telling the truth when she says that she owned compact discs containing some of the songs before she downloaded them and that she purchased others later. She concedes, however, that she has never owned legitimate copies of 30 songs that she downloaded. (How many of the remainder she owned is disputed.)

Instead of erasing songs that she decided not to buy, she retained them. It is these 30 songs about which there is no dispute concerning ownership that formed the basis of the damages award. This is not a form of time-shifting, along the lines of *Sony Corp. of America v. Universal Studios, Inc.*, 464 U.S. 417 (1984) (*Betamax*). A copy downloaded, played, and retained on one's hard drive for future use is a direct substitute for a purchased copy — and without the benefit of the license fee paid to the broadcaster. The premise of *Betamax* is that the broadcast was licensed for one transmission and thus one viewing. *Betamax* held that shifting the time of this single viewing is fair use. The files that Gonzalez obtained, by contrast, were posted in violation of copyright law; there was no license covering a single transmission or hearing — and, to repeat, Gonzalez kept the copies. Time-shifting by an authorized recipient this is not. See William M. Landes & Richard A. Posner, *The Economic Structure of Intellectual Property Law* 117-22 (2003).

Section 107 provides that when considering a defense of fair use the court must take into account "(1) the purpose and character of the use, including whether such use is of a commercial nature or is for nonprofit educational purposes; (2) the nature of the copyrighted work; (3) the amount and substantiality of the portion used in relation to the copyrighted work as a whole; and (4) the effect of the use upon the potential market for or value of the copyrighted work." Gonzalez was not engaged in a nonprofit use; she downloaded (and kept) whole copyrighted songs (for which, as with poetry, copying of more than a couplet or two is deemed excessive); and she did this despite the fact that these works often are sold per song as well as per album. This leads her to concentrate on the fourth consideration: "the effect of the use upon the potential market for or value of the copyrighted work."

As she tells the tale, downloading on a try-before-you-buy basis is good advertising for copyright proprietors, expanding the value of their inventory. The Supreme Court thought otherwise in *Grokster*, with considerable empirical support. As file sharing has increased over the last four years, the sales of recorded music have dropped by approximately 30%. Perhaps other economic factors contributed, but the events likely are related. Music downloaded for free from the Internet is a close substitute for purchased music; many people are bound to keep the downloaded files without buying originals. That is exactly what Gonzalez did for at least 30 songs. It is no surprise, therefore, that the only appellate decision on point has held that downloading copyrighted songs cannot be defended as fair use, whether or not the recipient plans to buy songs she likes well enough to spring for. See *A&M Records, Inc. v. Napster, Inc.*, 239 F.3d 1004, 1014-19 (9th Cir. 2001). See also *UMG Recordings, Inc. v. MP3.com, Inc.*, 92 F. Supp. 2d 349 (S.D.N.Y. 2000) (holding that downloads are not fair use even if the downloader *already* owns one purchased copy).

Although BMG Music sought damages for only the 30 songs that Gonzalez concedes she has never purchased, all 1,000+ of her downloads violated the statute. All created copies of an entire work. All undermined the means by which authors seek to profit. Gonzalez proceeds as if the authors' only interest were in selling compact discs containing collections of works. Not so; there is also a market in ways to introduce potential consumers to music.

Think of radio. Authors and publishers collect royalties on the broadcast of recorded music, even though these broadcasts may boost sales. See *Broadcast Music, Inc. v. Columbia Broadcasting System, Inc.*, 441 U.S. 1 (1979) (discussing the licenses available from performing rights societies for radio and television broadcasts). Downloads from peer-to-peer networks such as KaZaA compete with licensed broadcasts and hence undermine the income available to authors. This is true even if a particular person never buys recorded media. Cf. *United States v. Slater*, 348 F.3d 666 (7th Cir. 2003). Many radio stations stream their content over the Internet, paying a fee for the right to do so. Gonzalez could have listened to this streaming music to sample songs for purchase; had she done so, the authors would have received royalties from the broadcasters (and reduced the risk that files saved to disk would diminish the urge to pay for the music in the end).

Licensed Internet sellers, such as the iTunes Music Store, offer samples — but again they pay authors a fee for the right to do so, and the teasers are just a portion of the original. Other intermediaries (not only Yahoo! Music Unlimited and Real Rhapsody but also the revived Napster, with a new business model) offer licensed access to large collections of music; customers may rent the whole library by the month or year, sample them all, and purchase any songs they want to keep. New technologies, such as SNOCAP, enable authorized trials over peer-to-peer systems. See Saul Hansell, *Putting the Napster Genie Back in the Bottle*, New York Times (Nov. 20, 2005); see also http://www.snocap.com.

Authorized previews share the feature of evanescence: if a listener decides not to buy (or stops paying the rental fee), no copy remains behind. With all of these means available to consumers who want to choose where to spend their money, downloading full copies of copyrighted material without compensation to authors cannot be deemed "fair use." Copyright law lets authors make their own decisions about how best to promote their works; copiers such as Gonzalez cannot ask courts (and juries) to second-guess the market and call wholesale copying "fair use" if they think that authors err in understanding their own economic interests or that Congress erred in granting authors the rights in the copyright statute. Nor can she defend by observing that other persons were greater offenders; Gonzalez's theme that she obtained "only 30" (or "only 1,300") copyrighted songs is no more relevant than a thief's contention that he shoplifted "only 30" compact discs, planning to listen to them at home and pay later for any he liked.

[The District Court's decision was affirmed.]

COMMENTS AND QUESTIONS

1. On what basis does Judge Easterbrook distinguish Gonzalez's conduct from the "time shifting" conduct considered likely to be fair use in *Sony* (*supra*)? Do you find this distinction convincing?

2. Should "sampling" online music in order to decide whether to buy it later be protected by copyright law as a "fair use"? Is this question definitively settled in *BMG Music v. Gonzalez*?

3. Would it have affected the court's decision if Gonzalez had been able to establish that she owned legitimately purchased copies of all of the music she had downloaded?

4. Does a copyright holder's ability to stream music for a limited number of downloads solve the problems of online copying of music files? In other words, will technology overtake the law as the best way of protecting copyrights in the digital environment?

5. Fair use has remained a difficult challenge for law and policy makers in the digital age, particularly in the wake of anti-circumvention laws adopted in the DMCA (see *infra*). Various commentators have suggested new ways of looking at fair use in order to create a better balance between the rights of content owners and those of the general public. *See, for example*, Jessica Litman, *Lawful Personal Use*, 85 Tex. L. Rev. 1871 (2007) (suggesting side-stepping copyright law altogether — and thus avoiding the infringement versus fair use question — in cases of personal use that were probably not in the contemplation of legislators when drafting copyright legislation); Barton Beebe, *An Empirical Study of Fair Use*, 156 U. Pa. L. Rev. 549 (2008) (attempting to bring some balance to fair use debates through empirical evidence); Michael Carroll, *Fixing Fair Use*, 85 N.C. L. Rev. 1087 (2007) (advocating the establishment of a Fair Use Board in the U.S. Copyright

Office with power to declare a proposed use of another's copyrighted work to be a fair use).

b) Anti-Circumvention under the DMCA

As previously discussed, Congress adopted the DMCA in response to concerns that existing copyright law would not be up to the task of protecting intellectual property in a digital world. We have already examined the Internet service provider safe harbor provisions embodied in Section 512. In addition to encouraging Internet service providers to police their networks to combat copyright infringement, the DMCA's anti-circumvention provisions assist copyright owners who use technology to protect their works from copying. For example, Section 1201(a)(1)(A) provides that "no person shall circumvent a technological measure that effectively controls access to a work. . . ." Similarly, Section 1201(a)(2) prohibits the manufacture, import, offer to the public, provision, or otherwise trafficking in any technology, product, service, device, component, or part thereof, that:

(A) is primarily designed or produced for the purpose of circumventing a technological measure that effectively controls access to a work protected under this title;

(B) has only limited commercially significant purpose or use other than to circumvent a technological measure that effectively controls access to a work protected under this title [17 U.S.C.A. §§1 et seq.]; or

(C) is marketed by that person or another acting in concert with that person with that person's knowledge for use in circumventing a technological measure that effectively controls access to a work protected under this title.

To circumvent a technological measure "means to descramble a scrambled work, to decrypt an encrypted work, or otherwise to avoid, bypass, remove, deactivate, or impair a technological measure, without the authority of the copyright owner," and a technological measure effectively controls access to a work "if the measure, in the ordinary course of its operation, requires the application of information, or a process or a treatment, with the authority of the copyright owner, to gain access to the work."

According to the DMCA, "nothing in this section shall affect rights, remedies, limitations, or defenses to copyright infringement, including fair use, under this title [17 U.S.C.A. §§1 et seq.]."[23] Moreover, the DMCA provides for various exceptions including an exception for legitimate encryption research or to prevent the collection of personally identifying information.

---

23. 17 U.S.C. §1201(c).

What do the anti-circumvention provisions of the DMCA prevent? Is it fair to describe the DMCA anti-circumvention provisions as a law prohibiting lock picking or trading in lock picking tools? Do the anti-circumvention provisions prohibit a user from creating a program or device to circumvent technology to allow the user to make fair use of the work? Do they prevent such programs or devices from being marketed?

In light of the DMCA's exception for encryption research and privacy protection, would the publishing of a scientific paper outlining how to break encryption technology fall under an exception? In 2001, a Princeton University computer science professor and other researchers were threatened with prosecution under the anti-circumvention provisions for planning to present a paper on their success in breaking the protection regime employed by the music industry. While opposition to their paper was eventually dropped, could they have been prosecuted under the DMCA? What if the paper contained a step-by-step instruction on how they were able to break those measures? The source code for a program to defeat the protection measures?

Can the DMCA be applied against an individual for trafficking in a program or device if the program or device is created and marketed outside in another country and is legal in that country? Consider the case of Dmitri Sklyarov, a Russian software programmer, who wrote a program that permitted end users of Adobe eBook Readers to disable restrictions that certain Adobe formatted electronic books might establish. Sklyarov's employers sold the program on the Internet. The FBI was notified of this alleged DMCA violation. Although the software program was legal in Russia and in other countries, Sklyarov was arrested and indicted while attending a conference in the United States. He was later released in exchange for his testimony in an action against his employer. *See* United States v. Elcom, 203 F. Supp. 2d 1111 (2002).

As you study the following materials, to what extent do the anti-circumvention provisions alter or even replace copyright law?

REALNETWORKS, INC. V. STREAMBOX, INC.

No. 2:99CV02070 (W.D. Wash. Jan. 18, 2000)

PECHMAN, J.

Plaintiff RealNetworks, Inc. ("RealNetworks") filed this action on December 21, 1999. RealNetworks claims that Defendant Streambox has violated provisions of the Digital Millennium Copyright Act ("DMCA"), 17 U.S.C. §1201 et seq., by distributing and marketing products known as the Streambox VCR and the Ripper. RealNetworks also contends that another Streambox product, known as the Ferret, is unlawfully designed to permit consumers to make unauthorized modifications to a software program on which RealNetworks holds the copyright. . . .

FINDINGS OF FACT

RealNetworks

RealNetworks is a public company based in Seattle, Washington, that develops and markets software products designed to enable owners of audio, video, and other multimedia content to send their content to users of personal computers over the Internet.

RealNetworks offers products that enable consumers to access audio and video content over the Internet through a process known as "streaming." When an audio or video clip is "streamed" to a consumer, no trace of the clip is left on the consumer's computer, unless the content owner has permitted the consumer to download the file.

Streaming is to be contrasted with "downloading," a process by which a complete copy of an audio or video clip is delivered to and stored on a consumer's computer. Once a consumer has downloaded a file, he or she can access the file at will, and can generally redistribute copies of that file to others.

In the digital era, the difference between streaming and downloading is of critical importance. A downloaded copy of a digital audio or video file is essentially indistinguishable from the original, and such copies can often be created at the touch of a button. A user who obtains a digital copy may supplant the market for the original by distributing copies of his or her own. To guard against the unauthorized copying and redistribution of their content, many copyright owners do not make their content available for downloading, and instead distribute the content using streaming technology in a manner that does not permit downloading. . . .

RealNetworks' Products

The RealNetworks' products at issue in this action include the "RealProducer," the "RealServer" and the "RealPlayer." These products may be used together to form a system for distributing, retrieving and playing digital audio and video content via the Internet.

Owners of audio or video content may choose to use a RealNetworks product to encode their digital content into RealNetworks' format. Once encoded in that format, the media files are called RealAudio or RealVideo (collectively "RealMedia") files.

After a content owner has encoded its content into the RealMedia format, it may decide to use a "RealServer" to send that content to consumers. A RealServer is a software program that resides on a content owner's computer that holds RealMedia files and "serves" them to consumers through streaming.

The RealServer is not the only available means for distributing RealMedia files. RealMedia files may also be made available on an ordinary Web server instead of a RealServer. An end-user can download content from an ordinary

Web server using nothing more than a freely available Internet browser such as Netscape's Navigator or Microsoft's Internet Explorer.

To download streaming content distributed by a RealServer, however, a consumer must employ a "RealPlayer." The RealPlayer is a software program that resides on an end-user's computer and must be used to access and play a streaming RealMedia file that is sent from a RealServer.

RealNetworks' Security Measures

RealNetworks' products can be used to enable owners of audio and video content to make their content available for consumers to listen to or view, while at the same time securing the content against unauthorized access or copying.

The first of these measures, called the "Secret Handshake" by RealNetworks, ensures that files hosted on a RealServer will only be sent to a RealPlayer. The Secret Handshake is an authentication sequence which only RealServers and RealPlayers know. By design, unless this authentication sequence takes place, the RealServer does not stream the content it holds.

By ensuring that RealMedia files hosted on a RealServer are streamed only to RealPlayers, RealNetworks can ensure that a second security measure, which RealNetworks calls the "Copy Switch," is given effect. The Copy Switch is a piece of data in all RealMedia files that contains the content owner's preference regarding whether or not the stream may be copied by end-users. RealPlayers are designed to read this Copy Switch and obey the content owner's wishes. If a content owner turns on the Copy Switch in a particular RealMedia file, when that file is streamed, an end-user can use the RealPlayer to save a copy of that RealMedia file to the user's computer. If a content owner does not turn on the Copy Switch in a RealMedia file, the RealPlayer will not allow an end-user to make a copy of that file. The file will simply "evaporate" as the user listens to or watches it stream.

Through the use of the Secret Handshake and the Copy Switch, owners of audio and video content can prevent the unauthorized copying of their content if they so choose.

Content owners who choose to use the security measures described above are likely to be seeking to prevent their works from being copied without their authorization. RealNetworks has proffered declarations from copyright owners that they rely on RealNetworks security measures to protect their copyrighted works on the Internet. Many of these copyright owners further state that if users could circumvent the security measures and make unauthorized copies of the content, they likely would not put their content up on the Internet for end-users. . . .

RealNetworks' success as a company is due in significant part to the fact that it has offered copyright owners a successful means of protecting against unauthorized duplication and distribution of their digital works. . . .

Streambox

Defendant Streambox, Inc. is a Washington corporation which provides software products for processing and recording audio and video content, including but not limited to content which is streamed over the Internet. Streambox also maintains a searchable database of Internet Web addresses of various audio and video offerings on the Internet. The Streambox products at issue in this case are known as the Streambox VCR, the Ripper, and the Ferret.

Streambox VCR

The Streambox VCR enables end-users to access and download copies of Real Media files that are streamed over the Internet. While the Streambox VCR also allows users to copy RealMedia files that are made freely available for downloading from ordinary Web servers, the only function relevant to this case is the portions of the VCR that allow it to access and copy RealMedia files located on RealServers.

In order to gain access to RealMedia content located on a RealServer, the VCR mimics a RealPlayer and circumvents the authentication procedure, or Secret Handshake, that a RealServer requires before it will stream content. In other words, the Streambox VCR is able to convince the RealServer into thinking that the VCR is, in fact, a RealPlayer.

Having convinced a RealServer to begin streaming content, the Streambox VCR, like the RealPlayer, acts as a receiver. However, unlike the Real-Player, the VCR ignores the Copy Switch that tells a RealPlayer whether an end-user is allowed to make a copy of (i.e., download) the RealMedia file as it is being streamed. The VCR thus allows the end-user to download RealMedia files even if the content owner has used the Copy Switch to prohibit end-users from downloading the files.

The only reason for the Streambox VCR to circumvent the Secret Handshake and interact with a RealServer is to allow an end-user to access and make copies of content that a copyright holder has placed on a RealServer in order to secure it against unauthorized copying. In this way, the Streambox VCR acts like a "black box" which descrambles cable or satellite broadcasts so that viewers can watch pay programming for free. Like the cable and satellite companies that scramble their video signals to control access to their programs, RealNetworks has employed technological measures to ensure that only users of the RealPlayer can access RealMedia content placed on a RealServer. RealNetworks has gone one step further than the cable and satellite companies, not only controlling access, but also allowing copyright owners to specify whether or not their works can be copied by end-users, even if access is permitted. The Streambox VCR circumvents both the access control and copy protection measures.

The Streambox VCR can be distinguished from a third-party product sold by RealNetworks called GetRight. GetRight enables end-users to download

RealAudio files that have been placed on a Web server, but not RealAudio files placed on a RealServer.

A copyright owner that places a RealMedia file onto a Web server instead of a RealServer does not make use of protections offered by the RealNetworks security system. Thus, when GetRight is used to obtain such a file, it need not and does not circumvent RealNetworks' access control and copyright protection measures. GetRight cannot access materials available from a RealServer because it cannot perform the requisite Secret Handshake. Unlike GetRight, the Streambox VCR circumvents the Secret Handshake and enables users to make digital copies of content that the copyright owner has indicated that it should not be copied.

Once an unauthorized, digital copy of a RealMedia file is created it can be redistributed to others at the touch of a button.

Streambox's marketing of the VCR notes that end-users can "[d]ownload Real Audio and RealMedia files as easily as you would any other file, then reap the benefits of clean, unclogged streams straight from your hard drive" and that the product can be used by "savvy surfers who enjoy taking control of their favorite Internet music/video clips."

The Streambox VCR poses a threat to RealNetworks' relationships with existing and potential customers who wish to secure their content for transmission over the Internet and must decide whether to purchase and use RealNetworks' technology. If the Streambox VCR remains available, these customers may opt not to utilize RealNetworks' technology, believing that it would not protect their content against unauthorized copying. . . .

CONCLUSIONS OF LAW

. . . RealNetworks Has Demonstrated a Reasonable Likelihood of Success on its DMCA Claims with Respect to the Streambox VCR

The DMCA prohibits the manufacture, import, offer to the public, or trafficking in any technology, product, service, device, component, or part thereof that: (1) is primarily designed or produced for the purpose of circumventing a technological measure that effectively "controls access to" a copyrighted work or "protects a right of a copyright owner"; (2) has only limited commercially significant purpose or use other than to circumvent such technological protection measures; or (3) is marketed for use in circumventing such technological protection measures. 17 U.S.C. §§1201(a)(2), 1201(b).

Parts of the VCR Are Likely to Violate Sections 1201(a)(2) and 1201(b)

Under the DMCA, the Secret Handshake that must take place between a RealServer and a RealPlayer before the RealServer will begin streaming content to an end-user appears to constitute a "technological measure" that "effectively controls access" to copyrighted works. See 17 U.S.C. §1201(a)(3)(B) (measure "effectively controls access" if it "requires the application of information or a process or a treatment, with the authority of the copyright holder, to gain access to the work"). To gain access to a work protected by the Secret Handshake, a user must employ a RealPlayer, which will supply the requisite information to the RealServer in a proprietary authentication sequence.

In conjunction with the Secret Handshake, the Copy Switch is a "technological measure" that effectively protects the right of a copyright owner to control the unauthorized copying of its work. See 17 U.S.C. §1201(b)(2)(B) (measure "effectively protects" right of copyright holder if it "prevents, restricts or otherwise limits the exercise of a right of a copyright owner"); 17 U.S.C. §106(a) (granting copyright holder exclusive right to make copies of its work). To access a RealMedia file distributed by a RealServer, a user must use a RealPlayer. The RealPlayer reads the Copy Switch in the file. If the Copy Switch in the file is turned off, the RealPlayer will not permit the user to record a copy as the file is streamed. Thus, the Copy Switch may restrict others from exercising a copyright holder's exclusive right to copy its work.

Under the DMCA, a product or part thereof "circumvents" protections afforded a technological measure by "avoiding, bypassing, removing, deactivating or otherwise impairing" the operation of that technological measure. 17 U.S.C. §§1201(b)(2)(A), 1201(a)(2)(A). Under that definition, at least a part of the Streambox VCR circumvents the technological measures RealNetworks affords to copyright owners. Where a RealMedia file is stored on a RealServer, the VCR "bypasses" the Secret Handshake to gain access to the file. The VCR then circumvents the Copy Switch, enabling a user to make a copy of a file that the copyright owner has sought to protect.

Given the circumvention capabilities of the Streambox VCR, Streambox violates the DMCA if the product or a part thereof: (i) is primarily designed to serve this function; (ii) has only limited commercially significant purposes beyond the circumvention; or (iii) is marketed as a means of circumvention. 17 U.S.C. §§1201(a)(2)(A-C), 1201(b)(b)(A-C). These three tests are disjunctive. Id. A product that meets only one of the three independent bases for liability is still prohibited. Here, the VCR meets at least the first two.

The Streambox VCR meets the first test for liability under the DMCA because at least a part of the Streambox VCR is primarily, if not exclusively, designed to circumvent the access control and copy protection measures that RealNetworks affords to copyright owners. 17 U.S.C. §§1201(a)(2)(A), 1201(b)(c)(A).

The second basis for liability is met because the portion of the VCR that circumvents the Secret Handshake so as to avoid the Copy Switch has no significant commercial purpose other than to enable users to access and record protected content. 17 U.S.C. §§1201(a)(2)(B), 1201(b)(d)(B). There does not appear to be any other commercial value that this capability affords.

Streambox's primary defense to Plaintiff's DMCA claims is that the VCR has legitimate uses. In particular, Streambox claims that the VCR allows consumers to make "fair use" copies of RealMedia files, notwithstanding the access control and copy protection measures that a copyright owner may have placed on that file.

The portions of the VCR that circumvent the secret handshake and copy switch permit consumers to obtain and redistribute perfect digital copies of audio and video files that copyright owners have made clear they do not want copied. For this reason, Streambox's VCR is not entitled to the same "fair use" protections the Supreme Court afforded to video cassette recorders used for "time-shifting" in Sony Corp. v. Universal City Studios, Inc., 464 U.S. 417 (1984).

The *Sony* decision turned in large part on a finding that substantial numbers of copyright holders who broadcast their works either had authorized or would not object to having their works time-shifted by private viewers. See *Sony*, 464 U.S. at 443, 446. Here, by contrast, copyright owners have specifically chosen to prevent the copying enabled by the Streambox VCR by putting their content on RealServers and leaving the Copy Switch off.

Moreover, the Sony decision did not involve interpretation of the DMCA. Under the DMCA, product developers do not have the right to distribute products that circumvent technological measures that prevent consumers from gaining unauthorized access to or making unauthorized copies of works protected by the Copyright Act. Instead, Congress specifically prohibited the distribution of the tools by which such circumvention could be accomplished. The portion of the Streambox VCR that circumvents the technological measures that prevent unauthorized access to and duplication of audio and video content therefore runs afoul of the DMCA.

This point is underscored by the leading treatise on copyright, which observes that the enactment of the DMCA means that "those who manufacture equipment and products generally can no longer gauge their conduct as permitted or forbidden by reference to the Sony doctrine. For a given piece of machinery might qualify as a staple item of commerce, with a substantial noninfringing use, and hence be immune from attack under Sony's construction of the Copyright Act—but nonetheless still be subject to suppression under Section 1201." 1 Nimmer on Copyright (1999 Supp.), §12A.18[B]. As such, "[e]quipment manufacturers in the twenty-first century will need to vet their products for compliance with Section 1201 in order to avoid a circumvention claim, rather than under Sony to negate a copyright claim." Id.

Streambox also argues that the VCR does not violate the DMCA because the Copy Switch that it avoids does not "effectively protect" against the unauthorized copying of copyrighted works as required by §1201(a)(3)(B). Streambox claims this "effective" protection is lacking because an enterprising end-user could potentially use other means to record streaming audio content as it is played by the end-user's computer speakers. This argument fails because the Copy Switch, in the ordinary course of its operation when it is on, restricts and limits the ability of people to make perfect digital copies of a copyrighted work. The Copy Switch therefore constitutes a technological measure that effectively protects a copyright owner's rights under section 1201(a)(3)(B).

In addition, the argument ignores the fact that before the Copy Switch is even implicated, the Streambox VCR has already circumvented the Secret Handshake to gain access to an unauthorized RealMedia file. That alone is sufficient for liability under the DMCA. See 17 U.S.C. §1201(i)(e). . . .

As set forth above, the Streambox VCR falls within the prohibitions of sections 1201(a)(2) and 1201(b)(1). Accordingly, section 1201(c)(3) affords Streambox no defense. . . .

[The court concludes that RealNetworks has demonstrated that it is reasonably likely to succeed with respect to the VCR.]

UNIVERSAL CITY STUDIOS, INC. v. REIMERDES

111 F. Supp. 2d 294 (S.D.N.Y. 2000), *aff'd*, 273 F.3d 429 (2d Cir. 2001)

KAPLAN, J.

Plaintiffs, eight major United States motion picture studios, distribute many of their copyrighted motion pictures for home use on digital versatile disks ("DVDs"), which contain copies of the motion pictures in digital form. They protect those motion pictures from copying by using an encryption system called CSS. CSS-protected motion pictures on DVDs may be viewed only on players and computer drives equipped with licensed technology that permits the devices to decrypt and play — but not to copy — the films.

Late last year, computer hackers devised a computer program called DeCSS that circumvents the CSS protection system and allows CSS-protected motion pictures to be copied and played on devices that lack the licensed decryption technology. Defendants quickly posted DeCSS on their Internet Web site, thus making it readily available to much of the world. Plaintiffs promptly brought this action under the Digital Millennium Copyright Act (the "DMCA") to enjoin defendants from posting DeCSS and to prevent them from electronically "linking" their site to others that post DeCSS. Defendants responded with what they termed "electronic civil disobedience" — increasing their efforts to link their Web site to a large number of others that continue to make DeCSS available. . . .

Defendants argue first that the DMCA should not be construed to reach their conduct, principally because the DMCA, so applied, could prevent those who wish to gain access to technologically protected copyrighted works in order to make fair — that is, non-infringing — use of them from doing so. They argue that those who would make fair use of technologically protected copyrighted works need means, such as DeCSS, of circumventing access control measures not for piracy, but to make lawful use of those works.

Technological access control measures have the capacity to prevent fair uses of copyrighted works as well as foul. Hence, there is a potential tension between the use of such access control measures and fair use. Defendants are not the first to recognize that possibility. As the DMCA made its way through the legislative process, Congress was preoccupied with precisely this issue. Proponents of strong restrictions on circumvention of access control measures argued that they were essential if copyright holders were to make their works available in digital form because digital works otherwise could be pirated too easily. Opponents contended that strong anti-circumvention measures would extend the copyright monopoly inappropriately and prevent many fair uses of copyrighted material.

Congress struck a balance. The compromise it reached, depending upon future technological and commercial developments, may or may not prove ideal. But the solution it enacted is clear. The potential tension to which defendants point does not absolve them of liability under the statute. There is no serious question that defendants' posting of DeCSS violates the DMCA. . . .

D.   The Appearance of DeCSS

In late September 1999, Jon Johansen, a Norwegian subject then fifteen years of age, and two individuals he "met" under pseudonyms over the Internet, reverse engineered a licensed DVD player and discovered the CSS encryption algorithm and keys. They used this information to create DeCSS, a program capable of decrypting or "ripping" encrypted DVDs, thereby allowing playback on non-compliant computers as well as the copying of decrypted files to computer hard drives. Mr. Johansen then posted the executable code on his personal Internet web site and informed members of an Internet mailing list that he had done so. Neither Mr. Johansen nor his collaborators obtained a license from the DVD CCA.

Although Mr. Johansen testified at trial that he created DeCSS in order to make a DVD player that would operate on a computer running the Linux operating system, DeCSS is a Windows executable file; that is, it can be executed only on computers running the Windows operating system. Mr. Johansen explained the fact that he created a Windows rather than a Linux program by asserting that Linux, at the time he created DeCSS, did not support the file system used on DVDs. Hence, it was necessary, he said, to decrypt the DVD on a Windows computer in order subsequently to play the decrypted files on a Linux machine. Assuming that to be true, however, the fact remains that Mr. Johansen created DeCSS in the full knowledge that it could be used on computers running Windows rather than Linux. Moreover, he was well aware that the files, once decrypted, could be copied like any other computer files. . . .

E. The Distribution of DeCSS

In the months following its initial appearance on Mr. Johansen's web site, DeCSS has become widely available on the Internet, where hundreds of sites now purport to offer the software for download. A few other applications said to decrypt CSS-encrypted DVDs also have appeared on the Internet.

In November 1999, defendants' web site began to offer DeCSS for download. It established also a list of links to several web sites that purportedly "mirrored" or offered DeCSS for download. The links on defendants' mirror list fall into one of three categories. By clicking the mouse on one of these links, the user may be brought to a page on the linked-to site on which there appears a further link to the DeCSS software. If the user then clicks on the DeCSS link, download of the software begins. This page may or may not contain content other than the DeCSS link. Alternatively, the user may be brought to a page on the linked-to site that does not itself purport to link to DeCSS, but that links, either directly or via a series of other pages on the site, to another page on the site on which there appears a link to the DeCSS software. Finally, the user may be brought directly to the DeCSS link on the linked-to site such that download of DeCSS begins immediately without further user intervention. . . .

II. THE DIGITAL MILLENNIUM COPYRIGHT ACT

. . . The DMCA contains two principal anticircumvention provisions. The first, Section 1201(a)(1), governs "[t]he act of circumventing a technological protection measure put in place by a copyright owner to control access to a copyrighted work," an act described by Congress as "the electronic equivalent of breaking into a locked room in order to obtain a copy of a book."[131] The second, Section 1201(a)(2), which is the focus of this case, "supplements the prohibition against the act of circumvention in paragraph (a)(1) with prohibitions on creating and making available certain technologies . . . developed or advertised to defeat technological protections against unauthorized access to a work." As defendants are accused here only of posting and linking to other sites posting DeCSS, and not of using it themselves to bypass plaintiffs' access controls, it is principally the second of the anticircumvention provisions that is at issue in this case.

B. Violation of Posting of DeCSS

1. Anti-Trafficking Provision

. . . In this case, defendants concededly offered and provided and, absent a court order, would continue to offer and provide DeCSS to the public by making it available for download on the 2600.com Web site. DeCSS, a computer program, unquestionably is "technology" within the meaning of the statute.

---

131. H.R. Rep. No. 105-551(I), 105th Cong., 2d Sess. ("Judiciary Comm. Rep."), at 17 (1998).

"[C]ircumvent a technological measure" is defined to mean descrambling a scrambled work, decrypting an encrypted work, or "otherwise to avoid, bypass, remove, deactivate, or impair a technological measure, without the authority of the copyright owner," so DeCSS clearly is a means of circumventing a technological access control measure. In consequence, if CSS otherwise falls within paragraphs (A), (B) or (C) of Section 1201(a)(2), and if none of the statutory exceptions applies to their actions, defendants have violated and, unless enjoined, will continue to violate the DMCA by posting DeCSS. . . .

As CSS effectively controls access to plaintiffs' copyrighted works, the only remaining question under Section 1201(a)(2)(A) is whether DeCSS was designed primarily to circumvent CSS. The answer is perfectly obvious. By the admission of both Jon Johansen, the programmer who principally wrote DeCSS, and defendant Corley, DeCSS was created solely for the purpose of decrypting CSS — that is all it does. Hence, absent satisfaction of a statutory exception, defendants clearly violated Section 1201(a)(2)(A) by posting DeCSS to their web site. . . .

b. Section 1201(a)(2)(B)

As the only purpose or use of DeCSS is to circumvent CSS, the foregoing is sufficient to establish a prima facie violation of Section 1201(a)(2)(B) as well.

c. The Linux Argument

Perhaps the centerpiece of defendants' statutory position is the contention that DeCSS was not created for the purpose of pirating copyrighted motion pictures. Rather, they argue, it was written to further the development of a DVD player that would run under the Linux operating system, as there allegedly were no Linux compatible players on the market at the time. . . .

As noted, Section 1201(a) of the DMCA contains two distinct prohibitions. Section 1201(a)(1), the so-called basic provision, "aims against those who engage in unauthorized circumvention of technological measures. . . . [It] focuses directly on wrongful conduct, rather than on those who facilitate wrongful conduct. . . ." Section 1201(a)(2), the anti-trafficking provision at issue in this case, on the other hand, separately bans offering or providing technology that may be used to circumvent technological means of controlling access to copyrighted works. If the means in question meets any of the three prongs of the standard set out in Section 1201(a)(2)(A), (B), or (C), it may not be offered or disseminated.

[T]he question whether the development of a Linux DVD player motivated those who wrote DeCSS is immaterial to the question whether the defendants now before the Court violated the anti-trafficking provision of the DMCA. The inescapable facts are that (1) CSS is a technological means that effectively controls access to plaintiffs' copyrighted works, (2) the one and only function of DeCSS is to circumvent CSS, and (3) defendants offered and provided DeCSS by posting it on their web site. Whether defendants did so in order to infringe, or to permit or encourage others to infringe, copyrighted works in violation of other provisions of the Copyright Act simply does not matter for purposes of Section 1201(a)(2). The offering or provision of the program is the prohibited conduct — and it is prohibited irrespective of why the program was written, except to whatever extent motive may be germane to determining whether their conduct falls within one of the statutory exceptions.

2. Statutory Exceptions

[D]efendants rely on the doctrine of fair use. Stated in its most general terms, the doctrine, now codified in Section 107 of the Copyright Act, limits the exclusive rights of a copyright holder by permitting others to make limited use of portions of the copyrighted work, for appropriate purposes, free of liability for copyright infringement. For example, it is permissible for one other than the copyright owner to reprint or quote a suitable part of a copyrighted book or article in certain circumstances. The doctrine traditionally has facilitated literary and artistic criticism, teaching and scholarship, and other socially useful forms of expression. It has been viewed by courts as a safety valve that accommodates the exclusive rights conferred by copyright with the freedom of expression guaranteed by the First Amendment.

The use of technological means of controlling access to a copyrighted work may affect the ability to make fair uses of the work. Focusing specifically on the facts of this case, the application of CSS to encrypt a copyrighted motion picture requires the use of a compliant DVD player to view or listen to the movie. Perhaps more significantly, it prevents exact copying of either the video or the audio portion of all or any part of the film. This latter point means that certain uses that might qualify as "fair" for purposes of copyright infringement — for example, the preparation by a film studies professor of a single CD-ROM or tape containing two scenes from different movies in order to illustrate a point in a lecture on cinematography, as opposed to showing relevant parts of two different DVDs — would be difficult or impossible absent circumvention of the CSS encryption. Defendants therefore argue that the DMCA cannot properly be construed to make it difficult or impossible to make any fair use of plaintiffs' copyrighted works and that the statute therefore does not reach their activities, which are simply a means to enable users of DeCSS to make such fair uses.

Defendants have focused on a significant point. Access control measures such as CSS do involve some risk of preventing lawful as well as unlawful uses of copyrighted material. Congress, however, clearly faced up to and dealt with this question in enacting the DMCA.

The Court begins its statutory analysis, as it must, with the language of the statute. Section 107 of the Copyright Act provides in critical part that certain uses of copyrighted works that otherwise would be wrongful are "not . . . infringement[s] of copyright." Defendants, however, are not here sued for copyright infringement. They are sued for offering and providing technology designed to circumvent technological measures that control access to copyrighted works and otherwise violating Section 1201(a)(2) of the Act. If Congress had meant the fair use defense to apply to such actions, it would have said so. Indeed, as the legislative history demonstrates, the decision not to make fair use a defense to a claim under Section 1201(a) was quite deliberate.

Congress was well aware during the consideration of the DMCA of the traditional role of the fair use defense in accommodating the exclusive rights of copyright owners with the legitimate interests of noninfringing users of portions of copyrighted works. It recognized the contention, voiced by a range of constituencies concerned with the legislation, that technological controls on access to copyrighted works might erode fair use by preventing access even for uses that would be deemed "fair" if only access might be gained. And it struck a balance among the competing interests.

The first element of the balance was the careful limitation of Section 1201(a)(1)'s prohibition of the act of circumvention to the act itself so as not to "apply to subsequent actions of a person once he or she has obtained authorized access to a copy of a [copyrighted] work. . . ."[163] By doing so, it left "the traditional defenses to copyright infringement, including fair use, . . . fully applicable" provided "the access is authorized."[164]

Second, Congress delayed the effective date of Section 1201(a)(1)'s prohibition of the act of circumvention for two years pending further investigation about how best to reconcile Section 1201(a)(1) with fair use concerns. Following that investigation, which is being carried out in the form of a rule-making by the Register of Copyright, the prohibition will not apply to users of particular classes of copyrighted works who demonstrate that their ability to make noninfringing uses of those classes of works would be affected adversely by Section 1201(a)(1).

Third, it created a series of exceptions to aspects of Section 1201(a) for certain uses that Congress thought "fair," including reverse engineering, security testing, good faith encryption research, and certain uses by nonprofit libraries, archives and educational institutions.

Defendants claim also that the possibility that DeCSS might be used for the purpose of gaining access to copyrighted works in order to make fair use of those works saves them under Sony Corp. v. Universal City Studios, Inc. But they are mistaken. Sony does not apply to the activities with which defendants here are charged. Even if it did, it would not govern here. Sony involved a construction of the Copyright Act that has been overruled by the later enactment of the DMCA to the extent of any inconsistency between Sony and the new statute. . . .

When *Sony* was decided, the only question was whether the manufacturers could be held liable for infringement by those who purchased equipment from them in circumstances in which there were many noninfringing uses for their

---

163. Judiciary Comm. Rep. at 18.
164. *Id.*

equipment. But that is not the question now before this Court. The question here is whether the possibility of noninfringing fair use by someone who gains access to a protected copyrighted work through a circumvention technology distributed by the defendants saves the defendants from liability under Section 1201. But nothing in Section 1201 so suggests. By prohibiting the provision of circumvention technology, the DMCA fundamentally altered the landscape. A given device or piece of technology might have "a substantial noninfringing use, and hence be immune from attack under Sony's construction of the Copyright Act—but nonetheless still be subject to suppression under Section 1201."[170] Indeed, Congress explicitly noted that Section 1201 does not incorporate Sony.

The policy concerns raised by defendants were considered by Congress. Having considered them, Congress crafted a statute that, so far as the applicability of the fair use defense to Section 1201(a) claims is concerned, is crystal clear. In such circumstances, courts may not undo what Congress so plainly has done by "construing" the words of a statute to accomplish a result that Congress rejected. The fact that Congress elected to leave technologically unsophisticated persons who wish to make fair use of encrypted copyrighted works without the technical means of doing so is a matter for Congress unless Congress' decision contravenes the Constitution, a matter to which the Court turns below. Defendants' statutory fair use argument therefore is entirely without merit. . . .

III. The First Amendment

Defendants argue that the DMCA, at least as applied to prevent the public dissemination of DeCSS, violates the First Amendment to the Constitution. They claim that it does so in two ways. First, they argue that computer code is protected speech and that the DMCA's prohibition of dissemination of DeCSS therefore violates defendants' First Amendment rights. . . . They argue also that a prohibition on their linking to sites that make DeCSS available is unconstitutional for much the same reasons.

A. Computer Code and the First Amendment

The premise of defendants' first position is that computer code, the form in which DeCSS exists, is speech protected by the First Amendment. Examination of that premise is the logical starting point for analysis. And it is important in examining that premise first to define terms. . . .

---

170. [HOUSE COMM. ON JUDICIARY, SECTION-BY-SECTION ANALYSIS OF H.R. 2281 AS PASSED BY THE UNITED STATES HOUSE OF REPRESENTATIVES ON AUGUST 4, 1998] 9 ("The Sony test of 'capab[ility] of substantial non-infringing uses,' while still operative in cases claiming contributory infringement of copyright, is not part of this legislation. . . .").

It cannot seriously be argued that any form of computer code may be regulated without reference to First Amendment doctrine. The path from idea to human language to source code to object code is a continuum. As one moves from one to the other, the levels of precision and, arguably, abstraction increase, as does the level of training necessary to discern the idea from the expression. Not everyone can understand each of these forms. Only English speakers will understand English formulations. Principally those familiar with the particular programming language will understand the source code expression. And only a relatively small number of skilled programmers and computer scientists will understand the machine readable object code. But each form expresses the same idea, albeit in different ways.

There perhaps was a time when the First Amendment was viewed only as a limitation on the ability of government to censor speech in advance. But we have moved far beyond that. All modes by which ideas may be expressed or, perhaps, emotions evoked—including speech, books, movies, art, and music—are within the area of First Amendment concern. As computer code—whether source or object—is a means of expressing ideas, the First Amendment must be considered before its dissemination may be prohibited or regulated. In that sense, computer code is covered or, as sometimes is said, "protected" by the First Amendment. But that conclusion still leaves for determination the level of scrutiny to be applied in determining the constitutionality of regulation of computer code. . . .

Defendants first attack Section 1201(a)(2), the anti-trafficking provision, as applied to them on the theory that DeCSS is constitutionally protected expression and that the statute improperly prevents them from communicating it. Their attack presupposes that a characterization of code as constitutionally protected subjects any regulation of code to the highest level of First Amendment scrutiny. As we have seen, however, this does not necessarily follow.

Just as computer code cannot be excluded from the area of First Amendment concern because it is abstract and, in many cases, arcane, the long history of First Amendment jurisprudence makes equally clear that the fact that words, symbols and even actions convey ideas and evoke emotions does not inevitably place them beyond the power of government. The Supreme Court has evolved an analytical framework by which the permissibility of particular restrictions on the expression of ideas must be determined.

Broadly speaking, restrictions on expression fall into two categories. Some are restrictions on the voicing of particular ideas, which typically are referred to as content based restrictions. Others have nothing to do with the content of the expression—i.e., they are content neutral—but they have the incidental effect of limiting expression.

In general, "government has no power to restrict expression because of its message, its ideas, its subject matter, or its content. . . ." . . . "[S]ubject only to narrow and well-understood exceptions, [the First Amendment] does not countenance governmental control over the content of messages expressed by private individuals." In consequence, content based restrictions on speech are permissible only if they serve compelling state interests by the least restrictive means available.

Content neutral restrictions, in contrast, are measured against a less exacting standard. Because restrictions of this type are not motivated by a desire to limit the message, they will be upheld if they serve a substantial governmental interest and restrict First Amendment freedoms no more than necessary.

Restrictions on the nonspeech elements of expressive conduct fall into the conduct-neutral category. The Supreme Court long has distinguished for First Amendment purposes between pure speech, which ordinarily receives the highest level of protection, and expressive conduct. Even if conduct contains an expressive element, its nonspeech aspect need not be ignored. "[W]hen 'speech' and 'nonspeech' elements are combined in the same course of conduct, a sufficiently important governmental interest in regulating the nonspeech element can justify incidental limitations on First Amendment freedoms." The critical point is that nonspeech elements may create hazards for society above and beyond the speech elements. They are subject to regulation in appropriate circumstances because the government has an interest in dealing with the potential hazards of the nonspeech elements despite the fact that they are joined with expressive elements.

Thus, the starting point for analysis is whether the DMCA, as applied to restrict dissemination of DeCSS and other computer code used to circumvent access control measures, is a content based restriction on speech or a content neutral regulation. . . .

Given the fact that DeCSS code is expressive, defendants would have the Court leap immediately to the conclusion that Section 1201(a)(2)'s prohibition on providing DeCSS necessarily is content based regulation of speech because it suppresses dissemination of a particular kind of expression. But this would be a unidimensional approach to a more textured reality and entirely too facile.

The "principal inquiry in determining content neutrality . . . is whether the government has adopted a regulation of speech because of [agreement or] disagreement with the message it conveys." . . . The computer code at issue in this case, however, does more than express the programmers' concepts. It does more, in other words, than convey a message. DeCSS, like any other computer program, is a series of instructions that causes a computer to perform a particular sequence of tasks which, in the aggregate, decrypt CSS-protected files. Thus, it has a distinctly functional, non-speech aspect in addition to reflecting the thoughts of the programmers. It enables anyone who receives it and who has a modicum of computer skills to circumvent plaintiffs' access control system.

The reason that Congress enacted the anti-trafficking provision of the DMCA had nothing to do with suppressing particular ideas of computer programmers and everything to do with functionality—with preventing people from circumventing technological access control measures—just as laws prohibiting the possession of burglar tools have nothing to do with preventing people from expressing themselves by accumulating what to them may be attractive assortments of implements and everything to do with preventing burglaries. Rather, it is focused squarely upon the effect of the distribution of the functional capability that the code provides. Any impact on the dissemination of programmers' ideas is purely incidental to the overriding concerns of promoting the distribution of copyrighted works in digital form while at the same time protecting those works from piracy and other violations of the exclusive rights of copyright holders. . . .

Congress is not powerless to regulate content neutral regulations that incidentally affect expression, including the dissemination of the functional capabilities of computer code. A sufficiently important governmental interest in seeing to it that computers are not instructed to perform particular functions may justify incidental restrictions on the dissemination of the expressive elements of a program. Such a regulation will be upheld if:

> it furthers an important or substantial governmental interest; if the governmental interest is unrelated to the suppression of free expression; and if the incidental restriction on alleged First Amendment freedoms is no greater than is essential to the furtherance of that interest.

Moreover, "[t]o satisfy this standard, a regulation need not be the least speech-restrictive means of advancing the Government's interests." "Rather, the requirement of narrow tailoring is satisfied 'so long as the . . . regulation promotes a substantial government interest that would be achieved less effectively absent the regulation.'"

The anti-trafficking provision of the DMCA furthers an important governmental interest—the protection of copyrighted works stored on digital media from the vastly expanded risk of piracy in this electronic age. The substantiality of that interest is evident both from the fact that the Constitution specifically empowers Congress to provide for copyright protection and from the significance to our economy of trade in copyrighted materials. Indeed, the Supreme Court has made clear that copyright protection itself is "the engine of free expression." That substantial interest, moreover, is unrelated to the suppression of particular views expressed in means of gaining access to protected copyrighted works. Nor is the incidental restraint on protected expression—the prohibition of trafficking in means that would circumvent controls limiting access to unprotected materials or to copyrighted materials for noninfringing purposes—broader than is necessary to accomplish Congress' goals of preventing infringement and promoting the availability of content in digital form. . . .

C. LINKING

As indicated above, the DMCA reaches links deliberately created by a web site operator for the purpose of disseminating technology that enables the user to circumvent access controls on copyrighted works. The question is whether it may do so consistent with the First Amendment.

Links bear a relationship to the information superhighway comparable to the relationship that roadway signs bear to roads but they are more functional. Like roadway signs, they point out the direction. Unlike roadway signs, they take one almost instantaneously to the desired destination with the mere click of an electronic mouse. Thus, like computer code in general, they have both expressive and functional elements. Also like computer code, they are within the area of First Amendment concern. Hence, the constitutionality of the DMCA as applied to defendants' linking is determined by the same O'Brien standard that governs trafficking in the circumvention technology generally.

There is little question that the application of the DMCA to the linking at issue in this case would serve, at least to some extent, the same substantial governmental interest as its application to defendants' posting of the DeCSS code. Defendants' posting and their linking amount to very much the same thing. Similarly, the regulation of the linking at issue here is "unrelated to the suppression of free expression" for the same reason as the regulation of the posting. The third prong of the O'Brien test as subsequently interpreted — whether the "regulation promotes a substantial government interest that would be achieved less effectively absent the regulation" — is a somewhat closer call.

Defendants and, by logical extension, others may be enjoined from posting DeCSS. Plaintiffs may seek legal redress against anyone who persists in posting notwithstanding this decision. Hence, barring defendants from linking to sites against which plaintiffs readily may take legal action would advance the statutory purpose of preventing dissemination of circumvention technology, but it would do so less effectively than would actions by plaintiffs directly against the sites that post. For precisely this reason, however, the real significance of an anti-linking injunction would not be with U.S. web sites subject to the DMCA, but with foreign sites that arguably are not subject to it and not subject to suit here. An anti-linking injunction to that extent would have a significant impact and thus materially advance a substantial governmental purpose. In consequence, the Court concludes that an injunction against linking to other sites posting DeCSS satisfies the O'Brien standard. There remains, however, one further important point.

Links are "what unify the [World Wide] Web into a single body of knowledge, and what makes the Web unique." They "are the mainstay of the Internet and indispensable to its convenient access to the vast world of information." They often are used in ways that do a great deal to promote the free exchange of ideas and information that is a central value of our nation. Anything that would impose strict liability on a web site operator for the entire contents of any web site to which the operator linked therefore would raise grave constitutional concerns, as web site operators would be inhibited from linking for fear of exposure to liability. And it is equally clear that exposing those who use links to liability under the DMCA might chill their use, as some web site operators confronted with claims that they have posted circumvention technology falling within the statute may be more inclined to remove the allegedly offending link rather than test the issue in court. Moreover, web sites often contain a great variety of things, and a ban on linking to a site that contains DeCSS amidst other content threatens to restrict communication of this information to an excessive degree.

The possible chilling effect of a rule permitting liability for or injunctions against Internet hyperlinks is a genuine concern. But it is not unique to the issue of linking. The constitutional law of defamation provides a highly relevant analogy. The threat of defamation suits creates the same risk of self-censorship, the same chilling effect, for the traditional press as a prohibition of linking to sites containing circumvention technology poses for web site operators. Just as the potential chilling effect of defamation suits has not utterly immunized the press from all actions for defamation, however, the potential chilling effect of DMCA liability cannot utterly immunize web site operators from all actions for disseminating circumvention technology. And the solution to the problem is the same: the adoption of a standard of culpability sufficiently high to immunize the activity, whether it is publishing a newspaper or linking, except in cases in which the conduct in question has little or no redeeming constitutional value. . . .

Accordingly, there may be no injunction against, nor liability for, linking to a site containing circumvention technology, the offering of which is unlawful under the DMCA, absent clear and convincing evidence that those responsible for the link (a) know at the relevant time that the offending material is on the linked-to site, (b) know that it is circumvention technology that may not lawfully be offered, and (c) create or maintain the link for the purpose of disseminating that technology. Such a standard will limit the fear of liability on the part of web site operators just as the New York Times standard gives the press great comfort in publishing all sorts of material that would have been actionable at common law, even in the face of flat denials by the subjects of their stories. And it will not subject web site operators to liability for linking to a site containing proscribed technology where the link exists for purposes other than dissemination of that technology.

In this case, plaintiffs have established by clear and convincing evidence that these defendants linked to sites posting DeCSS, knowing that it was a circumvention device. Indeed, they initially touted it as a way to get free movies, and they later maintained the links to promote the dissemination of the program in an effort to defeat effective judicial relief. They now know that dissemination of DeCSS violates the DMCA. An anti-linking injunction on these facts does no violence to the First Amendment. Nor should it chill the activities of web site operators dealing with different materials, as they may be held liable only on a compelling showing of deliberate evasion of the statute. . . .

COMMENTS AND QUESTIONS

1.   As both the *Realnetworks* and *Reimerdes* decisions demonstrate, the anti-circumvention provisions of the DMCA may be interpreted as allowing copyright owners to prohibit the public from making fair use of those copyrighted works. Were these decisions compelled by the DMCA? Consider 17 U.S.C. §1201(c)(1), which provides that "[n]othing in this section shall affect rights, remedies, limitations, or defenses to copyright infringement, including fair use, under this title. . . ."

2.   Despite the wording of Section 1201(c)(1), subsequent courts have taken a similar approach to the *Reimerdes* courts in interpreting the DMCA in favor of copyright holders where fair use has been raised as a defense to the conduct in question. In the case involving the Russian programmer, Sklyarov (*supra*), the court noted that: "[W]ith regard to the argument that fair use rights are impaired [by the DMCA], the DMCA does not eliminate fair use or substantially impair the fair use rights of anyone. Congress has not banned or eliminated fair use and nothing in the DMCA prevents anyone from quoting from a work or comparing texts for the purpose of study or criticism. The fair user may find it more difficult to engage in certain fair uses with regard to electronic books, but nevertheless, fair use is still available." United States v. Elcom, 203 F. Supp. 2d 1111, 1134-35 (2002). Do you agree that making fair use more difficult to engage in is not the same as banning or eliminating fair use? How difficult would it have to be to engage in fair use before a court held that the defense had effectively been banned or eliminated?

3.   A subsequent judicial decision noted that even if fair use has been effectively banned or eliminated by the DMCA, this result would not be constitutionally invalid because fair use is not a guaranteed constitutional right. 321 Studios v. MGM Studios, 307 F. Supp. 2d 1085, 1101 (2004). Should fair use be accepted as a constitutionally guaranteed right in the age of digital information products?

4.   From the above cases, it seems clear that fair use is not a defense to a DMCA infringement claim (as distinct from a copyright infringement claim). Does it make sense to say that a person may have a fair use defense to a potential copyright infringement claim even though she is unable to *access* a relevant work to make a fair use of it? R. Anthony Reese has talked about the paradox created by the fact that digital encryption measures restricting access and use are usually technologically merged in practice, even though the DMCA regards them as separate issues. While it is not an infringement of the DMCA to circumvent a *copy control* measure, it is an infringement to circumvent an *access control* measure (17 U.S.C. §1201(a)(1)(A)).[24] This is a legislative attempt to preserve fair use under the DMCA. However, as Professor Reese points out, the attempt to preserve fair use in this way is relatively fruitless if most access

---

24. However, trafficking in both access-control and copy-control technologies are prohibited under the DMCA: 17 U.S.C. §§1201(a)(2), 1201(b)(1).

control measures are technologically merged with copy-control measures in practice. R. Anthony Reese, *Will Merging Access Controls and Rights Controls Undermine the Structure of Anticircumvention Law?*, 18 Berkeley Tech. L.J. 619 (2003).

5. The DMCA does include provision for the Librarian of Congress to periodically exempt certain classes of works from the access-control prohibitions: 17 U.S.C. §§1201(a)(1)(B)-(D). This provision was included to preserve access to digitally encrypted works for legitimate purposes. There have been several exemption hearings and orders made since the DMCA was enacted, although the scope of the exemptions granted to date has been fairly narrow.[25]

6. Many commentators have written about the need to better preserve fair use under the DMCA: for example, Pamela Samuelson has argued that the DMCA needs to be revised to include a general "legitimate purpose" exception. *See* Pamela Samuelson, *Intellectual Property and the Digital Economy: Why the Anti-Circumvention Regulations Need to Be Revised*, 14 Berkeley Tech. L.J. 519 (1999). *See also* Niva Elkin-Koren, *Cyberlaw and Social Change: A Democratic Approach to Copyright Law in Cyberspace*, 14 Cardozo Arts & Ent. L.J. 215, 273, 277 (1996) (arguing that users must be allowed "to do the same things they are able to do in a non-digitized environment"); Diane Leenheer Zimmerman, *Copyright in Cyberspace: Don't Throw Out the Public Interest with the Bath Water*, 1994 Ann. Surv. Am. L. 403, 405 (arguing for maintaining "some approximation of our current cheap and simple access to copyrighted works for research, scholarship, and pleasure"); Jacqueline Lipton, *Solving the Digital Piracy Puzzle: Disaggregating Fair Use from the DMCA's Anti-Device Provisions*, 19 Harv. J.L. & Tech. 111 (2005) (arguing for a new administrative procedure to allow fair users to bring complaints about lack of access to a protected work for fair use purposes); Jerome Reichman, Graeme Dinwoodie & Pamela Samuelson, *A Reverse Notice and Takedown Regime to Enable Public Interest Uses of Technically Protected Copyright Works*, 22 Berkeley Tech. L.J. 981 (2007), Jessica Litman, *Lawful Personal Use*, 85 Tex. L. Rev. 1871 (2007).

---

25. *See, e.g.*, Library of Congress, Copyright Office; Exemption to Prohibition on Circumvention of Copyright Protection Systems for Access Control Technologies, available at *http://www.copyright.gov/fedreg/2003/68fr2011.html*, last viewed on April 13, 2005 (exempting the following classes of works from the access control provisions: (a) Compilations consisting of lists of Internet locations blocked by commercially marketed filtering software applications that are intended to prevent access to domains, web sites or portions of web sites, but not including lists of Internet locations blocked by software applications that operate exclusively to protect against damage to a computer or computer network or lists of Internet locations blocked by software applications that operate exclusively to prevent receipt of e-mail; (b) Computer programs protected by dongles that prevent access due to malfunction or damage and which are obsolete; (c) Computer programs and video games distributed in formats that have become obsolete and which require the original media or hardware as a condition of access. A format shall be considered obsolete if the machine or system necessary to render perceptible a work stored in that format is no longer manufactured or is no longer reasonably available in the commercial marketplace; and (d) Literary works distributed in ebook format when all existing ebook editions of the work (including digital text editions made available by authorized entities) contain access controls that prevent the enabling of the ebook's read-aloud function and that prevent the enabling of screen readers to render the text into a specialized format.); 37 CFR 201 (available at *http://www.peer.org/docs/fs/02_19_09_USFS_Fed_Register_notice.pdf*, Dec. 29, 2008 exemption notice).

7. Over the years, a number of bills have been introduced into the United States Congress in an attempt to create a clearer balance between fair use and copyright interests. None of these bills has ultimately been enacted into law. However, interested readers may want to look at: Digital Media Consumers' Rights Act of 2003, H.R. 107, 108th Cong. (Section 5(b) would allow circumvention of a technological protection measure if it does not result in a copyright infringement); Digital Choice and Freedom Act of 2003, H.R. 1066, 108th Cong. (Section 5 would allow circumvention and/or trafficking in a circumvention device for the purposes of making a noninfringing use of a copyright work in certain circumstances).

8. Concerned about the problem of digital copyright law impinging on competing legitimate interests in digital works, the British Parliament built provisions into their DMCA-equivalent law to protect competing legitimate uses of copyright works in the digital age. Parliament added Section 296ZE(2) to the Copyright, Designs and Patents Act 1988 (Eng.). This section provides that where the application of an effective technological measure prevents a person from carrying out a permitted act in relation to a copyright work other than a computer program, then that person, or a person being a representative of a class of persons prevented from carrying out the permitted act, may issue a complaint to the Secretary of State. "Permitted act" is defined to include fair dealing for research and private study along with various other basic exemptions to copyright infringement relating to activities permitted by librarians and archivists, for parliamentary and judicial proceedings, and statutory enquiries. The provision gives discretion to the Secretary of State to order the owner or exclusive licensee of a copyright work to ensure that the owner or licensee makes available to the complainant the means of carrying out the permitted act to the extent necessary to benefit from the activity in question. The procedure is only available to persons who have "lawful access" to a protected copyright work. How effective is this approach likely to be in practice?

9. How does *Realnetworks* distinguish the Supreme Court's decision in *Sony*? In light of the DMCA, is copyright even relevant? *Consider* Glynn S. Lunney, Jr., *The Death of Copyright: Digital Technology, Private Copying, and the Digital Millennium Copyright Act*, 87 Va. L. Rev. 813 (2001) (arguing that the DMCA has killed copyright and created the possibility that the U.S. system for protecting creative works will serve primarily private interests).

10. How "effective" must a technological measure be under the DMCA anti-circumvention provisions to qualify for protection?

11. *Reimerdes* goes one step further than *Realnetworks* by concluding that Congress's interest in protecting copyright is sufficiently important to justify restricting speech. How is DeCSS speech? According to the court, are the DMCA's speech restrictions content based or content neutral?

12. Does the *Reimerdes* court treat links to DeCSS in the same manner as the program itself? What kind of liability does the court establish for individuals who may link to Web sites containing DeCSS?

13. For an argument that neither the DMCA nor copyright is necessary in the digital world, see Raymond Shih Ray Ku, *The Creative Destruction of Copyright: Napster and the New Economics of Digital Technology*, 69 U. Chi. L. Rev. 263 (2002). Professor Ku argues that copyright owners' exclusive rights were justified based upon the economics and limitations of Gutenberg's printing press in which substantial investments were required to distribute copyrighted works to the public. The printing press and other more modern distribution technologies were prone to free riding and were incapable of determining public preferences for works in the absence of a property-based regime. In contrast, digital technology in combination with the Internet as a means for distribution, eliminate free riding and concerns over the underproduction of creative works because the consuming public internalizes the costs of distribution by purchasing the computers, cables, and wires that make up the Internet. To the extent that the creation of certain works cannot be supported by alternative sources of revenue (e.g., ticket sales to concerts or movies), creation can now be funded in the same manner that most public goods are funded—taxation. Unlike other taxes, however, funding for creation can be disbursed based upon consumer preferences by monitoring aggregate Internet copying or usage of creative works and distributing government funding according to the popularity of a work. As such, Professor Ku suggests that the Internet and digital technology "promises a world in which no one is excluded from creations of the mind because he is unwilling or unable to pay. At the same time, it has the potential to encourage an independent and diverse community of artists who are directly connected to the public." If copyright is no longer necessary, does its continued recognition and expansion violate the U.S. Constitution by restricting freedom of expression or by exceeding the Congress's enumerated power under Art. I, §8, "To promote the Progress of Science and useful arts"?

Note: Unintended Applications of the DMCA's Anti-Circumvention Provisions

Anticircumvention infringements under the DMCA have been raised in some unusual contexts in recent years, at least in contexts that were outside the apparent legislative purposes of the statute. Manufacturers of physical goods that happen to incorporate computer software components have attempted to utilize the DMCA to restrict competition in aftermarket product replacement markets, such as markets involving printer toner cartridges and remote control devices for opening garage doors. At least one early judicial determination of this kind found in favor of the plaintiff, who argued that a competitor selling an interoperable replacement part (a toner cartridge) for one of its products (a laser printer) had infringed the DMCA. The plaintiff had utilized embedded software in its printers and toner cartridges to ensure that only authorized toner cartridges worked with the plaintiff's printers. The plaintiff argued that a competitor who circumvented the encryption code in the toner cartridges (to make its own toner cartridges interoperable with the plaintiff's printers) had infringed the DMCA by trafficking in a device that circumvented a technological protection measure restricting access to the operating software in the printer. While the plaintiffs were initially successful on this claim, the Sixth Circuit reversed on appeal on the basis that the encryption code was not an effective technological protection measure as required by the DMCA. Lexmark Int'l Inc. v. Static Control Components, 387 F.3d 522 (2004).

Other courts have disallowed DMCA anti-circumvention claims in similar cases by reading into the statute a requirement that the claimed DMCA infringement must have some connection with a realistic concern about copyright infringement, and cannot be simply for the purposes of locking a competitor out of a replacement product market. *See, e.g.*, Chamberlain Group v. Skylink Technologies, 381 F.3d 1178 (2004) (involving garage door remote control units with embedded software); Storage Technology Corp v. Custom Hardware Engineering & Consulting, 421 F.3d 1307, 1318 (2005) ("courts generally have found a violation of the DMCA only when the alleged access was intertwined with a right protected by the Copyright Act"); AGFA Monotype v. Adobe Systems Inc., 404 F. Supp. 2d 1030 (2005) (holding that there was no DMCA anti-circumvention infringement in the absence of an effective technical protection measure and with no purpose to infringe an underlying copyright).

The tenor of these judicial determinations appears to be sensible, given that the DMCA's anticircumvention provisions were enacted to protect copyright holders from those who hack encryption measures to access and make or distribute infringing copies of a protected work. However, commentators have pointed out that the literal wording of the statute does not require a DMCA infringement claim to be linked to a copyright infringement — or realistic threat of copyright infringement. Thus, there is no guarantee that future courts will not be convinced to allow plaintiffs to succeed on DMCA claims in markets for replacement parts that incorporate embedded software. *See, e.g.*, Jacqueline Lipton, *The Law of Unintended Consequences: The DMCA and Interoperability*, 62 Wash. & Lee L. Rev. 487 (2005) (arguing in favor of a legislative presumption against the applicability of the DMCA's anticircumvention provisions in disputes where the protection of a copyright work is not the central concern of the plaintiff).

Note: Copyright and the First Amendment

Because copyright law prevents the public from making certain uses of original expression, a tension exists between copyright law and freedom of speech as protected by the First Amendment. While this tension has always existed, it only began to be addressed in depth in the 1970s. For example, Melville Nimmer argued that the tension between copyright and the First Amendment is mitigated principally by the idea-expression dichotomy. *See* Melville B. Nimmer, *Does Copyright Abridge the First Amendment Guarantees of Free Speech and Press?*, 17 UCLA L. Rev. 1180, 1189-92 (1970). In other words, because copyright protects only an author's expression and not the underlying ideas expressed by the author, subsequent speakers are able to express those same ideas in their own words. According to Professor Nimmer, "It is exposure to ideas, and not to their particular expression, that is vital if self-governing people are to make informed decisions." *Id.* at 1191.

In addition to the idea-expression dichotomy, Professor Nimmer notes that to the extent that freedom of speech is in fact served by the verbatim communication of copyrighted expression, that interest is accommodated by limiting the length of copyright protection. *Id.* at 1193-96. Once the term expires, individuals are free to use the copyrighted work without copyright's restrictions. But what happens when Congress extends copyright's term especially when it does so retroactively? *Consider* Eldred v. Reno, 239 F.3d 372 (D.C. Cir. 2001), *aff'd*, 537 U.S. 186 (2003) (rejecting a challenge that the Copyright Term Extension Act violated the First Amendment). In *Eldred*, Judge Sentelle dissented from the court's opinion with respect to retroactive extensions of copyright protection arguing that:

> The clause is not an open grant of power to secure exclusive rights. It is a grant of a power to promote progress. The means by which that power is to be exercised is certainly the granting of exclusive rights — not an elastic and open-ended use of that means, but only a securing for limited times. *See Stewart v. Abend*, 495 U.S. 207, 228 (1990) ("The copyright term is limited so that the public will not be permanently deprived of the fruits of an artist's labors."). The majority acknowledges that "[i]f the Congress were to make copyright protection permanent, then it surely would exceed the power conferred upon it by the Copyright Clause." Maj. Op. at 377. However, there is no apparent substantive distinction between permanent protection and permanently available authority to extend originally limited protection. The Congress that can extend the protection of an existing work from 100 years to 120 years, can extend that protection from 120 years to 140; and from 140 to 200; and from 200 to 300; and in effect can accomplish precisely what the majority admits it cannot do directly.

Id. at 381-382 (Sentelle, J. dissenting).

The tension between copyright and free speech is further alleviated by the fair use doctrine. For example, Robert Denicola noted that while the idea-expression dichotomy is "the basic internal mechanism[, a] more broadly applicable restraint against the intrusion of copyright law into constitutional preserves is the doctrine of fair use." Robert C. Denicola, *Copyright and Free Speech: Constitutional Limitations on the Protection of Expression*, 67 Cal. L. Rev. 283, 293 (1979). For example, in Campbell v. Acuff-Rose Music, Inc., 510 U.S. 569 (1994), the Supreme Court concluded that 2 Live Crew's commercial parody of Roy Orbison's song, "Oh, Pretty Woman," may be a fair use. Fair use, however, does have its limits. In rejecting a magazine's defense of fair use for publishing excerpts from President Gerald R. Ford's memoirs, the Supreme Court noted that "it should not be forgotten that the

Framers intended copyright itself to be the engine of free expression. By establishing a marketable right to the use of one's expression, copyright supplies the economic incentive to create and disseminate ideas." Harper & Row Publishers v. Nation Enterprises, 471 U.S. 539, 558 (1985).

Does the Digital Millennium Copyright Act threaten to upset the balance created by the idea-expression dichotomy, copyright's limited term, and fair use? *Consider* Yochai Benkler, *Free as the Air to Common Use: First Amendment Constraints on Enclosure of the Public Domain*, 74 N.Y.U. L. Rev. 354, 445-46 (1999) (arguing that the DMCA and other efforts to extend intellectual property protection are suspect because they regulate the public's ability to engage in expression); Julie Cohen, *A Right to Read Anonymously: A Closer Look at "Copyright Management" in Cyberspace*, 28 Conn. L. Rev. 981, 1003-1119 (1996) (arguing that the First Amendment guarantees a right to read anonymously because of the "close interdependence between receipt and expression of information, and between reading and freedom of thought").

For more recent discussion on the relationship between copyright and the First Amendment in general, see Neil Weinstock Netanel, *Locating Copyright Within the First Amendment Skein*, 54 Stan. L. Rev. 1 (2001); Mark A. Lemley & Eugene Volokh, *Freedom of Speech and Injunctions in Intellectual Property Cases*, 48 Duke L.J. 147 (1998).

C. PATENTING CYBERSPACE

You have now studied how trademark law may preclude certain uses of words and symbols in cyberspace, and how copyright law may prevent the distribution of certain content. However, both trademark and copyright leave room for users to work around intellectual property restrictions through fair use, or additionally in the case of copyright, independently creating content. In contrast, patent law provides inventors with a limited monopoly over their inventions even if others arrive at them independently. In exchange for the broader scope of protection, patent law provides for a shorter term of protection, currently 20 years from the date the patent is filed.[26]

In the United States, "[W]hoever invents or discovers any new and useful process, machine, manufacture, or composition of matter, or any new and useful improvement thereof, may obtain a patent therefore. . . ."[27] To qualify for protection, the invention must fall within the preceding description of patentable subject matter and be novel, useful, and nonobvious. With respect to cyberspace, the principal issues are whether computer programs and the ideas contained within those programs may be patented. Originally, computer code was protected as original expression under the principles of copyright law. The question is to what extent should code be treated as patentable subject matter, and what

---

26. 35 U.S.C. §154(a).
27. 35 U.S.C. §101.

limitations, if any, should apply to the patenting of computer code? Given that cyberspace exists and functions solely because of computer code, the debate over whether and to what extent computer programs can be patented has had a tremendous impact on the development of cyberspace.

In early cases on the patentability of computer code, judges spent much time debating the appropriate questions to ask to determine the patentability or otherwise of software code. In particular, questions arose as to whether software code patents were patentable subject matter under 35 U.S.C. §101. If so, secondary questions would arise regarding the novelty and non-obviousness of the code under 35 U.S.C. §§102 and 103. In Diamond v. Diehr, 450 U.S. 175 (1981), the Supreme Court decided that a process of curing synthetic rubber, which included in several of its steps the use of a mathematical formula and a programmed digital computer, would be patentable subject matter under 35 U.S.C. §101. In so deciding, the majority judges noted that questions of "novelty" under 35 U.S.C. §102 were a different issue to the concept of "new and useful" in §101. Section 101 deals with whether an invention falls into the category of statutory subject matter, while the question of "novelty" in Section 102 is a wholly separate issue. An invention may be patentable subject matter under Section 101 and nevertheless fail the novelty test in Section 102. In this case, even though the claimed invention utilized a previously known mathematical formula and a digital computer, taken together the claimed process fell within statutory subject matter.

Later, in *In re Alappat*, 33 F.3d 1526 (Fed. Cir. 1994), a majority of judges read the scope of Section 101 equally broadly. This case related to a claimed invention for a means to create a smooth waveform display in a digital oscilloscope. It utilized digital technology to create an improvement in the picture produced in an oscilloscope. The majority cited with approval the famous comments of the Supreme Court from Diamond v. Chakrabarty, 447 U.S. 303, 309 (1980),[28] when citing Congress's intentions behind the drafting of Section 101. They noted with approval the Supreme Court's acknowledgment that Congress intended Section 101 to extend to "anything under the sun that is made by man." While acknowledging that a disembodied mathematical formula, equation, or algorithm which represents nothing more than a law of nature or abstract idea would not be patentable under Section 101, the majority felt that the claimed invention represented more than that. They held that the invention claimed was a specific machine that produced a useful, concrete, and tangible result, despite the use of a computer programmed to run certain mathematical algorithms.

What could qualify as patentable subject matter was once again expanded in State Street Bank & Trust Co. v. Signature Financial Group, 149 F.3d 1368 (Fed. Cir. 1998), in which the court held that a computer program for a method of doing business, monitoring, recording, and calculating the

---

28. S. Rep. No. 1979, 82d Cong., 2d Sess., 5 (1952); H.R. Rep No. 1923, 82d Cong., 2d Sess., 6 (1952).

values of a complex partnership of mutual funds, could be patented under Section 101. In so doing, it rejected the "mathematical algorithm exception," stating that:

> "Unpatentable mathematical algorithms are identifiable by showing they are merely abstract ideas constituting disembodied concepts or truths that are not 'useful.' From a practical standpoint, this means that to be patentable an algorithm must be applied in a 'useful' way. . . .
>
> Today, we hold that the transformation of data, representing discrete dollar amounts, by a machine through a series of mathematical calculations into a final share price, constitutes a practical application of a mathematical algorithm, formula, or calculation, because it produces 'a useful, concrete and tangible result' — a final share price momentarily fixed for recording and reporting purposes and even accepted and relied upon by regulatory authorities and in subsequent trades."

149 F.3d at 1373. The court also rejected the "business method exception" to patentability under Section 101, concluding that "Whether the claims are directed to subject matter within §101 should not turn on whether the claimed subject matter does 'business' instead of something else." *Id.* at 1377. Instead, a patent for a method of doing business "should be treated like any other process claim[]."*Id.* (quoting Examination Guidelines, 61 Fed. Reg. 7478, 7479 (1996)).

Later, the United States Court of Appeals for the Federal Circuit reexamined the question of "process" patents in In re Bilski, 545 F.3d 943 (2008), in the context of a patent claimed over a hedge fund method. In a split decision, the majority of the court neither expressly affirmed nor overruled *State Street* in coming to the conclusion that "process" claims should be treated differently to claims to patent machines, methods of manufacture, or matter. The majority adopted a "machine-or-transformation" test to be applied in determining whether an invention claimed over a process was patentable subject matter under 35 U.S.C. §101 (see following extract from the case). A number of the judges made obiter comments in the case about the continued application of the test in *State Street* for business method patents and software-implemented inventions. The case has therefore caused a significant amount of confusion and instability in the interpretation of the §101 subject matter requirements for patentability, set apart from questions about novelty and nonobviousness that are encountered in inquiries under §§102 and 103. Some of the relevant judicial comments are reproduced in the extract from the case that follows.

As you read through the following materials, consider the following questions. What are the risks of including computer programs and business methods within the concept of patentable subject matter for the purposes of 35 U.S.C. §101? What are the benefits? What are the limits to these process or business method claims? Before addressing the specific question of Internet-related patents, the following section examines the initial question of when and whether computer code should be protected by patent law.

Problem 8.0

StarttUp would like to build an online shopping site that would allow customers to compare the best prices available from various sellers for items they may be seeking to purchase. So far, your staff has manually searched the third-party comparison shopping sites each day for information about products and prices. Your head of technology, however, has written a program to use a robot or "spider" to search those sites automatically and record the relevant information. When you ask her how this came about, she explains that she read how other comparison shopping sites were using robots to collect information and decided to see if she could program one herself. Not only was she successful, but she believes that her program collects more information and is significantly faster than your competitors' comparable programs. Alan and Barbara are interested in finding out if StarttUp might patent this program.

Problem 8.1

Cora has become concerned about the "linear" nature of the Gals On-Line blog and is looking for a way to make the text much more easily searchable over time. Most blogs currently are organized in descending chronological order with older entries becoming increasingly difficult to locate as the blog gets bigger and bigger. She has started a sub-page of the blog for people with software engineering backgrounds to send in ideas for how to create a program that is more easily searchable over time. A number of software engineers and hobbyists have contributed ideas. Cora now wants to commission a software programmer to use the ideas to write a program for her. She is interested in finding out if she can — or should — attempt to patent any resulting program.

---

1. Patenting Code

DIAMOND V. DIEHR

450 U.S. 175 (1981)

Justice REHNQUIST delivered the opinion of the Court.

We granted certiorari to determine whether a process for curing synthetic rubber which includes in several of its steps the use of a mathematical formula and a programmed digital computer is patentable subject matter under 35 U.S.C. §101.

I

The patent application at issue was filed by the respondents on August 6, 1975. The claimed invention is a process for molding raw, uncured synthetic rubber into cured precision products. . . .

Respondents claim that their process ensures the production of molded articles which are properly cured. Achieving the perfect cure depends upon several factors including the thickness of the article to be molded, the temperature of the molding process, and the amount of time that the article is allowed to remain in the press. It is possible using well-known time, temperature, and cure relationships to calculate by means of the Arrhenius equation when to open the press and remove the cured product. Nonetheless, according to the respondents, the industry has not been able to obtain uniformly accurate cures because the temperature of the molding press could not be precisely measured, thus making it difficult to do the necessary computations to determine cure time. . . .

Respondents characterize their contribution to the art to reside in the process of constantly measuring the actual temperature inside the mold. These temperature measurements are then automatically fed into a computer which repeatedly recalculates the cure time by use of the Arrhenius equation. When the recalculated time equals the actual time that has elapsed since the press was closed, the computer signals a device to open the press. According to the respondents, the continuous measuring of the temperature inside the mold cavity, the feeding of this information to a digital computer which constantly recalculates the cure time, and the signaling by the computer to open the press, are all new in the art.

The patent examiner rejected the respondents' claims on the sole ground that they were drawn to nonstatutory subject matter under 35 U.S.C. §101. He determined that those steps in respondents' claims that are carried out by a computer under control of a stored program constituted nonstatutory subject matter under this Court's decision in Gottschalk v. Benson, 409 U.S. 63 (1972). The remaining steps — installing rubber in the press and the subsequent closing of the press — were "conventional and necessary to the process and cannot be the basis of patentability." The examiner concluded that respondents' claims defined and sought protection of a computer program for operating a rubber-molding press. . . .

III

[According to the court, "a physical and chemical process for molding precision synthetic rubber products falls within the §101 categories of possibly patentable subject matter."] Our conclusion regarding respondents' claims is not altered by the fact that in several steps of the process a mathematical equation and a programmed digital computer are used. This Court has undoubtedly recognized limits to §101 and every discovery is not embraced within the statutory terms. Excluded from such patent protection are laws of nature, natural phenomena, and abstract ideas. "An idea of itself is not patentable," Rubber-Tip Pencil Co. v. Howard, 20 Wall. 498, 507 (1874). "A principle, in the abstract, is a fundamental truth; an original cause; a motive; these cannot be patented, as no one can claim in either of them an exclusive right." Le Roy v. Tatham, 14 How. 156, 175 (1853). Only last Term, we explained:

> "[A] new mineral discovered in the earth or a new plant found in the wild is not patentable subject matter. Likewise, Einstein could not patent his celebrated law that $E = mc2$; nor could Newton have patented the law of gravity. Such discoveries are 'manifestations of . . . nature, free to all men and reserved exclusively to none.'" Diamond v. Chakrabarty, 447 U.S., at 309.

Our recent holdings . . . both of which are computer-related, stand for no more than these long-established principles. In *Benson*, we held unpatentable claims for an algorithm used to convert binary code decimal numbers to equivalent pure binary numbers. The sole practical application of the algorithm was in connection with the programming of a general purpose digital computer. We defined "algorithm" as a "procedure for solving a given type of mathematical problem," and we concluded that such an algorithm, or mathematical formula, is like a law of nature, which cannot be the subject of a patent.

Parker v. Flook, supra, presented a similar situation. The claims were drawn to a method for computing an "alarm limit." An "alarm limit" is simply a number and the Court concluded that the application sought to protect a formula for computing this number. Using this formula, the updated alarm limit could be calculated if several other variables were known. The application, however, did not purport to explain how these other variables were to be determined, nor did it purport "to contain any disclosure relating to the chemical processes at work, the monitoring of process variables, or the means of setting off an alarm or adjusting an alarm system. All that it provides is a formula for computing an updated alarm limit." 437 U.S., at 586.

In contrast, the respondents here do not seek to patent a mathematical formula. Instead, they seek patent protection for a process of curing synthetic rubber. Their process admittedly employs a well-known mathematical equation, but they do not seek to pre-empt the use of that equation. Rather, they seek only to foreclose from others the use of that equation in conjunction with all of the other steps in their claimed process. These include installing rubber in a press, closing the mold, constantly determining the temperature of the mold, constantly recalculating the appropriate cure time through the use of the formula and a digital computer, and automatically opening the press at the proper time. Obviously, one does not need a "computer" to cure natural or synthetic rubber, but if the computer use incorporated in the process patent significantly lessens the possibility of "overcuring" or "undercuring," the process as a whole does not thereby become unpatentable subject matter.

Our earlier opinions lend support to our present conclusion that a claim drawn to subject matter otherwise statutory does not become nonstatutory simply because it uses a mathematical formula, computer program, or digital computer. . . . As Justice Stone explained four decades ago:

> "While a scientific truth, or the mathematical expression of it, is not a patentable invention, a novel and useful structure created with the aid of knowledge of scientific truth may be." Mackay Radio & Telegraph Co. v. Radio of America, 306 U.S. 86, 94 (1939).[11]

We think this statement in Mackay takes us a long way toward the correct answer in this case. Arrhenius' equation is not patentable in isolation, but when a process for curing rubber is devised which incorporates in it a more efficient solution of the equation, that process is at the very least not barred at the threshold by §101.

In determining the eligibility of respondents' claimed process for patent protection under §101, their claims must be considered as a whole. . . . The "novelty" of any element or steps in a process, or even of the process itself, is of no relevance in determining whether the subject matter of a claim falls within the §101 categories of possibly patentable subject matter.

It has been urged that novelty is an appropriate consideration under §101. Presumably, this argument results from the language in §101 referring to any "new and useful" process, machine, etc. Section 101, however, is a general statement of the type of subject matter that is eligible for patent protection "subject to the conditions and requirements of this title." Specific conditions for patentability follow and §102 covers in detail the conditions relating to novelty. The question therefore of whether a particular invention is novel is "wholly apart from whether the invention falls into a category of statutory subject matter." . . .

Justice STEVENS, with whom Justice BRENNAN, Justice MARSHALL, and Justice BLACKMUN join, dissenting. . . .

I

Before discussing the major flaws in the Court's opinion, a word of history may be helpful. As the Court recognized in Parker v. Flook, 437 U.S. 584,

---

11. We noted in Funk Bros. Seed Co. v. Kalo Inoculant Co., 333 U.S. 127, 130 (1948):

> "He who discovers a hitherto unknown phenomenon of nature has no claim to a monopoly of it which the law recognizes. If there is to be invention from such a discovery, it must come from the application of the law of nature to a new and useful end."

Although we were dealing with a "product" claim in *Funk Bros.*, the same principle applies to a process claim. Gottschalk v. Benson, 409 U.S. 63, 68 (1972).

595 (1978), the computer industry is relatively young. Although computer technology seems commonplace today, the first digital computer capable of utilizing stored programs was developed less than 30 years ago. Patent law developments in response to this new technology are of even more recent vintage. The subject of legal protection for computer programs did not begin to receive serious consideration until over a decade after completion of the first programmable digital computer. It was 1968 before the federal courts squarely addressed the subject, and 1972 before this Court announced its first decision in the area.

Prior to 1968, well-established principles of patent law probably would have prevented the issuance of a valid patent on almost any conceivable computer program. Under the "mental steps" doctrine, processes involving mental operations were considered unpatentable. The mental-steps doctrine was based upon the familiar principle that a scientific concept or mere idea cannot be the subject of a valid patent. The doctrine was regularly invoked to deny patents to inventions consisting primarily of mathematical formulae or methods of computation. It was also applied against patent claims in which a mental operation or mathematical computation was the sole novel element or inventive contribution; it was clear that patentability could not be predicated upon a mental step. Under the "function of a machine" doctrine, a process which amounted to nothing more than a description of the function of a machine was unpatentable. This doctrine had its origin in several 19th-century decisions of this Court,[8] and it had been consistently followed thereafter by the lower federal courts. Finally, the definition of "process" announced by this Court in Cochrane v. Deener, 94 U.S. 780, 787-788 (1877), seemed to indicate that a patentable process must cause a physical transformation in the materials to which the process is applied.

[I]n 1968, a dramatic change in the law as understood by the Court of Customs and Patent Appeals took place. By repudiating the well-settled "function of a machine" and "mental steps" doctrines, that court reinterpreted §101 of the Patent Code to enlarge drastically the categories of patentable subject matter. This reinterpretation would lead to the conclusion that computer programs were within the categories of inventions to which Congress intended to extend patent protection. . . .

II

As I stated at the outset, the starting point in the proper adjudication of patent litigation is an understanding of what the inventor claims to have discovered. Indeed, the outcome of such litigation is often determined by the judge's understanding of the patent application. This is such a case.

8. The "function of a machine" doctrine is generally traced to Corning v. Burden, 15 How. 252, 268 (1854), in which the Court stated: "[I]t is well settled that a man cannot have a patent for the function or abstract effect of a machine, but only for the machine which produces it."

In the first sentence of its opinion, the Court states the question presented as "whether a process for curing synthetic rubber . . . is patentable subject matter." . . . Of course, that question was effectively answered many years ago when Charles Goodyear obtained his patent on the vulcanization process. The patent application filed by Diehr and Lutton, however, teaches nothing about the chemistry of the synthetic rubber-curing process, nothing about the raw materials to be used in curing synthetic rubber, nothing about the equipment to be used in the process, and nothing about the significance or effect of any process variable such as temperature, curing time, particular compositions of material, or mold configurations. In short, Diehr and Lutton do not claim to have discovered anything new about the process for curing synthetic rubber.

As the Court reads the claims in the Diehr and Lutton patent application, the inventors' discovery is a method of constantly measuring the actual temperature inside a rubber molding press. As I read the claims, their discovery is an improved method of calculating the time that the mold should remain closed during the curing process. If the Court's reading of the claims were correct, I would agree that they disclose patentable subject matter. On the other hand, if the Court accepted my reading, I feel confident that the case would be decided differently.

. . . I cannot accept the Court's conclusion that Diehr and Lutton claim to have discovered a new method of constantly measuring the temperature inside a mold. First, there is not a word in the patent application that suggests that there is anything unusual about the temperature-reading devices used in this process — or indeed that any particular species of temperature-reading device should be used in it. Second . . . devices for constantly measuring actual temperatures — on a back porch, for example — have been familiar articles for quite some time. . . .

A fair reading of the entire patent application, as well as the specific claims, makes it perfectly clear that what Diehr and Lutton claim to have discovered is a method of using a digital computer to determine the amount of time that a rubber molding press should remain closed during the synthetic rubber-curing process. There is no suggestion that there is anything novel in the instrumentation of the mold, in actuating a timer when the press is closed, or in automatically opening the press when the computed time expires. . . . What they claim to have discovered, in essence, is a method of updating the original estimated curing time by repetitively recalculating that time pursuant to a well-known mathematical formula in response to variations in temperature within the mold. Their method of updating the curing time calculation is strikingly reminiscent of the method of updating alarm limits that Dale Flook sought to patent. . . .

III

The Court misapplies Parker v. Flook because, like the Court of Customs and Patent Appeals, it fails to understand or completely disregards the distinction between the subject matter of what the inventor claims to have discovered — the §101 issue — and the question whether that claimed discovery is in fact novel — the §102 issue. If there is not even a claim that anything constituting patentable subject matter has been discovered, there is no occasion to address the novelty issue. Or, as was true in *Flook*, if the only concept that the inventor claims to have discovered is not patentable subject matter, §101 requires that the application be rejected without reaching any issue under §102; for it is irrelevant that unpatentable subject matter — in that case a formula for updating alarm limits — may in fact be novel.

Proper analysis, therefore, must start with an understanding of what the inventor claims to have discovered — or phrased somewhat differently — what he considers his inventive concept to be. It seems clear to me that Diehr and Lutton claim to have developed a new method of programming a digital computer in order to calculate — promptly and repeatedly — the correct curing time in a familiar process. In the §101 analysis, we must assume that the sequence of steps in this programming method is novel, unobvious, and useful. The threshold question of whether such a method is patentable subject matter remains.

If that method is regarded as an "algorithm" as that term was used in Gottschalk v. Benson, 409 U.S. 63 (1972), and in Parker v. Flook, 437 U.S. 584 (1978),[38] and if no other inventive concept is disclosed in the patent application, the question must be answered in the negative. In both *Benson* and *Flook*, the parties apparently agreed that the inventor's discovery was properly regarded as an algorithm; the holding that an algorithm was a "law of nature" that could not be patented therefore determined that those discoveries were not patentable processes within the meaning of §101. . . .

In Gottschalk v. Benson, we held that a program for the solution by a digital computer of a mathematical problem was not a patentable process within the meaning of §101. In Parker v. Flook, we further held that such a computer program could not be transformed into a patentable process by the addition of postsolution activity that was not claimed to be novel. That holding plainly requires the rejection of Claims 1 and 2 of the Diehr and Lutton application quoted in the Court's opinion. In my opinion, it equally requires rejection of Claim 11 because the presolution activity described in that claim is admittedly a familiar part of the prior art.

Even the Court does not suggest that the computer program developed by Diehr and Lutton is a patentable discovery. Accordingly, if we treat the program as though it were a familiar part of the prior art — as well-established

---

38. In *Benson*, we explained the term "algorithm" in the following paragraph:

"The patent sought is on a method of programming a general-purpose digital computer to convert signals from binary-coded decimal form into pure binary form. A procedure for solving a given type of mathematical problem is known as an 'algorithm.' The procedures set forth in the present claims are of that kind; that is to say, they are a generalized formulation for programs to solve mathematical problems of converting one form of numerical representation to another. From the generic formulation, programs may be developed as specific applications." 409 U.S., at 65.

precedent requires—it is absolutely clear that their application contains no claim of patentable invention. Their application was therefore properly rejected under §101 by the Patent Office and the Board of Appeals. . . .

COMMENTS AND QUESTIONS

1.   What was the invention in *Diehr*?

2.   According to the Court, why are ideas themselves not patentable? Under what circumstances is a computer program a mere idea versus patentable subject matter? Is it enough if the algorithm or software provides a mathematical result? Under *Diehr*, are all computer programs patentable?

3.   Justice Stevens notes that prior to 1968 the mental steps and function of a machine doctrine would have precluded the issuance of a valid patent. What limits would he apply in *Diehr*? Why did the Court reject prior efforts to patent programs in *Benson* and *Flook*?

4.   Is the majority correct when it characterizes the dissent's concern as a question of whether the invention is novel under 35 U.S.C. §102, rather than whether computer programs fall within 35 U.S.C. §101?

5.   Why should computer programs benefit from both copyright and patent protection? Recall that copyright does not preclude third-party rights in the independent development of a functionally equivalent program. Under what circumstances might copyright protection be preferred over patent protection?

In re Alappat

33 F.3d 1526 (Fed. Cir. 1994)

RICH, Circuit Judge, with whom NEWMAN, LOURIE, MICHEL, PLAGER and RADER, Circuit Judges, join.

Alappat's invention relates generally to a means for creating a smooth waveform display in a digital oscilloscope. The screen of an oscilloscope is the front of a cathode-ray tube (CRT), which is like a TV picture tube, whose screen, when in operation, presents an array (or raster) of pixels arranged at intersections of vertical columns and horizontal rows, a pixel being a spot on the screen which may be illuminated by directing an electron beam to that spot, as in TV. Each column in the array represents a different time period, and each row represents a different magnitude. An input signal to the oscilloscope is sampled and digitized to provide a waveform data sequence (vector list), wherein each successive element of the sequence represents the magnitude of the waveform at a successively later time. The waveform data sequence is then processed to provide a bit map, which is a stored data array indicating which pixels are to be illuminated. The waveform ultimately displayed is formed by a group of vectors, wherein each vector has a straight line trajectory between two points on the screen at elevations representing the magnitudes of two successive input signal samples and at horizontal positions representing the timing of the two samples.

Because a CRT screen contains a finite number of pixels, rapidly rising and falling portions of a waveform can appear discontinuous or jagged due to differences in the elevation of horizontally contiguous pixels included in the waveform. In addition, the presence of "noise" in an input signal can cause portions of the waveform to oscillate between contiguous pixel rows when the magnitude of the input signal lies between values represented by the elevations of the two rows. Moreover, the vertical resolution of the display may be limited by the number of rows of pixels on the screen. The noticeability and appearance of these effects is known as aliasing.

To overcome these effects, Alappat's invention employs an anti-aliasing system wherein each vector making up the waveform is represented by modulating the illumination intensity of pixels having center points bounding the trajectory of the vector. The intensity at which each of the pixels is illuminated depends upon the distance of the center point of each pixel from the trajectory of the vector. Pixels lying squarely on the waveform trace receive maximum illumination, whereas pixels lying along an edge of the trace receive illumination decreasing in intensity proportional to the increase in the distance of the center point of the pixel from the vector trajectory. Employing this anti-aliasing technique eliminates any apparent discontinuity, jaggedness, or oscillation in the waveform, thus giving the visual appearance of a smooth continuous waveform. In short, and in lay terms, the invention is an improvement in an oscilloscope comparable to a TV having a clearer picture. . . .

The plain and unambiguous meaning of §101 is that any new and useful process, machine, manufacture, or composition of matter, or any new and useful improvement thereof, may be patented if it meets the requirements for patentability set forth in Title 35, such as those found in §§102, 103, and 112. The use of the expansive term "any" in §101 represents Congress's intent not to place any restrictions on the subject matter for which a patent may be obtained beyond those specifically recited in §101 and the other parts of Title 35. Indeed, the Supreme Court has acknowledged that Congress intended §101 to extend to "anything under the sun that is made by man." Diamond v. Chakrabarty, 447 U.S. 303, 309 (1980), quoting S. Rep. No. 1979, 82nd Cong., 2nd Sess., 5 (1952); H.R. Rep. No. 1923, 82nd Cong., 2nd Sess., 6 (1952). Thus, it is improper to read into §101 limitations as to the subject matter that may be patented where the legislative history does not indicate that Congress clearly intended such limitations. See *Chakrabarty*, 447 U.S. at 308 ("We have also cautioned that courts 'should not read into the patent laws limitations and conditions which the legislature has not expressed.' "), quoting United States v. Dubilier Condenser Corp., 289 U.S. 178, 199 (1933).

Despite the apparent sweep of §101, the Supreme Court has held that certain categories of subject matter are not entitled to patent protection. In Diamond v. Diehr, 450 U.S. 175 (1981), its most recent case addressing §101, the Supreme Court explained that there are three categories of subject matter for which one may not obtain patent protection, namely "laws of nature, natural phenomena, and abstract ideas." *Diehr*, 450 U.S. at 185. Of relevance to this case, the Supreme Court also has held that certain mathematical subject matter is not, standing alone, entitled to patent protection. See *Diehr*, 450 U.S. 175; Parker v. Flook, 437 U.S. 584; Gottschalk v. Benson, 409 U.S. 63. A close analysis of *Diehr*, *Flook*, and *Benson* reveals that the Supreme Court never intended to create an overly broad, fourth category of subject matter excluded from §101. Rather, at the core of the Court's analysis in each of these cases lies an attempt by the Court to explain a rather straightforward concept, namely, that certain types of mathematical subject matter, standing alone, represent nothing more than abstract ideas until reduced to some type of practical application, and thus that subject matter is not, in and of itself, entitled to patent protection.

Diehr also demands that the focus in any statutory subject matter analysis be on the claim as a whole. . . . It is thus not necessary to determine whether a claim contains, as merely a part of the whole, any mathematical subject matter which standing alone would not be entitled to patent protection. Indeed, because the dispositive inquiry is whether the claim as a whole is directed to statutory subject matter, it is irrelevant that a claim may contain, as part of the whole, subject matter which would not be patentable by itself. "A claim drawn to subject matter otherwise statutory does not become nonstatutory simply because it uses a mathematical formula, [mathematical equation, mathematical algorithm,] computer program or digital computer." *Diehr*, 450 U.S. at 187. . . .

Given the foregoing, the proper inquiry in dealing with the so called mathematical subject matter exception to §101 alleged herein is to see whether the claimed subject matter as a whole is a disembodied mathematical concept, whether categorized as a mathematical formula, mathematical equation, mathematical algorithm, or the like, which in essence represents nothing more than a "law of nature," "natural phenomenon," or "abstract idea." If so, *Diehr* precludes the patenting of that subject matter. That is not the case here.

Although many, or arguably even all, of the means elements recited in claim 15 represent circuitry elements that perform mathematical calculations, which is essentially true of all digital electrical circuits, the claimed invention as a whole is directed to a combination of interrelated elements which combine to form a machine for converting discrete waveform data samples into anti-aliased pixel illumination intensity data to be displayed on a display means. This is not a disembodied mathematical concept which may be characterized as an "abstract idea," but rather a specific machine to produce a useful, concrete, and tangible result.

The fact that the four claimed means elements function to transform one set of data to another through what may be viewed as a series of mathematical calculations does not alone justify a holding that the claim as a whole is directed to nonstatutory subject matter. Indeed, claim 15 as written is not "so abstract and sweeping" that it would "wholly pre-empt" the use of any apparatus employing the combination of mathematical calculations recited therein. Rather, claim 15 is limited to the use of a particularly claimed combination of elements performing the particularly claimed combination of calculations to transform, i.e., rasterize, digitized waveforms (data) into anti-aliased, pixel illumination data to produce a smooth waveform. . . .

The reconsideration Board majority also erred in its reasoning that claim 15 is unpatentable merely because it "reads on a general purpose digital computer 'means' to perform the various steps under program control." *Alappat*, 23 USPQ2d at 1345. The Board majority stated that it would "not presume that a stored program digital computer is not within the §112 ¶6 range of equivalents of the structure disclosed in the specification." *Alappat*, 23 USPQ2d at 1345. Alappat admits that claim 15 would read on a general purpose computer programmed to carry out the claimed invention, but argues that this alone also does not justify holding claim 15 unpatentable as directed to nonstatutory subject matter. We agree. We have held that such programming creates a new machine, because a general purpose computer in effect becomes a special purpose computer once it is programmed to perform particular functions pursuant to instructions from program software.

Under the Board majority's reasoning, a programmed general purpose computer could never be viewed as patentable subject matter under §101. This reasoning is without basis in the law. The Supreme Court has never held that a programmed computer may never be entitled to patent protection. Indeed, the Benson court specifically stated that its decision therein did not preclude "a patent for any program servicing a computer." *Benson*, 409 U.S. at 71. Consequently, a computer operating pursuant to software may represent patentable subject matter, provided, of course, that the claimed subject matter meets all of the other requirements of Title 35. In any case, a computer, like a rasterizer, is apparatus not mathematics. . . .

REVERSED.

ARCHER, Chief Judge, with whom NIES, Circuit Judge, joins, concurring in part and dissenting in part. . . .

The requirement of the patent law that an invention or discovery reside in the application of an abstract idea, law of nature, principle, or natural phenomenon is embodied in the language of 35 U.S.C. §101. A patent can be awarded to one who "invents or discovers" something within the enumerated classes of subject matter — "process," "machine," "manufacture," "composition of matter." These terms may not be read in a strict literal sense entirely divorced from the context of the patent law. *Diehr*, 450 U.S. at 185. Rather they must be read as incorporating the longstanding and well-established limitation that the claimed invention or discovery must reside in a practical application. . . .

Consider for example the discovery or creation of music, a new song. Music of course is not patentable subject matter; a composer cannot obtain exclusive patent rights for the original creation of a musical composition. But now suppose the new melody is recorded on a compact disc. In such case, the particular musical composition will define an arrangement of minute pits in the surface of the compact disc material, and therefore will define its specific structure. Alternatively suppose the music is recorded on the rolls of a player piano or a music box.

Through the expedient of putting his music on known structure, can a composer now claim as his invention the structure of a compact disc or player piano roll containing the melody he discovered and obtain a patent therefor? The answer must be no. The composer admittedly has invented or discovered nothing but music. The discovery of music does not become patentable subject matter simply because there is an arbitrary claim to some structure.

And if a claim to a compact disc or piano roll containing a newly discovered song were regarded as a "manufacture" and within §101 simply because of the specific physical structure of the compact disc, the "practical effect" would be the granting of a patent for a discovery in music. Where the music is new, the precise structure of the disc or roll would be novel under §102. Because the patent law cannot examine music for "nonobviousness," the Patent and Trademark Office could not make a showing of obviousness under §103. The result would well be the award of a patent for the discovery of music. The majority's simplistic approach of looking only to whether the claim reads on structure and ignoring the claimed invention or discovery for which a patent is sought will result in the awarding of patents for discoveries well beyond the scope of the patent law. . . .

So what did Alappat invent or discover? Alappat's specification clearly distinguishes between an "oscilloscope" and a "rasterizer," and Alappat claims his invention in claims 15-19 to be only the "rasterizer." . . .

Alappat admits that each of the circuitry elements of the claimed "rasterizer" is old. He says they are merely "form." Thus, they are only a convenient and basic way of electrically representing the mathematical operations to be performed, that is, converting vector data into matrix or raster data. In Alappat's view, it is the new mathematic operation that is the "substance" of the claimed invention or discovery. Claim 15 as a whole thus claims old circuitry elements in an arrangement defined by a mathematical operation, which only performs the very mathematical operation that defines it. Rather than claiming the mathematics itself, which of course Alappat cannot do, Alappat claims the mathematically defined structure. But as a whole, there is no "application" apart from the mathematical operation that is asserted to be the invention or discovery. What is going on here is a charade. . . .

This is not to say that digital circuitry cannot be an element in an otherwise statutory machine. Under *Diehr*, it can.[26] . . .

Finally, a "general purpose computer" issue has been raised as an aside in this case. . . .

Getting back to the music analogy, Alappat is like a composer who claims his song on a compact disc, and then argues that the compact disc is equivalent to a player piano or a music box with the song on a roll or even sheet music because they all represent the same song. The composer is thus clearly asking for (and getting from the majority) a patent for the discovery of a song and a patent covering every physical manifestation of the song.

In any event, even if a programmed general purpose computer is "equivalent" to the rasterizer, it cannot be deemed to be within §101 by simply reasoning as does the majority that it is a "new machine." Alappat posits that a "programmed digital computer becomes a special purpose digital computer to perform the function specified by the software. The special purpose computer can be implemented likewise by digital components, or even by analog components." The majority casually agrees that a "general purpose computer in effect becomes a special purpose computer once it is programmed to perform particular functions from program software." *Id.* One cannot, however, just call a programmed computer a "new machine" without going through the §101 analysis required by the trilogy of Supreme Court decisions. Whether or not subject matter is a "new machine" within §101 is precisely the same question as whether or not the subject matter satisfies the §101 analysis I have described.

Thus, a known circuit containing a light bulb, battery, and switch is not a new machine when the switch is opened and closed to recite a new story in Morse code, because the "invent[ion] or discover[y]" is merely a new story, which is nonstatutory subject matter. An old stereo playing a new song on a compact disc is not a new machine because the invention or discovery is merely a new song, which is nonstatutory subject matter. The "perforated rolls [of a player piano] are parts of a machine which, when duly applied and properly operated in connection with the mechanism to which they are adapted, produce musical tones in harmonious combination." White-Smith Music Publishing Co. v. Apollo Co., 209 U.S. 1, 18 (1908). Yet a player piano playing Chopin's scales does not become a "new machine" when it spins a roll to play Brahms' lullaby. The distinction between the piano before and after different rolls are inserted resides not in the piano's changing quality as a "machine" but only in the changing melodies being played by the one machine. The only invention by the creator of a roll that is new because of its music is the new music. Because the patent law does not examine musical compositions to determine their relation to those that have gone before, the distinction between new

26. Likewise, but not present in this case, improved digital circuitry itself, such as faster digital processors, would be statutory subject matter. Unlike the "rasterizer" in this case, they are not simply a claimed arrangement of circuit elements defined by a mathematical operation which does nothing more than solve the operation that defines it.

and old music can never qualify for patent protection. . . . A programmed general purpose digital computer alleged to be patentable subject matter because of the program presents an independent §101 inquiry that is not resolved simply by calling the structure a "new machine."

Finally, a claim formally to a general purpose computer running a certain program cannot be deemed to satisfy §101 simply because the computer is a physical, tangible device. As the invalidated claims in *Flook* and *Benson* demonstrate, and consistent with my earlier discussion, a computer program for use in a physical electronic thing called a computer may nevertheless be held to be nonstatutory subject matter. It is illogical to say that although a claim to a newly discovered mathematical operation to be performed by a computer is merely a nonstatutory discovery of mathematics, a claim to any computer performing that same mathematics is a statutory invention or discovery. Our precedent has rejected reasoning that way. . . . Furthermore, the broad statement that a computer using any program is patentable subject matter trivializes the principles and distinctions wrestled with in *Benson*, *Flook*, and *Diehr*, and the case law thereunder.

In summary, it cannot be said that Alappat's circuit means each find equivalents in a programmed general purpose digital computer. If it can be said that Alappat's claimed circuit elements are each equivalent to a programmed general purpose computer just because they will perform the same claimed mathematics, then this demonstrates that Alappat's claimed circuitry does not represent the invention or discovery of statutory subject matter. As to the programmed general purpose computer itself, there is no justification for saying that it must constitute statutory subject matter. When a particular claim directed to an isolated general purpose digital computer instructed to store, compute, or retrieve information comes before us, the claimed invention or discovery must be analyzed as a whole by reference to the Supreme Court cases, cases of this court, and principles of §101, as has been done in this opinion with regard to Alappat's claimed rasterizer. Neither the recitation in the claim of structure nor the expedient label of "new machine" is sufficient for §101. . . .

[Additional concurring and dissenting opinions omitted.]

COMMENTS AND QUESTIONS

1. What must a computer program do to be considered patentable? In *Diehr*, the process led to the creation of rubber; what was created by the rasterizer?

2. The dissent characterizes Alappat's claim as a charade. Why?

3. *Alappat* expands upon *Diehr* by considering a program that can run on a general purpose computer patentable subject matter. Is the court's reasoning persuasive? If all the computer is doing is running a series of instructions based upon mathematical algorithms, why is the algorithm exception inapplicable? Is Judge Archer's analogy to music persuasive?

4. Under *Diehr* and *Alappat*, some computer programs can be considered patentable subject matter. What programming could be patented with respect to the Internet? Would the TCP/IP protocol be considered patentable subject matter? Would the code for banner ads or pop-up windows? What do these processes produce?

2. Internet Business Method Patents

Following *State Street* and concurrent with the growth of e-commerce, the filing of Internet business method patents increased significantly. One famous patent dispute occurred between Amazon.com and BarnesandNoble.com during the 1999 holiday shopping season after BarnesandNoble.com began to employ a "one-click" shopping function similar to one already employed by Amazon.com. Online businesses discovered that the more steps a customer was required to perform in order to complete a transaction, the more likely they were not to complete the transaction. In response to this dropout phenomenon, Amazon.com streamlined the purchasing process by allowing users to purchase products with a mouse click. When BarnesandNoble.com began using a similar process, Amazon.com successfully obtained a preliminary injunction to prevent its competitor from using the function during the lucrative holiday season.[29]

AMAZON.COM, INC. V. BARNESANDNOBLE.COM, INC.

239 F.3d 1343 (Fed. Cir. 2001)

CLEVENGER, Circuit Judge.

This is a patent infringement suit brought by Amazon.com, Inc. ("Amazon") against Barnesandnoble.com, Inc., and Barnesandnoble.com LLC. (together, "BN"). Amazon moved for a preliminary injunction to prohibit BN's use of a feature of its web site called "Express Lane." . . .

I

This case involves United States Patent No. 5,960,411 ("the '411 patent"), which issued on September 28, 1999, and is assigned to Amazon. On October 21, 1999, Amazon brought suit against BN alleging infringement of the patent and seeking a preliminary injunction.

Amazon's patent is directed to a method and system for "single action" ordering of items in a client/server environment such as the Internet. . . .

29. *See* Amazon.com, Inc. v. BarnesandNoble.com, Inc., 73 F. Supp. 2d 1228 (W.D. Wash. 1999).

The '411 patent describes a method and system in which a consumer can complete a purchase order for an item via an electronic network using only a "single action," such as the click of a computer mouse button on the client computer system. Amazon developed the patent to cope with what it considered to be frustrations presented by what is known as the "shopping cart model" purchase system for electronic commerce purchasing events. In previous incarnations of the shopping cart model, a purchaser using a client computer system (such as a personal computer executing a web browser program) could select an item from an electronic catalog, typically by clicking on an "Add to Shopping Cart" icon, thereby placing the item in the "virtual" shopping cart. Other items from the catalog could be added to the shopping cart in the same manner. When the shopper completed the selecting process, the electronic commercial event would move to the check-out counter, so to speak. Then, information regarding the purchaser's identity, billing and shipping addresses, and credit payment method would be inserted into the transactional information base by the soon-to-be purchaser. Finally, the purchaser would "click" on a button displayed on the screen or somehow issue a command to execute the completed order, and the server computer system would verify and store the information concerning the transaction.

As is evident from the foregoing, an electronic commerce purchaser using the shopping cart model is required to perform several actions before achieving the ultimate goal of the placed order. The '411 patent sought to reduce the number of actions required from a consumer to effect a placed order. . . .

[After concluding that the district court properly concluded that Amazon demonstrated that BN likely infringed the '411 patent, the court turned to whether the patent was valid.]

VII

The district court considered, but ultimately rejected, the potentially invalidating impact of several prior art references cited by BN. Because the district court determined that BN likely infringed all of the asserted claims, it did not focus its analysis of the validity issue on any particular claim. Instead, in its validity analysis, the district court appears to have primarily directed its attention to determining whether the references cited by BN implemented the single action limitation. . . .

In this case, we find that the district court committed clear error by misreading the factual content of the prior art references cited by BN and by failing to recognize that BN had raised a substantial question of invalidity of the asserted claims in view of these prior art references. . . .

. . . Here, we have several references that were urged upon the court as invalidating the asserted claims. The district court dismissed those references, for purposes of its invalidity analysis, because it did not perceive them to recite each and every limitation of the claims in suit. As we explain below in our review of the asserted prior art in this case, each of the asserted references clearly teaches key limitations of the claims of the patent in suit. BN argued to the district court that one of ordinary skill in the art could fill in the gaps in the asserted references, given the opportunity to do so at trial.

When the heft of the asserted prior art is assessed in light of the correct legal standards, we conclude that BN has mounted a serious challenge to the validity of Amazon's patent. We hasten to add, however, that this conclusion only undermines the prerequisite for entry of a preliminary injunction. Our decision today on the validity issue in no way resolves the ultimate question of invalidity. That is a matter for resolution at trial. It remains to be learned whether there are other references that may be cited against the patent, and it surely remains to be learned whether any shortcomings in BN's initial preliminary validity challenge will be magnified or dissipated at trial. All we hold, in the meantime, is that BN cast enough doubt on the validity of the '411 patent to avoid a preliminary injunction, and that the validity issue should be resolved finally at trial.

A

One of the references cited by BN was the "CompuServe Trend System." The undisputed evidence indicates that in the mid-1990s, CompuServe offered a service called "Trend" whereby CompuServe subscribers could obtain stock charts for a surcharge of 50 cents per chart. Before the district court, BN argued that this system anticipated claim 11 of the '411 patent. The district court failed to recognize the substantial question of invalidity raised by BN in citing the CompuServe Trend reference, in that this system appears to have used "single action ordering technology" within the scope of the claims in the '411 patent.

First, the district court dismissed the significance of this system partly on the basis that "[t]he CompuServe system was not a world wide web application." This distinction is irrelevant, since none of the claims mention either the Internet or the World Wide Web (with the possible exception of dependent claim 15, which mentions HTML, a program commonly associated with both the Internet and the World Wide Web). Moreover, the '411 patent specification explicitly notes that "[o]ne skilled in the art would appreciate that the single-action ordering techniques can be used in various environments other than the Internet." Col. 6, ll. 22-24.

More importantly, one of the screen shots in the record . . . indicates that with the CompuServe Trend system, once the "item" to be purchased (i.e., a stock chart) has been displayed (by typing in a valid stock symbol), only a single action (i.e., a single mouse click on the button labeled "Chart ($.50)") is required to obtain immediate electronic delivery (i.e., "fulfillment") of the item. Once the button labeled "Chart ($.50)" was activated by a purchaser, an electronic version of the requested stock chart would be transmitted to the purchaser and displayed on the purchaser's computer screen, and an automatic process to charge the purchaser's account 50 cents for the transaction would be initiated. . . .

The evidence before us indicates that the billing process for the electronic stock chart would not actually commence until the client system sent a message to the server system indicating that the electronic stock chart had been received at the client system. In its brief, Amazon argues that this feature of the CompuServe Trend system amounts to an additional "confirmation step necessary to complete the ordering process," and that the CompuServe Trend system therefore does not use "single action" technology within the scope of the claims in the '411 patent. However, all of the claims only require sending a *request* to order an item in response to performance of only a single action. In the CompuServe Trend system, this requirement is satisfied when a purchaser performs the single action of "clicking" on the button labeled "Chart ($.50)." The claims do not require that the billing process for the item must also be initiated in response to performance of the single action. Furthermore, in the CompuServe Trend system, the "action" of sending a message from the client system to the server system confirming successful reception of the electronic stock chart is performed automatically, without user intervention. . . .

In view of the above, we conclude that the district court erred in failing to recognize that the CompuServe Trend reference raises a substantial question of invalidity. Whether the CompuServe Trend reference either anticipates and/or renders obvious the claimed invention in view of the knowledge of one of ordinary skill in the relevant art is a matter for decision at trial.

B

In addition to the CompuServe Trend system, other prior art references were cited by BN, but ultimately rejected by the district court. For example, BN's expert, Dr. Lockwood, testified that he developed an on-line ordering system called "Web Basket" in or around August 1996. The Web Basket system appears to be an embodiment of a "shopping cart ordering component": it requires users to accumulate items into a virtual shopping basket and to check these items out when they are finished shopping. Because it is an implementation of a shopping cart model, Web Basket requires several confirmation steps for even pre-registered users to complete their purchases.

However, despite the fact that Web Basket is an embodiment of a shopping cart model, it is undisputed that Web Basket implemented the Internet Engineering Task Force ("IETF") draft "cookie" specification, and stored a customer identifier in a cookie for use by a web server to retrieve information from a database. In other words, when a user first visited the Web Basket site, a cookie (i.e., a file stored by the server system on the client system for subsequent use) was used to store an identifier on the user's computer. The first time that a user purchased an item on the Web Basket site, the information entered by the user necessary to complete the purchase (e.g., name, address) would be stored in a database on the server system indexed by an identifier stored in the cookie on the client system. On subsequent visits, the cookie could be used to retrieve the user identifier, which would serve as the key to retrieve the user's information from the database on the server system.

At the preliminary injunction stage, based on Dr. Lockwood's declaration and testimony during the hearing, BN argued that the Web Basket reference — combined with the knowledge of one of ordinary skill in the art at the relevant time — renders obvious the claimed invention.

The district court concluded that the Web Basket system was "inconsistent with the single-action requirements of the '411 patent" because "it requires a multiple-step ordering process from the time that an item to be purchased is displayed." However, as discussed earlier, the undisputed evidence demonstrates that the accused BN Express Lane feature also requires a multiple-step ordering process (i.e., at least two "clicks") *from the time that an item to be purchased is first displayed on the menu page*, yet the district court concluded that BN's Express Lane feature infringed all of the asserted claims of the '411 patent. The district court's failure to recognize the inconsistency in these two conclusions was erroneous.

Moreover, the district court did not address the "cookie" aspects of the Web Basket reference, and failed to recognize that a reasonable jury could find that the step of storing purchaser data on the server system for subsequent retrieval indexed by an identifier transmitted from the client system was anticipated and/or rendered obvious by the Web Basket reference. . . .

C

BN also presented as a prior art reference an excerpt from a book written by Magdalena Yesil entitled *Creating the Virtual Store* that was copyrighted in 1996. Before the district court, BN argued that this reference anticipated every limitation of claim 11. Before this court, BN also alleges that many other claim limitations are disclosed in the reference, but that there was insufficient time to prepare testimony concerning these limitations, given the district court's accelerated briefing and hearing schedule at the preliminary injunction stage.

In general terms, the reference apparently discusses software to implement a shopping cart ordering model. However, BN focuses on the following passage from Appendix F of the book:

Instant Buy Option
Merchants also can provide shoppers with an Instant Buy button for some or all items, enabling them to skip checkout review. This provides added appeal for customers who already know the single item they want to purchase during their shopping excursion.

The district court dismissed the significance of this passage, stating that "[r]ead in context, the few lines relied on by Defendants appear to describe only the elimination of the checkout review step, leaving at least two other required steps to complete a purchase." However, the district court failed to recognize that a reasonable jury could find that this passage provides a motivation to modify shopping cart ordering software to skip unnecessary steps. Thus, we find that this passage, viewed in light of the rest of the reference and the other prior art references cited by BN, raises a substantial question of validity with respect to the asserted claims of the '411 patent. . . . [The court's discussion of two additional examples of prior art is omitted.]

CONCLUSION

While it appears on the record before us that Amazon has carried its burden with respect to demonstrating the likelihood of success on infringement, it is also true that BN has raised substantial questions as to the validity of the '411 patent. For that reason, we must conclude that the necessary prerequisites for entry of a preliminary injunction are presently lacking. We therefore vacate the preliminary injunction and remand the case for further proceedings.

COMMENTS AND QUESTIONS

1. In *Amazon.com*, why did the Court of Appeals reverse the order granting Amazon.com a preliminary injunction? Did the court question whether the "one-click" function for online shopping could be considered patentable subject matter under Section 101?

2. Are the issues surrounding Internet business method patents different from those raised by patenting computer programs in general? If so how do they differ? What is the invention at issue in *Amazon.com*? As discussed in the preceding section on copyright, the recognition of intellectual property rights is often justified as necessary to provide sufficient incentives for invention or innovation. How would allowing Barnes and Noble to adopt one-click shopping without Amazon's authorization diminish Amazon's incentives to innovate? Does the propriety of recognizing such patents depend upon whether the patent holder is willing to license the invention to others?

3. Are the issues surrounding Internet business method patents different from those raised by patenting business methods more generally? Consider *In re Bilski* (below).

IN RE BILSKI

545 F.3d 943 (U.S. Court of Appeals for the Federal Circuit, 2008)

MICHEL, Chief Judge (DYK, Circuit Judge and LINN, Circuit Judge, concurring).

Bernard L. Bilski and Rand A. Warsaw (collectively, "Applicants") appeal from the final decision of the Board of Patent Appeals and Interferences ("Board") sustaining the rejection of all eleven claims of their U.S. Patent Application Serial No. 08/833,892 ("'892 application"). Specifically, Applicants argue that the examiner erroneously rejected the claims as not directed to patent-eligible subject matter under 35 U.S.C. §101, and that the Board erred in upholding that rejection. . . . We affirm the decision of the Board because we conclude that Applicants' claims are not directed to patent-eligible subject matter, and in doing so, we clarify the standards applicable in determining whether a claimed method constitutes a statutory "process" under §101.

I.

Applicants filed their patent application on April 10, 1997. The application contains eleven claims, which Applicants argue together here. Claim 1 reads:

> A method for managing the consumption risk costs of a commodity sold by a commodity provider at a fixed price comprising the steps of:
>
> (a) initiating a series of transactions between said commodity provider and consumers of said commodity wherein said consumers purchase said commodity at a fixed rate based upon historical averages, said fixed rate corresponding to a risk position of said consumer;
> (b) identifying market participants for said commodity having a counter-risk position to said consumers; and
> (c) initiating a series of transactions between said commodity provider and said market participants at a second fixed rate such that said series of market participant transactions balances the risk position of said series of consumer transactions.

In essence, the claim is for a method of hedging risk in the field of commodities trading. For example, coal power plants (i.e., the "consumers") purchase coal to produce electricity and are averse to the risk of a spike in demand for coal since such a spike would increase the price and their costs. Conversely, coal mining companies (i.e., the "market participants") are averse to the risk of a sudden drop in demand for coal since such a drop would reduce their sales and depress prices. The claimed method envisions an intermediary, the "commodity provider," that sells coal to the power plants at a fixed price, thus isolating the power plants from the possibility of a spike in demand increasing the price of coal above the fixed price. The same provider buys coal from mining companies at a second fixed price, thereby isolating the mining companies from the possibility that a drop in demand would lower prices below that fixed price. And the provider has thus hedged its risk; if demand and prices skyrocket, it has sold coal at a disadvantageous price but has bought coal at an advantageous price, and vice versa if demand and prices fall. Importantly, however, the claim is not limited to transactions involving actual commodities, and the application discloses that the recited transactions may simply involve options, i.e., rights to purchase or sell the commodity at a particular price within a particular timeframe.

The examiner ultimately rejected claims 1-11 under 35 U.S.C. §101, stating: "[r]egarding . . . claims 1-11, the invention is not implemented on a specific apparatus and merely manipulates [an] abstract idea and solves a purely mathematical problem without any limitation to a practical application, therefore, the invention is not directed to the technological arts." The examiner noted that Applicants had admitted their claims are not limited to operation on a computer, and he concluded that they were not limited by any specific apparatus.

On appeal, the Board held that the examiner erred to the extent he relied on a "technological arts" test because the case law does not support such a test. Further, the Board held that the requirement of a specific apparatus was also erroneous because a claim that does not recite a specific apparatus may still be directed to patent-eligible subject matter "if there is a transformation of physical subject matter from one state to another." Elaborating further, the Board stated: " 'mixing' two elements or compounds to produce a chemical substance or mixture is clearly a statutory transformation although no apparatus is claimed to perform the step and although the step could be performed manually." But the Board concluded that Applicants' claims do not involve any patent-eligible transformation, holding that transformation of "non-physical financial risks and legal liabilities of the commodity provider, the consumer, and the market participants" is not patent-eligible subject matter. The Board also held that Applicants' claims "preempt[] any and every possible way of performing the steps of the [claimed process], by human or by any kind of machine or by any combination thereof," and thus concluded that they only claim an abstract idea ineligible for patent protection. Finally, the Board held that Applicants' process as claimed did not produce a "useful, concrete and tangible result," and for this reason as well was not drawn to patent-eligible subject matter . . .

II.

Whether a claim is drawn to patent-eligible subject matter under §101 is a threshold inquiry, and any claim of an application failing the requirements of §101 must be rejected even if it meets all of the other legal requirements of patentability. . . .

A.

As this appeal turns on whether Applicants' invention as claimed meets the requirements set forth in §101, we begin with the words of the statute:

> Whoever invents or discovers any new and useful process, machine, manufacture, or composition of matter, or any new and useful improvement thereof, may obtain a patent therefor, subject to the conditions and requirements of this title.

35 U.S.C. §101. The statute thus recites four categories of patent-eligible subject matter: processes, machines, manufactures, and compositions of matter. It is undisputed that Applicants' claims are not directed to a machine, manufacture, or composition of matter. Thus, the issue before us involves what the term "process" in §101 means, and how to determine whether a given claim — and Applicants' claim 1 in particular — is a "new and useful process."

As several amici have argued, the term "process" is ordinarily broad in meaning, at least in general lay usage. In 1952, at the time Congress amended §101 to include "process," the ordinary meaning of the term was: "[a] procedure . . . [a] series of actions, motions, or operations definitely conducing to an end, whether voluntary or involuntary." WEBSTER'S NEW INTERNATIONAL DICTIONARY OF THE ENGLISH LANGUAGE 1972 (2d ed. 1952). There can be no dispute that Applicants' claim would meet this definition of "process." But the Supreme Court has held that the meaning of "process" as used in §101 is narrower than its ordinary meaning. See *Flook*, 437 U.S. at 588-89 ("The holding [in Benson] forecloses a purely literal reading of §101."). Specifically, the Court has held that a claim is not a patent-eligible "process" if it claims "laws of nature, natural phenomena, [or] abstract ideas." *Diamond v. Diehr*, 450 U.S. 175, 185 (1981) (citing *Flook*, 437 U.S. at 589, and *Gottschalk v. Benson*, 409 U.S. 63, 67 (1972)). Such fundamental principles are "part of the storehouse of knowledge of all men . . . free to all men and reserved exclusively to none." *Funk Bros. Seed Co. v. Kalo Inoculant Co.*, 333 U.S. 127, 130 (1948); see also *Le Roy v. Tatham*, 55 U.S. (14 How.) 156 (1852) ("A principle, in the abstract, is a fundamental truth; an original cause; a motive; these cannot be patented, as no one can claim in either of them an exclusive right."). "Phenomena of nature, though just discovered, mental processes, and abstract intellectual concepts are not patentable, as they are the basic tools of scientific and technological work." *Benson*, 409 U.S. at 67; see also *Comiskey*, 499 F.3d at 1378-79 (holding that "mental processes," "processes of human thinking," and "systems that depend for their operation on human intelligence alone" are not patent-eligible subject matter under *Benson*).

The true issue before us then is whether Applicants are seeking to claim a fundamental principle (such as an abstract idea) or a mental process. And the underlying legal question thus presented is what test or set of criteria governs the determination by the Patent and Trademark Office ("PTO") or courts as to whether a claim to a process is patentable under §101 or, conversely, is drawn to unpatentable subject matter because it claims only a fundamental principle.

The Supreme Court last addressed this issue in 1981 in *Diehr*, which concerned a patent application seeking to claim a process for producing cured synthetic rubber products. 450 U.S. at 177-79. The claimed process took temperature readings during cure and used a mathematical algorithm, the Arrhenius equation, to calculate the time when curing would be complete. *Id.* Noting that a mathematical algorithm alone is unpatentable because mathematical relationships are akin to a law of nature, the Court nevertheless held that the claimed process was patent-eligible subject matter, stating:

> [The inventors] do not seek to patent a mathematical formula. Instead, they seek patent protection for a process of curing synthetic rubber. Their process admittedly employs a well-known mathematical equation, but they do not seek to pre-empt the use of that equation. Rather, they seek only to foreclose from others the use of that equation in conjunction with all of the other steps in their claimed process.

Id. at 187 (emphasis added). The Court declared that while a claim drawn to a fundamental principle is unpatentable, "an application of a law of nature or mathematical formula to a known structure or process may well be deserving of patent protection." Id. (emphasis in original); see also *Mackay Radio & Tel. Co. v. Radio Corp. of Am.*, 306 U.S. 86, 94, 59 S. Ct. 427, 83 L. Ed. 506, 1939 Dec. Comm'r Pat. 857 (1939) ("While a scientific truth, or the mathematical expression of it, is not a patentable invention, a novel and useful structure created with the aid of knowledge of scientific truth may be.").

The Court in *Diehr* thus drew a distinction between those claims that "seek to pre-empt the use of" a fundamental principle, on the one hand, and claims that seek only to foreclose others from using a particular "application" of that fundamental principle, on the other. 450 U.S. at 187. Patents, by definition, grant the power to exclude others from practicing that which the patent claims. *Diehr* can be understood to suggest that whether a claim is drawn only to a fundamental principle is essentially an inquiry into the scope of that exclusion; i.e., whether the effect of allowing the claim would be to allow the patentee to pre-empt substantially all uses of that fundamental principle. If so, the claim is not drawn to patent-eligible subject matter.

In *Diehr*, the Court held that the claims at issue did not pre-empt all uses of the Arrhenius equation but rather claimed only "a process for curing rubber . . . which incorporates in it a more efficient solution of the equation." 450 U.S. at 188 . . .

In contrast to *Diehr*, the earlier *Benson* case presented the Court with claims drawn to a process of converting data in binary-coded decimal ("BCD") format to pure binary format via an algorithm programmed onto a digital computer. *Benson*, 409 U.S. at 65. The Court held the claims to be drawn to unpatentable subject matter:

> It is conceded that one may not patent an idea. But in practical effect that would be the result if the formula for converting BCD numerals to pure binary numerals were patented in this case. The mathematical formula involved here has no substantial practical application except in connection with a digital computer, which means that if the judgment below is affirmed, the patent would wholly pre-empt the mathematical formula and in practical effect would be a patent on the algorithm itself.

Id. at 71-72 (emphasis added). Because the algorithm had no uses other than those that would be covered by the claims (i.e., any conversion of BCD to pure binary on a digital computer), the claims pre-empted all uses of the algorithm and thus they were effectively drawn to the algorithm itself. See also *O'Reilly v. Morse*, 56 U.S. (15 How.) 62 (1853) (holding ineligible a claim pre-empting all uses of electromagnetism to print characters at a distance).

The question before us then is whether Applicants' claim recites a fundamental principle and, if so, whether it would pre-empt substantially all uses of that fundamental principle if allowed. Unfortunately, this inquiry is hardly straightforward. How does one determine whether a given claim would pre-empt all uses of a fundamental principle? Analogizing to the facts of *Diehr* or *Benson* is of limited usefulness because the more challenging process claims of the twenty-first century are seldom so clearly limited in scope as the highly specific, plainly corporeal industrial manufacturing process of *Diehr*, nor are they typically as broadly claimed or purely abstract and mathematical as the algorithm of *Benson*.

The Supreme Court, however, has enunciated a definitive test to determine whether a process claim is tailored narrowly enough to encompass only a particular application of a fundamental principle rather than to pre-empt the principle itself. A claimed process is surely patent-eligible under §101 if: (1) it is tied to a particular machine or apparatus, or (2) it transforms a particular article into a different state or thing. See *Benson*, 409 U.S. at 70 ("Transformation and reduction of an article 'to a different state or thing' is the clue to the patentability of a process claim that does not include particular machines."); *Diehr*, 450 U.S. at 192 (holding that use of mathematical formula in process "transforming or reducing an article to a different state or thing" constitutes patent-eligible subject matter); see also *Flook*, 437 U.S. at 589 n.9 ("An argument can be made [that the Supreme] Court has only recognized a process as within the statutory definition when it either was tied to a particular apparatus or operated to change materials to a 'different state or thing'"); *Cochrane v. Deener*, 94 U.S. 780, 788 (1876) ("A process is . . . an act, or a series of acts, performed upon the subject-matter to be transformed and reduced to a different state or thing."). A claimed process involving a fundamental principle that uses a particular machine or apparatus would not pre-empt uses of the principle that do not also use the specified machine or apparatus in the manner claimed. And a claimed process that transforms a particular article to a specified different state or thing by applying a fundamental principle would not pre-empt the use of the principle to transform any other article, to transform the same article but in a manner not covered by the claim, or to do anything other than transform the specified article. . . .

B.

Applicants and several amici have argued that the Supreme Court did not intend the machine-or-transformation test to be the sole test governing §101 analyses. As already noted, however, the Court explicitly stated in *Benson* that "[t]ransformation and reduction of an article 'to a different state or thing' is the clue to the patentability of a process claim that does not include particular machines." 409 U.S. at 70 (emphasis added). And the Court itself later noted in *Flook* that at least so far it had "only recognized a process as within the statutory definition when it either was tied to a particular apparatus or operated to change materials to a 'different state or thing.' " 437 U.S. at 589 n.9. Finally, the Court in *Diehr* once again applied the machine-or-transformation test in its most recent decision regarding the patentability of processes under §101. 450 U.S. at 184.

We recognize, however, that the Court was initially equivocal in first putting forward this test in *Benson*. As the Applicants and several amici point out, the Court there stated:

> It is argued that a process patent must either be tied to a particular machine or apparatus or must operate to change articles or materials to a 'different state or thing.' We do not hold that no process patent could ever qualify if it did not meet the requirements of our prior precedents.

Benson, 409 U.S. at 71. In *Flook*, the Court took note that this statement had been made in *Benson* but merely stated: "As in *Benson*, we assume that a valid process patent may issue even if it does not meet [the machine-or-transformation test]." 437 U.S. at 589 n.9 (emphasis added). And this caveat was not repeated in *Diehr* when the Court reaffirmed the machine-or-transformation test. See *Diehr*, 450 U.S. at 184 (quoting *Benson*, 409 U.S. at 70) ("Transformation and reduction of an article 'to a different state or thing' is the clue to the patentability of a process claim that does not include particular machines."). Therefore, we believe our reliance on the Supreme Court's machine-or-transformation test as the applicable test for §101 analyses of process claims is sound.

Nevertheless, we agree that future developments in technology and the sciences may present difficult challenges to the machine-or-transformation test, just as the widespread use of computers and the advent of the Internet has begun to challenge it in the past decade. Thus, we recognize that the Supreme Court may ultimately decide to alter or perhaps even set aside this test to accommodate emerging technologies. And we certainly do not rule out the possibility that this court may in the future refine or augment the test or how it is applied. At present, however, and certainly for the present case, we see no need for such a departure and reaffirm that the machine-or-transformation test, properly applied, is the governing test for determining patent eligibility of a process under §101.

C.

As a corollary, the *Diehr* Court also held that mere field-of-use limitations are generally insufficient to render an otherwise ineligible process claim patent-eligible. See 450 U.S. at 191-92 (noting that ineligibility under §101 "cannot be circumvented by attempting to limit the use of the formula to a particular technological environment"). We recognize that tension may be seen between this consideration and the Court's overall goal of preventing the wholesale pre-emption of fundamental principles. Why not permit patentees to avoid over-broad pre-emption by limiting claim scope to particular fields of use? This tension is resolved, however, by recalling the purpose behind the Supreme Court's discussion of pre-emption, namely that pre-emption is merely an indication that a claim seeks to cover a fundamental principle itself rather than only a specific application of that principle. See *id.* at 187; *Benson*, 409 U.S. at 71-72. Pre-emption of all uses of a fundamental principle in all fields and pre-emption of all uses of the principle in only one field both indicate that the claim is not limited to a particular application of the principle. See *Diehr*, 450 U.S. at 193 n.14 ("A mathematical formula in the abstract is nonstatutory subject matter regardless of whether the patent is intended to cover all uses of the formula or only limited uses.") (emphasis added). In contrast, a claim that is tied to a particular machine or brings about a particular transformation of a particular article does not pre-empt all uses of a fundamental principle in any field but rather is limited to a particular use, a specific application. Therefore, it is not drawn to the principle in the abstract.

The *Diehr* Court also reaffirmed a second corollary to the machine-or-transformation test by stating that "insignificant postsolution activity will not transform an unpatentable principle into a patentable process." *Id.* at 191-92; see also *Flook*, 437 U.S. at 590 ("The notion that post-solution activity, no matter how conventional or obvious in itself, can transform an unpatentable principle into a patentable process exalts form over substance."). The Court in *Flook* reasoned:

> A competent draftsman could attach some form of post-solution activity to almost any mathematical formula; the Pythagorean theorem would not have been patentable, or partially patentable, because a patent application contained a final step indicating that the formula, when solved, could be usefully applied to existing surveying techniques.

437 U.S. at 590. Therefore, even if a claim recites a specific machine or a particular transformation of a specific article, the recited machine or transformation must not constitute mere "insignificant postsolution activity."

D.

We discern two other important aspects of the Supreme Court's §101 jurisprudence. First, the Court has held that whether a claimed process is novel or non-obvious is irrelevant to the §101 analysis. *Diehr*, 450 U.S. at 188-91. Rather, such considerations are governed by 35 U.S.C. §102 (novelty) and §103 (non-obviousness). *Diehr*, 450 U.S. at 188-91. . . . So here, it is irrelevant to the §101 analysis whether Applicants' claimed process is novel or non-obvious.

Second, the Court has made clear that it is inappropriate to determine the patent-eligibility of a claim as a whole based on whether selected limitations constitute patent-eligible subject matter. *Flook*, 437 U.S. at 594 ("Our approach to respondent's application is, however, not at all inconsistent with the view that a patent claim must be considered as a whole."); *Diehr*, 450 U.S. at 188 ("It is inappropriate to dissect the claims into old and new elements and then to ignore the presence of the old elements in the analysis."). After all, even though a fundamental principle itself is not patent-eligible, processes incorporating a fundamental principle may be patent-eligible. Thus, it is irrelevant that any individual step or limitation of such processes by itself would be unpatentable under §101. See *In re Alappat*, 33 F.3d 1526, 1543-44 (Fed. Cir. 1994) (en banc) (citing *Diehr*, 450 U.S. at 187).

* * *

We hold that the Applicants' process as claimed does not transform any article to a different state or thing. Purported transformations or manipulations simply of public or private legal obligations or relationships, business risks, or other such abstractions cannot meet the test because they are not physical objects or substances, and they are not representative of physical objects or substances. Applicants' process at most incorporates only such ineligible transformations. As discussed earlier, the process as claimed encompasses the exchange of only options, which are simply legal rights to purchase some commodity at a given price in a given time period. The claim only refers to "transactions" involving the exchange of these legal rights at a "fixed rate corresponding to a risk position." Thus, claim 1 does not involve the transformation of any physical object or substance, or an electronic signal representative of any physical object or substance. Given its admitted failure to meet the machine implementation part of the test as well, the claim entirely fails the machine-or-transformation test and is not drawn to patent-eligible subject matter. . . .

. . . Applicants here seek to claim a non-transformative process that encompasses a purely mental process of performing requisite mathematical calculations without the aid of a computer or any other device, mentally identifying those transactions that the calculations have revealed would hedge each other's risks, and performing the post-solution step of consummating those transactions. Therefore, claim 1 would effectively pre-empt any application of the fundamental concept of hedging and mathematical calculations inherent in hedging (not even limited to any particular mathematical formula). And while Applicants argue that the scope of this pre-emption is limited to hedging as applied in the area of consumable commodities, the Supreme Court's reasoning has made clear that effective pre-emption of all applications of hedging even just within the area of consumable commodities is impermissible. See *Diehr*, 450 U.S. at 191-92 (holding that field-of-use limitations are insufficient to impart patent-eligibility to otherwise unpatentable claims drawn to fundamental principles). Moreover, while the claimed process contains physical steps (initiating, identifying), it does not involve transforming an article into a different state or thing. Therefore, Applicants' claim is not drawn to patent-eligible subject matter under §101.

CONCLUSION

Because the applicable test to determine whether a claim is drawn to a patent-eligible process under §101 is the machine-or-transformation test set forth by the Supreme Court and clarified herein, and Applicants' claim here plainly fails that test, the decision of the Board is

AFFIRMED.

[Separate concurring judgment by DYK, Circuit Judge and LINN, Circuit Judge omitted.]

NEWMAN, Circuit Judge, dissenting.

The court today acts en banc to impose a new and far-reaching restriction on the kinds of inventions that are eligible to participate in the patent system. The court achieves this result by redefining the word "process" in the patent statute, to exclude all processes that do not transform physical matter or that are not performed by machines. The court thus excludes many of the kinds of inventions that apply today's electronic and photonic technologies, as well as other processes that handle data and information in novel ways. Such processes have long been patent eligible, and contribute to the vigor and variety of today's Information Age. This exclusion of process inventions is contrary to statute, contrary to precedent, and a negation of the constitutional mandate. Its impact on the future, as well as on the thousands of patents already granted, is unknown.

This exclusion is imposed at the threshold, before it is determined whether the excluded process is new, non-obvious, enabled, described, particularly claimed, etc.; that is, before the new process is examined for patentability. For example, we do not know whether the Bilski process would be found patentable under the statutory criteria, for they were never applied.

The innovations of the "knowledge economy" — of "digital prosperity" — have been dominant contributors to today's economic growth and societal change. Revision of the commercial structure affecting major aspects of today's industry should be approached with care, for there has been significant reliance on the law as it has existed, as many amici curiae pointed out. Indeed, the full reach of today's change of law is not clear, and the majority opinion states that many existing situations may require reassessment under the new criteria.

Uncertainty is the enemy of innovation. These new uncertainties not only diminish the incentives available to new enterprise, but disrupt the settled expectations of those who relied on the law as it existed. I respectfully dissent.

DISCUSSION

The court's exclusion of specified process inventions from access to the patent system is achieved by redefining the word "process" in the patent statute. However, the court's redefinition is contrary to statute and to explicit rulings of the Supreme Court and this court. I start with the statute:

Section 101 is the statement of statutory eligibility

From the first United States patent act in 1790, the subject matter of the "useful arts" has been stated broadly, lest advance restraints inhibit the unknown future. The nature of patent-eligible subject matter has received judicial attention over the years, as new issues arose with advances in science and technology. The Supreme Court has consistently confirmed the constitutional and legislative purpose of providing a broadly applicable incentive to commerce and creativity, through this system of limited exclusivity. Concurrently, the Court early explained the limits of patentable subject matter, in that "fundamental truths" were not intended to be included in a system of exclusive rights, for they are the general foundations of knowledge. Thus laws of nature, natural phenomena, and abstract ideas are not subject to patenting. Several rulings of the Court have reviewed patent eligibility in light of these fundamentals. However, the Court explicitly negated today's restrictions. My colleagues in the majority are mistaken in finding that decisions of the Court require the per se limits to patent eligibility that the Federal Circuit today imposes. The patent statute and the Court's decisions neither establish nor support the exclusionary criteria now adopted.

The court today holds that any process that does not transform physical matter or require performance by machine is not within the definition of "process" in any of the patent statutes since 1790. All of the statutes contained a broad definition of patent-eligible subject matter, like that in the current Patent Act of 1952:

> 35 U.S.C §101 Whoever invents or discovers any new and useful process, machine, manufacture, or composition of matter, or any new and useful improvement thereof, may obtain a patent therefor, subject to the conditions and requirements of this title.

In *Diamond v. Diehr*, 450 U.S. 175 (1981), the Court explained that Section 101 is not an independent condition of patentability, but a general statement of subject matter eligibility. The Court stated:

> Section 101, however, is a general statement of the type of subject matter that is eligible for patent protection "subject to the conditions and requirements of this title." Specific conditions for patentability follow and §102 covers in detail the conditions relating to novelty. The question therefore of whether a particular invention is novel is "wholly apart from whether the invention falls in a category of statutory subject matter."

Id. at 189-90 (footnote omitted) (quoting *In re Bergy*, 596 F.2d 952, 961 (C.C.P.A. 1979)).

"Process" is defined in the 1952 statute as follows:

> 35 U.S.C. §100(b) The term "process" means process, art or method, and includes a new use of a known process, machine, manufacture, composition of matter, or material.

The 1952 Patent Act replaced the word "art" in prior statutes with the word "process," while the rest of Section 101 was unchanged from earlier statutes. The legislative history for the 1952 Act explained that "art" had been "interpreted by courts to be practically synonymous with process or method." S. Rep. No. 82-1979 (1952), reprinted in 1952 U.S.C.C.A.N. 2394, 2398, 2409-10. In Diehr the Court explained that a process "has historically enjoyed patent protection because it was considered a form of 'art' as that term was used in the 1793 Act." 450 U.S. at 182.

The definition of "process" provided at 35 U.S.C. §100(b) is not "unhelpful," as this court now states, maj. op. at 6 n.3, but rather points up the errors in the court's new statutory interpretation. Section 100(b) incorporates the prior usage "art" and the term "method," and places no restriction on the definition. This court's redefinition of "process" as limiting access to the patent system to those processes that use specific machinery or that transform matter, is contrary to two centuries of statutory definition.

The breadth of Section 101 and its predecessor provisions reflects the legislative intention to accommodate not only known fields of creativity, but also the unknown future. The Court has consistently refrained from imposing unwarranted restrictions on statutory eligibility, and for computer-implemented processes the Court has explicitly rejected the direction now taken. Nonetheless, this court now adopts a redefinition of "process" in Section 101 that excludes forms of information-based and software-implemented inventions arising from new technological capabilities, stating that this result is required by the Court's computer-related cases, starting with *Gottschalk v. Benson*, 409 U.S. 63, 93 S. Ct. 253, 34 L. Ed. 2d 273 (1972). However, the Court in *Benson* rejected the restriction that is imposed today:

This court's new definition of "process" was rejected in Gottschalk v. Benson

In *Benson* the claimed invention was a mathematical process for converting binary-coded decimal numerals into pure binary numbers. The Court explained that a mathematical formula unlimited to a specific use was simply an abstract idea of the nature of "fundamental truths," "phenomena of nature," and "abstract intellectual concepts," as have traditionally been outside of patent systems. 409 U.S. at 67. However, the Court explicitly declined to limit patent-eligible processes in the manner now adopted by this court, stating:

> It is argued that a process patent must either be tied to a particular machine or apparatus or must operate to change articles or materials to a "different state or thing." We do not hold

that no process patent could ever qualify if it did not meet the requirements of our prior precedents. It is said that the decision precludes a patent for any program servicing a computer. We do not so hold.

Id. at 71. The Court explained that "the requirements of our prior precedents" did not preclude patents on computer programs, despite the statement drawn from *Cochrane v. Deener*, 94 U.S. 780, 787-88 (1876), that "[t]ransformation and reduction of an article 'to a different state or thing' is the clue to the patentability of a process claim that does not include particular machines." *Benson*, 409 U.S. at 70. Although this same statement is now relied upon by this court as requiring its present ruling, maj. op. at 13 & n.11, the Court in Benson was explicit that: "We do not hold that no process patent could ever qualify if it did not meet [the Court's] prior precedents." The Court recognized that Cochrane's statement was made in the context of a mechanical process and a past era, and protested:

> It is said we freeze process patents to old technologies, leaving no room for the revelations of the new, onrushing technology. Such is not our purpose.

Benson, 409 U.S. at 71. Instead, the Court made clear that it was not barring patents on computer programs, and rejected the "argu[ment] that a process patent must either be tied to a particular machine or apparatus or must operate to change articles or materials to a 'different state or thing'" in order to satisfy Section 101. *Id.* Although my colleagues now describe these statements as "equivocal," there is nothing equivocal about "We do not so hold." *Benson*, 409 U.S. at 71. Nonetheless, this court now so holds. . . .

Evolution of process patents in the United States

. . . The United States Supreme Court has never held that "process" inventions suffered a second-class status under our statutes, achieving patent eligibility only derivatively through an explicit "tie" to another statutory category. The Court has repeatedly disparaged efforts to read in restrictions not based on statutory language. See *Diehr*, 450 U.S. at 182; *Chakrabarty*, 447 U.S. at 308. Yet second-class status is today engrafted on "process" inventions. There is plainly no basis for such restriction. . . .

The now-discarded criterion of a "useful, concrete, and tangible result" has proved to be of ready and comprehensible applicability in a large variety of processes of the information and digital ages. The court in *State Street Bank* reinforced the thesis that there is no reason, in statute or policy, to exclude computer-implemented and information-based inventions from access to patentability. The holdings and reasoning of *Alappat* and *State Street Bank* guided the inventions of the electronic age into the patent system, while remaining faithful to the *Diehr* distinction between abstract ideas such as mathematical formulae and their application in a particular process for a specified purpose. And patentability has always required compliance with all of the requirements of the statute, including novelty, non-obviousness, utility, and the provisions of Section 112.

The public has relied on the rulings of this court and of the Supreme Court

The decisions in *Alappat* and *State Street Bank* confirmed the patent eligibility of many evolving areas of commerce, as inventors and investors explored new technological capabilities. The public and the economy have experienced extraordinary advances in information-based and computer-managed processes, supported by an enlarging patent base. The PTO reports that in Class 705, the examination classification associated with "business methods" and most likely to receive inventions that may not use machinery or transform physical matter, there were almost 10,000 patent applications filed in FY 2006 alone, and over 40,000 applications filed since FY 98 when State Street Bank was decided. See Wynn W. Coggins, USPTO, Update on Business Methods for the Business Methods Partnership Meeting 6 (2007) (hereinafter "PTO Report"), available at http://www.uspto.gov/web/menu/pbmethod/partnership.pps. An amicus in the present case reports that over 15,000 patents classified in Class 705 have issued. See Br. of Amicus Curiae Accenture, at 22 n.20. The industries identified with information-based and data-handling processes, as several amici curiae explain and illustrate, include fields as diverse as banking and finance, insurance, data processing, industrial engineering, and medicine.

Stable law, on which industry can rely, is a foundation of commercial advance into new products and processes. Inventiveness in the computer and information services fields has placed the United States in a position of technological and commercial preeminence. The information technology industry is reported to be "the key factor responsible for reversing the 20-year productivity slow-down from the mid-1970s to the mid-1990s and in driving today's robust productivity growth." . . . By revenue estimates, in 2005 the software and information sectors constituted the fourth largest industry in the United States, with significantly faster growth than the overall U.S. economy. . . . A Congressional Report in 2006 stated:

> As recently as 1978, intangible assets, such as intellectual property, accounted for 20 percent of corporate assets with the vast majority of value (80 percent) attributed to tangible assets such as facilities and equipment. By 1997, the trend reversed; 73 percent of corporate assets were intangible and only 27 percent were tangible.

H.R. Rep. No. 109-673 (accompanying a bill concerning judicial resources).

This powerful economic move toward "intangibles" is a challenge to the backward-looking change of this court's ruling today. Until the shift represented by today's decision, statute and precedent have provided stability in the rapidly moving and commercially vibrant fields of the Information Age. Despite the economic importance of these interests, the consequences of our decision have not been considered. I don't know how much human creativity and commercial activity will be devalued by today's change in law; but neither do my colleagues.

MAYER, Circuit Judge, dissenting.

. . . Claim 1 of the application of Bernard L. Bilski and Rand A. Warsaw ("Bilski") is not eligible for patent protection because it is directed to a method of conducting business. Affording patent protection to business methods lacks constitutional and statutory support, serves to hinder rather than promote innovation and usurps that which rightfully belongs in the public domain. *State Street* and *AT&T* should be overruled.

I.

In discussing the scope of copyright protection, the Supreme Court has noted that " 'a page of history is worth a volume of logic.' " *Eldred v. Ashcroft*, 537 U.S. 186, 200 (2003) (quoting *New York Trust Co. v. Eisner*, 256 U.S. 345, 349 (1921)). The same holds true with respect to patent protection. From a historical perspective, it is highly unlikely that the framers of the Constitution's intellectual *property clause* intended to grant patent protection to methods of conducting business. To the contrary, "those who formulated the Constitution were familiar with the long struggle over monopolies so prominent in English history, where exclusive rights to engage even in ordinary business activities were granted so frequently by the Crown for the financial benefits accruing to the Crown only." *In re Yuan*, 188 F.2d 377, 380 (CCPA 1951). The Statute of Monopolies, enacted in 1624, curtailed the Crown's ability to grant "monopolies to court favorites in goods or businesses which had long before been enjoyed by the public." *Graham v. John Deere Co.*, 383 U.S. 1, 5 (1966). When drafting the Constitution, the framers were well aware of the abuses that led to the English Statute of Monopolies and therefore "consciously acted to bar Congress from granting letters patent in particular types of business." *In re Comiskey*, 499 F.3d 1365, 1375 (Fed. Cir. 2007); see also Malla Pollack, The Multiple Unconstitutionality of Business Method Patents: Common Sense, Congressional Consideration, and Constitutional History, 28 Rutgers Computer & Tech. L.J. 61, 90 (2002) ("[T]he ratifying generation did not agree to invention patents on advances in trade itself, because trade monopolies were odious.").

There is nothing in the early patent statutes to indicate that Congress intended business methods to constitute patentable subject matter. . . . By 1952, when Congress enacted the current Patent Act, it was widely acknowledged that methods of doing business were ineligible for patent protection. . . .

In passing the 1952 Act, Congress re-enacted statutory language that had long existed, thus signaling its intent to carry forward the body of case law that had developed under prior versions of the statute. Because there is nothing in the language of the 1952 Act, or its legislative history, to indicate that Congress intended to modify the rule against patenting business methods, we must presume that no change in the rule was intended. . . .

State Street's decision to jettison the prohibition against patenting methods of doing business contravenes congressional intent. Because (1) "the framers consciously acted to bar Congress from granting letters patent in particular types of business," *Comiskey*, 499 F.3d at 1375, and (2) Congress evidenced no intent to modify the long-established rule against business method patents when it enacted the 1952 Patent Act, it is hard to fathom how the issuance of patents on business methods can be supported.

II.

Business method patents have been justified, in significant measure, by a misapprehension of the legislative history of the 1952 Patent Act. In particular, proponents of such patents have asserted that the Act's legislative history states that Congress intended statutory subject matter to "include anything under the sun that is made by man." *AT&T*, 172 F.3d at 1355 (Fed. Cir. 1999) (citations and internal quotation marks omitted); see also *Diamond v. Chakrabarty*, 447 U.S. 303, 309 (1980). Read in context, however, the legislative history says no such thing. The full statement from the committee report reads: "A person may have 'invented' a machine or a manufacture, which may include anything under the sun that is made by man, but it is not necessarily patentable under section 101 unless the conditions of the title are fulfilled." S. Rep. No. 1979, 82d Cong., 2d Sess. 5 (1952) (emphasis added); H.R. Rep. No. 1923, 82d Cong., 2d Sess. 6 (1952) (emphasis added).

This statement does not support the contention that Congress intended "anything under the sun" to be patentable. To the contrary, the language supports the opposite view: a person may have "invented" anything under the sun, but it is "not necessarily patentable" unless the statutory requirements for patentability have been satisfied. Thus, the legislative history oft-cited to support business method patents undercuts, rather than supports, the notion that Congress intended to extend the scope of section 101 to encompass such methods.

Moreover, the cited legislative history is not discussing process claims at all. The quoted language is discussing "machines" and "manufactures"; it is therefore surprising that it has been thought a fit basis for allowing patents on business processes.

III.

. . . Before *State Street* led us down the wrong path, this court had rightly concluded that patents were designed to protect technological innovations, not ideas about the best way to run a business. We had thus rejected as unpatentable a method for coordinating firefighting efforts, *Patton*, 127 F.2d at 326-27, a method for deciding how salesmen should best handle customers, *In re Maucorps*, 609 F.2d 481 (CCPA 1979), and a computerized method for aiding a neurologist in diagnosing patients, *In re Meyer*, 688 F.2d 789 (CCPA 1982). We stated that patentable processes must "be in the technological arts so as to be in consonance with the Constitutional purpose to promote the progress of 'useful arts.'" *In re Musgrave*, 431 F.2d 882, 893 (CCPA 1970) (emphasis added).

Business method patents do not promote the "useful arts" because they are not directed to any technological or scientific innovation. Although business method applications may use technology — such as computers — to accomplish desired results, the innovative aspect of the claimed method is an entrepreneurial rather than a technological one. Thus, although Bilski's claimed hedging method could theoretically be implemented on a computer, that alone does not render it patentable. See *Diehr*, 450 U.S. at 192 n.14 (Patentability cannot be established by the "token" use of technology.); *Gottschalk v. Benson*, 409 U.S. 63, 64-66 (1972) (finding unpatentable a method of programming a general purpose digital computer to convert signals from binary-coded decimal to pure binary form). Where a claimed business method simply uses a known machine to do what it was designed to do, such as using a computer to gather data or perform calculations, use of that machine will not bring otherwise unpatentable subject matter within the ambit of section 101. See *Benson*, 409 U.S. at 67 (finding a process unpatentable where "[t]he mathematical procedures [could] be carried out in existing computers long in use, no new machinery being necessary"). . . .

Methods of doing business do not apply "the law of nature to a new and useful end." Because the innovative aspect of such methods is an entrepreneurial rather than a technological one, they should be deemed ineligible for patent protection. "[T]he primary purpose of our patent laws is not the creation of private fortunes for the owners of patents but is 'to promote the progress of science and useful arts.'" *Motion Picture Patents Co. v. Universal Film Mfg. Co.*, 243 U.S. 502, 511 (1917). Although business method patents may do much to enrich their owners, they do little to promote scientific research and technological innovation. . . .

V.

The majority's proposed "machine-or-transformation test" for patentability will do little to stem the growth of patents on non-technological methods and ideas. Quite simply, in the context of business method patent applications, the majority's proposed standard can be too easily circumvented. . . . Through clever draftsmanship, nearly every process claim can be rewritten to include a physical transformation. Bilski, for example, could simply add a requirement that a commodity consumer install a meter to record commodity consumption. He could then argue that installation of this meter was a "physical transformation," sufficient to satisfy the majority's proposed patentability test. . . .

Regardless of whether a claimed process involves a "physical transformation," it should not be patent eligible unless it is directed to an advance in science or technology. See *Benson*, 409 U.S. at 64-71 (finding a process unpatentable even though it "transformed" binary-coded decimals into pure binary numbers using a general purpose computer). Although the Supreme Court has stated that a patentable process will usually involve a transformation of physical matter, see *id.* at 70, it has never found a process patent eligible which did not involve a scientific or technological innovation. See *Diehr*, 450 U.S. at 192-93 (finding a process patentable where it involved new technology for curing rubber). . . .

Unlike a technological standard for patentability, the majority's proposed test will be exceedingly difficult to apply. The standard that the majority proposes for inclusion in the patentability lexicon — "transformation of any physical object or substance, or an electronic signal representative of any physical object or substance," ante at 28 — is unnecessarily complex and will only lead to further uncertainty regarding the scope of patentable subject matter. As noted in *In re Nuijten*, 500 F.3d 1346, 1353 (Fed. Cir. 2007), defining the term "physical" can be an "esoteric and metaphysical" inquiry. Indeed, although this court has struggled for years to set out what constitutes sufficient physical transformation to render a process patentable, we have yet to provide a consistent or satisfactory resolution of this issue.

We took this case en banc in a long-overdue effort to resolve primal questions on the metes and bounds of statutory subject matter. The patent system has run amok, and the USPTO, as well as the larger patent community, has actively sought guidance from this court in making sense of our section 101 jurisprudence. . . . The majority, however, fails to enlighten three of the thorniest issues in the patentability thicket: (1) the continued viability of business method patents, (2) what constitutes sufficient physical transformation or machine-implementation to render a process patentable, and (3) the extent to which computer software and computer-implemented processes constitute statutory subject matter. The majority's "measured approach" to the section 101 analysis, will do little to restore public confidence in the patent system or stem the growth of patents on business methods and other non-technological ideas.

VI.

Where the advance over the prior art on which the applicant relies to make his invention patentable is an advance in a field of endeavor such as law (like the arbitration method in *Comiskey*), business (like the method claimed by Bilski) or other liberal — as opposed to technological — arts, the application falls outside the ambit of patentable subject matter. The time is ripe to repudiate *State Street* and to recalibrate the standards for patent eligibility, thereby ensuring that the patent system can fulfill its constitutional mandate to protect and promote truly useful innovations in science and technology. I dissent from the majority's failure to do so.

[The dissenting opinion of Judge RADER is omitted.]

COMMENTS AND QUESTIONS

1. How does the majority of the Federal Circuit court define "process" in the context of 35 U.S.C. §101 in *Bilski*? What is excluded from the concept, according to the majority? Why?

2. What is the "machine-or-transformation" test? How does it apply to the invention claimed in *Bilski*?

3. What is the relationship between §§101, 102 and 103 of Title 35 according to the *Bilksi* court? Is there a disagreement between the majority and dissenting judges on this point?

4. Is there any way to reconcile the Federal Circuit court's decision in *Bilski* with *State Street*?

5. On what grounds does Judge Newman's dissent disagree with the majority's holding in *Bilski*? Do you find Judge Newman's position convincing?

6. What does Judge Newman mean by saying: "Uncertainty is the enemy of innovation"?

7. Judge Mayer suggests that the majority has failed to resolve key issues relating to the continued viability of business method patents and the extent to which software and software-implemented processes constitute patentable subject matter under 35 U.S.C. §101. Do you agree? How would you resolve these issues as a matter of policy? Is this a task for the courts, Congress, or the USPTO?

8. Does the *Bilski* case provide any useful guidance as to the future of Internet business method patents or patents claimed over software-related inventions?

9. In June 2009, the Supreme Court of the United States granted certiorari in *Bilski* so it is possible that a more cohesive view on the patentability of software related business methods will emerge in coming years in the United States. How do you think the Supreme Court should rule on this issue? Why?

10. In contrast to the American law on patentability of computer software and Internet business methods, the European approach has been much more cautious about extending patent protection in this direction. Article 52(2)(c) of the European Patent Convention specifically excludes both computer programs and business methods from the scope of patentable subject matter. However, Article 52(3) qualifies that exclusion to some

extent in providing that Article 52(2): "shall exclude patentability of the subject-matter or activities referred to in that provision only to the extent to which a European patent application or European patent relates to such subject-matter or activities *as such.*" (emphasis added). Thus, it is still technically possible in Europe to patent inventions that in some way incorporate software or business methods, provided that they are not regarded by the relevant patent office as software or a business method per se. How different does this approach seem in practice to the approach of Congress and the Courts to patentability of software and business methods in the United States?

Note: Trade Secrets in Cyberspace

For many innovators, particularly in science, technology, and business related fields, trade secret protection has historically been a viable alternative to patent protection. Trade secret law protects unauthorized misappropriation of a "trade secret" which is defined in the Uniform Trade Secrets Act to mean: "information, including a formula, pattern, compilation, program device, method, technique, or process, that: (i) derives independent economic value, actual or potential, from not being generally known to, and not being readily ascertainable by proper means by, other persons who can obtain economic value from its disclosure or use, and (ii) is the subject of efforts that are reasonable under the circumstances to maintain its secrecy." Uniform Trade Secrets Act, §1(4).

The advantages of relying on trade secrecy rather than patent protection are that trade secrecy is immediate and inexpensive as compared to applying for a patent. A trade secret can also last indefinitely provided that its secrecy can be maintained, unlike a patent which generally expires after 20 years. Trade secrets also cover information that is not novel or that may be obvious, such as customer and supplier lists, and day-to-day business policies and procedures. An innovator needs to take these issues into account and weigh up the likelihood and costs of obtaining a patent versus any potential benefits in relying on trade secrecy.

The challenge for trade secret law in the digital age is that much valuable information is now stored and distributed digitally. As digital formats can be easier to hack into than information locked in a physical filing cabinet in the real world, questions have arisen as to whether trade secrets law needs to be revised to take into account the realities of digital information storage and transmission. See discussion in Elizabeth Rowe, *Introducing a Take-Down for Trade Secrets on the Internet*, 2007 Wis. L. Rev. 1041 (2007); Elizabeth Rowe, *Saving Trade Secret Disclosures on the Internet Through Sequential Preservation*, 42 Wake Forest L. Rev. 1 (2007). In Chapter 6, we consider ways in which laws that protect network owners against illegal access might incidentally protect data stored within those networks.

D. *SUI GENERIS* PROTECTION

In addition to traditional intellectual property protection, this section explores the argument that cyberspace requires the recognition of new property rights in information. For example, many online businesses are built upon providing subscribers with access to databases containing vast amounts of information. Much of this information comes from other sources and is factual. Nonetheless, compiling the information in one location is both a costly and valuable enterprise. To what extent can others use that information without the authorization of the database owner? Can information be considered property outside the context of trademark, copyright, patent and trade secrets law?

There is no legislation in the United States that specifically protects property rights in databases as such. However, other non-U.S. jurisdictions have created such protections. In 1996, the European Union enacted the EU Directive on the Legal Protection of Databases, which will be examined *infra*. The Directive protects databases that result from the compiler's "substantial investment" where the selection or arrangement of the information is the compiler's own work. It provides protection for the EU country citizens. The *sui generis* right set forth in the Directive was based upon the catalogue rule in Scandinavian countries, which protects against unauthorized reproduction of a catalogue, table, or similar matter in which a large number of information items have been compiled. Originality is not a requirement. As you study the following materials, consider whether there is a need for such a law in the United States. Are there alternatives to legal regulation here? For example, might contractual licenses or technology provide appropriate solutions? Some of these alternatives will be examined in more detail in Chapter 7 (private ordering of cyberspace).

Problem 9.0

At a recent business luncheon for "General Counsel of Technology Firms," the General Counsel for a large online research company approached you to ask for your support. As a frequent user of his company's services, you know that such company provides one of the largest collections of legal research materials. In fact, since StarttUp does not want to spend money purchasing a library of books, you used this company's services to perform much of your legal research. However, with the rapid growth of the Internet, you are also aware that there are increasingly more Web sites that offer similar services. And, because many of these competing services are free, you often turn to them first.

The other General Counsel explains that the competing Web sites are hurting his business unfairly. Apparently, some of these sites subscribe to his service, download what they want, and then turn around and make those documents available to the public. He notes that several law professors are especially guilty of this, creating Internet law databases freely

---

available over the Internet. If this continues, he warns that his company may not be able to stay in business much longer, and the legal community will lose an important resource for legal research. He is thinking of forming a group to lobby Congress for a law that will protect the work of database compilers. He asks for your thoughts as to whether this is a good idea and, if so, how you think the law should be drafted.

Problem 9.1

Cora has approached you because someone has recently told her about the European Union Database Directive that creates intellectual property rights in databases and compilations—see *infra*. As you know, she has recently raised some concerns about unauthorized copying of GOL blog entries by bloggers on other blogs. She now seeks your advice as to whether she might be able to utilize the Database Directive as a weapon against these copyists as well as, or instead of, copyright law.

---

1. Constitutional Framework

FEIST PUBLICATIONS, INC. V. RURAL TELEPHONE SERV. CO.

499 U.S. 340 (1991)

Justice O'CONNOR delivered the opinion of the Court. . . .

I

Rural Telephone Service Company, Inc., is a certified public utility that provides telephone service to several communities in northwest Kansas. . . . [A]s a condition of its monopoly franchise, Rural publishes a typical telephone directory, consisting of white pages and yellow pages. . . . Rural distributes its directory free of charge to its subscribers, but earns revenue by selling yellow pages advertisements.

Feist Publications, Inc., is a publishing company that specializes in area-wide telephone directories. Unlike a typical directory, which covers only a particular calling area, Feist's area-wide directories cover a much larger geographical range, reducing the need to call directory assistance or consult multiple directories. The Feist directory that is the subject of this litigation covers 11 different telephone service areas in 15 counties and contains 46,878 white pages listings—compared to Rural's approximately

7,700 listings. Like Rural's directory, Feist's is distributed free of charge and includes both white pages and yellow pages. Feist and Rural compete vigorously for yellow pages advertising.

. . . To obtain white pages listings for its area-wide directory, Feist approached each of the 11 telephone companies operating in northwest Kansas and offered to pay for the right to use its white pages listings.

Of the 11 telephone companies, only Rural refused to license its listings to Feist. Rural's refusal created a problem for Feist, as omitting these listings would have left a gaping hole in its area-wide directory, rendering it less attractive to potential yellow pages advertisers. . . .

Unable to license Rural's white pages listings, Feist used them without Rural's consent. Feist began by removing several thousand listings that fell outside the geographic range of its area-wide directory, then hired personnel to investigate the 4,935 that remained. These employees verified the data reported by Rural and sought to obtain additional information. As a result, a typical Feist listing includes the individual's street address; most of Rural's listings do not. Notwithstanding these additions, however, 1,309 of the 46,878 listings in Feist's 1983 directory were identical to listings in Rural's 1982-1983 white pages. Four of these were fictitious listings that Rural had inserted into its directory to detect copying.

Rural sued for copyright infringement in the District Court for the District of Kansas taking the position that Feist, in compiling its own directory, could not use the information contained in Rural's white pages. Rural asserted that Feist's employees were obliged to travel door-to-door or conduct a telephone survey to discover the same information for themselves. . . .

II.

A.

This case concerns the interaction of two well-established propositions. The first is that facts are not copyrightable; the other, that compilations of facts generally are. Each of these propositions possesses an impeccable pedigree. That there can be no valid copyright in facts is universally understood. The most fundamental axiom of copyright law is that "[n]o author may copyright his ideas or the facts he narrates." Harper & Row, Publishers, Inc. v. Nation Enterprises, 471 U.S. 539, 556 (1985). . . . At the same time, however, it is beyond dispute that compilations of facts are within the subject matter of copyright. Compilations were expressly mentioned in the Copyright Act of 1909, and again in the Copyright Act of 1976.

There is an undeniable tension between these two propositions. Many compilations consist of nothing but raw data — i.e., wholly factual information not accompanied by any original written expression. On what basis may one claim a copyright in such a work? . . .

The key to resolving the tension lies in understanding why facts are not copyrightable. The sine qua non of copyright is originality. To qualify for copyright protection, a work must be original to the author. See *Harper & Row*, supra, at 547-549. Original, as the term is used in copyright, means only that the work was independently created by the author (as opposed to copied from other works), and that it possesses at least some minimal degree of creativity. 1 M. Nimmer & D. Nimmer, Copyright §§2.01[A], [B] (1990) (hereinafter Nimmer). To be sure, the requisite level of creativity is extremely low; even a slight amount will suffice. The vast majority of works make the grade quite easily, as they possess some creative spark, "no matter how crude, humble or obvious" it might be. Id., §1.08[C][1]. Originality does not signify novelty; a work may be original even though it closely resembles other works so long as the similarity is fortuitous, not the result of copying. To illustrate, assume that two poets, each ignorant of the other, compose identical poems. Neither work is novel, yet both are original and, hence, copyrightable. See Sheldon v. Metro-Goldwyn Pictures Corp., 81 F.2d 49, 54 (CA2 1936).

Originality is a constitutional requirement. The source of Congress' power to enact copyright laws is Article I, §8, cl. 8, of the Constitution, which authorizes Congress to "secur[e] for limited Times to Authors . . . the exclusive Right to their respective Writings." In two decisions from the late 19th century — *The Trade-Mark Cases*, 100 U.S. 82 (1879); and Burrow-Giles Lithographic Co. v. Sarony, 111 U.S. 53 (1884) — this Court defined the crucial terms "authors" and "writings." In so doing, the Court made it unmistakably clear that these terms presuppose a degree of originality. . . .

It is this bedrock principle of copyright that mandates the law's seemingly disparate treatment of facts and factual compilations. "No one may claim originality as to facts." Id., §2.11[A], p. 2-157. This is because facts do not owe their origin to an act of authorship. The distinction is one between creation and discovery: The first person to find and report a particular fact has not created the fact; he or she has merely discovered its existence. To borrow from *Burrow-Giles*, one who discovers a fact is not its "maker" or "originator." 111 U.S., at 58. . . .

Factual compilations, on the other hand, may possess the requisite originality. The compilation author typically chooses which facts to include, in what order to place them, and how to arrange the collected data so that they may be used effectively by readers. These choices as to selection and arrangement, so long as they are made independently by the compiler and entail a minimal degree of creativity, are sufficiently original that Congress may protect such compilations through the copyright laws. Nimmer §§2.11[D], 3.03; Denicola 523, n. 38. Thus, even a directory that contains absolutely no protectible written expression, only facts, meets the constitutional minimum for copyright protection if it features an original selection or arrangement. See *Harper & Row*, 471 U.S., at 547. Accord, Nimmer §3.03.

This protection is subject to an important limitation. The mere fact that a work is copyrighted does not mean that every element of the work may be protected. Originality remains the sine qua non of copyright; accordingly, copyright protection may extend only to those components of a work that are original to the author. . . . Thus, if the compilation author clothes facts with an original collocation of words, he or she may be able to claim a copyright in this written expression. Others may copy the underlying facts from the publication, but not the precise words used to present them. . . . Where the compilation author adds no written expression but rather lets the facts speak for themselves, the expressive element is more elusive. The only conceivable expression is the manner in which the compiler has selected and arranged the facts. Thus, if the selection and arrangement are original, these elements of the work are eligible for copyright protection. . . . No matter how original the format, however, the facts themselves do not become original through association. . . .

This inevitably means that the copyright in a factual compilation is thin. Notwithstanding a valid copyright, a subsequent compiler remains free to use the facts contained in another's publication to aid in preparing a competing work, so long as the competing work does not feature the same selection and arrangement. As one commentator explains it: "[N]o matter how much original authorship the work displays, the facts and ideas it exposes are free for the taking. . . . [T]he very same facts and ideas may be divorced from the context imposed by the author, and restated or reshuffled by second comers, even if the author was the first to discover the facts or to propose the ideas." Ginsburg 1868.

It may seem unfair that much of the fruit of the compiler's labor may be used by others without compensation. As Justice Brennan has correctly observed, however, this is not "some unforeseen byproduct of a statutory scheme." *Harper & Row*, 471 U.S., at 589, (dissenting opinion). It is, rather, "the essence of copyright," ibid., and a constitutional requirement. The primary objective of copyright is not to reward the labor of authors, but "[t]o promote the Progress of Science and useful Arts." Art. I, §8, cl. 8. Accord, Twentieth Century Music Corp. v. Aiken, 422 U.S. 151, 156 (1975). To this end, copyright assures authors the right to their original expression, but encourages others to build freely upon the ideas and information conveyed by a work. *Harper & Row*, supra, 471 U.S., at 556-557. This principle, known as the idea/expression or fact/expression dichotomy, applies to all works of authorship. As applied to a factual compilation, assuming the absence of original written expression, only the compiler's selection and arrangement may be protected; the raw facts may be copied at will. This result is neither unfair nor unfortunate. It is the means by which copyright advances the progress of science and art. . . .

B

As we have explained, originality is a constitutionally mandated prerequisite for copyright protection. The Court's decisions announcing this rule predate the Copyright Act of 1909, but ambiguous language in the 1909 Act caused some lower courts temporarily to lose sight of this requirement. . . .

[T]hese courts developed a new theory to justify the protection of factual compilations. Known alternatively as "sweat of the brow" or "industrious collection," the underlying notion was that copyright was a reward for the hard work that went into compiling facts. The classic formulation of the doctrine appeared in *Jeweler's Circular Publishing Co.*, 281 F., at 88:

> "The right to copyright a book upon which one has expended labor in its preparation does not depend upon whether the materials which he has collected consist or not of matters which are publici juris, or whether such materials show literary skill or originality, either in thought or in language, or anything more than industrious collection. The man who goes through the streets of a town and puts down the names of each of the inhabitants, with their occupations and their street number, acquires material of which he is the author." . . .

The "sweat of the brow" doctrine had numerous flaws, the most glaring being that it extended copyright protection in a compilation beyond selection and arrangement — the compiler's original contributions — to the facts themselves. Under the doctrine, the only defense to infringement was independent creation. A subsequent compiler was "not entitled to take one word of information previously published," but rather had to "independently wor[k] out the matter for himself, so as to arrive at the same result from the same common sources of information." Id., at 88-89 (internal quotation marks omitted). "Sweat of the brow" courts thereby eschewed the most fundamental axiom of copyright law — that no one may copyright facts or ideas. . . .

Without a doubt, the "sweat of the brow" doctrine flouted basic copyright principles. Throughout history, copyright law has "recognize[d] a greater need to disseminate factual works than works of fiction or fantasy." *Harper & Row*, 471 U.S., at 563. Accord, Gorman, *Fact or Fancy: The Implications for Copyright*, 29 J. Copyright Soc. 560, 563 (1982). But "sweat of the brow" courts took a contrary view; they handed out proprietary interests in facts and declared that authors are absolutely precluded from saving time and effort by relying upon the facts contained in prior works. In truth, "[i]t is just such wasted effort that the proscription against the copyright of ideas and facts . . . [is] designed to prevent." Rosemont Enterprises, Inc. v. Random House, Inc., 366 F.2d 303, 310 (CA2 1966), cert. denied, 385 U.S. 1009 (1967). "Protection for the fruits of such research . . . may in certain circumstances be available under a theory of unfair competition. But to accord copyright protection on this basis alone distorts basic copyright principles in that it creates a monopoly in public domain materials without the necessary justification of protecting and encouraging the creation of 'writings' by 'authors.' " Nimmer §3.04, p. 3-23 (footnote omitted).

[The Court's discussion of the 1976 Copyright Act is omitted.]

III

There is no doubt that Feist took from the white pages of Rural's directory a substantial amount of factual information. At a minimum, Feist copied the names, towns, and telephone numbers of 1,309 of Rural's subscribers. Not all copying, however, is copyright infringement. To establish infringement, two elements must be proven: (1) ownership of a valid copyright, and (2) copying of constituent elements of the work that are original. . . .

The question is whether Rural has proved the second element. In other words, did Feist, by taking 1,309 names, towns, and telephone numbers from Rural's white pages, copy anything that was "original" to Rural? Certainly, the raw data does not satisfy the originality requirement. Rural may have been the first to discover and report the names, towns, and telephone numbers of its subscribers, but this data does not " 'ow[e] its origin' " to Rural. . . .

The question that remains is whether Rural selected, coordinated, or arranged these uncopyrightable facts in an original way. As mentioned, originality is not a stringent standard; it does not require that facts be presented in an innovative or surprising way. It is equally true, however, that the selection and arrangement of facts cannot be so mechanical or routine as to require no creativity whatsoever. The standard of originality is low, but it does exist. . . .

The selection, coordination, and arrangement of Rural's white pages do not satisfy the minimum constitutional standards for copyright protection. As mentioned at the outset, Rural's white pages are entirely typical. Persons desiring telephone service in Rural's service area fill out an application and Rural issues them a telephone number. In preparing its white pages, Rural simply takes the data provided by its subscribers and lists it alphabetically by surname. The end product is a garden-variety white pages directory, devoid of even the slightest trace of creativity.

Rural's selection of listings could not be more obvious: It publishes the most basic information — name, town, and telephone number — about each person who applies to it for telephone service. This is "selection" of a sort, but it lacks the modicum of creativity necessary to transform mere selection into copyrightable expression. Rural expended sufficient effort to make the white pages directory useful, but insufficient creativity to make it original.

We note in passing that the selection featured in Rural's white pages may also fail the originality requirement for another reason. Feist points out that Rural did not truly "select" to publish the names and telephone numbers of its subscribers; rather, it was required to do so by the Kansas Corporation Commission as part of its monopoly franchise. See 737 F. Supp., at 612. Accordingly, one could plausibly conclude that this selection was dictated by state law, not by Rural.

Nor can Rural claim originality in its coordination and arrangement of facts. The white pages do nothing more than list Rural's subscribers in alphabetical order. This arrangement may, technically speaking, owe its origin to Rural; no one disputes that Rural undertook the task of alphabetizing the names itself. But there is nothing remotely creative about arranging names alphabetically in a white pages directory. It is an age-old practice, firmly rooted in tradition and so commonplace that it has come to be expected as a matter of course. . . . It is not only unoriginal, it is practically inevitable. This time-honored tradition does not possess the minimal creative spark required by the Copyright Act and the Constitution. . . .

COMMENTS AND QUESTIONS

1. According to the Supreme Court, why is "sweat of the brow" an insufficient justification for protecting compilations of fact? How did Rural's publication lack even the minimal level of creativity necessary to prevent the wholesale duplication of its directory? Would *Feist* have been decided differently if Rural's directory at issue had been organized by religious affiliation?

2. In light of *Feist*, could Congress amend the Copyright Act to provide greater protection for compilations? If Congress cannot protect compilations under Article I, §8 of the U.S. Constitution, could Congress create *sui generis* protection under the Commerce Clause? *Consider* In re Trademark Cases, 100 U.S. 82 (1879) (holding that Congress could not protect trademarks under either clause using the pre–New Deal Commerce Clause analysis). For arguments that Congress cannot create exclusive rights in compilations even under the Commerce Clause, see Malla Pollack, *Unconstitutional Incontestability? The Intersection of the Intellectual Property and Commerce Clauses of the Constitution: Beyond a Critique of Shakespeare Co. v. Silstar Corp.*, 18 Seattle U. L. Rev. 259 (1995) (arguing that the Intellectual Property Clause limits government's ability to create exclusive rights); Yochai Benkler, *Constitutional Bounds of Database Protection: the Role of Judicial Review in the Creation and Definition of Private Rights in Information*, 15 Berkeley Tech. L.J. 535 (2000) (same); Paul J. Heald & Suzanna Sherry, *Implied Limits on the Legislative Power: The Intellectual Property Clause as an Absolute Constraint on Congress*, 2000 U. Ill. L. Rev. 1119 (same).

3. If you were legal counsel for a provider of database information to businesses, what advice would you render to your client concerning possible alternative forms of legal protection for your valuable commercial information?

4. Subsequent to the *Feist* decision, the Canadian Federal Court of Appeals noted, in the context of a debate as to the copyrightability of compilations of certain legal research materials, that Canada does not follow the copyright law of the United States in terms of the standard of originality required to protect compilations of information. In CCH Canadian Ltd v. Law Society of Upper Canada, [2002] 4 F.C. 213, 2002 FCA 187, *http://www.canlii.org/ca/cas/fca/2002/2002fca187.html*, Judge Lingren noted that:

> [T]he American threshold for copyright protection, which [the trial judge] mistakenly adopted, does contain requirements of both originality and creativity. United States court

decisions must be scrutinized very carefully because of some fundamental differences in copyright concepts. The Trial Judge failed to conduct any substantive analysis of the American standard of originality. Therefore, by holding "imagination" or "creative spark" was essential to "originality" he inadvertently entangled the American standard with the Canadian touchstone of originality. There is no universal requirement of "creative spark" or "imagination" in Anglo-Canadian copyright law. Clearly, the crucial requirement for a finding of originality is that the work be more than a mere copy.

Do the divergences of judicial opinion on the standard of originality required to copyright a compilation create problems in cyberspace? Consider the increasingly global reach of the Internet.

5.   Should the United States Congress or judiciary revisit its position on the test for copyrighting compilations? How much of the problem is caused by the fact that the strongest American authority on the copyrightability of compilations (*Feist*) deals with one of the least "creative" compilations that could exist — i.e., a white pages telephone directory with subscriber numbers listed alphabetically? If the *Feist* court had given more guidance as to where the bar was to be placed to determine originality in compilations for copyright purposes, would there be less of a problem today? It would, in fact, appear that the *Feist* court felt that the bar should be set relatively low, without giving any precise guidance as to where that line was to be drawn. In delivering the opinion of the court in *Feist*, Judge O'Connor noted:

> Originality requires only that the author make the selection or arrangement independently (i.e., without copying that selection or arrangement from another work), and that it display some minimal level of creativity. Presumably, the vast majority of compilations will pass this test, but not all will. There remains a narrow category of works in which the creative spark is utterly lacking or so trivial as to be virtually non-existent. . . . Such works are incapable of sustaining a valid copyright.

Feist, 499 U.S. 340, 358-59 (1991). Could Congress or the American judiciary work from these comments to create clearer guidelines on the copyrightability of compilations of information, particularly electronic compilations whose value is in their comprehensiveness and ease of searching, rather than in any originality in the selection or arrangement of their contents?

2. Factual Information as Property

INTERNATIONAL NEWS SERVICE v. ASSOCIATED PRESS

248 U.S. 215 (1918)

Mr. Justice PITNEY delivered the opinion of the Court.

The parties are competitors in the gathering and distribution of news and its publication for profit in newspapers throughout the United States. The Associated Press, which was complainant in the District Court, is a co-operative organization, incorporated under the Membership Corporations Law of the state of New York, its members being individuals who are either proprietors or representatives of about 950 daily newspapers published in all parts of the United States. . . . Complainant gathers in all parts of the world, by means of various instrumentalities of its own, by exchange with its members, and by other appropriate means, news and intelligence of current and recent events of interest to newspaper readers and distributes it daily to its members for publication in their newspapers. The cost of the service, amounting approximately to $3,500,000 per annum, is assessed upon the members and becomes a part of their costs of operation, to be recouped, presumably with profit, through the publication of their several newspapers. . . . And each member is required to gather the local news of his district and supply it to the Associated Press and to no one else.

Defendant is a corporation organized under the laws of the state of New Jersey, whose business is the gathering and selling of news to its customers and clients, consisting of newspapers published throughout the United States, under contracts by which they pay certain amounts at stated times for defendant's service. It has widespread news-gathering agencies; the cost of its operations amounts, it is said, to more than $2,000,000 per annum; and it serves about 400 newspapers located in the various cities of the United States and abroad, a few of which are represented, also, in the membership of the Associated Press.

The parties are in the keenest competition between themselves in the distribution of news throughout the United States; and so, as a rule, are the newspapers that they serve, in their several districts. . . .

The bill was filed to restrain the pirating of complainant's news by defendant in three ways: First, by bribing employees of newspapers published by complainant's members to furnish Associated Press news to defendant before publication, for transmission by telegraph and telephone to defendant's clients for publication by them; second, by inducing Associated Press members to violate its by-laws and permit defendant to obtain news before publication; and, third, by copying news from bulletin boards and from early editions of complainant's newspapers and selling this, either bodily or after rewriting it, to defendant's customers. . . .

The only matter that has been argued before us is whether defendant may lawfully be restrained from appropriating news taken from bulletins issued by complainant or any of its members, or from newspapers published by them, for the purpose of selling it to defendant's clients. Complainant asserts that defendant's admitted course of conduct in this regard both violates complainant's property right in the news and constitutes unfair competition in business. And notwithstanding the case has proceeded only to the stage of a preliminary injunction, we have deemed it proper to consider the underlying questions, since they go to the very merits of the action and are presented upon facts that are not in dispute. As presented in argument, these questions are: (1) Whether there is any property in news; (2) Whether, if there be property in news collected for the purpose of being published, it survives the instant of its publication in the first newspaper to which it is communicated by the news-gatherer; and (3) whether defendant's admitted course of conduct in appropriating for commercial use matter taken from bulletins or early editions of Associated Press publications constitutes unfair competition in trade. . . .

In considering the general question of property in news matter, it is necessary to recognize its dual character, distinguishing between the substance of the information and the particular form or collocation of words in which the writer has communicated it.

No doubt news articles often possess a literary quality, and are the subject of literary property at the common law; nor do we question that such an article, as a literary production, is the subject of copyright by the terms of the act as it now stands. . . .

But the news element—the information respecting current events contained in the literary production—is not the creation of the writer, but is a report of matters that ordinarily are publici juris; it is the history of the day. It is not to be supposed that the framers of the Constitution, when they empowered Congress "to promote the progress of science and useful arts, by securing for limited times to authors and inventors the exclusive right to their respective writings and discoveries" (Const. art. 1, §8, par. 8), intended to confer upon one who might happen to be the first to report a historic event the exclusive right for any period to spread the knowledge of it.

We need spend no time, however, upon the general question of property in news matter at common law, or the application of the copyright act, since it seems to us the case must turn upon the question of unfair competition in business. And, in our opinion, this does not depend upon any general right of property analogous to the common-law right of the proprietor of an unpublished work to prevent its publication without his consent; nor is it foreclosed by showing that the benefits of the copyright act have been waived. We are dealing here not with restrictions upon publication but with the very facilities and processes of publication. The peculiar value of news is in the spreading of it while it is fresh; and it is evident that a valuable property interest in the news, as news, cannot be maintained by keeping it secret. Besides, except for matters improperly disclosed, or published in breach of trust or confidence, or in violation of law, none of which is involved in this stance of the case, the news of current events may be regarded as common property. What we are concerned with is the business of making it known to the world, in which both parties to the present suit are engaged. . . . The parties are competitors in this field; and, on fundamental principles, applicable here as elsewhere, when the rights or privileges of the one are liable to conflict with those of the other, each party is under a duty so to conduct its own business as not unnecessarily or unfairly to injure that of the other. . . .

Obviously, the question of what is unfair competition in business must be determined with particular reference to the character and circumstances of the business. The question here is not so much the rights of either party as against the public but their rights as between themselves. . . . Regarding the news, therefore, as but the material out of which both parties are seeking to make profits at the same time and in the same field, we hardly can fail to recognize that for this purpose, and as between them, it must be regarded as quasi property, irrespective of the rights of either as against the public. . . .

Not only do the acquisition and transmission of news require elaborate organization and a large expenditure of money, skill, and effort; not only has it an exchange value to the gatherer, dependent chiefly upon its novelty and freshness, the regularity of the service, its reputed reliability and thoroughness, and its adaptability to the public needs; but also, as is evident, the news has an exchange value to one who can misappropriate it.

The peculiar features of the case arise from the fact that, while novelty and freshness form so important an element in the success of the business, the very processes of distribution and publication necessarily occupy a good deal of time. Complainant's service, as well as defendant's, is a daily service to daily newspapers; most of the foreign news reaches this country at the Atlantic seaboard, principally at the city of New York, and because of this, and of time differentials due to the earth's rotation, the distribution of news matter throughout the country is principally from east to west; and, since in speed the telegraph and telephone easily outstrip the rotation of the earth, it is a simple matter for defendant to take complainant's news from bulletins or early editions of complainant's members in the eastern cities and at the mere cost of telegraphic transmission cause it to be published in western papers issued at least as early as those served by complainant. Besides this, and irrespective of time differentials, irregularities in telegraphic transmission on different lines, and the normal consumption of time in printing and distributing the newspaper, result in permitting pirated news to be placed in the hands of defendant's readers sometimes simultaneously with the service of competing Associated Press papers, occasionally even earlier.

Defendant insists that when, with the sanction and approval of complainant, and as the result of the use of its news for the very purpose for which it is distributed, a portion of complainant's members communicate it to the general public by posting it upon bulletin boards so that all may read, or by issuing it to newspapers and distributing it indiscriminately, complainant no longer has the right to control the use to be made of it; that when it thus reaches the light of day it becomes the common possession of all to whom it is accessible; and that any purchaser of a newspaper has the right to communicate the intelligence which it contains to anybody and for any purpose, even for the purpose of selling it for profit to newspapers published for profit in competition with complainant's members.

The fault in the reasoning lies in applying as a test the right of the complainant as against the public, instead of considering the rights of complainant and defendant, competitors in business, as between themselves. The right of the purchaser of a single newspaper to spread knowledge of its contents gratuitously, for any legitimate purpose not unreasonably interfering with complainant's right to make merchandise of it, may be admitted; but to transmit that news for commercial use, in competition with complainant — which is what defendant has done and seeks to justify — is a very different matter. In doing this defendant, by its very act, admits that it is taking material that has been acquired by complainant as the result of organization and the expenditure of labor, skill, and money, and which is salable by complainant for money, and that defendant in appropriating it and selling it as its own is endeavoring to reap where it has not sown, and by disposing of it to newspapers that are competitors of complainant's members is appropriating to itself the harvest of those who have sown. Stripped of all disguises, the process amounts to an unauthorized interference with the normal operation of complainant's legitimate business precisely at the point where the profit is to be reaped, in order to divert a material portion of the profit from those who have earned it to those who have not; with special advantage to defendant in the competition because of the fact that it is not burdened with any part of the expense of gathering the news. The transaction speaks for itself and a court of equity ought not to hesitate long in characterizing it as unfair competition in business. . . .

It is to be observed that the view we adopt does not result in giving to complainant the right to monopolize either the gathering or the distribution of the news, or, without complying with the copyright act, to prevent the reproduction of its news articles, but only postpones participation by complainant's competitor in the processes of distribution and reproduction of news that it has not gathered, and only to the extent necessary to prevent that competitor from reaping the fruits of complainant's efforts and expenditure, to the partial exclusion of complainant, and in violation of the principle that underlies the maxim "sic utere tuo," etc. . . .

The decree of the Circuit court of Appeals will be Affirmed.

Mr. Justice CLARKE took no part in the consideration or decision of this case.

[The dissenting opinion of HOLMES, J., in which McKENNA, J., concurred is omitted.]

Mr. Justice Brandeis, dissenting.

. . . News is a report of recent occurrences. The business of the news agency is to gather systematically knowledge of such occurrences of interest and to distribute reports thereof. The Associated Press contended that knowledge so acquired is property, because it costs money and labor to produce and because it has value for which those who have it not are ready to pay; that it remains property and is entitled to protection as long as it has commercial value as news; and that to protect it effectively, the defendant must be enjoined from making, or causing to be made, any gainful use of it while it retains such value. . . . But the fact that a product of the mind has cost its producer money and labor, and has a value for which others are willing to pay, is not sufficient to ensure to it this legal attribute of property. The general rule of law is, that the noblest of human productions — knowledge, truths ascertained, conceptions, and ideas — became, after voluntary communication to others, free as the air to common use. Upon these incorporeal productions the attribute of property is continued after such communication only in certain classes of cases where public policy has seemed to demand it. These exceptions are confined to productions which, in some degree, involve creation, invention, or discovery. But by no means all such are endowed with this attribute of property. The creations which are recognized as property by the common law are literary, dramatic, musical, and other artistic creations; and these have also protection under the copyright statutes. The inventions and discoveries upon which this attribute of property is conferred only by statute, are the few comprised within the patent law. . . .

The knowledge for which protection is sought in the case at bar is not of a kind upon which the law has heretofore conferred the attributes of property; nor is the manner of its acquisition or use nor the purpose to which it is applied, such as has heretofore been recognized as entitling a plaintiff to relief. . . .

Plaintiff further contended that defendant's practice constitutes unfair competition, because there is "appropriation without cost to itself of values created by" the plaintiff; and it is upon this ground that the decision of this court appears to be based. To appropriate and use for profit, knowledge and ideas produced by other men, without making compensation or even acknowledgment, may be inconsistent with a finer sense of propriety; but, with the exceptions indicated above, the law has heretofore sanctioned the practice. . . .

Such taking and gainful use of a product of another which, for reasons of public policy, the law has refused to endow with the attributes of property, does not become unlawful because the product happens to have been taken from a rival and is used in competition with him. The unfairness in competition which hitherto has been recognized by the law as a basis for relief, lay in the manner or means of conducting the business; and the manner or means held legally unfair, involves either fraud or force or the doing of acts otherwise prohibited by law. . . .

That competition is not unfair in a legal sense, merely because the profits gained are unearned, even if made at the expense of a rival, is shown by many cases besides those referred to above. He who follows the pioneer into a new market, or who engages in the manufacture of an article newly introduced by another, seeks profits due largely to the labor and expense of the first adventurer; but the law sanctions, indeed encourages, the pursuit. He who makes a city known through his product, must submit to sharing the resultant trade with others who, perhaps for that reason, locate there later. . . . He who has made his name a guaranty of quality, protests in vain when another with the same name engages, perhaps for that reason, in the same lines of business; provided, precaution is taken to prevent the public from being deceived into the belief that what he is selling, was made by his competitor. One bearing a name made famous by another is permitted to enjoy the unearned benefit which necessarily flows from such use, even though the use proves harmful to him who gave the name value. . . .

The means by which the International News Service obtains news gathered by the Associated Press is also clearly unobjectionable. It is taken from papers bought in the open market or from bulletins publicly posted. No breach of contract such as the court considered to exist in Hitchman Coal & Coke Co. v. Mitchell, 245 U.S. 229, 254; or of trust such as was present in Morison v. Moat, 9 Hare, 241; and neither fraud nor force is involved. The manner of use is likewise unobjectionable. No reference is made by word or by act to the Associated Press, either in transmitting the news to subscribers or by them in publishing it in their papers. Neither the International News Service nor its subscribers is gaining or seeking to gain in its business a benefit from the reputation of the Associated Press. They are merely using its product without making compensation. See Bamforth v. Douglass Post Card & Machine Co. (C.C.) 158 Fed. 355; Tribune Co. of Chicago v. Associated Press (C.C.) 116 Fed. 126. That they have a legal right to do, because the product is not property, and they do not stand in any relation to the Associated Press, either of contract or of trust, which otherwise precludes such use. The argument is not advanced by characterizing such taking and use a misappropriation. . . .

The great development of agencies now furnishing country-wide distribution of news, the vastness of our territory, and improvements in the means of transmitting intelligence, have made it possible for a news agency or newspapers to obtain, without paying compensation, the fruit of another's efforts and to use news so obtained gainfully in competition with the original collector. The injustice of such action is obvious. But to give relief against it would involve more than the application of existing rules of law to new facts. It would require the making of a new rule in analogy to existing ones. The unwritten law possesses capacity for growth; and has often satisfied new demands for justice by invoking analogies or by expanding a rule or principle. This process has been in the main wisely applied and should not be discontinued. Where the problem is relatively simple, as it is apt to be when private interests only are involved, it generally proves adequate. But with the increasing complexity of society, the public interest tends to become omnipresent; and the problems presented by new demands for justice cease to be simple. Then the creation or recognition by courts of a new private right may work serious injury to the general public, unless the boundaries of the right are definitely established and wisely guarded. In order to reconcile the new private right with the public interest, it may be necessary to prescribe limitations and rules for its enjoyment; and also to provide administrative machinery for enforcing the rules. It is largely for this reason that, in the effort to meet the many new demands for justice incident to a rapidly changing civilization, resort to legislation has latterly been had with increasing frequency. . . .

Courts are ill-equipped to make the investigations which should precede a determination of the limitations which should be set upon any property right in news or of the circumstances under which news gathered by a private agency should be deemed affected with a public interest. Courts would be powerless to prescribe the detailed regulations essential to full enjoyment of the rights conferred or to introduce the machinery required for enforcement of such regulations. Considerations such as these should lead us to decline to establish a new rule of law in the effort to redress a newly disclosed wrong, although the propriety of some remedy appears to be clear.

NATIONAL BASKETBALL ASS'N v. MOTOROLA, INC.

105 F.3d 841 (2d Cir. 1997)

WINTER, Circuit Judge:

I. BACKGROUND

The facts are largely undisputed. Motorola manufactures and markets the SportsTrax paging device while STATS supplies the game information that is transmitted to the pagers. The product became available to the public in January 1996, at a retail price of about $200. SportsTrax's pager has an inch-and-a-half by inch-and-a-half screen and operates in four basic modes: "current," "statistics," "final scores" and "demonstration." It is the "current" mode that gives rise to the present dispute. In that mode, SportsTrax displays the following information on NBA games in progress: (i) the teams playing; (ii) score changes; (iii) the team in possession of the ball; (iv) whether the team is in the free-throw bonus; (v) the quarter of the game; and (vi) time remaining in the quarter. The information is updated every two to three minutes, with more frequent updates near the end of the first half and the end of the game. There is a lag of approximately two or three minutes between events in the game itself and when the information appears on the pager screen.

SportsTrax's operation relies on a "data feed" supplied by STATS reporters who watch the games on television or listen to them on the radio. The reporters key into a personal computer changes in the score and other information such as successful and missed shots, fouls, and clock updates. The information is relayed by modem to STATS's host computer, which compiles, analyzes, and formats the data for retransmission. The information is then sent to a common carrier, which then sends it via satellite to various local FM radio networks that in turn emit the signal received by the individual SportsTrax pagers.

Although the NBA's complaint concerned only the SportsTrax device, the NBA offered evidence at trial concerning STATS's America On-Line ("AOL") site. Starting in January 1996, users who accessed STATS's AOL site, typically via a modem attached to a home computer, were provided with slightly more comprehensive and detailed real-time game information than is displayed on a SportsTrax pager. On the AOL site, game scores are updated every 15 seconds to a minute, and the player and team statistics are updated each minute. . . .

The NBA's complaint asserted six claims for relief: (i) state law unfair competition by misappropriation; (ii) false advertising under Section 43(a) of the Lanham Act, 15 U.S.C. §1125(a); (iii) false representation of origin under Section 43(a) of the Lanham Act; (iv) state and common law unfair competition by false advertising and false designation of origin; (v) federal copyright infringement; and (vi) unlawful interception of communications under the Communications Act of 1934, 47 U.S.C. §605. Motorola counterclaimed, alleging that the NBA unlawfully interfered with Motorola's contractual relations with four individual NBA teams that had agreed to sponsor and advertise SportsTrax.

The district court dismissed all of the NBA's claims except the first — misappropriation under New York law. The court also dismissed Motorola's counterclaim. . . .

II. THE STATE LAW MISAPPROPRIATION CLAIM

A. Summary of Ruling

Because our disposition of the state law misappropriation claim rests in large part on preemption by the Copyright Act, our discussion necessarily goes beyond the elements of a misappropriation claim under New York law, and a summary of our ruling here will perhaps render that discussion — or at least the need for it — more understandable.

The issues before us are ones that have arisen in various forms over the course of this century as technology has steadily increased the speed and quantity of information transmission. Today, individuals at home, at work, or elsewhere, can use a computer, pager, or other device to obtain highly selective kinds of information virtually at will. International News Service v. Associated Press, 248 U.S. 215 (1918) ("INS"), was one of the first cases to address the issues raised by these technological advances, although the technology involved in that case was primitive by contemporary standards. . . .

With the advance of technology, radio stations began "live" broadcasts of events such as baseball games and operas, and various entrepreneurs began to use the transmissions of others in one way or another for their own profit. In response, New York courts created a body of misappropriation law, loosely based on INS, that sought to apply ethical standards to the use by one party of another's transmissions of events.

Federal copyright law played little active role in this area until 1976. Before then, it appears to have been the general understanding — there being no case-law of consequence — that live events such as baseball games were not copyrightable. Moreover, doubt existed even as to whether a recorded broadcast or videotape of such an event was copyrightable. In 1976, however, Congress passed legislation expressly affording copyright protection to simultaneously-recorded broadcasts of live performances such as sports events. See 17 U.S.C. §101. Such protection was not extended to the underlying events.

The 1976 amendments also contained provisions preempting state law claims that enforced rights "equivalent" to exclusive copyright protections when the work to which the state claim was being applied fell within the area of copyright protection. See 17 U.S.C. §301. Based on legislative history of the 1976 amendments, it is generally agreed that a "hot-news" INS-like claim survives preemption. H.R. No. 94-1476 at 132 (1976), reprinted in 1976 U.S.C.C.A.N. 5659, 5748. However, much of New York misappropriation law after INS goes well beyond "hot-news" claims and is preempted.

We hold that the surviving "hot-news" INS-like claim is limited to cases where: (i) a plaintiff generates or gathers information at a cost; (ii) the information is time-sensitive; (iii) a defendant's use of the information constitutes free riding on the plaintiff's efforts; (iv) the defendant is in direct competition with a product or service offered by the plaintiffs; and (v) the ability of other parties to free-ride on the efforts of the plaintiff or others would so reduce the incentive to produce the product or service that its existence or quality would be substantially threatened. We conclude that SportsTrax does not meet that test. . . .

C. The State-Law Misappropriation Claim

The district court's injunction was based on its conclusion that, under New York law, defendants had unlawfully misappropriated the NBA's property rights in its games. The district court reached this conclusion by holding: (i) that the NBA's misappropriation claim relating to the underlying games was not preempted by Section 301 of the Copyright Act; and (ii) that, under New York common law, defendants had engaged in unlawful misappropriation. Id. at 1094-1107. We disagree.

1. Preemption Under the Copyright Act

a) Summary

When Congress amended the Copyright Act in 1976, it provided for the preemption of state law claims that are interrelated with copyright claims in certain ways. Under 17 U.S.C. §301, a state law claim is preempted when: (i) the state law claim seeks to vindicate "legal or equitable rights that are equivalent" to one of the bundle of exclusive rights already protected by copyright law under 17 U.S.C. §106—styled the "general scope requirement"; and (ii) the particular work to which the state law claim is being applied falls within the type of works protected by the Copyright Act under Sections 102 and 103—styled the "subject matter requirement."

The district court concluded that the NBA's misappropriation claim was not preempted because, with respect to the underlying games, as opposed to the broadcasts, the subject matter requirement was not met. 939 F. Supp. at 1097. The court dubbed as "partial preemption" its separate analysis of misappropriation claims relating to the underlying games and misappropriation claims relating to broadcasts of those games. *Id.* at 1098, n.24. The district court then relied on a series of older New York misappropriation cases involving radio broadcasts that considerably broadened INS. We hold that where the challenged copying or misappropriation relates in part to the copyrighted broadcasts of the games, the subject matter requirement is met as to both the broadcasts and the games. We therefore reject the partial preemption doctrine and its anomalous consequence that "it is possible for a plaintiff to assert claims both for infringement of its copyright in a broadcast and misappropriation of its rights in the underlying event." *Id.* We do find that a properly-narrowed INS "hot-news" misappropriation claim survives preemption because it fails the general scope requirement, but that the broader theory of the radio broadcast cases relied upon by the district court were preempted when Congress extended copyright protection to simultaneously-recorded broadcasts.

b) "Partial Preemption" and the Subject Matter Requirement

The subject matter requirement is met when the work of authorship being copied or misappropriated "fall[s] within the ambit of copyright protection." Harper & Row, Publishers, Inc. v. Nation Enter., 723 F.2d 195, 200 (1983), rev'd on other grounds, 471 U.S. 539 (1985). We believe that the subject matter requirement is met in the instant matter and that the concept of "partial preemption" is not consistent with Section 301 of the Copyright Act. Although game broadcasts are copyrightable while the underlying games are not, the Copyright Act should not be read to distinguish between the two when analyzing the preemption of a misappropriation claim based on copying or taking from the copyrightable work. We believe that:

> [O]nce a performance is reduced to tangible form, there is no distinction between the performance and the recording of the performance for the purposes of preemption under §301(a). Thus, if a baseball game were not broadcast or were telecast without being recorded, the Players' performances similarly would not be fixed in tangible form and their rights of publicity would not be subject to preemption. By virtue of being videotaped, however, the Players' performances are fixed in tangible form, and any rights of publicity in their performances that are equivalent to the rights contained in the copyright of the telecast are preempted.

Baltimore Orioles, 805 F.2d at 675 (citation omitted).

Copyrightable material often contains uncopyrightable elements within it, but Section 301 preemption bars state law misappropriation claims with

respect to uncopyrightable as well as copyrightable elements. In *Harper &
Row*, for example, we held that state law claims based on the copying of
excerpts from President Ford's memoirs were preempted even with respect
to information that was purely factual and not copyrightable. . . .

Adoption of a partial preemption doctrine—preemption of claims
based on misappropriation of broadcasts but no preemption of claims
based on misappropriation of underlying facts—would expand significantly
the reach of state law claims and render the preemption intended by
Congress unworkable. It is often difficult or impossible to separate the
fixed copyrightable work from the underlying uncopyrightable events or
facts. Moreover, Congress, in extending copyright protection only to the
broadcasts and not to the underlying events, intended that the latter be in
the public domain. Partial preemption turns that intent on its head by
allowing state law to vest exclusive rights in material that Congress intended
to be in the public domain and to make unlawful conduct that Congress
intended to allow. . . .

c)   The General Scope Requirement

Under the general scope requirement, Section 301 "preempts only those
state law rights that 'may be abridged by an act which, in and of itself, would
infringe one of the exclusive rights' provided by federal copyright law." Computer Assoc. Int'l, Inc. v. Altai, Inc., 982 F.2d 693, 716 (2d Cir. 1992) (quoting *Harper & Row*, 723 F.2d at 200). However, certain forms of commercial
misappropriation otherwise within the general scope requirement will survive
preemption if an "extra-element" test is met. As stated in Altai:

> But if an "extra element" is "required instead of or in addition to the acts of reproduction,
> performance, distribution or display, in order to constitute a state-created cause of action,
> then the right does not lie 'within the general scope of copyright,' and there is no
> preemption."

Id. (quoting 1 Nimmer on Copyright §1.01[B] at 1-15). . . .

We turn, therefore, to the question of the extent to which a "hot-news"
misappropriation claim based on INS involves extra elements and is not the
equivalent of exclusive rights under a copyright. Courts are generally agreed
that some form of such a claim survives preemption. Financial Information,
Inc. v. Moody's Investors Service, Inc., 808 F.2d 204, 208 (2d Cir. 1986),
cert. denied, 484 U.S. 820 (1987) ("*FII*"). This conclusion is based in part on
the legislative history of the 1976 amendments. The House Report stated:

> "Misappropriation" is not necessarily synonymous with copyright infringement, and thus
> a cause of action labeled as "misappropriation" is not preempted if it is in fact based neither
> on a right within the general scope of copyright as specified by section 106 nor on a right
> equivalent thereto. For example, state law should have the flexibility to afford a remedy

(under traditional principles of equity) against a consistent pattern of unauthorized appropriation by a competitor of the facts (i.e., not the literary expression) constituting "hot" news, whether in the traditional mold of International News Service v. Associated Press, 248 U.S. 215 [39 S. Ct. 68, 63 L. Ed. 211] (1918), or in the newer form of data updates from scientific, business, or financial data bases.

H.R. No. 94-1476 at 132, reprinted in 1976 U.S.C.C.A.N. at 5748 (footnote omitted), see also FII, 808 F.2d at 209 (" 'misappropriation' of 'hot' news, under *International News Service*, [is] a branch of the unfair competition doctrine not preempted by the Copyright Act according to the House Report" (citation omitted)). The crucial question, therefore, is the breadth of the "hot-news" claim that survives preemption. . . .

The theory of the New York misappropriation cases relied upon by the district court is considerably broader than that of INS. For example, the district court quoted at length from Metropolitan Opera Ass'n v. Wagner-Nichols Recorder Corp., 199 Misc. 786, 101 N.Y.S.2d 483 (N.Y. Sup. Ct. 1950), aff'd, 279 A.D. 632, 107 N.Y.S.2d 795 (1st Dep't 1951). *Metropolitan Opera* described New York misappropriation law as standing for the "broader principle that property rights of commercial value are to be and will be protected from any form of commercial immorality"; that misappropriation law developed "to deal with business malpractices offensive to the ethics of . . . society"; and that the doctrine is "broad and flexible." 939 F. Supp. at 1098-1110 (quoting *Metropolitan Opera*, 101 N.Y.S.2d at 492, 488-89).

However, we believe that *Metropolitan Opera*'s broad misappropriation doctrine based on amorphous concepts such as "commercial immorality" or society's "ethics" is preempted. Such concepts are virtually synonymous for wrongful copying and are in no meaningful fashion distinguishable from infringement of a copyright. The broad misappropriation doctrine relied upon by the district court is, therefore, the equivalent of exclusive rights in copyright law. . . .

Our conclusion, therefore, is that only a narrow "hot-news" misappropriation claim survives preemption for actions concerning material within the realm of copyright. . . .

INS is not about ethics; it is about the protection of property rights in time-sensitive information so that the information will be made available to the public by profit seeking entrepreneurs. If services like AP were not assured of property rights in the news they pay to collect, they would cease to collect it. The ability of their competitors to appropriate their product at only nominal cost and thereby to disseminate a competing product at a lower price would destroy the incentive to collect news in the first place. The newspaper-reading public would suffer because no one would have an incentive to collect "hot news."

We therefore find the extra elements — those in addition to the elements of copyright infringement — that allow a "hot news" claim to survive preemption are: (i) the time-sensitive value of factual information, (ii) the free-riding by a defendant, and (iii) the threat to the very existence of the product or service provided by the plaintiff.

2. The Legality of SportsTrax

We conclude that Motorola and STATS have not engaged in unlawful misappropriation under the "hot-news" test set out above. To be sure, some of the elements of a "hot-news" INS claim are met. The information transmitted to SportsTrax is not precisely contemporaneous, but it is nevertheless time-sensitive. Also, the NBA does provide, or will shortly do so, information like that available through SportsTrax. It now offers a service called "Gamestats" that provides official play-by-play game sheets and half-time and final box scores within each arena. It also provides such information to the media in each arena. In the future, the NBA plans to enhance Gamestats so that it will be networked between the various arenas and will support a pager product analogous to SportsTrax. SportsTrax will of course directly compete with an enhanced Gamestats.

However, there are critical elements missing in the NBA's attempt to assert a "hot-news" INS-type claim. As framed by the NBA, their claim compresses and confuses three different informational products. The first product is generating the information by playing the games; the second product is transmitting live, full descriptions of those games; and the third product is collecting and retransmitting strictly factual information about the games. The first and second products are the NBA's primary business: producing basketball games for live attendance and licensing copyrighted broadcasts of those games. The collection and retransmission of strictly factual material about the games is a different product: e.g., box-scores in newspapers, summaries of statistics on television sports news, and real-time facts to be transmitted to pagers. In our view, the NBA has failed to show any competitive effect whatsoever from SportsTrax on the first and second products and a lack of any free-riding by SportsTrax on the third. . . .

The NBA argues that the pager market is also relevant to a "hot-news" INS-type claim and that SportsTrax's future competition with Gamestats satisfies any missing element. We agree that there is a separate market for the real-time transmission of factual information to pagers or similar devices, such as STATS's AOL site. However, we disagree that SportsTrax is in any sense free-riding off Gamestats.

An indispensable element of an INS "hot-news" claim is free riding by a defendant on a plaintiff's product, enabling the defendant to produce a directly competitive product for less money because it has lower costs. SportsTrax is not such a product. The use of pagers to transmit real-time information about NBA games requires: (i) the collecting of facts about the games; (ii) the transmission of these facts on a network; (iii) the assembling of them by the particular service; and (iv) the transmission of them to pagers or an on-line computer site. Appellants are in no way free-riding on Gamestats. Motorola and STATS expend their own resources to collect purely factual information generated in NBA games to transmit to SportsTrax pagers. They have their own network and assemble and transmit data themselves.

To be sure, if appellants in the future were to collect facts from an enhanced Gamestats pager to retransmit them to SportsTrax pagers, that would constitute free-riding and might well cause Gamestats to be unprofitable because it had to bear costs to collect facts that SportsTrax did not. If the appropriation of facts from one pager to another pager service were allowed, transmission of current information on NBA games to pagers or similar devices would be substantially deterred because any potential transmitter would know that the first entrant would quickly encounter a lower cost competitor free-riding on the originator's transmissions. . . .

COMMENTS AND QUESTIONS

1.   What kind of protection for "hot news" does the Supreme Court recognize in *INS*? What is the basis for this form of protection? What are the limits of this protection? Is "hot news" the equivalent of "sweat of the brow"? If not, why not?

2.   How does Justice Brandeis disagree with the majority in *INS*? Does he believe that there is no protection for "hot news"? Does *INS* provide any guidance as to whether Congress can create exclusive rights in noncopyrightable expression? What are some of the reasons Justice Brandeis gives in support of his conclusion that courts in particular are ill-equipped to create new property rights in "hot news"?

3.   To what extent is *INS* preempted under copyright law? In *Motorola*, what must a plaintiff establish to state a claim for the protection of "hot news"? How do these elements differ from copyright law?

4.   What is the concept of "partial preemption"? Why did the court in *Motorola* reject partial preemption?

5.   In contrast to the concept of unfair competition, should data, regardless of its originality, be considered a form of property? *Consider* United States v. Riggs, 739 F. Supp. 414 (N.D. Ill. 1990), in which the court refused to dismiss charges against two hackers for transporting stolen goods under 18 U.S.C. §2314[30] when they obtained without authorization a computer file containing a telephone company's 911 procedures. In a motion to dismiss the charges, the defendants argued that the computer file could not be considered a good. According to the court:

The question this case presents, then, is not whether electronic impulses are "goods, wares, or merchandise" within the meaning of §2314, but whether the proprietary information contained in Bell South's E911 text file constitutes a "good, ware, or

30. 18 U.S.C. §2314, which provides, in relevant part:

Whoever transports, transmits, or transfers in interstate or foreign commerce any goods, wares, merchandise, securities or money, of the value of $5000 or more, knowing the same to have been stolen, converted or taken by fraud . . . [s]hall be fined not more than $10,000 or imprisoned not more than ten years, or both.

merchandise" within the purview of the statute. This court answers that question affirmatively. It is well-settled that when proprietary business information is affixed to some tangible medium, such as a piece of paper, it constitutes "goods, wares, or merchandise" within the meaning of §2314. . . .

Similarly, the defendants also relied upon a U.S. Supreme Court decision holding that pirated record albums did not fall under Section 2314 because copyright law did not provide the copyright owner with a legal interest that could be stolen. See Dowling v. United States, 473 U.S. 207 (1985). In rejecting this argument, the district court concluded:

> The instant case, however, is distinguishable from *Dowling* . . . This case involves the transfer of confidential, proprietary business information, not copyrights. As *Dowling* . . . recognized, the copyright holder owns only a bundle of intangible rights which can be infringed, but not stolen or converted. The owner of confidential, proprietary business information, in contrast, possesses something which has clearly been recognized as an item of *property.*

What kind of protection is afforded to information under *Riggs*? Is the district court's effort to distinguish confidential business information from copyrighted information persuasive? What is the argument that *Dowling* would preclude treatment of the E911 file as good? Under *Riggs*, would Section 2314 adequately protect the rights of database owners? On the broader question of whether information per se can amount to legal property, *see, e.g.*, Jacqueline Lipton, *Information Property: Rights and Responsibilities*, 56 Fla. L. Rev. 135 (2004); Jacqueline Lipton, *Mixed Metaphors in Cyberspace: Property in Information and Information Systems*, 35(1) Loy. U. Chi. L.J. 235 (2003); Patricia Bellia, *Defending Cyberproperty*, 79 N.Y.U. L. Rev. 2164 (2004); Michael Carrier, *Cabining Intellectual Property Through a Property Paradigm*, 54 Duke L.J. 1 (2004).

3. The EU Database Directive

In contrast to the current American approach toward protecting non-original information that relies heavily upon the concept of unfair competition, the European Union has taken steps to protect database owners. Directive 96/9/EC provides:

> Member States shall provide for a right for the maker of a database which shows that there has been qualitatively and/or quantitatively a substantial investment in either the obtaining, verification or presentation of the contents to prevent extraction and/or reutilization of the whole or of a substantial part, evaluated qualitatively and/or quantitatively, of the contents of that database.

Similarly,

> the repeated and systematic extraction and/or re-utilization of insubstantial parts of the contents of the database implying acts which conflict with a normal exploitation of that

database or which unreasonably prejudice the legitimate interests of the maker of the database shall not be permitted.

According to the Directive, this right "shall apply irrespective of the eligibility of that database for protection by copyright or by other rights. Moreover, it shall apply irrespective of eligibility of the contents of that database for protection by copyright or by other rights," and lasts 15 years from the first of January of the year following the date of the database's completion. However, subsequent additions and deletions to the database may qualify the database for a new 15-year term of protection, raising the possibility that many electronic databases will endure indefinitely provided that they are continually updated. The Database Directive has raised a number of concerns in relation to its practical operation and has led to confusion amongst European Union Member States in terms of its interpretation. In light of these confusions, and recent decisions of the European Court of Justice that conflict on significant points with national courts in EU Member States, the Commission of the European Communities issued an evaluation of the Directive that contemplates, amongst other things, significantly amending the Directive or potentially withdrawing it from operation. *See* DG Internal Market and Services Working Paper: First Evaluation of Directive 96/9/EC on the Legal Protection of Databases (Brussels, Dec. 12, 2005). The following extract summarizes some of the concerns about the operation of the Directive.

Jacqueline Lipton, Balancing Private Rights and Public Policies: Reconceptualizing Property in Databases

18 Berkeley Tech. L.J. 773 (2003)

. . .

3. The E.U. Approach

[T]he E.U. Directive is purely a proprietary rights model that expressly creates broad, generic rights in the exploitation of database contents, then carves out some fair use exemptions from liability. As set out below, there are many problems with this model. . . .

The European Union's original plan was more akin to a tort/misappropriation model that protected databases to prevent free riding in the database industry by competitors who unfairly extracted database contents. Early versions of the E.U. Directive also included provisions requiring compulsory licensing of databases that were the sole source of certain information within an industry. These provisions were designed to give database makers the head start they deserved for being the first players in the market, while allowing others to enter the market at a reasonable market cost. The provisions were not originally designed to give the database maker an exclusive property right in the fruits of its labors. However, determined lobbying by those in favor of protectionist strategies for the global information infrastructure — publishers and some E.U. and U.S. officials — successfully transformed the original E.U. proposal from "a relatively weak liability regime to a strong exclusive property right."

4. The Current E.U. Framework as Adopted in the United Kingdom

The final version of the E.U. Directive shows the advantages and disadvantages of its approach to sui generis rights in databases. Examining the operation of the Directive throughout the European Union, Professors Reichman and Samuelson have expressed various concerns:

1) The final version of the E.U. Directive moves away from notions of unfair or unauthorized uses of database contents, instead favoring the exclusive right of database makers to prevent extraction and re-use of a substantial part of a database's contents (evaluated quantitatively or qualitatively).

2) The Directive's fifteen-year term for the property right in a database can apparently be indefinitely extended.

3) The Directive does not require creativity or novel contribution to attract database protection only a substantial investment in obtaining, verifying, or presenting database contents.

4) The Directive offers no guidelines to determine the level of investment required to justify the property right in the database or to extend the duration of an existing right.

5) The Directive's database right potentially erodes the idea/expression dichotomy from copyright law.

6) The Directive's potentially unlimited term of protection, coupled with the strong proprietary nature of the protection and the lack of significant fair use exceptions to the property right, dramatically erodes the public domain and potentially over-commidifies information products.

7) The final Directive's deletion of the compulsory licensing provision for sole source providers of information creates nearly insurmountable barriers to entry for potential second-comers into information markets and secondary markets. The compulsory licensing provision had been the one aspect of government oversight contemplated in the E.U. database debate.

Looking at the way in which the E.U. Directive has been transposed into national law in various E.U. Member States, most of these concerns appear justified. For example, provisions in the United Kingdom's 1997 domestic legislative enactment — the Copyright and Rights in Databases Regulations 1997 ("CRDR") — raise precisely these concerns.

The CRDR defines a database broadly to include both paper-based and electronic databases. A "database right" is created in a database if there has been a "substantial investment in obtaining, verifying or presenting the contents of a database." Thus, in keeping with the aims of the legislation, there is no reference to creativity or innovation other than that required in section 3A(2) of the CDPA in relation to copyright protection for a database.

A person infringes a database right if that person extracts or reutilizes all or a substantial part of the contents of a database without the consent of the owner of the database right. In this context, the repeated and systematic extraction or reutilization of insubstantial parts of a database's contents may amount to the extraction or reutilization of a substantial part of those contents.

CDPA appears to give strong proprietary rights to database makers' The infringement provisions are broad, and the fifteen-year protection term is extendable upon "substantial" changes to the contents of the database, including changes from successive additions, deletions, or alterations. These provisions exemplify the operation of some of the concerns voiced by Professor Reichman, Professor Samuelson, and other commentators.

The English database right is limited by exceptions allowing a lawful user to use a database. The CDPA defines "lawful user," rather unhelpfully, in Rule 12(1) as a person who has a right to use the database, whether under a license to do any of the acts restricted by the database right or otherwise. For example, a lawful user of a database that has been made available to the public is entitled to extract or reutilize insubstantial parts of the database contents for any purpose. Additionally, a lawful user may extract a substantial part of such a database as an illustration for teaching or research but not for any commercial purpose provided that the source is indicated. . . .

Returning to the "lawful use" exceptions in English database law: there is no definition in either the CDPA or CRDR of "commercial purpose" relating to the "lawful use" provisions. Thus, difficult interpretative questions may arise as to whether particular teaching and research activities involving databases are permissible. A commercial purpose may be unclear in an era in which institutions such as universities have the potential to commercialize to an extent previously unpracticed research products and teaching materials in competition with other institutions.

In any event, it also seems possible that the CRDR provisions allowing extraction of database contents as illustration for teaching or research and not for any commercial purpose may have "illustration" interpreted narrowly. It is likely difficult to use database contents for illustration without also using them for broader research and educational purposes that led to the need for the illustration in the first place.

5. Critiquing the E.U. Approach

In summary, a brief look at the United Kingdom's transposition of the E.U. Directive into domestic law raises concerns about the creation of broad database rights with vague and narrow exceptions. The structural reason for this is the broad definition of database, leading to a potentially broad array of prohibited conduct, which is only tempered by vague "lawful use" exceptions.

Sui generis database protection law throughout the European Union is still in its nascent stages and time will tell how serious these problems will ultimately become in practice. Therefore, it may not be too late for some legislative changes to be made in the European Union if it can be demonstrated that a more desirable model of database protection legislation is possible, particularly if the United States subscribes to such a model.

Many of the commentators who have criticized the operation of the new database rules throughout the European Union hail from the United States. One reason for this is that recent moves by E.U. Member States to enact database legislation raise an imperative for the U.S. Congress to take similar action. If Congress fails to do so, businesses may perceive greater protection for their databases in Europe and may then set up operations in E.U. Member States rather than in the United States. Indeed, given the perceived problems with current E.U. measures, many American commentators hope that Congress does not "make the same mistakes" as the European Union.

COMMENTS AND QUESTIONS

1.   How does the European Union Directive protect databases? What conduct does the Directive prohibit? What rights does the public have under the Directive to make use of databases?

2.   Despite early concerns that American database producers would be at a disadvantage vis-à-vis their European Union counterparts, subsequent history has shown that the United States Congress has not felt an obvious need to act quickly to adopt *sui generis* database protection legislation. Several bills were introduced into Congress but were never enacted. Additionally, there appears to be no evidence that European Union database industries have gained an unfair advantage as a result of the Directive's protection. In the 1995 working paper, the Commission of the European Communities noted that the economic impact of the *sui generis* database right in the European Union is unproven and that, in particular, there has been no empirical evidence that it has enhanced the production and commercialization of databases throughout the European Union. Does this suggest that the Directive could now be withdrawn from operation to counteract some of the concerns raised about the overbroad reach of the Directive? For a post-E.U. Directive comparison of the European and American approaches to database protection, see Jacqueline Lipton, *Across the Pond and Back Again: Digital Database Protection in the European Union and the United States,* in *Information Property and Information Wealth* (P. Yu ed., 2007).

3.   Despite the lack of empirical evidence about the effect of the Directive on European Union database industries, the working paper also noted that an

overwhelming majority of respondents to an online survey about the Directive conducted by the Commission felt "protected" or "well protected" by the database right, and believed that database protection at the European Union level is important and presumably should be continued. Does this put pressure on the United States Congress to enact a similar law?

4. On appeal from a British Court, the European Court of Justice in effect limited the operation of the Database Directive by distinguishing between resources employed by a database producer in *creating* materials that make up a database from those expended on *obtaining* such data. The Court held that only the latter activity would be protected under the *sui generis* database right. The idea was to prevent bodies that create materials in the ordinary course of their operations from claiming proprietary protection in resulting information compilations. This is particularly applicable to the "sole source" information provider problem described *supra. See* The British Horse-racing Board and Others v. William Hill Organization, Ltd (Case C-203/02, Nov. 9, 2004). Does this alleviate some of the more significant concerns about the potentially overbroad reach of the Directive?

5. Copyright, misappropriation, and contracts, such as facility agreements and development and maintenance agreements, historically have been used to protect databases. What other means of protection could database owners employ?

6. Would the utilization of technological measures such as encryption, passwords, and gateways serve as additional protective measures?

5

PRIVACY

Since 1996, when Ann Branscomb wrote the essay you read in Chapter 3, the perceived anonymity of cyberspace has largely disappeared. Instead of a world in which all of our actions and communications may take place with complete anonymity, we have come to recognize that the network of networks makes it possible to monitor and record information about users to an unprecedented degree. As Scott McNealy, CEO of Sun Microsystems, Inc., put it, "You already have zero privacy. Get over it."

The initial disappearance of "privacy" in cyberspace was driven in large part by efforts to make cyberspace safe for commerce.[1] After all, buyers and sellers could not do business with confidence without some means of identifying with whom they were doing business and for promoting accountability. It is also the result of increased public awareness of the current architecture of cyberspace. While the Internet enables many new forms of communication, all of this communication occurs through data transmitted and stored on computer networks. In order to make this network and its applications function, a user's actions in cyberspace are recorded down to the minutest detail, such as the location of their mouse. As Paul Schwartz has written, this means that

> [t]he Internet's technical qualities also have a negative consequence: they make possible an intense surveillance of activities in cyberspace.... As a result of cyberspace code, surfing and other cyberspace behavior generate finely granulated data about an individual's activities — often without her permission or even knowledge.[2]

More recently, privacy has come under even greater attack as a result of efforts by copyright owners to identify copyright infringers. We discussed this in relation to the *Verizon* case in Chapter 3. Then, there is the rise of online social networking — utilizing services such as Facebook and YouTube. Outside

---

1. *See* Lawrence Lessig, *Code 2.0* (2006).
2. Paul Schwartz, *Privacy and Democracy in Cyberspace*, 52 Vand. L. Rev. 1609, 1620 (1999) (footnotes omitted).

of the economic and intellectual property contexts, privacy is threatened by the apparent willingness of individuals to post personal information on shared networks with little thought to the privacy risks involved.

In Chapter 3 we examined how the First Amendment guarantees certain rights to communicate, including the right of a speaker to maintain her anonymity, and in Chapter 4 we examined the extent to which avoiding consumer confusion or rewarding creativity or labor justified granting control of information to certain individuals. The following materials explore the arguments for and against regulating information based upon its personal nature. In a world in which everything from your e-mail and Web surfing habits to your individual keystrokes can be monitored, is there any information that should not be made public? In studying the following materials, should law recognize an individual's right to control truthful information about him- or herself? Under what circumstances should law intercede to protect expectations of privacy or require transparency?

Moreover, what are an individual's obligations to ensure privacy of her own personal information? If someone voluntarily posts information on a social networking Web site and it is later used without her permission, does she have a right to object to the ensuing loss of privacy? Certainly she was the person responsible for the original posting, but the viral nature of the Internet makes it extremely easy for someone to lose control of their information outside what may have been their initial expectations of the scope of the disclosure. And what of situations where a third party posts information about you on a social networking site without your permission? Should you have any rights to control subsequent dissemination of that information on the Internet?

As the following materials illustrate, much of the privacy debate is not over how technology impacts privacy, but what it means to speak of a right to privacy. Is privacy secrecy, or as Justice Brandeis described, the "right to be let alone"?[3] Is privacy a property right in information about oneself?[4] For example, Richard Murphy argues that personal information, "like all information, is property," and

> in many instances, privacy rules are in fact implied contractual terms. To the extent that information is generated through a voluntary transaction, imposing nondisclosure obligations on the recipient of the information may be the best approach for certain categories

---

3. Olmstead v. United States, *infra* (Brandeis, J., dissenting).
4. *See* Alan F. Westin, *Privacy and Freedom* 324-25 (1967); Lawrence Lessig, *The Architecture of Privacy*, 1 Vand. J. Ent. L. & Prac. 56, 63-65 (1999) (arguing that the law should grant individuals property rights in their personal data); Patricia Mell, *Seeking Shade in a Land of Perpetual Sunlight: Privacy as Property in the Electronic Wilderness*, 11 Berkeley Tech. L.J. 1, 26-41 (1996) (same); Richard S. Murphy, *Property Rights in Personal Information: An Economic Defense of Privacy*, 84 Geo. L.J. 2381, 2382 (1996) (same). *But see* Pamela Samuelson, *Privacy as Intellectual Property*, 52 Stan. L. Rev. 1125 (2000) (critiquing the property right's position and arguing for the adaptation of trade secrecy law); Jessica Litman, *Information Privacy/Information Property*, 52 Stan. L. Rev. 1283 (2000) (critiquing the property right's approach and arguing a tort-based remedy).

of information. The value that information has ex post is of secondary importance; the primary question is what is the efficient contract rule.[5]

Or, does privacy protect individual autonomy?[6] According to Julie Cohen:

> the data privacy debate is . . . about power over knowledge. It follows that mechanisms for accountability (a watchword for data privacy advocates) should concern at least this much. If categorization determines eligibility for rewards or opportunities, then we may have an interest in the algorithms used to categorize. More fundamentally, if preferences are subject to shaping and reshaping over time, then we may have an interest in the sorts of shaping that are permitted. . . .
>
> Better profiling enables discrimination in the broad sense, on any ground deemed reasonable, desirable, and not illegal. And even "benign" discrimination — say, a decision to market only to those subsets of consumers who are statistically more likely to buy — operates to categorize at least some individuals on a basis other than the one they would wish. . . .
>
> The data processing paradigm conceals a power relationship, and that relationship, in turn, is a crucial determinant of the truth that data processing constructs. In evaluating knowledge claims about the processing of personally-identified data, we are not simply concerned about predictability and risk tolerance, but more fundamentally with questions of behavior modification and free will.[7]

One's approach to how "private" information should be regulated in cyberspace will depend greatly upon how one defines the values and interests that "privacy" protects. To the extent that privacy is secrecy, once information is revealed it should no longer be considered private.[8] If we value this secrecy over other competing values including security and accountability, cyberspace can be designed to keep more information secret. Otherwise, we must find a way to balance the competing values. If privacy is a property right, the legal rules and the Internet's architecture should be designed to allow individuals to bargain over whether their information will be collected and how it will be used, and so on.

It is important to bear in mind that greater privacy protections may well impact on other important competing interests, notably free speech. The more the law is prepared to prohibit disclosures of truthful personal information, the more an impact will be felt on the right to speak freely in a democratic society.[9] Further, such impacts will play out differently in different jurisdictions. While

---

5. Murphy, *supra* note 4, at 2416-17.

6. *See* Paul Schwartz, *Privacy and Democracy in Cyberspace,* 52 Vand. L. Rev. 1609 (1999) (discussing the importance of privacy in democratic self-governance, and arguing for legislation protecting principles of fair information practice).

7. Julie E. Cohen, *Examined Lives: Informational Privacy and the Subject as Object,* 52 Stan. L. Rev. 1373, 1406-08 (2000).

8. *See generally* Bartnicki v. Vopper, 532 U.S. 514 (2001) (holding that media defendants had a First Amendment right to disclose the content of an illegally intercepted communication, in part, because they played no role in its interception); Eugene Volokh, *Freedom of Speech and Information Privacy: The Troubling Implications of a Right to Stop People from Speaking About You,* 52 Stan. L. Rev. 1049 (2000).

9. *See, e.g.,* Diane Leenheer Zimmerman, *Is There a Right to Have Something to Say? One View of the Public Domain,* 73 Fordham L. Rev. 297, 348-49 (2004).

the United States has no express constitutional protection for privacy, free speech is expressly guaranteed by the First Amendment. This may be contrasted with the European Convention on Human rights, which protects both privacy and free speech as important constitutional guarantees under Articles 8 and 10, respectively.

In studying the following materials, consider whether the answers to these questions about privacy depend upon the adoption of the appropriate metaphor for privacy. When it comes to privacy interests from surveillance, a common metaphor used by privacy advocates is that of Big Brother from George Orwell's *1984*. In contrast, with respect to data collection Daniel Solove argues that the Big Brother metaphor is misplaced and should be replaced by Franz Kafka's *The Trial*:

> The use of the Big Brother metaphor to understand the database privacy problem is hardly surprising. Big Brother has long been the metaphor of choice to characterize privacy problems, and it has frequently been invoked when discussing police search tactics, wiretapping and video surveillance, and drug testing. With regard to computer databases, however, Big Brother is the wrong metaphor.
>
> [T]he database problem cannot adequately be understood by way of the Big Brother metaphor — even when adapted to account for private sector databases. Although the Big Brother metaphor certainly describes particular facets of the problem, it neglects many crucial dimensions. This oversight is far from inconsequential, for the way we conceptualize a problem has important ramifications for law and policy. I argue that the Big Brother metaphor as well as much of the law that protects privacy emerges from an older paradigm for conceptualizing privacy problems. Under this paradigm, privacy is invaded by uncovering one's hidden world, by surveillance, and by the disclosure of concealed information. The harm caused by such invasions consists of inhibition, self-censorship, embarrassment, and damage to one's reputation. Privacy law has developed with this paradigm in mind, and consequently it has failed to adapt to grapple effectively with the database problem. The Big Brother metaphor merely reinforces this old paradigm, and impedes our understanding of the problem.
>
> I argue that the problem is best captured by Franz Kafka's depiction of bureaucracy in *The Trial* — a more thoughtless process of bureaucratic indifference, arbitrary errors, and dehumanization, a world where people feel powerless and vulnerable, without any meaningful form of participation in the collection and use of their information. . . .
>
> Franz Kafka's harrowing depiction of bureaucracy in *The Trial* is the most appropriate metaphor to capture the problem with databases. *The Trial* opens with the protagonist, Joseph K., awakening one morning to find a group of officials in his apartment, who inform him that he is under arrest. K. is bewildered at why he has been placed under arrest: "I cannot recall the slightest offense that might be charged against me. But even that is of minor importance, the real question is, who accuses me? What authority is conducting these proceedings?" When he asks why the officials have come to arrest him, an official replies: "You are under arrest, certainly, more than that I do not know." Instead of taking him away to a police station, the officials mysteriously leave.
>
> Throughout the rest of the novel, Joseph K. begins a frustrating quest to discover why he has been arrested and how his case will be resolved. A vast bureaucratic court has apparently scrutinized his life and assembled a dossier on him. The Court is clandestine and mysterious, and Court records are "inaccessible to the accused." In an effort to learn about this Court and the proceedings against him, Joseph K. scuttles throughout the city, encountering a maze of lawyers, priests, and others, each revealing small scraps of

knowledge into the workings of the Court. In a pivotal scene, Joseph K. meets a painter who gleaned much knowledge of the obscure workings of the Court while painting judicial portraits. The painter explains to K.:

> "The whole dossier continues to circulate, as the regular official routine demands, passing on to the highest Courts, being referred to the lower ones again, and then swinging backwards and forwards with greater or smaller oscillations, longer or shorter delays. . . . No document is ever lost, the Court never forgets anything. One day — quite unexpectedly — some Judge will take up the documents and look at them attentively. . . ." "And the case begins all over again?" asked K. almost incredulously. "Certainly" said the painter. . . .

As K. continues his search, he becomes increasingly perplexed at this unusual Court. The higher officials keep themselves hidden; the lawyers claim they have connections to Court officials but never offer any proof or results. Hardly anyone seems to have direct contact with the Court. In addition, its "proceedings were not only kept secret from the general public, but from the accused as well." Yet K. continues to seek an acquittal from a crime he hasn't been informed of and from an authority he cannot seem to find. As Joseph K. scurries through the bureaucratic labyrinth of the law, he can never make any progress toward his acquittal: "Progress had always been made, but the nature of the progress could never be divulged. The Advocate was always working away at the first plea, but it had never reached a conclusion. . . ." In the end, Joseph K. is seized by two officials in the middle of the night and executed.

Kafka's *The Trial* best captures the scope, nature, and effects of the type of power relationship created by databases. My point is not that *The Trial* presents a more realistic descriptive account of the database problem than Big Brother. Like *Nineteen Eighty-Four*, *The Trial* presents a fictional portrait of a harrowing world, often exaggerating certain elements of society in a way that makes them humorous and absurd. Certainly, most people are not told that they are inexplicably under arrest and they do not expect to be executed unexpectedly one evening. *The Trial* is in part a satire, and what is important for the purposes of my argument are the insights the novel provides about society through its exaggerations. In the context of computer databases, Kafka's *The Trial* is the better focal point for the discourse than Big Brother. Kafka depicts an indifferent bureaucracy, where individuals are pawns, not knowing what is happening, having no say or ability to exercise meaningful control over the process. This lack of control allows the trial to completely take over Joseph K.'s life. *The Trial* captures the sense of helplessness, frustration, and vulnerability one experiences when a large bureaucratic organization has control over a vast dossier of details about one's life. At any time, something could happen to Joseph K.; decisions are made based on his data, and Joseph K. has no say, no knowledge, and no ability to fight back. He is completely at the mercy of the bureaucratic process.

Daniel J. Solove, *Privacy and Power: Computer Databases and Metaphors for Informational Privacy*, 53 Stan. L. Rev. 1393, 1397-98, 1419-21 (2001) (footnotes omitted). What types of concerns are addressed by the Big Brother metaphor? What concerns are addressed by the Kafka metaphor? Are the metaphors mutually exclusive? As you study the materials in this chapter, consider whether these metaphors accurately describe the privacy issues surrounding communications and data, and how they may guide legal and policy decisions.

As we saw from Professor Dan Hunter's article in Chapter 2, metaphors can be very important in determining the direction of legal regulation in a given area. Might the metaphors we use for privacy impact on the way the law develops in this area? Might the focus on one particular metaphor skew legal developments to the detriment of other competing conceptions of privacy? In thinking about theories of privacy more generally, Professor Daniel Solove has suggested that we should jettison the search for a unifying theory of privacy and instead take a bottom-up approach drawing generalities from specific categories of privacy-related harms. *See, e.g.*, Daniel Solove, *Conceptualizing Privacy*, 90 Cal. L. Rev. 1087 (2002); Daniel Solove, *A Taxonomy of Privacy*, 154 U. Pa. L. Rev. 477-564 (2006). Do you agree with this view? Professor Jacqueline Lipton has made similar observations in favor of a bottom-up approach to privacy theory and has further advocated the development of an approach to digital privacy that attempts to identify the outside boundaries of online privacy. *See* Jacqueline Lipton, *Mapping Online Privacy*, 104 Nw. U. L. Rev. ____ (2010).

In the age of Web 2.0, it is also important to consider privacy issues in a global context. Online information exchanges — whether political, economic, or social — take place across international borders. We must also recognize that many privacy concerns today raise generation-specific concepts of privacy. It might be that the youth of today have completely different expectations and understandings of privacy than their parents' or grandparents' generations did. Patriciz Sánchez Abril, *A (My) Space of One's Own*, 6 Nw. J. Tech. & Intell. Prop. 73, 73 (2007); John Palfrey & Urs Gasser, *Born Digital: Understanding the First Generation of Digital Natives* (2008). To what extent should we take international and intergenerational issues into account when making decisions about the legal protection of privacy? How easy is it to accommodate these concerns in practice? Consider these issues as you examine the following materials.

A. PRIVACY OF COMMUNICATIONS

Problem 10.0

Having resolved, at least temporarily, some of the intellectual property questions for StarttUp, Alan and Barbara have now asked you to turn your attention to how StarttUp should deal with various privacy issues. Reports about governmental surveillance programs and the public's concern over data gathering and online profiling appear almost daily in the popular press, and Alan and Barbara want you to develop the company's internal and external privacy policies. While you have read a fair number of newspaper articles and watched television reports on privacy and the Internet, until now, you have not really explored the issue at work.

The first thing you discover upon meeting with your technology staff is the breadth of the information that is stored and accessible on your computer networks. From e-mail to computer keystrokes, everything that occurs on a computer and through a computer network can be saved and subsequently accessed. While much of this information is discarded, a tremendous amount is stored. For example, you are told that office e-mails are not only stored on individual computers, but are also stored in the office e-mail server. The e-mail server makes it possible for individuals to send e-mail to one another by acting as a digital post office. Unlike a brick-and-mortar post office, the e-mail server makes a copy of the message before delivering it to its recipient. This means that depending upon how your system is configured, someone with access to the server can gain access to all of the company's e-mails. Because all information in cyberspace is transmitted by multiple computers storing and transmitting data, you begin to see the potential privacy concerns.

Unfortunately, before you have had time to delve into these matters, a problem has arisen that demands your immediate attention. Alan is concerned that a recently hired employee is spending most of his time surfing the Web in search of pornography and MP3s, playing video games, and chatting with friends through e-mail and instant messaging. Unfortunately, Alan has not been able to catch this employee in the act. Every time Alan walks by the employee's cubicle, he appears to be hard at work on his computer. Because this employee has been exceptionally slow in completing projects, your head of technology expects that the employee has loaded a program onto his computer that allows the user to quickly "hide" items displayed on their computer monitor. Alan has already confronted the employee who denies any wrongdoing.

Concerned that this employee may be using company time and resources to search for pornography and copyrighted material—which in addition to wasting company resources may expose the company to civil and criminal liability, for, among other things, the creation of a potentially hostile work environment—Alan wants to know if you can search the employee's computer and network files. Given the demand letters Starttup received from the RIAA and the MPAA, Alan also wants to know if Starttup can monitor subscriber usage in chatrooms and bulletin boards to police for copyright infringing activity. In answering this question, consider the following materials.

Problem 10.1

To what extent does your advice change with respect to Cora's blog? Cora is concerned that a new blogger, Pat, is not who she claims to be.

Cora has not personally met Pat, and while Pat's initial posts seemed to fit right in with GOL, Pat's more recent posts have started to read as if they were written by some of GOL's harshest and abusive critics. As such, Cora is interested in Pat's identity both online and offline and wants to be sure that Pat genuinely shares the values and interests of GOL's existing bloggers. One possibility is to monitor all of Pat's online communications and online activities. Another is to have an outside service perform a background check on Pat, which would include prior online activities. Does Pat have a protected privacy interest in this information? If so, under what circumstances would that interests give way to Cora and GOL's competing interest?

1. Privacy and New Technology

That technological advances may threaten privacy is nothing new. Early in the twentieth century, the U.S. Supreme Court addressed the tapping of telephones, and at the turn of the twenty-first century, it examined the use of thermal imaging devices. Despite these decisions, there is still significant debate over how the law should protect privacy in response to new technology. From a constitutional perspective, the clearest and most powerful protection for privacy is the Fourth Amendment's prohibition of unreasonable searches and seizures. As you study how the Supreme Court grapples with interpreting this provision, what are the terms of this debate?

OLMSTEAD v. UNITED STATES

277 U.S. 438 (1928)

Mr. Chief Justice TAFT delivered the opinion of the Court.

[The appeals in this case are] confined to the single question whether the use of evidence of private telephone conversations between the defendants and others, intercepted by means of wire tapping, amounted to a violation of the Fourth and Fifth Amendments.

The petitioners were convicted in the District Court for the Western District of Washington of a conspiracy to violate the National Prohibition Act (27 USCA) by unlawfully possessing, transporting and importing intoxicating liquors and maintaining nuisances, and by selling intoxicating liquors. . . .

The information which led to the discovery of the conspiracy and its nature and extent was largely obtained by intercepting messages on the telephones of the conspirators by four federal prohibition officers. Small wires were inserted along the ordinary telephone wires from the residences of four of the petitioners and those leading from the chief office. The insertions were made without trespass upon any property of the defendants. They were made in the basement of the large office building. The taps from house lines were made in the streets near the houses. . . .

The Fourth Amendment provides:

> "The right of the people to be secure in their persons, houses, papers, and effects, against unreasonable searches and seizures, shall not be violated, and no warrants shall issue, but upon probable cause, supported by oath or affirmation, and particularly describing the place to be searched, and the persons or things to be seized."

And the Fifth:

> "No person . . . shall be compelled in any criminal case to be a witness against himself." . . .

There is no room in the present case for applying the Fifth Amendment, unless the Fourth Amendment was first violated. There was no evidence of compulsion to induce the defendants to talk over their many telephones. They were continually and voluntarily transacting business without knowledge of the interception. Our consideration must be confined to the Fourth Amendment.

The well-known historical purpose of the Fourth Amendment, directed against general warrants and writs of assistance, was to prevent the use of governmental force to search a man's house, his person, his papers, and his effects, and to prevent their seizure against his will. . . .

The amendment itself shows that the search is to be of material things — the person, the house, his papers, or his effects. The description of the warrant necessary to make the proceeding lawful is that it must specify the place to be searched and the person or things to be seized. . . .

. . . The Fourth Amendment may have proper application to a sealed letter in the mail, because of the constitutional provision for the Post Office Department and the relations between the government and those who pay to secure protection of their sealed letters. See Revised Statutes, §§3978 to 3988, whereby Congress monopolizes the carriage of letters and excludes from that business everyone else, and section 3929 (39 USCA §259), which forbids any postmaster or other person to open any letter not addressed to himself. It is plainly within the words of the amendment to say that the unlawful rifling by a government agent of a sealed letter is a search and seizure of the sender's papers or effects. The letter is a paper, an effect, and in the custody of a government that forbids carriage, except under its protection.

The United States takes no such care of telegraph or telephone messages as of mailed sealed letters. The amendment does not forbid what was done here. There was no searching. There was no seizure. The evidence was secured by the use of the sense of hearing and that only. There was no entry of the houses or offices of the defendants.

By the invention of the telephone 50 years ago, and its application for the purpose of extending communications, one can talk with another at a far distant place.

The language of the amendment cannot be extended and expanded to include telephone wires, reaching to the whole world from the defendant's house or office. The intervening wires are not part of his house or office, any more than are the highways along which they are stretched. . . .

[T]he Fifth Amendment and the Fourth Amendment were to be liberally construed to effect the purpose of the framers of the Constitution in the interest of liberty. But that cannot justify enlargement of the language employed beyond the possible practical meaning of houses, persons, papers, and effects, or so to apply the words search and seizure as to forbid hearing or sight. . . .

Congress may, of course, protect the secrecy of telephone messages by making them, when intercepted, inadmissible in evidence in federal criminal trials, by direct legislation, and thus depart from the common law of evidence. But the courts may not adopt such a policy by attributing an enlarged and unusual meaning to the Fourth Amendment. The reasonable view is that one who installs in his house a telephone instrument with connecting wires intends to project his voice to those quite outside, and that the wires beyond his house, and messages while passing over them, are not within the protection of the Fourth Amendment. Here those who intercepted the projected voices were not in the house of either party to the conversation. . . .

[The judgments of the Court of Appeals are] Affirmed.

Mr. Justice BRANDEIS (dissenting).

. . . The government makes no attempt to defend the methods employed by its officers. Indeed, it concedes that, if wire tapping can be deemed a search and seizure within the Fourth Amendment, such wire tapping as was practiced in the case at bar was an unreasonable search and seizure, and that the evidence thus obtained was inadmissible. But it relies on the language of the amendment, and it claims that the protection given thereby cannot properly be held to include a telephone conversation.

"We must never forget," said Mr. Chief Justice Marshall in McCulloch v. Maryland, 4 Wheat. 316, 407 4 L. Ed. 579, "that it is a Constitution we are expounding." Since then this court has repeatedly sustained the exercise of power by Congress, under various clauses of that instrument, over objects of which the fathers could not have dreamed. . . . We have likewise held that general limitations on the powers of government, like those embodied in the due process clauses of the Fifth and Fourteenth Amendments, do not forbid the United States or the states from meeting modern conditions by regulations which "a century ago, or even half a century ago, probably would have been rejected as arbitrary and oppressive." Village of Euclid v. Ambler Realty Co., 272 U.S. 365, 387; Buck v. Bell, 274 U.S. 200. Clauses guaranteeing to the individual protection against specific abuses of power, must have a similar capacity of adaptation to a changing world. . . .

When the Fourth and Fifth Amendments were adopted, "the form that evil had theretofore taken" had been necessarily simple. Force and violence were then the only means known to man by which a government could directly effect self-incrimination. It could compel the individual to testify — a compulsion effected, if need be, by torture. It could secure possession of his papers and other articles incident to his private life — a seizure effected, if need be, by breaking and entry. Protection against such invasion of "the sanctities of a man's home and the privacies of life" was provided in the Fourth and Fifth Amendments by specific language. Boyd v. United States, 116 U.S. 616, 630. But "time works changes, brings into existence new conditions and purposes." Subtler and more far-reaching means of invading privacy have become available to the government. Discovery and invention have made it possible for the government, by means far more effective than stretching upon the rack, to obtain disclosure in court of what is whispered in the closet.

Moreover, "in the application of a Constitution, our contemplation cannot be only of what has been, but of what may be." The progress of science in furnishing the government with means of espionage is not likely to stop with wire tapping. Ways may some day be developed by which the government, without removing papers from secret drawers, can reproduce them in court, and by which it will be enabled to expose to a jury the most intimate occurrences of the home. Advances in the psychic and related sciences may bring means of exploring unexpressed beliefs, thoughts and emotions. "That places the liberty of every man in the hands of every petty officer" was said by James Otis of much lesser intrusions than these. To Lord Camden a far slighter intrusion seemed "subversive of all the comforts of society." Can it be that the Constitution affords no protection against such invasions of individual security?

A sufficient answer is found in Boyd v. United States, 116 U.S. 616, 627-630, a case that will be remembered as long as civil liberty lives in the United States. . . .

> "The principles laid down in this opinion affect the very essence of constitutional liberty and security. They reach farther than the concrete form of the case there before the court, with its adventitious circumstances; they apply to all invasions on the part of the government and its employees of the sanctities of a man's home and the privacies of life. It is not the breaking of his doors, and the rummaging of his drawers, that constitutes the essence of the offense; but it is the invasion of his indefeasible right of personal security, personal liberty and private property, where that right has never been forfeited by his conviction of some public offense — it is the invasion of this sacred right which underlies and constitutes the essence of Lord Camden's judgment. Breaking into a house and opening boxes and drawers are circumstances of aggravation; but any forcible and compulsory extortion of a man's own testimony or of his private papers to be used as evidence of a crime or to forfeit his goods, is within the condemnation of that judgment. In this regard the Fourth and Fifth Amendments run almost into each other."

In *Ex parte Jackson*, 96 U.S. 727, it was held that a sealed letter entrusted to the mail is protected by the amendments. The mail is a public service furnished by the government. The telephone is a public service furnished by its authority. There is, in essence, no difference between the sealed letter and the private telephone message. As Judge Rudkin said below:

> "True, the one is visible, the other invisible; the one is tangible, the other intangible; the one is sealed, and the other unsealed; but these are distinctions without a difference."

The evil incident to invasion of the privacy of the telephone is far greater than that involved in tampering with the mails. Whenever a telephone line is tapped, the privacy of the persons at both ends of the line is invaded, and all conversations between them upon any subject, and although proper, confidential, and privileged, may be overheard. Moreover, the tapping of one man's telephone line involves the tapping of the telephone of every other person whom he may call, or who may call him. As a means of espionage, writs of assistance and general warrants are but puny instruments of tyranny and oppression when compared with wire tapping.

Time and again this court, in giving effect to the principle underlying the Fourth Amendment, has refused to place an unduly literal construction upon it. . . .

The narrow language of the amendment has been consistently construed in the light of its object, "to insure that a person should not be compelled, when acting as a witness in any investigation, to give testimony which might tend to show that he himself had committed a crime. The privilege is limited to criminal matters, but it is as broad as the mischief against which it seeks to guard." Counselman v. Hitchcock (12 S. Ct. 198). . . .

The protection guaranteed by the amendments is much broader in scope. The makers of our Constitution undertook to secure conditions favorable to the pursuit of happiness. They recognized the significance of man's spiritual nature, of his feelings and of his intellect. They knew that only a part of the pain, pleasure and satisfactions of life are to be found in material things. They sought to protect Americans in their beliefs, their thoughts, their emotions and their sensations. They conferred, as against the government, the right to be let alone — the most comprehensive of rights and the right most valued by civilized men. To protect that right, every unjustifiable intrusion by the government upon the privacy of the individual, whatever the means employed, must be deemed a violation of the Fourth Amendment. And the use, as evidence in a criminal proceeding, of facts ascertained by such intrusion must be deemed a violation of the Fifth.

Applying to the Fourth and Fifth Amendments the established rule of construction, the defendants' objections to the evidence obtained by wire tapping must, in my opinion, be sustained. It is, of course, immaterial where the physical connection with the telephone wires leading into the defendants' premises was made. And it is also immaterial that the intrusion was in aid of law enforcement. Experience should teach us to be most on our guard to protect liberty when the government's purposes are beneficent. Men born to freedom are naturally alert to repel invasion of their liberty by evil-minded rulers. The greatest dangers to liberty lurk in insidious encroachment by men of zeal, well-meaning but without understanding. . . .

[Justice Brandeis also concludes that the evidence should have been excluded because the wire tapping violated various provisions of state law.]

[Dissenting opinions of Justices HOLMES, BUTLER, and STONE omitted.]

COMMENTS AND QUESTIONS

1. What is Justice Taft's conception of privacy? How does Justice Brandeis's concept differ? How does each approach deal with advances in technology?

2. To what extent is the disagreement between Taft and Brandeis an issue of institutional competency? In other words, whose role is it to define the right of privacy: judges, legislators, state or federal government?

3. According to Justice Brandeis, "Discovery and invention have made it possible for the government, by means far more effective than stretching upon the rack, to obtain disclosure in court of what is whispered in the closet." In light of this statement, what matters are not considered private?

4. In 1934, as a response to *Olmstead*, Congress passed Section 605 of the Federal Communications Act, which made wiretapping a federal crime. In 1968, Congress passed a comprehensive federal statute for wiretapping which has been amended twice — in 1986 and again in 1994.

5. *Olmstead* was eventually overruled in Katz v. United States, 389 U.S. 347 (1967), in which the Supreme Court ruled that the tapping of a public telephone was a search and seizure subject to the Fourth Amendment. As noted by Justice Harlan in a concurring opinion:

> As the Court's opinion states, "the Fourth Amendment protects people, not places." The question, however, is what protection it affords to those people. Generally, as here, the answer to that question requires reference to a "place." My understanding of the rule that has emerged from prior decisions is that there is a twofold requirement, first that a person have [sic] exhibited an actual (subjective) expectation of privacy and, second, that the expectation be one that society is prepared to recognize as "reasonable." Thus a man's home is, for most purposes, a place where he expects privacy, but objects, activities, or statements that he exposes to the "plain view" of outsiders are not "protected" because no intention to keep them to himself has been exhibited. On the other hand, conversations in the open would not be protected against being overheard, for the expectation of privacy under the circumstances would be unreasonable. . . .

Does the reasonable expectation of privacy test resolve the debate in *Olmstead*? Leaving aside the circular nature of the *Katz* test, how would one define what is a reasonable expectation especially in regard to novel technology? Consider the Supreme Court's most recent statement on the subject.

Κʏʟʟο ᴠ. Uɴɪᴛᴇᴅ Sᴛᴀᴛᴇs

533 U.S.27 (2001)

Justice Sᴄᴀʟɪᴀ delivered the opinion of the Court.

This case presents the question whether the use of a thermal-imaging device aimed at a private home from a public street to detect relative amounts of heat within the home constitutes a "search" within the meaning of the Fourth Amendment.

I

In 1991 Agent William Elliott of the United States Department of the Interior came to suspect that marijuana was being grown in the home belonging to petitioner Danny Kyllo, part of a triplex on Rhododendron Drive in Florence, Oregon. Indoor marijuana growth typically requires high-intensity lamps. In order to determine whether an amount of heat was emanating from petitioner's home consistent with the use of such lamps, at 3:20 a.m. on January 16, 1992, Agent Elliott and Dan Haas used an Agema Thermovision 210 thermal imager to scan the triplex. Thermal imagers detect infrared radiation, which virtually all objects emit but which is not visible to the naked eye. The imager converts radiation into images based on relative warmth — black is cool, white is hot, shades of gray connote relative differences; in that respect, it operates somewhat like a video camera showing heat images. . . . The scan showed that the roof over the garage and a side wall of petitioner's home were relatively hot compared to the rest of the home and substantially warmer than neighboring homes in the triplex. Agent Elliott concluded that petitioner was using halide lights to grow marijuana in his house, which indeed he was. . . . Petitioner was indicted on one count of manufacturing marijuana, in violation of 21 U.S.C. §841(a)(1). He unsuccessfully moved to suppress the evidence seized from his home and then entered a conditional guilty plea. . . .

III

It would be foolish to contend that the degree of privacy secured to citizens by the Fourth Amendment has been entirely unaffected by the advance of technology. For example, as the cases discussed above make clear, the technology enabling human flight has exposed to public view (and hence, we have said, to official observation) uncovered portions of the house and its curtilage that once were private. See [California v. Ciraolo, 476 U.S. 207, 215 (1986)]. The question we confront today is what limits there are upon this power of technology to shrink the realm of guaranteed privacy.

The *Katz* test — whether the individual has an expectation of privacy that society is prepared to recognize as reasonable — has often been criticized as circular, and hence subjective and unpredictable. See 1 W. LaFave, Search and Seizure §2.1(d), pp. 393-394 (3d ed. 1996); Posner, The Uncertain Protection of Privacy by the Supreme Court, 1979 S. Ct. Rev. 173, 188; [Minnesota v. Carter, 525 U.S. 83, 97 (1998)] (Scalia, J., concurring). . . . While it may be difficult to refine *Katz* when the search of areas such as telephone booths, automobiles, or even the curtilage and uncovered portions of residences are at issue, in the case of the search of the interior of homes — the prototypical and hence most commonly litigated area of protected privacy — there is a ready criterion, with roots deep in the common law, of the minimal expectation of privacy that exists, and that is acknowledged to be reasonable. To withdraw protection of this minimum expectation would be to permit police technology to erode the privacy guaranteed by the Fourth Amendment. We think that obtaining by sense-enhancing technology any information regarding the interior of the home that could not otherwise have been obtained without physical "intrusion into a constitutionally protected area," [Silverman v. United States, 365 U.S. 505, 512 (1961)], constitutes a search — at least where (as here) the technology in question is not in general public use. This assures preservation of that degree of privacy against government that existed when the Fourth Amendment was adopted. On the basis of this criterion, the information obtained by the thermal imager in this case was the product of a search.[2]

The Government maintains, however, that the thermal imaging must be upheld because it detected "only heat radiating from the external surface of the house," Brief for United States 26. The dissent makes this its leading point, contending that there is a fundamental difference between what it calls "off-the-wall" observations and "through-the-wall surveillance." But just as a thermal imager captures only heat emanating from a house, so also a powerful directional microphone picks up only sound emanating from a house — and a satellite capable of scanning from many miles away would pick up only visible light emanating from a house. We rejected such a mechanical interpretation of the Fourth Amendment in *Katz*, where the eavesdropping device picked up only sound waves that reached the exterior of the phone booth. Reversing that approach would leave the homeowner at the mercy of advancing technology — including imaging technology that could discern all human

2. The dissent's repeated assertion that the thermal imaging did not obtain information regarding the interior of the home is simply inaccurate. A thermal imager reveals the relative heat of various rooms in the home. The dissent may not find that information particularly private or important, but there is no basis for saying it is not information regarding the interior of the home. The dissent's comparison of the thermal imaging to various circumstances in which outside observers might be able to perceive, without technology, the heat of the home — for example, by observing snowmelt on the roof — is quite irrelevant. The fact that equivalent information could sometimes be obtained by other means does not make lawful the use of means that violate the Fourth Amendment. The police might, for example, learn how many people are in a particular house by setting up year-round surveillance; but that does not make breaking and entering to find out the same information lawful. In any event, on the night of January 16, 1992, no outside observer could have discerned the relative heat of Kyllo's home without thermal imaging.

activity in the home. While the technology used in the present case was relatively crude, the rule we adopt must take account of more sophisticated systems that are already in use or in development. . . .

The Government also contends that the thermal imaging was constitutional because it did not "detect private activities occurring in private areas," Brief for United States 22. It points out that in *Dow Chemical* we observed that the enhanced aerial photography did not reveal any "intimate details." 476 U.S., at 238. *Dow Chemical*, however, involved enhanced aerial photography of an industrial complex, which does not share the Fourth Amendment sanctity of the home. The Fourth Amendment's protection of the home has never been tied to measurement of the quality or quantity of information obtained. In *Silverman*, for example, we made clear that any physical invasion of the structure of the home, "by even a fraction of an inch," was too much, 365 U.S., at 512, and there is certainly no exception to the warrant requirement for the officer who barely cracks open the front door and sees nothing but the nonintimate rug on the vestibule floor. In the home, our cases show, all details are intimate details, because the entire area is held safe from prying government eyes. . . .

Limiting the prohibition of thermal imaging to "intimate details" would not only be wrong in principle; it would be impractical in application, failing to provide "a workable accommodation between the needs of law enforcement and the interests protected by the Fourth Amendment," *Oliver v. United States*, 466 U.S. 170, 181 (1984). To begin with, there is no necessary connection between the sophistication of the surveillance equipment and the "intimacy" of the details that it observes — which means that one cannot say (and the police cannot be assured) that use of the relatively crude equipment at issue here will always be lawful. The Agema Thermovision 210 might disclose, for example, at what hour each night the lady of the house takes her daily sauna and bath — a detail that many would consider "intimate"; and a much more sophisticated system might detect nothing more intimate than the fact that someone left a closet light on. We could not, in other words, develop a rule approving only that through-the-wall surveillance which identifies objects no smaller than 36 by 36 inches, but would have to develop a jurisprudence specifying which home activities are "intimate" and which are not. And even when (if ever) that jurisprudence were fully developed, no police officer would be able to know in advance whether his through-the-wall surveillance picks up "intimate" details — and thus would be unable to know in advance whether it is constitutional. . . .

We have said that the Fourth Amendment draws "a firm line at the entrance to the house," *Payton*, 445 U.S., at 590. That line, we think, must be not only firm but also bright — which requires clear specification of those methods of surveillance that require a warrant. While it is certainly possible to conclude from the videotape of the thermal imaging that occurred in this case that no "significant" compromise of the homeowner's privacy has occurred, we must take the long view, from the original meaning of the Fourth Amendment forward.

"The Fourth Amendment is to be construed in the light of what was deemed an unreasonable search and seizure when it was adopted, and in a manner which will conserve public interests as well as the interests and rights of individual citizens."

Carroll v. United States, 267 U.S. 132, 149 (1925).

Where, as here, the Government uses a device that is not in general public use, to explore details of the home that would previously have been unknowable without physical intrusion, the surveillance is a "search" and is presumptively unreasonable without a warrant. . . .

Justice STEVENS, with whom THE CHIEF JUSTICE, Justice O'CONNOR, and Justice KENNEDY join, dissenting.

There is, in my judgment, a distinction of constitutional magnitude between "through-the-wall surveillance" that gives the observer or listener direct access to information in a private area, on the one hand, and the thought processes used to draw inferences from information in the public domain, on the other hand. . . .

I

There is no need for the Court to craft a new rule to decide this case, as it is controlled by established principles from our Fourth Amendment jurisprudence. One of those core principles, of course, is that "searches and seizures *inside a home* without a warrant are presumptively unreasonable." *Payton v. New York*, 445 U.S. 573, 586 (1980) (emphasis added). But it is equally well settled that searches and seizures of property in plain view are presumptively reasonable. See *id.*, at 586-587. Whether that property is residential or commercial, the basic principle is the same: " 'What a person knowingly exposes to the public, even in his own home or office, is not a subject of Fourth Amendment protection.' " *California v. Ciraolo*, 476 U.S. 207, 213 (1986) (quoting *Katz v. United States*, 389 U.S. 347, 351 (1967)); see *Florida v. Riley*, 488 U.S. 445, 449-450 (1989); *California v. Greenwood*, 486 U.S. 35, 40-41 (1988); *Dow Chemical Co. v. United States*, 476 U.S. 227, 235-236 (1986); *Air Pollution Variance Bd. of Colo. v. Western Alfalfa Corp.*, 416 U.S. 861, 865 (1974). That is the principle implicated here.

While the Court "take[s] the long view" and decides this case based largely on the potential of yet-to-be-developed technology that might allow "through-the-wall surveillance," this case involves nothing more than off-the-wall surveillance by law enforcement officers to gather information exposed to the general public from the outside of petitioner's home. All that the infrared camera did in this case was passively measure heat emitted from the exterior surfaces of petitioner's home; all that those measurements showed were relative differences in emission levels, vaguely indicating that some areas of the roof and outside walls were warmer than others. As still images from the infrared scans show, no details regarding the interior of petitioner's home were revealed. Unlike an X-ray scan, or other possible "through-the-wall" techniques, the detection of infrared radiation emanating from the home did not accomplish "an unauthorized physical penetration into the premises," *Silverman v. United States,* 365 U.S. 505, 509 (1961), nor did it "obtain information that it could not have obtained by observation from outside the curtilage of the house," *United States v. Karo,* 468 U.S. 705, 715 (1984).

Indeed, the ordinary use of the senses might enable a neighbor or passerby to notice the heat emanating from a building, particularly if it is vented, as was the case here. . . .

Thus, the notion that heat emissions from the outside of a dwelling is a private matter implicating the protections of the Fourth Amendment (the text of which guarantees the right of people "to be secure *in* their . . . houses" against unreasonable searches and seizures (emphasis added)) is not only unprecedented but also quite difficult to take seriously. Heat waves, like aromas that are generated in a kitchen, or in a laboratory or opium den, enter the public domain if and when they leave a building. A subjective expectation that they would remain private is not only implausible but also surely not "one that society is prepared to recognize as 'reasonable.'" *Katz,* 389 U.S., at 361 (Harlan, J., concurring).

To be sure, the homeowner has a reasonable expectation of privacy concerning what takes place within the home, and the Fourth Amendment's protection against physical invasions of the home should apply to their functional equivalent. But the equipment in this case did not penetrate the walls of petitioner's home, and while it did pick up "details of the home" that were exposed to the public . . . it did not obtain "any information regarding the *interior* of the home" . . . (emphasis added). . . .

Notwithstanding the implications of today's decision, there is a strong public interest in avoiding constitutional litigation over the monitoring of emissions from homes, and over the inferences drawn from such monitoring. Just as "the police cannot reasonably be expected to avert their eyes from evidence of criminal activity that could have been observed by any member of the public," *Greenwood,* 486 U.S., at 41, so too public officials should not have to avert their senses or their equipment from detecting emissions in the public domain such as excessive heat, traces of smoke, suspicious odors, odorless gases, airborne particulates, or radioactive emissions, any of which could identify hazards to the community. In my judgment, monitoring such emissions with "sense-enhancing technology," and drawing useful conclusions from such monitoring, is an entirely reasonable public service.

On the other hand, the countervailing privacy interest is at best trivial. After all, homes generally are insulated to keep heat in, rather than to prevent the detection of heat going out, and it does not seem to me that society will suffer from a rule requiring the rare homeowner who both intends to engage in uncommon activities that produce extraordinary amounts of heat, and wishes to conceal that production from outsiders, to make sure that the surrounding area is well insulated. . . .

II

In my judgment, the Court's new rule is at once too broad and too narrow, and is not justified by the Court's explanation for its adoption. As I have suggested, I would not erect a constitutional impediment to the use of sense-enhancing technology unless it provides its user with the functional equivalent of actual presence in the area being searched.

Despite the Court's attempt to draw a line that is "not only firm but also bright," the contours of its new rule are uncertain because its protection apparently dissipates as soon as the relevant technology is "in general public use." Yet how much use is general public use is not even hinted at by the Court's opinion, which makes the somewhat doubtful assumption that the thermal imager used in this case does not satisfy that criterion. In any event, putting aside its lack of clarity, this criterion is somewhat perverse because it seems likely that the threat to privacy will grow, rather than recede, as the use of intrusive equipment becomes more readily available. . . .

Because the new rule applies to information regarding the "interior" of the home, it is too narrow as well as too broad. Clearly, a rule that is designed to protect individuals from the overly intrusive use of sense-enhancing equipment should not be limited to a home. If such equipment did provide its user with the functional equivalent of access to a private place — such as, for example, the telephone booth involved in *Katz*, or an office building — then the rule should apply to such an area as well as to a home. See *Katz*, 389 U.S., at 351 ("[T]he Fourth Amendment protects people, not places"). . . .

COMMENTS AND QUESTIONS

1. According to Justice Scalia, what limits are there upon the "power of technology to shrink the realm of guaranteed privacy"?

2. Why is the public availability of surveillance relevant to the privacy analysis? If eyeglasses are developed that could see through clothing and are available to the public, does that mean that our unclad bodies are no longer private? How does this relate to Justice Stevens's argument that the defendant could have avoided this "search" by simply using better insulation?

3. In *Kyllo*, both the government and the dissenters argued that the use of thermal imaging was not a search in this case because the device did not penetrate the walls of the home. What concept of privacy is this position based upon? Is privacy tied to a particular location? If so, is this a return to *Olmstead*?

4. Justice Scalia concluded that "In the home, our cases show, all details are intimate details, because the entire area is held safe from prying government eyes. . . ." Are there any other areas in which all details are intimate? Why is intimacy relevant?

5. Which approach in *Olmstead* is Justice Scalia following? How is Justice Scalia's approach similar to Justice Brandeis's? How does it differ?

6.   How does an approach that focuses on preserving "that degree of privacy against government that existed when the Fourth Amendment was adopted" respond to new invasions of privacy? How could a historical approach be used to guarantee a broad right of privacy? A narrow right? For an argument that *Kyllo* represents a unique departure from existing Fourth Amendment doctrine, consider Raymond Shih Ray Ku, *The Founder's Privacy: The Fourth Amendment and New Technologies After* Kyllo, 86 Minn. L. Rev. 1325 (2002).

2. Intercepting Communications

As illustrated by *Olmstead*, one of the most significant privacy concerns is the confidentiality of communications. But just how private are communications in cyberspace? Who may access our e-mails or instant messages? Should Web pages be considered communications? In answering these questions, one must consider whether the individual has a reasonable expectation of privacy as exemplified by *Katz* and *Kyllo*.

One must also consider whether the monitoring violates any statutory protection of privacy. The principal statute that will be considered in the following materials is the U.S. Electronic Communications Privacy Act (ECPA),[10] which protects the privacy of communications in two ways. First, subject to several exceptions, the law generally prohibits the intentional interception and disclosure of wire, oral, or electronic communications.[11] Under what is commonly referred to as "Title I" or the "Federal Wire Tap Law," Section 2511 provides in pertinent part:

(1) Except as otherwise specifically provided in this chapter any person who —

(a) intentionally intercepts, endeavors to intercept, or procures any other person to intercept or endeavor to intercept, any wire, oral, or electronic communication; . . .

(c) intentionally discloses, or endeavors to disclose, to any other person the contents of any wire, oral, or electronic communication, knowing or having reason to know that the information was obtained through the interception of a wire, oral, or electronic communication in violation of this subsection; or . . .

shall be punished as provided in subsection (4) or shall be subject to suit as provided in subsection (5). . . .

(2) (a)(i) It shall not be unlawful under this chapter for an operator of a switchboard, or an officer, employee, or agent of a provider of wire or electronic communication service, whose facilities are used in the transmission of

10. Pub. L. 99-509, 100 Stat. 1860 (Oct. 21, 1986), codified as amended in scattered sections of 18 U.S.C.
11. See 18 U.S.C. §§2511-22.

a wire or electronic communication, to intercept, disclose, or use that communication in the normal course of his employment while engaged in any activity which is a necessary incident to the rendition of his service or to the protection of the rights or property of the provider of that service, except that a provider of wire communication service to the public shall not utilize service observing or random monitoring except for mechanical or service quality control checks.

(c) It shall not be unlawful under this chapter for a person acting under color of law to intercept a wire, oral, or electronic communication, where such person is a party to the communication or one of the parties to the communication has given prior consent to such interception.

(d) It shall not be unlawful under this chapter for a person not acting under color of law to intercept a wire, oral, or electronic communication where such person is a party to the communication or where one of the parties to the communication has given prior consent to such interception unless such communication is intercepted for the purpose of committing any criminal or tortious act in violation of the Constitution or laws of the United States or of any State. . . .

(g) It shall not be unlawful under this chapter or chapter 121 of this title for any person —

(i) to intercept or access an electronic communication made through an electronic communication system that is configured so that such electronic communication is readily accessible to the general public. . . .

Violation of Title I can result in damages of a minimum of $10,000 per violation as well as up to five years imprisonment.[13] If the government violates Title I, a criminal defendant "may move to suppress the contents" of the communication or "evidence derived therefrom."[14]

Second, the ECPA makes it unlawful to access communications in electronic storage. Section 2701 provides in pertinent part:

(a) Offense. — Except as provided in subsection (c) of this section, whoever —

(1) intentionally accesses without authorization a facility through which an electronic communication service is provided; or

(2) intentionally exceeds an authorization to access that facility; and thereby obtains, alters, or prevents authorized access to a wire or electronic communication while it is in electronic storage in such system shall be punished as provided in subsection (b) of this section. . . .

(c) Exceptions. — Subsection (a) of this section does not apply with respect to conduct authorized —

---

13. *See* 18 U.S.C. §§2511(4) & (5); 2520(c)(2)(B).
14. 18 U.S.C. §2518(10)(a).

(1) by the person or entity providing a wire or electronic communications service;

(2) by a user of that service with respect to a communication of or intended for that user. . . .[15]

Electronic storage is defined as: "(A) any temporary, intermediate storage of a wire or electronic communication incidental to the electronic transmission thereof; and (B) any storage of such communication by an electronic communication service for purposes of backup protection of such communication."[16] Violations of Section 2701 are subject to criminal and civil liability with a minimum of $1,000 per violation in damages and imprisonment up to two years.[17]

Title II also prohibits the disclosure of the contents of a communication in electronic storage subject except:[18]

A person or entity may divulge the contents of a communication —

(1) to an addressee or intended recipient of such communication . . .

(2) as otherwise authorized in by [Title I] or 2703 of this title;

(3) with the lawful consent of the originator or an addressee or intended recipient of such communication, or the subscriber in the case of remote computing service;

(4) to a person employed or authorized whose facilities are used to forward such communication to its destination;

(5) as may be necessarily incident to the rendition of the service or to the protection of the rights or property of the provider of that service. . . .[19]

In general, Title II requires the government to obtain a warrant or court order before it may obtain access to stored electronic communications.[20]

Because some of the Fourth Amendment and statutory protections differ depending upon who is doing the monitoring, the following materials are divided into government monitoring and private monitoring.

a) Government Monitoring

WARSHAK V. UNITED STATES

490 F.3d 455 (6th Cir. 2007)

Reversed En Banc, 532 F.3d 521 (holding claims not ripe for adjudication)

---

15. 18 U.S.C. §2701.
16. 18 U.S.C. §2510(17).
17. 18 U.S.C. §2701(b).
18. 18 U.S.C. §2702(a).
19. 18 U.S.C. §2702(b).
20. *See* 18 U.S.C. §2703.

BOYCE F. MARTIN, JR., Circuit Judge.

I.

In March 2005, the United States was engaged in a criminal investigation of Plaintiff Steven Warshak and the company he owned, Berkeley Premium Nutraceuticals, Inc. The investigation pertained to allegations of mail and wire fraud, money laundering, and related federal offenses. On May 6, 2005, the government obtained an order from a United States Magistrate Judge in the Southern District of Ohio directing internet service provider ("ISP") NuVox Communications to turn over to government agents information pertaining to Warshak's e-mail account with NuVox. The information to be disclosed included (1) customer account information, such as application information, "account identifiers," "[b]illing information to include bank account numbers," contact information, and "[any] other information pertaining to the customer, including set up, synchronization, etc."; (2) "[t]he contents of wire or electronic communications (not in electronic storage unless greater than 181 days old) that were placed or stored in directories or files owned or controlled" by Warshak; and (3) "[a]ll Log files and backup tapes." . . .

The order stated that it was issued under 18 U.S.C. §2703, part of the Stored Communications Act ("SCA"), and that it was based on "specific and articulable facts showing that there are reasonable grounds to believe that the records or other information sought are relevant and material to an ongoing criminal investigation." The order was issued under seal, and prohibited NuVox from "disclos[ing] the existence of the Application or this Order of the Court, or the existence of this investigation, to the listed customer or to any person unless and until authorized to do so by the Court." The magistrate further ordered that "the notification by the government otherwise required under 18 U.S.C. §2703(b)(1)(B) be delayed for ninety days." On September 12, 2005, the government obtained a nearly identical order pertaining to Yahoo, another ISP, that sought the same types of information from Warshak's Yahoo e-mail account and a Yahoo account identified with another individual named Ron Fricke. . . .

III.

B. Likelihood of Success on the Merits: Probable Cause versus Reasonableness and Fourth Amendment Implications of SCA Orders

1. Probable Cause versus Reasonableness

With respect to the merits of the preliminary injunction, the government argues that court orders issued under section 2703 are not searches but rather compelled disclosures, akin to subpoenas. As a result, according to the government, the more stringent showing of probable cause, a prerequisite to the issuance of a warrant under the Fourth Amendment, is inapplicable, and an order under section 2703 need only be supported by a showing of "reasonable relevance."

The government is correct that "whereas the Fourth Amendment mandates a showing of probable cause for the issuance of search warrants, subpoenas are analyzed only under the Fourth Amendment's general reasonableness standard." *Doe v. United States*, 253 F.3d 256, 263-64 (6th Cir. 2001). As this Court has explained, "[o]ne primary reason for this distinction is that, unlike 'the immediacy and intrusiveness of a search and seizure conducted pursuant to a warrant[,]' the reasonableness of an administrative subpoena's command can be contested in federal court before being enforced." *Id.* at 264. . . .

Phibbs makes explicit, however, a necessary Fourth Amendment caveat to the rule regarding third-party subpoenas: the party challenging the subpoena has "standing to dispute [its] issuance on Fourth Amendment grounds" if he can "demonstrate that he had a legitimate expectation of privacy attaching to the records obtained." . . . This language reflects the rule that where the party challenging the disclosure has voluntarily disclosed his records to a third party, he maintains no expectation of privacy in the disclosure vis-à-vis that individual, and assumes the risk of that person disclosing (or being compelled to disclose) the shared information to the authorities. *See, e.g., United States v. Jacobsen*, 466 U.S. 109, 117 (1984) ("[W]hen an individual reveals private information to another, he assumes the risk that his confidant will reveal that information to the authorities, and if that occurs the Fourth Amendment does not prohibit governmental use of that information.").

Combining this disclosure to a third party with the government's ability to subpoena the third party alleviates any need for the third-party subpoena to meet the probable cause requirement, if the challenger has not maintained an expectation of privacy with respect to the individual being compelled to make the disclosure. For example, in *Phibbs*, the documents in question were credit card and phone records that were "readily accessible to employees during the normal course of business." 999 F.2d at 1078. A similar rationale was employed by the Supreme Court in *Miller*. 425 U.S. at 442 ("The checks are not confidential communications but negotiable instruments to be used in commercial transactions. All of the documents obtained, including financial statements and deposit slips, contain only information voluntarily conveyed to the banks and exposed to their employees in the ordinary course of business."). . . . The government's compelled disclosure argument, while relevant, therefore begs the critical question of whether an e-mail user maintains a reasonable expectation of privacy in his e-mails vis-à-vis the party who is subject to compelled disclosure-in this instance, the ISPs. If he does not, as in *Phibbs* or *Miller*, then the government must meet only the reasonableness standard applicable to compelled disclosures to obtain the material. If, on the other hand, the e-mail user does maintain a reasonable expectation of privacy in the content of the e-mails with respect to the ISP, then the Fourth Amendment's probable cause standard controls the e-mail seizure.

2. Reasonable Expectation of Privacy in E-mail Content

Two amici curiae convincingly analogize the privacy interest that e-mail users hold in the content of their e-mails to the privacy interest in the content of telephone calls, recognized by the Supreme Court in its line of cases involving government eavesdropping on telephone conversations. *See Smith v. Maryland,* 442 U.S. 735 (1979); *Katz v. United States,* 389 U.S. 347 (1967); *Berger v. New York,* 388 U.S. 41 (1967). In *Berger* and *Katz,* telephone surveillance that intercepted the content of a conversation was held to constitute a search, because the caller "is surely entitled to assume that the words he utters into the mouthpiece will not be broadcast to the world," and therefore cannot be said to have forfeited his privacy right in the conversation. *Katz,* 389 U.S. at 352. This is so even though "[t]he telephone conversation itself must be electronically transmitted by telephone company equipment, and may be recorded or overheard by the use of other company equipment." *Smith,* 442 U.S. at 746 (Stewart, J., dissenting). On the other hand, in *Smith,* the Court ruled that the use of pen register, installed at the phone company's facility to record the numbers dialed by the telephone user, did not amount to a search. This distinction was due to the fact that "a pen register differs significantly from the listening device employed in *Katz,* for pen registers do not acquire the *contents* of communications." 442 U.S. at 741 (emphasis in original).

The distinction between *Katz* and *Miller* makes clear that the reasonable expectation of privacy inquiry in the context of shared communications must necessarily focus on two narrower questions than the general fact that the communication was shared with another. First, we must specifically identify the party with whom the communication is shared, as well as the parties from whom disclosure is shielded. Clearly, under *Katz,* the mere fact that a communication is shared with another person does not entirely erode all expectations of privacy, because otherwise eavesdropping would never amount to a search. It is true, however, that by sharing communications with someone else, the speaker or writer assumes the risk that it could be revealed to the government by that person, or obtained through a subpoena directed to that person. *See Miller,* 425 U.S. at 443 ("[T]he Fourth Amendment does not prohibit the obtaining of information revealed to a third party and conveyed by him to Government authorities."). The same does not necessarily apply, however, to an intermediary that merely has the ability to access the information sought by the government. Otherwise phone conversations would never be protected, merely because the telephone company can access them; letters would never be protected, by virtue of the Postal Service's ability to access them; the contents of shared safe deposit boxes or storage lockers would never be protected, by virtue of the bank or storage company's ability to access them.

The second necessary inquiry pertains to the precise information actually conveyed to the party through whom disclosure is sought or obtained. This distinction provides the obvious crux for the different results in *Katz* and *Smith,* because although the conduct of the telephone user in *Smith* "may have been calculated to keep the *contents* of his conversation private, his conduct was not and could not have been calculated to preserve the privacy of the number he dialed." 442 U.S. at 743. Like the depositor in *Miller,* the caller in *Smith* "assumed the risk" of the phone company disclosing the records that he conveyed to it. *Id.* Yet this assumption of the risk is limited to the specific information conveyed to the service provider, which in the telephone context excludes the content of the conversation. It is apparent, therefore, that although the government can compel disclosure of a shared communication from the party with whom it was shared, it can only compel disclosure of the specific information to which the subject of its compulsion has been granted access. It cannot, on the other hand, bootstrap an intermediary's limited access to one part of the communication (e.g. the phone number) to allow it access to another part (the content of the conversation).

This focus on the specific information shared with the subject of compelled disclosure applies with equal force in the e-mail context. Compelled disclosure of subscriber information and related records through the ISP might not undermine the e-mail subscriber's Fourth Amendment interest under *Smith,* because like the information obtained through the pen register in *Smith* and like the bank records in *Miller,* subscriber information and related records are records of the service provider as well, and may likely be accessed by ISP employees in the normal course of their employment. Consequently, the user does not maintain the same expectation of privacy in them vis-à-vis the service provider, and a third party subpoena to the service provider to access information that is shared with it likely creates no Fourth Amendment problems. The combined precedents of *Katz* and *Smith,* however, recognize a heightened protection for the *content* of the communications. Like telephone conversations, simply because the phone company or the ISP *could* access the content of e-mails and phone calls, the privacy expectation in the content of either is not diminished, because there is a societal expectation that the ISP or the phone company will not do so as a matter of course.

* * *

This analysis is consistent with other decisions that have addressed an individual's expectation of privacy in particular electronic communications. In *Guest v. Leis,* 255 F.3d 325, 333 (6th Cir. 2001), we concluded that users of electronic bulletin boards lacked an expectation of privacy in material posted on the bulletin board, as such materials were "intended for publication or public posting." Of course the public disclosure of material to an untold number of readers distinguishes bulletin board postings from e-mails, which typically have a limited, select number of recipients. . . . Although we stated that an e-mail sender would "lose a legitimate expectation of privacy in an e-mail that had already reached its recipient," analogizing such an e-mailer to "a letter-writer," this diminished privacy is only relevant with respect to the recipient, as the sender has assumed the risk of disclosure by or through the recipient. *Id.* at 333. . . .

Other courts have addressed analogous situations where electronic communications were obtained based on the sender's use of a computer network. In *United States v. Simons,* the Fourth Circuit held that a government employee lacked a reasonable expectation of privacy in electronic files on his office computer, in light of the employer's policy that explicitly notified the employee of its intention to "audit, inspect, and monitor," his computer files. 206 F.3d 392, 398 (4th Cir. 2000). In light of this explicit policy, the employee's belief that his files were private was not objectively reasonable. *Id.* On the other hand, in *United States v. Heckenkamp,* the Ninth Circuit held that a university student did have a reasonable expectation of privacy in his computer files even though he "attached [his computer] to the university network," because the "university policies do not eliminate Heckenkamp's expectation of privacy in his computer." 482 F.3d 1142, 1147 (9th Cir. 2007). Although the university did "establish limited instances in which university administrators may access his computer in order to protect the university's systems," this exception fell far short of a blanket monitoring or auditing policy, and the Ninth Circuit deemed it insufficient to waive the user's expectation of privacy.

Heckenkamp and *Simons* provide useful bookends for the question before us, regarding when the use of some intermediary provider of computer and e-mail services — be it a commercial ISP, a university, an employer, or another type of entity — amounts to a waiver of the user's reasonable expectation of privacy in the content of the e-mails with respect to that intermediary. In instances where a user agreement explicitly provides that e-mails and other files will be monitored or audited as in *Simons,* the user's knowledge of this fact may well extinguish his reasonable expectation of privacy. Without such a statement, however, the service provider's control over the files and ability to access them under certain limited circumstances will not be enough to overcome an expectation of privacy, as in *Heckenkamp.*

Turning to the instant case, we have little difficulty agreeing with the district court that individuals maintain a reasonable expectation of privacy in e-mails that are stored with, or sent or received through, a commercial ISP. The content of e-mail is something that the user "seeks to preserve as private," and therefore "may be constitutionally protected." *Katz,* 389 U.S. at 351. It goes without saying that like the telephone earlier in our history, e-mail is an ever-increasing mode of private communication, and protecting shared communications through this medium is as important to Fourth Amendment principles today as protecting telephone conversations has been in the past. *See Katz,* 389 U.S. at 352 ("To read the Constitution more narrowly is to ignore the vital role that the public telephone has come to play in private communication.")

The government asserts that ISPs have the contractual right to access users' e-mails. . . . [A] privacy interest in records held by a third party is only undermined where the documents are accessed by the third party or its employees "in the ordinary course of business." *Miller,* 425 U.S. at 442. [A]s explained in the Ninth Circuit's decision in *Heckenkamp,* mere accessibility is not enough to waive an expectation of privacy. . . . Where a user agreement calls for regular auditing, inspection, or monitoring of e-mails, the expectation may well be different, as the potential for an administrator to read the content of e-mails in the account should be apparent to the user. Where there is such an arrangement, compelled disclosure by means of an SCA order directed at the ISP would be akin to the third party subpoena directed at a bank. In contrast, the terms of service in question here, which the government has cited to in both the district court and this Court, clearly provide for access only in limited circumstances, rather than wholesale inspection, auditing, or monitoring of e-mails.[7] Because the ISPs right to access e-mails under these user agreements is reserved for extraordinary circumstances, much like the university policy in *Heckenkamp,* it is similarly insufficient to undermine a user's expectation of privacy. For now, the government has made no showing that e-mail content is regularly accessed by ISPs, or that users are aware of such access of content.

The government also insists that ISPs regularly screen users' e-mails for viruses, spam, and child pornography. Even assuming that this is true, however, such a process does not waive an expectation of privacy in the content of e-mails sent through the ISP, for the same reasons that the terms of service are insufficient to waive privacy expectations. The government states that ISPs "are developing technology that will enable them to scan user images" for child pornography and viruses. The government's statement that this process involves "technology," rather than manual, human review, suggests that it involves a computer searching for particular terms, types of images, or similar indicia of wrongdoing that would not disclose the content of the e-mail to any person at the ISP or elsewhere, aside from the recipient. But the reasonable expectation of privacy of an e-mail user goes to the *content* of the e-mail message. The fact that a computer scans millions of e-mails for signs of pornography or a virus does not invade an individual's content-based privacy interest in the e-mails and has little bearing on his expectation of privacy in the content. In fact, these screening processes are analogous to the post office screening packages for evidence of drugs or explosives, which does not expose the content of written documents enclosed in the packages. The fact that such screening occurs as a general matter does not diminish the well-established

---

7. *See* Gov't Br. at 34 (citing Yahoo terms of service which allow access where "reasonably necessary to: (a) comply with legal process; (b) enforce the [Terms of Service]; (c) respond to claims that any Content violates the rights of third parties; (d) respond to your requests for customer service; or (e) protect the rights, property or personal safety of Yahoo!, its users and the public."). As amicus Electronic Frontier Foundation points out, each instance involves outside prompting for an ISP to review content, and does not occur in the normal course of business. This type of accessibility by the service provider was rejected as diminishing the expectation of privacy in *Katz,* as well as in *Heckenkamp.*

reasonable expectation of privacy that users of the mail maintain in the packages they send.

It is also worth noting that other portions of the SCA itself strongly support an e-mail user's reasonable expectation of privacy in the content of his e-mails. Section 2701 prohibits unauthorized users from accessing e-mails. Section 2702 generally prohibits an ISP from disclosing e-mail content without the permission of the user. Further, section 2703 makes it easier for the government to get an order requiring the disclosure of records and subscriber information, in which the user does not maintain a privacy interest vis-à-vis the ISP, than to obtain an order requiring the disclosure of content. The statute also requires a warrant to search the content of e-mails that have been stored for 180 days or less. 18 U.S.C. 1703(a). Thus, even though the contested exception in section 2703(b) creates tension with the Fourth Amendment's requirements for a warrant, independent provisions support the proposition that a user maintains a reasonable expectation of privacy in the content of his e-mails.

COMMENTS AND QUESTIONS

1. As noted in *Warshak,* when dealing with Internet communications, courts distinguish between communication information routinely disclosed to third parties and the contents of those communications. As such, courts have held that individuals have no reasonable expectation of privacy in subscriber information such as their name, address, dates and times of Internet usage, or their IP addresses. *See* United States v. Allen, 53 M.J. 402 (C.A.A.F. 2000) (holding that such information was properly disclosed without a warrant); United States v. Butler, 151. F. Supp. 2d 82 (D. Me. 2001) (holding that a student had no reasonable expectation of privacy in university computer logs that recorded when he used the school's computers). Moreover, courts have reached this conclusion despite the fact that the ECPA creates statutory protection for this type of communications. As one court concluded, "Although Congress is willing to recognize that individuals have some degree of privacy in the stored data and transactional records that their ISP's retain, the ECPA is hardly a legislative determination that this expectation of privacy is one that rises to the level of 'reasonably objective' for Fourth Amendment purposes." United States v. Hambrick, 55 F. Supp. 2d 504, 507 (W.D. Va. 1999).

2. Does an individual have a reasonable expectation of privacy in an online alias? *See* United States v. Hambrick, 55. F. Supp. 2d 504 (W.D. Va. 1999) (concluding that a user had no reasonable expectation in the privacy of their online alias because, "When the defendant selected his screen name it became tied to his true identity in all [the ISP's] records."). In reaching this conclusion, the court relied heavily upon the argument that the ECPA does not prevent ISPs from disclosing a subscriber's identity to nongovernmental actors, and that ISPs commonly sell subscriber information to marketing firms.

Is disclosing Hambrick as a Mindspring subscriber the same as identifying him as "Blowuinva"? Can anyone request the identity of an anonymous Internet user and obtain that information? See Chapter 3, *supra*. If not, then why is there no reasonable expectation of privacy especially when the ECPA limits government access to such information?

3. Are the privacy interests in e-mail analogous to those respecting first-class mail and telephone calls?

4. In Commonwealth v. Proetto, 771 A.2d 823 (Super. Ct. Pa. 2001), the defendant was convicted of criminal solicitation, obscene and other sexual materials and performances, and corruption of minors resulting from chatroom conversations with a 15-year-old. The recipient of the e-mails forwarded them to the police, who then posed as the recipient and received further communications. With respect to the forwarded messages, the court concluded that the defendant could have no reasonable expectation of privacy because the recipient could forward them to whomever:

> Sending an e-mail or chat-room communication is analogous to leaving a message on an answering machine. The sender knows that by the nature of sending the communication a record of the communication, including the substance of the communication, is made and can be downloaded, printed, saved, or, in some cases, if not deleted by the receiver, will remain on the receiver's system. Accordingly, by the act of forwarding an e-mail or communication via the Internet, the sender expressly consents by conduct to the recording of the message.

Similarly, the court concluded that the defendant could have no reasonable expectation of privacy in his chatroom communications because "[w]hen Appellant engaged in chat-room conversations, he did not know to whom he was speaking. Oftentimes individuals engaging in chat-room conversations pretend to be someone other than who they are." *Id.* at 831. *See also* United States v. Charbonneau, 979 F. Supp. 1177 (S.D. Ohio 1997) (no reasonable expectation of privacy in the contents of online chats and emails sent to an undercover police officer).

5. In the preceding cases, any information intercepted by the government was "voluntarily" disclosed by the defendants, and the issues, therefore, revolved around the propriety of subsequent government access to stored information. As one court specifically noted "we can say that the transmitter of an e-mail message enjoys a reasonable expectation that police officials will not intercept the transmission without probable cause and a search warrant. However, once the transmissions are received by another person, the transmitter no longer controls its destiny." United States v. Maxwell, 45 M.J. 406, 418 (Armed Forces 1996). As the preceding cases make clear, this distinction is important, in part, because the ECPA suppresses illegally intercepted communications but does not provide for the suppression of stored information even when it is illegally obtained. But what does it mean to intercept an electronic communication?

STEVE JACKSON GAMES, INC. V. UNITED STATES SECRET SERVICE

36 F.3d 457 (5th Cir. 1994)

RHESA HAWKINS BARKSDALE, Circuit Judge:

The narrow issue before us is whether the seizure of a computer, used to operate an electronic bulletin board system, and containing private electronic mail which had been sent to (stored on) the bulletin board, but not read (retrieved) by the intended recipients, constitutes an unlawful intercept under the Federal Wiretap Act, 18 U.S.C. §2510, et seq., as amended by Title I of the Electronic Communications Privacy Act of 1986, Pub. L. No. 99-508, Title I, 100 Stat. 1848 (1986). . . .

Appellant Steve Jackson Games, Incorporated (SJG), publishes books, magazines, role-playing games, and related products. Starting in the mid-1980s, SJG operated an electronic bulletin board system, called "Illuminati" (BBS), from one of its computers. SJG used the BBS to post public information about its business, games, publications, and the role-playing hobby; to facilitate play-testing of games being developed; and to communicate with its customers and free-lance writers by electronic mail (E-mail).

Central to the issue before us, the BBS also offered customers the ability to send and receive private E-mail. Private E-mail was stored on the BBS computer's hard disk drive temporarily, until the addressees "called" the BBS (using their computers and modems) and read their mail. After reading their E-mail, the recipients could choose to either store it on the BBS computer's hard drive or delete it. In February 1990, there were 365 BBS users. Among other uses, appellants Steve Jackson, Elizabeth McCoy, William Milliken, and Steffan O'Sullivan used the BBS for communication by private E-mail.

In October 1988, Henry Kluepfel, Director of Network Security Technology (an affiliate Bell Company), began investigating the unauthorized duplication and distribution of a computerized text file, containing information about Bell's emergency call system. In July 1989, Kluepfel informed Secret Service Agent Foley and an Assistant United States Attorney in Chicago about the unauthorized distribution. In early February 1990, Kluepfel learned that the document was available on the "Phoenix Project" computer bulletin board, which was operated by Loyd Blankenship in Austin, Texas; that Blankenship was an SJG employee; and that, as a co-systems operator of the BBS, Blankenship had the ability to review and, perhaps, delete any data on the BBS.

On February 28, 1990, Agent Foley applied for a warrant to search SJG's premises and Blankenship's residence. . . . Among the items seized was the computer which operated the BBS. At the time of the seizure, 162 items of unread, private E-mail were stored on the BBS, including items addressed to the individual appellants. Despite the Secret Service's denial, the district court found that Secret Service personnel or delegates read and deleted the private E-mail stored on the BBS.

Appellants filed suit in May 1991 against, among others, the Secret Service and the United States, claiming, inter alia, violations of the Privacy Protection Act, 42 U.S.C. §2000aa, et seq.[1] the Federal Wiretap Act, as amended by Title I of the Electronic Communications Privacy Act (ECPA), 18 U.S.C. §§2510-2521 (proscribes, inter alia, the intentional interception of electronic communications); and Title II of the ECPA, 18 U.S.C. §§2701-2711 (proscribes, inter alia, intentional access, without authorization, to stored electronic communications). . . .

II.

As stated, the sole issue is a very narrow one: whether the seizure of a computer on which is stored private E-mail that has been sent to an electronic bulletin board, but not yet read (retrieved) by the recipients, constitutes an "intercept" proscribed by 18 U.S.C. §2511(1)(a).

. . . Prior to the 1986 amendment by Title I of the ECPA, [the Federal Wire Tap Act] covered only wire and oral communications. Title I of the ECPA extended that coverage to electronic communications. In relevant part, §2511(1)(a) proscribes "intentionally intercept[ing] . . . any wire, oral, or electronic communication," unless the intercept is authorized by court order or by other exceptions not relevant here. Section 2520 authorizes, inter alia, persons whose electronic communications are intercepted in violation of §2511 to bring a civil action against the interceptor for actual damages, or for statutory damages of $10,000 per violation or $100 per day of the violation, whichever is greater. 18 U.S.C. §2520.

The Act defines "intercept" as "the aural or other acquisition of the contents of any wire, electronic, or oral communication through the use of any electronic, mechanical, or other device." 18 U.S.C. §2510(4). The district court, relying on our court's interpretation of intercept in United States v. Turk, 526 F.2d 654 (5th Cir.), cert. denied, 429 U.S. 823 1976), held that the Secret Service did not intercept the communications, because its acquisition of the contents of those communications was not contemporaneous with their transmission. In Turk, the government seized from a suspect's vehicle an audio tape of a prior conversation between the suspect and Turk. (Restated, when the conversation took place, it was not recorded contemporaneously by the government.) Our court held that replaying the previously recorded conversation was not an "intercept," because an intercept "require[s] participation by the one charged with an 'interception' in the contemporaneous acquisition of the communication through the use of the device." *Id.* at 658.

---

1. Section 2000aa(a) provides that it is unlawful for a government officer or employee, in connection with the investigation . . . of a criminal offense, to search for or seize any work product materials possessed by a person reasonably believed to have a purpose to disseminate to the public a newspaper, book, broadcast, or other similar form of public communication. . . .

Appellants agree with Turk's holding, but contend that it is not applicable, because it "says nothing about government action that both acquires the communication prior to its delivery, and prevents that delivery." . . . They maintain that to hold otherwise does violence to Congress' purpose in enacting the ECPA, to include providing protection for E-mail and bulletin boards. . . .

Prior to the 1986 amendment by the ECPA, the Wiretap Act defined "intercept" as the "aural acquisition" of the contents of wire or oral communications through the use of a device. 18 U.S.C. §2510(4) (1968). The ECPA amended this definition to include the "aural or other acquisition of the contents of . . . wire, electronic, or oral communications. . . ." 18 U.S.C. §2510(4) (1986). The significance of the addition of the words "or other" in the 1986 amendment to the definition of "intercept" becomes clear when the definitions of "aural" and "electronic communication" are examined; electronic communications (which include the non-voice portions of wire communications), as defined by the Act, cannot be acquired aurally.

Webster's Third New International Dictionary (1986) defines "aural" as "of or relating to the ear" or "of or relating to the sense of hearing." *Id.* at 144. And, the Act defines "aural transfer" as "a transfer containing the human voice at any point between and including the point of origin and the point of reception." 18 U.S.C. §2510(18). This definition is extremely important for purposes of understanding the definition of a "wire communication," which is defined by the Act as:

> any aural transfer made in whole or in part through the use of facilities for the transmission of communications by the aid of wire, cable, or other like connection between the point of origin and the point of reception (including the use of such connection in a switching station) . . . and such term includes any electronic storage of such communication.

18 U.S.C. §2510(1). In contrast, as noted, an "electronic communication" is defined as "any transfer of signs, signals, writing, images, sounds, data, or intelligence of any nature transmitted in whole or in part by a wire, radio, electromagnetic, photoelectronic or photooptical system . . . but does not include . . . any wire or oral communication. . . ." 18 U.S.C. §2510(12).

Critical to the issue before us is the fact that, unlike the definition of "wire communication," the definition of "electronic communication" does not include electronic storage of such communications. *See* 18 U.S.C. §2510(12).[6] "Electronic storage" is defined as

(A) any temporary, intermediate storage of a wire or electronic communication incidental to the electronic transmission thereof; and

(B) any storage of such communication by an electronic communication service for purposes of backup protection of such communication. . . .

---

6. Wire and electronic communications are subject to different treatment under the Wiretap Act. The Act's exclusionary rule, 18 U.S.C. §2515, applies to the interception of wire communications, including such communications in electronic storage, *see* 18 U.S.C. §2510(1), but not to the interception of electronic communications. *See* 18 U.S.C. §2518(10)(a).

18 U.S.C. §2510(17). The E-mail in issue was in "electronic storage." Congress' use of the word "transfer" in the definition of "electronic communication," and its omission in that definition of the phrase "any electronic storage of such communication" (part of the definition of "wire communication") reflects that Congress did not intend for "intercept" to apply to "electronic communications" when those communications are in "electronic storage." . . .

Our conclusion is reinforced further by consideration of the fact that Title II of the ECPA clearly applies to the conduct of the Secret Service in this case. . . . Title II generally proscribes unauthorized access to stored wire or electronic communications. Section 2701(a) provides:

> Except as provided in subsection (c) of this section whoever —
> (1) intentionally accesses without authorization a facility through which an electronic communication service is provided; or
> (2) intentionally exceeds an authorization to access that facility; and thereby obtains, alters, or prevents authorized access to a wire or electronic communication while it is in electronic storage in such system shall be punished. . . .

18 U.S.C. §2701(a).

As stated, the district court found that the Secret Service violated §2701 when it:

> intentionally accesse[d] without authorization a facility [the computer] through which an electronic communication service [the BBS] is provided . . . and thereby obtain[ed] [and] prevent[ed] authorized access [by appellants] to a[n] . . . electronic communication while it is in electronic storage in such system.

18 U.S.C. §2701(a). The Secret Service does not challenge this ruling. We find no indication in either the Act or its legislative history that Congress intended for conduct that is clearly prohibited by Title II to furnish the basis for a civil remedy under Title I as well. Indeed, there are persuasive indications that it had no such intention.

First, the substantive and procedural requirements for authorization to intercept electronic communications are quite different from those for accessing stored electronic communications. For example, a governmental entity may gain access to the contents of electronic communications that have been in electronic storage for less than 180 days by obtaining a warrant. *See* 18 U.S.C. §2703(a). But there are more stringent, complicated requirements for the interception of electronic communications; a court order is required. *See* 18 U.S.C. §2518.

Second, other requirements applicable to the interception of electronic communications, such as those governing minimization, duration, and the types of crimes that may be investigated, are not imposed when the communications at issue are not in the process of being transmitted at the moment of seizure, but instead are in electronic storage. For example, a court order authorizing interception of electronic communications is required to include a directive that the order shall be executed "in such a way as to minimize the interception of communications not otherwise subject to interception." 18 U.S.C. §2518(5). Title II of the ECPA does not contain this requirement for warrants authorizing access to stored electronic communications. The purpose of the minimization requirement is to implement "the constitutional obligation of avoiding, to the greatest possible extent, seizure of conversations which have no relationship to the crimes being investigated or the purpose for which electronic surveillance has been authorized." James G. Carr, The Law of Electronic Surveillance, §5.7(a) at 5-28 (1994).

Obviously, when intercepting electronic communications, law enforcement officers cannot know in advance which, if any, of the intercepted communications will be relevant to the crime under investigation, and often will have to obtain access to the contents of the communications in order to make such a determination. Interception thus poses a significant risk that officers will obtain access to communications which have no relevance to the investigation they are conducting. That risk is present to a lesser degree, and can be controlled more easily, in the context of stored electronic communications, because, as the Secret Service advised the district court, technology exists by which relevant communications can be located without the necessity of reviewing the entire contents of all of the stored communications. For example, the Secret Service claimed (although the district court found otherwise) that it reviewed the private E-mail on the BBS by use of key word searches.

Next, as noted, court orders authorizing an intercept of electronic communications are subject to strict requirements as to duration. An intercept may not be authorized "for any period longer than is necessary to achieve the objective of the authorization, nor in any event longer than thirty days." 18 U.S.C. §2518(5). There is no such requirement for access to stored communications.

Finally, as also noted, the limitations as to the types of crimes that may be investigated through an intercept, see 18 U.S.C. §2516, have no counterpart in Title II of the ECPA. See, e.g., 18 U.S.C. §2703(d) (court may order a provider of electronic communication service or remote computing service to disclose to a governmental entity the contents of a stored electronic communication on a showing that the information sought is "relevant to a legitimate law enforcement inquiry").

In light of the substantial differences between the statutory procedures and requirements for obtaining authorization to intercept electronic communications, on the one hand, and to gain access to the contents of stored electronic communications, on the other, it is most unlikely that Congress intended to require law enforcement officers to satisfy the more stringent requirements for an intercept in order to gain access to the contents of stored electronic communications. . . .

For the foregoing reasons, the judgment is AFFIRMED.

COMMENTS AND QUESTIONS

1. Is there a difference in the distinction between interception of and access to electronic communications? Considering that all electronic communications, including electronic mail, must be stored before the data can be understood, under what circumstances can an electronic communication, including electronic mail, be intercepted?

2. Why does the court reject the argument that an electronic communication is intercepted if it has not yet reached the recipient? Compare *Steve Jackson Games* with Fraser v. Nationwide Mutual Ins. Co., *infra*, in which the court adopts this interpretation of interception? Does the language of the statute require the result reached by the court in *Steve Jackson Games*?

3. Is the Fifth Circuit's interpretation of interception consistent with Congress's intent? According to the legislative history, Congress enacted the ECPA specifically to provide, "comparable Federal statutory standards to protect the privacy and security of communications transmitted by new . . . forms of telecommunications and computer technology" and specifically to prevent the interception of electronic mail. *See* S. Rep. No. 99-541 (1986), reprinted in 1986 U.S.C.C.A.N. 3555 (noting the need to clarify that interception of electronic mail are covered by the federal wiretap law). In so doing, Congress specifically recognized that the minimization requirement of 18 U.S.C. §2815(5) would apply to electronic mail though it "would require a somewhat different procedure than that used to minimize a telephone call." *Id*.

4. In reaching its conclusion, the Fifth Circuit relied heavily on its belief that Congress did not intend "for conduct that is clearly prohibited by Title II to furnish the basis for a civil remedy under Title I as well." Compare this conclusion with the Ninth Circuit's decision in United States v. Smith, 155 F.3d 1051 (9th Cir. 1998) (concluding that the retrieval and recording of a voice-mail message was an interception subject to the ECPA). While distinguishing wire communications from electronic communications, the *Smith* court attempted to resolve the tension between access and interception by stating:

> The terms "intercept" and "access" are not, as the government claims, temporally different, with the former, but not the latter, requiring contemporaneity; rather, the terms are conceptually, or qualitatively, different. The word "intercept" entails *actually* acquiring the contents of a communication, whereas the word "access" merely involves *being in position* to acquire the contents of a communication. In other words, "access[ ]" is, for all intents and purposes, a lesser included offense (or tort, as the case may be) of "intercept[ion]." As applied to the facts of this case, Gore might have violated the Stored Communications Act's prohibition on "access[ing]" by simply making unauthorized use of Bravo's voice-mail password and roaming about PDA's automated voicemail system, even had she never recorded or otherwise "intercepted" the contents of any given message. Once she retrieved and recorded Smith's message, however, she crossed the line between

the Stored Communications Act and the Wiretap Act and violated the latter's prohibition on "intercept[ion]."

Id. at 1058 (emphasis in original). Could this reasoning be applied to electronic mail? Which approach is more consistent with the statute? With the statute's legislative history? For an interpretation of how the stored communications provisions should apply to e-mail in various means of storage consider the following excerpt from the Department of Justice explaining that "Whether a provider is a provider of 'electronic communication service (ECS),' a provider of 'remote computing service (RCS),' or neither depends on the nature of the particular communication sought. For example, a single provider can simultaneously provide 'electronic communication service' with respect to one communication and 'remote computing service' with respect to another communication."

An example can illustrate how these principles work in practice. Imagine that Joe sends an e-mail from his account at work ("joe@goodcompany.com") to the personal account of his friend Jane ("jane@localisp.com"). The e-mail will stream across the Internet until it reaches the servers of Jane's Internet service provider, here the fictional http://10.173.2.10/criminal/cybercrime/searchmanual.htm (58 of 122) [02/16/2001 b1:00:57 PM] LocalISP. When the message first arrives at LocalISP, LocalISP is a provider of ECS with respect to that message. Before Jane accesses LocalISP and retrieves the message, Joe's e-mail is in "electronic storage." See Steve Jackson Games, Inc. v. United States Secret Service, 36 F.3d 457, 461 (5th Cir. 1994). Once Jane retrieves Joe's e-mail, she can either delete the message from LocalISP's server, or else leave the message stored there. If Jane chooses to store the e-mail with LocalISP, LocalISP is now a provider of RCS with respect to the e-mail sent by Joe, not a provider of ECS. The role of LocalISP has changed from a transmitter of Joe's e-mail to a storage facility for the file on LocalISP's server. Joe's e-mail is now simply a file stored remotely for Jane by an RCS, in this case LocalISP. See H.R. Rep. No. 99-647, at 64-65 (1986) (noting Congressional intent to treat opened e-mail stored on a server under provisions relating to remote computing services, rather than services holding communications in "electronic storage").

Next imagine that Jane responds to Joe's e-mail. Jane's return e-mail to Joe will stream across the Internet to the servers of Joe's employer, Good Company. Before Joe retrieves the e-mail from Good Company's servers, Good Company is a provider of ECS with respect to Jane's e-mail (just like LocalISP was with respect to Joe's original e-mail before Jane accessed it). When Joe accesses Jane's e-mail message and the communication reaches its destination (Joe), Good Company ceases to be a provider of ECS with respect to that e-mail (just like LocalISP ceased to be a provider of ECS with respect to Joe's original e-mail when Jane accessed it). Unlike LocalISP, however, Good Company does not become a provider of RCS if Joe decides to store the opened e-mail on Good Company's server. Rather, for purposes of this specific message, Good Company is a provider of neither ECS nor RCS. Good Company does not provide RCS because it does not provide services to the public. See 18 U.S.C. §2711(2) ("[T]he term 'remote computing service' means the provision to the public of computer storage or processing services by means of an electronic communications system.") (emphasis added); Andersen Consulting, 991 F. Supp. at 1043. Because Good Company provides neither ECS nor RCS with respect to the opened e-mail in Joe's account, ECPA no longer regulates access to this e-mail, and such access is governed solely by the Fourth Amendment. Functionally speaking, the opened e-mail in Joe's account drops out of ECPA.

Finally, consider the status of the other copies in this scenario: Jane has downloaded a copy of Joe's e-mail from LocalISP's server to her personal computer at home, and Joe has downloaded a copy of Jane's e-mail from Good Company's server to his office desktop computer at work. ECPA governs neither. Although these computers contain copies of e-mails, these copies are not stored on the server of a third-party provider of RCS or ECS, and therefore ECPA does not apply. Access to the copies of the communications stored in Jane's personal computer at home and Joe's office computer at work is governed solely by the Fourth Amendment. . . .

Computer Crime and Intellectual Property Section, United States Department of Justice, Searching and Seizing Computers and Obtaining Electronic Evidence in Criminal Investigations 58-59 (Jan. 2001), available at *http://www.usdoj.gov/criminal/cybercrime/s&smanual/2002.htm*.

5. Compare the U.S. approach to reasonable expectations of privacy with the European Convention on Human Rights Article 8 which provides:

> 1. Everyone has a right to respect for his private and family life, his home and his correspondence.
>
> 2. There shall be no interference by a public authority with the exercise of this right except such as in accordance with the law and is necessary in a democratic society in the interests of national security, public safety or the economic well-being of the country, for the prevention of disorder or crime, for the protection of health or morals, or for the protection of the rights and freedoms of others.

Under these provisions, the European Court of Human Rights concluded in Copeland v. United Kingdom, ECHR (03/07/07), that the monitoring of a governmental employee to determine whether she was "making excessive use of College facilities for personal purposes" amounted to a violation of Article 8. According to the court:

> the collection and storage of personal information relating to the applicant's telephone, as well as to her e-mail and internet usage, without her knowledge, amounted to an interference with her right to respect for her private life and correspondence within the meaning of Article 8. . . .
>
> [In the absence of] domestic law regulating monitoring at the relevant time, the interference in this case was not "in accordance with the law" as required by Article 8 §2 of the Convention. The Court would not exclude that the monitoring of an employee's use of a telephone, e-mail or internet at the place of work may be considered "necessary in a democratic society" in certain situations in pursuit of a legitimate aim. However, having regard to its above conclusion, it is not necessary to pronounce on that matter in the instant case.

Aside from the result, how does the EU's approach differ from the approach taken by courts in the United States?

Note: Government Monitoring from Carnivore and the NSA

One technology that clearly involves the interception of electronic communications is the U.S. government's program formerly known as "Carnivore," now known as DCS1000. According to the Federal Bureau of Investigation:

> In recent years, the FBI has encountered an increasing number of criminal investigations in which the criminal subjects use the Internet to communicate with each other or to communicate with their victims. Because many Internet Service Providers (ISP) lacked the ability to discriminate communications to identify a particular subject's messages to the exclusion of all others, the FBI designed and developed a diagnostic tool, called Carnivore.
>
> The Carnivore device provides the FBI with a "surgical" ability to intercept and collect the communications which are the subject of the lawful order while ignoring those communications which they are not authorized to intercept. This type of tool is necessary to meet the stringent requirements of the federal wiretapping statutes.
>
> The Carnivore device works much like commercial "sniffers" and other network diagnostic tools used by ISPs every day, except that it provides the FBI with a unique ability to distinguish between communications which may be lawfully intercepted and those which may not. For example, if a court order provides for the lawful interception of one type of communication (e.g., e-mail), but excludes all other communications (e.g., online shopping) the Carnivore tool can be configured to intercept only those e-mails being transmitted either to or from the named subject.
>
> Carnivore serves to limit the messages viewable by human eyes to those which are strictly included within the court order. ISP knowledge and assistance, as directed by court order, is required to install the device.
>
> The use of the Carnivore system by the FBI is subject to intense oversight from internal FBI controls, the U.S. Department of Justice (both at a Headquarters level and at a U.S. Attorney's Office level), and by the Court. There are significant penalties for misuse of the tool, including exclusion of evidence, as well as criminal and civil penalties. The system is not susceptible to abuse because it requires expertise to install and operate, and such operations are conducted, as required in the court orders, with close cooperation with the ISPs.

Internet and Data Interception Capabilities Developed by the FBI, Statement for the Record, U.S. House of Representatives, the Committee on the Judiciary, Subcommittee on the Constitution, 07/24/2000, Laboratory Division Assistant Director Dr. Donald M. Kerr, available online at *http://www.cdt.org/security/carnivore/000724kerr.htm*. Previously available at the FBI's Web site (*www.fbi.gov*), the following diagram illustrates how Carnivore functions.

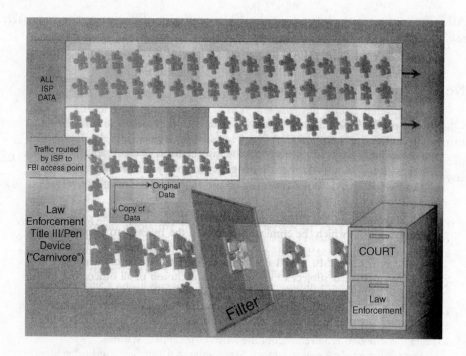

The top of the diagram shows all traffic through an Internet Service Provider (ISP). The FBI and ISP work together to identify an access point that contains all traffic from the suspect named in the court order, with as little other traffic as possible. In some cases, the ISP is able to provide the FBI with an access point that contains only the suspect's traffic.

The FBI connects a commercially available one-way tapping device at the ISP's access point. This tap produces an exact copy of all data at the access point. The tap also provides electrical isolation to prevent Carnivore from having any kind of impact on the ISP's network.

The copied network traffic then flows into the collection system where it is compared against a predefined filter. This filter only passes traffic authorized for capture by the court order. Traffic that passes through the filter continues on to be archived to permanent storage media. No other data is ever stored to permanent media, nor is any information recorded about traffic that does not match the filters.

All information collected is maintained and, in the case of full content interceptions, is sealed under the order of the court. This information, as well as information obtained pursuant to pen register and trap & trace authorities may subsequently be made available by the court to the defendant.

The existence of Carnivore raised significant public concern over the privacy of Internet communications and prompted congressional hearings on the subject. Prior to September 11, 2001, the validity of Carnivore was challenged, in part, because of the FBI's position that the use of Carnivore was authorized under Title III, which deals with pen registers and trap and trace devices used to record telephone numbers. *See* 18 U.S.C. §§3121-3127. In Smith v. Maryland, 442 U.S. 735 (1979), the Supreme Court concluded that there is no reasonable expectation of privacy in the telephone numbers that individuals dial because those numbers are revealed to the telephone company. Privacy advocates questioned whether the information gathered by Carnivore was comparable to the information gathered by pen registers. Unlike pen registers, which record only the telephone number an individual dialed, Carnivore records the entire electronic communication including the content of the communication. Moreover, unlike pen registers that record only the numbers dialed by a particular telephone subscriber, Carnivore records all of an ISP's electronic communication traffic in order to "filter" the communications sought by the government.

Following September 11, 2001, Congress adopted the USA Patriot Act of 2001, Pub. L. 107-56 (2001), which, among other things, amended Title III to include "routing" and "addressing" information. Moreover, Congress amended Section 3123(a) to provide in pertinent part:

> (3)(A) Where the law enforcement agency implementing an ex parte order under this subsection seeks to do so by installing and using its own pen register or trap and trace device on a packet-switched data network of a provider of electronic communication service to the public, the agency shall ensure that a record will be maintained which will identify—
> (i) any officer or officers who installed the device and any officer or officers who accessed the device to obtain information from the network;
> (ii) the date and time the device was installed, the date and time the device was uninstalled, and the date, time, and duration of each time the device is accessed to obtain information;
> (iii) the configuration of the device at the time of its installation and any subsequent modification thereof; and
> (iv) any information which has been collected by the device.
> To the extent that the pen register or trap and trace device can be set automatically to record this information electronically, the record shall be maintained electronically throughout the installation and use of such device.
> (B) The record maintained under subparagraph (A) shall be provided ex parte and under seal to the court which entered the ex parte order authorizing the installation and use of the device within 30 days after termination of the order (including any extensions thereof).

18 U.S.C. §3123(a). Do the procedures adopted by the USA Patriot Act alleviate the privacy concerns raised by Carnivore? Is Carnivore constitutional under *Smith*? For interesting discussions on Carnivore, see E. Judson Jennings, *Carnivore: U.S. Government Surveillance of Internet Transmissions*, 6 Va. J.L. & Tech. 10 (2001), at *http://www.vjolt.net*; *http://www.cdt.org/security/* (collecting various documents and statements on Carnivore).

In 2005, the public learned that President George W. Bush issued an executive order soon after September 11, 2001, authorizing the National Security Agency (NSA) to conduct surveillance of international communications on any person in the United States suspected of having links to terrorist organizations. Data from Verizon, BellSouth, and AT&T were placed in a database. This database of calls placed within the United States includes phone numbers, dates, and durations of the calls and was used for "data mining" — the process of analyzing large volumes of data for patterns. This has been called "the largest database ever assembled in the world."

The NSA gathered the information by installing splitters at communication traffic hubs and siphoning off a duplicate copy of all communication traffic going through the hub and routing it to a specialized piece of equipment, called a Narus STA 6400 "Semantic Traffic Analyzer," to detect suspect traffic according to parameters set by law enforcement. The Narus identifies, records, and reports questionable traffic including e-mail, VOIP/Skype, Web-browsing, and instant messaging. Since the three tapped U.S. telecom companies comprise the backbone of the U.S. telecommunications and Internet, any data sent from a nontapped network to a tapped network would be recorded.

In 2007 and again in 2008, Congress provided legislative authorization for what became known as the President's Surveillance Program. The Protect America Act, Pub. L. No. 110-55 (2007), amended the Foreign Intelligence Surveillance Act, 50 U.S.C. §§1801 et seq. (FISA), to exempt from FISA's definition of "electronic surveillance" and its warrant requirement from the Foreign Intelligence Surveillance Court, all communications "directed at" people outside the United States provided that Director of National Intelligence and the Attorney General believe that "there are reasonable procedures in place for determining that the acquisition foreign intelligence information . . . concerns persons reasonably believed to be located outside the United States, and such procedures will be subject to review of the Court pursuant to section 105C of this Act."

In 2008, Congress passed the FISA Amendment Act, which among other things, granted retroactive immunity to telecommunications companies for assisting in the President's Surveillance Program and essentially retroactively authorized that program. While the FAA did create some additional procedural safeguards, such as requiring court orders to eavesdrop on U.S. persons abroad, like the Protect America Act, the FAA permits the interception of foreign communications received in the U.S., and only requires judicial approval of the overall procedures employed by the government and does not provide for judicial review of individual cases and acts of surveillance.

There are a number of lawsuits challenging the legality of the U.S. Government's actions as well as class-action lawsuits against the telecoms seeking billions in damages for illegally turning over records under the Communications Act and various provisions of the Electronic Communications and Privacy Act, including the Stored Communications Act.

The legal issues include (1) violation of the Foreign Intelligence Surveillance Act, 50 U.S.C. §§1801 et seq., which requires the government, to obtain warrants from specialized FISA courts when engaging in such surveillance,

(2) violation of the doctrine of separation of powers, and (3) violation of the Fourth Amendment. Consider to what extent the legal issues presented by the President's Surveillance Program were anticipated in Professor Ku's article, *The Founders' Privacy: The Fourth Amendment and The Power of Technological Surveillance*, 86 Minn. L. Rev. 1325 (2002).

Should access to communication differ if the party intercepting or accessing the communication is not a representative of the government? Should employers, for example, be able to monitor their employees? Consider the following materials.

b) *Private Monitoring*

SMYTH V. PILLSBURY CO.

914 F. Supp. 97 (E.D. Pa. 1996)

WEINER, District Judge.

In this diversity action, plaintiff, an at-will employee, claims he was wrongfully discharged from his position as a regional operations manager by the defendant. . . .

Defendant maintained an electronic mail communication system ("e-mail") in order to promote internal corporate communications between its employees. Defendant repeatedly assured its employees, including plaintiff, that all e-mail communications would remain confidential and privileged. Defendant further assured its employees, including plaintiff, that e-mail communications could not be intercepted and used by defendant against its employees as grounds for termination or reprimand.

In October 1994, plaintiff received certain e-mail communications from his supervisor over defendant's e-mail system on his computer at home. In reliance on defendant's assurances regarding defendant's e-mail system, plaintiff responded and exchanged e-mails with his supervisor. At some later date, contrary to the assurances of confidentiality made by defendant, defendant, acting through its agents, servants and employees, intercepted plaintiff's private e-mail messages made in October 1994. On January 17, 1995, defendant notified plaintiff that it was terminating his employment effective February 1, 1995, for transmitting what it deemed to be inappropriate and unprofessional comments[1] over defendant's e-mail system in October 1994. . . .

Plaintiff claims that his termination was in violation of "public policy which precludes an employer from terminating an employee in violation of

---

1. Defendant alleges in its motion to dismiss that the e-mails concerned sales management and contained threats to "kill the backstabbing bastards" and referred to the planned Holiday party as the "Jim Jones Koolaid affair."

the employee's right to privacy as embodied in Pennsylvania common law." In support for this proposition, plaintiff directs our attention to a decision by our Court of Appeals in Borse v. Piece Goods Shop, Inc., 963 F.2d 611 (3d Cir. 1992). In *Borse*, the plaintiff sued her employer alleging wrongful discharge as a result of her refusal to submit to urinalysis screening and personal property searches at her work place pursuant to the employer's drug and alcohol policy. . . .

The Court of Appeals in *Borse* observed that one of the torts which Pennsylvania recognizes as encompassing an action for invasion of privacy is the tort of "intrusion upon seclusion." As noted by the Court of Appeals, the Restatement (Second) of Torts defines the tort as follows:

> One who intentionally intrudes, physically or otherwise, upon the solitude or seclusion of another or his private affairs or concerns, is subject to liability to the other for invasion of his privacy, if the intrusion would be highly offensive to a reasonable person.

Restatement (Second) of Torts §652B. Liability only attaches when the "intrusion is substantial and would be highly offensive to the 'ordinary reasonable person.'" *Borse*, 963 F.2d at 621 (citation omitted). . . . In determining whether an alleged invasion of privacy is substantial and highly offensive to a reasonable person, the Court of Appeals predicted that Pennsylvania would adopt a balancing test which balances the employee's privacy interest against the employer's interest in maintaining a drug-free workplace. *Id.* at 625. Because the Court of Appeals in *Borse* could "envision at least two ways in which an employer's drug and alcohol program might violate the public policy protecting individuals from tortious invasion of privacy by private actors," *id.* at 626, the Court vacated the district court's order dismissing the plaintiff's complaint and remanded the case to the district court with directions to grant Borse leave to amend the Complaint to allege how the defendant's drug and alcohol program violates her right to privacy.

Applying the Restatement definition of the tort of intrusion upon seclusion to the facts and circumstances of the case sub judice, we find that plaintiff has failed to state a claim upon which relief can be granted. In the first instance, unlike urinalysis and personal property searches, we do not find a reasonable expectation of privacy in e-mail communications voluntarily made by an employee to his supervisor over the company e-mail system notwithstanding any assurances that such communications would not be intercepted by management. Once plaintiff communicated the alleged unprofessional comments to a second person (his supervisor) over an e-mail system which was apparently utilized by the entire company, any reasonable expectation of privacy was lost. Significantly, the defendant did not require plaintiff, as in the case of an urinalysis or personal property search to disclose any personal information about himself. Rather, plaintiff voluntarily communicated the alleged unprofessional comments over the company e-mail system. We find no privacy interests in such communications.

In the second instance, even if we found that an employee had a reasonable expectation of privacy in the contents of his e-mail communications over the company e-mail system, we do not find that a reasonable person would consider the defendant's interception of these communications to be a substantial and highly offensive invasion of his privacy. Again, we note that by intercepting such communications, the company is not, as in the case of urinalysis or personal property searches, requiring the employee to disclose any personal information about himself or invading the employee's person or personal effects. Moreover, the company's interest in preventing inappropriate and unprofessional comments or even illegal activity over its e-mail system outweighs any privacy interest the employee may have in those comments.

In sum, we find that the defendant's actions did not tortiously invade the plaintiff's privacy and, therefore, did not violate public policy. As a result, the motion to dismiss is granted. . . .

COMMENTS AND QUESTIONS

1. As *Smyth* illustrates, in the absence of statutory protection, it can be quite difficult convincing a court to recognize a common law invasion of privacy. Would the result in *Smyth* be different if the *Katz* test were applied? Could Smyth argue that he had a reasonable expectation of privacy even if he could not prove that the invasion was highly offensive? *Consider* United States v. Simons, 206 F.3d 392 (4th Cir. 2000) (holding that employer's stated policy of monitoring all Internet use and e-mail communications defeated any reasonable expectation of privacy).

2. Of what relevance is the fact that Smyth communicated the message over the e-mail system that is used by the entire company? Is it the chance that he might inadvertently send it to the wrong recipients, or that the recipient may easily forward the message to others?

3. According to the court, even if Smyth had a reasonable expectation of privacy, why was the monitoring not highly offensive? Is it because the employer owned the computer network? If so, what about the assurances of privacy? Could Smyth sue for breach of contract or for unfair and deceptive business practices?

4. If it is difficult to establish a common law right of privacy, does the ECPA protect against the private interception of communications? For example, with respect to intercepting communications, 18 U.S.C. §2511(2)(a)(i) states:

> It shall not be unlawful . . . for an operator of a switchboard, or an officer, employee, or agent of a provider of wire or electronic communication service, whose facilities are used in the transmission of a wire or electronic communication, to intercept, disclose, or use that communication in the normal course of his employment while engaged in any activity which is a necessary incident to the rendition of his service or to the protection of the

rights or property of the provider of that service, except that a provider of wire communication service to the public shall not utilize service observing or random monitoring except for mechanical or service quality control checks.

Similarly, with respect to unauthorized access to stored communications, the ECPA exempts "the person or entity providing a wire or electronic communications service. . . ." 18 U.S.C. §2701(c)(1).

5.   In contrast with *Smyth*, France's highest court reportedly concluded that employees do have a right of privacy in their e-mail communications. In Nikon France v. Onos, Cour de cassation, Chambre Sociale, No. 41-6410/2/01, the employee, Frederic Onos was fired for engaging in unauthorized freelance activities during his working hours after management searched his computer and found various e-mail files. According to the French high court, "The employee has a right, even, during and at his place of work, to privacy," including "the right to secret correspondence." *See French Supreme Court Rules Employers Can't Read Employees' Personal E-mail*, 6 Electronic Com. & L. Rep. (BNA) 1049 (Oct. 10, 2001). Relying upon French labor law, Article 9 of the Civil Code, Article 9 of the Civil Law of Procedures Code, and Article 8 of the European Convention on Human Rights, the court stated that "the employer cannot without violating fundamental freedoms, discover personal messages emitted and received by an employee on computer equipment at his disposal . . . even in the case where the employer has forbidden non-professional use of the computer. . . ." *Id.* Are there comparable statutory and constitutional precedents for a U.S. court to rely upon to recognize a right of privacy in employee e-mail?

FRASER V. NATIONWIDE MUTUAL INS. CO.

135 F. Supp. 2d 623 (E.D. Pa. 2001)

[Richard Fraser, an employee of Nationwide Mutual Insurance, sued his employer for violation of federal and state wiretap laws. The alleged violation occurred when employees of Nationwide searched through the company's e-mail server and retrieved an e-mail sent by the plaintiff to another employee that had already been received and discarded.]

ANITA B. BRODY, District Judge.

A.   THE WIRETAP ACT AND THE STORED COMMUNICATIONS ACT (COUNTS I-IV)

. . . The ECPA has been noted for its lack of clarity. *See, e.g.*, United States v. Smith, 155 F.3d 1051, 1055 (9th Cir. 1998), *cert. denied*, 525 U.S. 1071 (1999) (citing Steve Jackson Games, Inc. v. United States Secret Service, 36 F.3d 457, 462 (5th Cir. 1994)). Courts and scholars have struggled to determine the precise boundaries of and also the intended relationship between the Wiretap Act and the Stored Communications Act by looking to the language of the statute, legislative history, and a basic understanding of communication technology. *See, e.g., Jackson*, 36 F.3d 457; Wesley College v. Pitts, 974 F. Supp. 375 (D. Del. 1997); Konop v. Hawaiian Airlines, Inc., 236 F.3d 1035 (9th Cir. 2001); Tatsuya Akamine, *Proposal for a Fair Statutory Interpretation: E-Mail Stored in a Service Provider Computer Is Subject to an Interception Under the Federal Wiretap Act*, 7 J.L. & Pol'y 519, 528 (1999). In this case, I am required to decide whether Nationwide's alleged conduct constitutes an "interception" of an electronic communication under the Wiretap Act, unlawful "access" to an electronic communication under the Stored Communications Act, a violation of both Acts, or a violation of neither Act. . . .

(1) "Interception" under the Amended Wiretap Act

The term "intercept" was interpreted under the original Wiretap Act to require that acquisition of the communication be contemporaneous with the transmission or transfer of information from the sender to the recipient. *See United States v. Turk*, 526 F.2d 654 (5th Cir. 1976), *cert. denied*, 429 U.S. 823 (1976) (holding that there was no interception when the police listened to a tape of a telephone conversation previously recorded by one of the parties to the conversation). "Intercept" is defined in the Wiretap Act as "the aural or other acquisition of the contents of any wire, electronic, or oral communication through the use of any electronic, mechanical, or other device." 18 U.S.C. §2510(4). "Electronic communication" is defined in the statute as "any *transfer* of signs, signals, writing, images," etc. 18 U.S.C. §2510(12) (emphasis added). Thus, by inserting the definition of "electronic communication" into the definition of "intercept," "intercept" is defined as the "acquisition" of the contents of any "transfer" of information from sender to recipient. As stated in *Turk*, under the terms of the statute, the acquisition must be during the transfer, or during the course of transmission.

This definition is consistent with the common meaning of "intercept." The common meaning of "intercept" is "to stop, seize, or interrupt in progress or course before arrival." *Webster's Ninth New Collegiate Dictionary* 630. With respect to communication, the "progress or course" is the transmission of a message from the sender to the recipient. Acquisition must occur "before arrival." Thus, interception of a communication occurs when transmission is interrupted, or in other words when the message is acquired after it has been sent by the sender, but before it is received by the recipient. The point in time when the message is acquired is the determining factor for whether or not interception has occurred. The Wiretap Act provides protection for private communication only during the course of transmission.

The meaning of "interception" does not change when the communication is indirect, passing through storage in the course of transmission for sender to recipient. For example, voice-mail communication is sent by recording a message into the recipient's voice-mail mailbox. The message then remains in storage in the recipient's mailbox until the recipient retrieves it from his or her personal mailbox by calling the voice-mail system. After listening to the message, the recipient may either delete it from the mailbox or save it for some period of time. If a third party obtains access to the recipient's personal mailbox and retrieves a saved message after the recipient has heard the message, there is no interception. The third party's acquisition of the message from storage occurred after the message had been transmitted from the sender to the recipient. On the other hand, if a third party obtains access to the recipient's mailbox and retrieves a message before it has been heard by the recipient, there is interception. *See Smith*, 155 F.3d 1051 (holding that interception had occurred when the defendant retrieved a voice-mail message from the recipient's personal mailbox before it had been received by the recipient and forwarded it to her own personal mailbox).

In an e-mail communication system, as in a voice-mail communication system, a message passes through intermediate storage in the course of transmission. In both an e-mail communication system and a voice-mail communication system, a message also may be saved in storage for period of time after transmission is complete. Retrieval of a message from storage while it is in the course of transmission is "interception" under the Wiretap Act; retrieval of a message from storage after transmission is complete is not "interception" under the Act. The only relevant difference between a voice-mail system and an e-mail system is that e-mail is stored in two different types of storage during the course of transmission — intermediate storage and back-up protection storage. Retrieval of an e-mail message from either intermediate or back-up protection storage is interception; retrieval of an e-mail message from post-transmission storage, where the message remains after transmission is complete, is not interception.

In this case, it is undisputed that Nationwide acquired Fraser's e-mail by retrieving it from Nationwide's electronic storage facility in Columbus, Ohio. At the time that Nationwide acquired Fraser's e-mail, the e-mail had already been received by the recipient. Fraser does not allege that Nationwide retrieved his e-mail communication before it was received and read by the recipient. Nationwide acquired Fraser's e-mail from post-transmission storage, after transmission was complete. Therefore, there was no "interception."

(2) Unauthorized "Access" under the Stored Communications Act

The Stored Communications Act, which prohibits unauthorized "access" to an electronic communication while it is in "electronic storage" similarly provides protection for private communication only during the course of transmission. "Electronic storage" is defined under the Act as:

"(A) any temporary, intermediate storage of a wire or electronic communication incidental to the electronic transmission thereof; and

(B) any storage of such communication by an electronic communication service for purposes of backup protection of such communication."

18 U.S.C. §2510(17). Part (A) of the definition fits what I previously defined as "intermediate storage." It is clear that the Stored Communications Act covers a message that is stored in intermediate storage temporarily, after the message is sent by the sender, but before it is retrieved by the intended recipient.

Part (B) of the definition refers to what I previously defined as back-up protection storage, which protects the communication in the event the system crashes before transmission is complete. The phrase "for purposes of backup protection of such communication" in the statutory definition makes clear that messages that are in post-transmission storage, after transmission is complete, are not covered by part (B) of the definition of "electronic storage." Therefore, retrieval of a message from post-transmission storage is not covered by the Stored Communications Act. The Act provides protection only for messages while they are in the course of transmission.

The facts of this case are that Nationwide retrieved Fraser's e-mail from storage after the e-mail had already been sent and received by the recipient. Nationwide acquired Fraser's e-mail from post-transmission storage. Therefore, Nationwide's conduct is not prohibited under the Stored Communications Act. . . .

COMMENTS AND QUESTIONS

1. According to the court in *Fraser*, how is an e-mail intercepted? Is this consistent with *Steve Jackson Games*?

2. Why was the employer's accessing of the plaintiff's e-mail not a violation of the stored communication provisions of the ECPA? Under this interpretation, is there any protection for an e-mail that has already been read?

3. Under the *Fraser* court's reasoning, are the stored communications provisions superfluous? Why did the employer not rely upon the argument that it is exempted under the ECPA as the provider of the e-mail service? *Compare Fraser with* Watkins v. L.M. Berry & Co., 704 F.2d 577, 583 (11th Cir. 1983) (concluding that an employer may only monitor an employee's telephone call under "the ordinary course of business under the exemption in section 2510(5)(a)(i) . . . to the extent necessary to guard against unauthorized use of the telephone or to determine whether a call is personal or not").

4. In Theofel v. Farey-Jones, 359 F.3d 1066 (9th Cir. 2004), the court noted the difficulty with the distinction between sections (A) and (B) stating:

> An obvious purpose for storing a message on an ISP's server after delivery is to provide a second copy of the message in the event that the user needs to download it again — if, for example, the message is accidentally erased from the user's own computer. The ISP copy of the message functions as a "backup" for the user. Notably, nothing in the Act requires that the backup protection be for the benefit of the ISP rather than the user. Storage under these circumstances thus literally falls within the statutory definition.

5. Should an employer's rights differ depending upon whether they are providing telephone service versus e-mail? Why?

6. Does an employer have a duty to monitor the electronic communications of employees? *Consider* Doe v. XYC Corp., 887 A.2d 1156 (N.J. Super. Ct. App. Div. 2005). XYC Corporation's network administrator discovered that an employee was visiting porn sites. The employee's supervisor confronted the employee who assured the supervisor that he would stop. The spouse of the employee, Jill Doe, sued XYC when she discovered that her husband had been videotaping and photographing his stepdaughter and using those images to gain access to a child porn Web site from his computer at work. In rejecting XYC's motion for summary judgment, the court stated:

> We hold that an employer who is on notice that one of its employees is using a workplace computer to access pornography, possibly child pornography, has a duty to investigate the employee's activities and to take prompt and effective action to stop the unauthorized activity, lest it result in harm to innocent third parties. No privacy interest of the employee stands in the way of this duty on the part of the employer. . . .

In reaching this conclusion, the court relied, in part, on XYC's written e-mail and Internet usage policies, and the fact that "Employee's office . . . did not have a door and his computer screen was visible from the hallway. . . ." According to the court, "Under those circumstances, we readily conclude that Employee had no legitimate expectation of privacy that would prevent his employer from accessing his computer to determine if he was using it to view adult or child pornography."

7. In the preceding cases, monitoring was accomplished by an employer who owned the computer network on which the communications were transmitted and stored. Should the results be different if the person intercepting or accessing the communications is a third party? Consider the following case.

KONOP v. HAWAIIAN AIRLINES, INC.

302 F.3d 868 (9th Cir. 2002)

BOOCHEVER, Circuit Judge.

Robert Konop brought suit against his employer, Hawaiian Airlines, Inc. ("Hawaiian"), alleging that Hawaiian viewed Konop's secure website without authorization, disclosed the contents of that website, and took other related actions in violation of the federal Wiretap Act, the Stored Communications Act, and the Railway Labor Act. Konop also alleged several state tort claims. . . .

Konop, a pilot for Hawaiian, created and maintained a website where he posted bulletins critical of his employer, its officers, and the incumbent union, Air Line Pilots Association ("ALPA"). Many of those criticisms related to Konop's opposition to labor concessions which Hawaiian sought from ALPA. Because ALPA supported the concessions, Konop, via his website, encouraged Hawaiian employees to consider alternative union representation.

Konop controlled access to his website by requiring visitors to log in with a user name and password. He created a list of people, mostly pilots and other employees of Hawaiian, who were eligible to access the website. Pilots Gene Wong and James Gardner were included on this list. Konop programmed the website to allow access when a person entered the name of an eligible person, created a password, and clicked the "SUBMIT" button on the screen, indicating acceptance of the terms and conditions of use. These terms and conditions prohibited any member of Hawaiian's management from viewing the website and prohibited users from disclosing the website's contents to anyone else.

In December 1995, Hawaiian vice president James Davis asked Wong for permission to use Wong's name to access Konop's website. Wong agreed. Davis claimed he was concerned about untruthful allegations that he believed Konop was making on the website. Wong had not previously logged into the website to create an account. When Davis accessed the website using Wong's name, he presumably typed in Wong's name, created a password, and clicked the "SUBMIT" button indicating acceptance of the terms and conditions.

Later that day, Konop received a call from the union chairman of ALPA, Reno Morella. Morella told Konop that Hawaiian president Bruce Nobles had contacted him regarding the contents of Konop's website. Morella related that Nobles was upset by Konop's accusations that Nobles was suspected of fraud and by other disparaging statements published on the website. From this conversation with Morella, Konop believed Nobles had obtained the contents of his website and was threatening to sue Konop for defamation based on statements contained on the website.

After speaking with Morella, Konop took his website offline for the remainder of the day. He placed it back online the next morning, however, without knowing how Nobles had obtained the information discussed in the phone call. Konop claims to have learned only later from the examination of system logs that Davis had accessed the website using Wong's name.

In the meantime, Davis continued to view the website using Wong's name. Later, Davis also logged in with the name of another pilot, Gardner, who had similarly consented to Davis' use of his name. Through April 1996, Konop claims that his records indicate that Davis logged in over twenty times as Wong, and that Gardner or Davis logged in at least fourteen more times as Gardner. . . .

I. ELECTRONIC COMMUNICATIONS PRIVACY ACT CLAIMS

We first turn to the difficult task of determining whether Hawaiian violated either the Wiretap Act, 18 U.S.C. §§2510-2522 (2000) or the Stored Communications Act, 18 U.S.C. §§2701-2711 (2000), when Davis accessed Konop's secure website. In 1986, Congress passed the Electronic Communications Privacy Act (ECPA), Pub. L. No. 99-508, 100 Stat. 1848, which was intended to afford privacy protection to electronic communications. Title I of the ECPA amended the federal Wiretap Act, which previously addressed only wire and oral communications, to "address[] the interception of . . . electronic communications." S. Rep. No. 99-541, at 3 (1986), *reprinted in* 1986 U.S.C.C.A.N. 3555, 3557. Title II of the ECPA created the Stored Communications Act (SCA), which was designed to "address[] access to stored wire and electronic communications and transactional records." *Id*.

As we have previously observed, the intersection of these two statutes "is a complex, often convoluted, area of the law." *United States v. Smith,* 155 F.3d 1051, 1055 (9th Cir. 1998). In the present case, the difficulty is compounded by the fact that the ECPA was written prior to the advent of the Internet and the World Wide Web. As a result, the existing statutory framework is ill-suited to address modern forms of communication like Konop's secure website. Courts have struggled to analyze problems involving modern technology within the confines of this statutory framework, often with unsatisfying results. . . . We observe that until Congress brings the laws in line with modern technology, protection of the Internet and websites such as Konop's will remain a confusing and uncertain area of the law.

A. The Internet and Secure Websites

While most websites are public, many, such as Konop's, are restricted. For instance, some websites are password-protected, require a social security number, or require the user to purchase access by entering a credit card number. . . . The legislative history of the ECPA suggests that Congress wanted to protect electronic communications that are configured to be private, such as email and private electronic bulletin boards. *See* S. Rep. No. 99-541, at 35-36, 1986 U.S.C.C.A.N. at 3599 ("This provision [the SCA] addresses the growing problem of unauthorized persons deliberately gaining access to . . . electronic or wire communications that are not intended to be available to the public."); H.R. Rep. No. 99-647 at 41, 62-63 (1986) (describing the Committee's understanding that the configuration of the electronic communications system would determine whether or not an electronic communication was readily accessible to the public). The nature of the Internet, however, is such that if a user enters the appropriate information (password, social security number, etc.), it is nearly impossible to verify the true identity of that user. . . .

We are confronted with such a situation here. Although Konop took certain steps to restrict the access of Davis and other managers to the website,[1] Davis was nevertheless able to access the website by entering the correct information, which was freely provided to Davis by individuals who were eligible to view the website.

B. Wiretap Act

Konop argues that Davis' conduct constitutes an interception of an electronic communication in violation of the Wiretap Act. The Wiretap Act makes it an offense to "intentionally intercept[] . . . any wire, oral, or electronic communication." 18 U.S.C. §2511(1)(a). We must therefore determine whether Konop's website is an "electronic communication" and, if so, whether Davis "intercepted" that communication.

An "electronic communication" is defined as "any transfer of signs, signals, writing, images, sounds, data, or intelligence of any nature transmitted in whole or in part by a wire, radio, electromagnetic, photoelectronic or photo-optical system." *Id.* §2510(12). As discussed above, website owners such as Konop transmit electronic documents to servers, where the documents are stored. If a user wishes to view the website, the user requests that the server transmit a copy of the document to the user's computer. When the server sends the document to the user's computer for viewing, a transfer of information from the website owner to the user has occurred. Although the website owner's document does not go directly or immediately to the user, once a user

1. Specifically, Konop configured the website to allow access when a person typed in the correct web address, received the home page of his website, entered the name of an eligible person, created a password, and clicked the "SUBMIT" button indicating acceptance of the terms and conditions of use. In addition, Konop displayed the following language on the home page of his website:

This is the gateway for NEWS UPDATES and EDITORIAL COMMENTS directed only toward Hawaiian Air's pilots and other employees, not including HAL management. By entering, you acknowledge and agree to the terms and conditions of use as specified below. You must read this entire page before entry. Others should simply find *something else* to do with their time.
If you are already a registered user, you may fill in your name along with the other information required below, then enter the system. If you want to visit the system, and you belong to the authorized group, you must supply the proper information before you will be allowed to enter. Make note of the password you enter for your first visit, otherwise future visits may be delayed. Visits by others will be strictly prohibited.

Beneath this language, Konop provided boxes for a person's name, occupation, email address and password. Below the boxes were two buttons: one said "SUBMIT," the other said "CLEAR." The advisement continued:

All name and contact information will be kept strictly confidential. Any effort to defeat, compromise or violate the security of this website will be prosecuted to the fullest extent of the law.
WARNING! The information contained herein is CONFIDENTIAL, and it is not intended for public dissemination! By requesting entry in the system, you must agree not to furnish any of the information contained herein to any other person or for any other use. Republication or redistribution of this information to any other person is strictly prohibited. Anyone found to disseminate this information to anyone other than those specifically named and allowed here will be banned from this website and held liable to prosecution for violation of the terms and conditions of use and for violation of this contract.

accesses a website, information is transferred from the website owner to the user via one of the specified mediums. We therefore conclude that Konop's website fits the definition of "electronic communication."

The Wiretap Act, however, prohibits only "interceptions" of electronic communications. "Intercept" is defined as "the aural or other acquisition of the contents of any wire, electronic, or oral communication through the use of any electronic, mechanical, or other device." *Id.* §2510(4). Standing alone, this definition would seem to suggest that an individual "intercepts" an electronic communication merely by "acquiring" its contents, regardless of when or under what circumstances the acquisition occurs. Courts, however, have clarified that Congress intended a narrower definition of "intercept" with regard to electronic communications. . . .

We agree with the *Steve Jackson* and *Smith* courts that the narrow definition of "intercept" applies to electronic communications. Notably, Congress has since amended the Wiretap Act to eliminate storage from the definition of wire communication, *see* USA PATRIOT Act §209, 115 Stat. at 283, such that the textual distinction relied upon by the *Steve Jackson* and *Smith* courts no longer exists. This change, however, supports the analysis of those cases. By eliminating storage from the definition of wire communication, Congress essentially reinstated the pre-ECPA definition of "intercept"—acquisition contemporaneous with transmission—with respect to wire communications. *See Smith*, 155 F.3d at 1057 n.11. The purpose of the recent amendment was to reduce protection of voice mail messages to the lower level of protection provided other electronically stored communications. *See* H.R. Rep. 107-236(I), at 158-59 (2001). When Congress passed the USA PATRIOT Act, it was aware of the narrow definition courts had given the term "intercept" with respect to electronic communications, but chose not to change or modify that definition. To the contrary, it modified the statute to make that definition applicable to voice mail messages as well. Congress, therefore, accepted and implicitly approved the judicial definition of "intercept" as acquisition contemporaneous with transmission.

We therefore hold that for a website such as Konop's to be "intercepted" in violation of the Wiretap Act, it must be acquired during transmission, not while it is in electronic storage. This conclusion is consistent with the ordinary meaning of "intercept," which is "to stop, seize, or interrupt in progress or course before arrival." *Webster's Ninth New Collegiate Dictionary* 630 (1985). More importantly, it is consistent with the structure of the ECPA, which created the SCA for the express purpose of addressing "access to *stored* . . . electronic communications and transactional records." S. Rep. No. 99-541 at 3 (emphasis added). The level of protection provided stored communications under the SCA is considerably less than that provided communications covered by the Wiretap Act. Section 2703(a) of the SCA details the procedures law enforcement must follow to access the contents of stored electronic communications, but these procedures are considerably less burdensome and less restrictive than those required to obtain a wiretap order under the Wiretap Act.

See Steve Jackson Games, 36 F.3d at 463. Thus, if Konop's position were correct and acquisition of a stored electronic communication were an interception under the Wiretap Act, the government would have to comply with the more burdensome, more restrictive procedures of the Wiretap Act to do exactly what Congress apparently authorized it to do under the less burdensome procedures of the SCA. Congress could not have intended this result. As the Fifth Circuit recognized in *Steve Jackson Games,* "it is most unlikely that Congress intended to require law enforcement officers to satisfy the more stringent requirements for an intercept in order to gain access to the contents of stored electronic communications." *Id.; see also Wesley Coll.,* 974 F. Supp. at 388 (same). . . .

REINHARDT, Circuit Judge, concurring in part, dissenting in part.

. . . I dissent, however, from Part B of Section I, which holds that the term "intercept" in the Wiretap Act, as applied to electronic communications, refers solely to *contemporaneous* acquisition. I conclude instead that "stored electronic communications" are subject to the statute's intercept prohibition as well.

Because I recognize that any reading of the relevant statutory provisions raises some difficulties and introduces some inconsistencies, the question becomes: which reading is more coherent and more consistent with Congressional intent? The majority reasons, and I agree, that stored electronic communications are covered under the definition of "electronic communications" in the Wiretap Act. However, having made that determination, the majority proceeds to introduce unnecessary confusion and incoherence into the statute by holding that "intercept" encompasses only *contemporaneous* acquisition of electronic communications, and thus that it is not possible to "intercept" a stored electronic communication. . . .

To read a contemporaneity requirement into the definition of "intercept" renders the prohibition against the electronic communication interception largely superfluous, and violates the precept against interpreting one provision of a statute to negate another. . . . The nature of electronic communication is that it spends infinitesimal amounts of time "en route," unlike a phone call. Therefore, in order to "intercept" an electronic communication, one ordinarily obtains one of the copies made en route or at the destination. These copies constitute "stored electronic communications," as acknowledged by the majority. 18 U.S.C. §2510(17)(A) ("'electronic storage' means . . . any temporary, intermediate storage of a wire or electronic communication incidental to the electronic transmission thereof"). If intercept is defined as solely contemporaneous acquisition, then in contravention of Congressional intent, at most all acquisitions of the contents of electronic communications would escape the intercept prohibition entirely. . . .

The majority asserts that it is reasonable that the term "intercept" would describe different conduct with respect to wire communications than with respect to electronic communications because different actions are required to intercept different kinds of communications. This reasoning fails because, although wire communications and electronic communications are quite different, stored wire communications are technologically equivalent to stored electronic communications. Thus it would make little sense to treat them differently. *See* 18 U.S.C. §2510(1) (defining "wire communication" as including "any *electronic storage* of [wire] communication"). While Congress may not always act sensibly, there is no reason for the majority to presume that it failed to do so in this instance. . . .

COMMENTS AND QUESTIONS

1. Even assuming that *Steve Jackson Games's* interpretation of the Wiretap Act is wrong with respect to e-mail, should a limited access Web site be considered an electronic communication in the same manner as an e-mail? Once a Web site has been viewed by someone other than the poster, should it be considered an interception when someone other than the authorized user logs in?

2. What if instead of creating a Web site, Konop allowed airline employees to remotely access his computer and gain access to: (a) read documents describing his complaints; (b) use a word processing program; (c) play a game of chess; or (d) use his computer? If someone other than a valid user obtained a password and accessed the computer for those various purposes would that person be intercepting communications, accessing stored communications, or neither? If your answer is not the same for each example, what distinguishes the examples?

3. When should the publisher of a Web site have a reasonable expectation of privacy with regard to the contents of the Web site? Could Konop argue that Davis's actions violated the anticircumvention provisions of the DMCA?

4. Following the terrorist attacks on September 11, 2001, Congress passed the USA Patriot Act of 2001, Pub. L. No. 107-56. Section 209 of the Act modifies the definition of "wire communication" by eliminating the phrase "any electronic storage of such communication" in 18 U.S.C. §2510(1) and amended 18 U.S.C. §§2703(a) & (b), Title II, by replacing "contents of electronic" communications with "contents of wire or electronic" communications. Under the Act, these amendments expired December 31, 2005. Do these amendments eliminate the confusion encountered by the courts with respect to when and how Title I and Title II of the Wiretap Act protect communications? Do the amendments clarify what it means to "intercept" an electronic or wire communication?

5. For a case on Title III, see In re Application for Pen Register, 396 F. Supp. 2d (S.D. Tex. 2005), where the court denied the government's request to obtain prospective cell site tower location information to turn a suspect's cellular phone into a real-time tracking device using the location of the signal towers to track the suspect's movements.

3. Technological Measures to Maintain Privacy: Encryption

In light of the potential for monitoring electronic communications, how can one ensure the confidentiality of electronic communications? In the world of computers, encryption is the key. As Lawrence Lessig suggests, "encryption technologies are the most important technological breakthrough in the last one thousand years. . . . Cryptography will change everything."[21] Cryptography is the mathematical science of "secret writing."[22] Through cryptography, encryption programs scramble electronic messages according to a complex mathematical formula so that only readers with the proper answer (or key, as it is commonly referred) can unscramble the message. The level of protection afforded by encryption varies depending upon the sophistication of the method used. A childhood decoder ring can be used to decrypt certain messages without the proper key. In contrast, today's most sophisticated encryption requires supercomputers to decrypt if it is possible to decrypt those messages at all.

While encryption may be seen as the solution to privacy in cyberspace, it is also a potential threat to other values. As discussed in *Bernstein* excerpted in Chapter 3, encryption can be used to shield criminal activities. Similarly, as you studied in Chapter 4, encryption may make it possible to protect intellectual property in a digital world. As you study the following materials, consider the various values and interests at stake.

BERNSTEIN v. UNITED STATES DEPARTMENT OF JUSTICE

176 F.3d 1132, *withdrawn*, 192 F.3d 1308 (9th Cir. 1999)

[The facts of *Bernstein* and the court's discussion on cryptography are excerpted in Chapter 3.]

FLETCHER, Circuit Judge:

. . . [W]e note that the government's efforts to regulate and control the spread of knowledge relating to encryption may implicate more than the First Amendment rights of cryptographers. In this increasingly electronic age, we are all required in our everyday lives to rely on modern technology to communicate with one another. This reliance on electronic communication, however, has brought with it a dramatic diminution in our ability to communicate privately. Cellular phones are subject to monitoring, e-mail is easily intercepted, and transactions over the internet are often less than secure. Something as commonplace as furnishing our credit card number, social

21. Lawrence Lessig, *Code and Other Laws of Cyberspace* 35-36 (1999).
22. Bernstein v. United States Department of Justice, 176 F.3d 1132, 1136 (9th Cir. 1999), *withdrawn*, 192 F.3d 1308 (9th Cir. 1999).

security number, or bank account number puts each of us at risk. Moreover, when we employ electronic methods of communication, we often leave electronic "fingerprints" behind, fingerprints that can be traced back to us. Whether we are surveilled by our government, by criminals, or by our neighbors, it is fair to say that never has our ability to shield our affairs from prying eyes been at such a low ebb. The availability and use of secure encryption may offer an opportunity to reclaim some portion of the privacy we have lost. Government efforts to control encryption thus may well implicate not only the First Amendment rights of cryptographers intent on pushing the boundaries of their science, but also the constitutional rights of each of us as potential recipients of encryption's bounty. Viewed from this perspective, the government's efforts to retard progress in cryptography may implicate the Fourth Amendment, as well as the right to speak anonymously, *see* McIntyre v. Ohio Elections Comm'n, 514 U.S. 334 (1995), the right against compelled speech, *see* Wooley v. Maynard, 430 U.S. 705, 714 (1977), and the right to informational privacy, *see* Whalen v. Roe, 429 U.S. 589, 599-600 (1977). While we leave for another day the resolution of these difficult issues, it is important to point out that Bernstein's is a suit not merely concerning a small group of scientists laboring in an esoteric field, but also touches on the public interest broadly defined.

COMMENTS AND QUESTIONS

1.   As recognized by the court in *Bernstein*, efforts to regulate cryptography have broad societal implications as we attempt to shield ourselves from what Jeffrey Rosen has described as the "unwanted gaze." *See* Jeffrey Rosen, *The Unwanted Gaze: The Destruction of Privacy in America* (Random House, 2000) (discussing modern privacy concerns). In light of the preceding materials on the monitoring of communications, to what extent does the use of encryption create a reasonable expectation of privacy? Consider the following:

> [Encryption] is armor around a communication much like a safe is armor around a possession. A person who puts something in a safe to which they have the only key or combination surely has both a subjective and objective reasonable expectation of privacy.

A. Michael Froomkin, *The Metaphor Is the Key: Cryptography, the Clipper Chip, and the Constitution*, 143 U. Pa. L. Rev. 709, 871 (1995). In contrast, Orin Kerr argues that because the government and individuals have access to encrypted messages even though they may have difficulty understanding them, encryption, like the use of an obscure language, does not create a reasonable expectation of privacy. *See* Orin S. Kerr, *The Fourth Amendment in Cyberspace, Can Encryption Create a Reasonable Expectation of Privacy?*, 33 Conn. L. Rev. 503, 505 (2001). According to Kerr:

> The Fourth Amendment simply does not recognize such expectations as "legitimate." Decoding communications by taping together shreds, finding someone who speaks a

foreign language, locating someone who has an encryption "key," or cracking the encryption using brute force methods merely affects the government's understanding of a communication, not the government's access to it. If the government obtains communications in a form that it does not understand, the Fourth Amendment does not require law enforcement to obtain a warrant before translating the documents into understandable English.

Id. at 518 (footnotes omitted). Which analogy do you find more persuasive? Should we treat encryption as an electronic envelope or the translation of a more sophisticated form of "pig Latin"?

2. How does the ECPA treat encrypted communications? *Consider* 18 U.S.C. §2511(2)(g), which exempts the interception of communications "made through an electronic communication system that is configured so that such electronic communication is readily accessible to the general public. . . ." Does encryption render a communication system not readily accessible to the general public?

3. How would the use of encryption fit under Justice Brandeis's approach in Olmstead? Justice Scalia's approach in *Kyllo?* Consider this question with respect to password protection of computers and files. Compare the following two cases. In Trulock v. Freeh, 275 F.3d 391, 403 (4th Cir. 2001), the court compared password protected files to a "locked footlocker inside the bedroom." As such, even though Nota Trulock and Linda Conrad shared a computer, Conrad could not consent to the FBI's warrantless search and seizure of Trulock's files. According to the court, "Conrad and Trulock both used a computer located in Conrad's bedroom and each had joint access to the hard drive. Conrad and Trulock, however, protected their personal files with passwords; Conrad did not have access to Trulock's passwords. Although Conrad had authority to consent to a general search of the computer, her authority did not extend to Trulock's password protected files."

In United States v. Andrus, 483 F.3d 711 (10th Cir. 2007), the police searched the defendant's computer using forensic software that bypassed any password protection put on the computer. The police did so with his father's consent even though the computer was located in the 51-year-old son's bedroom and his father did not know his son's password. The court distinguished Trulock because in that case Conrad informed the police that they each had password-protected files. Because the father did not give any indication, nor did the police inquire as to whether the password protection was enabled on the son's computer, the court concluded that under the "totality-of-the-circumstances analysis, the facts know to the officers at the time the computer search commenced created an objectively reasonable perception that [defendant's father] was, at least, *one* user of the computer."

The dissent argued that:

> The unconstrained ability of law enforcement to use forensic software such as the EnCase program to bypass password protection without first determining whether such passwords have been enabled does not "exacerbate[ ]" this difficulty; rather, it avoids it altogether, simultaneously and dangerously sidestepping the Fourth Amendment in the process.

Indeed, the majority concedes that if such protection were "shown to be commonplace, law enforcement's use of forensic software like EnCase . . . may well be subject to question." But the fact that a computer password "lock" may not be *immediately* visible does not render it unlocked. I appreciate that unlike the locked file cabinet, computers have no handle to pull. But, like the padlocked footlocker, computers do exhibit outward signs of password protection: they display boot password screens, username/password login screens, and/or screen-saver reactivation passwords. . . .

Accordingly, in my view, given the case law indicating the importance of computer password protection, the common knowledge about the prevalence of password usage, and the design of EnCase or similar password bypass mechanisms, the Fourth Amendment and the reasonable inquiry rule, mandate that in consent-based, warrantless computer searches, law enforcement personnel inquire or otherwise check for the presence of password protection and, if a password is present, inquire about the consenter's knowledge of that password and joint access to the computer. . . .

Which position do you find more persuasive?

4. For a survey of international responses to encryption, see Wayne Madsen et al., *Cryptography and Liberty: An International Survey of Encryption Policy*, 16 J. Marshall J. Computer & Info. L. 475 (1998).

5. What steps should the government take in countering encryption? How should we balance the legitimate needs of law enforcement with the public's need for privacy? Obviously, government could always use its computer capabilities to decipher encrypted messages. As encryption improves, however, this becomes an increasingly difficult task.

Note: The Battle over Encryption

In the past, the government has come up with several different proposals for responding to encryption, including the export controls of cryptography at issue in *Bernstein*. *See also* Junger v. Daley, 209 F.3d 481 (6th Cir. 2000) (examining the export controls for encryption) (see Chapter 3, *supra*). In addition to export controls, the Clinton Administration proposed two other approaches for responding to law enforcement concerns. The first approach involved the adoption of a single encryption standard to be embodied in the "clipper chip."

> Before a Clipper Chip is installed in a telephone, the government will permanently inscribe it with a unique serial number and a unique encryption key. The government will keep both of these numbers on file. In order to reduce the danger that the file might be stolen or otherwise compromised, the chip's unique encryption key will be split into two pieces, each held by a different "escrow agent." The escrow agents will be required to guard the segments and release them only to persons who can demonstrate that they will be used for authorized intercepts. Reuniting the pieces of a chip's unique key gives the government the capability to decrypt any Clipper conversations.

See A. Michael Froomkin, *The Metaphor Is the Key: Cryptography, the Clipper Chip, and the Constitution*, 143 U. Pa. L. Rev. 709, 752 (1995) (footnote omitted). The clipper chip would, therefore, create a "backdoor" that the government could always use to decrypt messages.

Another approach offered by the Clinton Administration involved "key escrow." Instead of mandating a uniform standard for encryption with government holding the key, "key escrow" would allow the adoption of any cryptographic algorithm while requiring that the keys necessary to decrypt the message be held by a third party. Upon a proper request, the government would then be able to obtain the key from the third party. *See* A. Michael Froomkin, *It Came from Planet Clipper: The Battle over Cryptographic Key "Escrow,"* 1996 U. Chi. Legal F. 15 (discussing the various proposals involving key escrow). What are the benefits and costs of these approaches? Do they adequately balance the government's need for access to information with the public's right of privacy? Are there other ways to design cyberspace to minimize the conflict?

More recently, the Department of Justice under the Bush Administration responded to the encryption problem with a new strategy. In order to defeat criminal use of encryption, the FBI chose to employ keystroke-logging devices that may be either physically or electronically installed on a suspect's computer. The keystroke-logger is then capable of recording all of the keystrokes entered on the computer, including a suspect's passwords and encryption keys. While these devices have apparently been used to combat international espionage, the first reported use of such a device in a domestic criminal investigation was upheld in United States v. Scarfo, C.A. No. 00-404 (NHP) (Dec. 26, 2001). In upholding the government's use of the keystroke logger, the court also agreed with the government that the details of how the keystroke logger operates were classified under the Classified Information Procedures Act, 18 U.S.C.A. App. 3 §1, and could not be revealed to the defense except in an unclassified summary.

As a complement to the keystroke logger, the FBI also acknowledged that as part of its Cyber Knight project, it had developed "Magic Lantern" software, which would record keystrokes much like the device/program used in *Scarfo*, but instead of requiring agents to physically install the device on a suspect's computer, the FBI would use techniques similar to those used by hackers to deliver Magic Lantern through the Internet. Is the use of keystroke loggers or Magic Lantern a search under the Fourth Amendment? To what extent should the use of these surveillance technologies be authorized and governed by statute before law enforcement may employ them? *See generally* Raymond Shih Ray Ku, *The Founders' Privacy: The Fourth Amendment and the Power of Technological Surveillance*, 86 Minn. L. Rev. 1325 (2002) (questioning government use of surveillance technologies under separation-of-powers principles).

B. DATA PRIVACY

As the preceding materials illustrate, one's activities in cyberspace leave an electronic trail that both the government and private parties can monitor. Part A examined the degree to which individuals can protect the privacy of their communications. The following examines the extent to which individuals can control the vast amount of other information about them and their activities in cyberspace, as well as the extent to which people can control the ways in which others use their personal information on blogs and online social networks.

Early Internet privacy concerns were effectively described by Jerry Kang.

> To focus that vague concern [over privacy], imagine the following two visits to a mall, one in real space, the other in cyberspace. In real space, you drive to a mall, walk up and down its corridors, peer into numerous shops, and stroll through corridors of inviting stores. Along the way, you buy an ice cream cone with cash. You walk into a bookstore and flip through a few magazines. Finally, you stop at a clothing store and buy a friend a silk scarf with a credit card. In this narrative, numerous persons interact with you and collect information along the way. For instance, while walking through the mall, fellow visitors visually collect information about you, if for no other reason than to avoid bumping into you. But such information is general — e.g., it does not pinpoint the geographical location and time of the sighting — is not in a format that can be processed by a computer, is not indexed to your name or another unique identifier, and is impermanent, residing in short-term human memory. You remain a barely noticed stranger. One important exception exists: The scarf purchase generates data that are detailed, computer-processable, indexed by name, and potentially permanent.
>
> By contrast, in cyberspace, the exception becomes the norm: Every interaction is like the credit card purchase. The best way to grasp this point is to take seriously, if only for a moment, the metaphor that cyberspace is an actual place, a computer-constructed world, a virtual reality. In this alternate universe, you are invisibly stamped with a bar code as soon as you venture outside your home. There are entities called "road providers," who supply the streets and ground you walk on, who track precisely where, when, and how fast you traverse the lands, in order to charge you for your wear on the infrastructure. As soon as you enter the cyber-mall's domain, the mall begins to track you through invisible scanners focused on your bar code. It automatically records which stores you visit, which windows you browse, in which order, and for how long. The specific stores collect even more detailed data when you enter their domain. For example, the cyber-bookstore notes which magazines you skimmed, recording which pages you have seen and for how long, and notes the pattern, if any, of your browsing. It notes that you picked up briefly a health magazine featuring an article on St. John's Wort, read for seven minutes a newsweekly detailing a politician's sex scandal, and flipped ever-so-quickly through a tabloid claiming that Elvis lives. Of course, whenever any item is actually purchased, the store, as well as the credit, debit, or virtual cash company that provides payment through cyberspace, takes careful notes of what you bought — in this case, a silk scarf, red, expensive.
>
> All these data generated in cyberspace are detailed, computer-processable, indexed to the individual, and permanent. While the mall example does not concern data that appear especially sensitive, the same extensive data collection takes place as we travel through other cyberspace domains — for instance: to research health issues and politics; to communicate to individuals, private institutions, and the state; and to pay our bills and manage our finances. Moreover, the data collected in these various domains can be aggregated to produce telling profiles of who we are, as revealed by what we do and say. The very technology that makes cyberspace possible also makes detailed, cumulative, invisible observation of our selves possible. One need only sift through the click-streams generated by our cyber-activity. The information we generate as a by-product of this activity is quite valuable. The private sector seeks to exploit it commercially, but individuals resist. Both sides lay powerful, clashing claims to this data generated in cyberspace. How we resolve this conflict warrants careful discussion.

Jerry Kang, *Information Privacy in Cyberspace Transactions*, 50 Stan. L. Rev. 1193, 1198 (1998).

As described by Kang, a troubling set of privacy concerns raised by cyber-space involves information or communications that individuals did not endeavor to keep secret. While we may not have initially been aware that this information was being recorded, let alone, used, we were not taking steps to keep our online activities hidden from others. Similarly, with certain exceptions, under cyberspace's current code, we do not have the option to withhold this information. What principles, if any, should be relied upon to regulate information in this context?

As Web 2.0 technologies — like blogs, online social networks, and multi-player online games — have developed in recent years, online privacy concerns become even broader in scope and nature. Individuals may easily lose control of content about them online, as others post information and images of them without their permission, or even their knowledge. Much of this information is harmless in the abstract, but can have wide-ranging consequences when dis-seminated in new contexts. For example, information that may only be known to a small group of people in the real world may attract a much greater audience as a result of dissemination over an online social network or blog. Consider the fact scenarios set out in Problems 11.0 and 11.1 as you read through the following materials.

Problem 11.0

Now that Starttup's subscriber base has grown to a significant size, your company has been approached by various businesses that are inter-ested in purchasing information about your subscribers. While some of these companies merely want to purchase the names and addresses of your subscribers, others would like more detailed information about their online usage. According to one representative, this detailed infor-mation is useful in targeting advertisements to consumers. For example, if a Starttup subscriber visits Web sites on pregnancy and baby care, that information is valuable to sellers of baby formula or strollers who can then market to that subscriber. Likewise, this information is potentially a very valuable asset to Starttup who can not only sell the information to outside marketers, but can use the information to better target advertising on your network. Through the use of "clickstream" data, the data transmit-ted from a user's computer to your network, you would be able to direct relevant third-party banner ads to your subscribers.

What are the limits to the gathering and use of this kind of infor-mation? Does it matter what type of information is collected or how information is used? Keep in mind that Starttup intends to create a global Internet community. Once your expansion in North America is well under way, the company intends to expand into Europe, Asia, and even-tually the rest of the world.

Problem 11.1

Cora has recently received complaints from several people that photographs, videos, and private information about them have been posted on the Gals Online blog. The complainants are predominantly men who made unflattering comments about women and feminist legal groups over online social networking services (OSNs) like Facebook and MySpace. Some of their online friends apparently distributed information about the men outside of the OSNs and it has found its way onto the Gals Online blog. Much of the information is innocuous, but some of it is quite embarrassing. One of the photographs on the blog depicts one of the complainants — a married man — holding hands with another man. Another is a video of one of the complainants dressed up as a turkey, presumably at a Thanksgiving parade. A rather unflattering caption has been attached to the photograph, suggesting that the man is, indeed, a turkey. Does Cora potentially face any liability for these postings?

---

1. Restrictions upon Government Data Collection and Disclosure

a) Collection

WHALEN v. ROE

429 U.S. 589 (1977)

Mr. Justice STEVENS delivered the opinion of the Court.

The constitutional question presented is whether the State of New York may record, in a centralized computer file, the names and addresses of all persons who have obtained, pursuant to a doctor's prescription, certain drugs for which there is both a lawful and an unlawful market.

The District Court enjoined enforcement of the portions of the New York State Controlled Substances Act of 1972 which require such recording on the ground that they violate appellees' constitutionally protected rights of privacy. . . .

[New York required doctors to complete an official form when proscribing certain "Schedule II" drugs, including opium and opium derivatives, cocaine, and methadone. "The completed form identifies the prescribing physician; the dispensing pharmacy; the drug and dosage; and the name, address, and age of the patient. One copy of the form is retained by the physician, the second by the pharmacist, and the third is forwarded to the New York State Department of Health in Albany."]

The District Court found that about 100,000 Schedule II prescription forms are delivered to a receiving room at the Department of Health in Albany each month. They are sorted, coded, and logged and then taken to another room where the data on the forms is recorded on magnetic tapes for processing by a computer. Thereafter, the forms are returned to the receiving room to be retained in a vault for a five-year period and then destroyed as required by the statute. The receiving room is surrounded by a locked wire fence and protected by an alarm system. The computer tapes containing the prescription data are kept in a locked cabinet. When the tapes are used, the computer is run "off-line," which means that no terminal outside of the computer room can read or record any information. Public disclosure of the identity of patients is expressly prohibited by the statute and by a Department of Health regulation. Willful violation of these prohibitions is a crime punishable by up to one year in prison and a $2,000 fine. . . .

II

Appellees contend that the statute invades a constitutionally protected "zone of privacy."[23] The cases sometimes characterized as protecting "privacy" have in fact involved at least two different kinds of interests. One is the individual interest in avoiding disclosure of personal matters, and another is the interest in independence in making certain kinds of important decisions. Appellees argue that both of these interests are impaired by this statute. The mere existence in readily available form of the information about patients' use of Schedule II drugs creates a genuine concern that the information will become publicly known and that it will adversely affect their reputations. This concern makes some patients reluctant to use, and some doctors reluctant to prescribe, such drugs even when their use is medically indicated. It follows, they argue, that the making of decisions about matters vital to the care of their health is inevitably affected by the statute. Thus, the statute threatens to impair both their interest in the nondisclosure of private information and also their interest in making important decisions independently.

---

23. As the basis for the constitutional claim they rely on the shadows cast by a variety of provisions in the Bill of Rights. Language in prior opinions of the Court or its individual Justices provides support for the view that some personal rights "implicit in the concept of ordered liberty" (*see* Palko v. Connecticut, 302 U.S. 319, 325, quoted in Roe v. Wade, 410 U.S., at 152), are so "fundamental" that an undefined penumbra may provide them with an independent source of constitutional protection. In Roe v. Wade, however, after carefully reviewing those cases, the Court expressed the opinion that the "right of privacy" is founded in the Fourteenth Amendment's concept of personal liberty, *id.*, at 152-153.

"This right of privacy, whether it be founded in the Fourteenth Amendment's concept of personal liberty and restrictions upon state action, as we feel it is, or, as the District Court determined, in the Ninth Amendment's reservation of rights to the people, is broad enough to encompass a woman's decision whether or not to terminate her pregnancy."

Id., at 153. *See also id.*, at 168-171 (Stewart, J., concurring); Griswold v. Connecticut, 381 U.S. 479, 500 (Harlan, J., concurring in judgment).

We are persuaded, however, that the New York program does not, on its face, pose a sufficiently grievous threat to either interest to establish a constitutional violation.

Public disclosure of patient information can come about in three ways. Health Department employees may violate the statute by failing, either deliberately or negligently, to maintain proper security. A patient or a doctor may be accused of a violation and the stored data may be offered in evidence in a judicial proceeding. Or, thirdly, a doctor, a pharmacist, or the patient may voluntarily reveal information on a prescription form.

The third possibility existed under the prior law and is entirely unrelated to the existence of the computerized data bank. Neither of the other two possibilities provides a proper ground for attacking the statute as invalid on its face. There is no support in the record, or in the experience of the two States that New York has emulated, for an assumption that the security provisions of the statute will be administered improperly. And the remote possibility that judicial supervision of the evidentiary use of particular items of stored information will provide inadequate protection against unwarranted disclosures is surely not a sufficient reason for invalidating the entire patient-identification program.

Even without public disclosure, it is, of course, true that private information must be disclosed to the authorized employees of the New York Department of Health. Such disclosures, however, are not significantly different from those that were required under the prior law. Nor are they meaningfully distinguishable from a host of other unpleasant invasions of privacy that are associated with many facets of health care. Unquestionably, some individuals' concern for their own privacy may lead them to avoid or to postpone needed medical attention. Nevertheless, disclosures of private medical information to doctors, to hospital personnel, to insurance companies, and to public health agencies are often an essential part of modern medical practice even when the disclosure may reflect unfavorably on the character of the patient. Requiring such disclosures to representatives of the State having responsibility for the health of the community, does not automatically amount to an impermissible invasion of privacy.

Appellees also argue, however, that even if unwarranted disclosures do not actually occur, the knowledge that the information is readily available in a computerized file creates a genuine concern that causes some persons to decline needed medication. The record supports the conclusion that some use of Schedule II drugs has been discouraged by that concern; it also is clear, however, that about 100,000 prescriptions for such drugs were being filled each month prior to the entry of the District Court's injunction. Clearly, therefore, the statute did not deprive the public of access to the drugs.

Nor can it be said that any individual has been deprived of the right to decide independently, with the advice of his physician, to acquire and to use needed medication. Although the State no doubt could prohibit entirely the use of particular Schedule II drugs, it has not done so. This case is therefore unlike those in which the Court held that a total prohibition of certain conduct was an impermissible deprivation of liberty. Nor does the State require access to these drugs to be conditioned on the consent of any state official or other third party. Within dosage limits which appellees do not challenge, the decision to prescribe, or to use, is left entirely to the physician and the patient.

We hold that neither the immediate nor the threatened impact of the patient-identification requirements in the New York State Controlled Substances Act of 1972 on either the reputation or the independence of patients for whom Schedule II drugs are medically indicated is sufficient to constitute an invasion of any right or liberty protected by the Fourteenth Amendment. . . .

IV

A final word about issues we have not decided. We are not unaware of the threat to privacy implicit in the accumulation of vast amounts of personal information in computerized data banks or other massive government files. The collection of taxes, the distribution of welfare and social security benefits, the supervision of public health, the direction of our Armed Forces, and the enforcement of the criminal laws all require the orderly preservation of great quantities of information, much of which is personal in character and potentially embarrassing or harmful if disclosed. The right to collect and use such data for public purposes is typically accompanied by a concomitant statutory or regulatory duty to avoid unwarranted disclosures. Recognizing that in some circumstances that duty arguably has its roots in the Constitution, nevertheless New York's statutory scheme, and its implementing administrative procedures, evidence a proper concern with, and protection of, the individual's interest in privacy. We therefore need not, and do not, decide any question which might be presented by the unwarranted disclosure of accumulated private data whether intentional or unintentional or by a system that did not contain comparable security provisions. We simply hold that this record does not establish an invasion of any right or liberty protected by the Fourteenth Amendment.

Reversed.

Mr. Justice BRENNAN, concurring. . . .

What is . . . troubling about this scheme . . . is the central computer storage of the data thus collected. Obviously, as the State argues, collection and storage of data by the State that is in itself legitimate is not rendered unconstitutional simply because new technology makes the State's operations more efficient. However, as the example of the Fourth Amendment shows the Constitution puts limits not only on the type of information the State may gather, but also on the means it may use to gather it. The central storage and easy accessibility of computerized data vastly increase the potential for abuse of that information, and I am not prepared to say that future developments will not demonstrate the necessity of some curb on such technology.

In this case, as the Court's opinion makes clear, the State's carefully designed program includes numerous safeguards intended to forestall the danger of indiscriminate disclosure. Given this serious and, so far as the record shows, successful effort to prevent abuse and limit access to the personal information at issue, I cannot say that the statute's provisions for computer storage, on their face, amount to a deprivation of constitutionally protected privacy interests, any more than the more traditional reporting provisions.

Mr. Justice STEWART, concurring.

In Katz v. United States, 389 U.S. 347, the Court made clear that although the Constitution affords protection against certain kinds of government intrusions into personal and private matters, there is no "general constitutional 'right to privacy.' . . . [T]he protection of a person's general right to privacy his right to be let alone by other people is, like the protection of his property and of his very life, left largely to the law of the individual States." *Id.*, at 350-351 (footnote omitted). . . .

Upon the understanding that nothing the Court says today is contrary to the above views, I join its opinion and judgment.

COMMENTS AND QUESTIONS

1. Does *Whalen* recognize a constitutional right to data privacy? Under what circumstances might such a right exist? How would it be violated?

2. What is Justice Brennan's position on the right to privacy? Justice Stewart's?

3. Does a person have a reasonable expectation of privacy with respect to the information collected in *Whalen*? If a doctor, pharmacist, and insurer all have access to this information, how can a patient have any expectation of privacy?

4. Does the medical nature of this information, as opposed to history of traffic violations or late child support payments, impact the privacy analysis? In other words, why do we care if others obtain this information?

5. Justice Brennan notes that: "The central storage and easy accessibility of computerized data vastly increase the potential for abuse of that information, and I am not prepared to say that future developments will not demonstrate the necessity of some curb on such technology." In fact, more recent technological capabilities have greatly increased concerns about storage and disclosure of health-related information in particular. The Health Insurance Portability and Accountability Act (HIPAA) has been implemented largely to address concerns about privacy of patients' health records. Commentators in recent years have expressed concerns about privacy even in the wake of HIPAA.

See, e.g., Sharona Hoffman & Andy Podgurski, *In Sickness, Health, and Cyber-space: Protecting the Security of Electronic Private Health Information*, 48 B.C. L. Rev. 331 (2007); Patricia Sánchez Abril & Anita Cava, *Health Privacy in a Techno-Social World: A Cyber-Patient's Bill of Rights*, 6 Nw. J. Tech. & Intell. Prop. 244 (2008). In the European Union, health information has obtained special protections under the European Union Directive on Data Protection, Art. 8, see *infra*. Are you convinced that the increased capabilities of digital technology with respect to storage and dissemination of health records creates particular privacy problems? Was Justice Brennan correct in expressing these particular concerns in *Whalen v. Roe*?

6. As the Supreme Court noted in *Whalen*, state and federal law prohibit government disclosure of certain information it collects. Consider the provision of the federal Privacy Act.

b) Disclosure

PRIVACY ACT OF 1974

5 U.S.C. §552a

. . .

(b) No agency shall disclose any record which is contained in a system of records by any means of communication to any person, or to another agency, except pursuant to a written request by, or with the prior written consent of, the individual to whom the record pertains, unless disclosure of the record would be:

(1) to those officers and employees of the agency which maintains the record who have a need for the record in the performance of their duties;

(2) required under section 552 of this title;

(3) for a routine use as defined in subsection (a)(7) of this section and described under subsection (e)(4)(D) of this section;

(4) to the Bureau of the Census for purposes of planning or carrying out a census or survey or related activity pursuant to the provisions of title 13;

(5) to a recipient who has provided the agency with advance adequate written assurance that the record will be used solely as a statistical research or reporting record, and the record is to be transferred in a form that is not individually identifiable;

(6) to the National Archives and Records Administration as a record which has sufficient historical or other value to warrant its continued preservation by the United States Government, or for evaluation by the Archivist of the United States or the designee of the Archivist to determine whether the record has such value;

(7) to another agency or to an instrumentality of any governmental jurisdiction within or under the control of the United States for a civil or

criminal law enforcement activity if the activity is authorized by law, and if the head of the agency or instrumentality has made a written request to the agency which maintains the record specifying the particular portion desired and the law enforcement activity for which the record is sought;

(8) to a person pursuant to a showing of compelling circumstances affecting the health or safety of an individual if upon such disclosure notification is transmitted to the last known address of such individual;

(9) to either House of Congress, or, to the extent of matter within its jurisdiction, any committee or subcommittee thereof, any joint committee of Congress or subcommittee of any such joint committee;

(10) to the Comptroller General, or any of his authorized representatives, in the course of the performance of the duties of the General Accounting Office;

(11) pursuant to the order of a court of competent jurisdiction; or

(12) to a consumer reporting agency in accordance with section 3711(e) of title 31.

Under the Act, "record" means "any item, collection, or grouping of information about an individual that is maintained by an agency, including, but not limited to, his education, financial transactions, medical history, and criminal or employment history and that contains his name, or the identifying number, symbol, or other identifying particular assigned to the individual, such as a finger or voice print or a photograph," 5 U.S.C. §552a(a)(4), and the term "routine use" means "the use of such record for a purpose which is compatible with the purpose for which it was collected." *Id*. at (a)(7).

In addition to the prohibition against disclosure, the Privacy Act requires Agencies to keep a record of disclosures, 5 U.S.C. §552a(c); to provide individuals with access to any information pertaining to them; *id*. at §552a(d); and to collect "only such information about an individual as is relevant and necessary." *id*. at 552a(e). Violations of the Act may be enforced by either civil or criminal penalties. *Id*. at 552(g).

COMMENTS AND QUESTIONS

1. How does the Privacy Act of 1974 protect individual privacy? Is the protection it affords sufficient?

2. Under what circumstances does the legislation prohibit the gathering of information? The disclosure of information?

3. Does the existence of the Privacy Act undermine any potential constitutional claim under *Whalen*?

4. The Privacy Act only applies to the federal government, and while most states have similar protections, to what extent can Congress prevent states from disclosing information that they would otherwise prefer to disclose? In Reno v. Condon, 528 U.S. 141 (2000), the U.S. Supreme Court upheld

the Driver's Privacy Protection Act of 1994 (DPPA) against a federalism challenge under the Tenth Amendment. The DPPA prohibited the states from disclosing or otherwise making available personal information about any individual obtained in connection with a motor vehicle record. 18 U.S.C. §2721(a). Prior to the DPPA, some states sold this information. While the Supreme Court did not address whether Congress could have enacted the DPPA in order to protect a constitutional right of privacy, the question was raised in the lower courts. Consider the Fourth Circuit's discussion in *Condon*:

> The United States asserts the individuals possess a Fourteenth Amendment right to privacy in their names, addresses, and phone numbers, and that the DPPA enforces that constitutional right. Neither the Supreme Court nor this Court, however, has ever recognized a constitutional right to privacy with respect to such information. Congress is granted a remedial power under Section 5 of the Fourteenth Amendment, not a substantive power. As a consequence, the DPPA is not a valid exercise if Congress's Enforcement Clause power.

Condon v. Reno, 155 F.3d 453, 456 (4th Cir. 1998), *rev'd*, 528 U.S. 141 (2000). Similarly, consider the district court's decision:

> While it is clear from the foregoing cases that at least in the Fourth Circuit there is a constitutional right to privacy in the nondisclosure of some form of personal information, the contours of this right are, as the Third Circuit has characterized, at best "murky." *Sheetz v. The Morning Call, Inc.*, 946 F.2d 202, 206 (3d Cir. 1991), *cert. denied*, 502 U.S. 1095 (1992). Further complicating the matter at hand is the fact that [none of the Fourth Circuit's decisions] involved the precise issue presented here. Each of those cases involved claims by individuals that they should not be *compelled to disclose* certain personal information to a governmental entity because of their right to privacy. Therefore, those cases presented a different question because the United States does not assert here that an individual's privacy right prohibits the States from requiring their citizens *to provide* the "personal information" specified in the DPPA to the State motor vehicle departments. Indeed, the United States (and the DPPA itself) implicitly concedes that an individual's privacy right in this information is outweighed by the States' interest in obtaining this information. The United States instead takes the privacy question one step further; that is, it asserts that the privacy interest at stake here is the right to have the government not *publicly disseminate* the validly obtained information contained in the State motor vehicle records. . . .
>
> [I]t seems certain that an individual's interest in not having certain personal information disseminated by the government is at least equal to, and probably greater than, his interest in merely avoiding disclosure of that information to the government. However the distinction to be made between the two interests likely lies in balancing to be done between the individual's privacy right and the government's need for disclosure. That is, the government likely would need to demonstrate a greater interest for disseminating personal information than it would for obtaining that same information. Of course, a prerequisite to either balancing process is an initial determination that the information is, in fact, the type of information that is protected under the Constitution.
>
> Therefore, in a case such as this one involving the *Whalen* right to privacy against the nondisclosure of personal information, the Court must, depending on the specific circumstances, potentially conduct a multi-pronged analysis. First, the Court must examine

the personal information at issue to determine whether, in fact, it is within a person's "reasonable expectation of confidentiality" and thus entitled to the constitutional right of privacy. If the information is not entitled to such protection, the inquiry ends. If the information is entitled to such protection, the Court next must determine whether the State's interest in obtaining the information from the individual outweighs the individual's privacy interest. . . . Again, if the answer here is negative, then the inquiry ends. However, if the answer is affirmative, then the Court must proceed to determine whether the State's interest in allowing the information to be made public outweighs the individual's privacy interest. As noted, this latter inquiry sorely requires the States to present a higher interest than they must show to obtain personal information. . . .

972 F. Supp. 977, 989-90 (D.S.C. 1997), *aff'd*, 155 F.3d 453, 456 (4th Cir. 1998), *rev'd*, 528 U.S. 141 (2000).

5. While the Privacy Act also applies to private companies that contract with the government to administer systems of records, 5 U.S.C. §552a(m), as Chris Hoofnagle observes, "a database of information that originates [from a commercial data broker] would not trigger the requirements of the Privacy Act." This limitation is critical because it allows the government to access huge databases that it would otherwise have been prohibited from creating. *See* Chris Jay Hoofnagle, *Big Brother's Little Helpers: How ChoicePoint and Other Commercial Data Brokers Collect and Package Your Data for Law Enforcement*, 29 N.C. J. Int'l L. & Com. Reg. 595, 623 (2004).

2. Restrictions upon Private Data Collection and Disclosure

a) Common Law

Before examining the issue as it has unfolded with respect to cyberspace, is data gathering anything new? In Jerry Kang's analogy to the shopping mall, would mall surveillance through video cameras or mall security violate an individual's privacy interests? What about tracking someone's purchasing habits through his or her credit cards?

DWYER v. AMERICAN EXPRESS CO.

273 Ill. App. 3d 742 (1995)

Justice BUCKLEY delivered the opinion of the court:

Plaintiffs, American Express cardholders, appeal the circuit court's dismissal of their claims for invasion of privacy and consumer fraud against defendants, American Express Company, American Express Credit Corporation, and American Express Travel Related Services Company, for their practice of renting information regarding cardholder spending habits.

On May 13, 1992, the New York Attorney General released a press statement describing an agreement it had entered into with defendants. The following day, newspapers reported defendants' actions which gave rise to this agreement. According to the news articles, defendants categorize and rank their cardholders into six tiers based on spending habits and then rent this information to participating merchants as part of a targeted joint-marketing and sales program. For example, a cardholder may be characterized as "Rodeo Drive Chic" or "Value Oriented." In order to characterize its cardholders, defendants analyze where they shop and how much they spend, and also consider behavioral characteristics and spending histories. Defendants then offer to create a list of cardholders who would most likely shop in a particular store and rent that list to the merchant.

Defendants also offer to create lists which target cardholders who purchase specific types of items, such as fine jewelry. The merchants using the defendants' service can also target shoppers in categories such as mail-order apparel buyers, home-improvement shoppers, electronics shoppers, luxury lodgers, card members with children, skiers, frequent business travelers, resort users, Asian/European travelers, luxury European car owners, or recent movers. Finally, defendants offer joint-marketing ventures to merchants who generate substantial sales through the American Express card. Defendants mail special promotions devised by the merchants to its cardholders and share the profits generated by these advertisements.

On May 14, 1992, Patrick E. Dwyer filed a class action against defendants. His complaint alleges that defendants intruded into their cardholders' seclusion, commercially appropriated their cardholders' personal spending habits, and violated the Illinois consumer fraud statute and consumer fraud statutes in other jurisdictions. Maria Teresa Rojas later filed a class action containing the same claims. . . .

Plaintiffs have alleged that defendants' practices constitute an invasion of their privacy and violate the Illinois Consumer Fraud and Deceptive Business Practices Act (Act or Consumer Fraud Act) (Ill. Rev. Stat. 1991, ch. 121 1/2, par. 261 et seq. (now 815 ILCS 505/1 et seq. (West 1992))). . . .

INVASION OF PRIVACY

There are four branches of the privacy invasion tort identified by the Restatement (Second) of Torts. These are: (1) an unreasonable intrusion upon the seclusion of another; (2) an appropriation of another's name or likeness; (3) a public disclosure of private facts; and (4) publicity which reasonably places another in a false light before the public. Restatement (Second) of Torts §§652B, 652C, 652D, 652E, at 378-94 (1977); W. Keeton, Prosser & Keeton on Torts §117, at 849-69 (5th ed. 1984). Plaintiffs' complaint includes claims under the first and second branches.

In *Melvin*, the court set out four elements which must be alleged in order to state a cause of action [for intrusion]: (1) an unauthorized intrusion or prying into the plaintiff's seclusion; (2) an intrusion which is offensive or objectionable to a reasonable man; (3) the matter upon which the intrusion occurs is private; and (4) the intrusion causes anguish and suffering. [Melvin v. Burling, 141 Ill. App. 3d 786, 789, 490 N.E.2d 1011, 1013-1014 (1986).] Since the third district set out the four elements in *Melvin*, this district has applied these elements without directly addressing the issue of whether the cause of action exists in this State. . . .

Plaintiffs' allegations fail to satisfy the first element, an unauthorized intrusion or prying into the plaintiffs' seclusion. The alleged wrongful actions involve the defendants' practice of renting lists that they have compiled from information contained in their own records. By using the American Express card, a cardholder is voluntarily, and necessarily, giving information to defendants that, if analyzed, will reveal a cardholder's spending habits and shopping preferences. We cannot hold that a defendant has committed an unauthorized intrusion by compiling the information voluntarily given to it and then renting its compilation.

Plaintiffs claim that because defendants rented lists based on this compiled information, this case involves the disclosure of private financial information and most closely resembles cases involving intrusion into private financial dealings, such as bank account transactions. . . .

However, we find that this case more closely resembles the sale of magazine subscription lists, which was at issue in Shibley v. Time, Inc. (1975), 45 Ohio App. 2d 69, 341 N.E.2d 337. In *Shibley*, the plaintiffs claimed that the defendant's practice of selling and renting magazine subscription lists without the subscribers' prior consent "constitut[ed] an invasion of privacy because it amount[ed] to a sale of individual 'personality profiles,' which subjects the subscribers to solicitations from direct mail advertisers." *Shibley*, 45 Ohio App. 2d at 71, 341 N.E.2d at 339. The plaintiffs also claimed that the lists amounted to a tortious appropriation of their names and "personality profiles." The trial court dismissed the plaintiffs' complaint and the Court of Appeals of Ohio affirmed. *Shibley*, 45 Ohio App. 2d at 71, 341 N.E.2d at 339.

The *Shibley* court found that an Ohio statute, which permitted the sale of names and addresses of registrants of motor vehicles, indicated that the defendant's activity was not an invasion of privacy. The court considered a Federal district court case from New York, Lamont v. Commissioner of Motor Vehicles (S.D.N.Y. 1967), 269 F. Supp. 880, aff'd (2d Cir. 1967), 386 F.2d 449, cert. denied (1968), 391 U.S. 915, to be insightful. In *Lamont*, the plaintiff claimed an invasion of privacy arising from the State's sale of its list of names and addresses of registered motor-vehicle owners to mail-order advertisers. The *Lamont* court held that however "noxious" advertising by mail might be, the burden was acceptable as far as the Constitution is concerned. *Lamont*,

269 F. Supp. at 883. The *Shibley* court followed the reasoning in *Lamont* and held:

> "The right to privacy does not extend to the mailbox and therefore it is constitutionally permissible to sell subscription lists to direct mail advertisers. It necessarily follows that the practice complained of here does not constitute an invasion of privacy even if appellants' unsupported assertion that this amounts to the sale of 'personality profiles' is taken as true because these profiles are only used to determine what type of advertisement is to be sent." *Shibley*, 45 Ohio App. 2d at 73, 341 N.E.2d at 339-40.

Defendants rent names and addresses after they create a list of cardholders who have certain shopping tendencies; they are not disclosing financial information about particular cardholders. These lists are being used solely for the purpose of determining what type of advertising should be sent to whom. We also note that the Illinois Vehicle Code authorizes the Secretary of State to sell lists of names and addresses of licensed drivers and registered motor-vehicle owners. (625 ILCS 5/2 — 123 (West 1992).) Thus, we hold that the alleged actions here do not constitute an unreasonable intrusion into the seclusion of another. We so hold without expressing a view as to the appellate court conflict regarding the recognition of this cause of action. . . .

CONSUMER FRAUD ACT

Plaintiffs' complaint also includes a claim under the Illinois Consumer Fraud Act. Ill. Rev. Stat. 1991, ch. 121 1/2, par. 261 et seq. (now 815 ILCS 505/1 et seq. (West 1992)). To establish a deceptive practice claim, a plaintiff must allege and prove (1) the misrepresentation or concealment of a material fact, (2) an intent by defendant that plaintiff rely on the misrepresentation or concealment, and (3) the deception occurred in the course of conduct involving a trade or commerce. Ill. Rev. Stat. 1991, ch. 121 1/2, par. 262 (now 815 ILCS 505/2 (West 1992)); Siegel v. Levy Organization Development Co. (1992), 153 Ill. 2d 534, 542, 607 N.E.2d 194, 198. . . .

According to the plaintiffs, defendants conducted a survey which showed that 80% of Americans do not think companies should release personal information to other companies. Plaintiffs have alleged that defendants did disclose that it would use information provided in the credit card application, but this disclosure did not inform the cardholders that information about their card usage would be used. It is highly possible that some customers would have refrained from using the American Express Card if they had known that defendants were analyzing their spending habits. Therefore, plaintiffs have sufficiently alleged that the undisclosed practices of defendants are material and deceptive.

As to the second element, the Act only requires defendants' intent that plaintiffs rely on the deceptive practice. Actual reliance is not required. *Siegel*, 153 Ill. 2d at 542, 607 N.E.2d at 198. . . . When considering whether this element is met, good or bad faith is not important and innocent misrepresentations may be actionable. *Warren*, 142 Ill. App. 3d at 566, 491 N.E.2d at 474. Defendants had a strong incentive to keep their practice a secret because disclosure would have resulted in fewer cardholders using their card. Thus, plaintiffs have sufficiently alleged that defendants intended for plaintiff's to rely on the nondisclosure of their practice.

The third element is not at issue in this case. However, defendants argue that plaintiffs have failed to allege facts that might establish that they suffered any damages. The Illinois Consumer Fraud Act provides a private cause of action for damages to "[a]ny person who suffers damage as a result of a violation of th[e] Act." Ill. Rev. Stat. 1991, ch. 121 1/2, par. 270a (now 815 ILCS 505/10a(a) (West 1992)). Defendants contend, and we agree, that the only damage plaintiffs could have suffered was a surfeit of unwanted mail. We reject plaintiffs' assertion that the damages in this case arise from the disclosure of personal financial matters. Defendants only disclose which of their cardholders might be interested in purchasing items from a particular merchant based on card usage. Defendants' practice does not amount to a disclosure of personal financial matters. Plaintiffs have failed to allege how they were damaged by defendants' practice of selecting cardholders for mailings likely to be of interest to them.

Plaintiffs argue that the consumer fraud statutes of other States allow recovery of mental anguish even if no other damages are pled or proved. Apparently, plaintiffs would like this court to assume that a third party's knowledge of a cardholder's interest in their goods or services causes mental anguish to cardholders. Such an assumption without any supporting allegations would be wholly unfounded in this case. Therefore, we hold that plaintiffs have failed to allege facts that might establish that they have suffered any damages as a result of defendants' practices.

Accordingly, for the reasons set forth above, we affirm the order of the circuit court of Cook County.

RAKOWSKI and CAHILL, JJ., concur.

COMMENTS AND QUESTIONS

1. *Dwyer* turns on the fact that American Express cardholders have voluntarily disclosed their shopping information to American Express. Does that resolve the question of whether American Express's conduct was authorized? Does it matter that American Express cardholders may have authorized only certain uses of their information? If not, why not?

2. *Dwyer* is based upon common law torts for the invasions of privacy. Assuming that the court considered American Express's conduct to be unauthorized, would the disclosure be offensive or objectionable to a reasonable person?

3. What kind of information, if any, does the court in *Dwyer* suggest is protected by the common law? In reaching its conclusion, *Dwyer* relies upon a

federal district court decision involving driver registration information. How would you distinguish the cases?

4.   Assuming that the facts of *Dwyer* could support a claim of invasion of privacy, would American Express be subject to liability if it disclosed its practices to cardholders? *Consider* United States v. Simons, 206 F.3d 392 (4th Cir. 2000) (holding that employer's stated policy of monitoring all Internet use and e-mail communications defeated any reasonable expectation of privacy). Why should such a disclosure constitute a defense to an invasion of privacy claim? Does this result suggest that the "reasonable expectation of privacy" test is meaningless in a world where entities who collect personal information can simply disclaim privacy rights and expectations as a matter of course?

5.   In light of the fact that American Express did not disclose its practices at the time, why did the court dismiss the consumer fraud claim? To what degree is information gathering an issue of privacy versus unfair business practices? For example, according to the Federal Trade Commission, Internet data collection should be governed by four principles:

1.   **Notice** — Web sites would be required to provide consumers clear and conspicuous notice of their information practices, including what information they collect, how they collect it (e.g., directly or through nonobvious means such as cookies), how they use it, how they provide Choice, Access, and Security to consumers, whether they disclose the information collected to other entities, and whether other entities are collecting information through the site.

2.   **Choice** — Web sites would be required to offer consumers choices as to how their personal identifying information is used beyond the use for which the information was provided (e.g., to consummate a transaction). Such choice would encompass both internal secondary uses (such as marketing back to consumers) and external secondary uses (such as disclosing data to other entities).

3.   **Access** — Web sites would be required to offer consumers reasonable access to the information a Web site has collected about them, including a reasonable opportunity to review information and to correct inaccuracies or delete information.

4.   **Security** — Web sites would be required to take reasonable steps to protect the security of the information they collect from consumers.

Federal Trade Commission, *Fair Information Practices in the Electronic Marketplace* at iii (May 2000), *http://www.ftc.gov/reports/privacy2000/privacy2000.pdf*.

6.   A good example of the FTC's treatment of these issues can be found in In the Matter of GeoCities, FTC Docket No. C-3850 (Feb. 5, 1999). In *GeoCities,* the FTC entered into a consent decree with a Web site requiring the site to disclose its information collection practices and to obtain parental consent before collecting information from children. At the time, GeoCities

provided numerous services including free and fee-based personal home pages and free e-mail to its members. To become a member, individuals were required to complete an online application form with certain information listed as mandatory and other as optional. Through its registration process:

> GeoCities created a database that included e-mail and postal addresses, member interest areas, and demographics including income, education, gender, marital status and occupation. According to the Federal Trade Commission (FTC), this information created target markets for advertisers and resulted in disclosure of personal identifying information of children and adults to third-party marketers.
>
> The FTC's complaint alleged that GeoCities misrepresented that the personal identifying information it collected through the membership application form was used only to provide members the specific advertising offers and products or services they requested, and that the "optional" information (education level, income, marital status, occupation, and interests) would not be released to anyone without the member's permission. The complaint also alleged that this information was disclosed to third parties, who used it to target members for solicitations beyond those agreed to by the member.
>
> The complaint also charged that GeoCities engaged in deceptive practices relating to its collection of information from children. According to the FTC, GeoCities promotes the Official GeoCities GeoKidz Club and contests for children in the Enchanted Forest neighborhood. Children wishing to join in these activities are required to complete forms that solicit personal identifying information. The agency charged that GeoCities misrepresented that GeoCities itself operated the GeoKidz Club and certain contests, and that the information collected online through the club and contests was maintained by Geo-Cities. In fact, according to the complaint, the Club and contests were run by third-party "community leaders" hosted on the GeoCities Web site, who collected and maintained the information.

See Internet Site Agrees to Settle FTC Charges of Deceptively Collecting Personal Information in Agency's First Internet Privacy Case (Aug. 13, 1998), *http://www.ftc.gov/opa/1998/08/geocitie.htm*. In its consent decree, the FTC ordered that GeoCities

> shall not make any misrepresentation, in any manner, expressly or by implication, about its collection or use of such information from or about consumers, including, but not limited to, what information will be disclosed to third parties and how the information will be used.

and

> shall not misrepresent, in any manner, expressly or by implication, the identity of the party collecting any such information or the sponsorship of any activity on its Web site.

In the Matter of GeoCities, FTC Docket No. C-3850 (Feb. 5, 1999). The consent decree required GeoCities to provide a clear and prominent notice of its privacy policies either at the location in which the information is collected or through a hyperlink or button. *Id.*

   7.   What concerns with respect to data privacy do the FTC's policies address? Is this approach sufficient? What other values might be implicated

by information gathering that are not addressed by an approach based upon fair information practices?

8.   To the extent to which a Web site is required to offer users a choice as to whether their information will be collected and how it will be used, how should that consent be manifested? Should Web site users be required to opt in to data collection, or is providing the user an opportunity to opt out of data collection sufficient? In other words, what should be the default position? For example, Jeff Sovern argues that an opt-in system is preferable because "it eliminates the incentives firms have to engage in strategic behavior and thus inflate consumer transaction costs." Jeff Sovern, *Opting In, Opting Out, or No Options at All: The Fight for Control of Personal Information*, 74 Wash. L. Rev. 1033, 1118 (1999). Is the benefit that opt-in would encourage Web sites to provide clearer privacy policies? If the concern is that users do not understand their rights or read privacy policies, which regime would encourage them to better inform themselves? What are the costs of making the default position consent to gather information?

9.   In addition to consent, are there other theories that may be used to control cyberspace data collection? Consider the following decision.

In re DoubleClick Inc. Privacy Litigation

154 F. Supp. 2d 497 (S.D.N.Y. 2001)

Buchwald, J.

Plaintiffs bring this class action on behalf of themselves and all others similarly situated against defendant DoubleClick, Inc. ("defendant" or "DoubleClick") seeking injunctive and monetary relief for injuries they have suffered as a result of DoubleClick's purported illegal conduct. Specifically, plaintiffs bring three claims under federal laws: (1) 18 U.S.C. §2701, et seq.; (2) 18 U.S.C. §2510, et seq.; (3) 18 U.S.C. §1030, et seq.; and four claims under state laws: (1) common law invasion of privacy; (2) common law unjust enrichment; (3) common law trespass to property; and (4) Sections 349(a) and 350 of Article 22A of the New York General Business Law.

Background

DoubleClick, a Delaware corporation, is the largest provider of Internet advertising products and services in the world. Its Internet-based advertising network of over 11,000 Web publishers has enabled DoubleClick to become the market leader in delivering online advertising. DoubleClick specializes in collecting, compiling and analyzing information about Internet users through proprietary technologies and techniques, and using it to target online advertising. DoubleClick has placed billions of advertisements on its clients' behalf and its services reach the majority of Internet users in the United States. . . .

DoubleClick's Technology and Services

DoubleClick provides the Internet's largest advertising service. Commercial Web sites often rent-out online advertising "space" to other Web sites. In the simplest type of arrangement, the host Web site (e.g., Lycos.com) rents space on its Webpages to another Web site (e.g., TheGlobe.com) to place a "hotlink" banner advertisement ("banner advertisement"). When a user on the host Web site "clicks" on the banner advertisement, he is automatically connected to the advertiser's designated Web site.

DoubleClick acts as an intermediary between host Web sites and Web sites seeking to place banner advertisements. It promises client Web sites that it will place their banner advertisements in front of viewers who match their demographic target. For example, DoubleClick might try to place banner advertisements for a Web site that sells golfclubs in front of high-income people who follow golf and have a track record of making expensive online purchases. DoubleClick creates value for its customers in large part by building detailed profiles of Internet users and using them to target clients' advertisements.

DoubleClick compiles user profiles utilizing its proprietary technologies and analyses in cooperation with its affiliated Web sites. DoubleClick is affiliated with over 11,000 Web sites for which and on which it provides targeted banner advertisements. A select group of over 1,500 of these Web sites form the "DoubleClick Network" and are among "the most highly trafficked and branded sites on the Web." . . .

When users visit any of these DoubleClick-affiliated Web sites, a "cookie" is placed on their hard drives. Cookies are computer programs commonly used by Web sites to store useful information such as usernames, passwords, and preferences, making it easier for users to access Web pages in an efficient manner. However, Plaintiffs allege that DoubleClick's cookies collect "information that Web users, including plaintiffs and the Class, consider to be personal and private, such as names, e-mail addresses, home and business addresses, telephone numbers, searches performed on the Internet, Web pages or sites visited on the Internet and other communications and information that users would not ordinarily expect advertisers to be able to collect." DoubleClick's cookies store this personal information on users' hard drives until DoubleClick electronically accesses the cookies and uploads the data.

How DoubleClick targets banner advertisements and utilizes cookies to collect user information is crucial to our analysis under the three statutes. Therefore, we examine both processes in greater detail.

A. Targeting Banner Advertisements

DoubleClick's advertising targeting process involves three participants and four steps. The three participants are: (1) the user; (2) the DoubleClick-affiliated Web site; (3) the DoubleClick server. For the purposes of this discussion, we assume that a DoubleClick cookie already sits on the user's computer with the identification number "# 0001."

In Step One, a user seeks to access a DoubleClick-affiliated Web site such as Lycos.com. The user's browser sends a communication to Lycos.com (technically, to Lycos.com's server) saying, in essence, "Send me your homepage." U.S. Patent No. 5,948,061 (issued September 7, 1999) ("DoubleClick Patent"), col. 3, ll. 6-9. This communication may contain data submitted as part of the request, such as a query string or field information.

In Step Two, Lycos.com receives the request, processes it, and returns a communication to the user saying "Here is the Web page you requested." The communication has two parts. The first part is a copy of the Lycos.com homepage, essentially the collection article summaries, pictures and hotlinks a user sees on his screen when Lycos.com appears. The only objects missing are the banner advertisements; in their places lie blank spaces. *Id.* at col. 3, ll. 28-34. The second part of the communication is an IP-address link to the DoubleClick server. *Id.* at col. 3, ll. 35-38. This link instructs the user's computer to send a communication automatically to DoubleClick's server.

In Step Three, as per the IP-address instruction, the user's computer sends a communication to the DoubleClick server saying "I am cookie # 0001, send me banner advertisements to fill the blank spaces in the Lycos.com Web page." This communication contains information including the cookie identification number, the name of the DoubleClick-affilated Web site the user requested, and the user's browser-type. *Id.* at col. 3, ll. 41-52.

Finally, in Step Four, the DoubleClick server identifies the user's profile by the cookie identification number and runs a complex set of algorithms based, in part, on the user's profile, to determine which advertisements it will present to the user. *Id.* at col. 3, ll. 52-57, col. 5, l. 11 — col. 6, l. 59. It then sends a communication to the user with banner advertisements saying "Here are the targeted banner advertisements for the Lycos.com homepage." Meanwhile, it also updates the user's profile with the information from the request. *Id.* at col. 6, l. 60 — col. 7, l. 14.

DoubleClick's targeted advertising process is invisible to the user. His experience consists simply of requesting the Lycos.com homepage and, several moments later, receiving it complete with banner advertisements.

B. Cookie Information Collection

DoubleClick's cookies only collect information from one step of the above process: Step One. The cookies capture certain parts of the communications that users send to DoubleClick-affiliated Web sites. They collect this information in three ways: (1) "GET" submissions, (2) "POST" submissions, and (3) "GIF" submissions.

GET information is submitted as part of a Web site's address or "URL," in what is known as a "query string." For example, a request for a hypothetical online record store's selection of Bon Jovi albums might read: http://record store.hypothetical.com/search? terms=bonjovi. The URL query string begins with the "?" character meaning the cookie would record that the user requested information about Bon Jovi.

Users submit POST information when they fill in multiple blank fields on a Webpage. For example, if a user signed up for an online discussion group, he might have to fill in fields with his name, address, e-mail address, phone number and discussion group alias. The cookie would capture this submitted POST information.

Finally, DoubleClick places GIF tags on its affiliated Web sites. GIF tags are the size of a single pixel and are invisible to users. Unseen, they record the users' movements throughout the affiliated Web site, enabling DoubleClick to learn what information the user sought and viewed.

Although the information collected by DoubleClick's cookies is allegedly voluminous and detailed, it is important to note three clearly defined parameters. First, DoubleClick's cookies only collect information concerning users' activities on DoubleClick-affiliated Web sites. Thus, if a user visits an unaffiliated Web site, the DoubleClick cookie captures no information. Second, plaintiff does not allege that DoubleClick ever attempted to collect any information other than the GET, POST, and GIF information submitted by users. DoubleClick is never alleged to have accessed files, programs or other information on users' hard drives. Third, DoubleClick will not collect information from any user who takes simple steps to prevent DoubleClick's tracking. As plaintiffs' counsel demonstrated at oral argument, users can easily and at no cost prevent DoubleClick from collecting information from them. They may do this in two ways: (1) visiting the DoubleClick Web site and requesting an "opt-out" cookie; and (2) configuring their browsers to block any cookies from being deposited.

Once DoubleClick collects information from the cookies on users' hard drives, it aggregates and compiles the information to build demographic profiles of users. Plaintiffs allege that DoubleClick has more than 100 million user profiles in its database. Exploiting its proprietary Dynamic Advertising Reporting & Targeting ("DART") technology, DoubleClick and its licensees target banner advertisements using these demographic profiles. . . .

Claim I. Title II of the ECPA

Title II ("Title II") of the Electronic Communications Privacy Act ("ECPA"), 18 U.S.C. §2701 et seq. ("§2701"), aims to prevent hackers from obtaining, altering or destroying certain stored electronic communications. . . . It creates both criminal sanctions and a civil right of action against persons who gain unauthorized access to communications facilities and thereby access electronic communications stored incident to their transmission. . . .

Plaintiffs contend that DoubleClick's placement of cookies on plaintiffs' hard drives constitutes unauthorized access and, as a result, DoubleClick's collection of information from the cookies violates Title II. However, Title II contains an exception to its general prohibition.

"(c) Exceptions. — Subsection (a) of this section does not apply with respect to conduct authorized. . . (2) by a user of that [wire or electronic communications] service with respect to a communication of or intended for that user;"

DoubleClick argues that its conduct falls under this exception. It contends that the DoubleClick-affiliated Web sites are "users" of the Internet and that all of plaintiffs' communications accessed by DoubleClick's cookies have been "of or intended for" these Web sites. Therefore, it asserts, the Web sites' authorization excepts DoubleClick's access from §2701(a)'s general prohibition. . . .

Assuming that the communications are considered to be in "electronic storage," it appears that plaintiffs have adequately pled that DoubleClick's conduct constitutes an offense under §2701(a), absent the exception under §2701(c)(2). Therefore, the issue is whether DoubleClick's conduct falls under §2701(c)(2)'s exception. This issue has three parts: (1) what is the relevant electronic communications service?; (2) were DoubleClick-affiliated Web sites "users" of this service?; and (3) did the DoubleClick-affiliated Web sites give DoubleClick sufficient authorization to access plaintiffs' stored communications "intended for" those Web sites?

A. "Internet Access" is the relevant electronic communications service

Obviously, in a broad sense, the "Internet" is the relevant communications service. However, for the purposes of this motion, it is important that we define Internet service with somewhat greater care and precision. Plaintiff, at turns, argues that the electronic communications service is "Internet access" and "the ISP [Internet Service Provider]." The difference is important. An ISP is an entity that provides access to the Internet; examples include America Online, UUNET and Juno. Access to the Internet is the service an ISP provides. Therefore, the "service which provides to users thereof the ability to send or receive wire or electronic communications" is "Internet access."

B. Web Sites are "users" under the ECPA

The ECPA defines a "user" as "any person or entity who (A) uses an electronic communication service; and (B) is duly authorized by the provider of such service to engage in such use." 18 U.S.C. §2510(13). On first reading, the DoubleClick-affiliated Web sites appear to be users — they are (1) "entities" that (2) use Internet access and (3) are authorized to use Internet access by the ISPs to which they subscribe. However, plaintiffs make two arguments that Web sites nevertheless are not users. Both are unpersuasive.

First, plaintiffs argue that "[t]he most natural reading of 'user' is the person who has signed up for Internet access, which means the individual plaintiffs and Class members — not the Web servers." Insofar as this argument implies that the statute meant to differentiate between human and non-human users, it is clearly contradicted by the statute's language that defines a "user" as "any person *or entity* . . ." (emphasis added). Furthermore, it rests on the erroneous assumption that only human users "sign[] up for Internet access," not Web sites or servers. This court takes judicial notice of the fact that all people and entities that utilize Internet access subscribe to ISPs or are ISPs. Although the vast majority of people who sign up for Internet access from consumer-focused ISPs such as America Online and Juno are individuals, every Web site, company, university, and government agency that utilizes Internet access also subscribes to an ISP or is one. These larger entities generally purchase "Internet access" in bulk from ISPs, often with value-added services and technologically advanced hardware. Nevertheless, they purchase the same underlying Internet access as individual users. Therefore, plaintiffs fail to distinguish class members from Web sites and servers based on whether they subscribe to an ISP for Internet access.

Second, plaintiffs argue that "[t]he individual plaintiff ('user') owns the personal computer ('facility'), while the Web sites she visits do not. [And that] [u]nder basic property and privacy notions, therefore, only she can authorize access to her own messages stored on that facility." Again, plaintiffs seem to ignore the statute's plain language. The general rule under §2701(a) embodies plaintiffs' position that only those authorized to use a "facility" may consent to its access. Nevertheless, Congress explicitly chose to make §2701(a)'s general rule subject to §2701(c)(2)'s exception for access authorized by authors and intended recipients of electronic communications. Thus, plaintiffs' argument is essentially that this Court should ignore §2701(c)(2) because Congress failed to take adequate account of "basic property and privacy notions." However, it is not this Court's role to revisit Congress' legislative judgments. . . .

C. All of the communications DoubleClick has accessed through its cookies have been authorized or have fallen outside of Title II's scope

Because plaintiffs only allege that DoubleClick accessed communications from plaintiffs to DoubleClick-affiliated Web sites, the issue becomes whether the Web sites gave DoubleClick adequate authorization under §2701(c)(2) to access those communications. This issue, in turn, has two parts: (1) have the DoubleClick-affiliated Web sites authorized DoubleClick to access plaintiffs' communications to them?; and (2) is that authorization sufficient under §2701(c)(2)?

1. The DoubleClick-affiliated Web sites have consented
    to DoubleClick's interception of plaintiffs' communications.

A plaintiff cannot survive a motion to dismiss a Title II claim based solely on the naked allegation that defendant's access was "unauthorized." A plaintiff must, "allege[ ] and proffer[ ] sufficient proofs to create a colorable claim that such access was 'unauthorized.'" *See Sherman & Co. v. Salton Maxim Housewares, Inc.*, 94 F. Supp. 2d 817, 820-821 (E.D. Mich. 2000) (denying motion to amend complaint because "proposed claim under the ECPA does not state a claim," despite the fact plaintiff alleged access was unauthorized); *cf. Hirsch v. Arthur Andersen & Co.*, 72 F.3d 1085 (2d Cir. 1995) ("General, conclusory allegations need not be credited, however, when they are belied by more specific allegations of the complaint.") (citation omitted). In the instant case, plaintiffs have proffered no proofs whatsoever to support their bare assertion that Doubleclick's access was unauthorized. What is more, every fact they do allege supports the inference that the DoubleClick-affiliated Web sites did authorize DoubleClick's access.

Examining DoubleClick's technological and commercial relationships with its affiliated Web sites, we find it implausible to infer that the Web sites have not authorized DoubleClick's access. In a practical sense, the very reason clients hire DoubleClick is to target advertisements based on users' demographic profiles. . . . Therefore, we find that the DoubleClick-affiliated Web sites consented to DoubleClick's access of plaintiffs' communications to them. . . .

3. To the extent that the DoubleClick cookies' identification
    numbers are electronic communications,
    (1) they fall outside of Title II's scope, and
    (2) DoubleClick's access to them is otherwise authorized.

Plaintiffs argue that even if DoubleClick's access to plaintiffs' GET, POST and GIF submissions is properly authorized under §2701(c)(2), the cookie identification numbers that accompany these submissions are not because they are never sent to, or through, the Web sites. However, this argument too is unavailing.

(a) The Cookies' Identification Numbers are not in "Electronic
     Storage" and Therefore are Outside Title II's Scope.

Putting aside the issue of whether the cookie identification numbers are electronic communications at all, DoubleClick does not need anyone's authority to access them. The cookies' long-term residence on plaintiffs' hard drives places them outside of §2510(17)'s definition of "electronic storage" and, hence, Title II's protection. Section 2510(17) defines "electronic storage" as:

> "(A) any *temporary, intermediate storage* of a wire or electronic communication incidental to the electronic transmission thereof; and

(B) any storage of such communication *by an electronic communication service* for the purpose of backup protection of such communication." (emphasis added)

Clearly, the cookies' residence on plaintiffs' computers does not fall into §2510(17)(B) because plaintiffs are not "electronic communication service" providers. . . .

(b) If the DoubleClick Cookies' Identification Numbers are Considered Stored Electronic Communications, They are "of or Intended for" DoubleClick and DoubleClick's Acquisition of them does not Violate Title II.

Even if we were to assume that cookies and their identification numbers were "electronic communication[s] . . . in electronic storage," DoubleClick's access is still authorized. Section 2701(c)(2) excepts from Title II's prohibition access, authorized by a "user," to communications (1) "of" (2) "or intended for" that user. In every practical sense, the cookies' identification numbers are internal DoubleClick communications — both "of" and "intended for" DoubleClick. DoubleClick creates the cookies, assigns them identification numbers, and places them on plaintiffs' hard drives. The cookies and their identification numbers are vital to DoubleClick and meaningless to anyone else. In contrast, virtually all plaintiffs are unaware that the cookies exist, that these cookies have identification numbers, that DoubleClick accesses these identification numbers and that these numbers are critical to DoubleClick's operations.

In this sense, cookie identification numbers are much akin to computer bar-codes or identification numbers placed on "business reply cards" found in magazines. These bar-codes and identification numbers are meaningless to consumers, but are valuable to companies in compiling data on consumer responses (e.g. from which magazine did the consumer get the card?). Although consumers fill-out business reply cards and return them to companies by mail, the bar-codes and identification numbers that appear on the cards are purely internal administrative data for the companies. The cookie identification numbers are every bit as internal to DoubleClick as the bar-codes and identification numbers are to business reply mailers. Therefore, it seems both sensible to consider the identification numbers to be "of or intended for" DoubleClick and bizarre to describe them as "of or intended for" plaintiffs. Accordingly, because the identification numbers are "of or intended for" DoubleClick, it does not violate Title II for DoubleClick to obtain them from plaintiffs' electronic storage. . . .

[The court then dismissed the plaintiffs' claim under Title I of the ECPA for intercepting the plaintiffs' communications. According to the court, because the Web sites authorized that interception, DoubleClick would only be subject to liability if it had acted with "criminal or tortious" purpose under 18 U.S.C. §2511(2)(d). While plaintiffs alleged that

DoubleClick had committed torts, they failed to allege that DoubleClick acted with a tortious purpose. The court also dismissed the plaintiffs' claims under the Computer Fraud and Abuse Act, 18 U.S.C. §§1030, et seq. The court's opinion with respect to the CFAA is excerpted in Chapter 6. Having dismissed the federal claims, the district court declined jurisdiction over the state law claims.]

COMMENTS AND QUESTIONS

1. Why did the plaintiffs raise claims under the ECPA? How did DoubleClick illegally intercept or access stored communications?

2. Why did the court reject the plaintiffs' claims under the ECPA? Why is the consent of DoubleClick's affiliated Web sites relevant? Who are the appropriate users under the statute?

3. Assuming that an affiliated Web site's consent to transfer user information is a defense to interception of electronic communications, why is DoubleClick's access to the cookie not an authorized access to stored communications if the individual who owns the computer objects?

4. Is there an argument that the plaintiffs authorized DoubleClick's access? Does it matter that Internet users can use programs including their Web browsers to block cookies?

5. Compare *DoubleClick* with *Dwyer*. In the absence of statutory damages, what injuries have the plaintiffs suffered? Is one of the problems of privacy law in its present form related to the requirement for the plaintiffs to establish economic harm in order to obtain a meaningful remedy? Should the law focus instead on other kinds of harms? If so, what kinds of harms should courts and legislatures take into account? Even if courts are only prepared to award nominal damages for privacy harms, might this serve an important communicative function about the need to protect privacy online?

6. Could plaintiffs argue that DoubleClick trespassed on their computers? See Chapter 6, *infra*.

7. Should data collectors bear some responsibility for the misuse of the information they collect? *Consider* Remsburg v. Docusearch, Inc., 816 A.2d 1001 (N.H. 2003), in which the New Hampshire Supreme Court ruled that information brokers and private investigators may be liable for foreseeable harms that result from the sale of personal information.

b) Statutory Protection

In response to growing public concern over private information gathering in cyberspace, governments throughout the world have enacted various statutory protections for privacy.[23] With the exception of the Children's Online

---

23. *See* Joel R. Reidenberg, *Resolving Conflicting International Data Privacy Rules in Cyberspace,* 52 Stan. L. Rev. 1315 (2000) (summarizing international data privacy principles).

Privacy Protection Act of 1998, 15 U.S.C. §§6501 et seq., which prohibits the collection and disclosure of personal information from children in the absence of express verifiable parental consent, 15 U.S.C. §6502(b), to date, the United States largely relies upon unfair and deceptive business practice law and self-regulation. In contrast, other nations, and most notably, the European Union, have taken more aggressive steps to protect individual privacy in data collection.

DIRECTIVE ON DATA PROTECTION

Directive 95/46/EC of the European Parliament and
of the Council of 24 October 1995

ARTICLE 6

Member States shall provide that personal data must be:

(a) processed fairly and lawfully;

(b) collected for specified, explicit and legitimate purposes and not further processed in a way incompatible with those purposes. Further processing of data for historical, statistical or scientific purposes shall not be considered as incompatible provided that Member States provide appropriate safeguards;

(c) adequate, relevant and not excessive in relation to the purposes for which they are collected and/or further processed;

(d) accurate and, where necessary, kept up to date; every reasonable step must be taken to ensure that data which are inaccurate or incomplete, having regard to the purposes for which they were collected or for which they are further processed, are erased or rectified;

(e) kept in a form which permits identification of data subjects for no longer than is necessary for the purposes for which the data were collected or for which they are further processed. Member States shall lay down appropriate safeguards for personal data stored for longer periods for historical, statistical or scientific use. . . .

ARTICLE 7

Member States shall provide that personal data may be processed only if:

(a) the data subject has unambiguously given his consent; or

(b) processing is necessary for the performance of a contract to which the data subject is party or in order to take steps at the request of the data subject prior to entering into a contract; or

(c)   processing is necessary for compliance with a legal obligation to which the controller is subject; or

(d)   processing is necessary in order to protect the vital interests of the data subject; or

(e)   processing is necessary for the performance of a task carried out in the public interest or in the exercise of official authority vested in the controller or in a third party to whom the data are disclosed; or

(f)   processing is necessary for the purposes of the legitimate interests pursued by the controller or by the third party or parties to whom the data are disclosed, except where such interests are overridden by the interests for fundamental rights and freedoms of the data subject which require protection under Article 1(1).

ARTICLE 8 — THE PROCESSING OF SPECIAL CATEGORIES OF DATA

Member States shall prohibit the processing of personal data revealing racial or ethnic origin, political opinions, religious or philosophical beliefs, trade-union membership, and the processing of data concerning health or sex life.

Paragraph 1 shall not apply where:

(a)   the data subject has given his explicit consent to the processing of those data, except where the laws of the Member State provide that the prohibition referred to in paragraph 1 may not be lifted by the data subject's giving his consent; or

(b)   processing is necessary for the purposes of carrying out the obligations and specific rights of the controller in the field of employment law in so far as it is authorized by national law providing for adequate safeguards; or

(c)   processing is necessary to protect the vital interests of the data subject or of another person where the data subject is physically or legally incapable of giving his consent; or

(d)   processing is carried out in the course of its legitimate activities with appropriate guarantees by a foundation, association or any other non-profit-seeking body with a political, philosophical, religious or trade-union aim and on condition that the processing relates solely to the members of the body or to persons who have regular contact with it in connection with its purposes and that the data are not disclosed to a third party without the consent of the data subjects; or

(e)   the processing relates to data which are manifestly made public by the data subject or is necessary for the establishment, exercise or defense of legal claims. . . .

Processing of data relating to offences, criminal convictions or security measures may be carried out only under the control of official authority, or if suitable specific safeguards are provided under national law, subject to derogations which may be granted by the Member State under national provisions providing suitable specific safeguards. However, a complete register of criminal convictions may be kept only under the control of official authority.

Member States may provide that data relating to administrative sanctions or judgments in civil cases shall also be processed under the control of official authority. Derogations from paragraph 1 provided for in paragraphs 4 and 5 shall be notified to the Commission.

Member States shall determine the conditions under which a national identification number or any other identifier of general application may be processed. . . .

ARTICLE 10 — INFORMATION IN CASES OF COLLECTION OF DATA FROM THE DATA SUBJECT

Member States shall provide that the controller or his representative must provide a data subject from whom data relating to himself are collected with at least the following information, except where he already has it:

(a) the identity of the controller and of his representative, if any;
(b) the purposes of the processing for which the data are intended;
(c) any further information such as the recipients or categories of recipients of the data, whether replies to the questions are obligatory or voluntary, as well as the possible consequences of failure to reply, the existence of the right of access to and the right to rectify the data concerning him in so far as such further information is necessary, having regard to the specific circumstances in which the data are collected, to guarantee fair processing in respect of the data subject. . . .

ARTICLE 11 — INFORMATION WHERE THE DATA HAVE NOT BEEN OBTAINED FROM THE DATA SUBJECT

1. Where the data have not been obtained from the data subject, Member States shall provide that the controller or his representative must at the time of undertaking the recording of personal data or if a disclosure to a third party is envisaged, no later than the time when the data are first disclosed provide the data subject with at least the following information, except where he already has it:

(a) the identity of the controller and of his representative, if any;
(b) the purposes of the processing;

(c) any further information such as
  • the categories of data concerned,
  • the recipients or categories of recipients,
  • the existence of the right of access to and the right to rectify the data concerning him
  in so far as such further information is necessary, having regard to the specific circumstances in which the data are processed, to guarantee fair processing in respect of the data subject.

2. Paragraph 1 shall not apply where, in particular for processing for statistical purposes or for the purposes of historical or scientific research, the provision of such information proves impossible or would involve a disproportionate effort or if recording or disclosure is expressly laid down by law. In these cases Member States shall provide appropriate safeguards.

ARTICLE 12 — RIGHT OF ACCESS

Member States shall guarantee every data right to obtain from the controller:

(a) without constraint at reasonable intervals and without excessive delay or expense: confirmation as to whether or not data relating to him are being processed and information at least as to the purposes of the processing, the categories of data concerned, and the recipients or categories of recipients to whom the data are disclosed, communication to him in an intelligible form of the data undergoing processing and of any available information as to their source, knowledge of the logic involved in any automatic processing of data concerning him at least in the case of the automated decisions referred to in Article 15(1);
(b) as appropriate the rectification, erasure or blocking of data the processing of which does not comply with the provisions of this Directive, in particular because of the incomplete or inaccurate nature of the data;
(c) notification to third parties to whom the data have been disclosed of any rectification, erasure or blocking carried out in compliance with (b), unless this proves impossible or involves a disproportionate effort. . . .

ARTICLE 14 — THE DATA SUBJECT'S RIGHT TO OBJECT

Member States shall grant the data subject the right:

(a) at least in the cases referred to in Article 7(e) and (f), to object at any time on compelling legitimate grounds relating to his particular situation to the processing of data relating to him, save where otherwise provided by national legislation. Where there is a justified objection, the processing instigated by the controller may no longer involve those data;

(b) to object, on request and free of charge, to the processing of personal data relating to him which the controller anticipates being processed for the purposes of direct marketing, or to be informed before personal data are disclosed for the first time to third parties or used on their behalf for the purposes of direct marketing, and to be expressly offered the right to object free of charge to such disclosures or uses.

Member States shall take the necessary measures to ensure that data subjects are aware of the existence of the right referred to in the first subparagraph of (b).

Article 15 — Automated Individual Decisions

Member States shall grant the right to every person not to be subject to a decision which produces legal effects concerning him or significantly affects him and which is based solely on automated processing of data intended to evaluate certain personal aspects relating to him, such as his performance at work, creditworthiness, reliability, conduct, etc. . . .

Article 25 — Principles

The Member States shall provide that the transfer to a third country of personal data which are undergoing processing or are intended for processing after transfer may take place only if, without prejudice to compliance with the national provisions adopted pursuant to the other provisions of this Directive, the third country in question ensures an adequate level of protection.

The adequacy of the level of protection afforded by a third country shall be assessed in the light of all the circumstances surrounding a data transfer operation or set of data transfer operations; particular consideration shall be given to the nature of the data, the purpose and duration of the proposed processing operation or operations, the country of origin and country of final destination, the rules of law, both general and sectoral, in force in the third country in question and the professional rules and security measures which are complied with in that country. . . .

Article 26 — Derogations

By way of derogation from Article 25 and save where otherwise provided by domestic law governing particular cases, Member States shall provide that a transfer or a set of transfers of personal data to a third country which does not ensure an adequate level of protection within the meaning of Article 25 (2) may take place on condition that:

(a) the data subject has given his consent unambiguously to the proposed transfer; or

(b) the transfer is necessary for the performance of a contract between the data subject and the controller or the implementation of precontractual measures taken in response to the data subject's request; or

(c) the transfer is necessary for the conclusion or performance of a contract concluded in the interest of the data subject between the controller and a third party; or

(d) the transfer is necessary or legally required on important public interest grounds, or for the establishment, exercise or defence of legal claims; or

(e) the transfer is necessary in order to protect the vital interests of the data subject; or

(f) the transfer is made from a register which according to laws or regulations is intended to provide information to the public and which is open to consultation either by the public in general or by any person who can demonstrate legitimate interest, to the extent that the conditions laid down in law for consultation are fulfilled in the particular case.

Without prejudice to paragraph 1, a Member State may authorize a transfer or a set of transfers of personal data to a third country which does not ensure an adequate level of protection within the meaning of Article 25(2), where the controller adduces adequate safeguards with respect to the protection of the privacy and fundamental rights and freedoms of individuals and as regards the exercise of the corresponding rights; such safeguards may in particular result from appropriate contractual clauses. . . .

COMMENTS AND QUESTIONS

1. As discussed above, the United States Federal Trade Commission requires Web sites to provide users with notice and choice. How does the EU Directive differ? What additional rights in personal information does the EU Directive recognize? What are the costs of adopting the EU Directive instead of the FTC's position?

2. How does the EU Directive limit the use of personal information?

3. How does the EU Directive deal with the transfer of information to third parties?

4. Does the EU Directive permit companies to collect personal information through an opt-out policy?

5. Why does the EU Directive "prohibit the processing of personal data revealing racial or ethnic origin, political opinions, religious or philosophical beliefs, trade-union membership, and the processing of data concerning health or sex life"? Does this protect an individual's privacy?

6. How does the EU Directive deal with the global nature of the Internet?

7. In response to the EU Directive and its provisions limiting the transfer of information to countries that do not adhere to the EU Directive, the United States has negotiated various safe harbor principles. According to the Department of Commerce:

Notice: An organization must inform individuals about the purposes for which it collects and uses information about them, how to contact the organization with any inquiries or complaints, the types of third parties to which it discloses the information, and the choices and means the organization offers individuals for limiting its use and disclosure. This notice must be provided in clear and conspicuous language when individuals are first asked to provide personal information to the organization or as soon thereafter as is practicable, but in any event before the organization uses such information for a purpose other than that for which it was originally collected or processed by the transferring organization or discloses it for the first time to a third party.[1]

Choice: An organization must offer individuals the opportunity to choose (opt out) whether their personal information is (a) to be disclosed to a third party[1] or (b) to be used for a purpose that is incompatible with the purpose(s) for which it was originally collected or subsequently authorized by the individual. Individuals must be provided with clear and conspicuous, readily available, and affordable mechanisms to exercise choice.

For sensitive information (i.e. personal information specifying medical or health conditions, racial or ethnic origin, political opinions, religious or philosophical beliefs, trade union membership or information specifying the sex life of the individual), they must be given affirmative or explicit (opt in) choice if the information is to be disclosed to a third party or used for a purpose other than those for which it was originally collected or subsequently authorized by the individual through the exercise of opt in choice. In any case, an organization should treat as sensitive any information received from a third party where the third party treats and identifies it as sensitive.

Onward Transfer: To disclose information to a third party, organizations must apply the Notice and Choice Principles. Where an organization wishes to transfer information to a third party that is acting as an agent, as described in the endnote, it may do so if it first either ascertains that the third party subscribes to the Principles or is subject to the Directive or another adequacy finding or enters into a written agreement with such third party requiring that the third party provide at least the same level of privacy protection as is required by the relevant Principles. If the organization complies with these requirements, it shall not be held responsible (unless the organization agrees otherwise) when a third party to which it transfers such information processes it in a way contrary to any restrictions or representations, unless the organization knew or should have known the third party would process it in such a contrary way and the organization has not taken reasonable steps to prevent or stop such processing.

---

1. It is not necessary to provide notice or choice when disclosure is made to a third party that is acting as an agent to perform task(s) on behalf of and under the instructions of the organization. The Onward Transfer Principle, on the other hand, does apply to such disclosures.

Security: Organizations creating, maintaining, using or disseminating personal information must take reasonable precautions to protect it from loss, misuse and unauthorized access, disclosure, alteration and destruction.

Data Integrity: Consistent with the Principles, personal information must be relevant for the purposes for which it is to be used. An organization may not process personal information in a way that is incompatible with the purposes for which it has been collected or subsequently authorized by the individual. To the extent necessary for those purposes, an organization should take reasonable steps to ensure that data is reliable for its intended use, accurate, complete, and current.

Access: Individuals must have access to personal information about them that an organization holds and be able to correct, amend, or delete that information where it is inaccurate, except where the burden or expense of providing access would be disproportionate to the risks to the individual's privacy in the case in question, or where the rights of persons other than the individual would be violated.

Enforcement: Effective privacy protection must include mechanisms for assuring compliance with the Principles, recourse for individuals to whom the data relate affected by non-compliance with the Principles, and consequences for the organization when the Principles are not followed. At a minimum, such mechanisms must include (a) readily available and affordable independent recourse mechanisms by which each individual's complaints and disputes are investigated and resolved by reference to the Principles and damages awarded where the applicable law or private sector initiatives so provide; (b) follow up procedures for verifying that the attestations and assertions businesses make about their privacy practices are true and that privacy practices have been implemented as presented; and (c) obligations to remedy problems arising out of failure to comply with the Principles by organizations announcing their adherence to them and consequences for such organizations. Sanctions must be sufficiently rigorous to ensure compliance by organizations.

U.S. Dep't of Commerce, Safe Harbor Privacy Principles (July 21, 2000). For information about the operation of the Safe Harbor, see *http://www.export.gov/safeharbor/eg_main_018236.asp.* Do the safe harbor provisions differ from the requirements set forth in the EU Directive? How different are they from the FTC's position in the United States? For an argument that the safe harbor provisions are *ultra vires, consider* Joel R. Reidenberg, *E-Commerce and Trans-Atlantic Privacy,* 38 Hous. L. Rev. 717 (2001) (arguing that an international treaty may be the only long-term solution).

8. Another approach to informational privacy is offered by the Canadian Personal Information Protection Act, 48-49 Elizabeth II, Chapter 5 (2000), which provides that, "An organization may collect, use or disclose personal information only for purposes that a reasonable person would consider are appropriate in the circumstances." Moreover, the Act requires organizations to obtain the consent of the individual in order to collect, use, or disclose information about an identifiable individual unless such collection, use, or disclosure falls under a specifically enumerated exception. Exceptions include such circumstances as protecting national security, investigation of a crime, protection of an individual's health and safety, or a news gathering. Available

at *http://www.parl.gc.ca/36/2/parlbus/chambus/house/bills/government/C-6/C-6_4/ C-6_cover-E.html*. How does the Canadian approach differ from the approaches taken by the United States and Europe?

3. Personal Privacy

As noted in Chapter 1, since the first edition of this book was published, we have moved into an age of technological development often described as "Web 2.0." This refers to increasingly community-based and participatory technologies. More people today actively participate online in more contexts than ever before. Web 2.0 technologies include social networking Web sites, blogs, virtual worlds, and wikis. As more people participate in these new contexts, is there a greater danger of privacy harm?

a) Collection and Dissemination of Personal Information

As we saw in Chapter 4 with respect to digital copyright issues, the Internet and other digital technology provides an unparalleled method for distributing content cheaply, quickly, and globally at the push of a button. The issue for copyright holders has been finding ways to protect their proprietary interests in the face of this unbridled online dissemination of the works. Similar issues arise with respect to online privacy. While advanced technology certainly makes the initial gathering of information easier, as we saw earlier in this chapter, many individuals are now more concerned with the viral online *dissemination* of personal information than with its initial collection.

Think back to the *Dwyer* case, *supra*. Many American Express customers probably didn't mind American Express having some of their personal information about purchasing preferences. Rather, they objected to American Express using that information in ways they didn't expect it to be used. This problem comes into sharp focus when we think about the possible global dissemination of snippets of private information that may be gathered in everyday situations, involving personal social interactions. To underline the increasingly global importance of the distinction between collection and dissemination of this kind of information, consider the following extract from a decision of the British House of Lords in 2004.

CAMPBELL v. MGN LIMITED

[2004] UKHL 22 The Lord Nicholls of Birkenhead

My Lords,

1.   Naomi Campbell is a celebrated fashion model. Hers is a household name, nationally and internationally. Her face is instantly recognisable. Whatever she does and wherever she goes is news.

2. On 1 February 2001 the 'Mirror' newspaper carried as its first story on its front page a prominent article headed 'Naomi: I am a drug addict.' The article was supported on one side by a picture of Miss Campbell as a glamorous model, on the other side by a slightly indistinct picture of a smiling, relaxed Miss Campbell, dressed in baseball cap and jeans, over the caption 'Therapy: Naomi outside meeting.' The article read:

> 'Supermodel Naomi Campbell is attending Narcotics Anonymous meetings in a courageous bid to beat her addiction to drink and drugs.
>
> The 30-year old has been a regular at counselling sessions for three months, often attending twice a day.
>
> Dressed in jeans and baseball cap, she arrived at one of NA's lunchtime meetings this week. Hours later at a different venue she made a low-key entrance to a women-only gathering of recovered addicts.
>
> Despite her £14million fortune Naomi is treated as just another addict trying to put her life back together. A source close to her said last night: "She wants to clean up her life for good.
>
> "She went into modelling when she was very young and it is easy to be led astray. Drink and drugs are unfortunately widely available in the fashion world.
>
> "But Naomi has realised she has a problem and has bravely vowed to do something about it. Everyone wishes her well."
>
> Her spokeswoman at Elite Models declined to comment.'

3. The story continued inside, with a longer article spread across two pages. The inside article was headed 'Naomi's finally trying to beat the demons that have been haunting her.' [The judgment continues with a more detailed description of the article.]

4. The article made mention of Miss Campbell's efforts to rehabilitate herself, and that one of her friends said she was still fragile but 'getting healthy.' The article gave a general description of Narcotics Anonymous therapy, and referred to some of Miss Campbell's recent publicised activities. These included an occasion when Miss Campbell was rushed to hospital and had her stomach pumped. She claimed it was an allergic reaction to antibiotics and that she had never had a drug problem: but 'those closest to her knew the truth.'

5. In the middle of the double page spread, between several innocuous pictures of Miss Campbell, was a dominating picture over the caption 'Hugs: Naomi, dressed in jeans and baseball hat, arrives for a lunchtime group meeting this week.' The picture showed her in the street on the doorstep of a building as the central figure in a small group. She was being embraced by two people whose faces had been pixelated. Standing on the pavement was a board advertising a named café. The article did not name the venue of the meeting, but anyone who knew the district well would be able to identify the place shown in the photograph.

6. The general tone of the articles was sympathetic and supportive with, perhaps, the barest undertone of smugness that Miss Campbell had been caught out by the 'Mirror.' The source of the newspaper's information was either an associate of Miss Campbell or a fellow addict attending meetings of

Narcotics Anonymous. The photographs of her attending a meeting were taken by a free lance photographer specifically employed by the newspaper to do the job. He took the photographs covertly, while concealed some distance away inside a parked car. . . .

The Proceedings and the Further Articles

8. On the same day as the articles were published Miss Campbell commenced proceedings against MGN Ltd, the publisher of the 'Mirror.' The newspaper's response was to publish further articles, this time highly critical of Miss Campbell. On 5 February 2001 the newspaper published an article headed, in large letters, 'Pathetic.' Below was a photograph of Miss Campbell over the caption 'Help: Naomi leaves Narcotics Anonymous meeting last week after receiving therapy in her battle against illegal drugs.' This photograph was similar to the street scene picture published on 1 February. The text of the article was headed 'After years of self-publicity and illegal drug abuse, Naomi Campbell whinges about privacy.' The article mentioned that 'the Mirror revealed last week how she is attending daily meetings of Narcotics Anonymous.' Elsewhere in the same edition an editorial article, with the heading 'No hiding Naomi,' concluded with the words: 'If Naomi Campbell wants to live like a nun, let her join a nunnery. If she wants the excitement of a show business life, she must accept what comes with it.'

[The judgment continues with descriptions of additional articles published by the defendant about the plaintiff.]

10. In the proceedings Miss Campbell claimed damages for breach of confidence and compensation under the Data Protection Act 1998. The article of 7 February formed the main basis of a claim for aggravated damages. Morland J [2002] EWHC 499 (QB) upheld Miss Campbell's claim. He made her a modest award of £2,500 plus £1,000 aggravated damages in respect of both claims. The newspaper appealed. The Court of Appeal, comprising Lord Phillips of Worth Matravers MR, Chadwick and Keene LJJ, allowed the appeal and discharged the judge's order: [2002] EWCA Civ 1373, [2003] QB 633. Miss Campbell has now appealed to your Lordships' House.

Breach of Confidence: Misuse of Private Information

11. In this country, unlike the United States of America, there is no over-arching, all-embracing cause of action for 'invasion of privacy': see *Wainwright v. Home Office* [2003] 3 WLR 1137. But protection of various aspects of privacy is a fast developing area of the law, here and in some other common law jurisdictions. The recent decision of the Court of Appeal of New Zealand in *Hosking v. Runting* (25 March 2004) is an example of this. In this country development of the law has been spurred by enactment of the Human Rights Act 1998.

12.   The present case concerns one aspect of invasion of privacy: wrongful disclosure of private information. The case involves the familiar competition between freedom of expression and respect for an individual's privacy. Both are vitally important rights. Neither has precedence over the other. The importance of freedom of expression has been stressed often and eloquently, the importance of privacy less so. But it, too, lies at the heart of liberty in a modern state. A proper degree of privacy is essential for the well-being and development of an individual. And restraints imposed on government to pry into the lives of the citizen go to the essence of a democratic state: see La Forest J in *R v. Dymont* [1988] 2 SCR 417, 426. . . .

LORD HOFFMAN

   . . .

122.   The photographs were taken of Miss Campbell while she was in a public place, as she was in the street outside the premises where she had been receiving therapy. The taking of photographs in a public street must, as Randerson J said in *Hosking v. Runting* [2003] 3 NZLR 385, 415, para 138, be taken to be one of the ordinary incidents of living in a free community. The real issue is whether publicising the content of the photographs would be offensive: Gault and Blanchard JJ in the Court of Appeal (25 March 2004), para 165. A person who just happens to be in the street when the photograph was taken and appears in it only incidentally cannot as a general rule object to the publication of the photograph, for the reasons given by L'Heureux-Dubé and Bastarache JJ in *Aubry v. Éditions Vice-Versa Inc* [1998] 1 SCR 591, para 59. But the situation is different if the public nature of the place where a photograph is taken was simply used as background for one or more persons who constitute the true subject of the photograph. The question then arises, balancing the rights at issue, where the public's right to information can justify dissemination of a photograph taken without authorisation: *Aubry*, para 61. The European Court has recognised that a person who walks down a public street will inevitably be visible to any member of the public who is also present and, in the same way, to a security guard viewing the scene through closed circuit television: *PG v JH v. United Kingdom*, App No. 44787/98, para 57. But, as the court pointed out in the same paragraph, private life considerations may arise once any systematic or permanent record comes into existence of such material from the public domain. In *Peck v. United Kingdom* [2003] 36 EHRR 719, para 62 the court held that the release and publication of CCTV forage which showed the applicant in the process of attempting to commit suicide resulted in the moment being viewed to an extent that far exceeded any exposure to a passer-by or to security observation that he could have foreseen when he was in that street. . . .

   [A majority of the Lords found in favor of the plaintiff that some of the information published by the defendant infringed her confidentiality interests under British law. The parties had conceded that the defendant was entitled to publish some information about the plaintiff's drug addiction in the public interest to counter her public claims that she did not have a drug problem. However, the House of Lords found that more information was published than was necessary towards this end.]

COMMENTS AND QUESTIONS

1. Lord Hoffman acknowledges that the dissemination of private information, even if gathered lawfully, could have extremely detrimental consequences to an individual — in this case, it could interfere with the plaintiff's efforts at rehabilitation from a drug addiction. Do you think Lord Hoffman's concerns are overstated? Do you think a distinction should be drawn between celebrities/public figures and private individuals with respect to the public dissemination of private facts?

2. These issues have taken on great significance in the context of recent Internet technologies. Google's Street View service, which is part of Google Maps, is a case in point. Google Street View involves Google using vehicles to take 360 degree videos of public places so they can map real life video images on to their Google Maps service. Street View has caused a public outcry in a number of countries, including Germany and Japan, because of concerns about intrusions into individual's private spaces. *See* Janet Lowe, *Google Speaks* 193-97 (2009). While individuals are no doubt concerned that Google's cameras potentially intrude into their living rooms or capture candid images of them walking in public streets, it seems more likely that the greatest concerns are about the widespread dissemination of the images over the Internet when they are uploaded to Google Maps. Google has so far successfully argued that it is not doing anything illegal because it is only taking pictures in public areas. It has also been prepared to blur license plate numbers and individuals' faces, and to remove pictures of individuals on request. Lowe, at 194. Does this policy support the argument that it is really mass dissemination of personal information that people are worried about, rather than initial information collection?

3. Lord Nicholls draws attention to concerns that resonate in both the United Kingdom and the United States about the need to find an appropriate balance between free speech and privacy. If more controls are put in place against unauthorized dissemination of private information, how much damage might this do to our concept of free speech under the First Amendment? Does it matter that much disclosure of private information online involves innocuous personal details, rather than particularly sensitive information collected and used by, say, government agencies? Consider the examples described in the following extract.

JACQUELINE LIPTON
"WE, THE PAPARAZZI": DEVELOPING A PRIVACY
PARADIGM FOR DIGITAL VIDEO

95 Iowa L. Rev. ____ (2010)

Are we all paparazzi now? Consider the story of "dog poop girl": Once upon a time, a passenger's dog defecated on the floor of a subway car in South Korea. While unremarkable in itself, this story quickly became an Internet sensation when the passenger refused to clean the mess. Someone on the train, an anonymous face in the crowd, took photos of the woman with a cellphone camera. These images were promptly posted on a popular Korean blog. The aim was to shame the unrepentant and socially irresponsible dog owner. Ultimately, the humiliation attached to this incident resulted in a firestorm of criticism that caused her to quit her job. This story is one of a number of recent episodes illustrating how a person's privacy can be destroyed at the push of a button, using the simplest and most ubiquitous combination of digital technologies — the cellphone camera and the Internet. While some may say that dog poop girl received her just desserts for being a socially irresponsible dog owner, others may well feel that the punishment far outweighed the crime.

Then there's the story of "Star Wars kid" — a Canadian teenager who filmed himself playing with a golf ball retriever as if it was a light-saber from the *Star Wars* movies. Embarrassing? Yes. Socially irresponsible? No. His video was posted to the Internet without his authorization. It was then adopted by a variety of amateur video enthusiasts on services such as YouTube. They created many popular, but extremely humiliating, mash-up videos of the youth. The young man ended up dropping out of school. He also required psychiatric care, including a period of institutionalization at a children's psychiatric facility. Even more worrying perhaps was the fate of "Bus Uncle" in Hong Kong. This man was physically assaulted in a targeted attack at the restaurant where he worked. The attack ensued after online posting of a video depicting him speaking loudly on his cellphone on a bus and ignoring requests of other passengers to be quiet.

We are witnessing the emergence of a worrying new trend: peers intruding into each other's privacy and anonymity with video and multi-media files in ways that harm the subjects of the digital files. There is a mismatch between these harms and available legal remedies, notably those arising out of privacy and defamation law. Even new laws such as the proposed Camera Phone Predator Alert bill would only notify a person that a picture of her may have been taken. It would do nothing to stem the tide of global online dissemination of a damaging image of a person. While it is now trite to say that the Internet poses significant risks to privacy, these risks have previously manifested themselves in the collection, use, and dissemination of text-based personal records by governments, businesses, health care providers, Internet intermediaries, and prospective employers. Today, we need to add concerns about unauthorized uses of our personal information by our peers over networks such as MySpace, Facebook, Flickr, and YouTube, much of it in video formats. An image of an individual in an embarrassing situation might well affect her chances of employment, education, or health insurance. As in the examples of Star Wars kid, dog poop girl, and Bus Uncle, the consequences of such unauthorized dissemination can be devastating.

COMMENTS AND QUESTIONS

1.   Professor Lipton draws a distinction between traditional data privacy concerns, such as those addressed earlier in this chapter, and privacy issues in the online social networking context. These latter concerns relate to unbridled dissemination of large amounts of seemingly innocuous personal information. Do you think the distinction drawn by Professor Lipton is useful or meaningful in considering privacy regulation in cyberspace?

2.   Should users of online services like Facebook and YouTube be expected to take full responsibility for all misuses or unauthorized uses of their own personal information? Is it reasonable to expect individuals to take responsibility for private information posted about them online by third parties, like friends and acquaintances? Who else might be asked to take responsibility? Online social network service providers?

3.   Another salient problem with privacy in the social networking context is that many of our current legal conceptions of privacy are linked with notions of physical space. Think back to the discussion of the *Olmstead*, *Katz*, and *Kyllo* cases at the beginning of this chapter. Many social contacts now occur completely online, and thus the link back to physical world concepts of privacy becomes increasingly difficult to apply. As Professor Patricia Sánchez Abril has noted:

> "Traditionally, privacy has been inextricably linked to physical space. In turn, space often defines our notions of personhood and identity. Consider, for example, the social stature ascribed to sitting in a corner office. Spatial concepts are interrelated with cultural norms prescribed social organization and human behavior, interaction, and expectations. The classic conceptions of privacy rely on spatial experiences, such as a room of one's own or a secluded hermitage."

Recasting Privacy Torts in a Spaceless World, 21 Harv. J.L. & Tech. 1, 3 (2007). Professor Sánchez Abril proceeds to describe ways in which the tort of public disclosure of private facts might be reworked to lessen the reliance on physical space metaphors. Do you think this is the right approach to privacy online? In what ways does this approach underline concerns raised by Professor Dan Hunter in Chapter 2 about the way in which over-reliance on inappropriate metaphors can skew legal developments in undesirable ways?

4.   What other problems may be faced by a plaintiff seeking to redress a privacy harm online? Professor Daniel Solove has raised concerns that private

individuals will often find litigation "expensive, imposing, and stressful" in the privacy context. Daniel J. Solove, *The Future of Reputation*, 120 (2007). Moreover, lawsuits can have a chilling effect on speech. Conversely, and perhaps somewhat paradoxically, the necessity to disclose all of the evidence of the privacy incursion in the public court record forces the plaintiff to relive all the shame and embarrassment of the original publication and may therefore deter many potential plaintiffs from seeking relief. In a recent decision on privacy in the United Kingdom that involved a wealthy public figure, the British High Court noted that: "[O]nce privacy has been infringed, the damage is done and the embarrassment is only augmented by pursuing a court action. Claimants with the degree of resolve (and financial resources) of Mr. Max Mosley are likely to be few and far between." (*Max Mosley v. News Group Newspapers Limited*, [2008] EWHC 1777 (QB), at para. 230).

b) Privacy in Multimedia Files

One thing that the current age of digital development has brought with it is an increased capacity for the uploading and sharing of large digital file formats including audio, video, and multimedia files. Much of the early digital privacy law and scholarship focused on text-based data aggregation. Think back to the *Dwyer* and *DoubleClick* cases discussed earlier in this chapter. However, audio, video, and multimedia files are qualitatively different from aggregated text records both in terms of the information they contain and in the ways they might be used online. For example, it is much easier to search text-based records than audio or visual records, at least with the current state of technology. However, richer file formats, once located, can be extremely damaging to an individual's privacy, particularly if taken out of context. Consider the following discussion from the British High Court drawing a distinction between text and video file formats with respect to privacy interests.

MAX MOSLEY v. NEWS GROUPS NEWSPAPERS LIMITED

[1008] EWHC 1777 (QB)

Mr. Justice EADY:

THE NATURE OF THE CLAIM

1. The claimant in this litigation is Mr. Max Mosley, who has been President of the Fédération Internationale de l'Automobile ("FIA") since 1993 and is a trustee of its charitable arm, the FIA Foundation. He sues News Group Newspapers Ltd as publishers of the *News of the World*, complaining of an article by Neville Thurlbeck in the issue for 30 March 2008 under the heading "F1 BOSS HAS SICK NAZI ORGY WITH 5 HOOKERS." It was claimed as an "EXCLUSIVE" and was accompanied by the subheading

"Son of Hitler-loving fascist in sex shame." It concerned an event which took place on 28 March, described variously as a "party" (by the Claimant and his witnesses) and "an orgy" (by the Defendant). He also complains of accompanying images published alongside the article.

2. He sues additionally over the same information and images on the newspaper's website, which also contained video footage relating to the same event. Reference is also made to a "follow up article" contained in the issue of 6 April headed "EXCLUSIVE: MOSLEY HOOKER TELLS ALL: MY NAZI ORGY WITH F1 BOSS." This consisted primarily of a purported interview with one of the women who had been present at the event in question and had filmed what took place clandestinely with a camera concealed in her clothing, which had been supplied by the *News of the World*. It is relied upon primarily in the context of aggravation of damages and in support of a claim for exemplary damages.

3. The cause of action is breach of confidence and/or the unauthorised disclosure of personal information, said to infringe the Claimant's rights of privacy as protected by Article 8 of the European Convention on Human Rights and Fundamental Freedoms ("the Convention"). There is no claim in defamation and I am thus not directly concerned with any injury to reputation. . . .

THE "NEW METHODOLOGY"

7. Although the law of "old-fashioned breach of confidence" has been well established for many years, and derives historically from equitable principles, these have been extended in recent years under the stimulus of the Human Rights Act 1998 and the content of the Convention itself. The law now affords protection to information in respect of which there is a reasonable expectation of privacy, even in circumstances where there is no pre-existing relationship giving rise of itself to an enforceable duty of confidence. That is because the law is concerned to prevent the violation of a citizen's autonomy, dignity and self-esteem. It is not simply a matter of "unaccountable" judges running amok. Parliament enacted the 1998 statute which *requires* these values to be acknowledged and enforced by the courts. In any event, the courts had been increasingly taking them into account because of the need to interpret domestic law consistently with the United Kingdom's international obligations. It will be recalled that the United Kingdom government signed up to the Convention more than 50 years ago.

8. The relevant values are expressed in Articles 8 and 10 of the Convention, which are in these terms:

"Article 8
1. Everyone has the right to respect for his private and family life, his home and his correspondence.

2. There shall be no interference by a public authority with the exercise of this right except such as is in accordance with the law and is necessary in a democratic society in the interests of national security, public safety or the economic well-being of the country, for the prevention of disorder or crime, for the protection of health or morals, or for the protection of the rights and freedoms of others.

Article 10
1. Everyone has the right to freedom of expression. This right shall include freedom to hold opinions and to receive and impart information and ideas without interference by public authority and regardless of frontiers. This article shall not prevent States from requiring the licensing of broadcasting, television or cinema enterprises.
2. The exercise of these freedoms, since it carries with it duties and responsibilities, may be subject to such formalities, conditions, restrictions or penalties as are prescribed by law, and are necessary in a democratic society, in the interests of national security, territorial integrity or public safety, for the protection of health or morals, for the protection of the reputation or rights of others, for preventing the disclosure of information received in confidence, or for maintaining the authority and impartiality of the judiciary."

9. It was recognised in *Campbell v. MGN Ltd* [2004] 2 AC 457 that these values are as much applicable in disputes between individuals, or between an individual and a non-governmental body such as a newspaper, as they are in disputes between individuals and a public authority: see e.g. Lord Nicholls at [17]-[18] and Lord Hoffmann at [50]. Indeed, ". . . in order to find the rules of the English law of breach of confidence we now have to look in the jurisprudence of articles 8 and 10": *per* Buxton LJ in *McKennitt v. Ash* [2008] QB 73 at [11]. . . .

THE SIGNIFICANCE OF VISUAL IMAGES

16. . . . Sometimes there may be a good case for revealing the fact of wrongdoing to the general public; it will not necessarily follow that photographs of "every gory detail" also need to be published to achieve the public interest objective. Nor will it automatically justify clandestine recording, whether visual or audio. So much is acknowledged in the relevant section of the Press Complaints Commission ("PCC") Editors' Code at Clause 10:

"i) The press must not seek to obtain or publish material acquired by using hidden cameras or clandestine listening devices; or by intercepting private or mobile telephone calls, messages or emails; or by the unauthorised removal of documents or photographs or by accessing digitally-held private information without consent.

ii) Engaging in misrepresentation or subterfuge, including by agents or intermediaries, can generally be justified only in the public interest and then only when the material cannot be obtained by other means."

17. Naturally, the very fact of clandestine recording may be regarded as an intrusion and an unacceptable infringement of Article 8 rights. That is one issue. Once such recording has taken place, however, a separate issue may need to be considered as to the appropriateness of onward publication, either on a limited basis or more generally to the world at large. In this case, the pleaded claim is confined to publication of the information; it does not include the intrusive method by which it was acquired. Yet obviously the nature and scale of the distress caused is in large measure due to the clandestine filming and the pictures acquired as a result.

18. The intrusive nature of photography has been fully discussed in the European Court of Human Rights in *Von Hannover v. Germany* (2004) 40 EHRR 1 and also in domestic jurisprudence. The point was articulated by Waller LJ in *D v. L* [2004] EMLR 1 at [23]:

"A court may restrain the publication of an improperly obtained photograph even if the taker is free to describe the information which the photographer provides or even if the information revealed by the photograph is in the public domain. It is no answer to the claim to restrain the publication of an improperly obtained photograph that the information portrayed by the photograph is already available in the public domain."

19. Later, in *Douglas v. Hello! Ltd (No 3)* [2006] QB 125 at [84] the Court of Appeal explored the underlying reasons in terms which resonate in the factual circumstances now before the court:

"This action is about photographs. Special considerations attach to photographs in the field of privacy. They are not merely a method of conveying information that is an alternative to verbal description. They enable the person viewing the photograph to act as a spectator, in some circumstances voyeur would be the more appropriate noun, of whatever it is that the photograph depicts. As a means of invading privacy, a photograph is particularly intrusive. This is quite apart from the fact that the camera, and the telephoto lens, can give access to the viewer of the photograph to scenes where those photographed could reasonably expect that their appearances or actions would not be brought to the notice of the public."

20. It was acknowledged by Lord Hoffmann in *Campbell*, at [60], that there could be a genuine public interest in the disclosure of the existence of a sexual relationship (in, for example, a situation giving rise to favouritism or advancement through corruption), but he went on to warn that the addition of salacious details or intimate photographs would be disproportionate and unacceptable. "The latter, even if accompanying a legitimate disclosure of the sexual relationship, would be too intrusive and demeaning."

21. At the Court of Appeal stage of *Campbell* [2003] QB 633 at [64], Lord Phillips stated that provided the publication of particular confidential

information is justifiable in the public interest, the journalist must be given reasonable latitude as to the manner in which the information is conveyed to the public: see too *Fressoz v. France* (1999) 31 EHRR 28. Yet, for the reasons given by Lord Hoffmann, it should not be assumed that, even if the subject-matter of the meeting on 28 March *was* of public interest, the showing of the film or the pictures was a reasonable method of conveying that information. In effect, it is a question of proportionality.

22. It is always important to remember that a number of the comments made about intrusion by photography or video recording in Strasbourg have been made in the context of images recorded in more or less public spaces. This was so in *Von Hannover v. Germany* itself and in *Peck v. United Kingdom* (2003) 36 EHRR 41. It was true also of the decision of the Supreme Court of Canada in *Aubry v. Éditions Vice-Versa Inc.* [1998] 2 SCR 591, in which it was held that there had been a violation of a young woman's right of privacy under Article 5 of the Quebec Charter of Human Rights and Freedoms, notwithstanding the fact that she had been sitting on the steps of a public building.

23. The present complaint relates to the recording on private property of sexual activity. The situation may be at the extreme of intimate intrusion, but the matter is by no means outside the scope of existing authority. An injunction was granted, for example, by Ouseley J in *Theakston v. MGN Ltd* [2002] EMLR 22 in respect of photographs taken inside a brothel, even though he recognised that it was not appropriate to restrain verbal descriptions of what the claimant did there. The passage in his judgment giving reasons for restraining publication of the photographs was cited and endorsed by the Court of Appeal in *Douglas v. Hello! Ltd (No 3)* at [85].

[The court went on to hold that in this case, both the text and visual images infringed the plaintiff's privacy rights.]

COMMENTS AND QUESTIONS

1. While British law protecting individual privacy historically revolved around the tortious action for breach of confidence, the enactment of the Human Rights Act of 1998, based on the principles set out in the European Convention on Human Rights, effectively added a new privacy-based cause of action to British law. The plaintiff in *Mosley* relied on this new privacy action. Note that Justice Eady sets out the full text of the relevant articles of the Convention — Articles 8 and 10 — dealing with privacy rights and speech rights respectively. The balancing act between privacy and speech in this context is a relatively new exercise for British courts. Historically, American courts have had more experience balancing speech and privacy interests. However, it should be noted that the new British law differs from American law in that the British law now expressly enshrines both personal privacy rights and speech rights as fundamental constitutional guarantees. In the United States, free speech is

expressly guaranteed by the First Amendment, but there is no express guarantee of privacy in the American federal Constitution.

2.   Judge Eady makes the point in *Mosley* that privacy values are "as much applicable in disputes between individuals, or between an individual and a non-governmental body such as a newspaper, as they are in disputes between individuals and a public authority" (at para. 9). Is this an important concession for privacy law in the digital age? How does this conception differ, if at all, from our conception of privacy rights in the United States?

3.   In what ways does Judge Eady distinguish photographs from text-based accounts of private information? Do you agree with the distinctions? *See* Jacqueline Lipton, *Mapping Online Privacy*, 104 Nw. U. L. Rev. ____ (2010) (providing a series of examples of disparate impacts on recipients of text, audio, video, and multimedia information).

4.   Judge Eady also distinguishes between information gathering and dissemination, reflecting the approach taken in the *Campbell* case, *supra*. Do you think this distinction is meaningful or important with respect to photography in particular? If an audio or video recording is legally made, do you think there should be any legal controls restricting its dissemination to the public?

5.   Judge Eady refers to the *Douglas v. Hello! Ltd* case, in which the well-known actors Michael Douglas and Catherine Zeta-Jones sued a British publication for unauthorized taking and publishing of photographs of their wedding. This case was decided on the base of the traditional British "breach of confidence" action rather than on the base of the new British privacy right. What do you understand to be the distinction between breach of confidence and privacy? Some would argue that while a breach of confidence action relies on relationships between parties to an action (i.e., relationships of confidence), a privacy right is enforceable against the whole world. Because of this, the privacy action arguably raises more pronounced free speech concerns because it is not simply a matter of a court enforcing a pre-existing relationship of confidence. Some American scholars have suggested that a breach of confidence action may be the answer to concerns about privacy rights impacting on First Amendment freedoms. Neil Richards & Daniel Solove, *Privacy's Other Path: Recovering the Law of Confidentiality*, 96 Geo. L.J. 123 (2007). Is this a plausible way forward for American privacy law?

c) Modes of Regulation

As we saw in Chapter 1, Professor Lawrence Lessig suggested four different modes of regulation for cyberspace generally: legal rules, social norms, market forces, and system architecture. His observations may be particularly useful for the protection of online privacy in the age of Web 2.0 technologies. As the previous materials demonstrate, legal rules alone may be particularly limited as a method of redressing online privacy harms. This is because the costs and embarrassment of litigation may deter injured parties from seeking legal redress. Additionally, once private information has been shared globally online, legal remedies are limited in their ability to effectively compensate a plaintiff. It is extremely difficult to quantify appropriate damages awards. Injunctions are also problematic in practice because of the permanent and viral nature of the Internet. Additionally, legal rules aimed at curbing truthful speech run into difficulties under the First Amendment, at least in the United States.

Other forms of regulation may address online privacy problems more effectively, either on their own or in concert with legal rules. Professor Patricia Sánchez Abril has stressed this point:

> "While reputational harms are more tangible and indelible than ever before, there is a dearth of support for the aggrieved. Our current law is ill-equipped to protect these injuries, ISPs are unwilling to mediate them, codes of ethics are scant, and technology is still too fragile to protect them. For digital immigrants, this lack of protection and redress is justified, after all, online, 'you have zero privacy — get over it.' While a prudent personal admonition, it is too simplistic and cynical to inform the law, public policy, ethics, or the future of technology.
>
> In order to analyze the shortcomings in this area, it is necessary to . . . understand the personal, relational, and social benefits of protecting privacy and personality on OSNs [online social networks] and beyond. Individuals need privacy to develop and sustain personality, strengthen interpersonal relationships, voice and test opinions, become producers of culture, and, ultimately, be free.
>
> The burden of protecting privacy on OSNs should not be solely borne by the OSN participants, rather it should be shared by the individuals, law, ethics, ISPs, and technology. Individuals should be cognizant of the reality of digital information and prudent in their selections of ISPs, privacy controls, and self-disclosure without assuming entitlement to selective anonymity. The law must also be updated to address modern harms, perhaps by incorporating a reasonable expectation of audience standard or a uniform code of privacy for adoption by state legislatures. Codes of ethics addressing dignitary harms on OSNs should be promulgated, perhaps encouraging employers to disclose the sources of an employee's background check and allow opportunity to refute any questionable online information.
>
> Finally, ISPs, who are perhaps the best situated actors to carry some of these burdens, should proactively educate their users as to the risks inherent in online disclosure, incorporate a code of online ethics to which participants can subscribe, and perhaps offer an active adjudication system for member privacy disputes. ISPs can also tailor the technology to protect situational personalities, perhaps allowing the online socializer to zone his personality as he can in real space. Protecting privacy and personality on OSNs from various angles and by several actors would ensure that the technology evolves in ways that encourage identity-building, intimacy, and social discourse, yet simultaneously protect and respect its participants."

A (My) Space of One's Own: On Privacy and Online Social Networks, 6 Nw. J. Tech. & Intell. Prop. 73, 87-88 (2007). Do you agree with Professor Sánchez Abril's analysis? What are some of the other modalities of regulation she favors for online privacy? Can any of these regulatory modalities be effective as stand-alone approaches to privacy, or do they have to work together? Who should adopt codes of ethics about privacy and how should they be enforced, if at all, in practice?

See also discussion in Jacqueline Lipton, *"We, the Paparazzi": Developing a Privacy Paradigm for Digital Video*, 95 Iowa L. Rev. _____ (2010); Lawrence Lessig, *The Architecture of Privacy*, 1 Vand. J. Ent. & Tech. L. 56 (1999).

Note: Privacy Harms and Remedies

Historically, one of the practical problems with legal claims for loss of privacy relates to identifying the nature of the harm and quantifying the appropriate level of damages. As we noted at the beginning of this chapter, there is no clearly accepted theoretical basis for a privacy right. A variety of different privacy metaphors have traditionally been used to explain the nature of the right. Professor Daniel Solove has suggested avoiding the search for a common unifying explanation for privacy and instead taking a "bottom up" pragmatic approach to privacy harms. Daniel Solove, *Conceptualizing Privacy*, 90 Cal. L. Rev. 1087 (2002); Daniel Solove, *A Taxonomy of Privacy*, 154 U. Pa. L. Rev. 477 (2006). *See also* Jacqueline Lipton, *Mapping Online Privacy*, 104 Nw. U. L. Rev. _____ (2010).

In the *Max Mosley* case, *supra*, the court awarded the unprecedented sum of £60,000 for infringement of the plaintiff's privacy rights. In coming to this conclusion, Justice Eady took great pains to identify the nature of the harms to be compensated:

> "... it is reasonable to suppose that damages for such an infringement may include distress, hurt feelings and loss of dignity. The scale of the distress and indignity in this case is difficult to comprehend. It is probably unprecedented. Apart from distress, there is another factor which probably has to be taken into account of a less tangible nature. It is accepted in recent jurisprudence that a legitimate consideration is that of vindication to mark the infringement of a right: see, e.g., *Ashley v. Chief Constable of Sussex* [2008] 2 WLR 975 at [21]-[22] and *Chester v. Afshar* [2005] 1 AC 134 at [87]. Again, it should be stressed that this is different from vindication of reputation (long recognised [sic] as a proper factor in the award of libel damages). It is simply to mark the fact that either the state or a relevant individual has taken away or undermined the right of another — in this case taken away a person's dignity and struck at the core of his personality. It is a relevant factor, but the underlying policy is to ensure that an infringed right is met with 'an adequate remedy.'"

Max Mosley v. News Group Limited, [2008] EWHC 1777 (QB), para. 216. What factors does Justice Eady take into account in assessing privacy-related damages? Do you agree with his approach? Do you think this approach could work in American privacy cases? Why/why not?

Some commentators have felt that privacy incursions should not be compensated in this way and have suggested that the better course of action would be to focus on redressing specific damages caused by breaches of privacy — such as loss of employment, health insurance, discrimination in employment and educational opportunities, etc. On this view, losses of privacy in the digital age are both inevitable and, to a significant extent, even desirable for a more transparent society, as long as particular resulting harms can be redressed. Do you agree with this view? *See* Lior Strahilevitz, *Reputation Nation: Law in an Era of Ubiquitous Personal Information,* 102 Nw. U. L. Rev. 1667 (2008) (arguing that basing decisions on real and accurate information rather than dangerous and discriminatory proxies such as race actually provides social benefits overall); David Brin, *The Transparent Society* (1999).

6

NETWORK OWNERSHIP AND ACCESS

We have now explored the extent to which information in cyberspace can be regulated under the principles of speech, intellectual property, and privacy. To what extent can the principles of real and/or personal property be applied to cyberspace? After all, information in cyberspace must travel through the private computers and computer networks that make up the Internet, and this hardware can be damaged and "occupied." Does ownership of the constituent parts of the network give the owner the right to control the electrons that pass through those parts? Does ownership entail a right to control access and exclude others?

Problem 12.0

With StarttUp's success, you begin to experience some unanticipated problems. First, because your subscriber base is now sizable, third-party businesses have begun to inundate your network with unsolicited bulk e-mail or "spam." These e-mails advertise everything from how to make money just by surfing the Internet to weight loss. Personally, you receive approximately 100 unsolicited messages each day in your StarttUp account. Some are filtered automatically by your e-mail system into your "junkmail" folder, but about 10 to 20 usually find their way into your "inbox."

These unsolicited e-mails are beginning to cause some problems. From a technical perspective, they are not significant, though they do increase the traffic that comes over your system, and as such take up computer time and storage space. The real problem is one of customer satisfaction. Subscribers are beginning to complain about these e-mails. Most of these complaints focus on the inconvenience created by having to wait for these messages to download, and then the time it takes to delete them.

Others are concerned that StarttUp sold their e-mail addresses to these third parties. (In some cases, StarttUp has sold this information after you consulted with Alan and Barbara.)

As part of its terms of service, StarttUp expressly prohibits spam.

Another problem you are experiencing stems from the actions of a former employee (yes, you have now been around long enough to have former employees). Disgruntled Employee was a member of your tech staff who was fired because he was spending too much time online and not completing his projects on time. Since then, Disgruntled Employee has been searching for ways into your network. So far, he has not been able to obtain access, but it may be only a matter of time. In addition to his hacking, Disgruntled Employee has also been sending e-mails to StarttUp's employees and management. These e-mails list his complaints against the company, and you in particular. The e-mails also encourage employees to quit, in particular, because of the company's policy of monitoring employee computer usage. While it does not appear that other employees are taking these complaints seriously, Alan and Barbara are concerned that they are impacting morale.

Your head of technology has informed you that the easiest way to deal with both problems is to block any e-mails coming from the relevant IP addresses. Alan and Barbara like this idea, but also want to pursue other options. What can you tell them?

Problem 12.1

Cora has asked your advice about spam "commenters." These "commenters" are posting messages unrelated to the blog, but instead advertise various products and services, including male enhancement drugs. While she and her co-bloggers can manually delete these comments as they become aware of them, it is a lot of work. It also annoys the bloggers and readers of the blog. Additionally, there are some "commenters" who write harassing, derogatory, and potentially threatening comments on the blog. Again, while these comments can be deleted manually some of the bloggers and readers are much less interested in participating and following the blog because of the environment created by the comments. While it is possible to block some of the IP addresses from which the undesired comments originate, the spammers and anti-feminist groups can quickly and easily make use of new IP addresses and start again. Advise Cora as to any legal or practical options she might have for controlling the unwanted comments.

A. STATUTORY PROHIBITIONS AGAINST ILLEGAL ACCESS

With the growth of computers in the 1970s and 1980s came a corresponding growth in "hacking"—efforts to electronically access a computer system without authorization. Hacking could be as innocuous as breaking in just to see whether it can be done, or as nefarious as the stealing or destruction of data. In response to concern over hacking, the U.S. Congress and state governments enacted laws to protect computer systems against hacking. As you study the following material, how does the Computer Fraud and Abuse Act protect a computer owner? What principles is this protection based upon? Damage to data or equipment? Proprietary rights in data? Or, a general right to control access to computer equipment?

COMPUTER FRAUD AND ABUSE ACT

18 U.S.C. §1030

(a) Whoever—

. . .

(2) intentionally accesses a computer without authorization or exceeds authorized access, and thereby obtains:

(A) information contained in a financial record of a financial institution, or of a card issuer as defined in section 1602(n) of title 15, or contained in a file of a consumer reporting agency on a consumer, as such terms are defined in the Fair Credit Reporting Act (15 U.S.C. 1681 et seq.);

(B) information from any department or agency of the United States; or

(C) information from any protected computer;

. . .

(4) knowingly and with intent to defraud, accesses a protected computer without authorization, or exceeds authorized access, and by means of such conduct furthers the intended fraud and obtains anything of value, unless the object of the fraud and the thing obtained consists only of the use of the computer and the value of such use is not more than $5,000 in any 1-year period;

(5) (A) knowingly causes the transmission of a program, information, code, or command, and as a result of such conduct, intentionally causes damage without authorization, to a protected computer;

(B) intentionally accesses a protected computer without authorization, and as a result of such conduct, recklessly causes damage; or

(C) intentionally accesses a protected computer without authorization, and as a result of such conduct, causes damage and loss;

(6) knowingly and with intent to defraud traffics (as defined in section 1029...) in any password or similar information through which a computer may be accessed without authorization, if—

(A) such trafficking affects interstate or foreign commerce; or

(B) such computer is used by or for the Government of the United States;

(7) with intent to extort from any person any money or other thing of value, transmits in interstate or foreign commerce any communication containing any—

(A) threat to cause damage to a protected computer;

(B) threat to obtain information from a protected computer without authorization or in excess of authorization or to impair the confidentiality of information obtained from a protected computer without authorization or by exceeding authorized access; or

(C) demand or request for money or other thing of value in relation to damage to a protected computer, where such damage was caused to facilitate the extortion;

shall be punished as provided in subsection (c) of this section.

(b) Whoever conspires to commit or attempts to commit an offense under subsection (a) of this section shall be punished as provided in subsection (c) of this section.

[Subsection (c) provides for various felony and misdemeanor penalties depending upon which provision of the CFAA is violated, and the motive for violation, or whether the defendant has already been convicted of violating the CFAA.]

. . .

(e) As used in this section—

(1) the term "computer" means an electronic, magnetic, optical, electrochemical, or other high speed data processing device performing logical, arithmetic, or storage functions, and includes any data storage facility or communications facility directly related to or operating in conjunction with such device, but such term does not include an automated typewriter or typesetter, a portable hand held calculator, or other similar device;

(2) the term "protected computer" means a computer—

(A) exclusively for the use of a financial institution or the United States Government, or, in the case of a computer not exclusively for such use, used by or for a financial institution or the United States Government and the conduct constituting the offense affects that use by or for the financial institution or the Government; or

(B) which is used in or affecting interstate or foreign commerce or communication, including a computer located outside the United States that is used in a manner that affects interstate or foreign commerce or communication of the United States;

. . .

(5) the term "financial record" means information derived from any record held by a financial institution pertaining to a customer's relationship with the financial institution;

(6) the term "exceeds authorized access" means to access a computer with authorization and to use such access to obtain or alter information in the computer that the accesser is not entitled so to obtain or alter;

. . .

(8) the term "damage" means any impairment to the integrity or availability of data, a program, a system, or information;

. . .

(11) the term "loss" means any reasonable cost to any victim, including the cost of responding to an offense, conducting a damage assessment, and restoring the data, program, system, or information to its condition prior to the offense, and any revenue lost, cost incurred, or other consequential damages incurred because of interruption of service; and

(12) the term "person" means any individual, firm, corporation, educational institution, financial institution, governmental entity, or legal or other entity.

(f) This section does not prohibit any lawfully authorized investigative, protective, or intelligence activity of a law enforcement agency of the United States, a State, or a political subdivision of a State, or of an intelligence agency of the United States.

(g) Any person who suffers damage or loss by reason of a violation of this section may maintain a civil action against the violator to obtain compensatory damages and injunctive relief or other equitable relief. A civil action for a violation of this section may be brought only if the conduct involves 1 of the factors set forth in subclauses (I), (II), (III), (IV), or (V) of subsection (c)(4)(A)(i). Damages for a violation involving only conduct described in subsection (c)(4)(A)(i)(I) are limited to economic damages. No action may be brought under this subsection unless such action is begun within 2 years of the date of the act complained of or the date of the discovery of the damage. No action may be brought under this subsection for the negligent design or manufacture of computer hardware, computer software, or firmware.

. . .

[The factors set forth in the relevant subclauses of subsection (c)(4)(A)(i) are:

(I) loss to 1 or more persons during any 1-year period (and, for purposes of an investigation, prosecution, or other proceeding brought by the United States only, loss resulting from a related course of conduct affecting 1 or more other protected computers) aggregating at least $5,000 in value;

(II) the modification or impairment, or potential modification or impairment, of the medical examination, diagnosis, treatment, or care of 1 or more individuals;

(III) physical injury to any person;

(IV) a threat to public health or safety;

(V) damage affecting a computer used by or for an entity of the United States Government in furtherance of the administration of justice, national defense, or national security; or

(VI) damage affecting 10 or more protected computers during any 1-year period.]

COMMENTS AND QUESTIONS

1. What types of "hacking" activities does the CFAA prevent? Does it apply to the facts set out in Problem 12.0 or 12.1?

2. Prior to the 2008 (and the earlier 1996) amendments to the CFAA, there was some concern over the *mens rea* requirements under the Act. For example, in the following case of United States v. Morris, the defendant was convicted under Section 1030(a)(5)(A) which originally applied to anyone who:

> (5) intentionally accesses a Federal interest computer without authorization, and by means of one or more instances of such conduct alters, damages, or destroys information in any such Federal interest computer, or prevents authorized use of any such computer or information, and thereby
>> (A) causes loss to one or more others of a value aggregating $1,000 or more during any one year period; . . .

While Morris intentionally released a computer virus, he argued that he did not intend to cause damage to any protected computers. Does the revised statute clarify this issue?

3. Could an employee who inadvertently crashes her company's computer network be prosecuted under the CFAA?

4. As we will see, violations of the CFAA turn upon whether a defendant's activities were authorized. Currently, the CFAA defines the term "exceeds authorized access" as accessing, "a computer with authorization and to use such access to obtain or alter information in the computer that the accesser is not entitled so to obtain or alter. . . ." 18 U.S.C. §1030(e)(6). Does it make a difference under the CFAA whether the defendant accesses a protected computer without authorization or by exceeding authorized access? When is a use unauthorized as opposed to exceeding authorization?

UNITED STATES V. MORRIS

928 F.2d 504 (2d Cir. 1991)

JON O. NEWMAN, Circuit Judge . . .

In the fall of 1988, Morris was a first-year graduate student in Cornell University's computer science Ph.D. program. Through undergraduate work at Harvard and in various jobs he had acquired significant computer experience and expertise. When Morris entered Cornell, he was given an account on the computer at the Computer Science Division. This account gave him explicit authorization to use computers at Cornell. Morris engaged in various discussions with fellow graduate students about the security of computer networks and his ability to penetrate it.

In October 1988, Morris began work on a computer program, later known as the INTERNET "worm" or "virus." The goal of this program was to demonstrate the inadequacies of current security measures on computer networks by exploiting the security defects that Morris had discovered. The tactic he selected was release of a worm into network computers. Morris designed the program to spread across a national network of computers after being inserted at one computer location connected to the network. Morris released the worm into INTERNET, which is a group of national networks that connect university, governmental, and military computers around the country. The network permits communication and transfer of information between computers on the network. . . .

Morris identified four ways in which the worm could break into computers on the network:

1. through a "hole" or "bug" (an error) in SEND MAIL, a computer program that transfers and receives electronic mail on a computer;
2. through a bug in the "finger demon" program, a program that permits a person to obtain limited information about the users of another computer;
3. through the "trusted hosts" feature, which permits a user with certain privileges on one computer to have equivalent privileges on another computer without using a password; and
4. through a program of password guessing, whereby various combinations of letters are tried out in rapid sequence in the hope that one will be an authorized user's password, which is entered to permit whatever level of activity that user is authorized to perform.

On November 2, 1988, Morris released the worm from a computer at the Massachusetts Institute of Technology. MIT was selected to disguise the fact that the worm came from Morris at Cornell. Morris soon discovered that the worm was replicating and reinfecting machines at a much faster rate than he had anticipated. Ultimately, many machines at locations around the country either crashed or became "catatonic." When Morris realized what was happening, he contacted a friend at Harvard to discuss a solution. Eventually, they sent an anonymous message from Harvard over the network, instructing programmers how to kill the worm and prevent reinfection. However, because the network route was clogged, this message did not get through until it was too late. Computers were affected at numerous installations, including leading universities, military sites, and medical research facilities. The estimated cost of dealing with the worm at each installation ranged from $200 to more than $53,000. . . .

DISCUSSION

Section 1030(a)(5)(A) penalizes the conduct of an individual who "intentionally accesses a Federal interest computer without authorization." Morris contends that his conduct constituted, at most, "exceeding authorized access" rather than the "unauthorized access" that the subsection punishes. Morris argues that there was insufficient evidence to convict him of "unauthorized access," and that even if the evidence sufficed, he was entitled to have the jury instructed on his "theory of defense."

We assess the sufficiency of the evidence under the traditional standard. Morris was authorized to use computers at Cornell, Harvard, and Berkeley, all of which were on INTERNET. As a result, Morris was authorized to communicate with other computers on the network to send electronic mail (SEND MAIL), and to find out certain information about the users of other computers (finger demon). The question is whether Morris's transmission of his worm constituted exceeding authorized access or accessing without authorization.

The Senate Report stated that section 1030(a)(5)(A), like the new section 1030(a)(3), would "be aimed at 'outsiders,' *i.e.*, those lacking authorization to access any Federal interest computer." Senate Report at 10, U.S. Code Cong. & Admin. News at 2488. But the Report also stated, in concluding its discussion on the scope of section 1030(a)(3), that it applies "where the offender is completely outside the Government, . . . *or where the offender's act of trespass is interdepartmental in nature.*" *Id*. at 8, U.S. Code Cong. & Admin. News at 2486 (emphasis added).

Morris relies on the first quoted portion to argue that his actions can be characterized only as exceeding authorized access, since he had authorized access to a federal interest computer. However, the second quoted portion reveals that Congress was not drawing a bright line between those who have some access to any federal interest computer and those who have none. Congress contemplated that individuals with access to some federal interest computers would be subject to liability under the computer fraud provisions for gaining unauthorized access to other federal interest computers. *See, e.g., id*. (stating that a Labor Department employee who uses Labor's computers to access without authorization an FBI computer can be criminally prosecuted).

The evidence permitted the jury to conclude that Morris's use of the SEND MAIL and finger demon features constituted access without authorization. While a case might arise where the use of SEND MAIL or finger demon falls within a nebulous area in which the line between accessing without authorization and exceeding authorized access may not be clear, Morris's conduct here falls well within the area of unauthorized access. Morris did not use either of those features in any way related to their intended function. He did not send or read mail nor discover information about other users; instead he found holes in both programs that permitted him a special and unauthorized access route into other computers.

Moreover, the jury verdict need not be upheld solely on Morris's use of SEND MAIL and finger demon. As the District Court noted, in denying Morris's motion for acquittal,

> Although the evidence may have shown that defendant's initial insertion of the worm simply exceeded his authorized access, the evidence also demonstrated that the worm was designed to spread to other computers at which he had no account and no authority, express or implied, to unleash the worm program. Moreover, there was also evidence that the worm was designed to gain access to computers at which he had no account by guessing their passwords. Accordingly, the evidence did support the jury's conclusion that defendant accessed without authority as opposed to merely exceeding the scope of his authority.

In light of the reasonable conclusions that the jury could draw from Morris's use of SEND MAIL and finger demon, and from his use of the trusted hosts feature and password guessing, his challenge to the sufficiency of the evidence fails. . . .

COMMENTS AND QUESTIONS

1. What is the argument that Morris's use of SEND MAIL or finger demon exceeded his authorized access as opposed to being unauthorized? Is there a coherent distinction between unauthorized access and exceeding authorized access? What example could be used to illustrate this difference?

2. Both the Court of Appeals and the District Court in *Morris* framed the issue as Morris was not authorized to unleash the worm program. Under this interpretation of authorization are there any acts that would be considered exceeding authorized access?

3. Is the distinction between insiders and outsiders helpful? How would it apply in *Morris*? While other provisions of the CFAA prohibit both unauthorized access and exceeding authorized access, Section 1030(a)(5) only prohibits defendants from causing damage to a protected computer if the defendant's access was unauthorized. Is there a justification for treating outsiders differently from insiders under those circumstances?

4. While the insider and outsider distinction may make sense with respect to proprietary networks, can it be applied to Internet communications? How might that distinction work on the Internet?

5. What if a defendant merely accesses information for his or her own curiosity? *Consider* United States v. Czubinski, 106 F.3d 1069 (1st Cir. 1997). Czubinski, who had been employed by the Internal Revenue Service, used his access to the IRS's computers to obtain the tax returns of various people including individuals working for the David Duke campaign, an assistant-district attorney who was prosecuting his father in an unrelated case, and various local officials. Czubinski was convicted under the CFAA, Section 1030(a)(4). The conviction was subsequently overturned on appeal because the court concluded that Czubinski had not obtained "anything of value." According to the court:

> The plain language of section 1030(a)(4) emphasizes that more than mere unauthorized use is required: the "thing obtained" may not merely be the unauthorized use. It is the showing of some additional end — to which the unauthorized access is a means — that is lacking here. The evidence did not show that Czubinski's end was anything more than to satisfy his curiosity by viewing information about friends, acquaintances, and political rivals. No evidence suggests that he printed out, recorded, or used the information he browsed. No rational jury could conclude beyond a reasonable doubt that Czubinski intended to use or disclose that information, and merely viewing information cannot be deemed the same as obtaining something of value for the purposes of this statute.
>
> The legislative history further supports our reading of the term "anything of value." . . . Here, a Senate co-sponsor's comments suggest that Congress intended section 1030(a)(4) to punish attempts to steal valuable data, and did not wish to punish mere unauthorized access:

>> The acts of fraud we are addressing in proposed section 1030(a)(4) are essentially thefts in which someone uses a federal interest computer to wrongly obtain something of value from another. . . . Proposed section 1030(a)(4) is intended to reflect the distinction between the theft of information, a felony, and mere unauthorized access, a misdemeanor.

> 132 Cong. Rec. 7128, 7129, 99th Cong., 2d. Sess. (1986). The Senate Committee Report further underscores the fact that this section should apply to those who steal information through unauthorized access as part of an illegal scheme:

>> The Committee remains convinced that there must be a clear distinction between computer theft, punishable as a felony [under section 1030(a)(4)], and computer trespass, punishable in the first instance as a misdemeanor [under section 1030(a)(2)]. The element in the new paragraph (a)(4), requiring a showing of an intent to defraud, is meant to preserve that distinction, as is the requirement that the property wrongfully obtained via computer furthers the intended fraud.

> S. Rep. No. 432, 99th Cong., 2d Sess., reprinted in 1986 U.S.C.C.A.N. 2479, 2488. For the same reasons we deemed the trial evidence could not support a finding that Czubinski deprived the IRS of its property . . . we find that Czubinski has not obtained valuable information in furtherance of a fraudulent scheme for the purposes of section 1030(a)(4). . . .

106 F.3d at 1078-79. This case was decided under the 1996 version of the CFAA. Could Czubinski have been convicted under any provisions of the 2008 version?

6. While the crashing of computer networks can clearly be considered damage under the CFAA, what else may be considered damage? As demonstrated by the following cases, the question of damages is muddled by the CFAA's separate references to damages in Sections 1030(a)(5) and 1030(g) with only a single definition under Section 1030(e)(8).

**SHURGARD STORAGE CENTERS, INC. v.
SAFEGUARD SELF STORAGE, INC.**

119 F. Supp. 2d 1121 (W.D. Wash. 2000)

ZILLY, District Judge.

INTRODUCTION

Shurgard Storage Centers, Inc. (plaintiff) and Safeguard Self Storage, Inc. (defendant) are competitors in the self-storage business. The plaintiff alleges that the defendant embarked on a systematic scheme to hire away key employees from the plaintiff for the purpose of obtaining the plaintiff's trade secrets. The plaintiff also alleges that some of these employees, while still working for the plaintiff, used the plaintiff's computers to send trade secrets to the defendant via e-mail. The plaintiff's complaint alleges misappropriation of trade secrets, conversion, unfair competition, violations of the Computer Fraud and Abuse Act (CFAA), tortious interference with a business expectancy, and seeks injunctive relief and damages. The defendant has moved to dismiss the CFAA claim pursuant to Fed. R. Civ. P. 12(b)(6). . . .

DISCUSSION

B. Does the Plaintiff State a Claim under 18 U.S.C. §1030(a)(2)(C)?

Under §1030(a)(2)(C), "[w]hoever . . . intentionally accesses a computer without authorization or exceeds authorized access, and thereby obtains . . . information from any protected computer if the conduct involved an interstate or foreign communication . . . shall be punished" as provided in section (c) of the statute. 18 U.S.C. §1030(a)(2)(C). . . .

The defendant contends the plaintiff's complaint does not state a claim for relief under 18 U.S.C. §1030(a)(2)(C) for two reasons. First, the defendant asserts that the plaintiff has not alleged that the employees in question accessed the trade secrets without authorization. Second, the defendant argues that the plaintiff has not alleged facts showing that the alleged behavior by the defendant impacts the national economy.

i. Did Plaintiff Allege That its Former Employees were Without Authorization or That They Exceeded Authorized Access?

The defendant's first ground for challenging the plaintiff's claim under §1030(a)(2)(C) is that the plaintiff has not alleged that its former employees did not have authorized access to the information in question. The defendant notes that the plaintiff alleged that Mr. Leland had full access to all the information allegedly transferred to the defendant. Accordingly, the defendant argues that the plaintiff cannot maintain an action under §1030(a)(2)(C) because it has not alleged that anyone accessed its computers without authorization or exceeded authorized access to those computers.

The plaintiff responds by arguing that the authorization for its former employees ended when the employees began acting as agents for the defendant. The plaintiff cites to the Restatement (Second) of Agency §112 (1958) and argues that when Mr. Leland or other former employees used the plaintiff's computers and information on those computers in an improper way they were "without authorization."

Under the Restatement (Second) of Agency . . . :

> Unless otherwise agreed, the authority of an agent terminates if, without knowledge of the principal, he acquires adverse interests or if he is otherwise guilty of a serious breach of loyalty to the principal.

Restatement (Second) of Agency §112 (1958). Under this rule, the authority of the plaintiff's former employees ended when they allegedly became agents of the defendant. Therefore, for the purposes of this 12(b)(6) motion, they lost their authorization and were "without authorization" when they allegedly obtained and sent the proprietary information to the defendant via e-mail. The plaintiff has stated a claim under 18 U.S.C. §1030(a)(2)(C). *See United States v. Morris*, 928 F.2d 504, 510 (2d Cir. 1991) (holding that a computer user, with authorized access to a computer and its programs, was without authorization when he used the programs in an unauthorized way).

ii. Did the Plaintiff have to Allege that the Violation of 18 U.S.C. §1030(a)(2)(C) Affected the National Economy?

The defendant's second argument challenging the plaintiff's claim under §1030(a)(2)(C), as well as its other claims under the CFAA, is that the CFAA was only intended to protect information in large businesses where information, if released or stolen, could affect the public. The defendant maintains that since information from the storage business is not of the type that the CFAA was intended to protect (as opposed to the transportation or power-supply industries), the CFAA does not apply.

Nowhere in language of §1030(a)(2)(C) is the scope limited to entities with broad privacy repercussions. The statute simply prohibits the obtaining of information from "*any* protected computer if the conduct involved an inter-state or foreign communication." 18 U.S.C. §1030(a)(2)(C) (emphasis added). According to the statute, a protected computer is a computer used in interstate or foreign commerce. *See* 18 U.S.C. §1030(e)(2)(B). This lan-guage is unambiguous. There is no reasonable implication in any of these terms that suggests only the computers of certain industries are protected. Therefore, the defendant's argument on this issue is unpersuasive. . . .

D. Does the Plaintiff State a Claim under 18 U.S.C. §1030(a)(5)(C)?

Under 18 U.S.C. §1030(a)(5)(C), "[w]hoever . . . intentionally accesses a protected computer without authorization, and as a result of such conduct, causes damage" violates the CFAA. 18 U.S.C. §1030(a)(5)(C). The only new issue under this portion of the statute is whether the plaintiff has alleged that "damage" occurred. "The term 'damage' means any impairment to the integ-rity or availability of data, a program, a system, or information, that . . . causes loss aggregating at least $5,000 in value during any 1-year period to one or more individuals. . . ." 18 U.S.C. §1030(e)(8)(A). . . .

[T]he defendant argues that the plaintiff has not pled that it incurred "damage" as defined in the statute. Specifically, the defendant argues that the alleged loss of information by the plaintiff is not "damage" under the statute. The statute says damage is "*any impairment* to the integrity . . . of data . . . or information." 18 U.S.C. §1030(e)(8)(A) (emphasis added). The unambigu-ous meaning of "any" clearly demonstrates that the statute is meant to apply to "any" impairment to the integrity of data. However, the word "integrity" is ambiguous in this context. Webster's New International Dictionary (3d ed. 1993), defines "integrity" as, "an unimpaired or unmarred condition: entire correspondence with an original condition." The word "integrity" in the con-text of data necessarily contemplates maintaining the data in a protected state. Because the term may be ambiguous, the Court examines the legislative history to determine if "integrity" and thus "damage" could include the alleged access and disclosure of trade secrets in this case.

The term "damage" was addressed in the Senate Report regarding the 1996 amendments to the CFAA:

> The 1994 amendment required both "damage" and "loss," but it is not always clear what constitutes "damage." For example, intruders often alter existing log-on programs so that user passwords are copied to a file which the hackers can retrieve later. After retrieving the newly created password file, the intruder restores the altered log-on file to its original condition. Arguably, in such a situation, neither the computer nor its information is damaged. Nonetheless, this conduct allows the intruder to accumulate valid user passwords to the system, requires all system users to change their passwords, and requires the system administrator to devote resources to resecuring the system.

Thus, although there is arguably no "damage," the victim does suffer "loss." If the loss to the victim meets the required monetary threshold, the conduct should be criminal, and the victim should be entitled to relief.

The bill therefore defines "damage" in new subsection 1030(e)(8), with a focus on the harm that the law seeks to prevent.

S. Rep. No. 104-357, at 11 (1996). This example given in the report is analogous to the case before the Court. The "damage" and thus violation to the "integrity" that was caused in the example is the accumulation of passwords and subsequent corrective measures the rightful computer owner must take to prevent the infiltration and gathering of confidential information. Similarly, in this case, the defendant allegedly infiltrated the plaintiff's computer network, albeit through different means than in the example, and collected and disseminated confidential information. In both cases no data was physically changed or erased, but in both cases an impairment of its integrity occurred. From the legislative history it is clear that the meaning of "integrity" and thus "damage" apply to the alleged acts of the defendant in this case and thus the plaintiff has stated a claim under 18 U.S.C. §1030(a)(5)(C).

COMMENTS AND QUESTIONS

1. Following *Morris*, the court in *Shurgard* concludes that the employees' access to the company's trade secrets was unauthorized. The court reaches this conclusion by relying upon the Restatement (Second) of Agency. Did the court have to reach this conclusion in order to find that the complaint stated a cause of action against the defendants? Subsequent courts have taken a similar view that an employee who authorizes a computer with access but who uses that access to obtain information that she knows she is not entitled to obtain or alter satisfied the "exceeds authorized access" criterion of the CFAA:

> "In *Int'l Airports Center, LLC v. Citrin*, 440 F.3d 418 (7th Cir. 2006), the Seventh Circuit considered what constitutes unauthorized access by an employee who has been granted access to protected computers. The court held that an employee who breaches her duty of loyalty to an employer or acquires an adverse interest to her employer is no longer authorized to access the employer's computers. *Id.* at 420-21. Under the CFAA, the phrase "'exceeds authorized access' means to access a computer with authorization and to use such access to obtain or alter information in the computer that the accesser is not entitled to obtain or alter." 18 U.S.C. §1030(e)(6). Allegations that an employee e-mailed and downloaded confidential information for an improper purpose are sufficient to state a claim that the employee exceeded her authorization. *Mintel Int'l Group, Ltd. v. Neergheen*, No. 08 C 3939, 2008 U.S. Dist. LEXIS 54119, 2008 WL 2782818, at *3 (N.D. Ill. July 16, 2008)."

Motorola v Lemko, 609 F. Supp. 2d 760 (2009). Do you agree with this interpretation as a matter of policy? Even though the *Motorola* case was decided in 2009, the court applied the 1996 version of the CFAA as it was the applicable law at the time the facts arose in the case. Does anything in the 2008 version of the act change your views?

2. According to the *Shurgard* court, how did the defendant "damage" plaintiff's computer network or information? What is the defendant's position? Is the legislative history cited by the court relevant to interpreting "damage" under Section 1030(a)(5)? Does the court's interpretation of the CFAA protect against hacking or does it create a new property right in information?

3. What are the consequences, if any, of adopting the defendant's interpretation of damages under Section 1030(a)(5)? Would the plaintiff still have a claim against the defendant? A private cause of action?

4. What other kinds of "damage" might be covered by the CFAA? Might the use of cookies on private computers to obtain personally identifying information and spending preferences of users give rise to a claim for damages under the CFAA? The court in In re DoubleClick Inc. Privacy Litigation, 154 F. Supp. 2d 497 (S.D.N.Y. 2001), held that such activities did not satisfy the "damage or loss" requirements of the 1996 version of the CFAA:

> as counsel demonstrated at oral argument, users may easily and at no cost prevent DoubleClick from collecting information by simply selecting options on their browsers or downloading an "opt-out" cookie from DoubleClick's Web site. . . . Similarly, they have not pled that DoubleClick caused any damage whatsoever to plaintiffs' computers, systems or data that could require economic remedy. Thus, these remedial economic losses are insignificant if, indeed, they exist at all.
>
> Plaintiffs also contend that they have suffered economic damages consisting of the value of: (1) the opportunity to present plaintiffs with advertising; and (2) the demographic information DoubleClick has collected. . . . Essentially, they argue that because companies pay DoubleClick for plaintiffs' attention (to advertisements) and demographic information, the value of these services must, in some part, have rightfully belonged to plaintiffs. . . .
>
> Even assuming that the economic value of plaintiffs' attention and demographic information could be counted towards the monetary threshold—a dubious assumption—it would still be insufficient. We do not commonly believe that the economic value of our attention is unjustly taken from us when we choose to watch a television show or read a newspaper with advertisements and we are unaware of any statute or caselaw that holds it is. We see no reason why Web site advertising should be treated any differently. A person who chooses to visit a Web page and is confronted by a targeted advertisement is no more deprived of his attention's economic value than are his off-line peers. Similarly, although demographic information is valued highly (as DoubleClick undoubtedly believed when it paid over one billion dollars for Abacus), the value of its collection has never been considered a economic loss to the subject. Demographic information is constantly collected on all consumers by marketers, mail-order catalogues and retailers. However, we are unaware of any court that has held the value of this collected information constitutes damage to consumers or unjust enrichment to collectors. Therefore, it appears to us that plaintiffs have failed to state any facts that could support a finding of economic loss from DoubleClick's alleged violation of the CFAA. [The facts of this case and the court's discussion of claims raised under the ECPA are excerpted in Chapter 5—EDS.]

Do you agree that this is not the kind of damage or loss that should be compensated under the CFAA? Is this approach to damage under the

CFAA consistent with the discussion of damage in *Shurgard*? In *DoubleClick*, the court notes that the plaintiffs could easily have prevented DoubleClick from accessing their computers by setting their browsers to reject cookies. Does the CFAA require a "victim" to take such self-help measures? Is it possible to argue that in the absence of such measures, courts should imply authorization?

5.   What if the defendant's acts do not affect the information stored on a computer at all, but simply occupy space or computer processing?

MOULTON v. VC3

2000 WL 33310901 (N.D. Ga. Nov. 7, 2000)

[In *Moulton*, the plaintiff, a computer contractor for the county's 911 center, performed security tests on the City of Canton Police Department's computer networks without the authorization of the Department. Moulton was allegedly concerned about the Department's security following discussions with the defendant, a computer contractor hired by the City of Canton. As a result, he "performed a series of remote access tests on Defendant's servers. These tests included a port scan and a throughput test. A port scan is a method of checking a computer to see what ports are open by trying to establish a connection to each and every port on the target computer. If used by a network administrator on his own network, the scan is a method of determining any possible security weaknesses. If used by an outsider, the scan indicates whether a particular port is used and can be probed for weakness. A throughput test sends information across a network to test the speed with which a computer processes data." At no time did Moulton otherwise gain access to the Department's computers or information. After he was subsequently arrested for this testing, he brought suit against the defendant, and the defendant counterclaimed against Moulton for violations of Georgia's Computer Systems Protection Act and the 1996 version of the CFAA.]

THRASH, D.J. . . .

III.   DISCUSSION

4.   Georgia Computer Systems Protection Act

Defendant also brings a claim under the Georgia Computer Systems Protection Act. O.C.G.A. §16-6-90 *et seq.* This criminal statute makes illegal the use of a computer with the intention of "obstructing, interrupting, or in any way interfering with the use of a computer program or data; or altering, damaging or in any way causing the malfunction of a computer, computer network, or computer program, regardless of how long the alteration, damage, or malfunction persists." O.C.G.A. §16-9-93(b)(2) and (3). When damage results from the criminal activity, the section also authorizes a civil suit for monetary recovery. O.C.G.A. §16-9-93(g). According to the Court's research, no case construing the section exists. The Court holds that Defendant does not have a civil damages claim for violation of the Computer Systems Protection Act. Defendant argues that Plaintiff Moulton's activities constituted a violation of the Computer Systems Protection Act because a throughput test and a ping flood can slow down a network. In this way, Defendant asserts, Plaintiff Moulton's actions "interfered" with Defendant's network. However, Defendant itself admits that any slow down was negligible at best and not noticeable to the company or its customers. . . . No reasonable jury could conclude that this constituted interfering with Defendant's network. Additionally, Defendant argues that it does not matter that the slow down was not noticeable because the statute states that an activity in violation of the statute can be actionable no matter how long it persists. However, the language that allows a claim for actions that are not noticeable to the victim apply only to activities which alter, damage or malfunction a network. There is no evidence that Plaintiff Moulton's activities resulted in any alteration, damage or malfunction of Defendant's network. . . .

5. Computer Fraud and Abuse Act

Finally, Plaintiffs seek summary judgment on Defendant's claim for violation of the Computer Fraud and Abuse Act. The Act forbids the "intentional . . . accessing [of] a protected computer without authorization, [that] as a result of such conduct, recklessly causes damage." 18 U.S.C. §1030(a)(5)(B). There is a dispute over whether the Defendant can make out the element of damage. Damage is defined in the Act as "any impairment to the integrity or availability of data, a program, a system, or information. . . ." 18 U.S.C. §1030(e)(8). . . . However, this damage does not fit the statutory definition of damage. Defendant agrees that no structural damage to their network resulted from Plaintiff's activities. The statute clearly states that the damage must be an impairment to the *integrity* and *availability* of the network. Defendant's network security was never actually compromised and no program or information was ever unavailable as a result of Plaintiff Moulton's activities. . . . Therefore, Defendant can not make out the damage element for a claim pursuant to the Computer Fraud and Abuse Act. Plaintiff's Motion for Summary Judgment is granted as to this claim.

AMERICA ONLINE, INC. v. NATIONAL HEALTH CARE DISCOUNT, INC.

121 F. Supp. 2d 1255 (N.D. Iowa 2000)

Zoss, United States Magistrate Judge. . . .

AOL is a Delaware corporation, with its principal place of business in Virginia. AOL provides a variety of services to its customers, or "members," as they are called by AOL. These services include the transmission of electronic mail ("e-mail") to and from other members and across the Internet.

NHCD is an Iowa corporation with administrative offices in Sioux City, Iowa, and sales offices in Atlanta, Kansas City, Phoenix, Dallas, and Denver. NHCD is engaged in the business of selling discount optical and dental service plans. NHCD membership entitles members to discounts from participating dentists and optical care providers.

This lawsuit concerns advertising via the Internet. . . . These messages, called "unsolicited bulk e-mail" or "UBE," are often referred to pejoratively as "junk e-mail" or "spam." It is undisputed that at times relevant to this lawsuit, a large volume of e-mail messages was sent through AOL's computer system to generate leads for NHCD's products.

AOL has put in place various "filtering programs" in an attempt to block UBE. By using these programs, AOL attempts to identify UBE coming into AOL's computer systems so that it can be rejected. These filtering programs have had only limited success, however, because bulk e-mailers have developed counter-programs to thwart the filtering programs. . . .

AOL has adopted policies applicable to its members in an effort to prevent them from sending UBE over AOL's computer system or from facilitating the sending of UBE over AOL's computer system by others. As bulk e-mail has become increasingly problematic, AOL's policies have been revised and strengthened to make it clear that members are not authorized to use AOL for bulk e-mail purposes. . . .

AOL argues the evidence in this case is sufficient to establish NHCD's liability to AOL under the Computer Fraud and Abuse Act, 18 U.S.C. §1030 *et seq.* Specifically, AOL argues NHCD violated 18 U.S.C. §§1030(a)(5) and (a)(2)(C). . . .

The elements of a civil claim under section 1030(a)(5)(C) are as follows: (1) the person or entity must intentionally access a computer; (2) the computer must be a "protected computer"; (3) the access must be without authorization; and (4) the access must cause damage. There is no question that AOL's computers are "protected computers." However, it remains for the court to determine whether NHCD's contract e-mailers intentionally accessed AOL's computers, whether any such access was "without authorization," and whether such access caused damage to AOL.

The CFAA does not define "access," but the general definition of the word, as a transitive verb, is to "gain access to." MERRIAM-WEBSTER'S COLLEGIATE DICTIONARY (hereinafter "Webster's") 6 (10th ed. 1994). As a noun, "access," in this context, means to exercise the "freedom or ability to . . . make use of" something. *Id.* The question here, therefore, is whether NHCD's e-mailers, by harvesting e-mail addresses of AOL members and then sending the members UBE messages, exercised the freedom or ability to make use of AOL's computers. The court finds they did. For purposes of the CFAA, when someone sends an e-mail message from his or her own computer, and the message then is transmitted through a number of other computers until it reaches its destination, the sender is making use of all of those computers, and is therefore "accessing" them. This is precisely what NHCD's e-mailers did with respect to AOL's computers.

The next disputed element of AOL's claim under section 1030(a)(5)(C) is whether the access was "without authorization." Again, the CFAA . . . gives no direct guidance on the meaning of the phrase "without authorization." In a case similar factually to the present one, the United States District Court for the Eastern District of Virginia found an e-mailer's actions constituted "unauthorized access" because they violated AOL's Terms of Service. *See America Online, Inc. v. LCGM, Inc.*, 46 F. Supp. 2d 444, 450-51 (E.D. Va. 1998); *see also Hotmail Corp. v. Van$ Money Pie, Inc.*, 1998 WL 388389 (N.D. Cal. Apr. 16, 1998). No other reported opinion contains precisely this interpretation of the statute.

Although AOL clearly advised its members they were not authorized to harvest member e-mail addresses from its system or to use its system to send UBE to its members . . . it is not clear that a violation of AOL's membership agreements results in "unauthorized access." If AOL members are "insiders" rather than "outsiders" for purposes of section 1030(a)(5), then subparagraph (C) does not apply at all, and this inquiry ends for purposes of AOL's motion. . . . AOL members, such as Dayton, obviously have "authorization" to access the AOL network. Having done so, is a member's authorized access converted into unauthorized access when the member violates one of the terms and conditions of membership? Similarly, is the member converted from an "insider" to an "outsider" for purposes of the CFAA by violating AOL's policies? On the other hand, if AOL members are "outsiders," then why would AOL's membership policies apply to them at all? Furthermore, by imposing restrictions on its members, can AOL deny or restrict the rights of non-member Internet users with respect to sending any type or volume of e-mail to AOL members, including UBE? These unanswered questions represent mixed issues of fact and law, requiring further factual development before the court can rule. This record is not clear enough on these issues for the court to grant summary judgment.

Even assuming *arguendo* that NHCD's e-mailers accessed AOL's system "without authorization," the question still remains whether such access caused AOL "damage" for purposes of the CFAA. . . .

Section 1030(e)(8)(A) provides, in relevant part: "the term 'damage' means any *impairment* to the *integrity* or *availability* of *data*, a *program*, a *system*, or *information*. . . ." . . . [I]t can be concluded that when a large volume of UBE causes slowdowns or diminishes the capacity of AOL to serve its customers, an "impairment" has occurred to the "availability" of AOL's "system."

. . .

A disturbing issue is whether subsection (a)(5)(c) is intended to address UBE at all. The original statute, enacted in 1984, was directed at protecting classified information in government computer systems, and protecting financial records and credit histories in financial institution computers. *See* S. Rep. No. 99-432, at §I (1986 W.L. 31918), 1986 U.S.C.C.A.N. 2479 (discussing the 1986 amendments to the statute). When the statute was amended in 1986, the Senate Judiciary Committee expressly rejected the approach of enacting a comprehensive, sweeping statute that would leave "no computer crime . . . potentially uncovered," opting instead "to limit Federal jurisdiction over computer crime to those cases in which there is a compelling Federal interest, *i.e.*, where computers of the Federal Government or certain financial institutions are involved, or where the crime itself is interstate in nature." *Id.*

The statute provided only criminal penalties until enactment of the Computer Abuse Amendments Act of 1994, which added the civil remedies subsection 1030(g). *See* S. Rep. No. 104-357, §IV(1)(E) (1996 W.L. 492169) ("1996 S. Rep."); H.R. Conf. Rep. No. 103-711, §290001(d) (1994 W.L. 454841), 1994 U.S.C.C.A.N. 1839. At the same time, subsection 1030(a)(5) was amended "to further protect computers and computer systems covered by the statute from damage both by outsiders, who gain access to a computer without authorization, and by insiders, who intentionally damage a computer." In discussing the amendments to subsection (a)(5), the Senate Judiciary Committee noted:

> In sum, under the bill, insiders, who are authorized to access a computer, face criminal liability only if they intend to cause damage to the computer, not for recklessly or negligently causing damage. By contrast, outside hackers who break into a computer could be punished for any intentional, reckless, or other damage they cause by their trespass.

1996 S. Rep., §IV(1)(E). AOL does not claim NHCD's e-mailers were "outside hackers," or that NHCD "intend[ed] to cause damage to the computer." Rather, NHCD's e-mailers (or at least Dayton) were members of AOL, accessing AOL's system as a result of that membership. Realistically, no federal statute currently exists which would prohibit a non-AOL member from sending UBE to any number of AOL members' e-mail addresses, without ever accessing AOL directly. . . .

In Count III of its Complaint, AOL claims NHCD violated the Virginia Computer Crimes Act, Virginia Code Annotated §18.2-152.1 *et seq.* ("VCCA"), specifically section 18.2-152.3, which provides:

> Any person who uses a computer or computer network without authority and with the intent to: . . .
>   (3) Convert the property of another shall be guilty of the crime of computer fraud. . . .

Va. Code Ann. §18.2-152.3 (1999). The VCCA provides a civil remedy in section 18.2-152.12, for the recovery of damages. The section provides its remedies are in addition to other available civil remedies, and prescribes damages applicable to AOL's claim, as follows:

> If the injury arises from the transmission of unsolicited bulk electronic mail, an injured electronic mail service provider may also [in addition to damages and costs of suit] recover attorneys' fees and costs, and may elect, in lieu of actual damages, to recover the greater of ten dollars for each and every unsolicited bulk electronic mail message transmitted in violation of this article, or $25,000 per day.

Va. Code Ann. §18.2-152.12(C) (1999).

Application of the VCCA to the facts of this case is a simpler matter than application of the CFAA, largely because of the VCCA's specific definition of relevant terms. The Virginia statute seems to have been crafted for just the type of injury alleged by AOL in this case. The statute specifically defines "without authority" as follows:

> A person is "without authority" when (i) he has no right or permission of the owner to use a computer *or he uses a computer in a manner exceeding such right or permission or (ii) he uses a computer, a computer network, or the computer services of an electronic mail service provider to transmit unsolicited bulk electronic mail in contravention of the authority granted by or in violation of the policies set by the electronic mail service provider.*

Va. Stat. Ann. §18.2-152.2 (1999) (emphasis added).

The court finds Dayton and other e-mailers violated the Virginia statute; however, they are not parties to this lawsuit. Whether NHCD is liable for Dayton's actions still remains to be determined, as discussed below. If NHCD is liable for its e-mailers' actions, then AOL is entitled to summary judgment on this claim, with damages to be determined at trial.

COMMENTS AND QUESTIONS

1. In *Moulton*, how did Moulton allegedly damage the police department's computers? Did the court accept this view of damage?

2. In *America Online*, how did the unsolicited mail allegedly damage AOL's computer network? Should reduced network speeds be considered damage?

3. According to the court in *America Online*, does a violation of a network's terms of service constitute unauthorized use? What argument can be made that such a violation should not be considered a lack of authorization? Does *DoubleClick* provide an answer? *See also* Register.com v. Verio, Inc., 126 F. Supp. 2d 238 (S.D.N.Y. 2000) (concluding that violation of terms of use constituted unauthorized use).

4. Why does the court in *American Online* suggest that, "[r]ealistically, no federal statute currently exists which would prohibit a non-AOL member from sending UBE to any number of AOL members' e-mail addresses, without

ever accessing AOL directly"? What difference does it make whether the sender is a member of AOL or not? Subsequently, Congress has enacted the CAN-SPAM Act of 2003. ("CAN-SPAM" stands for "Controlling the Assault of Non-Solicited Pornography and Marketing".) This legislation creates civil and criminal sanctions related to spam. It also requires spammers to include accurate e-mail transmission information and identification of their physical location, as well as provisions for recipients of unwanted e-mails to opt-out of further mailings. The provisions of the CAN-SPAM Act can be enforced by a combination of federal agencies, including the Federal Trade Commission and the Department of Justice. Although the legislation has been criticized for not having the preventative impact on spam that some people had hoped for,[1] the Federal Trade Commission issued a report in December of 2005, suggesting that overall the legislation has made some significant inroads into the spam problem, including creating e-mail "best practices" that legitimate commercial e-mail services are now adopting and providing a useful tool against spam to law enforcement agencies and Internet service providers: Federal Trade Commission, Effectiveness and Enforcement of the CAN-SPAM Act (December 2005), available at *http://www.ftc.gov/reports/canspam05/051220canspamrpt.pdf.*

5.   Are there circumstances when we may not want Internet service providers or other network owners to block unsolicited e-mail? Do we object to presidential and other political candidates sending bulk unsolicited e-mails? Or subscribers who were unhappy with an ISP's services?

6.   Other than *Morris* and *Shurgard*, is there an argument that the CFAA is not applicable to any of the other cases? On what grounds? Consider the argument that the question of damages is inextricably combined with the question of whether the computer owner has a property right in information. *See* Maureen A. O'Rourke, *Shaping Competition on the Internet: Who Owns Product and Pricing Information?* 53 Vand. L. Rev. 1965, 1992 (2000) (arguing that the CFAA should not be used "to deal with developing issues in e-commerce"). Consider the issue of *sui generis* protection for information. Could the CFAA be used in lieu of a property right to protect factual compilations contained in computer databases? A privacy right in clickstream data? How would you make such an argument?

B. COMMON LAW TRESPASS

In addition to the protection provided by the Computer Fraud and Abuse Act and its state law equivalents, can computer owners assert property interests akin to those of real property owners? Can unauthorized access be considered trespass? Trotter Hardy, for example, argues that common law principles of

---

1. *See, e.g.,* discussion in Peter Maggs et al., *Internet and Computer Law* 476 (2005) (suggesting that the CAN-SPAM Act has been a "total failure" and that the amount of spam e-mails has increased steadily since the passage of the Act).

trespass to real property should be applied to Web sites. *See* I. Trotter Hardy, *The Ancient Doctrine of Trespass to Web Sites*, 1996 J. Online L. art. 7. According to Hardy, by considering Web sites a species of property, trespass is a more "straightforward and intuitively sensible means of controlling access to 'sites,'" than copyright. What does the principle of trespass add to regulating information in cyberspace? Is it a useful idea, or an anachronism in a world made up of electrons? How does property in cyberspace differ from real space?

1. Access to Users

Before examining this question in the context of cyberspace, consider the following cases discussing the limits of land owners' rights to control access to their property. To what extent does a land owner's bundle of rights include the right to exclude others from communicating on real property? How should these rights be applied, if at all, to Web sites and computer networks?

a) Real Property Cases

MARSH v. ALABAMA

326 U.S. 501 (1946)

Mr. Justice BLACK delivered the opinion of the Court.

In this case we are asked to decide whether a State, consistently with the First and Fourteenth Amendments, can impose criminal punishment on a person who undertakes to distribute religious literature on the premises of a company-owned town contrary to the wishes of the town's management. The town, a suburb of Mobile, Alabama, known as Chickasaw, is owned by the Gulf Shipbuilding Corporation. Except for that it has all the characteristics of any other American town. . . . There is nothing to stop highway traffic from coming onto the business block and upon arrival a traveler may make free use of the facilities available there. In short the town and its shopping district are accessible to and freely used by the public in general and there is nothing to distinguish them from any other town and shopping center except the fact that the title to the property belongs to a private corporation.

Appellant, a Jehovah's Witness, came onto the sidewalk we have just described, stood near the post-office and undertook to distribute religious literature. In the stores the corporation had posted a notice which read as follows: "This Is Private Property, and Without Written Permission, No Street, or House Vendor, Agent or Solicitation of Any Kind Will Be Permitted." Appellant was warned that she could not distribute the literature without a permit and told that no permit would be issued to her. She protested that the company rule could not be constitutionally applied so as to prohibit her from distributing religious writings. When she was asked to leave the sidewalk and Chickasaw she declined. The deputy sheriff arrested her and she was charged in the state court with violating Title 14, Section 426 of the 1940 Alabama Code which makes it a crime to enter or remain on the premises of another after having been warned not to do so. Appellant contended that to construe the state statute as applicable to her activities would abridge her right to freedom of press and religion contrary to the First and Fourteenth Amendments to the Constitution. This contention was rejected and she was convicted. . . .

We do not agree that the corporation's property interests settle the question. The State urges in effect that the corporation's right to control the inhabitants of Chickasaw is coextensive with the right of a homeowner to regulate the conduct of his guests. We can not accept that contention. Ownership does not always mean absolute dominion. The more an owner, for his advantage, opens up his property for use by the public in general, the more do his rights become circumscribed by the statutory and constitutional rights of those who use it. . . . Thus, the owners of privately held bridges, ferries, turnpikes and railroads may not operate them as freely as a farmer does his farm. Since these facilities are built and operated primarily to benefit the public and since their operation is essentially a public function, it is subject to state regulation. . . .

Many people in the United States live in company-owned towns. These people, just as residents of municipalities, are free citizens of their State and country. Just as all other citizens they must make decisions which affect the welfare of community and nation. To act as good citizens they must be informed. In order to enable them to be properly informed their information must be uncensored. There is no more reason for depriving these people of the liberties guaranteed by the First and Fourteenth Amendments than there is for curtailing these freedoms with respect to any other citizen.

When we balance the Constitutional rights of owners of property against those of the people to enjoy freedom of press and religion, as we must here, we remain mindful of the fact that the latter occupy a preferred position. As we have stated before, the right to exercise the liberties safeguarded by the First Amendment "lies at the foundation of free government by free men" and we must in all cases "weigh the circumstances and appraise . . . the reasons . . . in support of the regulation of (those) rights." Schneider v. State, 308 U.S. 147, 161. In our view the circumstance that the property rights to the premises where the deprivation of liberty, here involved, took place, were held by others than the public, is not sufficient to justify the State's permitting a corporation to govern a community of citizens so as to restrict their fundamental liberties and the enforcement of such restraint by the application of a State statute. Insofar as the State has attempted to impose criminal punishment on appellant for undertaking to distribute religious literature in a company town, its action cannot stand. The case is reversed and the cause remanded for further proceedings not inconsistent with this opinion.

Reversed and remanded.

Mr. Justice JACKSON took no part in the consideration or decision of this case.

[Concurring opinion of Justice FRANKFURTER omitted.]

Mr. Justice REED, dissenting.

... A state does have the moral duty of furnishing the opportunity for information, education and religious enlightenment to its inhabitants, including those who live in company towns, but it has not heretofore been adjudged that it must commandeer, without compensation, the private property of other citizens to carry out that obligation. ...

Our Constitution guarantees to every man the right to express his views in an orderly fashion. An essential element of "orderly" is that the man shall also have a right to use the place he chooses for his exposition. The rights of the owner, which the Constitution protects as well as the right of free speech, are not outweighed by the interests of the trespasser, even though he trespasses in behalf of religion or free speech. We cannot say that Jehovah's Witnesses can claim the privilege of a license, which has never been granted, to hold their meetings in other private places, merely because the owner has admitted the public to them for other limited purposes. Even though we have reached the point where this Court is required to force private owners to open their property for the practice there of religious activities or propaganda distasteful to the owner, because of the public interest in freedom of speech and religion, there is no need for the application of such a doctrine here. Appellant, as we have said, was free to engage in such practices on the public highways, without becoming a trespasser on the company's property.

The CHIEF JUSTICE and Mr. Justice BURTON join in this dissent.

COMMENTS AND QUESTIONS

1. Justice Black states that ownership of property "does not always mean absolute dominion." What does this statement acknowledge? How else is the dominion of a landowner circumscribed?

2. Why is the company in this instance denied the right to control how its property will be used? Is it because it is the functional equivalent of a municipality? Because it opened its property to third parties? Because the right to speak was at issue?

3. *Marsh* is often interpreted for the proposition that when private property serves a "public function" it becomes subject to state regulation. Does state regulation necessarily mean constitutional regulation? The Constitution's protection of freedom of speech only applies to state actors. Does opening

one's property to the public make one a state actor? Reconsider the Supreme Court's decision in *PruneYard* in Chapter 3.

4. If, as Justice Black suggests, freedom of expression and religion occupy a preferred place in our Constitution, why does Justice Reed dissent? What other interests are also protected by the Constitution?

5. *Marsh* could be considered a unique case in which a private property owner actually owned the entire town; what other circumstances might justify limiting the property owner's right to control access? Consider Justice Marshall's conclusion that the owner of a shopping mall could not prohibit picketing on mall property:

> The economic development of the United States in the last 20 years reinforces our opinion of the correctness of the approach taken in *Marsh*. The largescale movement of this country's population from the cities to the suburbs has been accompanied by the advent of the suburban shopping center, typically a cluster of individual retail units on a single large privately owned tract. . . .
>
> These figures illustrate the substantial consequences for workers seeking to challenge substandard working conditions, consumers protesting shoddy or overpriced merchandise, and minority groups seeking nondiscriminatory hiring policies that a contrary decision here would have. Business enterprises located in downtown areas would be subject to on-the-spot public criticism for their practices, but businesses situated in the suburbs could largely immunize themselves from similar criticism by creating a cordon sanitaire of parking lots around their stores. Neither precedent nor policy compels a result so at variance with the goal of free expression and communication that is the heart of the First Amendment.
>
> Therefore, as to the sufficiency of respondents' ownership of the Logan Valley Mall premises as the sole support of the injunction issued against petitioners, we simply repeat what was said in Marsh v. State of Alabama, 326 U.S. at 506, "Ownership does not always mean absolute dominion. The more an owner, for his advantage, opens up his property for use by the public in general, the more do his rights become circumscribed by the statutory and constitutional rights of those who use it." Logan Valley Mall is the functional equivalent of a "business block" and for First Amendment purposes must be treated in substantially the same manner.

Amalgamated Food Employees Union Local 590 v. Logan Valley Plaza, Inc., 391 U.S. 308, 324-25 (1968). *Logan Valley* was subsequently overruled in Hudgens v. N.L.R.B., 424 U.S. 507, 518 (1976).

STATE V. SHACK

58 N.J. 297 (1971)

WEINTRAUB, C.J.

Defendants entered upon private property to aid migrant farmworkers employed and housed there. Having refused to depart upon the demand of the owner, defendants were charged with [criminal trespass]. . . .

Complainant, Tedesco, a farmer, employs migrant workers for his seasonal needs. As part of their compensation, these workers are housed at a camp on his property.

Defendant Tejeras is a field worker for the Farm Workers Division of the Southwest Citizens Organization for Poverty Elimination, known by the acronym SCOPE, a nonprofit corporation funded by the Office of Economic Opportunity. . . . The role of SCOPE includes providing for the "health services of the migrant farm worker."

Defendant Shack is a staff attorney with the Farm Workers Division of Camden Regional Legal Services, Inc., known as "CRLS," also a nonprofit corporation funded by the Office of Economic Opportunity. . . . The mission of CRLS includes legal advice and representation for these workers.

Differences had developed between Tedesco and these defendants prior to the events which led to the trespass charges now before us. Hence when defendant Tejeras wanted to go upon Tedesco's farm to find a migrant worker who needed medical aid for the removal of 28 sutures, he called upon defendant Shack for his help with respect to the legalities involved. Shack, too, had a mission to perform on Tedesco's farm; he wanted to discuss a legal problem with another migrant worker there employed and housed. Defendants arranged to go to the farm together. Shack carried literature to inform the migrant farmworkers of the assistance available to them under federal statutes, but no mention seems to have been made of that literature when Shack was later confronted by Tedesco.

Defendants entered upon Tedesco's property and as they neared the camp site where the farmworkers were housed, they were confronted by Tedesco who inquired of their purpose. Tejeras and Shack stated their missions. In response, Tedesco offered to find the injured worker, and as to the worker who needed legal advice, Tedesco also offered to locate the man but insisted that the consultation would have to take place in Tedesco's office and in his presence. Defendants declined, saying they had the right to see the men in the privacy of their living quarters and without Tedesco's supervision. Tedesco thereupon summoned a State Trooper who, however, refused to remove defendants except upon Tedesco's written complaint. Tedesco then executed the formal complaints charging violations of the trespass statute.

I.

The constitutionality of the trespass statute, as applied here, is challenged on several scores.

It is urged that the First Amendment rights of the defendants and of the migrant farmworkers were thereby offended. Reliance is placed on Marsh v. Alabama, 326 U.S. 501 (1946), where it was held that free speech was assured by the First Amendment in a company-owned town which was open to the public generally and was indistinguishable from any other town except for the fact that the title to the property was vested in a private corporation. Hence a Jehovah's Witness who distributed literature on a sidewalk within the town could not be held as a trespasser. Later, on the strength of that case, it was held that there was a First Amendment right to picket peacefully in a privately owned shopping center which was found to be the functional equivalent of the business district of the company-owned town in *Marsh*. Amalgamated Food Employees Union Local 590 v. Logan Valley Plaza, Inc., 391 U.S. 308 (1968). See, to the same effect, the earlier case of Schwartz-Torrance Investment Corp. v. Bakery and Confectionery Workers' Union, 61 Cal. 2d 766, 40 Cal. Rptr. 233 (Sup. Ct. 1964), cert. denied, 380 U.S. 906 (1964). Those cases rest upon the fact that the property was in fact opened to the general public. There may be some migrant camps with the attributes of the company town in *Marsh* and of course they would come within its holding. But there is nothing of that character in the case before us, and hence there would have to be an extension of *Marsh* to embrace the immediate situation. . . .

These constitutional claims are not established by any definitive holding. We think it unnecessary to explore their validity. The reason is that we are satisfied that under our State law the ownership of real property does not include the right to bar access to governmental services available to migrant workers and hence there was no trespass within the meaning of the penal statute. The policy considerations which underlie that conclusion may be much the same as those which would be weighed with respect to one or more of the constitutional challenges, but a decision in nonconstitutional terms is more satisfactory, because the interests of migrant workers are more expansively served in that way than they would be if they had no more freedom than these constitutional concepts could be found to mandate if indeed they apply at all.

II.

Property rights serve human values. They are recognized to that end, and are limited by it. Title to real property cannot include dominion over the destiny of persons the owner permits to come upon the premises. Their well-being must remain the paramount concern of a system of law. Indeed the needs of the occupants may be so imperative and their strength so weak that the law will deny the occupants the power to contract away what is deemed essential to their health, welfare, or dignity.

Here we are concerned with a highly disadvantaged segment of our society. We are told that every year farmworkers and their families numbering more than one million leave their home areas to fill the seasonal demand for farm labor in the United States. . . . The migrant farmworkers come to New Jersey in substantial numbers. . . .

The migrant farmworkers are a community within but apart from the local scene. They are rootless and isolated. Although the need for their labors is evident, they are unorganized and without economic or political power. It is their plight alone that summoned government to their aid. In response, Congress provided under Title III-B of the Economic Opportunity Act of

1964 (42 U.S.C.A. §2701 et seq.) for "assistance for migrant and other seasonally employed farmworkers and their families." Section 2861 states "the purpose of this part is to assist migrant and seasonal farmworkers and their families to improve their living conditions and develop skills necessary for a productive and self-sufficient life in an increasingly complex and technological society." Section 2862(b)(1) provides for funding of programs "to meet the immediate needs of migrant and seasonal farmworkers and their families, such as day care for children, education, health services, improved housing and sanitation (including the provision and maintenance of emergency and temporary housing and sanitation facilities), legal advice and representation, and consumer training and counseling." As we have said, SCOPE is engaged in a program funded under this section, and CRLS also pursues the objectives of this section although, we gather, it is funded under §2809(a)(3), which is not limited in its concern to the migrant and other seasonally employed farmworkers and seeks "to further the cause of justice among persons living in poverty by mobilizing the assistance of lawyers and legal institutions and by providing legal advice, legal representation, counseling, education, and other appropriate services."

These ends would not be gained if the intended beneficiaries could be insulated from efforts to reach them. It is in this framework that we must decide whether the camp operator's rights in his lands may stand between the migrant workers and those who would aid them. The key to that aid is communication. Since the migrant workers are outside the mainstream of the communities in which they are housed and are unaware of their rights and opportunities and of the services available to them, they can be reached only by positive efforts tailored to that end. . . .

A man's right in his real property of course is not absolute. It was a maxim of the common law that one should so use his property as not to injure the rights of others. Broom, Legal Maxims (10th ed. Kersley 1939), p. 238; 39 Words and Phrases, "Sic Utere Tuo ut Alienum Non Laedas," p. 335. Although hardly a precise solvent of actual controversies, the maxim does express the inevitable proposition that rights are relative and there must be an accommodation when they meet. Hence it has long been true that necessity, private or public, may justify entry upon the lands of another. For a catalogue of such situations, see Prosser, Torts (3d ed. 1964), §24, pp. 127-129; 6A American Law of Property (A. J. Casner ed. 1954) §28.10, p. 31; 52 Am. Jur., "Trespass," §§40-41, pp. 867-869. See also Restatement, Second, Torts (1965) §§197-211; Krauth v. Geller, 31 N.J. 270, 272-273, 157 A.2d 129 (1960).

The subject is not static. . . . The process involves not only the accommodation between the right of the owner and the interests of the general public in his use of this property, but involves also an accommodation between the right of the owner and the right of individuals who are parties with him in consensual transactions relating to the use of the property. Accordingly substantial alterations have been made as between a landlord and his tenant. See Reste Realty

Corp. v. Cooper, 53 N.J. 444, 451-453, 251 A.2d 268 (1969); Marini v. Ireland, 56 N.J. 130, 141-143, 265 A.2d 526 (1970).

The argument in this case understandably included the question whether the migrant worker should be deemed to be a tenant and thus entitled to the tenant's right to receive visitors . . . or whether his residence on the employer's property should be deemed to be merely incidental and in aid of his employment, and hence to involve no possessory interest in the realty. . . .

We see no profit in trying to decide upon a conventional category and then forcing the present subject into it. That approach would be artificial and distorting. The quest is for a fair adjustment of the competing needs of the parties, in the light of the realities of the relationship between the migrant worker and the operator of the housing facility.

Thus approaching the case, we find it unthinkable that the farmer-employer can assert a right to isolate the migrant worker in any respect significant for the worker's well-being. The farmer, of course, is entitled to pursue his farming activities without interference, and this defendants readily concede. But we see no legitimate need for a right in the farmer to deny the worker the opportunity for aid available from federal, State, or local services, or from recognized charitable groups seeking to assist him. Hence representatives of these agencies and organizations may enter upon the premises to seek out the worker at his living quarters. So, too, the migrant worker must be allowed to receive visitors there of his own choice, so long as there is no behavior hurtful to others, and members of the press may not be denied reasonable access to workers who do not object to seeing them.

It is not our purpose to open the employer's premises to the general public if in fact the employer himself has not done so. We do not say, for example, that solicitors or peddlers of all kinds may enter on their own; we may assume "for" the present that the employer may regulate their entry or bar them, at least if the employer's purpose is not to gain a commercial advantage for himself or if the regulation does not deprive the migrant worker of practical access to things he needs.

And we are mindful of the employer's interest in his own and in his employees' security. Hence he may reasonably require a visitor to identify himself, and also to state his general purpose if the migrant worker has not already informed him that the visitor is expected. But the employer may not deny the worker his privacy or interfere with his opportunity to live with dignity and to enjoy associations customary among our citizens. These rights are too fundamental to be denied on the basis of an interest in real property and too fragile to be left to the unequal bargaining strength of the parties. . . .

It follows that defendants here invaded no possessory right of the farmer-employer. Their conduct was therefore beyond the reach of the trespass statute. The judgments are accordingly reversed and the matters remanded to the County Court with directions to enter judgments of acquittal.

COMMENTS AND QUESTIONS

1. Unlike *Marsh*, *Shack* does not rely upon the Constitution, but instead interprets the common law rights of property owners. According to the court, why is this a more satisfactory means of analysis? Could the U.S. Supreme Court have taken this approach?

2. According to *Shack*, why does the farmer have no possessory right in this context?

3. In reaching its conclusion, the court relies upon the common law maxim that property should not be used to injure the rights of others. How did Tedesco use his property to injure his farmworkers? Did Tedesco actually isolate his employees from the outside world, from aid workers, or their families?

4. Under the court's reasoning in *Shack*, are farm owners required to allow Jehovah's Witnesses onto their land?

5. As you study the following Internet cases, consider whether *Marsh* and *Shack* have any place in cyberspace.

b) Internet Cases

COMPUSERVE, INC. v. CYBER PROMOTIONS, INC.

962 F. Supp. 1015 (S.D. Ohio 1997)

GRAHAM, District Judge.

This case presents novel issues regarding the commercial use of the Internet, specifically the right of an on-line computer service to prevent a commercial enterprise from sending unsolicited electronic mail advertising to its subscribers.

Plaintiff CompuServe Incorporated ("CompuServe") is one of the major national commercial on-line computer services. It operates a computer communication service through a proprietary nationwide computer network. In addition to allowing access to the extensive content available within its own proprietary network, CompuServe also provides its subscribers with a link to the much larger resources of the Internet. This allows its subscribers to send and receive electronic messages, known as "e-mail," by the Internet. Defendants Cyber Promotions, Inc. and its president Sanford Wallace are in the business of sending unsolicited e-mail advertisements on behalf of themselves and their clients to hundreds of thousands of Internet users, many of whom are CompuServe subscribers. CompuServe has notified defendants that they are prohibited from using its computer equipment to process and store the unsolicited e-mail and has requested that they terminate the practice. Instead, defendants have sent an increasing volume of e-mail solicitations to CompuServe subscribers. CompuServe has attempted to employ technological means to block the flow of defendants' e-mail transmissions to its computer equipment, but to no avail. . . .

I.

... Internet users often pay a fee for Internet access. However, there is no per-message charge to send electronic messages over the Internet and such messages usually reach their destination within minutes. Thus electronic mail provides an opportunity to reach a wide audience quickly and at almost no cost to the sender. It is not surprising therefore that some companies, like defendant Cyber Promotions, Inc., have begun using the Internet to distribute advertisements by sending the same unsolicited commercial message to hundreds of thousands of Internet users at once. Defendants refer to this as "bulk e-mail," while plaintiff refers to it as "junk e-mail." In the vernacular of the Internet, unsolicited e-mail advertising is sometimes referred to pejoratively as "spam." . . .

Over the past several months, CompuServe has received many complaints from subscribers threatening to discontinue their subscription unless Compu-Serve prohibits electronic mass mailers from using its equipment to send unsolicited advertisements. CompuServe asserts that the volume of messages generated by such mass mailings places a significant burden on its equipment which has finite processing and storage capacity. CompuServe receives no payment from the mass mailers for processing their unsolicited advertising. However, CompuServe's subscribers pay for their access to CompuServe's services in increments of time and thus the process of accessing, reviewing and discarding unsolicited e-mail costs them money, which is one of the reasons for their complaints. CompuServe has notified defendants that they are prohibited from using its proprietary computer equipment to process and store unsolicited e-mail and has requested them to cease and desist from sending unsolicited e-mail to its subscribers. Nonetheless, defendants have sent an increasing volume of e-mail solicitations to CompuServe subscribers.

In an effort to shield its equipment from defendants' bulk e-mail, CompuServe has implemented software programs designed to screen out the messages and block their receipt. In response, defendants have modified their equipment and the messages they send in such a fashion as to circumvent CompuServe's screening software. . . .

Defendants assert that they possess the right to continue to send these communications to CompuServe subscribers. CompuServe contends that, in doing so, the defendants are trespassing upon its personal property. . . .

IV.

... Trespass to chattels has evolved from its original common law application, concerning primarily the asportation [sic] of another's tangible property, to include the unauthorized use of personal property:

> Its chief importance now, is that there may be recovery . . . for interferences with the possession of chattels which are not sufficiently important to be classed as conversion,

and so to compel the defendant to pay the full value of the thing with which he has interfered. Trespass to chattels survives today, in other words, largely as a little brother of conversion.

Prosser & Keeton, Prosser and Keeton on Torts, §14, 85-86 (1984).

The scope of an action for conversion recognized in Ohio may embrace the facts in the instant case. The Supreme Court of Ohio established the definition of conversion under Ohio law in Baltimore & O.R. Co. v. O'Donnell, 49 Ohio St. 489, 32 N.E. 476, 478 (1892) by stating that:

> [I]n order to constitute a conversion, it was not necessary that there should have been an actual appropriation of the property by the defendant to its own use and benefit. It might arise from the exercise of a dominion over it in exclusion of the rights of the owner, or withholding it from his possession under a claim inconsistent with his rights. If one takes the property of another, for a temporary purpose only, in disregard of the owner's right, it is a conversion. Either a wrongful taking, an assumption of ownership, an illegal use or misuse, or a wrongful detention of chattels will constitute a conversion.

Id. at 497-98, 32 N.E. 476; see also Miller v. Uhl, 37 Ohio App. 276, 174 N.E. 591 (1929); Great American Mut. Indem. Co. v. Meyer, 18 Ohio App. 97 (1924); 18 O. Jur. 3d, Conversion §17. While authority under Ohio law respecting an action for trespass to chattels is extremely meager, it appears to be an actionable tort. . . .

The Restatement §217(b) states that a trespass to chattel may be committed by intentionally using or intermeddling with the chattel in possession of another. Restatement §217, Comment e defines physical "intermeddling" as follows:

> . . . intentionally bringing about a physical contact with the chattel. The actor may commit a trespass by an act which brings him into an intended physical contact with a chattel in the possession of another[.]

Electronic signals generated and sent by computer have been held to be sufficiently physically tangible to support a trespass cause of action. Thrifty-Tel, Inc. v. Bezenek, 46 Cal. App. 4th 1559, 1567, 54 Cal. Rptr. 2d 468 (1996); State v. McGraw, 480 N.E.2d 552, 554 (Ind. 1985) (Indiana Supreme Court recognizing in dicta that a hacker's unauthorized access to a computer was more in the nature of trespass than criminal conversion); and State v. Riley, 121 Wash. 2d 22, 846 P.2d 1365 (1993) (computer hacking as the criminal offense of "computer trespass" under Washington law). It is undisputed that plaintiff has a possessory interest in its computer systems. Further, defendants' contact with plaintiff's computers is clearly intentional. Although electronic messages may travel through the Internet over various routes, the messages are affirmatively directed to their destination. . . .

A plaintiff can sustain an action for trespass to chattels, as opposed to an action for conversion, without showing a substantial interference with its right to possession of that chattel. Thrifty-Tel, Inc., 46 Cal. App. 4th at

1567, 54 Cal. Rptr. 2d 468 (quoting Zaslow v. Kroenert, 29 Cal. 2d 541, 176 P.2d 1 (Cal. 1946)). Harm to the personal property or diminution of its quality, condition, or value as a result of defendants' use can also be the predicate for liability. Restatement §218(b).

> An unprivileged use or other intermeddling with a chattel which results in actual impairment of its physical condition, quality or value to the possessor makes the actor liable for the loss thus caused. In the great majority of cases, the actor's intermeddling with the chattel impairs the value of it to the possessor, as distinguished from the mere affront to his dignity as possessor, only by some impairment of the physical condition of the chattel. There may, however, be situations in which the value to the owner of a particular type of chattel may be impaired by dealing with it in a manner that does not affect its physical condition. . . . In such a case, the intermeddling is actionable even though the physical condition of the chattel is not impaired.

The Restatement (Second) of Torts §218, comment h. In the present case, any value CompuServe realizes from its computer equipment is wholly derived from the extent to which that equipment can serve its subscriber base. Michael Mangino, a software developer for CompuServe who monitors its mail processing computer equipment, states by affidavit that handling the enormous volume of mass mailings that CompuServe receives places a tremendous burden on its equipment. . . . Defendants' more recent practice of evading CompuServe's filters by disguising the origin of their messages commandeers even more computer resources because CompuServe's computers are forced to store undeliverable e-mail messages and labor in vain to return the messages to an address that does not exist. . . . To the extent that defendants' multitudinous electronic mailings demand the disk space and drain the processing power of plaintiff's computer equipment, those resources are not available to serve CompuServe subscribers. Therefore, the value of that equipment to CompuServe is diminished even though it is not physically damaged by defendants' conduct.

Next, plaintiff asserts that it has suffered injury aside from the physical impact of defendants' messages on its equipment. Restatement §218(d) also indicates that recovery may be had for a trespass that causes harm to something in which the possessor has a legally protected interest. Plaintiff asserts that defendants' messages are largely unwanted by its subscribers, who pay incrementally to access their e-mail, read it, and discard it. Also, the receipt of a bundle of unsolicited messages at once can require the subscriber to sift through, at his expense, all of the messages in order to find the ones he wanted or expected to receive. These inconveniences decrease the utility of CompuServe's e-mail service and are the foremost subject in recent complaints from CompuServe subscribers. . . .

Many subscribers have terminated their accounts specifically because of the unwanted receipt of bulk e-mail messages. . . . Defendants' intrusions into CompuServe's computer systems, insofar as they harm plaintiff's business reputation and goodwill with its customers, are actionable under Restatement §218(d).

The reason that the tort of trespass to chattels requires some actual damage as a prima facie element, whereas damage is assumed where there is a trespass to real property, can be explained as follows:

> The interest of a possessor of a chattel in its inviolability, unlike the similar interest of a possessor of land, is not given legal protection by an action for nominal damages for harmless intermeddlings with the chattel. In order that an actor who interferes with another's chattel may be liable, his conduct must affect some other and more important interest of the possessor. Therefore, one who intentionally intermeddles with another's chattel is subject to liability only if his intermeddling is harmful to the possessor's materially valuable interest in the physical condition, quality, or value of the chattel, or if the possessor is deprived of the use of the chattel for a substantial time, or some other legally protected interest of the possessor is affected as stated in Clause (c). Sufficient legal protection of the possessor's interest in the mere inviolability of his chattel is afforded by his privilege to use reasonable force to protect his possession against even harmless interference.

Restatement (Second) of Torts §218, Comment e. Plaintiff CompuServe has attempted to exercise this privilege to protect its computer systems. However, defendants' persistent affirmative efforts to evade plaintiff's security measures have circumvented any protection those self-help measures might have provided. In this case CompuServe has alleged and supported by affidavit that it has suffered several types of injury as a result of defendants' conduct. The foregoing discussion simply underscores that the damage sustained by plaintiff is sufficient to sustain an action for trespass to chattels. However, this Court also notes that the implementation of technological means of self-help, to the extent that reasonable measures are effective, is particularly appropriate in this type of situation and should be exhausted before legal action is proper.

Under Restatement §252, the owner of personal property can create a privilege in the would-be trespasser by granting consent to use the property. A great portion of the utility of CompuServe's e-mail service is that it allows subscribers to receive messages from individuals and entities located anywhere on the Internet. Certainly, then, there is at least a tacit invitation for anyone on the Internet to utilize plaintiff's computer equipment to send e-mail to its subscribers. Buchanan Marine, Inc. v. McCormack Sand Co., 743 F. Supp. 139 (E.D.N.Y. 1990) (whether there is consent to community use is a material issue of fact in an action for trespass to chattels). However, in or around October 1995, CompuServe employee Jon Schmidt specifically told Mr. Wallace that he was "prohibited from using CompuServe's equipment to send his junk e-mail messages." . . . There is apparently some factual dispute as to this point, but it is clear from the record that Mr. Wallace became aware at about this time that plaintiff did not want to receive messages from Cyber Promotions and that plaintiff was taking steps to block receipt of those messages. . . .

Defendants argue that plaintiff made the business decision to connect to the Internet and that therefore it cannot now successfully maintain an action for trespass to chattels. Their argument is analogous to the argument that because an establishment invites the public to enter its property for business purposes, it cannot later restrict or revoke access to that property, a proposition which is erroneous under Ohio law. See, e.g., State v. Carriker, 5 Ohio App. 2d 255, 214 N.E.2d 809 (1964) (the law in Ohio is that a business invitee's privilege to remain on the premises of another may be revoked upon the reasonable notification to leave by the owner or his agents); Allstate Ins. Co. v. U.S. Associates Realty, Inc., 11 Ohio App. 3d 242, 464 N.E.2d 169 (1983) (notice of express restriction or limitation on invitation turns business invitee into trespasser). On or around October 1995, CompuServe notified defendants that it no longer consented to the use of its proprietary computer equipment. Defendants' continued use thereafter was a trespass. Restatement (Second) of Torts §§252 and 892A(5); see also Restatement (Second) of Torts §217, Comment f ("The actor may commit a new trespass by continuing an intermeddling which he has already begun, with or without the consent of the person in possession. Such intermeddling may persist after the other's consent, originally given, has been terminated."); Restatement (Second) of Torts §217, Comment g.

Further, CompuServe expressly limits the consent it grants to Internet users to send e-mail to its proprietary computer systems by denying unauthorized parties the use of CompuServe equipment to send unsolicited electronic mail messages. . . . This policy statement, posted by CompuServe on-line, states as follows:

> CompuServe is a private on-line and communications services company. CompuServe does not permit its facilities to be used by unauthorized parties to process and store unsolicited e-mail. If an unauthorized party attempts to send unsolicited messages to e-mail addresses on a CompuServe service, CompuServe will take appropriate action to attempt to prevent those messages from being processed by CompuServe. Violations of CompuServe's policy prohibiting unsolicited e-mail should be reported to. . . .

Defendants Cyber Promotions, Inc. and its president Sanford Wallace have used plaintiff's equipment in a fashion that exceeds that consent. The use of personal property exceeding consent is a trespass. City of Amsterdam v. Daniel Goldreyer, Ltd., 882 F. Supp. 1273 (E.D.N.Y. 1995); Restatement (Second) of Torts §256. It is arguable that CompuServe's policy statement, insofar as it may serve as a limitation upon the scope of its consent to the use of its computer equipment, may be insufficiently communicated to potential third-party users when it is merely posted at some location on the network. However, in the present case the record indicates that defendants were actually notified that they were using CompuServe's equipment in an unacceptable manner. To prove that a would-be trespasser acted with the intent required to support liability in tort it is crucial that defendant be placed on notice that he is trespassing. . . .

In response to the trespass claim, defendants argue that they have the right to continue to send unsolicited commercial e-mail to plaintiff's computer systems under the First Amendment to the United States Constitution. The First Amendment states that "Congress shall make no law respecting an establishment of religion, or prohibiting the free exercise thereof; or abridging the freedom of speech, or of the press." The United States Supreme Court has recognized that "the constitutional guarantee of free speech is a guarantee only against abridgement by government, federal or state." Hudgens v. NLRB, 424 U.S. 507, 513 (1976). Indeed, the protection of the First Amendment is not a shield against "merely private conduct." Hurley v. Irish-American Gay Group of Boston, 515 U.S. 557, 115 S. Ct. 2338, 2344 (1995) (citation omitted). . . .

In the present action, CompuServe is a private company. Moreover, the mere judicial enforcement of neutral trespass laws by the private owner of property does not alone render it a state actor. Rotunda & Nowak, Treatise on Constitutional Law §16.3, 546 (West 1992). Defendants do not argue that CompuServe is anything other than a private actor. Instead, defendants urge that because CompuServe is so intimately involved in this new medium it might be subject to some special form of regulation. Defendants cite Associated Press v. United States, 326 U.S. 1 (1945), and Turner Broadcasting Sys., Inc. v. FCC, 512 U.S. 622 (1994), which stand for the proposition that when a private actor has a certain quantum of control over a central avenue of communication, then the First Amendment might not prevent the government from enacting legislation requiring public access to private property. No such legislation yet exists that is applicable to CompuServe. Further, defendants' discussion concerning the extent to which the Internet may be regulated (or should be regulated) is irrelevant because no government entity has undertaken to regulate the Internet in a manner that is applicable to this action. Indeed, if there were some applicable statutory scheme in place this Court would not be required to apply paradigms of common law to the case at hand. . . .

Defendants in the present action have adequate alternative means of communication available to them. Not only are they free to send e-mail advertisements to those on the Internet who do not use CompuServe accounts, but they can communicate to CompuServe subscribers as well through on-line bulletin boards, web page advertisements, or facsimile transmissions, as well as through more conventional means such as the U.S. mail or telemarketing. Defendants' contention, referring to the low cost of the electronic mail medium, that there are no adequate alternative means of communication is unpersuasive. There is no constitutional requirement that the incremental cost of sending massive quantities of unsolicited advertisements must be borne by the recipients. The legal concept in Lloyd that private citizens are entitled to enforce laws of trespass against would-be communicators is applicable to this case. . . .

In the present case, plaintiff is physically the recipient of the defendants' messages and is the owner of the property upon which the transgression is occurring. As has been discussed, plaintiff is not a government agency or state actor which seeks to preempt defendants' ability to communicate but is instead a private actor trying to tailor the nuances of its service to provide the maximum utility to its customers.

Defendants' intentional use of plaintiff's proprietary computer equipment exceeds plaintiff's consent and, indeed, continued after repeated demands that defendants cease. Such use is an actionable trespass to plaintiff's chattel. The First Amendment to the United States Constitution provides no defense for such conduct.

COMMENTS AND QUESTIONS

1. What property interest or interests of CompuServe is the court protecting? Is the court protecting CompuServe or its customers?

2. As the court notes, common law trespass to chattels requires that the defendant use the chattel even temporarily to the exclusion of the rightful owner. How does sending e-mail over a system designed to deliver e-mail messages exclude CompuServe from its computers?

3. Even assuming that electronic signals can constitute a physical invasion, how does spam harm CompuServe? Is this damage to CompuServe's computer network or to CompuServe's business?

4. For a critique of the *CompuServe* decision see Dan L. Burk, *The Trouble with Trespass*, 4 J. Small & Emerging Bus. L. 27 (2000). Burk suggests that "It is nearly impossible to recognize trespass to chattels in . . . *CompuServe*, since the owners of the equipment were not in any way dispossessed of its use by the passage of electrons through the equipment in exactly the way the equipment was designed to carry them." *Id.* at 34. Instead, trespass in this context should be viewed as an effort to create a new form of intellectual property right, *id.* at 28, and that the imposition of such a theory may "lead to the detrimental over-propertization of the Internet." *Id.* at 53. What additional benefits are generated by recognized trespass to networks? What are the costs?

5. Should the computer network owner's authorization end the inquiry? While the court rejects the defendant's First Amendment argument because CompuServe is a private actor, can a *Shack* argument be made?

INTEL CORP. V. HAMIDI

1 Cal. Rptr. 3d 32 (Cal. 2003)

WERDEGAR, J.

Intel Corporation (Intel) maintains an electronic mail system, connected to the Internet, through which messages between employees and those outside the company can be sent and received, and permits its employees to make reasonable nonbusiness use of this system. On six occasions over almost two years, Kourosh Kenneth Hamidi, a former Intel employee, sent e-mails criticizing Intel's employment practices to numerous current employees on Intel's electronic mail system. Hamidi breached no computer security barriers in order to communicate with Intel employees. He offered to, and did, remove from his mailing list any recipient who so wished. Hamidi's communications to individual Intel employees caused neither physical damage nor functional disruption to the company's computers, nor did they at any time deprive Intel of the use of its computers. The contents of the messages, however, caused discussion among employees and managers.

On these facts, Intel brought suit, claiming that by communicating with its employees over the company's e-mail system Hamidi committed the tort of trespass to chattels. The trial court granted Intel's motion for summary judgment and enjoined Hamidi from any further mailings. A divided Court of Appeal affirmed.

After reviewing the decisions analyzing unauthorized electronic contact with computer systems as potential trespasses to chattels, we conclude that under California law the tort does not encompass, and should not be extended to encompass, an electronic communication that neither damages the recipient computer system nor impairs its functioning. Such an electronic communication does not constitute an actionable trespass to personal property, i.e., the computer system, because it does not interfere with the possessor's use or possession of, or any other legally protected interest in, the personal property itself. . . . The consequential economic damage Intel claims to have suffered, i.e., loss of productivity caused by employees reading and reacting to Hamidi's messages and company efforts to block the messages, is not an injury to the company's interest in its computers—which worked as intended and were unharmed by the communications—any more than the personal distress caused by reading an unpleasant letter would be an injury to the recipient's mailbox, or the loss of privacy caused by an intrusive telephone call would be an injury to the recipient's telephone equipment.

Our conclusion does not rest on any special immunity for communications by electronic mail; we do not hold that messages transmitted through the Internet are exempt from the ordinary rules of tort liability. To the contrary, e-mail, like other forms of communication, may in some circumstances cause legally cognizable injury to the recipient or to third parties and may be actionable under various common law or statutory theories. . . . Intel's claim fails not because e-mail transmitted through the Internet enjoys unique immunity, but because the trespass to chattels tort—unlike the causes of action just mentioned—may not, in California, be proved without evidence of an injury to the plaintiff's personal property or legal interest therein.

Nor does our holding affect the legal remedies of Internet service providers (ISP's) against senders of unsolicited commercial bulk e-mail (UCE), also known as "spam." . . . A series of federal district court decisions, beginning with *CompuServe, Inc. v. Cyber Promotions, Inc.* (S.D. Ohio 1997) 962 F. Supp. 1015, has approved the use of trespass to chattels as a theory of spammers' liability to ISP's, based upon evidence that the vast quantities of mail sent by spammers both overburdened the ISP's own computers and made the entire computer system harder to use for recipients, the ISP's customers. In those cases, discussed in greater detail below, the underlying complaint was that the extraordinary *quantity* of UCE impaired the computer system's functioning. In the present case, the claimed injury is located in the disruption or distraction caused to recipients by the *contents* of the e-mail messages, an injury entirely separate from, and not directly affecting, the possession or value of personal property. . . .

DISCUSSION

I. Current California Tort Law

Dubbed by Prosser the "little brother of conversion," the tort of trespass to chattels allows recovery for interferences with possession of personal property "not sufficiently important to be classed as conversion, and so to compel the defendant to pay the full value of the thing with which he has interfered." (Prosser & Keeton, Torts (5th ed. 1984) §14, pp. 85-86.)

Though not amounting to conversion, the defendant's interference must, to be actionable, have caused some injury to the chattel or to the plaintiff's rights in it. Under California law, trespass to chattels "lies where an intentional interference with the possession of personal property *has proximately caused injury*." . . . In cases of interference with possession of personal property not amounting to conversion, "the owner has a cause of action for trespass or case, *and may recover only the actual damages suffered by reason of the impairment of the property or the loss of its use*." . . . In modern American law generally, "[t]respass remains as an occasional remedy for minor interferences, *resulting in some damage*, but not sufficiently serious or sufficiently important to amount to the greater tort" of conversion. (Prosser & Keeton, Torts, *supra*, §15, p. 90, italics added.)

The Restatement, too, makes clear that some actual injury must have occurred in order for a trespass to chattels to be actionable. . . .

In this respect, as Prosser explains, modern day trespass to chattels differs both from the original English writ and from the action for trespass to land: "Another departure from the original rule of the old writ of trespass concerns the necessity of some actual damage to the chattel before the action can be maintained. Where the defendant merely interferes without doing any harm — as where, for example, he merely lays hands upon the plaintiff's horse, or sits in his car — there has been a division of opinion among the writers, and a surprising dearth of authority. *By analogy to trespass to land there might be a technical tort in such a case. . . . Such scanty authority as there is, however, has considered that the dignitary interest in the inviolability of chattels, unlike that as to land, is not sufficiently important to require any greater defense than the privilege of using reasonable force when necessary to protect them. Accordingly it has been held that nominal damages will not be awarded, and that in the absence of any actual damage the action will not lie.*" (Prosser & Keeton, Torts, *supra,* §14, p. 87, italics added, fns. omitted.) . . .

The dispositive issue in this case, therefore, is whether the undisputed facts demonstrate Hamidi's actions caused or threatened to cause damage to Intel's computer system, or injury to its rights in that personal property, such as to entitle Intel to judgment as a matter of law. To review, the undisputed evidence revealed no actual or threatened damage to Intel's computer hardware or software and no interference with its ordinary and intended operation. Intel was not dispossessed of its computers, nor did Hamidi's messages prevent Intel from using its computers for any measurable length of time. Intel presented no evidence its system was slowed or otherwise impaired by the burden of delivering Hamidi's electronic messages. Nor was there any evidence transmission of the messages imposed any marginal cost on the operation of Intel's computers. In sum, no evidence suggested that in sending messages through Intel's Internet connections and internal computer system Hamidi used the system in any manner in which it was not intended to function or impaired the system in any way. Nor does the evidence show the request of any employee to be removed from FACE-Intel's mailing list was not honored. The evidence did show, however, that some employees who found the messages unwelcome asked management to stop them and that Intel technical staff spent time and effort attempting to block the messages. A statement on the FACE-Intel Web site, moreover, could be taken as an admission that the messages had caused "[e]xcited and nervous managers" to discuss the matter with Intel's human resources department.

Relying on a line of decisions, most from federal district courts, applying the tort of trespass to chattels to various types of unwanted electronic contact between computers, Intel contends that, while its computers were not damaged by receiving Hamidi's messages, its interest in the "physical condition, quality or value" (Rest. 2d Torts, §218, com. e, p. 422) of the computers was harmed. We disagree. The cited line of decisions does not persuade us that the mere sending of electronic communications that assertedly cause injury only because of their contents constitutes an actionable trespass to a computer system through which the messages are transmitted. Rather, the decisions finding electronic contact to be a trespass to computer systems have generally involved some actual or threatened interference with the computers' functioning.

In *Thrifty-Tel, Inc. v. Bezenek,* the California Court of Appeal held that evidence of automated searching of a telephone carrier's system for authorization codes supported a cause of action for trespass to chattels. The defendant's automated dialing program "overburdened the [plaintiff's] system, denying some subscribers access to phone lines" showing the requisite injury.

Following *Thrifty-Tel,* a series of federal district court decisions held that sending UCE through an ISP's equipment may constitute trespass to the ISP's computer system. . . .

In each of these spamming cases, the plaintiff showed, or was prepared to show, some interference with the efficient functioning of its computer system. In *CompuServe*, the plaintiff ISP's mail equipment monitor stated that mass UCE mailings, especially from nonexistent addresses such as those used by the defendant, placed "a tremendous burden" on the ISP's equipment, using "disk space and drain[ing] the processing power," making those resources unavailable to serve subscribers. (*CompuServe, supra*, 962 F. Supp. at p. 1022.) Similarly, in *Hotmail Corp. v. Van$ Money Pie, Inc.*, the court found the evidence supported a finding that the defendant's mailings "fill[ed] up Hotmail's computer storage space and threaten[ed] to damage Hotmail's ability to service its legitimate customers." *America Online, Inc. v. IMS*, decided on summary judgment, was deemed factually indistinguishable from *CompuServe;* the court observed that in both cases the plaintiffs "alleged that processing the bulk e-mail cost them time and money and burdened their equipment." (*America Online, Inc. v. IMS, supra*, 24 F. Supp. 2d at p. 550.) . . .

Building on the spamming cases . . . three even more recent district court decisions addressed whether unauthorized robotic data collection from a company's publicly accessible Web site is a trespass on the company's computer system. (*eBay, Inc. v. Bidder's Edge, Inc., supra*, 100 F. Supp. 2d at pp. 1069-1072; *Register.com, Inc. v. Verio, Inc.* (S.D.N.Y. 2000) 126 F. Supp. 2d 238, 248-251; *Ticketmaster Corp. v. Tickets.com, Inc., supra*, 2000 WL 1887522, at p. *4.) The two district courts that found such automated data collection to constitute a trespass relied, in part, on the deleterious impact this activity could have, especially if replicated by other searchers, on the functioning of a Web site's computer equipment. . . .

That Intel does not claim the type of functional impact that spammers and robots have been alleged to cause is not surprising in light of the differences between Hamidi's activities and those of a commercial enterprise that uses sheer quantity of messages as its communications strategy. Though Hamidi sent thousands of copies of the same message on six occasions over 21 months, that number is minuscule compared to the amounts of mail sent by commercial operations. The individual advertisers sued in *America Online, Inc. v. IMS, supra*, 24 F. Supp. 2d at page 549, and *America Online, Inc. v. LCGM, Inc., supra*, 46 F. Supp. 2d at page 448, were alleged to have sent more than 60 million messages over 10 months and more than 92 million messages over seven months, respectively. Collectively, UCE has reportedly come to constitute about 45 percent of all e-mail. The functional burden on Intel's computers, or the cost in time to individual recipients, of receiving Hamidi's occasional advocacy messages cannot be compared to the burdens and costs caused ISP's and their customers by the ever-rising deluge of commercial e-mail.

Intel relies on language in the *eBay* decision suggesting that unauthorized use of another's chattel is actionable even without any showing of injury: "Even if, as [defendant] BE argues, its searches use only a small amount of eBay's computer system capacity, BE has nonetheless deprived eBay of the ability to use that portion of its personal property for its own purposes. The law recognizes no such right to use another's personal property." But as the *eBay* court went on immediately to find that the defendant's conduct, if widely replicated, *would* likely impair the functioning of the plaintiff's system, we do not read the quoted remarks as expressing the court's complete view of the issue. In isolation, moreover, they would not be a correct statement of California or general American law on this point. While one may have no *right* temporarily to use another's personal property, such use is actionable as a trespass only if it "has proximately caused injury." . . . "[I]n the absence of any actual damage the action will not lie." (Prosser & Keeton, Torts, *supra*, §14, p. 87.) Short of dispossession, personal injury, or physical damage (not present here), intermeddling is actionable only if "the chattel is impaired as to its condition, quality, or value, or [¶] . . . the possessor is deprived of the use of the chattel for a substantial time." (Rest. 2d Torts, §218, pars. (b), (c).) In particular, an actionable deprivation of use "must be for a time so substantial that it is possible to estimate the loss caused thereby. A mere momentary or theoretical deprivation of use is not sufficient unless there is a dispossession. . . ." That Hamidi's messages temporarily used some portion of the Intel computers' processors or storage is, therefore, not enough; Intel must, but does not, demonstrate some measurable loss from the use of its computer system.

In addition to impairment of system functionality, *CompuServe* and its progeny also refer to the ISP's loss of business reputation and customer goodwill, resulting from the inconvenience and cost that spam causes to its members, as harm to the ISP's legally protected interests in its personal property. . . . Intel argues that its own interest in employee productivity, assertedly disrupted by Hamidi's messages, is a comparable protected interest in its computer system. We disagree.

Whether the economic injuries identified in *CompuServe* were properly considered injuries to the ISP's possessory interest in its personal property, the type of property interest the tort is primarily intended to protect (see Rest. 2d Torts, §218 & com. e, pp. 421-422; Prosser & Keeton, Torts, *supra*, §14, p. 87), has been questioned. "[T]he court broke the chain between the trespass and the harm, allowing indirect harms to CompuServe's business interests — reputation, customer goodwill, and employee time — to count as harms to the chattel (the server)." (Quilter, *The Continuing Expansion of Cyberspace Trespass to Chattels*, *supra*, 17 Berkeley Tech. L.J. at pp. 429-430.) "[T]his move cuts trespass to chattels free from its moorings of dispossession or the equivalent, allowing the court free reign [*sic*] to hunt for 'impairment.'" (Burk, *The Trouble with Trespass* (2000) 4 J. Small & Emerging Bus. L. 27, 35.) But even if the loss of goodwill identified in *CompuServe* were the type of injury that would give rise to a trespass to chattels claim under California law, Intel's position would not follow, for Intel's claimed injury has even less connection to its personal property than did CompuServe's.

CompuServe's customers were annoyed because the system was inundated with unsolicited commercial messages, making its use for personal communication more difficult and costly. . . . Their complaint, which allegedly led some to cancel their CompuServe service, was about *the functioning of* CompuServe's *electronic mail service.* Intel's workers, in contrast, were allegedly distracted from their work not because of the frequency or quantity of Hamidi's messages, but because of assertions and opinions the messages conveyed. Intel's complaint is thus about *the contents of the messages* rather than the functioning of the company's e-mail system. Even accepting CompuServe's economic injury rationale, therefore, Intel's position represents a further extension of the trespass to chattels tort, fictionally recharacterizing the allegedly injurious effect of a communication's *contents* on recipients as an impairment to the device which transmitted the message.

This theory of "impairment by content" (Burk, *The Trouble with Trespass, supra,* 4 J. Small & Emerging Bus. L. at p. 37) threatens to stretch trespass law to cover injuries far afield from the harms to possession the tort evolved to protect. Intel's theory would expand the tort of trespass to chattels to cover virtually any unconsented-to communication that, solely because of its content, is unwelcome to the recipient or intermediate transmitter. . . . ". . . After all, '[t]he property interest protected by the old action of trespass was that of possession; and this has continued to affect the character of the action.' (Prosser & Keeton on Torts, *supra,* §14, p. 87.) Reading an e-mail transmitted to equipment designed to receive it, in and of itself, does not affect the possessory interest in the equipment. Indeed, if a chattel's receipt of an electronic communication constitutes a trespass to that chattel, then not only are unsolicited telephone calls and faxes trespasses to chattel, but unwelcome radio waves and television signals also constitute a trespass to chattel every time the viewer inadvertently sees or hears the unwanted program." We agree. While unwelcome communications, electronic or otherwise, can cause a variety of injuries to economic relations, reputation and emotions, those interests are protected by other branches of tort law; in order to address them, we need not create a fiction of injury to the communication system. . . .

Intel connected its e-mail system to the Internet and permitted its employees to make use of this connection both for business and, to a reasonable extent, for their own purposes. In doing so, the company necessarily contemplated the employees' receipt of unsolicited as well as solicited communications from other companies and individuals. That some communications would, because of their contents, be unwelcome to Intel management was virtually inevitable. Hamidi did nothing but use the e-mail system for its intended purpose — to communicate with employees. The system worked as designed, delivering the messages without any physical or functional harm or disruption. These occasional transmissions cannot reasonably be viewed as impairing the quality or value of Intel's computer system. We conclude, therefore, that Intel has not presented undisputed facts demonstrating an injury to its personal property, or to its legal interest in that property, that support, under California tort law, an action for trespass to chattels.

II. Proposed Extension of California Tort Law

We next consider whether California common law should be *extended* to cover, as a trespass to chattels, an otherwise harmless electronic communication whose contents are objectionable. We decline to so expand California law. Intel, of course, was not the recipient of Hamidi's messages, but rather the owner and possessor of computer servers used to relay the messages, and it bases this tort action on that ownership and possession. The property rule proposed is a rigid one, under which the sender of an electronic message would be strictly liable to the owner of equipment through which the communication passes — here, Intel — for any consequential injury flowing from the *contents* of the communication. The arguments of amici curiae and academic writers on this topic, discussed below, leave us highly doubtful whether creation of such a rigid property rule would be wise.

Writing on behalf of several industry groups appearing as amici curiae, Professor Richard A. Epstein of the University of Chicago urges us to excuse the required showing of injury to personal property in cases of unauthorized electronic contact between computers, "extending the rules of trespass to real property to all interactive Web sites and servers." The court is thus urged to recognize, for owners of a particular species of personal property, computer servers, the same interest in inviolability as is generally accorded a possessor of land. In effect, Professor Epstein suggests that a company's server should be its castle, upon which any unauthorized intrusion, however harmless, is a trespass.

Epstein's argument derives, in part, from the familiar metaphor of the Internet as a physical space, reflected in much of the language that has been used to describe it: "cyberspace," "the information superhighway," e-mail "addresses," and the like. Of course, the Internet is also frequently called simply the "Net," a term, Hamidi points out, "evoking a fisherman's chattel." A major component of the Internet is the World Wide "Web," a descriptive term suggesting neither personal nor real property, and "cyberspace" itself has come to be known by the oxymoronic phrase "virtual reality," which would suggest that any real property "located" in "cyberspace" must be "virtually real" property. Metaphor is a two-edged sword.

Indeed, the metaphorical application of real property rules would not, by itself, transform a physically harmless electronic intrusion on a computer server into a trespass. That is because, under California law, intangible intrusions on land, including electromagnetic transmissions, are not actionable as trespasses (though they may be as nuisances) unless they cause physical damage to the real property. . . . Since Intel does not claim Hamidi's electronically transmitted messages physically damaged its servers, it could not prove a trespass to land even were we to treat the computers as a type of real property. Some further extension of the conceit would be required, under which the electronic signals Hamidi sent would be recast as tangible intruders, perhaps as tiny messengers rushing through the "hallways" of Intel's computers and bursting out of employees' computers to read them Hamidi's missives. But such fictions promise more confusion than clarity in the law. . . .

The plain fact is that computers, even those making up the Internet, are—like such older communications equipment as telephones and fax machines—personal property, not realty. Professor Epstein observes that "[a]lthough servers may be moved in real space, they cannot be moved in cyberspace," because an Internet server must, to be useful, be accessible at a known address. But the same is true of the telephone: to be useful for incoming communication, the telephone must remain constantly linked to the same number (or, when the number is changed, the system must include some forwarding or notification capability, a qualification that also applies to computer addresses). Does this suggest that an unwelcome message delivered through a telephone or fax machine should be viewed as a trespass to a type of real property? We think not: As already discussed, the contents of a telephone communication may cause a variety of injuries and may be the basis for a variety of tort actions (e.g., defamation, intentional infliction of emotional distress, invasion of privacy), but the injuries are not to an interest in property, much less real property, and the appropriate tort is not trespass.

More substantively, Professor Epstein argues that a rule of computer server inviolability will, through the formation or extension of a market in computer-to-computer access, create "the right social result." In most circumstances, he predicts, companies with computers on the Internet will continue to authorize transmission of information through e-mail, Web site searching, and page linking because they benefit by that open access. When a Web site owner does deny access to a particular sending, searching, or linking computer, a system of "simple one-on-one negotiations" will arise to provide the necessary individual licenses.

Other scholars are less optimistic about such a complete propertization of the Internet. Professor Mark Lemley of the University of California, Berkeley, writing on behalf of an amici curiae group of professors of intellectual property and computer law, observes that under a property rule of server inviolability, "each of the hundreds of millions of [Internet] users must get permission in advance from anyone with whom they want to communicate and anyone who owns a server through which their message may travel." The consequence for e-mail could be a substantial reduction in the freedom of electronic communication, as the owner of each computer through which an electronic message passes could impose its own limitations on message content or source. As Professor Dan Hunter of the University of Pennsylvania asks rhetorically: "Does this mean that one must read the 'Terms of Acceptable Email Usage' of every email system that one emails in the course of an ordinary day? If the University of Pennsylvania had a policy that sending a joke by email would be an unauthorized use of their system, then under the logic of [the lower court decision in this case], you commit 'trespass' if you emailed me a . . . cartoon." (Hunter, *Cyberspace as Place, and the Tragedy of the Digital Anticommons* (2003) 91 Cal. L. Rev. 439, 508-509.)

Web site linking, Professor Lemley further observes, "would exist at the sufferance of the linked-to party, because a Web user who followed a 'disapproved' link would be trespassing on the plaintiff's server, just as sending an e-mail is trespass under the [lower] court's theory." . . . A leading scholar of Internet law and policy, Professor Lawrence Lessig of Stanford University, has criticized Professor Epstein's theory of the computer server as quasi-real property, previously put forward in the *eBay* case (*eBay, supra,* 100 F. Supp. 2d 1058), on the ground that it ignores the costs to society in the loss of network benefits: "eBay benefits greatly from a network that is open and where access is free. It is this general feature of the Net that makes the Net so valuable to users and a source of great innovation. And to the extent that individual sites begin to impose their own rules of exclusion, the value of the network as a network declines. If machines must negotiate before entering any individual site, then the costs of using the network climb." . . .

We discuss this debate among the amici curiae and academic writers only to note its existence and contours, not to attempt its resolution. Creating an absolute property right to exclude undesired communications from one's e-mail and Web servers might help force spammers to internalize the costs they impose on ISP's and their customers. But such a property rule might also create substantial new costs, to e-mail and e-commerce users and to society generally, in lost ease and openness of communication and in lost network benefits. In light of the unresolved controversy, we would be acting rashly to adopt a rule treating computer servers as real property for purposes of trespass law. . . .

[Concurring opinion by KENNARD, J. omitted.]

Dissenting opinion of BROWN, J.

Candidate A finds the vehicles that candidate B has provided for his campaign workers, and A spray paints the water soluble message, "Fight corruption, vote for A" on the bumpers. The majority's reasoning would find that notwithstanding the time it takes the workers to remove the paint and the expense they incur in altering the bumpers to prevent further unwanted messages, candidate B does not deserve an injunction unless the paint is so heavy that it reduces the cars' gas mileage or otherwise depreciates the cars' market value. Furthermore, candidate B has an obligation to permit the paint's display, because the cars are driven by workers and not B personally, because B allows his workers to use the cars to pick up their lunch or retrieve their children from school, or because the bumpers display B's own slogans. I disagree.

Intel has invested millions of dollars to develop and maintain a computer system. It did this not to act as a public forum but to enhance the productivity of its employees. Kourosh Kenneth Hamidi sent as many as 200,000 e-mail messages to Intel employees. The time required to review and delete Hamidi's messages diverted employees from productive tasks and undermined the utility of the computer system. "There may . . . be situations in which the value to the owner of a particular type of chattel may be impaired by dealing with it in a manner that does not affect its physical condition." (Rest. 2d Torts, §218, com. h, p. 422.) This is such a case. . . .

The majority endorses the view of the Court of Appeal dissent, and review a finding of a trespass in this case as a radical decision that will endanger almost every other form of expression. Contrary to these concerns, the Court of Appeal decision belongs not to a nightmarish future but to an unremarkable past — a long line of cases protecting the right of an individual not to receive an unwanted message after having expressed that refusal to the speaker. It breaks no new legal ground and follows traditional rules regarding communication. . . .

It is well settled that the law protects a person's right to decide to whom he will speak, to whom he will listen, and to whom he will not listen. . . . As the United States Supreme Court observed, "we have repeatedly held that individuals are not required to welcome unwanted speech into their homes" (*Frisby v. Schultz* (1988) 487 U.S. 474, 485), whether the unwanted speech comes in the form of a door-to-door solicitor, regular "snail" mail, radio waves, or other forms of amplified sound. . . .

Of course, speakers have rights too, and thus the result is a balancing: speakers have the right to initiate speech but the listener has the right to refuse to listen or to terminate the conversation. This simple policy thus supports Hamidi's right to send e-mails initially, but not after Intel expressed its objection. . . .

Those who have contempt for grubby commerce and reverence for the rarified heights of intellectual discourse may applaud today's decision, but even the flow of ideas will be curtailed if the right to exclude is denied. As the Napster controversy revealed, creative individuals will be less inclined to develop intellectual property if they cannot limit the terms of its transmission. Similarly, if online newspapers cannot charge for access, they will be unable to pay the journalists and editorialists who generate ideas for public consumption. . . .

The principles of both personal liberty and social utility should counsel us to usher the common law of property into the digital age.

Dissenting opinion by MOSK, J.

. . . In my view, the repeated transmission of bulk e-mails by appellant Kourosh Kenneth Hamidi (Hamidi) to the employees of Intel Corporation (Intel) on its proprietary confidential e-mail lists, despite Intel's demand that he cease such activities, constituted an actionable trespass to chattels. The majority fail to distinguish open communication in the public "commons" of the Internet from unauthorized intermeddling on a private, proprietary intranet. Hamidi is not communicating in the equivalent of a town square or of an unsolicited "junk" mailing through the United States Postal Service. His action, in crossing from the public Internet into a private intranet, is more like intruding into a private office mailroom, commandeering the mail cart, and dropping off unwanted broadsides on 30,000 desks. Because Intel's security measures have been circumvented by Hamidi, the majority leave Intel, which has exercised all reasonable self-help efforts, with no recourse unless he causes a malfunction or systems "crash." Hamidi's repeated intrusions did more than merely "prompt[] discussions between '[e]xcited and nervous managers' and the company's human resource department" (maj. opn., *ante,* 1 Cal. Rptr. 3d at p. 38, 71 P.3d at p. 301); they also constituted a misappropriation of Intel's private computer system contrary to its intended use and against Intel's wishes.

The law of trespass to chattels has not universally been limited to physical damage. I believe it is entirely consistent to apply that legal theory to these circumstances—that is, when a proprietary computer system is being used contrary to its owner's purposes and expressed desires, and self-help has been ineffective. Intel correctly expects protection from an intruder who misuses its proprietary system, its nonpublic directories, and its supposedly controlled connection to the Internet to achieve his bulk mailing objectives—incidentally, without even having to pay postage. . . .

[I] believe that existing legal principles are adequate to support Intel's request for injunctive relief. But even if the injunction in this case amounts to an extension of the traditional tort of trespass to chattels, this is one of those cases in which, as Justice Cardozo suggested, "[t]he creative element in the judicial process finds its opportunity and power" in the development of the law. (Cardozo, Nature of the Judicial Process (1921) p. 165.)

The law has evolved to meet economic, social, and scientific changes in society. The industrial revolution, mass production, and new transportation and communication systems all required the adaptation and evolution of legal doctrines.

The age of computer technology and cyberspace poses new challenges to legal principles. . . .

Before the computer, a person could not easily cause significant disruption to another's business or personal affairs through methods of communication without significant cost. With the computer, by a mass mailing, one person can at no cost disrupt, damage, and interfere with another's property, business, and personal interests. Here, the law should allow Intel to protect its computer-related property from the unauthorized, harmful, free use by intruders. . . .

As the Court of Appeal observed, connecting one's driveway to the general system of roads does not invite demonstrators to use the property as a public forum. Not mindful of this precept, the majority blur the distinction between public and private computer networks in the interest of "ease and openness of communication." By upholding Intel's right to exercise self-help to restrict Hamidi's bulk e-mails, they concede that he did not have a right to send them through Intel's proprietary system. Yet they conclude that injunctive relief is unavailable to Intel because it connected its e-mail system to the Internet and thus, "necessarily contemplated" unsolicited communications to its employees. Their exposition promotes unpredictability in a manner that could be as harmful to open communication as it is to property rights. It permits Intel to block Hamidi's e-mails entirely, but offers no recourse if he succeeds in breaking through its security barriers, unless he physically or functionally degrades the system. . . .

COMMENTS AND QUESTIONS

1. How does the majority in *Hamidi* distinguish cases like CompuServe v. Cyber Promotions (*supra*) and eBay v. Bidder's Edge (*infra*)? Do you find the distinction convincing? Is there a substantive difference between making unauthorized access to a system to criticize an ex-employer versus to disseminate commercial spam? Do you think the result in *Hamidi* would have been different if Hamidi had sent so many messages critical of Intel that his activities had significantly impacted on Intel's server capacity and slowed down Intel's system?

2. Is there a difference between the way the majority and dissenting judges conceptualize a computer system in terms of the "property" analogy? Do the dissenting judges give greater weight to the private property-like attributes of a computer system? If so, in what ways does this impact on their conclusions as to liability for computer trespass?

3. Does the *Hamidi* case illuminate ways in which rights to freedom of expression might be balanced against private property rights in cyberspace in the future?

4. One commentator has suggested that the reliance on trespass to chattel doctrine is misplaced with respect to cases involving spam e-mails. Professor Mossoff has suggested that the tort of nuisance is a more appropriate legal avenue for dealing with these cases because nuisance focuses more squarely on conduct that substantially interferes with a plaintiff's commercial operations, as opposed to trespass to chattels with its inherent focus on property injury. *See* Adam Mossoff, *Spam: Oy What a Nuisance!* 19 Berkeley Tech. L.J. 625 (2004).

2. Restricting Access to Data

eBay, Inc. v. Bidder's Edge, Inc.

100 F. Supp. 2d 1058 (N.D. Cal. 2000)

WHYTE, District Judge.

I. Background

eBay is an Internet-based, person-to-person trading site. eBay offers sellers the ability to list items for sale and prospective buyers the ability to search those listings and bid on items. . . .

Users of the eBay site must register and agree to the eBay User Agreement. Users agree to the seven page User Agreement by clicking on an "I Accept" button located at the end of the User Agreement. The current version of the User Agreement prohibits the use of "any robot, spider, other automatic device, or manual process to monitor or copy our web pages or the content contained herein without our prior expressed written permission." It is not clear that the version of the User Agreement in effect at the time BE began searching the eBay site prohibited such activity, or that BE ever agreed to comply with the User Agreement. . . .

A software robot is a computer program which operates across the Internet to perform searching, copying and retrieving functions on the web sites of others. A software robot is capable of executing thousands of instructions per minute, far in excess of what a human can accomplish. Robots consume the processing and storage resources of a system, making that portion of the system's capacity unavailable to the system owner or other users. Consumption of sufficient system resources will slow the processing of the overall system and can overload the system such that it will malfunction or "crash." A severe malfunction can cause a loss of data and an interruption in services.

BE is a company with 22 employees that was founded in 1997. The BE web site debuted in November 1998. BE does not host auctions. BE is an auction aggregation site designed to offer on-line auction buyers the ability to search for items across numerous on-line auctions without having to search each host site individually. . . .

[eBay initially allowed BE to access its site, but subsequently requested that it stop. BE, nonetheless, continued to access eBay's site.]

The parties agree that BE accessed the eBay site approximate 100,000 times a day. eBay alleges that BE activity constituted up to 1.53% of the number of requests received by eBay, and up to 1.10% of the total data transferred by eBay during certain periods in October and November of 1999. BE alleges that BE activity constituted no more than 1.11% of the requests received by eBay, and no more than 0.70% of the data transferred by eBay. eBay alleges that BE activity had fallen 27%, to 0.74% of requests and 0.61% of data, by February 20, 2000. eBay alleges damages due to BE's activity totaling between $45,323 and $61,804 for a ten month period including seven months in 1999 and the first three months in 2000. However, these calculations appear flawed in that they assume the maximal BE usage of eBay resources continued over all ten months. Moreover, the calculations attribute a pro rata share of eBay expenditures to BE activity, rather than attempting to calculate the incremental cost to eBay due to BE activity. eBay has not alleged any specific incremental damages due to BE activity.

It appears that major Internet search engines, such as Yahoo!, Google, Excite and AltaVista, respect the Robot Exclusion Standard.

eBay now moves for preliminary injunctive relief preventing BE from accessing the eBay computer system based on nine causes of action: trespass, false advertising, federal and state trademark dilution, computer fraud and abuse, unfair competition, misappropriation, interference with prospective economic advantage and unjust enrichment. However, eBay does not move, either independently or alternatively, for injunctive relief that is limited to restricting how BE can use data taken from the eBay site.

III. ANALYSIS

A. Balance of Harm

eBay asserts that it will suffer four types of irreparable harm if preliminary injunctive relief is not granted: (1) lost capacity of its computer systems resulting from BE's use of automated agents; (2) damage to eBay's reputation and goodwill caused by BE's misleading postings; (3) dilution of the eBay mark; and (4) BE's unjust enrichment. The harm eBay alleges it will suffer can be divided into two categories. The first type of harm is harm that eBay alleges it will suffer as a result of BE's automated query programs burdening eBay's computer system ("system harm"). The second type of harm is harm that eBay alleges it will suffer as a result of BE's misrepresentations regarding the information that BE obtains through the use of these automated query programs ("reputational harm").

As noted above, eBay does not seek an injunction that is tailored to independently address the manner in which BE uses the information it obtains from eBay. . . .

According to eBay, the load on its servers resulting from BE's web crawlers represents between 1.11% and 1.53% of the total load on eBay's listing servers. eBay alleges both economic loss from BE's current activities and potential harm resulting from the total crawling of BE and others. In alleging economic harm, eBay's argument is that eBay has expended considerable time, effort and money to create its computer system, and that BE should have to pay for the portion of eBay's system BE uses. eBay attributes a pro rata portion of the costs of maintaining its entire system to the BE activity. However, eBay does not indicate that these expenses are incrementally incurred because of BE's activities, nor that any particular service disruption can be attributed to BE's activities. eBay provides no support for the proposition that the pro rata costs of obtaining an item represent the appropriate measure of damages for unauthorized use. In contrast, California law appears settled that the appropriate measure of damages is the actual harm inflicted by the conduct:

> Where the conduct complained of does not amount to a substantial interference with possession or the right thereto, but consists of intermeddling with or use of or damages to the personal property, the owner has a cause of action for trespass or case, and may recover only the actual damages suffered by reason of the impairment of the property or the loss of its use.

Zaslow v. Kroenert, 29 Cal. 2d 541, 551, 176 P.2d 1 (1946). Moreover, even if BE is inflicting incremental maintenance costs on eBay, potentially calculable monetary damages are not generally a proper foundation for a preliminary injunction. See e.g., Sampson v. Murray, 415 U.S. 61, 90 (1974). Nor does eBay appear to have made the required showing that this is the type of extraordinary case in which monetary damages may support equitable relief. See In re Estate of Ferdinand Marcos, Human Rights Litigation, 25 F.3d 1467, 1480 (9th Cir. 1994) ("a district court has authority to issue a preliminary injunction where the plaintiffs can establish that money damages will be an inadequate remedy due to impending insolvency of the defendant or that defendant has engaged in a pattern of secreting or dissipating assets to avoid judgment").

eBay's allegations of harm are based, in part, on the argument that BE's activities should be thought of as equivalent to sending in an army of 100,000 robots a day to check the prices in a competitor's store. This analogy, while graphic, appears inappropriate. Although an admittedly formalistic distinction, unauthorized robot intruders into a "brick and mortar" store would be committing a trespass to real property. There does not appear to be any doubt that the appropriate remedy for an ongoing trespass to business premises would be a preliminary injunction. See e.g., State v. Carriker, 5 Ohio App. 2d 255, 214 N.E.2d 809, 811-12 (1964) (interpreting Ohio criminal trespass law to cover a business invitee who, with no intention of making a purchase, uses the business premises of another for his own gain after his invitation has been revoked); General Petroleum Corp. v. Beilby, 213 Cal. 601, 605, 2 P.2d 797 (1931). More importantly, for the analogy to be accurate, the robots would have to make up less than two out of every one-hundred customers in the store, the robots would not interfere with the customers' shopping experience, nor would the robots even be seen by the customers. Under such circumstances, there is a legitimate claim that the robots would not pose any threat of irreparable harm. However, eBay's right to injunctive relief is also based upon a much stronger argument.

If BE's activity is allowed to continue unchecked, it would encourage other auction aggregators to engage in similar recursive searching of the eBay system such that eBay would suffer irreparable harm from reduced system performance, system unavailability, or data losses. BE does not appear to seriously contest that reduced system performance, system unavailability or data loss would inflict irreparable harm on eBay consisting of lost profits and lost customer goodwill. Harm resulting from lost profits and lost customer goodwill is irreparable because it is neither easily calculable, nor easily compensable and is therefore an appropriate basis for injunctive relief. See, e.g., People of California ex rel. Van De Kamp v. Tahoe Reg'l Planning Agency, 766 F.2d 1316, 1319 (9th Cir. 1985). Where, as here, the denial of preliminary injunctive relief would encourage an increase in the complained of activity, and such an increase would present a strong likelihood of irreparable harm, the plaintiff has at least established a possibility of irreparable harm. . . .

B. Likelihood of Success

As noted above, eBay moves for a preliminary injunction on all nine of its causes of action. These nine causes of action correspond to eight legal theories: (1) trespass to chattels, (2) false advertising under the Lanham Act, 15 U.S.C. §1125(a), (3) federal and state trademark dilution, (4) violation of the Computer Fraud and Abuse Act, 18 U.S.C. §1030, (5) unfair competition, (6) misappropriation, (7) interference with prospective economic advantage and (8) unjust enrichment. The court finds that eBay has established a sufficient likelihood of prevailing on the trespass claim to support the requested injunctive relief. Since the court finds eBay is entitled to the relief requested based on its trespass claim, the court does not address the merits of the remaining claims or BE's arguments that many of these other state law causes of action are preempted by federal copyright law. The court first addresses the merits of the trespass claim, then BE's arguments regarding copyright preemption of the trespass claim, and finally the public interest.

1. Trespass

Trespass to chattels "lies where an intentional interference with the possession of personal property has proximately cause injury."

Thrifty-Tel v. Bezenek, 46 Cal. App. 4th 1559, 1566, 54 Cal. Rptr. 2d 468 (1996). Trespass to chattels "although seldom employed as a tort theory in California" was recently applied to cover the unauthorized use of long distance telephone lines. *Id.* Specifically, the court noted "the electronic signals generated by the [defendants'] activities were sufficiently tangible to support a trespass cause of action." *Id.* at n. 6. Thus, it appears likely that the electronic signals sent by BE to retrieve information from eBay's computer system are also sufficiently tangible to support a trespass cause of action.

In order to prevail on a claim for trespass based on accessing a computer system, the plaintiff must establish: (1) defendant intentionally and without authorization interfered with plaintiff's possessory interest in the computer system; and (2) defendant's unauthorized use proximately resulted in damage to plaintiff. See *Thrifty-Tel*, 46 Cal. App. 4th at 1566, 54 Cal. Rptr. 2d 468; see also Itano v. Colonial Yacht Anchorage, 267 Cal. App. 2d 84, 90, 72 Cal. Rptr. 823 (1968) ("When conduct complained of consists of intermeddling with personal property 'the owner has a cause of action for trespass or case, and may recover only the actual damages suffered by reason of the impairment of the property or the loss of its use.'") (quoting Zaslow v. Kroenert, 29 Cal. 2d 541, 550, 176 P.2d 1 (1946)). Here, eBay has presented evidence sufficient to establish a strong likelihood of proving both prongs and ultimately prevailing on the merits of its trespass claim.

a. BE's Unauthorized Interference

eBay argues that BE's use was unauthorized and intentional. eBay is correct. BE does not dispute that it employed an automated computer program to connect with and search eBay's electronic database. BE admits that, because other auction aggregators were including eBay's auctions in their listing, it continued to "crawl" eBay's web site even after eBay demanded BE terminate such activity.

BE argues that it cannot trespass eBay's web site because the site is publicly accessible. BE's argument is unconvincing. eBay's servers are private property, conditional access to which eBay grants the public. eBay does not generally permit the type of automated access made by BE. In fact, eBay explicitly notifies automated visitors that their access is not permitted. "In general, California does recognize a trespass claim where the defendant exceeds the scope of the consent." Baugh v. CBS, Inc., 828 F. Supp. 745, 756 (N.D. Cal. 1993).

Even if BE's web crawlers were authorized to make individual queries of eBay's system, BE's web crawlers exceeded the scope of any such consent when they began acting like robots by making repeated queries. . . . Moreover, eBay repeatedly and explicitly notified BE that its use of eBay's computer system was unauthorized. The entire reason BE directed its queries through proxy servers was to evade eBay's attempts to stop this unauthorized access. The court concludes that BE's activity is sufficiently outside of the scope of the use permitted by eBay that it is unauthorized for the purposes of establishing a trespass. . . .

eBay argues that BE interfered with eBay's possessory interest in its computer system. Although eBay appears unlikely to be able to show a substantial interference at this time, such a showing is not required. Conduct that does not amount to a substantial interference with possession, but which consists of intermeddling with or use of another's personal property, is sufficient to establish a cause of action for trespass to chattel. See *Thrifty-Tel*, 46 Cal. App. 4th at 1567, 54 Cal. Rptr. 2d 468 (distinguishing the tort from conversion). Although the court admits some uncertainty as to the precise level of possessory interference required to constitute an intermeddling, there does not appear to be any dispute that eBay can show that BE's conduct amounts to use of eBay's computer systems. Accordingly, eBay has made a strong showing that it is likely to prevail on the merits of its assertion that BE's use of eBay's computer system was an unauthorized and intentional interference with eBay's possessory interest.

b. Damage to eBay's Computer System

A trespasser is liable when the trespass diminishes the condition, quality or value of personal property. See CompuServe, Inc. v. Cyber Promotions, 962 F. Supp. 1015 (S.D. Ohio 1997). The quality or value of personal property may be "diminished even though it is not physically damaged by defendant's conduct." *Id.* at 1022. . . .

eBay is likely to be able to demonstrate that BE's activities have diminished the quality or value of eBay's computer systems. BE's activities consume at least a portion of plaintiff's bandwidth and server capacity. Although there is some dispute as to the percentage of queries on eBay's site for which BE is responsible, BE admits that it sends some 80,000 to 100,000 requests to plaintiff's computer systems per day. Although eBay does not claim that this consumption has led to any physical damage to eBay's computer system, nor does eBay provide any evidence to support the claim that it may have lost revenues or customers based on this use, eBay's claim is that BE's use is appropriating eBay's personal property by using valuable bandwidth and capacity, and necessarily compromising eBay's ability to use that capacity for its own purposes. See *CompuServe*, 962 F. Supp. at 1022 ("any value [plaintiff] realizes from its computer equipment is wholly derived from the extent to which that equipment can serve its subscriber base").

BE argues that its searches represent a negligible load on plaintiff's computer systems, and do not rise to the level of impairment to the condition or value of eBay's computer system required to constitute a trespass. However, it is undisputed that eBay's server and its capacity are personal property, and that BE's searches use a portion of this property. Even if, as BE argues, its searches use only a small amount of eBay's computer system capacity, BE has nonetheless deprived eBay of the ability to use that portion of its personal property for its own purposes. The law recognizes no such right to use another's personal property. Accordingly, BE's actions appear to have caused injury to eBay and appear likely to continue to cause injury to eBay. If the court were to hold otherwise, it would likely encourage other auction aggregators to crawl the eBay site, potentially to the point of denying effective access to eBay's customers. If preliminary injunctive relief were denied, and other aggregators began to crawl the eBay site, there appears to be little doubt that the load on eBay's computer system would qualify as a substantial impairment of condition or value. California law does not require eBay to wait for such a disaster before applying to this court for relief. The court concludes that eBay has made a strong showing that it is likely to prevail on the merits of its trespass claim, and that there is at least a possibility that it will suffer irreparable harm if preliminary injunctive relief is not granted. eBay is therefore entitled to preliminary injunctive relief.

2. Copyright Preemption

BE argues that the trespass claim, along with eBay's other state law causes of action, "is similar to eBay's originally filed but now dismissed copyright infringement claim, and each is based on eBay's assertion that Bidder's Edge copies eBay's auction listings, a right within federal copyright law." Opp'n at 8:10-12. BE is factually incorrect to the extent it argues that the trespass claim arises out of what BE does with the information it gathers by accessing eBay's computer system, rather than the mere fact that BE accesses and uses that system without authorization. . . .

IV. Order

Bidder's Edge, its officers, agents, servants, employees, attorneys and those in active concert or participation with them who receive actual notice of this order by personal service or otherwise, are hereby enjoined pending the trial of this matter, from using any automated query program, robot, web crawler or other similar device, without written authorization, to access eBay's computer systems or networks, for the purpose of copying any part of eBay's auction database. . . .

Nothing in this order precludes BE from utilizing information obtained from eBay's site other than by automated query program, robot, web crawler or similar device. . . .

COMMENTS AND QUESTIONS

1. If Bidder's Edge's activities accounted for less than 2 percent of eBay's network usage, was the injury irreparable? According to the court in *eBay*, how did Bidder's Edge damage eBay's computer network?

2. How is Bidder's Edge's use of robots relevant to a trespass analysis? Would the court's conclusion be the same if Bidder's Edge hired real people to conduct searches on eBay's site?

3. How does *eBay* address the issue of substantial interference? Should the fact that eBay invites anyone with Internet access to come to their site to shop and browse impact this analysis?

4. Following the decision in *eBay*, a District Court in New York applied trespass to chattels in Register.com, Inc. v. Verio, Inc., 126 F. Supp. 2d 238 (S.D.N.Y. 2000). Register.com is a registrar of Internet domain names. As part of its contract with the Internet Corporation for Assigned Names and Numbers (ICANN), Register.com is required to provide a WHOIS database, which contains the names and contact information for customers who register domain names through the registrar, and to make the database freely available to the public. As part of its terms of use, Register.com forbade those accessing the WHOIS database from using the information for commercial solicitations. Verio, a provider of Internet services, used robots to access Register.com's WHOIS database in order to market its services to new registrants. The district court issued an injunction against Verio prohibiting it from using the WHOIS data and from using robots to gather information from the database. The court concluded that the use of the data was contractually limited by Register.com's terms of use, that Verio was on notice that the use of robots was prohibited and its continued use of robots constituted trespass, and that both its means of access and use of the data violated the CFAA. With respect to the trespass claim, the court found in favor of Register.com even though Register.com was unable to quantify the extent to which Verio's robots occupied its system resources. According to the district court "evidence of mere possessory

interference is sufficient to demonstrate the quantum of harm necessary to establish a claim for trespass to chattels."

5. Unlike *CompuServe*, is the real issue in *eBay* whether eBay has an intellectual property right to the bidding information? Why is that claim not preempted by copyright law? *Consider* Ticketmaster Corp. v. Tickets.Com, Inc., 2000 WL 1887522 (C.D. Cal. Aug. 10, 2000):

> . . . The trespass aspects of the case have taken on new significance in the light of Judge Whyte's opinion in eBay. . . . The computer is a piece of tangible personal property. It is operated by mysterious electronic impulses which did not exist when the law of trespass to chattels was developed, but the principles should not be too different. If the electronic impulses can do damage to the computer or to its function in a comparable way to taking a hammer to a piece of machinery, then it is no stretch to recognize that damage as trespass to chattels and provide a legal remedy for it. . . . A basic element of trespass to chattels must be physical harm to the chattel (not present here) or some obstruction of its basic function (in the court's opinion not sufficiently shown here). TM has presented statistics showing an estimate of the number of hits by T.Com spiders in its own computers and has presented rough comparisons with the total use of the computers by all users of the computers. The comparative use by T.Com appears very small and there is no showing that the use interferes to any extent with the regular business of TM. If it did, an injunction might well issue, but should not with a showing of lack of harm or foreseeable harm. Nor here is the specter of dozens or more parasites joining the fray, the cumulative total of which could affect the operation of TM's business. Further, the showing here is that the effect of T.Com's taking of factual data from TM is not to operate in direct competition with TM—it is not selling the data or the tickets. While TM sees some detriment in T.Com's operation (possibly in the loss of advertising revenue), there is also a beneficial effect in the referral of customers looking for tickets to TM events directly to TM. (In fact, other companies, who presumably pay a fee, are allowed to refer customers directly to the internal web pages of TM, presumably leading to sale of TM tickets despite hypothetical loss of advertising revenue by not going through the TM home web page.) Accordingly, while the trespass theory has some merit, there is insufficient proof of its elements in this case to justify a preliminary injunction. . . .

How does the analysis employed in *Ticketmaster* differ from *CompuServe* and *eBay*? Which approach is more consistent with trespass?

6. If computer network owners are entitled to rely upon real property rights in dealing with users, should they be required to satisfy real property duties as well? For example, America Online was sued by the National Federation for the Blind under the Americans with Disabilities Act because its proprietary software was not compatible with existing Braille translating programs. While the parties eventually settled the lawsuit with AOL agreeing to make its AOL 6.0 compatible with screen access software for the blind, should AOL be considered a place of public accommodation required to reasonably accommodate individuals with disabilities? Is AOL required to prevent discrimination against its users?

7
PRIVATE ORDERING OF CYBERSPACE

The preceding chapters explored how freedom of speech, property, and privacy could be used to control the flow of information in cyberspace. This chapter explores how and to what extent those principles and rules can be modified, supplemented, or replaced by private ordering. By private ordering we do not mean to suggest decision making in the absence of law or in some form of cyberspace state of nature. Rather, private ordering examines the question of when government should allow individual decision making—either made jointly or unilaterally—to regulate cyberspace. In other words, to what extent should contracts and self-help replace or supplement the laws that regulate cyberspace?

From the Internet's beginnings, commentators have suggested that contracts are an ideal means for regulating cyberspace.[1] As noted in Chapter 2, private agreements may avoid many of the difficult issues of notice and avoid the difficult question of what state may legitimately regulate the global information network. Moreover, according to one school of thought, because the Internet facilitates easy and relatively inexpensive communications, the transaction costs associated with brick and mortar negotiations are absent (or at least greatly reduced) in what one author has described as the "frictionless" environment of cyberspace.[2] In the absence of transaction costs, these commentators suggest that individuals should be allowed to order their relationships as they see fit.[3]

In the United States, the federal and state governments have taken steps to recognize the validity of electronic agreements in general. For example, under the Electronic Signatures in Global and National Commerce Act, the validity of

---

1. *See, e.g.,* I. Trotter Hardy, *Property (and Copyright) in Cyberspace,* 1996 U. Chi. Legal F. 217. *But see* Julie E. Cohen, *Lochner in Cyberspace: The New Economic Orthodoxy of "Rights Management,"* 97 Mich. L. Rev. 462 (1998).

2. Robert P. Merges, *The End of Friction? Property Rights and Contract in the "Newtonian" World of On-line Commerce,* 12 Berkeley Tech. L.J. 115 (1997).

3. Hardy, *supra* note 1, at 259-60.

signatures and contracts cannot be denied simply because they are in electronic form.[4] This chapter, however, does not focus on the general effort to translate signatures or other aspects of contract law for an electronic world. Instead, the following materials address the central questions for private ordering in cyberspace, namely, what constitutes an agreement in this digital universe, and what are the limits to those agreements?

Similarly, to what extent can individuals control behavior in cyberspace through self-help? In cyberspace, self-help is accomplished through the computer code that runs the network of networks and all its applications. As Lawrence Lessig suggests, in cyberspace, code regulates conduct.[5] For example, Microsoft Windows XP was programmed to self-destruct after 30 days if it is installed on an unauthorized computer. To what extent should individuals be allowed to use code to regulate conduct and to protect interests that might not otherwise be protected by law?

As the preceding chapters suggest, the questions of consent and self-help are universal, and how we resolve these questions will have a significant impact on how we deal with jurisdiction, freedom of speech, intellectual property, privacy, and network ownership. In some cases, consent and self-help may supplant other doctrines, while in others they may only represent the beginning of the inquiry.

Problem 13.0

Having finished work on StarttUp's Privacy Policy, Alan and Barbara want you to examine all of the company's agreements. To date, they assumed that the Web site's Privacy Policy, Terms and Conditions of Use, and Subscriber Agreement represented legal and binding contracts. Your discussions about modifying StarttUp's Privacy Policy in light of the consent requirements of the European Union Data Protection Directive have unnerved them. As noted in Problem 1.0, StarttUp provides users with several levels of access:

1. **Free Access.** Anyone coming to the Web site will have access to an extremely limited amount of content and no access to services. This level is primarily a means of exposing interested subscribers to the service.
2. **Registered Free Access.** By providing certain personal and demographic information, registered users will be able to access more of StarttUp's content, and will be able to view message boards and enter chatrooms.

---

4. 15 U.S.C. §7001. This legislation at the federal level is largely intended as a "gap filler" on this issue for states that have not enacted the Uniform Electronic Transactions Act, which is an attempt at a relatively harmonized state law to achieve the same ends.

5. *See generally* Lawrence Lessig, *Code 2.0* (2006).

3. **Regular Subscriber Access.** For a monthly fee and after agreeing to an online subscription agreement, subscribers are given access to all of StarttUp's content and services, including e-mail and instant messaging. Certain premium services such as streaming music and video are available on a pay-per-use basis.

4. **Premium Subscriber Access.** For a higher monthly fee and after agreeing to an online subscription agreement, premium subscribers are given access to all of the services as regular subscribers plus unlimited access to the premium services.

How a user's consent is obtained varies depending upon the level of access.

Free Access users are considered to have agreed to the terms of both the Privacy Policy and Terms and Conditions of Use simply by continuing to use the site. Links to these documents are provided at the bottom of each Web page with a note to "Please read the following. . . ." If a user does not agree to the terms, they are told to stop using the site.

Registered Free Access users are presented with a window containing the Terms and Conditions of Use and are asked to click on either an "I Agree" or "I Disagree" button. If they disagree, the registration process ends and their access is limited to that of a Free Access user. The Terms and Conditions of Use incorporate the terms of the Privacy Policy. Users may simply click the "I Agree" button without scrolling through the document.

Regular and premium subscribers must go through the same process as Registered Free Access users, plus they are required to enter into a subscription agreement. The user is presented with another screen containing the agreement, but unlike the Terms and Conditions of Use, the user must scroll to the bottom of the subscription agreement before they can click "I Agree."

Alan and Barbara are particularly concerned about three provisions. All three clauses appear in the Terms and Conditions of Use as well as the subscription agreement. The first is the choice of forum and choice of law clause that you recommended. The second is a clause that prohibits users from publicly criticizing and disparaging StarttUp and/or its officers. The third provision states that the services provided to the user are conditioned upon the user maintaining good standing as a StarttUp user. If a user violates any of the StarttUp agreements or fails to make a required payment, StarttUp reserves the right to cancel the user's service and deactivate any products the user may have obtained from StarttUp. Are these provisions enforceable?

Problem 13.1

In light of your discussions with Cora about the unwanted comments on her blog (see Problem 12.1), Cora has decided to revisit the terms of use on the blog. She would like to include terms that she and her co-bloggers are entitled to actively monitor comments and remove any that they do not believe are in keeping with the overall tone of the blog. She also wants to prevent commenters from disparaging or criticizing Cora and her co-bloggers, and the feminist ideals that they espouse on the blog. How might Cora most effectively incorporate these issues as terms of use on the blog? Will they be contractually binding on commenters?

A. Shrinkwrap, Click-Wrap, and Browser Agreements

The very heart of the debate over private ordering is the question of what constitutes a meeting of the minds in cyberspace. Does clicking the "I Agree" button on the Web page or during the installation of software bind the consumer? Does the browsing of a Web page bind the surfer to the site's terms of use? Beginning with the sale of computer programs and so-called "shrinkwrap agreements," courts have been confronted with the task of determining what constitutes a binding agreement with respect to new technologies. As you study the following materials, consider what is at stake in this debate. What values support each side in the debate? Are they the same values or are they conflicting values? Also, consider whether contracts are a more efficient or satisfactory means for regulating conduct in comparison to statutory or common laws.

ProCD, Inc. v. Zeidenberg

86 F.3d 1447 (7th Cir. 1996)

Easterbrook, Circuit Judge . . .

I

ProCD, the plaintiff, has compiled information from more than 3,000 telephone directories into a computer database. We may assume that this database cannot be copyrighted, although it is more complex, contains more information (nine-digit zip codes and census industrial codes), is organized differently, and therefore is more original than the single alphabetical directory at issue in Feist

Publications, Inc. v. Rural Telephone Service Co., 499 U.S. 340 (1991). . . . ProCD sells a version of the database, called SelectPhone (trademark), on CD-ROM discs. (CD-ROM means "compact disc — read only memory." The "shrinkwrap license" gets its name from the fact that retail software packages are covered in plastic or cellophane "shrinkwrap," and some vendors, though not ProCD, have written licenses that become effective as soon as the customer tears the wrapping from the package. Vendors prefer "end user license," but we use the more common term.) . . .

The database in SelectPhone (trademark) cost more than $10 million to compile and is expensive to keep current. It is much more valuable to some users than to others. The combination of names, addresses, and SIC codes enables manufacturers to compile lists of potential customers. Manufacturers and retailers pay high prices to specialized information intermediaries for such mailing lists; ProCD offers a potentially cheaper alternative. People with nothing to sell could use the database as a substitute for calling long distance information, or as a way to look up old friends who have moved to unknown towns, or just as an electronic substitute for the local phone book. ProCD decided to engage in price discrimination, selling its database to the general public for personal use at a low price (approximately $150 for the set of five discs) while selling information to the trade for a higher price. It has adopted some intermediate strategies too: access to the SelectPhone (trademark) database is available via the America Online service for the price America Online charges to its clients (approximately $3 per hour), but this service has been tailored to be useful only to the general public.

If ProCD had to recover all of its costs and make a profit by charging a single price — that is, if it could not charge more to commercial users than to the general public — it would have to raise the price substantially over $150. The ensuing reduction in sales would harm consumers who value the information at, say, $200. They get consumer surplus of $50 under the current arrangement but would cease to buy if the price rose substantially. If because of high elasticity of demand in the consumer segment of the market the only way to make a profit turned out to be a price attractive to commercial users alone, then all consumers would lose out — and so would the commercial clients, who would have to pay more for the listings because ProCD could not obtain any contribution toward costs from the consumer market.

To make price discrimination work, however, the seller must be able to control arbitrage. An air carrier sells tickets for less to vacationers than to business travelers, using advance purchase and Saturday-night-stay requirements to distinguish the categories. A producer of movies segments the market by time, releasing first to theaters, then to pay-per-view services, next to the videotape and laserdisc market, and finally to cable and commercial TV. Vendors of computer software have a harder task. Anyone can walk into a retail store and buy a box. Customers do not wear tags saying "commercial user" or "consumer user." Anyway, even a commercial-user-detector at the door would not work, because a consumer could buy the software and resell to a commercial user. That arbitrage would break down the price discrimination and drive up the minimum price at which ProCD would sell to anyone.

Instead of tinkering with the product and letting users sort themselves — for example, furnishing current data at a high price that would be attractive only to commercial customers, and two-year-old data at a low price — ProCD turned to the institution of contract. Every box containing its consumer product declares that the software comes with restrictions stated in an enclosed license. This license, which is encoded on the CD-ROM disks as well as printed in the manual, and which appears on a user's screen every time the software runs, limits use of the application program and listings to non-commercial purposes.

Matthew Zeidenberg bought a consumer package of SelectPhone (trademark) in 1994 from a retail outlet in Madison, Wisconsin, but decided to ignore the license. He formed Silken Mountain Web Services, Inc., to resell the information in the SelectPhone (trademark) database. The corporation makes the database available on the Internet to anyone willing to pay its price — which, needless to say, is less than ProCD charges its commercial customers. . . .

II

Following the district court, we treat the licenses as ordinary contracts accompanying the sale of products, and therefore as governed by the common law of contracts and the Uniform Commercial Code. Whether there are legal differences between "contracts" and "licenses" (which may matter under the copyright doctrine of first sale) is a subject for another day. See Microsoft Corp. v. Harmony Computers & Electronics, Inc., 846 F. Supp. 208 (E.D.N.Y. 1994). . . . Zeidenberg [argues], and the district court held, that placing the package of software on the shelf is an "offer," which the customer "accepts" by paying the asking price and leaving the store with the goods. Peeters v. State, 154 Wis. 111, 142 N.W. 181 (1913). In Wisconsin, as elsewhere, a contract includes only the terms on which the parties have agreed. One cannot agree to hidden terms, the judge concluded. So far, so good — but one of the terms to which Zeidenberg agreed by purchasing the software is that the transaction was subject to a license. Zeidenberg's position therefore must be that the printed terms on the outside of a box are the parties' contract — except for printed terms that refer to or incorporate other terms. But why would Wisconsin fetter the parties' choice in this way? Vendors can put the entire terms of a contract on the outside of a box only by using microscopic type, removing other information that buyers might find more useful (such as what the software does, and on which computers it works), or both. . . . Notice on the outside, terms on the inside, and a right to return the software for a refund if the terms are unacceptable (a right that the license expressly extends), may be a means of doing business valuable to buyers and sellers alike. . . .

Doubtless a state could forbid the use of standard contracts in the software business, but we do not think that Wisconsin has done so.

Transactions in which the exchange of money precedes the communication of detailed terms are common. Consider the purchase of insurance. The buyer goes to an agent, who explains the essentials (amount of coverage, number of years) and remits the premium to the home office, which sends back a policy. On the district judge's understanding, the terms of the policy are irrelevant because the insured paid before receiving them. Yet the device of payment, often with a "binder" (so that the insurance takes effect immediately even though the home office reserves the right to withdraw coverage later), in advance of the policy, serves buyers' interests by accelerating effectiveness and reducing transactions costs. Or consider the purchase of an airline ticket. The traveler calls the carrier or an agent, is quoted a price, reserves a seat, pays, and gets a ticket, in that order. The ticket contains elaborate terms, which the traveler can reject by canceling the reservation. To use the ticket is to accept the terms, even terms that in retrospect are disadvantageous. See Carnival Cruise Lines, Inc. v. Shute, 499 U.S. 585 (1991); see also Vimar Seguros y Reaseguros, S.A. v. M/V Sky Reefer, 515 U.S. 528 (1995) (bills of lading). Just so with a ticket to a concert. The back of the ticket states that the patron promises not to record the concert; to attend is to agree. A theater that detects a violation will confiscate the tape and escort the violator to the exit. One could arrange things so that every concertgoer signs this promise before forking over the money, but that cumbersome way of doing things not only would lengthen queues and raise prices but also would scotch the sale of tickets by phone or electronic data service.

Consumer goods work the same way. Someone who wants to buy a radio set visits a store, pays, and walks out with a box. Inside the box is a leaflet containing some terms, the most important of which usually is the warranty, read for the first time in the comfort of home. . . .

Next consider the software industry itself. Only a minority of sales take place over the counter, where there are boxes to peruse. A customer may place an order by phone in response to a line item in a catalog or a review in a magazine. Much software is ordered over the Internet by purchasers who have never seen a box. Increasingly software arrives by wire. There is no box; there is only a stream of electrons, a collection of information that includes data, an application program, instructions, many limitations ("MegaPixel 3.14159 cannot be used with BytePusher 2.718"), and the terms of sale. The user purchases a serial number, which activates the software's features. On Zeidenberg's arguments, these unboxed sales are unfettered by terms—so the seller has made a broad warranty and must pay consequential damages for any shortfalls in performance, two "promises" that if taken seriously would drive prices through the ceiling or return transactions to the horse-and-buggy age.

According to the district court, the UCC does not countenance the sequence of money now, terms later. One of the court's reasons—that by proposing as part of the draft Article 2B a new UCC §2-2203 that would explicitly validate standard-form user licenses, the American Law Institute and the National Conference of Commissioners on Uniform Laws have conceded the invalidity of shrinkwrap licenses under current law, see 908 F. Supp. at 655-56 — depends on a faulty inference. To propose a change in a law's text is not necessarily to propose a change in the law's effect. New words may be designed to fortify the current rule with a more precise text that curtails uncertainty. To judge by the flux of law review articles discussing shrinkwrap licenses, uncertainty is much in need of reduction — although businesses seem to feel less uncertainty than do scholars, for only three cases (other than ours) touch on the subject, and none directly addresses it. See Step-Saver Data Systems, Inc. v. Wyse Technology, 939 F.2d 91 (3d Cir. 1991); Vault Corp. v. Quaid Software Ltd., 847 F.2d 255, 268-70 (5th Cir. 1988); Arizona Retail Systems, Inc. v. Software Link, Inc., 831 F. Supp. 759 (D. Ariz. 1993). As their titles suggest, these are not consumer transactions. *Step-Saver* is a battle-of-the-forms case, in which the parties exchange incompatible forms and a court must decide which prevails. See Northrop Corp. v. Litronic Industries, 29 F.3d 1173 (7th Cir. 1994) (Illinois law); Douglas G. Baird & Robert Weisberg, Rules, Standards, and the Battle of the Forms: A Reassessment of §2-207, 68 Va. L. Rev. 1217, 1227-31 (1982). Our case has only one form; UCC §2-207 is irrelevant. *Vault* holds that Louisiana's special shrinkwrap-license statute is preempted by federal law, a question to which we return. And *Arizona Retail Systems* did not reach the question, because the court found that the buyer knew the terms of the license before purchasing the software.

What then does the current version of the UCC have to say? We think that the place to start is §2-204(1): "A contract for sale of goods may be made in any manner sufficient to show agreement, including conduct by both parties which recognizes the existence of such a contract." A vendor, as master of the offer, may invite acceptance by conduct, and may propose limitations on the kind of conduct that constitutes acceptance. A buyer may accept by performing the acts the vendor proposes to treat as acceptance. And that is what happened. ProCD proposed a contract that a buyer would accept by using the software after having an opportunity to read the license at leisure. This Zeidenberg did. He had no choice, because the software splashed the license on the screen and would not let him proceed without indicating acceptance. So although the district judge was right to say that a contract can be, and often is, formed simply by paying the price and walking out of the store, the UCC permits contracts to be formed in other ways. ProCD proposed such a different way, and without protest Zeidenberg agreed. Ours is not a case in which a consumer opens a package to find an insert saying "you owe us an extra $10,000" and the seller files suit to collect. Any buyer finding such a demand can prevent formation of the contract by returning the package, as can any consumer who concludes that the terms of the license make the software worth less than the purchase price. Nothing in the UCC requires a seller to maximize the buyer's net gains.

Section 2-606, which defines "acceptance of goods," reinforces this understanding. A buyer accepts goods under §2-606(1)(b) when, after an opportunity to inspect, he fails to make an effective rejection under §2-602(1). ProCD extended an opportunity to reject if a buyer should find the license terms unsatisfactory; Zeidenberg inspected the package, tried out the software, learned of the license, and did not reject the goods. We refer to §2-606 only to show that the opportunity to return goods can be important; acceptance of an offer differs from acceptance of goods after delivery, see Gillen v. Atlanta Systems, Inc., 997 F.2d 280, 284 n.1 (7th Cir. 1993); but the UCC consistently permits the parties to structure their relations so that the buyer has a chance to make a final decision after a detailed review.

. . . In the end, the terms of the license are conceptually identical to the contents of the package. Just as no court would dream of saying that Select-Phone (trademark) must contain 3,100 phone books rather than 3,000, or must have data no more than 30 days old, or must sell for $100 rather than $150 — although any of these changes would be welcomed by the customer, if all other things were held constant — so, we believe, Wisconsin would not let the buyer pick and choose among terms. Terms of use are no less a part of "the product" than are the size of the database and the speed with which the software compiles listings. Competition among vendors, not judicial revision of a package's contents, is how consumers are protected in a market economy. Digital Equipment Corp. v. Uniq Digital Technologies, Inc., 73 F.3d 756 (7th Cir. 1996). ProCD has rivals, which may elect to compete by offering superior software, monthly updates, improved terms of use, lower price, or a better compromise among these elements. As we stressed above, adjusting terms in buyers' favor might help Matthew Zeidenberg today (he already has the software) but would lead to a response, such as a higher price, that might make consumers as a whole worse off. . . .

COMMENTS AND QUESTIONS

1. In *ProCD*, the Seventh Circuit concludes that shrinkwrap agreements can be used to limit a user's fair use of a product under copyright law. In general, courts have held that software contracts (often referred to as End User License Agreements, or "EULAs") are enforceable even if they involve users agreeing to give up rights that they would otherwise have under copyright law. In Blizzard v. Jung, 422 F.3d 630 (2005), for example, the United States Court of Appeals for the Eighth Circuit held with respect to the reverse engineering exception to copyright infringement that: " 'Private parties are free to contractually forego the limited ability to reverse engineer a software product under the exemptions of the Copyright Act[,]' Bowers v. Baystate Techs, Inc., 320 F.3d 1317, 1325-26 (Fed. Cir. 2003), and 'a state can permit parties to contract away a fair use defense or to agree not to engage in uses of copyrighted material that are permitted by the copyright law if the contract is

freely negotiated.' *Id.* at 1337 (Dyk, J., dissenting). *See also Nat'l Car Rental Sys., Inc.*, 991 F.2d at 434 (holding that the Copyright Act does not preempt a breach of contract action based on prohibited use of software contained in a license agreement). While *Bowers* and *Nat'l Car Rental* were express preemption cases rather than conflict preemption, their reasoning applies here with equal force. By signing the TOUs and EULAs, Appellants expressly relinquished their rights to reverse engineer. Summary judgment on this issue was properly granted in favor of Blizzard and Vivendi." (422 F.3d 630, 639 (2005)). *See also* Robert W. Gomulkiewicz, *Getting Serious About User-friendly Mass Market Licensing For Software*, 12 Geo. Mason L. Rev. 687, 687 (2004) ("EULAs are here to stay for the foreseeable future. Courts, by and large, have enforced EULAs, provided the software publisher gives the user a reasonable opportunity to review and the user makes a meaningful manifestation of assent").

2. Might shrinkwrap licenses and clickwrap licenses (see below) be useful in incorporating publicly beneficial terms into software contracts: for example, in the context of open source licensing and perhaps also in incorporating terms that protect an individual's privacy? On privacy, see discussion in Chapter 5. *See also* Robert W. Gomulkiewicz, *Getting Serious About User-friendly Mass Market Licensing For Software*, 12 Geo. Mason L. Rev. 687, 690-91 (2004) ("Software publishers use EULAs for a variety of important reasons. First, EULAs allow them to license various packages of rights to users at various price points. For example, a software publisher might license word processing software to business users for one price, to home users for a lower price, academic institutions for an even lower price, and to charitable organizations for free. Certain types of software, such as server software and developer tools, must be licensed to be useful — a Copyright Act 'first sale' does not provide sufficient rights. Software publishers use licensing to foster innovative software developments such as 'open source' software. Open source EULAs grant broad rights to make and distribute derivative works. EULAs also serve the practical purpose of explaining to users what can and cannot be done with the software. Even unfriendly EULAs do this to a degree . . .").

3. In his book, *Free Culture*, Professor Lawrence Lessig describes the operation of the Creative Commons license project, which facilitates the use of licenses by copyright holders who want to give certain freedoms to users of their work beyond fair use: Lawrence Lessig, *Free Culture*, 282-86 (2004). A licensor has the flexibility to choose amongst different licenses which give varying rights to users such as: (a) the right to make any use of a licensed work provided that attribution is given; (b) the right to make any *noncommercial* use of a licensed work; (c) the right to make any use of a licensed work so long as any sub-licenses of the new work are granted with the same freedoms as the original work; (d) the right to sample the work as long as permanent copies are not made; or (e) the right to use the work provided that no derivative works are made without the copyright owner's permission. For more details, see *http://creativecommons.org/* (full license terms available).

4. According to *ProCD*, is the law relating to shrinkwrap licenses clear? On its face, is the court's approach in *ProCD* dictated by the law of contracts or does it represent a policy choice within what Justice Cardozo described as interstices of the law?

5. According to Zeidenberg, when was the contract formed? What authority does Judge Easterbrook rely upon in rejecting Zeidenberg's argument that ProCD's additional terms are not part of their agreement? Are his illustrations persuasive?

6. How, according to Judge Easterbrook, is the enforcement of shrinkwrap agreements ultimately good for consumers? What would be the result of clarifying the current uncertainty in favor of the purchaser?

7. The court in *ProCD* distinguishes the agreement in the case from one in which the shrinkwrap terms provided that the purchaser owe the seller an additional $10,000. If the purchaser has the option to return the purchase, what makes the terms limiting the purchaser's ability to use the product different from the demand for additional payment? Does it depend upon whether the subsequent terms are material to the purchaser? If so, why is the fair use of intellectual property immaterial to a consumer?

8. According to Judge Easterbrook, " 'Terms of Use' are no less a part of 'the product' than are the size of the database and the speed with which the software compiles the listing." What does he mean by this statement? To the extent that a consumer's remedy is competition, does it matter whether such competition actually exists?

9. The approach taken by *ProCD* was critized in Kloceck v. Gateway, Inc., 104. F. Supp. 2d 1332 (D. Kan. 2000). In *Kloceck*, the court rejected Gateway's argument that the purchaser of its computer was bound by Gateway's Terms and Conditions Agreement contained in the computer's packing box. According to the court:

> Disputes under §2-207 often arise in the context of a "battle of forms," see, e.g., Diatom, Inc. v. Pennwalt Corp., 741 F.2d 1569, 1574 (10th Cir. 1984), but nothing in its language precludes application in a case which involves only one form. . . . By its terms, §2-207 applies to an acceptance or written confirmation. It states nothing which requires another form before the provision becomes effective. . . .
>
> Under §2-207, the Standard Terms constitute either an expression of acceptance or written confirmation. As an expression of acceptance, the Standard Terms would constitute a counter-offer only if Gateway expressly made its acceptance conditional on plaintiff's assent to the additional or different terms. K.S.A. §84-2-207(1); V.A.M.S. §400.2-207(1). "[T]he conditional nature of the acceptance must be clearly expressed in a manner sufficient to notify the offeror that the offeree is unwilling to proceed with the transaction unless the additional or different terms are included in the contract." *Brown Machine*, 770 S.W.2d at 420. Gateway provides no evidence that at the time of the sales transaction, it informed plaintiff that the transaction was conditioned on plaintiff's acceptance of the Standard Terms. Moreover, the mere fact that Gateway shipped the goods with the terms attached did not communicate to plaintiff any unwillingness to proceed without plaintiff's agreement to the Standard Terms. . . .
>
> Because plaintiff is not a merchant, additional or different terms contained in the Standard Terms did not become part of the parties' agreement unless plaintiff expressly agreed to them. . . .

Section 2-207 of the UCC provides that:

> Additional Terms in Acceptance or Confirmation.
>
> (1) A definite and seasonable expression of acceptance or a written confirmation which is sent within a reasonable time operates as an acceptance even though it states terms additional to or different from those offered or agreed upon, unless acceptance is expressly made conditional on assent to the additional or different terms.
>
> (2) The additional terms are to be construed as proposals for addition to the contract. Between merchants such terms become part of the contract unless:
>
> > (a) the offer expressly limits acceptance to the terms of the offer;
> >
> > (b) they materially alter it; or
> >
> > (c) notification of objection to them has already been given or is given within a reasonable time after notice of them is received.
>
> (3) Conduct by both parties which recognizes the existence of a contract is sufficient to establish a contract for sale although the writings of the parties do not otherwise establish a contract. In such case the terms of the particular contract consist of those terms on which the writings of the parties agree, together with any supplementary terms incorporated under any other provisions of the Act.

10.   This discussion highlights the problems inherent in applying legal default rules governing pre-digital sales and license transactions to contracts involving computer software. Article 2 of the UCC, for example, is drafted with physical sales of goods in mind, and there has been some question as to the extent to which applying its provisions to computer software contracts makes logical sense. It has never been particularly clear whether software transactions should be regarded as sales or licenses, or a combination of both. *See, e.g.,* Nancy Kim, *The Software Licensing Dilemma,* (2008) BYU L. Rev. 1103 (2008). Over the years, various attempts have been made to draft new sets of legal default rules that would be a better fit for software transactions. Earlier attempts, such as the proposed Article 2B of the UCC, and its immediate successor, the Uniform Computer Transactions Act (UCITA), met with very limited success. UCITA was ultimately only adopted in two states — Virginia and Maryland. A number of states, in fact, adopted "anti-UCITA" laws. Patrick Thibodeau, *Mass. Could Be Fifth State to Adopt Anti-UCITA Law* (Computerworld, 2003, available at *http://www.computerworld.com/action/article.do?command=viewArticleBasic&articleId=81812*). Thibodeau expresses some of the objections to UCITA as follows:

> According to opponents, UCITA sets default contract terms that favor software vendors and free them of liability for any software problems. Supporters say companies are free to negotiate terms and conditions, and they have attempted, unsuccessfully, to ameliorate

concerns by removing some controversial provisions, such as "self-help," which would have allowed a vendor to disable a system during a dispute.

More recently, the American Law Institute has approved a new set of Principles of the Law of Software Contracts (*see* Bob Hillman, *American Law Institute Approves the Principles of the Law of Software Contracts*, June 2, 2009, Concurring Opinions, available at *http://www.concurringopinions.com/ archives/2009/06/american-law-institute-approves-the-principles-of-the-law-of-software-contracts.html#more-16731*). It remains to be seen whether these Principles will be adopted in practice by those engaged in software transactions. One lawyer has said that he is advising clients to disclaim the operation of these new Principles. Sean Hogle has blogged that:

> I'm recommending to all of my clients that they insert into their operative software license agreements the following or something close to it in the choice of law clause: "This Agreement and all related disputes shall be governed by the laws of __, without regard to the United Nations Convention on Contracts for the International Sale of Goods or the American Law Institute's Principles of the Law of Software Contracts ("Principles"). The parties agree that (i) the Principles shall have no application whatsoever to the interpretation or enforcement of this Agreement, and (ii) neither party shall invoke the Principles in whole or in part in any judicial or arbitral proceeding relating to this Agreement."
>
> But, aren't many of the rules stated in the Principles, especially the controversial ones like the implied warranty of no hidden material defects and the implied indemnification obligation, not excludable or disclaimable, or disclaimable only with specific prescribed language?
>
> Well, that's what the Principles say. The Principles dictate, for example, that the newly-discovered warranty of no hidden defects cannot be excluded or disclaimed.
>
> Here's the thing: the Prinicples have no force of law whatsoever. They have persuasive authority only. They are not the equivalent of a statute or judicial decision. If the parties agree in their contract that the Principles will have no effect, why would a court feel free to disregard that?

Concurring Opinions, June 8, 2009, available at *http://www. concurringopinions.com/archives/2009/06/american-law-institute-approves-the-principles-of-the-law-of-software-contracts.html#more-16731*.

Mr. Hogle notes that the Principles state that certain implied warranties cannot be disclaimed under the terms of the Principles, but that the Principles themselves have no particular force of law. How do you think a court should deal with this problem in practice? Should a court hold, for example, that certain warranties cannot be disclaimed only in cases where the Principles have been expressly incorporated into a given software contract? If so, would this be a deterrent to parties incorporating the Principles at all in cases where they are uncomfortable with one or more of the non-disclaimable terms?

11. What other forms of software contracts have courts been prepared to enforce? Consider the following cases.

Specht v. Netscape Communications Corp.

150 F. Supp. 2d 585 (S.D.N.Y. 2001), *aff'd*, 306 F.3d 17 (2d Cir. 2002)

Hellerstein, District Judge.

Promises become binding when there is a meeting of the minds and consideration is exchanged. So it was at King's Bench in common law England; so it was under the common law in the American colonies; so it was through more than two centuries of jurisprudence in this country; and so it is today. Assent may be registered by a signature, a handshake, or a click of a computer mouse transmitted across the invisible ether of the Internet. Formality is not a requisite; any sign, symbol or action, or even willful inaction, as long as it is unequivocally referable to the promise, may create a contract.

The three related cases before me all involve this timeless issue of assent, but in the context of free software offered on the Internet. If an offeree downloads free software, and the offeror seeks a contractual understanding limiting its uses and applications, under what circumstances does the act of downloading create a contract? On the facts presented here, is there the requisite assent and consideration? My decision focuses on these issues.

In these putative class actions, Plaintiffs allege that usage of the software transmits to Defendants private information about the user's file transfer activity on the Internet, thereby effecting an electronic surveillance of the user's activity in violation of two federal statutes, the Electronic Communications Privacy Act, 18 U.S.C. §2510 *et seq.*, and the Computer Fraud and Abuse Act, 18 U.S.C. §1030. Defendants move to compel arbitration and stay the proceedings, arguing that the disputes reflected in the Complaint, like all others relating to use of the software, are subject to a binding arbitration clause in the End User License Agreement ("License Agreement"), the contract allegedly made by the offeror of the software and the party effecting the download. Thus, I am asked to decide if an offer of a license agreement, made independently of freely offered software and not expressly accepted by a user of that software, nevertheless binds the user to an arbitration clause contained in the license.

I. Factual and Procedural Background

Defendant Netscape, a provider of computer software programs that enable and facilitate the use of the Internet, offers its "SmartDownload" software free of charge on its web site to all those who visit the site and indicate, by clicking their mouse in a designated box, that they wish to obtain it. Smart-Download is a program that makes it easier for its users to download files from the Internet without losing their interim progress when they pause to engage in some other task, or if their Internet connection is severed. Four of the six named Plaintiffs—John Gibson, Mark Gruber, Sean Kelly and Sherry

Weindorf—selected and clicked in the box indicating a decision to obtain the software, and proceeded to download the software on to the hard drives of their computers. . . .

Visitors wishing to obtain SmartDownload from Netscape's web site arrive at a page pertaining to the download of the software. On this page, there appears a tinted box, or button, labeled "Download." By clicking on the box, a visitor initiates the download. The sole reference on this page to the License Agreement appears in text that is visible only if a visitor scrolls down through the page to the next screen. . . .

Visitors are not required affirmatively to indicate their assent to the License Agreement, or even to view the license agreement, before proceeding with a download of the software. But if a visitor chooses to click on the under-lined text in the invitation, a hypertext link takes the visitor to a web page entitled "License & Support Agreements." The first paragraph on this page reads in pertinent part:

> The use of each Netscape software product is governed by a license agreement. You must read and agree to the license agreement terms BEFORE acquiring a product. Please click on the appropriate link below to review the current license agreement for the product of interest to you before acquisition. For products available for download, you must read and agree to the license agreement terms BEFORE you install the software. If you do not agree to the license terms, do not download, install or use the software.

Below the paragraph appears a list of license agreements, the first of which is "*License Agreement for Netscape Navigator and Netscape Communicator Product Family* (Netscape Navigator, Netscape Communicator and Netscape SmartDownload)." If the visitor then clicks on that text, he or she is brought to another web page, this one containing the full text of the License Agreement.

The License Agreement, which has been unchanged throughout the period that Netscape has made SmartDownload available to the public, grants the user a license to use and reproduce SmartDownload, and otherwise contains few restrictions on the use of the software. The first paragraph of the License Agreement describes, in upper case print, the purported manner in which a user accepts or rejects its terms.

BY CLICKING THE ACCEPTANCE BUTTON OR INSTALLING OR USING NETSCAPE COMMUNICATOR, NETSCAPE NAVIGATOR, OR NETSCAPE SMARTDOWNLOAD SOFTWARE (THE "PRODUCT"), THE INDIVIDUAL OR ENTITY LICENSING THE PRODUCT ("LICENSEE") IS CONSENTING TO BE BOUND BY AND IS BECOMING A PARTY TO THIS AGREEMENT. IF LICENSEE DOES NOT AGREE TO ALL OF THE TERMS OF THIS AGREEMENT, THE BUTTON INDICATING NON-ACCEPTANCE MUST BE SELECTED, AND LICENSEE MUST NOT INSTALL OR USE THE SOFTWARE.

The License Agreement also contains a term requiring that virtually all disputes be submitted to arbitration in Santa Clara County, California. . . .

III. Did Plaintiffs Consent to Arbitration?

Unless the Plaintiffs agreed to the License Agreement, they cannot be bound by the arbitration clause contained therein. My inquiry, therefore, focuses on whether the Plaintiffs, through their acts or failures to act, manifested their assent to the terms of the License Agreement proposed by Defendant Netscape. More specifically, I must consider whether the web site gave Plaintiffs sufficient notice of the existence and terms of the License Agreement, and whether the act of downloading the software sufficiently manifested Plaintiffs' assent to be bound by the License Agreement. . . .

In order for a contract to become binding, both parties must assent to be bound. "[C]ourts have required that assent to the formation of a contract be manifested in some way, by words or other conduct, if it is to be effective." E. Allan Farnsworth, *Farnsworth on Contracts* §3.1 (2d ed. 2000). "To form a contract, a manifestation of mutual assent is necessary. Mutual assent may be manifested by written or spoken words, or by conduct." *Binder v. Aetna Life Ins. Co.*, 75 Cal. App. 4th 832, 850, 89 Cal. Rptr. 2d 540, 551 (Cal. Ct. App. 1999) (citations omitted). "A contract for sale of goods may be made in any manner sufficient to show agreement, including conduct by both parties which recognizes the existence of such a contract." Cal. Com. Code §2204.

These principles enjoy continuing vitality in the realm of software licensing. The sale of software, in stores, by mail, and over the Internet, has resulted in several specialized forms of license agreements. For example, software commonly is packaged in a container or wrapper that advises the purchaser that the use of the software is subject to the terms of a license agreement contained inside the package. The license agreement generally explains that, if the purchaser does not wish to enter into a contract, he or she must return the product for a refund, and that failure to return it within a certain period will constitute assent to the license terms. These so-called "shrink-wrap licenses" have been the subject of considerable litigation. . . .

For most of the products it makes available over the Internet (but not SmartDownload), Netscape uses another common type of software license, one usually identified as "click-wrap" licensing. A click-wrap license presents the user with a message on his or her computer screen, requiring that the user manifest his or her assent to the terms of the license agreement by clicking on an icon.[12] The product cannot be obtained or used unless and until the icon is clicked. For example, when a user attempts to obtain Netscape's Communicator or Navigator, a web page appears containing the full text of the Communicator/Navigator license agreement. Plainly visible on the screen is the query, "Do you accept all the terms of the preceding license agreement? If so, click on the Yes button. If you select No, Setup will close." Below this text are

---

12. In this respect, click-wrap licensing is similar to the shrink-wrap license at issue in *ProCD, supra,* which appeared on the user's computer screen when the software was used and could not be bypassed until the user indicated acceptance of its terms. *See ProCD,* 86 F.3d at 1452.

three button or icons: one labeled "Back" and used to return to an earlier step of the download preparation; one labeled "No," which if clicked, terminates the download; and one labeled "Yes," which if clicked, allows the download to proceed. Unless the user clicks "Yes," indicating his or her assent to the license agreement, the user cannot obtain the software. The few courts that have had occasion to consider click-wrap contracts have held them to be valid and enforceable. *See, e.g., In re RealNetworks, Inc. Privacy Litigation*, No. 00C1366, 2000 WL 631341 (N.D. Ill. May 8, 2000); *Hotmail Corp. v. Van$ Money Pie, Inc.*, No. C 98-20064, 1998 WL 388389 (N.D. Cal. April 16, 1998).

A third type of software license, "browse-wrap," was considered by a California federal court in *Pollstar v. Gigmania Ltd.*, No. CIV-F-00-5671, 2000 WL 33266437 (E.D. Cal. Oct. 17, 2000). In *Pollstar*, the plaintiff's web page offered allegedly proprietary information. Notice of a license agreement appears on the plaintiff's web site. Clicking on the notice links the user to a separate web page containing the full text of the license agreement, which allegedly binds any user of the information on the site. However, the user is not required to click on an icon expressing assent to the license, or even view its terms, before proceeding to use the information on the site. The court referred to this arrangement as a "browse-wrap" license. The defendant allegedly copied proprietary information from the site. The plaintiff sued for breach of the license agreement, and the defendant moved to dismiss for lack of mutual assent sufficient to form a contract. The court, although denying the defendant's motion to dismiss, expressed concern about the enforceability of the browse-wrap license:

> Viewing the web site, the court agrees with the defendant that many visitors to the site may not be aware of the license agreement. Notice of the license agreement is provided by small gray text on a gray background. . . . No reported cases have ruled on the enforceability of a browse wrap license. . . . While the court agrees with [the defendant] that the user is not immediately confronted with the notice of the license agreement, this does not dispose of [the plaintiff's] breach of contract claim. The court hesitates to declare the invalidity and unenforceability of the browse wrap license agreement at this time.

Id. at *5-6.

The SmartDownload License Agreement in the case before me differs fundamentally from both click-wrap and shrink-wrap licensing, and resembles more the browse-wrap license of *Pollstar*. Where click-wrap license agreements and the shrink-wrap agreement at issue in *ProCD* require users to perform an affirmative action unambiguously expressing assent *before* they may use the software, that affirmative action is equivalent to an express declaration stating, "I assent to the terms and conditions of the license agreement" or something similar. For example, Netscape's Navigator will not function without a prior clicking of a box constituting assent. Netscape's SmartDownload, in contrast, allows a user to download and use the software without taking any action that plainly manifests assent to the terms of the associated license or indicates an understanding that a contract is being formed.

California courts carefully limit the circumstances under which a party may be bound to a contract. "[A]n offeree, regardless of apparent manifestation of his consent, is not bound by inconspicuous contractual provisions of which he was unaware, contained in a document whose contractual nature is not obvious. . . . This principle of knowing consent applies with particular force to provisions for arbitration." *Windsor Mills, Inc. v. Collins & Aikman Corp.,* 25 Cal. App. 3d 987, 993, 101 Cal. Rptr. 347 (Cal. Ct. App. 1972). . . .

Netscape argues that the mere act of downloading indicates assent. However, downloading is hardly an unambiguous indication of assent. The primary purpose of downloading is to obtain a product, not to assent to an agreement. In contrast, clicking on an icon stating "I assent" has no meaning or purpose other than to indicate such assent. Netscape's failure to require users of SmartDownload to indicate assent to its license as a precondition to downloading and using its software is fatal to its argument that a contract has been formed.

Furthermore, unlike the user of Netscape Navigator or other click-wrap or shrink-wrap licensees, the individual obtaining SmartDownload is not made aware that he is entering into a contract. SmartDownload is available from Netscape's web site free of charge. Before downloading the software, the user need not view any license agreement terms or even any reference to a license agreement, and need not do anything to manifest assent to such a license agreement other than actually taking possession of the product. From the user's vantage point, SmartDownload could be analogized to a free neighborhood newspaper, readily obtained from a sidewalk box or supermarket counter without any exchange with a seller or vender. It is there for the taking.

The only hint that a contract is being formed is one small box of text referring to the license agreement, text that appears below the screen used for downloading and that a user need not even see before obtaining the product. . . .

Couched in the mild request, "Please review," this language reads as a mere invitation, not as a condition. The language does not indicate that a user *must* agree to the license terms before downloading and using the software. While clearer language appears in the License Agreement itself, the language of the invitation does not require the reading of those terms or provide adequate notice either that a contract is being created or that the terms of the License Agreement will bind the user.

The case law on software licensing has not eroded the importance of assent in contract formation. Mutual assent is the bedrock of any agreement to which the law will give force. Defendants' position, if accepted, would so expand the definition of assent as to render it meaningless. Because the user Plaintiffs did not assent to the license agreement, they are not subject to the arbitration clause contained therein and cannot be compelled to arbitrate their claims against the Defendants. . . .

COMMENTS AND QUESTIONS

1.   According to the court in *Specht*, why are the users of SmartDownload not bound by the license agreement? Does the court follow the approach taken by *ProCD*?

2.   What acts would evidence mutual assent in *Specht*? Would the court reach the same result if instead of a download button, Netscape's Web page stated that users must agree to the License Agreement in order to download the software and required the user to click on an "I Agree" button to download the program? If so, why should these two procedures lead to such disparate results?

3.   To what extent does it matter whether a user actually reads the License Agreement? If the plaintiffs in *Specht* read the agreement before downloading the program, why were the acts of downloading and use of the program not evidence that they agreed to the terms of the License Agreement? Correspondingly, if a user could simply click on a button labeled "I Agree" without being required to review the License Agreement, would she be bound to its terms?

4.   Apply the reasoning of *Specht* to the facts of *ProCD*, or *Kloceck*. Does *Specht* lead to a different result in those cases?

Note on Electronic Self-Help

Related to the issue of electronic consent is the issue of electronic self-help. Because the Internet and electronic devices in general operate according to their computer programming, user behavior is ultimately governed by that code. Rather than relying upon contract or other legal doctrine, to what extent can programmers build their terms into code itself? As we have already seen in Chapter 4, one method of preventing users from freely copying digital works is to use encryption to prevent those works from being copied regardless of whether they are being copied for fair or foul uses. Similarly, while users may have the option to reject cookies, Web sites may be programmed to function only when cookies are accepted. Likewise, computer programs and files can be programmed to expire or self-destruct after a certain number of uses or after a certain date. To what extent should self-help be permitted in cyberspace?

In American Computer Trust Leasing v. Jack Farrell Implement Co., 763 F. Supp. 1473 (D. Minn. 1991), the plaintiff, Automatic Data Processing, Inc (ADP), and defendants, Boerboom International, Inc. and Jack Farrell Implement Co. (Farrell), entered into an agreement for the defendants to lease computer services from the plaintiff. When the defendants defaulted on their payments, ADP stopped providing services and, in the case of Farrell, ADP deactivated the computer software leased by Farrell. The court held that

ADP had a contractual right to deactivate the software under its contract with the defendants, and the deactivation was not wrongful. The court also dismissed claims against ADP under various federal statutes, including the ECPA (see *supra*), and the Minnesota statute relating to the torts of trespass to chattels and nuisance.

In Clayton X-Ray Co. v. Profession Systems Corp., 812 S.W.2d 565 (Mo. Ct. App. 1991), the plaintiff, Clayton X-Ray Corp. (Clayton), purchased a computer system from defendant, Profession Systems Corp. (PSC). Unknown to Clayton, PSC had inserted a lockup program into the computer system which could lock up the machine and prevent the plaintiff's access to its files on nonpayment of a bill. When Clayton failed to pay a bill, PSC activated the lockup provision. The court held that PSC had no legal right to do so and ordered punitive damages against PSC.

Can these approaches be reconciled with each other? What are the policy arguments in favor of, and against, permitting self-help of the kind utilized in these two cases?

B. LIMITATIONS UPON PRIVATE ORDERING

Part A of this chapter explored the procedural requirements for recognizing private ordering. This section explores limitations, if any, upon the substance of private ordering, even when the procedural requirements have been satisfied. In considering this issue you may want to review the materials dealing with jurisdiction and forum selection in Chapter 2, part B.5.

1. Freedom of Expression

COHEN v. COWLES MEDIA CO.

501 U.S. 663 (1991)

Justice WHITE delivered the opinion of the Court.

The question before us is whether the First Amendment prohibits a plaintiff from recovering damages, under state promissory estoppel law, for a newspaper's breach of a promise of confidentiality given to the plaintiff in exchange for information. We hold that it does not.

During the closing days of the 1982 Minnesota gubernatorial race, Dan Cohen, an active Republican associated with Wheelock Whitney's Independent-Republican gubernatorial campaign, approached reporters from the St. Paul Pioneer Press Dispatch (Pioneer Press) and the Minneapolis Star and Tribune (Star Tribune) and offered to provide documents relating to a candidate in the upcoming election. Cohen made clear to the reporters that he would provide the information only if he was given a promise of confidentiality. Reporters from both papers promised to keep Cohen's identity anonymous and Cohen turned over copies of two public court records concerning Marlene Johnson, the Democratic-Farmer-Labor candidate for Lieutenant Governor. The first record indicated that Johnson had been charged in 1969 with three counts of unlawful assembly, and the second that she had been convicted in 1970 of petit theft. Both newspapers interviewed Johnson for her explanation and one reporter tracked down the person who had found the records for Cohen. As it turned out, the unlawful assembly charges arose out of Johnson's participation in a protest of an alleged failure to hire minority workers on municipal construction projects, and the charges were eventually dismissed. The petit theft conviction was for leaving a store without paying for $6 worth of sewing materials. The incident apparently occurred at a time during which Johnson was emotionally distraught, and the conviction was later vacated.

After consultation and debate, the editorial staffs of the two newspapers independently decided to publish Cohen's name as part of their stories concerning Johnson. In their stories, both papers identified Cohen as the source of the court records, indicated his connection to the Whitney campaign, and included denials by Whitney campaign officials of any role in the matter. The same day the stories appeared, Cohen was fired by his employer.

Cohen sued respondents, the publishers of the Pioneer Press and Star Tribune, in Minnesota state court, alleging fraudulent misrepresentation and breach of contract. The trial court rejected respondents' argument that the First Amendment barred Cohen's lawsuit. A jury returned a verdict in Cohen's favor, awarding him $200,000 in compensatory damages and $500,000 in punitive damages. . . .

Respondents rely on the proposition that "if a newspaper lawfully obtains truthful information about a matter of public significance then state officials may not constitutionally punish publication of the information, absent a need to further a state interest of the highest order." *Smith v. Daily Mail Publishing Co.*, 443 U.S. 97, 103 (1979). That proposition is unexceptionable, and it has been applied in various cases that have found insufficient the asserted state interests in preventing publication of truthful, lawfully obtained information. See, e.g., *Florida Star v. B.J.F.*, 491 U.S. 524 (1989); *Smith v. Daily Mail, supra; Landmark Communications, Inc. v. Virginia*, 435 U.S. 829 (1978).

This case, however, is not controlled by this line of cases but, rather, by the equally well-established line of decisions holding that generally applicable laws do not offend the First Amendment simply because their enforcement against the press has incidental effects on its ability to gather and report the news. As the cases relied on by respondents recognize, the truthful information sought to be published must have been lawfully acquired. The press may not with impunity break and enter an office or dwelling to gather news. Neither does the First Amendment relieve a newspaper reporter of the obligation shared by all citizens to respond to a grand jury subpoena and answer questions relevant to a criminal investigation, even though the reporter might be required to reveal a confidential source. *Branzburg v. Hayes*, 408 U.S. 665 (1972). The press, like others interested in publishing, may not publish copyrighted material without obeying the copyright laws. See *Zacchini v. Scripps-Howard Broadcasting Co.*, 433 U.S. 562, 576-579 (1977). Similarly, the media must obey the National Labor Relations Act, *Associated Press v. NLRB*, 301 U.S. 103 (1937), and the Fair Labor Standards Act, *Oklahoma Press Publishing Co. v. Walling*, 327 U.S. 186, 192-193 (1946); may not restrain trade in violation of the antitrust laws, *Associated Press v. United States*, 326 U.S. 1 (1945); *Citizen Publishing Co. v. United States*, 394 U.S. 131, 139 (1969); and must pay non-discriminatory taxes, *Murdock v. Pennsylvania*, 319 U.S. 105, 112 (1943); *Minneapolis Star & Tribune Co. v. Minnesota Comm'r of Revenue*, 460 U.S. 575, 581-583 (1983). . . . It is, therefore, beyond dispute that "[t]he publisher of a newspaper has no special immunity from the application of general laws. He has no special privilege to invade the rights and liberties of others." *Associated Press v. NLRB, supra*, 301 U.S., at 132-133. Accordingly, enforcement of such general laws against the press is not subject to stricter scrutiny than would be applied to enforcement against other persons or organizations.

There can be little doubt that the Minnesota doctrine of promissory estoppel is a law of general applicability. It does not target or single out the press. Rather, insofar as we are advised, the doctrine is generally applicable to the daily transactions of all the citizens of Minnesota. The First Amendment does not forbid its application to the press.

Justice Blackmun suggests that applying Minnesota promissory estoppel doctrine in this case will "punish" respondents for publishing truthful information that was lawfully obtained. . . . This is not strictly accurate because compensatory damages are not a form of punishment, as were the criminal sanctions at issue in *Smith v. Daily Mail, supra*. If the contract between the parties in this case had contained a liquidated damages provision, it would be perfectly clear that the payment to petitioner would represent a cost of acquiring newsworthy material to be published at a profit, rather than a punishment imposed by the State. The payment of compensatory damages in this case is constitutionally indistinguishable from a generous bonus paid to a confidential news source. In any event, as indicated above, the characterization of the payment makes no difference for First Amendment purposes when the law being applied is a general law and does not single out the press. Moreover, Justice Blackmun's reliance on cases like *Florida Star v. B.J.F., supra*, and *Smith v. Daily Mail* is misplaced. In those cases, the State itself defined the content of publications that would trigger liability. Here, by contrast, Minnesota law simply requires those making promises to keep them. The parties themselves, as in this case, determine the scope of their legal obligations, and any restrictions that may be placed on the publication of truthful information are self-imposed. . . .

Respondents and *amici* argue that permitting Cohen to maintain a cause of action for promissory estoppel will inhibit truthful reporting because news organizations will have legal incentives not to disclose a confidential source's identity even when that person's identity is itself newsworthy. Justice Souter

makes a similar argument. But if this is the case, it is no more than the incidental, and constitutionally insignificant, consequence of applying to the press a generally applicable law that requires those who make certain kinds of promises to keep them. Although we conclude that the First Amendment does not confer on the press a constitutional right to disregard promises that would otherwise be enforced under state law, we reject Cohen's request that in reversing the Minnesota Supreme Court's judgment we reinstate the jury verdict awarding him $200,000 in compensatory damages. . . . The Minnesota Supreme Court's incorrect conclusion that the First Amendment barred Cohen's claim may well have truncated its consideration of whether a promissory estoppel claim had otherwise been established under Minnesota law and whether Cohen's jury verdict could be upheld on a promissory estoppel basis. Or perhaps the State Constitution may be construed to shield the press from a promissory estoppel cause of action such as this one. These are matters for the Minnesota Supreme Court to address and resolve in the first instance on remand. Accordingly, the judgment of the Minnesota Supreme Court is reversed, and the case is remanded for further proceedings not inconsistent with this opinion.
So ordered.

Justice BLACKMUN, with whom Justice MARSHALL and Justice SOUTER join, dissenting.

I agree with the Court that the decision of the Supreme Court of Minnesota rested on federal grounds and that the judicial enforcement of petitioner's promissory estoppel claim constitutes state action under the Fourteenth Amendment. I do not agree, however, that the use of that claim to penalize the reporting of truthful information regarding a political campaign does not violate the First Amendment. Accordingly, I dissent.

The majority concludes that this case is not controlled by the decision in *Smith v. Daily Mail Publishing Co.*, 443 U.S. 97 (1979), to the effect that a State may not punish the publication of lawfully obtained, truthful information "absent a need to further a state interest of the highest order." *Id.*, at 103. Instead, we are told, the controlling precedent is "the equally well-established line of decisions holding that generally applicable laws do not offend the First Amendment simply because their enforcement against the press has incidental effects on its ability to gather and report the news." . . . I disagree.

I do not read the decision of the Supreme Court of Minnesota to create any exception to, or immunity from, the laws of that State for members of the press. In my view, the court's decision is premised, not on the identity of the speaker, but on the speech itself. Thus, the court found it to be of "critical significance," that "the promise of anonymity arises in the classic First Amendment context of the quintessential public debate in our democratic society, namely, a political source involved in a political campaign." 457 N.W.2d 199, 205 (1990); see also *id.*, at 204, n.6 ("*New York Times v. Sullivan*, 376 U.S.

254 . . . (1964), holds that a state may not adopt a state rule of law to impose impermissible restrictions on the federal constitutional freedoms of speech and press"). Necessarily, the First Amendment protection afforded respondents would be equally available to nonmedia defendants. See, e.g., *Lovell v. Griffin*, 303 U.S. 444, 452 (1938) ("The liberty of the press is not confined to newspapers and periodicals. . . . The press in its historic connotation comprehends every sort of publication which affords a vehicle of information and opinion"). The majority's admonition that " '[t]he publisher of a newspaper has no special immunity from the application of general laws,' " and its reliance on the cases that support that principle, are therefore misplaced.

In *Branzburg*, for example, this Court found it significant that "these cases involve no intrusions upon speech or assembly, no . . . restriction on what the press may publish, and no express or implied command that the press publish what it prefers to withhold. . . . [N]o penalty, civil or criminal, related to the content of published material is at issue here." 408 U.S., at 681. Indeed, "[t]he sole issue before us" in *Branzburg* was "the obligation of reporters to respond to grand jury subpoenas as other citizens do and to answer questions relevant to an investigation into the commission of crime." *Id.*, at 682. . . . In short, these cases did *not* involve the imposition of liability based upon the content of speech.

Contrary to the majority, I regard our decision in *Hustler Magazine Inc. v. Falwell*, 485 U.S. 46 (1988), to be precisely on point. There, we found that the use of a claim of intentional infliction of emotional distress to impose liability for the publication of a satirical critique violated the First Amendment. There was no doubt that Virginia's tort of intentional infliction of emotional distress was "a law of general applicability" unrelated to the suppression of speech. Nonetheless, a unanimous Court found that, when used to penalize the expression of opinion, the law was subject to the strictures of the First Amendment. In applying that principle, we concluded, *id.*, at 56, that "public figures and public officials may not recover for the tort of intentional infliction of emotional distress by reason of publications such as the one here at issue without showing in addition that the publication contains a false statement of fact which was made with 'actual malice,'" as defined by *New York Times Co. v. Sullivan*, 376 U.S. 254 (1964). In so doing, we rejected the argument that Virginia's interest in protecting its citizens from emotional distress was sufficient to remove from First Amendment protection a "patently offensive" expression of opinion. 485 U.S., at 50.

As in *Hustler*, the operation of Minnesota's doctrine of promissory estoppel in this case cannot be said to have a merely "incidental" burden on speech; the publication of important political speech *is* the claimed violation. Thus, as in *Hustler*, the law may not be enforced to punish the expression of truthful information or opinion. In the instant case, it is undisputed that the publication at issue was true.

To the extent that truthful speech may ever be sanctioned consistent with the First Amendment, it must be in furtherance of a state interest "of the highest order." *Smith*, 443 U.S., at 103. Because the Minnesota Supreme Court's opinion makes clear that the State's interest in enforcing its promissory estoppel doctrine in this case was far from compelling, see 457 N.W.2d, at 204-205, I would affirm that court's decision.

I respectfully dissent.

[Justice SOUTER, with whom Justice MARSHALL, Justice BLACKMUN, and Justice O'CONNOR join, dissenting on the grounds that "the State's interest in enforcing a newspaper's promise of confidentiality insufficient to outweigh the interest in unfettered publication of the information revealed in this case. . . ."]

COMMENTS AND QUESTIONS

1. Is *Cohen* merely a case in which those who make promises are required to keep those promises or does it represent as the dissent suggests a content-based restriction upon speech?

2. Under *Cohen*, could a software provider or Web site operator prohibit a user from criticizing the service by including a provision in its subscriber or licensing agreement against such criticism?

3. Why does the majority return the case to the Minnesota courts rather than reinstating the jury's verdict? Is the question of contractual limitations upon speech an issue for state common law?

2. Intellectual Property Preemption

Both the U.S. Constitution and federal intellectual property law prohibit the states from protecting certain interests that are the subject of federal copyright or patent law. For example, in Bonito Boats, Inc. v. Thunder Craft Boats, Inc., the Supreme Court held that a Florida statute protecting boat hull designs was preempted by federal patent law.[6] Similarly, Section 301 of the Copyright Act expressly preempts state laws that (1) pertain to "works of authorship that are fixed in a tangible medium of expression and come within the subject matter of copyright"; and (2) protect rights "equivalent to any of the exclusive rights within the general scope of copyright."[7] The following materials explore whether rights created by contract can be considered preempted.

6. 9 U.S. 141 (1989).
7. 17 U.S.C. §301(a).

VAULT CORP. v. QUAID SOFTWARE LTD.

847 F.2d 255 (5th Cir. 1988)

REAVLEY, Circuit Judge:

Vault brought this copyright infringement action against Quaid seeking damages and preliminary and permanent injunctions. The district court denied Vault's motion for a preliminary injunction, holding that Vault did not have a reasonable probability of success on the merits. *Vault Corp. v. Quaid Software Ltd.*, 655 F. Supp. 750 (E.D. La. 1987). By stipulation of the parties, this ruling was made final and judgment was entered accordingly. We affirm.

I

Vault produces computer diskettes under the registered trademark "PROLOK" which are designed to prevent the unauthorized duplication of programs placed on them by software computer companies, Vault's customers. Floppy diskettes serve as a medium upon which computer companies place their software programs. To use a program, a purchaser loads the diskette into the disk drive of a computer, thereby allowing the computer to read the program into its memory. The purchaser can then remove the diskette from the disk drive and operate the program from the computer's memory. This process is repeated each time a program is used.

The protective device placed on a PROLOK diskette by Vault is comprised of two parts: a "fingerprint" and a software program ("Vault's program").[1] The "fingerprint" is a small mark physically placed on the magnetic surface of each PROLOK diskette which contains certain information that cannot be altered or erased. Vault's program is a set of instructions to the computer which interact with the "fingerprint" to prevent the computer from operating the program recorded on a PROLOK diskette (by one of Vault's customers) unless the computer verifies that the *original* PROLOK diskette, as identified by the "fingerprint," is in the computer's disk drive. While a purchaser can copy a PROLOK protected program onto another diskette, the computer will not read the program into its memory from the copy unless the original PROLOK diskette is also in one of the computer's disk drives. The fact that a fully functional copy of a program cannot be made from a PROLOK diskette prevents purchasers from buying a single program and making unauthorized copies for distribution to others. . . .

---

1. A PROLOK diskette contains two programs, the program placed on the diskette by a software company (e.g., word processing) and the program placed on the diskette by Vault which interacts with the "fingerprint" to prevent the unauthorized duplication of the software company's program. We use the term "software program" or "program" to refer to the program placed on the diskette by one of Vault's customers (a computer company) and "Vault's program" to refer to the program placed on the diskette by Vault as part of the protective device. We collectively refer to the "fingerprint" and Vault's program as the "protective device."

Each version of PROLOK has been copyrighted and Vault includes a license agreement with every PROLOK package that specifically prohibits the copying, modification, translation, decompilation or disassembly of Vault's program. Beginning with version 2.0 in September 1985, Vault's license agreement contained a choice of law clause adopting Louisiana law.

Quaid's product, a diskette called "CopyWrite," contains a feature called "RAMKEY" which unlocks the PROLOK protective device and facilitates the creation of a fully functional copy of a program placed on a PROLOK diskette. The process is performed simply by copying the contents of the PROLOK diskette onto the CopyWrite diskette which can then be used to run the software program *without* the original PROLOK diskette in a computer disk drive. RAMKEY interacts with Vault's program to make it appear to the computer that the CopyWrite diskette contains the "fingerprint," thereby making the computer function as if the original PROLOK diskette is in its disk drive. A copy of a program placed on a CopyWrite diskette can be used without the original, and an unlimited number of fully functional copies can be made in this manner from the program originally placed on the PROLOK diskette. . . .

II

Vault brought this action against Quaid seeking preliminary and permanent injunctions to prevent Quaid from advertising and selling RAMKEY, an order impounding all of Quaid's copies of CopyWrite which contain the RAMKEY feature, and monetary damages in the amount of $100,000,000. . . .

IV. VAULT'S LOUISIANA CLAIMS

Seeking preliminary and permanent injunctions and damages, Vault's original complaint alleged that Quaid breached its license agreement by decompiling or disassembling Vault's program in violation of the Louisiana Software License Enforcement Act (the "License Act"), La. Rev. Stat. Ann. §51:1961 *et seq.* (West 1987), and that Quaid misappropriated Vault's program in violation of the Louisiana Uniform Trade Secrets Act, La. Rev. Stat. Ann. §51:1431 *et seq.* (West 1987). On appeal, Vault abandons its misappropriation claim, and, with respect to its breach of license claim, Vault only seeks an injunction to prevent Quaid from decompiling or disassembling PROLOK version 2.0.

Louisiana's License Act permits a software producer to impose a number of contractual terms upon software purchasers provided that the terms are set forth in a license agreement which comports with La. Rev. Stat. Ann. §§51:1963 & 1965, and that this license agreement accompanies the producer's software. Enforceable terms include the prohibition of: (1) any copying of the program for any purpose; and (2) modifying and/or adapting the program in any way, including adaptation by reverse engineering, decompilation or disassembly. La. Rev. Stat. Ann. §51:1964. The terms "reverse engineering, decompiling or disassembling" are defined as "any process by which computer software is converted from one form to another form which is more readily understandable to human beings, including without limitation any decoding or decrypting of any computer program which has been encoded or encrypted in any manner." La. Rev. Stat. Ann. §51:1962(3).

Vault's license agreement, which accompanies PROLOK version 2.0 and comports with the requirements of La. Rev. Stat. Ann. §§51:1963 & 1965, provides that "[y]ou may not . . . copy, modify, translate, convert to another programming language, decompile or disassemble" Vault's program. Vault asserts that these prohibitions are enforceable under Louisiana's License Act, and specifically seeks an injunction to prevent Quaid from decompiling or disassembling Vault's program.

The district court held that Vault's license agreement was "a contract of adhesion which could only be enforceable if the [Louisiana License Act] is a valid and enforceable statute." *Vault*, 655 F. Supp. at 761. The court noted numerous conflicts between Louisiana's License Act and the Copyright Act, including: (1) while the License Act authorizes a total prohibition on copying, the Copyright Act allows archival copies and copies made as an essential step in the utilization of a computer program, 17 U.S.C. §117; (2) while the License Act authorizes a perpetual bar against copying, the Copyright Act grants protection against unauthorized copying only for the life of the author plus fifty years, 17 U.S.C. §302(a); and (3) while the License Act places no restrictions on programs which may be protected, under the Copyright Act, only "original works of authorship" can be protected, 17 U.S.C. §102. *Vault*, 655 F. Supp. at 762-63. The court concluded that, because Louisiana's License Act "touched upon the area" of federal copyright law, its provisions were preempted and Vault's license agreement was unenforceable. *Id.* at 763.

In *Sears, Roebuck & Co. v. Stiffel Co.*, 376 U.S. 225 (1964), the Supreme Court held that "[w]hen state law touches upon the area of [patent or copyright statutes], it is 'familiar doctrine' that the federal policy 'may not be set at naught, or its benefits denied' by the state law." *Id.* at 229 (quoting *Sola Elec. Co. v. Jefferson Elec. Co.*, 317 U.S. 173, 176, 63 S. Ct. 172, 173, 87 L. Ed. 165 (1942)). . . . Section 117 of the Copyright Act permits an owner of a computer program to make an adaptation of that program provided that the adaptation is either "created as an essential step in the utilization of the computer program in conjunction with a machine," §117(1), or "is for archival purpose only," §117(2). The provision in Louisiana's License Act, which permits a software producer to prohibit the adaptation of its licensed computer program by decompilation or disassembly, conflicts with the rights of computer program owners under §117 and clearly "touches upon an area" of federal copyright law. For this reason, and the reasons set forth by the district court, we hold that at least this provision of Louisiana's License Act is preempted by federal law, and thus that the restriction in Vault's license agreement against decompilation or disassembly is unenforceable. . . .

ProCD, Inc. v. Zeidenberg

86 F.3d 1447 (7th Cir. 1996)

[The facts of *ProCD* are excerpted *supra*.]

III

The district court held that, even if Wisconsin treats shrinkwrap licenses as contracts, §301(a) of the Copyright Act, 17 U.S.C. §301(a), prevents their enforcement. 908 F. Supp. at 656-59. The relevant part of §301(a) preempts any "legal or equitable rights [under state law] that are equivalent to any of the exclusive rights within the general scope of copyright as specified by section 106 in works of authorship that are fixed in a tangible medium of expression and come within the subject matter of copyright as specified by sections 102 and 103." ProCD's software and data are "fixed in a tangible medium of expression," and the district judge held that they are "within the subject matter of copyright." The latter conclusion is plainly right for the copyrighted application program, and the judge thought that the data likewise are "within the subject matter of copyright" even if, after *Feist*, they are not sufficiently original to be copyrighted. 908 F. Supp. at 656-57. Baltimore Orioles, Inc. v. Major League Baseball Players Ass'n, 805 F.2d 663, 676 (7th Cir. 1986), supports that conclusion, with which commentators agree. E.g., Paul Goldstein, III Copyright §15.2.3 (2d ed.1996); Melville B. Nimmer & David Nimmer, Nimmer on Copyright §101[B] (1995); William F. Patry, II Copyright Law and Practice 1108-09 (1994). One function of §301(a) is to prevent states from giving special protection to works of authorship that Congress has decided should be in the public domain, which it can accomplish only if "subject matter of copyright" includes all works of a type covered by sections 102 and 103, even if federal law does not afford protection to them. Cf. Bonito Boats, Inc. v. Thunder Craft Boats, Inc., 489 U.S. 141 (1989) (same principle under patent laws).

But are rights created by contract "equivalent to any of the exclusive rights within the general scope of copyright"? Three courts of appeals have answered "no." National Car Rental System, Inc. v. Computer Associates International, Inc., 991 F.2d 426, 433 (8th Cir. 1993); Taquino v. Teledyne Monarch Rubber, 893 F.2d 1488, 1501 (5th Cir. 1990); Acorn Structures, Inc. v. Swantz, 846 F.2d 923, 926 (4th Cir. 1988). The district court disagreed with these decisions, 908 F. Supp. at 658, but we think them sound. Rights "equivalent to any of the exclusive rights within the general scope of copyright" are rights established by law—rights that restrict the options of persons who are strangers to the author. Copyright law forbids duplication, public performance, and so on, unless the person wishing to copy or perform the work gets permission; silence means a ban on copying. A copyright is a right against the world. Contracts, by contrast, generally affect only their parties; strangers may do as they please, so contracts do not create "exclusive rights." Someone who found a copy of SelectPhone (trademark) on the street would not be affected by the shrinkwrap license — though the federal copyright laws of their own force would limit the finder's ability to copy or transmit the application program.

Think for a moment about trade secrets. One common trade secret is a customer list. After *Feist*, a simple alphabetical list of a firm's customers, with address and telephone numbers, could not be protected by copyright. Yet Kewanee Oil Co. v. Bicron Corp., 416 U.S. 470 (1974), holds that contracts about trade secrets may be enforced — precisely because they do not affect strangers' ability to discover and use the information independently. If the amendment of §301(a) in 1976 overruled Kewanee and abolished consensual protection of those trade secrets that cannot be copyrighted, no one has noticed — though abolition is a logical consequence of the district court's approach. Think, too, about everyday transactions in intellectual property. A customer visits a video store and rents a copy of Night of the Lepus. The customer's contract with the store limits use of the tape to home viewing and requires its return in two days. May the customer keep the tape, on the ground that §301(a) makes the promise unenforceable?

A law student uses the LEXIS database, containing public-domain documents, under a contract limiting the results to educational endeavors; may the student resell his access to this database to a law firm from which LEXIS seeks to collect a much higher hourly rate? Suppose ProCD hires a firm to scour the nation for telephone directories, promising to pay $100 for each that ProCD does not already have. The firm locates 100 new directories, which it sends to ProCD with an invoice for $10,000. ProCD incorporates the directories into its database; does it have to pay the bill? Surely yes; Aronson v. Quick Point Pencil Co., 440 U.S. 257 (1979), holds that promises to pay for intellectual property may be enforced even though federal law (in *Aronson*, the patent law) offers no protection against third-party uses of that property. See also Kennedy v. Wright, 851 F.2d 963 (7th Cir. 1988). But these illustrations are what our case is about. ProCD offers software and data for two prices: one for personal use, a higher price for commercial use. Zeidenberg wants to use the data without paying the seller's price; if the law student and Quick Point Pencil Co. could not do that, neither can Zeidenberg.

Although Congress possesses power to preempt even the enforcement of contracts about intellectual property — or railroads, on which see Norfolk & Western Ry. v. Train Dispatchers, 499 U.S. 117 (1991) — courts usually read preemption clauses to leave private contracts unaffected. American Airlines, Inc. v. Wolens, 513 U.S. 219 (1995), provides a nice illustration. A federal statute preempts any state "law, rule, regulation, standard, or other provision . . . relating to rates, routes, or services of any air carrier." 49 U.S.C. App. §1305(a)(1). Does such a law preempt the law of contracts — so that, for example, an air carrier need not honor a quoted price (or a contract to reduce the price by the value of frequent flyer miles)? The Court allowed that it is possible to read the statute that broadly but thought such an interpretation would make little sense. Terms and conditions offered by contract reflect private ordering, essential to the efficient functioning of markets. 513 U.S. at ___, 115 S. Ct. at 824-25. Although some principles that carry the name of contract law are designed to defeat rather than implement consensual transactions, id. at ___ n.8, 115 S. Ct. at 826 n.8, the rules that respect private choice are not preempted by a clause such as §1305(a)(1). Section 301(a) plays a role similar to §1301(a)(1): it prevents states from substituting their own regulatory systems for those of the national government. Just as §301(a) does not itself interfere with private transactions in intellectual property, so it does not prevent states from respecting those transactions. Like the Supreme Court in *Wolens*, we think it prudent to refrain from adopting a rule that anything with the label "contract" is necessarily outside the preemption clause: the variations and possibilities are too numerous to foresee. *National Car Rental* likewise recognizes the possibility that some applications of the law of contract could interfere with the attainment of national objectives and therefore come within the domain of §301(a). But general enforcement of shrinkwrap licenses of the kind before us does not create such interference.

Aronson emphasized that enforcement of the contract between Aronson and Quick Point Pencil Company would not withdraw any information from the public domain. That is equally true of the contract between ProCD and Zeidenberg. Everyone remains free to copy and disseminate all 3,000 telephone books that have been incorporated into ProCD's database. Anyone can add SIC codes and zip codes. ProCD's rivals have done so. Enforcement of the shrinkwrap license may even make information more readily available, by reducing the price ProCD charges to consumer buyers. To the extent licenses facilitate distribution of object code while concealing the source code (the point of a clause forbidding disassembly), they serve the same procompetitive functions as does the law of trade secrets. Rockwell Graphic Systems, Inc. v. DEV Industries, Inc., 925 F.2d 174, 180 (7th Cir. 1991). Licenses may have other benefits for consumers: many licenses permit users to make extra copies, to use the software on multiple computers, even to incorporate the software into the user's products. But whether a particular license is generous or restrictive, a simple two-party contract is not "equivalent to any of the exclusive rights within the general scope of copyright" and therefore may be enforced.

COMMENTS AND QUESTIONS

1. Is it possible to reconcile *Vault* and *ProCD*? Does it matter that Louisiana enacted legislation specifically authorizing the type of licensing agreement at issue in *Vault*? To what extent are the different conclusions regarding preemption influenced by each court's view of the legitimacy of the process in which the agreements were entered?

2. According to the court in *Vault*, how does Vault's license create rights equivalent to the exclusive rights of copyright law? What is the argument that the contractual rights at issue in *ProCD* are equivalent to copyright law?

3. In *ProCD*, Judge Easterbrook concludes that contractual rights are not the equivalent to the exclusive rights created by copyright. According to Easterbrook, "A copyright is a right against the world. Contracts, by contrast, generally affect only their parties; strangers may do as they please, so contracts do not create 'exclusive rights.'" Is this distinction between parties to a contract and strangers persuasive? Should the size of the licensor and whether it ever varies the terms of the license be relevant? Can an argument be made that copyright law often applies only to parties in a specific transaction?

4. In Bowers v. Baystate Technologies, Inc., 320 F.3d 1317 (2003), the Federal Circuit Appeals Court took a similar view to Judge Easterbrook in *ProCD* on the question as to whether federal copyright law preempts a contractual agreement, in this case an agreement to exclude fair use privileges relating to reverse engineering. In *Bowers*, a software manufacturer utilized shrinkwrap license terms to prevent unauthorized reverse engineering of its software to create a new software product. Although this conduct would likely have been permitted as a fair use under copyright law, the court held that the shrinkwrap license term was enforceable on this point. The Court considered both the *Vault* case and the *ProCD* case in making its determination. It distinguished *Vault* on the basis that *Vault* concerned a state law prohibiting unauthorized copying, while *Bowers* concerned private contractual agreements. Under the principles of freedom of contract, the Court held that private parties are free to contract as they see fit and can contractually forego the ability to reverse engineer software that might otherwise be protected as a fair use under the copyright act. The holding in *Bowers* was followed by the Eighth Circuit Court of Appeal in Blizzard v. Jung, 422 F.3d 630, 639 (2005), *supra*.

3. Antitrust

Perhaps some of the most important restraints upon private ordering in the United States are those imposed by antitrust law. For example, Section 1 of the Sherman Act states that "[e]very contract, combination . . . or conspiracy, in restraint of trade or commerce . . . is declared to be illegal."[8] Similarly, Section 2 prohibits unilateral and joint efforts to monopolize or attempt to monopolize trade or commerce.[9] According to the U.S. Supreme Court:

> The Sherman Act was designed to be a comprehensive charter of economic liberty aimed at preserving free and unfettered competition as the rule of trade. It rests on the premise that the unrestrained interaction of competitive forces will yield the best allocation of our economic resources, the lowest prices, the highest quality and the greatest material

8. 15 U.S.C. §1.
9. 15 U.S.C. §2.

progress, while at the same time providing an environment conducive to the preservation of our democratic political and social institutions. But even were that premise open to question, the policy unequivocally laid down by the Act is competition.[10]

As you study the following decision involving Microsoft, consider whether and to what extent antitrust law should limit Microsoft's ability to enter into contracts with computer suppliers and/or limit its ability to determine how its operating system will function. Consider what public interests are at stake in the outcome of this decision.

UNITED STATES V. MICROSOFT CORP.

253 F.3d 34 (D.C. Cir. 2001)

PER CURIAM:

Microsoft Corporation appeals from judgments of the District Court finding the company in violation of §§1 and 2 of the Sherman Act and ordering various remedies.

The action against Microsoft arose pursuant to a complaint filed by the United States and separate complaints filed by individual States. The District Court determined that Microsoft had maintained a monopoly in the market for Intel compatible PC operating systems in violation of §2; attempted to gain a monopoly in the market for internet browsers in violation of §2; and illegally tied two purportedly separate products, Windows and Internet Explorer ("IE"), in violation of §1. *United States v. Microsoft Corp.*, 87 F. Supp. 2d 30 (D.D.C. 2000) (*"Conclusions of Law"*). . . .

I. INTRODUCTION

A. Background

In July 1994, officials at the Department of Justice ("DOJ"), on behalf of the United States, filed suit against Microsoft, charging the company with, among other things, unlawfully maintaining a monopoly in the operating system market through anticompetitive terms in its licensing and software developer agreements. The parties subsequently entered into a consent decree, thus avoiding a trial on the merits. *See United States v. Microsoft Corp.*, 56 F.3d 1448 (D.C. Cir. 1995) (*"Microsoft I"*). . . .

On May 18, 1998, shortly before issuance of the *Microsoft II* decision, the United States and a group of State plaintiffs filed separate (and soon thereafter consolidated) complaints, asserting antitrust violations by Microsoft and seeking preliminary and permanent injunctions against the company's allegedly unlawful conduct. The complaints also sought any "other preliminary and

10. Northern Pacific Railway v. United States, 356 U.S. 1, 4 (1958).

permanent relief as is necessary and appropriate to restore competitive conditions in the markets affected by Microsoft's unlawful conduct." Gov't's Compl. at 53, *United States v. Microsoft Corp.*, No. 98-1232 (D.D.C. 1999). Relying almost exclusively on Microsoft's varied efforts to unseat Netscape Navigator as the preeminent internet browser, plaintiffs charged four distinct violations of the Sherman Act: (1) unlawful exclusive dealing arrangements in violation of §1; (2) unlawful tying of IE to Windows 95 and Windows 98 in violation of §1; (3) unlawful maintenance of a monopoly in the PC operating system market in violation of §2; and (4) unlawful attempted monopolization of the internet browser market in violation of §2. The States also brought pendent claims charging Microsoft with violations of various State antitrust laws. . . .

B. Overview

Before turning to the merits of Microsoft's various arguments, we pause to reflect briefly on two matters of note, one practical and one theoretical.

The practical matter relates to the temporal dimension of this case. The litigation timeline in this case is hardly problematic. Indeed, it is noteworthy that a case of this magnitude and complexity has proceeded from the filing of complaints through trial to appellate decision in a mere three years. . . .

What is somewhat problematic, however, is that just over six years have passed since Microsoft engaged in the first conduct plaintiffs allege to be anticompetitive. As the record in this case indicates, six years seems like an eternity in the computer industry. By the time a court can assess liability, firms, products, and the marketplace are likely to have changed dramatically. This, in turn, threatens enormous practical difficulties for courts considering the appropriate measure of relief in equitable enforcement actions, both in crafting injunctive remedies in the first instance and reviewing those remedies in the second. Conduct remedies may be unavailing in such cases, because innovation to a large degree has already rendered the anticompetitive conduct obsolete (although by no means harmless). And broader structural remedies present their own set of problems, including how a court goes about *restoring* competition to a dramatically changed, and constantly changing, marketplace. That is just one reason why we find the District Court's refusal in the present case to hold an evidentiary hearing on remedies — to update and flesh out the available information before seriously entertaining the possibility of dramatic structural relief — so problematic. . . .

We do not mean to say that enforcement actions will no longer play an important role in curbing infringements of the antitrust laws in technologically dynamic markets, nor do we assume this in assessing the merits of this case. Even in those cases where forward-looking remedies appear limited, the Government will continue to have an interest in defining the contours of the antitrust laws so that law-abiding firms will have a clear sense of what is permissible and what is not. And the threat of private damage actions will remain to deter those firms inclined to test the limits of the law.

The second matter of note is more theoretical in nature. We decide this case against a backdrop of significant debate amongst academics and practitioners over the extent to which "old economy" §2 monopolization doctrines should apply to firms competing in dynamic technological markets characterized by network effects. In markets characterized by network effects, one product or standard tends towards dominance, because "the utility that a user derives from consumption of the good increases with the number of other agents consuming the good." Michael L. Katz & Carl Shapiro, *Network Externalities, Competition, and Compatibility*, 75 Am. Econ. Rev. 424, 424 (1985). For example, "[a]n individual consumer's demand to use (and hence her benefit from) the telephone network . . . increases with the number of other users on the network whom she can call or from whom she can receive calls." Howard A. Shelanski & J. Gregory Sidak, *Antitrust Divestiture in Network Industries*, 68 U. Chi. L. Rev. 1, 8 (2001). Once a product or standard achieves wide acceptance, it becomes more or less entrenched. Competition in such industries is "for the field" rather than "within the field." *See* Harold Demsetz, *Why Regulate Utilities?*, 11 J.L. & Econ. 55, 57 & n.7 (1968) (emphasis omitted).

In technologically dynamic markets, however, such entrenchment may be temporary, because innovation may alter the field altogether. *See* Joseph A. Schumpeter, Capitalism, Socialism and Democracy 81-90 (Harper Perennial 1976) (1942). Rapid technological change leads to markets in which "firms compete through innovation for temporary market dominance, from which they may be displaced by the next wave of product advancements." Shelanski & Sidak, at 11-12 (discussing Schumpeterian competition, which proceeds "sequentially over time rather than simultaneously across a market"). Microsoft argues that the operating system market is just such a market.

Whether or not Microsoft's characterization of the operating system market is correct does not appreciably alter our mission in assessing the alleged antitrust violations in the present case. As an initial matter, we note that there is no consensus among commentators on the question of whether, and to what extent, current monopolization doctrine should be amended to account for competition in technologically dynamic markets characterized by network effects. . . . Indeed, there is some suggestion that the economic consequences of network effects and technological dynamism act to offset one another, thereby making it difficult to formulate categorical antitrust rules absent a particularized analysis of a given market. . . .

With this backdrop in mind, we turn to the specific challenges raised in Microsoft's appeal.

II. MONOPOLIZATION

Section 2 of the Sherman Act makes it unlawful for a firm to "monopolize." 15 U.S.C. §2. The offense of monopolization has two elements: "(1) the possession of monopoly power in the relevant market and (2) the willful acquisition or maintenance of that power as distinguished from growth or development as a consequence of a superior product, business acumen, or historic accident." *United States v. Grinnell Corp.*, 384 U.S. 563, 570-71 (1966). The District Court applied this test and found that Microsoft possesses monopoly power in the market for Intel-compatible PC operating systems. Focusing primarily on Microsoft's efforts to suppress Netscape Navigator's threat to its operating system monopoly, the court also found that Microsoft maintained its power not through competition on the merits, but through unlawful means. Microsoft challenges both conclusions. . . .

A. Monopoly Power

While merely possessing monopoly power is not itself an antitrust violation, *see Northeastern Tel. Co. v. AT&T*, 651 F.2d 76, 84-85 (2d Cir. 1981), it is a necessary element of a monopolization charge, *see Grinnell*, 384 U.S. at 570. The Supreme Court defines monopoly power as "the power to control prices or exclude competition." *United States v. E.I. du Pont de Nemours & Co.*, 351 U.S. 377, 391 (1956). More precisely, a firm is a monopolist if it can profitably raise prices substantially above the competitive level. 2A Phillip E. Areeda et al., Antitrust Law §501, at 85 (1995); *cf. Ball Mem'l Hosp., Inc. v. Mut. Hosp. Ins., Inc.*, 784 F.2d 1325, 1335 (7th Cir. 1986) (defining market power as "the ability to cut back the market's total output and so raise price"). Where evidence indicates that a firm has in fact profitably done so, the existence of monopoly power is clear. . . . Because such direct proof is only rarely available, courts more typically examine market structure in search of circumstantial evidence of monopoly power. 2A Areeda et al., Antitrust Law §531a, at 156; *see also, e.g., Grinnell*, 384 U.S. at 571. Under this structural approach, monopoly power may be inferred from a firm's possession of a dominant share of a relevant market that is protected by entry barriers. *See Rebel Oil*, 51 F.3d at 1434. "Entry barriers" are factors (such as certain regulatory requirements) that prevent new rivals from timely responding to an increase in price above the competitive level. *See S. Pac. Communications Co. v. AT & T*, 740 F.2d 980, 1001-02 (D.C. Cir. 1984).

The District Court considered these structural factors and concluded that Microsoft possesses monopoly power in a relevant market. Defining the market as Intel-compatible PC operating systems, the District Court found that Microsoft has a greater than 95% share. It also found the company's market position protected by a substantial entry barrier. *Conclusions of Law*, at 36.

Microsoft argues that the District Court incorrectly defined the relevant market. It also claims that there is no barrier to entry in that market. Alternatively, Microsoft argues that because the software industry is uniquely dynamic, direct proof, rather than circumstantial evidence, more appropriately indicates whether it possesses monopoly power. Rejecting each argument, we uphold the District Court's finding of monopoly power in its entirety. . . .

[The court affirms the district court definition of the market as "the licensing of all Intel-compatible PC operating systems worldwide," finding that there are "currently no products—and . . . there are not likely to be any in the near future—that a significant percentage of computer users worldwide could substitute for [these operating systems] without incurring substantial costs." *Conclusions of Law*, at 36.]

b. Market Power

Having thus properly defined the relevant market, the District Court found that Windows accounts for a greater than 95% share. *Findings of Fact* §35. The court also found that even if Mac OS were included, Microsoft's share would exceed 80%. *Id.* Microsoft challenges neither finding, nor does it argue that such a market share is not predominant. . . .

Instead, Microsoft claims that even a predominant market share does not by itself indicate monopoly power. Although the "existence of [monopoly] power ordinarily may be inferred from the predominant share of the market," *Grinnell*, 384 U.S. at 571, we agree with Microsoft that because of the possibility of competition from new entrants, *see Ball Mem'l Hosp., Inc.*, 784 F.2d at 1336, looking to current market share alone can be "misleading." *Hunt-Wesson Foods, Inc. v. Ragu Foods, Inc.*, 627 F.2d 919, 924 (9th Cir. 1980); *see also Ball Mem'l Hosp., Inc.*, 784 F.2d at 1336 ("Market share reflects current sales, but today's sales do not always indicate power over sales and price tomorrow."). In this case, however, the District Court was not misled. Considering the possibility of new rivals, the court focused not only on Microsoft's present market share, but also on the structural barrier that protects the company's future position. *Conclusions of Law*, at 36. That barrier—the "applications barrier to entry"—stems from two characteristics of the software market: (1) most consumers prefer operating systems for which a large number of applications have already been written; and (2) most developers prefer to write for operating systems that already have a substantial consumer base. *See Findings of Fact* §§30, 36. This "chicken-and-egg" situation ensures that applications will continue to be written for the already dominant Windows, which in turn ensures that consumers will continue to prefer it over other operating systems. *Id.*

Challenging the existence of the applications barrier to entry, Microsoft observes that software developers do write applications for other operating systems, pointing out that at its peak IBM's OS/2 supported approximately 2,500 applications. *Id.* §46. This misses the point. That some developers write applications for other operating systems is not at all inconsistent with the finding that the applications barrier to entry discourages many from writing for these less popular platforms. Indeed, the District Court found that IBM's difficulty in attracting a larger number of software developers to write for its platform seriously impeded OS/2's success. *Id.* §46.

Microsoft does not dispute that Windows supports many more applications than any other operating system. It argues instead that "[i]t defies common sense" to suggest that an operating system must support as many applications as Windows does (more than 70,000, according to the District Court, *id.* §40) to be competitive. Appellant's Opening Br. at 96. Consumers, Microsoft points out, can only use a very small percentage of these applications. *Id.* As the District Court explained, however, the applications barrier to entry gives consumers reason to prefer the dominant operating system even if they have no need to use all applications written for it:

> The consumer wants an operating system that runs not only types of applications that he knows he will want to use, but also those types in which he might develop an interest later. Also, the consumer knows that if he chooses an operating system with enough demand to support multiple applications in each product category, he will be less likely to find himself straitened later by having to use an application whose features disappoint him. Finally, the average user knows that, generally speaking, applications improve through successive versions. He thus wants an operating system for which successive generations of his favorite applications will be released — promptly at that. The fact that a vastly larger number of applications are written for Windows than for other PC operating systems attracts consumers to Windows, because it reassures them that their interests will be met as long as they use Microsoft's product.

Findings of Fact §37. Thus, despite the limited success of its rivals, Microsoft benefits from the applications barrier to entry. . . .

Microsoft next argues that the applications barrier to entry is not an entry barrier at all, but a reflection of Windows' popularity. It is certainly true that Windows may have gained its initial dominance in the operating system market competitively — through superior foresight or quality. But this case is not about Microsoft's initial acquisition of monopoly power. It is about Microsoft's efforts to maintain this position through means other than competition on the merits. Because the applications barrier to entry protects a dominant operating system irrespective of quality, it gives Microsoft power to stave off even superior new rivals. The barrier is thus a characteristic of the operating system market, not of Microsoft's popularity, or, as asserted by a Microsoft witness, the company's efficiency. . . .

B.   Anticompetitive Conduct

As discussed above, having a monopoly does not by itself violate §2. A firm violates §2 only when it acquires or maintains, or attempts to acquire or maintain, a monopoly by engaging in exclusionary conduct "as distinguished from growth or development as a consequence of a superior product, business acumen, or historic accident." *Grinnell*, 384 U.S. at 571; *see also United States v. Aluminum Co. of Am.*, 148 F.2d 416, 430 (2d Cir. 1945) (Hand, J.) ("The successful competitor, having been urged to compete, must not be turned upon when he wins.").

In this case, after concluding that Microsoft had monopoly power, the District Court held that Microsoft had violated §2 by engaging in a variety of exclusionary acts (not including predatory pricing), to maintain its monopoly by preventing the effective distribution and use of products that might threaten that monopoly. Specifically, the District Court held Microsoft liable for: (1) the way in which it integrated IE into Windows; (2) its various dealings with Original Equipment Manufacturers ("OEMs"), Internet Access Providers ("IAPs"), Internet Content Providers ("ICPs"), Independent Software Vendors ("ISVs"), and Apple Computer; (3) its efforts to contain and to subvert Java technologies; and (4) its course of conduct as a whole. Upon appeal, Microsoft argues that it did not engage in any exclusionary conduct.

Whether any particular act of a monopolist is exclusionary, rather than merely a form of vigorous competition, can be difficult to discern: the means of illicit exclusion, like the means of legitimate competition, are myriad. The challenge for an antitrust court lies in stating a general rule for distinguishing between exclusionary acts, which reduce social welfare, and competitive acts, which increase it.

From a century of case law on monopolization under §2, however, several principles do emerge. First, to be condemned as exclusionary, a monopolist's act must have an "anticompetitive effect." That is, it must harm the competitive *process* and thereby harm consumers. In contrast, harm to one or more *competitors* will not suffice. "The [Sherman Act] directs itself not against conduct which is competitive, even severely so, but against conduct which unfairly tends to destroy competition itself." *Spectrum Sports, Inc. v. McQuillan*, 506 U.S. 447, 458 (1993); *see also Brooke Group Ltd. v. Brown & Williamson Tobacco Corp.*, 509 U.S. 209, 225 (1993) ("Even an act of pure malice by one business competitor against another does not, without more, state a claim under the federal antitrust laws. . . .").

Second, the plaintiff, on whom the burden of proof of course rests . . . must demonstrate that the monopolist's conduct indeed has the requisite anticompetitive effect. . . .

Third, if a plaintiff successfully establishes a *prima facie* case under §2 by demonstrating anticompetitive effect, then the monopolist may proffer a "procompetitive justification" for its conduct. *See Eastman Kodak*, 504 U.S. at 483. If the monopolist asserts a procompetitive justification—a nonpretextual claim that its conduct is indeed a form of competition on the merits because it involves, for example, greater efficiency or enhanced consumer appeal— then the burden shifts back to the plaintiff to rebut that claim. . . .

Fourth, if the monopolist's procompetitive justification stands unrebutted, then the plaintiff must demonstrate that the anticompetitive harm of the conduct outweighs the procompetitive benefit. In cases arising under §1 of the Sherman Act, the courts routinely apply a similar balancing approach under the rubric of the "rule of reason." The source of the rule of reason is *Standard Oil Co. v. United States*, 221 U.S. 1 (1911), in which the Supreme

Court used that term to describe the proper inquiry under both sections of the Act. . . .

Finally, in considering whether the monopolist's conduct on balance harms competition and is therefore condemned as exclusionary for purposes of §2, our focus is upon the effect of that conduct, not upon the intent behind it. Evidence of the intent behind the conduct of a monopolist is relevant only to the extent it helps us understand the likely effect of the monopolist's conduct. *See, e.g., Chicago Bd. of Trade v. United States*, 246 U.S. 231, 238 (1918) ("knowledge of intent may help the court to interpret facts and to predict consequences"); *Aspen Skiing Co. v. Aspen Highlands Skiing Corp.*, 472 U.S. 585, 603 (1985). . . .

1. Licenses Issued to Original Equipment Manufacturers

The District Court condemned a number of provisions in Microsoft's agreements licensing Windows to OEMs, because it found that Microsoft's imposition of those provisions (like many of Microsoft's other actions at issue in this case) serves to reduce usage share of Netscape's browser and, hence, protect Microsoft's operating system monopoly. The reason market share in the browser market affects market power in the operating system market is complex, and warrants some explanation.

Browser usage share is important because, as we explained in Section II.A above, a browser (or any middleware product, for that matter) must have a critical mass of users in order to attract software developers to write applications relying upon the APIs it exposes, and away from the APIs exposed by Windows. Applications written to a particular browser's APIs, however, would run on any computer with that browser, regardless of the underlying operating system. "The overwhelming majority of consumers will only use a PC operating system for which there already exists a large and varied set of . . . applications, and for which it seems relatively certain that new types of applications and new versions of existing applications will continue to be marketed. . . ." *Findings of Fact* §30. If a consumer could have access to the applications he desired—regardless of the operating system he uses—simply by installing a particular browser on his computer, then he would no longer feel compelled to select Windows in order to have access to those applications; he could select an operating system other than Windows based solely upon its quality and price. In other words, the market for operating systems would be competitive.

Therefore, Microsoft's efforts to gain market share in one market (browsers) served to meet the threat to Microsoft's monopoly in another market (operating systems) by keeping rival browsers from gaining the critical mass of users necessary to attract developer attention away from Windows as the platform for software development. Plaintiffs also argue that Microsoft's actions injured competition in the browser market—an argument we will examine below in relation to their specific claims that Microsoft attempted to monopolize the browser market and unlawfully tied its browser to its operating system so as to foreclose competition in the browser market. In evaluating the §2 monopoly maintenance claim, however, our immediate concern is with the anticompetitive effect of Microsoft's conduct in preserving its monopoly in the operating system market. . . .

a. Anticompetitive Effect of the License Restrictions

The restrictions Microsoft places upon Original Equipment Manufacturers are of particular importance in determining browser usage share because having an OEM pre-install a browser on a computer is one of the two most cost-effective methods by far of distributing browsing software. (The other is bundling the browser with internet access software distributed by an IAP.) *Findings of Fact* §145. The District Court found that the restrictions Microsoft imposed in licensing Windows to OEMs prevented many OEMs from distributing browsers other than IE. *Conclusions of Law*, at 39-40. In particular, the District Court condemned the license provisions prohibiting the OEMs from: (1) removing any desktop icons, folders, or "Start" menu entries; (2) altering the initial boot sequence; and (3) otherwise altering the appearance of the Windows desktop. *Findings of Fact* §213.

The District Court concluded that the first license restriction — the prohibition upon the removal of desktop icons, folders, and Start menu entries — thwarts the distribution of a rival browser by preventing OEMs from removing visible means of user access to IE. *Id.* §203. The OEMs cannot practically install a second browser in addition to IE, the court found, in part because "[p]re-installing more than one product in a given category. . . can significantly increase an OEM's support costs, for the redundancy can lead to confusion among novice users." *Id.* §159; *see also id.* §217. That is, a certain number of novice computer users, seeing two browser icons, will wonder which to use when and will call the OEM's support line. Support calls are extremely expensive and, in the highly competitive original equipment market, firms have a strong incentive to minimize costs. *Id.* §210.

Microsoft denies the "consumer confusion" story; it observes that some OEMs do install multiple browsers and that executives from two OEMs that do so denied any knowledge of consumers being confused by multiple icons. . . .

Other testimony, however, supports the District Court's finding that fear of such confusion deters many OEMs from pre-installing multiple browsers. . . . Most telling, in presentations to OEMs, Microsoft itself represented that having only one icon in a particular category would be "less confusing for end users." *See* Government's Trial Exhibit ("GX") 319 at MS98 0109453. Accordingly, we reject Microsoft's argument that we should vacate the District Court's Finding of Fact 159 as it relates to consumer confusion.

As noted above, the OEM channel is one of the two primary channels for distribution of browsers. By preventing OEMs from removing visible means of user access to IE, the license restriction prevents many OEMs from pre-installing a rival browser and, therefore, protects Microsoft's monopoly from the competition that middleware might otherwise present. Therefore, we conclude that the license restriction at issue is anticompetitive. We defer for the moment the question whether that anticompetitive effect is outweighed by Microsoft's proffered justifications.

The second license provision at issue prohibits OEMs from modifying the initial boot sequence — the process that occurs the first time a consumer turns on the computer. Prior to the imposition of that restriction, "among the programs that many OEMs inserted into the boot sequence were Internet sign-up procedures that encouraged users to choose from a list of IAPs assembled by the OEM." *Findings of Fact* §210. Microsoft's prohibition on any alteration of the boot sequence thus prevents OEMs from using that process to promote the services of IAPs, many of which — at least at the time Microsoft imposed the restriction — used Navigator rather than IE in their internet access software. . . . Microsoft does not deny that the prohibition on modifying the boot sequence has the effect of decreasing competition against IE by preventing OEMs from promoting rivals' browsers. Because this prohibition has a substantial effect in protecting Microsoft's market power, and does so through a means other than competition on the merits, it is anticompetitive. Again the question whether the provision is nonetheless justified awaits later treatment.

Finally, Microsoft imposes several additional provisions that, like the prohibition on removal of icons, prevent OEMs from making various alterations to the desktop: Microsoft prohibits OEMs from causing any user interface other than the Windows desktop to launch automatically, from adding icons or folders different in size or shape from those supplied by Microsoft, and from using the "Active Desktop" feature to promote third-party brands. These restrictions impose significant costs upon the OEMs; prior to Microsoft's prohibiting the practice, many OEMs would change the appearance of the desktop in ways they found beneficial. . . .

The dissatisfaction of the OEM customers does not, of course, mean the restrictions are anticompetitive. The anticompetitive effect of the license restrictions is, as Microsoft itself recognizes, that OEMs are not able to promote rival browsers, which keeps developers focused upon the APIs in Windows. *Findings of Fact* §212 (quoting Microsoft's Gates as writing, "[w]inning Internet browser share is a very very important goal for us," and emphasizing the need to prevent OEMs from promoting both rival browsers and IAPs that might use rivals' browsers); *see also* 01/13/99 Tr. at 305-06 (excerpts from deposition of James Von Holle of Gateway) (prior to restriction Gateway had pre-installed non-IE internet registration icon that was larger than other desktop icons). This kind of promotion is not a zero-sum game; but for the restrictions in their licenses to use Windows, OEMs could promote multiple IAPs and browsers. By preventing the OEMs from doing so, this type of license restriction, like the first two restrictions, is anticompetitive: Microsoft reduced rival browsers' usage share not by improving its own product but, rather, by preventing OEMs from taking actions that could increase rivals' share of usage.

b. Microsoft's Justifications for the License Restrictions

Microsoft argues that the license restrictions are legally justified because, in imposing them, Microsoft is simply "exercising its rights as the holder of valid copyrights." Appellant's Opening Br. at 102. Microsoft also argues that the licenses "do not unduly restrict the opportunities of Netscape to distribute Navigator in any event." *Id.*

Microsoft's primary copyright argument borders upon the frivolous. The company claims an absolute and unfettered right to use its intellectual property as it wishes: "[I]f intellectual property rights have been lawfully acquired," it says, then "their subsequent exercise cannot give rise to antitrust liability." Appellant's Opening Br. at 105. That is no more correct than the proposition that use of one's personal property, such as a baseball bat, cannot give rise to tort liability. As the Federal Circuit succinctly stated: "Intellectual property rights do not confer a privilege to violate the antitrust laws." *In re Indep. Serv. Orgs. Antitrust Litig.*, 203 F.3d 1322, 1325 (Fed. Cir. 2000).

Although Microsoft never overtly retreats from its bold and incorrect position on the law, it also makes two arguments to the effect that it is not exercising its copyright in an unreasonable manner, despite the anticompetitive consequences of the license restrictions discussed above. In the first variation upon its unqualified copyright defense, Microsoft cites two cases indicating that a copyright holder may limit a licensee's ability to engage in significant and deleterious alterations of a copyrighted work. *See Gilliam v. ABC*, 538 F.2d 14, 21 (2d Cir. 1976); *WGN Cont'l Broad. Co. v. United Video, Inc.*, 693 F.2d 622, 625 (7th Cir. 1982). The relevance of those two cases for the present one is limited, however, both because those cases involved substantial alterations of a copyrighted work, *see Gilliam*, 538 F.2d at 18, and because in neither case was there any claim that the copyright holder was, in asserting its rights, violating the antitrust laws, *see WGN Cont'l Broad.*, 693 F.2d at 626; *see also Cmty. for Creative Non-Violence v. Reid*, 846 F.2d 1485, 1498 (D.C. Cir. 1988) (noting, again in a context free of any antitrust concern, that "an author . . . may have rights against" a licensee that "excessively mutilated or altered" the copyrighted work).

The only license restriction Microsoft seriously defends as necessary to prevent a "substantial alteration" of its copyrighted work is the prohibition on OEMs automatically launching a substitute user interface upon completion of the boot process. . . . We agree that a shell that automatically prevents the Windows desktop from ever being seen by the user is a drastic alteration of Microsoft's copyrighted work, and outweighs the marginal anticompetitive effect of prohibiting the OEMs from substituting a different interface automatically upon completion of the initial boot process. We therefore hold that this particular restriction is not an exclusionary practice that violates §2 of the Sherman Act.

In a second variation upon its copyright defense, Microsoft argues that the license restrictions merely prevent OEMs from taking actions that would reduce substantially the value of Microsoft's copyrighted work: that is, Microsoft claims each license restriction in question is necessary to prevent OEMs from so altering Windows as to undermine "the principal value of Windows as a stable and consistent platform that supports a broad range of applications and that is familiar to users." Appellant's Opening Br. at 102. Microsoft, however, never substantiates this claim, and, because an OEM's altering the appearance of the desktop or promoting programs in the boot sequence does not affect the code already in the product, the practice does not self-evidently affect either the "stability" or the "consistency" of the platform. *See Conclusions of Law*, at 41; *Findings of Fact* §227. Microsoft cites only one item of evidence in support of its claim that the OEMs' alterations were decreasing the value of Windows. . . . That document, prepared by Microsoft itself, states: "there are quality issues created by OEMs who are too liberal with the pre-install process," referring to the OEMs' installation of Windows and additional software on their PCs, which the document says may result in "user concerns and confusion." To the extent the OEMs' modifications cause consumer confusion, of course, the OEMs bear the additional support costs. *See Findings of Fact* §159. Therefore, we conclude Microsoft has not shown that the OEMs' liberality reduces the value of Windows except in the sense that their promotion of rival browsers undermines Microsoft's monopoly — and that is not a permissible justification for the license restrictions.

Apart from copyright, Microsoft raises one other defense of the OEM license agreements: It argues that, despite the restrictions in the OEM license, Netscape is not completely blocked from distributing its product. That claim is insufficient to shield Microsoft from liability for those restrictions because, although Microsoft did not bar its rivals from all means of distribution, it did bar them from the cost-efficient ones.

In sum, we hold that with the exception of the one restriction prohibiting automatically launched alternative interfaces, all the OEM license restrictions at issue represent uses of Microsoft's market power to protect its monopoly, unredeemed by any legitimate justification. The restrictions therefore violate §2 of the Sherman Act. . . .

2. Integration of IE and Windows

Although Microsoft's license restrictions have a significant effect in closing rival browsers out of one of the two primary channels of distribution, the District Court found that "Microsoft's executives believed . . . its contractual restrictions placed on OEMs would not be sufficient in themselves to reverse the direction of Navigator's usage share. Consequently, in late 1995 or early

1996, Microsoft set out to bind [IE] more tightly to Windows 95 as a technical matter." *Findings of Fact* §160.

Technologically binding IE to Windows, the District Court found, both prevented OEMs from pre-installing other browsers and deterred consumers from using them. In particular, having the IE software code as an irremovable part of Windows meant that pre-installing a second browser would "increase an OEM's product testing costs," because an OEM must test and train its support staff to answer calls related to every software product preinstalled on the machine; moreover, pre-installing a browser in addition to IE would to many OEMs be "a questionable use of the scarce and valuable space on a PC's hard drive." *Id.* §159.

Although the District Court, in its Conclusions of Law, broadly condemned Microsoft's decision to bind "Internet Explorer to Windows with . . . technological shackles," *Conclusions of Law*, at 39, its findings of fact in support of that conclusion center upon three specific actions Microsoft took to weld IE to Windows: excluding IE from the "Add/Remove Programs" utility; designing Windows so as in certain circumstances to override the user's choice of a default browser other than IE; and commingling code related to browsing and other code in the same files, so that any attempt to delete the files containing IE would, at the same time, cripple the operating system. As with the license restrictions, we consider first whether the suspect actions had an anticompetitive effect, and then whether Microsoft has provided a procompetitive justification for them.

a. Anticompetitive Effect of Integration

As a general rule, courts are properly very skeptical about claims that competition has been harmed by a dominant firm's product design changes. *See, e.g., Foremost Pro Color, Inc. v. Eastman Kodak Co.*, 703 F.2d 534, 544-45 (9th Cir. 1983). In a competitive market, firms routinely innovate in the hope of appealing to consumers, sometimes in the process making their products incompatible with those of rivals; the imposition of liability when a monopolist does the same thing will inevitably deter a certain amount of innovation. This is all the more true in a market, such as this one, in which the product itself is rapidly changing. *See Findings of Fact* §59. Judicial deference to product innovation, however, does not mean that a monopolist's product design decisions are per se lawful. . . .

The District Court first condemned as anticompetitive Microsoft's decision to exclude IE from the "Add/Remove Programs" utility in Windows 98. *Findings of Fact* §170. Microsoft had included IE in the Add/Remove Programs utility in Windows 95, *see id.* §§175-76, but when it modified Windows 95 to produce Windows 98, it took IE out of the Add/Remove Programs utility. This change reduces the usage share of rival browsers not by making Microsoft's own browser more attractive to consumers but, rather, by discouraging OEMs from distributing rival products. *See id.* §159. Because Microsoft's conduct, through something other than competition on the merits, has the effect of significantly reducing usage of rivals' products and hence protecting its own operating system monopoly, it is anticompetitive; we defer for the moment the question whether it is nonetheless justified.

Second, the District Court found that Microsoft designed Windows 98 "so that using Navigator on Windows 98 would have unpleasant consequences for users" by, in some circumstances, overriding the user's choice of a browser other than IE as his or her default browser. *Id.* §§171-72. Plaintiffs argue that this override harms the competitive process by deterring consumers from using a browser other than IE even though they might prefer to do so, thereby reducing rival browsers' usage share and, hence, the ability of rival browsers to draw developer attention away from the APIs exposed by Windows. Microsoft does not deny, of course, that overriding the user's preference prevents some people from using other browsers. Because the override reduces rivals' usage share and protects Microsoft's monopoly, it too is anticompetitive.

Finally, the District Court condemned Microsoft's decision to bind IE to Windows 98 "by placing code specific to Web browsing in the same files as code that provided operating system functions." *Id.* §161; *see also id.* §§174, 192. Putting code supplying browsing functionality into a file with code supplying operating system functionality "ensure[s] that the deletion of any file containing browsing-specific routines would also delete vital operating system routines and thus cripple Windows. . . ." *Id.* §164. As noted above, preventing an OEM from removing IE deters it from installing a second browser because doing so increases the OEM's product testing and support costs; by contrast, had OEMs been able to remove IE, they might have chosen to pre-install Navigator alone. *See id.* §159.

Microsoft denies, as a factual matter, that it commingled browsing and non-browsing code, and it maintains the District Court's findings to the contrary are clearly erroneous. According to Microsoft, its expert "testified without contradiction that '[t]he very same code in Windows 98 that provides Web browsing functionality' also performs essential operating system functions—not code in the same files, but the very same software code." Appellant's Opening Br. at 79 (citing 5 J.A. 3291-92).

Microsoft's expert did not testify to that effect "without contradiction," however. A Government expert, Glenn Weadock, testified that Microsoft "design[ed][IE] so that some of the code that it uses co-resides in the same library files as other code needed for Windows." Direct Testimony §30. Another Government expert likewise testified that one library file, SHDOCVW.DLL, "is really a bundle of separate functions. It contains some functions that have to do specifically with Web browsing, and it contains some general user interface functions as well." 12/14/98 Am Tr. at 60-61 (trial testimony of Edward Felten), *reprinted in* 11 J.A. at 6953-54. One of Microsoft's own documents suggests as much. . . .

In view of the contradictory testimony in the record, some of which supports the District Court's finding that Microsoft commingled browsing and non-browsing code, we cannot conclude that the finding was clearly erroneous. *See Anderson v. City of Bessemer City*, 470 U.S. 564, 573-74 (1985) ("If the district court's account of the evidence is plausible in light of the record viewed in its entirety, the court of appeals may not reverse it even though convinced that had it been sitting as the trier of fact, it would have weighed the evidence differently."). Accordingly, we reject Microsoft's argument that we should vacate Finding of Fact 159 as it relates to the commingling of code, and we conclude that such commingling has an anticompetitive effect; as noted above, the commingling deters OEMs from pre-installing rival browsers, thereby reducing the rivals' usage share and, hence, developers' interest in rivals' APIs as an alternative to the API set exposed by Microsoft's operating system.

b. Microsoft's Justifications for Integration

Microsoft proffers no justification for two of the three challenged actions that it took in integrating IE into Windows — excluding IE from the Add/ Remove Programs utility and commingling browser and operating system code. Although Microsoft does make some general claims regarding the benefits of integrating the browser and the operating system, *see, e.g.*, Direct Testimony of James Allchin §94, *reprinted in* 5 J.A. at 3321 ("Our vision of deeper levels of technical integration is highly efficient and provides substantial benefits to customers and developers."), it neither specifies nor substantiates those claims. Nor does it argue that either excluding IE from the Add/Remove Programs utility or commingling code achieves any integrative benefit. Plaintiffs plainly made out a *prima facie* case of harm to competition in the operating system market by demonstrating that Microsoft's actions increased its browser usage share and thus protected its operating system monopoly from a middleware threat and, for its part, Microsoft failed to meet its burden of showing that its conduct serves a purpose other than protecting its operating system monopoly. Accordingly, we hold that Microsoft's exclusion of IE from the Add/Remove Programs utility and its commingling of browser and operating system code constitute exclusionary conduct, in violation of §2.

As for the other challenged act that Microsoft took in integrating IE into Windows — causing Windows to override the user's choice of a default browser in certain circumstances — Microsoft argues that it has "valid technical reasons." Specifically, Microsoft claims that it was necessary to design Windows to override the user's preferences when he or she invokes one of "a few" out "of the nearly 30 means of accessing the Internet." Appellant's Opening Br. at 82. According to Microsoft:

> The Windows 98 Help system and Windows Update feature depend on ActiveX controls not supported by Navigator, and the now-discontinued Channel Bar utilized Microsoft's Channel Definition Format, which Navigator also did not support. Lastly, Windows

> 98 does not invoke Navigator if a user accesses the Internet through "My Computer" or "Windows Explorer" because doing so would defeat one of the purposes of those features — enabling users to move seamlessly from local storage devices to the Web *in the same browsing window.*

Id. (internal citations omitted). The plaintiff bears the burden not only of rebutting a proffered justification but also of demonstrating that the anticompetitive effect of the challenged action outweighs it. In the District Court, plaintiffs appear to have done neither, let alone both; in any event, upon appeal, plaintiffs offer no rebuttal whatsoever. Accordingly, Microsoft may not be held liable for this aspect of its product design. . . .

[The remainder of the court's discussion with respect to Microsoft's abuse of its monopoly power, attempted monopolization of the Internet browser market, and the behavior of the trial judge are omitted.

With respect to the District Court's conclusion that Microsoft's contractual and technological bundling of the IE Web browser with its Windows operating system was per se unlawful, the court concluded that arrangement should be examined under the real reason instead of considered per se illegal. According to the court, a per se analysis with respect to software may "stunt valuable innovation."] . . .

VII. CONCLUSION

The judgment of the District Court is affirmed in part, reversed in part, and remanded in part. . . .

COMMENTS AND QUESTIONS

1. Despite the fact that the Department of Justice signaled that it would no longer ask for the company to be broken into separate entities, *Microsoft* represents an important limit to private ordering in an information economy. Students who are not familiar with antitrust law must remember, however, that the decision against Microsoft is based entirely upon the conclusion that Microsoft is considered to have a monopoly on the market for PC operating systems.

2. *Microsoft* also raises questions about institutional competency. Are courts capable of addressing the equitable concerns raised by anticompetitive behavior in a market as dynamic as the computer industry? According to the Court of Appeals, "six years seems like an eternity in the computer industry. By the time a court can assess liability, firms, products, and the marketplace are likely to have changed dramatically." Similarly, to what extent should new developments, like the growth of Linux as a competing operating system, be considered when those facts are not part of the trial record? *See* Stuart M. Benjamin, *Stepping into the Same River Twice: Rapidly Changing Facts and*

the Appellate Process, 78 Tex. L. Rev. 269 (1999) (recommending appellate updating of facts).

3.   What is the "network effect"? In the context of Microsoft how does it challenge traditional ideas about monopolization? According to the Court of Appeals, how does Microsoft have monopoly market power in the market for operating systems for PCs? What prevents competitors from entering the market? For an excellent discussion of network effects see Mark A. Lemley & David McGowan, *Legal Implications of Network Effects*, 86 Cal. L. Rev. 479 (1998).

4.   To what extent is antitrust law applicable to the new economy? Like the network effects discussed in *Microsoft*, the Internet, computer, communications, and electronics industries are driven to a significant degree by the adoption of uniform standards. For example, the agreement among network providers and software providers to adopt the TCP/IP protocols makes widespread Internet communications possible. Of course, keep in mind that the adoption of a standard means those who would prefer a competing standard are unable to compete. To what extent does standardization lead to antitrust liability? *Consider* Mark A. Lemley, *The Internet Standardization Problem*, 28 Conn. L. Rev. 1041 (1996), and Frank H. Easterbrook, *Information and Antitrust*, 2000 U. Chi. Legal F. 1.

5.   The *Microsoft* decision also raises the fundamental question of what represents permissible innovation in the information age versus anticompetitive conduct. According to the plaintiffs, what did Microsoft do to unfairly maintain its monopoly? Which of these acts did the Court of Appeals consider anticompetitive?

6.   Does it matter whether the conduct manifested in contracts was deemed anticompetitive or whether the conduct was Microsoft's writing of computer code? Could Microsoft design its operating system to only allow the programs it sells to operate under this decision? Could America Online program its Internet software to prohibit a user from accessing competing Internet service providers?

7.   What other areas of cyberspace raise antitrust concerns? Open access? Text messaging? Online social networks?

8.   More recently, courts and commentators have considered refining and potentially expanding the copyright misuse doctrine in the cyberlaw area. This is a doctrine based on the earlier developed doctrine of patent misuse. The idea is to prevent those holding intellectual property rights from utilizing them in an anticompetitive way. Patent and copyright misuse can be raised as defenses for claims to infringement in circumstances where the rights-holder is arguably utilizing its intellectual property rights to stifle competition in an anticompetitive manner. A copyright misuse defense was initially raised in Lexmark v. Static Control Components, 387 F. 3d 522 (2004). However, the appeal court held that it was unnecessary to discuss copyright misuse because the plaintiff had not made out a clear case of copyright or DMCA infringement (see discussion in Chapter 4, *supra*). For more detail

on the copyright misuse doctrine and its potential application in the cyberlaw area, see Brett Frischmann & Dan Moylan, *The Evolving Common Law Doctrine of Copyright Misuse: A Unified Theory and its Application to Software*, 15 Berkeley Tech. L.J. 865 (2000) (describing the development and contours of the copyright misuse doctrine); Lydia Pallas Loren, *Slaying the Leather-Winged Demons in the Night: Reforming Copyright Owner Contracting with Clickwrap Misuse*, 30 Ohio N.U. L. Rev. 495 (2004) (arguing for the development of copyright misuse principles to stem the tide of enforcement of unfair contractual provisions restricting uses that can be made of copyright works); Dan Burk, *Anticircumvention Misuse*, 50 UCLA L. Rev. 1095 (2003) (arguing for the development of an "anticircumvention misuse" doctrine to apply as a defense to infringements of the anti-circumvention provisions of the DMCA, on the assumption that copyright misuse may not be a defense to such infringements if fair use is not a defense to such infringements — see discussion in Chapter 4, *supra*).

TABLE OF CASES

Principal cases are indicated by italics.

INDEX